Congressional Practice and Procedure

Congressional Practice and Procedure

A Reference, Research, and Legislative Guide

Charles Tiefer

Greenwood Press
New York • Westport, Connecticut • London

Library of Congress Cataloging-in-Publication Data

Tiefer, Charles.
  Congressional practice and procedure : a reference, research, and
legislative guide / Charles Tiefer.
    p. cm.
  Bibliography: p.
  Includes index.
  ISBN 0-313-26355-8 (lib. bdg. : alk. paper)
    1. United States. Congress—Rules and practice. 2. Legislation—
United States. I. Title.
  KF4937.T54 1989
  328.73'05—dc19   88-25104

British Library Cataloguing in Publication Data is available.

Library of Congress Catalog Card Number: 88-25104
ISBN: 0-313-26355-8

First published in 1989

Greenwood Press, Inc.
88 Post Road West, Westport, Connecticut 06881

Printed in the United States of America

The paper used in this book complies with the
Permanent Paper Standard issued by the National
Information Standards Organization (Z39.48-1984).

10 9 8 7 6 5 4 3 2 1

Copyright Acknowledgments

The author and publisher wish to thank the following for
permission to use quotations from the following works:

From the book *The American Congress: The First Branch* by
Abner J. Mikva and Patti B. Saris. Copyright © 1983 by Abner J.
Mikva and Patti B. Saris. Reprinted with permission of the
publisher, Franklin Watts.

From *The Ralph Nader Congress Project* by Ralph Nader.
Copyright © 1975 by Ralph Nader. All rights reserved. Reprinted
by permission of Viking Penguin Inc.

From *Majority Leadership in the U.S. House* by Barbara Sinclair,
1983, by permission of The Johns Hopkins University Press.

From *The United States Congress: Organization and Procedure* by
Floyd M. Riddick, 1949, published by National Capital Publishers,
Inc. Reprinted by permission of Floyd M. Riddick.

From articles appearing in the 1982 and 1983 *Congressional
Quarterly Almanac*. Reprinted by permission of Congressional
Quarterly Inc.

Contents

Introduction

Congress wields enormous power. It directs taxing
and spending of a trillion dollar budget;
prescribes the federal laws regarding crime,
finance, welfare, natural resources, energy,
environment, and agriculture; commands creation of
public works; establishes civil rights through
statutes and proposed constitutional amendments;
conducts regular oversight of the executive
departments and occasional major investigations;
and functions as an active partner with the
President in making diplomatic, trade, and
military policy. For purposes of this book, it
does one other thing of importance: by deciding
what to take up and what not to take up, it sets
the nation's agenda.

In our democracy, the world's oldest
constitutional government, Congress has provided
the forum for two centuries of national debate.
Although we see Congress most clearly when it
acts, its greatest role may be when it does not
act. Impassioned arguments for change pour into
it from grievants in all regions, economic
spheres, and walks of life; from all officials
from the President and the Cabinet to the meanest
state and local governments. In the body politic,
some would change our foreign policy; some,
redistribute wealth; some, stimulate the economy;
some, roll back the federal government's say in
private and local matters; others, reshape our
health or criminal justice systems; and still

others, impose general codes of morality.
Conversely, upholders of the status quo in all
these areas rally to its defense. To all these
desires for change, Congress serves as the great
traffic cop. It defeats or stalls the vast
majority of proposals, sifts out the particular
changes supported at any time by the general will,
and puts these few changes through an obstacle
course that exposes them to all manner of
limitation and compromise to make them fit the
desires of interested groups and the public.

As Congress matters for the nation, so
procedure matters for Congress. The first chapter
of this book delves into the importance of
procedure. Procedure governs both the maintenance
of stability and the possibility of change. It
holds back proposals for new legislation by
imposing a thousand obstacles, stumbling blocks,
and filters. The committee system entrenches
present interests, forcing proposals for change
past a gauntlet of Members with specialization,
experience, and incentives to represent the status
quo interests.

Many of the procedures on the floor of the
House and Senate exist to preclude by-passing that
committee system. Other floor procedures exist to
make it difficult even for committee-blessed
measures to reach enactment. The tightly
organized House floor, with the filter of the
Rules Committee and the strict barrier of the
germaneness rule for amendments, blocks some types
of changes. The more loosely organized Senate,
with its hundred separate centers of objection and
filibuster, ambushes others.

Nevertheless, the system also creates the
possibility of change, even massive change. For
example, by its budget process, each year the
House and Senate may order their committees to
make major cuts in existing entitlement programs,
or they may require major changes in taxing and
spending. The very procedures which protect the
committee system have their exceptions, from the
House discharge petition to the Senate non-germane
amendment, which allow the House and Senate to
move legislation blocked in committee.

The importance of Congress and its procedure
might lead one to expect to find books
illuminating the subject. Without belittling the
existing literature addressing Congress as a whole

(as distinct from specific subtopics), it largely falls into two limited categories. On the one hand, Congress itself generates massive tomes collecting its procedural precedents. In the House, these are called the Hinds, Cannon, and Deschler precedents, and a unified collection of rules and precedents updated each Congress by the Parliamentarian is called the House Manual. In the Senate, the collection of Riddick's precedents has roughly a similar role.

These collections of precedents serve a vital function. They enable each chamber to maintain a steady course following the procedures it has established in the past. However, these collections simply have not been prepared to be useful except to the individual who already has a detailed understanding of Congressional procedure. For others, learning procedure from the books of precedents is like trying to learn English by reading a dictionary; the raw material is all there, but you have to know the language already to know how to put it together.

On the other hand, there are short popular works describing Congress.[1] These provide the general reader with a useful introduction to how Congress works. However, these works cannot lead the reader through the detail and complexity of Congressional procedure. The limitations of space and depth prevent the inclusion of much of the rules, history, applications, and exceptions.

In some areas, the gap between popular short works, and encyclopedic but difficult internal collections of precedents, is partly bridged over by specialized works. However, in many areas, no easy means for follow-up exists. Often, no specialized work exists. For example,[2] in the budget process, for most of the 1980s the best

---

[1] The most notable of these are W. Oleszek, <u>Congressional Procedure and the Policy Process</u> (3d ed. 1988), and L. A. Froman, <u>The Congressional Process</u>: Strategies, Rules, and Procedures (1967).

[2] That 1980 work was A. Schick, <u>Congress and Money:</u> <u>Budgeting, Spending and Taxing</u> (1980). The subsequent study was R. G. Penner and A. J. Abramson, <u>Broken Purse Strings:</u> <u>Congressional Budgeting, 1974-88</u> (1988).

specialized study was a work published in 1980.
For all its value, it did not, of course, address
any of the major changes in the process
subsequently, in the 1980s, in so rapidly evolving
a process. In the area of filibuster and cloture,
no existing specialized work seeks to explain
systematically the most striking development since
1975, the postcloture filibuster.

Other subjects have plenty of more
specialized works, but these do not focus on
procedure. For example, any number of historians
have written histories of the House of
Representatives which cover the better-known
historical episodes. However, such histories of
Congress often focus on dramatic substantive
enactments, not on the matters key for
understanding Congressional procedure. The arcane
House floor procedure can be better understood
from a study of how it arose in both the first and
second halves of the nineteenth century, but few
books examine the first half's procedural
contribution, or bring this together with current
procedure.

According, this work has an ambitious
scope. It covers procedure in the strict sense --
the rules and precedents for floor procedure,
including the budget and appropriations rules. In
addition, it seeks to describe <u>practice</u> in the
Congress -- how a bill passes, how an agenda is
carried out, how the budget proceeds. Such
practice matters more in many areas than the rules
and precedents. The rules tell little about the
functioning of the elected party leaderships of
either chamber or of the internal functioning of
committees. Rules and precedents by themselves
tell little about the daily use in the Senate of
unanimous consent agreements or in the House of
flexibly shaped special rules from the House Rules
Committee. They suggest nothing of how conference
committees function internally.

Describing practice requires going to sources
beyond the rules, the collections of precedents,
and the Congressional Record. It requires
descriptions of history, for the origins of
practices tell much about them. It requires using
books and articles by political scientists. It
requires massive use of Congressional Quarterly's
articles and annual almanacs, which provide a
running account by Members and observers about the

informal aspects of legislative action.

There is a special reason for making heavy use of citable primary and secondary sources. For much of what this book says, the author could perhaps have skipped use of such sources, and relied upon observation over the period since 1979 that he has worked in Congress. Many books about Congress have been written from just such personal observation. However, citation and quotation from the broad range of sources offers greater reliability. It draws together the wisdom of many rather than the beliefs of one. Moreover, it allows the interested reader to follow up with the range of sources on Congress.[3]

In Chapter 1, the book begins with an introduction to Congressional procedure. It opens with some of the underlying questions that haunt the subject: whether "procedure" in any rigorous sense even matters, or whether Congress simply acts by the exercise of power. Then, the chapter covers two overall perspectives, the "cast" -- executive and legislative figures and the sources of rules -- and the "temporal" perspective of the life of a Congress or a bill. While the history of particular aspects of Congressional procedure is discussed throughout the book, here an overall history of the central points in Congressional procedure is provided.

Chapter 2 addresses committee organization and jurisdiction. Congress organizes itself through rules establishing the jurisdiction of each committee, through assigning Members to each committee and subcommittee, and through choosing chairs for these bodies. These means of organization continue to operate dynamically after the structure is established, through referral of each bill, pursuant to these rules (and to the discretion they leave) to one or more committees. The 1970s and 1980s have witnessed

---

[3]   There is an additional reason for reliance on these sources. As lawyer for the Senate in 1979-84 and for the House since then, the author has been privy to a large number of descriptions by legislative "clients" of particular aspects of practice. Reliance on objective sources precludes the appearance or reality of revelation of privileged information.

many shakeups in these areas, including increasing
authority of subcommittees, greater use of
multiple referrals in the House, and
reorganization of the mechanisms for assigning
Members to committees.

Committees have been called "little
legislatures," and they have their own procedure,
described in Chapter 3. The power of committee
chairs and the influence of committee rules impose
a structure on committee and subcommittee
activity. Three familiar stages dominate
committee action: hearings, meetings for markup of
bills, and reporting. Here, too, the 1970s and
1980s have seen shifts in the balance of power
between full committee chairs and junior Members.

With this introduction and committee-level
foundation, the next three chapters, as a unit,
deal with House procedure. Chapter 4 begins with
an overview of how the House is run. Above all,
this addresses the procedural and political roles
of the Speaker, Majority Leader, Majority Whip
system, minority leadership, and similar party
organs. It deals with floor speeches, and the
mechanics of action on bills -- how bills get
introduced, referred, reported, calendared,
engrossed and enrolled.

Next, Chapter 5 looks at how the House sets
its agenda and structures its procedure. This is
largely the province of the Rules Committee, with
its many functions from deciding what amendments
to allow for any bill, to resolving turf battles
between committees. This has been the scene of
rapid evolution since the 1960s. The nuances of
the Rules Committee's use of special rules --
open, closed, or in-between ("complex") -- have
much to do with how the House operates. Besides
special rules, the House uses other enactment
processes: suspension of the rules, discharge, and
the specialized calendars.

When a bill comes to the House floor pursuant
to a "special rule," it sets out on the elaborate
procedural journey described in Chapter 6. That
chapter describes the mechanics of voting and
quorum calls, as well as the prologue to bill
passage: the adoption of a special rule.
Following such adoption comes amending of the bill
in the Committee of the Whole under the five
minute rule. Towering over other rules, the
germaneness rule sets the boundaries for how

tightly the House restricts its agenda and how
little the House permits tacking together of
dissimilar proposals.   After amending, the
Committee of the Whole rises, and the House
completes additional procedures before final
passage of a bill.   In all these steps, numerous
strategies and tactics have been devised to
advance and defeat variations from the reported
bill.
     Chapters 7, 8, 9, and 10 concern Senate
procedure.   This unit begins with an overview of
how the Senate is run, in Chapter 7.   The Majority
and Minority Leaders serve critical functions
here.   In the Senate, the Chair plays a small
role, not allowed the discretion in recognition
and the political tools possessed by the House
Speaker.   This chapter closes with mechanics of
speeches, quorum calls, and voting.
     An elaborate if informal system structures
the   agenda   of   the   Senate,   as   Chapter   8
describes.   The Majority Leader determines when a
new "legislative day" begins, when to move to
proceed to particular bills, and when to propose
complex unanimous consent agreements that may
structure a bill's consideration.   Conversely,
individual Senators can move legislative proposals
by   the   option   of   offering   non-germane
amendments.   Additionally, the Senate has a whole
separate procedure for "Executive Business,"
namely, advising and consenting to the President's
nominations and treaties.   The Senate parts
company with the House on most aspects of
management of its agenda, providing a major source
of diversity within Congress.
     Chapter 9 describes Senate amending on the
floor, which occurs through a largely consensual
system of managing floor progress.   Senators
possess a variety of tools in this process, the
most potent being the motion to table which brings
a swift kill to an amendment without a clear ("up-
or-down") vote, as well as the complex limits on
numbers and postures of pending amendments known
as the "amendment tree".
     Unique to the Senate is the procedure of
filibustering and cloture, described in Chapter
10.   The basic filibuster procedure consists
simply of talking a bill to death, but even at its
most basic, a filibuster must contend with many
rules and tactics.   Opponents of a filibuster may

impose cloture, with its complex procedures.
After 1976, the "postcloture" filibuster assumed
great importance.   Few areas involve so many
special situations, from filibusters on motions to
proceed, to the use of appeals as a dilatory
tactic.   The procedure of filibuster and cloture
has changed again and again since the early 1960s,
producing a current system that incorporates many
layers of historical evolution.

The existence of a bicameral legislature
necessitates means for the two chambers to agree
on bills, addressed in Chapter 11.   A bill can
simply be sent back and forth, the process known
as "amendments between houses," until the chambers
agree.   On important bills, the two chambers
create conference committees.   Since conference
outcomes depend largely on who attends conference,
the choice of conferees has much importance.   The
conference itself has few rules to restrict it,
but the House and Senate have special procedures
for adopting the report of the conference.   They
even have increasingly important "postconference"
procedures to maneuver around a conference report.

Finally, the last two chapters deal with the
procedures for money decisions.   Chapter 12
describes the budget process enacted into law in
1974 and rewritten by the Gramm-Rudman act in
1985.   Few areas of such importance change so
rapidly and involve such technicality as this
process.   The budget process starts with the
formulation of a budget resolution containing
tools such as aggregates, functions, committee
allocations (in the accompanying reports) and
reconciliation instructions.   Reconciliation
serves as the procedure for Congress to direct its
own committees to cut entitlement spending or to
increase taxes.   Especially after Gramm-Rudman,
budget procedure includes many points of order
and, not surprisingly, means to waive those points
of order.

Chapter 13 discusses the appropriations
process.   It describes how appropriations
coordinate with the budget process, through
procedures known as crosswalking and
suballocation. The appropriations process has its
own restrictions, such as the requirement of
authorizations -- other bills making the policy
decisions intended to precede the spending
decisions in the appropriation bills themselves.

Appropriations bills also face ambushes on the floor, through the offering of amendments that either add legislation directly, or impose limitations on the purposes of spending. This chapter ends with two creatures that have grown increasingly important, continuing resolutions and supplemental appropriations. These last two chapters on budget and appropriations serve to bring together all the preceding procedure and to confirm, by practical illustration, the importance of the procedures described in the prior chapters.

The writing of this book depended heavily upon the help of others. As a historic matter, the writer today stands on the shoulders of the giants of the past who created and systematized Congressional procedure. These started with Thomas Jefferson, who wrote the classic procedural manual in 1797-1801 still authoritative in the House today. On the House side, Asher Hinds and Clarence Cannon developed compilations of precedents (and in Cannon's case, an unequalled one volume description of House procedure). More recently, two House parliamentarians, Lewis Deschler and Wm. Holmes Brown, similarly created the post-1936 collections known as Deschler's precedents. On the Senate side, the figure of Floyd Riddick towers over all, both for his well-known thousand-page collection of Senate precedents, and for his 1949 book on both House and Senate procedure.

At a more personal level, I owe my training to Walter Kravitz, whose course in Congressional procedure shown a powerful light through the thick fog. Over the years, Alan Frumin, now Senate Parliamentarian, has devoted a generous share of his time to purging or at least combatting my misconceptions about Senate procedure. The numbers of Members and staff who have explained to me how particular procedures worked could not be counted. Among Members, Richard Bolling stands out; as the author of two books of his own, former chair of the House Rules Committee, inventor of the new system of complex special rules, leader of the House committee on reorganization of the committee system, and co-author of the 1974 budget act, his discussions with me shed great light on the whole range of procedural subjects.

Members whom I have served under and learned from in the Senate would include Robert Byrd, the unmatched master of Senate procedure and the hidden hand behind many careful modernizations since 1970, and Strom Thurmond, one of the wiliest of Senators, who chaired the Judiciary Committee during much of my representation of the Senate. In the House, my regular duties, and my service as Special Deputy Chief Counsel on the Iran-contra committee staff, allowed me to learn most from Tom Foley, an exceptionally learned as well as gifted leader, who could expound upon the parallels between a current situation and one in Parliament four centuries ago as easily as he could make a speech or debate an amendment; from Jack Brooks, whose piercing and tough commentary taught in pithy observations much of what these chapters laboriously detail; from Henry Hyde, admired user of the minority's prerogatives; and from Dick Cheney, author of his own work on House history.

Among staff, special mention is owed to George Van Cleve, Jim Horney, Hyde Murray, Gerry Siegel, Mike Epstein, and Charles Kinney. Wm. Holmes Brown, the House Parliamentarian, and Charles Johnson, the Deputy Parliamentarian, took much time from their heavy schedules to work over parts of a draft of the House procedure chapters. They offered invaluable suggestions on every level, from adjustments in footnoted descriptions of exceptions to technical rules, up to philosophical illumination about the role of the germaneness tests. Working with them is always a humbling experience, and much as I hope this book is helpful, no one should doubt that the Parliamentarian is the real fount of knowledge about House procedure.

I also received invaluable help from William Shook, a former staff attorney on both the House and Senate sides now in private practice, who took upon himself the prodigious labor of reading the entire manuscript; from Michael Harrison, an attorney working for the House Rules Committee who examined with care the House and conference chapters; and from Robert Keith, pre-eminent Congressional Research Service expert on the budget process, who gave a close and critical reading to the budget chapter. None of the aforementioned Members or staff bear any responsibility for any mistakes or inadequacies of the text, which solely belongs to the author, but they deserve much of the credit for what is right.

My debt is great to Georgetown University Law Center, at which I have taught a seminar on Congressional procedure each year (but one) since 1982. The scores of students who took that seminar over the years would be wrong if they indulged in the common student belief that professors crib their books from student term papers, but they would be right if they recognized how much the process of give and take with such a lively, irreverant and intelligent crew contributed to the thoughts in the book. I received precious and good-natured secretarial help from Beth Dutko, while my user-friendly assistant in wrestling with my word processor was the redoubtable Barbara Thoreson.

Much is owed to my two superiors in the Congress, Michael Davidson, Senate Legal Counsel, and Steven R. Ross, General Counsel to the Clerk of the House. Under them, I represented the Congress in litigation -- defending lawsuits against Members and staff, filing briefs ;for the Senate and House in separation of powers cases, advising investigations -- as Assistant Senate Legal Counsel in 1979-1984, and since 1984 as Deputy General Counsel to the Clerk of the House. In both offices, I was allowed and encouraged to continue this avocation of studying Congressional procedure notwithstanding our litigation responsibilities. Their assignments over the years, from defending the legislative veto, the Gramm-Rudman act, and the independent counsel statute, have provided a precious opportunity to live and feel the Congress's life as well as to study it. Michael Davidson and I came to the Senate at about the same time, and learned some of its mysterious ways together. Steven Ross, as a knowledgeable long-standing denizen of the House, led me in many journeys through the House maze, analyzing the most complicated and subtle of maneuvers down to what I could understand. In some hard times he was a true friend. Most helpful of all experiences was service as Special Deputy Chief Counsel on the House Iran-contra committee, in which it often seemed that whole lifetimes of experience were crammed into months or weeks.

During the major effort to complete this book, I received much help from the staff of Greenwood Press, notably Meg Fergusson, Nick

Allison, Neil Kraner, Margaret Brezicki, Maureen Melino, and especially Mildred Vasan, the Politics and Law Editor. Modern technology in the form of the word processor, although it seems sometimes to have made tremendous contributions to producing works of this length and documentation, at other times seems to intensified the production burden on the author past the supportable. Only the creative suggestions of these editors made that technology a servant (if at times a surly, manuscript-destroying one) rather than a master, and thereby made producing this manuscript possible.

My sister, Leonore Tiefer, herself a much-published author on psychology, applied her most therapeutic insights to encourage me many times to complete the long road to this work. My mother, Rosalind Tiefer, not only provided much additional support toward the same end, but used her background as an instructor in American history to prepare the index for this work, mastering some challenging word processing skills to produce it. She put a tremendous effort into the index, which I hope the reader will find a contribution in itself by one perfectly at home with historic Thomases from Jefferson to Wilson (who, the indexer learnedly correct me, is properly addressed as Thomas Woodrow Wilson). I also owe a great debt to Eva Kleederman, who somehow lived with a person whose idea of a good time for years seemed to be writing yet another hundred footnotes, as well as to supportive experts and friends who discussed the work many times, including Jeffrey Hoffstein, Yardena Mansoor, Peggy McFadden, Tambrey Matthews, Johnathan Cuneo, and Vicky Szerko.

Finally, the book owes a great deal to my father, Abraham David Tiefer. Throughout his life and labors, he cultivated an inquiring soul about national events. The text of his lesson to me was that public affairs is an ennobling as well as entertaining study. This book is for him.

Congressional Practice and Procedure

1
Basic Themes of Congressional Procedure

A. THE MYSTERY OF CONGRESSIONAL PROCEDURE[1]

Does Congressional Procedure Exist?

To start by asking whether the subject of congressional procedure even exists may seem strange. However, one may well ask whether organized procedure really matters, or whether mere arbitrary and irregular exercise of power runs the Capitol. A skeptic about congressional procedure can contrast it with civil procedure in the federal courts. Judicial procedure has numerous factors reinforcing its orderliness and stability: the judges have lifetime tenure and complete disinterest in the cases; they act with the aid of trained lawyers, and the parties cannot exert pressure to obtain favoritism.

---

[1] Sources frequently cited in this chapter include R. H. Davidson and W. J. Oleszek, Congress and its Members (1981) (Davidson and Oleszek); How Our Laws Are Made, H. Doc. No. 158, 99th Cong., 2d Sess. (1966) (How Our Laws Are Made) Congressional Quarterly, Origins and Development of Congress (1976) (Origins and Development); G. B. Galloway, History of the House of Representatives (1976) (Galloway); J. H. Birnbaum and A. S. Murray, Showdown at Gucci Gulch: Lawmakers, Lobbyists, and the Unlikely Triumph of Tax Reform (1987) (Birnbaum and Murray).

Congress operates quite differently. Many key congressional procedures operate without procedural rulings at all, only through what political figures decide -- for instance, Members' assignments to committees, deciding the floor agenda, and bargaining in conference committees. The presiding officers of the House and Senate either possess power because, in the case of the Speaker of the House, they lead the majority party, or are quite weak because, in the case of the Vice President who presides over the Senate, other leaders -- the party leaders -- have the real power. In either chamber, no one would confuse party leaders with judges. Far from having lifetime tenure, they are always accountable to their political organizations. Far from being disinterested, they are vitally interested in keeping sharp the tools of politics -- sensitivity to public opinion, rewarding of loyalty and punishment of opposition, readiness to make deals, and skill in handling the application of influence. Members of Congress do not approach proceedings like trial lawyers, with a requirement of training and a general standard of procedural expertise. Some know procedure well, but many do not, for the primary concern of Members is politics, not procedure.

A skeptic knowledgeable about Congress operations would challenge its orderliness in countless ways. While the federal courts follow written Federal Rules of Civil Procedure, the Senate and House often honor their own written rules only in the breach. The Senate and House have not followed their formal scheduling rules, which read like tracts from a bygone era, for decades.[2] In both chambers, extraordinary deviations from ordinary procedure are common: major bills that zip through in minutes without

---

[2]   When bills come to the floor, the chambers tend to devise ad hoc procedures rather than following their rules; Senate bills proceed by unanimous consent, House bills by "special rules" from the Rules Committee. The Senate, in particular, is notorious for ignoring violations of the rules, waiving the rules by unanimous consent, and overruling the Chair on the occasions when it makes procedural rulings.

debate, greased by special arrangments; Senate
filibusters disorganizing the chamber's operation;
unrelated riders jammed onto omnibus bills;
strained bill drafting and other pressures used to
circumvent committee jurisdictional rules; and a
host of other extraordinary practices.

Does this mean there is no congressional
procedure, only the arbitrary exercise of power?
It must be remembered that even judicial
procedure, with its ordered and regular aspects,
only sets the stage for relatively arbitrary
decisions by that other great democratic
institution, the jury.[3] Regular and orderly
procedure exists outside the courthouse; there is
procedure through international law in the game of
nations, procedure through commercial law in the
economic jungle, and procedure through labor law
in the conflict of labor and management. The
metaphor of boxing applies here: procedure can
serve a vital function in merely "holding the
ring" -- establishing an orderly framework around
an arena, and certain limited rules within the
arena -- even though within that arena
arbitrariness, power, and force decide outcomes.

Moreover, notwithstanding the difference
between courts (and even sports) and legislatures,
powerful needs push the Congress into maintaining
a somewhat regular procedure. The author of a
leading short work on Congressional procedure
notes the basic functions such procedure serves:
"to provide stability, legitimize decisions,
divide responsibilities, reduce conflict, and
distribute power."[4] Thomas Jefferson, in writing
his great manual two centuries ago, emphasized the
importance of procedure both as "a shelter and

---

[3]   Trial lawyers well know that juries, however
conscientious and however much harangued by courts with
(unintelligible) instructions, often act on the basis of
irrelevant factors, evidence that they were told to
disregard, prejudiced stereotypes, and methods of compromise
that they were told not to use.

[4]   W.J. Oleszek, Congressional Procedure and the Policy
Process 5 (3d ed. 1989).

protection to the minority, against the attempts of power," and "that there may be uniformity of proceeding in business."[5]   The scale of Congress business, the need for public acceptance of its legitimacy, the requirement that the same Members do business with each other year after year, provide potent incentives for order.

Most important of all, procedural order solves a fundamental problem in the American political system.   While the national parties organize national politics, individual Members follow their states' and districts' interests and their own perspectives, rather than the party line.   In other words, the United States has a "weak" party system.   Thus, although the majority party leaderships must run the chambers, frequently the opposition, not the majority party leadership, has an actual voting majority on particular propositions.   In either chamber, a conservative coalition of southern Democrats and Republicans often outvotes the "national" Democratic leadership; conversely, moderate coalitions, or for that matter regional or issue-specific coalitions, may outvote any leadership.

Congressional procedure provides stability despite this weak party system.   Very simply, both sides, or all sides, can win occasionally, without the government falling, because congressional procedure provides for easy alternation in success.   Congressional procedure favors certain powerful institutions that play functional roles within the Congress, in fact that procedure gives those institutions much of their strength -- institutions like the party leaderships, the committees, and the managers of bills.   At the same time, orderly procedure provides safety valves for successful opposition coalitions.   Such safety valves include offering of Senate non-germane amendments, getting amendments adopted in either chamber, Senate "holds," filibusters, committee discharge, defeat of House special rules, and defeating bills on final passage.

---

[5]   House Manual § 284 (first section of Jefferson's Manual, quoting a Speaker of the House of Commons).

Thus, the majority party leadership can set an agenda for the chamber without falling over defeats; the opposition can resist and win, at times, without being oppressed. Congressional procedure keeps a dynamic balance, with majority advantages and yet minority rights, powers of control and yet tolerance of resistance, preservation of past patterns and yet responsiveness to change. The heart of congressional procedure consists of the various procedures by which the majority's powers -- agenda control and bill management -- balance against the legitimate means for opposition resistance.

Moreover, this dynamic balance legitimates the government, and its new laws. It legitimates the government because the source of legitimacy in our democracy is, firstly, the will of the majority, and the Congress' procedures allow the representatives of the majority to work their will -- to do what the people want. At the same time, the system consists of many and varied obstacles and screens. Before a majority in each chamber passes a bill, both the majority, and the bill, must run a veritable marathon -- through committees, past the party-controlled gates to the floor, across the battlefield of floor consideration and the many techniques for stalling, changing, or killing bills.

In the end, the majority which backs a bill can differ substantially from the one which backed it originally. The bill may get larger in scope, or more modest; more or less expensive; more or less pointed in its ideology; more or less helpful to a particular region or to interest groups. As the bill changes, so does the coalition which supports it. Thus not only is the bill as finally passed the will of the majority, but the majority which passes it has itself metamorphosed during the consideration process, making it the current expression of a vast array of competing political considerations and hence an eminently legitimate expression of the current political balance.

If the enactment process is to legitimize both the passage of new laws and the retention of old ones, it must satisfy expectations on all sides of fair play -- both in techniques of control, and techniques of resistance -- and must meet standards by which both sides judge whether those expectations are being fulfilled. Although both chambers know their leaders are partisan, both chambers expect rulings from the Chair with objectivity and neutrality. Each chamber has written rules supplemented by precedents and practices which it expects its Chair to follow. Each chamber has an expert and neutral Parliamentarian to hold those rulings together despite their often confused and heated context.

It is true that a great deal of Congress operation does not occur on the floor, and that many floor actions follow other than written rules. That is part of why there has not previously been a full-length treatise attempting, as here, to explore the interaction of formal procedures and the informal operating practices. However, procedure exists despite the deviations and uncodified practices; those just make description more challenging. The Senate and House leaderships may arrange their scheduling outside their chambers' outdated written rules on the subject, but they do so through regular and orderly channels. The Senate and House may devise ad hoc procedures for each bill, but as might be expected for a system that handles hundreds of bills each Congress, the ad hoc procedures themselves follow standard forms with limited variations.[6] In sum, not every aspect of congressional procedure is orderly, but there is something orderly in every aspect of congressional procedure -- and a great deal of order and regularity in the system as a whole.

---

[6] "Extraordinary" deviations from ordinary procedures may occur all the time, but even "extraordinary" deviations often can be seen to follow patterns laid down by precedent and standard forms: bills "zipped" through often follow particular channels long provided for certain bills, Senate filibusters have a long history and classic patterns, "riders" jammed onto omnibus bills get on by familiar rules and arrangements, and the twists and turns of manipulation of committee jurisdiction occur within an elaborate system to steer thousands of bills.

Importance

Another question is how much procedure matters. A short answer begins by examining the key screens and decision points in Congress, which promote or retard legislation in quite different ways: committee jurisdiction, floor scheduling, bill management on the floor, conference, and the budget and appropriations cycle.

The press often presents congressional procedure as a matter of lost trivia collected by antiquarians. Press accounts depict congressional procedure as divorced from the real world and as a mere screen for the operationof power which is overriden by political will whenever inconvenient. For example, the Washington _Post_ took an episode in the evolution of the Senate's two-speech rule (described below as a minor element in filibuster and cloture battles) and painted it thusly:

> The Senate stumbled over a 50-year-old precedent last week, became ensnared in it and, in a debate studded with flares of bad temper, struggled for six hours and 10 minutes to free itself . . . .
>
> [After the Chair cited an old precedent, Senator] Hollings erupted: "I respectfully, disrespectfully I should say, object to that ruling. That is babble from the parliamentarian . . . ."
>
> The precedent had been set, the parliamentarian disclosed, on June 12, 1935 . . . . And it was all set down, said the chair, in footnote 487 on page 626 of the book, "Senate Procedure."
>
> [After a new precedent was made, the article concluded:] [A] precedent, hidden in a footnote for 51 years, was put to rest.[7]

---

[7]   Knutson, _Senate Stumbles, Breaks Precedent_, Washington Post, Oct. 1, 1986, at A17.   The citation mocked in the article could not be clearer:
(footnote continued)

To be sure, congressional procedure includes enormous numbers of obscure precedents collected in the many volumes of House precedents compiled by Hinds, Cannon, and Deschler, and in the thousand-page compendium of Senate precedents authored by Dr. Riddick. However, most of those precedents are not at the heart of congressional procedure. The parliamentarians must compile them all to maintain correctly the system, but at the heart of congressional procedure lie a few actively followed rules and practices, dealing with the major loci of powers mentioned above.

The first of these loci of power over bills consists of the committees. Disputes over which committees control what bills could be dismissed as trivial "turf battles" if the subject lacked importance. Yet committee jurisdiction rules divide up power in a very tangible way, like jurisdictional rules for federal and state courts or the rules separating military and civilian control. These rules distribute power to particular groups, which differ ideologically and regionally. Which committee controls a subject determines who will possess power, what -- if anything -- will be done, and who will benefit.

For example, civil rights bills live or die on whether they circumvent hostile committees. The fate of a strict pesticide safety bill depends on whether it goes to a friendly environmental committee, or a hostile agricultural committee. The jurisdiction of committees over bills aimed at imports decides whether the nation follows free trade or protectionist policies. Multi-billion

---

If a Senator in possession of the floor yields to another Senator to make a motion to recess or makes such a motion himself he would lose the floor, and would have no prior right to recognition, and if recognized again, it would be his second speech.[487/]

[487/] See June 12, 1935, 74-1, Record, p. 9127.

Riddick at 626 & n.487.

dollar arms programs, with major strategic importance, and with national redistribution of profits and jobs, get adopted or shelved, depending on whether control comes to lie in the armed services committees, the defense appropriation subcommittees, or the military construction subcommittees.

A second locus of power, "floor scheduling" could be and will be described as "agenda control." Congress sets national priorities, and determines national issues, above all by its agenda system -- its decisions about what national issues to take up at any particular time out of the enormous variety of political issues mooted. Agenda control by pro-business forces meant that little economic welfare legislation passed after the Progressive Era until the New Deal; agenda control by southern Members meant that little in the way of strong civil rights legislation passed during the three quarters of a century from the Force Bills in the 1890s until the Civil Rights Act of 1964; agenda control in the House by pro-labor forces prevented a rollback of labor legislation even at the peak of President Reagan's authority in 1981-82.

The other branches of government have their agenda power: the President focuses national attention on a handful of issues, the Supreme Court picks a relative handful of legal questions to take up. Even compared to these, Congress' agenda control is one of the greatest powers in the government. The House and the Senate each have elaborate procedures and practices determining how much the party leaderships control national priorities through floor scheduling. Such seemingly technical institutions and procedures as the House Rules Committee and suspension calendar, and the Senate motion to proceed, unanimous consent agreement, and non-germane amendment, play major roles in this process of setting national priorities.

On the floor of the House and Senate, power is balanced between the bill managers, typically committee chairs, who "manage" and promote a bill as reported, and their opponents who seek to amend or defeat the bill. Always lurking behind these figures are the party leaders, who may, when they choose, have a strong impact on floor proceedings, supporting -- or not -- the bill managers. The rules concerning amendments, such as the germaneness rule in the House or the "amendment trees" in each chamber, include many of the hoariest, driest, and most obscure of precedents. Yet those procedures often determine what kinds of alternatives the Congress will consider, and which ones will be favored for passage. On issues where national sentiment -- and congressional sentiment -- is divided, those rules can tip the balance on what Congress does. For example, for years in the early 1980s the House found itself closely divided on bills to fund the Nicaraguan contras; what it decided each time hinged to a considerable degree on the floor procedures for amendments on each bill that came up -- and on the skill of the two sides in using those procedures.

"The conference committee is sometimes popularly referred to as the 'Third House of Congress.'"[8] Whatever the House and Senate do on an important bill, the conference committee will write a third version, which has a very high probability of being the last word. Conference bargaining does not follow any procedure -- it is as pure an exercise in negotiation as can be found. However, a number of crucial procedures surround the conference committee, to decide who picks conferees, how the bill goes to conference, how the chambers adopt conference reports, the limits on what conference committees can do -- and the end runs around those limits -- and the rules that limit those end runs -- and so on in an extraordinarily complex process.

Finally, the budget and appropriations cycle has a surpassing importance and a procedure of its own to match. Its importance comes from the enormous size of the federal budget, and from the massive amounts of legislation attached to money bills.[9] Appropriations bills, as the annual

---

[8]   How Our Laws are Made at 38.

(footnote continued)

spending bills, follow a special procedure that
has evolved over two centuries, yet has passed
through many changes in the past two decades.
Since the 1970s, the increasing use of continuing
resolutions which wrap many appropriation bills
together in one package has, at times, altered the
very nature of legislating, from a piecemeal
exercise subject to floor amendments and
Presidential veto challenge, to an exercise in
backstage creation of an omnibus measure
impervious to floor tampering and too massive for
Presidential impact.

   In sum, the existence of vast congeries of
old and obscure precedents no more trivializes all
of procedure than the existence of thousands of
obscure words in comprehensive dictionaries
trivializes the English language. Congressional
procedure is the language of legislative action;
its central aspects can be separated from the
details, and they have at least the meaningfulness
and the importance -- if not more -- possessed by
civil procedure as the language of the courts and
international law as the language of diplomacy.
   Later sections in this chapter will lay the
groundwork for a detailed exploration of that
procedure in subsequent chapters. The next
section summarizes the background of procedure:
the structures, the executive and legislative
"cast," and the sources of rules. After that, the
following section provides some temporal
perspectives on procedure, looking at a whole
Congress, the passage of a "regular" bill, and the
passage of an "irregular" bill. Finally, the last
section provides a unified overview of the history
of congressional procedure, to set the context for
the histories of particular procedures in the
chapters that follow.

---

9 The budget process itself dates back only to 1974, yet it
has evolved at a furious pace, with late-1970s procedure
unrecognizable in the 1980s, and 1980s procedure changed by
the Gramm-Rudman bills in 1985 and 1987.

B.   THE BACKGROUND

This section describes the basic background of congressional operations -- the roles of the President and agencies, the nature of the two chambers, the leaders and committees, and the various sources of rules. All this was assumed in the previous section and will be assumed throughout. The goal here is not completeness, which would require a whole treatise on American politics, or special insight, but merely a basic minimum statement of the underlying constitutional and political elements. Given the brevity of this section, most of what is said should be very familiar.

The Executive "Cast"

The American government derives its structure from the doctrines established in 1789 by the Framers of the Constitution of separation of powers, and checks and balances. As the Constitution establishes the government, Congress functions quite independently of the other two branches, the executive and the judiciary. This is very different from other countries, as one commentator noted in contrasting American government with the parliamentary system:

> The strength and independence of Congress contrast sharply with the position of legislatures in other democratic countries. In most, policy making is concentrated in the hands of a prime minister and cabinet who are normally elected members of the legislature and are leaders of the majority party. . . .
>
> The U.S. Congress, by contrast, is elected separately from the president and has independent policy-making authority.[10]

A classic legal statement of each branch's function is that the Congress makes the laws, the

---

[10]   W. J. Oleszek, supra, at 5.

President executes them, and the courts interpret them.[11] Yet Congress' function has evolved not to be merely lawmaking but, more broadly, "representation."   As a political scientist observes, Congress is the

> forum where the interests and demands of all groups in society are expressed. A member of Congress is expected to act as a spokesperson for the ethnic, economic, religious, political, and professional groups within his or her geographic district . . . .
>
> [It is] the duty of members of Congress not only to . . . vot[e] . . . but also to express the interests of electoral minorities when participating in debate, casework, and other activities.   Associated with this conception of representation are the ideas of decentralization, access of a vast number of groups to the government, and predominance of local interests over some national interest expressed through presidential elections and national parties . . . .[12]

Contrasting the President and the Congress shows the significance of Congress' representational function. The President is a single elected national leader, chosen in a national referendum, who addresses the national audience as a whole. As one individual, he has physical limits preventing him from dealing directly with any but a very tiny portion of the diverse population. The President develops a national program which constitutes his balance of

---

[11] For discussions of separation of powers, see, e.g., L. Fisher, Constitutional Dialogues (1988); L. Fisher, Constitutional Conflicts Between Congress and the President (1985); W. T. Reveley, War Powers of the President and Congress (1981); L. Henkin, Foreign Affairs and the Constitution (1972); A. M. Schlesinger, Jr., The Imperial Presidency (1974); The Tethered Presidency: Congressional Restraints on Executive Power (T. M. Franck ed. 1981).

[12] D. J. Vogler, The Politics of Congress 11-12 (4th ed. 1983).

the aggregate needs of the nation.   While the
President, assisted by those who work for him,
know of many of the local or particular interests,
their primary task is to establish unified
positions and to carry out goal-oriented missions,
both through a hierarchical structure.   Such a
hierarchical organization cannot be expected to
carry out well its primarily unified tasks, and at
the same time to convey the diversity of
perspectives of numerous localities to represent
faithfully the nation's enormous multiplicity of
interests.

In contrast, Congress has 535 Members, most
chosen in relatively local elections.   The Members
remain attuned to the varieties of interest groups
through their individual campaigning and the
thousands of committee hearings and more informal
meetings each year.   Congress provides a diverse
focus for the media, which can cover the countless
actions of the individual Members and committees,
as well as numerous hours of debates of the whole
chamber, particularly because the Members largely
address specialized, or local, rather than
national audiences.   Thus Congress, rather than
the President, primarily satisfies the desire of
local or particular interests to separately make
their position felt in the formulation of
policy.   A President can best handle a swift
response to a foreign country's aggression, but he
can hardly be expected to devise a farm law, or a
procedure for formulating such a law, that will
respond to all the multitudinous interests at
stake in such a law.

Besides the separation of powers with its
independence and differentiation of President and
Congress, a second chief characteristic of the
American government relevant to congressional
procedure is the "weak party" system, as noted in
the previous section.   Most democratic governments
in the world follow the strong party system, in
which individual legislators vote as their party
directs, and a majority party (or coalition) wins
all the important votes as long as it is in
power.   As soon as the majority party in a
parliamentary system loses an important vote, a
"vote of confidence," the government falls,
requiring either a new election or at least a new
government (perhaps by a rearranged coalition of
the elements of the prior government).

By contrast, in the weak party system of the
United States, substantive votes occur less often
along strict party lines. Rather, Members return
to Congress as long as they can persuade their own
state or district to reelect them.   Voters pay
only   limited   attention   to   party   labels   or
positions, being as much or more interested in the
Members' image (presented in personal campaigning
and   in   the   media),   representation   of   the
district's   economic   and   other   interests,   and
constituent service.   Substantive defeats by the
majority party leadership on particular bills have
much   less   significance   than   in   parliamentary
systems.   Defeats do not represent any loss of
"confidence" and do not lead to new elections or
to any significant reorganization; majority party
leadership   successes,   defeats,   and   compromises
occur on the floor in rapid succession while the
structure of the government and the operation of
the Congress continue unchanged.   As discussed,
the   weak   party   system   gives   congressional
procedure much of its importance as the balance
between the organizational prerogatives of party
and committee leaders, and opposition rights.
     This discussion of separation of powers and
the weak party system has emphasized that the
President   does   not   control   Congress   either
formally   through   legal   powers,   or   informally
through party organization. Law and politics both
keep Congress independent of the President, and
the   President   has   only   such   influence   over
Congress as he earns. Nevertheless, the President
has formidable means for earning such influence,
which give him a major role. His public stature,
ability to command media attention, direction of
the executive agencies, control over the details
of spending, patronage powers, position in his own
party, and numerous other resources for rewarding
and punishing all serve to induce Congress to pay
him heed.
     Moreover,   the   Constitution   gives   him   one
potent control over legislation: each bill enacted
by the Congress comes to him for signature or
veto, providing him with considerable power to
negate Congressional action he does not want and
to bargain for what he wants. Since Congress can
only override a veto by a two-thirds vote of each
House, which is a high burden, it can rarely pass
bills over Presidential resistance.   On the other

hand, the President can only veto bills as a whole, and not items. Thus, his veto often creates a bargaining situation when Congress combines items he opposes by attaching them to bills he supports. This has created part of the dynamics of congressional procedure in the 1980s, in which much legislation passes in the form of a few giant omnibus bills, like budget reconciliation bills and continuing resolutions. By packaging much legislation into omnibus bills, Congress forces the President to accept or to reject the product as a whole, making it more difficult for him to bargain over particular items.

As a result of the President's many sources of power, his program is usually, though not always, the single greatest influence on the congressional agenda. The congressional leadership's relationship with him is a major source of its own authority. Views of the Administration are given weight in the consideration of all legislation. In particular, the budget and appropriation cycle starts with the President's budget, and often follows it in many aspects. Still, in all the operations of Congress, the President is off-stage. His influence occurs through many channels, particularly the party leaderships, but he does not act directly on legislation (except at the veto stage).

Below the President are the host of executive agencies which administer the laws -- departments headed by Cabinet members, and various free-standing and independent agencies, government corporations, and other governmental entities. In his three-sided relationship with the agencies and Congress, the President possesses many tools for keeping the agencies in line with his own legislative agenda, notably the system of central clearance of all agencies' formal expressions of views on proposed legislation, run by the Office of Management and Budget.

Nevertheless, to some extent, the agencies have their own policy agendas distinct from the President's. Agencies want to avoid restrictive or "interfering" legislation, to continue and to

expand their missions, and to secure funding that
is at least constant and hopefully increased.
Agencies and interest groups often come together
with the congressional committees of jurisdiction
to form "subgovernments" or "iron triangles" --
strong alliances to promote shared interests that
resist control by the President, the rest of the
Congress, or the general public.[13]

The Legislative "Cast"

Turning to Congress, and especially the
significance of its structure for this book's
sequence, the Constitution created a bicameral
legislature with a separate Senate and House.
Each chamber debates bills for itself in committee
and on the floor, paying only such heed to
developments in the other chamber as it wishes.
Large numbers of bills pass one chamber but die in
the other, and it is a rare bill of importance
that passes the two chambers in the same form.
Thus, a conference committee or other mechanism to
work out a compromise version of the two chambers'
product is often necessary.

To do its own work, each chamber has its own
leaders, committees, staff, rules, precedents, and
informal operating mechanisms. A fundamental fact
of life of congressional procedure is that Senate
and House procedure are completely different,
necessitating one set of chapters to describe
House floor procedure, while another set describes
Senate floor procedure. Even those aspects of
procedure that run sufficiently similarly in both

---

[13] For example, a President may propose a budget cut for
some agency, and can require that the agency publicly
testify in favor of that budget cut, but in private, agency
administrators may cooperate with sympathetic Members of
Congress in preventing the budget cut. Presidential
directions or suggestions to the agencies can be delayed or
diluted, particularly with the cooperation of outside
interest groups and the congressional committees of
jurisdiction. Davidson & Oleszek at 349-50, and sources
cited; M. Fiorina, Congress: Keystone of the Washington
Establishment (1977).

chambers to be described in single chapters for the whole Congress -- committee jurisdiction and procedure, conference procedure, and budget and appropriations procedure -- have separate sections or units to address differences between the House and Senate.

Each chamber's distinctive procedure reflects that chamber's unique genius.   The House of Representatives consists of 435 Representatives, each from a district of uniform population (now over half a million persons).   Each Representative is elected for two years, and the entire House is up for election every two years, giving many Representatives a never-ending preoccupation with impending reelection and thus with the political concerns of the moment.   The House's size and the Members' preoccupation with current concerns would lead to anarchy if House procedure did not provide strongly centralized direction.   Thus, the House defers considerably to its committees, screens all bills through the Rules Committee, vests its majority leadership with much control, and processes bills on the floor under tight procedures that move bills quickly.

The Senate consists of 100 Senators, two from each of the 50 states, with six-year terms staggered so that only one-third of the Senate is up for election every two years.   The Framers modeled the Senate to some extent on the British House of Lords, with the expectation that Senators' longer terms would insulate them from passions of the moment.   When the Senate established its procedure, it expected Senators to be free from a need or desire for discipline.   Due to the smaller size of the Senate, and this expected insulation, Senate procedure does not give the majority a free hand to carry out its will, but allows much greater rights than in House procedure for the minority party and for individual Senators.   Individual Senators not in the leadership, even junior Senators in the minority party, may have a say in the agenda through their ability to offer non-germane amendments, to withhold the unanimous consent necessary for many procedural steps, and ultimately to filibuster.

In recent years, many Senators have felt keenly the pressures of reelection, and the Senate as a whole has become somewhat like the House in sensitivity to popular will and media attention. There has been some breakdown in traditions of deference and comity, and the Senate has appeared at times to face a real crisis in governance, manifested in frequent filibusters on less important bills, greater difficulty in obtaining unanimous consent, and difficulty in processing even vital bills such as appropriations. Some of the tasks that the Senate floor could handle have instead been shifted to a later phase, the conference committee deliberations. The chapters on Senate procedure address these problems in detail.

Within each legislative chamber, the Members organize themselves in their two parties by the election of party leaders. The party leaders play a visible and highly important role in congressional procedure. In the House, the most important party leaders are the Speaker, the Majority Leader, and the Majority Whip, and the Minority Leader and Minority Whip. In the Senate, the most important party leaders are the Majority Leader and Majority Whip, and the Minority Leader and Minority Whip.

Politically, the leaders serve as spokesmen to the media, liaison to the President, and articulators of their Members' consensus. Within the chambers, they control scheduling, direct the daily operation of the floor, give party cues on substantive voting, and exercise some control over committee assignments. The particular procedures of the Senate and House endow the leaders in each chamber with various powers, such as the Speaker's powers to make bill referrals and his influence over the Rules Committee, and the Senate Majority Leader's prerogatives of priority in recognition and making of the motions to proceed. In light of the major role of the leadership, most of the chapter on House organization is devoted to the House leadership, and most of the chapter on Senate organization is devoted to the Senate leadership.

Congress' enormous work and power and its

representational role necessitate a division of labor by which particular subjects go to particular committees. In each chamber there are about 15 major committees, each with a separately defined jurisdiction. These divide, in turn, into a hundred or more subcommittees, also generally having defined jurisdictions. Each committee and subcommittee has both majority and minority members, with a chair from the majority party and a ranking minority member from the minority party who lead the committee.

Each bill starts when a Member introduces it, then goes by referral of the Presiding Officer to a committee (sometimes to more than one). The committees allow most bills to die, study a limited number at hearings, and "mark up" (amend) and report a select group for consideration by the full House or Senate on the floor. Even after reporting bills to their full chambers, the committees continue to have a significant voice, both in floor proceedings, and then in resolving differences with the other chamber through conference committees. In light of the dominant influence of committee operations on congressional actions, a chapter is devoted to committee jurisdiction, another to committee procedure, and a third to conference procedure.

Serving the committees and individual Members are thousands of congressional staff. The staff do much of the low-level legislative work in Congress: organizing the committee hearings and meetings; dealing with interest groups and the media; drafting the bills and reports; preparing floor speeches; keeping track of the tangled course of legislation; and handling much of the bargaining on minor points. While political science commentators have given congressional staff increasing attention,[14] the staff have virtually no formal role in Congress' floor operations, and accordingly do not receive

---

[14] For studies regarding the importance of congressional staff see M. J. Malbin, Unelected Representatives (1980); H. W. Fox & S. W. Hammond, Congressional Staffs: the Invisible Force in American Lawmaking (1977).

separate   attention   in   the   discussion   of
congressional procedure.

The Sources of Rules

Analytically, congressional procedure flows
from the Constitution.   As alluded to above, the
Constitution   sets   the   stage   by   prescribing   a
separate President and Congress, and separate
House of Representatives and Senate.[15]   More
directly, on a number of key points the
Constitution itself sets forth the procedure to be
followed   in   Congress.   Article   I   of   the
Constitution explicitly requires a majority of
each chamber as a quorum to do business; specifies
that   one-fifth   of   the   Members   can   demand   a
recorded vote; requires the keeping of a journal;
and gives the Congress control over its own
adjournment.[16]   It lets the House choose its own
Speaker, but puts the Vice President over the
Senate,[17] a difference which has led to a strong
presiding officer in the former and a weak one in
the   latter.   The   first   article   provides   the
procedure for enacting legislation by the same
bill passing both chambers and then being
submitted to the President, who can veto it, in
which case it will become law only "if approved by

---

[15] The Constitution prescribes most of the powers of the
President in Article II, and most of the powers of the
Congress in Article I (leaving aside various shared and
miscellaneous powers).   It sets forth the basic procedures
for presidential elections in Article II, section 1, which
have been modified by the XIIth (separate election of
President and Vice President) and XXth ("lame duck")
amendments.   It sets forth the basis for election of
Congressmen in Article I, section 2 (House) and Amendment
XIX (Senate).   The basic natures of the two chambers are set
forth in Article I, sections 2 (House) and 3 (Senate).

[16] The provision regarding quorums is in Art. I, sec. 5,
cl. 1; regarding recorded votes and the Journal, in cl. 3;
and regarding adjournment, in cl. 4.

[17] Art. I, sec. 2, cl. 5 (Speaker); sec. 3, cl. 4 (Vice
President and Senate).

two thirds of [both] House[s]."[18]   Most important,
it provides that "Each House may determine the
Rules of its Proceedings,"[19] which authorizes each
chamber to establish the details of its procedure
in written rules and precedents.

Turning to these sources of detailed
procedure, at the beginning the Senate and House
borrowed their formal procedure largely from the
British Parliament (primarily the House of
Commons).[20]   Thomas Jefferson prepared his Manual
of Parliamentary Practice, for use when he
presided over the Senate as Vice President from
1797 to 1801, by citation to the rulings and
actions of Parliament.[21]   Both chambers have
relied on Jefferson's Manual,[22] as well as on

---

[18]   Art I, sec. 7, cl.2.

[19]   Art. I, sec. 5, cl. 2 (which also gives the force to
back this up: each House may also "punish its Members for
disorderly Behaviour, and, with the concurrence of two
thirds, expel a Member").

[20]   Members of Congress followed Parliament's procedure both
by directly taking Parliament as a guide, and indirectly by
following colonial and state legislatures which themselves
took Parliament as a guide.   For a discussion of some
aspects of colonial legislatures, see M. P. Clarke,
Parliamentary Privilege in the American Colonies (1943).

[21]   In fact, Jefferson's "Manual is regarded by English
parliamentarians as the best statement of what the law of
Parliament was at the time Jefferson wrote it."   House
Manual § 284.   Jefferson relied principally on the best
contemporary eighteenth-century treatise, J. Hatsell's
Precedents of Proceedings in the House of Commons.

[22]   The House of Representatives officially endorsed
Jefferson's Manual as its procedure in 1837, by a rule still
in effect as amended, Rule XLII:

The rules of parliamentary practice comprised in
Jefferson's Manual and the provisions of the
Legislative Reorganization Act of 1946, as amended,
shall govern the House in all cases to which they are
applicable, and in which they are not inconsistent with
(footnote continued)

other treatises on Parliament.[23]

However, the first House and Senate soon set about developing procedures quite different from Britain's, and the chambers developed their procedures in three ways. The House and Senate promulgated their own written rules, starting with short initial sets in the first Congress. Each chamber made many major changes in the procedure through changes in the rules, such as the House's perfection of the motion for the previous question in 1890, or the Senate's adoption of a cloture rule in 1917. Scarcely a Congress went by without at least minor changes in the written rules, and both chambers made periodic large-scale revisions: the House in 1811, 1822, 1837, 1860, 1880, 1911, 1931, 1946, and 1970;[24] the Senate in 1806, 1820, 1828, 1868, 1877, 1884, 1946, 1970, and 1979.[25]

---

the standing rules and orders of the House and joint rules of the Senate and House of Representatives.

The Senate does not follow Jefferson's Manual as controlling (see Riddick, "Debate: Jefferson's Manual Does not Control Senate Debate," at 603), but as Dr. Riddick himself noted, "the procedure of both bodies [Senate and House] is basically founded on Jefferson's Manual of Parliamentary Practice," F. Riddick, The United States Congress 328 (1949).

[23]   A commentator wrote in 1896 regarding other procedural reference works that "[s]ince the Speakership of Mr. Winthrop, 1847-49, May's Parliamentary Practice has been kept on the Speaker's table as a guide and authority on all difficult points of parliamentary administration . . . . Lex Parliamentaria was for many years referred to as an authority."   M. Follett, The Speaker of the House of Representatives 122 n.2 (1896).   The two books cited by Follett are both treatises on law and procedure of the British Parliament.

[24]   R. E. Damon, The Standing Rules of the United States House of Representatives 11 (1971).

[25]   The changes in 1946 and 1970 were pursuant to the two Legislative Reorganization Acts of those years.   The others are cited in History of the Committee on Rules and Administration, United States Senate, S. Doc. No. 27, 96th (footnote continued)

Some rules, like those prescribing committee
jurisdictions, grew to contain extensive and
detailed guidance followed closely by their
chambers; others were minor.

The written rules never settled all, or even
most, questions of procedure: the earliest rules
were short and simple, and later compilations
often skirted major issues and retained outdated
procedures. For example, the Senate Rules barely
mention several of the various key motions in the
Senate, and do not discuss what they are or what
they do.[26] The House Rules do not specify the
variations on control of procedure possible
through special rules, other than placing a few
subjects off-limits. Both chambers chose, instead
of attempting to codify procedures in
comprehensive rules, to establish and follow
precedents, much like common law courts and
Parliament. Starting with the First Congress,
whenever a question of procedure ("point of
order") arose, the Chair in each chamber decided
it by making a ruling. These rulings served
thereafter as precedents; on subsequent occasions
when the same question arose, the Chair sought to
decide it the same way ("follow the precedent"),
and when new questions arose, the Chair reasoned
from analogous precedents, trying to keep all
rulings as consistent as possible.

Pursuant to standard parliamentary procedure,
when the Chair decides a point of order, any
Member can challenge the decision by appealing it
to the full chamber, which then votes on the
appeal. The chamber's vote either sustains the
ruling, or overrules it. In the House, appeals
are exceedingly rare, even during the most heated
and partisan disputes between the Speaker and
Members; an appeal is certain to lose because of

Cong., 1st Sess. 7 (1980). Some of these revisions made
major changes in how the chamber's procedure worked; others
simply pruned obsolete provisions and organized
systematically the retained ones.

[26] Senate Rule XXII (1) simply lists types of motions
(e.g., "To adjourn," "To lay on the table"), states their
precedence, and notes which ones are not debatable.

the strong responsibility of majority party Members to support the Speaker,[27] and an appeal today is considered as a personal insult to the Speaker. By contrast, in the Senate, appeals occur often, and succeed with some frequency; the Senate views overruling the Chair as a legitimate way to break certain rules when they are inconvenient, as discussed in the chapter on Senate organization.

When the Chair must rule, it looks to the pertinent precedents. The Chair in each chamber can refer back to the actual record (in the House or Senate Journals or the Congressional Record) for past proceedings, but the number of precedents grew so vast in the nineteenth and twentieth centuries as to require secondary reference sources. The Chair in each chamber, and others with parliamentary interests, have come to rely on certain authoritative compilations and digests of precedents, which have served as major sources for this book. The Senate relies on one key thousand-page compilation, Senate Procedure ("Riddick"), originally written by Dr. Floyd Riddick, and published in updated editions by the office of the Senate Parliamentarian.[28] The House relies on several multivolume compilations: Hinds' Precedents of the House of Representatives (precedents from 1789 to 1907), Cannons' Precedents of the House of Representatives (precedents from 1908 to 1936), and Deschler's Precedents of the United States (precedents since 1937; only some volumes have yet been published).[29] For short reference, the House

---

[27] There does not appear to have been a successful appeal from a ruling of the Speaker since 1927. See T. Siff & A. Weil, Ruling Congress 47 (1975).

[28] Originally Senate Procedure was authored by Riddick and by Charles Watkins, then Senate Parliamentarian, who supplied the collected precedents.

To keep the Senate updated, the Senate Parliamentarian's office maintains a computerized reference system (named "Rules and Precedents," in the LEGIS system) for all the rulings in recent years.
(footnote continued)

relies on a periodically updated one-volume compilation of precedents since 1937, Deschler's Procedure in the U.S. House of Representatives (1982), and on the House Manual updated each Congress, both prepared by the Office of the House Parliamentarian.[30]

Supplementing the rules and precedents are an elaborate network of traditions, customs, and patterns. For example, the fundamental structure of modern Senate procedure starts with certain prerogatives of the Majority Leader, including some unwritten ones, such as that he alone may make successful motions to proceed to bills. The multitude of ways in which such practices start, prosper, become incorporated in formal procedure, or die out will become clear in countless examples throughout this book.

C.   TEMPORAL PERSPECTIVES

The structure already described shows one type of cycle that Congress goes through: the two-year cycle from election to election, the life of each "Congress" from the First Congress in 1789-91 on up. Another key cycle is the "regular" pattern

---

[29]   These published sets are not complete sets of precedents. Of these there is only one copy in the world, the unprinted, hand-compiled and hand-assembled versions for each chamber: the set of House precedents belonging to the House Parliamentarian, and the set of Senate precedents belonging to the Senate Parliamentarian. Ruling Congress, supra, at 29-30 (set of House precedents), and at 52 (Senate precedents).

[30]   The House Manual reprints the Constitution, Jefferson's Manual, and the House Rules; it breaks each into numerous sections, and sets forth relevant precedents after each section.

To keep the House updated, the House Parliamentarian's office publishes an updated edition of the House Manual each Congress, and publishes periodic supplements to the one-volume Deschler.

for passage of a bill -- what some might call the "civics text" model. A third perspective comes from an "irregular" pattern for passage of a bill. Looking at temporal cycles provides the only way to bring together meaningfully the individual procedural pieces.

One Congress

Regarding the two-year life cycle of the Congress, as a formal matter, all bills either receive enactment in a Congress, or lapse at the Congress's end. However, for practical purposes, issues often mature more slowly, taking three, five, ten, or more years before they receive legislative solutions or lose importance. Hence, a slowly-maturing issue like civil rights, or nuclear waste, or tax reform, may see some proceedings in successive Congresses before a bill finally passes. Such an issue loses some ground at the end of each Congress, as the bills must be reintroduced in the next Congress and likely must recapitulate other steps, such as hearings, reporting to the floor, and floor proceedings in each chamber. However, some progress may be saved, simply by the requisite hearings and other proceedings occurring more quickly in successive Congresses.

In any event, the electorate selects a new Congress in November of each even-numbered year, although, of course, two thirds of the Senators do not stand for election but continue the rest of their six-year term, and of the Senators and Representatives who do stand for election, a large majority of incumbents tend to be reelected. The new Congress convenes formally in January,[31] but

---

[31]   The new Congress convenes pursuant to the Twentieth Amendment of the Constitution two months later, on January 3 (or some other day set by law) of the following odd-numbered year. Section 2 of Amendment XX prescribes: "The Congress shall assemble at least once in every year, and such meeting shall begin at noon on the 3d day of January, unless they shall by law appoint a different day." Other days frequently are set by law. See House Manual § 243 (listing (footnote continued)

practically speaking, a new Congress starts
earlier, in the December following the election,
when each chamber's parties hold organizational
meetings.   These meetings deal with vacancies or
challenges in leadership positions and with rules
changes.   They also start the allocation of
committee seats to newly elected Members, and to
reelected Members seeking transfers to different
committees than their prior ones.   These committee
appointments greatly influence the subsequent
course of legislation.

On January 3, the House and Senate assemble
to organize themselves formally.   In recent times,
the events involved in organizing the House and
Senate on opening day mostly have symbolic and
ceremonial rather than practical significance.[32]
The committee assignments of each party, and rules
changes, may be formally ratified by the chambers
on opening day, or this may be deferred awhile.

---

such laws).

[32]   Members commonly bring their families to watch (it is
the occasion when Members' children play on the chamber
floors) and the media often report fluffy pieces about the
new Congress.   The convening may also occasion some degree
of procedural struggle, such as the beginning of an election
contest over a disputed seat, or a rules dispute such as the
clashes over the Senate's cloture rule that occurred often
on opening days in the 1960s and early 1970s.   Historically,
on rare occasion, major conflicts erupt on opening day over
leadership successions when no party has clear control, and
the potential for such conflict underlines the potential
significance of the organizing events.

The basic steps in each chamber on opening day, not
necessarily in order, consist of swearing in the newly
elected Members (the whole House and one-third of the
Senate), establishing a quorum, electing the Speaker and
President Pro Tempore as well as the officers like the Clerk
of the House and Secretary of the Senate, in the House
adopting the rules, and formally giving various notices such
as announcing to the President that the chamber is ready.
Because these and other lesser steps involved in organizing
the chambers are quite involved and technical and occur only
once per Congress largely without incident in recent times,
they will not be discussed in detail.

Once the chambers elect their committees, then each committee holds its own organizational meeting, which includes adopting committee rules and establishing subcommittees.   By assigning Members to committees, organizing subcommittees, and choosing the chairs for committees and subcommittees, the parties distribute key power bases and to a significant degree shape what occurs legislatively over the next two years.

Since the mid-1960s, Congress has tended to meet all year long, and rather than taking one or two lengthy breaks, Congress has adjourned for about a half-dozen breaks mostly ten days to a month in duration.[33]   One of the leadership's major functions in each chamber, as it sets the floor schedules, is to make progress towards clearing the calendar of urgent pending business before each adjournment.   The leadership must keep a balance between the Members who consider some uncompleted measure vital and who would continue in session (either to pass the measure or to stall passage), and the many Members unconvinced of the need to stay and eager to get away.[34] Understandably, Members complain audibly about the forces that break schedules.   Much of the need for investing power in congressional leadership comes from the collective desire, which cannot be overestimated, that someone enforce schedules on powerful and clashing Members, when the Constitution puts the congressional schedule beyond the control of outsiders.[35]

---

[33] Typically, these include breaks around the birthdays of Washington and Lincoln in February, Easter in April, the Fourth of July, and an extended Labor Day break in August and September, plus a couple of others.

[34] Members depend on a leadership-devised schedule to plan crucial political events at home -- campaigning, fund-raising, party-support, and just measuring the constituents' mood -- and also to see their oft-neglected families.

[35] Article I, section 5, clause 2 prescribes that both Houses must decide together on adjournments over three days: "Neither House, during the Session of Congress shall, without the Consent of the other, adjourn for more than (footnote continued)

During the first few months of the year, the least legislative work gets done on the floor. The annual budget cycle does begin during this time, when the President submits his proposed budget by the first Monday after January 3. If Congress followed the timetable in the Gramm-Rudman budget act, Congress would complete enactment of a budget resolution by April 15, of a reconciliation bill by June 15, and of all appropriations by the Fourth of July adjournment. In reality, it is a certainty that Congress will not meet this ambitious schedule, but the act's schedule does reflect the preoccupation of the Congress with the budget in the early months.

Congress moves much of its legislation in the second half of that first year of the Congress. Committees attempt to move annual authorization and appropriation bills in the summer and fall. Whatever other major bills are on the agenda for a particular year -- packaged budget cuts (called "budget reconciliation" bills), tax, civil rights, energy, treaties in the Senate -- often gather speed at the approach of the major adjournments in the latter part of the year, for the completion of a bill allows Members to return to their states and districts without facing criticism for failure to act. Particular pushing occurs at year's end, on the eve of the end of the session. This may occur in November, or the session may go even later and only break in December for Christmas and New Year's Day. That break constitutes the end of

---

three days . . . ." The Framers gave the President power to schedule adjournments if Congress could not; Article II, section 3, states that "in Case of Disagreement between [the two houses], with Respect to the Time of Adjournment, [the President] may adjourn them to such Time as he shall think proper." Congress has never failed to decide its own adjournment, and the President has never exercised that power.

The President can convene special sessions pursuant to the same section ("he may, on extraordinary Occasions, convene both Houses, or either of them," Art. II, sec. 3). Historically, there have been many special sessions, though none since President Truman.

the "first session" of the Congress.   After an
"intersession" adjournment, the "second session"
starts in January of the following even-numbered
year.[36]

The second session brings a new dynamic into
play.   It is the election year, and Members are
looking   closely   at   what   legislative
accomplishments they can show the voters at year's
end, and at how the voters will understand their
Member's voting record.   Legislation continues in
the second session without dying or abating.   The
second session starts a new annual budget cycle
with a new presidential budget and congressional
budget resolution and the need to pass a new set
of appropriations.   As in the first session, the
spring and early summer tend to be slower times on
the floor, and the appropriations usually do not
achieve completion until the fall.   However, when
the pace picks up later in the summer and fall of
the second year, it is truly forced, for all the
work of the Congress must be completed or die.

Late in the second session, Members finally
reach the choice between getting a bill passed in
some   form,   or   not   getting   it   at   all   that
Congress.   The crush of business produces perhaps
the   most   important   bottleneck   in   national
government.   As floor managers insist on getting
their bills onto the floor, "[l]ate in the session
there is a tendency to placate floor managers by
overscheduling."[37]

Toward the Congress' end, major bills may
rush   through   the   floor   with   abbreviated
consideration -- in the House under tight special

---

[36]   All   other   adjournments   during   the   Congress   are
"intrasession."   In   practice   there   is   virtually   no
difference   between   "intrasession"   and   "intersession"
adjournments, except that something of a rush to complete
business occurs at the end of the first session of a
Congress,   partly   to   complete   the   annual   budget   and
appropriations cycle.

[37]   B. Sinclair, Majority Leadership in the U.S. House 43
(1983).

rules, in the Senate under goading of leadership
direction and late night sessions.   Numerous
conference reports pass at breakneck speed, as the
calendar pressure combines with other forces to
push through conference compromises that would
otherwise be utterly unpalatable. At this point,
Members cannot depend on their own ability to
examine the conference reports and other detailed
explanations.   They have no choice but to trust
almost completely their own "representatives,"
such as the Members on committees who come from
the same state or the same party wing as they do,
and who they consider reliable. When the session
ends,[38] all bills not enacted into law die.
Educated by the fall campaign, instructed by the
election's outcome, and altered by the departure
of former Members and the arrival of freshmen, the
next Congress starts anew.

One "Regular" Bill

A second temporal perspective, perhaps the
commonest one for viewing the Congress, is the
life cycle of the process for passing a "regular"
bill.   Although terming this the "civics text"
model of enactment may make it sound like it
exists only in the thoughts of the naive, in fact
many bills, including some of the most important,
pass by a fairly regular process. The tax
overhaul of 1985-86 furnishes a good example of a
bill that marched, step by step, along a path much
like that proclaimed in the civics text.   In
general, the process can be followed from the
House of Representatives' publication, How Our
Laws Are Made, quoted below.[39]   The regular
process may be viewed in five successive parts:
committee   consideration,   and   then   floor

---

[38] The second session ends in October before the election,
unless the Congress takes an extended election break in
October and November and returns for a lame duck session
after Election Day. that Congress ends, taking its "final
adjournment" until the next Congress starts the following
year.

[39] H. Doc. No. 158, 99th Cong., 2d Sess. (1966).

consideration, in the bill's first chamber; committee and floor consideration in the second chamber; and finally conference.

Consideration of a bill in its first chamber begins formally with its introduction:

> Any Member . . . in the House of Representatives may introduce a bill at any time while the House is actually sitting by simply placing it in the "hopper" provided for the purpose at the side of the Clerk's desk in the House chamber. . . .
>
> In the Senate, a Senator usually introduces a bill or resolution by presenting it to the clerks at the Presiding Officer's desk, without commenting on it from the floor of the Senate.[40]

Often, informal but extensive debate on an issue precedes introduction of the bill that ultimately resolves that issue. In the case of the tax overhaul bill, the concept of a "flat tax" received attention for years, until President Reagan announced it in a plan in May 1985.[41] The tax overhaul plan received its extensive initial legislative analysis in the House Ways and Means Committee, where interest groups took sides and the Congress's debating and trading began. In June and July of 1985, the House Ways and Means Committee conducted marathon (and tedious) hearings, and in October Ways and Means began work on a version of the plan endorsed by Chairperson Dan Rostenkowski (D-Ill.) The committee "marked up" the plan in October and November, "mark up" being the drafting sessions in which the committee's Members debate and propose changes. Ultimately, the committee "reported" a version of the bill (H.R. 3838, 99th Cong., 1st Sess.) to the House floor[42] by a committee vote of 12-24.[43]

---

[40] How Our Laws Are Made at 8.

[41] 1985 Congressional Quarterly Almanac 481, 488-92.

[42] 1985 Congressional Quarterly Almanac 492 (start of (footnote continued)

The House leadership may watch a bill during its committee consideration -- as with the tax bill, which from the earliest stages drew the Speaker's general interest. Still, a bill only becomes a central leadership concern when it leaves committee, and needs scheduling for the House floor. The House schedules major bills primarily by the House Rules Committee giving the bill a "special rule," which requires House approval to take effect. A special rule makes the bill in order for consideration on the House floor and establishes the procedure for that consideration: "The Committee on Rules reports a special resolution or 'rule' allowing for immediate consideration of a measure by the Committee of the Whole."[44]

H.R. 3838 ran into a brief but high-profile legislative detour at this point. On December 10 the Rules Committee reported a special rule for the bill. Generally the House adopts what the Rules Committee recommends, but this time the the House Republican leadership successfully attacked and defeated the special rule, with support from conservative Democrats disliking what the bill did to corporations and investors.[45] To put out the

---

consideration), 495 (later numbering). The bill had not followed the "regular" model of being introduced and referred to committee before hearings and markup; rather, the hearings and markup concerned a plan, and only when they were done was a bill drafted, introduced, referred, and reported in short order. This is the fairly common gambit of a committee completing proceedings and then reporting a "clean bill," discussed in the chapter on committee procedure. For a description of the hearings and markup, see Birnbaum and Murray at 107-151.

[43] Reporting means that the committee supports the bill and considers it ready for the full House, and that the committee staff prepare a lengthy description of the bill, the "committee report."

[44] "After adoption of the resolution by the House . . . the Speaker declares the House resolved into the Committee of the Whole without intervening motion." How Our Laws Are Made at 24.

(footnote continued)

fire, President "Reagan made an unusual trip to
Capitol Hill Dec. 16 to meet with recalcitrant
Republicans" promising to assure the bill's final
version better protected Republican interests,[46]
and the next day the Rules Committee reported a
second special rule which the House adopted.

Adoption of the special rule clears the way
for floor action, with the House's hallmark being
its controlled floor proceedings with limited
debate and amendment.   Pursuant to the special
rule, the House considered H.R. 3838 on December
17, going into "Committee of the Whole," a
parliamentary device used for purposes of debate
and amendment.[47] The special rule allowed several
hours of floor debate, and allowed the Republicans
to offer a single comprehensive alternative to the
committee version, but otherwise virtually
foreclosed floor amendments.[48]   As usual, the
chair of the committee (here, Representative
Rostenkowski) served as majority manager for floor
proceedings, and the ranking minority member of

---

[45]   1985 Congressional Quarterly Almanac 496-97.   Although
the administration supported House passage of the bill, the
House Republican leadership successfully fought the special
rule, reflecting Republican unhappiness over the bill's
contents and the sense that the committee had not taken
minority views into account.   Birnbaum and Murray at 158-
165.

[46]   1985 Congressional Quarterly Almanac 497; Birnbaum &
Murray at 169-171.

[47]   "When the House resolves into the Committee of the
Whole, the Speaker leaves the chair after appointing a
Chairman to preside."   How Our Laws Are Made at 24.   The
House uses the Committee of the Whole procedure because of
the Committee's fast-paced and smooth amendment process that
(1) basically allots only five minutes' debate on each side
per amendment (apart from   additions through "pro forma"
amendments) and (2) can end debate through the motion to
close or to limit debate.   Also the Committee has a reduced
quorum of 100.

[48]   It also deleted a controversial provision of the bill,
and made some other procedural changes discussed in 1985
Congressional Quarterly Almanac 497.

the committee (here, Representative John J. Duncan
(R-Tenn.)) served as minority manager. The two
managers coordinate the sequence of debate and
other floor action.

In this case, floor action consisted
principally of the key vote in which the Committee
of the Whole rejected the Republican
alternative.   "At the conclusion of the
consideration of a bill for amendment, the
Committee of the Whole 'rises' and reports the
bill to the House with the amendments that have
been adopted,"[49] and after certain steps the vote
occurs on final passage. For H.R. 3838,
strangely, no Members made a timely demand for a
recorded vote,[50] and so the House held only a
voice vote when it passed this major bill.

After passage in the first chamber, a bill is
messaged over to the second chamber, where by the
"regular" model, consideration starts all over
again by referral to committee: "The Presiding
Officer of the Senate refers the [House-passed]
bill to the appropriate standing committee of the
Senate . . . Senate committees give the bill the
same kind of detailed consideration as it received
in the House, and may report it with or without
amendment or 'table' it."[51] The tax bill's
progress responded to the biennial Congressional
cycle by taking a lengthy pause (for the Christmas
intersession break, and for early-spring

---

[49] "[A]nd the Chairman of the Committee is replaced in the
chair by the Speaker of the House." How Our Laws Are Made
at 25-26.

[50] This was an odd lapse. The Speaker "called first for a
voice vote, expecting the Republicans would then demand a
recorded vote . . . . He then looked to the Republican side
of the chamber, expecting to see a Republican member rise
and call for a roll call, but no one moved. The speaker
banged his gavel, and it was done . . . . A few Republicans
made a show of complaining that the speaker had gaveled too
quickly, but any fair witness could see that the Republicans
had simply made a mistake." Birnbaum and Murray at 175.

[51] How Our Laws Are Made at 34.

preoccupation with budget). Following House passage on December 17, the Senate referred H.R. 3838 to the Senate Finance Committee on December 18, but the committee did not commence marking up Chairman Robert Packwood's (R-Oreg.) own version until March, and markup proceeded slowly in following months. After a disastrous early period when the committee caved in to many requests for preserving tax breaks,[52] Senator Packwood put forth a tougher version, doing away with more tax breaks in return for bigger cuts in general tax rates, which the committee adjusted somewhat and then approved and reported in May.[53]

As in the House, the Senate leadership plays its chief role in scheduling for floor proceedings, where Majority Leader Dole and Minority Leader Byrd moved the bill along promptly. On the floor, the majority manager for the bill was Senator Packwood, and the minority manager was the Finance Committee's ranking minority member, Senator Russell Long (D-La.).[54] In a typical contrast, whereas the House had completed floor consideration of this bill in a single floor day with virtually no amendments, in the Senate the bill stayed on the floor for 12 days of debate, with votes on a host of amendments. The Senate procedure felt some constraint from the tight budget process imposed by the Gramm-Rudman law.[55] Following a standard

---

[52] Fessler, Packwood's Senate Colleagues Already Fighting Over Tax Bill, 44 Cong. Q. Week. Rep. 646 (1986); Birnbaum and Murray at 176-203.

[53] Shanahan, Finance Panel OKs Radical Tax Overhaul Bill, 44 Cong. Q. Week. Rep. 1007 (1986).

[54] The usually open Senate floor rules regarding amendments did not apply fully because the newly adopted Gramm-Rudman budget procedure barred revenue-losing amendments (absent a waiver by 60 Senators). Wehr, Tax Bill Could Face Procedural Hurdles on Senate Floor, 44 Cong. Q. Week. Rep. 1013 (1986). "It was the requirement of revenue-neutrality that caused most of the amendments offered to go down." Shanahan, Senate Nears Tax Bill Passage, Adheres to No-Change Rule, 44 Cong. Q. Week. Rep. 1311 (1986).
(footnote continued)

practice, the Senate eventually settled the
procedures on the bill under pressure from the
Majority Leader by a unanimous consent agreement,
which set a final vote for June 24, on which date
the bill was adopted.[56]

With Senate passage, attention immediately
focused on the conference to resolve the
differences between the two chambers' versions.
The conference committee consisted of a delegation
of Representatives led by Representative
Rostenkowski, and a delegation of Senators led by
Senator Packwood. For conference, the key choice
is often the picking of the conferees, as it was
for the tax conference, where each chair picked
conferees looking for "demonstrated personal
loyalty to himself."[57] The conference began

---

[55]   Under the Gramm-Rudman act's amendments to the budget
law:

> amendments that increased the budget deficit could be
> blocked by an objection from any member of the
> Senate. For technical reasons, that portion of the
> budget law was not in place in the early summer of
> 1986 when the tax debate began, but the spirit of
> Gramm-Rudman prevailed, and the senators were under
> pressure to keep all amendments revenue neutral.
> This meant senators wishing to restore a tax break
> would also have to propose a way to pay for the
> break.

Birnbaum and Murray at 237.

[56]   Shanahan, Panel's Tax Bill Largely Intact as Senate
Nears Final Passage, 44 Cong. Q. Week. Rep. 1377 (1986);
Birnbaum and Murray at 235-252.

[57]   Shanahan, Tax Bill Wins Senate Approval; Post-Recess
Conference Next, 44 Cong. Q. Week. Rep. 1452 (1986);
Shanahan, Tax Conferees Start Work, Highlight Problems, 44
Cong. Q. Week. Rep. 1599, 1601 (1986) ("Handpicked
Conferees"); Birnbaum and Murray at 256-258:

> The first step for both chairmen was to choose their
> fellow conferees . . . . Rostenkowski then combed
> the committee list, choosing those most likely to
(footnote continued)

serious work on July 24, and largely by leaving
most of the unresolved differences to the two
chairs, reached a rough agreement August 17.[58]

   "When the conferees, by majority vote of each
group, have reached complete agreement . . . they
embody their recommendations in a report . . .
that must be signed by a majority of the conferees
appointed by each body."[59]   The tax overhaul
conference formally reported (that is, filed the
completed draft of the final agreed-upon bill) on
September 18, 1986, and votes on House and Senate
passage occurred September 25 and 27. As with the
overwhelming majority of conference reports, what
the conference committee approved won acceptance
in both chambers.[60]   "When the bill has been
agreed to in identical form by both bodies . . .
[such as] by agreement in both bodies to the
conference report -- a copy of the bill is
enrolled for presentation to the President,"[61] and
President Reagan signed the tax bill into law.

   In the "regular" process, the role of
procedure often is taken for granted, with the
focus of public attention being the policy issues,
political forces, and the personalities of the key
individuals. Even in understanding the workings
of the most regular aspects of the process,

---

support reform, tossing out those most likely to
oppose it, regardless of their seniority . . . .
Packwood too decided to lay aside seniority to get
members of his committee who were most loyal to his
package.

[58] "'We gave carte blanche to the chairmen.'" Shanahan,
Congress Expected to OK Tax Overhaul Bill, 44 Cong. Q. Week.
Rep. 1947, 1949 (1986) (quoting Senator John C. Danforth (R-
Mo.), a conferee); Birnbaum and Murray at 268.

[59] How Our Laws Are Made at 40.

[60] Shanahan, House Overwhelmingly OKs Tax Overhaul Bill, 44
Cong. Q. Week. Rep. 2255 (1986); Shanahan, Senate Clears
Massive Tax Overhaul Measure, 44 Cong. Q. Week. Rep. 2344
(1986); Birnbaum and Murray at 284.

[61] How Our Laws Are Made at 43.

procedure plays a significant part. Regular procedures were much of the reason Speaker Thomas P. O'Neill (D-Mass.) and the two chairs, Rostenkowski and Packwood, were the key figures. Regular procedures led to critical policy and political decisions occurring during consideration in the two committees, and in conference.

Moreover, procedure had its own sphere in numerous incidents that happened along the bill's path. Procedure explains, among other points, what happened in the House when H.R. 3838 hit its major snag before floor consideration, in the House Republicans' defeat of the first special rule; how it happened that the House had no record vote on passage of the bill; why the House had only one day of consideration with few amendments, while the Senate had many days and many amendments; how the budget process constrained Senate floor consideration; how the choice of chair-loyal conferees occurred and why it mattered; and why there was so little chance for serious opposition to the final conference agreement. In sum, even "regular" progress of a bill reflects much procedure of interest.

One "Irregular" Bill

Regular congressional procedures put agenda control and bill management in the hands of the party and committee leaderships. The most "irregular" procedures occur when large blocs of Members revolt against their own leadership, such as when an avalanche of complaining letters comes in from constitutents. A classic example consists of the 1983 repeal of the provision for withholding of taxes on interest and dividends. In 1982, Congress had extended withholding of income taxes from payrolls to interest-bearing bank accounts. The banks had not accepted the provision, and they launched a repeal effort. To provide the muscle for repeal, the banks generated "one of the most massive mail-in campaigns in Capitol Hill history . . . . [T]he pressure became too much, with literally millions of letters demanding repeal pouring into congressional offices."[62] In turn, this effort met potent top-level resistance: "Congressional leaders, including House Speaker Thomas P. O'Neill Jr., D-Mass., and Senate Finance Chairman Robert Dole, R-Kan., used their legislative powers to block repeated attempts to bring the issue up for floor votes."[63]

Repeal proponents skipped committee proceedings in the Senate -- i.e., moved the bill without hearings or markup or reporting -- because of the hostility toward the bill of the chair of the Senate Finance Committee, Senator Dole. Repeal proponents skipped the "regular" process of committee consideration by offering the repeal provision as a "non-germane" (i.e., irrelevant) floor amendment to unrelated bills, since the Senate has no general germaneness rule (only the House does). Repeal opponents responded with threats of filibusters that would tie up those key unrelated bills, particularly a jobs bill. "To keep the issue from tying up the jobs bill, Senate leaders agreed in March that repeal proponent Bob Kasten, R-Wis., would be allowed to offer an amendment to repeal withholding when S.144 reached the floor."[64] This was a compromise. It let a vote occur on attaching the repeal provision to S. 144, an unrelated trade bill, but without any relaxation of efforts of opponents to stall repeal after that vote.

Accordingly, repeal proponents then faced a variety of opposition tactics. They faced a filibuster on S. 144, necessitating a cloture motion to cut off debate. Cloture requires more than the usual majority; it requires the support of 60 Senators. It is rare for cloture to succeed on matters opposed by the leadership, but there is no rule against it, and this time repeal proponents had the needed votes.[65]

---

[62] 1983 Congressional Quarterly Almanac 261.

[63] 1983 Congressional Quarterly Almanac 261.

[64] 1983 Congressional Quarterly Almanac 262.

[65] "Senate Finance Committee Chairman Robert Dole, R-Kan., a strong supporter of withhholding, planned to filibuster (footnote continued)

"With a cloture vote pending on Kasten's amendment, the Senate leadership attempted to adjourn early April 19 to avoid defeat."[66] Adjournment is usually a leadership prerogative, which the acting leader invoked as one of his tools for controlling the Senate agenda. While it is customary for the Senate majority party to back its leader on adjournment motions, this time the Senate refused to back the acting leader, and the motion to adjourn was defeated.[67]   This demonstrated strikingly that the leadership would not be able to restrain the repeal provision. Shortly thereafter the Senate agreed on some minor compromises in the measure and adopted it.

Repeal of withholding of interest and dividends followed an "irregular" course in the House as well.   There, too, implacable hostility on the committee of jurisdiction precluded the regular route of committee consideration, and so repeal proponents again sought to go directly to the floor.   Repeal proponents were required to use a discharge petition, a powerful but infrequently used tool which requires the signature of a majority of Representatives on a petition to bring a bill out of committee and onto the floor. Because of the strong House norm of respect for committee jurisdiction, few discharge petitions obtain the requisite 218 signatures.

However, this petition did.   "Success of the

Kasten's amendment but agreed to accept the compromise plan April 19 after discovering he had only 28 votes -- not enough to prevent cloture on the amendment or to uphold an expected presidential veto."   1983 Congressional Quarterly Almanac 262.

[66]   1983 Congressional Quarterly Almanac 262.

[67]   As one Senator observed the next day, Senator Kasten had "prevailed against tremendous opposition . . . . to the point of even winning by a substantial margin on defeating a motion to adjourn yesterday which traditionally, I think, would be viewed as simply a leadership prerogative."   129 Cong. Rec. S4977 (daily ed. April 20, 1983) (Sen. Danforth); see id. at S4842 (actual 63-31 defeat of the motion to adjourn).

discharge petition, a rarely used device to circumvent the will of the leadership or a strong committee chairman, was a major blow to the House leadership which had kept the bill bottled up in committee for almost four months."[68] The Ways and Means committee bowed to the inevitable, and reported a repeal bill, H.R. 2973.   The House considered and passed the bill under the procedure of suspension of the rules, usually reserved for lesser bills than this, which precludes amendments, truncates debate, and requires a two-thirds vote to pass.   "The step was taken by the House leadership in part to ensure that the bill would be passed with enough votes to show that a presidential veto could easily be overridden. Such action required a two-thirds majority in both houses."[69]

In the "regular" or "civics text" model, once the Senate and House have passed versions of a bill, they go to conference. However, instead of going immediately to conference, the Senate and House may maneuver by continuing to amend a bill, passing it back and forth.   In this case, the Senate took the House-passed bill, and amended it by "load[ing] the package with a number of unrelated amendments, some of which were intended to make the bill more palatable to the administration" -- "[a] portion of the administration's Caribbean Basin Initiative," a "trade 'reciprocity' measure," "[t]he administration's enterprise zone plan," and "[a] controversial measure to make permanent an existing law allowing for tax-exempt mortga[g]e revenue bonds."[70] The Senate frequently engages in such loading of bills with extraneous amendments, particular bills like the tax bill

---

[68] 1983 Congressional Quarterly Almanac 263.

[69] 1983 Congressional Quarterly Almanac 263-64.   For the full account, see Fessler, Interest Withholding Repeal Sails Through House, 382-41, 41 Cong. Q. Week. Rep. 988 (1983); 129 Cong. Rec. H2991 (daily ed. May 17, 1983)(vote on passage).

[70] 1983 Congressional Quarterly Almanac 264.

that are clearly fated for passage. Only with
that load did the bill go to a conference
committee, which scrapped trade reciprocity,
enterprise zones, and tax-exempt bonds -- such
scrapping being a frequent outcome when House
conferees confront Senate baggage. The House and
Senate then quickly approved the conference
report.

In sum, when powerful political forces back
an insurgency against the position of party or
committee leaders, they may use a variety of
"irregular" procedures. When Members use these
channels, procedure takes on great significance,
for it defines the terms of combat between
powerful opposed forces.

D.   ESSENTIAL HISTORY OF PROCEDURE

The history of Congressional procedure has greatly
affected its current shape. In fact, most of the
most visible features of Congressional procedure
trace to historical trends or key incidents. In
the Congress's first century, the growing House
put itself under increasingly centralized control,
while the Senate established an opposing pattern
of individual power amounting at times almost to
anarchy. During the twentieth a powerful
conservative coalition which had exercised its
power through key devices such as the power of
senior committee chairs, bottlenecks on the House
floor such as the Rules Committee, and the
unavailability of cloture on the Senate floor. In
both chambers, history has bequeathed to the
present a number of devices concerning whether
Members can be forced to visibly go on record on
key issues, from the House germaneness rule of
1822 to the partisan Senate tabling motions of the
1980s.

That history does not always fall into
orderly or even trends. Three rough divisions
stand out. From the First Congress in 1789 to the
1930s, the two chambers established their basic
organization. From the 1930s to the 1970s, the
conservative coalition rose and fell, leaving in
place a complex procedural balance. In the 1980s,

a unique legislative process grew up around omnibus bills, complex special rules in the House, extensive use of filibuster and cloture in the Senate, and other developments.

House and Senate Evolution to the 1930s

The modern observer would find the First Congress as it met in New York City in 1789, with its 26 Senators elected by state legislatures and its 65 Representatives from districts of 40,000 people, procedurally rudimentary. As James Madison (D-Va.) complained: "in every step the difficulties arising from novelty are severely experienced, and are an ample as well as just source of apology. Scarcely a day passes without some striking evidence of the delays and perplexities springing merely from the want of precedents."[71] The House and Senate began without any significant standing committee system, and without any clear leadership structure. By the basic theory advocated by Jeffersonians, the legislature was to formulate the principles of each bill by discussion on the floor among its general membership.[72]

Congress' first step toward modern organization came in the immediate rise of party politics, as the First Congress divided between Federalists and Democratic-Republicans. Even in its first two years, Congress' "driving power" was "furnished by the Hamiltonian or Federalist party organization . . . . [T]he real work of legislation was put in shape, not in the legislature, but in secret session of the majority party."[73] In the House, the party system at first

---

[71] V Writings of James Madison 373 (G. Hunt ed. 1906).

[72] For the early philosophy that the House of Representatives was to formulate principles on the floor (in Committee of the Whole), and then use select committees only for reducing its decisions to writing, see J. Cooper, The Origins of the Standing Committees and the Development of the Modern House 3-15 (1970); R. V. Harlow, The History of Legislative Methods in the Period Before 1825 127-28 (1917).

(footnote continued)

served administration leadership, but then
developed its own internal leadership in the form
of a stronger and partisan Speakership starting
with Speaker Henry Clay in 1811.[74] In the Senate,
although there were periods of significant party
leadership, "[t]hroughout most of the eighteenth
and nineteenth centuries, there was no one
leader . . . .   Partisan floor leadership was
fragmented, decentralized, and occasional."[75]

Within the first decades, Congress groped
toward the division of labor and power of a system
of standing committees.   The House first
established its initial standing committees over
several decades from the 1790s to the 1820s, while
the Senate created a set of standing committees in
1816.   Committees gained the power to receive
referral of all bills in their jurisdiction and to
report by bill, and thereby exercised the
screening function for the floor.[76]   Party and
committee systems reinforced each other, as a
major strength and function of the party system
came to be assigning Members to committees.[77]
Seniority gradually became the criterion for
Members to retain committee slots and to advance

---

[73]   R. V. Harlow, supra, at 144-45.

[74]   The strength of the early party system should not be
overestimated.   Both parties suffered severe internal
divisions and the absence of the modern structures, and an
examination of the disorganized voting for Speakers suggests
that "nothing approaching a stable party system in Congress
emerged in Congress until the Jacksonian era." J. S. Young,
The Washington Community 1800-1828 119 (1966).

[75]   R. L. Peabody, Leadership in Congress: Stability,
Succession, and Change 327 (1976).

[76]   J. Cooper, supra, at 46-56 (bill referral) and 56-59
(bill reporting).

[77]   The majority party in the House chose a Speaker who
appointed committees; the majority party in the Senate made
its committee decisions itself, not through a leader (though
with the aid of evolving party organs).   Origins and
Development at 83, 89 (Speaker appointment in House), 195-96
(Senate).

within committees toward the chair.

A major prop for the committee system came with the evolution of the conference committee procedure for resolving differences between chambers. The First Congress had inherited the basic tool of conference committees from Parliament and the colonial legislatures, both of which had used them to resolve differences between chambers.[78] It was not until the 1850s, however, that the major pieces of the congressional conference system were in place, above all the practice that the Presiding Officer would appoint conferees from the committee of jurisdiction.[79] That practice joined in the committees the power of preparing bills before floor consideration and the further power to rewrite them in conference after the floor, an overwhelming combination.

Floor procedure and scheduling took on greater importance after the Civil War as the volume of legislative business grew. The House and Senate irrevocably parted ways at this point in their internal organizational structures. In the 1880s and 1890s, the House responded to minority party obstruction by creating powerful mechanisms for majority party control: the use of "special rules" from the Rules Committee as the means for scheduling and for controlling floor proceedings, and an array of powers in the Speaker for overcoming minority resistance.[80] The Speaker grew powerful enough to be accounted temporarily the President's equal in the conduct of domestic government. In 1909, the House revolted against

---

[78] See House Manual §§ 530-559 (Thomas Jefferson's description of conference procedure, drawn from Parliament); A. S. McCown, The Congressional Conference Committee (1927), at 23-33 (British antecedents), 33-37 (colonial antecedents).

[79] A. S. McCown, supra, at 62-64 (trend by 1850s toward committee role on conference).

[80] Committee on Rules, 97th Cong., 2d Sess., A History of the Committee on Rules 61-79 (Comm. Print 1983) (Rules Committee History).

the last of the autocratic Speakers, "Czar" Cannon, deciding to shift much power to a newly independent Rules Committee and Majority Leader. Still, the House retained its basic system of majority-controlled floor proceedings unyielding to wishes of individual Members or the minority party.

In contrast, by and large the Senate did not vest much constricting power in its leadership in the nineteenth century.[81] The latter part of the century saw the rise of the unchecked filibuster, the ultimate symbol of the resistance powers of individual Senators and the minority party. Only near the turn of the century did effective party leadership and floor organization emerge in the Senate, with the development of the position and prerogatives of the Majority Leader and of binding unanimous consent agreements. Initial adoption of a cloture rule in 1917 presaged later constraints on individual rights in the Senate, but the loopholes in the rule made it largely ineffective for many years. Whether this made the Senate stronger or weaker may be debated. It clearly established the chamber's character as a place where otherwise outnumbered factions could still hold up and defeat legislation, such as, most visibly, where Southern Senators could keep civil rights for blacks at bay for a century after Reconstruction.

The early twentieth century brought a new influence on congressional procedure in the shape of enhanced presidential status in legislating. Presidents Theodore Roosevelt and Wilson augmented Presidential status and prerogatives in legislating, and congressional party leaders took on, in part, the role of intermediaries between President and Congress. This shift accelerated, after the relatively quiet 1920s, with the extensive New Deal program of President Franklin Roosevelt, shepherded through both chambers by loyal party leaders.

---

[81]   Origins and Development at 184, 188-89.

1930s-1970s "Conservative Coalition" Control

The unprecedented scale of New Deal liberal economic legislation produced a backlash with special importance in the history of congressional procedure. Starting in 1937, and continuing for decades, conservative Democrats joined Republicans in a "conservative coalition" successfully opposing any further extension of national economic legislation.[82] Conservative coalition control depended on the disproportionate share of conservative southern Democrats in committee chairs, which they obtained and kept through seniority. These chairs wielded enormous power within their committees by tight control over agendas and refusals to delegate to junior Members or subcommittees.

On the floor, these chairs often avoided recorded calls on amendments that would mobilize majorities against them, in the House through the unavailability of recorded votes in Committee of the Whole, and in the Senate through the systematic refusal to give a sufficient "second" for a recorded vote. Both chambers decided committee appointments through organs in which conservative senior Members had a strong voice: the House Ways and Means Committee's Democratic caucus, and the Senate's Democratic Steering Committee. Retaliation crushed junior Members, who found they would not "get along" if they did not "go along."

In the House, conservative chairs reinforced their control through their command center, the Rules Committee.[83] Speaker Sam Rayburn (D-Tex.), who served with brief interruptions from 1940 to 1961, delicately balanced the liberal majority

---

[82] See J. T. Patterson, Congressional Conservatism and the New Deal: The Growth of the Conservative Coalition in Congress, 1933-1939 (1967).

[83] The Rules Committee denied special rules to bills and even to conference reports, and controlled the floor consideration of those bills that it allowed to come up. Rules Committee History, supra, at 136-77.

within the party against the powerful senior
conservatives, to a considerable degree ceding
agenda control to the latter.   Similarly, in the
Senate,   conservative   chairs   reinforced   their
control with the informal system known as the
Senate "club," meaning a distinction between
insiders and outsiders, which penalized junior
Members and insubordinate "mavericks." As the New
York Times commented later, in "the 1950s, [the]
Senate was run with an iron hand by a small group
of barons led by Lyndon Johnson [(D-Tex.)] as the
majority leader."[84]   The filibuster against civil
rights measures reigned supreme as the Senate
failed to vote cloture on any bill from 1937 to
1962.   Expanded use of unanimous consent
agreements precluded the usual weapon of the
individual Senator, the non-germane amendment.

Through these and other control techniques,
the conservative coaltion blunted President
Franklin Roosevelt's late 1930s efforts to
continue enacting New Deal legislation, blocked
most of President Truman's 1940s Fair Deal
program, helped President Eisenhower resist 1950s
liberal Democratic initiatives, and resisted or
toned down much of President Kennedy's 1960s New
Frontier agenda. The appropriations system of the
era also maintained tight control in the interests
of fiscal conservatism.   Appropriations
Committees' internal organization strengthened
antispending subcommittee chairs -- within
committee, on the floor, and in conference.[85]

1970s Breakdown of the Old Structure

The conservative coalition's tight control
began weakening in the 1960s. For civil rights

---

[84]   Tolchin, Senators Assail Anarchy in New Chamber of
Equals, New York Times, Nov. 25, 1984, at 40.   For the
contemporary description, see W. S. White, Citadel: The
Story of the United States Senate (1957); J. S. Clark, et
al., The Senate Establishment (1963).

[85]   R. F. Fenno, The Power of the Purse: Appropriations
Politics in Congress (1966).

bills, the Senate voted cloture, and in committees, liberals accumulated sufficient seniority to obtain positions of importance.   A powerful Democratic majority in 1965-66 led by President Johnson, a master parliamentarian, pushed through a large share of the agenda that had long been held back in such areas as civil rights, education, welfare, immigration, and Medicare.[86]

Still, the conservative coalition retained and even regained procedural power in the late 1960s, and it was not until the 1970s that a major wave of formal procedural changes occurred, particularly when Watergate brought a swollen crew of junior Democrats to Congress.[87]   Parallel developments in each chamber allowed Members to easily obtain roll call votes on the floor, that is, to force their colleagues to go on record by voting on controversial propositions.   This encouraged liberals and conservatives alike to offer and to enact floor amendments in record numbers over the opposition of committee chairs. Meanwhile, committee chairs gave way to more open committee procedures and delegated power to subcommittees headed by junior Members.   The procedural apparatus for fiscal conservatism crumbled, as the appropriations committees lost their power to resist spending requests and as authorizing committees enacted new spending programs as "entitlements" requiring no appropriations.[88]

---

[86]   See D. M. Berman, A Bill Becomes A Law: Congress Enacts Civil Rights Legislation (2d ed. 1966) (comparing procedurally the means by which President Johnson pushed through a strong civil rights bill in 1964 in the face of resistance from the House Rules Committee and a Senate filibuster, with the gutting of the weak bill in 1960).

[87]   An example of the regained power of the conservative coalition in the late 1960s was the repeal in 1967 of the House's twenty-one-day rule, which had checked the Rules Committee during the "Great Society" Congress of 1965-66. Rules Committee History at 202-03.   For an overview of the 1970s changes, see L. M. Schwab, Changing Patterns of Congressional Politics (1980).
(footnote continued)

The House saw a host of formal procedural changes. Junior Democrats used the party caucus to assault the citadels of control directly, remaking the Rules Committee into an arm of the leadership, and overthrowing the seniority rule to depose three chairmen and tame those allowed to remain in power. The caucus shifted decision making on committee appointments to the Steering and Policy Committee, another arm of the leadership. Thus, a new legislative system arose in place of the former committee chair control, relying on subcommittee chairs and party leadership. In the Senate, change began in the 1960s and continued in the 1970s in evolutionary fashion with the slow dissolution of the "club." Junior liberal and moderate Senators gained in seniority and power; leadership style evolved under Majority Leaders Mansfield (1961-76) and Byrd (1977-80) toward service for all Senators; and decades of struggle against the filibuster culminated finally in 1975 with a relaxation of the requirements for voting cloture.[89]

These major 1970s changes produced a powerful swing in the opposite direction from the previous era, from the prior tight control by committee chairs toward a condition at times verging on anarchy. "As the number of roll calls increas[ed] so d[id] the difficulties committees encounter[ed] in protecting their bills on the floor."[90] Record numbers of surprise floor amendments eroded the position of bill managers; examples included foreign affairs amendments like aid cutoffs and conditions that were politically irresistible because of their appeal to particular interest groups, but were unconsidered hasty floor innovations incompatible with long-term national interests.[91] Endless jurisdictional disputes

---

[88]   A. Schick, Congress and Money: Budgeting, Spending and Taxing 424-40 (1980).

[89]   M. Foley, The New Senate: Liberal Influence on a Conservative Institution, 1952-1972 (1980); Origins and Development at 259-65.

[90]   B. Sinclair, supra, at 10.
(footnote continued)

occurred among the numerous subcommittees eager to stake turf claims. In the Senate, the breakdown of control led to filibustering on minor bills, and to the "postcloture filibuster," a technique for painfully stalemating the chamber despite even supermajority votes to proceed.

1980s Procedure

Congressional procedure in the 1980s took shape from three principal forces. First, the election of a Republican President and a Republican Senate produced a sharp party clash in 1981-86.[92] The two chambers had opposed partisan interests, putting their agenda-control devices into opposition; neither wanted to move the other's preferred legislation. This constricted the passage of legislation, particularly because the tight finances of the era after passage of the great tax cut in 1981 left no money to spend.

This conflict between the two chambers produced a procedure relying on "omnibus bills" -- a few large bills on which the two chambers must act, with struggles to attach other legislation as riders to these. A leading observer cited the Members' nickname for this, the "four bill system":

> Many members like to refer to the current legislative process in the House as the "four bill" system. What they mean is that in the average year, there may be only four important domestic legislative vehicles -- the budget resolution, continuing appropriations, supplemental appropriations, and the reconciliation package of spending cuts that the budget dictates. Sometimes legislation to raise the federal debt limit is another.

---

[91]   C. Whalen, The House and Foreign Policy (1980).

[92]   There had only been four prior years in this century of divided Congresses, in 1911-13 and 1931-33.

"The only way to get things done in recent years," says Leon E. Panetta, a California Democrat, "has been to attach them to bills the Senate and the president cannot refuse."[93]

Second, fiscal policy became the chief consideration in the Congress as the succession of inflation and recession in the early 1980s and budget and trade deficits in the late 1980s dominated the agenda. Congress had enacted the Congressional Budget Act, with its new budget procedure, in 1974, but the procedure had limited effect in the 1970s. In the 1980s it took on far greater importance, with the rise of the powerful technique of reconciliation, and the availability of the budget resolution and reconciliation bills as focuses of national policy conflict. After budget procedures evolved rapidly in the 1980s, the Congress further completely revised it in the Gramm-Rudman acts of 1985 and 1987.

Appropriations procedure changed, too. The loosening of floor procedures in the 1970s had brought the rise and fall of the "limitation" rider. The post-Watergate era of greater congressional influence had brought the rise and fall of the annual authorization, a vehicle for close control of government agencies. In the 1980s, continuing resolutions, the tool for forcing many late appropriations through in a single package, took on significance. The complex interplay around budget and appropriations bills produced its own unique procedure.[94]

---

[93] Ehrenhalt, Media, Power Shifts Dominate O'Neill's House, 44 Cong. Q. Week. Rep. 2131, 2136 (1986).

[94] In the House, complex special rules structuring the consideration of those financial bills became the centerpiece of floor action. In the Senate, the techniques by which floor managers handled such bills became crucial, such as increased and partisan use of the motion to table and of procedures for ordering and stacking amendments. Conferences on budget measures took on amazing elaboration, with attendance by record numbers of conferees dividing into subconferences.

Finally, a third factor in procedure of the late 1970s and early 1980s was a reaction, to a limited extent, against the reforms of the prior decade where they had created excessive disorganization. The House majority party developed a number of techniques for fending off controversial amendments, from expanded reliance on suspension of the rules to a strengthened whip system.[95] The Senate struggled with the postcloture filibuster, adopting rule changes in 1979 and 1986 and developing strategies for containing and breaking such filibusters.

It would be an error, however, to stress overly the reaction against the 1970s. Committee chairs never regained their previous power: committee procedure remained largely open, subcommittees retained their decentralized power, and the seniority rule continued to be subordinate to majority will. As Congressional Quarterly noted, "[t]he House of 1986 -- as opposed to the one of 1976 -- [was] a place where literally any member who wants to publicize his issues or himself c[ould] do so with relatively little effort,"[96] and the same was even truer in the Senate. The 1970s and 1980s produced a uniquely complex but highly dynamic and publicly accessible system of congressional procedure.

---

[95] Also, the House coped with committee jurisdiction problems through multiple referrals that gave only limited rights to committees, and through management by the Rules Committee. The Senate reorganized its committees in a major way in 1977 and trimmed back its subcommittees again in the 1980s.

[96] Ehrenhalt, Media, Power Shifts Dominate O'Neill's House, 44 Cong. Q. Week. Rep. 2131, 2134 (1986).

2
Committee Organization and Jurisdiction[1]

A. OVERVIEW AND HISTORY

Overview

Woodrow Wilson wrote in 1885 that "Congress in session is Congress on public exhibition, whilst Congress in its committee-rooms is Congress at work," and that is as true today as then.[2] Congress divides up its work -- and its power -- by the committee system, ceding control over each subject to the relatively few Members on the committee of jurisdiction. Committees receive bills by referral as soon as they are introduced. Thereafter, committees control the bills at hearings, markup, and reporting, greatly influence the bills' progress in scheduling and floor proceedings, and control them again at conference.[3] Committees decide with respect to

---

[1] Sources most frequently cited in this chapter include Congressional Quarterly, Origins and Development of Congress (1976) (Origins and Development); S.S. Smith & C.J. Deering, Committees in Congress (1984) (Smith & Deering).

[2] W. Wilson, Congressional Government 69 (1956 ed.).

[3] To take that one step at a time, after a bill is (footnote continued)

legislation what will be buried, what will barely come out of committee, and what will come out with a favored likelihood of enactment.

Moreover, apart from legislation, committees consult on administrative actions in their areas and determine what issues will be highlighted by hearings and reports. Whenever Presidents and party leaders concern themselves with a particular area, they deal with the committee of jurisidiction. Agencies and interest groups devote most of their congressional efforts to their relationship with their particular committee of jurisdiction.

All this means that to understand congressional action, one must understand the basic jurisdictional lines. However, the jurisdictional structure is far from simple. To be sure, some committees parallel the well-known structure of the executive departments -- the Agriculture committees have jurisdiction largely parallel to what the Agriculture Department does, and the Armed Services committees largely parallel the Defense Department. However, some committees have a complexly mixed jurisdiction, and many subjects are shared among several committees.

Members have an enormous interest in winning assignment to a preferred committee during the period at the beginning of each Congress when new Members receive initial assignments and some previously elected Members seek reassignments. In each chamber, each party starts with a limited number of assignments on each committee, depending on the committee sizes and the party ratio. Each party has an elaborate apparatus for making

---

referred, it goes through hearings, mark-up, and reporting, as discussed in the chapter on committee procedure. After reporting, the bill comes to the floor, where it is managed, almost invariably, by the chair of the committee or subcommittee of jurisdiction, as discussed in the chapters on House and Senate floor procedure. An important bill that passes both chambers usually goes to a conference committee, consisting of members from the House and Senate committees of jurisdiction, as discussed in the chapter on conference procedure.

assignment decisions, focused on a special committee on committees usually with an important role for the party leadership. The committees on committees tend to take into account a wide range of factors in making their decisions, including the Members' desires, geographical balance, the loyalty of previously elected Members to the party, and Members' sponsorship by powerful figures.

The parties not only assign Members to committees, but also determine who will chair the committee, a vast grant of power. The historic shift in the 1970s in this regard reshaped all of congressional procedure, when the previous iron rule of seniority was overthrown in the House by the deposing of three committee chairs, and the power of chairs in the Senate was quietly but similarly reduced. Since then, committee chairs have had to remain particularly responsive to their Members. Committees themselves organize into subcommittees at the beginning of each Congress. This includes not only confirming or redrawing subcommittee lines and assigning Members to subcommittee, but also the selection of subcommittee chairs, posts of increased importance.

Committee jurisdictional lines, assignment, and organization at the beginning of the Congress set the stage for the bill referral process that occurs during the Congress. While bill referral is often simple and straightforward, endemic jurisdictional uncertainties can often make it far from clear which committee will take jurisdiction of a particular bill. Subjects of newly increased importance and changed contexts -- national defense in the 1950s, pension reform and energy in the 1970s, international trade and nuclear waste in the 1980s -- often raise the greatest disputes over jurisdiction. Committees have several arenas for contesting jurisdiction: drafting bills to fit within their jurisdiction rather than another committee's; obtaining help from the leadership, particularly in arranging multiple referrals; negotiating special floor arrangements through House complex rules or Senate unanimous consent agreements; and securing the appointment of multiple-committee conferees.[4]

A   specific   example   illustrates   the importance, and some of the techniques, of jurisdictional struggle.   In 1981, when the automobile industry sought protection from foreign competition, two House committees vied for jurisdiction of the subject: the Ways and Means Committee, oriented toward free trade, and the more protectionist Energy and Commerce Committee chaired by Representative John Dingell (D-Mich.) of Detroit.   The Ways and Means Committee had traditional jurisdiction over tariffs and import quotas, which the Energy and Commerce Committee countered with a focus on commerce, by drafting a "domestic content" bill providing that automobiles sold in United States commerce would have to include   a   high   percentage   of   domestically manufactured parts. Ultimately, the Speaker gave the domestic content bill a multiple referral to both committees.

The two committees accorded the bill very different treatment.[5]   Since the Energy and Commerce Committee favored the bill, it held early hearings that reflected support and conferred

---

[4] Moreover, to maintain jurisdiction, committees struggle not only against each other, but against the various devices, discussed in detail in subsequent chapters, by which legislation may bypass the committee and come directly to the House or Senate floor. These devices are legion: in the Senate, non-germane amendments, and the Rule XIV procedure; in the House, special rules waiving germaneness, and the discharge petition; in both chambers, legislative riders on appropriations and, to some extent, budget reconciliation.

[5] Just as the House refers a bill to committee, a committee usually (though not always) refers a bill to subcommittee. The chapter on committee procedure includes a discussion of subcommittee   jurisdiction,   for   often   subcommittee proceedings influence a bill as much as, if not more than, full committee proceedings. Regarding the domestic content bill, both House committees of jurisdiction referred the bill   to   subcommittee: Energy   and   Commerce   to   its Subcommittee on Commerce, Transportation and Tourism; Ways and Means to its Subcommittee on Trade. These subcommittees held the respective two-day and nine-day hearings.

legitimacy without unduly belaboring any faults in
the bill.[6]   By contrast, the Ways and Means
Committee was highly unsympathetic to the bill,
holding nine days of thorough hearings with 104
witnesses to probe and publicize every possible
problem with the bill.[7] It presumably would have
bottled up and killed the bill if it could have,
and being unable to, prepared major floor
amendments against the bill.

   After Energy and Commerce reported the bill,
the Rules Committee, which makes the primary
decisions about scheduling bills for House floor
proceedings, held a scheduling hearing where
Energy and Commerce testified in favor of the
bill, and Ways and Means opposed it.   The Rules
Committee allowed the bill to come to the floor.
Energy and Commerce managed the bill on the House
floor, meaning that its chair shaped the order of
debate and made central strategic decisions.[8] The
House passed the bill, though with a major floor
amendment from Ways and Means.   The Senate never
took up the bill, so the bill never went to
conference; if it had, the House conference
delegation would probably have included conferees
from both Energy and Commerce, and Ways and

---

[6] The Energy and Commerce hearings on the bill only lasted
two hours with 11 witnesses, after which the Committee
marked up the bill in supportive fashion. Most important,
Energy and Commerce then reported the bill, rather than
exercising the greatest power of a committee, to bury a bill
without reporting and thereby kill it. Hearings, markup,
and reporting are discussed in the chapter on committee
procedure.

[7] Because Ways and Means did not have time, during the
short referral period allowed by the House leadership, to
mark up the bill formally, the amendments of its members
were not reported as committee amendments. However, much
the same effect was achieved when its members offered their
amendments on the floor. The Ways and Means Committee was
automatically discharged from consideration of the bill when
the time ran out on its multiple referral.

[8] The Rules Committee and floor management are each
discussed in separate chapters.

Means.   In short, at every stage of the bill's
progress, its course was shaped by the committee
jurisdictional structure and the struggle between
committees.   This is not an uncommon process for
highly important bills.

Besides   such   straight-out   jurisdictional
battles, other types of struggles include efforts
by Members of Congress to use the various methods
of   forcing   floor   consideration   to   end-run   a
committee that has bottled up a bill.   Another
type of struggle occurs between the appropriation
and budget committees handling money bills, and
the   other   ("legislative"   or   "authorization")
committees, over the making of policy.   However,
the dramatic "turf war" aspects of committee
jurisdiction   should   not   overshadow   the   more
important   quiet,   undisputed,   but   important
machinery by which committees organize to control
their core areas of jurisdiction.

History

Congress'   standing   committee   system   dates
almost from the beginning of the republic.   The
House   first   established   its   initial   standing
committees over several decades from the 1790s to
the 1820s, while the Senate established a set of
standing committees in 1816.   During the first
half of the eighteenth century, the committees
developed   their   key   prerogatives   and   features:
receiving   referral   of   bills,   reporting   bills   to
their   chambers,   filling   conference   committees,
obtaining staff and office space, and centralizing
authority in their chairs.[9]   In both chambers,

---

[9]   The historic evolution of the congressional committee
system is a subject that cannot be treated here fully.   The
two most extensive studies are J. Cooper, The Origins of the
Standing Committees and the Development of the Modern House
(1970), which develops in an exceptional way the political
philosophies that lay behind the rise of the House committee
system, and G. L. Robinson, The Development of the Senate
Committee System (unpublished Ph.D. dissertation, New York
University, 1954), which traces the various reorganizations
of Senate committees.   An overview of the Senate history is
(footnote continued)

during the nineteenth century seniority gradually
became the primary criterion for members to retain
committee slots and advance within committees
toward the chairmanships.[10]

In the House, committee chairs took on
considerable authority in the late nineteenth
century, and that authority grew with the early
twentieth century demise of the autocratic
Speakers.[11]   The 1911 revolt against Speaker

Kravitz, Evolution of the Senate's Committee System, 411
Ann. Am. Acad. of Poli. Sci. 27 (1974).   For brief
discussions of the early origins of the committee system,
see Origins and Development at 90-91 (House) and 181-82, 187
(Senate); Smith & Deering at 10-18.

[10]   For accounts of the nineteenth century committee system,
see Origins and Development at 110 (House), 202-3
(Senate). In the Senate, seniority as the ground for chairs
became established before the Civil War, as a neutral way
"to avoid fierce inter-party struggles for committee
control." Origins and Development at 196.   See G. H.
Haynes, The Senate of the United States 294-306
(1938)(discussing seniority and chairs, and the few historic
exceptions); R. P. Ripley, Congress: Process and Policy 64
(1975)(suggesting seniority hardened in the Senate shortly
after the return of a substantial post-Civil War Democratic
party in 1877).

In the House, seniority as the ground for retaining
prior committee seats and achieving chairs gradually became
generally accepted in the nineteenth century.   However,
"Speakers were struggling to get contrtol of the House in
the 1880s and 1890s and they frequently ignored seniority in
the appointment of committee chairmen," R.P. Ripley, supra,
at 64.   Seniority did not become an absolute rule until the
revolt against "Czar" Cannon in 1909-11.   See Polsby, The
Institutionalization of the House of Representatives, 62 Am.
Poli. Sci. Rev. 144 (1968).

[11]   Wilson wrote in 1885 that "[t]he leaders of the House
are the chairmen of the principal Standing Committees." W.
Wilson, supra, at 58.   By contrast, "[t]he [Senate]
committee chairman is a leader of secondary importance, much
less privileged on the floor of the Senate than on the floor
of the House." L. G. McConachie, Congressional Committees
326 (1898).   For a discussion of both House and Senate
(footnote continued)

"Czar" Cannon led to assignments to committees in each party by a Committee on Committees, the same system that had developed in the Senate.[12] Subcommittees also burgeoned by the twentieth century.[13]

The hardening of the seniority rule in the twentieth century, plus the rise of the conservative coalition after the late 1930s, lent special power and importance to the committee system and committee chairs. Junior Members found it impossible to depose chairs, and almost impossible to bring legislation to the floor against their will or to challenge them within committees. Chairs of full committees restrained subcommittee chairs during this era by keeping subcommittees in the minimal status of being "special" or "numbered." "Special" subcommittees just worked on one bill and then lapsed;[14]

---

committees in the late nineteenth and early twentieth centuries, see Smith & Deering at 18-22.

[12] Until 1911 the Speaker had assigned committee seats. See Origins and Development at 110-13 (House history), 187, 195-97 (Senate history).

[13] French, Subcommittees of Congress, 9 Am. Poli. Sci Rev. 68 (1915).

[14] A "special" subcommittee was "organized to conduct hearings, in many cases, on one piece of legislation and cease[d] to exist when that task [was] completed," so it "could not develop the same kind of identification [as a standing subcommittee could] with a broad issue area." Haeberle, The Institutionalization of the Subcommittee in the United States House of Representatives, 50 J. of Politics 1054, 1058-59 (1978).

For example, the standing General Education Subcommittee of the House Education and Labor Committee, which periodically handled the major federal school aid legislation contrasted with special subcommittees of the House Foreign Relations Committee, such as "the Subcommittee on the Toll Bridge Across the Rainy River at Baudette, Minnesota and the Subcommittee on the Return to Mexico of Flags Captured in the Mexican War. Obviously, these narrowly defined special subcommittees could not develop the (footnote continued)

"numbered" subcommittees (i.e., a committee's "Subcommittee No. 1" or "Subcommittee No. 2") had no fixed jurisdiction and received bills at the full committee chairs' discretion. [15]

The Senate began evolving out of the era of domination by full committee chairs in the 1960s, as the balance among Senate Democrats shifted from South to North and from conservative to liberal. Junior northern Democrats could not, and did not, depose the full committee chairs, but they pressed for creation of more subcommittees with greater autonomy.[16]   As subcommittees grew in number from

---

same kind of identification with a broad issue area as did the General Education Subcommittee." Id.

[15]   As one observer noted, "For a conservative chairman, perhaps the next best thing to having no subcommittees is to have numbered subcommittees without specified jurisdiction and to assign bills to them according to their responsiveness to his desires." Goodwin, Subcommittees: the Miniature Legislatures of Congress, 56 Am. Poli. Sci. Rev. 596, 598 (1962).   Concerning numbered subcommittees, see also Ornstein, "The Democrats Reform Power in the House of Representatives, 1969-75," in America in the Seventies 2, 24 (A. P. Sindler ed. 1977).

All the House subcommittees from 1947 to 1974 are listed by committee and by type of subcommittee in Appendix B of H.R. Rept. No. 916, 93d Cong., 2d Sess., Part I, at 214-34 (1974) (report of the Bolling Committee).   The list shows the large number of special, special investigating, and numbered subcommittees.   Of the big three House committees other than Appropriations, none had autonomous subcommittees in that era: Ways and Means and Rules had no subcommittees, and the Armed Services Committee had only numbered subcommittees.   T. Siff & A. Weil, Ruling Congress (1975).

[16]   "In the Labor and Public Welfare Committee, which contained more liberals than any other committee, the number of subcommittees doubled from 7 in 1959 to 14 in 1972. . . .   [In the Senate as a whole,] [t]hirteen subcommittee chairmanships were held by liberals in 1959, at a time when there were 18 liberal members in the Senate.   In 1972, liberals held 40 subcommittee chairmanships when their overall membership stood at 24." M. Foley, The New Senate: (footnote continued)

107 in 1955 to 140 in 1975, Majority Leader
Mansfield commented that "I think this body is
getting subcommittee-happy."[17] The shift in power
toward junior Senators was reflected in changes
(discussed in chapters on Senate procedure) in
Majority Leader styles from Lyndon Johnson (D-
Tex.) in the 1950s to Mike Mansfield (D-Mont.),
Robert Byrd (D-W. Va.), Howard Baker (R-Tenn.),
Robert Dole (R-Kans.), and George Mitchell (D-
Maine) in the 1960s to 1990s.

Change in the House was more traumatic.[18] It
started later, in the 1970s, and occurred through
formal rules changes. In 1971, the Democratic
Caucus adopted a rule that spread subcommittee
chairs more widely; in 1973 the Caucus adopted a
"Subcommittee Bill of Rights"; and in December
1974 the Caucus purged three chairs partly for
failing to implement subcommittee rights.[19]

Liberal Influence on a Conservative Institution 1959-1972
242 (1980).

[17] Oleszek, "Overview of the Senate Committee System," in
Commission on the Operation of the Senate, Committees and
Senate Procedures: A Compilation of Papers 1, 6 (Comm. Print
1976). It was apparent that many of these subcommittees
were dormant, holding no meetings and serving only to
provide staff and office space for support of a chairman's
constituent services or his race for President. A 1976
study by the Library of Congress reported that 28 Senate
subcommittees never met in 1975 and that 67 held four or
fewer meetings that year. Congressional Quarterly, Guide to
Congress 384 (2d ed. 1976). Of an eight-part series on the
Washington Post concerning congressional practices, most
parts concerned diversion of staff from committee and
subcommittee work. See Senate Committee System: Hearings
Before the Temporary Select Comm. to Study the Senate
Committee System, 94th Cong., 2d Sess. 283-97 (1976)
(reprinting the series).

[18] House changes were spearheaded by junior Democrats led
by the Democratic Study Group. Democratic Study Group: A
Winner on House Reforms, Cong. Q. Week. Rep. 1366, 1368
(1973). For a vigorous defense of the outcome of the
reforms by the executive director of the Democratic Study
Group, see "Response by Richard P. Conlon" in The United
States Congress 239 (D. Hale ed. 1983).
(footnote continued)

That same revolt shifted the committee
assignment function to the party's Steering and
Policy Committee. Steering and Policy reflected
decision making by the leadership and regional
caucuses. It contrasted with the prior Committee
on Committees (which had been the Democratic
caucus of the Ways and Means Committee), composed
of senior and not very accountable Members.

These evolutionary and revolutionary steps in
both chambers produced an effect described
sometimes as "subcommittee government." The large
number of junior Members who chaired subcommittees
collectively held major control, particularly in
the mid-1970s. Subcommittee chairs held bills
hostage or killed them, scrapped with each other
for turf, and managed bills on the floor.

Such "subcommittee government" spawned a
number of changes and reactions, from the weakened
ability of the Ford and Carter administrations to
manage the Congress to a wide-open floor where
amendments were adopted in unprecedented
numbers. After some experience with the extremes
of this era, each chamber curbed somewhat the
growth of subcommittees: the Senate by its 1977
committee reorganization, the House by a 1981
cap.[20] In both chambers, as discussed in other

---

[19] The 1971 change reduced "the ability of chairmen to
'stockpile' power positions themselves or to assign several
such positions to each of a few committee allies."
Ornstein, supra, in America in the Seventies at 14. This
created the momentum for more reform, since it "made it
possible for younger, liberal, nonsouthern members to become
subcommittee chairmen," and to begin feeling the limitations
of that role. R. H. Davidson & W. J. Oleszek, Congress and
Its Members 226 (1981). The "Subcommittee Bill of Rights,"
now Rule 33 of the House Democratic Caucus, provides that
the Democratic members of each committee -- not the chair --
"shall establish the number of subcommittees, shall fix the
jurisdiction of each subcommittee, and shall determine the
size of each subcommittee."

[20] By 1979 the Senate again had only 105 subcommittees. R.
H. Davidson & W. J. Oleszek, supra, at 225. To take a
particular example, while the Commerce Committee had eight
(footnote continued)

chapters, the reactions included other means for recentralizing power in the party leaderships more than in committee chairs, leaving committee and subcommittee relations in a dynamic balance.

B.   COMMITTEE JURISDICTION

The House and Senate started with initial standing committee systems in place by the 1820s and created or split off new committees as new subjects took on increased importance, such as manufactures in the 1820s, banking and revenues in the 1860s, civil service in the 1870s, overseas territories at the turn of the century, unified armed services in 1940s, aeronautics in the 1950s, and budget in the 1970s. General jurisdictional reorganizations to weed out obsolete committees and to straighten out tangled lines of authority occurred in the Senate[21] and, to a lesser extent, in the House.[22]

---

regular and five special subcommittees in 1976, in 1983 it had seven regular and no special subcommittees, and most of its regular subcommittees had fairly regular jurisdictions. Oleszek, supra, in Committees and Senate Procedures at 5. For the 1981 House cap, see Smith & Deering at 128.

[21] In both chambers, committee reorganization was tied to available perquisites. The Senate's committee reorganization history to 1946 is summarized by the leading commentator as follows: "The Senate's overall pattern of standing committee creation and destruction falls rather neatly into two eras. The first, from 1789 to 1920, was one of accelerating creation and ever larger numbers. The second began with a cataclysmic destruction of committees in 1921, followed by a further reduction in 1946." Kravitz, supra, at 33. The 1921 reorganization consisted of abolishing 41 largely moribund "sinecure" committees, which existed chiefly to allow their chairs perquisites. "When the Senate eventually began to provide every senator with reasonable clerical staff, office space and other allowances, the chief raison d'etre for sinecure committees vanished." Id. at 34.

(footnote continued)

Both Houses engaged in their greatest reorganization pursuant to the Legislative Reorganization Act of 1946, when they radically reduced the number of committees (from 33 to 15 in the Senate and from 48 to 19 in the House), and codified in standing rules the jurisdictional structure, previously a matter of scattered precedent.[23] Since then, the House has not engaged in major committee jurisdictional reorganization. In 1974 and 1980, the House attempted such reorganization, but made only limited adjustments.[24]

---

[22] For a general overview, see Galloway, Development of the Committee System in the House of Representatives, LXV Am. Hist. Rev. 17 (1959). In the House, after summarizing the origins of the committees in the nineteenth century, a commentator adds: "Several of [the House] committees seemed to exist for no other purpose than to furnish rooms for their chairmen -- a highly prized perquisite in the absence of an office building. But after its erection (1909) the House dropped the Committees on Ventilation and Acoustics, Militia, Manufactures, Private Land Claims, Pacific Railroads, and Levee Improvements, leaving a total of fifty-five." DeA. S. Alexander, History and Procedure of the House of Representatives 233 (1916). No major cutback in House committees occurred after 1909 until 1946, when there were still 48 committees.

House reorganizations tended to be less frequent and thoroughgoing than the Senate's, perhaps because of the more intense investment of House members in their assignments, which were fewer in number than Senators'.

[23] Origins and Development at 136. The Legislative Reorganization Act sought to "define the jurisdiction of each reorganized committee so as to avoid jurisdictional disputes between them." S. Rept. No. 1400, 79th Cong., 2d Sess. 3 (1946). The 1946 act reacted to a number of factors, from the untidy proliferation of investigating committees in the 1930s to recognition after World War II of the need to meet larger responsibilities. Much intellectual credit is due to Dr. George H. Galloway, a leading commentator on congressional affairs who served as staff director in 1945-46 of the Joint Committee on the Organization of Congress which produced the 1946 act.

(footnote continued)

By contrast, in the late 1970s, the Senate recognized that overlapping committee jurisdictions and soaring numbers of subcommittees[25] necessitated a major reorganization. Accordingly, in 1977 the Senate followed the recommendations of a Temporary Select Committee on Committees, the Stevenson Committee, and reorganized its committee jurisdictions, considerably reducing the number of subcommittees and clarifying the lines of committee jurisdiction.[26]   The Senate gave some

---

[24]   The Bolling Committee effort in 1974 is chronicled in R. H. Davidson & W. J. Oleszek, Congress Against Itself (1977).   The Patterson Committee in 1980 received little attention.   It produced a fine study of several procedural issues, H. Rept. No. 866, 96th Cong., 2d Sess. (1980), and it did reshape the House's handling of energy bills, but otherwise it "le[ft] behind barely a trace of its 13-month-long effort to change House procedures." 1980 Congressional Quarterly Almanac 562.

[25]   "In 1945, the 33 full committees of the Senate had 34 standing subcommittees.   In 1976, the standing committees had no fewer than 140 subcommittees." Temporary Senate Select Committee to Study the Senate Committee System, 94th Cong., 2d Sess., The Senate Committee System: Jurisdictions, Referrals, Numbers and Sizes, and Limitations on Membership 6 (Comm. Print 1976) (staff report) (The Senate Committee System).   That staff study noted that federal energy authorities were "answerable to no fewer than 14 standing committees of the Senate, not to mention 2 select committees and 31 subcommittees or panels," and concluded that while "[e]nergy is probably the most striking current example of jurisdictional overlap[,] the picture is not very different for environmental protection, economic policy, research and development, transportation, health, and other such topics." Id. at 103.

[26]   For a discussion of the 1977 reorganization, see Parris, The Senate Reorganizes Its Committees, 1977, 94 Poli. Sci. Q. 319 (1979).   Of the topics where the overlaps had been greatest, S. Res. 4 attempted to put most urban affairs jurisdiction in Banking, Housing, and Urban Affairs; most science and transportation jurisdiction in Commerce, Science, and Transportation; most energy jurisdiction in Energy and Natural Resources; most environmental jurisdiction in Environment and Public Works; most (footnote continued)

consideration in 1985 to another reorganization to trim the number of subcommittees, but ultimately left them largely untouched.[27]

"Regular" Committees

The House and Senate both establish their committee jurisdictions by standing rules, Senate Rule XXV and House Rule X.   For example, the Senate establishes its Committee on Foreign Relations in Senate Rule XXV(1)(j), which provides "[t]he following standing committees shall be appointed at the commencement of each Congress . . . .   (j) Committee on Foreign Relations, to which committee shall be referred all proposed legislation . . . relating to . . . [r]elations of the United States with foreign nations generally [among other subjects]."   Each chamber supplements these rules with a host of precedents of past referrals of legislation.

While the the details of committee jurisdictional divisions take up whole volumes,[28] certain basic concepts provide considerable guidance.   The House and Senate have roughly matching structures, both of which correspond very roughly to the organization of the executive

---

international economic policy jurisdiction in Foreign Relations; and most health and education jurisdiction in Labor and Human Resources.

[27] Senate Cuts Committee Slots; Members Assigned to Panels, 43 Cong. Q. Week. Rep. 348, 349 (1985) ("Opposition to cutting subcommittees has come chiefly from Republicans who are up for re-election in 1986 . . . .   [who] weren't exactly standing in line to give up their subcommittee chairs") (quotation omitted).

[28] For the House, the best study is House Select Committee on Committees, 93d Cong., 2d Sess., Monographs on the Committees of the House of Representatives (Comm. Print 1974).   For the Senate, the equally unrivaled study is: Temporary Senate Select Committee to Study the Senate Committee System, 94th Cong., 2d Sess., The Senate Committee System: Jurisdictions, Referrals, Numbers and Sizes, and Limitations on Membership (Comm. Print 1976) (staff report).

departments. Most of the 13 executive departments report primarily to one committee in each chamber; most major committees primarily oversee one executive department.

Eight committees each have jurisdiction primarily over areas for which there is one executive department:

-- the foreign relations and armed services committees have jurisdiction over foreign relations and military affairs, paralleling the State and Defense departments;
-- the agriculture committees have jurisdiction over the nation's agricultural affairs, paralleling the Agriculture Department;

-- the judiciary committees have jurisdiction over the criminal laws, immigration,[29] and the federal courts, paralleling the Justice Department's enforcement of the criminal and immigration laws;

-- the education and labor committees (House Education and Labor, Senate Labor and Human Resources) have jurisdiction over federal educational and labor programs, paralleling the Education Department and the Labor Department;
-- the public land committees (House Interior, Senate Energy and Natural Resources) have jurisdiction over public land matters paralleling the Interior Department;[30]

---

[29] However, in the House, immigration reform presents an example of jurisdictional overlap. While House Judiciary handles most normal immigration legislation, omnibus immigration reform bills have been multiply referred to other interested committees, namely Agriculture (because of the farm labor role of aliens) and Labor and Human Resources (because of aliens' other labor roles and the potential for employer sanctions to enforce immigration laws).

[30] Following a nineteeth-century division, a large portion of the public lands, primarily acquired lands in the East, are national forests administered by the Forest Service in the Agriculture Department, which fall into the jurisdiction (footnote continued)

-- the banking committees (House Banking, Finance, and Urban Affairs; Senate Banking, Housing, and Urban Affairs) have jurisdiction over the nation's housing and urban programs, paralleling the Department of Housing and Urban Affairs.

The accompanying chart illustrates both these straightforward parallels and the more complex areas.

The chart points to serious overlaps, grey areas, and fragmentation in the jurisdictional structure for the five remaining executive departments.   Obviously, there are some basic parallels suggesting the core jurisdiction of many of the remaining committees:

-- the tax committees (House Ways and Means, Senate Finance) have jurisdiction over taxes and public borrowing, paralleling the Treasury Department;

-- the energy committees (House Energy and Commerce for nonresearch aspects, House Science, Space, and Technology for research aspects; Senate Energy and Natural Resources) have jurisdiction over energy, paralleling the Energy Department;

-- the maritime committees (House Merchant Marine and Fisheries, Senate Commerce, Science, and Transportation) have jurisdiction over maritime affairs, paralleling the maritime components of the Commerce Department and of the independent Federal Maritime Commission;

-- the transportation committees (House Public Works and Transportation for highways, Energy and Commerce for rail; Senate Environment and Public Works for highways, Commerce, Science, and Transportation for rail) have jurisdiction over transportation, paralleling the Department of Transportation and the Interstate Commerce

---

of the agriculture committees.   Such matters as mining in national forests raise complex jurisdictional questions both administratively and for the congressional committees.

CHART OF JURISDICTIONAL PARALLELS
FOR CABINET DEPARTMENTS

Executive Department	House Committee	Senate Committee
Agriculture	Agriculture	Agriculture
Commerce	*	*
Defense	Armed Services	Armed Services
Education	Education and Labor	Labor and Human Resources
Energy	1. Energy and Commerce 2. Science, Space, and Technology	Energy and Natural Resources
Health and Human Services	1. Ways and Means 2. Education and Labor 3. Energy and Commerce	1. Finance 2. Labor and Human Resources
Housing and Urban Development	Banking	Banking
Interior	Interior	Energy and Natural Resources
Justice	Judiciary	Judiciary
Labor	Education and Labor	Labor and Human Resources
State	Foreign Affairs	Foreign Relations
Transportation	Public Works and Transportation	1. Environment and Public Works 2. Commerce, Science, and Transportation
Treasury	1. Ways and Means 2. Banking	1. Finance 2. Banking

Commission.

However, each of these committees and areas presents complex overlaps. Transportation presents a classic overlap, because the Transportation Department brings together different transportation modes, but Congress does not. The Secretary of Transportation reports to one pair of committees regarding highways and other committees concerning maritime, rail, and mass transit programs.[31] Moreover, the aforementioned committees only control spending and regulation, while the tax committees control the earmarked taxes that provide funding for improvements (the highway gasoline tax and the airplane ticket tax).[32]

The Treasury Department reflects another jurisdictional split. Its tax matters are handled by the tax committees (House Ways and Means, Senate Finance). Its banking matters are handled by the banking committees. Its role in international trade and finance is split largely between the tax and banking committees.[33]

---

[31] Highways are overseen by House Public Works and Transportation and Senate Energy and Public Works. Shipping is overseen by the maritime committees (House Merchant Marine and Fisheries; Senate Commerce, Science and Transportation). Mass transit is overseen by House Banking and Senate Banking.

[32] For example, a jurisdictional dispute occurred in 1982 between House Ways and Means and House Public Works and Transportation concerning jurisdiction over the bill to increase the gasoline tax to fund public works, since Ways and Means controls the earmarked tax, and Public Works and Transportation controls the spending.

[33] Trade jurisdiction splits in a complex way. The tax committees (House Ways and Means, Senate Finance) set tariff rates and import quotas and oversee reciprocal trade agreements. However, the banking committees devise export controls. The foreign affairs committees have a nebulous role: for example, Senate Foreign Relations' jurisdiction under Senate Rule XXV(1)(j) includes the International Monetary Fund, and "Measures to foster commercial (footnote continued)

The huge Department of Health and Human Services reports to a host of committees on one matter or another. Its primary job, the administration of Social Security, Medicare, and disability insurance programs, falls under the jurisdiction of the tax committees because of the earmarked payroll taxes that fund those programs, a jurisdictional line laid down in the 1930s and confirmed in the 1960s. On social welfare matters, HHS reports to the social welfare committees (House Education and Labor, Senate Labor and Human Resources). The department's health matters are split complexly.[34]

The Energy Department also presents some fragmentation, although in general it reflects an achievement of administrative and congressional reorganization efforts. The 1977 Senate reorganization consolidated most energy jurisdiction in the Energy and Natural Resources Committee (formerly the Interior Committee). In 1980, the House consolidated most of its nonresearch energy jurisdiction in the Energy and Commerce Committee (formerly the Interstate and Foreign Commerce Committee). It consolidated energy research jurisdiction in Science, Space and Technology.

Finally, the Commerce Department presents the extreme case of jurisdictional overlap, for it is essentially a "holding company" for unrelated functions, with the parallel committee jurisdictions badly split. Its international trade functions fall under the different committees with overlapping roles regarding trade matters, principally the tax and banking committees. Its maritime functions fall under the maritime committees (House Merchant Marine and

---

intercourse with foreign nations and to safeguard American business interests abroad," while House Banking, not House Foreign Affairs, covers the International Monetary Fund.

[34] Medicare, as noted, belongs to the tax committees. Medicaid is handled in the Senate by Finance, in the House by Ways and Means together with Energy and Commerce. Health facilities are handled in the Senate by Labor and Human Resources, in the House by Energy and Commerce.

Fisheries; Senate Commerce, Science, and Transportation). Its research, census, and patent components all fall under different sets of congressional committees.[35]

In addition to the 13 cabinet departments, there are a number of other important governmental bodies, the reporting relations of which are summarized in the accompanying chart.

"Special" Committees

Although the overlaps render the above-denominated jurisdictions complex, they bear a recognizably "regular" pattern of jurisdiction over particular executive departments. There are also a wide variety of committees that do not fit under that rubric and may loosely be called "special,"[36] coming in five kinds: government-wide, specialized, internal, select, and joint.

---

[35] The scientific components are overseen by House Science, Space, and Technology and Senate Commerce, Science, and Transportation. The Patent Office is overseen by House Judiciary and Senate Judiciary. The Census Bureau is overseen by House Post Office and Civil Service and by Senate Governmental Affairs.

[36] This should not be confused with the very limited class of committees actually named "special," which are similar to "select" committees. The purpose here is not to launch a new nomenclature into a field already full of patterns, none of which easily fit the varied facts, but simply to separate the easiest-to-describe "regular" committees from the others.

CHART OF JURISDICTIONAL PARALLELS FOR
INDEPENDENT EXECUTIVE OFFICES

Body	House Committee	Senate Committee
Intelligence Agencies	Intelligence	Intelligence
District of Columbia	D.C. Committee	Governmental Affairs
Environmental Protection Agency	1. Energy and Commerce 2. Science, Space and Technology	Environment and Public Works
Federal Reserve	Banking	Banking
NASA	Science, Space and Technology	Commerce, Science, and Transportation
Postal Service	Post Office and Civil Service	Governmental Affairs
Veterans' Administration	Veterans' Affairs	Veterans' Affairs
Independent Regulatory Agencies	Commerce and Energy	Commerce, Science, and Transportation

First, the chart does not address the Appropriations, Budget, and Governmental Affairs[37] committees. These exercise a government-wide jurisdiction over, respectively, spending, budgeting, and oversight. For example, the

---

[37] These are Senate Governmental Affairs and House Government Operations. The Senate committee has legislative jurisdiction over the District of Columbia and the Postal Service, which was given it in the 1977 reorganization to allow the abolition of the committees with those jurisdictions.

spending for all the departments must come from
the Appropriations Committee (apart from
entitlement legislation). Appropriations and
Budget are each the subject of a separate chapter.

Second, several committees have specialized
jurisdiction built around the needs of a
particular constituency. These committees look
into those needs, regardless of which agency is
involved. For example, the Small Business
committees look out for the small business
community, which takes in some of the farm
regulations of the Agriculture Department, the
procurement policies of the Defense Department,
the antitrust enforcement practices of the Justice
Department, and whatever else concerns the small
business community. Typically, constituency-
oriented committees are select rather than
standing, and their jurisdiction is largely
limited to oversight rather than legislation.[38]
Then, there are internal committees, which concern
themselves with the rules, housekeeping, and
ethics of their chambers. The House Rules
Committee controls the House's floor operations
for the legislation in all areas; it is the
subject of much of the chapter on House
scheduling.

The accompanying chart summarizes the
government-wide, specialized, and internal
committees by subject (rather than department).

Supplementing the standing committee system
are two minor adjuncts, select committees (or
special committees)[39] and joint ones. Select

---

[38]   The distinction between oversight and legislative
jurisdiction is discussed in a separate section.

[39]   Once there were differences between select and special
committees, but now the terms are virtually interchangeable.

SPECIALIZED COMMITTEES

Subject	House Committee	Senate Committee
Budgeting	Budget	Budget
Spending	Appropriations	Appropriations
Taxing	Ways and Means	Finance
Oversight	Government Operations	Governmental Affairs
Elderly	Aging	Aging
Children	Children, Youth, and Families	----
Indians	Interior	Indian Affairs
Small Business	Small Business	Small Business
Civil Service	Post Office and Civil Service	Governmental Affairs
Drugs	Narcotics	----

INTERNAL

Rules	Rules	Rules and Administration
Housekeeping	House Administration	Rules and Administration
Ethics	Standards of Official Conduct	Ethics

committees typically derive their authority from Senate or House resolutions rather than from the standing rules.   For   example,   the   Senate established its Select Committee on Intelligence, not in Senate Rule XXV, but in Senate Resolution 400,   94th   Cong.,   2d   Sess.   (1976).[40] Traditionally,   the   grant   of   authority   by resolution rather than by rule meant that select committees   were   intended   to   be   temporary   in duration, but now some select committees have no durational limit.[41]

Select committees typically combine a limited legislative jurisdiction (or none at all) with a broad   oversight   jurisdiction.   For   example, neither   the   Senate   nor   the   House   Select   Aging Committees can report legislation.   However, they can investigate the problems of the elderly and make proposals for the consideration of standing committees which do have legislative jurisdiction.

Currently,   the   Senate   has   three   select   or special   committees   with   no   time   limit   on   their lives: Ethics,   Intelligence,   and   Aging.[42] Similarly,   the   House   has   four   select   committees with   no   time   limit[43]   on   their   lives: Aging;

---

[40]   Two   House   select   committees   are   established   by   rule rather than by resolution, Intelligence (House Rule XLVIII) and Aging (House Rule X(6)(i)).   Technically, the House, as a body, appoints the members of standing committees, while the Speaker appoints the members of select committees under House Rule X(6)(f).

[41]   The Senate Study Group established under S. Res. 392, 97th Cong., 2d Sess. (1982) proposed that Intelligence be absorbed by Appropriations, Armed Services, and Foreign Relations; Ethics, by Rules; Aging, by Labor and Human Resources;   and   Indian   Affairs,   by   Energy   and   Natural Resources.   This recommendation was not acted upon by the Senate but reflects the potential for treating the select committees as temporary.

[42]   A   fourth   committee,   the   Select   Committee   on   Indian Affairs, has a temporary mandate which has been periodically renewed.

(footnote continued)

Children, Youth and Families (created in 1983); Intelligence; and Narcotics. Besides the long-term select committees, from time to time the House or Senate creates temporary select committees for special investigations, such as the Watergate, Assassinations, and Billy Carter committees in the 1970s, the Abscam Committee in 1982, and the Iran arms deal committees in 1987.

Finally, there are a few joint committees, which are unique bodies because they have members from both the House and the Senate. These derive their authority from public laws rather than one-chamber rules or resolutions. The 1970s saw a trend against joint committees, with the abolition of the powerful Joint Committee on Atomic Energy and some minor entities. Of the current joint committees, only the Joint Economic Committee stands out as having a significant public presence through its wide-ranging hearings on the economy. The Joint Tax Committee provides staff support to the House and Senate tax committees.

Oversight Jurisdiction

Besides legislating, committees conduct oversight: even when they do not have any bill before them on a particular subject, they investigate, obtain information, hold hearings, and write reports on the subjects if it is of interest. Committees have "oversight jurisdiction" -- the power to conduct oversight -- for areas of their legislative jurisdiction,[44]

---

[43] Technically, the House must readopt all rules at the start of each Congress, and it thus recreates its standing committees every two years. For practical purposes, that does not constitute a time limit on the life of committees, the way an expiration date in a resolution creating a select committee does, since readoption of the jurisdictional rule is standard.

[44] For example, when the Senate Committee on Labor and Human Resources uses its jurisdiction to legislate regarding elderly assistance, it can put existing programs under the spotlight by investigating.

AREAS OF OVERSIGHT JURISDICTION ADDED IN 1970s REORGANIZATIONS[45]

House Committee	Oversight Area	Senate Committee	Oversight Area
Armed Services	arms control, military schools	Armed Services	defense policy
Budget	budget outlays tax expenditures	Budget	budget outlays tax expenditures
Education and Labor	educational programs	Labor and Human Resources	education and training, public welfare, health
Foreign Affairs	customs intelligence int'l financial organizations	Foreign Relations	nat'l security, foreign policy, int'l economic policy
Energy and Commerce	nuclear and other energy	Energy and Natural Resources	energy, resources development
Interior	nonmilitary nuclear waste disposal and energy	Environment and Public Works	environmental protection, resource conservation
Science, Space and Technology	nonmilitary research	Science, Commerce, and Transportation	science transportation communications consumer affairs
		Agriculture	food and nutrition
		Banking	international economic policy, credit, financial institutions, economic affairs, urban growth

---

54 House Rule X(3), Senate Rule XXV(1).

beyond the areas where they have legislative jurisdiction,[45] and even when they have no legislative jurisdiction at all. For example, the Senate Select Committees on Aging's authorizing resolution specifies that "No proposed legislation shall be referred to such committee, and such committee shall not have power to report by bill, or otherwise have legislative jurisdiction."[46] The Senate authorizes the Aging Committee only to "conduct a continuing study of any and all matters pertaining to problems and opportunities of older people."[47] That means it can conduct oversight, but cannot legislate.

Oversight jurisdiction has two historical roots. The House and Senate have appointed hundreds of special investigating committees since 1792 that could investigate though not legislate.[48] Famous ones include the Senate committee that investigated the Teapot Dome scandal, the Kefauver Crime Committee, the McClellan Labor Racketeering Committee, and the Watergate (Ervin) Committee.[49] Second, in the

---

[45] For example, the House Foreign Affairs Committee does not have legislative jurisdiction over international financial and monetary institutions, which is vested in the House Banking Committee. See House Rule X(1)(d)(8)(Banking), X(3)(d)(Foreign Affairs). However, the House Foreign Affairs Committee does have oversight jurisdiction over international financial and monetary organizations.

[46] Section 104(b)(1) of S. Res. 4, 95th Cong., 1st Sess. (1977).

[47] Id.

[48] See Chalou, "St. Clair's Defeat, 1792," in Congress Investigates: 1792-1974 1-18 (A. Schlesinger & R. Bruns. eds. 1975) (describing first investigation, in 1792). "No writer has made a complete tabulation of investigations to date. Dimock, however, found 330 concluded between 1792 and 1928 . . . . From 1929 to 1938, 146 more were authorized." McGeary, Congressional Investigations: Historical Development, 18 U. Chi. L. Rev. 425, 425 n.4 (1951).
(footnote continued)

nineteenth century the House and Senate created standing audit committees, the descendants of which were renamed Government Operations in 1952, with the Senate committee later renamed Governmental Affairs.[50] Besides some legislative jurisdiction, these committees have essentially unlimited power to investigate and to conduct oversight anywhere in the government.[51]

Based on these historic examples, the Legislative Reorganization Act of 1946 moved to confirm and strengthen oversight jurisdiction of

---

[49] These committees had power to summon witnesses, report conclusions, and even recommend legislation. However, no bills could be referred to them, and they could not report legislation. For example, the Watergate Committee concluded its investigation with a report with various legislative recommendations such as for ethics laws. It could not report a bill with such ethics provisions. Only the Senate Governmental Affairs Committee could send such a bill to the floor.

[50] In 1814, the House created a Committee for Public Expenditures; the Senate created a similar committee in 1884. The House and Senate divided their expenditure committees into several committees, then reassembled them into single committees in the 1920s. See L. Fisher, Presidential Spending Power 14 (1975); History 1911-1971, Committee on Government Operations of the United States Senate, S. Doc. No. 31, 92d Cong., 1st Sess. 2, 4 (1971); House Manual § 679. As Woodrow Wilson wrote in 1884 of those committees, "[b]esides exercising these functions of careful audit, they are, moreover, required to . . . . ferret out all abuses that may make their appearance." W. Wilson, Congressional Government 125-26 (1956 ed.). Regarding the Senate Governmental Affairs Committee, see S. Doc. No. 31, supra, at 17; regarding the House Government Operations Committee, see House Manual § 679.

[51] Even when some committee exercises total legislative jurisdiction, as the armed services committees exercise over the military, the government operations committees can, and do, investigate waste and fraud, hold hearings, write reports, and make legislative recommendations, though they cannot report bills outside their limited legislative jurisdiction.

standing committees within their legislative
jurisdiction, by conferring subpoena authority on
all standing Senate committees and duly authorized
subcommittees, a step which the House ultimately
took in 1975.[52]   Following that 1946 act,
committee claims to oversight jurisdiction
proliferated.[53]   In the 1970s, both Houses
augmented committees' oversight jurisdiction to
let them look at matters systematically and
comprehensively, even when they lacked
comprehensive legislative jurisdiction.   The
accompanying table shows the House grants of
"special oversight jurisdiction" and the Senate's
grants of the equivalent jurisdiction to "study
and review."

Committees that lack legislative jurisdiction
but have some claim to oversight jurisdiction,
real or tenuous, often stake jurisdictional claims
by holding hearings and influencing the
development of policy. A dramatic example came
during the Senate's consideration of the SALT II
treaty in 1979.   Only the Foreign Relations
Committee had legislative jurisdiction over the
treaties, but the Armed Services Committee could
claim oversight jurisdiction for the treaty's
military implications.   Accordingly, the Armed
Services Committee held hearings, with more
dramatic and more "intense questioning" than in
Foreign Relations' hearings, since a "much larger
number of senators on this panel was hostile to
the treaty than was the case on Foreign

---

[52] Section 133 of the Legislative Reorganization Act of
1946, which conferred the subpoena power, is now Senate Rule
XXVI. The House's conferral of subpoena power is discussed
in House Manual § 718. Prior to these standing rules, the
House and Senate conferred subpoena power on standing
committees by adopting resolutions providing that power.

[53] As the Stevenson Committee noted in 1976: "Oversight
jurisdiction necessarily flows from specific legislative
enactments, but it also emanates from broader and more
vaguely defined jurisdiction which committees may exercise
in particular subject matter areas. Hence oversight
jurisdiction is more subject to overlap than is legislative
jurisdiction." The Senate Committee System, supra, at 104.

Relations."[55]

Later, the Armed Services Committee captured public attention in another way. It "adopted a report concluding that the SALT II treaty 'as it now stands, is not in the national security interests of the United States,'" after a jurisdictional dispute. "The committee battle over the report focused almost exclusively on the question of whether the panel had a right to adopt a formal report on the treaty which was under the jurisdiction of the Foreign Relations Committee."[56]

C.   COMMITTEE ASSIGNMENT

The system of committee jurisdiction gives Members a strong incentive to obtain positions on desirable committees, and makes the assignment of Members to particular committees critical for what happens to legislation in each area. This section addresses in turn the two distinguishable aspects that determine assignments: how many seats there are to assign (a product of committee size and the proportion of seats for each party, or "party ratio"); and who gets which seats (the machinery for "member assignment").

Committee Size and Party Ratio

Of course, committees come in all sizes, from the House's compact Rules Committee with 13 Members to its Appropriations Committee with over 50 Members. For assignment purposes, the key House trend regarding committee size has been the slow but steady tendency for growth, as the easiest solution to demands by Members for more assignments. In effect, the House "inflated" the currency of committee membership over time to pay off irresistible demands for more committee

---

[55]   1979 Congressional Quarterly Almanac 417.

[56]   Id. at 428.

slots.[57]   As recent academic observers described that historical change:

> In the 1950s only about a third of all House Democrats had two assignments, but that number rose gradually in the 1970s under Speaker John McCormack and then shot upward in the early 1970s under Speaker Carl Albert . . . .   With Albert's help, reformers successfully pushed for caucus rules guaranteeing all Democrats two assignments, except for members of the three exclusive committees.[58]

The House grew from 484 committee seats in the 80th Congress to 771 seats in the 94th Congress; some of the increase was in new committees, but most of the increase was due to the enlargement of existing committees.[59]

---

[57]   For various theories about the purpose of House leaders in allowing committee expansion, see Ray & Smith, Committee Size in the U.S. Congress, 9 Legis. Stud. Q. 679 (1984); Westefield, Majority Party Leadership and the Committee System in the House of Representatives, 69 Am. Poli. Sci. Rev. 1593 (1974).

[58]   Smith & Deering at 235.   House Democratic Caucus Rule 18 states in part:

Rule 18.   Restrictions on Committee Memberships

A.   Except with respect to service on the Committee on the Budget, no Democratic member of an exclusive committee shall also serve on another exclusive, major, or non-major committee.

B.   Each Democratic Member shall be entitled to serve on one but only one exclusive or one major committee.

C.   No Democratic Member shall serve on more than one major and one non-major committee or two non-major committees.

[59]   Final Report of the House Select Committee on Committees, H.R. Rept. No. 866, 96th Cong., 2d Sess. 489 (1980).

"Committee assignments per member [rose] from nearly 1.3 slots in 1959 to better than 1.6 slots in 1975."[60]   A dramatic example of committee expansion was the House Ways and Means Committee, which the Democratic Caucus forcibly increased from 25 to 37 seats in 1975.[61]

Combined with the increase in autonomous subcommittees, this expansion in the number of committee slots has greatly increased the number of demands on House Members.   As a House subcommittee staff director commented,

> Everyone is familiar with the pinball existence of members of Congress, bouncing between several subcommittees, at least two committees, conferences, office work, constituent visits and the floor schedule. For example, "in 1977-78, there were 7,000 committee and subcommittee meetings, 5,000 of which presented scheduling conflicts for the members."[62]

Or as one Representative described his existence, "You are a piece of meat shoved from one meeting to another."[63]
The other component defining the available House committee seats for assignment is the ratio of the seats for each party.   Until the mid-1970s, the party ratio in the House as a whole generally determined the party ratio for each committee. For example, if the Democrats had 55% of the seats

---

[60]   K. A. Shepsle, The Giant Jigsaw Puzzle: Democratic Committee Assignments in the Modern House 242 (1978).

[61]   Rudder, Committee Reform and the Revenue Process, in Congress Reconsidered 117, 120 (L. C. Dodd & B. I. Oppenheimer eds. 1977).

[62]   Wolanin, "A View from the Trench: Reforming Congressional Procedures," in The United States Congress 209, 225 (ed. D. Hale 1983), quoting Frenzel, House Reforms and Why They Haven't Worked, Commonsense 3 (1980), at 32.

[63]   Congress Off the Record: The Candid Analyses of Seven Members 13 (ed. J. F. Bibby 1983).

in the House, then on each committee they would assign 55% of the slots to themselves, and 45% to the Republicans.   Only   for   a   few   critical committees, such as the Rules Committee,[64] did the Democrats   assign   themselves   more   seats   in committee than their proportion of the House.

Breaking from this pattern, the Democratic Caucus in 1975 allocated more seats to Democrats than their proportion in the House.[65]   In 1981, Republican Members sued the Democratic leadership in federal court challenging the party ratios, but the courts dismissed the case as an internal congressional matter.[66]   The large Democratic success in the 1982 election, with a limited loss in 1984, closed the gap somewhat between House and committee ratios, and in 1985, the matter was largely laid to rest by Democratic allocation of additional seats to Republicans.[67]

---

[64]   "Even when one party has held a bare House majority (as in the 65th, 72nd, and 83rd Congresses among others), the majority has maintained at least a two-to-one advantage on the Rules Committee since 1917."   House Committee on Rules, 97th Cong., 2d Sess., A History of the Committee on Rules 234 (Comm. Print 1983).

[65]   The change's purpose was to break the voting power on committees of the coalition of Republicans and conservative Democrats, by opening new seats for Democrats not members of that coalition.   The Democratic Caucus accepted a Democratic Study Group proposal to set the party ratio on all committees at "2 to 1 plus 1."   This meant that the Democrats would receive twice as many seats on each committee, plus one additional seat, as the Republicans. Id. at 491.   House Democratic Caucus Rule 11 stated that "Committee ratios should be established to create firm working majorities on each committee.   In determining the ratio on the respective standing committees, the Speaker should provide for a minimum of three Democrats for each two Republicans."

[66]   Vander Jagt v. O'Neill, 699 F.2d 1166 (D.C. Cir. 1983).

[67]   1985 Congressional Quarterly Almanac 17-G.

The Senate has fought back from time to time against its own trend toward growth in committee size. In 1946 it imposed limits on assignments to major committees,[68] and in 1970 to minor committees.[69] By 1976, despite these limits, the number of assignments, particularly subcommittee assignments, had zoomed again.[70] Accordingly, in 1977 the Senate cut back a second time, limiting Senators, in most cases, to serve on only three

---

[68] The 1921 change was noted in the historical discussion. The Legislative Reorganization Act of 1946 limited Senators to membership on no more than two of the standing committees. Section 103 of the Legislative Reorganization Act, Rule XXV(2)(4), provided: "Each Senator shall serve on two standing committees and no more; except that Senators of the majority party who are members of the Committee on the District of Columbia or of the Committee on Expenditures in the Executive Departments may serve on three standing committees and no more."

[69] By 1970, the Members had inflated their memberships by adding many assignments to minor committees, which were not counted in the Rule XXV limit. Accordingly, the Legislative Reorganization Act of 1970 imposed limits on minor committee assignments as well. Section 132 of the Legislative Reorganization Act of 1946 imposed a complex system by adding several paragraphs to Senate Rule XXV. Rule XXV(6) limited Senators to two seats on major standing committees, one seat on a minor standing committee, one seat on a select or special committee, and one seat on a joint committee. The rule granted elaborate "grandfather" rights to permit Senators holding extra seats before 1970 to keep them.

[70] Compared to 1947, the Senate had six more select and special committees and eight joint committees, and it had 171 subcommittees (compared to 44 in 1947). Temporary Select Committee to Study the Senate Committee System, 94th Cong., 2d Sess., First Staff Report: The Senate Committee System 6 (1976). The number of standing committee assignments had grown slowly, from 2.1 per Senator in 1947 to 2.56 in 1976. Meanwhile the number of subcommittee assignments mushroomed from 2.5 per Senator in 1947 to 11.4 in 1976. Id. That figure counted only subcommittees of standing committees. If subcommittees of select, special, and joint committees were counted, the figure went up further to 14.3 subcommittee assignments per Senator.

subcommittees of each of their major committees, and two subcommittees of each of their minor committees.[71]

Thereafter, again the pressures arose for inflating committee and subcommittee memberships. As a task force noted in 1984, "[b]efore the [1977] reforms efforts . . . there were 240 slots on standing committees. For the 98th Congress there [were] 292 slots on standing committees."[72]

The task force noted the resulting strains: "When senators acquire additional committee and subcommittee commitments, it becomes increasingly difficult for them to attend all of the meetings scheduled for each of their panels. This situation frustrates not only each individual senator, but the chairs of committees when they try to muster a quorum to conduct business."[73] The task force, chaired by Senator Quayle, recommended another pruning back of subcommittee memberships, which the Senate carried out in 1985, cutting back the slots on major committees from 231 to 214.[74]

---

[71] This cutback in the number of subcommittee assignments per member produced a drop in the number of subcommittees, as Senators eliminated or consolidated subcommittees not worth their limited number of assignments. The subcommittee limitation is Rule XXV(4)(b). For a full description of the labyrinthian assignment rules, see J. Schneider, Senate Rules and Practices on Committee, Subcommittee, and Chairmanship Assignment Limitations, as of April 30, 1982 (Cong. Res. Serv. Print 1982).

[72] Report of the Temporary Select Committee to Study the Senate Committee System, S. Prt. No. 254, 98th Cong., 2d Sess. 6 (1984).

[73] Report of the Temporary Select Committee, supra, at 7.

[74] The Quayle Committee noted that while Senate Rule XXV limited Senators to service on no more than two major committees and one minor committee, "Rule XXV also provides 55 exceptions to these assignment limitations covering (footnote continued)

Thus, the Senate kept some restraint on the sizes of committees. The other component determining the number of seats available to each party, the party ratio, was not significantly varied in the Senate, which consistently uses roughly the same party ratio on each committee that the parties have in the whole body, subject to some fine-tuning by negotiations between party leaderships at the beginning of each Congress.

House Assignments [75]

The formal sequence in the House for committee assignments starts following the congressional election in November of each even-numbered year when the two parties engage in a flurry of committee assignment planning. Each party has a committee on committees that serves as the arena for thrashing out assignment decisions: the Democratic Steering and Policy Committee, and the executive committee of the Republican Committee on Committees (whose decisions are ratified by the full Republican Committee on Committees). Once these committees make the initial decisions regarding committee assignments, those decisions go to the party caucus for ratification. When the new House convenes in January, or if decisions have not yet been made, then at an early point (typically late in January) in the new session, the House ratifies these caucus decisions by adopting House resolutions formally making the assignments.

---

additional committee assignments for 50 senators during the 98th Congress." Report of the Temporary Select Committee, supra, at 6.

See also Committee Slots May be Cut; Filibuster Change Considered, 43 Cong. Q. Week. Rep. 108 (1985); Senate Cuts Committee Slots; Members Assigned to Panels, 43 Cong. Q. Week. Rep. 348 (1985).

[75] For a review of the literature on the subject, see Eulau, Legislative Committee Assignments, 9 Legis. Stud. Q. 587 (1984).

In the 1970s, House Democrats changed their mechanism for assigning Members to seats, as noted above, from the Democratic caucus of the Ways and Means Committee to the leadership-influenced Steering and Policy Committee. The new assignment structure has helped junior Members somewhat to obtain desirable positions. In 1983-84, the 79 freshmen (18 per cent of the House) racked up proportionate levels on important House committees such as Armed Services, Energy and Commerce, Foreign Affairs, Banking, and a high of 17 seats out of the total of 49 on Public Works.[76] However, the exclusive committees -- Appropriations, Ways and Means, and Rules -- still remained largely for senior Members.[77]

The virtually ironclad rule called by observers the "property-right norm" is that reelected Members hold the seats assigned in previous Congresses unless they ask for transfer. Because of the "property-right norm," the assignment process begins with requests by newly-elected freshmen for seats but, from reelected Members, requests only for transfers to new seats.

Members making their requests must balance a number of factors. The main consideration is how they can help their reelection, and this chiefly means obtaining seats on committees with "jurisdiction over specific segments of federal activity to benefit [the] locale"[78] of their

---

[76] The freshman portions on these committees were (freshman seats/total committee seats): Armed Services, 8/44; Energy and Commerce, 6/42; Foreign Affairs, 6/37; Banking, 10/47.

[77] In 1975-76 "the three most powerful House committees -- Appropriations, Rules and Ways and Means -- had only seven freshmen among their 73 Democratic members." Congressional Quarterly, Guide to Congress 375 (2d ed. 1976). Eight years later, in 1983-84, there was only one freshman apiece on Appropriations and Rules, and none on Ways and Means. In part, this reflects the willingness of senior Members to give up other committee seats to take any openings on these committees.

(footnote continued)

districts, such as the Agriculture Committee for
farm districts or the Armed Services Committee for
districts with military bases and contracts.
Other considerations are the Members' interests in
policy areas and in gaining influence and prestige
within the chamber,[79] and their calculations about
what they can best obtain from the assignment
machinery.

Pursuant to party rules, the Democratic
Steering and Policy Committee has 30 Members.[80]
It has ten leadership Members: its chair, the
Speaker; its two vice-chairs, the Majority Leader
and Caucus Chairman; and seven other leaders

---

[78]   Ray, _Federal Spending and the Selection of Committee
Assignments in the U.S. House of Representatives_, 24 Am. J.
Poli. Sci. 494 (1980) (presenting a sophisticated version of
this theory and a review of the literature).

[79]   Smith & Deering, at 83-124, analyze Members' goals in
general terms and on a committee-by-committee basis.

[80]   Rule 42 of the Democratic Caucus specifies these
membership of the Steering and Policy Committee. See 1985
Congressional Quarterly Almanac 74-G (listing of members).
Pursuant to Rule 42, the regional divisions are reviewed
following each election, so as "to maintain, as near as
practicable, an equal number of Members in each region."
For the 12 regional divisions at one particular time, see
Democratic Study Group, _Democratic Campaign Committee and
Democratic Steering & Policy Committee_ 7-18 (1982).

Rule 42 specifies the procedure of the Steering and
Policy Committee and its functions: "to report its
nominations for committee memberships and chairmen and
resolutions regarding party policy, legislative priorities,
scheduling of matters for House or Caucus action, and other
matters as appropriate to further Democratic programs and
policies."

The Steering Committee had a venerable history but
lapsed from the 1950s to the 1970s before its revival under
Speaker Thomas P. O'Neill (D-Mass.).   See Loomis,
_Congressional Careers and Party Leadership in the
Contemporary House of Representatives_, 28 Am. J. Poli. Sci.
180, 185-87 (1984); B. Sinclair, _Majority Leadership in the
U.S. House_ 67 (1983).

(Majority Whip, caucus secretary, chief deputy whip, and chairs of Appropriations, Rules, Budget, and Ways and Means committees). It also has eight Members appointed by the Speaker, and 12 chosen by regional caucuses.

Membership on Steering and Policy confers a good deal of inside influence. This derives from the importance of the appointment function and also the inside information provided by the committee's discussions during the Congress. Accordingly, Members compete in lively fashion to get on in the two available ways: favor with the Speaker (for his eight seats) and election by the regional delegation (for those 12 seats).

In deciding on committee assignments, the Committee starts with a desire to accommodate as many requests as possible. Therefore, the first determinant of whether requests are granted is competition. Members who ask for uncontested seats obtain them. Members asking for seats sought by others take their chances.[81]

In the 1980s, the Democratic leadership made party loyalty (of reelected Members seeking transfer) a critical consideration, rewarding with choice assignments those who had voted with the leadership on key votes such as the 1981 budget and tax votes.[82] A host of other considerations also enter into decisions, such as the power of state delegations, the need for geographical balance on the committees, the "inheritance" by

---

[81] Smith & Deering at 240.

[82] Congressional Quarterly, Politics in America: Members of Congress in Washington and at Home (1985), in describing individual Members, notes frequently the influence of the loyalty factor on committee assignments. See, e.g., id. at 25 (obtaining Ways and Means); id. at 86 (obtaining Ways and Means); id. at 388 (not obtaining Appropriations); id. at 402 (obtaining Appropriations); id. at 626 (not obtaining choice assignments); id. at 634 (not obtaining choice assignments); id. at 663 (not obtaining Appropriations); id. at 674 (obtaining Appropriations with help from powerful sponsor).

Members of seats vacated by predecessors from
their states, the Members' personal qualifications
and lobbying, and some complex horsetrading.[83]

On the side of Republican assignments, the
Republicans start, from consultation and
negotiation with the Democratic leadership, with
the number of assignments they will have on each
committee.[84] The executive committee of the
Republican Committee on Committees, which makes
the initial assignment decisions, consists of one
Member from each large state, plus a few Members
representing the smaller states.[85] Each Member
casts as many votes in decision making as his
state has Republican Members, so the "big-state
members of the executive committee [are] likely to
dominate assignments."[86] The committee tends to

---

[83] The relevant factors are canvassed by Smith & Deering at
240-46; a brief account for one year is Shapiro, House
Democrats Assign Committee Seats, Washington Post, Jan. 23,
1985, at A4. For specific examples, see, e.g., Politics in
America, supra, at 178 ("California" seat on
Appropriations); id. at 268 (the lack of a strong state
delegation); id. at 385 (inheriting predecessor's chair on
Ways and Means).

[84] This is the conceptual sequence. In practice, the
Democrats and Republicans may well make provisional
assignments and then consult on how large to make the
committees in order to accommodate those provisional
assignments.

[85] In the 98th Congress, the executive committee consisted
of 12 Members representing states with four or more
Republicans; two Members representing all the states with
three Republicans; two Members representing all the states
with two Republicans; one Member representing all the states
with one Republican; and one Member each representing the
freshmen of the 97th and 98th Congresses.

The Republicans first devised their committee on
committees when they regain control of the House in 1919,
after the decade of "Czar" Cannon's defeat and subsequent
Democratic control. For a description of that origin, see
R. B. Cheney & L. V. Cheney, Kings of the Hill: Power and
Personality in the House of Representatives 145-46 (1983).
(footnote continued)

defer somewhat to the Republican party leader.[87]

Just as membership on the Democratic Steering and Policy Committee confers significant authority, so too does membership on the Republican Committee on Committees.[88] In general, the Republicans appear to apply criteria for requesting seats and deciding among requests comparable to those on the Democratic side, although there is less public discussion about the Republican process.

Senate Assignments

As noted in the historical discussion above, the Senate settled in the nineteenth century on the "property right" and seniority norms: that

---

[86]   R.H. Davidson & W.J. Oleszek, Congress and its Members 212 (1982). In 1979, the Committee on Committees enlarged the role of the Member representing the smallest states:

> Before, the senior guy from each of the big states -- like Bob Wilson [of California] -- would sit on the committee and cast seventeen votes because there are seventeen Republicans from California, whereas the members from states with only one Republican had only one member, Don Young . . . . and he might represent fifteen single-state members, but he had only one vote, instead of fifteen . . . . [N]ow it is one man, one vote. The guy from the one-member state will cast fifteen votes if that is how many members he represents . . . .

Congress Off the Record: The Candid Analyses of Seven Members 8 (ed. J. F. Bibby 1983) (explanation of anonymous freshman Republican).

[87]   Smith & Deering at 239 (quoting leadership assistants).

[88]   See Politics in America, supra, at 198 (noting that the Member who was "California's chief representative in the party's committee assignment process[, a]s the voice of the single biggest bloc of Republicans in the House [is] likely to be a power broker in the institution for years to come.").

Senators would keep committee seats unless they requested transfers and that the most senior member would be chair.[89]   By the second half of the twentieth century, the seniority system had begun to chafe junior Members in the Senate as in the House.   Instead of the kind of revolutionary changes in assignment and selection of chairs made by the House in the 1970s, junior Senators achieved some relief through gradual evolutionary trends.

From the 1950s to the 1980s, Senate assignment evolution took the direction of a specific policy: distributing vacant seats on the choice committees to junior as well as senior Members.   Until 1953, seniority determined who got committee vacancies, and senior Members monopolized seats on the desirable committees.[90] When Lyndon Johnson became Democratic leader (then, minority leader) in 1953, to forge an alliance with the junior Democrats, he used his influence over the party committee on committees, the Steering Committee, to impose the "Johnson Rule."   This provided that all Democrats receive one major committee assignment before the senior Members receive a second.[91]

---

[89] Origins and Development at 187, 195-97.

[90] As one observer described the resulting situation:

> The Foreign Relations and Appropriations committees, for example, are made up largely of chairmen of other committees . . . .   Thus the caste system tends to feed on and perpetuate itself; the most influential committees tend to be composed of the most esteemed senators, which lends the committee even more prestige . . . .   [Low-prestige committees] tend to be staffed almost entirely by Senate newcomers.   Turnover is high, skill is lacking, and morale among those members covetously eyeing other committee posts is frequently low.

D. R. Mathews, U.S. Senators and Their World 151 (1973 ed.) (first published in 1960).   The effects of the "Johnson Rule" were still "rather limited" when Professor Mathews wrote in 1960. Id. at 152.
(footnote continued)

The trend toward junior membership on choice committees was uneven in the 1960s.[92] With the expanded role of government and the national media, and the larger issue agenda, in the 1960s and 1970s, came a transformation driving Senators to expect and to obtain better distribution of choice assignments.[93]   In 1970, the Legislative Reorganization Act prescribed that a Senator could only serve on one of the four exclusive committees: Appropriations, Armed Services, Finance, and Foreign Relations.[94]   Meanwhile, the Republicans adopted policies similar to the Democrats.   Starting informally in 1959, and formally in 1965, Senator Everett Dirksen (R-Ill.), the Minority Leader, adopted a version of the "Johnson rule" to guarantee choice positions to junior Republicans.[95]

---

[91]   By so doing, Senator Johnson "collected political IOU's from the freshman Democrats whom he helped.   In one blow he had accomplished a multiple increase in the power of his office."   R. Evans & E. Novak, Lyndon B. Johnson: The Ascent to Leadership 75 (1966).

[92]   In 1961, southerners maintained disproportionate membership on the Steering Committee.   Senator Mansfield, the new Majority Leader, was not inclined to challenge them, and junior liberals suffered a number of setbacks in committee assignments.   Rosenthal, Toward Majority Rule in the U.S. Senate, Eagleton Institute Cases in Practical Politics No. 25, at 29.   In 1963, the Steering Committee penalized junior liberals who had attempted to reform the cloture rule to pave the way for civil rights legislation. J. S. Clark, Congress: The Sapless Branch 127 (1964) (written by a leading maverick Senator).

[93]   Sinclair, The Distribution of Committee Positions in the U.S. Senate: Explaining Institutional Change, 32 Am. J. Poli. Sci. 276, 297-98 (1988).

[94]   Section 132 of the Act, Senate Rule XXV(6)(d).   The rule had a grandfather exception.   As of 1983, Senator John Stennis (D-Miss.) was the last Senator who was a member of two exclusive committees (Appropriations and Armed Services).

[95]   R. H. Davidson & W. J. Oleszek, Congress and Its Members (footnote continued)

By the 1980s, the effect of the trend had become dramatic, particularly with the turnover of party control, which brought two large junior classes of Republicans (1978 and 1980) to importance. In 1983, the Senate's 43 freshmen[96] held 41 percent of the seats on the four exclusive committees, virtually a proportional share. Indeed, the freshmen were actually overrepresented on the committee with arguably the broadest jurisdiction, Finance.[97] This result was starkly different from the House, where junior Members were underrepresented on the three most desirable committees.

As for the mechanics of particular assignments, there is less public information about Senate than House assignments. The Senate Republican "party makes its committee selections strictly on the basis of seniority," so that "assignments [are] routinely handed out."[98] Their organ is a Committee on Committees appointed by the Conference Chairman (an elected party position), with an elected chair.[99]

The Senate Democratic Steering Committee is "chaired by the Democratic floor leader and has about 25 members."[100] While the party leader traditionally chose the Steering Committee members, an agreement made in 1977 provided that

---

213 (1982).

[96] The periods of service of Senators are listed in the Congressional Directory 251-53 (1981).

[97] The figures were (freshman members, total seats): Appropriations, 8/29; Armed Services, 11/18; Finance, 10/20; Foreign Relations, 6/17; all four committees, 35/84.

[98] Cohen, The Mysterious Ways Congress Makes Committee Assignments, National Journal, February 3, 1979, at 183, 188. See Smith & Deering at 242.

[99] Ornstein, Peabody, & Rohde, "The Contemporary Senate: Into the 1980s," in Congress Reconsidered 13 (ed. L. C. Dodd & B. I. Oppenheimer 1977); Smith & Deering at 238.

[100] Smith & Deering at 238.

future choices of members for the Steering Committee would be submitted to the party membership.[101] The Steering Committee has served in the past as a ruling tool, for Lyndon Johnson in the 1950s and for southern conservatives in the early 1960s. It became more democratic in the later Mansfield years and individual decisions tended to turn on a host of particularized factors.[102]

D.   CHOICE OF CHAIRS AND SUBCOMMITTEE ORGANIZATION

Choice of Chairs

In the period leading up to the 1970s, the iron rule of seniority made selection of the most senior Member as chair automatic. For the House in the 1960s, this meant dominance of the committees by senior conservative douthern Democrats, who had accumulated the maximum seniority by virtue of their election from safe districts and who became legendary barriers to legislation.[103] A lesser share of chairs went to

---

[101] Ornstein, Peabody, and Rohde, supra, at 26.

[102]   See Ornstein, Peabody, and Rohde, supra, at 26 (history, and recent democratization); Smith & Deering at 243 (importance of a Senator's own membership on Committee on Committees for his obtaining a good assignment for himself); Cohen, supra, at 184, 186 (accounts of 1979 decisions, including one overruling by the Democratic caucus of a Steering Committee decision on the urging of a committee chair).

[103]   The 1960s southern chairs included: (1) Rep. Howard Smith (D-Va.) and Rep. William Colmer (D-Mass.), chairs of the Rules Committee, who kept large numbers of important bills off the floor; (2) Rep. Mendel Rivers (D-S.C.) and Rep. Edward Hebert (D-La.), chairs of the Armed Services Committee, who blocked floor votes on the Vietnam War for many years; (3) Rep. Wilbur Mills (D-Ark.), chair of the Ways and Means Committee, whose power was said to be so great that when he sought a nomination for President, a (footnote continued)

northern Members from districts made safe by big-city machines.

In theory, the selection of these chairs, although made initially by seniority, was subject to ratification by the Democratic Caucus. However, the Caucus' procedure involved a single open ballot on "a single, full, and uncontested slate. To vote against any one chair, members would have to vote against them all,"[104] a foolhardy gesture considering the inevitability of defeat and the likelihood of retaliation.

The revolt against these chairs began in 1971 when the Democratic Caucus, under pressure from junior Members led by the Democratic Study Group, began allowing separate votes on individual chairs on the demand of any ten Members. In December 1974, a rambunctious post-Watergate class of Democratic freshmen arrived to organize the next Congress. At that time, in a coup perhaps greater than any in the House since the 1909 revolt against "Czar" Joseph Cannon (R-Ill.), the caucus deposed the chairs of the Agriculture, Armed Services, and Banking committees, replacing them with Members with less seniority.

Thereafter, no chair was deposed until 1985, because it was not necessary. Chairs yielded to pressures from junior Members or from the leadership that they would have resisted in the past, rather than face the loss of their position. As one freshman noted in 1979:

The biggest change, I think . . . is the fact

---

colleague asked "Wilbur, why do you want to run for President and give up your grip on the country?" See M. Green, J. M. Fallows, & D. R. Zwick, Who Runs Congress 80 (1972); (4) Rep. John McMillan (D-S.C.), chair of the District of Columbia Committee, who delayed home rule in the District for many years; and (5) Rep. Jamie Whitten (D-Miss.), chair of the Agriculture Committee, and a powerful opponent of food stamp legislation. Id. at 71.

[104] Ornstein, The Democrats Reform Power in the House of Representatives, 1969-75, in America in the Seventies 5 (ed. A. P. Sindler 1977).

> that the leadership is all elected.   I just
> think   that   that   is   an   extraordinarily
> important change -- electing subcommittee
> chairmen in real elections, where you have
> fights, and electing committee chairmen with
> real elections . . . .   They are much more
> inclined to look upon that new group [of
> freshmen] as potential constituents in their
> election.[105]

A second, quieter trend also changed the
complexion of the House chairs.   Whereas southern
Members held a disproportionate share of the
committee chairs in the 1950s and 1960s, in the
1970s northern and western Members took a sizable
share of the chairs, as the rise in the South of
primary challenges and of the Republican Party
eliminated its consistent reelection of senior
Democrats and as the Democratic party strengthened
itself in other regions.[106]

The Senate never experienced a dramatic purge
of committee chairs as the House did in 1974.
Rather, some measure of control over ranking
positions was assumed quietly.   In 1973, the
Republican Caucus agreed that the Republican
Members of each committee would choose their
ranking member.   However, in 1987, when the
Republican Members of the Foreign Relations
Committee voted to have Senator Richard Lugar (R-
Ind.) as their ranking minority member, the
Republican Caucus overruled them, and followed
strict seniority in making Senator Jesse Helms (R-
N.C.) the ranking minority member.[107]   In 1975,

---

[105]   Congress Off the Record, supra, at 8-9.

[106]   For example, in 1983, northern and western chairs held
most of the important committees: Armed Services (Rep. Mel
Price (D-Ill.)); Banking (Rep. Ferdinand St. Germain (D-
R.I.)); District of Columbia (Rep. Ronald Dellums (D-Cal.));
Energy and Commerce (Rep. John Dingell (D-Mich.)); Foreign
Affairs (Rep. Clem Zablocki (D-Wisc.)); Interior (Rep.
Morris Udall (D-Ariz.)); Judiciary (Rep. Peter Rodino, (D-
N.J.)); Post Office and Civil Service (Rep. William Ford (D-
Mich.)); Public Works (Rep. James Howard (D.N.J.)); and Ways
and Means (Rep. Daniel Rostenkowski (D-Ill.)).
(footnote continued)

the Senate Democratic Caucus agreed to permit secret ballot votes by the caucus on any committee chair if one-fifth of the Democratic Members requested it.[108]

Within the framework of seniority, the Republican ascendancy as majority party in 1981 led to an unprecedented bestowing of chairs on junior Senators. This was in part because the rapid growth of the Republican membership meant that many of the Senators were junior, making junior chairs inevitable. In 1981, two Senate committees were chaired by freshman, and four by second-term Members.[109] Still, only Members with three terms or more chaired the four exclusive committees. Because Senators serve on a number of committees, senior Senators often have a choice as to which committee they will lead, and the movement of one such Senator may have a reverberating effect as a string of others change chairs.[110]

---

[107] Felton, In Victory for Seniority System, Helms Wrests Post from Lugar, 45 Cong. Q. Week. Rep. 143 (1987); 1987 Congressional Quarterly Almanac 7.

[108] Ornstein, Peabody & Rohde, The Changing Senate: From the 1950s to the 1970s, in Congress Reconsidered, supra.

[109] The two freshmen were Senators Orrin Hatch (R-Utah) (Labor and Human Resources) and Alan Simpson (R-Wyo.) (Veterans' Affairs); the four second-term members were Senators Helms (Agriculture), Jake Garn (R-Utah) (Banking), Peter Domenici (R-N.Mex.) (Budget), and James McClure (R-Idaho) (Energy and Natural Resources).

[110] For example, in 1979, Senator Strom Thurmond (R-S.C.) chose to be ranking minority member of Judiciary rather than Armed Services, displacing Senator Charles Mathias (R-Md.) on Judiciary. This prevented Senator Mathias, one of the most liberal Members of the party, from achieving an influential post where he could have worked with the Judiciary chair, Senator Edward Kennedy (D-Mass.). M. Barone & B. Ujifusa, The Almanac of American Politics 1982 999 (1981). In 1983, Senator Stennis chose to be ranking minority Member on Appropriations, relinquishing Armed Services to Senator Henry Jackson (D-Wash.) (and later (footnote continued)

House Organization into Subcommittees

At the beginning of each Congress, each committee of the House and Senate holds an organizational session. These sessions are preceded by some of the least visible and most intense political maneuvers, as members assess their interests in the assignment of themselves and others to subcommittees and the choice of subcommittee chairs. Both for the Members and for legislation, organization can have great significance. For example, in any session, one Judiciary Committee subcommittee may handle vital legislation concerning civil rights, another may handle vital legislation of economic interest to well-heeled lobbies handling issues such as video copyright legislation, and a third may only handle matters of peripheral interest. Which Members end up on which subcommittees determines both the balance of power on that legislation, and the Members' ability to promote their policy goals, serve their constituencies, and raise campaign contributions from interest groups.

In the House, Democratic Caucus rules specify the method of organization. Caucus Rule 30 specifies that majority members who served on the committee in the preceding Congress "bid" at the committee caucus either "to retain one subcommittee assignment held on that committee in the preceding Congress," or "to select a new subcommittee assignment." The first round of bidding occurs "in order of their rank on the full committee." After all previous members bid, new committee members bid for an assignment.

After that first round, there are "further

Senator Sam Nunn (D-Ga.)); Senator Ernest Hollings (D-S.C.) chose Commerce, relinquishing Budget to Senator Lawton Chiles (D-Fla.). Senator Stennis thereby took Appropriations, while leaving Armed Services in the hands of strong military supporters. Senator Hollings thereby took Commerce, a committee traditionally important to interest groups that may make campaign contributions, at a time when he was a presidential candidate in need of contributions.

rounds of selection in order of Members' rank on
the full committee until remaining subcommittee
vacancies are filled." The system neatly balances
the claims of senior Members for priority, and the
availability to junior Members of some choices.
Democratic Caucus rules limit Members to service
on five subcommittees, and in 1987, the party made
it harder for Members to get waivers to serve on
more than that.[111]

Caucus Rule 27 provides for similar bidding
for subcommittee chairs, again "in order of full
committee seniority." However, "[a]ny request for
a subcommittee chairmanship shall be subject to
approval by a majority of those present and voting
by secret ballot in the committee caucus." In
contrast to committee chairs, where there have
been few dramatic purges since 1975, there have
been a number of subcommittee chair battles.[112]

In an early example in 1975, Representative
John Moss (D-Calif.) orchestrated an elaborate
restructuring of subcommittee jurisdictions of the
House Commerce Committee, accompanied by his own
installation as chair of the powerful
Investigations subcommittee in place of full

---

[111] House Democrats Tighten Rules on Subcommittees, 109
Cong. Q. Week. Rep. 499 (1987); 1987 Congressional Quarterly
Almanac 53.

[112] Besides instances discussed below:

Frank Annunzio of Illinois beat Leonor K. Sullivan of
Missouri for a subcommittee on Banking in 1975; Joe D.
Waggonner, Jr., was sidestepped by Ways and Means
members to prevent him from getting a chair in 1977;
Michael E. Barnes of Maryland beat Gus Yatron of
Pennsylvania for a subcommittee on Foreign Affairs in
1981; Jerry M. Patterson beat out Henry B. Gonzalez of
Texas for a subcommittee on Banking in 1981; James H.
Scheuer was deprived of a subcommittee by the Commerce
Committee in 1981; and Samual S. Stratton of New York
was beaten by Charles E. Bennett of Florida for a
subcommittee on Armed Services in 1983.

Smith and Deering at 202 n.45.

Committee Chair Harley Staggers (D-W.Va.).[113]   The
subcommittee then awakened into active oversight,
first   under   Chairperson   Moss,   then   under
Chairperson Dingell.[114]

    In 1979, liberal junior Members defeated more
senior   conservative   Members   for   three   different
House subcommittee chairs.[115]   No two subcommittee

---

[113]   See Ornstein & Rohde, supra, at 216-18.

    Sometimes, as in the 1975 Commerce Committee example,
committee organization involves not merely assignment, but
completely   restructuring   the   subcommittee   jurisdictions.
For example, in 1975 the House Foreign Affairs Committee
(then   "International   Relations")   restructured   its
subcommittees.   These had previously been organized by areas
(Africa, Europe, Near East, etc.), but were reorganized by
subject (International Economic Policy, International Trade
and Commerce, etc.).   The result was to liberate issue-
oriented junior Members for such matters as human rights on
a world-wide basis.   See Ornstein & Rohde, supra, at 223-26,
252-61.

[114]   Rep. Moss "held 25 days of hearings through the first
10 months of 1975.   Under [the subcommittee's] previous
chairman, it held only 18 days of hearings in the entire
93rd Congress.   The subcommittee issued seven reports in
1975 compared to one in 1973."   Guide to Congress, supra, at
385.

[115]   The three races were described thusly:

    In at least three cases, all in 1979, the member
    considered more liberal defeated a senior colleague.
    California's Henry A. Waxman [(D-Calif.)] was elected
    over North Carolina's Richardson Preyer [(D-N.C.)] for
    the Health Subcommittee of the Commerce Committee
    . . . .   At the same time, Texas's Bob Eckhardt [(D-
    Tex.)] defeated New York's John M. Murphy [(D-N.Y.)] to
    become chair of Commerce's Oversight Subcommittee and
    Connecticut's Toby Moffett [(D-Conn.)] was elected to
    chair Government Operation's Environment, Energy, and
    Natural Resources Subcommittee after three more senior
    colleagues had been rejected.

Smith & Deering at 198.

races follow the same pattern, and sometimes observers find that a race has turned on varied factors.   Representative Henry Waxman (D-Cal.) became chair of the highly important Energy and Commerce Committee's Subcommittee on Health by the following approach:

> When he wanted to run for Health Subcommittee chairman in 1979 against the highly respected Richardson Preyer of North Carolina, Waxman raised money from his own wealthy campaign contributors, and distributed it to Democrats on the full Commerce Committee who would be making the decision.   It led to the charge that   Waxman   was   buying   himself   a chairmanship, but he prevailed, 15-12.[116]

Senate Organization into Subcommittees

In the Senate, there are no rules comparable to   the   House   Caucus   rules,   so   that   the organizational process at the beginning of each Congress   varies   from   committee   to   committee. Senate   committee   organization   also   tends,   in general, to be less frenetic than in the House; turnover is generally less in the Senate since only   one-third   of   the   members   are   up   for reelection any particular year.   In a year like 1983, when the preceding November's election changed only five seats, the new organization may be barely noticeable; in years like 1981 and 1987, when   the   chamber   changed   party,   there   is considerably greater activity.

On some Senate committees, the rules specify that   the   committee   establishes   subcommittees   by majority vote, while on other committees, chairs establish   the   subcommittees,   either   subject   to committee   approval   or   in   consultation   with   the ranking minority member.[117]   As for assignment,

---

116   _Politics in America: Members of Congress in Washington and at Home_ 137 (A. Ehrenhalt ed. 1981).

117   Compare   Banking   Rule   3(a)   (majority   establishes subcommittees) with Finance Rule 16(a) (chair establishes (footnote continued)

the Senate adopted a resolution in 1977 declaring its "sense" -- not a binding rule -- that assignments should occur by bidding in order of seniority.[118] A number of committees have rules providing for such bidding for assignments, while others still vest assignment in the chair, acting in consultation with the ranking minority Member.[119]

E.   REFERRAL

Once the committees have been organized, they receive all bills in their area of jurisdiction by referral, and the bills are not considered on the floor unless and until the committee reports them out.[120] The fruits of committee jurisdiction -- hearings, mark-up, reporting, scheduling influence, floor management, and conference committee membership -- largely follow from the pattern of referral.

Referral is the one of the most "iceberg"-like aspects of congressional procedure: massive in importance, it lies almost entirely below the surface. All that the public record reflects for referral of a bill is a brief notation in a portion of the Congressional Record -- a portion that is a pure formal written record, there usually being no oral proceedings on the House or Senator floor -- that the Presiding Officer has referred Bill So-and-So to such-and-such committee or committees. Underneath the surface, the complexities of referral may involve jurisdictional gray areas and the techniques of

---

subcommittees with approval of committee).

[118]   Section 201(f) of S. Res. 4, 95th Cong., 1st Sess.

[119]   Compare the committee rules in effect in 1983: Agriculture Committee Rule 3 (bidding) with Governmental Affairs Committee Rule 7(c) (chair acts in consultation with the ranking minority member).

[120]   The mechanics of referral in the House and the Senate chamber are discussed in the chapters on each chamber.

committee struggle to gain influence over those areas.

Jurisdictional Ambiguity

Overlaps, grey areas, and fragmentation occur often in committee jurisdiction.[121] Newly recognized legislative issues offer the greyest of the grey areas, since their newness means they have not been settled conclusively by prior rules or precedents. A number of areas of 1980s committee jursidictional overlap were pointed out above, such as international trade, health, and transportation.

The House in particular suffers from a chronic case of jurisdictional ambiguities.[122] In 1973, the Bolling Committee examination of the House jurisdictional lines found "disarray" and "endemic" jurisdictional conflict, of which "hundreds of such cases, involving virtually every committee, were detailed in the staff-prepared monographs."[123] A classic 1980s example was

---

[121] Of course, there are many areas of clear jurisdictional division. No artful drafting will keep tax bills from the tax committees or appropriation bills from the appropriations committees.

[122] When the Legislative Reorganization Act of 1946 codified House committee jurisdictions, "[m]ost of the jurisdictional provisions of the Act were borrowed verbatim from Hinds' and Cannon's Precedents, perpetuating all of the ambiguities of the earlier language." R. H. Davidson & W. J. Oleszek, Congress Against Itself 52 (1977). After 1946, "there were innumerable de facto and statutory jurisdictional shifts through referral decision. Neither formal nor de facto changes were made with any consideration of their overall rationale or their work load implications." Id. at 52-53.

[123] As a result, there was "a vast de facto structure of responsibilities that often bore only the vaguest resemblence to the House rules . . . . [T]he long-term result for the House as a whole was conflict and confusion, a triumph of politics over logic." Id. at 53.

nuclear waste disposal, an area that was claimed by Energy and Commerce (with jurisdiction over nuclear energy), Science and Technology (technology), and Interior (public lands, where the disposal sites would be), among others.

When the issue came to a head in 1982, the bill referrals reflected the overlap. The Chair referred one bill, H.R. 3809, to Interior;[124] another bill, H.R. 6598, to Energy and Commerce; and a third, H.R. 5016, to Science and Technology. All three committees reported their bills and sought rules from the Rules Committee. Ultimately, the Rules Committee arranged that the Interior Committee bill come to the floor with an amendment in the nature of a substitute reflecting a compromise among the three committees' versions.

Technically, responsibility for interpreting the jurisdictional rules and precedents lies in the presiding officer of each chamber -- the Speaker of the House, and the President of the Senate -- who, as a formal matter, takes bills that have been introduced and refers them. However, as a practical matter, the Chair rarely devotes much attention personally to the referral decision. Rather, the responsibility falls to the Parliamentarians in each chamber, an office discussed in the chapters on organization of the House and Senate.

Routine referrals may be made by the Parliamentarian with little discussion, but more complex or controversial ones often cause Members and staff to consult with the Parliamentarian's office for an advance indication of the likely referral. Advance contact gives the Parliamentarian an opportunity to review the voluminous and obscure precedents and sometimes to consult with the House (or Senate) and committee leadership before making a nonroutine referral. Advance contact also facilitates negotiations over multiple referrals, as discussed below, as well as

---

[124] The bill was also referred to Armed Services because of early concerns that it might control the disposal of the military's nuclear waste.

advice on how redrafting a bill might change the referral.

Although the Parliamentarians usually keep confidential the internal workings of the referral process, one historic series of Senate referrals has been analyzed on the public record by Dr. Floyd Riddick, Senate Parliamentarian Emeritus, which sheds light on the players, the stakes, and the factors considered in major referrals. The series of referrals concerned the perennial question in the Senate of whether jurisdiction over international banking lies in Foreign Relations or Banking:

> [I]n the 80th Congress, Senator [Arthur] Vandenberg [R-Mich.] was the President Pro Tem. He was also the chairman of the Foreign Relations Committee, and under the rules at that time, all foreign banking legislation was to be referred to the Committee on Foreign Relations; Bretton Woods, for example, should have gone to Foreign Relations.

> But it didn't work out that way, because Vandenberg was then President Pro Tem, the former Vice President, Harry Truman, being in the White House as President . . . . [Vandenberg] instructed Mr. Watkins [Dr. Riddick's predecessor as Senate Parliamentarian] to refer all international banking legislation to the Banking and Currency Committee. He didn't like handling banking legislation, he wanted it to go to Banking and Currency, so that's where we referred it.

> It went that way until Senator [J. William] Fulbright [(D-Ark.)] who had been chairman of the Banking and Currency Committee, wanted it to go to Foreign Relations when he became chairman of the Foreign Relations Committee. Because of his insistence, and conferences with the leadership, that's what occurred. So without any rule change at all, we went back to following the written rule of the Senate that said that all foreign banking legislation

would go to Foreign Relations.[125]

Theoretically, each chamber may overrule the referral decision of the Chair, made on the advice of the Parliamentarian.[126]   Actually, motions or appeals of this kind virtually never occur in the House and are rare in the Senate.   Rather, disagreements with a referral surface in other ways: drafting of an alternative bill to get a different referral, efforts to keep a controversially referred bill off the floor, or if one such reaches the floor, efforts to amend massively or defeat it.

Drafting

One of the main reflections of jurisdictional lines is the drafting of bills.   It is no secret that "members may attempt to draft a bill which could go to one of several committees in such a way as to make it easier for the Speaker to send the bill to the desired committee."[127]   To begin with, referral depends in part on the drafting of the symbolic and hortatory elements of a bill -- the bill's title, stated goals, structure and subheadings, and the introductory speech of its sponsor -- as distinguished from its substantive contents.   Members can give their draftsman a relatively freer hand to shape those elements to support a referral, insofar as Members seriously interested in moving legislation usually care much more about getting a referral to the right committee than about the details of the bill.

For example, in the early 1970s Senator Sam

---

[125] Oral History Interview of Dr. Floyd Riddick, on file in the Senate Library.

[126] Overruling votes would occur in the House "on motion of a committee claiming jurisdiction," House Rule XXII(4)(a); in the Senate, by appeal from the Chair's decision under Senate Rule XVII(1).

[127] L. A. Froman, The Congressional Process: Strategies, Rules and Procedures 37 (1967).

Ervin (D-N.C.) investigated Army intelligence-
gathering about civilians. When he first
introduced a bill to prohibit such military
practices, it was naturally referred to the Armed
Services Committee, where it died. The following
Congress, Senator Ervin introduced another bill
with the same objective. However, this time, the
bill's title and stated goals concerned
enforcement of the first and fourth amendments and
the constitutional rights of privacy. Senator
Ervin accompanied the bill with an introductory
speech emphasizing those constitutional rights
aspects.[128]

This time, the Chair referred the bill to the
Judiciary Committee, a more sympathetic
environment. As the Chief Counsel of Senator
Ervin's subcommittee concluded, "[b]y careful
drafting of a bill's short title, by use of
introductory findings and purpose, and by an
introductory speech, a bill's author has great
influence over its referral."[129] Another example
would be the House bills noted above regarding
disposal of nuclear waste, with preambles drafted
to favor particular referrals.[130]

---

[128] The bill's substance also inclined it a particular way:
it included judicial remedies -- criminal provisions and
provisions for civil lawsuits.

[129] Baskir, Reflections on the Senate Investigation of Army
Surveillance, 49 Ind. L. J. 618, 649 (1974).

[130] Science and Technology drafted the preamble of its
bill, H.R. 5016, to emphasize national policy: the bill was
"[t]o establish a Federal policy with respect to the
disposal of high-level radioactive waste . . . ." Interior
drafted the preamble of its bill, H.R. 3809, to emphasize
where the waste was going (i.e., public lands): the bill was
"[t]o provide for repositories for the disposal of high-
level radiocative waste. . . ." Energy and Commerce drafted
the preamble of its bill, H.R. 6598, to focus on the nuclear
energy aspect: the bill was "[t]o provide for the
development of repositories for the disposal of high-level
radioactive waste and spent nuclear fuel, and for other
purposes." (Emphasis supplied.)

Notwithstanding the significance of symbolic and hortatory elements, the most important aspect of drafting consists of the bill's practical elements, such as what title of the United States code the bill amends, what agency will administer it, and how it is to be enforced.   To take a hypothetical example, a narcotics bill may amend Title 18 of the United States Code to add a new criminal law administered by the Department of Justice.   The Parliamentarian will refer such a bill to the Judiciary Committee.

However, that is only one option.   The would-be authors of a narcotics bill may not be on the Judiciary Committee and may desire to get a narcotics bill for their own committee.   They may draft a bill to amend Title 21 to add a new element to the food and drug law administered by the Food and Drug Administration, or to amend Title 42 to add a new rehabilitation service to be administered by the Secretary of Health and Human Services.   The Parliamentarian might refer such bills, respectively, to the commerce (House Energy and Commerce; Senate Commerce, Science and Transporation) and social welfare (House Education and Labor; Senate Labor and Human Resources) committees.

Alternatively, the Members may amend the foreign aid law to cut off aid to some nations, or the intelligence law to facilitate narcotics intelligence-gathering, sending bills to foreign relations and intelligence committees.   They may create a new agency altogether, sending the bill to the governmental operations committees with their jurisdiction over government organization. The Members may create a congressional investigatory committee with oversight power, sending a resolution to the rules committees.

One famous example of tilted drafting was the Civil Rights Act of 1964.   As introduced, the civil rights bill relied, not on the Congress' constitutional power to enforce civil rights under the Fourteenth Amendment, but on its constitutional power to regulate interstate commerce, such as by its prohibiting discrimination in public accommodations, like motels, that participate in interstate commerce.

This drafting twist, with sympathetic help from the presiding officers in each chamber, led to a very important set of referrals:

> In the Senate the bill was referred to the Commerce Committee, chaired by Warren Magnuson of Washington, rather than to the Judiciary Committee with James Eastland of Mississsippi as Chairman.   In the House the bill was referred to the Judiciary Committee, Emanual Celler of New York, Chairman, rather than to the Interstate and Foreign Commerce Committee which was chaired by Oren Harris of Oklahoma.   The strategy in each instance was obvious.[131]

However, there are both formal and informal limits to the extent to which tilted drafting may affect legislative outcomes, and, in particular, there are limits to the obtaining of what may be called "exotic" referrals.   As a formal matter, some types of provision are almost manipulation-proof.   No matter what the subject, constitutional amendments go through the judiciary committees, changes in the tax law go through the tax committees, and appropriations go through the appropriation committees.

More important than the formal limits, there are informal limits set by the leaderships and the committees regarding jurisdictional "raids."   A bill that has been drafted peculiarly for a referral to a "wrong" committee may be kept off the floor, even after reporting, by complaints to the leadership.   As discussed below, the House Rules Committee routinely denies rules to many bills ensnared in jurisdictional disputes.

The Senate Majority Leader will similarly resolve such a dispute by refusing to move to proceed to such bills.   This happens, not out of some moral sense of jurisdictional rectitude, but because jurisdictional raids elicit protests from the committee leaderships and result in embarrassing floor fights.   If a bill that had an

---

[131]   L. A. Froman, supra, at 37.

exotic referral does reach the floor, its
opponents will use the often-potent argument that
the bill violates their jurisdiction, and has not
"received adequate consideration" by those who
"know the problem best."[132]

F. MULTIPLE REFERRALS

House History

In the last decade, the House transformed
significantly its referral practices through use
of multiple referrals. Multiple referral means
the bill goes to two or more committees, each of
which shares in the fruits of referral. Each
committee can hold hearings, propose committee
amendments, and write reports. Each committee may
testify regarding the special rule for the bill,
and may have a stake in floor management of the
bill and in conference.

For example, in 1982, H.R. 5447, the Futures
Trading Act of 1982, resolved whether the newly
emerging futures and options for securities would
be regulated by the Securities and Exchange
Commission (SEC), or the Commodities Futures
Trading Commission (CFTC). In the House, the
Agriculture Committee oversees the CFTC, while the

---

[132] Claims of expertise may be bolstered by substantive
amendments reflecting the specialized field of the hostile
committee. For example, the Energy and Commerce Committee
drafted the domestic content bill, discussed above, to fall
within its interstate commerce jurisdiction rather than as
an orthodox import-restriction bill that would fall within
Ways and Means' jurisdiction. House leadership sympathies
led to the bill's obtaining a rule. Yet on the House floor,
fierce opposition from Ways and Means defanged the bill by
an amendment peculiarly within Ways and Means' trade
expertise: an amendment that the measure would not
"supersede" any "treaty, international convention or
agreement on tariffs and trade." Observers believed "[t]hat
provision would enable U.S. courts to invalidate the measure
for violating the General Agreement on Tariffs and Trade
(GATT)." 1982 Congressional Quarterly Almanac 55.

Energy and Commerce Committee oversees the SEC.
When the Agriculture Committee reported a bill on
May 17, it was sequentially referred to the Energy
and Commerce Committee, which reported its own
view on June 21.[133] The Rules Committee gave each
committee a role in floor management,[134] and
during floor consideration of that bill and a
companion H.R. 6156, significant Energy and
Commerce amendments were adopted.   As conferees,
the   Speaker   appointed   Members   from   both
committees.[135]

Until 1975, the Speaker could only refer a
bill to one committee.[136] In 1974, Representative
Bolling's Select Committee on Committees proposed

---

[133]   An agency-devised compromise found favor with the
Agriculture Committee, but Energy and Commerce Committee
"Chairman John D. Dingell, D-Mich., disapproved strongly of
the accord" at an Energy and Commerce subcommittee hearing
that "signaled deep skepticism in and out of Congress about
the wisdom of the CFTC-SEC agreement." 1982 Congressional
Quarterly Almanac 367-68.

[134]   H. Res. 566 provided for one hour of general debate to
be controlled by managers from Agriculture, and a half hour
to be controlled by managers from Energy and Commerce.

[135]   Representatives Dingell, Timothy E. Wirth (D-Colo.),
and James Broyhill (R-N.C.) of Energy and Commerce were
appointed   as   conferees,   with   their   role   limited   to
consideration of Title I and section 237 of H.R. 5447 and
section 3 of the Senate amendment.   Multiple-committee
participation was necessary since there were major
differences in the House and Senate versions.   1982
Congressional Quarterly Almanac 369.

[136]   For example, before 1975 the domestic content bill,
discussed in the previous section, could only have been
referred to one committee, presumably the Energy and
Commerce Committee, however great the interest of another
committee, such as Ways and Means.   Occasionally, some
cumbersome procedure was worked out to ease particularly
awkward single-committee referrals.   See Deschler 17 §§
16.3-16.7; H.R. Rept. No. 916, 93d Cong., 2d Sess., Part I.
at 57, 59 (1974) (Speaker's testimony before Bolling
Committee).

a wide-ranging reform of House committee
jurisdictions. As part of a comprehensive package
of procedural changes, the committee proposed that
the Speaker have power to make multiple
referrals.[137]   The House largely adopted the
Bolling Committee's proposal for multiple
referrals in an amendment of House Rule
X(5)(b).[138]

---

[137] In retrospect, it appears that the the House did not
anticipate the importance of that change:

> The Bolling Committee thought that such multiple
> referrals would be relatively rare because they had
> also proposed grouping major policy areas within
> individual committees. However, most of the Bolling
> jurisdictional realignments were diluted by House floor
> action, while the multiple referral provisions
> remained. Without jurisdictional consolidation, the
> number of multiple referrals was substantially higher
> than anticipated, and has continued to increase over
> time.

Final Report of the House Select Committee on Committees,
H.R. Rept. No. 866, 96th Cong., 2d Sess. 223 (1980).

[138] Early in the Bolling Committee's proceedings, "Bolling
wanted to institutionalize the Speaker's power to refer
bills, perhaps in tandem with some body like the Rules
Committee. Whatever the mechanism, there should be constant
review and renewal of work loads and jurisdictions.   'I
believe more in process than in plan,' he said,
significantly."   R. H. Davidson & W. J. Oleszek, Congress
Against Itself 128 (1977).

The House took much, but not all, of the Bolling
Committee proposal. It accepted the Speaker's role, but not
the Rules Committee role:

> Additionally the Bolling Committee established a
> pr[o]cedure whereby the Rules Committee would serve as
> arbitrator of conflicting jurisdictional claims in the
> bill referral process. The Hansen Committee resolution
> coincided with the Bolling Committee proposal with one
> exception -- the Caucus unit rejected any arbitrator
> role for the Rules Committee. During floor debate, an
(footnote continued)

House rules now provide that referrals shall "assure to the maximum extent feasible that each committee which has jurisdiction . . . will have responsibility for considering such provision . . . ." (Emphasis supplied). The proportion of multiply referred bills has become between ten and fifteen percent of all bills.[139]

More important than the gross proportion is the proportion of measures of importance. As a rough measure, the House's most important bills may be considered those for which a special rule was sought. In 1981-82, special rules were sought for approximately 180 bills, of which 29, or one-sixth, had received a multiple referral.[140] The

---

amendment to delete the Speaker's authority to refer bills jointly, in parts, or sequentially -- or to an ad hoc unit -- was defeated by voice vote.

H.R. Rept. No. 866, supra, at 125. For the details of the role proposed for the Rules Committee, and for a procedure for appealing referrals, see H.R. Rept. No. 816, 93d Cong., 2d Sess., Part I, at 60-61 (1974).

[139] "In the 94th Congress, approximately 1200 bills were referred to more than one House committee; in the 95th Congress, the number rose to 1800 multiple referrals." H.R. Rept. No. 866, supra, at 223. Thereafter, while the number of multiply referred bills fell with the drop in the total number of introduced bills, the proportion remained relatively constant. Rough unpublished data provided by Judy Schneider of the Congressional Research Service indicated the following about bills introduced in the House:

Congress	Multiply Referred Bills	Singly Referred Bills
95th	1,734	14,209
96th	1,174	8,211
97th	838	7,559

[140] Among the major multiply referred bills receiving rules were those concerning immigration reform, domestic content of automobiles, nuclear waste disposal, gasoline tax increase for public works construction, coal slurry (footnote continued)

massive omnibus reconciliation bills may also be
considered much like a multiply referred bill,
since different House committees contributed to
each of the titles of the bill as reported, and to
floor management and conference.

House Types of Multiple Referrals

House Rule X(5)(c) provides for three types
of multiple referrals: joint ("the Speaker may
refer the matter simultaneously to two or more
committees for concurrent consideration"),
sequential (the Speaker may refer a measure "for
consideration in sequence"), and split (he may
"divide the matter into two or more parts
reflecting different subjects and jurisdictions
and refer each such part to a different
committee").

Looking more closely, in a joint referral,
the committees of referral may all consider the
bill at the same time. The committees report
amendments to the underlying bill, not to each
other's version, and no committee controls the
timing of when the others get the bill. This is
particularly appropriate when various committees
have roughly comparable claims to the whole
bill. For example, in 1980 and 1981 the Speaker
referred bills to control transportation of
hazardous materials jointly to Energy and Commerce
and to Public Works and Transportation.[141]

---

pipelines, authorizations for the State Department and for
the intelligence agencies, airport development, and, in a
manner of speaking, the 1982 reconciliation bill boosting
taxes by $98 billion and cutting Medicare-Medicaid
expenditures. Technically, no rule was sought for the House
version of that tax/Medicare-Medicaid bill. Rather, a rule
was sought for the Senate version, which had not been
referred at all. However, in conference, the version that
had been devised by House committees was used as the House's
negotiating benchmark. The bill received a multiple
referral because of Energy and Commerce's Medicaid
jurisdiction.

[141] Energy and Commerce has jurisdiction over interstate
commerce and railroads under Rule X(1)(h)(11), and Public
Works and Transportation has jurisdiction over highways
(footnote continued)

In a sequential referral, the second committee only begins consideration of the bill when the first committee is done. Sometimes the second committee can amend only the underlying bill, and sometimes it can propose amendments to the first committee's amendments, depending on the Speaker's wording of his multiple referral. A sequential referral is more suitable than a joint referral in two cases: when one committee's interests overshadow the other's; or when one committee, having received a bill on a single referral, reports it with an amendment falling within another committee's interests.

For example, in 1981 the Speaker initially referred the State Department authorization bill, H.R. 3518, to Foreign Affairs on May 19. The bill, as reported by the committee, contained provisions concerning location of foreign government offices, which concerned the District of Columbia Committee. Accordingly, the Speaker sequentially referred the bill to that committee, which reported it June 19.[142]

Finally, in a split referral, different committees receive the bill with instructions only to report amendments to certain sections. It is as if the bill were split into parts, and the different parts were sent to different committees. This is particularly appropriate when a committee has a claim only to part of the bill, such as when a bill concerns both civilian and military aspects of a problem, with Armed Services having an exclusive claim to the military aspects but no claim to the civilian aspects.

An extreme example of a split referral

_____

under Rule X(1)(p)(10). The bills were H.R. 7103 and H.R. 3403. In 1980, the Speaker referred H.R. 7103 to them jointly on April 22, Commerce reported it on May 13, and Public Works reported it on May 16. It was defeated on the floor. In 1981, the Speaker referred H.R. 3403 to them jointly on May 4, and they both reported it on May 19. This time, the House passed the bill.

[142] The House defeated the bill. See 1981 _Congressional Quarterly Almanac_ 159.

occurred in 1975: "H.R. 2633, the Energy
Independence Act of 1975, was divided and
initially referred as follows: Title I to the
Committee on Armed Services, Titles II, III, IV,
V, VI, VII, VIII, XII, and XIII to the Committee
on Interstate and Foreign Commerce, Title IX to
the Committee on Ways and Means; and Titles X and
XI to the Committee on Banking, Currency and
Housing."[143]

Multiple referrals can include limits on
duration of committee consideration, which deprive
a committee of referral of one of its greatest
powers, the power to kill a bill by refusing
indefinitely to report it. Rule X(5)(c) provides
that the Speaker can limit the time for
consideration of sequential referrals.[144] He may
specify that the bill will be automatically
discharged a specified number of days after
whenever the second committee receives the bill,
or he may list a date on which the second
committee will be automatically discharged. In
1983, the Speaker also began using authority to
limit the time on joint referrals.[145]

The domestic content bill illustrates time
limits in both types of referrals. In 1982,
Energy and Commerce reported the bill on September

---

[143] H.R. Rept. No. 866, supra, at 470-71.

[144] The rule specifies that "the Speaker may refer the
matter . . . for consideration in sequence (subject to
appropriate time limitations in the case of any
committee)." When first adopted in 1975, it allowed time
limits on the second consideration in sequence; in 1977, it
was amended to allow time limits on the first consideration
in sequence.

[145] Rule X(5)(c) provided, besides its express arrangements
for multiple referral, that the Speaker could "make such
other provision as may be considered appropriate."
Accordingly the Speaker implemented an old suggestion of the
Patterson Committee staff and began making joint referrals
in which one committee was "primary," and the other,
"secondary" one had a time limit on its consideration. See
H.R. Rept. No. 866, supra, at 465.

21, 1982, and the Speaker sequentially referred it
"to the Committee on Ways and Means for a period
ending not later than October 1, 1982." In 1983,
the Speaker jointly referred the reintroduced
domestic content bill to Energy and Commerce and
"concurrently to the Committee on Ways and Means
for a period ending not later than 30 calendar
days following the date on which the Committee on
Energy and Commerce files its report in the
House." The joint referral allowed Ways and Means
a fuller time period and an earlier start, but did
not let Ways and Means kill the bill by declining
for an indefinite time period to report it.

Members and staff of the concerned committees
may themselves negotiate the terms of a multiple
referral prior to introducing a bill. The
Parliamentarian then checks their arrangement and
implements it. While the elaborate multiple
referral process is sometimes criticized as an
inadequate substitute for clear jurisdictional
lines, it has also been defended as maximizing
perspectives and competition.[146]

---

[146] One commentator on the subject has quoted from a
classic of political science: "'[a]bove everything,' E. E.
Schattschneider once wrote, 'the people are powerless if the
political enterprise is not competitive. It is the
competition of political organizations that provides the
people with the opportunity to make a choice.'" MacKenzie,
"Committee Coordination and Policy Integration in the
Senate," in Commission on the Operation of the Senate, 94th
Cong., 2d Sess., Committees and Senate Procedure, 74, 89
(Comm. Print 1977) (quoting E. E. Schattschneider, The
Semisovereign People 140 (1960)).

Mr. MacKenzie argues that "[f]or every committee
involved in the consideration of a complex issue, another
multiplier is added to the number of public and private
interests included in the process of deliberation." Id.
Jurisdictional competition "involves fundamental questions
of social welfare and economic prosperity and political
power. It is too easy in discussing jurisdictional
conflicts to categorize them as anomalies of democracy when
in fact, they are fundamentals of democracy." Id.

(footnote continued)

It should be mentioned that the Speaker has other jurisdictional resources besides multiple referrals. Under House Rule X(5)(c) the Speaker may "refer the matter to a special <u>ad hoc</u> <u>committee</u> appointed by the Speaker with the approval of the House (from the members of the committees having legislative jurisdiciton) for the specific purpose of considering that mater and reporting to the House thereon." (Emphasis supplied.) The power to create ad hoc committees is an old one.[147] A major example was the Speaker's referral of President Carter's energy program in 1977 to the new Ad Hoc Committee on Energy.[148]

Senate Multiple Referral

The Legislative Reorganization Act's provision for Senate referral, still in effect as Rule XVII(1), provides that the presiding officer decide questions of committee jurisdiction without

---

It was similarly argued that committee overlaps "maximize congressional bargaining operations" and force executive agencies to deal with "differing interest perspectives." W. L. Morrow, <u>Congressional Committees</u> 22-23 (1969).

[147] Historically, the Speaker's power to create ad hoc committees traces back to his power from 1789 to 1911 to make all appointments to committees; the power was taken away regarding standing committees but not ad hoc committees.

[148] The Ad Hoc Committee was created by H. Res. 508, which the House adopted by voice vote. In a sophisticated juggling action run by Speaker O'Neill and the ubiquitous Representative Bolling, five standing committees with jurisdiction over energy completed action on the Carter energy program, the Ad Hoc Committee readied the bill for floor action, and the House adopted a complex rule providing for debate of the bill. See Stanley Bach, <u>Complexities of the Legislative Process: A Case Study of Congressional Consideration of National Energy Legislation During the 95th Congress</u> at 2-9 (Cong. Res. Serv. 1979); Entin, <u>Energy Politics in the House of Representatives: The National Energy Plan</u>, 11 Conn. L. Rev. 403, 418-27 (1979).

debate, "in favor of the committee which has jurisdiction over the subject matter which predominates in such proposed legislation."[149] Rule XVII(1) purported to allow jurisdictional appeals, but these are quite rare.[150] In contrast to the House, where the Speaker makes multiple referrals, in the Senate, multiple referrals occur only by unanimous consent.

After study by the Senate's temporary committee on jurisdictional reform,[151] Senate Rule

---

[149] The rule was apparently a reaction to lax referral practices prior to 1946. The Joint Committee on the Organization of Congress, whose recommendations were embodied in the 1946 act, had commented: "We recommend the exercise of more care in the reference of Senate bills. A bill should be referred without regard to the author's service on any particular committee seeking jurisdiction when its subject matter does not normally lie in the defined province of that committee." S. Rept. No. 1011, 79th Cong., 2d Sess. 5 (1946).

[150] In an illuminating debate in 1977, the Senate Judiciary and Commerce committees disputed referral of a bill to deregulate the trucking industry and to subject it to the antitrust law. Judiciary has jurisdiction over the antitrust laws, while modification of trucking regulation was a matter for the Commerce Committee. Senator Howard Metzenbaum (D-Ohio) noted that "going back more than 20 years, I have been unable to find any record of a successful appeal of a Parliamentarian's referral of a particular piece of legislation." 125 Cong. Rec. S1232 (daily ed. Feb. 7, 1979) (emphasis supplied). He explained that "appealing the Parliamentarian's decision . . . opens a Pandora's box for those who would like to raise issues." Id. The outcome was eventually a multiple referral to both committees by unanimous consent.

[151] The 1976 Temporary Senate Select Committee on Committees' staff study found that "the Senate permits joint referral of measures under unanimous consent procedures"; the Committee found that the Senate had multiply referred 68 bills and joint resolutions in 1975. Temporary Select Committee to Study the Senate Committee System, 94th Cong., 2d Sess, First Staff Report: The Senate Committee System: Jurisdiction, Referrals, Numbers and Sizes, and Limitations (footnote continued)

XVII(3) was amended in 1977 to allow the leadership to move for multiple referrals.[152] However, Majority Leader Byrd opposed use of the mechanism, and it languished unused.[153]

In 1977, the Senate engaged in a general jurisdictional reorganization based on the recommendations of a Temporary Select Committee on Committees, the "Stevenson Committee;" because of this reorganization, which eliminated committee jurisdiction overlaps and ambiguities, and the other sources of Senate opposition to multiple referrals, the number of multiple referrals in the Senate is lower than in the House. In the 96th Congress, only 8.2 percent of all Senate bills were referred to more than one committee, well below the level in the House.[154] Still, some key

---

on Membership 98 (1976). That study considered multiple referrals a mixed blessing, since they can "enlarge the potential for jurisdictional conflict between committees . . . touching off protracted negotiations among chairmen, party leaders, and the Parliamentarian as to which panel should receive the measure." Id. at 97.

The Select Committee made proposals regarding multiple referrals, which the Senate Rules Committee revised with a detailed report. See S. Rept. No. 2, 95th Cong., 1st Sess. 59-60 (1977).

[152] As adopted by the Senate, the mechanism authorizes the majority and minority leaders, together, to make a motion for a joint or sequential referral. That rule invested the motion with great potential power, as the motion could limit the portions of the bills each committee could consider and the time allowed to each committee.

[153] Majority Leader Byrd warned "that increased use of multiple referrals would unnecessarily delay committee action on legislation, and that it would tend to blur the jurisdictional boundaries among committees." H. Rept. No. 866, supra, at 224. Following the acrimonious trucking deregulation dispute of 1977, Majority Leader Byrd "announced that he would henceforth oppose. . . . all but the most vital multiple referrals in the future." H.R. Rept. No. 866, supra, at 224.

[154] Id.

bills[155] do receive multiple referrals by
unanimous consent, due to the persistence of many
jurisdictional overlaps, some in vital areas.[156]

One example of how one is worked out, through
the traditional negotiated agreement, concerns
"leasing" of arms to other countries. The
Pentagon expanded this activity into a means for
controversial transfers of major equipment such as
jets and helicopters.[157] While the Foreign

---

[155] Key bills receiving multiple referrals in 1981-82, for
example, included the bills for nuclear waste disposal, the
gasoline tax increase for highway construction, the
intelligence authorization, and the regulatory reform bill,
as well as, for practical purposes, the budget
reconciliation bills. These were respectively S.1662,
S.3044, S.2487, and S.1080. As in the House, technically
only the Budget Committee reports the budget reconciliation
bill, but in fact that committee assembled provisions
reported by several committees in reporting the 1981
reconciliation bill, S.1377, and the 1982 bill, S.2774.

Minor bills receiving multiple referrals concerned such
matters as leasing of naval vessels to foreign countries,
which resolved a jurisdictional battle between Armed
Services and Foreign Affairs; extradition reform, involving
Judiciary and Foreign Affairs; and payment for cleanup of
the Three Mile Island reactor, involving Energy and Natural
Resources, and Environment and Public Works. These were
respectively S.2965, S.1940, and S.1606.

[156] The Stevenson Committee left untouched the widespread
jurisdiction of the Finance Committee, which had a share in
virtually every policy area through the Internal Revenue
Code's policy-laden credits and deductions, and through the
Finance Committee's jurisdiction over programs paid for by
earmarked taxes like Social Security, Medicare, and highway
and airport development. For the sparing of the Finance
Committee, see Parris, The Senate Reorganizes its
Committees, 1977, 94 Poli. Sci. Q. 319 (1979). Similarly,
the Stevenson Committee left untouched the jurisdiction of
the Armed Services Committee, with its widespread overlaps
due to military aspects of many matters, such as military
dependents' overseas education, military research, and
military aspects of nuclear energy.

(footnote continued)

Relations Committee legislates concerning arms
sales, the arms leasing provision was in the armed
services title (Title 10) of the U.S. Code, giving
the   Armed   Services   Committee   its   own
jurisdictional claim.

In 1981, the Foreign Relations Committee
tried   to   obtain   jurisdiction   by   reporting
provisions in its annual foreign aid authorization
putting arms leasing restrictions under the arms
sales law.   Armed Services countered with a floor
amendment to retain existing law and its existing
jurisdiction.   After a test vote on the floor and
extensive   negotiations,   a   complex   understanding
was   reached   sharing   jurisdiction   between   Foreign
Affairs   and   Armed   Services.[158]   In   accord   with

---

157   The   Stevenson   Committee,   appointed   to   study   the
committee   system   in   1976,   reported   on   how   committees
obtained "gradual accretions" of jurisdictional power over
time   by   an   almost   invisible   web   of   "precedents   and
agreements,"   partly   by   making   arrangements   with   other
committees, partly by inserting provisions in the areas of
the U.S. Code under their jurisdiction:

   The   formal   provisions   of   [Rule   XXV,   defining
committee jurisdictions] are supplemented by a complex
series   of   precedents   and   agreements   governing   the
reference   of   bills.   In   general,   once   a   piece   of
legislation   is   referred   to   a   given   committee,   it
remains there in perpetuity, as do any amendments that
may   be   proposed   to   it.   Thus,   committees   often   utilize
statutes   as   springboards   for   enlarging   their   span   of
authority.   These gradual accretions of responsibility
greatly   complicate   the   jurisdictional   picture   in   the
Senate.

First Staff Report, supra, at 103.

158   Senator   John   Tower   (R-Tex.),   chairperson   of   Armed
Services, "explained to the Senate that, under an agreement
between [the chair of Foreign Relations] and himself, 'the
Foreign   Relations   Committee   will   continue   to   have   its
present   review   of   transfers   to   foreign   countries   [with
regard   to   leases   as   well]   .   .   .   .   The   Armed   Services
Committee would have legislative jurisdiction over . . . the
ceiling [for the fund paying for equipment for leasing] and
procurements . . . .'" 1981 Congressional Quarterly Almanac
176.

that agreement, the following year the Parliamentarian smoothly referred S.2965, a bill concerning naval vessel leasing, first to Armed Services, then to Foreign Relations.[159]

The regulatory reform bill, S.1080, offers another illustration of contemporary Senate practice. For years, Judiciary and Governmental Affairs competed for control of "regulatory reform" (revision of administrative procedure). Neither committee's version could get to the floor over the jurisdictional opposition of the other committee.

Accordingly, Judiciary and Governmental Affairs worked out a unanimous consent referral, under which the Chair jointly referred S.1080 to them in April, 1981. Each reported out a version, and laborious negotiations produced a "staff compromise [that] ironed out many technical differences" -- a "consensus version" that left "only the most significant issues open for further resolution."[160]. With the path thus smoothed, the Senate resolved those issues and passed the bill in March, 1982.

As in the House, though to a lesser extent, the Senate often follows multiple referrals with multiple-committee participation in other legislative stages. For example, in consideration of the 1982 Surface Transportation Act, the gasoline tax increase to fund public works, the administration bill received a multiple referral to four committees. The Senate referred the administration bill, S.3044, to Finance (tax); Environment and Public Works (highways); Banking, Housing, and Urban Affairs (mass transit); and

---

[159] The Speaker had referred the parallel House measure, H.R.7115, jointly to Armed Services and Foreign Affairs. Both chambers passed the bill, which became law.

[160] 1981 Congressional Quarterly Almanac 406 ("staff compromise"); 127 Cong. Rec. S15129 (daily ed. Dec. 11, 1981) (statement of Sen. Paul Laxalt (R-Nev.), chair of the Judiciary subcommittee working on the bill) ("consensus version").

Commerce, Science, and Transportation (trucking regulation).[161] All four committees participated in floor management of the act, and all four committees contributed members to the conference committee.

The Senate uses a number of other techniques besides multiple referrals for resolving jurisdictional overlaps, to a greater extent than the House. Such other techniques include select committees which may have memberships drawn from regular committees of competing jurisdiction. Classic examples of select committees to solve jurisdictional disputes were the Kefauver Committee to study organized crime, with Senators drawn from Commerce and from Judiciary, and the McClellan Labor Racketeering Committee, with Senators drawn from Labor and from the Permanent Subcommittee on Investigations.[162]

Elaborate consultation methods may be used, such as non-binding recommedations from one committee to another, or participation by off-committee Senators in matters of competing jurisdictional interest. For example, the Senate used such methods, instead of multiple referral, to resolve the jurisdictional competition[163] over

---

[161] Although technically the Senate used the House bill, H.R.6211, which received a single referral to Finance as its basis for legislation, the first amendment offered, which essentially acted as the basis for action, was a joint amendment offered by the Majority Leader and the four chairs of the four committees listed above.

[162] Another example was the Billy Carter Subcommittee in 1980, with Members from Judiciary and Foreign Relations.

[163] As for other techniques, for one example, when the Senate took up President Carter's energy program, it split the program into two packages. Each was referred only to a single committee, a much tighter referral pattern than the House. One bill was referred to Finance (taxes), the other, S.1469, to Energy and Natural Resources. When Senator Jackson, chair of that committee, introduced S. 1469, he noted that his committee and other committees -- Banking, Commerce, Environment and Public Works, Labor and Human (footnote continued)

the energy legislation of the 1970s.

Resources, and Governmental Affairs -- all had some interest, but that those interests could be accommodated by a single referral and consultation:

> If title I is referred to the Committee on Energy and Natural Resources in this way, we would be prepared to work with other committees in any way which seems desirable. Some committees may wish to hold hearings and make formal legislative recommendations. Others may wish to participate in markups. In some cases, less formal arrangements may be satisfactory. In the course of our energy work over the past 5 years we have worked with several committees on legislation and would hope to continue this kind of cooperative effort.

See S. Bach, supra, at 10.

3
Committee Procedure[1]

Since Congress does most of its work in committees, the procedure it follows at the committee level has considerable importance. The basic sequence is familiar enough. Chairs have considerable influence over committees, although they are far from dominating as they did some decades ago. Most committees divide themselves into subcommittees, and farm out greater or lesser amounts of their work to those subcommittees.

Either at the full committee or subcommittee level, bills start their progress when the chairs schedule hearings on them, at which witnesses testify on their views of the bills. A chairperson may schedule a bill for mark-up, a session for amending the bill. Ultimately, the full committee votes on whether to report the bill to the floor, sending it off toward enactment.

---

[1] Sources most frequently cited in this chapter include A. J. Mikva & P. B. Sarris, The American Congress (1983) (Mikva & Sarris); S. S. Smith & C. J. Deering, Committees in Congress (1984) (Smith & Deering); House Comm. on Science and Technology, 99th Cong., Legislative Manual (4th ed. 1985) (Legislative Manual).

The simplicity of this basic process masks the elaborate struggles and tactics at committee level.   Chairs do not possess a fixed quantum of authority; their authority has changed over time and reflects both procedural and political aspects. Similarly, the distribution of authority between committees and subcommittees has changed dynamically over time.   The hearing process has as many layers of subtlety and maneuver as its nearest equivalent, trial procedure, while mark-up and reporting have much of the complexity of action on the Senate and House floors.   This chapter examines each of these steps in turn.

Chairs: How Much Control

The starting point for committee procedure is an assessment of the position of the chair. Each chair has the basic functions of a presiding officer: to maintain order during committee proceedings, decide questions of procedure, and set the schedule.   However, the function of presiding only begins to suggest the chair's role.   During the era of conservative coalition domination, particularly in the House, committee chairs tended to completely control committees:

> [The chairs] can, in most cases, establish subcommittees, determine their size, establish party ratios, appoint the members, maintain ex officio membership, control the referral of bills and either assign or hold back staff and money for subcommittee operations.[2]

Accordingly, one commentator wrote that "the chairman deals from a stacked deck. He should be able to maintain control even against rank-and-file rebellion, unless he is politically inept."[3]

Dramatic change came in the House in the

---

[2]   Goodwin, Subcommittees: The Miniature Legislatures of Congress, 56 Am. Poli. Sci. Rev. 596, 602 (1962).

[3]   Id., 56 Am. Poli. Sci. Rev. at 600-601.

1970s, as discussed in part in the chapter on committee organization. By deposing three chairs in 1975, the Democratic Caucus established that committee chairs would have to be responsive to junior Members to retain their posts. Moreover, the "Subcommittee Bill of Rights," first adopted in 1973 and now incorporated in the Rules of the Democratic Caucus, established the autonomy of subcommittees and preserved a number of rights for subcommittee chairs and junior Members. The caucus rules specify methods of assignments to subcommittees; methods of choice of subcommittee chairs, discussed below; and that chairs of committees "shall insofar as practicable, permit subcommittee chairmen to handle on the floor legislation from their respective subcommittees."[4] The Senate accomplished somewhat similar results, in terms of the rights of subcommittee chairs and junior Members, through evolution rather than specific rules changes.[5]

Nonetheless, full committee chairs still have considerable authority over their committees, and subcommittee chairs have considerable authority over their subcommittees. Like the House Speaker, who combines authority as presiding officer and party leader, committee chairs both preside in committee and lead the majority party Members of their committees. Hence, as outside observers stated in 1984 of House chairs:

> the same personal resources that were important in the 1970s are still important today. Subject matter expertise, knowledge of House procedure, friendship with party leaders, and associations with interest group representatives and other personal resources still give chairs an advantage

---

[4]   House Democratic Caucus Rule 40.

[5]   Compare Smith & Deering at 30 (in the 1947-64 period, "[i]n many respects, House and Senate leadership resembled confederations of committee chairs, each acting as the sovereign over a committee's jurisdiction") with id. at 188 (in the 1980s, "[f]ew Senate chairs seem to dominate their committees").

over more junior members.   Moreover, chairs
still control large full committee staffs
and can, within limits, manipulate the full
committee schedule enough to gain some
influence over committee activities.[6]

Apart from these political sources of
strength, the various procedural activities of
full committee chairs provide a constant theme in
a number of chapters in this book: leading
jurisdictional struggles; directing full committee
hearings, mark-up, and reporting as discussed
below; often managing on the floor the committees'
most important bills; and choosing and leading
conference delegations.   Similarly, subcommittee
chairs often play a role in jurisdictional
struggles, they have the major role in
subcommittee proceedings discussed below, they
floor manage many bills, and they play a
significant role in conference.

Committee Rules

Just as the House and Senate adopt standing
rules as the core of their internal self-
regulation, so committees formally regulate their
operations through adopting committee rules.
Committee rules are an old practice; some early
nineteenth-century investigating committees had
written rules concerning examination of
witnesses.[7]   However, as late as 1970, important

---

[6]   Smith & Deering at 177. As two insiders noted in 1983:

Party discipline is a constant factor in committee
operation, especially on important bills. . . . A
committee chairman and a ranking minority member
display their displeasure with errant committee
members in a variety of ways: they are awarded smaller
budgets, their subcommittees are eliminated,
legislation is not referred to their subcommittees,
they are not recognized at committee meetings, the
rooms they request are not available, and so on.

Mikva & Sarris at 147-48.

[7]   3 A. Hinds & C. Cannon, Precedents of the House of
(footnote_continued)

committees still had no formal rules of procedure.[8] The Legislative Reorganization Act of 1970 required that all committees adopt and publish their own written rules of procedure: Senate committees must publish their rules every year, House committees every odd-numbered year, to give public access to committee rules and to make Members accountable for the fairness of the rules.[9] The rules for all House committees are compiled each Congress into a committee print of the Rules Committee. The rules for all Senate committees are compiled each Congress by the Office of Senate Legal Counsel.

Typically, committees change their rules, if at all, only when they adopt the rules at their first organizational meeting in each Congress. More often than not they simply retain their rules from the previous Congress: when the Senate changed majority parties in 1981 and 1987, the new majority parties hardly altered any committee rules at all. On the other hand, when junior House Democrats made the dramatic revolts discussed above in the 1970s establishing autonomous subcommittees and other restrictions on committee chairs, they sealed the victory by changes in committee rules.[10]

Representatives § 1841 (1907, 1936) (rules of procedure of committee in 1838).

[8]   Nine Senate committees lacked written rules in 1970, including Agriculture, Appropriations, Finance, Foreign Relations, Interior, Labor, and Rules. 116 Cong. Rec. 35009 (1970) (table inserted by Sen. Metcalf).

[9]   The requirement to publish committee rules is now in House Rule XI(2)(a) and Senate Rule XXVI(2). In hearings on legislative organization in the 1960s, members and others advocated uniform rules of procedure for all committees, partly as a way of checking arbitrary chairs. Organization of Congress: Hearings Before the Jt. Comm. on the Organization of Congress, 89th Cong., 1st Sess. 261, 505, 894, 974 (1965). However, committees and their chairs varied too much in operating styles to adopt uniform rules. For a discussion of the origin and purposes of the publication requirement, see United States v. Reinecke, 524 F.2d 435, 438-39 (D.C. Cir. 1975).
(footnote continued)

Committee rules cover only a portion of committee procedure, just as the written rules of the Senate and House cover only a portion of floor procedure. The most typical subjects covered by rules are scheduling of meetings (days for regular meetings and the procedures for calling special meetings); how closed sessions are held; broadcasting of hearings; and procedures for voting (quorums, proxies, demands for recorded votes, and reporting). Committee rules may also discuss the rights of witnesses at hearings; the status of subcommittees (particularly for House committees); and the procedures for authorizing investigations and issuing subpoenas.

B.   SUBCOMMITTEES

Activity at Full Committee and Subcommittee Levels

Enormous activity occurs in committee and subcommittee. Thousands of bills are referred to committee and, usually, to subcommittee. As for hearings, in 1983, for example, House committees and subcommittees held 3,274 hearings; Senate committees and subcommittees held 2,008 hearings.[11] As the New York Times noted in 1988,

---

[10] Ornstein & Rohde, "Shifting Forces, Changing Rules, and Political Outcomes: The Impact of Congressional Change on Four House Committees," in New Perspectives on the House of Representatives (3d ed., ed. by R. L. Peabody & N. W. Polsby 1977) at 207, 218.

[11] Davidson & Kephart, Indicators of House of Representatives Workload and Activity (Cong. Res. Serv. 1985), at 32; Davidson & Cook, Indicators of Senate Activity and Workload (Cong. Res. Serv. 1984), at 59 (the Senate figure only covers hearings in Washington, D.C., not field hearings, and the figures may include meetings as well as hearings).

A Senate study found "[d]uring the 93rd Congress [1973-74], for example, 4,067 meetings were held for the 100 Senators, compared with 5,888 meetings for the 435 House (footnote continued)

"[d]ay in and day out, committees of Congress conduct a dozen or more hearings."[12]   Hundreds of mark-up meetings also occurred.

There is a complex and uneven distribution of authority between full committees and subcommittees. At one extreme on the spectrum, subcommittees may play a maximum role. The appropriations committees of both chambers allow their subcommittees such a role. The full appropriations committees do not conduct the hearings or primary mark-up of appropriations bills. Rather, the subcommittees hold the hearings, conduct the primary mark-up, and report a bill to full committee in a form that the full committee usually accepts with little change after a short mark-up. The subcommittee chairs then manage "their" bills on the floor and take the lead on "their" bills in conference; the conference committee membership is drawn from the subcommittee (plus the committee leadership). In practical terms, this means that when a Secretary of the Interior needs funding to start a program, for example, and interest groups wish to support or oppose it, the most important leaders for them to see may not be those of the full Appropriations Committees, but those of the Subcommittees on Interior and Related Appropriations.

In the House, as a result of the 1970s reforms, the tendency has been to give subcommittees something tending toward such a maximum role, though with a greater full committee share on most committees than on the

---

Members." Commission on the Operation of the Senate, 94th Cong., 2d Sess., Toward a Modern Senate, S. Doc. No. 278, 94th Cong., 2d Sess. 4 (1976). The underlying data indicated that Senate committees and subcommittees had held 1,024 "meetings" in 1975; a House study found that committees and subcommittees had held 6,771 "meetings" in 1977-78. Commission on the Operation of the Senate, 94th Cong., 2d Sess., Legislative Activity Sourcebook: United States Senate 26 (Comm. Print 1976); H.R. Rept. No. 866, 96th Cong., 2d Sess. 68 (1980).

[12] Hershey, Hearings on Capitol Hill and Who They Attract, New York Times, May 6, 1988, at A22.

Appropriations Committee:

> Nearly all House hearings now are held by
> subcommittees . . . . [While] a majority of
> the meetings at which substantive policy
> decisions are made also now are held in
> subcommittee . . . . full committee meetings
> still are not greatly outnumbered by
> subcommittee meetings, even though
> subcommittees outnumber House full
> committees by more than six to one. The
> pattern of meetings indicates, therefore,
> that while the House clearly has moved
> toward subcommittee government, existing
> committee activities represent a mixed
> pattern of subcommittee and full committee
> involvement.[13]

A 1983 House housing bill illustrates
concretely how House full committees defer to
subcommittees. The House Committee on Banking,
Finance and Urban Affairs referred the 1983 $24
billion housing authorization bill to its
Subcommittee on Housing and Community
Development. The subcommittee completed hearings
and mark-up and reported the bill with amendments
back to the full committee. Then, the full
committee's "members essentially ratified the bill
approved by the Housing subcommittee"; "[i]n
contrast to the five-day subcommittee mark-up, the
full Banking Committee swept through HR 1 in about
three hours . . . ."[14]

Senate committees tended in the 1970s to
give their subcommittees a greater role, but after
then, a somewhat lesser role:

> Senate subcommittees are very active in
> holding hearings, but on most committees
> they play virtually no formal role in
> writing legislation. Even on Judiciary and

---

[13] Smith & Deering at 133.   For a committee-by-committee
survey, see id. at 134-48.

[14] House Committee Approves New Housing Rental Program, 41
Cong. Q. Week. Rept. 947 (1983).

Labor, committees often cited as among the
Senate's most "decentralized," a clear
majority of meetings in which legislation is
written are held by the full committee.[15]

At the other extreme end of the spectrum
from appropriations committees, some Senate
committees allocate only a minimal role to
subcommittees, denying them separate funding or
staff, and holding mark-up and even hearings at
full committee level. The Senate Budget Committee
and the Rules and Administration Committee have no
subcommittees,[16] while some committees, such as

---

[15] Smith & Deering at 151.   For a committee-by-committee
survey, see id. at 153-61.

As for the 1970s pattern, Minority Leader Howard Baker
(R-Tenn.) commented that "In most committees, whatever the
subcommittee sends up, the full committee generally stamps
and sends to the floor." B. Asbell, The Senate Nobody Knows
338 (1978).   In raw numbers a Senate study found that 55
percent of markup sessions in 1975 took place at the
subcommittee level, and only 45 percent at the full
committee level. S. Doc. No. 278, 94th Cong., 2d Sess. 36
(1976).

A 1978 study of seven Senate committees' operations
concluded that

[t]he committees differ in their use of
subcommittees. The chairman's style, the committee
membership, numbers of staff, and the legislative
jurisdiction often are determining factors in whether
a committee delegates legislative responsibility and
initiative to a subcommittee.

Samuelson, "Senate Committee Operations," in Commission on
the Operation of the Senate, 94th Cong., 2d Sess.,
Committees and Senate Procedure 44 (1977).

[16] In each case there are special reasons. The Senate
Rules and Administration Committee has a number of senior
Senators, including chairs of full committees, who would
much rather have a subcommittee chair on a major committee
than on Rules.   The Senate Budget Committee cannot have
formal subcommittees, any more than the House Budget
(footnote continued)

Finance and Foreign Relations, use their
subcommittees only for hearings, with no
subcommittee mark-ups, separate budgets, or
staffs. Indeed, the Senate altered its budget
systems in 1970 and 1980 to impose greater
committee control over subcommittees.[17]

Committee, without appearing to take line-item scrutiny of
areas that would encroach on the authorizing and
appropriating committees.

[17]   In the 1960s, some Senate subcommittees apparently
received authorizations from the Senate for separate
subcommittee budgets. In 1966, the Joint Committee on the
Organization of the Congress found that committees should
control subcommittees better, and that

> [t]he most practical means of exercising full
> committee supervision is in connection with annual
> requests for funds. . . . [A] single committee
> resolution for such funding -- designating the
> subcommittees to be funded -- furnishes the best
> annual mechanism for evaluating subcommittee
> operations.

The Legislative Reorganization Act implemented the Joint
Committee's proposal for Senate committees, but not House
committees. Section 110(a) of the act, codified at 2 U.S.C.
§ 190(g), provided

> Each standing committee. . . shall offer one annual
> authorization resolution to procure such
> authorization. . . . [which] shall include a
> specification of the amount of all such funds sought
> by such committee for expenditure by all subcommittees
> thereof during that year and the amount so sought for
> each such subcommittee.

In 1979, when the Senate recodified its rules by adopting S.
Res. 274, 96th Cong., 1st Sess., it moved 2 U.S.C. § 190(g)
into Senate Rule XXVI(9).

By 1980, the monopoly of funding by full committees
took a further step, as amended by S. Res. 281, 96th Cong.,
2d Sess. Now, not only did funds only flow in
authorizations to full committees, but in addition, the
authorization resolutions were no longer supposed to
specify, as line items, "the amount so sought for each
(footnote continued)

The Senate Foreign Relations Committee also illustrates this pattern.   It has a set of subcommittees devoted to different world regions: the Subcommittee on African Affairs, the Subcommittee on East Asian and Pacific Affairs, and so on.[18]   These subcommittees do not have separate budgets or staff and do not conduct mark-ups.   Their functions are to conduct hearings and consultations with executive officials, and to give their chairs an area of specialization, and even these limited roles may not be fully carried out.   For example, in 1982 the full committee, rather than the Subcommittee on Western Hemisphere Affairs, not only marked up the bill to implement President Reagan's Carribean Basin Initiative, but even conducted the hearings.[19]

Initial Referral of Bills

The first step with a bill, once it has been referred by the chamber to committee, is to keep the bill at full committee or refer it to subcommittee (and if so, to choose the subcommittee or subcommittees of referral).   As former Representative, now Judge, Mikva notes:

> [a]s a bill can be referred to a friendly or
> unfriendly committee, so also can its fate
> be sealed by the subcommittee to which it is
> referred . . . .   The decision by Judiciary
> Committee Chairman Peter Rodino to refer
> revision of the criminal code to the
> subcommittee chaired by Michigan Congressman

---

subcommittee" (a requirement often not heeded anyway). Senate Rule XXVI(9) simply provided for each committee to report an annual authorization resolution.   Contrast House Rule XI(5)(d).

[18] One subcommittee handles international economic policy; another, arms control, oceans, international operations and environment.

[19] Senate Panel Votes Changes in Caribbean Basin Aid Plan, 40 Cong. Q. Week. Rep. 1186 (1982); Year-End Report of the 2d Session of the 97th Congress, S. Doc. No. 28, 97th Cong., 2d Sess. 104 (1982).

John Conyers, Jr., boded ill for any comprehensive rewrite of the code in the Ninety-seventh Congress, for Conyers was a known opponent of the legislation.[20]

In the House, the Democratic Caucus rules prescribe that "[a]ll legislation . . . shall be referred to all subcommittees of appropriate jurisdiction within 2 weeks unless, by majority vote of the Democratic Members of the full committee, consideration is to be by the full committee."[21] Accordingly, House chairs refer most bills to subcommittee.[22] The House Committee on Space, Science and Technology noted in its manual of committee procedure that a referral is announced by a letter from the committee staff director to the subcommittee chair.[23] This information then goes into the committee's periodically issued calendar, and into the LEGIS computer system maintained for the Congress. A bill may be multiply referred, i.e., referred to more than one subcommittee.[24] Several House committees have explicit rules authorizing

---

[20] Mikva & Sarris at 206. By contrast, "[i]n the previous Congress the code legislation, referred to a friendlier subcommittee chaired by Massachusetts Congressman Father Robert Drinan, had come close to passage." Id.

[21] House Democratic Caucus Rule 33(D).

[22] "Until the 1970s, many full committee chairs did not bother to refer to a subcommittee legislation that was not likely to be taken up by the full committee," but by the 96th Congress, almost 80 percent of all bills referred to standing committees were referred to subcommittees. Smith & Deering at 132.

[23] Legislative Manual at 27.

[24] The manual notes that "[i]f a subcommittee feels a joint or sequential referral of a bill is warranted, request should be made to the General Counsel. This usually takes the form of a memorandum, so that such justification of referral can be made part of the permanent record." Legislative Manual at 27.

multiple referrals.

Because of the House Democratic Caucus
rules, House committee chairs do not tend to hold
any large proportion of their bills at full
committee level.   Instead, House full committee
chairs can lead one subcommittee in their
committee, and refer bills to (or handle the most
interesting oversight subjects in) that
subcommittee:

> [Chairman Jack Brooks (D-Tex.) of the
> Committee on Govenrment Operations] chaired
> the Legislation and National Security
> Subcommittee -- which handles nearly all
> committee legislation . . . .   [Chairman
> John Dingell (D-Mich.) of the Energy and
> Commerce Committee] moved to chair the
> Oversight and Investigations Subcommittee.
> The new subcomittee would give Dingell broad
> oversight powers over all subject matter
> within the committee's jurisdiction.   The
> Dingell and Brooks examples show how
> aggressive chairs, lacking great formal
> authority, can still shape their committees'
> work environment as committee and
> subcommittee chairs . . . .[25]

The Senate had no revolt against chairs in
the 1970s and therefore never developed hard and
fast party rules on the subject.   This has left
its committee chairs with much more flexibility
about referring bills to subcommittees.   Often
Senate chairs do not refer bills to subcommittees
at all.   "A Senate chairman often keeps
legislation he supports at full committee to keep
a firm rein on its course,"[26] as Senate committee
calenders reflect.[27]   Observers have catalogued

---

[25]   Smith & Deering at 181.

[26]   Mikva & Sarris at 206.   In contrast to the 80 percent of
House bills referred to subcommittee in the 96th Congress,
only 41 percent of Senate bills were so referred.   Smith &
Deering at 132.

[27]   The 1983 Senate Judiciary Committee calendar reflected a
wide range of bills that the chair had kept for full
(footnote continued)

examples of this.[28]
   When Senate chairs do refer bills to subcommittee, they may refer without following fixed jurisdictional lines, either because of the chairs' own wishes or because of the personal interests of subcommittee chairs. For example, in 1983, reflecting the subcommittee chair's own interests, the Judiciary Committee's Subcommittee on Separation of Powers "consider[ed] a diverse range of issues," including "consideration of the United States-Communist China communique of 1982 concerning United States-Taiwan relations," "division of powers between the National and State governments," "government information (except Freedom of Information and Privacy Acts)," and the authorization for the Civil Rights Commission.[29]

---

committee consideration, with no subcommittee role, including all nominations and major antitrust bills, and some bankruptcy court reorganization, anticrime and gun decontrol bills. Senate Committee on the Judiciary, 98th Cong., 1st Sess., Legislative and Executive Calendar No. 1 (S. Prt. 98-5 1983).

[28]   To take some particular examples:

As the new chairman of the Senate Judiciary Committee, Strom Thurmond [(R-S.C.)] insisted on keeping the death penalty and the criminal code legislation at full committee. Senator William Roth [(R-Del.)] of Delaware, chairman of the Governmental Affairs Committee, refused to refer his regulatory reform legislation to the appropriate subcommittee even though its chairman, Senator Charles Percy [(R-Ill.)] favored the bill. Depriving a subcommittee of rightful jurisdiciton carries some risk, however, and a chairman does not take such action if antagonizing a powerful committee member might result. Senator Harrison Williams [(D-Pa.)], for example, did not claim jurisdiction of health-care issues, which rightfully belonged to the subcommittee.

Mikva & Sarris at 209. A similar catalog is in Smith & Deering at 157.

[29]   Senate Committee on the Judiciary, 98th Cong., 1st Sess. Committee on the Judiciary: Program for the First Session of the 98th Congress 4, 14 (S. Prt. 98-23 1983). On the other (footnote continued)

As in the House, though perhaps to a lesser
extent, some Senate committees engage in multiple
referrals to different subcommittees.[30]

C. HEARINGS

Significance

Holding hearings is perhaps Congress' single most
extensive activity, as suggested by the figures
cited above. In a legislative hearing, the focus
is on a particular bill or bills. For example,
the Foreign Relations Committee may hold
legislative hearings on a bill to reform the
Foreign Service retirement system.   In an
oversight hearing, the focus is on the functioning
of some federal program or agency -- its
efficiency, obedience to statutory mandate, or new
policies -- or some private sector problem. Not
legislation, but merely congressional and public
attention, may be sought as a response to the
situation.   For example, the Foreign Relations
Committee may hold oversight hearings on American
foreign relations in Central America, even without
a bill, just to ventilate administration policies
and provide a forum for committee and public
views.[31]

---

hand, a chair may respect relatively regular jurisdictional
lines for subcommittees. For example, in the same Judiciary
Committee, the Subcommittee on Immigration and Refugee
Policy received referrals of all legislation congruent with
its name and tradition.

[30]   A 1983 calendar of the Senate Judiciary Committee
reflected nine jointly referred bills, including a major
alternative anticrime bill.   An example of a significant
intracommittee referral pattern occurred in Senate Judiciary
in 1981, where referrals of anti-abortion measures to two
different subcommittees meant that the two "subcommittees
approved separate anti-abortion measures": one a bill, the
other a constitutional amendment. "[A]nti-abortion groups
were . . . badly split over which legislation to support
. . . .   The divisions within the anti-abortion ranks
contributed to delays in further action on either
measure." 1982 Congressional Quarterly Almanac 403.
(footnote continued)

Following referral of a bill to subcommittee (or keeping it at the full committee), the next key decision is whether to have hearings on the bill. That decision separates a bill out from the vast majority which receive no attention and just die. A much-mooted point is how much the content of hearings matters. Sometimes the record created has minimal importance, since committees can find out through informal means where the key players stand, and the hearing may merely observe the formalities and allow interested persons to "blow off steam." However, sometimes the hearings themselves serve as critical moments in the development of a congressional and public judgment because of the positions taken and the publicity provided.

A concrete example shows how important a witness's testimony may be. In 1965, when the Ways and Means Committee called representatives of the American Medical Association to an executive session hearing on Medicare -- this being legislation of the greatest importance, and AMA opposition being the principal resistance -- the witnesses took a hard-line position. That position had great influence, though not as the AMA wished: "AMA representatives refused to discuss the bill at hand or to recommend marginal changes -- the only kind that might conceivably have been accepted." Chairperson Wilbur Mills (D-Ark.) commented that the witnesses were "amazing," insofar as "[t]hey haven't learned a thing." Another member summed up the impact of the testimony: "The behavior of the AMA witnesses was the greatest favor that could have been done for the medicare cause. Their refusal to cooperate relieved us of any obligation to them."[32]

---

[31] Of course, hearings may combine both legislative and oversight functions. For example, the Senate Foreign Relations Committee may hold hearings on the annual foreign aid authorization bill. Part of the testimony would concern the specifics of the foreign aid bill -- the need to increase or decrease suggested amounts, or to write in legislative changes. Part of the testimony would concern the administration's general conduct of foreign relations.

(footnote continued)

Scheduling and Notice

Each hearing begins with the chair's initial decision to schedule it, sometimes for the chair's own reasons, sometimes as a favor for another Member.[33]   Timing is everything, giving significance to the chair's decision on when to schedule a hearing. The chair may time it to suit the convenience of herself or another interested Member, to catch an issue about which the press is hot, to move pending legislation, to delay pending legislation, to accommodate Administration spokesmen or interest groups requesting a current forum, to exhibit the results of an investigation that has finally matured, to take advantage of a gap in the schedule of a busy hearing room, or for any of a hundred other reasons.

Once she picks the date, notice is given directly to committee or subcommittee Members, to all members and staff through the Daily Digest of the Congressional Record, which, in turn, puts it

---

[32] The quotes are all from D. E. Price, Who Makes the Laws? 113-14 (1972).

[33] For example, a deceptive packaging bill began moving in the 89th Congress when Senator Philip Hart (D-Mich.), a member of the Commerce Committee, wanted the chair, Senator Warren Magnuson (D-Wash.), to schedule hearings. Senator Magnuson agreed to do so. "[T]he scheduling of hearings did not necessarily indicate great interest on Magnuson's part. He was not particularly close to Hart, knew little about his bill, and had slightly negative first impressions." Rather, Senator Magnuson scheduled hearings because "such generosity with junior members" was, for him, "standard operating procedure." D. E. Price, supra, at 25-26.

Classic examples occur when chairs allow Members to hold field hearings in their home states, which let constituents see their Senators at work. Examples can be found in the 1982 field hearings of the Senate Small Business and Aging Committees, described in Year-End Report of the 2d Session of the 97th Congress, S. Doc. No. 38, 97th Cong., 2d Sess. 143, 145, 146, 154 (1982).

in the House and Senate computer information systems.[34]   Formal publication of notice must occur one week in advance in the Congressional Record. Notifying the press, interest groups, and the public receives great attention:

> A committee can alert the news media to upcoming hearings days in advance by supplying press releases and other printed announcements to the House and Senate news galleries and by direct mailing to news organizations with a possible interest in the subject matter of the hearings. On short notice, the committee can keep a smaller list of "must-contact" reporters to notify in person or by telephone.[35]

---

[34] In the House, a scheduling service was created by H. Res. 988, 93d Congress, and was made mandatory at the beginning of 1981. House Rule X(4)(d)(3) specifies that the Committee on House Administration must provide "through the House Information Systems a scheduling service which shall be used by all the committees and subcommittees of the house to eliminate, insofar as possible, any meeting and scheduling conflicts."

In the Senate, section 401 of S. Res. 4, 95th Cong., 1st Sess. (1977), provided that committees were to give notice of meetings to an office designated by the Rules Committee, which has been the Daily Digest office. The Daily Digest is printed at the end of the Congressional Record, in pages with numbers after the letter D (as distinguished from S for Senate, H for House, and E for Extension of Remarks). These notices are also the basis for a computerized schedule "to assist committees in minimizing conflicts of meetings for their members by providing comprehensive and constantly updated information about the scheduled meetings of all committees and subcommittees." S. Rept. No. 2, 95th Cong., 2d Sess. 60 (1977).

On Mondays and Wednesdays, a long-term schedule of committee meetings is printed in the section for Extension of Remarks of the Congressional Record.

[35] R. C. Sachs, Conducting Committee Hearings: A Guide for Preparation and Procedure 14 (Cong. Res. Serv. 1982).

Members' and Witnesses' Statements

The chair and his staff dominate the tone of the hearing. They select the subject and timing, decide what will be said in the chair's opening statement, and select and sequence the witnesses. As Congressman (now Judge) Mikva says, "At both the full and subcommittee level, hearings are seldom a paragon of spontaneity. They are carefully mapped out and scripted in advance."[36]

Physically, a hearing consists typically of Members arrayed in line on a raised podium, all facing a witness table, often with microphones, and with a space behind them for the staff. The witness table is successively occupied by each witness during the hearing. Further back is an area for the public to sit, and in the audience, or at a table off to the side, are the press.

Each hearing begins with the chair calling the hearing in session (often by the classic symbol of banging the gavel) and reading an opening statement. The courts regard these opening statements as essential expressions of the subject of the hearings.[37] A former staffer tells the story of preparing the opening statement for Senator Ralph Yarborough (D-Tex.) on a 1970 bill to establish a National Health Service Corps. Although the chair started with the staffer's dry statement,

> Yarborough warmed to his text . . . . speaking emphatically and departing freely from the prepared statement to make his points more clearly . . . . [Chairperson

---

[36] Mikva & Sarris at 210.

[37] In investigative hearings, witnesses have a right to know the subject of the hearing, so that they can determine whether the questions being asked of them are pertinent. They can be convicted for contempt only for refusing to answer "pertinent" questions. The chair's opening statement may serve to inform them of the subject of the hearing. See, e.g., Hutcheson v. United States, 369 U.S. 599, 620 (1962).

Yarborough extemporized:]

> Unfortunately, the Administration
> has declined this Committee's
> invitation to present testimony on
> this important health bill. They
> have been invited . . . . They
> didn't see fit to come . . . .
> [We] grow increasingly weary of
> [this] Administration which, after
> almost two years in office, still
> finds itself unable to take
> forthright positions on vital
> domestic health issues . . . .

Yarborough, his prepared statement
abandoned, . . . excoriated the
Administration.[38]

If other Members come, they often deliver
their own opening statements; when there are
several, a common pattern is for them to speak in
order of descending party seniority, with
alternation between parties, so that after the
chair comes the ranking minority member, then the
ranking majority member, and so on. As an example
of such a statement, once Chairperson Yarborough
finished the statement noted above, the highly
impatient lead-off witness, Senator Magnuson, had
to endure "a long and equally deferential welcome
from Senator Jacob Javits of New York, the ranking
Republican on Yarborough's Committee."[39] However,
particularly in the Senate, "for hearings that are
neither controversial nor exciting, the chairman
is frequently the only Member present. Absent
Members submit statements, which are recorded in
the hearing documents as if the members had been
present."[40]

---

38   E. Redman, The Dance of Legislation 115, 117 (1973).

39   Id. at 121. Members are occasional witnesses,
particularly when they sponsor a bill that comes before a
committee on which they do not sit.

40   Mikva & Sarris at 210.

When the Members are done, the witnesses give their testimony, which starts with their own prepared statement. House and Senate rules require that witnesses' written statements be submitted in advance. Witnesses frequently submit them at the last minute in their rush to prepare (or to forestall advance preparation of questioning), but congressional staff go to considerable lengths to try nonetheless to obtain the testimony in time to prepare their Members.[41]

This part of hearings can be tedious to watch, as witnesses drone through their prepared statements. Observers speak of chairpersons who have rear ends of "iron," or ones with "novocaine" in them, when the chairs can sit listening to many days of hearings. As the hearings on the "flat tax" reform bill of 1985 were described:

> The hearings droned on throughout the summer, as the [House Ways and Means] committee heard from well over four hundred special pleaders, who once again demonstrated the intensity of opposition to tax reform. Committee members grew weary of the harangues and tried to avoid the meetings, but [Chairperson Dan] Rostenkowski [D-Ill.] ordered his staff to assign at least a few members the choree of sitting with him through every hearing. While the members paid half-attention to the numbing parade of witnesses, the Ways and Means staff listened intently for hints of where compromises might lie, where allies could be enlisted.[42]

---

[41] There is no set penalty to force timely submission, other than staff nagging about delays, and the occasional exasperated chair who recesses the hearing to allow time to review a late statement. See Workshop on Congressional Oversight and Investigations, H. Doc. No. 217, 96th Cong., 1st Sess. 27 (1979).

[42] J.H. Birnbaum and A.S. Murray, Showdown at Gucci Gulf: Lawmakers, Lobbyists, and the Unlikely Triumph of Tax Reform 107-08 (1987).

Witnesses fall into several categories, summarized in a Senate survey of 8,500 witnesses testifying in one year.[43]   Of these, 2,500 were from the Executive Branch.   Some 1,800 came from business generally -- companies, trade associations, banks, industrial research firms, law firms and professional associations.   About 700 came from state governments, and about 500 were from unions, public interest and consumer groups, and nonprofit institutions.   Another 600 were academics, consultants, or from nonprofit research groups.   That left only 2,400 either from miscellaneous institutions or unaffiliated -- the "citizen witnesses," the celebrated "John Q. Publics."   Another study concluded that of roughly 10,000 to 12,000 witnesses in House hearings in 1974, only 1,200 were citizen witnesses.[44] Clearly, testifying is the activity of representatives of the executive and interested institutions much more than of individual citizens.

Congress attaches great importance to the testimony of executive branch witnesses: they often have the power to act under current law and to shape the implementation of changes in the law, provide the main focus of press attention, deliver the key political cues for administration supporters, and may have the most information.   In light of this importance, the executive branch uses an elaborate process to determine its bosition, particularly on proposed legislation. Typically, agencies and bureaus have their own congressional liaison officers, who work with other agency personnel to formulate the initial reaction to a proposed bill, and to write the actual prepared testimony.   However, agencies must clear their positions with the Office of Management and Budget (OMB), and often with the

---

[43]   The Senate survey was in Legislative Activity Sourcebook, supra, at 26, for 1975.

[44]   Van der Slik & Stenger, Citizen Witnesses Before Congressional Committees, 92 Poli. Sci. Q. 465, 466-67 (1977).

White House's own staff.

Clearance began in the 1920s and 1930s, when the Bureau of the Budget, OMB's predecessor, began formulating a unified executive budget and began determining which agency proposals for legislation fit the President's program -- and which did not.[45] From the 1960s to the 1980s, the clearance process increasingly centralized control of the Executive position in OMB and the White House staff.[46]

An example illustrates how clearance and intra-executive bargaining produce layers of overtones in testimony. At Senate hearings in 1979 on the SALT II treaty, the executive witnesses all took the position required by the White House of supporting the treaty. Yet once the Senators started questioning the Joint Chiefs of Staff using leaked internal materials, an observer could read four distinct levels in the testimony. The White House had instructed the Chiefs to say one thing; the Chiefs were willing to testify to something else regardless of their instructions; the Chiefs had said a lot more in "private" internal memoranda that had been leaked; and of course, the Chiefs were willing to say even more when truly speaking in private, a matter to which some Senators could allude.[47]

---

[45] During that initial period, the clearance process only determined which proposals would be submitted to Congress. S. J. Wayne, The Legislative Presidency 71 (1979). Beginning in 1947, congressional committees "started requesting the president's position on pending legislation that did not originate in the executive departments and agencies." Id. at 74. The clearance process grew, until "[b]y the end of the Eisenhower period, over 13,000 separate congressional requests, agency reports, legislative drafts, and private bills were being regularly processed through the clearance mechanism during each Congress." Id. at 74.

[46] Id. at 78-96.

[47] See W. S. Cohen, Roll Call: One Year in the United States Senate 259 (1981).

Another set of nuances in a hearing concerns what the chair and staff have done to point it in a particular direction. Decades ago, an observer pointed out the ways in which, when "the committee chairman or other influential committee members . . . are already committed to the passage of a bill," the staff may carry out the "delicate" task of "slanting the hearings":

> This the staff can do by several means: by inviting the strongest, most persuasive witnesses to testify on behalf of the measure; by endeavoring to limit the number of strong opposition witnesses to a minimum; by asking "proper" questions of "friendly" witnesses and embarrassing ones who are "unfriendly"; by arranging to close the hearing at a propitious time . . . .[48]

To this list must be added the staff's arranging the sequence of witnesses, a matter of considerable importance, particularly to the media.[49]

---

[48]   Cohen, Hearing on a Bill: Legislative Folklore, 37 Minn. L. Rev. 34, 38 (1952).

[49]   Witnesses frequently argue over the order in which they will testify. Ralph Nader has refused to go on a panel with other witnesses and often insists on going first.   An elaborate etiquette of witness order involves such questions as: Should a federal judge or a cabinet secretary testify first?   Should the chairman of the Council of Economic Advisors testify before the director of the Food and Drug Administration?   To maximize his opportunity for media coverage as well as the value of his comments, a witness strives to be placed early on the agenda.   The last witnesses in a three-hour hearing are indeed fortunate to find even one committee member still present.

Mikva & Sarris at 211.

Questioning

Once the witness finishes his statement, the Members can question him. Typically, the chair starts. If other Members come, their questioning follows, either in descending order of seniority with alternation between parties, or, under the "early bird" rule, in order of their arrival at the hearing.[50] Commonly, in each round of questioning, each Member gets a fixed period of time. In the House, Rule XI(2)(j)(2) prescribes five minutes per Member. In the Senate, a common custom is to allow ten minutes per Member. On controversial subjects, these time limits aid the obfuscating witness greatly. One House chief counsel observed:

> In point of fact, the witness dominates the hearings, and why is that? . . .   5 minutes . . . . is not time enough to lay the predicate for one question. It is clearly not time enough to follow up with two or three questions.

> If your Congressman is unprepared . . . the 5-minute rule is a blessing . . . . On the other hand, if your Congressman is prepared to followup and the person who comes after them is not, it is a disaster . . . .[51]

---

[50] House freshman express great enthusaism about "early bird" procedures. Often, the important questions are obvious, and the number of things the witness will say is limited. Waiting for more senior members relegates junior members to eliciting trivia or repetitions. Two freshmen commented in 1979:

> On the Interior Committee, the chairman has a standard rule that whoever gets there first gets to ask questions first . . . .

> We do that on the Foreign Affairs Committee, too . . . . That is a great rule . . . a very practical rule. The people show up, and we start on time. All the committees ought to have it.

Congress Off the Record, supra, at 17.
(footnote continued)

Senate Rule XXVI(4)(d) and House Rule XI(2)(j)(1) empower the minority party to call formally for additional witnesses when it is unsatisfied with those of the majority. In practice, the minority rarely make formal invocation of that rule, due to factors such as limited time and staff to prepare, basic acceptance of the majority's choice of witnesses, and the minority's ability to informally negotiate the addition of witnesses when necessary. The majority party's power does not lie so much in excluding witnesses with whose position it disagrees, particularly since important witnesses who have been unfairly excluded may get sympathetic coverage in the press. Rather, it lies in the majority's control over the timing of hearings, the topic, and the sequence of witnesses.

Open Hearings and Media Coverage

Besides the Members and the witnesses, there may be one other crucial participant in the hearings: the public and press. In the nineteenth century, committees frequently held closed hearings, even when they intended eventually to publish the transcript and the report. Since then, there has been a long trend from closed hearings (also called hearings in "executive session"[52]) to open ones. Steady pressure for

---

[51] Oversight Workshop, supra. For example, when Secretary of Defense Harold Brown testified before the Senate Armed Services Committee on the SALT II treaty in 1979, Senator Cohen found him easily able to evade questioning because of the ten minute rule. W. S. Cohen, supra. Speaker O'Neil explained how the rule arose: in the 1950's, "committee members spoke in order of seniority," and on one committee, the chair "would monopolize two or three hours of the committee's time before he finally turned things over to the ranking Republican . . . . It was situations like this that later prompted the House to institute a new system, allowing each committee member five minutes of questions on a rotating basis." T. O'Neill, Man of the House 159 (1987).

(footnote continued)

open hearings ultimately resulted in Senate and House sunshine rules in the 1970s limiting when hearings could be closed.[53] These rules require that a committee affirmatively vote to close a session.   They restrict closings to particular grounds, such as that the testimony will defame persons or will concern national security. Partly because of these rules, the frequency of closed committee sessions fell off markedly, from 30 to 40 percent before 1973 to seven percent in 1975.[54]

Committees sometimes evade the sunshine rules -- for example, by meeting in the back room, with or without witnesses, to thrash matters out before a public hearing, or by holding a session in a room that, although open, is so small that few besides Members and staff can squeeze in.[55] Although there is no enforcement mechanism

---

[52] The term "executive session" derives from the Senate's having two types of business: lawmaking, done in legislative session, and advice and consent to treaties and nominations, done in executive session. Traditionally the latter was done in closed session, and so the two became equated. However, there is no necessary equivalence. Legislative work must sometimes be closed, as in intelligence authorization markups, while executive work will usually be open, as in virtually all nominations. The House never has "executive session" in the technical sense, but it does have "closed legislative sessions," as does the Senate.

[53] House Rule XI(2)(g)(2); Senate Rule XXVI(5)(b). Individual committees have their own rules on closing sessions, which usually just echo their chamber's rules.

[54] The figures refer to meetings and hearings together. Congressional Quarterly, Guide to Congress, supra, at 370.

[55] Sometimes committees systematically close their sessions, as the House Appropriations subcommittees did in the difficult days following the Gramm-Latta budget cutbacks in 1981. "Seven of the 13 subcommittees of the House Appropriations Committee have closed -- or plan to close -- the markups of their fiscal 1982 appropriations bills . . . . 'I find that committee members can do a better job in closed meetings,' said Appropriations Chairman Jamie L. Whitten, D-Miss." Some Appropriations Panels Shy of Public, 39 Cong. Q. Week. Rep. 1140 (1981).

triggered when a committee violates the sunshine
rule, excluded reporters may counterattack with
hostile publicity, and by finding out anyway from
leakers what transpired. As for who attends, a
1988 survey by the New York Times of 85 persons
attending   hearings   on   health   care   found
journalists,   committee   staffers,   government
employees, trade association and interest group
representatives, all with an interest in the
subject.[56]

House Rule XI(3) and Senate Rule XXVI(5)(e)
allow committees to decide whether to admit
television and radio to hearings. An occasional
set of hearings may be televised live and capture
the nation's attention, such as the Kefauver
hearings in the 1950s on organized crime, the
Fulbright   hearings   in   1966   on   Vietnam,   the
Watergate hearings in 1973, and the Iran arms deal
hearings in 1986-87.

Committees eventually publish the records
of   most   hearings,   though   there   are   notable
exceptions.[57]   Publication   began   in   the   late
nineteenth century, and currently Congress pours
out a veritable Niagara of printer's ink: "[e]ach
year Senate committees and subcommittees produce
more   than   500,000   pages   of   hearings   and
reports."[58]   Before   a   committee   publishes   a

---

[56] It also found "several [attendees] turned out to have no
interest at all in the matter at hand," who had come simply
because federal agencies considered hearings "a valued
training ground" to send employees as a "civics lesson."
Hershey, Hearings on Capitol Hill and Who They Attract, New
York Times, May 6, 1988, at A22.

[57] The House Rules Committee does not publish its vitally
important hearings on granting special rules for major
bills, even though the hearings themselves are in open
session.   It would be virtually impossible for the Rules
Committee to publish hearings prior to floor consideration
of its special rules, and the Rules Committee may defer to
committees   of   jurisdiction   for   making   the   legislative
history on bills.   The Intelligence Committees hold many
unpublished hearings on classified matters.

(footnote continued)

hearing transcript, each participating Member's staff may revise it to polish its member's words.   The sensitivity of that revision was illustrated when House Republicans raised a minor scandal over "Altergate" in 1983 upon discovering that someone had made unauthorized and unflattering revisions in one committee's published hearings.   Witnesses may also correct their testimony, to the extent committees allow.

Hearings usually take some months to be published: indeed, while "[t]he original transcript of testimony is usually available for examination in the committee office soon after the conclusion of hearings . . . .   Except for appropriations hearings, they are seldom printed prior to floor action on a bill."[59]   Congress does not index current committee hearings, although there are past published indexes up to the late 1970s.   The need for a current index has been met by CIS/Annual, which indexes published hearings by committee and by subject.

D.   MEETINGS AND MARKUP

When a subcommittee or committee completes hearings on a bill, the next key decision is whether to bring the bill up at a subcommittee or committee meeting.   While the committee holds

---

[58]   Toward a Modern Senate, supra, at 4.   As for history, in the last century McConachie noted that "[a] beginning has been made of preserving hearings in the annual series of public documents."   L. G. McConachie, Congressional Committees 61 n.1 (1898).   In 1922 it was noted that committees commonly printed the transcript of hearings that had been held in closed session, providing "[d]elayed publicity" that "d[id] not go far enough."   R. Luce, Legislative Procedure 145 (1922).

[59]   Zwirn, Congressional Committee Hearings, 7A Gov't Pub. Rev. 453, 458 (1980).   Each committee has its own printing staff which compiles the hearing for the Government Printing Office to print.   The printing staff collects the edited transcripts, and adds the voluminous inserted materials that make up the bulk of published hearings.

hearings just to take testimony, it holds meetings to act.   Several rules and practices reflect the heightened seriousness of meetings.   Committees and subcommittees may hold hearings with only one member present in the Senate, or two in the House, while it requires at least a third of the body's members to attend for a quorum at a meeting.[60] Also, chairs often let other members preside over hearings, but rarely relinquish the chair at meetings.   In sum, a bill virtually moves to a new kind of body when the chair moves it from the hearing stage to the meeting stage; it goes from being a little investigatory commission to a little legislature.

Ordinarily, chairs determine when to convene meetings, and what to put on the agenda. These are among the chair's greatest powers. Matters never put on a meeting agenda die the same death as matters never scheduled for hearings.   As with hearings, timing is everything, and a chair will schedule a meeting on a matter, or add a particular matter to an agenda for a regularly scheduled meeting, for any of a hundred reasons: enthusiasm for the measure; pressure from Members, the leadership, the press, the administration, or interest groups; a race with competing committees in the same chamber or the other; a judgment about the current mood of the committee or the floor; the completion of lengthy hearings; or the approaching end of the session.

---

[60]   House Rule XI(2)(h)(1) and Senate Rule XXVI(7)(a)(2). These rules responded to Christoffel v. United States, 338 U.S. 84 (1949), in which the Supreme Court reversed a conviction for perjury before a House committee by requiring the prosecution to prove affirmatively that a quorum was present at the moment of perjury.   The reduced quorum rules allow committees to compel witnesses to tell the truth, on penalty of perjury, even at hearings where few members attend.

The quorum requirements for meetings are set in House Rule XI(2)(h)(2) and Senate Rule XXVI(7)(a)(1).   A higher quorum -- a majority of the members -- is necessary to report a matter to the floor, as discussed in the next section.

Both chambers have had to deal with chairs'
abuse of the near-absolute control over scheduling
of meetings. The story is often told of how the
conservative Chairperson Howard W. Smith (D-Va.)
of the House Rules Committee failed in the late
1950s to convene meetings concerning civil rights
bills he opposed. Supposedly, he was busy
returning to Virginia where his barn had burned
down. Speaker Sam Rayburn (R-Tex.) commented that
"I knew that Chairman Smith did not want to hold
meetings to consider these amendments or bills,
but I never thought he would resort to arson."[61]
What is less often noted is how old that tradition
is.   In 1806, a Member denounced one of the
Founding Fathers, Chairman Edmund Randolph of the
House Ways and Means Committee, by offering
resolutions

> to prevent in future the most important
> business of the nation from being retarded
> by a Chairman of the Committee of Ways and
> Means, or any other committee, from going to
> Baltimore or elsewhere, without leave of
> absence, and staying six days or more,
> either for his pleasure or his
> interest . . . .[62]

In the 1970s, as part of the revolt against
chairs, Congress limited their powers in this
regard in two ways. First, the standing
committees have regular meeting days, usually
listed in the committee rules.[63] Second, Senate
Rule XXVI(3) and House Rule VI(2)(c)(2) provide
that a sufficient number of committee members may
trigger the calling of a special meeting without
the chair's approval. Although infrequently used,
this provision does provide members with a rule
they can cite when pressuring a recalcitrant

---

[61] T. Siff & A. Weil, Ruling Congress 121 (1975).

[62] J. Cooper, The Origins of the Standing Committees and
the Development of the Modern House 27 (1970).

[63] Senate Rule XXVI(3); House Rule XI(2)(b). The rule
dates back to the Legislative Reorganization Act of 1946,
but was not always obeyed.

chair.[64]

Minor matters may go on the agenda of a
committee meeting without preliminary
consideration. These include such matters as
noncontroversial bills, where the staff may work
out the details, and committees' internal
business, such as budgets, staff hiring, rules,
and scheduling. Also on the agenda may be
interlocutory procedural steps regarding bills --
referring to subcommittee, discharging from
subcommittee, and fancier maneuvers.

In contrast, major matters -- important
legislation -- requires two additional steps:
markup and reporting. A legislative manual
describes the following format for these steps, by
saying that

> A typical agenda for the consideration of a
> bill at a [full committee] legislative
> markup would be as follows:
>
> I. Convene Meeting -- Opening Remarks
> (Chairman)
>
> II. Presentation of Subcommittee
> Report (Subcommittee Chairman).
>
> III. Motion to Adopt Subcommittee
> Report.
>
> IV. Discussion of Bill and Report.
>
> V. Bill and Report open for
> amendment. (If Committee Print is used in
> lieu of bill, a unanimous consent request
> must be made to do so.)
>
> VI. Motion to report the bill. (The
> House Rules require the presence of a

---

[64]   An example was that members of the Senate Foreign
Relations Committee forced a meeting on the nuclear freeze
in 1983 after the House adopted a freeze resolution.

majority of the committee to report the bill.)[65]

Markup and reporting, in committee, are like amending and final passage on the floor. Markup is when committees make particular changes in the language of bills, like amending on the floor; reporting is when committees decide whether to approve the bill in its final form, like final passage on the floor. This section discusses markup; the next section discusses reporting.

Markup

Markup starts with an initial version or "vehicle," sometimes referred to as "the mark." Typically, the chair selects the mark, although the committee or subcommittee may undo the choice.[66] Sometimes, the chair's choice is simple: one bill on a particular subject has been referred to the committee or subcommittee, and that becomes the mark. Sometimes, however, the choice of mark represents a significant decision, as illustrated by the choice of marks by the House and Senate Budget Committees for their annual budget resolutions in the late 1970s. By rejecting the President's budget as their mark and using their own, they established their budget process's independence from the President.[67] Senate consideration of the Clean Air Act reauthorization in 1982, and the flat tax bill in 1986, illustrate the tactical role of choice of mark. Regarding the Clean Air Act, Chairperson Robert T. Stafford (R-Vt.) believed "that nothing

---

[65] Legislative Manual at 49-50.

[66] For example, when the House Subcommittee on Health and the Environment took up the reauthorization of the Clean Air Act described above, Chairperson Henry Waxman (D-Calif.) selected his own bill as the mark, but the subcommittee then rewrote the bill to correspond largely to the industry bill. 1982 Congressional Quarterly Almanac 431.

[67] A. Schick, Congress and Money: Budgeting, Spending and Taxation 222-23 (1980).

more than a 'fine-tuning' of the existing law was needed."[68]   Accordingly, he chose not to use any new bill as the mark, but used the Clean Air Act itself.   Thus, "the panel plowed through the existing law section by section, a procedure that forced members who favored changes to muster a majority of the panel each time they wanted to propose a modification."[69]   In contrast, for the flat tax bill in 1986, Chairperson Robert Packwood (R-Ore.) devised a new bill, different from the recommendations of either President Reagan or the House, which itself incorporated months of unofficial discussions among committee members.[70]

Once the chair selects the mark, typically the committee or subcommittee then proceeds through the bill line by line, section by section, or page by page.   This is an old process, familiar to Thomas Jefferson, who wrote of the distinction between markup and the final vote in committee:

> In every case the whole paper is read first by the Clerk, and then by the chairman, by paragraphs, pausing at the end of each paragraph, and putting questions for amending, if proposed . . . . but no question on agreeing to the paragraphs separately; this is reserved to the close, when a question is put on the whole, for agreeing to it as amended or unamended.[71]

Sometimes markup is quick and informal.[72]

---

[68]   1982 Congressional Quarterly Almanac 425.

[69]   Id.

[70]   Those discussions lasted from January through March, 1986, and they involved a total reconsideration of tax reform.   See Birnbaum and Murray at 191-99 (describing that period).

[71]   House Manual § 412.

[72]   Members or staff may prenegotiate the changes they wish to make in the language of a bill prior to the mark-up session.   "Subcommittee markup sessions tend to be less (footnote continued)

Members can both exchange views, and give guidance for staff revision of a draft to resolve any matters left after the markup session. In the House, markup may sometimes be slow and formal at the subcommittee level, when that is where all the details are worked out, and then quick and informal at the full committee level which just ratifies the subcommittee product. The Senate tends not to use subcommittee markups as much, perhaps because Senators are difficult to round up for subcommittee meetings.[73]

In the fullest form, markup may be lengthy and formal both at the subcommittee and at the full committee level. The Clean Air Act reauthorization in 1982 illustrates the extreme possibilities for formality. On the Senate side, markup was done only at the full committee, and it took the Environment and Public Works Committee nine months of markups before ordering S.3041 reported on August 19. On the House side, the Health and Environment Subcommittee, chaired by Representative Waxman, began markup on February 25. The subcommittee first voted on a proposed amendment on March 4, and continued subcommittee markups for several weeks, finally approving the bill on March 24.

That sent the bill up to the full committee, Energy and Commerce, where the struggle began all over again. Full committee markup began on March 30, and then, after intense disputes, was broken off on April 29. It resumed in August, but without success, and the bill died. During these periods, interested groups carried on the most intense lobbying and maneuvering based on calculations of the relative forces at subcommittee and full committee levels.[74]

---

formal than full committee markup sessions," just as committee mark-up tends to be less formal than floor amending; "[m]embers and staff may, for instance, prefer [in subcommittee markup] to conduct a roundtable discussion on the bill," leaving precise drafting of an amended bill to subsequent staff or small group negotiations. Legislative Manual at 41.

[73] Smith & Deering at 151.
(footnote continued)

Chairs and Members may employ a broad range of strategies in markups. For example, Senator Warren Magnuson (D-Wash.), as chair of the Commerce Committee in the early 1970s, often accepted minority proposals to obtain a consensus bill: "Affable, compromising, anxious to avoid conflict and to take a united committee to the floor, Magnuson's relationships with the minority were generally cooperative."[75] In contrast, when the House Energy and Commerce Committee took up reauthorization of the Clean Air Act in 1982, "comity soon disappeared," "[t]empers flared," and the bill ultimately came to "a test of strength that proved to be the death knell."[76]

Several House and Senate rules shape the context of these strategies, notably the limited application of floor procedure, the voting procedure, the proxy rules, and the rules concerning "permission to sit." First, as to the application of floor procedure, House Rule XI(1)(a)(1) provides that "[t]he Rules of the House are the rules of its committees and subcommittees so far as applicable . . . ." No Senate rule so provides, but committees often follow some Senate floor procedure where applicable, if only because there has to be some way to settle procedural disputes and the Senate's rules are the most proximate model. Still, House committees tend to follow the floor procedures more than Senate committees do: there are more pertinent House floor procedures, such as the germaneness requirement for amendments, and the House floor generally follows its rules more strictly than the Senate floor, where so much is done by unanimous consent. Ultimately, the committee determines its procedure for itself, as neither chamber allows noncommittee members much leverage to interfere with committee procedure.[77]

---

74   See 1982 _Congressional Quarterly Almanac_ 425-34.

75   D. E. Price, _supra_, at 32.

76   1982 _Congressional Quarterly Almanac_ 431-32.

77   Technically, House Rule XI(2)(g)(5) would allow "a point
(footnote continued)

Voting and Proxies

Just as a call for a recorded vote on the
floor requires a "sufficient second," so a
committee may require that several members support
a rollcall demand for there to be a "sufficient
second" to have such a vote.[78] Like floor demands
for recorded votes, demands in committee markup
represent a tactical judgment about factors such
as whether a strong favorable vote, or a vote that
is unfavorable but close, will strengthen a
Member's hand if the question of an amendment
arises again on the floor, in the other chamber or
in conference. For example, during the House Ways
and Means Committee's 1985 consideration of the
flat tax bill, Chairperson Rostenkowski crafted a
deal on a controversial question. Committee
Democrats:

> would allow him to pass his package intact
> -- with the 35-percent corporate rate and
> the taxation of life insurance fringes --
> but only if the Republicans permitted a
> voice vote, so the Democrats would not have
> to go on record by name opposing labor. If
> the Republicans insisted on a roll-call
> vote, Rostenkowski said, the Democrats could

---

of order" on the ground "that hearings on [a] measure were
not conducted in accordance with the provisions" concerning
open and closed hearings, but in practice, the only points
of order that lie in either chamber for violation of
committee procedure concern failure to obtain a quorum for
reporting.

[78] For example, House Rules Committee's Rule 3(b)(2)
provides that "A rollcall vote of the Committee shall be
provided on any question before the Committee upon the
request of any member of the Committee." In contrast, House
Ways and Means Committee's Rule 14 provides that "A record
vote on an issue shall be required on the request of a
member which is supported by at least one-fifth of a
quorum." The latter rule tracks the constitutional
provision for yeas and neas. In a committee of 35 members
that requires a majority for a quorum, this means it takes
three members to demand a record vote.

> feel free to retain tax-free life insurance
> benefits.   "If there are recorded votes,"
> the chairman repeated, "all bets are off."
> The Democrats left the library [where this
> deal was struck] like a football team
> charging onto the field from the locker
> room, ready for the second half.[79]

The committee procedure which differs most
markedly from floor procedure is the use of
proxies.   On the floor of the Senate and House,
only the Members present can vote.[80]   By contrast,
in committee, both House and Senate rules allow
absent Members to give proxies -- authorizations
for Members who are present to cast votes for the
absent.   Proxies often make a big difference,
usually strengthening the chair, who can push
through the majority position with his members'
proxies even when minority members attend more
faithfully.   As one freshman commented: "[i]n the
[House] Education and Labor Committee . . . I find
[the Chair's] real strength is that he has the
proxies.   We have had some votes when he has ten,
twelve proxies, and he goes through with it.[81]
Less often, another member can get proxies, when,
for example, absentees see him as "the person who
has the energy and the drive and who does his
homework."[82]

Minority party members and reformers often
criticize proxies for excessively strengthening
the chair and encouraging absenteeism.   As one
report said, "You cannot argue with a proxy; a
proxy cannot consider an offered amendment; a
proxy cannot compromise."[83]   On the other hand,

---

[79]   Birnbaum and Murray, _supra_, at 150.

[80]   There is a method for limiting the significance of
absence, "pairing," discussed in the chapters on House and
Senate floor procedure.

[81]   _Congress Off the Record_, _supra_, at 16.

[82]   _Id._ at 17.

[83]   Organization of Congress, Final Report of the Jt. Comm.
(footnote continued)

members' time is in short supply, and there has to be some way for members to deal with conflicting schedules for committee meetings. The elimination of proxies, if the members continued to be absent, would simply eliminate the mechanism for them -- and their constituents -- to be represented in decisions.

House Rule XI(2)(f) provides that committees can permit proxies, but the proxies must be in writing and must be limited "to a specific measure or matter and any amendments or motions pertaining thereto." This is the result of much tugging back and forth in the 1970s over the permissible use of proxies, and it has led to use by many House committees of a fairly strict proxy form.[84] House committees may make less use of proxies even than the rule allows; some do not allow proxies at all.[85] Senate Rule XXVI(7)(a)(3) is somewhat looser, only specifying that "proxies may not be voted when the absent committee member has not been informed of the matter on which he is being recorded and has not affirmatively requested that he be so recorded." Through this rule, the Senate essentially leaves the regulation of proxies to individual committees, some of which may accept oral proxies, more of which use written proxies, and a few of which have rules restricting proxies to when a majority of Members are present or to votes other than to report a bill.

Watching proxies being voted -- often a dramatic moment when the vote is close -- is not a part of congressional procedure calculated to reassure the political idealist. A written proxy may confer authority on some member, with the

---

on the Organization of the Congress, H.R. Rept. No. 1414, 89th Cong., 2d Sess. 9 (1966).

[84] See H.R. Rept. No. 96-866, 96th Cong., 2d Sess. 571-81 (1980) (memorandum by Richard Sachs of the Congressional Research Service tracing the history of proxies).

[85] House Appropriations Committee Rule 7(a) provides: "No vote by any Member of the Committee or any of its subcommittees with respect to any measure or matter may be cast by proxy."

unwritten understanding that the member will vote
it as suggested by the staffer of the absentee
member -- leaving a nervous staffer making the
legislative decisions about how to apply
instructions to new propositions. The looseness
of proxy use poses other perils. The story is
told of the Senate chair on the verge of losing a
vote in committee, who announced he had won
because a particular absent Senator had given him
an oral proxy. Another Senator complained "that's
impossible -- he told me he wanted to vote my way,
and gave me this written proxy." Not a bit
abashed, the chair blandly responded, "Well, he
must have changed his mind after we talked."

Both the House and Senate create tactical
opportunities for opposition Members to stop
committee proceedings by invocation of rules
concerning "permission to sit." The longstanding
rule, articulated by Thomas Jefferson, was that
"so soon as the House sits, and a committee is
notified of it, the chairman is in duty bound to
rise instantly, and the members to attend the
service of the House."[86]   House Rule XI(2)(i)
forbids committees to sit while it "is reading a
measure for amendment under the five-minute rule,"
and exempts several important committees. Senate
Rule XXVI(5)(a) forbids committees to sit during
any kind of Senate business, starting two hours
after the session begins; when Senate sessions
begin at 10:00 a.m., as is common, the "two hour
rule" is referred to as the "noon rule."

Committee sessions terminate in some cases
when members go to the floor, such as in a 1988
Senate committee markup of a controversial
bill.[87]   However, notwithstanding the rules,

---

[86]   House Manual § 324.

[87]   On May 12, 1988, the Senate Judiciary Committee marked
up a bill to limit the use of the federal anti-racketeering
("RICO") statute. In the debate over a controversial
amendment to subject certain firearms offenses to RICO
prosecutions, several Senators "argued about the amendment
for 20 minutes, but the committee had to break off its
markup so senators could go to the Senate floor to vote."
(footnote continued)

chairs routinely carry on committee meetings and
hearings during floor sessions, breaking up to go
to the floor when the buzzers, bells, and lights
warn of floor votes and live quorum calls, then
resuming afterwards, with the committee members
perhaps a little distracted if the meeting is
broken up repeatedly this way. This produces part
of the "pin-ball" sense of Members, as they bounce
back and forth between the bumpers of the
committee and the floor.   To continue sitting
while the floor is at work requires "permission to
sit" from the chamber.   In the Senate, such
permission is granted only by unanimous consent,
so that a single Member can block it; in the
House, Rule XI(2)(i) provides that ten Members can
block it. Although blocking is unusual, it can be
used when Members want to filibuster a committee
to prevent action.

Blocking fits well with other filibuster
techniques, such as extended debate, offering of
numerous amendments, demands for numerous roll
calls, and absences intended to deny a quorum.[88]
In fact, even without filibuster techniques,
mustering the minimum quorum to do business -- a
third of the committee members -- can be hard:

Cohodas, Senate Committee Moves to Limit RICO Suits, 46
Cong. Q. Week. Rep. 1283 (1988).

[88]   A bill may be filibustered to death in the exec [i.e.,
the executive session of the committee, where a bill
may be marked up].   In some committees limits are
placed on the amount of time a senator can speak.
Rules sometimes specify that a majority vote,
including at least one vote of a minority member, can
cut off debate. Limiting debate, however, does not
limit the numbers of amendments that can be
introduced, and the procedural maneuvering in an exec
is as complicated as that on the floor. In the House,
because the Rules Committee does not act to limit
debate in committee, members are allowed to debate
infinite numbers of amendments. Debates are ended
only when the chair musters a majority to move the
previous question on the bill and report it out.

Mikva & Sarris at 215.

In the Senate, the lobbying, begging, pleading, and strategizing to obtain a quorum are hard to believe. A minority that desires to block legislation simply boycotts the exec [the meeting] . . . . To reach a quorum, the busy schedules of the members must be synchronized. A chairman frequently sits alone in a mark-up, with staff members milling around, until one by one the other members gradually drift in. To implement a boycott, the minority members designate a watchdog, or spy, to let them know when the majority finally has its quorum. At that point, the minority files in, ready to do battle. As soon as a majority member leaves, the minority too marches out. No quorum, no proceedings . . . .

House subcommittees frequently adopt rules to accommodate the difficulty of obtaining and keeping a quorum. Consideration of the proposed new criminal code involved many, many days of mark-up sessions. The subcommittee adopted a rule, which became known as the "Drinan quorum rule," that allowed the mark-up to proceed as long as Chairman Drinan and at least one other member were present.[89]

E.   REPORTING

After hearings and markup for a bill comes the climax: reporting. The reporting process has three components, each important. First, the committee or subcommittee meets, achieves a quorum, and votes to report: at this point the bill has been "ordered reported." Then, the staff prepares the formal written description of the bill -- the "report." Finally, the bill (with any committee amendments) and the report are filed at the desk on the floor: now the bill has "been reported."

The vote to "order [a bill] reported"

---

[89]   Mikva & Sarris at 212-13.

matters for several reasons. This is the final
make-or-break point in committee for the bill. If
the bill is not reported, it survives only by the
use, which is infrequent, of some form of
discharge, direct or indirect.   Reporting also
marks a major change in the relevant cast of
players involved with the bill. Before the vote
to   report,   the   outside   world   of   media,
administration, and interest groups focus their
attention almost exclusively on the committee.
After that vote, much attention shifts to the
scheduling machinery and the floor.

Thus, the outcome of the vote matters
greatly. So, too, the vote's size may matter as a
cue for further proceedings. The bill's next stop
will   be   the   scheduling   machinery   of   the
leadership, who often have not paid much attention
to the bill prior to reporting. A unanimous or
near-unanimous vote to report suggests to the
leadership   that   the   bill   is   largely
noncontroversial, either because of its subject or
because the committee forged a consensus. If so,
it may be a candidate for the quicker, simpler
floor routes, such as suspension of the rules in
the House and unanimous consent in the Senate. On
the floor, Members may take unanimous or near-
unanimous votes in committee as a signal they can
accept the bill without extensive study.   In
contrast, a sharply divided vote on reporting the
bill signals, as nothing else does, that the bill
is controversial.   When scheduling such a bill,
the leadership must handle it carefully.[90]

Because of the critical importance of the
vote to order a bill reported, both chambers'
rules, and some committees' rules, hedge that vote

---

[90] In the House such care may requires close scrutiny by
the Rules Committee, in the Senate such care may require
calling up the bill only when there is ample time for it and
possibly with readiness for a filibuster. Both chambers may
activate their whip mechanisms to provide more information
and guidance to members and perhaps to get vote counts, and
the administration may step in more. Individual Members,
too, must handle the bill more carefully, by having a
staffer study it, by preparing for floor amendments, or
perhaps by taking soundings from the leadership, in the home
district or state, or from interest groups.

with safeguards, notably a tough quorum
requirement. Both the Senate and the House
require that a bill be reported by a committee
meeting at which a majority of the committee is
actually present. That means a majority of warm
bodies, not by using "polls," not by counting
proxies, and not by keeping the vote open
afterwards.

Of course, this rule is not always obeyed.
Particularly in the Senate, committees often poll
out matters by a written (occasionally even oral)
survey of members without a committee meeting, or
they report out matters with an inadequate
quorum.[91] So long as no one raises a point of
order on the floor, the matter will glide through,
but the point of order is there. Any Member can
raise that point on the floor, at which point the
presiding officer will ask the committee chair if
a quorum was present, and the chair must confess
if there was not.[92]

As a threat, that point of order may have
real effectiveness at the end of a session, when
there may not be time for a committee meeting to
report out the matter properly. In the House,
there are ways to protect against a point of order
on quorum grounds, either by a special rule
waiving the point of order, or by taking up the
bill under suspension of the rules.[93] In the
Senate, the system of "holds" serves a comparable
purpose. A Member who would raise the point of
order about lack of a quorum will simply put a
"hold" on instead, until the committee leadership
deals with the Member's substantive complaint
about the bill.

The quorum rule's main effect is to enhance

---

[91] "In the Senate, by unanimous consent of the members,
legislation is 'polled out,' reported out by written ballot
or telephone. Another approach is the 'rolling quorum,'
which permits legislation to be reported out as long as a
quorum appeared at some time during a mark-up." Mikva &
Sarris at 212.

[92] Deschler 17 § 14.10.

[93] The point of order will not lie under suspension.
Deschler 17 § 14.3.

further the significance of the vote to order
reporting. A committee can handle other matters
-- hearings, markup -- with a chair, a skeleton
crew of members representing both parties, and
staff. Only this quorum requirement forces
otherwise uninterested members to take part in
each reported bill: to become informed, to reach a
decision, and to become motivated enough to
attend.

The previous discussion about quorums in
committee mark-ups applies with double force to
the quorum requirement for reporting. Chairs
often have great difficulty obtaining the quorum
need for reporting. Absentees may be either
genuinely busy, or calculating nicely whether
their interest lies in staying away to break the
quorum or arriving and earning a chair's
gratitude. One staffer quotes Senator Magnuson
describing in 1970 how a minority boycott to deny
a quorum brought a bill to create a National
Health Service Corps to a perilous point:

> [Senator Magnuson told me:] "Our problem is
> that [Senator] Yarborough can't get a quorum
> in his Committee . . . . The problem is
> that the Republicans are boycotting
> Yarborough's Committee meetings to prevent
> him from reporting out the 'Occupational
> Health and Safety' bill. And if blocking
> that one bill means blocking every other
> bill before the Committee, the Republicans
> will do it."[94]

Both chambers treat gingerly the role of
proxies in reporting. In neither chamber can
proxies be counted toward the quorum for
reporting; a majority of the members must be
physically present for a vote to report. House
Rule XI(2)(f) and Senate Rule XXVI(7)(a)(3) allow
committees to decide whether proxies will be
counted at all on a vote to report, and some
committees have provided by rule that they will
not count proxies on such a vote.[95] Finally, the

---

94   E. Redman, The Dance of Legislation 137 (1973).

95   For example, Senate Appropriations Committee Rule III
(footnote continued)

Senate, but not the House, imposes an additional requirement, in Senate Rule XXVI(7)(a)(1), that the "vote of any committee to report a measure or matter shall require the concurrence of a majority of the members of the committee who are present." This could creates situations where the members present determine the outcome, contrary to the outcome if proxies counted.[96]

Committee Report

Once the committee orders a bill reported, it must prepare a print of the bill "as reported" to reflect all the amendments voted by the committee in markup. More important, it also must prepare a report. Historically, the House came generally to use written reports by the Civil War, and the Senate caught up by the twentieth century.[97]

This report serves two purposes. Internally, within Congress, it serves as a source of information for floor proceedings. It is more intelligible than the bill itself, is "presented in a politically useful form,"[98] and is also

---

provides: "Except for the reporting of a bill, votes may be cast by proxy when any member so requests."

[96] For example, in an 11 member committee, six members may attend of whom two favor a measure and four oppose it, and three members may vote by proxy in favor of the measure. In both House and Senate, the six members attending make a quorum for reporting. If this is a House committee, the two members present who favor the measure, plus the three proxies who favor, report the measure. If this is a Senate committee, the four members present who oppose the measure defeat reporting, since a motion to report lacks "the concurrence of a majority of the members of the committee who are present."

[97] Broden, Congressional Committee Reports: Their Role and History 33 Notre Dame Law. 209, 229, 237-38 (1958).

[98] Zwirn, Congressional Committee Reports, 7A Gov. Pub. Rev. 319, 320 (1980). Members may also receive whip advisory notices, "Dear Colleague" letters, floor speeches, and circulars from specialized caucuses.

generally more complete than the other in-house sources. Observers disagree on how seriously it is taken within Congress. Congressman Mikva commented that "[t]he report, however, is relatively insignificant for purposes of floor action. At best, it serves to educate the legislative assistants of non-committee members."[99]

Externally, the committee report serves a more important purpose as the central guide for courts and agencies looking into the "legislative history" of a bill for clues on interpreting it. As the House Republican Manual explains to "the staff as it works on committee reports," committee reports "are often the repository of important legislative history to supplement the written text of the bill. The creation of legislative history should be done with some degree of reverence . . . ."[100] That Manual notes the open secret that staff, not Members, prepare reports. A 1982 colloquy between Senators William L. Armstrong (R-Colo.) and Robert Dole (R-Kans.) discussed the Members' limited contact with a singularly important report, the Senate Finance Committee report on a $98 billion tax increase:

> Sen. Armstrong: Does the Senator know of any Senator who wrote the committee report?
>
> Sen. Dole: I might be able to identify one, but I would have to search. I . . . . worked carefully with the staff as they worked. As I recall, during the July 4 recess week there were about five different working groups of staff from both parties, the joint committee [on Internal Revenue, which has staff tax experts], and the Treasury working on different provisions.
>
> Sen. Armstrong: Mr. President, has the Senator from Kansas, the chairman of the Finance Committee, read the committee report in its entirety?

---

99 Mikva & Sarris at 216.

100 House Republican Manual at 116-17.

Sen. Dole: I am working on it.   It is not a
bestseller, but I am working on it.

Sen. Armstrong: Mr. President, did members
of the Finance Committee vote on the
committee report?

Sen. Dole: No.[101]

Staff may look to outsiders in writing the
report.   The interested executive agencies may
draft part of the report, unless they oppose the
bill, in which case they may draft the separate
views.   As Congressman Mikva comments:

Staff members use the language in a report
as a significant bargaining tool.   An
interest group is sometimes content to get
its language into the report, knowing that
somewhere down the line it can point to the
language in a court challenge or in an
agency proceeding.[102]

The interpreters of legislative history
have become increasingly cognizant of the limited
role of Members in writing reports, and the lack
of opportunity for Members to amend reports in
committee or on the floor.   Justice (then Judge)
Antonin Scalia wrote in 1985 that "routine
deference to the detail of committee reports
. . . [is] converting a system of judicial

---

[101]   128 Cong. Rec. S8659 (daily ed. July 19, 1982).

[102]   Mikva & Sarris at 216.   The House Republican Manual
warns about lobbyists' offers:

[P]rivate groups and persons or government agencies
. . . are usually enthusiastic in volunteering their
"expert" assistance.   Staff should be alert to the
fact that the material as suggested often either may
not be in harmony with the language of the bill
. . . or was not examined thoroughly by the
committee or its subcommittees . . . .

House Republican Manual at 102.

construction into a system of committee-staff
prescription."   In   reaction,   the   courts,
interpreting   general   legislation,   and   the
Comptroller General, interpreting appropriations,
have   emphasized   that   bill   language   alone   is
controlling, while report language is not.[103]

Nevertheless,   report   language   can   matter
greatly, particularly because it can illuminate
matters left silent in the bill language, and
because committee staff may carefully use reports
in an ongoing dialogue with expert audiences.
Typically,   for   example,   the   annual   military
authorization and appropriation bills only contain
"lump sums" for accounts such as research and
development,   without   stating   what   particular
weapon or facility should be purchased.   Only the
reports address this.   Even though the Defense
Department need not treat such reports as binding,
it follows them when it can, rather than force the
committees to tie its hands in subsequent years by
explicit bill language.   In this way, such reports
influence the expenditure of hundreds of billions
of dollars.

Because of the importance of reports, House
and Senate rules protect minority rights and
provide "sunshine" on committee processes in
reports.   Most notably, both House and Senate

---

[103] The Scalia quote is from _Hirschey v. Federal Energy
Regulatory Comm'n_, 777 F.2d 1, 7-8 (D.C. Cir. 1985)
(concurring opinion).   In recent years, the Supreme Court
repeatedly used Justice Powell's aphorism, "The starting
point in every case involving construction of a statute is
the language itself," _Blue Chip Stamps v. Manor Drug Stores_,
421 U.S. 723, 756 (1975) (concurring opinion), to minimize
the   role   of   committee   reports   and   other   legislative
history.   This does not prevent the Supreme Court and other
courts from resorting on countless occasions to committee
reports for guidance.   The Comptroller General's leading
opinions on the nonbinding nature of committee reports for
appropriations are the "LTV case," 55 Comp. Gen. 307 (1975),
and the "Newport News" case, 55 Comp. Gen. 812 (1976),
discussed   in   Office   of   General   Counsel,   U.S.   General
Accounting Office, _Principles of Federal Appropriations Law_
at 5-97 (1982).

rules allow members of committees to file "supplemental, minority, or additional views." House Rule XI(2)(5) and Senate Rule XXVI(10)(c) guarantee members three calendar days to file those views, and require that the covers of reports reflect that they contain such views. These views function somewhat like concurring and dissenting opinions, except that their effect is much more immediate since the report sets the stage for floor action. As one commentator noted, "[the dissenting representative or senator puts all of his colleagues . . . on notice that this legislation has a controversial aspect to it . . . ."[104]

Like the vote to order reporting described above, part of the views' message goes to the leadership, putting it "on notice that this is not 'consent calendar' business, which can be passed by unanimous consent with no real debate."[105] Another part of the message goes to Members and their staff, telling them "what the amendments offered on the floor will be . . . [and that staff] will have to study a question and advise their congressmen . . . ."[106] Members can join in separate views, sending signals, as in cosponsorship, about where the lines have been drawn, such as by party, ideology, or geography.

Besides the descriptions of the bill and the other views, reports contain a number of other significant contents, as well as some useless filler.[107] Committee reports include the recorded

---

104   F. Cummings, Capitol Hill Manual 56 (1975).

105   Id.

106   Id.

107   One list of a House report's format is:

    1.   Amendments.
    2.   Table of contents.
    3.   Summary of Committee Actions (including summary table, as appropriate).
    4.   Purpose of the bill.
(footnote continued)

votes taken in committee, including who voted by proxy, which tell the astute reader much about what issues mattered and what were the lineups. They show the changes the bill will make in existing law, by reprinting existing law with indications of insertions and deletions -- the "Ramseyer" print (in the House) or "Cordon" print (in the Senate).[108] Reports typically make their descriptions of the bill both overall, and

---

5.   Committee Actions (hearings, markup).

6.   Background and Need for the Legislation.

7.   Explanation of the bill.

8.   Sectional Analysis of the bill.

9.   Committee Views.

10.   Committee cost estimate on bills or joint resolutions of public character (Rule XIII, Clause 7) (Optional . . . .)

11.   Inflation Impact on bills and joint resolutions of public character (Rule XI, Clause 2(1)(4)).

12.   Committee oversight findings and recommendations (Rule XI, Clause 2(1)(3)).

13.   Summary of Government Operations Committee Findings and Recommendations (Rule XI, Clause 2(1)(3)).

14.   Budget Analysis and Projection (on legislation containing new budget authority or tax expenditures) (Rule XI, Clause 2(1)(3)).

15.   Congressional Budget Office estimates and comparisons timely submitted to committee) (Rule XI, Clause 2(1)(3)).

16.   Administration Position.

17.   Changes in Existing Law (Ramseyer) (Rule XIII, Clause 3).

18.   Recital of Record Vote on Reporting -- Committee Recommendation (Rule XI, Clause 2(1)(2)(B)).

19.   Supplemental, Minority, or Additional Views (if their inclusion is requested and they are submitted within 3 days) (Rule XI, Clause 2(1)(5)).

Legislative Manual at 48.

---

[108]   Senate Rule XXVI(12); House Rule XIII(3). The Speaker will not uphold a point of order for a failure to provide a Ramseyer print if the committee has substantially complied with the rule. Deschler 14 § 41.13.

section-by-section.   They   may   summarize   the
hearings and the executive's view, sometimes by
reprinting   an   OMB   letter.   The   Congressional
Budget   Office   provides   cost   estimates   on   the
bill.[109]   Various flotsam largely ignored, such as
regulatory   impact   statements   and   oversight
findings, also go in.[110]

        Once   the   committee   has   ordered   a   bill
reported, and prepared its report, committee staff
file the report with the legislative clerks on the
floor.   The procedural mechanics of such reporting
are discussed in the chapters on House and Senate
floor procedure.

---

[109]   House   Rule   XI(2)(1)(3)(C);   Senate   Rule   XXVI(11)(a).
These estimates can slay efforts to slip through quietly a
very costly bill.

[110]   Senate Rule XXVI(11)(b); House Rule XI(2)(1)(3)(A).

4
Running the House[1]

A. OVERVIEW AND HISTORY

The House is special in its organization. In the
Senate, the Majority Leader has considerable

---

[1] Sources commonly cited in this chapter include House
Committee on Rules, 97th Cong., 2d Sess., A History of the
Committee on Rules (Comm. Print 1983) (written with the
assistance of Professor Bruce I. Oppenheimer) (hereafter
Rules Committee History); R. E. Damon, The Standing Rules of
the United States House of Representatives (Ph.D.
dissertation, 1971) (available from University Microfilms)
(Damon); G. B. Galloway, History of the House of
Representatives (rev. ed. S. Wise 1976) (Galloway);
Congressional Quarterly, Origins and Development of Congress
(1976) (Origins and Development); B. Sinclair, Majority
Leadership in the U.S. House (1983) (Sinclair); L. G.
McConachie, Congressional Committees (1898) (McConachie); R.
B. Ripley, Party Leaders in the House of Representatives
(1967) (Ripley); M. P. Follett, The Speaker of the House of
Representatives (1896) (Follett); N. MacNeil, Forge of
Democracy: The House of Representatives (1963) (MacNeil);
DeA. S. Alexander, History and Procedure of the House of
Representatives (1916) (Alexander); R. B. Cheney & L. V.
Cheney, Kings of the Hill: Power and Personality in the
House of Representatives (1983) (Cheney & Cheney); Calmes,
The Hill Leaders: Their Places on the Ladder, 45 Cong. Q.
Week. Rep. 5 (1987) (Hill Leaders).

power, but he and his party face sharp limits in
their procedural control: the unanimous consent
requirements, the ability of Senators to offer
non-germane amendments, the necessity to consult
with the Minority Leader, and the filibuster.
These make the theme of Senate procedure a balance
between majority and individual. In contrast, the
House runs like a machine, with procedural control
vested in its majority party leadership and
particularly its Speaker.   As Speaker O'Neill
commented in 1987, the Speaker's "most important
power is to set the agenda, and if he doesn't want
a certain bill to come up, it usually doesn't."[2]

For a time, in the middle of the twentieth
century, the majority leadership lost control of
the House to a coalition of conservative Democrats
and Republicans, who used the Rules Committee and
committee chairs to take away much of the
scheduling power.   However, since 1961, and
particularly from the 1970s on, the majority
leadership regained and reinforced its control.
The 1980s became a period of particularly strong
procedural dominance.

Under the House system, only the majority
party and its leadership, not individual Members
or the minority, can ordinarily put bills on the
House agenda or keep them off.   No unanimous
consent is needed, no filibusters can succeed, and
no unwanted items can come to the floor except
through certain carefully constrained safety
valves (such as by a discharge petition).
Ultimately, the majority leadership's limit is
that, while it can lead the House "horse" to
water, it cannot make it drink; while it puts the
agenda before the House, the Members decide
collectively for themselves what bills or
amendments to accept.

For an example of how the agenda control
system works, in the early 1980s, a major issue
for the nation was immigration reform. The House
leadership controlled the timing of this issue
coming to the House floor; as a compromise between
the wings of the majority party supporting and

---

[2]   T. O'Neill, <u>Man of the House</u> 327 (1987).

opposing immigration reform, the leadership kept the bill off the floor until 1984, which delayed ultimate enactment until 1986. Also, the leadership framed the issue: it brought the bill up in 1984 through a special rule allowing opponents no fewer than 73 amendments, and then proffered it in 1986 under procedures that led to initial defeat. Finally, the leadership controlled significant party cues: when the bill came up, the Speaker bluntly announced that the bill was not a Democratic party measure, releasing Democrats from any party loyalty to the bill.[3] Ultimately, at the end of 1986, a bipartisan consensus developed that enacted the bill.

History explains a great deal about how the House has come to organize itself in this fashion, and what control systems and safety valves it employs. Accordingly, this chapter begins with sections on the history and nature of the control by the leadership. The final sections of this chapter address how the House conducts its routine floor business -- speeches, voting, quorum calls, and bill introduction, referral, and calendaring. With this background, the following three chapters discuss in detail the Rules Committee's role; the House floor management and amendment of bills that come up through the main route; and the other routes to the floor, notably suspension of the rules.

Historic Origins of House Leadership and Basic Procedure

This section discusses how the Speaker's current role and the House's procedure result from two centuries of House experimentation; it will foreshadow but not duplicate later detailed descriptions of procedures. Four general phases chararacterize that lengthy history: early

---

[3] Similarly, the House leadership and the Rules Committee quietly killed a regulatory reform bill in 1982, notwithstanding its having been passed by the Senate and reported by the House Judiciary Committee, simply by refusing to schedule it.

development, rise, and fall of the autocratic
Speakers of the turn of the century, rise and fall
of the conservative coalition in the mid-twentieth
century, and the revival of the Speakership in the
1970s and 1980s.[4]

As noted in the introductory chapter, the
House began its operation in 1789 with a procedure
very rudimentary compared to today's.   The
Constitution prescribed in Article I, section 2,
clause 5, that "[t]he House of Representatives
shall chuse [sic] their Speaker" as presiding
officer, following the traditions of a Speaker of
the   House   of   Commons   and   of   colonial
legislatures. In theory, the early House expected
to formulate bills without preliminary committee
assistance or strong party leadership, through
floor discussions by the whole membership of each
bill.[5] Since unstructured mass decision making
was unworkable, in practice the early House
largely succumbed to administration control.[6]

---

[4] There have been large-scale revisions of the House rules
in 1811, 1822, 1837, 1860, 1880, 1890, 1911, 1931, 1946, and
1970, and on these and other occasions one observer counted
"over four hundred amendments to the rules in the course of
one hundred eighty years." Damon at 11 (dates of major
revisions), and 10 & n.12 (counting over 400 "substantive
amendments" which "change[d] the text, and not just the
number" or grammar of the rule).

[5]   Following British tradition, early House Speakers
exercised little power and served largely as neutral
arbiters in the chair.   See Follett 3-25 (British and
colonial progenitors of the Speaker), 25-26 and 31-32
(Speakership clause in the Constitution), 64-69 (early
Speakers); Galloway at 109 (early Speaker "mere
figurehead").   Colonial antecedents had often been run by
party organizations (then nicknamed "Juntos"), out of which
came the leadership of the Continental Congress. Harlow at
24-60; Follett at 12-20. Hence it was natural for the first
House to divide into parties. Galloway at 20. However,
early House parties were not highly organized. J. S. Young,
The Washington Community 1800-1828 110-31 (1966).

[6]   During parts of the early congressional period, House
floor procedure consisted of preliminary consideration of
(footnote continued)

Starting in 1811, Speaker Henry Clay (D-Ky.)
established the pattern of the Speaker as a
powerful head of the House's majority party, which
has endured (with ups and downs) through the many
shifts in House party control.[7] The House needed
to establish a basic procedure for controlling
action on bills once they came to the floor as it
expanded from a mere 65 Members in 1789 to 243 in
1860, amid fierce struggles between pro- and
antislavery factions.[8]   In 1822, the House

---

the general principles of legislation in Committee of the
Whole, followed by drafting of bill language by a select
committee, with the House then taking up that bill.   At
first there were not many significant standing committees:
Ways and Means, the first, was not created as an enduring
standing committee until 1795, and it took another decade to
create a number of important standing committees. Gradually
initial consideration of principles in Committee of the
Whole, and use of select committees, gave way to initial
consideration in the standing committees and reporting by
bill. See generally J. Cooper, The Origins of the Standing
Committees and the Development of the Modern House (1970);
R. V. Harlow, The History of Legislative Methods Before 1825
(1917).

Absent internal party and committee leadership, the
early House was largely controlled by strong executive
leadership of its majority party, first by Alexander
Hamilton as Secretary of the Treasury, later by Thomas
Jefferson as President.

[7] Speaker Clay founded his office's strength on his power
to appoint the standing committees that were rising in
importance, and on his maintenance of order including
pushing through measures over delay by firm rulings.
Galloway at 111.   For accounts of Clay's brilliant capture
of control of the House, see Harlow at 199-208; Cheney &
Cheney at 1-21.

[8] Galloway at 22 (growth in size) and 45-50 (factional
struggles).   Galloway summarizes the alternation in party
control of the House as follows:

From 1801 down to the eve of the Civil War, the
Democrats kept control of the House of Representatives
in all but four Congresses.   Then, during the Civil War
and Reconstruction period, the Republicans were in
(footnote continued)

constricted the amending process by adopting its germaneness rule, and by 1841, delay was being prevented in the House through an hour cap on Members' floor speeches and by effective use of the motion for the previous question.   To curb stormy filibustering during the amending process, in 1840-60 the House established an orderly procedure for its Committee of the Whole starting with general debate and finishing with amendment under the "five minute" rule subject to motions to limit debate.

Rise and Fall of the All-Powerful Speakers

These orderly procedures only moved bills along once they reached the floor; they did not provide the Speaker with much power to decide what would come to the floor.   That lack of agenda control had been endurable before the Civil War, when no one "anticipate[d] that [the] business [of the House] would increase fivefold in twenty years."[9]   Such an increase overwhelmed the House.   Its calendaring rule, which remains on the books as House Rule XXIV, proved unworkable, as in practice it depended on the House to vote by two-thirds majority to move bills up on the agenda.[10]   By the 1880s, "the House of

---

power for sixteen years (1859-1875).   Thereafter the political pendulum swung back and forth between the two major parties, with the Republicans controlling the house for two long periods: from 1895 to 1911 and from 1919 to 1933 . . . .   Since 1933, the Republicans have controlled the House only during 1947-48 and 1953-54.

Id. at 38.

[9]   Alexander at 193.

[10]   "Beginning in 1828 the motion to suspend the rules came to be used as a means of hastening the passage of legislation which was otherwise stymied.   A rule adopted in 1828 permitted the order of business to be altered by two-thirds vote, and this was used as a device to secure immediate consideration of legislation."   Damon at 177; see V Hinds § 6790, at 902 (wording of 1828 rule).   What the House was doing was adopting a "special order of the day," (footnote continued)

Representatives had been reduced to a condition of
legislative impotence by abuses of its then
existing rules of procedure . . . . mak[ing] the
House an object of public ridicule and
condemnation."[11]

In response, the majority party established
the powerful modern machinery for scheduling
bills. The Rules Committee first assumed in 1883
its major modern function of making particular
bills in order, by reporting "special rules" for
those bills. That committee's own privileged
status, by which it can bring to the floor at any
time proposed resolutions on the rules, allowed
privileged scheduling resolutions to come to the
floor. Such privileged scheduling resolutions --
"special rules" -- needed only a majority vote for
adoption, unlike the previous two-thirds
requirements for scheduling. Once adopted, the
special rules both made bills privileged and
thereby moved them up the agenda, and specified
the procedure for the bills and thereby provided
floor control.

Through major rules revision in 1880 and
1890, and dramatic rulings particularly by Speaker
Thomas Reed (R-Maine), the House strengthened its
new scheduling system, crushed delaying tactics,

---

or "special order," giving bills precedence and thereby
moving them up the agenda, by the two-thirds vote to suspend
the rules. "Special orders for disposing of particular
matters of legislation, such as appropriation bills and
other important measures, began to be used quite frequently
in the first session of the Twenty-fourth Congress (1836),
and the index of the Journal shows a considerable number of
them proposed and adopted." IV Hinds § 3158 (footnote
omitted).

[11]   Galloway at 165. As a contemporary observer noted,
"[e]xperience has shown that two-thirds and unanimous
consent requirements in lawmaking put too much power in the
hands of small and irresponsible minorities." McConachie at
190-91. Until 1890, as the Republican and Democratic
parties alternated in office, "[i]t was a period
characterized by intense resistances within Congress both to
organizational change and to legislation of any sort."
Alexander at 164.

and put its Speaker and the Rules Committee into dominant control of its agenda.[12]   The Speaker now possessed three great powers, among others:[13] to appoint the chairs and Members of committees; to chair and control the Rules Committee; and to recognize -- or not -- whomsoever he chose for motions and other requests.[14]

By 1910, "the speaker came to be considered as an officer second only in power and influence to the President of the United States himself, and so far as the enactment of legislation was concerned to exercise powers superior to his."[15]

---

[12]   Speaker Reed made a further revision in the rules in 1890, known as the "Reed rules"). Also Speaker Reed took two steps of major historical interest, though not actively employed in current procedure. He ruled that he could count a quorum by including Members present but not voting, thereby ending the minority's chief stalling tactic, its refusal to be counted on quorum calls -- the so-called "disappearing quorum." See Cheney & Cheney at 104-7. He announced, and wrote into the rules, that he could refuse to entertain motions he deemed dilatory. See Cheney & Cheney at 99, 107; Galloway at 167-68.

[13]   The Speakers enhanced their power in many other ways. Rules changes also gave the Speaker automatic power to refer bills without floor proceedings, and discretion over calendars. Damon at 169, 187. Then (unlike now), calendaring control led to "the domination of leaders who used their control of the calendar system as a lever . . . ," id. at 188, because of the vast flow of pensions and claims bills vital to Members as political favors.

[14]   Full assumption of recognition power came in 1880-81 when the Speaker took discretionary control over recognizing for the vital motion to suspend the rules, and declined any longer to entertain appeals from decisions on recognition. Follett at 258-60. The Speakers enlarged their recognition power by asking prior to recognizing a Member, "For what purpose does the gentleman seek recognition?" -- a power never possessed by the chair in the Senate, which "fortifies the presiding officer against unexpected moves by individual Members of the House." F. Riddick, The United States Congress 3 (1949).
(footnote continued)

Speaker "Czar" Joseph Cannon's (R-Ill.) arbitrary exercise of these enormous powers pushed the progressive wing of his party to join the Democrats in successful revolt on March 16, 1910. The revolt and the ensuing rewriting of the rules in 1911, when the Democrats won a majority, cut back on all three of the Speaker's chief powers: he lost his power to appoint standing committees, left the Rules Committee, and was restricted in his recognition power.[16]

The new system enhanced the post of Majority Leader, previously a mere lieutenant of the Speaker. A Majority Leader elected by, and responsive to, the majority caucus exercised political powers superior to the diminished Speaker. The leader led the majority party on the floor, established the House's daily schedule, and influenced the Committee on Committees which now decided committee appointments, subject to the strengthened seniority rule. Majority party agenda control came also through the Rules Committee. After some revival in the 1920s of the Speaker's authority, it was this system which, in the 1930s, enacted the enormous New Deal legislative program.

That unprecedented surge of national liberal economic legislation brought a backlash that

---

[15]   W. F. Willoughby, Principles of Legislative Organization and Administration 540 (1934). As Galloway sums up the two decades after Reed:

> The net effect of the Reed rules was a great increase in the powers of the Speaker. Reed ruled the House with an iron hand for six years . . . . When Speaker Cannon succeeded to the scepter in 1903, he continued and expanded the Reed techniques until by 1909 the power of the Speaker had been extended to a quasi dictatorship.

Galloway at 168-69.

[16]   For discussions of the 1910 revolt and 1911 rules change, see Cheney & Cheney at 131-35; Galloway at 57-58; Rules Committee History at 88-99.

created a new House configuration.   Starting in
1937, a bipartisan "conservative coalition" sought
to put a stop to that surge.   Control by the
conservative coalition relied on senior southern
Democratic committee chairs[17] possessing vast
power within their jurisdiction, and on a
coalition of southern Democrats and Republicans on
the Rules Committee which blocked or controlled
floor consideration.   Speaker Sam Rayburn (D-
Tex.), who held the post (with two brief
interludes of Republican control) from 1940 to
1961, held fairly strong personal power, but
depended on his individual stature rather than
institutionalized procedural changes and often
ceded much control of the floor agenda to the
conservative coalition.   Ultimately, somewhat
reluctantly, in 1961 he led the revolt against the
Rules Committee that relaxed somewhat the
conservative coalition's grip on the floor.[18]
However, Rayburn's successors, Speakers John
McCormack (D-Mass.) and Carl Albert (D-Okla.),
largely refused to lead confrontations against the
coalition in the 1960s, even while moving
President Johnson's "Great Society" Program.
Accordingly, the majority party took another
decade to break the conservative constraints.

Change accelerated starting in 1970, when the
chamber first established the holding of recorded
votes in the Committee of the Whole, which firmed
the position of junior Members on floor amendment
votes against pressure from committee chairs.   A
major revolt against committee chairs occurred

---

[17] During the 1920s, the Republican party had made inroads
into northern Democratic ranks. Thus, the senior Democrats,
from whose ranks the chairs were drawn due to the seniority
rule, were largely southern when the House began its modern
period of Democratic control in 1931 (a period broken only
by Republican control in 1947-48 and 1952-54).   Southern
districts tended then to retain the same members for long
periods, keeping southern Democratic chairs in office and
tending to make their replacements other southern Democrats.

[18] See Cheney & Cheney at 170-81 (Speaker Rayburn's
coexistence with the Rules Committee) and 182-89 (his
leading of the successful effort to enlarge the committee).

when the 1974 "Watergate" election swept in a
large and irreverent class of seventy-five
freshmen Democrats, who deposed three chairs and
adopted a "Subcommittee Bill of Rights."
Accession in 1977 of Speaker Thomas P. "Tip"
O'Neill, Jr. (D-Mass.), a strong Speaker bolstered
by the institutional reforms, led to a more
powerful and complex leadership operation. As
previously discussed, this included enhanced
influence by the Speaker over committee
appointments through the Steering and Policy
Committee, and over bill movement through multiple
referrals (based on a rule change in 1975).
Elements discussed below include the
extraordinarily supple tool of the new complex
special rules from the Rules Committee; more
sophisticated floor work, including a stronger
whip system and rules on postponing votes and
quorum calls; and expanded use of suspension of
the rules.

B. HOUSE LEADERSHIP

The Speaker: Procedural Role

Roles of the key majority leadership -- Speaker,
Majority Leader, and Majority Whip -- may be
divided into procedural, and political. Starting
at the top of the leadership, "[t]he office of
speaker of the House of Representatives is the
second most powerful in the land [after the
President]."[19] The Speaker often presides over
the House, and when not in the Chair, chooses the
officers who act in his stead: the Speakers Pro
Tempore, and the Chairs of the Committee of the
Whole.[20]

---

[19] A. J. Mikva & P. B. Sarris, The American Congress: The
First Branch 86 (1983).

[20] The Chairs of the Committee of the Whole preside during
the amending of bills in Committee of the Whole; the
Speakers Pro Tempore preside over the House when the Speaker
is absent. Both are chosen by the Speaker. House Rule
XXIII(1)(a) provides that "in forming a Committee of the
(footnote continued)

The first task of the Speaker and his stand-ins is to keep order. As Rule I(2) instructs, the Speaker "shall preserve order and decorum, and, in case of disturbance or disorderly conduct in the galleries, or in the lobby, may cause the same to be cleared." Members must constantly be reminded to keep down the noise level, to clear the aisles, and to stay within certain bounds of decorum in debate. When floor debate becomes fractious, the presiding officer calls Members to order for personal accusations such as that other Members are lying, as discussed in the section below on debate.

Of more parliamentary significance, the presiding officer decides points of order regarding the proper mode of procedure, such as that a motion is out of order as not privileged at that time. Rule I(4) states that the Speaker shall "decide all questions of order, subject to an appeal by any Member . . . ." Members can raise points of order at any time except during a vote, even when another is speaking. The Member simply states, "Mr. Speaker, I make a point of order against . . ." or "I make a point of order that . . . ."

A Speaker's power regarding points of order is far greater than that of the presiding officer in the Senate. The Speaker rarely refers points of order for a vote of the House, and is rarely appealed from, as appeals invariably fail -- the majority party always supports the Chair -- and in modern practice may be taken by the Speaker as a personal insult.[21]   A Member may ask a

---

Whole House, the Speaker shall leave his chair after appointing a Chairman to preside . . . ." House Rule I(7) provides that the Speaker "shall have the right to name any Member to perform the duties of the Chair," i.e., appoint the Speaker Pro Tempore. The rule further provides that in the "absence and omission to make such appointment, the House shall proceed to elect a Speaker pro tempore to act during his absence."

[21]   The last successful appeal was apparently in the 1920s. Appeals in the House (but not in Committee of the Whole) may be tabled rather than debated and voted upon.

parliamentary inquiry to receive an answer on a procedural point without actually pressing a point of order. On certain procedures, such as when an amendment is offered, a Member may reserve a point of order, allowing an explanation of the meaning of the amendment; other points of order, such as against a provision in an appropriations bill, are ruled upon at once.

Decisions by the Speaker on procedure encompass two aspects of particular importance: referrals of bills to committee, and germaneness. Regarding referrals, as previously discussed, the Speaker's decisions on which committees shall receive which bills define the all-important boundaries of committee jurisdiction. The Speaker's multiple referrals, which can impose deadlines for reporting by the various committees, amount to a power to discharge committees.[22] Regarding germaneness, the Speaker rules on which amendments offered to a bill on the floor are in order as relevant, and which ones are out of order as irrelevant ("non-germane"). Germaneness acts as a highly important screen concerning what subjects will come onto the floor of the House, and is the subject of several sections in a later chapter.

The Speaker does not exercise arbitrarily his referral, germaneness, and other responsibilities for ruling on procedural questions. By tradition, he is constrained to follow precedents, which are rarely overruled,[23] and acts with guidance from the Parliamentarian, a non-Member whose role includes many duties:

---

[22] In the example discussed in the committee jurisdiction chapter, the leadership supported the 1981 domestic content bill for automobiles, and gave the bill a multiple referral to Energy and Commerce, and Ways and Means, with a time limit preventing the Ways and Means Committee from bottling the bill up.

[23] House Manual § 627. The House Manual also lists the various types of questions on which the Speaker generally does not rule.

> referring all bills to the proper committee;
> advising the speaker or chair on all points
> of order or parliamentary inquiries; checking
> for procedural problems all legislative
> drafts of bills, resolutions, and rules
> coming out of the Rules Committee; and
> offering members of the House technical
> assistance for preparing motions and other
> legislative measures.[24]

Having a Parliamentarian resolves the tension
between the interests of all in procedural
regularity, legitimacy about actions, and
excessive engagement of leadership authority in
disputes, on the one hand, and the majority
party's procedural control, on the other. What
the Speaker and chamber need, and the
Parliamentarian provides, are rulings which
implement the rules in predictable, stable, and
orderly fashion; the rules themselves, implemented
neutrally, provide the majority party with the
tools for control.

As presiding officers, the Speaker and his
stand-ins make the decisions on recognition. This
is not the supremely unbridled recognition power
developed and possessed by the turn-of-the-century
Speakers until the revolt against "Czar" Cannon in
1910; its limits will become apparent below.
Still, it is a considerably less constrained power
than that of the Senate's presiding officer, and
it continues to play an important part in floor
maneuvering. The Speaker's recognition power
enables him to control the hour-by-hour schedule
on the floor; it gives him control over the
secondary route for bills to the floor, the motion

---

[24] Ruling Congress, supra, at 29. Before the 1920s, there
were clerks who assisted the chair in its procedural rulings
before there was a formal office of Parliamentarian. The
first House Parliamentarian, Lehr Fess, was named in the
1920s. From 1928 to 1974, Lewis Deschler served as House
Parliamentarian for no fewer than nine Speakers of both
parties. Ruling Congress, supra, at 28. A general account
of the House and Senate parliamentarians is in Hook,
Parliamentarians: Procedure and Pyrotechnics, 45 Cong. Q.
Weekly Rep. 1951 (1987).

to suspend the rules; it gives the majority managers one of their key tools in bill management; and it often serves to give the majority party some tactical advantage in debate and amendment.

Among the ultimate powers of the Speaker as presiding officer is to put an end to dilatory tactics. The powerful Speakers of the 1880s established the principle, enshrined in 1890 in what is now Rule XVI(10), that "No dilatory motion shall be entertained by the Speaker." Among the pillars of this principle are that Speakers will not allow appeals from their actions on certain matters, such as recognition; that Rule XI(4) provides that when a Rules Committee report is under consideration, "the Speaker shall not entertain any other dilatory motion until the report shall have been fully disposed of"; and that Rule XXIII(6) provides that even for amendments on which debate time is guaranteed by printing, "such time for debate shall not be allowed when the offering of such amendment is dilatory."

In practice, Speakers rarely invoke their power to deem motions and amendments dilatory. They do not have to. Attempts by the minority to filibuster in the House are rare, although they have occurred.[25] When debates drag, the

---

[25]   As Galloway describes:

Speaker Rayburn, who had occupied the Chair since 1940 except during [1947-48], told the House on July 25, 1949, that "since the present Speaker has occupied the Chair he has yet to hold a motion to be dilatory, and will not until it becomes obvious to everybody that dilatory tactics are being indulged in and that a filibuster is being conducted." The Speaker made this statement after five roll calls had been held on motions to adjourn, for the previous questions and approval of the Journal: motions that were apparently designed to prevent the House from taking up the anti-poll-tax bill.

G. Galloway, The Legislative Process in Congress 529 (footnote continued)

leadership has other tools for moving them along, such as special rules from the Rules Committee, the motion for the previous question, and the motion to close or limit debate in Committee of the Whole.

The Speaker: Political Role

Turning from the procedural to the political powers, the reforms of the 1970s have given the Speaker much greater levers for control within the majority party.   He reappoints each Congress the Members of the Rules Committee (by a recommendation to the Democratic Caucus, which sends the party's appointment choices to the floor); this, in an era when Members of the committee have been selected for loyalty, means the Speaker possesses floor control through that committee.[26]   Through the Speaker's large voice on

---

(1953).   A late effort at a filibuster occurred when Representative James Weaver (D-Oreg.) attempted to block a bill concerning power in the northwest single-handedly:

> When the bill's managers brought it to the floor in October, Weaver assaulted it with a vengeance beyond the bounds of normal House procedure.   He prepared 73 amendments to the legislation, including one that was 56 pages long and took 90 minutes to read on the House floor after Weaver objected to its routine inclusion in the Congressional Record. . . .

> [Weaver] only succeeded in delaying passage for a month.   But the Oregon Democrat appeared to enjoy the scene, pointing proudly to his effort as the first filibuster by amendment in House memory.

Congressional Quarterly, Politics in America 1294 (1985).

[26] This is not to suggest that the Speaker constantly gives instructions to the Rules Committee.   On the contrary, as Congressional Quarterly observed, "on most bills, the [Rules] committee gets no word from the leadership. 'Ninety-nine percent of the time, the Speaker never communicates at all,' [Chairperson Claude] Pepper says. 'Only when there's something he has strong feelings about.'"   Plattner, Rules Under Chairman Pepper Looks Out (footnote continued)

the Steering and Policy Committee, which recommends the appointments of chairs and committee Members for Democrats, and in the Democratic Caucus, which ratifies the choice, the Speaker has the ability at the beginning of each Congress to reward the faithful and to punish the disloyal.[27]   In addition, the Speaker appoints conferees, largely following the decisions of committee chairs but with some discretion particularly from the rise of off-committee and multicommittee conferees.   The Speaker may constitute his own informal but highly important groupings.[28]   He draws on a variety of miscellaneous resources, such as enhanced staff and information resources, numerous minor

---

for the Democrats, 43 Cong. Q. Week. Rep. 1671 (1985). However, as "Rules member Anthony C. Beilenson [(D-Cal.)] . . . says, 'The Speaker does not ask much of us, partly because we mostly do what we think he wants.'" Id.

[27] Thus, for example, in 1981 most chairs, even those from conservative districts, voted with the leadership on the key budget votes rather than jeopardize their chair, and after the 1982 election some southern Democrats who had failed to do so found their access to desired committee appointments blocked.

[28] Historically, a famous example of this was the "Board of Education," established by Speaker Nicholas Longworth (R-Ohio) and continued for two-score years through the time of Speaker Rayburn.   It was an informal group of leaders who "invited colleagues for a drink -- [John Nance] Garner [(D-Tex.)] always called it 'striking a blow for liberty' -- and talked over the business coming before the House." MacNeil at 81.   There a Speaker

> learned all the gossip of the House and there he planned much of the House's operations . . . .   These private sessions . . . . enormously helped the Speakers -- Longworth, Garner, and Rayburn -- to re-establish the old prestige of their office . . . .   [I]nfluential men of the House were invited to these sessions . . . .   [to] participate in developing the Speaker's strategy.   They often left the sessions carrying the Speaker's orders.

Id. at 83.

appointments to boards and commissions, and ability to influence election fundraising.[29]

Perhaps the single most clearly defining political characteristic of each twentieth-century Speaker has been his relationship with the President. In the late nineteenth century, that was much less true: Presidents did not submit systematic legislative programs to the Congress, and the powerful Speakers managed legislative affairs with only limited consultation.[30] However, with the growth of the twentieth century presidency's role in leading the Congress, leaders of the same party as the President came to see themselves as his lieutenant in enacting the administration program.[31] More recently, Speakers with the task of passing their President's program included Speaker Joseph Martin (R-Mass.) (for President Eisenhower in 1953-54), Speaker McCormack (for Presidents Kennedy and Johnson) and Speaker O'Neill (for President Carter). In working with a same-party President, the Speaker receives the benefits of Administration support, from presidential command of the media to patronage.

Conversely, when the Speaker and Majority Leader are of the other party than the President, they may become leading national opposition figures. They may enjoy the prerogatives of a key

---

[29] For example, Speaker O'Neill "visit[ed] the districts of thirty to forty Democrats each year . . . . customarily appear[ing] at members' fund-raisers . . . . [b]ecause the Speaker is a good draw, the member is likely to raise more money." Sinclair at 40. For an extensive treatment of the Speaker's current informal powers, see id. at 34-41.

[30] Early in the twentieth century, the House majority leaderships were "heirs to a tradition that allowed them to view themselves as at least equal to the President . . . a tradition of inactive . . . Presidents and firmly control-ling . . . leaders in Congress." Ripley at 172.

[31] Early examples of this were Majority Leader Oscar Underwood (D-Ala.) (for President Wilson) and Speaker Henry Rainey (D-Ill.) (for President Franklin Roosevelt).

national leader in their ability to focus press
and party attention on issues and in performing
the key bargaining on compromises with the
administration. Many observers would contend that
the chief role of Speaker O'Neill in 1981-86 and
Speaker Wright in from 1987 on was to define the
national opposition position of the Democrats to
Presidents Reagan and Bush. This was a role in
keeping with past opposition Speakers.[32]
Alternatively, some opposition Speakers may keep a
low profile vis-a-vis their President, as Speaker
Albert did under Presidents Nixon and Ford.

From the formal and political status of the
Speaker flows a resource of immense importance in
the 1970s and 1980s, his position as a media
spokesman. As a leading observer chronicled in
1986, "[a] decade ago, and for most of its history
before that, the House was a relatively insular
place outside the circle of national publicity and
attention." With the rise of televised politics,
"it [was] [Speaker] O'Neill who ha[d] become the
first media celebrity in the history of the
speakership." Making a historical comparison,
then-Majority Whip Thomas Foley commented:

> Sam Rayburn could have walked down the
> streets of Spokane, Wash., without anybody

---

[32] Similarly, Speaker Martin (in opposition to President
Truman) and Speaker Rayburn (sometimes in opposition to
President Eisenhower) often defined the national opposition
position, sometimes passing legislation opposed by the
President at least through the House if not to enactment.
Speaker Martin passed the Taft-Hartley Act restricting labor
unions over President Truman's consistent opposition and
eventual veto. Ripley at 150-55 (regarding Speaker Martin).

Speaker Rayburn cooperated more in the period 1957-58
when the Democratic majority margin was thin, than in 1959-
60 when the party had a large margin. See Ripley at 162-65
(1959-60). The large Democratic margin in the later period
proved illusory due to resistance from the Rules Committee,
committee chairs, and conservative Democrats. For example,
the House adopted the Republican version of the current
labor law bill, the Landrum-Griffin Act, after Speaker
Rayburn and President Eisenhower each made nationwide
broadcasts. Id. at 163.

> noticing him . . . . Tip O'Neill couldn't do
> that . . . . And it is very unlikely that
> any future Speaker will be anonymous to the
> country. The Speaker is going to join the
> vice president, the chief justice and a few
> Cabinet members in the forefront of public
> recognition.[33]

This has great significance in House operations:

> A decade ago, nearly all influential House
> members would have said that legislative
> arguments are won on the floor . . . .

> Nowadays, many of them say that sort of work
> is only part of the story. Increasingly,
> they believe, floor fights are won by
> orchestrating a campaign aimed over the heads
> of the members, at the country at large
> . . . .

Particularly this proved true in the context of 1980s procedure, which, as discussed above, can fall into a "four bill" pattern in which a few highly publicized omnibus bills, like budget resolutions and reconciliation, continuing resolutions, debt increases, tax bills, and a few key issue bills such as on foreign affairs, may consolidate much of the Congress' work for a year. Such concentrated agendas produce major media struggles between the President and congressional leaders.

The Majority Leader and Scheduling

In contrast to the Speaker, at least some of whose powers have formal bases in House and Caucus rules, the Majority Leader's powers derive almost solely from informal practice. Nonetheless, his power is as real and potent as that of the Senate leadership, whose powers are also the creatures of informal practice.

---

[33] This quote, and the others in this paragraph, are drawn from Ehrenhalt, _Media, Power Shifts Dominate O'Neill's House_, 44 Cong. Q. Week. Rep. 2131-34 (1986).

Historically, parties needed another official besides the Speaker to lead the party on the floor, since the Speaker presided from the Chair and by custom appeared on the floor to vote or to speak only infrequently. Prior to 1910, the Speaker chose the majority leader.[34] In reaction to "Czar" Cannon's Speakership, the majority party caucus took over the choice of Majority Leader and enhanced his power.[35] Today, first, the Majority Leader is the heir apparent to the position of Speaker, as Majority Leader Jim Wright (D-Tex.) was heir apparent before he became Speaker in 1987. The Majority Leader has been consciously elected by the party with that probability in the Members' minds: "[o]f the 15 Speakers in this century, Wright is the 12th -- and the 11th in a row since 1925 -- to advance from the post of party floor leader."[36]   When the Majority Leader

---

[34]   During the earliest periods of House history, when Alexander Hamilton (then Secretary of the Treasury) and Thomas Jefferson (then President) dominated the House, they chose their floor leaders. Harlow, supra, at 176-77. The rise of the Speakership with Speaker Clay encompassed internal choice of the floor leader. "During the nineteenth century the majority floor leader was customarily selected by the Speaker who often designated either his leading opponent within the party or the chairman of Ways and Means or of the Appropriations Committee or one of this faithful lieutenants." Galloway at 135-36. See F. Riddick, The United States Congress 86n. (1949); McConachie at 159-60.

[35]   In 1911 the Democrats named a leader, Underwood, who "was supreme, [and] the Speaker [was] a figurehead." Galloway at 136. Restoration of the Speaker to a position superior to Majority Leader came in the mid-1920s with Speaker Longworth, whose effective maneuvers are described in Cheney & Cheney at 154-55. Since then the Majority Leader has typically been subordinate to the Speaker.

[36]   Hill Leaders at 5.

As a result, elections of Majority Leaders may be highly charged affairs. A major contest occurred in 1976, when Representative Wright was chosen as Majority Leader over Representatives Phillip Burton (D-Calif.) and Richard Bolling (D-Mo.). For an unusual account of the race by one (footnote continued)

seeks to influence voting, committee appointments, and like matters, other Members must deal with him on the assumption that to cross him very likely is to cross the next Speaker.

Second, the Majority Leader has the role "of field marshal on the floor of the House"[37] for the majority party. When the leader so indicates, the position he takes constitutes the party position, which is decisive on procedural matters and influential on substantive matters. As one Representative said in 1928, in words applicable today:

> The floor leader, especially the leader of the majority side, has much to do with the legislative program. The majority leader, of course, represents the majority on the floor. Motions he makes are usually passed. He endeavors to represent the majority view and the majority follow his leadership. He leads in debate on administration matters and gives the House and the country the viewpoint of his party on the legislative program.[38]

Majority Leaders implement this role through speeches, amendments, and even tactically timed votes. "A speech by the majority leader puts the imprimatur upon the legislation . . . . From 1977 to 1980 [Majority Leader Wright] averaged forty major floor statements a year in his capacity as floor leader."[39] Even when he makes no speech and

---

of the losers, see Bolling, Learn from My Losses How Not to Run for Speaker, Washington Post, July 27, 1986, at D1.

[37]   Galloway at 139.

[38]   Galloway at 139, quoting Cong. Rec., 70th Cong., 1st Sess. 8439 (1928) (Rep. Hardy). The majority leader usually receives priority in recognition; however, others may obtain priority by offering motions of higher precedence, and it is possible that the Chair might give priority to the manager, or another majority member from the committee of jurisdiction, to offer amendments in Committee of the Whole.

[39]   Sinclair at 49.

offers no amendment, the Majority Leader's vote itself may constitute a key signal. Since usually the Speaker does not vote, the Majority Leader's is the vote by the highest-ranking voting majority party member.   "[H]ow and when he votes can influence others . . . ."[40]   Finally, like the Speaker, the Majority Leader holds keys to positioning with regards to the President, and to coverage by the media.

Third, the Majority Leader prescribes and announces the schedule of the House.   "Control over floor scheduling is probably the majority party leadership's single most important power."[41]   The leadership and its staff watch the bills proceeding on each of the routes to the floor, the subject of the next chapters.[42]

While the whole leadership, including the Speaker, the Majority Whip, and the chairman of the Rules Committee, have a say in the schedule,

---

[40]   "Members will frequently ask [the Majority Leader] to vote early during the fifteen-minute roll call [when he is on their side] . . . .   Alternatively, members who know [that the Majority Leader] will vote against their position may ask that he do so as unobtrusively as possible," i.e., late, after most members have voted and left and before his vote could be taken as a party position.   Sinclair at 51.

[41]   Sinclair at 158.

[42]   When committees report bills, they go onto the House's various calendars, and "the majority leader's staff go through the calendars every morning to check what has been reported."   Sinclair at 43.   Once a bill of importance is reported and calendared, its chair must almost inevitably ask for floor consideration in one of two ways.   He may write to the Rules Committee requesting a special rule for the bill, and the majority leader's "aides also work closely with the Rules Committee staff director, who sends copies of all letters requesting rules to the majority leader's office."   Sinclair at 43.   Or, he may ask the Speaker to schedule the bill for consideration under suspension of the rules.   Those letters must be sent to the Speaker, whose staff can review them together with the other leadership staff.

the Majority Leader has the primary role in devising short-term schedules.[43] Devising the actual schedule is "an extremely complex process," because of "the desire to accommodate floor managers, the necessity of meeting various deadlines, the difficulty of predicting how much floor time a given measure will take, and the dictates of strategic scheduling."[44]

The Majority Leader reveals the final schedule at the regular Thursday weekly announcement, the Majority Whip sends a printed copy out to Democratic members, and the Majority Leader shares it with the Minority Leader. Starting in 1920, the Majority Leader by custom has formally announced the schedule for the following week.[45] Each Thursday, the Majority Leader releases the schedule on the floor Thursday afternoon in a time-honored ritual. The Minority Leader obtains recognition and asks the Majority Leader to tell the schedule, then yields him time

---

[43]   The process of devising such a schedule begins as the majority leader's staff track bills as they go through committee, are reported onto the calendar, and receive special rules. "[T]he majority leader's staff go through the calendars every morning to check what has been reported. The aides also work closely with the Rules Committee staff director, who sends copies of all letters requesting rules to the majority leader's office." Sinclair at 43. "The majority leader's office may prepare up to twelve tentative schedules (called 'tentatives') before a final schedule is announced." Sinclair at 44. As the Majority Leader and his staff start to draw up the next week's schedule, they receive lobbying from floor managers and staff, the White House and interest groups, although, as in other internal matters, "direct interest group lobbying has a relatively minor impact on scheduling." Sinclair at 45.

[44]   Sinclair at 44.

[45]   This started in 1920 "by word of mouth," then in the following Congress with "a little bulletin with the tentative program . . . posted where it could be consulted." P. D. Hasbrouck, Party Government in the House of Representatives 110 (1927).

to do so.   Often, the Minority Leader, or his surrogate, will press questions, some practical -- "so the Members should not expect any votes on Monday?" -- and some with a partisan bite -- "then next week the Members still will not see the long-promised budget reconciliation legislation?"

In scheduling, the first question is whether a bill will come up at all.   This question dominates the President's relations with the House leadership, as the President seeks to push through his program, and the leadership either helps, temporizes, or resists.   A prime example was the immigration reform bill discussed earlier, which the leadership chose not to allow to come up in 1982 or 1983.   Another example was Social Security reform: the majority leadership quietly avoided compromises in 1981-82 to preserve the unpopular administration position as an issue in the 1982 congressional election.   Even when there is extreme opposition, the leadership may bend to a presidential demand for an opportunity to get a vote, as on the 1981 budget bills.   Because the chief place major bills get screened out is the Rules Committee, the screening out of bills is discussed in the next chapter.

Scheduling Rhythms

Besides the question of whether to bring a bill to the floor at all, the key question is when.   The leadership's scheduling falls loosely into two types -- the routine "housekeeping" scheduling to keep the House operating smoothly from day to day, and "strategic" scheduling to facilitate passage of key elements of the majority party's program.   Each type of scheduling involves certain recognizable rhythms -- annual, weekly, and daily.   Looking first at the annual level, the House leadership takes care to schedule the breaks of a week or more around various holidays throughout the year facilitating planning of campaigning, fundraising, and other activities.[46]   For the Members, the predictable

---

[46]   These occur around Christmas and New Year's Day in (footnote continued)

schedule of such breaks has great importance.[47]

On the strategic level, the leadership may make important general decisions regarding the year's program. For example, Speaker O'Neill reacted to criticism about congressional delay in appropriation bills by having the House take up such bills early in 1983 and 1984, in late spring or early summer. The Budget Act also forces a certain amount of annual scheduling,[48] as do the crushes of business at the end of the first session and especially at the end of the Congress. The leadership must balance its obligations to move along bills for which there are deadlines or promises to the administration, committees, or particular groups.[49] When

---

December and January, the birthdays of Washington and Lincoln in February, Easter in April, the Fourth of July, an extended Labor Day break in August and September, and, in election years, an extended election break in October and November. Barring the unusual lame duck session, in election years the House does not meet formally after election day in November.

[47] The lack of such a predictable schedule under Speaker Albert irritated the Members constantly. In reaction:

> When he became Speaker, O'Neill adopted an Obey Commission recommendation that has immensely increased predictability [in scheduling]. In January a schedule of Washington work periods and district work periods [adjournment breaks] for the year is made up. Except for the adjournment date, which is given as a target, the House follows this schedule closely.

Sinclair at 46.

[48] The House must take up the budget resolution in the spring; under the act's schedule, not always followed, the House and Senate must agree on a concurrent budget resolution by April 15. The House also is supposed, when it is doing a reconciliation bill under the Gramm-Rudman amended system, to pass that bill in the summer, but that schedule cannot be expected to be followed.

[49] Leadership staff track legislation at a number of levels, including both reported and unreported bills, to (footnote continued)

particular bills come up can determine whether
supporters or opponents will have time for
grassroots lobbying campaigns.[50]

---

anticipate what the leadership will have to schedule.

> The staff of the Steering and Policy Committee [who]
> in effect works for the Speaker . . . . prepare
> periodic reports on the status of various bills and
> provide check lists of legislation that must be
> passed -- authorizations that are expiring, for
> example.

> "Just for the leadership we have got to keep a
> complete list of all bills in every one of our
> committees and where they are," a staff[er]
> explained. "A background, how the bill originated,
> what the bill does, and what the issues are."

Sinclair at 76.

[50] "Sometimes a bill is scheduled quickly so as to prevent
a full-scale campaign by unfriendly interest groups."
Sinclair at 159. For example, in 1981, the omnibus budget
reconciliation act came up after a considerable delay, which
allowed the President successfully to rally enormous
national pressure for his proposal. In 1982, the House
leadership moved its budget reconciliation bills suddenly,
without allowing time for counterlobbying.

The potency of interest group grassroots lobbying has
become a key factor in moving legislation. For example, the
Chamber of Commerce, which "during 1981 had more than 4,000
organization members -- local, state, and regional chambers
as well as trade and professional associations . . . in
particular, was noted for pioneering sophisticated
[grassroots] lobbying techniques using computer technology
that facilitated constituent participation." Congressional
Quarterly, Guide To Congress 798 (3d ed. 1982).

> As a staffer explained: "The Chamber of Commerce says
> they can trigger 50,000 people and they in turn trigger
> 25 [letters to Members] apiece. They can inundate you
> but it takes about six weeks to get the flow started.
> If you give them six weeks, they can kill almost any
> bill if it['s] controversial. So, clearly, if you've
> got one like that, the thing to do is to move before
> they move -- before they've got time to gin up."

(footnote continued)

Weekly, particularly in the early part of the session, the leadership often attempts to make Monday and Friday days of debate and consensual matters only, without recorded votes or with as few as possible. This allows Members to take an extended weekend in their districts without missing votes. Partly, the leadership does this through its prerogatives in scheduling and in control of certain votes; partly, it does this through the cooperation of the membership.[51] Rule I(3) allows the Speaker to postpone recorded votes for two legislative days on most matters. For example, when a bill is controversial but the special rule on it is not, the leadership can have the House debate and pass the special rule on a Monday, but wait to call up the bill until Tuesday. In taking up suspension bills on Monday, the leadership will enact the noncontroversial bills, and conduct debate on the others while using Rule I(3) to postpone the vote until Tuesday.

Daily events on the floor can affect a bill, from unrelated partisan controversies that lead to polarized votes, to a conjunction of several spending measures that make Members leery of adding the final ones to the early ones. If the majority leadership loses control on one key vote, it may have difficulty immediately after in regaining control on another tough one. Countless legislative struggles illustrate the impact of daily timing. For example, in the classic struggle to expand the Rules Committee in 1961, southern Democrats previously on Speaker Rayburn's

---

Sinclair at 159.

[51] Avoiding votes requires the general cooperation of the minority party and the House membership, since there is no way, when the House is in session, from stopping a Member from offering one of the privileged motions (such as to adjourn) and, at least once during the day, from demanding a quorum call, which could trigger a roll-call vote. However, a member who so acts risks antagonizing colleagues of both parties who went back to their districts, if, to their surprise, a call for a recorded vote spoils their attendance record on such votes.

side seemed to drift away during the week prior to the scheduled vote. Accordingly,

> Speaker Rayburn announced abruptly that he
> had postponed the vote on the Rules Committee
> from Thursday until the following Tuesday,
> January 31. Rayburn, doubtful about the
> outcome of the vote, had used his prerogative
> as Speaker to delay the vote. He wanted to
> give his own men more time to try to line up
> an absolute majority of the members.[52]

Conversely, the leadership may push a bill quickly when it has the support it needs and fears delay. In 1979, on a bill to authorize a synfuels program,

> Originally the majority leader's office had
> scheduled HR 3930 for Friday, 29 June, the
> last day before the 4 July recess. A mass of
> major legislation was awaiting consideration,
> and that seemed to be the only possible day
> to take up the synfuels bill. But as a
> senior staffer explained, that late date
> would have worked to the advantage of the
> bill's opponents. By some judicious juggling
> of the schedule, HR 3930 was moved up to
> Tuesday 26 June.[53]

Daily, the House proceeds on a path somewhat foreshadowed by the Majority Leader when he announced the week's schedule. After completing the open formalities and the one-minute speeches (discussed below), it takes up either a scheduled calendar or list of suspensions, or a bill to be brought up by special rule. During the day, the House typically takes up only one bill at a time until it completes action on that bill. Few bills take more than one day on which votes occur, apart from the common pattern of having general debate on one day (Friday or Monday) and amendment action or voting on another (the next midweek). When the House finishes working on bills for the day, it

---

[52] MacNeil at 436.

[53] Sinclair at 228.

allows Members to conduct "special orders," or longer speeches (discussed below), until it adjourns for the night.

The Whip System

The third member of the majority leadership triumvirate is the Majority Whip. While the whip function informally dates back to the early nineteenth century, its formal development occurred in the twentieth century.[54]   Its importance grew[55] in the 1970s and 1980s with the increasing number of floor votes,[56] and it now

---

[54] "In 1811, John Eppes of Virginia . . . acted as whip in rounding up votes to approve the Previous Question rule, the first great limit on House debate . . . .   [Thereafter,] [w]hen the House stood in tenuous balance between two parties, every vote became important and the unofficial whips reappeared." MacNeil at 97-98. The Democrats created an elaborate whip system to push through New Deal legislation in the 1930s. Ripley at 70-71.

[55] After the first burst of activity during the New Deal, Speaker Rayburn made little use of whips during the 1940s and 1950s, and the White House liaison office under Presidents Kennedy and Johnson largely supplanted the whip function in the 1960s.   Also during the 1960s, the Democratic Study Group played a whip-like role in rounding up liberal Democratic votes on measures opposed by conservatives.   For example, during the debate over the Civil Rights Act of 1964, "[f]or all practical purposes, the [Democratic] Study Group took over the functions of the regular Democratic whip organization."   D. Berman, A Bill Becomes a Law 113 (2d ed. 1967).

[56] The revival of the leadership's whip system occurred in response to President Nixon. Dodd, The Expanded Roles of the House Democratic Whip System: The 93rd and 94th Congresses, 7 Cong. Studies 27, 28-29 (1979); Sinclair at 55. The revival of the whip function in the 1970s appears to have been the work of then-Majority Whip O'Neill, who explained "We made the [whip] meetings on Thursday mornings attractive . . . by having chairmen come down and explain the legislation, and . . . by insisting that [Speaker] Albert and [Majority Leader] Boggs be there. In the old (footnote continued)

constitutes one of the party's major responses to decentralization of power in the House. "In 1986, for the first time, the whip was elected rather than hand-picked by the leadership." The change from appointive to elected whip was explained thusly: "Making the office elective was a concession to junior members. Since the 1970s, they had demanded a voice in picking the officer who seemed to be in line for Speaker. Also, they said the whip should act as a liaison officer between them and the leaders, not merely the leaders' enforcer and intelligence agent."[57] The change reinforces the Majority Whip's potential for succession to be Majority Leader and Speaker.[58]

Serving the Majority Whip is a whip system consisting of three segments: (1) a chief deputy whip and a number of other deputy whips appointed by the leadership; (2) a number of geographic or "zone" whips, "selected by the 19 regional subcaucuses into which the whip system divides the Democratic Caucus"; and (3) a number of "at large" whips, chosen by the leadership as links to groups such as "the black caucus, the women's caucus, and the freshman caucus."[59] This whole system meets

---

days, the leadership never came. There was no incentive for anyone else to come." P. Clancy & S. Elder, Tip: A Biography of Thomas P. O'Neill 124 (1980) (quoting O'Neill); see T. O'Neill, Man of the House 264 (1987).

[57]   Hill Leaders at 6.   See 1988 Congressional Quarterly Almanac 4.

[58]   As that succession was described: "Of the six Democratic floor leaders since 1949, [Thomas] Foley [(D-Wash.)] is the fifth to move up from whip. The exception was Wright; he was a deputy whip in 1976 when he beat Majority Whip John McFall of California and two other men to become leader". Hill Leaders at 5.

[59]   Dodd & Sullivan, "Majority Party Leadership and Partisan Vote Gathering: The House Democratic Whip System," in Understanding Congressional Leadership 227, 228, 231 (F. H. Mackaman ed. 1981).   The role of one regional whip was described this way:

(footnote continued)

with the Speaker and Majority Leader every Thursday, in a formalized echo of the old smaller "Board of Education," to discuss controversial legislation and general party matters.

Principally, the Majority Whip and his system poll the party on upcoming propositions, conducting about 80 whip polls each Congress in recent years.[60] The commodity of intelligence with which to shape party strategy is priceless, considering the basic logistics of the House: 435 Members who vote in 15 minutes or less, making it necessary to persuade the changeable votes early. Whip counts tend to be accurate -- in contrast the varying quality of counts or estimates by outside lobbyists -- because Members level with fellow party Members, who conduct the poll, as they need not with outsiders.[61] The importance of counts shows most on the occasions of the great test votes. Accounts of such struggles as expansion of the Rules Committee in 1961, and enactment of budget legislation in 1981, show the pivotal role of such counts.[62]

[Rep. Charles O.] Whitley [(D-N.C.)] is also a regional whip, and while that office is not important in some cases, it does seem to be here. The North Carolina Democratic delegation's record in the first two years of the Reagan administration was mostly one of support for the Democratic leadership, and Whitley must take some of the credit (or blame) for this. His own instincts seem solidly conservative, yet on the big votes he stayed with the Democrats and helped persuade others to do so.

M. Barone & G. Ujifusa, The Almanac of American Politics: 1984 877 (1983). In 1985 there were eight deputy whips (besides the chief deputy), and 32 assistant whips. 1985 Congressional Quarterly Almanac 73-G.

[60] Sinclair at 56.

[61] "The whip counts on the key roll calls in 1981 reportedly were accurate to within one vote." Sinclair at 64.

[62] For an account of the 1981 whip count's importance, see Sinclair at 195, 202. An account of the 1961 count is even (footnote continued)

     To conduct a poll, the system acts "only on
instruction from the Speaker, who is usually
responding to a request from the committee
chairman."[63]   The office of the Majority Whip
formulates the question to be asked, seeking to
identify what the "principal problem is, whether
it's an amendment or the passage of a bill or
adoption of the rule."[64] Sometimes a question is

---

more dramatic. Congressman Frank Thompson (D-N.J.) had
become chief counter for the forces of Speaker Rayburn
seeking to enlarge the Rules Committee, to add
proleadership, anticonservative coalition Members. The day
before the vote,

> Sam Rayburn likewise called a meeting of the "Board of
> Education" . . . . For an hour and a half, they
> scrutinized Thompson's list of Representatives
> committed to Rayburn. Thompson detailed the vote,
> state by state, as he had it calculated on his tally
> sheet. Thompson's calculations had been checked,
> rechecked, and rechecked again to make certain that
> every member listed as committed to Rayburn really
> would stand firm. Thompson's final total for Rayburn
> stood at 217 . . . .

MacNeil at 442. The count proved exact. Speaker Rayburn's
side won by 217 to 212.

[63] Sinclair at 62.

[64] Id. at 63. An academic observer explains that

> [t]o the leadership, depending on the phrasing of
> question, responses can indicate:
>
>   a. core support for a bill as reported by
> committee;
>   b. general support without specification of the
> nature of that support;
>   c. attendance for the vote;
>   d. potentiality for passage.

The richness of the information that can be gleaned
from whip counts obviously makes them extremely useful
to the leadership, and puts a premium on the manner in
which they are conducted.

(footnote continued)

simple; sometimes it can be as complicated as
"Will you support Chairman Staggers in voting
against the previous question on the rule for
consideration of S. 2589, the Energy Emergency
Act, so that a substitute rule can be considered
permitting separate votes on the question of
rating authority, price rollbacks, and energy
conservation plans?"[65]   Once the question is
formulated, the Majority Whip's office then
"transmits the written questions to the regional
whips . . . [who] are then supposed to talk with
each member in their zone, using information
provided in the [Majority Whip office's]
memorandum to explain the bill if necessary, and
report their results to the whip's office."[66]

Besides these counts, the whip system has a
host of other functions, the most traditional
being to ensure that Members turn up for
votes.[67] The whip system provides advance written
information on legislation in the form of "whip
advisories" on current and upcoming bills and
conference reports.[68] Members often rely heavily

Dodd, supra, at 38.

[65] Dodd, supra, at 39, quoting a question asked in a whip
count in the 93rd Congress.

[66] Id. at 63. Although the ideal is a poll of Members by
Members, often staff ask and/or answer the poll.

[67] At one time, this consisted of the Majority Whip's being
able to round up absent Members by knowing "'their habits,
the recreations, their loafing-places, the condition of
their health, and that of their families . . . ; what
churches they attend; what theaters they frequent -- in
short , all about them.'"   MacNeil at 98, quoting II C.
Clark, My Quarter Century of American Politics 337 (1920).
That function fell off in importance as recorded votes
became available on amendments in Committee of the Whole,
for Members sensitive to their attendance records did not
need to be rounded up for recorded votes.   Dodd at 36.

[68] Sinclair at 65-66; see Dodd, supra, at 34-36. A Whip
Advisory highlights the following:

1. Committee and Rules Committee action on the
(footnote continued)

on the whip advisory for guidance, particularly on less controversial legislation.[69]

A final major function of the whip system is in persuading other Members to go along with the party on votes, through "a variety of approaches: legislative logrolling, policy persuasion, party loyalty and esprit de corps, and use of concrete incentives."[70]   The Majority Whip and assistant whips may play a last-minute key persuasive function in "working the door" -- standing by floor entrances during votes, to make a brief pitch on the current floor proposition. Ordinarily, the manager of the bill, or other particularly interested members, work the door; the participation of the whips signals greater leadership and party interest. Working the door may be highly important, particularly during hectic periods when Members rush to the floor from committees or their offices without detailed knowledge of the proposition before the House, and the words of those working the door constitute a major voting cue.[71]   In its persuasive role, the

---

    bill, and any previous congressional action;
2. Who will be the floor manager;
3. Summary and background of the legislation (in
    several paragraphs);
4. Cost estimates; and
5. Minority views and anticipated amendments.

After the Majority Leader tentatively schedules a bill for floor action, the Majority Whip's office will request a draft whip advisory from the committee, and the committee, or a subcommittee handling the bill, prepares a draft. House Committee on Science and Technology, 99th Cong., Legislative Manual 90 (Comm. Print 4th ed. 1985).

[69]   The Majority Whip's office also distributes other forms of information: "whip-grams" ("shorter and more partisan than advisories"), and "a weekly leadership information pack" or "whip packet." Sinclair at 65-66.

[70]   Dodd & Sullivan, supra, at 241.

[71]   To take a 1987 example, Representative Timothy J. Penny (D-Minn.) described unhappily how Members did not hear the subtleties of his amendment when they came to vote. "At the
(footnote continued)

whip system may work closely with outside lobbies (or with the administration when their positions coincide).

Minority Leader and Minority Whip

The role of the House minority leadership warrants a briefer discussion than the majority leadership. Historically, the Minority Leader (whom Republicans call the Republican Leader) has occupied a clearly established post since 1883, when the tradition began that the minority signaled their choice of leader by putting up a losing candidate for Speaker.[72]   The minority party elects its leader in caucus, and has deposed leaders the same way.[73]

A Minority Leader's political powers come from being the party's floor leader, from relations with the majority party, and from outside status with the President and media. As

---

door [when Members enter the chamber to vote], all they hear is 'it's a 2 percent cut, or it's a 4 percent cut.'" 1988 Congressional Quarterly Almanac 455.

[72] Ripley at 28. The minority party had floor leaders before then only intermittently; "[b]etween 1861 and 1883, the identity of the minority floor leader is often unclear." Id. at 28 n.31.

[73]   Continuity -- the 1980's evidence notwithstanding -- is not as much a leadership tradition for House Republicans as it is for Democrats. While no House Democratic leader has been unseated in modern times, two Republicans have. Charles Halleck of Indiana (1935-69) ousted Joseph W. Martin Jr. of Massachusetts (1925-67) as minority leader in 1959, and Halleck in turn was defeated by Gerald R. Ford of Michigan in 1965 . . . .

[Minority Leaders have] none of the Speaker's powers over lower-level leadership posts, committee staffing and assignments, or the floor fate of members' bills, so he cannot compel allegiance like the Democrats' leader.

Hill Leaders at 8.

floor leader, the Minority Leader's role parallels the Majority Leader's: they give tactical signals to their side through speeches, amendments, and votes. In a favorable context, where they can draw on support from Democratic conservatives, Republican Leaders can win important floor battles. For example, in 1981, Minority Leader Robert Michel triumphed on the vote on the omnibus budget reconciliation bill that included much of President Reagan's legislative program. Similarly, in 1986, the Minority Leader led the forces that defeated the tax overhaul bill until the President came to terms with his disaffected House party.

As leader of the minority party, the Minority Leader "is expected to put forth legislative alternatives to [majority] proposals and to publicize these alternatives to the country."[74] When the House minority party is the same as the President's, as in 1955-60, 1969-76, and in the 1980s, those proposals usually are worked out together with the Administration. While the majority party controls the House's agenda, a Minority Leader has a number of means for putting forth these alternatives. Regular means include floor amendments and the motion that is the minority's prerogative, the motion to recommit. Special means include the "safety valves" such as defeating the previous question on special rules, and discharge petitions.

Within the party, the Minority Leader exercises influence by the stature of an elected leader. A Republican Leader's additional source of influence within the party comes from chairing the Executive Committee of the Committee on Committees, and from a major voice in the allocation of committee assignments to minority Members.

In relating to the majority party, the Minority Leader makes the critical strategic calls: whether to obstruct and defeat the majority

---

[74] Ripley at 29. The minority leader is aided by the "changes in House operations adopted in the 1970s [that] provided additional committee staffing for the Republican minority," Congressional Quarterly, Guide to Congress 386 (3d ed. 1982).

program, if possible, or to bargain for
compromise. Minority Leaders such as Joseph W.
Martin Jr. (R-Mass.), in the 1950s, and Robert
Michel (R-Ill.), in the 1980s, have maintained a
relationship with their Speakers at the same time
adversarial and yet friendly. They exchange
information about party preferences regarding
substance and scheduling, and work out deals when
possible, while fighting when that serves
better. The Minority Leader can "oppose outright
the majority party and its leadership, or use
parliamentary rules and procedures to win
concessions from the majority to thwart its
will."[75]
     Outside the House, a Minority Leader may
serve as a principal intermediary between the
President and the Congress. When the minority
party does not have a President as its chief, the
House minority leader, along with his opposite
number in the Senate, may become one of principal
national opposition figures. Either way, a leader
has a high status as a media spokesman. A symbol
of the position's prominence in the party and the
country was Minority Leader Gerald Ford's
selection to be appointed Vice President in 1974,
from which he succeeded to the Presidency.
     The Minority Whip carries out a function much
like the Majority Whip's. Like the Democrats, the
Republicans use an elaborate whip system with
regional and assistant whips to sound out in
advance, inform, persuade, and round up votes in
their party.[76] Also, the Minority Whip is elected
by his party, conferring on him a sure footing as
a voice of the party and as heir apparent if the
Minority Leader's post becomes vacant.[77] Still,

---

[75] R. H. Davidson & W. J. Oleszek, Congress and its Members
171 (1981).

[76] Ripley at 36. In 1985, the Republican Whip was assisted
by a chief deputy whip, two other deputy whips, four
regional whips, and one whip each for the sophomore and
freshmen classes. 1985 Congressional Quarterly Almanac 75-
G.

[77] For example, Representative Michel, who had been elected
Whip in 1974, won the leadership contest in 1980 to become
(footnote continued)

the post has its frustrating limits. Representative Trent Lott (R-Miss.) chose to give it up
in 1988 to run (successfully) for the Senate,
whereupon it was won by Representative Dick Cheney
(R-Wyo.), himself a former White House chief of
staff and distinguished author on House history.

Party Caucuses and Committees

Each House party uses its caucus and party
committees to provide additional leadership. The
House Democratic Caucus, consisting of all the
House Democrats, meets in its most important
session at the beginning of the Congress. It
chooses the party leaders -- not only the Speaker,
Majority Leader, and Majority Whip, but its own
head, the Caucus Chairman, who is assisted by a
Vice Chair (formerly secretary) of the Caucus (the
party position from which Representative Geraldine
Ferraro (D-N.Y.) ran for Vice President in
1984). Also, the caucus ratifies the
recommendations for committee appointments and
chairs, and decides on any rules changes.
Thereafter, the caucus, by its rules, meets at
least once a month, in closed session.

The Democratic Caucus has had ups and downs
in importance since its founding in 1796, with
intervals of significant power in the early 1800s,
in the early twentieth century following the
revolt against "Czar" Cannon, and in the early
1970s as the tool of the party's revolt against
conservative chairs. It became quiescent in the
late 1970s, and then revived to a limited extent
as a forum for debate in the 1980s under Caucus
Chairs Gillis Long (D-La.) and Richard Gephardt
(D-Mo.).[78] As described in the chapter on

Minority Leader, beating the campaign committee chair,
Representative Guy Vander Jagt (R-Mich.). The Minority Whip
in the 1980s, Representative Trent Lott (R-Miss.), added to
his position by occupying a seat on the Rules Committee,
providing a prominent position both to gather information
and to articulate the minority position.

[78] For an account of the caucus, see Granat, Democratic
Caucus Renewed as Forum for Policy Questions, 41 Cong. Q.
Week. Rep. 2115 (1983).

committee organization, the Steering and Policy Committee makes the party's basic decisions about committee appointments. The party also has a Democratic Congressional Campaign Committee to provide funding and other election support.[79]

Similarly, the Republican party meets collectively as the Republican Conference for functions like those of the Democratic Caucus. As in the Senate, where the Republican leadership includes a larger number of figures than the Democratic leadership, so in the House the Republicans elect not only a leader and a whip, but also elect for their Conference a chair, vice chair, and secretary; a chair of the Republican Policy Committee, which provides party direction; a chair of the Republican Research Committee; and a chair of the campaign committee.[80]

C.   FLOOR BUSINESS: THE ORDER OF BUSINESS, SPEECHES, VOTING, AND QUORUM CALLS

The next two sections address the mechanics of the House which set the stage each day for bill scheduling and management. This section addresses basic floor action: the daily order of business, speeches, voting, and quorum calls. These fill up much of the Congressional Record and a fair part of the House's day. The next section addresses the basic mechanics of bill processing: introduction, referral, calendaring, engrossment and enrollment. Procedural rules and tactics discussed in each of the following chapters make the most sense against the background of these underlying mechanics.

Daily Order of Business

---

[79]   Democratic Study Group, Democratic Campaign Committee and Democratic Steering & Policy Committee (1982).

[80]   Contested elections for most of these posts occurred in 1980. See Arieff, House Democrats, GOP Elect Leaders, Draw Battle Lines, 38 Cong. Q. Week. Rep. 3549 (1980).

Rule XXIV, the "Order of Business," seeks to
establish an orderly procedure for the House: It
begins with "Prayer by the Chaplain," and then
"[r]eading and approval of the Journal, unless
postponed."[81]   It continues with two matters that
rarely take any floor time.   "Correction of
reference of public bills" rarely occurs in the
manner suggested in the rule.[82]   "Disposal of
business on the Speaker's table," referring to the
procedure for messages to the House from the
President or the Senate,[83] goes as Hinds recites:

---

[81]   This consists of the Speaker announcing that "[t]he
Chair has examined the Journal of the last day's proceedings
and announces to the House his approval thereof," and
pausing.   If someone wants a recorded vote on that approval,
it occurs, most often when the minority party wants to see
what Members are in town.   Pursuant to Rule I(5)(b)(1), the
Speaker can postpone "the question of agreeing to the
Speaker's approval of the Journal" to another "place in the
legislative schedule on that legislative day."   This avoids
embarrassing Members who did not anticipate a need to be
present early on a day for roll calls.

Rule I(1) provides that a "motion that the Journal be
read" is in order "only if the Speaker's approval of the
Journal is not agreed to."   This does not occur.

[82]   Correction of reference is discussed in the next section
on the mechanics of bill processing.   It usually occurs by
unanimous consent at a convenient time, not the time fixed
in Rule XXIV.

[83]   See House Manual §§ 560 - 566 (receipt of messages
during sittings).   Rule XXIV(2) notes the types of messages
received: "[m]essages from the President," "[r]eports and
communications from heads of departments," "other
communications addressed to the House," and "bills,
resolutions, and messages from the Senate."   Messages from
the President are laid before the House by the Speaker, and
read in full (though the accompanying documents are not
read).   House Manual § 884; Deschler 34 § 1.

The Committee of the Whole House does not receive
messages; it rises (usually informally, but on occasion
formally), receives the message, and then goes back into
(footnote continued)

The messenger is introduced by the Doorkeeper
at the bar of the House, with the words, "Mr.
Speaker, a message from the President" (or
the Senate, as the case may be).   Thereupon
the messenger bows and addresses the Speaker
as "Mr. Speaker." The Speaker, with a slight
inclination, addresses the messenger as "Mr.
Secretary," since such is his title whether
he be from the President or the Senate.
Thereupon the messenger delivers the message
in a distinct voice that should be heard by
all the Members present.[84]

During adjournments the Clerk receives the message
and provides it to the Speaker.[85] Either way, the
Speaker lays the message before the House, and
sends it to the "Speaker's table," from which most
messages are referred to committee by the
automatic referral mechanisms.[86]

The following matter mentioned in Rule XXIV,
"[u]nfinished business," occurs infrequently.[87]

Committee of the Whole.   Deschler 32 §§ 1.8-1.10 (Senate
messages); House Manual §§ 330, 563.

[84]   V Hinds § 6591.

[85]   When the House is not sitting, the Clerk receives the
message, and transmits it to the Speaker with a covering
letter, who lays it before the House at the earliest
opportunity.   House Rule III(5); Deschler 34 § 1.6.

[86]   Some conference-related matters stay on the Speaker's
Table until timely, as discussed in the chapter on
conferences, but in any event, they take up no floor time.
House Manual § 883; Deschler 34 § 2 (referral of
presidential messages); Deschler 32 § 3.12 (conditions for
exceptional handling of Senate bill on Speaker's table);
Deschler 32 § 5.7 (holding at Speaker's Table until timely).

[87]   House Rule XXIV(3) and House Manual §§ 886-887 discuss
the procedure for unfinished business. See also Deschler 21
§ 1.3.   Votes that the Speaker has postponed (such as on
suspensions, or on approving special rules) constitute
"unfinished business," but these votes are brought up on
succeeding days at convenient time, not the beginning of the
(footnote continued)

Then, Rule XXIV prescribes the procedure developed in the nineteenth century for scheduling bills, the morning call of the calendar, which simply never occurs anymore.[88]   Instead, as discussed below, the House has evolved away from this Rule XXIV system.   It interrupts the procedure set forth in Rule XXIV to take up matters made privileged, either by unanimous consent, or by one of the routes by which bills or questions come to the floor discussed in the next chapter.

Recognition

The immediate question of what happens -- and the question of what happens moment by moment, as the day proceeds -- depends on who the Speaker recognizes.   That recognition power took a century to develop.   In 1789 the House adopted the rule, still on the books as Rule XIV(2), that "[w]hen two or more Members rise at once, the Speaker shall name the member who is first to speak."[89] With the rise in the late nineteenth century of the majority party control, the Speaker began exercising complete discretion regarding whom he would, and would not, recognize.[90]   In 1881 the

---

day. Rarely are there other kinds of "unfinished business," because most of the chamber's business that takes more than one day consists of major bills receiving consideration in Committee of the Whole, and "unfinished business" only means business unfinished at day's end in the House, not in Committee of the Whole. See House Manual § 886. Business in the House (as opposed to Committee of the Whole) rarely lasts more than one day, owing to the previous question and the Hour Rule. Still, something such as consideration of a presidential veto in the House might last more than one day, and thus become "unfinished business."

[88]   Rule XXIV(4) describes the morning hour.   See House Manual §§ 889, 890.   Rule XXIV(5) describes motions to go into Committee of the Whole. See House Manual § 892.

[89]   The rule's wording reflects how "[i]n the early history of the House, when business proceeded on presentation by individual Members, the Speaker recognized the Member who arose first; and in case of doubt there was an appeal from his recognition." House Manual § 753.
(footnote continued)

Speaker declined to entertain an appeal from his
decision on a question of recognition, cementing a
mighty power.[91]

---

[90]   In the first half of the nineteenth century, the custom
had already grown up that during debate on bills, the
Speaker would have "before him a list of the men desiring to
speak," and would recognize Members by following this list."
Follett at 253. Prior to the 1880s, the Speakers apparently
recognized members of both parties freely to move to suspend
the rules, thus allowing minority members to embarrass the
majority by shaping propositions and then forcing votes. It
was charged that minority members frequently offered
"resolutions on subjects of no practical standing in the
House, sometimes so artfully worded as to be political
traps, condemning many Members to political danger in their
districts, whether they voted for or against them." Bach at
25, quoting article by Hinds inserted in the Congressional
Record, January 7, 1909, p. 589.

In Hinds' precedents, "the first cited instance of the
Speaker's discretionary power occurred in 1881."   Bach,
supra, at 47, citing V Hinds § 6791. "About that time
[1880], Speaker Randall, without complaint of the House,
began to exercise the right to determine when he would
recognize for the motion [to suspend the rules], thus still
further placing it under control."   Bach, supra, at 25,
quoting article by Hinds inserted in the Congressional
Record, January 7, 1909, p. 589.

[91]   House Manual § 753. With the strengthening of such
Speakers, Follett could say in 1896 that "the practice has
gradually grown up of the Speaker's using this ordinary
parliamentary duty for political purposes, and recognizing
only such persons as he pleases." Follett at 250.

Once consolidated, the Speaker's recognition power was
potent indeed. Follett recounts the ends of sessions, when
recognition vel non determined whether Members would pass
their vital bills, and the House would "stop" time itself to
keep let that power continue its sway. At that point,

the power of the Speaker is at its height. Tremendous
pressure is brought to bear upon him. Day and night
his   room   is   crowded   with   members   begging   for
recognition. The struggle on the floor is severe. The
time is brief. Twice on March 3, 1887, [Speaker John
(footnote continued)

Part of the revolt against "Czar" Cannon in 1910 consisted of placing constraints on the Speaker's recognition power, which have endured. As the House Manual states:

> Although there is no appeal from the Speaker's recognition, he is not a free agent in determining who is to have the floor. The practice of the House establishes rules from which he may not depart. When the order of business brings before the house a certain bill he must first recognize, for motions for its disposition, the Member who represents the committee which has reported it.[92]

Hence, the rules regarding the relative levels of privilege govern the Speaker's recognition. Elaborate tables have been created reflecting which matters have highest privilege, which have high privilege, and which are privileged.

Of the principles of recognition, the ones which most affect the daily conduct of business concern the privilege of majority manager. "The order of recognition to offer amendments is within the discretion of the Chair, but practice indicates that he should recognize members of the committee handling the bill in the order of their seniority on the committee."[93] Through that practice, the majority manager, the "Member in charge" from the committee, controls the progress of floor proceedings. The majority manager ordinarily opens and closes debate, has priority to speak and to offer amendments and motions, and decides when to move to cut off further debate, as discussed in the chapter on bill management.[94]

G.] Carlisle [(D-Ky.)] had the minute-hand of the clock turned back.

Follett at 253-54.

[92] House Manual § 754.

[93] Deschler 29 § 5.1.

[94] For an example of the tactical value, after the Chair recognizes a minority Member to offer an amendment, the (footnote continued)

However, "when an essential motion made by
the Member in charge is decided adversely the
right to prior recognition passes to the leading
opponent of motion."[95]   Essential motions only
include a select few, primarily the motion for the
previous question, not mere defeat on amendments
or even on adoption of a conference report.
Defeat on "an essential motion" on the House floor
can be a matter of secondary significance, if it
occurs on a trivial bill, or can be a dramatic
moment -- a climax of a high-stakes procedural
battle over an important bill, marking the limit
of the majority leadership's power.   It opens up
the safety valves by which the majority leadership
must relinquish control of the agenda temporarily
when the opposition has the votes to seize
control.

Decorum in Debate

As noted above, pursuant to Rule I the
Speaker has responsibility for maintaining order
and decorum, including proper attire and no
smoking.[96]   House Rule XIV establishes the basic
procedures for debate in the House:

> When any Member desires to speak or deliver
> any matter to the House, he shall rise and
> respectfully address himself to "Mr.
> Speaker," and, on being recognized, may
> address the House from any place on the floor
> or from the Clerk's desk, and shall confine
> himself to the question under debate,
> avoiding personality.

---

chair may tactically choose to recognize a majority Member
for a substitute counteramendment.

[95]   Cannon at 153.   See House Manual § 755; Deschler 29 §§
5.14 - 5.16.

[96]   Rule XIV(7).   The Speaker maintains standards of proper
attire for Members ("coats and ties for male Members and
appropriate attire for female Members") by requesting
inappropriately attired Members to remove themselves and
appear in appropriate attire, and by refusing to recognize
them until they do so.   House Manual §§ 622, 763.

The rule requires Members to address themselves to "Mr. (or Madam) Speaker," or during debate in Committee of the Whole, to "Mr. (or Madam) Chairman" (referring to the Chairman of the Committee of the Whole). A number of limits are placed on what Members can say. A Member is to "confine himself to the question under debate," and to speak only once on each question, although there are ways to make multiple speeches.[97] In 1987, the House relaxed the previous ban on speaking of proceedings in the Senate (habitually referred to in debate only as "the other body"); Rule XIV(1) now provides that "Debate may include references to actions taken by the Senate or by committees thereof which are a matter of public record, and to the pendency or sponsorship in the Senate of bills, resolutions and amendments." The rule still forbids "other references to individual Members of the Senate, expressions of opinion concerning Senate action, or quotations from Senate proceedings." Presumably, Members should still avoid making inflammatory references to Senators, such as by telling them to "get off their butts."[98]

"[R]eferences to other Members may not be by familiar name," and certainly not by use of the pronoun "you," but "must be in the third person, by state designation."[99] Hence, Members constantly refer to each other in the third-person fashion: "Will the gentlelady from Nebraska yield for a question?"

House Rule XIV(5) provides the procedure for dealing with remarks out of order, principally personal insults such as accusations that another

---

[97] Rule XIV(6) limits Members other than the movers of matters to one speech, but they can speak again after amendments. House Manual § 762. The more complex situation in Committee of the Whole is discussed in House Manual § 873a.

[98] Deschler 29 § 14.1. See House Manual §§ 371-72.

[99] House Manual §§ 749, 354.

Member has engaged in hypocrisy, deception, intentional misrepresentation, or plain lying.[100] The procedure in the rule is called having the words "taken down":

> If a Member is called to order for words
> spoken in debate, the Member calling him to
> order shall indicate the words excepted to,
> and they shall be taken down in writing at
> the Clerk's desk and read aloud to the House;
> but he shall not be held to answer, nor be
> subject to the censure of the House therefor,
> if further debate or other business has
> intervened.

If a Member takes offense during Committee of the Whole, the words are taken down as in the House and read at the Clerk's desk, and the Committee rises automatically, for the matter to be dealt with in the House.[101]

Often the Member called to order will withdraw his objectionable statements by unanimous consent, or the Chair may rule them to have been in order. However, if the Chair rules the Member's words transgressed the rules of the House, he cannot proceed unless permitted by the House.[102] A classic example occurred in 1984, when the Speaker, angrily protesting on the floor how Members had challenged the Americanism of other Members before an empty House during special orders (when there was no one there to reply), described that as "the lowest thing that I have ever seen in my 32 years in Congress." The Minority Whip raised a point of order regarding the Speaker's comment (i.e., that accusing Members of "the lowest thing" was unparliamentary), and on his demand the Speaker's words were taken down and ruled out of order by the Speaker pro tempore.[103]

---

[100]   House Manual § 363.

[101]   House Manual § 761.

[102]   House Rule XIV(4).

[103]   Deschler 29 § 16.8.

Congressional Record and Time Control

What Members say is taken down by the House's official reporters and transcribed for the Congressional Record,[104] which records both speeches and actions, and the other components of House floor activity -- texts of legislation; roll calls; notations of bills introduced, referred, calendared, engrossed, enrolled, and signed; lists of messages received; and a host of other matters. Elaborate practices govern the preparation of the Congressional Record, which is compiled by staffs of the House and Senate and printed overnight by the Government Printing Office.

The most important practice is the privilege of "revising and extending."[105] Using this privilege, a Member can put in additional parts of speeches, or take out or change what she said. Thus, for example, a Member may rise during debate, comment that "I rise in support of the Jones amendment and ask unanimous consent to revise and extend my remarks," and sit down; later, a full-length speech text may be inserted in the Congressional Record at that point. Some critics express disappointment that the Record is not a verbatim transcript, fearing this misleads agencies and courts regarding legislative history. However, the privilege of revising and extending conserves much precious floor time, and allows Members to express their minds simply and directly, and then lay out a full technical treatment in the Record. The reporters under the Chief of Reporters who transcribe and compile the Record deliver raw transcript of speeches back to

---

[104] House Rule XXXIV provides for official reports of the House. For discussions of the precedents regarding the Congressional Record, see House Manual §§ 924-929.

[105] In Committee of the Whole, Members can request leave to revise and extend their own remarks; in the House, Members can request general leave that all Members involved in a certain debate be allowed to revise and extend their remarks. House Manual § 929.

Members who revise and edit.[106]

There is one major constraint on putting
undelivered speeches into the Record. Under rules
adopted in the 1970s and 1980s, when a Member
inserts in the Record a speech of which no part
was delivered orally, the speech gets marked off
in the Record by printing in a different
typeface. The reader who sees such print knows
the Member did not present any of it aloud. The
Record also includes a section entitled
"Extensions of Remarks," consisting of speeches,
almost all by House Members, that were not
delivered at all, mostly remarks unrelated to a
particular day's proceedings.[107]

Numerous House rules and procedures limit
time, such as the Hour Rule for debate in the
House, the five-minute rule during amending in
Committee of the Whole, and the limits in special
rules for general debate in Committee of the
Whole. When the Chair recognizes a Member for the
limited time pursuant to such rules and
procedures, the Member controls that time. Under
the Hour Rule, a Member may yield specified
amounts of that time to another Member, who then
controls it, as in the custom when the Chair
recognizes the majority manager of a special rule
for an hour and that majority manager yields half
the hour to the minority manager.[108] The minority
manager may, in turn, further yield time to the

---

[106] Much of the time this is the staff's job -- personal
staff for speeches, committee staff for "remarks of Members
of the committee who serve as floor managers on a specific
piece of legislation." House Republican Manual at 43.

[107] Also included in Extensions are speeches made during
the period for one-minute speeches that went on more than
300 words, and speeches that were sent to a Member to revise
and extend and not returned before the 9:00 p.m. deadline.
See Advisory Committee on Automation and Standardization of
Congressional Proceedings to the Joint Committee on
Printing, 95th Cong., Current Procedures and Production
Processes of the Congressional Record (Comm. Print 1978).

[108] Deschler 29 § 8.10.

various minority Members wishing to speak.   The
controller of time must be careful to yield time
for debate only, for if he yields time to another
Member to offer an amendment, he may lose control
of the floor.[109]   In contrast, Members obtaining
recognition under the five minute rule cannot
yield time.[110]

Members who control time may be asked by
others to yield for debate, the format being for
the would-be interrupter to ask the Chair ("Mr.
Speaker, will the gentleman yield?").[111]   The
controller of time has discretion whether to
yield, or having done so, whether to reclaim his
time.[112]   The Member yielding for debate must
remain on his feet absent unanimous consent.[113]

One Minute and Special Order Speeches

On most days, what the House does immediately
after its first preliminaries -- usually prayer
and handling of the Journal and messages -- is
that by unanimous consent, the Speaker recognizes
Members for "one minute speeches."[114]   There is no
rule governing this; the practice occurs by
unanimous consent, under arrangements between the
parties regularized in 1937.[115]   During the period

---

[109]   Deschler 29 § 12.1

[110]   House Manual § 872.

[111]   Deschler 29 § 11.1.

[112]   House Manual § 750.

[113]   Deschler 29 §§ 8.2-8.6.

[114]   On occasion, the Chair will allow one minute speeches
at other times during the day, such as when important
business has not yet arrived, but is expected soon, and the
leadership does not want to start any other serious matter
until that business arrives.

[115]   In 1937, Majority Leader Rayburn established the basic
practice that he would object to early-morning speeches
(footnote continued)

for one minute speeches, a Member will line up to "address himself to the House on almost any subject that comes to mind."[116]   Usually his only live audience is the other Members waiting to give their own one minute speeches, but the speech goes into the Congressional Record, out over the closed circuit television, and out to the audience reached by the C-SPAN cable television network.

The period for one minute speeches provides a convenient forum to let many Members quickly get their views back to constituents.   Whether the press reports the speeches, a Member can have extracts from the Congressional Record printed and sent back home almost immediately.   Some one minute speeches concern topical issues, such as reactions to an administration position or to an upcoming legislative item.   Some have nothing at all to do with government, and speak to the mundane concerns of the district, such as historical anniversaries, personal tragedies, high school basketball championships, and the like.

At the end of the day the Speaker will recognize Members for "special orders."   These resemble one minute speeches in that they occur outside the time for consideration of pending legislation; the difference is that one-minute speeches come early in the day and last only a minute or less, while special orders come late in the day and can last much longer, 60 minutes being the maximum period.   Some Members become known for taking pains over the years to deliver many serious and thoughtful speeches during special orders.   The House arranges special orders well in advance, by unanimous consent approval of requests for special order time.   It is implicit that the special order will give way to any legislative business that happens still to be going on when the scheduled time arrives.[117]   Once special

---

unless they were limited in duration to one minute.   See F. Riddick, The United States Congress: Organization and Procedure 98 (1949); VI Deschler § 6.1.

[116]   House Republican Manual at 41.   The procedures for one minute speeches are discussed in Deschler 21 § 7.

(footnote continued)

orders begin, usually no further legislative business is conducted, so that the Members know they can leave that day.[118]

In 1984, controversy arose over special orders, after a group of conservative Republican Members began making extensive use of them to attack the Democratic Party. The majority responded with a direction that the chamber's cameras, which provide live broadcasts of House proceedings, periodically give wide-angle coverage of the entire House chamber, which showed that no Members were present to listen to the speeches.[119] Also, a trailer, like a subtitle, would be run from time to time announcing that the House had finished its legislative business for the day. Finally, the Speaker established a policy on special order speeches:

> (1) alternate recognition between majority and minority members in the order in which they seek recognition; (2) recognize Members for special-order speeches first who want to address the House for five minutes or less, alternating between majority and minority members, otherwise in the order in which permissions were granted; (3) then recognition of Members who wish to address the House for longer than five minutes and up to one hour, alternating between majority and minority members in the order in which permissions were granted by the House.[120]

---

[117] See VI Deschler § 7.1.

[118] On occasion when the House awaits some development, such as on the eve of recess when the only remaining business is action on some matter which the Senate has not messaged over yet, special orders occur while the House is waiting and thus before legislative business is finished. VI Deschler § 7.4.

[119] For the precedent that began the wide-angle coverage, see 4 Deschler § 6.13.

[120] Deschler 21 § 8.10; House Manual § 753.

D. BILL PROCESSING

As the House processes its thousands of bills each Congress, it moves them along a path that includes both the key political processes, in committee and on the floor, discussed in detail herein, and also through a number of relatively routine steps that provide the background structure.   In the nineteenth century, these routine steps took up much of the House's time.   As the press of business required time-saving methods, the House "automated" these steps by having them occur without requiring floor time or Member attention.   Currently, staff conduct these processes, producing lists printed in the Congressional Record after the end of the day's proceedings.   The mechanical processes each deserve brief mention.

Bill Processing: Introduction, Cosponsorship, And Referral

A bill starts when a Member introduces it. In the early years of the House, a Member needed leave, on motion, to introduce a bill, and did so by obtaining recognition on the floor.   As the House began to consider Member introduction largely noncontroversial, leave became routine in minor cases and timeconsuming in major ones and was dropped late in the nineteenth century.[121] Today, Rule XXII(4)(a) simply requires that bills "be delivered, indorsed with the names of Members introducing them, to the Speaker . . . ."

The prime sponsor of the bill must himself sign the bill before placing it in the "hopper," the term used to describe the receptacle for legislation.[122]   Upon   introduction,   Rule

---

[121] In 1887, "[i]t was provided that private bills could be introduced by simply filing them in a box on the Clerk's desk," which "removed a great bottleneck . . . .   An entire stage in the legislative process was dropped."   Damon at 167.   In 1890, the House extended that simplified procedure to public bills as well.

(footnote continued)

XXII(4)(a) provides that the next day's Congressional Record include the title of the bill, and the committee of reference. Typically, the Record includes, after the end of the day's proceedings, a section entitled "Public Bills and Resolutions" listing newly introduced bills by title and sponsor. Members can introduce bills "by request," as "a way of limiting the responsibility of the introducer, and of notifying other members that his heart was not in it."[123]

Cosponsorship did not exist in the House (although it had started in the Senate) as late as 1967. Only one Member could sponsor a bill, and other Members supporting the bill had to signal their support by the wasteful dodge of introducing an identical bill. Starting in 1967, first 25 Members, and now any number of Members, may cosponsor a bill; Rule XXII(4)(a) provides that "[t]wo or more Members may introduce jointly any bill, or resolution."[124] They may either cosponsor it at the time of introduction, or later at any time until it is reported, and by unanimous consent (which is routinely given) may delete cosponsorship.[125]

---

[122] Deschler 16 § 2.1.

[123] Damon at 169. For example, the chair of a committee may introduce a draft bill of the administration "on request." This gives the administration bill the dignity of a high-level sponsor, without preventing the chair from favoring his own changes or version. A rule of 1888 first provided for introduction "on request," Damon at 169, presumably because the automatic filing eliminated the opportunity for a Member to explain on the floor, when introducing the bill, any reservations he had.

[124] Deschler 16 §§ 2.2, 2.9.

[125] Rule XXII(4)(b)(1) provides that "The name of any Member shall be added as a sponsor of any bill or resolution . . . and shall appear as a sponsor in the next printing of that bill or resolution: Provided, That a request signed by such Member is submitted by the first sponsor to the Speaker . . . ." If the bill receives a multiple referral, consponsorship may occur until "the day on which the last committee authorized to consider and (footnote continued)

A Member does not formally bind himself by cosponsorship -- he may freely vote to amend or even to defeat a measure he cosponsors, just as, for that matter, a sponsor is free to criticize or disinherit his brainchild -- but cosponsorship counts as a statement of political support. A cosponsor receives praise or criticism from persons interested in the bill, and a bill that obtains a large number of cosponsors appears to have widespread support. Under Rule XXII(4)(b), the Congressional Record lists cosponsors at the time of introduction when it announces the introduction of the bill; it lists post-introduction cosponsorships the day after they occur, typically in a list after the end of the day's proceedings under a heading, "Additional Sponsors"; and the bill goes through multiple printings, which list new and deleted cosponsors.[126]

---

report such bill or resolution reports it to the House." Rule XXII(4)(b)(1).

Rule XXII(4)(b)(2) provides for deleting cosponsorship: "The name of any Member listed as a sponsor of any such bill or resolution may be deleted by unanimous consent, but only at the request of such Member, and such deletion shall be indicated in the next printing of the bill or resolution (together with the date on which such name was deleted)." As with cosponsorship, so too deletion of consponsorship may occur until "the last committee authorized to consider and reports such bill or resolution reports it to the House." Rule XXII(4)(b)(2). The same provision specifies that "the Speaker shall not entertain a request to delete the name of the first sponsor of any bill or resolution."

[126] Rule XXII(4)(b)(3) provides that "The addition of the name of any Member, or the deletion of any name by unanimous consent, of a sponsor of any such bill or resolution shall be entered on the Journal and printed in the Record of that day." New bill printings, with the new or deleted cosponsors, occur pursuant to Rule XXII(4)(b)(4), which provides that "Any such bill or resolution shall be reprinted (A) if the Member whose name is listed as the first sponsor submits to the Speaker a written request that it be reprinted, and (B) if twenty or more Members have been added as sponsors of the bill or resolution since it was (footnote continued)

Every bill, once introduced, is referred to
committee by the Speaker, pursuant to Rule
X(5)(a): "Each bill, resolution or other matter
which relates to a subject listed under any
standing committee named in [Rule X(1)] shall be
referred by the Speaker . . . ." As discussed in
the chapter on committee jurisdiction, often
Members and staff consult in advance with the
Speaker or Parliamentarian, and then the
Parliamentarian makes the referral on behalf of
the Speaker, which may be a referral to single or
multiple committees. The Congressional Record
states, in the column on "Public Bills and
Resolutions," the committees to which bills have
been referred. Subsequent to referral, the
Speaker may change an original multiple referral,
which the Congressional Record will list in a
column with a heading such as "Subsequent Action
on a Reported Bill Sequentially Referred."

Formerly, there had been floor contests over
referrals, and Rule XXII(4)(a) still provides for
them.[127] However, typically any changes or
corrections approved by the Speaker (in reality,
the Parliamentarian) are made by having the
pertinent committee chairman rise during one of
the periods the House is handling unanimous
consent business, and ask unanimous consent to
make the change.

---

last printed."

[127]   The traditional mechanism for contesting referral was
the motion for a change of reference, which became
privileged when authorized by the committee claiming
jurisdiction. Rule XXIV sets aside, as the third matter in
the daily order of business, "Correction of reference of
public bills." Rule XXII(4)(a) provides that "correction in
case of error of reference may be made by the House, without
debate, in accordance with Rule X [which specifies the
committee jurisdictions] on any day immediately after the
reading of the Journal, by unanimous consent, or on motion
of a committee claiming jurisdiction, or on the report of
the committee to which the bill has been erroneously
referred." For the privileged nature of the committee-
authorized motion to correct reference, on those rare
occasions of a real dispute, see House Manual § 854.

Reporting and Calendaring

Like introduction, reporting and calendaring now also occur automatically. The early House allowed committees a specific time period to make their reports, but floor congestion made it increasingly difficult for many committees to report.[128] Accordingly, the 1890 rules eliminated the need for a floor report. Rule XIII(2) provides that "[a]ll reports of committees . . . shall be delivered to the Clerk for printing and reference to the proper calendar under the direction of the Speaker."[129] When time is short, Members often ask unanimous consent for permission that their committees may report outside of House hours, such as "until midnight" or "during the adjournment."[130]

Reported bills go onto the House calendars. The calendar system in its current form resulted from the rules revision of 1880.[131] Physically,

---

[128] Thomas Jefferson explained that "[t]he chairman of the committee, standing in his place, informs the House that the committee . . . have directed him to report the same . . . which he is ready to do when the House pleases to receive it." House Manual § 418. By the end of the nineteenth century, floor congestion had become so great that even the provision of a special period, the "morning hour" for reports of committees, failed to alleviate it, "and unprivileged reports were buried under a mass of more privileged legislation." Damon at 69.

[129] Today, only those committees privileged to report, principally the Rules and Appropriations committees, and on certain matters, the Budget and House Administration committees, actually make floor reports, not so much out of any preference for a live report, as because they can receive immediate consideration of their resolutions and bills.

[130] See Deschler 17 § 43.

[131] While in 1820 a system of five "calendars" was established for use in Committee of the Whole, those were only categories for matters, not true calendars in the sense (footnote continued)

calendars consist of lists of bills and other matters maintained by the office of the Clerk of the House.   When the Speaker (actually, staff acting under the direction of the Parliamentarian) refers a bill or other matter to a calendar, the Clerk's office adds that matter to the pertinent calendar in chronological order of referral.

Each bill reported goes to one of three calendars specified in Rule XIII.   First and foremost is the Union Calendar, the "Calendar of the Committee of the Whole House on the state of the Union."   Most bills go on the Union Calendar, the exceptions being private bills and certain House Calendar matters.   Under Rule XXIII(3), bills on the Union Calendar require consideration in Committee of the Whole.[132]

Second is the House Calendar.   At one time, the House Calendar included a sizable fraction of the work of the House of Representatives. However, today few matters go on it,[133] primarily

---

of complete listings of all items in the category.   "The first actual calendar under the present meaning of the term," i.e., "a complete listing of items awaiting consideration," was a "calendar of private bills committed to the Committee of the Whole which was established in 1839." Damon at 187.

In 1879, the House "instructed a committee of its most skillful parliamentarians" to revise its rules, which the House debated "[f]rom time to time for two months . . . in great detail," producing "a labor brilliant and far-reaching." McConachie at 38.   This 1880 rules revision produced the calendar system of Union, House, and Private calendars.   Initially, the House itself decided motions to refer matters to each calendar, but the Reed Rules of 1890 gave the Speaker authority to automatically refer matters to calendars. Damon at 191.

[132] Exceptions occur when bills are considered under suspension of the rules, since among the rules suspended are those requiring consideration in Committee of the Whole, or under a special rule that waives consideration in Committee of the Whole.

[133] Rule XIII has provided since 1880 for the referral of (footnote continued)

special rules, changes in the House rules, ethics resolutions (such as those providing for censure of misbehaving Members), and some constitutional amendments. Matters on the House Calendar usually do not receive consideration in Committee of the Whole.[134]   Third is the Private Calendar, for private bills such as those for the relief of individual aliens seeking to stay in the country, and individual citizens injured by the government.

Besides these three calendars, to which all reported bills are referred, there are two derivative calendars. The Consent Calendar consists of bills on the House and Union calendars, which a Member places on the Consent Calendar as well, in anticipation that the House will pass them by unanimous consent. The Discharge Calendar consists of motions to discharge bills or special rules still pending in committee. The private, consent, and discharge procedures each receive separate discussion below.

Under Rule XIII(2), the Congressional Record typically includes a list of bills reported and calendared after the end of the day's proceedings

---

bills to the Union or House calendar. The Union Calendar receives bills involving money or property: "bills raising revenue, general appropriation bills, and bills of a public character directly or indirectly appropriating money or property." The House Calendar receives bills not involving money or property: "bills of a public character not raising revenue nor directly or indirectly appropriating money or property."

Although the rule has not changed in this respect since 1880, the House calendar has declined in importance. "Comparison of the calendars for Dec. 1, 1890, shows a ratio of about five bills on that of the House to twelve on that of the Committee of the Whole on the State of the Union." McConachie at 101. Today the proportion of bills referred to the House Calendar is far smaller. This has resulted from a broadening of the interpretation of what is included in bills "indirectly" affecting money.

[134]   They receive consideration in Committee of the Whole only by unanimous consent or by a special rule so providing. See House Manual § 867 (noting procedure for Legislative Reform Act of 1970).

under a heading, "Reports of Committees on Public
Bills and Resolutions."   Each day that the House
is   in   session,   the   Clerk   prints   out   revised
calendars in a key reference source, the <u>Calendars
of the United States House of Representation and
History of Legislation</u>.[135]

Engrossment and Enrollment

When the House passes a bill, it has the bill
prepared formally to be messaged to the Senate, a
process known as "engrossment."   Technically, the
House makes a decision whether to order the bill
to be engrossed.   In fact, almost invariably the
Speaker simply states that "[t]he question is on
the engrossment and third reading of the bill,"
and immediately thereafter, "The bill is ordered
to be engrossed and read a third time . . . . "[136]

In engrossment, "a bill is printed on special

---

[135]   Today it is as true as in 1949, when Riddick stated it
(apparently   quoting   an   even   older   source)   that   "the
calendars of business and the indexes of legislation are
constantly being changed and represent a great volume of
work."   F. Riddick, <u>The United States Congress</u> 204 (1949).
Besides   the   calendars,   this   publication   includes   an
invaluable background on bills (the "History of Legislation"
in the publication's title).

[136]   The Speaker recites this formula after the House acts
on the amendments reported by the Committee of the Whole,
and before the opportunity for a motion to recommit.   In
Jefferson's   time,   "the   question   whether   it   shall   be
engrossed and read a third time" was "usually the most
interesting   contest . . . . the   main   trial   of   strength
between [the bill's] friends and opponents."   House Manual §
429.   Members used to be able to delay final passage by
demanding a reading in full, which had to wait until the
bill was engrossed.   See D. M. Berman, <u>A Bill Becomes a Law</u>
111-112 (3d ed. 1966) (Mississippi Congressman delayed final
passage of civil rights bill for one day by demanding a
third reading).   However, rarely does anyone now ask for a
recorded vote on engrossment (although it is available; see
Deschler 24 § 8.2), and Rule XXI(1) now provides that the
third reading only be "by title."

paper by direction of the enrolling clerk under supervision of the Clerk of the House."[137]   The enrolling clerk prints House bills, and House amendments to Senate bills, on blue paper. Often, immediately after passage, the bill manager makes a unanimous consent request that in the course of engrossment, the Clerk may make technical corrections in section numbers and cross-references to make the bill come out neat and consistent when prepared.[138]   The Congressional Record does not list when engrossment is completed (only the formal House Journal lists the Clerk's certification at that time), but engrossment is usually swift. When completed, the bill is messaged over to the Senate where the Congressional Record notes the presentation of the message.

When both the House and Senate have passed a bill in identical form, they have the bill formally prepared for signature and presentation to the President, a process known as "enrollment." The officer of the chamber that originated the particular measure -- the Clerk of

---

[137]   Deschler 24 § 8.1. The preparation of the copy for printing is more fully described thusly:

> [The enrolling clerk] receives all the papers relating to the bill, including the official Clerk's copy of the bill as reported by the standing committee and each amendment adopted by the House. From this material he prepares the engrossed copy of the bill as passed, containing all the amendments agreed to by the House . . . . At this point the measure ceases technically to be called a bill and is termed "an act" signifying that it is the act of one body of the Congress, although it is still popularly referred to as a bill. The engrossed copy is printed on blue paper and a certificate that it passed the House of Representatives is signed by the Clerk of the House.

How Our Laws are Made, H. Doc. No. 97-120, 97th Cong., 1st Sess. 34 (1981).

[138]   That request must be made in the House, not in Committee of the Whole. Deschler 24 §§ 8.4-8.7.

the House, or the Secretary of the Senate, as the
case may be -- performs the enrollment.   In
enrollment, the bill is printed on parchment in
its final form.[139]   At this stage, technical
corrections can still be made (and, on rare
occasions, major amendments), but only by the
House and Senate passing a concurrent resolution
directing the Clerk to make the correction.[140]

---

[139]   House Manual § 574, citing 1 U.S.C. § 106.   In
exceptional circumstances, such as when a continuing
resolution must be signed by the President immediately to
close a period when the government has gone unfunded, the
two Houses can waive the printing on parchment.

The process has been described fully thus:

The enrolling clerk of the House (with respect to
bills originating in the House) receives the original
engrossed bill, the engrossed Senate amendments, the
signed conference report, the several messages from
the Senate, and a notation of the final action by the
House, for the purpose of preparing the enrolled
copy.   From these he must prepare meticulously the
final form of the bill . . . .

The enrolled bill is printed on parchment paper,
with a certificate on the reverse side of the last
page, to be signed by the Clerk of the House stating
that the bill originated in the House of
Representatives . . . .

How Our Laws Are Made, supra, at 44.

[140]   Deschler 24 § 6.   By Rule X(4)(d), the House vests in
the Committee on House Administration the function of
"examining all bills and joint resolutions which shall have
passed both Houses to see that they are correctly
enrolled."   Thus, the enrolled bill "is examined for
accuracy by the Committee on House Administration . . . .
When the Committee is satisfied with the accuracy of the
bill the Chairman of the Committee attaches a slip stating
that it finds the bill truly enrolled and sends it to the
Speaker of the House for his signature." How Our Laws are
Made, supra, at 45.

Once the bill is enrolled, it is delivered to
the Speaker for his signature. Rule I(4)
authorizes the Speaker "to sign enrolled bills
whether or not the House is in session."[141] First
the Speaker, and then the Senate's President
(either the Vice President or the President Pro
Tempore) sign the bill. Then it is presented to
the President for signature or veto.

---

[141] Speakers Pro Tempore chosen by the Speaker's
designation do not sign enrolled bills, House Manual § 634,
in contrast to Senate Presidents Pro Tempore who do,
Deschler 6 § 4.5.

5
Agenda Setting and Structuring House Proceedings[1]

A. OVERVIEW AND HISTORY

Overview

House Rule XXIV provides an "Order of Business"

---

[1] Sources cited frequently in this chapter include R. E.
Damon, The Standing Rules of the United States House of
Representatives (Ph.D. dissertation, 1971) (available from
University Microfilms) (Damon); G. B. Galloway, History of
the House of Representatives (rev. ed. S. Wise 1976)
(Galloway); B. Sinclair, Majority Leadership in the U.S.
House (1983) (Sinclair); L.G. McConachie, Congressional
Committees (1898) (McConachie); M.P. Follett, The Speaker of
the House of Representatives (1896) (Follett); DeA. S.
Alexander, History and Procedure of the House of
Representatives (1916) (Alexander); J. Robinson, The House
Rules Committee (1963) (Robinson); S. M. Matsunaga & P.
Chen, Rulemakers of the House (1976) (Matsunaga & Chen);
House Committee on Rules, 97th Cong., 2d Sess., A History of
the Committee on Rules (Comm. Print 1983) (Rules Committee
History); Bach, The Structure of Choice in the House of
Representatives: The Impact of Complex Special Rules, 18
Harv. J. Legis. 553 (1981) (cited as Bach, with page numbers
in Harv. J. Legis.); Plattner, Rules Under Chairman Pepper
Looks Out for the Democrats, 43 Cong. Q. Week. Rep. 1671
(footnote continued)

for the House to schedule its proceedings, which, as previously noted, the House never follows. Rather, the modern House has evolved two major and various minor routes to the floor for bills (and other matters). Approximately 150 to 200 bills per Congress, including most of the important ones, come by a "special rule" from the Rules Committee. As Speaker Thomas P. "Tip" O'Neill explained in 1987, "What makes the Rules Committee so important is that it sets the agenda for the flow of legislation in the House and ensures that the place runs smoothly and doesn't get bogged down."[2] The Rules Committee's powers include screening out of some controversial bills, structuring floor consideration including deciding what amendments to allow, and settling jurisdictional disputes. Several hundred more bills of some importance come to the floor by suspension of the rules, a procedure that allows no floor amendments and requires a two-thirds vote for passage.

Bills also come to the floor by a variety of lesser-used routes. The discharge petition, although infrequently used, may be the most important of these lesser routes for the balance in the House. Through it, a majority of the total membership of the House (i.e., 218) can force any measure onto the floor for consideration, no matter how intense the resistance of the committee of jurisdiction or the party leadership. In 1982, for example, the administration succeeded in forcing the House to take up the balanced budget amendment, over the strenuous resistance of the majority leadership, by use of the discharge procedure.

(1985)(Rules Under Chairman Pepper); Cooper, House Use of Suspensions Grows Drastically, 36 Cong. Q. Week. Rep. 2694 (1978) (Cooper); Oppenheimer, Legislative Reform 91, 99 (L. N. Rieselbach ed. 1978) (Oppenheimer); S. Bach, Suspension of the Rules in the House of Representatives (Cong. Res. Serv. May 12, 1986) (Bach); Richard S. Beth, Outline and Historical Development of the Discharge Rule in the House of Representatives (Cong. Res. Serv. Dec. 30, 1982) (Beth); F. Riddick, The United States Congress: Structure and Organization (1940) (F. Riddick (1949)).

[2] T. O'Neill, Man of the House 158 (1987).

The Consent and Private Calendars, the routes for very minor bills, have subsided in importance with the modern shift of most pension and claims work to agencies and courts. "Privileged committees," most significantly the Appropriations Committee, can move their bills directly onto the floor under Rule XI(4)(a); so can conference committees under Rule XXVIII(1)(a). Members can raise directly on the floor a "question of privilege" under Rule IX when it affects the chamber and its Members. A final miscellaneous route not used in recent times is Calendar Wednesday under Rule XXIV(4).

The routes by which the House moves reported bills onto the floor matter greatly. These routes determine which bills come to the floor, and how they proceed on the floor: whether passage takes a majority vote or two-thirds; what amendments are in order; and what debate is allowed. Such determinations are the essence of procedural power. Some of that power lies in the hands of the chairs of the committees of jurisdiction, and the committee Members with whom the chairs consult, as they consider what route to request. However, much of that power lies with those who determine what moves along the routes, namely, the Rules Committee and the majority party leadership. Conversely, the safety valves in these routes, such as the means for defeating or changing special rules, and the discharge procedure, provide the House rank and file and the minority party with countervailing power.

History of House Scheduling

For two centuries, the House has experimented with a variety of scheduling mechanisms. In the nineteenth century, faced with a crush of business, the House sought to develop a "morning hour for the consideration of bills called up by committees," an orderly calendar call procedure by which each committee would call up, in turn, bills of its choice.[3] This system never really worked,

---

[3] Earliest procedure gave the Speaker discretion to decide what questions the House should address, unless the House (footnote continued)

for when the minority party stalled, it took too long to work through calendar calls.[4] Although House Rule XXIV, which codifies the House's "Order of Business," still provides for new business to come up through the morning call of the calendar, the last "morning hour" call occurred in 1933, and even then it was a throwback.[5]

Instead of calendar calls, the majority party turned in the late nineteenth century to conferring special status directly on the bills it wanted to reach. At first it used the motion to suspend the rules by a two-thirds vote.[6]

---

itself decided to take up a particular subject. House Manual § 349 (Jefferson's description, based on British precedents). The House adopted its first rules on the subject in 1811 and 1822, prescribing an order of business with specific periods for presentation of various kinds of business. Alexander at 214; IV Hinds § 3056 at 142, and § 3155 at 193; House Manual § 878. For the later evolution, see IV Hinds § 3056, at 142-44; House Manual § 878; Damon at 181-86. The morning call of the calendar would be for bills on the House Calendar. After that, Members would move to take up bills on the Union Calendar by going into Committee of the Whole. Damon at 184.

[4] "Here came the opportunity of the minority, which got to be so expert in preventing important bills from being reached by simply filibustering away the two hours upon minor measures, that the sixty-minute period came to be called the 'nine-holes,' an allusion to the familiar noughts and crosses of school-boys." McConachie at 168.

[5] See 6 Deschler 21 § 4. A 1927 writer called the "morning hour" a "dead letter." P. D. Hasbrouck, Party Government in the House of Representatives 100 (1927). The morning hour for a call of the calendar should not be confused with Calendar Wednesday, a separate procedure.

[6] In 1822, the House had adopted a rule providing: "Nor shall any rule be suspended, except by a vote of at least two-thirds of the Members present." V Hinds § 6790, at 902. "A Member would introduce a resolution to make a bill or bills -- say from the Committee on Naval Affairs -- a special order for an advanced date . . . . When its turn came in the Morning Hour the Naval Affairs would present this resolution, and try to get for it the necessary two-thirds vote." McConachie at 191.

Eventually, the majority turned to a hitherto
unusued[7] but more promising tool, the Rules
Committee chaired by the Speaker, with its
privileged right to report.[8]   In 1882,
Representative Thomas B. Reed (R-Maine)
established a key precedent that when the Rules
Committee reported a resolution to change the
rules, dilatory tactics were out of order.[9]   The
following year, the Rules Committee reported a
resolution -- the first "special rule" -- to make
privileged, and to create a special procedure for,
a single bill, the tariff bill which was the major
bill of the year.[10]

---

[7]   For the early history of the Rules Committee, see Rules
Committee History at 33-52.   From 1789 on, the House used
first select, and then standing, Committees on Rules to
recommend amendments and rewritings of the House rules.
Notwithstanding its potentially great assets, until the
1880s the Rules Committee continued to concern itself only
with amending the general House rules and not with procedure
for individual bills.   Its role was much like today's Senate
Committee on Rules and Administration, which concerns itself
with the Senate rules, not individual bills.

[8]   In 1841, the Rules Committee gained the right to report
"at any time," the essence of its privileged status, and in
that year the House established an isolated but significant
precedent of emergency use of a resolution from the Rules
Committee to change procedures to get through a particular
matter.   See V Hinds § 5221; Rules Committee History at 45;
Alexander at 191-92.   The 1841 incident, part of the origin
of debate limitations in Committee of the Whole, is
discussed in the chapter on bill management.   In 1853 the
Rules Committee enhanced its privilege by gaining the right
for its reports to "be acted upon by the House until
disposed of, to the exclusion of other business," in 1859
the Speaker became chair of the committee, and in 1880 it
became a standing committee.   Rules Committee History at 46,
51.

[9]   Rules Committee History at 62; R. B. Cheney & L. V.
Cheney, Kings of the Hill: Power and Personality in the
House of Representatives 99 (1983).

[10]   See Rules Committee History at 63; A. S. McCown, The
Congressional Conference Committee 104-23 (1927).   The
(footnote continued)

Thereafter the House began relying with increasing frequency on the Rules Committee to report special rules to make particular bills privileged. A series of rules changes and rulings by the Chair vested enormous ability in the Rules Committee to overcome obstruction.[11]   In particular, with the triumph of majority party scheduling, the old means for the majority to protect itself against considering undesired minority initiatives -- the "question of consideration" -- fell into disuse.[12]

The Rules Committee served as the tool, first of the powerful Speakers, and later, after the revolt against "Czar" Joseph Cannon (R-Ill.) of the majority party.[13]   Then, from 1937 through the

---

majority party's invention of this tactic for moving the tariff bill met with "indignant opposition" on the ground that the special rule was "no rule at all but simply a revolutionary party expedient." Id. at 117.

[11]   After a brief hiatus in 1883-89, when there was little resort to special rules, Representative Reed became Speaker in 1890. That year he established the precedent that broke the chief dilatory tactic of the minority, the disappearing quorum, and then rewrote the House rules; in the following four years he and his successors established a series of key precedents strengthening the Rules Committee. Rules Committee History at 69-79.

[12]   Under Rule XVI(3), "When any motion or proposition is made, the question, Will the House now consider it? shall not be put unless demanded by a Member." Traditionally, by voting down the question of consideration, the House avoided taking up the agenda of the minority or dissidents (even if privileged) without having to vote down the matters on their merits, which would be embarrassing in the case of popular matters.   See House Manual §§ 779-81 (discussing the question of consideration).

Special rules can include language providing for immediate consideration, which precludes the question of consideration.   House Manual § 780.   The strengthening of the Speaker's discretion regarding recognition, particularly regarding motions to suspend the rules, made rare the occasions when minority members were recognized for matters on which the question of consideration would be called for.

(footnote continued)

1960s, conservative Democrats on the committee, mostly southern, joined with Republicans to forge working control against the majority party, under the active leadership (after 1955) of conservative Chairperson Howard Smith (D-Va.).[14] Representative Smith controlled the committee's operations both through having a working majority, until the 1961 committee expansion, and through a variety of tools: refusals to schedule committee meetings, to put items on agendas, or to recognize for motions; quorum-breaking; and allowing endless testifying at hearings and other stalling tactics. He was considered at times "even more powerful than the Speaker himself."[15]

In this period, the Rules Committee led the conservative coalition[16] in blunting President

---

[13]   Rules Committee History at 80-84 (autocratic Speakers), 84-101 (revolt and 1911 aftermath), 101-31 (service to majority party through 1936).

[14]   The chair under whom conservative coalition control started in 1937-38 was the victim of a purge effort by President Franklin Roosevelt in the 1938 election. Rules Committee History at 140. The conservatives then continued control against the wishes of the new chair, Adolph Sabath (D-Ill.). Sabath was loyal to Roosevelt and the party leadership, but proved largely impotent in the face of a conservative majority on the committee led skillfully by Eugene Cox (D-Ga.). Id. at 140, 145, 162.

[15]   Matsunaga & Chen at 107. "Confident in the belief that the committee would not take the extraordinary step of overruling him, out of respect for committee tradition and the lack of sufficient opposing votes . . . Smith refused to schedule an average of thirty bills per Congress from 1955-60, as compared to Chairman Leo Allen's [(R-Ill.)] twenty measures (83rd Congress) and Chairman Sabath's eleven measures (82nd Congress)." Id. at 104.

[16]   Rules Committee History at 133-212 (rise and fall of the Rules Committee as tool of the conservative coalition). Only during two Congresses when the Republicans were in the majority did the Rules Committee serve the majority party's interests. Rules Committee History at 155-58, 164-67. The bills blocked from the late 1930s to the 1960s came to include a host of the priority legislation in the Democratic party's campaign platforms: civil rights, labor laws, (footnote continued)

Roosevelt's efforts to continue enacting New Deal legislation, defeating many of President Truman's Fair Deal initiatives, helping President Eisenhower resist Democratic initiatives, and stalling President Kennedy's program.[17] Efforts to break its hold were largely bootless.[18]

---

federal aid to education and housing, and other federal aid programs. What the Rules Committee did not block, it allowed to Speaker Sam Rayburn (D-Tex.) only in return for concessions on his part.

[17] The peak of frustration for the Democratic party came in 1959-60. Despite a commanding House majority of 283 out of 435 (and 64 out of 100 in the Senate), the Democrats could not move legislation, with a major factor being Rules Committee "actions [that were] a source of continual frustration for liberal Democrats." Rules Committee History at 175. Thereafter, the "Rules Committee was a bottleneck for a number of bills on [President] Kennedy's legislative agenda." Id. at 191, citing Fox & Clapp, The House Rules Committee and the Programs of the Kennedy and Johnson Administration, Midwest J. Poli. Sci. 667-672 (1970).

[18] The Democratic majority tried the old Calendar Wednesday procedure (devised in 1909 as an ineffectual control on "Czar" Cannon); this is discussed below as a miscellaneous route to the floor. It also frequently sought adoption of a "twenty-one-day" rule, which was actually adopted in 1949-50 and 1965-66, to let bills come to the floor even when the Rules Committee held them up. Galloway at 67-68 (twenty-one-day rule); Rules Committee History at 158-165 (twenty-one-day rule in 1949-50), and 198-99 and 202-3 (twenty-one-day rule in 1965-66).

The Rules Committee sometimes wrote rules that fixed the procedure on bills to aid the conservative side in controversial ways. In one classic case, its rule for a World War II price control bill made antistrike legislation in order as an amendment to the bill -- in essence, discharging the committee that had not reported such legislation. Speaker Rayburn himself denounced the rule on the floor, and it was defeated. Rules Committee History at 149-50. Similarly, occasional fights occurred in the late 1960s when liberals sought without success to obtain recorded votes on the Vietnam War, which necessitated changing rules reported by the Rules Committee. Id. at 208. However, in general, few rules were defeated or (footnote continued)

Starting in the 1960s, the majority party gradually cut back the Rules Committee's independence, expanding the committee in 1961 to create a tenuous party-loyal majority,[19] and later constraining the committee's conservative chair by adopting written rules.[20]   In 1975, the "Watergate"-elected Democrats established a new

---

amended on the floor.

[19] For the enlargement of the Rules Committee, see Cummings & Peabody, "The Decision to Enlarge the Committee on Rules: An Analysis of the 1961 Vote", in New Perspectives on the House of Representatives 253-80 (2d ed. R. L. Peabody & N. W. Polsby 1969); R. B. Cheney & L. V. Cheney, Kings of the Hill: Power and Personality in the House of Representatives 182-89 (1983).

[20] In 1965, the House created a mechanism (in Rule XX) for sending bills to conference without a special rule, a permanent change discussed in the chapter on conference procedure, and revived the twenty-one-day rule (a change that endured only for that Congress). Rules Committee History at 198; Matsunaga & Chen at 26. In 1967, after Chairperson Smith was defeated for reelection, the equally conservative heir apparent, Representative William Colmer (D-Miss.), "in a successful effort to undercut a potential challenge to his becoming chairman, accepted the first set of committee rules." Oppenheimer at 92. These rules curtailed the chair's ability to block bills by refusing to hold committee meetings to decide on requests for special rules. See Rules Committee History at 201-2.

Still, the Rules Committee retained a considerable role in blocking on behalf of the conservative coalition until the 1970s. As late as the 91st Congress (1969-70), the committee "upheld Chairman Colmer's stubborn refusal to take any action on the Equal Employment Opportunity Act, despite repeated pleadings from the Speaker and majority leader to schedule the nationally significant measure for committee action." Matsunaga & Chen at 20. (Senator Spark Matsunaga (D-Hawaii) had been a member of the House Rules Committee during this time.) For a list of bills killed by the Rules Committee from the 87th to the 93d Congress, see id. at 171-76. What clinched the evolution of the committee toward majority leadership loyalty was the filling of further vacancies by Members loyal to the leadership. Oppenheimer at 92.

Caucus rule that the Speaker would decide afresh
each Congress whether to reappoint former
committee Members -- a stark exception to the
seniority norm which cemented the Speaker's
control.[21]

The Speaker did not in fact depose any
particular committee Members, for he did not need
to; he just continued to exercise care in filling
vacancies as they arose, and the potential for
non-reappointment obviated the need for any actual
purges. This new loyalty did not end the
importance or the judgmental role of the Rules
Committee. After some initial mistakes, the newly
loyal Rules Committee "regain[ed] the image of
independence" by walking a skillful line between
resisting the leadership and reporting unpopular
special rules.[22]

In place of the old role of obstructing on
behalf of the conservative coalition, new primary
roles emerged for the Rules Committee in reporting
complex rules, resolving jurisdictional disputes,
screening out overly divisive bills, and doling
out waivers for the authorization-appropriation
process.[23] The majority leadership relied on the
Rules Committee in the 1980s for structuring the
floor fights over key issues, particularly
budgetary legislation. During this period, the
Rules Committee enjoyed great success on the
floor; from 1981 to 1985 "only six rules [were]

---

[21] For the adoption of the new procedure in January, 1985,
see Rules Committee History at 214. Rule 14 of the
Democratic Caucus puts nominations for Rules Committee on
the same plane as nominations for open seats on other
committees:

> The Democratic nominee for Speaker (or Speaker, as
> the case may be) shall recommend to the Caucus
> nominees for membership to the Committee on Rules.
> Debate and balloting on any such nomination shall be
> subject to the same provisions as apply to the
> nominations of Members of other committees, as set
> forth in Caucus Rule 13.

[22] Matsunaga & Chen at 116-18.

[23] Rules Under Chairman Pepper at 1674-75.

rejected by the House."[24]

The end of obstructionism did not mean indiscriminate reporting of rules on request, which brief experience showed to be disastrous.[25]   Rather, the Rules Committee performed a delicate minuet between the leadership, the floor, the standing committees and the parochial interests of its own Members.

Respecting the Speaker, as Congressional Quarterly noted in 1985, "[m]ore than any other standing committee, the strictly partisan panel is an arm of the Speaker . . . .   But because [the Speaker] seldom gets involved with the details of bills, the committee's members, particularly the Democrats, have great leeway to act as legislative brokers within the House."[26]   Cases even occurred "in which a minority of Rules Democrats (not including the committee chairman) opposed granting the type of rule the Speaker wanted," but these ended, when the Speaker applied sufficient pressure, in committee acquiescence.[27]

Meanwhile, the House put the old motion to suspend the rules to a new use.   Rather than using it for scheduling alone, as in the 1800s, the House established the practice of adopting bills by this motion.[28]   Through most of the twentieth

---

[24]   Rules Under Chairman Pepper at 1674.

[25]   For one unusual Congress in 1973-74 the committee overreacted, indiscriminately reporting out special rules at upon the requests of other committees.   The House responded with an unprecedented series of rejections.   "In the 93d Congress, 16 rules were defeated on the House floor, a number larger than the combined total for the preceding six Congresses."   Oppenheimer, supra, at 97.   "Led by Richard Bolling [D-Mo.] . . . Rules Democrats persuaded the leadership that it was necessary to tighten the rein on granting rules if the House were to function more effectively in making legislative policy decisions."   Id.

[26]   Rules Under Chairman Pepper at 1671.

[27]   Sinclair at 84.   See id. at 189, and Rules Under Chairman Pepper at 1674.

[28]   House Manual §§ 903   In the early 1800s, "suspension (footnote continued)

century, the majority chose measures for
suspension with care so that very few would be
defeated, sometimes through consultation with the
minority, although there were exceptions when it
was used for important matters.[29]

In the late 1970s, Speaker Thomas P. O'Neill
(D-Mass.) expanded the use of suspensions so that
large numbers of bill, including some highly
important ones, came up under suspension.[30]
Considerable controversy ensued. "A variety of
House members -- from liberal Democrats to
conservative Republicans -- ha[d] seized the
suspension procedure as an argument for voting
against bills they oppose"; "[t]he argument often

---

motions related primarily to the order of business on the
House floor." Bach at 58. However, in 1868, in voting on
the impeachment resolution for President Andrew Johnson, the
House established a precedent that it did not have "to vote
separately on suspending the rules and then on agreeing to
the [impeachment] resolution." Id. at 15. "[T]he practice
developed of offering motions to suspend the rules and
dispose of a measure by one vote," id. at 58, meaning, in
short, both to schedule and to adopt with one vote. Hinds
provides three major examples in the late 1870s: two major
silver bills (in 1877 and 1878) and a major appropriation
bill (in 1879). V Hinds § 6821, at 916.

[29] It "came to be used principally to enable the House to
take up and dispose of measures which did not evoke
substantial opposition, especially along partisan lines."
Bach at 18; id. at 50-51 (consultation with minority on
use). As Speaker Nicholas Longworth (R-Ohio) claimed in
1931, "I think the Chair is safe in saying that not more
than three or four times since his incumbency of this office
for the past six years has the motion to suspend the rules,
out of hundreds of cases, received less than the necessary
two-thirds." Bach, at 30, quoting Cong. Rec., March 2,
1931, p. 6735. There were exceptions in the 1920s, 1940s,
and 1950s, when important measures came up under suspension
to preclude amendments. Bach at 70-71. By the early 1970s,
the House passed hundreds of measures each Congress by
suspension, defeating almost nothing brought up that way.

[30] The House increased the opportunity for suspensions in
1977 by providing for them to be in order on suspension days
two days each week, four times as many suspension days as
only a few years before. House Manual § 902.

work[ed],"[31] and in 1977-78 the House defeated a record 35 suspensions. In 1979 the Democratic Caucus adopted guidelines limiting the use of suspension, but on occasion major matters continued to come up that way.

B. RULES COMMITTEE FUNCTIONS

Today, special rules from the Rules Committee serve three main functions each discussed in turn below. The Rules Committee performs its historic function of screening bills before granting the rule that admits them to the floor.   More important, the Committee structures the floor consideration by the type of special rule it grants, and by the particular provisions it writes into the special rule.   Finally, the Committee settles jurisdictional disputes, including authorization-appropriation issues.

---

[31]   Cooper at 2694.

A particularly important bill was defeated after opponents termed its offering under suspension a "calculated affront to the over 200 Members who support [tuition] tax credits," 124 Cong. Rec. 7526 (1978) (Rep. Tom Corcoran (R-Ill.)).   The bill was the Middle Income Student Assistance Act, an alternative to tuition tax credits which "authorize[d] the expenditure of $1.5 billion of the taxpayers' money;" the leadership let the motion to suspend be offered on short notice and over the objection to the legislation by the Budget Committee. 124 Cong. Rec. 7526 (1978)(Rep. William Frenzel (R-Minn.)). The bill did not even receive a majority, being denied a second by 156-218. Id. 7536.

For proposals to limit suspensions, see Bach at 67 (quoting an August 1978 proposal of the New Members Caucus of Democratic Representatives first elected to the 95th Congress, that a suspension not be in order "if it makes or authorizes appropriations which may be in excess of $ 100,000,000 for any fiscal year."); Cooper, House Use of Suspensions Grows Drastically, 36 Cong. Q. Weekly Rep. 2694, 2695 (1978) ($100 million restriction proposed in H. Res. 1332.)

Screening bills

Historically, the Rules Committee's most formidable power was its power to kill a bill by refusing to report a special rule for it. Since the mid-1970s, the Rules Committee's responsiveness to the majority leadership has led it to exercise sparingly the power to kill bills by denying them special rules, in contrast to the prior reign of the conservative coalition. Still, each Congress furnishes some prominent examples of major bills screened out by the Rules Committee, usually bills considered divisive within the majority party.

For example, in 1982, the Rules Committee killed H.R. 746, the regulatory reform bill, a major measure to limit federal agency promulgation of regulations, by imposing procedural requirements. The bill's prospects for enactment, apart from the Rules Committee's resistance, were excellent: the Senate had passed a companion bill, the House Judiciary Committee had reported this one, and in all probability a solid majority waited on the House floor to pass it. Nevertheless, the bill died at the end of 1982 when the Rules Committee chair, Representative Richard Bolling (D-Mo.), gaveled a motion to report a rule for it out of order and adjourned the committee meeting on the bill without taking action. As is often the case, behind the scenes extensive bargaining and calculating preceded the decision to kill.[32]

---

[32] The Rules Committee held two hearings on the bill. In the first, there was a "lethal dose of talking by committee and subcommittee chairmen opposed to the measure," 1982 Congressional Quarterly Almanac 523, particularly by Representative John Dingell (D-Mich.), chair of Energy and Commerce. Then came the election recess, and in the post-election lame duck session the Democratic victories in the election encouraged bill opponents to want to kill the bill, as they assumed the next Congress would be less favorable to regulatory reform. Despite extensive behind-the-scene negotiations involving the Speaker's staff, there was still "a lack of enthusiasm by House Democratic leaders," including Rules Chairperson Bolling. Id. at 523.

In this same 1981-82 period, the Rules Committee denied a special rule to a bill authorizing coal slurry pipelines. While two House committees had reported the bill, they both did so by narrow votes and the bill would have produced intense conflict within the majority party.[33]

The next Congress, in 1986, the Rules Committee threatened to kill the Appropriations Committee's version of the continuing resolution. Appropriations had included $3.4 billion to fund revenue sharing, otherwise due to expire. According to one Rules Committee member, "'a howl literally went up' at a party caucus as members insisted that they be spared a public choice on whether to let the popular program die, continue it in violation of budget limits, or continue it by cutting into other programs."[34] Accordingly, the Rules Committee refused to let the committee bill come to the House floor unless revenue sharing was excised. "Confronted with an adamant Rules Committee, a displeased [Appropriations Chairperson Jamie] Whitten [(D-Miss.)] introduced a new version of the continuing

---

[33] The controversy over the coal slurry bill, H.R. 4230, is described in 1982 Congressional Quarterly Almanac 341-42. In 1983, when the Rules Committee let the bill come to the floor, the House defeated it in the vote on final passage.

In the following Congress, the Rules Committee killed a compromise bill reforming natural gas regulation. The compromise had sufficient backing that 218 Members wrote the Speaker asking that the Rules Committee consider it. However, the issue was notoriously divisive: "at a Democractic caucus . . . members complained that they would be forced to vote on a no-win issue, one that would hurt the Democratic presidential ticket in the Southwest. Gettinger, Divisive Natural Gas Bill Scrapped in House, 42 Cong. Rec. 2409 (1984). A majority of Rules Committee Members apparently oppesed a special rule, and the bill simply disappeared from the Rules Committee's agenda, with the Speaker later announcing that the bill was just too controversial.

[34] Wehr, Omnibus Spending Bill Wins House Approval by One Vote, 44 Cong. Q. Week. Rep. 2261, 2263 (1986).

resolution, identical to that reported by his Appropriations Committee, except that it excluded the revenue sharing money . . . ."[35]

What also may occur is that a reporting committee deals with the Rules Committee, precisely to avoid such screening. For example, "[i]n preparing the fiscal 1985 supplemental appropriations bill (HR 2577 - PL 99-88), the Appropriations Committee kept Rules firmly in mind. The spending measure was loaded with water projects, including several for key Rules members."[36]

Apart from individual prominent bills, the Rules Committee screens out a fair number of other bills. Surveying the years 1981-82 as an example, committees asked during those years for special rules for approximately 180 bills. Thirty-three requests were not granted, of which 24 concerned bills which failed to be enacted by the House and which the Rules Committee may be said to have killed.[37] These 24 included many bills representing committees' parochial viewpoints but not general House interests: bills fostering foreign language instruction, enlarging the federal payment to the District of Columbia, controlling Canadian maritime competition, and regulating state and local pension plans.[38]

Also, the committee screened out about a half-dozen bills that came up too late in the Congress. In the period just before the election recess at the end of a Congress, the House runs

---

[35] Id. The only other difference was that the new version funded anti-drug programs by across-the-board cuts.

[36] Rules Under Chairman Pepper at 1673.

[37] The statistics are based on the Rules Committee's final calendar for the 97th Congress. Of the nine bills enacted without rules, five were adopted under suspension of the rules, and four under unanimous consent.

[38] These were respectively H.R. 3231, H.R. 4127, H.R. 3637, and H.R. 4929. Other measures apparently the subject of such decisions were bills concerning Defense Department organization, H.R. 4448, and to reform disability payments procedure (a bill which disabled groups opposed), H.R. 6181.

short on time and Members become restless to
adjourn for campaigning.   The Rules Committee
husbands the House's limited time for action,
denying special rules to controversial or
dispensable bills.   Former Chairperson Bolling
commented that "[i]n the last six months of every
two-year Congress . . . [whoever is chair] has the
same relative power as the president or the
Speaker has, because you can delay things for six
months, particularly if you're just a little bit
clever."[39]

Similarly, the committee screens out bills
for which a better vehicle is available than the
one for which the special rule has been
requested.   In 1981-82, about eight such bills
were denied rules.   These included bills which
were loaded into various "omnibus" vehicles, such
as budget reconciliation or supplemental
appropriation bills, or continuing resolutions.
For example, for years the Congress failed to
enact an authorization bill for the Department of
Energy.   In 1981, the Rules Committee did not

---

[39]   Rules Under Chairman Pepper at 1675.   As an observer
commented, "During most of the Congressional session the
Rules Committee can delay legislation but not kill it, yet
the approach of adjournment makes delay and death
legislatively synonymous. The Committee decides which bills
in the "adjournment crush" shall receive the life-giving
rule and which shall perish."   E. Redman, The Dance of
Legislation 240 (1973).

An example in 1981-82 of such a bill that died for lack
of time was H.R. 8444 to extend the term of patents.   This
bill clearly had the support of a majority, for a majority
voted for its passage when it came up under suspension of
the rules; it fell short of the two-thirds needed for
enactment that way.   Its sponsors had recognized the
lateness problem, explaining that they sought suspension of
the rules "in view of the period of time that we have
remaining in this Congress. . . ." 128 Cong. Rec. H6919
(daily ed. Sept. 13, 1982)(Rep. Robert Kastenmeier (D-
Wisc.)).   Similarly, H.R. 6258, authorizing the Travel
Administration, received a majority but not a two-thirds
majority under suspension of the rules, but a rule was
sought on August 23, 1982, when the House was already
feeling the adjournment crush.

grant a rule sought for such an authorization, H.R. 3146; instead, a three-year authorization was loaded onto the omnibus reconciliation bill.

The committee has another power, the opposite of its power to kill bills. It can make bills in order which have not been reported from committee, a process once known as "extraction," and dating back to an 1895 precedent.[40]   When the Rules Committee in 1986 eliminated revenue sharing from the continuing resolution, it did so by not only threatening to kill the Appropriation Committee's version of the continuing resolution, but also threatening to report to the floor (i.e., to extract) the Rules Committee's own version.[41]   A complex rule which makes a bill in order as a non-germane amendment to some other bill acts similarly to the classic "extraction" making a

---

[40]   VIII Cannon § 3389; Rules Committee History at 79 (original 1895 precedent); 21 Deschler § 20 (giving examples).

> Mindful of the House's reluctance to circumvent its traditional ways of handling business through the committee system, the Rules Committee has been, throughout its history, extremely cautious in [in]voking this power. From 1944 to 1974, the committee sent only four bills to the floor for House consideration which were not first acted upon favorably by their respective jurisdictional legislative committees. Although none of these bills had support from the leadership, they all received decisive majorities for passage.

Matsunaga & Chen at 24. One of these four was in 1964, when conservatives sought to overcome the Supreme Court's state reapportionment decisions with a bill cutting off the jurisdiction of the Supreme Court or federal courts. Both the leadership and the Judiciary Committee opposed the bill, but the Rules Committee "extracted" it to the floor, where the House passed it in amended form, though the Senate did not approve it. Rules Committee History at 197. In 1972, the Rules Committee similarly extracted a bill concerning a dock strike. Id. at 209.

[41]   Wehr, Omnibus Spending Bill Wins House Approval by One Vote, 44 Cong. Q. Week. Rep. 2261 (1986).

bill in order on its own; both amount to the equivalent of a discharge power. Together with the Speaker's power to include time limits as part of multiple referrals, these give the leadership some leverage against recalcitrant committee chairs, though the leadership makes limited use of these powers to avoid crippling the committee system and to preclude having the leadership take the responsibility for all unpopular events.

The Rules Committee may report self-executing rules. These are resolutions which provide, not merely the terms for debate over some other bill, but themselves provide for action on the bill. For example, a self-executing rule may provide that upon the rule's adoption, an amendment to a bill is "considered" adopted, and that the bill itself is "considered" to have been passed. The House most often uses such rules for rushing through bills either in light of some question of House-Senate timing, or as a way of forcefully pushing a leadership arrangement.

Structuring Floor Consideration

Since the 1970s, the Rules Committee's most important function has been structuring floor consideration of bills through complex special rules. "Complex" rules can be defined most simply as rules that define what amendments are in order or set up some complex arrangement for debate, without being completely open or completely closed (allowing no amendments). The Rules Committee, which had not previously written many complex rules, first began doing so in large numbers in the mid-1970s with the ascendancy of Representative Bolling, a scholar of procedure and an effective champion of strong majority party leadership.[42]

---

[42] Bolling was the author of two books on procedure while serving as a Representative. R. Bolling, House Out of Order (1965); R. Bolling, Power in the House (2d ed. 1974).

"Prior to the 93d Congress, most rules that the committee granted specified whether amendments could be offered (open versus closed rules) . . . . [and] could (footnote continued)

Bolling stepped in with the theory and practice of complex rules at a timely moment, when the old floor control by the conservative coalition broken down due to the weakening of committee chairs, the floods of floor amendments, and the incessant jurisdictional disputes. As the leading analyst of the Rules Committee noted:

> Given that Richard Bolling is the committee's acknowledged leader, it is not suprprising that committee efforts have focused on many of the same problems addressed directly and indirectly by the select committee [on committees] Bolling chaired in the 93d Congress: jurisdictional overlap, duplication of effort, competition for policy turf, isolation of decision-making environments, and lack of integrative approaches to policy problems.[43]

Other reformers agreed with Bolling that complex rules could help the decentralized House of the 1970s pull itself together, particularly if the special rules satisfied both parties by allowing the minority to offer its own considered alternatives to bills.[44]

---

generally be called _simple_ rules. Only on rare occasions would a rule be more complex and require lengthy explanation on the floor." Oppenheimer, "Policy Implications of Rules Committee Reforms", in _Legislative Reform_ 91, 99 (L.N. Rieselbach ed. 1978). Oppenheimer provides a table counting only 9 complex rules, out of 204, in the 92d Congress (1971-72), but 24 complex rules, out of 255, in the 93d Congress (1973-74), and 35 out of 300, in the 94th (1975-76), _id._; the number increased to 53 out of 256 in the 95th (1977-78). _Rules Committee History_ at 219. Bach counts slightly differently, but agrees that the number of complex rules "increased tenfold from the Ninetieth through the Ninety-sixth Congress, from four in 1967-68 to forty-three in 1977-78 and forty in 1979-80." Bach, 18 Harv. J. Legis. at 555.

[43] Oppenheimer, _supra_, at 98.

[44] In 1979, a group of 35 Democrats wrote to the Speaker proposing that the House leadership continue its "expansion of the use of the modified open rule" to increase "the efficiency and quality of the body's work product." Frank (footnote continued)

A first role for complex rules was to deal with jurisdictional disputes, a Rules Committee function discussed below. However, complex rules went beyond this, not only structuring choices among competing committee versions, but restricting the amendment process to a few key alternatives. The consideration of President Jimmy Carter's energy program in 1977 provided a showcase for the use of complex rules by the new Speaker O'Neill and by the new Rules Chair Bolling. Speaker O'Neill organized an Ad Hoc Committee on Energy to coordinate the numerous proposals and suggested variations which fell under various committees' jurisdiction. Then, the Rules Committee provided a special rule presented by its chair:

> Bolling announced, ". . . this is a very complicated rule on a very complicated subject which came to the Committee on Rules in a very complicated way." The rule limited the amendments to be offered to those specified in the bill, including 20 to be offered en bloc by the Ad Hoc Committee and approximately 12 others to be offered by

---

Annunzio, et al., "Dear Colleague Letter: Greater Use of Modified Rule," Sept. 12, 1979, quoted in C. Whalen, The House and Foreign Affairs: The Irony of Congressional Reform 167 (1981).

Representative Whalen, the former ranking minority Member of the Foreign Affairs Committee, offered similar support on the other side of the aisle in his book-length study of the impact of House rules changes. Whalen contended that loose and hasty consideration of floor amendments wreaked havoc on sensitive foreign policy issues, and he picked increased use of restrictive rules as one of his chief proposals for reform. Noting the destructive effect of surprise amendments on the foreign aid bill, he urged "a modified open rule that provided for floor consideration of only those amendments that had previously been submitted to the committee of jurisdiction during its mark-up of the bill." Id. at 169. Such a rule, he explained, "would afford the occasion for a thorough review by committee members and administration officials," while still "preserv[ing] the author's right to present the amendment during floor debate." Id. at 169-70.

> individual House members. . . . Because of
> the tight design of the rule, opponents of
> the energy package were prevented from
> loading it down or delaying it with last-
> minute amendments. But they were given the
> opportunity to vote on controversial
> provisions, to substitute the language of the
> Republican program, and to recommit the bill
> with or without instructions.[45]

The complex role evolved further, and took on
a major annual role, with new procedures for
budget resolutions. Until 1979, the House
considered budget resolutions in an open process,
which increasingly tied up the floor for days in
inconclusive voting on dozens of uncoordinated
amendments. A different procedure for budget
resolutions dates from the second resolution for
1979, which failed to be passed on its first
try. For the second try, the Rules Committee
provided an essentially restrictive rule, pursuant
to which the House would consider first the
Democratic alternative, then, if that was voted
down, the Republican alternative.[46] By 1980, both

---

[45] Oppenheimer, supra, at 101. The organized floor process
contrasted starkly with the process without a complex
rule. "Compared to the more limited energy proposals of the
94th Congress, which tied up the House floor for weeks and
resulted in passage of several heavily amended pieces of
legislation . . . the House was able to complete action on
the 1977 legislation in five legislative days." Id.

[46] The rule provided only "That upon the adoption of this
resolution it shall be in order to consider the concurrent
resolution [on the budget] in the House." This made the
resolution subject to the hour rule and made the motion for
the previous question in order, since the resolution was
going to be considered "in the House," not in Committee of
the Whole. (A small irony is that the particular function
of Committee of the Whole, as opposed to the House, is money
matters.) It was agreed that the budget committee chairman
would be recognized for one hour and would move the previous
question on his version. If he failed, the ranking minority
member would be recognized for one hour and would move the
previous question on his version. See 125 Cong. Rec. H8577
(daily ed. Sept 27, 1979).

party leaderships favored a complex rule to let
each party put forward a comprehensive position
without minor distracting amendments. The Rules
Committee reported a rule allowing only eight
amendments, principally three chief
alternatives.[47]

Chairperson Bolling defended his proposal:

> we felt that a majority of the Members of the
> institution wish to vote on the broad
> issues. . . . rather than the
> specifics. . . . [Thus,] virtually everything
> [allowed as an amendment by the rule] is a
> real substitute. The line that we drew on
> the rule is at the individual particular
> interests; and very frankly, they are not
> given an opportunity for a single shot.[48]

When the first effort to pass a first budget
resolution in 1982 failed under a special rule
which made dozens of amendments in order, one of
which proved to be a killer, the Rules Committee
provided for the second effort a tightly
restrictive special rule. This time, the House
chose one of the alternatives proffered and
adopted a budget resolution.[49]

In this way, complex rules took on their
greatest importance in the 1980s because of what
was nicknamed the "four bill" system in which a
few omnibus bills each year became the major
elements of an otherwise somewhat stalemated
legislative process. When the House considered

---

[47] The move to a complex rule in 1980 is discussed in
Sinclair at 183.

[48] 126 Cong. Rec. H2804 (daily ed. April 23, 1980).

[49] 1982 Congressional Quarterly Almanac 192-95. The first
rule for the 1982 first resolution allowed seven main
alternatives and 68 perfecting amendments. That rule led
the budget resolution to defeat, when the main alternatives
died beneath the burden of a popular but lethal second-
degree amendment. The conservatives could not defeat the
Oakar amendment shifting funds from defense to Medicare, but
they would not then support a resolution combining a high
deficit and low defense. Id. at 193.

each of the few key annual vehicles -- typically a
budget resolution, reconciliation bill, continuing
resolution, and supplemental appropriation -- the
Rules Committee structured the floor consideration
each time by a complex special rule. The
leadership, the Rules Committee, and the key
committees of jurisdiction defined what
alternatives will be considered and created a
procedure for the bills. How controversial such
special rules are is discussed in the section on
restrictive rules below.

Resolving Jurisdictional Disputes

Through its powers to screen bills, and to
report complex rules, the Rules Committee performs
an important function in resolving jurisdictional
disputes. These disputes arise when different
committees report bills on the same subject, or
report different versions of a bill multiply
referred to them. The ultimate power of the Rules
Committee in such a situation is to choose one
committee's bill or version and to kill the
others' bills by denying them special rules. For
example, three House committees sought special
rules in the 97th Congress for nuclear waste
disposal bills: Science and Technology, Energy and
Commerce, and Interior. The Rules Committee
granted the special rule to the Interior bill, and
denied rules to the bills of the other
committees.[50]
Alternatively, the Rules Committee may work
out a solution harmonizing the differing
committees.[51] It may deny all of them a special

---

[50] It granted a special rule to H.R. 7187 and denied rules
to H.R. 6598 and H.R. 5016. This bill is discussed further
below.

[51] For example, the Interior Committee, and the Interstate
and Foreign Commerce Committee, reported out different
versions of a Nuclear Regulatory Commission authorization
bill in 1979. The two committees devised a "substitute
bill" as a "mutually acceptable vehicle for floor
consideration," and the Rules Committee reported a special
rule which allowed "consideration of the substitute bill as
an original bill for purpose of amendment. . . ." Bach, 18

rule until they agree to negotiate a joint
version. It may report a complex rule which
shares the floor among them, such as one which
allows several committees to share in the time for
general debate. Complex rules splitting general
debate time have became increasingly common in the
1970s: "Since [the early 1970s] control of time by
other than one committee has become more common:
such provisions were included in nineteen special
rules of the Ninety-fourth Congress, twenty-seven
of the Ninety-fifth, and twenty-five reported
during the Ninety-sixth."[52] In 1981-82, about 20
reported special rules gave general debate time to
more than one committee.[53]

An example of a division of general debate
time was the special rule which ended a
jurisdictional dispute dealt with the issue
discussed in the committee jurisdiction chapter,
the dispute between Ways and Means, and Energy and
Commerce, over the "domestic content" bill
restricting automobile imports. After three hours
of "unusually detailed" Rules Committee debate,[54]
the Rules Committee reported a special rule giving
one hour of general debate time to the chair and
ranking minority Member of Energy and Commerce,
and one hour to the chair and ranking minority
Member of Ways and Means.

Besides dividing up general debate time, the

Harv. J. Legis at 586, quoting 125 Cong. Rec. H11206 (daily
ed. Nov. 27, 1979)(Rep. Anthony Beilenson (D-Cal.)).

[52]   Bach, 18 Harv. J. Legis. at 562.

[53]   A striking example in those years, apart from budget
reconcilation bills, was a relatively minor bill, H.R. 4326,
setting aside research funding for small business. This
touched on the jurisdiction of a number of committees with
authority regarding different kinds of research funding.
The Speaker referred the bill to seven committees, and when
they reported it out, the Rules Committee reported a rule
that gave two hours each to the chair and ranking minority
Member of the Committee on Small Business, and 30 minutes
each to the chairs and ranking minority Members of Energy
and Commerce, Veterans' Affairs, Science and Technology,
Foreign Affairs, Armed Services, and Intelligence.

[54]   Washington Post, Dec. 8, 1982.

Rules Committee may take steps to resolve
jurisdictional disputes that are more complex. It
may have to devise a system to allow the House to
intelligently choose between different versions of
a bill reported by different committees. For
example, the Rules Committee faced a real
challenge in the most highly publicized
jurisdictional fight of the 97th Congress over the
bill to increase the gasoline tax (in Ways and
Means' jurisdiction) primarily to pay for highway
construction (in Public Works' jurisdiction). A
rule compromising the dispute and bringing up the
controversial tax increase bill was adopted by the
razor-thin margin of 197 to 194.[55]

From Request to Special Rule

Rules Committee consideration of a special
rule begins with a letter from a committee
formally requesting that the Rules Committee set a
hearing on the bill.[56] A requesting committee

---

[55] Under intense pressure in the lame duck session of 1982
to create jobs, the two committees achieved a compromise and
the Rules Committee reported out a special rule. The rule
made the Public Works bill in order and gave that committee
control of general debate time. However, the rule made in
order as an amendment a new title approved by the Ways and
Means Committee, and prohibited any amendments except those
of Ways and Means itself. It also gave that title two hours
of debate time, making up for the exclusion of Ways and
Means from general debate time.

For discussions of the use of complex rules for
resolving jurisdictional problems, see Bach, 18 Harv. J.
Legis. at 559-64 (jurisdictional problems), 568-71
(restrictive rules), and 585-93 (expansive rules).

[56] Under Rules Committee Rule 7(c)(3):

a rule is considered as formally requested when the
chairman of a committee which has reported a bill or
resolution (or a member of such committee authorized
to act on the chairman's behalf) (A) has requested in
writing to the Chair, that a hearing be scheduled on
(footnote continued)

furnishes copies of the bill and the committee
report on the bill for Rules Committee Members and
staff to study before the hearing.   Request
letters usually describe what waivers the
requesting committee seeks, and what else it seeks
in the special rule, such as prohibitions on
amendments.[57]
    Once the Rules Committee has received a
request letter, the Chair decides whether, and
when, to set the bill for a hearing. In the late
1960s, the Committee adopted elaborate committee
rules "to restrain the powers of the chairman in
such areas as calling meetings, ascertaining
quorums, etc."[58] Nevertheless, the committee
deferred considerably to Chairpersons Bolling and
his successor, Claude Pepper (D-Fla.), and the
chair of Rules remains one of the party leaders in
the House.[59] Moreover, alone among standing House

---

a rule for the consideration of the bill or
resolution, and (B) has supplied the Committee with
an adequate number of copies of the bill or
resolution, as reported, together with the final
printed committee report thereon.

[57] One such request letter is reprinted in Legislative
Manual at 73. As the manual suggests:

The letter to the Chairman of the Rules Committee
should contain the following information:
    1. A brief description of the legislation to be
considered;
    2. The amount of time requested for general
debate;
    3. Request as to whether the bill will be open
for amendment;
    4. Requests for waivers of points of order, if
any, which might be raised of specific provisions of
the bill; and
    5. Date the legislative report will be
available to Members.

Legislative Manual at 70.

[58] Matsunaga & Chen at 109.

[59] Bolling, considered a brilliant political strategist,
had run the committee as a fiefdom, according to a
(footnote continued)

committees, the Rules Committee is heavily stacked in favor of the majority party, with nine Democrats and only four Republicans. Individual Members of the Rules Committee themselves possess considerable authority, due to the committee's powers, its small size, and its "inside" position providing information and access as well as power.[60]

One description of a scheduling exercise captures the roles of leadership and Rules Committee chair in scheduling the House through the Rules Committee:

> In 1980, after the 4 July recess, senior staffers from Rules and from the leadership made up a list of legislation for which Rules had requests and legislation still in the pipeline. The Speaker, the majority leader, the majority whip, the chairman of the

---

number of members and staff. At caucuses of committee Democrats before public meetings, Bolling would present other members with what he wanted the committee to do and there were rarely any changes made, they said.

"We were there to ratify what Bolling had decided," says one Rules Democrat.

Things are much looser under Pepper, Democratic committee members say, noting that most decisions are reached by consensus, not dictate.

Rules Under Chairman Pepper at 1672. Pursuant to Democratic Caucus Rule 42, the chair of the Rules Committee is a Member of the Steering and Policy Committee which decides committee appointments.

[60] Paradoxically, the committee's size shrank to 13 from 16 in 1983 because the Speaker was "[u]nable to persuade any senior members to take vacant seats on Rules," because such Members cared more for "attracting money and media," which other committees can provide, than for the "'inside game'" at Rules. Ehrenhalt, The Unfashionable House Rules Committee, 41 Cong. Q. Week. Rep. 151 (1983). The Rules Committee is an exclusive assignment, pursuant to Democratic Caucus Rule 17, except that several Members serve on the Budget Committee.

caucus, and the chairman of Rules met to review the list and to decide on a shorter list of priorities. According to a staffer, ". . . . that basically has become the so-called priority list."[61]

Pursuant to Rules Committee Rule 2(a)(1), the Committee's regular meeting day is Tuesday of each week that the House is in session. The committee chair decides which requests to take up each week, circulating an agenda for the meeting to the members. Typically, before the meeting, the Democratic Members of the committee hold a private caucus to reach agreement.[62]

At the hour appointed for the hearing, the Rules Committee meets on the third floor of the Capitol, a high-status location directly opposite the House galleries. The room is a small one, with forty seats, half of which are reserved for the witnesses, press, and committee staff, and the other half of which are obtained by spectators willing to come early. When the committee comes to order, the spectator observes a unique hearing, for unlike hearings anywhere else in the Congress, the Rules Committee hears only one type of witnesses: other Members of the House.

Typically the lead-off witness is the bill's majority manager (usually a committee or subcommittee chair), who delivers a prepared statement.[63] Professor Oppenheimer, a leading

---

[61] Sinclair at 80.

[62] Rules Under Chairman Pepper at 1671. As these meetings have been described:

> A half hour before the [committee] meeting, the Democrats meet in the chairman's office. There's a specific discussion of the items on the agenda. Just a last shakedown before going in to make sure there are no big problems that are going to surface. And occasionally you'll have a case where the chairman comes back in the room at the beginning of the meeting and the agenda changes.

Sinclair at 81 (quoting observer).
(footnote continued)

observer of the Rules Committee, identifies these
Rules Committee hearings as serving a special
"dress rehearsal" function for the manager. After
the initial statement, Rules Committee Members may
pepper the witnesses with questions. The
questioning and judgments reflect well what will
be be heard later on the floor, since the
political parties have put some of their shrewdest
Members on the Rules Commmittee -- e.g., Minority
Whip Trent Lott (R-Miss.) -- and since the
committee Members gain experience from seeing all
the important bills:

> One Rules member calls it an 'early warning
> system,' and another calls it a 'preview
> movie.' But in essence it is no different
> from a theatre critic's review of a play in
> Boston before it goes to New York. It
> provides a good indicator of strengths and
> weaknesses; the main difference is that the
> director learns that the first act needs a
> rewrite, whereas the floor manager learns
> that he might have to accept an amendment to
> Title I.[64]

Bill managers need this "dress rehearsal"
more today than in the past, because bill managers
often are subcommittee chairs who may not manage
many bills. Bills they have marked up in
subcommittee have faced a limited sample of House
opinion in their formulation, particularly
depending on the reaction at full committee mark-

---

[63]   [Committee] [s]taff may be requested to appear before
the Rules Committee. Staff may be requested to
prepare a statement for the Member before the Rules
Committee.
1.   Brief description of legislation;
2.   Provisions contained therein;
3.   Open, closed or modified Rule request; and
4.   Waivers of points of order, if any.

Legislative Manual at 70.

[64]   Oppenheimer, "The Rules Committee: New Arm of Leadership
in a Decentralized House," in Congress Reconsidered 96, 107
(L.C. Dodd & B.I. Oppendheimer eds. 1977 ed.).

up, so that the Rules hearing could be a bill's first broad airing. Preparation for the hearing, and the grilling at the hearing itself, tune the managers up for the floor. Moreover, while the managers understand the substance of their bill, the Rules Committee hearing forces them to focus more on the procedural background of a bill.[65]

The Rules Committee Members may do much with this information. They may bargain at the hearing for changes in the bill.[66] They serve as an important intelligence network, alerting the leadership and other Members if a bill is in trouble and will need delay, rewriting, or coordination with other committees. They can alert other Members about which amendments are particularly promising.

Depending on how controversial the rule is, the manager, or the majority and minority managers, may be the only witnesses, or there may

---

[65] The witness at a Rules Committee hearing learns to draw on the previous procedural history of her bill or amendment -- that it passed the House in a previous session, that there were many hearings or a bipartisan vote in committee, or that it was introduced with many cosponsors. She may explain how the bill fits into the budget, or how the committee worked out jurisdictional problems with other committees. Conversely, the minority Members of the Rules Committee, when they doubt they support the bill, will dig out procedural weaknesses: that Administration testimony was skipped or ignored, that there were no field hearings, that the committee split on partisan lines, or that there is a high CBO cost estimate.

[66]   The Rules Committee has no direct power to amend bills upon which Rules are requested; it can report a Rule for a bill or it can refuse to do so. As a practical matter, however, proponents of a bill being considered for a Rule, to ensure favorable consideration by the Committee, will sometimes agree at the hearing to offer on the Floor what a committee majority considers to be a desireable amendment.

Legislative Manual at 70. Actually, the Rules Committee could report special rules to amend bills, but this step would rarely be taken over opposition by the committee of jurisdiction.

be others such as the potential offerors of floor amendments. In effect, the witnesses produce a mini-version of what the floor debate will look like if the rule is reported: the majority manager explaining the merits of the bill, the opponents the demerits, and the amendment-offerors the need for their amendments. These functions are so important that offerors of major amendments often come to the Rules Committee hearing even when they need no expansive rule provision for their amendment, just to get the word-of-mouth advertising from the committee for their amendments.

Each meeting day the Rules Committee will hear about one or more bills and then vote on the special rules. A committee Member offers a motion that a rule with such-and-such provisions be adopted, either as requested by the bill's committee, or in some other form. The chair may entertain the motion, or, on occasion, may refuse to do so, deferring consideration and placing a roadblock before the rule. It was by refusing to entertain such a motion, after two full hearings, that Chairperson Bolling killed the regulatory reform bill in the 97th Congress.

Once the committee votes to report a rule, under Committee Rule 7(a)(1) "the Chair or Acting Chair shall report it to the House or designate a member of the Committee to do so." The Member who reports the rule typically manages it on the floor, as discussed in the next chapter. This choice of a rule manager may make involve tactical judgments: a conservative may shepherd through a rule that would raise ideological hackles if managed by a liberal, and the opportunity (or penalty) of managing a popular (or unpopular) rule may bind committee Members to the chair.[67]

---

[67] In one dramatic case, the 1957 civil rights bill, the committee almost revolted against Chairperson Howard Smith (D-Va.) on this point:

Having learned that the chairman might stop at nothing to kill the bill and even floor manage the rule himself, Congressman Richard Bolling, with the support of all the non-Southerners on the committee, threatened to move to restrict Smith's exercise of this

(footnote continued)

Ordinarily, once the Rules Committee reports a rule, the rule lies on the House Calendar for a short time before being considered. The chair cannot kill a bill by keeping the rule on the House Calendar indefinitely. Under House Rule XI(4)(c), if a rule is not called up within seven legislative days, any Rules Committee member (not just the chair or designated manager) may call it up upon notice to the House.[68]

More important, a rule can be called up very quickly, if need be. Under House Rule XI(4)(b), the House can call up a rule after only one day's delay. Dramatically, the House can call up any rule without that one day's delay "by a vote of not less than two-thirds of the Members voting."[69]   Under House Rule XI(2)(1)(6), the

---

prerogative by specifying that [Representative Ray Madden (D-Ind.), a supporter of the bill] manage the rule.

Matsunaga & Chen at 101.   Representative Smith agreed informally to let Representative Madden manage the rule for that bill rather than face a revolt.

[68] Rule XI(4)(c) was adopted in 1924 to deal with Rules Chairperson Philip Campbell.   Rep. Campbell buried any special rules reported by the Committee which he disliked, by refusing to call them upon the floor. His response to outraged complaints from Committee Members had been something of a classic: "You can go to hell, it makes no difference what a majority of you decide, if it meets with my disapproval, it shall not be done; I am the Committee, in me reposes absolute obstructive power."   F. Riddick, The United States Congress: Organization and Procedures 123 (1949).

In 1987, the House amended the rule to provide that "if [the rule is] not called up by the Member making the report within seven legislative days thereafter, any member of the Rules Committee may call it up as a question of privilege (but only on the day after the calendar day on which such Member announces to the House his intention to do so) . . . ." The new requirement of one day's notice aimed to quell the minority's surprise invocation of special rules which the majority had a reason for leaving dormant.

[69] The two-thirds requirement was added in 1924, to prevent (footnote continued)

House can call up a rule without either one day's delay or a two-thirds vote, when the rule simply waives the three day layover for another measure.   These techniques provide the general escape hatch for the House when it must move quickly.   When the House must pass a bill right away, the Rules Committee can hold an emergency meeting on little or no notice, immediately report a rule, and have the rule adopted by a two-thirds vote bare minutes later.

In a 1985 example of the use of a rule for quick movement, the House considered the conference report on a budget resolution on the eve of the August recess.   "[A] senior Democrat, Neal Smith of Iowa objected, [and] the leadership flexed its muscle.   It ordered the Rules Committee to meet and send the resolution to the floor with a waiver of the three-day rule."   In response, "Rules acted quickly, approving the necessary waivers, and members were able to depart for vacation having voted for a deficit-cutting budget."[70]

C. TYPES OF RULES

Until the 1970s, describing special rules was easy, as the vast majority were either open or closed, but the great variety of provisions in special rules starting in the mid-1970s eludes easy classification. Loosely speaking, provisions in special rules still tend in the two directions of open and closed. Provisions that are open include those in open rules, waivers, and expansive provisions; provisions that close include those in closed and in restrictive rules.

---

the majority from bringing out measures without notice. "[W]hen `anything that can be designated as an emergency [is reported], two-thirds of the Members will recognize that fact and can agree that the matter be taken up immediately.'" Rules Committee History at 118 (quoting Rep. R. Walton Moore (D-Va.)).

[70] Rules Under Chairman Pepper at 1671.

Open Rules, Waivers, and Expansive Provisions

Rules to open floor consideration can be classified as one of three types: open rules, waivers, and rules with expansive provisions. Simple "open rules" just make a bill in order, with certain boilerplate language governing their consideration. The next chapter discusses in detail the operation of that boilerplate. In a nutshell, the open rule makes it in order for the House to resolve into Committee of the Whole, controls general debate time, provides for the normal amendment process, and provides for final passage in the House. The simplest open rule does not waive points of order against the bill or amendments and does not foreclose any amendments.

Historically, open rules predominated. Today there are relatively few of the pure and simple open rules because so many special rules have at least one waiver provision or make special arrangements for general debate or amendments. In 1981-82, of 150 special rules, there were only 33 of these pure and simple open rules with no special provisions. They attracted little fuss, with few serious fights or even roll call votes on adoption.[71]

"Waivers" are provisions in special rules that eliminate points of order against bills. The Rules Committee

> has the power to grant a waiver on any point of order which may be raised on the House floor against a bill, or any provisions thereof, for the reason that its consideration would be in violation of the House rules. . . . In essence, this device enables the committee and the House to circumvent certain rules of the House by

---

[71] For those 33, only four roll call votes took place, none of which had more than ten votes in opposition. Ordinarily it takes a very noncontroversial bill to need only the pure open rule. Moreover, the open rule itself allows the minority full opportunity to press its views on the floor, and since the minority thus does not find it unfair, such rules tend to be even less controversial than the bills they accompany.

> proposing the necessary exemptions to these
> rules on a temporary basis.[72]

Often, the impetus for waivers comes from
early consultation between the committee of
jurisdiction for the bill, and the
Parliamentarian, who advises what points of order
require waivers. The committee of jurisdiction
tells the Rules Committee in its request letter
what waivers it needs, and the Parliamentarian may
provide a draft special rule to the Rules
Committee. After the Rules Committee reports a
special rule containing the waivers, the manager
of the rule tells the House about the waivers when
he presents the rule.

The Rules Committee puts waiver provisions on
one of two vehicles. They can go on special rules
with the usual boilerplate language regarding
Committee of the Whole, general debate, and so
forth. Alternatively, the Rules Committee can
report resolutions that contain nothing but waiver
language without any boilerplate, where the
underlying legislation has its own privilege and
requires only the waiver; such "naked" waivers
occur often for appropriations and occasionally
for conference reports. Either way, the waiver
provisions usually name the House rule being
waived, and the parts of the bill for which that
rule is waived. On occasions, waiver provisions
may just say broadly that some rule or point of
order is waived for a whole bill or even that all
points of order are waived for the whole bill.

As late as the mid-1970s, analysts gave only
passing mention to waivers.[73] After that, waivers
mushroomed in number, particularly if the several
waiver provisions that may be incorporated in one
special rule are counted separately. In 1981-82,
"[t]he 152 rules recommended by the Committee
contained 127 waivers of Rules of the House" and
"98 waivers of the requirements of the Budget

---

[72]   Matsunaga & Chen at 23.

[73]   Matsunaga and Chen only mention waivers briefly, at
23. Robinson discusses appropriation waivers at 47-51,
noting 47 such in 1939-56 and 18 in 1957-60; none were
defeated.

Act."[74]

In that period, the House adopted 50 special rules that consisted of open rules plus waivers, or naked waivers (without any expansive or restrictive provisions regarding amendments). Seventeen of the rules were for appropriation bills, as discussed above. Waivers for non-appropriation bills have grown greatly in number in recent years, mainly to fill two needs: compliance with the technical provisions of the Budget Act[75] and with the increasingly technical authorization-appropriation process. Of 127 provisions waiving rules of the House, 41 waived the rule against appropriations on legislative bills, House Rule XXI(5). Almost all concerned the technical situation of minor adjustments made by bills in the applicability of previously passed appropriations.[76]

---

[74] Survey of Activities of the House Committee on Rules, 97th Congress, H. Rept. No. 1007, 97th Cong., 2d Sess. 15, 16. (1983)("Rules Activity Survey"). Before adding these numbers up, it must be remembered that many special rules contained more than one waiver, and many waivers were in expansive or restrictive rules, the non-waiver portions of which mattered more than the waivers. Still, it appears that a majority of special rules include at least one waiver provision.

[75] In 1981-82, of the 98 provisions waiving the requirements of the Budget Act, 42 waived section 401(a), which required at that time that authorizations be reported by May 15 of each year. Rules Activity Survey, supra, at 15. The Gramm-Rudman act in 1985 eliminated that point of order.

[76] Rules Activity Survey, supra, at 16. Many legislative bills that change a program or agency must include provisions adjusting the previous appropriations to reflect the new situation. For example, when a bill abolishes an old program, and replaces it with a new one, there must be provisions allowing the agency to spend previous appropriations for the old program on the new program. Technically, these provisions count as appropriations, as they divert existing appropriations to new purposes, and they require a waiver of Rule XXI(5). See House Manual § 846a.

(footnote continued)

While most waivers are technical, some matter considerably. Some bring up bills on an emergency basis, despite Rule XI(2)(1)(6) requiring a three day layover for reports. Some bring up bills that exceed the budget ceiling, despite section 311 of the Congressional Budget Act, or bring up conference reports in which the conferees have included new legislation, despite Rule XXVIII.[77] This means that the Rules Committee holds the key that releases bills from compliance with layover, budget, or conference rules.

Members do not fight most special rules that simply waive House rules to open up floor consideration, but there are more roll calls and more fights over waivers than over simple open rules.[78] That somewhat increased likelihood of a fight or a roll call partly reflects the increased likelihood that a bill needing a waiver is a controversial bill, and that its opponents may choose to fight on the rule. Occasionally the waiver provision itself is controversial, as illustrated by the one open waiver defeated in 1981-82. The 1982 appropriation bill containing funds for the Federal Trade Commission (FTC), H.R. 6957, came to the floor with a rule waiving the point of order against the FTC funds for being unauthorized.

That waiver offended FTC critics, who wanted to require the FTC to obtain an authorization, especially since such an authorization bill would

---

Another 15 were of the Rule XXI(6) forbidding reappropriations, a similar technical appropriations rule making provisions that carry over unexpended balances "appropriations."

[77] Budget and conference waivers are discussed in the chapters on these subjects. In 1981-82, there were nine waivers of the layover rule, four of the rule concerning conference report scope, and 15 of section 911's spending ceiling and revenue floor.

[78] Of the approximately 20 rules with waiver provisions in 1981-82, 20 had roll call votes. On most of the roll call votes there was more than token opposition. One such rule was defeated, and on two a switch of 30 votes would have defeated the rule.

serve as a vehicle for imposing a legislative veto on FTC rulemaking. The FTC critics revolted against the special rule with its waiver, beating it on a test vote of 208-144.[79] Clearly, a waiver can produce a fight where opponents can portray it as involving a controversial substantive issue.

Besides open rules and waivers, the "expansive rule" is the third type of special rule which opens up floor consideration. While a waiver removes a point of order against a bill, an expansive rule removes impediments or points of order against amendments. In 1981-82, the Rules Committee reported 19 rules containing just expansive provisions and the usual boilerplate.[80]

Some types of expansive rules resemble waivers, and are often noncontroversial.[81] In

---

[79] 128 Cong. Rec. H5898 (daily ed. Aug. 13, 1982). The test vote came on the motion for the previous question. After some sophisticated procedural maneuvering, the special rule was referred back to the Rules Committee. Id. at H5901. When the Rules Committee eventually called up another rule for the same appropriation bill, on December 8, the rule did not include an FTC waiver, and the FTC funds were struck on a point of order. The FTC survived that year only by coverage in the continuing resolution.

[80] This figure does not count the expansive provisions in restrictive rules, discussed below, or in the seventeen rules resolving jurisdictional disputes.

[81] An expansive rule may waive points of order against a noncontroversial committee amendment. For example, both a bill, and the committee amendments to it, may technically violate the technical appropriation requirements of Rule XXI(5) as just discussed. The expansive provision making the committee amendments in order will be no more controversial than a waiver making the underlying bill in order.

Also, often the rules which resolve jurisdictional disputes among committees are expansive, because a common solution to such disputes requires making one committee's version in order as an amendment to the other committee's version. For example, Public Works, and Energy and Commerce, disputed jurisdiction over toxic waste bills. The Rules Committee made the Public Works bill in order, but (footnote continued)

fact, some expansive rules may even settle otherwise controversial disputes. In 1987, the House defeated a special rule on the airport and airway reauthorization measure. The Rules Committee then hastily approved a special rule as sought by the chair of the Public Works and Transportation Committee, which expansively made in order that chair's amendment to remove an important trust fund from the budget. This special rule then passed easily.[82]

On the other hand, some expansive rules are very controversial. "The most controversial waivers of House rules in expansive rules tend to be those that set aside the germaneness requirement of Rule XVI, clause 7."[83] In 1981-82, there were 27 waivers of the germaneness rule.[84] Non-germane amendments offer one of those ways -- like legislative riders on appropriations, multiple referrals with time limits, discharge, and extraction -- to get around a committee of jurisdiction when it is bottling up a bill. The bottled-up bill can be freed by offering it as a non-germane amendment so long as there is a special rule "permitting a non-germane amendment to be offered to a measure that has been reported."[85]

For example, in 1982 the rule for the Defense Department authorization, H.R. 6030, waived the germaneness rule for several amendments, and the House adopted one, an amendment barring aid to students failing to register with the draft. If introduced as a bill, that provision would presumably have received a referral to the Committee on Education and Labor which would have

---

waived a point of order against a substitute amendment to be offered by the Energy and Commerce committee. Expansive rules may also offer more complex ways for considering various versions from competing committees. See Bach, 18 Harv. J. Legis at 585-93.

[82]   1987 Congressional Quarterly Almanac 342.

[83]   Bach, 18 Harv. J. Legis. at 595.

[84]   Rules Activity Survey, supra, at 16.

[85]   Bach, 18 Harv. J. Legis. at 596.

bottled up or at least slowed it down.   It is not surprising that special rules which allow such provisions to come to the floor in violation of the germaneness rules should sometimes be the subject of floor fights, roll calls, and partisan splits.[86]

Closed and Restrictive Provisions

Common use of closed or restrictive rules for diverse types of bills is a recent matter.   The authoritative survey of special rules between 1939 and 1960 showed that 1128 were open and 87 were closed.[87]   Of the closed rules, the Ways and Means Committee took the lion's share for its tax and tariff bills.   These bills received closed rules due to the committee's power,[88] the closed rule's

---

[86]   A centerpiece of the procedural strategy in 1947 of the Republican House for dismantling old programs was for the Rules Committee to waive points of order against riders on appropriations bills to deauthorize or restrict the programs. Rules Committee History at 157.

[87]   Robinson at 44.   At two points during this period, the House used bursts of closed rules in ways which presaged the current use of complex rules.   In 1933, the Democrats used closed rules to steer through key New Deal legislation. Rules Committee History at 127.   In 1947-48, the Republicans, upon obtaining their brief postwar control of the House, used closed rules to steer through legislation. "Just as the Democrats in the Seventy-third [New Deal] Congress had relied on closed rules to avoid internal dissension and expedite passage of their measures, so now in the Eightieth Congress the Republicans did likewise." Galloway at 185; Rules Committee History at 156.

[88]   Ways and Means' committee power had a host of pillars: its Democratic members functioned as the Democratic Committee on Committees from 1911 to 1975; it controlled the new benefits included in each of the tax bills that came to the floor under closed rules; the closed rule protected from floor amendments the existing tax preferences (notably those of the oil industry, beloved of Speaker Sam Rayburn and key to the flow of campaign contributions to the Democratic party until the 1970s); and the committee had broad (footnote continued)

protection of established tax benefits from
change, the technical nature of the bills, and the
danger that open floor consideration would produce
"Christmas trees" loaded with giveaway
provisions.[89]

By the early 1970s, the closed rule for tax
bills received increasing protest, particularly
from liberals, as a "'gag' rule," "'a legislative
abomination,'" which "'insults not only Members of
Congress but also the constituents who have
elected them.'"[90] The Democratic Caucus reduced
the power of Ways and Means in 1973[91], as it did

---

jurisdiction in non-tax areas, including Social Security,
Medicare, and welfare programs.   See J. F. Manley, The
Politics of Finance: The House Committee on Ways and Means
(1970).

[89]   "Nearly one-third of the closed rules [from 1939 to
1960] governed fiscal matters, either taxation or
appropriation items.   Bills on tariffs, the simplification
of customs, and social security typically carry closed
rules."   Robinson at 44.   This probably evolved from the
nineteenth-century view of tariff bills as matters for
binding caucus decisions.   The very first special rule, in
1883, had sent a tariff bill to conference without floor
amendments.   For discussion of closed rules and tariff
bills, see S. McCall, The Business of Congress 112 (1911).

A typical explanation of why the House would handle
such bills through closed rules was that "these issues are
especially allergic to local and regional vote trading, less
elegantly known as logrolling . . . [M]any amendments, with
no apparent relation to any conception of the 'national
interest,' doubtless would be proposed if open rules
prevailed."   Robinson at 44.

[90]   Ruling Congress at 123-36 (quoting Representatives).   At
earlier times, closed rules had gone largely undefeated.
"In spite of the usual criticism of 'gag rules,' none of the
twenty-four rules defeated by the House in the two decades
between 1937 and 1960 was a closed rule."   Robinson at 45.
As battles over the closed rules increased, Ways and Means
Chairman Wilbur Mills (D-Ark.) won the first rounds by
threatening, and demonstrating, that if denied a closed rule
he would not report vitally needed legislation to the
floor.   Ruling Congress at 124-25 (1970 controversy); Rules
Committee History at 208 (1969 and 1971 controversies).
(footnote continued)

again in 1975,[92] and since then the committee has often had to face floor amendments on a fair number of its bills.

The demise of Ways and Means' absolute right to a totally closed rule ushered in the rise of the restrictive or "modified closed" rule, which the Rules Committee, in its new role as loyal majority party organ, provided for diverse kinds of bills. Restrictive rules, allowing a few select amendments but no others, were seen in the 1970s as "a compromise between the harsh, undemocratic closed rule and the time-consuming, democratic open rule."[93]

Restrictive special rules lie on a spectrum of degrees of closure. Some restrictive rules are virtually open, allowing large numbers of amendments. These rules do not so much restrict

---

[91] In January 1973, the Democratic Caucus adopted a rule empowering itself to influence the formulation of closed rules by specifying amendments that had to be allowed. Rule 9 of the House Democratic Caucus provides that before the Rules Committee can support a closed rule, there has to be notice in the Congressional Record. Fifty members can give written notice that they wish to offer a particular germane amendment, in which case the Caucus meets to decide whether the amendment should be considered.

Chairman Mills continued to fight even after adoption of the Caucus rule. In 1974, the Caucus, in the first battle over its rule, demanded two amendments on an oil and energy tax bill, H.R. 14462, one of them an amendment to repeal the oil depletion allowance. Rep. Mills responded by withdrawing the request for a rule, killing the bill. Matsunaga & Chen at 41.

[92] Representative Mills had become enmeshed in the scandal over his relationship with a stripper, Fanne Fox, weakening the committee's ability to fight. By 1975, the Caucus had shifted the function of Democratic Committee on Committees to the Steering and Policy Committee, expanded the Ways and Means Committee to add a dozen new Members, and required the committee to create subcommittees. These steps all opened the committee and reduced the institutional power of its chair and senior Members.

[93] Id. at 22.

amendments as make them visible in advance, to
prevent surprises during floor debate. Some rules
provide a long list of amendments, like the 1982
nuclear waste bill, H.R. 3809 (18 amendments) and
the 1982 first budget resolution, for which the
first rule allowed seven major alternatives and
scores of minor amendments. Other restrictive
rules allow any amendments printed in the
Congressional Record by a specified deadline to be
in order.

Another type of restrictive rules limits
amendments, but still allows floor amendments both
for majority party and minority party purposes.
On key budget matters, such rules focus floor
consideration on the parties' major alternatives,
serving as a centralizing force that brings the
House to clear-cut decisions. Often the minority
supports such complex rules[94] when they give the
minority the right to offer its chosen
alternatives.[95]

Finally, some restrictive rules are almost
completely closed, allowing only amendments
proposed by the committee of jurisdiction or only

---

[94] "The possibility of bipartisan support for a restrictive
rule is likely to be greatest when the Rules Committee
accepts the recommendations of the reporting committee and
permits amendments to be offered by Members of both
parties." Bach, 18 Harv. J. Legis. at 574. For example, on
the first budget resolution in 1981, only four amendments
were in order; in June 1982, on the second attempt to pass a
first budget resolution, only two amendments were in order;
on the 1981 tax cut bill only two amendments were in
order. All three times the rule sailed through, and all
three times the Republican alternatives won, marking a high-
water mark of Republican influence in the House -- and of
general acceptance of restrictive rules.

[95] Such complex rules help the minority leadership, in two
ways. By focusing on the minority's chief alternative, they
may actually help the minority leadership corral dissidents
and maintain its internal organization. Also, technically,
the waivers in the complex rule make alternatives possible
that had never been possible on the minority's traditional
tool, the motion to recommit with instructions, because such
motions were subject to points of order, such as for
germaneness.

amendments for majority party purposes.   For
example, the 1982 surface transportation bill,
H.R. 6211, allowed no amendments to the tax title
except Ways and Means Committee amendments, being
little different from an old-style closed rule.[96]
    Special rules that only allowed amendments
for majority party purposes can elicit complaints
and resistance from the minority.   Examples of
major battles included the complex rule for the
reconciliation bill in 1981, when the Republicans
defeated the Democratic version of the rule
because it denied them a single up-or-down vote on
the President's program; and the special rule for
the omnibus continuing resolution in 1986, which
passed, but just barely, when it allowed virtually
no floor amending of the year's appropriations.[97]
    By the late 1980s, increasing use of
restrictive rules had become a controversial
issue.   In 1987, Minority Whip Trent Lott (R-
Miss.) charged that "The Democratic leadership is
trying to turn the Rules Committee into the
stranglehold on this institution that it was 30
years ago."[98]   That year, "[i]t took four attempts

---

[96]   Opponents wished to offer alternative tax approaches to
those of Ways and Means, such as capping the income tax
cut.   Combined in their opposition to the rule with outright
opponents of the tax increase, they came within a hair of
defeating the rule, which squeaked by 197-194.   1982
Congressional Quarterly Almanac 323-34.

[97]   Wehr, Omnibus Spending Bill Wins House Approval by One
Vote, 44 Cong. Q. Week. Rep. 2261 (1986); id. at 2314 (vote
number 382 on the special rule, which was adopted by the
close margin of 216-202.).

[98]   Lott is quoted in Hook, GOP Chafes Under Restrictive
House Rules, 45 Cong. Q. Weekly Rep. 2449 (1987).   "The
remarkable unity demonstrated by House Republicans on a
number of votes to order the previous question on complex
rules certainly demonstrates their belief that those rules
organized the amending process in a fashion that operated to
their clear disadvantage."   Bach, 18 Harv. J. Legis. at
576.   The Republicans would oppose the previous question as
the only way to amend a complex rule, as discussed in the
next chapter.

(footnote continued)

by the Democratic leadership before welfare reform legislation passed the full House in December, largely because of controversy over the rule."[99] In the first attempt, a coalition of Republicans and conservative Democrats defeated the special rule which sought to join the welfare reform bill and the budget reconciliation bill.

At the second attempt, Democrats complained that a proposed restrictive rule amounted to a "gag rule." The third attempt to move welfare reform suffered much the problem of the second.[100] On the fourth try, a restrictive rule passed, as did the bill.

D.   SUSPENSION OF THE RULES

When Used

The procedure of suspension of the rules under Rule XXVII allows the House to act swiftly and directly, but it allows very limited debate, no amendments, and no motions, and it requires a two-thirds vote for adoption. As described above, in the 1970s the House began making increasing use of suspensions to move lesser legislation. Thereafter, the House used suspensions when bills

---

In 1982 House Democrats used a restrictive rule to allow only one amendment to a reconciliation bill to cut government retirees' cost of living increase. The rule put the Republicans to the unpalatable dilemma of offering that one allowed amendment, which would have required them to vote for a very visible and unpopular cut, or drop their economic program. The Republicans fought hard against that rule, but lost, 240-170, and chose not to offer the one amendment allowed.

[99]   1987 Congressional Quarterly Almanac 555.

[100]   This "was the latest in a string of bills to be sent to the House floor under highly restrictive rules that precluded members from offering amendments. Republicans had long protested such rules and they were now joined by scores of Democrats who resented being cut off from any opportunity to shape major legislation moving through the House." 1987 Congressional Quarterly Almanac 556.

meet three criteria.

First, a committee must have considered and approved the bill. By tradition, the Speaker only recognizes the mover of a motion to suspend the rules after the committee of jurisdiction reports the bill. Otherwise the motion would constitute a new form of discharge, with major injury to the committee system. It should be noted, though, that this tradition is not an explicit requirement for the motion in Rule XXVII, and House precedents establish that a motion to suspend the rules can be used, as it has been used on rare occasions, for a bill that has not been considered in committee.[101] The tradition does not mean that the committee must report the bill out in exactly the form put forth in the motion to suspend, as discussed below, just that it have reported the bill out.

Once a committee reports out a bill, the committee chair makes the initial judgment about whether to request the Speaker to entertain a motion to suspend, as opposed to requesting the Rules Committee to grant a special rule. Committee chairs may consult with others on the committee, and in fact usually do consult the minority, but some disputes in this regard may well occur, as reflected in a 1983 contretemps. Chairperson E. "Kika" de la Garza (D-Tex.) of the Agriculture Committee moved under suspension a farm bill reported unanimously by the committee.[102]

Chairperson de la Garza admitted that "[u]sually we make mention of this at the committee meeting, but this time we did not."[103]

---

[101] Deschler 21 §§ 10.5, 10.6.

[102] The subcommittee chair and ranking minority member had asked for suspension treatment, but the ranking minority Member of the full committee, Representative Edward R. Madigan (R-Ill.), complained on the floor that he "was never consulted about this bill being placed on the Suspension Calendar," and he had wanted "the opportunity to try to work out some compromise or a resolution of the differences that exist between the administration and this body with regard to this bill." 129 Cong. Rec. H6102 (daily ed. Aug. 1, 1983).

(footnote continued)

As the argument continued on a later occasion,
Chairperson de la Garza emphasized that the votes
for reporting the bills had been unanimous. "What
do you do with something unanimous out of the
committee? You go on suspension." The ranking
minority member responded with a list of reasons
that unanimity might not be all that it
appeared.[104] Still, the ranking minority member's
only procedural recourse for the asserted breach
in comity was to try to defeat the bill.[105] He
could not make any point of order that suspension
was improper.[106]

---

[103] 129 Cong. Rec. H6107 (daily ed. Aug. 1, 1983).

[104] Representative Madigan explained that one bill was
reported unanimously "while the gentleman from Texas and I
were in the back room with the Secretary of Agriculture and
we did not even know the committee was voting it out." A
second was reported when he (Representative Madigan) was
"stuck in the elevator of the Longworth Building." The
third was reported when Representative Madigan was told by
another Member they would "continue to work on this bill
after it was passed out of the committee. Then, it was
placed on the Suspension Calendar. . . ." Chairman de la
Garza responded, "So now I am accused because the elevator
get[s] stuck in the Longworth Building." 129 Cong. Rec.
H8294 (daily ed. Oct. 18, 1983).

[105] The House adopted H.R. 3564 under suspension. Since
the differences with the Administration had never been
worked out, the President killed the bill by veto on August
12. After some adjustments, a new bill on the subject, H.R.
3914, was passed under suspension on September 20, and
became Public Law 98-100.

[106] The House had declined in 1977 to take up a Republican
proposal that suspensions only be "authorized by rollcall
vote of the committee having jurisdiction or by joint
request of the chairman and ranking minority member". Bach,
quoting 123 Cong. Rec. H10 (daily ed. Jan. 4,
1977)(amendment to rules change that the Minority Leader
would have offered if allowed). Historically, there were
two types of suspension days, one for suspensions approved
by committee, and ones for suspensions sought by
individuals, and on the committee day, the measure had to
have been referred to committee, and both the motion, and
(footnote continued)

Second, the Speaker must grant the request for consideration of the measure under suspension. The Speaker retains the absolute power first claimed in 1880 not to recognize Members to move bills under suspension. The Speaker's decision reflects political and scheduling calculations of the types discussed in the previous chapter regarding the roles of the Speaker and Majority Leader. It also reflects the guidelines in Democratic Caucus Rule 39 which provide that "[t]he Speaker . . . shall not schedule any bill or resolution for consideration under the Suspension of the Rules . . . in any case where a request . . . contains a cost estimate in excess of $100,000,000 in any fiscal year," except when authorized by the Steering and Policy Committee. The guidelines aimed to cut back on the controversial use of the suspension procedure,[107] and they have done so in the main, although the House continues to consider large numbers of bills under suspension.

Even so, the Speaker occasionally entertains major bills under suspension. In 1984, the House passed the bill repealing the withholding of tax from interest and dividends under suspension. The bill was expected to "reduc[e] revenues by roughly $13.4 billion over the next 5 fiscal years."[108] The bill was highly controversial because it reduced revenues that the government sought to collect from tax evaders. Not only did the Ways and Means Committee strongly oppose the bill,[109]

---

the amendments included in the motion, had to have been authorized by the committee. V Hinds §§ 6805 ("informal assent" by the committee, without a meeting, ruled to be insufficient), 6812 (only authorized amendments), 6813 (only measures referred, not committee-originated). However, the distinction between committee days and individual days withered away, and with it the strict requirements for formal committee approval.

[107] It was estimated that if there had been an absolute bar to suspensions of that kind (involving over $100,000,000) in 1978, "21 bills considered under suspension would not have been allowed on the calendar." Cooper at 2695.

[108] 129 Cong. Rec. H2992 (daily ed. May 17, 1984)(Rep. Daniel Rostenkowski (D-Ill.)).

but the President had threatened that he would veto it (but in the end, did not). The House adopted the measure under suspension by an overwhelming vote.

In 1987, the Public Works Committee brought up its airline consumer protection bill, an important measure, under suspension, from fear of amendments:

> Because of concern that members would offer even more controversial amendments to reimpose controls on the industry, Public Works leaders successfully pushed to have the bill considered by the full House under suspension of the rules, a procedure that did not allow for any amendments.[110]

Some such major measures brought up under suspension have been defeated. A prominent example was the consideration in 1983 under suspension of the Equal Rights Amendment. In bringing the ERA under suspension of the rules, the majority leadership precluded opponents from offering amendments on subjects the opponents considered major issues, concerning abortion, veterans preferences, and the drafting of women for the armed services. It also restricted the debate on the constitutional amendment to 20 minutes on a side. The Speaker took the floor, and defended the procedure, explaining bluntly:

> The power of the Speaker of the House is the power of scheduling . . . Why is [the ERA] here today? Because I have been asked by the people who are interested in this, that it not get log-jammed . . . . [T]here is no way this [constitutional] amendment would pass under an open rule with either one of those

---

[109] The committee reported the measure to the floor only after a discharge petition had gathered the necessary signatures anyway to force a floor vote. It reported the measure without opinion, to show its lack of support. Both the committee chair and its ranking minority member spoke and voted against the bill.

[110] 1987 Congressional Quarterly Almanac 337.

amendments [regarding abortion and the
draft]."[111]

The ERA fell short of the two-thirds needed for
passage, losing by the slim margin of 278-147,
with some Members voting against it because of the
use of the suspension procedure.[112]
    Third, once the committee reports the bill,
and the Speaker recognizes a motion to suspend,

Congressional Quarterly Almanac 381 (antitrust exemption
bill protected from non-germane amendment to expand consumer
antitrust rights).

[111] 129 Cong. Rec. H9856 (daily ed. Nov. 15, 1984). The
Speaker was alluding to the fact that the sponsors of the
ERA would not support it had anti-abortion amendments been
attached, and although the sponsors of such amendments might
have the strength to attach them to the ERA, they might not
support the ERA on final passage even with such amendments
on board. In a nutshell, the Speaker took the ERA up under
suspension to preclude "killer" amendments. Some observers
also believed that if the ERA was going to be defeated,
tactically it made a cleaner election issue against those
who opposed it for them to have to vote against it on a
straight up-or-down vote than for there to be a complex
amendment situation.

[112] The vote is at 129 Cong. Rec. H9865 (daily ed. Nov. 15,
1984). A switch of six votes would have sufficed for
passage.

    Strong opponents of the measure, who naturally
denounced the suspension procedure, were joined by
Representative Romano L. Mazzoli (D-Ky.). He was a
cosponsor of the ERA who had voted for it in committee, but
who said that he would vote against it under suspension,
explaining that he "must oppose this procedure that we are
engaged in today because it perverts and is contemptuous of
the legislative process." 129 Cong. Rec. H9854 (daily ed.
Nov. 15, 1984).

    Consideration of a constitutional amendment under
suspension posed a subtle issue because under the
Constitution, constitutional amendments always require a
two-thirds vote in the House (and Senate) for adoption when
being submitted to the states. Thus, the normal restraint
on resorting to suspension -- the larger requirement for
adoption of a two-thirds, not majority, vote -- does not
increase the voting requirement for constitutional
amendments.

then after the procedure described below, the House must adopt it by a two-thirds vote. The House may deny a two-thirds vote for all sorts of reasons. Of course, the House may object to the bill itself: many debates on controversial suspensions include no comments at all about procedure, only substantive criticism of the bill.

Alternatively, the House may object to the procedure, particularly the bar against amendments. Representative Edward R. Madigan (R-Ill.) complained during the dispute previously discussed that suspension "is the same as if the bill had a closed rule . . . which denies to me or to any other Member of the House any opportunity to be a legislator."[113] As he elaborated:

> Members . . . who are not members of the House Agriculture Committee are not given the opportunity to be legislators in the sense that they are given an opportunity to offer amendments . . . . There are 390 Members of this House that want the opportunity to debate, that want the opportunity to offer amendments, that want the opportunity to be legislators and it is being denied to them again one more time tonight.[114]

In another instance, in 1982 the House considered under suspension a bill to lengthen the terms of patents for government-approved products. Representative Barney Frank (D-Mass.) argued vigorously against consideration under suspension:

> Allusion was made to the fact that opponents to the bill . . . were overwhelmed. Mr. Speaker, we were 'whelmed,' but I am not sure

---

[113]   129 Cong. Rec. H6102 (daily ed. Aug. 1, 1983).

[114]   129 Cong. Rec. H8294 (daily ed. Oct. 18, 1983). On this occasion the bill had come up through another route than suspension, but his remarks concerned suspension as well, as he complained that "Every bill that has been coming from the House Agriculture Committee has been coming to the floor either under a circuitous procedure like this or on the suspension calendar or in some other way . . . ." Id.

that we were overwhelmed. We got better than
a third of the committee that supported some
fairly substantial amendments, and we lost by
votes of 16 to 10 and 16 to 9. That seems to
me to justify a chance to deal with the bill
in a form that allows amendment.[115]

The House found the argument persuasive, and
rejected the motion to suspend the rules and pass
the bill.

Procedure

The procedure for a measure under suspension
begins when the committee reports the measure out
and the committee chair writes a letter to the
Speaker requesting consideration of the measure
under suspension.[116] Under the Democratic Caucus
guidelines discussed in the previous section, when
the chair sends the letter requesting suspension
treatment, he includes a cost estimate.   While
most such letters note that the cost estimate

---

[115] 128 Cong. Rec. H6922 (daily ed. Sept. 13, 1982). The
amendments concerned such matters as whether the regulatory
delay for which the patent term would be lengthened had been
the fault of inadequate patent applicant testing, or had
been otherwise the patenter's own fault.

[116] Democratic Caucus Rule 39 requires that "any committee
chairman requesting that a bill or resolution be brought up
under the suspension of the Rules of the House must make
this request in writing and include any cost
estimate . . . ."

For various scheduling reasons, there may be a hiatus
after the bill is reported and before suspension is
requested.   For example, a committee may first request a
special rule.   In 1981 the Science and Technology Committee
reported its annual authorization for the National Oceanic
and Atmospheric Administration (NOAA), H.R. 2803, on May 19,
1981, and a week later requested a hearing from the Rules
Committee.   The Rules Committee did not act on the
request.   Only after six weeks of waiting, on July 8, did
Science and Technology send its letter to the Speaker
requesting suspension treatment.

shows the measure is under the $100 million guideline, it is not at all unusual for a letter to note that the measure is over the guideline but request suspension consideration anyway.[117]

Staff of the Speaker and Majority Leader who coordinate the preparation of tentative schedules watch over the requests for suspensions. When the leadership approves a request, it joins a list mentioned by the Majority Leader in his announcement of the next week's schedule.[118] Technically, the House has no "Suspension Calendar," the way it has its five formal calendars (Union, House, Private, Consent, and Discharge), but Members and observers often refer to the leadership's informal list that way.

Rule XXVII (1) provides now that the Speaker shall not "entertain a motion to suspend the rules except on Mondays and Tuesdays . . . ." During the period 1880-1974, the House only considered motions to suspend the rules on two Mondays each month. As Majority Leader and then Speaker, Tip O'Neill favored the use of suspensions by increasing the available days from two days per month to eight.[119]

---

[117] For example, the letter seeking suspension for the 1981 NOAA authorization pointed out that the bill authorized $ 498 million in expenditures, which "does exceed the $100 million ceiling guideline . . . " The letter, signed by both the chair and ranking minority Member of the committee, explained that "the bill is non-controversial and has strong bipartisan support, and we feel that action by the House can be expedited by its consideration under the Suspension of Rules." The letter is reproduced as a sample in House Committee on Science and Technology, 97th Cong., Legislative Manual 94 (Comm. Print. 1982).

[118] For example, the NOAA request letter, dated July 8, led to consideration of the bill on July 27. When the Majority Whip sends out his weekly letter announcing the schedule, and the Majority Leader announces that schedule on the floor each Thursday, they announce which bills are expected to be taken up under suspension of the rules the following week.

[119] In 1880 the motion was restricted to the first and third Mondays of each month. This represented a holdover from the period before 1880, when the minority had used the (footnote continued)

Rule XXVII also makes suspension in order "during the last six days of a session," because of the enormous crush of business toward the end of the session.   For example, for the week in November, 1983, when the ERA was brought up, the Majority Leader announced 26 bills for suspension on Monday and 20 for suspension on Tuesday.[120]   On December 13, 1983, the House passed 14 bills under suspension, and defeated five.[121]   The House often fixes the period at the end of session when suspensions are in order by unanimous consent or by resolution.[122]   Also, the House occasionally provides for other suspension days by unanimous consent or by resolution.[123]

Typically, when the House finishes its preliminaries on a day on which suspensions have been scheduled, the managers of the bills bring them up in the sequence informally settled by the Majority Leader's list, unless some last-minute consideration changes the schedule.   As with management of other bills, the manager may be the

---

motion to embarrass the majority; the 1880 rule had limited the number of days on which the motion could be offered to limit the opportunity for such minority efforts.   In 1973 the following first and third Tuesdays were added, and in 1977 the window was expanded to Monday and Tuesday of every week.   House Manual § 902.

[120]   129 Cong. Rec. H9703 (daily ed. Nov. 10, 1984).   The bills are listed in the Daily Digest.   129 Cong. Rec. D1528-29 (daily ed. Nov. 11, 1983).

[121]   Deschler 21 § 11.9.

[122]   Rule XXVII's terms concerning the end of a session sometimes present a technical problem, because the House does not know formally what are "the last six days of a session" until both Houses adopt an adjournment resolution.   The uncertainties of processing the last key items, particularly when they are subject to a filibuster in the Senate, often push the adoption of such a resolution to the very eve of adjournment, requiring earlier fixing by unanimous consent or other action of a date after which suspensions are in order each day.   Deschler 21 §§ 11.3, 11.5, 11.9.

[123]   Deschler 21 § 11.

chair of either the committee or the subcommittee
(and the minority manager may be ranking at either
level).[124]   On unusual occasions, some other
interested Member may manage, such as when
Chairperson Morris Udall (D-Ariz.) let another
Democratic Member from Arizona move to suspend the
rules for an Arizona wilderness bill.

When his bill's turn comes, managers rise and
state either "Mr. Speaker, I move to suspend the
rules and pass the bill (H.R. ----)," or "Mr.
Speaker, I move to suspend the rules and pass the
bill (H.R. ----) as amended."   In making the
motion, the managers decide whether to include
amendments, and if so what ones.   That is up to
the managers; the amendments need not have been
formally recommended by the committee reporting
the bill.[125]   Thus, the managers exercises
considerable power, for they alone decide what
will be put before the House.   The only
opportunity for decision will be whether to vote
for or against the motion as it is offered,
without anyone but the managers offering
amendments.[126]

Since most suspensions pass, the managers
effectively write the final versions of bill by
what they put in their motions.   Moreover, the
managers have no obligation even to commit
themselves in advance as to what they will include
in his motion.   Thus, up to the last moment,
managers may bargain with dissidents within their
committees or potential floor opponents by
including or altering amendments in their motion
as they deem appropriate.   Frenzied last-minute
bargaining among interest groups is far from
unknown.

Once the manager makes the motion, it is the

---

[124]   For example, for the ERA, Chairman Peter Rodino (D-
N.J.) of the full Judiciary Committee was the majority
manager; Representative F. James Sensenbrenner (R-Wis.),
ranking minority member of the Subcommittee on Civil and
Constitutional rights, was the minority manager.   129 Cong.
Rec. H9850 (daily ed. Nov. 15, 1983).

[125]   Deschler 21 §§ 10.10, 17.14.

[126]   Deschler 21 §§ 16, 17.3.

Clerk's turn to read the bill, but "[u]nder the
modern practice . . . only the title of the bill
is normally read by the Clerk . . . "[127] Members
may, at this point, demand a second -- a vote to
determine whether a majority wishes to take up the
matter.[128]   Under current rules, a Member can
demand a second if and only if the bill being
brought up by the motion being offered has not
been "printed" and available.[129]

---

[127]   House Manual § 903.   An exception may be made when
members would get surprised by what the manager includes in
the motion as amendments.   "[A]mendments included in the
motion are not reported separately, but the Chair may, in
his discretion, where objection is made to that procedure,
require the reading of an amendment which is not printed or
otherwise available," Id.

[128]   This requirement dates from 1880, when the majority
party created it to fend off use of the motion by the
majority.   In 1880, the suspension procedure was revised to
require that "[a]ll motions to suspend the rules shall,
before being submitted to the House, be seconded by a
majority by tellers, if demanded." Bach at 38. A vote by
tellers, like a division vote, does not record which members
vote each way, only how many, so that majority members could
vote down a proposition (by denying it a second) without
having to go on record against it.

     Thus, the majority could avoid "trick" minority motions
by refusing to second the motion.   The motion was made a
tool only for the majority.   Once the Speaker established
his discretion in recognition for making the motion,
minority use was no longer a problem.

[129]   A 1979 rules change eliminated the vote on the second,
which the majority had come to see as a dilatory demand by
the minority, since its original purpose (discussed in the
preceding section) was now amply served by the Speaker's
power not to recognize disfavored movants.   With that
change, Rule XVII(2) now provides that

     a second shall not be required on a motion to suspend
     the rules where printed copies of the measure or matter
     as proposed to be passed or agreed to by the motion
     have been available for one legislative day before the
     motion is considered.
(footnote continued)

When the manager moves suspension with last-minute changes or compromises included, as is often the case, opponents can demand a second as a last stalling tactic, for the manager's changes mean the bill has not been "printed" in the form being offered. In a throwback to old procedures, the vote on a second takes place by tellers, not by a recorded vote, meaning that the Members voting for or against are counted, but only total votes, not the ways individual Members voted, are announced.

As for debate, currently Rule XXVII(3) provides that "it shall be in order, before the final vote is taken thereon, to debate the proposition to be voted upon for 40 minutes, one-half of such time to be given to debate in favor of, and one-half to debate in opposition to, such proposition."[130] Accordingly, after the motion is put (and any request for a second is resolved), the Chair announces that two Members will each be recognized for 20 minutes, one of them being the mover of the motion. The ranking minority Members on the full or subcommittee are favored to be recognized for the other 20 minutes, but when they support the measure, as is often the case for suspensions because of their noncontroversiality, actual opponents have the option of inquiring whether the minority managers "qualify."

If the managers cannot state that they oppose the measure "in its present form," the Speaker will recognize other minority Members for the 20 minutes.[131] While some in the minority urge such

---

The Speaker may announce that "Pursuant to the rule, a second is not required on this motion." However, the Speaker, when he knows that the motion being offered includes changes from the bill as printed, will inquire whether a second is demanded, and if the Chair learns this after debate has begun, he will inquire at that point whether a second is demanded. Deschler 21 § 13.1.

[130] Prior to 1880, at this point, the motion came immediately to a vote, without debate. Once the House began in the 1870s to use the motion not only to schedule, but also to pass measures, the need for some debate became palpable.

(footnote continued)

replacement of a bill-supporting manager,[132] often
no one bothers, as the manager's role is limited
to debate and time control; even bill supporters
usually dole out time fairly. As for the 40
minute limit on debate, it is permissible to
extend the limit by unanimous consent, but such
consent is rare, as the House prefers to keep
debate short on all suspensions.[133]

After the debate on each bill, the vote may
occur. However, often the Speaker will put the
vote off if a recorded vote is demanded. Monday
is one of the two days on which Rule XXVII makes
suspensions in order, and for most of the year,
the leadership avoids floor votes on Monday to
allow Members to conduct business elsewhere,
particularly in their districts or in committee.
Accordingly, it is frequent for the Chair to
invoke for suspensions House Rule I(5), which

---

[131]   The House Republican Manual, at 121-22 (citations
omitted), summarizes the precedents about recognition:

A member of the minority party who is opposed to the
bill is given preference in recognition over a Member
of the majority party who is opposed to the bill.
However, the Speaker will give preference to any Member
who states that he or she is opposed to the bill, even
if he or she is a Member of the majority party, if the
other Members seeking recognition are not actually
opposed to the bill. If two minority Members opposed
to the bill seek recognition, the chair will recognize
the one with the most seniority. Once a Member is
recognized, no Member may rise, declare himself or
herself in opposition to the bill and win recognition,
even though the Member previously recognized is not
actually opposed. It's too late once recognition is
granted.

[132]   The House Republican Manual, at 121-22, urges:

To insure control of the time for debate when no
committee Memmbers on your side are opposed to the
bill, a Member not on the commmittee who is opposed
should seek recognition. He or she can then yield to
committee Members. This precludes opponents on the
other side of the aisle from controlling the time.

[133]   Deschler 21 § 15.3.

provides that "whenever a recorded vote is ordered
. . . the Speaker may, in his discretion, postpone
further proceedings on each such question to a
designated time . . . within two legislative
days." This produces, on the subsequent day when
the vote is held, a string of recorded votes on
various suspensions, with no intervening
debates. Usually the string of votes occurs in
the order in which the motions to suspend were
previously presented.

Suspensions require a two-thirds vote for
adoption.[134] This may be a voice vote, for often
suspensions are so noncontroversial that no Member
demands a recorded vote. When a Member wishes to
demand a recorded vote, she must follow a careful
procedural plan at the end of the debate on the
motion. She may ask for the yeas and nays, if she
expects one fifth of those present (however few
they may be) to support her. Alternatively, she
may let a voice vote occur, and then object to the
vote on the ground that a quorum is not present.
The Speaker may postpone a yea and nay vote, and
may postpone further proceedings following the
objection for lack of a quorum.[135] When such

---

[134] The two-thirds is two-thirds of the Members present and
voting yea or nay; the total does not include Members who
vote present. "Members voting 'present' are only counted to
establish a quorum and not to determine a two-thirds
majority." 129 Cong. Rec. H 9849 (daily ed. Nov. 15,
1984)(response of the Chair on parliamentary inquiry prior
to consideration of the ERA).

[135] If a Member demands a recorded vote before the Speaker
announces that further proceedings on the motion will be
postponed, the demand requires a second of 44, hard to
obtain during the sparsely-attended debates on suspension.
Deschler 21 §§ 17.2, 17.6, 17.10, 17.11. See, e.g. 129
Cong. Rec. H 1476 (daily ed. March 22, 1983)(refusal, for
lack of a sufficient second, of Representative Ron Paul's
(R-Tex.) demand for recorded vote on adoption of H.R. 2112
extending the Defense Production Act). Moreover, if she
makes a demand for the yeas and neas which is rejected for
lack of a second, the demand cannot be repeated during
"further proceedings." Deschler 21. § 17.11. The matter is
discussed further in the section on voting and quorum calls.

(footnote continued)

further proceedings occur for lack of a quorum, usually on a later day, the vote is put de novo.[136]   At this time, she demands a yea and nay or recorded vote, looking to her colleagues for a sufficient second.[137]

When that string of record votes occurs, not only do Members vote without having heard the preceding debate, but they may also vote quickly.   Usually, the Speaker reduces the time for taking votes on suspension votes after the first one to five minutes.[138]   These rapid-succession, debate-free votes sometimes justify the saying that "no one should watch sausage or laws being made."   Many Members admit they do not attend closely to the considerations regarding large numbers of suspensions voted in a row.   One journalist's account of proceedings during such a

---

If a Member seeks to obtain an automatic roll call prior to the putting of the question (for a voice vote), she will be frustrated, because the Speaker will postpone further proceedings.   An automatic roll call can only be obtained by making a point of order that a quorum is not present; under Rule XV(6)(e)(1), "it shall not be in order to make or entertain a point of order that a quorum is not present unless the Speaker has put the pending motion or proposition to a vote."   Postponing further proceedings means the Speaker has not yet put the pending motion to a vote, so there can be no point of order about quorums, and no automatic roll call vote.   Deschler 21 § 17.15.   Also, by postponing further proceedings, the Speaker precludes any subsequent immediate demand for a recorded vote.   Deschler 21 §§ 17.7 - 17.9.

[136]   House Manual §631.

[137]   Usually the postponed proceedings consist of a series of votes on suspension.   With all the Members coming to the floor to vote on that series, a Member can usually find enough supportive colleagues to obtain a sufficient second.   Often during such a series, an automatic roll call could not be obtained merely by objecting to the vote on the ground that a quorum is not present, because during such a series, a quorum is generally present.   In those instances when a quorum is not present, a Member could obtain an automatic roll call vote.

[138]   Deschler 21 § 17.13.

string was the following:

> One House Democrat paused last week on the
> way to cast his fourth in a rapid-fire series
> of votes.
>
> "I don't know a goddamn thing about the
> Amateur Sports Act of 1978," he said,
> referring to a bill he was about to vote
> on. "So I'll just have to ask someone on the
> floor. And frankly I couldn't care less."
>
> Another young Democrat dashed onto the
> House floor to record his vote on one bill in
> the series, then emerged a minute later and
> admitted, "I can't tell you what the next
> vote is." Scanning his Democratic Study
> Group summary of bills, he added ruefully,
> "Normally I do better than I'm doing
> today."[139]

In 1988, at the end of the 101st Congress,
the House set new records for voting on a string
of suspensions in what the press described as a
"frantic voting binge":

> In the spirit of the Olympics, the House
> shattered all previous records in roll-call
> voting last Tuesday -- 36 votes in just two
> hours, two minutes -- in a session marked by
> raucous applause, catcalls, and Bronx
> cheers . . . .
>
> It all happened because Rep. Bob Walker (R-
> Pa.) Monday demanded roll-call votes on 43
> resolutions brought up under suspension of
> the rules . . . .
>
> Rep. John Murtha (D-Pa.), who was scheduled
> to preside that day, made a similarly
> stunning and unprecedented request. He
> proposed that after the first 15-minute roll-
> call vote, the House pare down the voting
> periods for each vote to two minutes.[140]

---

[139]   Cooper at 2693.

(footnote continued)

Virtually no motions are in order under
suspension. The motion cannot be divided, tabled,
or amended (apart from the amendments included in
the motion itself). One motion to adjourn may be
offered during consideration under Rule XXVII, and
a motion to suspend that is adopted (but not one
rejected) can be reconsidered, but rarely are
either of those steps taken.

The motion for suspension of the rules has
another function besides moving minor bills
quickly and major ones, on occasion, without
amendment. It can be used like a special rule
waiving points of order, since no points of order
against the underlying measure may be raised under
suspension.[140]   For example, managers may use
suspension of the rules to bring up conference
reports, or measures previously passed by the
House and then passed in some form by the
Senate. Managers do so not to get these scheduled
-- conference reports are privileged in their own
right, and previously-passed measures usually come
to the floor by unanimous consent -- but to avoid
a point of order because the conferees exceeded
the scope of disagreement, or because some budget
rule has been violated.[141]

---

[140] Frazier, House Goes on Record-Setting Spree, Passes 36
Bills in 2 Hours, Roll Call, Oct. 16, 1988, at 1, 24.

[140] The only points of order that can be raised -- the only
"rules" not "suspended" by the motion -- are those from Rule
XXVII itself, such as that the motion has been raised on a
day when the rule does not make such motions in order.

[141] In a complex version of this approach, in 1983 the
House adopted under suspension of the rules a resolution, H.
Res. 293, which provided that the House adopt (1) the
conference report on a bill providing small business with
access to federal procurement information (S. 272), and (2)
a concurrent resolution changing some of the matters in that
conference report (by directing the Secretary of the Senate
to change the enrolled bill). As explained by the chair of
the Small Business Committee, Parren Mitchell (D-Md.), the
matter was

handled on the suspension calendar . . . "to avoid any
possible point o[f] order for exceeding the scope of
(footnote continued)

When a measure fails under suspension, that is often the end.   However, if the measure falls short of two thirds but receives more than a majority, its proponents may then ask the Rules Committee for a rule.   Indeed, sometimes the proponents just try suspension first, hoping to avoid compromising or weakening amendments, and when that fails, they then face the amendment problems.   For example, in 1979, proponents of a national holiday for Martin Luther King's birthday brought a bill up under suspension of the rules. They fell short by four votes.   When they obtained a special rule, the House attached such weakening amendments that sponsors pulled the bill off the floor, until 1983, when the House passed the bill under suspension by 338-90.[142]

The other problem with post-suspension resort to a special rule is the delay.   At the end of the session, there may not be time to get a special rule.   On the other hand, there are examples of swift action such as H.R. 3191, to modify the North American Convention on tax rules.   The bill received a majority but not two-thirds vote of 219-164, failing under suspension on December 13.[143]   On December 15, after an emergency hearing, the Rules Committee reported out H. Res. 630, a special rule for the bill.   On December 16, the House adopted the rule and the bill.

E. DISCHARGE

The House's restrictive procedure can sometimes create intense tension by clamping strict control

---

conference;" the concurrent resolution was used because "conference reports cannot be amended on the floor . . . . The procedure needed to accomplish the changes is for the House and Senate to adopt a resolution for the Secretary of the Senate to make the changes."

129 Cong. Rec. H6059 (daily ed. Aug. 1, 1983)(Rep. Mitchell).

142 See 41 Cong. Q. Weekly Rep. 2178 (1983).

143 129 Cong. Rec. H 9571 (daily ed. Dec. 13, 1984).

from the top over what can come to the floor --
tension made all the more explosive because the
representatives of the "people's body" have no
buffer from surges of public opinion.   Without a
"safety valve," sooner or later that explosive
pressure would produce a revolution in the House
-- as, in fact, it did in 1909 against "Czar"
Cannon.   The House's most prominent "safety valve"
allowing bottled-up bills to come to the floor
over the resistance of the majority leadership,
the   Rules   Committee,   and   the   committee   of
jurisdiction, is its discharge procedure.   Because
the discharge procedure represents this ultimate
release   point,   it   looms   much   larger   in   public
debate surrounding the House and in House history
than would be expected from the infrequency of its
successful use.   The   discharge   rule's   complex
provisions and the House's subtle attitudes toward
its use derive from its lengthy development and
the two modern eras of use.

Development of the Discharge Rule

Prior   to   strong   leadership   control   of   the
schedule,   there   was   no   need   for   a   discharge
procedure, and the strong late-nineteenth century
Speakers who established such control refused to
allow any effective discharge procedure.[144]   After
the revolt against Czar Cannon demonstrated the
necessity for House majority recourse against the
leadership,   the   House   created   a   discharge
procedure   in   1910.[145]   However,   the   new   procedure

---

[144]   Beth at 5-6.

[145]   Just as "Czar" Cannon had controlled consideration of
bills in the House, "[l]ikewise, many chairmen of standing
committees has played the part of little autocrats over
their respective committees."   F. Riddick, The United States
Congress 238 (1949).   "This rule was offered by the Rules
Committee in 1910 as a sop to liberal pressures within the
House."   Damon at 217.   Its enactment is described in P.
DeW.   Hasbrouck,   Party   Government   in   the   House   of
Representatives 139-42 (1927).   At the time, the rule was
considered "purely experimental" but "a long step forward."
Id. at 141 (quoting congressional leaders).

languished unused after it proved vulnerable to obstructionist tactics,[146] particularly by one legendary obstructionist.[147]

In 1924, progressive Republicans forced reforms in the discharge rule.[148] The new rule

---

[146] That early discharge procedure depended on a written motion by a Member, which could be called up on a particular day; adoption of the motion discharged the bill from committee and placed it on the appropriate calendar. The text of the rule is in Hasbrouck, supra, at 141.

For the uselessness of the early rule, see Beth at 7-9; Damon at 217-20; Riddick (1949) at 237-8.

[147] The early rule "was open to perversion in a number of ways, and James R. Mann (Rep.) of Illinois, one of the most clever parliamentarians in the House, set out to pervert it." Hasbrouck, supra, at 143. Mann's tactics resembled the postcloture filibuster tactics used in the Senate in the 1970s; they included insisting on the reading at full length of the bills for which motions were made, offering of up to 107 discharge motions (none serious) by one Member (all of which had to be processed before serious motions further down the calendar were reached), and standard dilatory tactics such as quorum calls and motions to adjourn. Id.

In 1911, the House attempted to stop this obstruction, by revising the rule's provisions. Id. at 145. Rep. Mann then adopted the opposite tactic, pushing forward motions to discharge popular bills before the majority Democrats were ready to act on them. Thereby he embarrassed the majority by forcing it to vote against motions regarding propositions it supported. After the majority party suffered one day of thus being assaulted with its own program, it made sure that "the discharge rule remained for ten years a 'dead letter', -- until the session following Mr. Mann's death." Id. at 147. It did so in part by 1912 changes in the discharge rule, which reduced the priority of discharge motions. Id.

[148] In terms of its origin, the discharge rule is kin to other Progressive Era procedures, like the initiative, recall, and referendum, intended to allow popular rule in the face of "machine" control. The rule change was the Progressives' price for ending a deadlock over the choice of Speaker. See Hasbrouck, supra, at 148-55 (describing the pressures in 1922-24 leading to revision of the discharge (footnote continued)

provided for a petition to discharge, signed by a
sufficient number of Members, as the prerequisite
to a House vote on a motion to discharge a
committee.   The discharged matter did not just go
on   the   calendars   (where   it   might   lie
unconsidered), but was subject to a motion for
immediate consideration.   Also, the new rule
provided an important alternative channel for
getting a bill to the floor: discharging a special
rule tailored for consideration of the bill.[149]
In 1931, Depression-era Democrats, chafing over
the   restrictions   of   the   1920s,   plugged   the
remaining loopholes that had allowed filibusters
and put the rule in virtually its present form.[150]
     Since the revision of the rule in the 1920s
and 1930s, its use has been divided into roughly
two eras.   The first, from the late 1930s to the
early 1970s, consisted largely of efforts by

---

rule).   For a description of the 1923 contest over the
Speakership that paved the way to changing the rule, see C.
A. Moser, The Speaker and the House: Coalitions and Power in
the United States House of Representatives 45-48 (1979)
(print of the Free Congress Research and Education
Foundation).

[149]   Under this new rule, in 1924 for the first time a
discharged bill, which concerned arbitration of railroad
labor disputes, reached the House floor.   However, even the
new discharge rule still had loopholes, and opponents of the
bill killed it by a filibuster.   Beth at 11; Hasbrouck,
supra,   at   158-63.   Establishment   (non-Progressive)
Republicans regained control in the next election and
restrained the discharge procedure further in 1925, by
raising the required number of petition signatories to 218,
and by changing other provisions of the rule.   Damon at 222-
23.

[150]   Beth at 12-13; Damon at 223-4.   The 1931 changes
restored the details of the rule that had been altered in
1925.   Also, in 1931 the Democrats flirted with a minimal
signatory requirement of 145.   After some experience with
this, the Democrats "recognized that allowing fewer
signatures was too big a concession to either a political or
party minority," Rules Committee History at 122, and in 1935
restored the rule's present requirement of signatures by "a
majority of the total membership of the House," or 218
votes.   House Manual § 908.

liberals to free legislation bottled up by the conservative coalition domination of the Rules Committee and the committee chairs. This era began in 1937 when the newly-established conservative coalition denied a special rule to the bill to establish a national minimum wage and maximum number of hours.[151] Liberals responded by achieving an incredible record of "requir[ing] only two and one-half hours to obtain the 218 signatures" for the petition to discharge a special rule for the bill,[152] and the bill became law. During the following 35 years, liberals obtained sufficient signatures to force release of bills on lynching in the 1930s, civil rights and federal pay increases in 1960, civil rights again in 1964, home rule for the District of Columbia in 1965, and the Equal Rights Amendment in 1970.[153]

---

[151]   In 1937, President Franklin Roosevelt "gave top priority to legislation to set national minimum wage and maximum hours provisions and to provide certain child labor standards." Rules Committee History at 138. This legislation took priority after the Supreme Court retreated from its holding the previous year that state minimum wage laws were unconstitutional, the famous "switch in time that saved the nine" by heading off President Roosevelt's threatened plan to pack the Court.

[152]   Rules Committee History at 139. The speed came because there had been a preliminary round. In October, 1937, President Roosevelt called a special session of Congress to enact the bill. The bill was discharged but labor opposed the committee version and recommitted it. The House leadership waited for proof of popular support for the bill before bringing it out again. Rules Committee History at 139.

[153]   Rules Committee History, at 141 (anti-lynching); Deschler, 18 § 2.1.; Robinson at 5 (federal pay act); D. Berman, A Bill Becomes a Law 91 (1966 ed.)(civil rights bill); id. (1964 civil rights bill); Deschler 18 § 2.2 (home rule); L. A. Froman, The Congressional Process: Strategies, Rules, and Procedures 91 (1967); Deschler 18 §§ 2.3, 2.4 (Equal Rights Amendment). "Release" includes both formal discharge, and also reporting by a committee after accumulation of enough signatures on a petition for discharge shows that formal discharge might be imminent.

Yet overall, successful enactment through discharge was rare.[154]

By the 1970s, as previously discussed, the House broke the power of the Rules Committee and of committee chairs to block the majority party agenda. This began a second era of use of the discharge rule consisting largely of use by the minority party, with conservative Democratic assistance, to release bills bottled up by the majority leadership. This era's beginning may be set in 1971, when conservatives discharged a constitutional amendment regarding school prayer from the Judiciary Committee, followed in 1979 and 1982 by discharge from the same committee of constitutional amendments regarding busing and a balanced budget.[155] All three constitutional amendments failed on the House floor. In contrast the failure of those "social agenda" bills, discharge won success for some economic measures during this era: a 1980 antitrust exemption for soft-drink bottlers, and a 1983 repeal of withholding of taxes on interest and dividends.[156]

---

[154] Usually it required an election when the ranks of liberal Democrats were swollen, particularly the 1936, 1958, and 1964 elections, for the liberals to muster the numbers needed for discharge. Even then, actual enactment of legislation, as opposed to mere tactical gains, could be thwarted; the delay inherent in discharge in the House often increased the opportunity of conservatives in the Senate to filibuster or emasculate liberal bills.

A table of the history of discharge petitions can be found in Congressional Quarterly, Guide to Congress 426 (3d ed. 1982).

[155] There was some overlap in the eras; as early as 1964, conservatives used a discharge petition to pressure the Judiciary Committee into holding hearings on a constitutional amendment on public school prayer. L.A. Froman, supra, at 93. See Deschler 18 § 2.5 (1971 school prayer); H.J. Res. 74, 96th Cong., discussed in Congrssional Quarterly, Guide to Congress 425 (3d ed. 1982)(busing); H.J. Res. 350, 97th Cong. (balanced budget).

[156] Guide to Congress, supra, at 426 (soft drinks); Fessler, Interest Withholding Repeal Sails Through House, 382–41, 41 (footnote continued)

In 1982, the House Democratic Caucus proposed raising the number of petition signatories needed to discharge a constitutional amendment from half of the House to two-thirds. That proposal represented a reaction against the 1982 discharge of the balanced budget amendment, regarded by the House leadership as an Administration attempt to embarrass Democrats on the eve of election. Initially, on December 8, 1982, the House Democratic Caucus adopted the proposal, but the leadership withdrew the proposal the following month.[157]

Procedural and Tactical Aspects of Discharge

Rule XXVII(4) provides the elaborate procedures for discharge: filing of a petition, then a motion, then consideration of the bill. In filing a petition, proponents of discharge must choose whether to seek to discharge the bill itself, or to discharge a special rule for the bill.[158] Discharging a special rule, instead of

---

Cong. Q. Week. Rev. 988 (1983); 129 Cong. Rec. H2991 (daily ed. May 17, 1983).

[157] Plattner, Democrats Set Stage for House Rules Battle, 40 Cong. Q. Week. Rep. 3031, 3032 (Dec. 11, 1982)(117-83 Caucus vote in favor of the proposal). Proponents of the new rule argued that since a constitutional amendment itself required a two-thirds rather than simple majority to adopt, it should require more to discharge, lest the House force itself by discharge to deal with matters lacking any chance of enactment. The proposal drew fire both from conservatives and also, surprisingly, "from liberals, led by Don Edwards, D-Calif," id. at 3032, chairman of the Judiciary subcommittee with jurisdiction over constitutional amendments, who might have been expected to lead the criticism of the discharge procedure chiefly being used to invade his turf. However, Representative Edwards recalled that only by a discharge petition had the Equal Rights Amendment come to the floor, and said the discharge rule "has served the House well. It is a tool for the little guy," id., and a "safety valve, a very democratic procedure." Roberts, Altering the Way the House Operates, New York Times, Dec. 13, 1982, at D16.

(footnote continued)

the bill, has the advantage that the special rule can prescribe floor procedures more flexible than those prescribed for bills in Rule XXVII(4) itself.

Either way, the proponents can file the petition only after a waiting period, to give the committee of jurisdiction thirty days to consider the bill.[159] If the proponents seek to discharge a special rule, their wait must also allow seven days after referral of the special rule to the Rules Committee.[160] This cooling-off period avoids overhasty floor consideration of legislation. Also, the committee of jurisdiction obtains time to deal with pressure, either by generating counter-pressure or by giving some ground through hearings or meetings on the bottled-up bill.

After that waiting period, Rule XXVII(4) provides that any Member can file the petition with the "Clerk, who shall arrange some convenient place for the signature of Members." The petition is not public during this phase. While a Member

---

[158]   Rule XXVII(4) provides for discharge from the Rules Committee of three types of special rules for bills. The first is a "resolution providing [for] a special order of business," an old-fashioned route no longer used. Second is "a special rule for the consideration of any public bill or resolution favorably reported by a standing committee," usable when only the Rules Committee, not a standing committee, is bottling up the bill. Third is "a special rule for the consideration of a public bill or resolution which has remained in a standing committee thirty or more days without action," which uses the Rules Committee's power of "extraction" of bills bottled up by a committee.

[159]   Rule XXVII(4) provides regarding discharge of a bill: "A Member may present to the Clerk a motion in writing to discharge a committee from the consideration of a public bill or resolution which has been referred to it thirty days prior thereto." Similarly, the rule provides regarding discharge of a special rule for a bill bottled up in committee that the petition may be filed only for "a special rule for the consideration of a public bill or resolution which has remained in a standing committee thirty or more days without action."

[160]   See Rule XXVII(4).

can look at it, "for the purpose of signing it or withdrawing his signature -- or refreshing his memory as to whether he has already signed,"[161] no one else can. This gives opponents of discharge an important advantage. Members can often avoid pressures to sign by supporting the bill publicly, such as through cosponsoring it, but not signing the discharge petition.

Proponents of discharge have ways to breach the secrecy. In a classic 1960 maneuver, Democratic liberals sought to force the hand of Republicans who publicly favored a civil rights bill but would not sign the discharge petition. Individual liberal Members took advantage of their right to look at the petition.[162] Once the proponents had thereby assembled an accurate equivalent of the petition list, "the complete list of signatories was turned over to a grateful New York Times, which at once proceeded to publish it." Shortly thereafter, "a flock of belated converts were finding their way to the Speaker's desk" to sign the petition.

During the signature phase, the Members have the opportunity to weigh their reluctance in general to discharge committees against their interest in the particular measure. That general reluctance has several roots. Above all, discharge grossly breaches the jurisdiction of the committee controlling the bill. Discharging a committee nullifies the committee's most essential power, its control over its own turf, expressed in its decision what and when to report, and thus violates the norms of comity and reciprocity. Discharge signatories do not respect the jurisdiction of others' committees; others ask why they should respect that of the signatories' committees.

---

161   D. Berman, supra, at 90.

162   "[T]here seemed to be an epidemic of forgetfulness among liberal Democrats as to whether they had already subscribed to the petition." Meanwhile, "[e]ach member was made responsible for a group of names . . . to see whether [the petition] contained any of the names he had been assigned to track down." The quotes are all from D. Berman, supra, at 90.

The House majority leadership often join a committee in resisting discharge petitions.[163] Together with political persuasion come arguments such as the complexity of the bill; the need for study and refinement, which discharge cuts off; and the divisiveness of a bill on the floor which pits diverse party elements against each other. Even when signatures mount up on a petition, a counter-campaign by the House leadership often keeps the number low, by putting strongly to past signatories the necessity to withdraw their names.[164]

Once a petition receives the requisite 218 signatures, Rule XXVII(4) provides that "it shall be entered on the Journal, printed with the signatures thereto in the Congressional Record, and referred to the Calendar of Motions to Discharge Committees." At or before this point, usually the committee of jurisdiction, or the Rules Committee, opts out of the discharge process by surrendering, and reporting the hitherto bottled-up matter. This allows it to keep control of the procedure, and to develop tactical

---

[163] In the first era of the use of discharge (from 1937 through the 1960s), sometimes the House leadership looked kindly on discharge as a counterbalance to the Rules Committee and the committee chairs. See, e.g., D. Berman, supra, at 91 (regarding the civil rights bill in 1960, "[t]here was no question that the Speaker [Rayburn] was throwing his considerable weight on the side of discharge"). In the current era, the majority leadership has other, better ways to release bills from committee when it wishes -- such as using the Rules Committee, discharge, to obtain a special rule making a bill in order.

[164] In 1982, the supporters of discharge for the balanced budget amendment devised a strategem to deal with this: when they needed only 13 more signatures, instead of letting them trickle in (allowing time for a counter-campaign to withdraw other signatures), a "group [of thirteen] marched en masse onto the House floor, signed the petition, and put it over the top. So organized was the 'coup' that Vice President George Bush was on hand to greet the 13 in a Capitol meeting room." W. J. Oleszek, Congressional Procedures and the Policy Process 136 (3d ed. 1989), quoting Christian Science Monitor, Oct. 4, 1982, at 4.

approaches, instead of ceding control to the discharge proponents.

For example, regarding the balanced budget amendment in 1982, the placing of the discharge motion on the calendar came as a stunning shock to the House leadership. However, the leadership recovered, and quickly had the Rules Committee report a special rule with a number of tactical advantages.[165] Regarding repeal of withholding of interest and dividends in 1983, once proponents obtained enough signatures for discharge, the Ways and Means Committee brought the matter up under suspension of the rules, which also had tactical advantages.[166]

If, nevertheless, the committee lets the matter be brought out by the discharge procedure, the discharge motion waits on its special Discharge Calendar at least seven days, and until the next discharge day.[167] The elaborate terms of the discharge rule then act to prevent filibusters.[168] On the discharge day, when a

---

[165] Because the rule brought the constitutional amendment up literally overnight, it cut off the Administration's lobbying before there was time to build irresistable pressure for passage. The rule also made in order an amendment to the constitutional amendment. Members could vote for that amendment, but (after the amendment's defeat) vote against the constitutional amendment on final passage. This allowed the Members to show their constituents they supported at least the idea of a balanced budget.

[166] It required a two-thirds vote to pass this way. That meant that passage would signal the President of the futility of a veto, avoiding a bruising two-round match over an issue which had already been lobbied through a record-breaking letter campaign.

[167] These come on the second and fourth Mondays of each month except during the last six days of the session.

[168] As described above, the rule required extensive work in 1911, 1924, and 1931 to prevent filibusters, a natural problem since the discharge process operates without assistance from the scheduling power of the House leadership and Rules Committee. Among other restrictions, the rule (footnote continued)

signatory of the petition calls up the motion,
there is "twenty minutes' debate, one-half in
favor of the proposition and one-half in
opposition thereto," and the House votes on the
motion.[169]

At this point, the House votes on the motion
to discharge, and if adopted, the House proceeds
immediately to the consideration of the bill.[170]
A motion to discharge a special rule, rather than
a bill itself, causes the House to proceed first
to the special rule, and only pursuant to that
rule, later to consideration of the underlying
bill.[171] Rule XXVII(4) provides that the House
take up consideration of the bill, absent a
special rule, "under the general rules of the
House."

Of course, these general rules can be
disadvantageous to passage. A matter on the House
Calendar -- such as some constitutional
amendments, like a school prayer amendment --

---

provides that the Speaker "shall recognize" the Member
seeking recognition "for the purpose of calling up the
motion" (precluding the Speaker from using his discretion
regarding recognition); that the motion is considered
"without intervening motion except one motion to adjourn";
that "the bill or resolution shall be read by title only";
and that Members can only be called up for such motions when
"they have been entered on the Journal," i.e., after they
have received the 218 signatures, precluding blocking by
numerous frivolous motions.

[169] Traditionally the chair of the committee of
jurisdiction, if opposed to the bill, receives the time in
opposition on a motion to discharge a bill. Deschler 18 §§
3.3, 3.4.

[170] Rule XXVII(4) provides that a signatory to the petition
can "move that the House proceed to the immediate
consideration of such bill." The House must adopt the
motion to proceed (a nondebatable motion), and if it does,
"the bill shall be immediately considered . . . ."

[171] For discharge of a special rule, Rule XXVII(4) provides
that adoption of the motion to discharge causes the House to
"immediately vote on the adoption of said resolution," and
if the House adopts the special rule, then it "shall
immediately proceed to its execution."

receives consideration under the Hour Rule.[172]   A matter on the Union Calendar faces all the problems normally cured by a special rule.   Thus, discharge of a special rule, which organizes consideration of the bill, rather than discharge of the bill itself, has often been favored.[173]

In the last analysis, few bills become enacted into law by discharge.   Only two have formally followed that route: the Fair Labor Standards Act of 1938 and the Federal Pay Raise Act of 1960.   In other instances, the discharge petition has forced the release of a bill, which may be enacted into law without having formally been discharged.[174]   Some bills are discharged, or their release is forced, and then they either fail on the House floor or later in the process (in the Senate, or in or after conference, or when vetoed).   Nevertheless, the discharge rule serves as the safety valve, for under it, the majority of the House, when its will is steeled sufficiently, can always work that will.

F.   CONSENT AND PRIVATE CALENDARS, PRIVILEGED COMMITTEES, AND MISCELLANEOUS ROUTES

Besides the main routes discussed above, the House uses a variety of other routes to the floor that confer the necessary privileged status.   For legislation even less controversial than the hundreds of bills passed by suspension of the rules, the House has several special calendars, which had much greater significance historically than currently.   Also, certain committees themselves have privileged reporting status.

---

[172]   Deschler 18 § 4.3.

[173]   Rule XXVII(4) also provides that if a motion to discharge is acted on, no other motions to discharge substantially similar matters come up and substantially similar motions to discharge are stricken from the Discharge Calendar.

[174]   The repeal of withholding of taxes on interest and dividends is an example.

Finally, certain questions of privilege, and
Calendar Wednesday, provide routes to the floor.

Consent and Private Calendars and District of Columbia Day

In the early twentieth century, House Members
craved a mechanism for moving the vast number of
bills to which no member had any objection.   To
take an example, on one day in 1926, Members moved
to the floor 55 noncontroversial bills: "19 were
bridge bills . . . [m]any of the remainder had to
do with Indian affairs, but some laid down rules
of administration which were general in their
application, while others amended the immigration
act or the judicial code."[175]   Absent a formal
mechanism, the Members had to rise and seek
recognition from the Speaker to ask unanimous
consent to pass such bills. Particularly during
the reign of "Czar" Cannon, the Speaker could use
his complete discretion to punish his foes by
refusing such recognition, cutting such Members
off from the ability to do necessary, if minor,
business on behalf of their constituencies.
     In reaction to the exercise of such power, in
1909 the House created a Unanimous Consent
Calendar, later renamed the Consent Calendar.[176]
At the time, it was "classed as one of the
principal changes in the House rules of that
time."[177] Since then, the need for such bills has
fallen off with the enactment of general
legislation and the creation of administrative

---

[175] P. DeW. Hasbrouck, Party Government in the House of
Representatives 128 (1927).

[176] This was not created by the insurgents who toppled
"Czar" Cannon from his great power, but earlier, in an
attempt by the pro-Speaker faction to head off the
insurgency. See P. DeW. Hasbrouck, supra, at 5.

[177] F. Riddick, The United States Congress: Organization
and Procedure 228 (1949). "Members rebelled against the
necessity of going, as they said, 'hat in hand', to the
Speaker's office before they could so much as voice their
requests." P. DeW. Hasbrouck, supra, at 126.

agencies; members perform most work for constituents now by persuasion of Executive departments rather than by moving limited-scope bills. However, the Consent Calendar still serves for some limited purpose bills. Pursuant to guidelines incorporated each Congress into a unanimous consent agreement, the Consent Calendar shall be used for only for a bill which does not involve "an aggregate expenditure of more than $1 million," which does not make changes in "national or international policy," and which "should not be approved without the membership being fully informed of its contents."[178]

Under Rule XIII(4), "[a]fter a bill has been favorably reported and shall be upon either the House or Union Calendar any Member may file with the Clerk a notice that he desires such bill placed upon a special calendar to be known as the 'Consent Calendar.'"[179] There it stays only a minimum of three legislative days, until the next Consent Calendar Day, which comes on the first and third Mondays of each month. Then, the rule provides that "the Speaker shall direct the Clerk to call the bills in numerical order."

Usually, only a few Members (if any) attend during the call of the Consent Calendar. The two parties each choose three Members, called "official objectors," who screen the bills to be sure they merit consent calendar treatment. If no one objects to the bill, it is enacted, and the Clerk reads the next bill. If there is an objection, the rule provides for the bill to "be carried over on the calendar without prejudice to the next day when the 'Consent Calendar' is again called.'"[180] At that second date, it takes three

---

[178] 129 Cong. Rec. H 2122 (daily ed. April 19, 1983)(Rep. Dyson).

[179] Usually a committee or subcommittee chair invokes the procedure. Standard forms are available at the Clerk's Document Room for requesting the Clerk to place measures on the Consent Calendar. House Republican Manual at 53.

[180] The revision to allow bills a second chance on the calendar occurred in April, 1911, after an incident in January of that year when one Member who "became disgruntled (footnote continued)

objections to stop the bill, but if three objections are made, the bill is stricken from the Consent Calendar for that Congress, and must be brought up again, if at all, by one of the other mechanisms.[181]

Not surprisingly, a sponsor can best move his bill by "getting in touch with [the official objectors] at least 24 hours in advance of the time the legislation is called up," to "clear away questions which the objectors may have . . . "[182] If the way is cleared, it is a remarkably easy way to pass legislation. For example, on May 3, 1983, Representative Sam Hall (D-Tex.) secured adoption through the Consent Calendar of a bill, H.R. 594, to authorize the Secretary of Commerce to settle claims under $2,500. Representative Hall was apparently not even on the floor at the time.[183]

It should be noted that a fair number of measures each year pass by unanimous consent, without formally going through the Consent Calendar. For example, the chair of the subcommittee which deals with ceremonial and commemorative resolutions may seek recognition to ask, by unanimous consent, for consideration of a resolution establishing "National Congressional

---

. . . because he was not allowed to extend his remarks . . . . objected to most of the bills which were called up during the remainder of the day." P. DeW. Hasbrouck, supra, at 127.

[181] "In practice, however, the procedure usually followed is that an individual Member will ask that the bill be passed over 'without prejudice' so that it can remain on the Consent Calendar." House Republican Manual at 53.

[182] 129 Cong. Rec. H2122 (daily ed. April 19, 1983)(Rep. Roy Dyson (D-Md.)). The objectors will want to know the department or agency position on the bill. It used to be (but no longer is) that objection to a bill by the Administration was one of the guidelines for not allowing it on the Consent Calendar, Deschler 22 § 3.1.

[183] The Congressional Record reports the adoption of the bill without objection, and with only a bulleted statement by the Congressman (signifying his absence). 129 Cong Rec. H2532 (daily ed. May 3, 1983).

Procedure Month." The ranking minority Member may
reserve the right to object, and under that
reservation, ask for the resolution to be
explained. When all sides have explained why they
support the resolution, it passes by unanimous
consent. Other kinds of business may also be done
by this free-form unanimous consent, notably the
sending of bills to conference, as discussed in
the chapter on conference. Pursuant to his
recognition power, the Speaker does not recognize
for such unanimous consent requests unless the
Member has cleared them with both the majority and
minority leaderships.[184]

Similar to the Consent Calendar is the
Private Calendar, for handling private bills.[185]
Private bills grant "relief" from the law,
typically to a single or a few individuals; most
often they provide either relief from the
immigration laws, or grant a monetary claim for
some government-caused mishap. Upon enactment,
the private bills become "Private Laws," codified
separately from the regular public laws. The 97th
Congress in 1981-82 enacted 56 of these private
laws. This number is far smaller than the number
being enacted 100 or 40 or even 20 years before:
creation of administrative procedures regarding
government civil and military pensions,
immigration, and federal tort claims markedly
diminished the need for private laws. Private
immigration bills continued in large numbers until
the prosecution of Representative Henry Helstoski
(D-N.J.) for alleged sale of private bills, the
Abscam scandal, and Senate opposition reduced
their numbers dramatically.[186]

---

[184]   Deschler 21 § 2.1.

[185]   For a full treatment of the general topic of private
bills, see Congressional Quarterly, Guide to Congress 349-61
(3d ed. 1982).

[186]   In 1949, Dr. Riddick noted that "in the past nearly
half, or more, of the laws enacted in each session of
Congress have been passed from this Calendar," with 892
passed in the 79th Congress. F. Riddick (1949), at 231.
For a 1960s discussion of the Private Calendar's importance,
see L.A. Froman, The Congressional Process: Strategies,
(footnote continued)

Under Rule XIII(1), there is a separate Private Calendar, so that appropriate reported bills are placed on it as other bills are placed on the Union and House Calendars. Under Rule XXIV(6), the first Tuesday, and (at the discretion of the Speaker) the third Tuesday, of each month is a Private Calendar day. For private bills, as for consent calendar bills, the two parties each appoint three objectors (not the same ones for the two calendars).

Pursuant to the rule, on Private Calendar days "the Speaker shall direct the Clerk to call the bills and resolutions on the Private Calendar." Upon objection "by two or more Members to the consideration of any bill or resolution so called, it shall be recommitted to the committee which reported the bill or resolution . . . ." The rule provides details of consideration, including procedures for considering "omnibus" private bills consolidating many private bills onto one vehicle.[187] However, in general the bills on the calendar go through with virtually no debate or procedural activity.[188]

Rules, and Procedures 44-45 (1967). The number of private laws had been high even recently -- e.g., 170 in the 95th Congress. Then, first, in 1976 the Justice Department indicted Rep. Helstoski for bribery in the introduction of private immigration bills. The prosecution was dismissed after one trip to the Supreme Court and a second to the Court of Appeals, but nevertheless it chilled the ardor of the potential offerors of such bills. Second, the new chair (in 1981-86) of the Senate Subcommitee on Immigration and Refugee Policy, Senator Alan Simpson (R-Wyo.), through whose subcommittee almost all private bills had to go, took a restrictive view regarding such bills. Finally, in the Abscam scandal, the Justice Department indicted and convicted several Representatives and one Senator, using a scam built around bribes for a promise of future private immigration bill help.

[187] Rule XXIV(6) gives preference to omnibus bills on the third Tuesday of the month, and prescribes the procedure by which they are read for amendment, and upon passage, resolved into individual bills. See House Manual § 895; Deschler 22 § 7.

[188] For a discussion of Private Calendar procedure, see F. (footnote continued)

Since 1870, the House has set aside a day for District of Columbia legislation. Since the Constitution gives the Congress special governing power over the District, the House needed a mechanism to insure that the necessary laws could get floor time, particularly since the District has no voting representative on the floor (just its Delegate, who votes only in committee) to push for necessary measures. However, since enactment of home rule legislation in 1973, the volume of District of Columbia legislation that Congress must move has diminished, although the need has not ended. Under Rule XXIV(8), the second and fourth Mondays in each month are District of Columbia days, on which legislation relating to the District will be heard, without needing a special rule, when the day is "claimed by the Committee on the District of Columbia."[189]

For example, on June 27, 1983, the committee claimed District of Columbia Day so that the House would consider H.R.2637, increasing the authorization for the annual federal payment to the District of Columbia from $361 million to $386 million. The chair, the ranking minority Member, and the District of Columbia Delegate spoke briefly in favor of the bill. As with unobjected-to bills generally considered on D.C. Day, the bill was considered under the procedures of the House "as in Committee of the Whole," and the House passed it.[190]

Privileged Committees and Conference Committees

Rule XI(4)(a) gives several committees

Riddick, supra, at 231-35.

[189] For the history of the rule, see House Manual § 899. The rule applies only to legislation from the District of Columbia Committee, so it does not apply to the Appropriation Committee's annual District of Columbia Appropriation Bill.

[190] Deschler 22 § 4.1 (consideration of unobjected-to bills under the procedure of the House "as in Committee of the Whole"); 129 Cong. Rec. H4479 (daily ed. June 27, 1983).

besides the Rules Committee the privilege of reporting at any time, and thus obtaining privileged consideration of their bills, thus obviating these committees' need to obtain special rules for all their bills.[191]   By far the most important is the Appropriations Committee, which can obtain privileged consideration of general appropriation bills and continuing resolutions. Politically, this means that the Appropriations Committee need not have the same close, dependent relationship to the Rules Committee as other committees.

However, the Appropriations Committee must still come to the Rules Committee for waivers on points of order.   This means that in most years only about half the appropriation bills, and the lesser ones at that, come to the floor without first stopping at the Rules Committee.   The same is true of the Budget Committee: it has a privilege to report its resolutions, but they stop at the Rules Committee anyway for a complex rule restricting amendments.

Two other committees, House Administration, and Standards of Official Conduct (the ethics committee), can go directly to the floor.   House Administration uses its privilege for the resolutions providing funding for committees. Standards of Official Conduct uses its privilege for resolutions disciplining Members.   Formerly a number of other committees had such privileges, but they were cut back in 1975.[192]

---

[191]   The rule does not free all the committees from layover requirements.   The only committees whose reports are not required to lay over for three days (absent waiver of the layover by a special rule, suspension of the rules, or unanimous consent) are the Rules Committee and the House Administration Committee (with its own one-day layover for committee funding resolutions).   See Rule XI(2)(6); House Manual § 726; Deschler 17 § 44.

[192]   Among the obscure questions of procedure in the House is the continuing significance of Rule XVI(9), which provides for privileged motions by the Ways and Means Committee to take up "bills raising revenue."   The 1975 rules change eliminated the provision in Rule XI(4)(a) that had conferred privilege on the Ways and Means Committee, but (footnote continued)

Similarly, presentation of a report of a conference committee has its own privilege pursuant to House Rule XXVIII.[193]   The House confers high privilege on such presentation, which has precedence even over reports from the Rules Committee.[194]   Once presented, the conference report then lays over pursuant to Rule XXVIII(2)(a) for three calendar days before its consideration is in order.   The House sometimes uses special rules (or suspension of the rules or even unanimous consent) for conference reports either to waive the three-day layover,[195] or to waive some other point of order such as when the conferees exceeded their scope.   Because of the House's favorable view on moving conference reports as rapidly as possible, when the Majority Leader announces his schedule for the week he either mentions, or it is taken for granted, that the schedule may be interrupted at any time to bring up conference reports.   Procedure for conference reports is discussed in a separate chapter.

Questions of Privilege and Calendar Wednesday

The House considers certain "questions of

---

not this separate provision.   All that is known, since there has been no floor test of Rule XVI(9) alone, is that the Rule XVI(9) privilege "was derived from and was dependent upon the former privilege conferred upon the Committee on Ways and Means under Rule XI, clause 4(a)," House Manual § 802.

[193]   The rule provides: "The presentation of reports fo committees of conference shall always be in order, except when the Journal is being read, while the roll is being called, or the House is dividing on any proposition."

[194]   House Manual § 909.

[195]   See House Rule XXVIII(a)(special rule can make conference report in order without layover); House Manual § 729a (although two-thirds vote required for special rules making bills in order the same day, a special rule making a conference report in order immediately needs only majority vote).

privilege" intrinsically privileged so that they can be raised from the floor without requiring a special rule, suspension of the rules, or inclusion on any of the special calendars. Genuine questions of privilege occur infrequently, but when they occur it is commonly during sharp in-fighting.

As Deschler's Procedure notes, "[t]here are two classes of questions of privilege -- the first pertaining to the House collectively, the second pertaining to the Members individually."[196] House Rule IX distinguishes these two classes:

> Questions of privilege shall be, first those affecting the rights of the House collectively, its safety, dignity, and the integrity of its proceedings; second, the rights, reputation, and conduct of Members, individually, in their representative capacity only; and shall have precedence of all other questions, except motions to adjourn.

Looking first at the questions of privilege concerning the House as a whole, these start with matters that threaten the constitutional powers of the House, such as its power to originate revenue and spending bills, and its contempt power. They also include questions relating to the organization of the House; to Members' title to their seats such as contested elections and vacancies due to death or resignation; admission to the floor; and broadcasting and the accuracy of the Congressional Record.[197] Lawsuits and subpoenas to Members, officers, and staff often raise questions of the privileges of the House.[198] Privileges of individual Members in their highest form concern the Members' constitutional rights to freedom of speech or debate, and to immunity from civil arrest. Rule IX's inclusion of the "reputation" of Members

---

[196] Deschler 11 § 1.1.

[197] House Manual § 662; Riddick (1949) at 303.

[198] Deschler 11 §§ 2-12.

allows Members to raise charges in newspapers as questions of privilege, giving Members a particularly dignified way of responding to such charges.[199]

Procedurally, Members may raise questions of privilege by offering the House a resolution to adopt (although they may simply avail themselves of the opportunity to discuss the matter). Pursuant to the Hour Rule, the Speaker will recognize a Member raising such a question for an hour to debate her resolution. Questions of privilege cannot be raised in Committee of the Whole. Although a question of privilege has high precedence pursuant to Rule IX, it is subject to disposition by the ordinary motions such as the motion to refer, and the motion to table, which provide convenient means to fend off awkward issues brought to the floor through this out-of-channels method.[200]

A final miscellaneous route is Calendar Wednesday. Historically, Speaker "Czar" Cannon allowed the creation of Calendar Wednesday in 1909, in what turned out to be a futile effort to deflect the gathering revolt. Under Rule XXIV(4), the Calendar Wednesday procedure prescribes that every Wednesday, the House has a call of the committees, during which successive committees can call up their bills from the calendar. During the period when the Rules Committee acted for the conservative coalition in refusing special rules to liberal bills, efforts were made to use Calendar Wednesday to bring bills up without special rules, but these rarely worked.[201]

For almost 20 years after 1963, Calendar

---

[199] House Manual § 663; Deschler 11 § 15; Riddick (1949) at 303-04.

[200] House Manual § 665.

[201] See Galloway at 140-41 (Calendar Wednesday). Only on two occasions did the House enact bills through Calendar Wednesday procedure: the Fair Employment Practices Bill in 1950, and an area redevelopment bill in 1960. For discussions of each, see Rules Committee History at 163, 175. The procedure "proved to be a very costly way to circumvent the Rules Committee." Id. at 175.

Wednesday lay dormant; the Majority Leader routinely waived it by unanimous consent. In 1982-84, several militantly conservative Republicans, under the name "Conservative Opportunity Society," insisted on occasional calls of the calendar under the rule to dramatize their claim that the Democrats were refusing to handle their important agenda (such as the balanced budget amendment).[202] However, the call accomplished little other than the passage of one minor bill, since only by authorization of a committee can a motion to call up a bill be made on Calendar Wednesday. The majority party declined to have any committees provide such authorization. Accordingly, Calendar Wednesday still remained an unused House procedure.

---

[202] For any other such procedure, the majority might respond by reporting a special rule to eliminate the obstruction, but Rule XI(4)(b) uniquely forbids the Rules Committee to "report any rule or order which provides that business under clause 7 of Rule XXIV shall be set aside by a vote of less than two-thirds of the Members present." Thus, as long as the protesting Members had backing from more than one-third of the House and firmly resisted a vote to waive Calendar Wednesday, they could insist on the procedure being followed.

6

Bills Under Special Rules in the House[1]

A. HISTORY AND OVERVIEW

The House's procedure for considering bills on the floor is probably what most observers have in mind by Congressional procedure: daily action cloaked in many historic ritualistic forms, extensive maneuvering, and motions with a large number of governing rules and precedents. As the foregoing two chapters reflect, much House procedural

---

[1] Sources cited frequently in this chapter include F. Riddick, The United States Congress, Organization and Procedure (1949) (cited as "F. Riddick (1949)"); R. Luce, Legislative Procedure (1922) (Luce); DeA. S. Alexander, History and Procedure of the House of Representatives (1916) (Alexander); R. E. Damon, The Standing Rules of the House of Representatives (1971) (Damon); L. Froman, The Congressional Process: Strategies, Rules and Procedures (1967) (Froman); S. S. Smith & C. J. Deering, Committees in Congress (1984) (Smith & Deering); Bach, Parliamentary Strategy & the Amendment Process: Rules & Case Studies of Congressional Action, Polity, Summer 1983 (Bach); B. Sinclair, Majority Leadership in the U.S. House (1983) (Sinclair); G. B. Galloway, History of the House of Representatives (rev. ed. S. Wise 1976) (Galloway); Also, this section draws on papers submitted in the author's seminar by Janet A. Nuzum, Kenneth J. Kahn, and Gaye L. Hume.

decision making occurs either before bills come to the floor, as in Rules Committee decisions, or in the implementation of majority leadership decisions to schedule bills for special routes, such as suspension of the rules.

Still, House procedure for considering bills on the floor matters enormously. Most of the rest of House procedure serves as the opening act for this. The votes on the House floor decide what bills will pass and with what amendments, and establish the chamber's views as guidance for the rest of the processes in committee, scheduling, and conference. To the extent House floor procedure gives advantages to the majority or committee leaderships, this augments their other powers; to the extent the procedure gives free rein to floor majorities, it decentralizes power. In this regard the changes in treatment of floor amendments since 1970 have had a major effect on Congress.

This section starts with a brief history of floor procedure, emphasizing the developments since 1970. The next section continues with a description of the rules of procedure applying generally in the "House" (as opposed to Committee of the Whole). Following that are three sections which address procedure in Committee of the Whole, including amending under the five-minute rule and the tactical uses of the amendment process. The last three sections address the germaneness rule and how proceedings occur in the "House" leading to final passage of a bill as amended.

History

The House inherited its basic procedure from the British Parliament. For example, the Committee of the Whole procedure, the heart of the chamber's operations, dates back to the House of Commons in the 1600s.[2] Committee of the Whole

---

[2] The first great chronicler of House procedure, L. G. McConachie, told in 1898 the story of the procedure's old roots. "In the reign of James I, the [House of] Commons [in the English Parliament] invented the Committee of the Whole . . . . The tyrannical Stuart stood ready to single out and (footnote continued)

procedure was used by the House from its beginning
in 1789[3] to provide a relatively informal process
for amending bills.[4]

---

crush that member who dared to speak freely to his fellows;
and the officers of the House, including the Speaker, an
appointee of the crown, were the king's tattling minions."
McConachie at 7-8. Parenthetically, that unhappy experience
explains the explicit provision in the Constitution, Art. I,
sec. 2, cl. 5, that "The House of Representatives shall
chuse [sic] their Speaker," rather than the President or
some other outsider making the choice.

As McConachie explains, "in order to protect their
precious right of untrammelled deliberation, the members [of
the House of Commons] began to hold secret and informal
sessions with a chairman of their own choosing. These so-
called Grand Committees met in the afternoons, when the
spies were gone." Id. at 8. It was as if the House of
Representatives today were to slip off in the evenings to
some hideaway when meeting to discuss challenging the
President. "Upon the ancient rolls half a dozen words and a
dotted line in place of the spokesman's name are all that
indicate the report to the House [of Commons] of their
momentous proceedings." Id. at 8.

In America, "the Continental Congress used the
Committee of the Whole frequently," IV Hinds § 4705, at 986,
as did the Constitutional Convention. Id. at 986-87.

[3] Thomas Jefferson wrote that "matters of great concernment
are usually referred to a Committee of the Whole House,
where general principles are digested . . . [and] debated
and amended till they get into a shape which meets the
approbation of a majority. These [are then] reported and
confirmed by the House . . . ." House Manual § 326.

[4] The House's actual procedure in the first Congresses was
much more different from today's than the prior quotation
from Jefferson suggests. The Committee of the Whole, and
the House, were "digest[ing]" not a bill, but a resolution
regarding general principles. When Committee and House were
done, the resolution would be given to a select committee to
draft a bill. This meant that the early House relied on
Committee of the Whole to do much of the work of formulating
legislative proposals for which the House began relying in
the nineteenth century on standing committees. See J.
Cooper, The Origin of the Standing Committees and the
(footnote continued)

Following British antecedents, the chamber's earliest procedures provided for a systematic reading for amendment.[5]   Since the rules set no time limit on speeches, and in the Committee of the Whole there was no motion for the previous question (i.e, motion for ending debate), opponents could easily stall bills.[6]   In 1822, the House constricted the amending process by adopting a germaneness rule, and by 1841, delay was being prevented through an hour cap on Members' floor speeches in the "House" and by effective use of the motion for the previous question.   In 1841, the majority party broke a filibuster by providing that debate in the Committee of the Whole could be cut off by majority vote.[7]

Development of the Modern House 8-17 (1970).

[5]   The rule adopted in 1789 provided:

> Upon bills committed to a Committee of the Whole House, the bill shall be first read throughout by the Clerk, and then again read and debated by clauses . . . . [A]ll amendments, noting the page and line, shall be duly entered by the Clerk, on a separate paper, as the same shall be agreed to by the committee, and so reported to the House.   After report, the bill shall again be subject to be debated and amended by clauses before a question to engross it be taken.

V Hinds § 5221, at 125.

[6]   Compare House Manual §§ 461-63 (early history of motion for the previous question in the House) with _id._ § 333 ("[n]o previous question can be put in a committee [of the Whole]").

[7]   A public land bill sent by the majority Whig party to Committee on the Whole "was still being debated in Committee on July 6, when the Committee on Rules, after much opposition," V Hinds § 5221, at 126, passed a rule that broke the filibuster.   The Rules Committee action had followed by a month the adoption by the House of a rule authorizing the Rules Committee "to report at any time" -- a crucial step in the committee's evolution.   See Alexander at 191; House Committee on Rules, 97th Cong., 2d Sess., _A History of the Committee on Rules_ 45 (1983).   The rule "provid[ed] that by vote of the majority . . . the House (footnote continued)

By the time of the Civil War, having invented the techniques for breaking filibusters[8] and made use of those techniques routine,[9] the procedures for Committee of the Whole were consolidated by the "five-minute" rule for amending, and the motion to close debate on "any section or paragraph of the bill."[10]   After the late

---

might suspend the rules for the purpose of discharging the Committee of the Whole from the consideration of any bill referred to them after acting without debate upon all amendments pending and that might be offered." V Hinds § 5221, at 126.

As one observer said, "The result was cataclysmal," for "[i]t not only gave a majority power to control debate in Committee of the Whole, but made it master of the House." Alexander at 191.

[8]   In 1854, there was no motion to close proceedings in Committee of the Whole, and opponents of the Kansas-Nebraska Bill filibustered it indefinitely by the offering of amendments. To break the filibuster, proponents of the bill adopted a motion to rise and report with the recommendation that the enacting clause be stricken, which brought the bill out of Committee of the Whole and into the House. "[T]his [motion] has played an important part in the parliamentary history of the House," V Hinds § 5326, at 172; see Alexander at 270.   Then, "after fifteen roll calls" on dilatory motions, V Hinds § 5342, at 181, the House disagreed with the recommendation, keeping the enacting clause in place.   With the bill now out of Committee and into the House, "the previous question could be used to cut off the obstructive amendments which threatened the bill in Committee of the Whole." V Hinds § 5326, at 173.

[9]   "This device [of moving to strike, then disagreeing to the recommendation] came into quite frequent use," V Hinds § 5326, at 173; see McConachie at 105.   Use of the maneuver was ended in 1860, after the development of the straightforward motion to close debate in Committee of the Whole rendered the maneuver no longer necessary.   Damon at 202; Alexander at 270-71.

[10]   Alexander at 267-68; V Hinds § 5221, at 127 (rule changes in 1847 and 1850) (for five-minute rule); V Hinds § 5221, at 128 (1860 rule for motion to limit debate).   Today these are in Rule XXVIII(5)(a) (five-minute rule) and (5)(b) (footnote continued)

nineteenth-century development of the special rule, the House included boilerplate language in the special rule speeding along the enactment process.

In the twentieth century, powerful unwritten norms plus the impact of certain rules sharply curbed the amending process. Particularly in the peak eras of conservative coalition dominance, "there existed a strong presumption in favor of the committee's bill. 'Go with the committee on the floor' was the watchword; 'the committee has exhaustively examined the matter and has brought its expertise to bear.'"[11]

Reinforcing the informal norm was the rule, from 1789 until 1970, that there would be no recorded votes in Committee of the Whole.[12] Committee chairs could retaliate when they saw Members on the floor voting against them, but the Members' constituents knew nothing because of the lack of a recorded vote. Hence, prudent Members either voted with the chairs or skipped votes.[13] "[T]he only amendments that passed during floor consideration were those presented by conservatives with 'establishment' blessings."[14]

Three key factors in the 1970s caused a

(closing debate on a provision).

[11]   Sinclair at 9; see Froman at 70-71.

[12]   "Before passage of the Legislative Reorganization Act of 1970, members of Congress were able to hide their votes by walking up an aisle between two tellers, on one side of the question or the other, who counted their number but did not take down their names." T. Siff & A. Weil, Ruling Congress 158 (1975).

[13]   "Northern Democrats [were] notoriously poor attenders on the floor during Committee of the Whole proceedings." Froman at 77. Northern Democrats, being from more insecure seats, had poorer attendance levels generally because they had to pay more district campaigning visits. Attendance was particularly poor during days of Committee of the Whole proceedings, because the absence of recorded votes meant absenteeism did not create a bad attendance record.

[14]   C. Whalen, The House and Foreign Policy: The Irony of Congressional Reform 35 (1981).

massive change in the number and success rate of
floor amendments.   The 1970 rules change made
recorded votes available in the Committee of the
Whole.   The recording of their votes made Members
accountable to constituents for votes against
popular amendments.[15]   Starting in 1973, when the
House deposed three chairs and thereby overturned
the iron rule of seniority, chairs possessed less
security, and had to court junior Members, even
those who offered or voted for amendments.
Finally, junior Members developed independent
methods of winning elections,[16] like developing
large treasuries of campaign contributions, and
depended less on being "team players" for
chairs.[17]

---

[15]   In the Senate, the same tactical use of amendments (for
which, unlike the House, there had always been recorded
votes) spread as well:

> Regularly, [Senator Jesse] Helms [R-N.C.] offers
> controversial social amendments (abortion, school
> prayer, etc.) and forces votes on them.   "His
> amendments," wrote Elizabeth Drew, "gave him a kind of
> publicity that was useful, firmed up his relationships
> with a cluster of 'New Right' groups, helped him raise
> money, and provided material with which he and his
> allies could try to defeat opponents."

R. Davidson & W. Oleszek, Congress and its Members 351
(1981), quoting Drew, A Reporter at Large, Jesse Helms, The
New Yorker, July 20, 1981, at 80.

[16]   "The reciprocity norm is weaker now and there is a
greater tendency to 'mark-up' bills on the floor.   Younger
members are simply not willing to defer to the committee."
Sinclair at 10.   Much more today than a decade ago, the
combination of PAC money, purchased media, campaign
consultants, and constituent operations (personal staff
doing mail, casework and newsletters) matter in reelection
of incumbents.   As Speaker Thomas P. "Tip" O'Neill (D-Mass.)
commented, Democratic Members "no longer have to follow the
national philosophy of the party.   They can get re-elected
on their newsletter, or on how they serve their
constituents."   Arrieff, House, Senate Chiefs Attempt to
Lead a Changed Congress, 38 Cong. Q. Week. Rep. 2695, 2696
(1980).
(footnote continued)

Accordingly, as Representative Charles Whalen (R-Ohio) noted, "recorded votes on amendments offered in the Committee of the Whole moved from zero in 1969 to 295 in 1979."[18] The total number of recorded votes, including amendments in Committee of the Whole, zoomed from 443 in 1969-70 to 1540 in 1977-78, before falling back somewhat in the 1980s.[19] A comparison of appropriation bills on the House floor from 1963 to 1982 found striking increases in the numbers of amendments offered and the numbers that won over managers' opposition.[20] Another study found a similar increase in amendments to key foreign affairs bills.[21]

---

[17] While national electoral trends are beyond the scope of this book, two trends merit mention for giving the majority less resistance to minority floor amendments than the party ratio would suggest, particularly in comparison to ratios that were seemingly less favorable to the Democrats before 1970. First, the Democratic party's gains in 1974 and 1982 often came in districts with a natural Republican base. "[J]unior members elected from districts previously held by Republicans are particularly troublesome to the [Democratic] party leadership." Sinclair at 17. Second, the majority leadership's ability to gain Republican votes against amendments fell through a reduction in the swing bloc of moderate Republicans. "Republicans who first entered the House in the 1970s, then, are more likely than members first elected earlier to oppose strongly the Democratic position across the whole range of issues." Sinclair at 19 (analyzing Member voting surveys).

[18] C. Whalen, supra, at 58.

[19] R. H. Davidson & T. Kephart, Indicators of House of Representatives Workload and Activity 62 (1985) (combining yea nay and recorded votes). In the 1980s, the number of recorded votes fell off somewhat, to 906 in 1983-84. Id.

[20] "There has been a concomitant increase in the number of contested amendments that won: from 9 in 1963-1966 to 29 and then 22 in 1967-1970 and 1971-1974, and, most recently, to 56 and 59 in 1975-1978 and 1979-1982." Bach, Representatives and Committee on the Floor: Amendments to Appropriations Bills in the House of Representatives, 1963-1982, 13 Congress & The Presidency 41, 47 (1986). (footnote continued)

"[T]he floor role of a bill manager has become increasingly frustrating and often embarrassing."[22] It became a struggle against the Members' willingness to adopt floor amendments. Congressional Quarterly described in 1980 how "[m]ajor bills are pulled from the floor after crippling amendments spring from nowhere to win adoption on the floor. Appropriations bills are weighted down with riders."[23]

In reaction, the House majority party took a number of steps in the late 1970s and 1980s to regain control of floor amending. Many have been detailed above: restrictive special rules; more use of suspension of the rules, which bars amendments; strengthening of the leadership; and development of an elaborate whip system. With these came other developments, notably a new tactical sophistication in floor amendment fights, as described in this chapter.

A second curb on amendments consists of the increased importance of the House's great restriction, its rule of germaneness. Germaneness is not a new factor, as the rule dates back to the 1820s. However, it has taken on special significance in defining the limits of what floor amendments could be offered and thus how much change from committee-reported bills could be made on the floor.

---

[21] In 1969, 18 floor amendments were adopted on 14 foreign policy bills; in 1979, 104 floor amendments were adopted on 30 such bills. Representaive Whalen found a "decline in the committee of jurisdiction's floor 'batting average' from .591 in 1969, to .329 in 1979." C. Whalen, supra, at 58. Many of the adopted amendments went to the heart of major issues, such as bans on arms sales to Turkey, or refusals to abide by international trade sanctions against Rhodesia. Those 104 floor amendments represented a vast shift in power toward sponsoring Members who were junior in status, not on the committee, and often from the minority party.

[22] Whalen, supra, at 58.

[23] Arrieff, House, Senate Chiefs Attempt to Lead a Changed Congress, 38 Cong. Q. Week. Rep. 2695 (1980).

"House" and "Committee of the Whole"

"House" procedure differs from "Committee of the Whole" procedure. The chamber reserves "Committee of the Whole" procedure for two tasks: general debate and amending bills under the five-minute rule. These tasks take up most of the House's time (leaving aside the virtually unattended speeches in special orders), but they are quite focused, with only a limited number of motions and actions possible. Apart from debating and amending bills under the five-minute rule, the chamber conducts the rest of its business in the "House." That includes adopting special rules; proceedings on final passage of bills after amending in the Committee of the Whole; the specialized calendar days such as for suspension of the rules; one-minute and special order speeches; relations with the Senate and the President, such as receipt of messages, steps for going to conference, conference reports, and veto overrides; and a host of other matters. There is a rarely-used variant procedure called "House as in Committee of the Whole."[24]

The most visible differences between "House" and Committee of the Whole procedure are that the Speaker presides in the House, while his appointee, the Chairman of the Committee of the Whole, presides in Committee of the Whole; and that the Committee of the Whole cannot conduct business apart from the narrow range noted above.[25] There are three other basic differences,

---

[24] This is rarely seen now, except in odd situations such as bills brought up on District of Columbia Day or on the Private Calendar. It consists of the basic rules of "House" procedure, except that amendments are debated under a five-minute rule. The House only uses it by unanimous consent, or pursuant to language in a special rule. For discussions, see House Manual §§ 424, 427; Riddick (1949) at 212-213.

[25] As Dr. Riddick comments:

A few of the more outstanding actions beyond the jurisdiction of the Committee of the Whole are: general questions of privilege, the right to grant leaves of absence, the control of admission to the floor,
(footnote continued)

each discussed in detail at some point below.

First, and most important, the Committee of the Whole cannot cut off amendments. The House relies on the motion for the previous question both to stop debate and to cut off amendments, while the Committee's motion to close or limit debate puts a limit to talking but does not avoid pending amendments. This critical factor means that the limiting of amendments must occur in more complicated ways, such as by the adoption of closed or complex special rules, and by the operation of the germaneness rule.

Second, they have different debate patterns. The House follows the Hour Rule; the Committee of the Whole has general debate and debate of amendments under the five-minute rule. Third, the House and the Committee of the Whole have different rules regarding voting and quorum calls, as discussed next.

B.   VOTING AND QUORUM CALLS

Voting Methods

In theory, all kinds of matters may be decided by unanimous consent, "such as leave to print, to vacate actions already taken by the House, to make special orders, to change the regular order of business prescribed by the rules, to bring a bill before the House for immediate action and the like."[26]   However, these only get resolved by

---

questions of considerations, and the disposition of words taken down in debate in the Committee . . . .

[T]he following actions are not in order in the Committee of the Whole: to appoint or discharge a committee, to originate legislation, to order a call of the hosue in the absence of a quorum, to recess, to limit general debate except by unanimous consent and then when it was not fixed by the House, to send matters to conference, to recommed a conference, to instruct conferees, or to reconsider an issue. These are matters to be attended to by the House.

Riddick (1949) at 215-26.
(footnote continued)

unanimous consent when they are utterly without
controversy; apart from a very few matters
customarily decided this way,[27] the House lacks
the Senate's tradition of proceeding by unanimous
consent.   Instead,   the   chamber   must   decide
propositions, from routine procedural motions to
the final passage of major legislation, by vote.
     Since the vote is the bottom line for all
parliamentary efforts, rules regarding voting are
no   minor   matter.   The   ability   of   amendment
offerors to obtain a record vote in Committee of
the   Whole   with   a   minimal   seconding   by   24
colleagues greatly changed the dynamics of the
House floor in the 1970s.   Between record votes
and other factors, many more floor amendments came
up, with a higher chance of success.[28]
     The   chamber   has   four   principal   methods   of
voting: voice,   division,   teller,   and   record
vote. First, if no other method is requested, the
Chair will ask for a voice vote.   Rule I(5)(a)
states   the   procedure: "[The   Chair]   shall   put
questions in this form, to wit; "as many as are in
favor (as the question may be), say 'Aye'."; and
after the affirmative voice is expressed, "As many
as are opposed, say 'No'."   "This is the fastest
method, but the least accurate."[29]   Sometimes the

---

[26]   Riddick (1949) at 266.

[27]   Unanimous consent is freely given to bring commemorative
bills and resolutions to the floor; to take bills for which
both House and Senate versions have been passed and go
through either amendments between Houses, or conference; and
to obtain leave to revise and extend remarks.

[28]   Representative   Charles   Whalen   (R-Ohio),   a   liberal
Republican,   saw   the   process   as   so   demoralizing   that   he
proposed to raise the number for obtaining a recorded vote
in Committee of the Whole from 25 to 44.   "The present 6-
percent   (25-member)   requirement   denigrates   the   amending
process   by   failing   to   differentiate   between   what   is
important and what is unimportant.   Any amendment, however
mischievous, is practically guaranteed a recorded vote under
current rules." Whalen, supra, at 166.

[29]   House Republican Manual at 237.   There is a possibility
of the Chair hearing with particular clarity the voices on
(footnote continued)

Chair recites this procedure in one swift breath, clearly to get a matter out of the way with minimal attention: "all-in-favor-say-aye-all-opposed-nay-the-ayes-have-it." At other times there may well be a real voice vote, with the Members on each side lustily cheering their proposition and the Chair listening to the volume and pondering which side included more voices (the test being number of voting Members, not number of decibels).

The second method is that any Member may demand a division vote. Rule I(5)(a) describes this procedure: "those in the affirmative of the question shall first rise from their seats, and then those in the negative." The Chair counts the Members standing each time. As with a voice vote, the Chair's count is not subject to question or appeal. The division vote has advantages and disadvantages: "[A division vote] generally takes only a few minutes. It is a reasonably accurate way of determining the number of votes on the floor at the time. However, it does not allow time for absent Members to get to vote; nor does it provide a record of how each Member voted."[30] Since in a division vote the votes of individual Members are not recorded, and the vote ends quickly, Members not on the floor rarely come to the floor. Often division votes reflect that only a dozen or two Members are on the floor at any particular moment.

Third, on rare occasions, such as when a second is demanded under suspension of the Rules, the House votes by tellers.[31]

---

the side it supports, but this leaves the other side its perfect right to insist on the more precise voting methods if it cares.

[30] House Republican Manual at 238.

[31] The requirement that the vote on seconding a motion to suspend the rules be by tellers is in Rule XXVII(2); House Manual § 906.

It requires one-fifth of a quorum to demand a teller vote. Rule I(5)(a). Rule I(5)(a) specifies that in a teller vote, the Chair "shall name one or more from each side of the question to tell the Members in the affirmative (footnote continued)

Finally, and most important, a Member may obtain a record vote. The House rules preserve several old methods for conducting such votes. These include calling of the roll[32] -- the term that is habitually used (in this book as well) for a record vote however taken -- and recorded votes by clerks,[33] in which the Members vote by ballot cards.[34]

---

and negative; which being reported, he shall rise and state the decision." "A teller vote (clause 5 Rule I) is a voting procedure wherein the Members cast their votes by passing through the center aisle to be counted by Member tellers, but not recorded. First the Members voting 'aye' are counted, and then the Members voting 'no' are counted." Deschler 30 § 8.1.

"This method produces accurate vote totals but does not provide a record of how individual Members voted." House Republican Manual at 238.

[32] The recorded vote by roll call was the main pre-electronic method, and is still used in the Senate. Rule XV(1) prescribes:

upon every roll call the names of the Members shall be called alphabetically by surname, except when two or more have the same surname, in which case the name of the State shall be added . . . ; and after the roll has been once called, the Clerk shall call in their alphabetical order the names of those not voting. Members appearing after the second call, but before the result is announced, may vote or announce a pair.

Roll calls take nearly 30 minutes generally. House Republican Manual at 239.

[33] Rule I(5)(a) prescribes certain votes

shall be taken by electronic device, unless the Speaker in his discretion orders clerks to tell the names of those voting on each side of the question, and such names shall be recorded by electronic device or by clerks, as the case may be, and shall be entered in the Journal, together with the names of those not voting. Members shall have not less than fifteen minutes to be counted from the . . . ordering of clerks to tell the vote.

(footnote continued)

However, since the adoption of the system for electronic voting in 1972, virtually all record votes have occurred by that system, provided for in Rule XV(5).[35]   The House electronic voting system has ten voting stations on the House floor.   Each Member -- and only that Member[36] -- inserts his or her special voting card into the voting station and pushes the button for yes or no.

There is a display board on one wall towering over the floor, so Members can see the votes of anyone who has voted already.   Watching the board, a Member or observer knowledgeable about where various Members stand can make running estimates as to which blocs are voting which way.   Also, a running tally, not only of the totals but also of the breakdown of the vote by party, can be seen on the House's closed-circuit television.   Further information is available at computer consoles.

---

[34]   The procedure is:

> In this case a Members signs his name on a green card if voting in the affirmative and on a red card if voting in the negative.   Then Members voting in the affirmative and Members voting in the negative file up designated aisles so that they can be counted by clerks and drop the cards into ballot boxes.   Members have no less than 15 minutes to vote by this method.   Accurate vote totals are available immediately.   This method also provides a record of how each Member voted.

House Republican Manual at 238.

[35]   The rule provides:

> Unless, in his discretion, the Speaker orders the calling of the names of members in the manner provided for under the preceding provisions of this rule, upon any roll call or quorum call the names of such Members voting or present shall be recorded by electronic device . . . .

[36]   In response to voting irregularities, in 1981 the House adopted Rule VIII(3), prohibiting Members from having anyone else, Member or non-Member, cast their vote or record their presence.

Ordinarily, an electronic vote takes at least 15 minutes. The vote can be shortened to five minutes in two situations. First, Rule I(5)(b)(3) allows the Chair to postpone or "cluster" a number of votes, such as votes from a number of suspensions, with the expectation that after the first full-length (15 minute) vote, the other votes will occur in a cluster of rapid-fire votes of five minutes' duration each.[37] In fact, in 1988, the House held several dozen votes of two minutes' duration each, when working through lengthy lists of end-of-session votes on suspension of the rules.[38] Second, Rule XV(5) allows the Chair, after a full length (15) vote on a motion to recommit, to follow with a short vote on final passage.[39] On rare occasions the Speaker holds a vote open to obtain needed late votes or vote changes, such as on a 1987 budget reconciliation bill, where Speaker "Wright eked out his controversial victory by delaying announcement of the vote's outcome for several minutes until fellow Texas Democrat Jim Chapman

---

[37] Rule I(5)(b)(3) allows the Chair, after one full-length (15 minute) vote on a postponed matter, to

> reduce to not less than five minutes the period of time within which a rollcall vote by electronic device on the question may be taken without any intervening business on any or all of the additional questions on which the Speaker has postponed further proceedings under this paragraph.

[38] Hook, End-of-Session Vote Spree Inflames Tempers, 46 Cong. Q. Week. Rep. 2787 (1988)(the House conducted "40 votes, a record number for an afternoon's work . . . . Members were asked every two or five minutes to register their votes.")

[39] Rule XV(5) specifies:

> The Speaker may, in his discretion, announce after a rollcall vote has been ordered on a motion to recommit . . . that he may reduce to not less than five minutes the period of time in which a rollcall vote, if ordered, will be taken by electronic device on the question of passage or adoption.

switched his vote -- and the results."[40]

Quorum Calls

Article I, sec. 5, cl. 1 provides that "a Majority of each [House] shall constitute a Quorum to do Business." With the full complement of the House at 435, a quorum in the "House" is normally 218. When a Member makes the point of order that a majority is not present, the Chair must see if the House has that majority present to continue "to do Business." If not, the House must either take the steps that summon Members, or adjourn.[41]   In the nineteenth century, the combination of difficult transportation from distant districts and minority party tactics often deprived the House of a quorum.

Today, the quorum call is not a test of whether the House can do business, but nevertheless it is an important tactical tool. When a serious proposition will soon come to the floor, a quorum call may be used to gain time to handle it, and to summon supporters. The minority may use it to see who is in town in its party and in the majority party. Sometimes, Members use it as a delaying or harassing tactic, to even the score for some slight by taking up the time of several hundred others with a trip to the floor, and by impairing the attendance record of Members out of town.[42]

Starting in 1890, when Speaker Reed was

---

[40]   1987 Congressional Quarterly Almanac 622.

[41]   In practice, the House rarely resorts any more to the special methods for summoning, namely, compelling the attendance of absent Members by having them arrested by the Sergeant-at-Arms.   Rule XV(2)(a) and (4); House Manual § 768-70, 774a.

[42]   Confidential interviews of Members by one of the author's students found a number who attributed some quorum calls and meaningless votes to the working out of grudges; for example, Member A held a vote in committee on a day when Member B was away, embarrassing him, so Member B had a floor vote occur on another day when Member A was away.

chopping down all the other techniques for blocking majority action, the majority party cut down the availability of quorum calls. At that time, it amended House Rule XXIII(2)(a) to create the reduced quorum in Committee of the Whole (as distinguished from the full quorum in the "House").   Rule XXIII(2)(a) prescribes that "A quorum of a Committee of the Whole shall consist of one hundred Members."[43] A demand for a quorum call in Committee of the Whole may sometimes[44] end after the first 100 Members show up, without even a record of who came.[45] The same rule limits in other ways the requests for quorum calls in

---

[43] The rule was adopted in 1890 to expedite proceedings. House Manual § 863.

[44] Sometimes Members can be sluggish about coming around for such a "notice quorum" call, expecting that they will lose nothing by letting others constitute the necessary 100.   This has limited the willingness of the House leadership to use this procedure. If the Committee of the Whole cannot produce its quorum of 100 by this easy method, the Chair goes to a quorum call that produces a record. In the unusual situation that the Committee of the Whole still cannot develop its quorum of 100, the Committee would rise pursuant to this rule. All further proceedings would occur in the House.

[45] Rule XXIII(2)(a), regarding quorum calls in Committee of the Whole, allows the Chair to choose between electronic voting methods (or calling the roll), and using the teller procedure of Rule XV(2)(b), pursuant to which Members may simply deposit "quorum tally cards with clerk tellers." House Manual § 771b. Rule XXIII(2)(a) further provides:

> If, at any time during the conduct of any quorum call in a Committee of the Whole, the Chairman determines that a quorum is present, he may, in his discretion and subject to his prior announcement, declare that a quorum is constituted. Proceedings under the call shall then be considered as vacated, and the Committee shall not rise but shall continue its sitting and resume its business.

Vacating proceedings prevents any further record of who came (and who was absent).

Committee of the Whole.[46]

Subsequently, particularly in 1981, the House adopted further rules limiting the availability of quorum calls. Most important, Rule XV(6)(e)(1) prevents a point of order that a quorum is not present "unless the Speaker has put the pending motion or proposition to a vote."[47] As the House Manual explains, "[i]n adopting this rule, the House has presumably determined that the mere conduct of debate in the House, where the Chair has not put the pending motion or proposition to a vote, is not such business as requires a quorum" under the Constitution.[48]

Obtaining Roll-Call Votes: Recorded, "Yea and Nay," and Automatic

There are three methods for obtaining a roll-call vote in the "House" (as opposed to Committee of the Whole): "recorded votes," "Yea and Nay" votes, and "automatic roll-call" votes. All are conducted the same way, almost invariably by

---

[46] The rule allows the Chairman to "refuse to entertain a point of order that a quorum is not present during general debate only." The rule further provides that after a quorum has been established, either by a quorum call, or by a recorded vote on an amendment, Deschler 20 § 11.11, "the Chairman may not entertain a point of order that a quorum is not present unless the Committee is operating under the five-minute rule and the Chairman has put the pending motion or proposition to a vote."

[47] Rule XV(e)(2) allows the Speaker to recognize a Member to move a call of the House even absent the putting of the pending matter to a vote. Other elements of Rule XV limiting points of order regarding quorums are Rule XV(c) and (d), that "[a]fter the presence of a quorum is once ascertained on any day . . . a point of order of no quorum may not be made or entertained -- (1) during the reading of the Journal"; after the Committee of the Whole has risen and before its Chairman reports; during special order speeches; and after the presence of a quorum has been ascertained, before "additional business intervenes."

[48] House Manual § 774c.

electronic device; the difference is in the requirements to obtain that roll call vote. First, a "recorded vote" can be obtained pursuant to Rule I(5)(a) by demand of at least one-fifth of a quorum.[49] Since the full complement of the House is 435, a quorum (one-half) is 218, and a "recorded vote" demand requires the support of 44 (one-fifth of 218). A Member seeking a "recorded vote" says, either before or after a voice vote, "Mr. Speaker, on that vote I request a recorded vote." The Speaker counts those who second the request (by standing) and announces whether there is a sufficient second (of 44 Members) and, accordingly, whether there will be a recorded vote.

Second, the Constitution prescribes that "the Yeas and Nays of the Members of either House on any question shall, at the Desire of one fifth of those Present, be entered on the Journal."[50] When fewer than a quorum are present, it is easier to obtain a "Yea and Nay" vote than a "recorded vote," while the opposite is true when more than a quorum are present. For example, if ten Members are on the floor, and later 300 show up, at all times the requirement of support for a "Yea and Nay" vote would remain 44 (one-fifth of a quorum), but the requirement of support for a "recorded vote" would go up from an easy two Members (one-fifth of the ten initially present) to a hard 60 Members (one-fifth of the 300 present later). To obtain a "Yea and Nay" vote, the Member says regarding a vote, "Mr. Speaker, on that vote I demand the yeas and nays."

Finally, a Member can take advantage of the lack of a quorum to invoke the provision for an "automatic roll-call vote." Rule XV(4) provides that: "[W]henever a quorum fails to vote on any question, and a quorum is not present and objection is made for that cause, unless the House shall adjourn there shall be a call of the House

---

[49] The rule provides: "[I]f any Member requests a recorded vote and that request is supported by at least one-fifth of a quorum, such vote shall be taken by electronic device . . . ."

[50] Art. I, sec. 5, cl. 3.

. . . ." The sequence is that a question is voted upon by voice vote or division vote. Then a Member states, "Mr. Speaker, I object to the vote on the ground that a quorum is not present, and I make a point of order that a quorum is not present."

The Speaker, upon seeing that fewer than 218 present, responds, "Evidently a quorum is not present," and directs that a roll-call vote occur. The roll-call vote on the question brings most of the House Members in, and since that vote shows more than a quorum are present, it satisfies the point of order regarding the quorum.[51] This automatic roll call represents a boon to individual Members, who need no support -- not 44 Members, not a fifth of those present, just themselves -- to obtain a roll call vote on their proposition.

In Committee of the Whole, the requirements for obtaining a roll call vote are entirely different. The "Yeas and Nays" are not taken in Committee of the Whole.[52] Also, there are no automatic roll-call votes. Rather, the sole type of roll-call is the recorded vote.

Rule XXIII(b) allows, in Committee of the Whole, "a recorded vote on request supported by at least twenty-five Members." As a practical matter, only a few Members have such far-out views that they cannot get 24 colleagues -- less than six percent of the House -- to support them if they want a recorded vote. The only problem is to make enough Members show up as to provide those 24.

The method used by the minority to obtain enough Members is a choreographic number referred to by the House Republican Manual as the "dance of the swans and the ducks."[53] The unique "dance of the swans" occurs when few Members are present and an opposition Member wants a roll call vote. For

---

[51] "In this case a simultaneous determination is made as to the presence of a quorum and as to the vote on the question." House Republican Manual at 240.

[52] House Manual § 76.

[53] House Republican Manual at 243.

example, a Member would begin by reciting the
formula, "Mr. Chairman, I request a recorded vote
. . . and pending that vote, I make a point of
order that a quorum is not present." That formula
places the recorded vote demand before the
Committee, and stalls it while the Chair counts
for a quorum. Meanwhile the Member "[m]ove[s]
hands and arms in gentle upward motion resembling
the beginning flight of a graceful swan."[54] This
signals to supporters to stand, so that when the
Chair counts to see if a sufficient second
supports a recorded vote, enough will be standing
to obtain one, particularly if the majority
consents and supports the request.[55]

Otherwise, the opposition Member continues to
demand that a quorum show up.[56] Once "there are
100 or more Members present [the Member can] say:
'I insist on my request for a recorded vote,'"[57]
and by this time, hopefully, the Member has enough
supporters present. Seen less often is the
opposite of the Swan Dance, "the Duck Dance," to
avoid a recorded vote.[58]

---

[54] House Republican Manual at 244.

[55] "If the [majority] side responds to the Swan Dance," by
agreeing to a recorded vote, the Member can "say: 'Mr.
Chairman, I withdraw my point of order.'" House Republican
Manual at 244.

[56] On the other hand, "if the other side does not respond
to the Swan Dance, and the division vote [the Chair's count
of Members present] showed 99 or fewer Members, [the Member
may] insist on [the] point of order that a quorum is not
present." House Republican Manual at 244.

[57] Id.

[58] In the "Duck Dance," the minority Member p. 245:
"mov[es] his hands and arms in a vigorous downward motion,
resembling a diving duck." House Republican Manual at
245. This signals to the other minority Members not to
second the demand for a recorded vote, as when the quorum
call brings in many minority and few majority Members. The
minority may then avoid a recorded vote (which would bring
in the absent majority Members) and can hope to win on a
division by using its temporary advantage in numbers.

When a Member demands a quorum call in Committee of the Whole and then obtains a recorded vote, this provides yet another occasion on which the Chair may shorten the time for votes. Rule XXIII(2)(a) allows the Chair to announce that "following a regular quorum call" in such circumstances, he "will reduce to not less than five minutes the period of time within which a recorded vote on the pending question may be taken if such a vote is ordered."

Tactical Considerations in Voting

As noted above, the allowance of recorded votes in Committee of the Whole, on a seconding by a mere 25 Members, boosted the ability of offerors of floor amendments to defeat chairs. Such tactical nuances of voting may not matter on some votes, because votes with strong substantive interest to Members will be made only with regard to that interest and not to such nuances. On votes which matter a great deal to Members, like decisions on major budget alternatives, or decisions on industries located in their particular districts, Members vote their interest no matter what.

However, on many votes, the outcome may not matter too much to most Members, and their votes can be influenced by tactical considerations. One tactical consideration of particular interest has been the existence of the board displaying votes as Members make them. Since Members no longer vote in alphabetical order (as in the days when the roll was actually called), the trend of their voting can provide significant information. Tacticians may structure that voting trend in order to persuade Members who have not voted yet.

Several common approaches may be noted. Most common is getting the supporters on one side to "hit the boards" first. A minor bill may have only 150 natural supporters and an equal number of natural opponents. Yet if its proponent can get 100 of the 150 supporters ready to vote right when the vote starts, while others just trickle in at a normal rate, the undecided Member who comes in sees an overwhelming margin for the proposition, like 95 to six.   Such an undecided Member may conclude that the side with the "95" is the sensible side, add his vote to the 95, and leave the floor without further ado.

This tactic may be particularly effective for the minority.   Ninety-five minority Members voting early may look like a general favorable consensus to the undecided majority Member, at least without inspecting the display boards to find out who the 95 are.   (The running tally displayed visible on the floor -- unlike the one displayed on closed-circuit television -- does not show a party breakdown.)

Conversely, both leaderships can use the electronic displays to pinpoint the Members to be lobbied immediately.   As the House Republican Manual states:

> With the voting display board and the computer console the leadership can determine the votes of individual Members during the vote. With such information the leadership or floor manager might elect to make direct personal contact with a Member in order to convince him to either change his or her vote, or, if he or she has not yet voted, to urge a particular position.[59]

All sorts of other approaches to voting may be found.   In a close vote, each side may have votes "in its pocket" -- Members who prefer to vote one way, but will switch if their leadership strongly requests their vote.[60]   Or, one party may hold back its votes on an unpopular but necessary matter to be sure that the other party is fulfilling its pledge to vote the necessary way. For example, in 1981, Democrats held back their vote on a debt limit increase until the Republicans had shown by their votes that they would break with their past position and support

---

[59]   House Republican Manual at 252.

[60]   "[S]carcely a single controversial bill has come to the House floor in modern times without both party floor leaders having at least two or three such 'pocket' votes ready for switching."   MacNeil at 359.

the increase.[61]

C.   "HOUSE" PROCEDURE

Adopting a Noncontroversial Rule

Although the chamber does most of its work on bills in Committee of the Whole, "House" procedure still matters from several perspectives. The key role of special rules was discussed in the previous chapter. For each bill, the House adopts a special rule before proceedings begin in Committee of the Whole, so it is in the House that the key test motions and votes occur on proposed special rules. A potpourri of other matters may come up in the "House," from the organization of the House at the beginning of each Congress, to the disposition of veto messages and conference reports.

Moreover, each bill considered in Committee of the Whole must emerge for proceedings in the "House" before final passage. Because basic "House" procedure can be somewhat dry if viewed in the abstract, an illustration is provided of the most important use of "House" procedure: adopting a special rule. After this, the motions and rules are described, followed by two other illustrations from battles over adopting controversial special rules.

Adoption of the open rule for the 1981 Justice Department authorization bill, H.R. 3462, was noncontroversial and simple. On June 4, 1981, the Rules Committee ordered the special rule reported. The rule's manager reported the rule, that is, stood up in the chamber and filed it with the Clerk, whereupon the Speaker referred it to the House Calendar. On June 9, the majority manager of the rule, Representative Leo Zeferetti (D-N.Y.), rose and obtained recognition from the Speaker pro tempore, and announced in the standard formula, "Mr. Speaker, by direction of the Committee on Rules, I call up House Resolution 147 and ask for its immediate consideration," thereby

---

[61]   Sinclair at 233.

bringing it off the calendar and onto the floor, and the Clerk then read the special rule.[62]

The Speaker pro tempore recognized Representative Zeferetti, as majority manager of the open rule, for one hour, and he yielded the customary half of that time to the minority manager, Representative John Rhodes (R-Ariz.). In yielding, the majority manager specified that he yielded time "for debate only," meaning that Representative Rhodes, and Members to whom he in turn yielded time, could only debate and not offer amendments to the special rule.

As per usual, the two managers discussed the rule and the bill, a discussion that often includes such matters as waivers and amendment restrictions in the special rule, and the bill's merits and procedural history. Those who attend the Rules Committee hearing on any special rule will hear echoes from that hearing in the floor statements by the rule's managers. When the managers of the special rule have spoken, they yield time to those of their parties who wish to speak. Often, on noncontroversial rules, less than the whole hour is needed, and time can be yielded back. On the rule for H.R. 3462, no one other than the rule managers wanted to speak.

When the managers finished discussing the rule for H.R. 4242, Representative Zeferetti moved the previous question. No one sought a record vote, and the motion carried on a voice vote without apparent opposition; in the words of the Congressional Record, "[t]he previous question was ordered."[63] Once the motion carried, no more debate could occur, nor could amendments be offered.

Since the pending question was on adoption of the rule, the Speaker pro tempore put that question. Again, no one sought a record vote or apparently offered opposition, and in the words of the Congressional Record, "[t]he resolution was agreed to," and the traditional pro forma motion to reconsider was "laid on the table."[64] If any

---

[62] 127 Cong. Rec. H2787 (daily ed. June 9, 1981).

[63] 127 Cong. Rec. H2788 (daily ed. June 9, 1981).

(footnote continued)

Members had wanted a record vote on either the motion for the previous question, or the adoption of the rule, or both, they could probably have obtained it, as Members usually can, pursuant to the previously described "automatic roll-call" procedure of Rule XV(4).

The Hour Rule, Adjourning, and Tabling

Basic "House" procedure begins with Speaker recognition. Any Member who seeks to make a motion or to request other action stands up and "actively seek[s] recognition by addressing the Chair at the appropriate time," which is once the prior speaker finishes.[65] The Speaker decides whether to recognize, following the precedents as to the rights of Members with privileged business to receive priority in recognition. When the Speaker recognizes a Member, he grants the Member recognition for a particular period of time, generally for an hour, as the Speaker pro tempore recognized Representative Zeferetti for an hour in the example.

Recognition for an hour occurs pursuant to Rule XIV(2), which provides that "no Member shall occupy more than one hour in debate on any question in the House or in committee, except as further provided in this rule." The Hour Rule dates back to 1840, when it "was necessitated by the rising membership of the House".[66] It applies

---

[64] Id. These are customary formulas rattled off so rapidly by the Speaker that they may pass unheard unless one is listening for them.

[65] Deschler 29 § 4.1

[66] Damon at 195. The old rule of Parliament had been: "if any one . . . be long and out of the matter, then may the Speaker gently admonish him of the shortness of the time or the business of the House, and pray him to make as short as may be." Luce at 262. For the history of the Hour Rule in the House, see id. at 263-64; Damon at 195; McConachie at 167. The most well-known difference between House and Senate procedure, the Senate's unlimited debate and associated opportunity for filibuster, traces to the Senate's refusal to adopt anything like the hour rule until (footnote continued)

across the board to all motions in the House unless some other rule applies (for example, the limit of 20 minutes on a side for motions to suspend the rules).

The Member who seeks and obtains recognition as manager of a matter typically shares half of his hour with another Member who manages the other side (most often, the minority manager), as Representative Zeferetti shared with Representative Rhodes, by announcing "I yield 30 minutes for debate only to the gentleman from ---."[67] So long as the manager yields time "for debate only," no motions can be made during the yielded time. Any Member who wishes to speak must request and receive time from one of the managers, by an exchange such as: "Mr. Speaker, will the gentleman from Florida yield?" -- "Mr. Speaker, I yield three minutes to the gentleman from Alaska."

In theory, at the end of the first hour, the Speaker would recognize another Member for another hour. As in most matters of recognition, the tendency would be to alternate as a matter of fairness between majority and minority.[68]   In practice, because of the House's tight scheduling practices, debate under the Hour Rule usually does not go beyond the first recognition for one hour (unless the House votes down a motion for the previous question and thereby decides not to cut off debate).

House Rule XVI(4) lists the motions available in the House, (the bracketed numbers reflect the discussion below):

> When a question is under debate, no motion shall be received but [1] to adjourn, [2] to lay on the table, [3] for the previous question (which motions shall be decided without debate), [4] to postpone to a day certain, [5] to refer, [6] or to amend, or

---

cloture came in 1917.

[67]   "Debate on a privileged resolution is under the hour rule and the Member recognized to call it up has control of the time." Deschler 29 § 20.5.

[68]   See generally Deschler 29 § 5.1 (alternation during amending under the five minute rule).

> postpone indefinitely; which several motions
> shall have precedence in the foregoing
> order . . . .

Taking these in the order listed in the rule, the motion to adjourn, known since 1789, ends the House's sitting for that day.[69]   It has the highest precedence of all motions, meaning that even after some other motion -- any other motion -- has been made, a motion to adjourn can still be made and will be voted on before the other motion. Thus, the motion to adjourn can be made at almost any time to stop proceedings cold, except when a Member has the floor during a vote, or during Committee of the Whole.[70]   It can even be made in the absence of a quorum, since the Quorum Clause of the Constitution states that "a Majority of each [House] shall constitute a Quorum to do Business; but a smaller Number may adjourn from day to day."[71]

Starting in 1973, the House created an equally privileged variation, the motion to fix "a day and time certain" to which the House shall adjourn instead of just adjourning until the regular convening hour the next day.[72] Generally a majority Member makes the motion to adjourn when the business scheduled by the Majority Leader is over.[73]

The motion to table, known more formally as the motion to lay on the table, provides "a final,

---

[69]   See House Manual §§ 585 (Jefferson's discussion of the motion), 783-84 (discussion of motion in modern times).

[70]   House Manual § 783; Deschler 37 § 5.

[71]   U.S. Const., Art. I, sec. 5, cl.; see Deschler 20 § 8 and 37 § 6.

[72]   Rule XVI(4) (last clause); see House Manual § 784; Deschler 37 § 5.13. This version may even be used when a vote on a pending question has been objected to for lack of a quorum. Deschler 37 § 5.2.

[73]   On occasion, a minority Member offers the motion at the end of special orders when no majority Members remain. Deschler 37 § 5.13.

adverse disposition of a matter without debate,"
or in other words, a quick kill.[74] It can be used
either against another motion (e.g., tabling an
amendment), or against the pending matter
itself.[75] Motions to table are seen occasionally
in the House, such as in stopping oddball floor
actions.[76] The motion to table cannot be used in
Committee of the Whole,[77] and is thus unavailable

---

[74]   House Manual § 785. Although known since the early
practice of the House, at the time it had a different use
then, of deferring rather than killing matters. Jefferson
noted that the chamber may "order [legislation] to lie on
their table. It may then be called for at any time." House
Manual § 445 (Jefferson).

[75]   As Dr. Floyd Riddick noted:

> Senate bills, House bills with Senate amendments,
> vetoed bills, motions to reconsider, postpone to a day
> certain, and discharge committees from resolutions of
> inquiry, resolutions presenting questions of privilege,
> appeals from the decisions of the chair, and like
> matters may be laid on the table. Conference reports,
> previous questions, motions to recommit, to suspend the
> rules to go into Committee of the Whole, and generally
> motions relative to the order of business may not be
> laid on the table. A motion to discharge a committee
> can be laid on the table.

Riddick (1949) at 308.

[76]   For example, when Representative Father Robert Drinan
(D-Mass.) put in an impeachment resolution for President
Nixon in July, 1973, which centrist Democrats considered
premature, the majority leadership planned that "[i]n the
event that any member of the House called for a vote on
Drinan's motion, we would immediately move to table it." T.
O'Neill, Man of the House 297 (1987). The successful use of
a motion to table on amendments in the "House" has the
paradoxical effect of killing not only the amendment but the
bill as well. House Manual § 785. In the usual situation,
the previous question is ordered, or the yeas and nays are
ordered on a motion for the previous question, and in either
case the motion to table is no longer in order. House
Manual §§ 785, 809.

(footnote continued)

for most amendments.

This contrasts significantly with the motion's availability, and very frequent use, in the Senate, where it kills controversial amendments that lack sufficient support -- and does so without creating a clear substantive record on them like an "up-or-down" vote. The Committee of the Whole lacks any corresponding way to defeat controversial amendments once they are offered without creating a clear record. Thus, the House majority party, to avoid going on record on germane amendments, must resort to means which absolutely forbid the amendments from even being offered, such as restrictive special rules, and suspension of the rules.

The Previous Question and Other Motions

Of all the motions in the "House" (as distinguished from the Committee of the Whole), the most important by far is the motion for the previous question, which the House in the nineteenth century "perfected into a highly useful tool for ending obstructive debate."[78] Rule XVII(1) provides: "There shall be a motion for the

---

[77] Deschler 23 § 4.4.

[78] Damon at 200. The previous question was first introduced in Parliament in 1604. House Manual § 463. In the House's early years it took a form very different from its modern one, being debatable until 1811, and not cutting off amendments until 1840. McConachie traces the 1811 reshaping of the previous question to "five years of turmoil" during which "a main feature of opposition tactics was long and wearisome speech-making," and the particular need of the House for "a bridle for the eccentric Virginian" John Randolph, with his rambling bizarre speeches. Interestingly, just as cloture came to the Senate on the eve of World War I, so "after an all-night struggle between supporters and opposers of the coming war [of 1812], the cloture [i.e., the motion for the previous question] fastened itself upon the House of Representatives -- as its enemies would express themselves, -- unlike Sinbad's Old Man of the Sea, never to be shaken off." McConachie, supra, at 104. For the further history of the motion, see Luce at 270-73; Damon at 197-200; House Manual § 804.

previous question, which, being ordered by a majority of Members voting, if a quorum be present, shall have the effect to cut off all debate and bring the House to a direct vote upon the immediate question or questions on which it has been asked and ordered." The motion for the previous question belongs largely to the manager, who can use the motion Representative Zeferetti used it in the example above,[79] while opponents cannot use the motion against the manager.[80]

Once the manager moves the previous question on an underlying matter that has been debated, a vote occurs immediately on the manager's motion

---

[79]   The manager can demand the motion for the previous question over the efforts of others:

> The Member in charge of the bill and having the floor may demand the previous question although another Member may propose a motion of higher privilege, but the motion of higher privilege must be put first . . . and the Member in charge is entitled to recognition to move the previous question even after he has surrendered the floor in debate.

House Manual § 807.

[80]   [I]f the Member in charge of the bill claims the floor in debate another Member may not demand the previous question; but having the floor any Member may make the motion although the effect may be to deprive the member in charge of the bill. And if, after debate, the member in charge of the bill does not move the previous question, another Member may; but where a Member intervenes on a pending proceeding to make a preferential motion, such as the motion to recede from a disagreement with the Senate, he may not move the previous question on that motion as against the rights of the Member in charge . . . .

House Manual § 807. The exception is that even when a manager allows an amendment, another Member may use the previous question to cut the amendment off: "Where a Member controlling the time on a bill or resolution in the House yields for the purpose of amendment, another Member may move the previous question before the Member offering the amendment is recognized to debate it." Id.

without further debate.[81]   If the motion passes,
or if the previous question is otherwise ordered
(such as by language in a special rule), it cuts
off further debate on the underlying matter and
virtually all motions, and brings the matter to a
final vote.[82]   On most occasions, such as the
adoption of the vast majority of special rules,
the combination of the Hour Rule, plus at the end
of the hour or earlier a motion for the previous
question, together suffice to produce the tightly
scripted procedure that is the House's hallmark.
The motion for the previous question is not
available in Committee of the Whole, where cutting
off amendments requires a closed rule.[83]

Because managers routinely use the previous
question to bar all motions, any Member who wants
to offer motions in the House must typically start
by defeating the motion for the previous
question.   Defeat of a motion for the previous
questions invokes a special practice regarding
recognition.   Ordinarily, the majority manager
controls the progress of floor proceedings through
his right to prior recognition.[84]

However, "when an essential motion made by
the Member in charge is decided adversely the
right to prior recognition passes to the leading
opponent of motion."[85]   Defeat on "an essential
motion" on the House floor, such as defeating the

---

[81]   It is typical to move the previous question after debate
on a matter, in which case it cuts off further debate.
However, if the previous question is successfully moved
before any debate has even begun on a matter, 40 minutes of
debate is allowed.   House Manual § 805.

[82]   The previous question cuts off motions to amend, to
table, and to postpone, House Manual §§ 806, 808, although
by Rule XVII's terms, of course, the previous question may
be moved on an amendment or amendments, in which case it
brings votes on them without further amendment.

[83]   House Manual §§ 333, 334 (as in Jefferson's time, no
previous question in Committee of the Whole).

[84]   House Manual § 754.

[85]   Cannon, 153; House Manual § 755; Deschler 29 §§5.14-16.

previous question, is a dramatic moment, marking the limit of the manager's power, often even the limit of the power of the majority leadership.[86] It also marks the strength of the underlying democratic process in the House, for the process smoothly mediates the temporary passage of power to those who have shown, for the moment, that they have the power.

When the previous question is defeated, or for some reason is not moved, the other motions of lower precedence listed in Rule XVI(4) can be offered. The motion to postpone is rarely seen.[87] The motions to commit, refer, or recommit, which are substantially equivalent, send matters to committee. This motion has an important role after the Committee of the Whole reports a bill to the House for proceedings leading to final passage, as discussed in this chapter's last section; in that context Rule XVI(4) protects the motion to recommit from the previous question. For example, when the Committee of the Whole finishes amending an appropriation bill, and sends the bill back to the "House," the minority may offer a motion to recommit the bill with instructions to lop five percent off every item. Other uses are occasionally made of this motion.[88]

---

[86] An example is when a House select committee sought to seat Adam Clayton Powell, the controversial black chair of the Education and Labor Committee, with a resolution which would censure him for ethical transgressions. When it offered a motion for the previous question on that resolution, the House defeated the motion, amending the resolution to exclude Powell. Powell v. McCormack, 395 U.S. 486, 492 (1969). (See also id. at 510 n.31, the Supreme Court's description of the motion for the previous question, a rare foray of the Justices into congressional procedure.) For a description of another similar floor revolt regarding Powell, and a parliamentary inquiry regarding a Powell matter, see 7 Deschler 23 §§ 23.3, 23.5.

[87] For discussion of the motion to postpone, see House Manual § 786.

[88] The motion to refer may be used on other matters in the House, such as by the majority party to send to committee a (footnote continued)

House Rule XIX provides a motion to amend, and allows a variety of amendments of different types to be pending at the same time. The mover of an amendment in the "House" can withdraw his amendment (unlike in Committee of the Whole, where withdrawal requires unanimous consent).[89] Opponents who wish to change a complex special rule amend it after defeating the previous question. However, the germaneness rule, which applies in the House just as it does in Committee of the Whole, prevents non-germane amendments to special rules as well as to bills.

Thus, Members who wish to tack non-germane amendments onto a bill, and who seek to prepare by tacking a waiver for germaneness onto the special rule, may find that they cannot amend the special rule, for the waivers for a non-germane amendment may themselves be non-germane to the special rule. For example, to a special rule that contains no waivers at all, an amendment to add a germaneness waiver for offering a major irrelevant substitute for the bill may itself be non-germane. In this situation, the Members cannot amend the special rule as they would like, even when they have defeated the previous question.[90]

For example, on August 18, 1982, anti-Federal

---

question of privilege. For example, the majority may refer to committee an inconvenient minority resolution to seat the minority contender in a contested election.

Also, the Rules Committee may use the motion to refer as a means to pull a special rule off the floor after opponents achieve a rare victory and defeat the previous question. For example, if the special rule for an appropriations bill waives points of order for the FTC being unauthorized, the minority might defeat the previous question on that special rule and threaten to amend it differently. To keep control, the majority might refer the special rule back to the Rules Committee for study. For discussion of the motion, see House Manual §§ 787-88; Deschler 23 § 11-16.

[89] House Manual §§ 823 (types of amendments) and 824 (modification and withdrawal).

[90] House Manual § 794.

Trade Commission forces defeated the previous question on a special rule for an appropriation bill providing FTC funds.   However, their alternative expansive rule for attaching legislative riders to that appropriation was held non-germane and out of order.   This is a serious limit on the extent to which the minority party can alter the agenda of the House.   Even if it wins a fight over a special rule, it cannot perform the equivalent of discharge and call wholly new subjects onto the floor by grafting unrelated germaneness waivers onto rules.   Thus, the minority party may not be able to offer its version of a bill when that includes non-germane aspects.   Because the motion to amend receives heavy use in Committee of the Whole, it will be discussed below.

Finally, Rule XVIII provides for the venerable motion to reconsider.[91]   After a vote occurs, making a motion to reconsider suspends that vote.   If the motion carries, it nullifies that first vote, and a second vote on the matter occurs.   Usually in House consideration of a special rule or bill, pro forma motions to reconsider are made and then tabled, just as was done in the example of Representative Zeferetti's rule, because once one motion to reconsider has been made and tabled, no other motion to reconsider can be made, and the decision on the matter has been "locked in."[92]   The motion cannot

---

[91]   The motion has been allowed in the House since 1789, and Jefferson devoted a whole section in his manual to reconsideration, citing its old English precedents.   House Manual §§ 513-18, 812.

[92]   Deschler 23 § 19.2.   For discussion of the motion to reconsider see House Manual §§ 812-19; Deschler 23 §§ 17-20.

As the rule's wording suggests, regarding how the motion "shall not be withdrawn . . . and thereafter any Member may call it up for consideration," a motion to reconsider can be entered, but not called up until later. Entry of a motion to reconsider is a matter of high privilege, whereas actual calling up of the motion may wait.   House Manual § 814.   There does not appear to be as much use in the House of entry of motions to reconsider as a (footnote continued)

be made in Committee of the Whole,[93] and real (as opposed to <u>pro forma</u>) motions to reconsider are relatively infrequent.

A Controversial Special Rule

Traditionally, the House adopts the vast majority of special rules reported by the Rules Committee in precisely the form reported, as discussed in the chapter on the Rules Committee. That trend does not rob the procedure for adopting or defeating special rules of its significance. On the contrary, such procedure has significance out of all proportion to the number of special rules amended or defeated. The pattern of House acceptance or rejection of special rules reflects acutely the balance of forces in the House, serving as a sensitive indicator of leadership control. Moreover, while effective attempts to beat special rules are few in number, often they occur over rules for the bills of the highest importance, such as budget reconciliation bills or continuing resolutions.

For example, in 1981-82, the House rejected the Rules Committee's recommendation on only a handful of occasions: the House defeated outright only one special rule, referred (essentially defeated) another, and amended a third. There were not even ten occasions when a shift of 40 or fewer votes would have defeated a rule. Yet these few close fights mattered greatly.

The one special rule amended on the floor established the procedure for the book-length wide-ranging Omnibus Budget Reconciliation Act of 1981. In winning the fight over that special rule, the Republicans won much of their legislative program for the entire Congress. Significant rules fights occurred over the rules for all three major tax bills of 1981-82, as well as over budget reconciliation legislation again in

---

device for keeping votes from becoming final, as in the Senate.

[93]   House Manual § 416.

1982.[94]

Accordingly, a second example, this time of a controversial rule, will illustrate the procedure in a tough rule fight. The Omnibus Budget Reconciliation Act of 1981, H.R. 3982, was the most important bill of 1981-82. The budget chapter discusses its budget aspects; here, it suffices to say that a coalition of Republicans and conservative Democrats sought to enact the "Gramm-Latta II" substitute for the bill as the vehicle for President Reagan's whole budget-cutting program. That coalition had its best chance if Gramm-Latta II were presented in a single vote -- a vote that could be portrayed as being for, or against, the program of the popular new President. The coalition put in the substitute some provisions, termed "sweeteners," such as oil industry subsidies to attract uncommitted Members from Texas and Louisiana.

On June 25, 1981, the Speaker recognized Rules Chair Richard Bolling (D-Mo.) under the Hour Rule to manage the reported special rule, which cut the Republican substitute into pieces, and dropped the sweeteners.[95] In turn, he yielded 30 minutes to the minority manager, Representative Delbert Latta (R-Ohio). In the illuminating

---

[94] For the $98 billion tax increase of 1982, the Tax Equity and Fiscal Responsibility Act, H.R. 4961, the motion for the previous question on the rule waiving points of order against the conference report barely won adoption by 220-210, and the rule itself was adopted 253-176. For the public works/gas tax increase in the Surface Transportation Act of 1982, the rule was adopted by the cliffhanging vote of 197-194. For the massive tax cut bill of 1981, the Economic Recovery Tax Act, H.R. 4242, the motion for the previous question on the special rule was adopted 282-148, and the rule itself was adopted 280-150.

[95] The Rules Committee reported a rule providing for Gramm-Latta to be voted on in six pieces, minus the sweeteners, and the conservative coalition readied an alternative rule providing for a single vote on the whole package, including the sweeteners. Both versions included comprehensive waivers of points of order against the bill and the amendments allowed. Both versions were highly restrictive, allowing no extra amendments.

debate that followed, the Democratic leadership's side argued its rule was necessary because "Gramm-Latta went way beyond the budget process," and the conservatives responded that the Democratic leadership's rule violated the "restraint which is necessary and traditional in a democratic republic" because the majority sought "to dictate to the minority what amendments they can offer."[96]

At the end of the hour, Chairperson Bolling moved the previous question. The Gramm-Latta coalition wished to amend the special rule, and since the motion for the previous question cuts off amendments, the coalition had to defeat that motion. Accordingly, it demanded a roll-call vote, and defeated the motion for the previous question by 217-210.[97]

As the leading opponent of the motion for the previous question, Representative Latta had earned the right, upon defeat of that leading motion, to prior recognition, and the Speaker recognized him for one hour pursuant to the Hour Rule. Representative Latta offered an amendment to the special rule to recast it as the conservative coalition had sought. In a rare instance, the Speaker left the chair to speak on the floor; Representative Latta yielded him half of that hour.[98]

At the close of the hour, Representative Latta took the necessary steps to adopt the rule in the form he sought. First, he moved the previous question on both his amendment, and on the resolution, precluding other amendments or debate.[99] This motion for the previous question

---

[96]   127 Cong. Rec. H3382 (daily ed. June 25, 1981) (Rep. Bolling); id. at H3373 (Rep. Barber Conable (R-N.Y.)).

[97]   Id. at H3382.

[98]   Representative Latta at first "yield[ed] the Speaker whatever time he may need." 127 Cong. Rec. H3383 (daily ed. June 25, 1981). At the end of the Speaker's speech, Rep. Latta stated that he had yielded 30 minutes to the Speaker, id. at H3385, meaning the Speaker could yield time to others on his side.

[99]   "The previous question may be asked and ordered upon a (footnote continued)

carried, 219-208.   Then Representative Latta's amendment to the rule, recasting the rule into the form he sought, carried by 216-212, and the rule as amended carried, 214-206, all without further debate pursuant to the ordering of the previous question.   With that special rule adopted, the next day the House adopted the Gramm-Latta II substitute version of the reconciliation bill.

Sometimes rule fights can be either much simpler, or much more complex.   Commonly, opponents of a rule do not seek to amend it, but merely to defeat it, a much simpler maneuver which joins those who oppose the rule because of its form, and those who oppose the bill because of its content.   For example, opponents almost defeated the rule for the surface transportation bill in 1982, which squeaked through 197-194, when opponents of the bill joined forces with opponents of the rule's provision preventing amendment of the tax aspects of the bill.[100]

Complex maneuvering occurs when opponents of a special rule defeat the previous question on the majority's version, but cannot continue to keep control.   For example, the House defeated the motion for the previous question on the special rule for the State-Justice-Commerce Appropriation in 1982, due to opposition to waiving the point of order against funding for the Federal Trade Commission.   In response to that defeat, the majority, through the manager of the special rule, moved to refer the special rule back to the Rules Committee.   The minority could not maintain control; it tried to table that motion to refer, but was defeated.   Then the manager moved the previous question on the motion to refer.   If that had been defeated, a minority motion to recommit with instructions would have been in order (with some germaneness restrictions).   However, the manager prevailed: the House adopted the previous

---

single motion, a series of motions allowable under the rules, or an amendment or amendments, or may be made to embrace all authorized motions or amendments and include the bill to its passage or rejection."   Rule XVII(1).   In complex maneuvering in the House, it is not uncommon to see the motion for the previous question used repeatedly.

[100]   Id. at 324.

question and then also adopted the motion to refer. As a result of this see-saw battle, the Rules Committee won the opportunity to take back the special rule and reshape it into something the majority could control.[101]

D. FLOOR MANAGING AND THE START OF BILL CONSIDERATION IN COMMITTEE OF THE WHOLE

With the adoption of a special rule, a bill becomes privileged, and the spotlight shifts from the manager of the special rule, to the manager of the bill itself. A bill's floor manager is "king for a day." As political observers noted about the role of the bill manager, "[f]or some bills, especially the more controversial ones, [that role] also may mean the difference between passage unamended, significant amendments, or defeat. Therefore, the skill of the bill manager may play an important role in determining the fate of a piece of legislation."[102]

The bill managers' role on the floor is an extension of their place in the committee and conference process, since they typically chair either the subcommittee or committee of jurisdiction, as discussed below. Thus, would-be floor managers may have drafted the bills originally, or secured their referral. Very likely they chaired the hearings on the bills, led the markups in subcommittee or committee, supervised the writing of the reports, testified for the bills at the Rules Committee hearings on their special rules, and coordinated with the leadership the scheduling of the rules and the bills. If the bills pass on the floor, the erstwhile floor managers can anticipate again taking control: often they recommend the choice of the House conferees and lead the conference delegation, or handle nonconference ("amendment between Houses") negotiations. Thus, while floor

---

[101]   128 Cong. Rec. H5899-5901 (daily ed. Aug. 13, 1982).

[102]   Smith & Deering at 195.

management is the moment of highest visibility, it represents only the tip of the iceberg for the manager's role in moving and shaping a bill.   All these reasons combine to make the manager the chief Member on the bill for interest groups and administration who lobby, and for the public when it assigns credit or blame for the measure's form and fate.

Who Manages

The selection of bill managers today changed sharply as a result of the revolt against chairs in the 1970s.   In the nineteenth century,[103] as the House depended more on its committee structure, chairs monopolized management of the most important bills, like appropriations and tariffs.[104]   In the twentieth century, full

---

[103]   In the House's very earliest days, "[t]here was indifference as to which member of a committee should report its measures to the House" and thereby manage the bill.   At this early point, the chairs of the standing committees initially reported all their committee's bills, but for lesser bills, a chair might well allow "charge of the floor [to] fall by courtesy to the author, or as the chairman called him, the father of the bill."   McConachie at 156, 163.

[104]   The regularity of the floor management role for the chairs of Ways and Means, and Appropriations, gave rise to their posting as majority leaders:

[T]he early titular floor leaders were at the same time the chairmen of the Ways and Means Committee.   Before the division of the work of that committee, the duties of its chairmen were so numerous that they automatically became the actual [majority] leaders, since as chairmen of that committee they had to direct the consideration of most of the legislation presented to the House.   [Ways and Means handled both the revenue and the appropriations bills down to 1865].

From 1865 to 1896 the burden of handling most of the legislation was shifted to the chairman of the Appropriations Committee, who then was designated most

(footnote continued)

committee chairs tended to monopolize floor management of all committee bills. Floor management by chairs reinforced their other control over bills and denied junior Members the visibility and credit for which they hungered.[105]   While in theory, a chair would "subordinat[e] his personal views and devot[e] every effort to securing [a bill's] consideration and passage in the form in which reported to the House,"[106] in fact, chairs often managed bills with their own views rather than the committee's in mind.[107]

Accordingly, as part of the 1970s revolt against full committee chairs, junior Members demanded and received a greater share in the role of floor manager. Democratic Caucus Rule 39 was amended in 1974 to provide that "[t]he chairmen of full committees shall, insofar as practicable, permit subcommittee chairmen to handle on the floor legislation from their respective

---

frequently as the [majority] leader. From 1896 to 1910 once again the chairmen of the Ways and Means Committee were usually sought as the floor leaders.

Galloway at 136. For appropriations, the manager came to be the chair of the pertinent appropriations subcommittee, rather than chair of the full committee.

[105] "Still another major power is the chairman's automatic choice of managing a committee bill on the chamber floor or appointing others to do so. In this way, the chairman controls debate time on the chamber floor, a power which can limit true dissent." T. Siff & A. Weil, Ruling Congress: How the House and Senate Rules Govern the Legislative Process 99 (1975).

[106] Cannon at 220.

[107] Here, as in other contexts, comes to mind the famous dictum of Chairperson Philip Campbell of the Rules Committee in the 1920s, in response to complaints of junior committee members at his (successful) refusal to report a measure they had voted out: "You can go to ---- . . . [I]t makes no difference what a majority of you decide; if it meets with my disapproval, it shall not be done; I am the Committee; in me reposes absolute obstructive powers." F. Riddick (1949) at 123.

subcommittees."   Within   a   few   years,   floor
management shifted dramatically in a number of
committees.   Full   committee   chair   management   of
bills   of   the   Commerce   Committee   fell   from   100
percent to 7.6 percent; of the Banking Committee,
from 96.4 percent to 15.9 percent.[108] While "most
full   committee   chairs   remain   very   active
participants,"   "[n]onetheless, House subcommittee
chairs are much more active than they were before
the reforms."[109]

The House's increase in subcommittee chairs
as managers in the 15 years after 1970 changed
significantly   the   complexion   of   floor
proceedings.   Thereafter, the House often tooks
its lead from a large pool of relatively junior
Members   --   subcomittee chairs who had been in the
House only six or eight or ten years, many in
their thirties or forties.   They contrasted with
the   small   circle   of   relatively   senior   full
committee   chairs,   some   of   them   septua-   or
octogenarians.

Thus, floor management often fell upon junior
new subcommittee chairs, who lacked a record of
managing   similar   bills   if,   indeed,   they   had
managed   any   bills   at   all.   As   has   been   noted
above,   this   trend   spurred   other   major   House
trends: jockeying for subcommittee chairs, and for
expanded subcommittee jurisdictions; weakening of
the barriers against floor amendments; and the
compensating rise of complex special rules and
stronger majority leadership.

Boilerplate   in   special   rules   always   gives
time control to the full committee leaders, but
then the political processes within each committee
decide, separately for majority and minority, on
managers   from   the   level   of   full   committee   or
subcommittee.   For example, in 1982 the domestic
content bill for automobiles, H.R. 5133, received
a multiple referral to Energy and Commerce, and

---

[108]   Deering & Smith at 283.   For the House committees
averaged overall, the statistics were less dramatic, since
some committees has previously given subcommittee chairs a
role, and many committees continued to give full committee
chairs a role.

[109]   Deering & Smith at 196.

Ways and Means. Accordingly, the language in the
special rule provided one hour of general debate
for the chair and ranking minority Member of Ways
and Means, and the same for Energy and Commerce.
This was just to settle the committees' roles on
the floor, not who each committee would send to
manage.   Of the four managers (majority and
minority from each committee), three came from the
subcommittee level.[110]

Going into Committee of the Whole

The boilerplate first part of each special
rule provides for going into Committee of the
Whole.[111]   In 1983, the House adopted Rule
XXIII(1)(b)[112] to provide that once a special rule

---

[110] The managers for Ways and Means were the chair and
ranking minority member of the Subcommittee on Trade,
Representatives Sam Gibbons (D-Fla.) and William Frenzel (R-
Minn.). The managers for Energy and Commerce were the chair
of the Subcommittee on Commerce, Transportation, and
Tourism, Representative James J. Florio (D-N.J.), and the
ranking minority member for the full committee,
Representative James T. Broyhill (R-N.C.). Chairperson John
Dingell (D-Mich.) of the full committee also played an
important role, as the chief mover behind the legislation.

[111] The language reads: "Resolved, that at any time after
the adoption of this resolution the Speaker may, pursuant to
clause 1(b) of rule XXIII, declare the House resolved in the
Committee of the Whole House on the State of the Union for
the consideration of [the particular measure]."

[112] From 1789 until then, the House had gone into Committee
of the Whole by adopting a motion, often by recorded vote.
"The form of going from the House into committee, is for the
Speaker, on motion, to put the question that the House do
now resolve itself into a Committee of the Whole to take
into consideration such a matter naming it." House Manual §
328 (from Jefferson's Manual). Such motions led to needless
recorded votes, since if the House had not wanted to
consider a bill, it would have defeated the special rule.
Elimination of this vote accords with the House's ruling
long ago not to vote on the question of consideration for
bills taken up under a special rule: the modern House relies
(footnote continued)

has been adopted, the House can go into Committee of the Whole without a motion or vote.[113]   The Speaker chooses a time consistent with the schedule announced by the Majority Leader -- sometimes immediately after adoption of a rule, sometimes a day or more later[114] -- and declares that pursuant to the previously-passed rule, the House shall resolve into Committee of the Whole for consideration of the bill.

House Rule XXIII(3) lists the matters that "shall be first considered in a Committee of the Whole," which covers anything concerning money, and conforms to the broad standards for matters placed on the Union Calendar (as opposed to the House Calendar).[115]   Following the ancient formula, to this day Rules XXIII(1)(a) provides that "in forming a Committee of the Whole House,

---

solely on the vote to adopt a special rule as the test of its willingness to take up a bill.

[113]   Rule XXIII(1)(b) provides that "[a]fter the House has adopted a special order of business resolution," i.e., a special rule, "the Speaker may at any time within his discretion, when no question is pending before the House, declare the House resolved into the Committee of the Whole House on the State of the Union for the consideration of that measure without intervening motion. . . ."

[114]   A common reason for delay is when a rule for a bill is completely noncontroversial and can be adopted on a Friday or Monday without a vote, while consideration of the bill itself waits until Tuesday through Thursday, the days when Members expect record votes.

[115]   Rule XXIII(3) provides:

All motions or propositions involving a tax or charge upon the people, all proceedings touching appropriations of money, or bills making appropriations of money, or property, or requiring such appropriation to be made, or authorizing payments out of appropriations already made, or releasing any liability to the United States for money or property, or referring any claim to the Court of Claims, shall be first considered in a Committee of the Whole, and a point of order under this rule shall be good at any time before the consideration of a bill has commenced.

the Speaker shall leave his chair after appointing
a Chairman to preside."[116]   Meanwhile,   the
majority and minority managers of the bill take up
their positions at the tables provided for them,
each table having its own microphone.

General Debate

Immediately   upon   the   Chairman   of   the
Committee of the Whole assuming the Chair, the
Chairman follows the language in the special rule
dispensing with reading of the bill and providing
for general debate, by announcing that "pursuant
to the rule, the first reading has been dispensed
with.   Under the rule, Mr. -- is recognized for
one half hour, and Mr. -- is recognized for one
half hour."[117]   General debate consists of a
period of pure debate about the bill without
amendments or motions of any kind.[118]

---

[116] As Thomas Jefferson wrote almost two centuries ago, the
Speaker   "leaves   the   Chair   and   takes   a   seat
elsewhere . . . . and the person appointed chairman seats
himself . . . ." House Manual § 328.

[117] Boilerplate language in the rule invariably dispenses
with   the   first   reading   of   the   bill.   Absent   such
boilerplate, the first action of the Chair would be to
direct the Clerk to read the bill. Rule XXI(1) provides
that "Bills and joint resolutions on their passage shall be
read   the   first   time   by   title   and   the   second   time   in
full . . . ." The reading of the bill by title, which
formerly occurred at the time of introduction, now occurs in
Committee of the Whole. "As the processes of handling bills
have been shortened, the second reading now occurs . . . for
bills considered in Committee of the Whole, when they are
taken up in that committee . . . . before general debate
begins." House Manual § 831.

The   special   rule   typically   provides   for   "general
debate, which shall be confined to the bill and shall
continue not to exceed one hour, to be equally divided and
controlled by the chairman and ranking minority member of
the Committee on -- ."

[118] The typical rule includes boilerplate language that
(footnote continued)

Consideration in Committee of the Whole is the dominant phase in the chamber's consideration of a bill.   Dr. Floyd Riddick estimated in 1941 that the House of Representatives spent "from only five to thirty minutes for each bill" in "House" procedure (as distinguished from "Committee of the Whole" procedure) while it was "the common practice for the Committee of the Whole House on the State of the Union to spend anywhere from two to twenty hours' consideration on each bill, debating and amending it";[119] this continues to be a fair estimate.

Majority managers usually prepare in some depth for their role in Committee of the Whole on major matters.   They gather intelligence on their own and by use of whip polls, trying to anticipate the likely floor amendments and opposition arguments.   They negotiate potential problems, seeking to position favorably or at least neutralize the party factions, the administration, and interest groups.   They foreshadow their floor themes in speaking before the Rules Committee, and perhaps elsewhere -- in press contacts, the committee report, and "Dear Colleague" letters. All this may involve consultation with the leadership, and extensive staff preparation.

On the floor, the managers lead off with the opening statements during general debate.   The House Republican Manual reminds staff to "give particular attention to the following" in drafting material for general debate:

> (a)   Establishing clear Congressional intent by the Floor debate which becomes a part of the legislative history of the legislation;

> (b) Explaining difficult or controversial sections of the legislation and their effects;

---

general debate shall be "confined to the bill," i.e., relevant (and not, say, about the latest administration statement on some exiguous topic.)   Absent such boilerplate, "during this general debate the Members can talk on any subject under the sun."   F. Riddick (1949) at 221.

[119] F. Riddick (1949) at 213-14.

(c) Explaining the position of the
Majority and/or Minority of the committee and
their intentions with respect to any
amendments to be offered.[120]

During the preparation for floor
consideration, and then prominently at the outset
of general debate, the minority manager announces
his position on the bill. That is a very
significant choice. Minority managers can
position themselves along a spectrum from
providing wholehearted support, to accepting the
bill as a general matter while supporting
amendments, all the way to a tough partisan
opposition seeking to defeat the bill. Of course,
the minority manager typically does not arrive at
a position only by solitary introspection. That
position may result from extensive consultation
between the ranking minority members on committee
and subcommittee, other minority Members on the
committee and off it, the minority leadership, and
outside forces.
It may be surprising how frequently the
minority manager supports the bill, such as when
the bill represents a constituency interest shared
by the whole committee (such as in agriculture,
armed service, and merchant marine matters) or a
deal where both sides received something (such as
in appropriations and tax bills). Conversely,
though not often, a majority manager may oppose a
bill. Thus, for example, on the domestic content

----

[120] House Republican Manual at 124. These floor statements
are important enough that staff must prepare "sufficient
copies for appropriate floor and press distribution . . .
[and sometimes] mimeographed copies of major statements to
be made on the Floor should be distributed." Id. at 125.

As the Manual notes, those floor statements constitute
important legislative history for the bill. Indeed, they
usually constitute the most complete description of the key
elements of the bill outside the committee report. When
floor amendments of importance come up that were not the
subject of committee consideration, the floor debate
beginning with any discussion in general debate may
constitute the sole legislative history.

bill, H.R. 5133, three managers -- both minority managers, and one majority manager -- took an opposition position, while only one majority manager supported the bill. The majority manager who opposed the bill, Representative Sam Gibbons (D-Fla.) of Ways and Means, commented that "trying to patch up this bill is like trying to put a band-aid on a rattlesnake. There is not much way you can improve a rattlesnake and there is no way you can improve this bill."[121] As is typical, that manager yielded time to Members of his party even when they held opposing views to his.[122]

After the speeches by the majority and minority managers, the managers yield time to other Members wishing to speak. A majority manager trying to push his bill lines up impressive Members on and off the committee to endorse it during general debate, and sees that as many persuasive themes are touched as possible.[123] "Time control," mentioned above for House proceedings, is also essential to Committee of the Whole proceedings. A Member speaks during the period of controlled time when he gets two different "nods" -- recognition by the Chair, and the "yielding" of time by the managers.

Technically, those are two separate nods. Practically, the Chair recognizes whoever the managers choose to yield time to; in a smoothly flowing debate, a Member seeking recognition simply asks a manager "Will the gentleman yield?" without any explicit act of recognition by the Chair. Also, as a matter of comity, managers usually do not refuse a Member time to speak during general debate.[124]

---

[121]   128 Cong. Rec. H9863 (daily ed. Dec. 15, 1982).

[122]   128 Cong. Rec. H9394 (daily ed. Dec. 10, 1982) (Rep. Gibbons yields to Rep. Don Pease (D-Ohio)).

[123]   A majority manager mentions, if applicable, that the committee gave the measure unanimous, bipartisan, or at least widespread support; that similar support came from outside interest groups, the administration or the party leadership; that the measure did well previously in the House, or in the Senate; that it resolves a major problem; that it adheres to the budget; and like matters.
(footnote continued)

General debate continues until both managers use up all their time, or "yields back" to the Chair any unused time. Managers who still have time, and are not yielding it out, may tell the Chair they are "reserving" their time, meaning they keep it to yield it later. For most bills, few Members stay on the floor to watch general debate. However, they may keep an eye on it in their offices through watching the House television, or monitor it through staff.

E. AMENDING UNDER THE FIVE-MINUTE RULE

With the close of general debate comes the third step provided in the special rule, that "the bill shall be read for amendment under the five-minute rule."

Reading For Amendment

Military metaphors abound in comments on the amending process. As the various sides "fight" the "battle" of amendments, the floor managers serve as the "generals" who "marshal the forces," decide when to "retreat," and ultimately announce the "victory" or "defeat." As they plan and execute their "strategy" and "tactics," they may keep various amendments "in reserve," go for the "weak points" in the bill, and launch "attacks," especially "surprise attacks." To paraphrase Clausewitz, amending appears to be the execution of military tactics by political means.

Physically, the managers take up positions at the two desks with microphones, one for the majority, the other for the minority. Members who speak may go to the well of the House; brief comments, and especially those of the managers in colloquies, can be made from those desks. Rule

---

[124] Even when both managers support the bill, they are expected to yield a fair amount of time to the bill's opponents. However, a Member may have to make do with a short period, perhaps as little as a minute, if time is short or the managers have some reason to be restrictive.

XXXII, regulating admission to the floor, has been interpreted to allow a committee to have five staff members on the House floor to help during its bills' consideration.[125]   Once a vote comes on, the managers often leave their desks and "work the doors," informing arriving Members in abbreviated phrases of the issue and asking for their support.

Except when the bill as a whole has been opened for amendment, amending consists of a repeated cycle: reading a unit of the bill, offering amendments to that unit, debating and then voting on the amendments, and moving on to the next unit.   The cycle begins with reading the bill, unit by unit.[126]   Most bills are read section by section, but by tradition, appropriation and revenue bills are read paragraph by paragraph.[127]   Bills to which few amendments are expected may be read, either by a special rule or by a manager's unanimous consent request, by titles or even by the whole bill at once (which is the practice in the Senate).   In this way, the size of the unit for reading is chosen, be it paragraph, section, title, or whole bill.

Typically, the reading itself is dispensed with, either by language in the special rule or, absent such language, by a unanimous consent request as soon as the Clerk starts reading each portion.   Points of order against particular portions of a bill must be raised immediately after the Clerk reads the portion, and before Members are recognized to offer amendments.[128]

---

[125]   The rule provides that "[t]he persons hereinafter named, and none other, shall be admitted to the Hall of the House . . . clerks of committees when business from their committee is under consideration."   See House Manual § 919 (limit of five).

[126]   "The reading of the bill for amendment is not specifically required by the present form of [Rule XXIII]; but is done under a practice which was originally instituted by the rule of 1789 and has continued, although the rule was eliminated . . . ."   House Manual § 872.

[127]   House Manual § 872.

(footnote continued)

For example, once the Clerk reads or designates each paragraph in an appropriation bill, an opponent must immediately challenge that paragraph as unauthorized, or legislation, or otherwise not in order, or else he will lose his right to do so.[129]

Offering the Amendment

Once the Clerk finishes reading the portion, and any points of order have been stated and resolved (or reserved), Members offer their amendments. The amendments for each unit come after the reading of that unit.[130] First come the committee amendments, which have priority and which the Chair puts without motion from the floor. Then come the floor amendments.[131]

Bill opponents must make some tactical choices regarding what floor amendments to offer. For an example, on the domestic content bill, opponents had lined up scores of hostile amendments. Their decisive move came in having an amendment adopted that significantly gutted the bill, by subordinating it to international treaties and agreements. Once that amendment passed 195 - 194, the two minority managers notified the floor that they would not offer any of the 36 amendments they had in reserve which they had been prepared to introduce.[132]

---

[128] Deschler 31 § 4.2. If a bill is deemed read and open to amendment at any point, points of order should be stated before any amendments are offered. Id. § 4.3. An exception is that Rule XXI(5) provides points of order against appropriations carried by bills not from the appropriations committee, or appropriations offered as amendments to bills not from the appropriations committee, can be made "at any time." See House Manual § 846a.

[129] Such points of order must also be reserved in the House prior to referral of the bill to Committee of the Whole. House Manual § 835.

[130] Deschler 27 §§ 10 (title), 10.11 (part), 11 (bill as a whole).

[131] Deschler 27 §§ 9.1, 10.1; House Manual § 423.
(footnote continued)

The "window" for offering the amendment is narrow. An amendment cannot be offered before the Clerk reads the portion to which it applies, but if Members miss that reading, they also cannot offer the amendment after the Clerk moves on to reading subsequent sections.[133] Many is the time when a Member patiently waits to offer his amendment or point of order to a particular section, becomes distracted by conversation just when that section goes by, and misses his "window." Such a Member cannot go back to the passed section to get his amendment or point of order considered, except by unanimous consent, which is frequently denied.[134] Members with this problem attempt to solve it by redrafting their amendment to fit another section, but often they can only do so in strained ways that make both the managers and themselves uncomfortable.

To offer an amendment, Members stand up, obtain recognition from the Chair, and usually announces that they offer an amendment "at the desk," meaning an amendment in writing left with

---

[132]   128 Cong. Rec. H9899 (daily ed. Dec. 15, 1982). Representative Millicent Fenwick (R-N.J.) offered the amendment. The Ways and Means Committee opponents of the bill believed that amendment crippled the bill because the bill conflicted directly with the General Agreement on Tariffs and Trade, and would necessarily by invalidated if subordinated to that agreement. This amendment is a "killer" amendment in one of the two meanings of the term, discussed in the next section.

[133]   Deschler 27 § 8. "When a paragraph or section has been passed it is not in order to return thereto . . . ." House Manual § 873. Members may be able to say they were standing on their feet and seeking recognition to offer an amendment to the previous portion, and the Chair failed to notice them. Deschler 27 § 8.9.

An amendment cannot even be offered after a vote to insert a new portion, which would occur before the reading of the next portion. Deschler 27 §§ 7.12, 8.6. Therefore, amendments to pending sections take precedence of amendments proposing new sections. VIII Cannon §§ 2358, 2868.

[134]   Deschler 27 § 8.

the clerks.[135] The Chair then instructs the Clerk
to report the amendment; a reading clerk starts
reading the amendment, unless someone (typically
the offeror) asks unanimous consent to dispense
with the reading.[136] Rather than require Members
to follow the amendment from its reading, Rule
XXIII(5)(a) provides for copies to be distributed
to the majority and minority committee tables and
cloakrooms.[137]

By putting their amendments, Members
relinquish control over the amendments: once
offered to the Committee of the Whole, they cannot
withdraw or modify the amendments except by
unanimous consent.[138] Thus, Members may bargain

---

[135] Rule XVI(1) prescribes that "Every motion made to the
House and entertained by the Speaker shall be reduced to
writing on the demand of any Member." On occasion a Member
will offer some minor amendment orally, such as to add a few
words to another's amendment, without anyone demanding that
it be reduced to writing. Preprinting of amendments in the
Congressional Record does not supplant the necessity of
providing the amendment in writing to the Clerk at the time
of offering, insofar as the Clerk cannot be required to hunt
through back copies of the Record to find a preprinted
amendment. House Republican Manual at 152-53.

[136] A stalling tactic that used to be available was to
object to such unanimous consent, slowing down the Committee
of the Whole as each amendment was laboriously read. In
1981, the House adopted Rule XXIII(b), making it "in order
to move in the Committee of the Whole to dispense with the
reading of an amendment" under various circumstances, which
"motion shall be decided without debate."

[137] Because of the need to quickly distribute copies and
inform the Members, Members and staff are admonished that
"[a]ll amendments which might conceivably be offered should
be carefully prepared in advance in proper legislative form,
preferably being mimeographed to provide sufficient copies
for distribution to appropriate persons on the Floor."
House Republican Manual at 125.

[138] Deschler 27 §§ 18, 19. This practice of the Committee
of the Whole contrasts with the procedure in the House,
where by Rule XVI(2) first adopted in 1789, "a motion . . .
may be withdrawn at any time before a decision or
(footnote continued)

extensively with the committee leadership or floor
factions prior to offering key amendments;
however, once they offer their amendments, they
can express only willingness on their part to ask
unanimous consent to withdraw or modify the
amendments (e.g., to withdraw them in return for
committee hearings on the subject), while any
other Members, by objecting, can force a vote on
the amendments. Before debate begins, Members
must state (or reserve) any points of order
against the amendment, such as for lack of
germaneness.[139]

Upon the offering of an amendment under the
"five-minute rule," Rule XXIII(5)(a) gives the
proponent just that: "five minutes" of debate time
"to explain any amendment he may offer . . . ."
The rule states that "the Member who shall first
obtain the floor shall be allowed to speak five
minutes in opposition to it." Since the managers
of the bill have priority in recognition, this
means that usually the five minutes to respond
goes to the majority manager if he chooses to
oppose the amendment. The offeror and the
opponent (usually the majority manager) may yield
to others to speak,[140] but others usually enter
the debate on an amendment by "offering a pro
forma amendment." The oft-repeated formula is for
the Member to rise and say "I move to strike the
last word" or "I move to strike the requisite
number of words."[141] For making this motion

---

amendment." As part of the general tightening of procedure
in Committee of the Whole in the period 1840-60 discussed
above, the Committee put a stop to the practice of
filibustering by offering and withdrawing amendments. See V
Hinds § 5221.

[139] Deschler 31 § 5.

[140] Deschler 29 § 25.12. Members do not yield time during
debate under the five-minute rule. House Manual § 872.

[141] The Member does not actually discuss "the last word"
and no actual action occurs on the "pro forma motion"
itself. In theory, the Committee of the Whole implicitly
defeats the motion without action, such disposition of the
motion occurring when its proponent is done speaking. As a
general matter, when a motion is defeated, it is not in
(footnote continued)

Members get five minutes. They cannot make a
second pro forma amendment.[142] Members can extend
their five minutes (obtained either by being the
principal offeror or opponent, or by pro forma
motion) only by a unanimous consent request for
additional time.[143]

With the amendment offered and under debate,
the majority manager makes his key decisions. As
Professor Lewis Froman, a studious analyst of
these tactics, summed up, the manager "can accept
the amendment (in which case the amendment will
almost always be adopted, usually by a quick voice
vote)[,] attempt to change it by proposing a
substitute, or try to defeat it."[144] Accepting an
amendment is akin to a committee having reported
the amendment out with the bill. As a formal
matter, the House must vote to adopt committee
amendments, but in practice, they start with a
presumption of acceptance. Similarly, as a formal
matter, the announcement by the bill manager that
he accepts an amendment still requires that the
House vote to adopt it,[145] but in practice,
manager acceptance usually foreshadows adoption
without contest.

Offering of an amendment often triggers a
host of tactical and informational reactions:
counteramendments for tactical purposes; taped
messages to Members from their party leadership
over an automatic telephone system; and
dissemination by party leadership staff of "the

---

order to offer an identical one again. Thus, after one
Member moves to strike the last word, a procedural purist
would insist that the next Member cannot make this same
motion; he must move differently, e.g., to strike the last
two words. For those not keeping track of how many such
motions have been offered, the phrase used is to strike "the
requisite number of words." In practice, no one worries
about identical pro forma motions, and frequently several
Members identically move to strike the last word.

[142] Deschler 29 § 25.6.

[143] Deschler 29 § 25.2.

[144] Froman at 70.

[145] Deschler 27 § 20.15.

'bullet,' a mimeographed, one-page summary of an amendment."[146]   A manager's decision whether to accept, try to change, or oppose an amendment "depends upon a host of complicated factors including how much the amendment changes the bill, and how much support [the bill manager] thinks the amendment has."[147]

The manager approaches each amendment, not only on its own merits, but as part of his general control of the floor.   If managers win consistently when they oppose amendments, then they "develo[p] the reputation for getting what they want," making winning easier each time.[148] If they lose consistently, they continue to lose, and when they start losing on a particular bill, they lose the intangible but very vital "control of the floor" for that bill;[149] if a "rout" develops, the bill may even have to be pulled from the floor.

Several motions available in the House are not available in Committee of the Whole.   Besides there being no motion for the previous question, there is also no motion to recommit, no motion to reconsider, and no motion to table.   The lack of a

---

[146]   B. Sinclair, Majority Leadership in the U.S. House 163 (1983).   The role of the party leadership was described in the previous chapter on running the House.

[147]   Froman at 70.   A manager faces all kinds of pitfalls:

> He could, for example, accept an amendment which would not have carried, thereby changing the bill and possibly losing some support for the bill which he had before the amendment was added.   The manager could attempt to propose a substitute and perhaps win, but the change would not have been necessary because the original amendment would have been lost.

Froman at 70.

[148]   Froman at 73.

[149]   "The manager could attempt to defeat the amendment and lose.   This latter alternative is especially costly because when one amendment carries, it opens the possibility that others may also."   Froman at 70.

motion to table means that the proponent of an
allowed amendment has a guarantee of a vote on
that amendment (and, with 24 colleagues, of a
recorded vote).   Some counteramendment may
overtake the original amendment, but even then the
amendment may be rewritten for reoffering.[150]

Amendments that contain more than one
substantive proposition may be divided for voting
on demand of a single Member.[151]   In a classic
defensive use of the division procedure in 1983,
Majority Leader Jim Wright (D-Tex.) offered an
amendment to provide additional funding to a
series of education and domestic programs.
Representative Robert Walker (R-Pa.) asked for a
division of the amendment into 17 categories, and
some with narrow bases of support were
defeated.[152]   This weakened the overall support
for the resolution just enough for it to be
defeated by the narrow vote of 203-206.[153]

---

[150]   In contrast, in the Senate, the availability of the
motion to table during the amendment process means that the
opposition or minority amendments often get disposed of
without a vote on the amendments themselves, only on the
"procedural" motion to table, which creates a much less
clear record.

[151]   House Rule XVI(6) provides: "On the demand of any
Member, before the question is put, a question shall be
divided if it includes propositions so distinct in substance
that one being taken away a substantive proposition shall
remain . . . ." Division applies to all kinds of questions,
but most importantly to amendments.   The procedure of
division began with a House Rule in 1789 contrasting with
old English rules.   Compare House Manual § 481 (Jefferson's
rule) with id. § 791 (history of House rule).

[152]   For example, the portion to provide money for higher
education facilities at three particular universities, of
which one was in Boston, lost 122-286.   129 Cong Rec. H9472
(daily ed. Nov. 8, 1983).

[153]   129 Cong. Rec. H9476 (daily ed. Nov. 8, 1983) (defeat
of H.J.Res. 403). Two days later, the continuing resolution
came back, this time with more organization by the majority,
and it passed.   On November 10, the House considered H. J.
Res. 413.   On this round, Majority Leader Wright offered the
(footnote continued)

Conversely, when a Member seeks to offer an amendment to more than one portion, he asks unanimous consent to do so.

Motion to Strike the Enacting Clause

One particular tactic faced by the bill manager, which goes not to amendments but to the very passage of the bill, deserves mention. Rule XXIII(7) provides for "[a] motion to strike out the enacting words of a bill," available only during the amendment process.[154] To be precise, the motion is not to strike the enacting clause, but for the Committee of the Whole to rise and report to the House with the recommendation that the enacting clause be stricken.[155] The House

---

parts of his amendment that the House had adopted the previous time. 129 Cong. Rec. H9617 (daily ed. Nov. 10, 1983). He offered his parts in the form of a motion to strike all after the enacting clause and insert an amendment in the nature of a substitute.

Rule XVI(7) provides that "A motion to strike out and insert is indivisible." As Rules Chairperson Claude Pepper (D-Fla.) explained, "Unlike the last time this House considered the Wright amendment, Mr. Wright will offer a motion to strike and insert and that question, in this instance, is not divisible." 129 Cong. Rec. H9610 (daily ed. Nov. 10, 1983). This time the continuing resolution passed.

[154] Deschler 19 § 11.1.

[155] For example, in 1964, a coalition of conservative Members ambushed the bill for an antipoverty program, by offering a motion to strike the enacting clause at a moment when bill opponents had been told to be present but when few supporters were on the floor. The Committee of the Whole adopted the motion, and rose and reported with the recommendation that the enacting clause be struck, but "the leadership was now in full gear attempting to get its supporters back to the floor for a vote . . . . A roll-call vote normally takes about 25 minutes. On this roll-call, 50 minutes were consumed, as the Democratic reading clerk called each name slowly and deliberately." Froman at 81. Enough bill supporters appeared in time for the House to
(footnote continued)

then decides whether to accept this
recommendation.[156]   Since a bill without its
enacting clause is a nullity, the adoption of such
a motion amounts to killing the bill.   By
tradition, the motion is considered a rough and
ungentle form of execution, and its to kill a bill
is a high-stakes gamble by bill opponents.

"A motion to strike the enacting clause is an
unusual event, but when used is surrounded by
drama."[157]   For example the motion was used when
the House considered the controversial bill to
create a Department of Education.   Representative
David Obey (D-Wis.) capitalized on a mood of
frustration that developed at 10:00 p.m. after
more than 15 hours of debate.   "Although Obey, a
shrewd legislative strategist, had doubts about
whether he had the votes to kill the bill, he
thought that in the madness of the late hour, his
colleagues might be angry enough to vote no in
order to be able to go home for the night."[158]
The threat was serious enough to bring Speaker
O'Neill back to the Capitol, just before a
midnight vote defeated the motion.

More often, the motion to strike the enacting
clause is used to obtain debate time.   The motion
has "precedence of a motion to amend," so someone
who wants to talk can stand, even when an
amendment is pending, and demand recognition for
this preferential motion.   That Member then gets
five minutes, even when debate has been closed on
amendments.[159]   Thus, "the motion may be used by a

---

overturn the recommendation of the Committee of the Whole to
strike the enacting clause.

[156]   Under today's Rule XXIII(7), when a recommendation to
strike is disagreed to, "the bill shall stand recommitted to
the said committee [of the Whole] without further action by
the House."   This change was made in 1860 to end the prior
technique (adopting the motion, then disagreeing to the
recommendation to strike) by which the motion was used to
get filibustered bills out of Committee of the Whole and
into the House.

[157]   Froman at 80.

[158]   P. Clancy & S. Elder, Tip: A Biography of Thomas P.
O'Neill 209 (1980).
(footnote continued)

Member to secure five minutes to debate a pending amendment notwithstanding a limitation of time."[160] Applicability of such a limitation depends on its wording,[161] and only a very broadly worded limitation of time would cut off this motion.[162] Then, the bill manager also receives five minutes,[163] in theory to respond to the

---

[159] Deschler 19 § 12.10.

[160] Deschler 19 § 12.11. The motion can be used a second time for the same purpose, but only after "there has been a material modification of the bill subsequent to the defeat of the first motion." Deschler 19 § 13.5.

[161] As the House Republican Manual carefully notes, whether a time limitation applies to a motion to strike the enacting clause depends on the precise wording. If a time limitation applies to:

> "an amendment and all amendments thereto" or to "all amendments to the bill and amendments thereto," it applies only to the amendments and not to the bill itself. Hence, a motion to strike the enacting clause of the bill is outside the time limitation and the mover is entitled to a full 5 minutes. On the other hand, if the limitation is for "the bill and all amendments thereto" then the motion is subject to the time limitation (see generally Deschler's Procedure 19:10-13, and specifically section 12 on debate).

House Republican Manual at 201.

[162] Moreover, even under a time limitation, the mover may still get a more generous helping of time than anyone else:

> When the motion is subject to the time limitation, discussions with the Parliamentarian indicate that a Member will be given half of the remaining time under the limitation agreement if the time remaining is less than 10 minutes. If, on the other hand, 11 or more minutes remain under a time limitation when the motion is made, it is expected that the mover would be recognized for the entire 5 minutes.

Id.

(footnote continued)

motion, in practice to do whatever seems helpful
in waning moments under a time limit.   Members
generally let the motion then be rejected on a
voice vote without bothering with a record vote.

Closing and Limiting Debate

As the Committee on the Whole resolves one
amendment, another can be offered regarding the
same bill section, and so on _ad infinitum_.   To end
debate and amending, the House developed in 1841-
1860, and perfected in 1890, the motion to close
or limit debate.[164]   In contrast to the bludgeon
of the motion for the previous question (available
only in the House, not in Committee of the Whole),
the motion to close or limit debate has a great
deal of flexibility.

Often, instead of using the motion, the bill
manager makes a unanimous consent request;
typically, the manager looks around the House
chamber and says something to the effect of "there
are only about six Members who still want to offer
amendments to this section, and so I ask unanimous
consent to end debate on this section in an
hour."   Opposing Members may reserve the right to
object to such a request, and under that
reservation, discuss how much time they want.[165]
"Motions, rather than unanimous consent requests
are avoided, if possible, because they have the
appearance of shutting off the opposition from
debate."[166]

However, if the manager cannot devise a

---

[163]   Deschler 19 §§ 12.12, 12.15.

[164]   The 1841-60 development was discussed above.   The 1890
change allowed the motion to be used to close or limit
debate on an individual section of the bill, rather than
having to shut off the whole bill.

[165]   "If unanimous consent is not granted the floor manager
generally looks to the Republican floor manager (or to the
mover of the amendment) . . . . [who] may then signal the
number of minutes desired and the Democratic floor manager
will modify his request."   Froman at 74.

[166]   Froman at 74.

satisfactory arrangement by unanimous consent and resorts to a motion, Rule XXIII(6) gives two options. Managers can close debate "upon the pending amendments only"; this is the gentler way to proceed which allows debate on further amendments. Alternatively, managers can close debate "upon such section or paragraph," cutting off debate on the pending amendments and on any further amendments that are made. In either case, Rule XXIII(6) provides that such a motion "shall not preclude further amendment, to be decided without debate, which may produce a situation in which Members vote on amendments without much discussion of what they are voting on. For example, in 1987, a successful motion by appropriations subcommittee chair William H. Natcher (D-Ky.) to close debate on the huge Labor-HHS appropriation "effectively prevented amendments from being offered on sensitive social topics that in years past mired the funding bill in controversy," such as amendments on abortion research, AIDS-patients partner location, and funding cuts.[167]

Under a debate limit, the Chairman of the Committee of the Whole has several ways to parcel out the time left under the debate limit.[168] A

---

[167] 1987 _Congressional Quarterly Almanac_ 455. In general, motions to close debate have these drawbacks for the process of sound legislating:

> When that time is reached [when] amendments may still be voted on but . . . cannot be debated[,] [t]he only notion that members have of what is being voted on is from the clerk's reading the amendment, and through informal discussion among the members. This procedure gets very involved and members are even more in the dark about what they are voting on than they usually are . . . . The practice probably favors the committee bill since members are reluctant to support amendments to the committee bill (majority party members, anyway) unless they have good reason. In the absence of debate, "good reason" is difficult to establish.

Froman at 79.

(footnote continued)

complex overlay to this results from the provision
of the Legislative Reorganization Act of 1970, now
Rule XXIII(6), that guarantees debate time to
Members who print their amendments "in the
Congressional Record after the reporting of the
bill by the committee but at least one day prior
to floor consideration of such amendment."[169]
Often amendment offerors like to round up support
through publication, so advance printing in the
Congressional Record, although a chore, is
agreeable.[170]   However, for tactical reasons,
offerors sometimes prefer surprise, and then must
weigh the risk to an unprinted amendment that a
motion to close debate may preclude it.

---

[168] A common pattern when the Committee adopts a unanimous
consent request or motion to close debate is for the Members
who will want time to stand up and be counted, and for the
Chair to divide the remaining time equally among them --
shutting out absentees entirely (unless someone present
yields absentees who arrive later some of his time). "[T]he
Chair may, in his discretion, either permit continued debate
under the five-minute rule, or divide the remaining time
among all those desiring to speak, or divide the remaining
time between a proponent and an opponent to be yielded by
them to other Members . . .   The Chair may also in his
discretion give priority of recognition under a limitation
to those Members seeking to offer amendments, over other
Members" just seeking to debate. House Manual § 874 (1977
and 1982 rulings).

[169] Even "if debate is closed on any section or paragraph,"
the rule provides that such Members "shall be given five
minutes in which to explain such amendment, after which the
first person to obtain the floor shall be given five minutes
in opposition to it." Thus, the rule prevents a motion to
close debate from cutting off a preprinted amendment, and
Members can protect their right to offer an amendment by
such preprinting.

[170] The House Republican Manual admonishes that "Staff
should be aware of this provision and work with Members to
protect debate time on important amendments. Amendments
should be written and printed ahead of time, with proper
care given to drafting details." House Republican Manual at
152.

F.   TACTICAL USE OF AMENDMENTS

Two levels of tactics may be distinguished in the offering of amendments: political and parliamentary.   Political calculation include the choice of subject and offeror for an amendment, as well as timing and drafting.   Parliamentary calculation concerns the choice of sequence and form for offering the amendment.   In light of the procedural focus here, only a brief mention will be made of political calculation before looking at parliamentary considerations.

Some political uses of amendments are relatively straightforward.   As one observer summed up:[171]

> [Some are] offered in deference to pressure groups, executive branch officials, or constituents; others are designed to attract public notice, to stall the legislative process, to demonstrate concern for an issue, or to test sentiment for or against a bill. Some amendments are more technical than substantive; they may renumber sections of a bill or correct typographical errors.

An example discussed further below illustrates political calculation on controversial amendments.   In a key 1983 debate, the House took up a bill concerning a cutoff of covert action in Nicaragua.   That covert action had become a key issue between the parties and between the Democratic-controlled House and the Republican administration.   The first round of amending of the bill reflected each side's political calculations regarding offeror, subject, and drafting.

On the administration side, Representative Dan Mica (D-Fla.) offered the key amendment. Representative Mica, as a Democrat from Florida, could be expected to propose amendments that would draw support from the most important wavering bloc, the conservative southern Democrats.   His

---

[171]   W. J. Oleszek, <u>Congressional Procedures and the Policy Process</u> 156 (3d ed. 1989).

amendment's subject and drafting focused on the administration's best issue, Nicaraguan aid to guerrillas in El Salvador.[172]

On the Democratic leadership side, Chairperson Edward Boland (D-Mass.) offered the key amendment. Representative Boland commanded considerable respect as the chair of the House Select Committee on Intelligence, and was known as usually supportive of intelligence operations. His amendment's subject and drafting countered the administration focus on Nicaraguan aid to guerrillas, by focusing on having the process for decisions on aid include the Congress instead of being unilaterally presidential. This typical pattern showed each side choosing a particular subject, and an offeror from a particular region and a particular ideological wing, to give that side the best shot at winning.[173]

"Saving" and "Killer" Amendments

Two sophisticated political uses of amendments deserve special mention because, as discussed below, they can involve parliamentary complexities: the "saving" amendment and the "killer" amendment. A saving amendment makes a bill more likely to pass in a form acceptable to its supporters, typically because it compromises with some bill opponents without alienating bill supporters. Often the House or committee leadership propose a "saving" amendment, and uses the leadership's resources to line up support for it.

---

[172] The amendment added the requirement of a plan to interdict Nicaraguan aid to guerrillas in El Salvador, to an underlying amendment (of Rep. Young) to cut off covert action upon Nicaraguan agreement not to aid those guerrillas anymore. See 129 Cong. Rec. H5742 (Representative C. W. Young's (R-Fla.) Amendment), H5820 (Mica Amendment) (daily ed. July 27 and 28, 1983).

[173] The amendment offered a resumption of covert action if Nicaragua continued to support the guerrilas, if Congress enacted a joint resolution providing for such resumption. 129 Cong. Rec. H5822 (daily ed. July 28, 1983).

For example, in 1979 the House considered the bill to implement the Panama Canal Treaty, a controversial bill that started out with a high probability either of being defeated or of being amended to a point unacceptable to Panama and to the administration. The majority leadership knew Representative George Hansen (R-Idaho), the leading opponent of the bill, would offer key unacceptable amendments. "Instead of attempting to defeat Hansen on an up-or-down vote," the leadership had Representative John "Murphy [D-N.Y.] offer 'a Zablocki-Foreign Affairs type substitute' -- one keeping much of the Hansen language but leaving its implementation to the President's discretion."[174] The strategy of adopting this saving amendment worked.[175] The "saving" Murphy amendment attracted 25 Republican votes; it had been estimated that 20 Republican votes to support the bill were needed for passage.

The "killer" amendment is one which either (1) leads to defeat of the underlying bill, typically because it appeals to enough bill supporters to be adopted, but renders the bill objectionable to others; or (2) impairs the operation of the bill for its supporters' purposes, rendering passage useless (absent further change in the Senate or in conference). To look at an example from the Senate side, when the Senate considered the Panama Canal Treaty, "what were openly referred to by Senator [Robert] Byrd [(D-W.Va.)], Senator [Howard] Baker [(R-Tenn.)] and others as 'killer' amendments employed the strategy of attempting to alter the treaties in any way possible to bring about rejection of them by Panama."[176] One killer amendment of Senator James Allen's (D-Ala.), with much floor

---

174 Sinclair at 221.

175 "As expected, the showdown came on the Murphy substitute to the Hansen amendment. When the Murphy substitute was adopted on a 220 to 200 vote, the most severe test had been passed." Sinclair at 222.

176 Enelow & Koehler, The Amendment in Legislative Strategy: Sophisticated Voting in the U.S. Congress, 42 J. Pol. 396, 409 (1980).

appeal but unacceptable to Panama, "provided that
the U.S. could '. . . maintain military bases in
the former Canal Zone after December 31, 1999, if
the United States was at war with a country that
might attempt to send its ships through the
canal . . . .'"[177]

As political observers have shown, "saving"
and "killer" amendments can lead to paradoxical
floor voting patterns. Numerous supporters and
opponents of the bill may vote opposite to their
normal preferences regarding an amendment because
of calcuations about the amendment's impact on
final passage.[178] Opponents may vote against an
otherwise attractive "saving" amendment, and
proponents may vote against an otherwise
attractive "killer" amendment, respectively to
weaken or to strengthen the bill's chances on
final passage.[179]

Amendment in the Nature of a Substitute

An "amendment in the nature of a substitute"
is one that completely replaces a bill with an

---

[177] Id., 42 J. Pol. at 411.

[178] Political scientists found, in a close analysis of
voting on amendments on the common situs picketing bill in
1977, that at least 59 percent of the voting body voted
against their own preference on amendments because of the
expected impact on final passage. Id., 42 J. Pol. at 404.

[179] For example, in response to Senator Allen's killer
amendment quoted above, "Senator [Frank] Church [(D-Id.), a
Panama Canal treaty supporter] reacted "It reminds me of
that passage from the Godfather, 'I'll make him an offer he
can't refuse.'"" Id., 42 J. Pol. at 411. Nevertheless,
Senator Church refused the offer and voted against the
attractive but lethal amendment, and "the 'Godfather'
amendment was tabled by a 57-38 vote." Id. History
confirmed the irony in Senator Church's characterization.
Part of the reason for Senator Church's electoral defeat in
1980 was thought to be his espousal of the Panama Canal
Treaty. As can sometimes be the case regarding killer
amendments, the opposition had indeed made him an offer he
could not refuse.

alternative text, by striking all after the enacting clause and inserting the new material. The term produces endless confusion because when someone just refers to a "substitute," they may be talking about a substitute amendment, or an amendment in the nature of a substitute, which are very different and bear no necessary relation.[180] This type of amendment turns up in several areas of procedure, because Congress conducts much business by such amendments, and often they are covered by special procedures.[181]

Very often, when a committee reports a bill with committee changes (as opposed to a "clean bill" without amendments), instead of reporting a series of particular committee amendments, the committee reports one comprehensive committee amendment in the nature of a substitute. The normal rules about such a comprehensive substitute produce several anomalies, resulting mainly from the "lock-out" rule, that language, once completely amended, cannot be amended again.[182]   A

---

[180]   An "amendment in the nature of a substitute" means an amendment that strikes all after the enacting clause and replaces it with new text.   It may be offered as an amendment to the text -- as a first-degree amendment.   A "substitute" amendment is offered when an amendment is already pending; the substitute is an amendment to replace that pending amendment.   A substitute amendment can vary in extent.   It may be very localized -- an amendment to put in a different word would be a perfect substitute to an amendment to change one word in the bill -- or it may be as big as the whole text of the bill (in which case it is also an amendment in the nature of a substitute, besides being a substitute amendment).

[181]   For example, when the House adopts a bill on a subject for which the other chamber has already adopted and sent over a bill, to iron out the differences typically the House takes the bill from the Senate and replaces its text with the text of its own bill; it does this by adopting the language of its own bill as an amendment in the nature of a substitute to the Senate bill.

[182]   Deschler 27 § 27.   This has particular impact regarding figures, such as appropriation figures, which once amended, get locked in.   Deschler 27 § 31.

chief way around the "lock-out" problem is the
"bigger bite" principle, which allows changing a
larger piece than the previously amended text,[183]
but since there is no "bigger bite" than a
complete substitute, that exception cannot be used
for amendments in the nature of a substitute.

Usually, the Rules Committee includes
language in the special rule to cure the various
problems with a committee amendment in the nature
of a substitute: portion-by-portion reading,[184]
the number of degrees of amendment that can be
offered,[185] the occasional reporting of revised

---

[183] Deschler 7 §§ 27-29. For example, when a figure in a
budget resolution has been amended, that figure could not,
by itself, be changed again; however, a more comprehensive
amendment could be offered changing that figure and other
unamended figures. Deschler 27 § 31.9.

Another method is to adopt an inconsistent amendment
somewhere else on the bill, trusting to an eventual cleanup
of the inconsistency. See Deschler 27 § 27.9. For example,
after amending a figure in an appropriation bill, additional
language can be inserted adding funds for the program "in
addition thereto." Deschler 27 § 31.6.

A rule similar to the lockout rule prevents offering
amendments identical to those previously rejected. However,
an amendment worded differently and yet having the same
effect as a previously rejected amendment is quite in
order. Deschler 27 § 33.

[184] Ordinarily an amendment, like the smallest unit in a
bill, must be read from beginning to end before it can be
amended, and once read, it is open to amendment at all
points. This is true of any amendment, but in a
comprehensive substitute, it produces the disorderly
situation that an amendment text which is, in effect, like a
whole bill, is opened all at once for amending. Often,
therefore, a rule will provide about a committee substitute
that it shall be deemed read, or that it shall be read by
sections.

[185] The legislative committee "will normally seek from the
Rules Committee as part of the 'rule' on the bill a
provision 'making the committee amendment in the nature of a
substitute printed in the bill in order as an original bill
(footnote continued)

versions of a bill,[186] and the separate vote on
amendments which occurs in the House after
proceedings in Committee of the Whole.[187]

Naturally, when a Member wants to offer from
the floor an amendment in the nature of a
substitute -- such as a minority Member wishing to
propose a comprehensive alternative to the
committee bill -- there are complications, since
no special rule has prepared the ground. The
"precedents are that he can do so only at two

---

for the purpose of amendment.'" House Republican Manual at
157. This "permits the amending process on the Floor to
proceed normally, without having amendments to an amendment
to the text ruled out of order as being in the third degree
as would be the case if a committee substitute were not so
design[at]ed." Id. at 157-58. Compare Deschler 27 § 5.15
(no rule language) with id. § 5.19 (rule language). This
may allow the full four-amendment tree on both the amendment
in the nature of a substitute and the bill itself, although
eight pending amendments at once are rare.

[186] Sometimes, prior to the Rules Committee's reporting of
a rule for the bill, the committee chair completes
negotiations to increase a bill's chances of passage, which
may involve other substantive committees, the Rules
Committee, the majority leadership, the administration, or a
group of House opponents. The committee chair then prepares
a revised bill representing the result of the
negotiations. The rule makes that newly introduced bill in
order as an amendment in the nature of a substitute,
avoiding the delay -- and risk -- in first referring the
bill to committee, and then reporting it out.

[187] Ordinarily an amendment in the nature of a substitute
would negate the "separate vote" in the House following
proceedings in Committee of the Whole. The separate vote
occurs only on amendments adopted to the bill, and cannot be
demanded on second-degree amendments. When an amendment in
the nature of a substitute is adopted, it is the only
amendment actually adopted to the bill itself -- other
amendments being second-degree amendments offered to that
substitute.

Accordingly, a special rule often provides regarding
the "separate vote" that it will be allowed, both on
amendments, and also on amendments to the committee
amendment in the nature of a substitute.

points,"[188] at the very beginning and very end of
the amendment process.[189]   Because of the "bigger
bite" principle, once such a floor amendment in
the nature of a substitute has been adopted, no
further amendments are in order.   Thus, Members
must choose whether to try to amend that floor
substitute before being "locked out."

Basic Amendment Types

Under Rule XIX, the House has long permitted

---

[188]   House Republican Manual at 158; Deschler 27 § 12.5.
The Manual explains in detail:

> The first comes after the close of general debate, when
> the clerk has completed the reading of the first
> paragraph, section or title of the bill.   The second
> comes at the conclusion of the reading of the bill for
> amendment if perfecting amendments have not changed the
> bill entirely . . . .   At other times, the amendment in
> the nature of a substitute is subject to a point of
> order . . . unless the bill is considered as having
> been read and open for amendment at any point.

House Republican Manual at 158 (citations omitted).

[189]   See Deschler 27 § 12.   The House Republican Manual, at
158-59, advises further:

> As a parliamentary device it is generally preferable to
> offer the amendment in the nature of a substitute first
> rather than last; this gives Members the opportunity to
> make their choice at the close of general debate when
> the issues between the committee bill and the amendment
> in the nature of a substitute have been clearly drawn
> and before the committee bill has been perfected and
> objectionable features removed.

As a technical matter, when a bill is being read by
paragraphs, at the beginning of reading an amendment cannot
strike all after the enacting clause -- only the first
paragraph.   Hence, Members offering an amendment in the
nature of a substitute at that point give notice that if it
is agreed to, they will move to strike all the other
paragraphs later. Deschler 27 §§ 12.6-12.9.

four types of amendments to be pending simultaneously (plus motions to strike).[190] Before turning to their tactical use, the four types and their relations should be set forth.

First, Rule XIX provides that "[w]hen a motion or proposition is under consideration a motion to amend . . . shall be in order." That first type of amendment -- very simply called "the amendment to the text" -- can change ("perfect") the text either by adding language ("inserting") to the text, or by taking out some language and add new language ("striking out and inserting") in its place. If a Member proposes only to take out language, that is a "motion to strike." For example, if a committee brought up a fly-the-flag bill consisting of an enacting clause plus one section saying "All flags shall be flown in September, October, and November," a flag expert could offer an amendment to the text inserting the words and December, or striking the words October and November and inserting the words January and February.

Second, Rule XIX provides that "a motion to amend that amendment shall be in order." This amendment to the amendment is a second-degree amendment. It perfects the first degree amendment to the text, just as that amendment perfects the text. For example, once the flag expert offered his first degree amendment to insert the words and December, the flag critic could offer a second degree amendment to insert the words every other, so that, if the second degree amendment won, the pending first degree amendment to the text would then be and every other December.

----

190 Rule XIX itself dates to the major recodification of House Rules in 1880. As for the earlier evolution of the tree, Jefferson's Manual proposes a somewhat different type of amendment structure than today's. See House Manual §§ 468-69. After an 1822 ruling that a substitute amendment was not in order, the House that year changed its rule regarding substitute amendments (into the modern germaneness rule, discussed elsewhere) to clearly permit them. By the mid-1830s, substitute amendments seem to have been offered as a matter of course, and by 1836 it was held that amendments may be proposed to the substitute. V Hinds § 5753.

Third, Rule XIX provides that "it shall also be in order to offer a further amendment by way of substitute." A substitute for an amendment necessarily replaces it completely. Thus, for example, once the flag expert offered his first degree amendment to insert the words and December, a rival July Caucus could offer a substitute amendment to insert instead the words and July. Approval of the substitute amendment would not yet change the text, but would replace the flag expert's amendment. After such approval, the amendment to insert the words and July would then be the pending first-degree amendment to the text.

Fourth, Rule XIX provides that when a substitute amendment has been offered, "one amendment may be offered" to that substitute. The flag critic could propose an amendment to the July caucus substitute to insert the words almost every other, which, if approved, would make the substitute amendment read and almost every other July. Since all these amendments "branch off" the text and some branch off each other, the plotter of multiple amendment situations usually diagrams them by an "amendment tree." A figure would show the classic four-amendment tree that would result from the four amendments to the fly-the-flag bill. That is the limit. No amendments can be offered in the third degree.[191]

Several rules govern in a multiple amendment situation. "There is no set order in which amendments must be offered; once an amendment to the text has been offered, either a substitute amendment or a perfecting amendment is in order."[192] However, there is a set order for

---

[191]   House Manual § 454; Deschler 27 § 6.

[192]   House Republican Manual at 155. In the fly-the-flag example, once the flag expert offered the amendment to the text, and December, there is no set order for the flag critic or July Caucus amendments. That means that either the flag critic could offer his second degree amendment next (to insert every other) or the July Caucus could offer its substitute next (to replace with and July). If the July Caucus offered its substitute next, then after that either the Flag Critic could offer his second degree amendment next (to insert every other to the flag expert's amendment), or
(footnote continued)

disposition of amendments, of considerable importance, since, as discussed below, much of the tactical point lies in what amendment gets the first vote. "[F]irst, perfect the amendment to the text: then, perfect the substitute amendment: then, vote on the substitute amendment, then, vote on the amendment to the text."[193]

Thus, in the example, after all four amendments were offered, the required order for disposition would be: (1) the flag critic's second degree amendment (every other) perfecting the flag expert's amendment to the text; then, (2) the flag critic's second degree amendment (almost every other) perfecting the July Caucus substitute; then, (3) the July Caucus substitute (originally, and July, and then either amended to include almost every other or not); and finally, (4) the flag expert's amendment to the text (amended or not, and substituted-for or not).

The precedents impose various restrictions on the amendments. Just as an amendment to the text must be germane to the text, so the other types of amendment must be germane to what they amend. Moreover, to qualify as a substitute amendment, an amendment must not only be germane, but must also treat the same subject matter in the same manner and must propose a related objective.[194]

---

the flag critic could offer his second degree amendment to the substitute next (to insert almost every other to the July Caucus' amendment).

[193] Id. (capitalization changed). This order derives from several sources. Both the amendment to the amendment and the amendment to the substitute are disposed of prior to disposition of the substitute (as amended) because, as Thomas Jefferson wrote, "When it is proposed to amend by inserting a paragraph, or part of one, the friends of the paragraph may make it as perfect as they can by amendments before the question is put for inserting it." House Manual § 469. Rule XIX provides that while "it shall also be in order to offer a further amendment by way of substitute . . . [this] shall not be voted on until the original matter is perfected."

[194] Thus, for example, the July Caucus could not have qualified, as a substitute, an amendment to strike the words October and November from the bill and insert July. Such a
(footnote continued)

Also, a motion to strike can be offered, but only at certain times and with a particular precedence. Traditional parliamentary law holds that a text should be perfected before resolving a motion to strike.[195]   Thus, a trim-the-flag faction could move to strike from the text the words October and November. However, the faction could only offer its motion before the flag expert offered his perfecting amendment; after that, the perfecting amendment would have to be resolved before the House could entertain a motion to strike.[196]

---

strike-and-insert amendment would not have qualified as a substitute because it failed to treat the bill the same way as the flag expert's amendment to the text treated the bill.   For an amendment to the text that merely inserts language, an amendment that would strike and insert does not qualify as a substitute.   VIII Cannon §§ 2879 - 81; see also VIII Cannon § 3430 (substitute must have related objective).   A motion to strike out text is not a substitute for a perfecting amendment, nor may it be offered as a second-degree amendment to a perfecting amendment.   Deschler 27 §§ 14.8 - 14.10, 14.13 - 14.16, 15.4, 16.10.

[195]   As Jefferson wrote, "if it is proposed to amend by striking out a paragraph, the friends of the paragraph are first to make it as perfect as they can by amendments, before the question is put for striking it out."   House Manual § 469.

[196]   See Deschler   27 §§ 13.17, 14.1, 14.5.

Motions to strike must wait before disposition.   If the trim-the-flag faction did get its motion to strike offered first, then nevertheless the other amendments could be offered and would have to be disposed of before the House would come back to the motion to strike.   See Deschler 27 §§ 13.1-13.6, 13.8, 14.20, 22.   Also, big motions to strike must wait for little ones.   A motion to strike out a lesser portion of words (for example, a motion by the moderate wing of the trim-the-flag caucus, just to strike the words and November) could be offered before or after a motion to strike out more words (October and November), Deschler 27 §§ 13.7, 14.4, in which case the motion to strike out fewer words gets voted on first, Deschler 27 § 22.9.

Tactical Use of the Amendment Tree

Looked at systemically, this structure seeks to set up for the House two rival choices on the floor at once -- the amendment to the text, and the substitute amendment. Members perfect each of the rival choices by second-degree amendments until each fits the sense of the House. Then, by a vote on the substitute, they choose between the two rivals.

Beyond this systemic goal, Members have their own tactical objectives. Each floor situation creates its unique tactical complexities and key objectives: (1) pre-empting -- getting one side the first vote on a proposition, on the general belief that success on the first vote captures control of the whole process; (2) blocking out -- using additional amendments to preclude rival factions from offering theirs;[197] (3) nullifying -- using an amendment to take the teeth out of a rival faction's amendment, particularly a rival's effective saving or killer amendment; and (4) recouping -- trying a second time to approve a

---

[197] An example shows the use of blocking out. When the House took up in 1974 the proposals of the Committee on Committees (Bolling Committee), opponents immediately offered an amendment (the Hansen amendment) and a substitute amendment (the Martin substitute). "Under House procedure, members could now offer and vote on amendments to either Martin or Hansen, switching back and forth at will." R. H. Davidson & W. J. Oleszek, Congress Against Itself 239 (1977). As a result, "[t]he original (Bolling) measure could not be amended directly until the substitutes had been disposed of . . . . Only then would the House actually have a chance to consider and perfect the Select Committee's plan -- assuming, of course, that the substitutes were defeated." Id.

In retrospect, "[s]trategically, perhaps, the [Bolling] Committee erred by not preempting Martin with a substitute amendment of its own." Id. Had the committee offered a substitute similar to its underlying measure, and thereby "blocked out" the Martin substitute, it would have kept the House's attention focused on amending its own measure, rather than being partly ignored and thrown on the defensive while the House focused on rival proposals.

previously defeated proposition.

Two concrete situtations illustrate these amendment tactics in action. When the House took up the foreign aid appropriation bill in 1979, Representative Bill Young (R-Fla.) offered an amendment to cut it from $887 million to $150 million.[198] Rep. Trent Lott (R-Miss.) offered an amendment to the amendment, to cut only from $887 million to $763 million.   "Under these circumstances, Lott's amendment might appear to be a   reasonable   compromise . . .   "[199]   Then, Representative David Obey (D-Wis.) offered a substitute for the Young amendment to reduce the appropriation much less, to $870 million (a cut of only about 2 percent).

By offering his substitute, Representative Obey offered a "saving" amendment, in the terminology previously discussed, and as a parliamentary strategy sought a "nullifying" objective.   A Member could "vote for the Lott amendment" but then vote "to nullify the effect of that vote by voting also for the Obey amendment."[200] A Member who voted that way could show his seeming eagerness to cut the budget by voting in favor of two amendments to cut.   Yet, since the adoption of a substitute replaces the amendment, the vote for the Obey substitute would lead to replacement of the large cuts in the Young and Lott amendments with the higher level of spending in the Obey substitute.

At that point, Representative Matthew McHugh (D-N.Y.) offered a second-degree amendment to the Obey amendment, very similar to it, to cut to $869.5 million.   "[T]he McHugh amendment was designed to block other possible amendments to the Obey substitute."[201]   Once it took up the last

---

[198]   Representative Young, the ranking minority member on the Subcommittee on Foreign Operations, "noted the magnitude of his proposed cut, and explained that his purpose was to eliminate that part of the [international development] bank's appropriation that had not yet been authorized by law." Bach at 579.

[199] Id. at 580.

[200] Id. at 581.
(footnote continued)

place on the amendment tree, no member could offer "an amendment to the substitute to decrease the funding level from $870.0 million to $763.7 million."[202]   There would have been a real incentive for a sympathizer of the Young amendment to offer such an amendment, because by doing so, he would accomplish "pre-empting."   A Member who voted for such an amendment, as his first vote, would have difficulty later voting against the Young amendment: "[f]or this figure to be accepted in the first instance but then rejected in the second, some members would have been compelled to reverse their positions on successive votes."[203] This does not readily occur: "such a voting strategy can be difficult to explain to constituents and equally difficult to communicate quickly and successfully on the floor."[204]

Another example of massive use of multiple amendments with high political stakes occurred during the 1983 debate mentioned above over a cutoff of covert action in Nicaragua, with the administration favoring continuation of the covert action.   The debate began with an amendment to the text by Representative Young (pro-administration), and a second-degree amendment by Representative Michael Barnes (D-Md.) (anti-administration). Then, Representative Mica offered his substitute (pro-administration) for the Young amendment, and Representative Boland offered a second-degree amendment (anti-administration) to the Mica substitute.[205]

By this sequence, the anti-Administration forces accomplished pre-empting.   The first votes necessarily came on their two second-degree amendments, the Barnes and Boland amendments,

---

201   Id. at 582.

202   Id. at 582.

203   Id.

204   Id.

205   The amendments were offered at 129 Cong. Rec. H5742 (Young), H5755 (Barnes), H5820 (Mica), and H5822 (Boland) (daily ed. July 27 and 28, 1983).

allowing them to try out positions on the undecided Members and get them committed to one before a vote on the pro-administration positions (of the Young and Mica amendments). On the first vote, the House rejected the Barnes amendment by the cliff-hanging vote of 213-214. Then, "the House reversed itself -- and set the pattern for the rest of its action on HR 2760 -- by approving, 221-205, a complicated amendment sponsored by Boland."[206]

There is no necessity that votes on all the multiple amendments immediately follow each other, unless all debate has ben cut off. Rather, when the House disposes of some amendments in a tree, the emptied positions can be filled by other amendments. Thus, in the Nicaragua debate, once the Barnes and Boland second-degree positions were emptied by the votes on those amendments, Representative William Broomfield (R-Mich.) offered a second-degree amendment (pro-administration), akin in content to the early Mica amendment, as a second-degree amendment to the Young amendment (now amended by Boland). This constituted an attempt at recoupment.[207] The House defeated the amendment, in a "vote [that] sealed the outcome of the legislation,"[208] but after the amendments pending were disposed of, another round of amendments was tried.[209] Through

_____

[206] Felton, House Quashes Covert Nicaragua Aid, 41 Cong. Q. Week. Rep. 1536 (1983).

[207] As the press noted, "[t]hrough [this] parliamentary maneuvering, Administration supporters managed to get a second vote on the same issue later in the evening . . . ." Roberts, House Votes Down Effort to Weaken Ban on Covert Aid, New York Times, July 29, 1983, at 1.

[208] House Quashes Covert Nicaragua Aid, supra, at 149.

[209] After the House defeated the Broomfield amendment and dealt with a perfecting amendment, it adopted the Mica substitute (amended by Boland), meaning that it replaced the language of Young's amendment with Mica's (as amended), and then it adopted the "Young amendment" (actually, the Mica amendment, as amended -- but in the position first taken by the Young amendment). 129 Cong. Rec. H5869-70 (daily ed. (footnote continued)

these methods, "both sides," which "estimated the vote to be extremely close," tried to "advanc[e] moderating amendments designed to bring defectors from the other camp."[210]

G. GERMANENESS: SUBSTANTIVE STANDARDS

Rule XVI(7) states the House's germaneness rule in 19 words -- "no motion or proposition on a subject different from that under consideration shall be admitted under color of amendment." The brevity of this rule masks the difficulty in testing whether a subject is "different," and a bafflingly complex set of tests and precedents. The House Republican Manual, the only source outside the compilations of the Parliamentarian's office that has tried to explore the germaneness rule,[211] explains that "In the course of time, the rule of germaneness has become much more difficult to interpret. In short, there is no precise response to the question of what 'germaneness' means."[212]

The germaneness tests "can sometimes take on the appearance of empty sayings, always there after the fact, but not necessarily always there before hand to help and guide,"[213] with what the Chair once called "twilight zones."[214] However, a

---

July 28, 1983).

As for the second tree, Majority Leader Wright offered an amendment, Representative Henry Hyde (R-Ill.) offered a second-degree amendment, Representative Douglas Bereuter (R-Neb.) offered a substitute, the House rejected the Hyde and Bereuter amendments and agreed to the Wright amendment. Id. at 5873-80.

[210]   Roberts, supra.

[211]   This section relies heavily on the analysis of the Parliamentarian in the House Manual §§ 794-800 and in chapter 28 of Deschler's procedure, and an independent examination of Hinds and Cannon.

[212]   House Republican Manual at 174.

[213]   House Republican Manual at 187-88.
(footnote continued)

key means of analysis starts with how generally the Chair will see a particular bill's subject. This can be determined from the breadth and diversity of the bill's contents. With a sense of how general is the bill's subject, the tests for whether an amendment's subject is germane to the bill's can be applied with greater confidence.

Historically, the germaneness rule evolved virtually solely by rulings of the Speaker and the Chairman of the Committee of the Whole.[215] In the period prior to the Constitution, general parliamentary law allowed non-germane amendments.[216] The House's first set of rules, in 1789, created a limited germaneness rule by requiring that substitute amendments relate to the same subject as the pending amendment; after an era of obstructionist tactics, an 1822 rules revision extended the requirement of germaneness to all amendments.[217] Since 1822, the House has

---

[214] As the Chair commented in 1919, "[t]he matter of germaneness, of course, is one that is filled at times with some uncertainty. There are frequently twilight zones. . . ." 8 Cannon § 2916. Often, though, what might appear to be two Speakers or Chairs seeing matters differently may instead be the application of subtle tests to complex but distinguishable situations.

[215] Since the House takes up most amendments to bills in Committee of the Whole, most rulings on germaneness are by Chairmen of Committees of the Whole. For simplicity, this section will simply refer to "the House" as considering amendments (whether in Committee of the Whole or in the House) and "the Chair" as making all rulings on germaneness (whether by the Chairman of the Committee of the Whole or the Speaker).

[216] "Amendments may be made so as totally to alter the nature of the proposition." House Manual § 467 (Jefferson's Manual, 1797-1801).

[217] The original 1789 rule provided: "[n]o new motion or proposition shall be admitted under color of amendment as a substitute for the motion or proposition under consideration." V Hinds § 5767 (emphasis supplied). See Alexander at 184-89 (obstructive era); House Committee on Rules, 97th Cong., 2d Sess., A History of the Committee on
(footnote_continued)

not changed the text of the rule.[218]

Although the germaneness rule's wording has not changed, individual rulings of the Chair have elaborated, modified, or even overruled previous doctrines applying the rule. For example, in 1904 the Chair took a formal view of the germaneness of motions to strike, holding that a motion simply to strike out language would always be germane.[219] However, in 1920 the Chair reconsidered that precedent. Faced with the problems of the previous formalistic doctrine, the Chair held that even a motion simply to strike words could be non-germane when, through it, "the scope of the legislation under consideration is broadened beyond that contemplated in the bill."[220]

Rules 41 (Comm. Print 1983) ("Another technique used to check obstruction was to prohibit debate . . . on motions or propositions on subjects that were not germane to the proposal under debate.").

[218] In 1911-24, the House had a rule specifying particularly restrictive germaneness for revenue bills. VIII Cannon § 2908.

[219] The Chair stated that "Form, and not effect, should be considered. Germaneness refers to words added rather than to those taken away." V Hinds § 5805. As the rule was repeated in 1914, "it "is always in order -- to strike anything out of anything." VIII Cannon § 2973, at 538.

[220] As Representative James R. Mann (R-Ill.), a brilliant parliamentarian, hypothesized, if someone took up a bill which, by its wording, concerned tariffs on goods coming from the Phillipines and struck out those particular words, "that would have made it a universal tariff bill" -- which would make that motion to strike a classic example of a non-germane amendment broadening a specific bill into a general one. 8 Cannon § 2920. The 1920 principle remains the rule today. To a bill relaxing the Hatch Act for civilian employees, an amendment striking the words "but does not include a member of the uniformed services" and thereby extending it to military servicemen as well, was held non-germane. The rule was that "an amendment simply striking out words already in a bill may not be attacked as not germane unless such action would change the scope and meaning of the text." 123 Cong. Rec. 17714 (1977) (ruling of the Chair)(emphasis supplied).

Functions of Germaneness Rule

The germaneness rule profoundly shapes House action according to certain major purposes. Officially, the House explains that the rule seeks "to prevent hasty and ill-considered legislation, to prevent propositions being presented for the consideration of the body which might not be reasonably anticipated and for which the body might not be properly prepared."[221]   Also, the rule aims to take advantage of committees' expertise, experience, and ability;   it "preclude[s] consideration of subjects that were not considered by the appropriate committee."[222] However, germaneness does much more than that, since it bars amendments even when they received full consideration in committee.[223]   The "rule [is one] that favors the majority and hinders the minority in its attempt to introduce alternate proposals."[224]

Thus, the rule has three main deeper functions.   First and by far most important, the

---

[221]   VIII Cannon § 2993 (comment of the Chair in 1914).

[222]   House Republican Manual at 173.   It prevents bills from being "rewritten on the floor" on terms "which ha[ve] never been reported by any committee." VIII Cannon § 2912 at 479.

[223]   For example, the Judiciary Committee may consider a civil rights problem involving both voting and employment. The committee may consider both aspects of the problem in committee hearings, debating both in committee meetings, and then decide only to send a voting bill to the floor.   At that point, if a Member offered an employment provision as a floor amendment, the chamber would have the benefits of committee specialization regarding employment: it would have the hearing record, the course of committee debate, and the signal of committee views.   However, the germaneness rule means that the chamber cannot take those benefits of specialized attention and come to a different view; it can only legislate regarding voting when the only bill before it is a voting bill.

[224]   House Republican Manual at 173.

rule ensures control of the House's agenda.[225]
Those who control what bills come up, control the
issues before the House, so long as the
germaneness rule precludes bringing up new issues
by amendment. The germaneness rule implements the
preference of the majority controlling the House,
and the committee and leadership organs through
which it acts, for keeping some issues off the
floor -- issues that belong to the minority
party's agenda, or that would painfully divide the
majority party. The germaneness rule implements
that preference -- not because it is interpreted
in a partisan or biased way, but simply because,
interpreted neutrally, it limits the subjects on
the floor to those reported in bills.

To take both old and new examples, in the
1890s two populist battle cries were that "the
tariff was the mother of trusts," and for free
coinage of silver to relieve debt-burdened
farmers. The majority did not want to face either
of these issues, and of course did not report out
bills regarding them. The germaneness rule took
care of the rest. When the House took up the
Sherman Anti-Trust Act, the Speaker ruled out, as
non-germane, an amendment to suspend tariff duties
on items produced by trusts. When the House took
up a tariff bill, the Chair ruled out of order, as
non-germane, an attempt to raise the silver
issue.[226]

Similarly, in the decades following the
1950s, divisive national issues have included
civil rights and busing to integrate schools. Of
course, at certain times the House has considered
legislation on these matters. However, apart from
those specific times when it is ready to act, the

---

[225]   The rule does not determine who exercises that
control. Traditionally, the majorities on committees, who
decide whether to report bills, share control with the
majority leadership and the Rules Committee members, who
decide what reported bills come to the floor. How these and
other centers of power share their control has changed many
times since the adoption of the germaneness rule in the
1820s. Nevertheless, regardless of who shares what control,
the germaneness rule implements that control.

[226]   V Hinds § 5865; see also id. § 5835.

majority has preferred not to bring up bills on
these issues, and the germaneness rule often keeps
the issues from coming up as amendments. The rule
kept out amendments to broaden limited civil
rights bills into more general ones;[227] it kept
out busing amendments on bills regarding energy
conservation or the criminal code.[228]

In this respect, House procedure contrasts
strongly with Senate procedure, which lacks a
general germaneness rule, so that the minority
party, and individual mavericks, can bring up
issues in the form of proposed non-germane
amendments. As one observer notes, "[w]ithout
doubt, the right to offer non-germane amendments
is the most potent leverage that individual
Senators have to place matters on the floor agenda
. . . in terms of the issues that Senators can
compel [the Senate] to confront."[229]

Secondly, besides giving committees control
over what comes up, the germaneness rule gives
them some control, after subjects come up, over
how much the House can do with them. A committee
can report a narrow bill on a particular subject
-- or a bill taking a particular approach -- and
the germaneness rule prevents the House from
broadening the bill or adding other approaches.
For example, when the Education and Labor
Committee reported a bill narrowly drafted to
permit "common situs" picketing in the
construction industry, the germaneness rule
prevents amending the bill to create other rules
and remedies for picketing.[230] When a committee
brings up an annual authorization bill, the
germaneness rule prevents amending the bill to

---

[227] Deschler 28 § 5.3.

[228] Deschler 28 §§ 5.26 (energy conservation), 7.10
(imprisonment).

[229] S. Bach, Senator and Senate: Influence on the
Legislative Agenda (Cong. Res. Serv. Nov. 12, 1983).

[230] Deschler 28 §§ 28.6, 28.59. See also 123 Cong. Rec.
52507-08 (1977) (bill amending procedural rules governing
labor elections and organizations; amendment creating new
unfair labor practice not germane).

change the agency's permanent law. The germaneness rule confines amendments on such limited bills "to the agencies, authority, and funds addressed by the bill."[231] As a repeated example, when the House gets ready to do something about the farm problem, whether the year is 1924[232] or 1981, the germaneness rule forces it to consider only the type of approach favored by the committee of jurisdiction reporting the bill.[233]

Thirdly, the rule prevents committees from raiding other committees' jurisdiction. When House committees report bills to the floor with committee amendments, these committee amendments must meet the test of germaneness, like any other amendments.[234] Because both committee and floor

---

[231]   28 Deschler § 27.19.

[232]   In 1924, the committee proposed a relief corporation with emergency authority to buy products; the Chair ruled amendments non-germane that proposed other approaches, such as cooperative marketing and export encouragement. VIII Cannon § 2912; see also id. §§ 2967, 2969. Ironically, nine years later, Representative Henry Thomas Rainey (D-Ill.), the offeror of the non-germane amendment in 1924, sat in the Chair as Speaker when a similar point arose on a motion to recommit, and he reminisced about it. He recalled that his 1924 amendment's:

> method was much better than the method provided in that bill; but that did not make any difference . . . . Mr. [Clarence] Cannon [D-Mo.] of Missouri, the author of Cannon's Precedents . . . convinced the Chairman [in 1924] . . . that my amendment was not germane, although he did not convince me then, that my amendment was not germane . . . . The Chair, therefore, feels constrained to and does sustain the point of order.

VIII Cannon § 2969.

[233]   In 1981, the committee proposed price supports; the Chair ruled out an amendment to restrict imports. House Manual § 798b.

[234]   V Hinds § 5806; 28 Deschler § 17.1. A committee can attempt to beat the germaneness rule by deciding what it wants to report, introducing that in the form of a bill, and (footnote continued)

amendments must be germane, and committee
jurisdictional lines provide one of the tests for
germaneness, amendments to bills from one
committee cannot invade subjects belonging to
another.

As discussed elsewhere, the House does have
several safety valves regarding agenda control.
The Rules Committee can provide a special rule
waiving the point of order for germaneness; it can
also make legislation in order as an amendment to
an appropriation bill. With enough support, the
minority can defeat special rules on the floor for
failing to make adequate alternatives in order, or
can discharge a measure it desires to vote on.
Each of these techniques poses its separate
problems, and thus the germaneness rule remains a
highly significant constraint on floor amendments.

With those general purposes sketched out, we
may turn to the tests of germaneness. There are
two main batteries of germaneness tests. One
looks at "subject relatedness" -- at whether the
bill and the amendment have subjects that are
sufficiently related. These are the tests of
subject matter, purpose and method, and
jurisdiction. The other main battery of tests
looks at "formal generality," both of the bill and
the amendment. These tests look at whether the
amendment excessively broadens the generality of
the bill, particularly in terms of whether the
bill starts out diverse and broad, or narrow.
Finally, there are certain specific principles for
recurrent problems, such as restrictive
amendments.

Germaneness Tests I: Subject Relatedness
-- Subject Matter

The first battery of tests has three ways of
looking at subject relatedness: the "subject
matter" of the bill, such as sex discrimination,

---

then reporting that out as a "clean bill" (without
amendments). However, when a committee does this, other
checks on it can operate: another committee whose
jurisdiction is being raided can ask the Speaker for a
multiple referral, or the Rules Committee can hold the bill
up or give special floor procedures to the other committee.

agency reorganization, or "common situs" picketing; the "fundamental purpose" of the bill, including the similarity between the bill's and amendment's methods -- creation of a new agency, regulatory standards, civil penalties, or tax rebates; and "committee jurisdiction," or whether the amendment falls within the jurisdiction of the committee that reported the bill -- e.g., for an Energy and Commerce bill, whether the amendment adds matter that would go through that committee, or through Banking, or Judiciary, or Ways and Means.

Of these, the first test looks at the bill's "subject matter."[235]   As the House Republican Manual comments, "[i]n preparing an argument in support or opposition to an amendment['s] germaneness, one must determine 'what is the subject matter under consideration?'   The arguments pro and con will frequently revolve around this question."[236]   A few examples show the test in action.   For a highway program bill, an amendment is non-germane, as not on the same subject, that would divert funds to urban mass transportation.[237]   For a sex discrimination (equal pay) bill, an amendment is non-germane that concerns race discrimination.[238]   However, for a bill providing for an interoceanic canal through Nicaragua, an amendment is germane that provides for a route through Panama.[239]

---

[235]   For precedents under this test, see House Manual § 798a; Deschler 28 § 3.   Although many of the precedents in Hinds and Cannon illustrate this test, it is not articulated as a particularly distinct test in those precedents.   The first distinct articulation appears in the one-volume work by Clarence Cannon on procedure which went through many editions, e.g., Cannon's Procedure in the House of Representatives, H. Doc. No. 122, 86th Cong., 1st Sess. 208-9 (1959), which provides examples of related subjects.

[236]   House Republican Manual at 181.

[237]   Deschler 28 § 3.4; see 118 Cong. Rec. 34115 (1972) (citing two previous highway trust/mass transit precedents).

[238]   Deschler 28 § 3.1.

(footnote continued)

Obviously, this test depends greatly on how generally the Chair sees a bill's subject for which the key is the breadth and diversity of the bill's contents.[240]   In two of the above examples, the   Chair   saw   narrow   subjects: highway transportation (rather than transportation in general) and sex discrimination (rather than discrimination in general).   In one, it saw a broad subject: interoceanic canal (not Nicaraguan canals).

An instance of extensive application of the germaneness tests illustrates this.   In December, 1973, during the Arab oil boycott, the House took up an Energy Emergency Act with provisions ranging from enhancement of production to mandatory energy conservation and rationing.[241]   Faced with a very broad bill, the Chair took a very broad view of the bill's subject for germaneness purposes.

The bill modified the Clean Air Act regarding energy production, and so the Chair held germane an amendment to modify Clean Air Act enforcement of auto emissions, since "the Clean Air Act is comprehensively amended by the bill."[242]   The bill had a provision for allocation (rationing) of petroleum products, and so the Chair held germane an   amendment   blocking   exports   of   allocated products, since the amendment "refers to total allocation within the United States and to the relation between those allocations and export."[243]   However, even with this very broad

---

[239]   V Hinds § 5909.

[240]   This may seem like an overlap with the second battery of tests concerning the generality of the bill and the amendment.   That is the way these precedents are cited and applied; they overlap.

[241]   The bill brought up matters of the greatest partisan and regional differences, triggering a host of related and not-so-related amendments; at one point, 68 amendments were ready for consideration.   119 Cong. Rec. 41683 (1973).   In the Chair was the redoubtable Representative Richard Bolling (D-Mo.), entrusted by the leadership with supervising a debate of much more than usual procedural challenge.

[242]   Id. at 41689.

(footnote continued)

bill for which the floodgates of germaneness had been opened wide, the Chair found a completely unrelated subject when it came to an amendment to create a homeowners' insulation loan program.[244] Similarly, the Chair ruled out an amendment to prohibit non-returnable bottles.[245]

Fundamental Purpose and Method, and Committee Jurisdiction

The second test looks at the bill's "fundamental purpose." Among other aspects,[246] this test compares the bill's methods with the amendment's methods. If a bill proposes to deal with an issue by one method, such as providing funds, then an amendment to deal with the same issue by other methods, such as regulation, tax

---

[243] Similarly, the bill's allocation provision favored petroleum needed for extraction of essential minerals (e.g., for coal mining), and the Chair held germane an amendment for exemptions from the coal mine safety law, saying that the bill's language "urging full production by the domestic energy industry, justifies the offering of this amendment which deals with coal production." Id. 41748.

[244] The proponent called the bill's subject "a national energy proposal" with provisions "as broad as ranging from car-pools to hydroelectric projects." However, the Chair thought the homeowner loan amendment "introduces a subject not before the committee." Id. at 41738-39.

[245] Deschler 28 § 6.18.

[246] In Deschler's Procedure, the precedents for fundamental purpose, Deschler 28 § 5, are separated from those for different method, Deschler 28 § 6. However, the House Manual combines the two, in § 798b, and many of the precedents cited in Deschler regarding "fundamental purpose" address different methods, see Deschler 28 §§ 5.16- 5.21. Although there are a number of fundamental purpose precedents that do not address methods, they do not reflect any clear overarching test distinct from other tests.

For early precedents regarding the nongermaneness of amendments proposing different methods, see VIII Cannon §§ 2978-80, 2988.

credits, loans,[247] civil penalties, criminal prosecutions, or international agreements, may be non-germane. "The arguments against the [germaneness of the] amendment would attempt to show that the methods were not 'closely allied' or related."[248]

In a 1918 precedent, the House considered a bill to defray wartime expenditures by raising revenue, and the Chair held non-germane an amendment to create a joint committee on war expenditures.[249] In another example in 1975, the House considered a bill to raise gas mileage of automobiles being sold, by imposing civil penalties on auto manufacturers, and the Chair held non-germane an amendment to raise that gas mileage by selective tax rebates to auto purchasers.[250] Both precedents held amendments non-germane that proposed entirely different methods than the underlying bills. As a general rule, to a bill proposing a study of something, an amendment proposing actually to do something is not germane. Conversely, to bills proposing action, amendments proposing study are germane.[251]

---

[247]   However, to a bill providing loan guarantees, an amendment providing direct loans was germane, as proposing a closely related method. Deschler 28 § 6.26.

[248]   House Republican Manual at 183.

[249]   VIII Cannon § 2911.

[250]   121 Cong. Rec. 18696 (1975). Similarly, in a bill to promote energy conservation, an amendment was nongermane to repeal the oil depletion allowance. Deschler 28 § 5.24. Sometimes the distinguishing among methods can go very far, perhaps reflecting how often particular committees have control over particular methods (e.g., tax credits, appropriations, criminal laws, and changes in House rules). For example, to a bill to enforce Prohibition by injunction for which the penalty was contempt, an amendment was not germane to specify trial of violations by jury, VIII Cannon § 2977 -- then a big issue (particularly in light of the impact of convictions without jury of union leaders for violating labor injunctions).

[251]   Compare Deschler 28 § 3.25 (nongermane amendment (footnote continued)

On the other hand, an amendment may be germane, even when it contains a provision for a different method, when the bill and amendment are both comprehensive and the particular provision proposing a new method merely "incidental."[252] For example, the House considered a bill and a committee amendment in the nature of a substitute which both provided comprehensive schemes for the construction of the Alaska pipeline. The committee amendment expedited court actions challenging pipeline permits, which the bill did not. The Chair held the amendment germane, deeming the permit provision "merely incidental to the purpose of the original bill."[253]

The third subject test concerned with relatedness looks at committee jurisdiction: whether the same committee that reported the bill would have jurisdiction over the amendment.[254] This test invokes the vast store of precedents under House Rule X regarding the past referrals of bills. This test brings in the established (if sometimes arbitrary) distinctions upon which the lines dividing committee jurisdiction often depend.

Committee jurisdiction must be a key test of germaneness to avoid letting committees usurp others' jurisdictions. For example, the House distributes transportation issues over several committees. While the Committee on Public Works has jurisdiction over highway construction, the Banking Committee and Commerce Comittee have jurisdiction, respectively, over urban mass transit and railroads.[255] To let amendments for

---

proposing action) with id. § 5.14 (germane amendment proposing study). On the other hand, to a bill proposing to study something, an amendment requiring that the study be followed up with submission of proposed legislation is germane. Id. § 3.18.

252   Deschler 28 §§ 5.16, 5.19, 5.25.

253   119 Cong. Rec. 27675 (1973).

254   Deschler 28 § 4; House Manual § 798c.

(footnote continued)

funding these alternative transportation modes come up on Public Works bills would place "in the jurisdiction of the Committee on Public Works a subject matter heretofore not within that committee's jurisdiction."[256] Accordingly, as mentioned above, the Chair has held amendments non-germane that would take funds accumulated in the Highway Trust Fund and apply them to non-highway transportation issues.[257] A similar pattern has held regarding energy jurisdiction: the House distributes jurisdiction over several committees, and amendments regarding one committee's area may be non-germane to bills from another committee.[258]

However, the test of committee jurisdiction, more than any other test, evokes frequent warnings by the Chair that it is not the exclusive test of jurisdiction.[259] "In short, the subject matter of the bill is the controlling factor, not the description in the Rules of the House of the various committees' jurisdiction."[260] Comprehensive amendments to bills from a variety of committees might contain some provision reorganizing federal departments, since new

---

[255] Deschler 28 § 4.20. The Ways and Means Committee controls the raising of revenue for the Highway Trust Fund, and so shares jurisdiction over the Fund with Public Works.

[256] 118 Cong. Rec. 4116 (1972)(ruling of the Chair).

[257] Deschler 28 §§ 3.4, 4.25, and 5.11.

[258] In the consideration of the comprehensive Energy Emergency Act of 1973 discussed above, some of the amendments crossing committee lines were held non-germane, such as changes in the federal employee workweek (a matter for the Committee on Post Office and Civil Service), creation of homeowner conservation loan programs (a matter for the Banking Committee) (Deschler 28 §§ 4.29 -4.31) and creation of user fee programs as part of rationing (a matter for the Ways and Means Committee) (119 Cong. Rec. 41750 (1973)). The same lines on germaneness have held for other energy acts (Deschler 28 §§ 4.41-4.43).

[259] Deschler 28 § 4.27.

[260] House Republican Manual at 181-82.

programs require new organizations. Departmental reorganization is a matter that, standing alone, falls in the Government Operations Committee's jurisdiction, but the amendments do not thereby become non-germane.[261]

Germaneness Tests II: Formal Generality -- Particular and General Propositions

Besides the above-described three "subject relatedness" tests, there is quite a different battery of tests that looks at the "formal generality" of the bill and amendment. These tests look at whether the amendment, even if related to the bill, excessively broadens the generality of the bill. These tests' difficulty comes in defining levels of formal generality, such as in "identify[ing] what is or is not an individual proposition."[262]

In simple and concrete bills, these tests can produce clear results. A nineteenth-century test still applied today holds that when a bill contains one specific "proposition," an amendment that would add another, even of the same class, is non-germane as broadening the bill.[263] When a bill provides monetary relief to a single person or institution or creates a single post (each a specific proposition), an amendment is non-germane that would relieve or create another;[264] when a

---

[261]   An amendment to a Commerce Committee bill that, among other matters, reorganized an energy agency was germane; although "a bill containing the substance of the amendment [was] jointly referred to [the Committee on Government Operations] and to the Committee on Interstate and Foreign Commerce in this Congress, the Chair would point out that committee jurisdiction is not the sole or exclusive test of germaneness." 122 Cong. Rec. 16025 (1976) (ruling of the Chair).

[262]   House Republican Manual at 183.

[263]   See House Manual § 798e; Deschler 28 §§ 7, 10; Hinds and Cannon precedents listed in Cannon at 202-3.

[264]   V Hinds §§ 181-30, 5833.   "For a time [1852-57] a (footnote continued)

bill insures, pays, aids, or awards medals to one group, an amendment would be non-germane to do the same for another.[265]

Similarly, when a bill contains a specific proposition, an amendment to add a general one is non-germane.[266] To a bill suspending Clean Air Act requirements temporarily during a fuel shortage, an amendment adding a general suspension from "other environmental protection requirements" was non-germane.[267] To a bill implementing sanctions against Rhodesia for violating human rights, an amendment generalizing sanctions to all countries for such violations was non-germane.[268] To an amendment regarding one budget function in a resolution, an amendment regarding several functions was non-germane.[269]

Conversely, longstanding principles hold that when a bill contains several "propositions," an amendment that would add another of the same class is germane; and, for a bill containing a general proposition, an amendment that would add a specific one is germane.[270] Germaneness is

---

different principle prevailed." Id. § 5831.

[265]   VIII Cannon §§ 2951-3, 2958-62. When the House considered a bill to relax the Hatch Act for federal civilian employees (a specific proposition), an amendment was deemed non-germane that would do the same for servicemen (another specific proposition). 123 Cong. Rec. 17714 (1977). For a convict labor bill, a child labor amendment was non-germane. VIII Cannon § 2963. To a bill regulating interstate buses, an amendment is non-germane regulating intrastate ones. VIII Cannon § 2964.

[266]   House Manual § 798f; Deschler 28 § 8; Hinds and Cannon precedents listed in Cannon at 203.

[267]   Deschler 28 § 8.16.

[268]   Deschler 28 § 8.27.

[269]   125 Cong. Rec. 9564 (1979).

[270]   House Manual § 798g; Deschler 28 § 9; Hinds and Cannon precedents listed in Cannon at 203-5. This is "that familiar rule where a bill provides for more than one class, a third class may be added." VIII Cannon 3013 (ruling of (footnote continued)

clearest when the bill's several propositions are diverse or unrelated.[271]   To a bill providing generally for prison sites, study of public lands, road repairs, and study of the relation of pollution to disease, amendments were germane that specified particular states, areas, roads, and study of the impact of smoking on the relation of pollution to disease.[272]

The recurrent problem of arms shipments to Turkey produced a nice example of these contrasting principles in action.   To a matter that delayed arms shipments pending progress on one problem with Turkey (regarding Cyprus) (one individual proposition), an amendment was non-germane regarding progress with another problem (opium control) (another individual proposition).[273]   Yet to a bill to promote strong relations with Turkey in several ways (several individual propositions), an amendment was germane regarding negotiations over opium control (one more individual proposition).[274]

Of course, the difficulty comes when bills act more abstractly and complexly.   For example, the Emergency Energy Act described above included many methods for conserving energy.   The Chair could have responded regarding amendments to add other conservation methods that they were germane as adding an individual proposition to several others.   Instead, the Chair relied on the subject relatedness test that the amendments proposed methods not "closely allied" with those in the bill.

The apparent discretion of the Chair is

---

the Chair).

[271]   28 Deschler §§ 9.16-17, 9.20-21, 9.27-32, 9.35.

[272]   VIII Cannon §§ 3006, 3007, 3020; 122 Cong. Rec. 30498 (1976);   To a bill listing three identification requirements for cold-storage goods, providing flood relief to two areas, or putting several restrictions on an expenditure, an amendment adding another requirement, area for relief, or restriction is germane.   VIII Cannon §§ 3002-3, 3010.

[273]   Deschler 28 § 7.19.

[274]   Deschler 28 § 9.30.

subject, always, to the drive to keep the precedents consistent, and the Parliamentarian, familiar with the multitudinous precedents, thus is more confined than a recital of the rules would reflect. As the House Republican Manual concludes, "[t]hese 'tests' essentially do not yield answers as much as they tend to organize analysis and facilitate the marshalling of precedents . . . . There is no substitute in debate for the closest analogy."[275]

A recurrent problem concerns amendments containing restrictions or limitations. Typically, these involve a natural political gambit: trying to block the effectiveness of a pending bill that has too much support for it to be defeated directly by conditioning the bill's effectiveness on enactment of some other legislation. Conditions generally on legislation resemble appropriations "riders," discussed separately in the chapter on appropriations, and as there, the test differentiates between "related" and "unrelated" conditions, contingencies, and limitations.

Limitations may bring in major issues while still being "related." To a military authorization bill, an amendment was germane that declared it "to be the sense of the Congress that none of the funds authorized by this Act shall be used to carry out military operations in or over North Vietnam."[276] To a bill authorizing agency activity, an amendment is germane that conditions that activity on congressional approval or disapproval, so long as the amendment does not also alter House rules.[277]

---

[275] House Republican Manual at 187-88.

[276] 113 Cong. Rec. 5143 (1967).

[277] House Manual § 800. Although the legislative veto has been declared unconstitutional, a provision requiring congressional approval can be perfectly constitutional so long as the vehicle for approval or disapproval is a joint resolution or bill that requires presidential signature. Often, the proponent of such provisions wants to change House rules to assure expedited treatment of the vehicle for approval or disapproval. However, such changes in House (footnote continued)

The germaneness rule admits one particular political solution to jurisdictional disputes: restrictions limiting what a bill does to subsequently adopted authorizations. For example, to an Interior Committee bill establishing petroleum reserves, an amendment was germane providing conditionally for placing such reserves in strategic storage facilities, even though such facilities fall within the jurisdiction of the Armed Services Committee. The amendment conditioned such placement that it be "pursuant to any program subsequently authorized by Congress."[278] Congress compromises many difficulties between two committees of competing jurisdictions this way, by making effectiveness of action under a bill of the first committee conditional on an authorization from the second.[279]

On the other hand, the Chair deems conditions regarding enactment of other bills "unrelated," and hence non-germane,[280] when their link is only political, and not operational. In the classic examples, to a bill for relief for war victims, an amendment was non-germane which conditioned effectiveness on enactment of veterans' compensation.[281] To an appropriation bill funding energy assistance, an amendment was non-germane that conditioned effectiveness on enactment of an oil windfall profits tax.[282]

---

rules belong to the particular jurisdiction of the Rules Committee.

[278] Deschler 28 § 23.15.

[279] Similarly, a Member can play political hardball against an official by a condition that funds in a bill shall not be expended "so long as the present . . . Commissioner of Education [or some other targeted official] occupies that office." Deschler 28 § 24.8. Such indirection is necessary because cutting off funds directly for a particular official's salary raises constitutional questions under the Bill of Attainder Clause. United States v. Lovett, 328 U.S. 303 (1946).

[280] Deschler 28 § 24.

[281] VIII Cannon § 3035; see also id. § 3037.
(footnote continued)

H.   GERMANENESS: PROCEDURE

Germaneness issues arise only when Members raise points of order against amendments.   Several important rules govern those points.   The previously stated germaneness tests make sense in any situation only with an understanding of how germaneness points are raised, and how comparisons are made.

General Procedure for Raising Germaneness Points

Germaneness procedure begins with the principle that no points of order can be raised against the bill itself, only against amendments.   In other words, a bill on one subject can contain wildly unrelated provisions on totally different subjects, without being subject to a point of order.[283]   Members offer amendments, as a bill is read for amendments, only to the portion being read, and the point of order for germaneness can only be made against the amendment as it is read.   The point of order comes too late if the Member waits until after the amendment is read (or the reading is waived) and debate has begun.[284]

---

[282]   125 Cong. Rec. 29639 (1979).   See Deschler 28 § 4.11.

[283]   Deschler 28 §§ 12.1, 12.3.   "A committee may report a bill embracing different subjects, such as would not be admitted under color of amendment."   P. DeW. Hasbrouck, Party Government in the House of Representatives 115 (1927).   For such a bill, an opponent's remedy, if any, lies only in seeking a multiple referral or trying to persuade the Rules Committee not to clear the bill for floor consideration.

[284]   Deschler 28 §§ 35.8, 35.9, 35.11-14.   However, a Member who attempts to make a point of order by standing up and seeking recognition can insist on it even if the Chair does not at first notice him and recognizes another.   Id. §§ 35.1, 35.4.

To soften the rudeness of killing an amendment before its offeror can even explain his creation, often Members do not "make" the point of order while the amendment is read, but "reserve" it. Then the offeror and others can discuss the amendment, until the objecting Member "insists" on his point of order. Sometimes at that point, upon reflection, the offeror will "concede" the point. If not, the objector can offer to the Chair to discuss the point of order, and the Chair, in its discretion, can allow the two sides to debate the germaneness issue before ruling. The burden is on the proponent of the amendment to show germaneness, not on the Member raising the point of order to refute it.[285]

Most commonly, Members seek to anticipate germaneness points. Committee chairs check with the Parliamentarian informally -- the Chair does not give formal rulings in advance[286] -- to be sure that the committee amendments will not be subject to points of order; minority members check their alternatives, too, unless they prefer the highly risky tactic of surprising the Chair.[287] Usually a warning that the amendment is non-germane leads to its being junked, but on occasion, the Rules Committee will include a waiver of the point of order in its special

---

[285]   VIII Cannon § 2995.

[286]   28 Deschler § 37.

[287]   One study suggested:

In certain circumstances, however, surprise may be the best resource . . . . The minority counsel to the House Agriculture Committee, Hyde Murray [later counsel to the Minority Leader] has explained the occasional need for surprise:

"Lew [i.e., Lewis Deschler, then Parliamentarian] loves this House and would never do anything to hurt it. But sometimes I know viscerally that if I show this to Lew he's going to knock it down and rebut it. Only in that kind of situation is surprise an alternative."

T. Siff & A. Weil, supra, at 36.

rule.[288]   As discussed above, expansive rules
containing such waivers can represent high
political strategy.   For example, when the House
took up expansion of the Superfund in 1984, the
Rules Committee provided a germaneness waiver so
that a whole new program, a Superfund for oil
spills, could be considered.[289]

Germaneness procedure tests the amendment,
not against the bill as introduced or reported,
but against the bill as amended.[290]   Often, a bill
starts out narrow, but is broadened by amendment,
and amendments previously not in order become
germane.   For example, a bill that narrowly
amended one section of the Food Stamp Act was
broadened by amendment to alter another section of
the Act.   At that point, a further amendment to
change a third section of the Act was held
germane.[291]

When the Committee of the Whole considers a
bill, it reads the bill section by section, or by
some other unit, amending each unit before going
on to the next.   An amendment's germaneness must
be tested against the portion of the bill being
read,[292] and the portion to which offered.[293]

---

[288]   Deschler 28 § 36.4.

[289]   130 Cong. Rec. H8737 (daily ed. Aug. 9, 1984). Also in
1984, when the leadership decided to link two bills, one
regarding the new drug approval process and another
regarding drug patent extension, it did so with a rule
waiving the germaneness point of order against an amendment
incorporating the second bill. 130 Cong. Rec. H8702 (daily
ed. Aug. 8, 1984).

[290]   Deschler 28 §§ 1.1, 2.4, 4.16, 28.13; VIII Cannon §
2910. A more precise statement would note that technically
the Committee of the Whole does not itself amend the bill,
only reports it to the House with the certain recommended
amendments that the House must then itself pass. Thus, to
be precise, germaneness tests the amendment against the bill
as the Committee of the Whole recommends to modify it.

[291]   Deschler 28 §§ 28.13-14.

[292]   For a bill being read by sections, amendments must be
germane to the section being read; for one being read by
(footnote continued)

This "portion being read" principle gives way to a principle regarding the "scale of the amendment," which allows amendments in the nature of a substitute, and amendments creating new titles, sections, and paragraphs to be judged against something larger than the immediate portion of the bill.[294]   Still,   the   "portion   being   read" principle   creates   an   obstacle   when   Members desiring to amend a bill fail to watch the floor closely. Once the House goes past the section the Member wants to amend, the House can only return to that section by unanimous consent.[295]

Rule   XVI(7)   applies   to   "motion[s]   or proposition[s]" generally, not just to bills, and

---

titles, to the title being read; and for a bill deemed (by special rule or unanimous consent) read in full and open to amendment at any point, to the bill as a whole. Deschler 28 § 2.25.

[293]   Deschler 28 §§ 1.3, 2.5 - 2.6, 13, 14. For example, the House considered a tax bill and began the amending process at the beginning, with the definitional section. The Chair held non-germane an amendment requiring that municipal securities be taxed like other matter, even though that amendment might have been germane to later provisions in the bill, because it was more than definitional, and "amendments to be germane must not only be germane to the subject matter of the bill but also to the paragraph where offered." VIII Cannon § 2922.

[294]   "Sometimes, an amendment which would be held not germane when offered to a particular title of a bill would be considered germane if offered as a new title." Deschler 28 § 14.2. An amendment in the nature of a substitute id. § 2.13, or an amendment adding a new title, or adding a new section at the end of a bill, need only be germane to the bill as a whole. Id. §§ 2.9, 14.4, 14.12. Similarly, an amendment adding a new section or paragraph need not necessarily be germane to the section or paragraph immediately preceding it. Id. § 14.14; VIII Cannon § 2932.

[295]   VIII Cannon § 2930. If the House refuses that consent and goes on to later sections, the same amendment may not be germane to them. Members may attempt to redraft and reoffer their amendments, but they may either not be germane to those sections, or may have to be altered into strained and undesirable forms to achieve germaneness.

it has some important applications other than to
bills.   It applies to amendments offered to other
amendments rather than to the bill itself: to
second   degree   amendments   or   substitute
amendments.[296]   For   example,   often   a   committee
reports out a bill with a committee amendment in
the nature of a substitute, and everyone offering
a floor amendment offers it to that amendment in
the   nature   of   a   substitute   --   and   so   all
amendments must be germane to that amendment, not
to the bill.[297]   Likewise, the germaneness rule
applies to motions to strike language.[298]   It also

---

[296]   Deschler 28 §§ 2.10, 8.19, 16.

[297]   Deschler 28 § 2.9.   Similarly, when the imperatives of
floor maneuvering lead to offering a substitute amendment to
"de-fang" a killer amendment, the substitute must be germane
to the killer amendment.   Thus, for example, during debate
on a budget resolution, an amendment sought to increase the
figure for defense.   (The amendment was actually a
substitute for another amendment.   125 Cong. Rec. 9562
(1979).)   To beat it, an amendment was offered to it
regarding the figures for several other functions, including
veteran's benefits.   The Chair held that this proposed
second-degree amendment was non-germane, since it "deals not
only with defense but with several other functional
categories and is more general in scope."   Id. at 9564.

For another example, during debate on a bill to raise
the pay of Members and other government officials, an
amendment was offered to give a raise only to the other
government officials.   An amendment was offered to that
amendment, adding language which barred pay raises for
Members voting to limit their own pay.   (Only by a
circuitous route could the second degree amendment be other
than a redundancy in that particular situation, but there is
no parliamentary rule against such amendments.)   The Chair
held that second degree amendment germane, as "a further
selective restriction" to an amendment that already
"contains a selective restriction."   Id. at 26143.

[298]   As discussed in the previous section, generally such
motions are germane.   However, the motion to strike may be
nongermane if, by striking language, it expands the bill's
scope to new subjects -- as when qualifiers such as that a
bill only concerns imports "from the Phillipines" would be
(footnote continued)

applies, in some complex situations discussed in the chapter on conference procedure, to House amendments to Senate amendments,[299] when a non-germane amendment would otherwise almost certainly become law.[300]

The germaneness rule also applies to resolutions -- resolutions proposing constitutional amendments, and special rules.[301] For example, when a special rule makes one bill in order, an amendment would be non-germane making another in order.[302] Also, the germaneness rule

---

struck.

[299] Deschler 28 §§ 21.11, 21.12.   The regular germaneness rule does not apply to the Senate amendment itself.   For handling non-germane Senate amendments, the House has a special procedure in Rule XXVIII(5), discussed in the chapter on conference procedure.

Only occasionally, but nevertheless on some significant occasions (because of the significance of the post-conference procedures discussed elsewhere) such amending occurs, and only germane amendments can be offered in motions to concur. As discussed in the chapter on resolving differences between Houses, what happens most often is that any amending is done by unanimous consent as a preliminary step to agreement between the Houses or to conference, without any elaborate floor amendment process.

[300] To take a hypothetical example, in a common postconference appropriation pattern, the Senate may have tacked a wholly new limitation onto the appropriation bill, such as a cutoff on covert action in Nicaragua. The House manager may move to concur with a limited amendment adding further requirements of notification to Congress. The minority may wish to offer a broad second-degree amendment to that motion to concur, such as conditioning any cutoff on certification of an end to Cuban interference. If the minority gets to offer any amendment at all (it may be precluded from offering amendments by moving the previous question on the motion to concur with an amendment), it can only offer an amendment germane to the one in the motion to concur.

[301] VIII Cannon § 2995 (constitutional amendments); V Hinds § 5882 (same); House Manual § 762 (special rules).

(footnote continued)

applies to motions to recommit, even though the minority has a right to make that motion and the germaneness rule constrains this minority right.[303] The germaneness test for special rules and motions to recommit constitutes a major check on the minority's ability to bring up its favored alternative agenda, as discussed in the chapter on rules.[304] On the other hand, an amendment to a motion to recommit need only be germane to the bill as a whole, and as amended. Thus, in some situations, such as a continuing resolution for which highly diverse amendments were made in order by a special rule, a bill may be open to almost any motion to recommit with instructions, without that motion being subject to a germaneness point of order.

Amendments to Existing Law

---

[302] V Hinds §§ 5834-36; VIII Cannon § 2956.

[303] Although the minority party receives preference in using the motion to recommit with instructions as its channel for offering major alternatives, the germaneness rule limits those alternatives to the subjects in the bill. Deschler 28 § 18.1; V Hinds § 5834. For example, after the failure to end World War I formally by ratifying the Treaty of Versailles, the House considered in 1921 a joint resolution simply repealing its declaration of war against Germany. The minority offered a motion to recommit which instead authorized treaty negotiations. While the Chair "appreciate[d] the force of the suggestion that a motion to recommit is intended to allow the minority to express its views . . . [this] is an entirely different proposition . . . [and] the motion to recommit is not in order." VIII Cannon § 2987.

[304] For example, in 1984, on the interior appropriation bill, the minority wished to make in order an amendment to cut synfuels funding. It could not do so by defeating the previous question on the bill's special rule and putting in a provision making such a cut in order, because that provision would have been nongermane to the special rule. Instead, it could only defeat the rule, and await the reporting of a new rule -- by which time the majority had regrouped behind a compromise proposal, which made only a limited synfuel cut.

A recurrent problem concerns amendments to a bill that address the terms of existing (previously enacted) law, rather than the bill.[305]   In general, to be germane an amendment must concern the same subject as the bill, not the existing law that the bill amends.[306]   For example, the House considered a bill amending the labor law to require new agency regulations regarding representation.   The Chair held non-germane an amendment to the existing labor law to require new agency regulations against unreasonable union discipline.[307]

As an exception, a bill may amend existing law so broadly as to open up all of it, even the parts not amended by the bill, to amendments.[308] A bill revised the Rail Reorganization Act in "so comprehensive" a fashion" "as to permit germane amendments to any portion of the law,"[309] even

---

[305]   House Manual § 799; Deschler 28 §§ 28-32.

[306]   VIII Cannon § 2909.

[307]   123 Cong. Rec. 32508 (1978).

[308]   Compare Deschler 28 §§ 28.43-4, 28.46-7, 28.51, 28.55-8, 28.60 (all involving sufficiently broad or diverse revisions to accommodate amendments to existing law as germane) with id. § 28.45 (bill too limited to accommodate amendment to existing law).   In the classic 1921 statement, the Chair said it

> does not think that the general rule can be laid down that where several portions of a law are amended by a bill reported by a committee, it is not in any case in order to amend another section of the [law] not included in the bill reported by the committee, nor does the Chair think that the opposite rule can be laid down and rigidly applied in every instance.   The Chair thinks that a question of this kind must be determined in every instance in the light of the facts which are presented in the case.

VIII Cannon § 2938, at 503-04.

[309]   121 Cong. Rec. 3596 (1975).

matters unchanged by the law, such as approval <u>vel</u>
<u>non</u> by Congress of the finalized railroad system
plan.   A bill changed the Airport and Airway
Development Act "in several respects and with some
depth and breadth,"[310] making amendments germane
even to a particular innovative development
program in the Act not touched by the bill.
     An important closely related problem concerns
"permanent" amendments of "temporary" bills.[311]
The rise of multiyear and annual authorizations
(as opposed to permanent ones) and of "sunset"
provisions increases the frequency with which the
House   passes   "temporary"   bills   --   limited-term
authorizations and extensions.   Thus, what types
of   amendments   can   be   tacked   onto   such   bills
determines a significant part of what can be done
on the floor.   Temporary or limited laws,[312] or
bills that merely reauthorize agency funding like
the annual Justice authorization, do not open the
whole permanent law to amendment or repeal.[313]
However, when a bill extends an existing law which
would otherwise expire -- a "sunsetted" law -- the
bill opens that law up to amendment.   To a bill
extending   the   term   of   the   Federal   Energy

---

[310]   124 Cong. Rec. 29488 (1978).

[311]   House Manual § 799.   For discussion of the role of
periodic   authorizations,   see   the   chapter   on   the
authorization-appropriation cycle.

[312]   Temporary debt limit increases, do not make germane
amendments that would make permanent changes in law.   119
Cong. Rec. 36240 (1973)(debt limit); VIII Cannon § 2913 (to
a one year increase in salaries, a two year increase is not
germane).

[313]   House Manual § 799; 28 Deschler §§ 29, 30, 32.   To a
bill reauthorizing the Veteran's Administration to set loan
interest rates, an amendment was not germane to adjust
various existing laws regarding the VA's life insurance
funds.   The particular reauthorization "d[id] not 'extend
existing law' in the sense that it reenacts it and could
possibly open up the basic law to modification."   119 Cong.
Rec. 27343 (1969).   See VIII Cannon § 2949 (bill amending
law in one respect does not make germane an amendment
repealing the law).

Administration, an amendment was germane which proposed an extensive reorganization of the agency. In the case of such an extension, "the basic law which created the [agency] is before the committee [of the Whole]."[314]

I. HOUSE PROCEDURE AFTER COMMITTEE OF THE WHOLE

Completion of Committee of the Whole Proceedings

Section by section, the Committee on the Whole thus works through amendments and completes or closes debate. Proceedings in Committee of the Whole may be interrupted either momentarily for various reasons,[315] or longer to do some other activity (e.g., take up the Consent Calendar), by the Committee "rising" (that is, for proceedings to resume in the "House"). An informal momentary rising occurs with a few words.[316] For a longer rising, the bill manager moves that the Committee rise, a motion almost invariably adopted by voice vote. "[T]he chairman [of the Committee of the Whole] reports that the Committee of the Whole have, according to order, had under their consideration such a matter, and have made progress therein; but not having had time to go through the same,"[317] he explains that the Committee has "come to no resolution thereon."
    The majority manager makes the basic

---

[314]   122 Cong. Rec. 16025 (1976). See VIII Cannon 2941 (Committee of the Whole, overruling Chair, decides that an extension of the Federal Radio Act opens that act to amendment), overruling V Hinds 5806.

[315]   The Committee of the Whole may rise at any "time to receive special messages, as messages from the President and the Senate. It may rise and report any disorderly words spoken during debate. It may rise to adjourn until the next day's sitting." F. Riddick (1949) at 225.

[316]   House Manual § 563.

[317]   House Manual § 333.

decisions previously discussed, of whether to stop
proceedings in Committee of the Whole along the
way, either just to allow other business to be
conducted in the House, or strategically to gain
time to regroup or prepare. The House then goes
about its other business. When the House finishes
whatever it wishes to do, either the same day, or
on a later day, the Speaker simply announces again
that, pursuant to the special rule, the House is
declared resolved into Committee of the Whole to
consider the bill.   "Generally, the Committee
rises at the close of each day and reports the
situation to the House until the particular bill
has been completed; at the next meeting of the
House, it is reconstituted to resume that
unfinished business."[318]

When the Committee of the Whole reaches the
end of the bill, it considers any amendments
offered to add new sections at the end. The Chair
asks, "Are there any further amendments?"   For
appropriation bills, at this point, can come test
votes regarding limitation riders.[319]   If there
are no further amendments, the time has come for a
motion to rise (which has its variations),[320] or

---

[318]   Riddick (1949) at 225.

[319]   House Rule XXI(2)(d) regarding this is discussed in the
chapter on appropriations.

[320]   Its variations include:

> Consideration of the bill in Committee having been
> finished, the motion to rise is in order, and it is not
> debatable. The motion to rise has precedence over a
> motion to proceed to the consideration of another
> measure; the simple motion to rise has precedence over
> the motion to amend; and the motion to report a measure
> back to the House with recommendations that it be
> recommitted has precedence over a motion to rise and
> report with recommendations that the bill pass. The
> Committee may make a report to the House with
> recommendations that the measure be postponed; such a
> recommendation has precedence over a recommendation
> that it pass.

Riddick (1949) at 226. Rule XV(b) provides that "[a] quorum
(footnote continued)

for the Chair to follow boilerplate in a special rule and intone, "if not, then under the rule, the Committee rises."[321]   Following the ancient formula, "the chairman rises, the Speaker resumes the chair,"[322] the House mace is raised, and the Chairman informs the Speaker that the Committee reported back the bill, with amendments. When the Chairman has reported, the Speaker announces pursuant to the boilerplate in the special rule, if there has been one:[323] "the previous question shall be considered as ordered on the bill and amendments thereto to final passage without intervening motion except one motion to recommit."   Absent the ordering of the previous question, all kinds of motions would be in order.[324]

There then ensue opportunities for three steps in the House: the separate vote on amendments, the motion to recommit, and the vote

---

shall not be required in Committee of the Whole for agreement to a motion that the Committee rise."

[321]   Special rules include the boilerplate language that "[a]t the conclusion of the consideration of the bill for amendment, the Committee shall rise and report the bill to the House with such amendments as may have been adopted . . . ." The language in the special rule avoids a motion to rise much as the rule language described earlier avoids a motion to go into Committee.   Absent such boilerplate (such as with appropriation bills taken up without a special rule), the process is as Jefferson described: "[I]f they have gone through the matter referred to them, a member moves that the committee may rise, and the chairman report their proceedings to the House; which being resolved, the chairman rises . . . ." House Manual § 334.

[322]   House Manual § 334.

[323]   Where there is no special rule, such as on appropriation bills taken up without one, the bill manager moves the previous question.

[324]   Motions to table, to postpone, and to offer further amendments would be in order until the manager moved a motion for the previous question. As in previously noted boilerplate language of special rules, the effect of this is to obviate the need for an actual motion.

on final passage.   Each of these steps involves important rules and tactics.

Separate Vote on Amendments

At this point the procedure first occurs for a "separate vote on amendments."   Although the Committee of the Whole has sifted the amendments to the bill, technically no amendments have yet been adopted.   Only the House, not a committee -- not even the Committee of the Whole -- can formally amend bills.   All a committee can do, all the Committee of the Whole has done, is recommend to the House that it amend the bill.   Immediately after announcing that under the rule the previous question has been ordered, the Speaker asks if anyone demands a separate vote on any particular amendment (in the form it was perfected in Committee of the Whole).   If no one asks for a separate vote, all the amendments adopted by Committee of the Whole are put before the House en bloc.   Typically, the House adopts them all in one voice vote.[325]

A Member may choose to demand a separate vote when the vote in Committee of the Whole for an amendment was close; in effect, the separate vote serves as the equivalent of a motion to reconsider.   Such a second chance to defeat an amendment can "giv[e] a double advantage to the [majority] leadership."[326]   An amendment by the minority or bill opponents may get adopted in Committee of the Whole that surprises the leadership.   The separate vote procedure gives the leadership at least some time, and sometimes several days, to prepare for an attempt to reverse the adoption, by rounding up absentees or even changing votes the second time.

This process has some weaknesses.   The adoption of one amendment in Committee of the Whole may trigger the adoption of others, and a reversal by separate vote thus comes too late to prevent that trend from running its course.[327]

---

[325]   See House Manual §§ 336-337.

[326]   Froman at 85.
(footnote continued)

Moreover, leadership lobbying for Members to change their votes grates on Members' sensibilities, because it requires a complete about-face of their vote on an identical proposition in a short period of time. Accordingly, while "if the amendment is particularly serious . . . the House will reverse the action taken by the Committee of the Whole," "[i]t should be noted, however, that rarely are amendments adopted in Committee of the Whole defeated in the House."[328]

The fact that the House is proceeding under the previous question means that a "separate vote" occurs without further debate. It also means that only the amendments adopted in Committee of the Whole come up for the separate vote. An amendment defeated in Committee of the Whole, even by a cliff-hanger vote, cannot be brought up in the House because of the previous question procedure. Finally, House precedents only allow separate votes on amendments as perfected (unless a special rule provides otherwise).[329]   No

---

[327]   For example, on a standby gas rationing bill in 1979, an amendment to reinstate restrictive review proceedures for the rationing plan was unexpectedly adopted in Committee of the Whole when offered by a liberal Republican. The House leadership then chose the path for response:

> An amendment approved in the Committee of the Whole may be voted on again in the House after the amending process is completed. Alternatively, one can negate the effect of an amendment by passing another carefully drafted amendment. The leaders decided to adopt the latter course because they did not want to wait until the amendment process was completed . . . . "We felt it important to establish a pattern of victory." . . . The committee staff quickly drafted . . . [and] the majority leader offered the amendment . . . . [which] was approved 234 to 189 . . . . The next day . . . the House passed the bill.

Sinclair at 168-69.

[328]   Froman at 85.

[329]   If the Committee on the Whole amends amendment A by (footnote continued)

separate   votes   occur   on   second-degree
amendments.[330] Once the House completes action on
the amendments reported by the Committee of the
Whole,   the   Speaker   puts   the   question   "on
engrossment and third reading of the bill."[331]
Third reading, under Rule XX, is by title only,
and very rarely does anyone demand a vote on the
question of engrossment.[332]

---

adopting a perfecting amendment A-1, in the House the
separate amendment procedure is only on whether to accept
amendment A as amended by A-1. Amendment A in its original
(unamended by A-1) form cannot be resuscitated.

[330]   The Committee of the Whole can adopt an amendment in
the nature of a substitute as amended, and in fact, it
frequently does so when a committee reports the bill with an
amendment in the nature of a substitute.   This would
virtually eliminate the separate vote procedure, as the
Committee of the Whole only reports the bill to the House
with one amendment -- the amendment in the nature of a
substitute, as amended.   Accordingly, when a committee
reports a bill with an amendment in the nature of a
substitute, frequently the special rule includes language
that a separate vote may be demanded on amendments to the
amendment in the nature of a substitute.   In that event,
during the separate vote procedure, the individual
amendments adopted in Committee of the Whole may be voted on
again. See Deschler 27 § 34.

[331]   In Jefferson's time, this was "the main trial of
strength between [the bill's] friends and its opponents."
House Manual § 429.   After engrossment and before third
reading, any amendments to the preamble are offered. House
Manual § 414.   The old rule had allowed Members to demand a
delay while the engrossed copy was physically prepared. It
was invoked for example, during consideration of the Civil
Rights Bill of 1960, D. Berman, A Bill Becomes a Law 111-12
(2d ed. 1967), and again during consideration of the Civil
Rights Bill of 1964, Froman at 85-86, by which time the
House leadership had had enough.   In 1965 the language
allowing a delay for physical preparation was deleted from
the rule. Id.

[332]   Engrossment consists of preparing the certified copy of
the legislation as it has finally been approved by one House
of Congress. (It contrasts with enrollment, which occurs
after both Houses approve the bill.) The Clerk of the House
(footnote continued)

Motion to Recommit

There then ensues the opportunity for a
motion to recommit, a flexible instrument for
either killing or amending a bill. In this motion
the minority party possesses one of its most
important formal procedural prerogatives under the
House rules. Former Minority Leader John Rhodes
(R-Ariz.) noted in 1981, during the debate on the
rule for the key budget reconciliation bill, that
"I have known for 28 years that the motion to
recommit is probably the best weapon that the
minority has."[333] As Speaker Gillett said in
1919: "the whole purpose of the motion to recommit
is to provide a record vote on the program of the
minority."[334] This makes the motion a "safety
valve" of House procedure, allowing the minority,
however else it is restricted, a chance to put
forth a germane alternative version of a bill.
The House first safeguarded the motion in 1848,[335]
then cemented it in 1909.[336]

---

may be authorized by unanimous consent to make technical
corrections in the engrossment of a bill, such as by
correcting punctuation, section and title numbers, and cross
references. Deschler 24 §§ 8-9.

[333] 127 Cong. Rec. H3373 (daily ed. June 25, 1981).

[334] See Cannon at 307.

[335] In 1845, when the joint resolution for the admission of
Texas was under consideration, the Whigs sought by motion to
recommit to amend the resolution to include a proviso
prohibiting slavery. The Democratic majority overruled the
Speaker and held on an appeal that the motion for the
previous question could cut the minority off even from
offering a motion to recommit. When the Whigs were in the
majority in 1848, they retained their distaste for what had
happened to them, and wrote into the rule that the previous
question would not bar the motion to recommit. See R. E.
Damon, The Standing Rules of the U.S. House of
Representatives 198 (1971).

(footnote continued)

When the moment comes when the motion is in
order, the Speaker looks first to minority members
of the committee of jurisdiction, in order of
seniority, to make the motion.[337] The mover of
the motion to recommit must qualify by being able
to say, if asked, that he is opposed to the bill
(at least in its "present form").[338] The offerors
of the motion can offer one of two kinds:
straight, or with instructions. The "straight"
motion simply recommits the bill to the committee
of jurisdiction. It amounts to a gentle way to
kill the bill at least temporarily (with the
possibility left open that the committee could
report the bill again, perhaps with amendments to
make it more palatable).

More important, the motion to recommit "with
instructions" amounts to a means of amending the
bill. The instructions usually direct the
committee of jurisdiction to report the bill
"forthwith" with amendments. The amendment may be
short and simple, or may be a whole minority
alternative to the bill -- a large and complex
amendment in the nature of a substitute.

---

[336] In the latter year, the House formally stated in Rule
XVI(4) that "[a]fter the previous question shall have been
ordered . . . one motion to recommit shall be in order, and
the Speaker shall give preference in recognition for such
purpose to a Member who is opposed to the bill . . . ."
This excepted the motion to recommit from the Speaker's
otherwise unchallengeable discretion in recognition.

The provision was put forth as a compromise move by
Speaker "Czar" Cannon in an (unsuccessful) attempt to head
off insurgency. House Committee on Rules, 97th Cong., 2d
Sess. A History of the Committee on Rules 86 (Comm. Print
1983).

[337] House Republican Manual at 209 n.l. If no minority
Member on the committee wishes to offer such a motion, the
Speaker then has discretion regarding who he will recognize
off the committee, allowing games to be played sometimes;
for example, knowing that a minority Member wishes to offer
a motion to recommit with instructions that will embarrass
the majority party, the Speaker may recognize some other
minority Member to offer a straight motion to recommit.

[338] House Manual § 788.

Considerable discretion and power lies in the hands of the Member who decides what kind of motion to recommit will be made. In essence, that Member stakes the minority party's position on his choice.

Rule XVI(4) provides for ten minutes of debate, five minutes per side, on a motion to recommit with instructions (which may be extended by special rule), although pursuant to a 1985 amendment, the majority manager can extend the debate to half an hour on a side.[339] The previous question must be separately moved on the motion to recommit; a recorded vote is usually foregone, but can be obtained,[340] and the previous question must be defeated for altering of any amendments included in the motion.[341] If the House adopts

---

[339]   Under the previous question, straight (without instructions) motions to recommit are not debated. Debate on motions to recommit had been allowed by special rule provisions for tax and similar bills where recommittal might be the key test vote; also, in 1984, the minority had rewritten the entire federal criminal code on a motion to recommit that had gotten only ten minutes of debate.

[340]   It is possible (but rare) to demand a recorded vote on the motion for the previous question, and even to defeat it and amend the motion. The amendment need only be germane to the bill, not to the original motion, and it can add or change instructions. Usually, the Chair simply recites that "the previous question is ordered" with no vote.

[341]   If the majority does not like the proposed amendments in the motion to recommit, it can offer amendments to those amendments, which the minority can prevent if and only if the previous question is voted on the minority version. Deschler 23 § 14.6 - 14.7. A paradoxical example occurred on the Omnibus Budget Reconciliation Act of 1981. The Republicans had won their version of the rule and of the bill. Nevertheless, because the Republicans were the minority party, priority in offering a motion to recommit belonged to them. Thus, a Republican Member, Representative Claudine Schneider (R-R.I.), perhaps the only Republicans who could qualify by saying that she opposed the bill, offered a motion to recommit with instructions. Majority Leader Wright sought to amend Representative Schneider's motion to include some majority-party instructions, but the (footnote continued)

the motion to recommit with instructions to report forthwith with an amendment, the chair of the committee of jurisdiction immediately[342] comes forward to be recognized and announces that the bill is reported with an amendment (the amendment in the recommittal instructions), and the House votes on that amendment.

The motion to recommit has taken on renewed importance primarily because of the increasing use of complex restrictive special rules.[343] A complex restrictive rule may not allow the minority to offer some amendments it wants. The minority can then put forth its amendments in the form of a motion to recommit with instructions. "[I]n a 'closed rule' scenario it can be the only opportunity for the minority to amend a bill."[344] Thus, for example, when the Ways and Means Committee brings a tax bill to the floor

---

motion for the previous question was adopted, cutting him off from such amending.   127 Cong. Rec. H4034 (daily ed. June 26, 1981).

The minority mover of the motion to recommit may accommodate others by yielding for the offering of amendments to the motion to recommit, prior to the moving of the previous question. House Manual § 788.

[342] "Instructions to report 'forthwith' accompanying a motion to recommit must be complied with immediately." Deschler 23 § 15.2.   The committee does not convene; the chair does not consider the amendment; all that happens is that the committee chair immediately puts forth the amendment in the motion to recommit.

[343] In contrast, before 1970, the motion to recommit mattered most because it allowed a recorded vote on minority amendments defeated in Committee of the Whole (where no recorded vote had been allowed).   The House Republican Manual states at 212: "With the advent of recorded teller votes in the Committee of the Whole, the motion to recommit seemed to have lost some of its earlier importance.   In recent years however, the ability of individual Members to spontaneously offer amendments has been more limited, so the importance of their parliamentary process has been re-established."

[344] House Republican Manual at 212.

under a closed rule, the minority can offer a substitute for the bill in the form of a motion to recommit with amendments. Paradoxically, since the minority has priority in offering the motion to recommit, this means that "the opposition has an opportunity to amend the bill but the proponents do not."[345]

This may lead to some strategic jockeying within the minority party: a minority Member may make a motion to recommit that cuts off other potential motions that would represent more aggressive minority strategies. For example, in 1984, the House took up an ethics resolution to reprimand Representative Hansen, who had been convicted and sentenced for false statements on his financial disclosure form. Some of his sympathizers might have wanted to offer a motion to recommit with instructions that would divert attention to the less serious but somewhat analogous alleged infractions of the financial disclosure rules by Representative Geraldine Ferraro (D-N.Y.), the Democratic vice presidential candidate. However, Representative Barber Conable (R-N.Y.), a senior minority member on the ethics committee, firmly opposed to such maneuvers, and invoked his seniority to offer the motion to recommit. He offered only a straight motion, cutting off the sympathizers' options to seek to recommit with instructions; the House defeated the straight motion on a voice vote.[346]

---

[345]   Froman at 87.

[346]   "Mr. Hansen's is the only case before us today, Consequently, any . . . attempt to draw a parallel now to any other matter involving any other Member is . . . unfair to that Member . . . [and] premature and I believe inappropriate . . . ." 130 Cong. Rec. H8059-60 (daily ed. July 31, 1984) (Rep. Conable); see id. at 8062 (vote on motion).

Technically, Representative Conable qualified, as he voted "no" on the reprimand. Id. at H 8063. It may be questioned as to whether that upright Congressman voted no out of real sympathy with the convicted Member, or did so as Members sometimes seem to -- in order to qualify to offer a motion to recommit -- in this case preserving the House (footnote continued)

The minority does not have complete freedom on the motion to recommit. As with any amendments, the amendments it proposes through a motion to recommit must be germane, although, as discussed in the section on germaneness, the motion need only be germane to the bill as a whole, and as amended; for bills which emerge from Committee of the Whole with diverse and broad amendments, this test may therefore be a relaxed one. The House subjects recommittal instruction amendments to the other House rules, such as the rule against legislation on an appropriation bill.[347] Moreover, the most important limitation on the motion to recommit is simply that the motion has the reputation of being the minority motion, and it is disfavored for majority Members to vote for it.

Thus, few such motions ever get adopted. An observer found that in 1964 only one bill had been recommitted.[348] However, on occasion, "[b]y skillfully phrasing the motion to recommit, with instructions, it was possible to detach members from the majority coalition and thereby affect the outcome."[349] In 1984, for example, the Republicans attached an entire revamping of the federal criminal code to the continuing resolution on a motion to recommit, skillfully timing that "anticrime" proposition to confront the House on the eve of the election.

Rule XI(4) prohibits a special rule "which

---

ethics debate from the injection of presidential campaign politics.

[347] House Manual § 808. Ordinarily, House rules would prohibit further amendments when the House has adopted an amendment in the nature of a substitute, but when a rule includes the boilerplate language making in order "a motion to recommit with instructions," this language is held to waive that restriction. Deschler 23 § 15.4, 15.6.

[348] Froman at 87.

[349] Damon at 235. In 1977, a motion to recommit succeeded in attaching a provision for a legislative veto to the Federal Trade Commission reauthorization -- 123 Cong. Rec. 33624 (1977) -- an early harbinger of what soon became repeatedly expressed antipathy to FTC rulemaking.

would prevent the motion to recommit from being made as provided in clause 4 of Rule XVI." Thus, the majority cannot adopt a special rule cutting off the motion to recommit.[350]   While the Rules Committee has the power to curb what the minority may offer by way of a motion to recommit with instructions, that step is not taken very often.[351]

Final Passage

After the opportunity for a motion to recommit, the House finally faces the vote on final passage.   While this may be the focus of great effort and planning in assembling votes, the

---

[350]   A 1912 incident reinforced the rule.   When the Rules Committee reported a rule that did not provide for a motion to recommit, even the Speaker supported the immediate sharp objection of the minority leader.   "[T]he inexperienced majority on Rules [had] overstepped its authority and was forced to retreat."   House Committee on Rules, supra, at 103.

[351]   It was taken in 1934, when the rule for a New Deal bill precluded amendments either in Committee of the Whole or in the House.   House Manual § 729b.   That was for a unique bill.   See House Committee on Rules, 97th Cong., 2d Sess. A History of the Committee on Rules 129 (Comm. Print 1983).

When the Democrats offered their restrictive rule for the Omnibus Budget Reconciliation Act of 1981, it not only restricted what amendments could be offered, but what motion to recommit could be offered.   Outraged Republicans denounced the rule.   Former Minority Leader Rhodes, drawing on his 28 years of experience, stated "I have never seen this happen before."   127 Cong. Rec. H3373 (daily ed. June 25, 1981).   Representative Conable, the ranking minority Member on the Ways and Means Committee, said that "the power of the majority" should be "exercised with the restraint which is necessary and traditional in a democratic republic like ours . . . .   It is not restraint if the majority specifies what will be in the motion to recommit, the last recourse of the minority."   Id.   The Republicans defeated that Democratic special rule, and adopted their own without such a restriction on the motion to recommit.

procedure itself could not be simpler. The Speaker just announces that the question is on the passage of the bill. A recorded vote occurs if demanded and adequately seconded.

One observer noted that "[f]or the overwhelming majority of measures that reach a vote on final passage on the floor, approval in some form by the House or Senate has been a foregone conclusion."[352] He explained: "The final outcome of the legislative process in Congress rarely is in doubt. During the 95th and 96th Congresses, the House passed 3,013 measures and defeated 72; in the Senate, 2,626 measures were passed and only 8 were defeated."[353] To some extent, those figures overstate the assurance for major scheduled bills of final passage,[354] but real uncertainty over final passage is still very much the exception rather than the rule.

Once the result of the vote is announced, almost invariably the Speaker announces that "a motion to reconsider is laid on the table." However, any Member who voted with the victorious side may offer a motion to reconsider. It is rarely offered except when the vote is extremely close.

---

[352]   Bach at 573-74.

[353]   Id. at 573.

[354]   These figures reflect inflated success because so many of the bills passed are minor matters that come up under unanimous consent, such as commemmorative days, or that come up under suspension of the rules and do not even involve a recorded vote. Defeated bills are much more likely to be not only controversial, but important. Also, even after the leadership schedules a bill for floor consideration, once the bill seems headed for defeat in either House or for Senate filibuster, the leadership is likely to pull that bill without seeking a vote on final passage.

7
Running the Senate[1]

A. OVERVIEW AND HISTORY

Balance Between Members and Leadership

The Senate's allocation of authority to its
leadership differs sharply from that of the
House.   In the House, the majority leadership
controls the agenda fairly tightly, determining

---

[1] Sources cited frequently in this chapter include Peabody,
"Senate Party Leadership: From the 1950s to the 1980s," in
Understanding Congressional Leadership (ed. F. H. Mackaman
1981) ("Peabody, Senate Party Leadership: From the 1950s to
the 1980s"); Ehrenhalt, In the Senate of the '80s, Team
Spirit has Given Way to the Rule of Individuals, 40 Cong. Q.
Week. Rep. 2175 (1982) (Senate of the '80s'); Davidson,
"Senate Leaders: Janitors for an Untidy Chamber?", in
Congress Reconsidered (3d ed. by L. C. Dodd & B. I.
Oppenheimer 1985) (Davidson); Munk, Origin and Development
of the Party Floor Leadership in the United States Senate, 2
Capitol Studies J. 23 (1974) (Munk); D. J. Rothman, Politics
and Power: The United States Senate 1869-1901 (1966)
(Rothman); Majority and Minority Leaders of the Senate: S.
Doc. No. 12, 97th Cong., 1st Sess. (1981)(prepared by Dr.
Riddick); Keith, "The Use of Unanimous Consent in the
Senate", in Commission on the Operation of the Senate, 94th
Cong., 2d Sess., Committees and Senate Procedures (1977)
(Keith).

what individual Members may act upon.   In the
Senate, the majority leadership must consult with
the minority leadership, and both must accommodate
the individual Senators who can have a large say
in the agenda.   As a matter of daily scheduling,
this institutional style puts on the leadership a
major   task   in   accommodating   each   Senator   on
scheduling of bills, votes, speeches, and other
matters.   In essence, the Senate allows each
Senator's intense time burdens -- her large number
of constituents to reach, national audiences to
address, and issues to cover -- to triumph over
central control and regularity.
     Looking   beyond   scheduling,   on   other   key
matters   the   individual   Senators   possess   major
procedural resources lacking in the more rigidly
controlled House.   The most famous, of course, is
the   filibuster   --   the   ability   of   individual
Senators to delay a measure, often even to kill
it, despite its having majority support, simply by
talking about it without stopping.   The Senate
requires "unanimous consent" to do almost anything
-- giving each of the hundred Senators power, by
objecting   to   the   matters   requiring   unanimous
consent,   virtually   to   bring   the   process   to   a
halt.   Less well known, but very important, the
Senate lacks a germaneness rule, meaning that
Senators can bring up whatever issues they wish as
amendments to any bill on the floor, absent an
agreement to forego this right.   Armed by these
rights, individual Senators can stake claims to
agenda power against the desires of the leadership
and of a majority in the chamber.
     In the 1940s and 1950s, observers considered
the   Senate   to   be   run   by   an   inner   circle,   a
bipartisan (but largely conservative) "club," of
senior   committee   chairs   and   ranking   minority
members.   The club was led in the later part of
the period by the legendary Majority Leader (later
President),   Lyndon   Johnson   (D-Tex.).   Junior
Members and outsiders, particularly liberals, were
quite subordinate.[2]

---

[2]   A retrospective comment was that in "the 1950s, [the]
Senate was run with an iron hand by a small group of barons
led by Lyndon Johnson as the majority leader."   Tolchin,
Senators Assail Anarchy in New Chamber of Equals, New York
(footnote continued)

In the subsequent 30 years, that "inner club" system ended.   As a noted columnist observed in the title of an essay, "In the Senate of the '80s, Team Spirit has Given Way to the Rule of Individuals."[3]   In 1984, the New York Times noted that "[a] decade of diffusion of authority has steadily eroded the powers of seniority and leadership, creating near anarchy."[4]   Then-Minority Whip Alan Cranston (D-Calif.) commented that "[a] lot of leadership is just housekeeping now . . . .   The weapons to keep people in line just aren't there."[5]

Senators' emphasis on individual prerogatives ranged from filibustering on the eve of the hitherto sacrosanct Christmas vacation in 1982, to a large-scale frustration of the majority party agenda through filibuster in 1987-88.   In some years, Senators refused to yield on controversial non-germane amendments blocking the most vital funding bills.   In what was perhaps hyperbole but reflected the comments of many, Senator Dan Quayle (R-Ind.) commented, "We are witnessing the disintegration of the U.S. Senate."[6]

Still, such individuation does not mean that the Senate suffers yet from anarchy.   The authority of the Senate leadership varies from Congress to Congress with the chamber's balance and the leaders' personalities, but even faced with the strong individual tendencies, Majority Leaders Robert Byrd (D-W.Va.) in 1977-80 and 1987-88, Howard Baker (R-Tenn.) in 1981-84, Robert Dole

---

Times, Nov. 25, 1984, at 40.   For the contemporary description, see W. S. White, Citadel: The Story of the United States Senate (1956); J. S. Clark, et al., The Senate Establishment (1963).

[3]   Senate of the '80s.

[4]   Tolchin, Senators Assail Anarchy in New Chamber of Equals, New York Times, Nov. 25, 1984, at 40.

[5]   Senate of the '80s at 2181.

[6]   Tolchin, supra, at 1.   As Senator Dale Bumpers (D-Ark.) commented, "Unless we recognize that things are out of control and procedures have to be changed . . . we'll never be an effective legislative body again."   Ehrenhalt at 2182.

(R-Kan.) in 1985-86, and George Mitchell (D-Maine) after 1989 developed means to direct their chamber. These included complex unanimous consent agreements, use of the motion to table against amendments, swift cloture responses to filibusters, and trimming back of some of the deference to individual Senators such as "holds," in combination with the essential leadership qualities of diplomacy, patience, and persuasiveness. The Senate equips its leadership with a number of subtle means of procedural direction. To understand the balance between leadership and individuals, Senate procedure can be traced through several historic movements: the rise of the leadership, and of unanimous consent agreements, and the evolution over time of filibustering and cloture. Each of these points will be addressed in greater detail below, but a general overview now will assist in understanding the Senate procedure as a system.

Overview

The particular role of the Majority Leader and other leadership figures will be discussed in detail in the next section, and their agenda-setting mechanisms in the next chapter. This section provides an overview of the system in historic context. Historically, the Senate refused to confer power on its formal chair, the Vice President, and conferral of power on an informal leader occurred late. "[I]dentifiable Senate leadership dates only from the late nineteenth century, and in modern form from Woodrow Wilson's day,"[7] with formal choice of designated "leaders" only in the 1910s and 1920s. These leaders have a purely political component, as the spokesman for their party in key respects: for example, Majority Leader Dole took a lead in formulating a Republican budget proposal in 1985. This role involves acting as a conduit to the President, and serving as a focus for media attention.[8]

---

[7] Davidson at 226.

(footnote continued)

Regarding procedure, the Majority Leader, by custom and by his party's support, directs the basic steps for moving the Senate's business -- both the scheduling of legislation and the daily direction of the floor. The Majority Leader, together with the Minority Leader, provides direction by formulating formal requests submitted to the Senate for "unanimous consent," which guide the floor. These include the unanimous consent request (or, when necessary, the motion) to "proceed to consider" a bill -- that is, to take up a particular bill, the request (or motion) that most essentially defines the Senate's agenda. Complex "unanimous consent agreements" also define how each bill will be considered, such as what amendments will be in order. This does not mean the Majority Leader invariably succeeds in his unanimous consent requests, or wields authority comparable to what the House leadership does through special rules, just that no one else will conduct these steps except the Majority Leader.

At the level of daily functioning, the Senate operates with great flexibility. On a typical day, it may proceed from early speeches, through partial consideration of one bill, to passage of minor legislation, on to partial consideration of another bill, through consideration of a nomination of an executive officer or back to the first bill, and so on from matter to matter until recessing in the evening. The Senate conspicuously lacks many of the House's firm scheduling mechanisms, such as the House's pattern of persisting on one pending major bill at a time, and the House's rules setting aside calendar days.

In considering each particular major bill, the Senate also follows a more flexible procedure

---

8   These components depend heavily on the leader's character and personal relation to his party and President. For example, although Senator Mike Mansfield (D-Mont.) held the majority leadership for sixteen years, from 1961-77, he preferred not to seize the limelight. He allowed Presidents Kennedy and Johnson to define, and to a considerable extent manage, their legislative programs themselves; he rarely took a highly visible lead in opposition to Presidents Nixon and Ford. In essence, he portrayed himself as just one Senator among many, chiefly with a function of coordinating rather than directing.

than the House, without the adoption of a
procedural instrument as elaborate as the special
rule or use of a precise system like the five-
minute rule.   Rather, first, the Senate proceeds
to consider the bill, either by unanimous consent
or on the Majority Leader's motion.   To the extent
that it adopts any procedural instrument, it
adopts a unanimous consent agreement (also
referred to as "UCAs" or "time agreements"), most
often in a form proposed by the Majority Leader
(as modified to accommodate the minority party and
individual Senators).   While UCAs vary
considerably, they tend to have certain common
elements.[9]   Necessarily, a time agreement is less
restrictive than a special rule can be, since no
UCA can be adopted over even a single Senator's
objection.

Then, either with or without a UCA, once the
Senate proceeds to consider the bill, it engages
freely in debating and amending.   Debate and
amendments are intermingled without time limits
(other than those provided by unanimous consent
agreements) such as apply to House general debate
and debate under the five-minute rule, and there
are no motions to close or limit debate or for the
previous question (other than cloture, discussed
separately, which is largely restricted to
filibuster situations).   Debating and amending
simply continue until no Senator has any more to
offer.

The Senate's underlying loose procedure dates
from the nineteenth century; the structuring role
of the leadership evolved largely in the
twentieth.   In the nineteenth century, the slower
pace of business seems generally to have allowed
the Senate simply to work through whatever bills
its committees reported, at whatever pace the
Senators wished.[10]   Some guidance, largely behind

---

[9]   These can include specification of a time for beginning
of consideration; time limits on debates on the bill itself,
and on amendments and motions; restrictions on amendments
(such as allowing only specific named amendments plus any
other germane amendments); and a time for a vote on final
passage.

[10]   Even as late as the early 1920s, "[t]he Senate was
(footnote continued)

the scenes, came from the steering committees of
each party.[11]   The Senate leadership visibly grew
in importance from the beginning of the twentieth
century, and ultimately Lyndon Johnson as Majority
Leader in the 1950s set the pace for leadership-
pushed drive toward completion of business rather
than speechifying.   In the 1960s and early 1970s,
as the "Inner Club" broke down, and in the 1980s,
as the system sometimes seemed to move toward
anarchy in some respects, the Senate accepted
increased prerogatives of the leadership and floor
managers as a counterbalance.

The procedures for filibusters and clotures
have evolved, setting the ultimate balance in each
era between individual Senators and institutional
control.   Filibustering -- the tactic of talking
without end and otherwise delaying a bill, perhaps
to death -- first became a major factor in the
late nineteenth century.   In 1917, the Senate
adopted a cloture rule allowing a vote to end a
filibuster, but filibusters remained relatively
infrequent -- and successful invocation of cloture
remained extremely infrequent -- until the early
1960s, when the Senate overcame, through cloture,
filibusters of the key civil rights bills.

In the 1970s and 1980s, the patterns of
filibuster and cloture evolved rapidly.
Filibusters occurred more often and on more varied
matters, including categories such as minor bills
and necessary funding bills.   In 1975, the Senate
made it easier to vote cloture by reducing the
necessary vote to 60.   However, on occasion
Senators began using various delaying tactics for
a "post-cloture filibuster," which let them delay

---

rarely under time pressure," and indeed, Senator Daniel P.
Moynihan (D-N.Y.) commented regarding the New Deal era that
until then "[t]here was nobody, for practical purposes, in
the history of the U.S. Senate who had ever run out of
time." Oppenheimer, "Changing Time Constraints on Congress:
Historical Perspectives on the Use of Cloture," in Congress
Reconsidered (3d ed. by L.C. Dodd & B.I. Oppenheimer 1985),
at 402-3 (quoting a speech by Senator Moynihan).   A more
detailed discussion is provided below.

[11]   Starting in the 1910s, formally chosen and designated
party "leaders" began defining, together with those steering
committees, the program and pace of floor business.

a bill even after the Senate voted for cloture. The Senate's difficulties in dealing with "post-cloture" filibusters in the late 1970s and 1980s contributed powerfully to the impression it was out of control.

In the 1980s, Senate floor action came increasingly to be concerned with vital funding bills as "vehicles" for action. Different parties controlled the House and the Senate in 1981-86, making the chambers less than willing to agree on nonvital legislation. Accordingly, Senators focused on vital bills such as appropriations, continuing resolutions, increases in the national debt limit, and budget reconciliation bills as "vehicles" for amendments on a range of issues.

With that overview, the following sections in this chapter address the majority leader and other leadership, the Chair, and the floor mechanics. The next chapter addresses agenda setting, and the following two chapters address floor management and filibusters.

B.   MAJORITY LEADERSHIP

Historic Origins

Senate majority leadership has changed at different times and among different leaders. A recent analyst summed up the Majority Leader as having five roles, which might be further broken down into two types: political (overall relations with his party, President, and media), and procedural (setting the agenda for bill consideration, and daily scheduling).[12]   Perhaps

---

[12]   The full description of the five functions is as follows. First are the three political roles:

> The floor leaders' jobs now embrace the following responsibilities: (1) managing the affairs of the senatorial party . . . (4) serving as a conduit between the Senate, the White House, and the House; and (5) acting as a public voice of the Senate through the media.

(footnote continued)

the best sense of majority leadership can be obtained by looking at its origins and then at recent Majority Leaders, cataloguing separately the political and the procedural roles.

Starting with historic origins and the Majority Leader's political role, that role dates back only to the early twentieth century.[13] "Throughout most of the eighteenth and nineteenth centuries, there was no one leader . . . . Partisan floor leadership was fragmented, decentralized, and occasional."[14]

There are also the two procedural roles:

> (2) scheduling Senate floor business in accord with workload needs and individual senators' desires; (3) monitoring floor deliberations, which includes seeking unanimous consent agreements governing debates and votes.

Davidson at 236.

[13] As Professor (later President) Woodrow Wilson put it in 1885, "No one is the Senator . . . . [N]o one exercises the special trust of acknowledged leadership. The Senate is merely a body of individual critics . . . . " W. Wilson, Congressional Government 147 (Meridian ed. 1956).

In the late nineteenth century, each party chose caucus chairs, but these lacked clear authority; sometimes such chairs led their parties, sometimes they were simply the most senior Senator of that party. Regarding the position of caucus chair, its lack of power, and the general absence of leadership, see Ripley at 25-26; Munk at 27; Rothman at 29-30, 35; but see L. G. McConachie, Congressional Committees 339 (1898) (contending that there have been "powerful" caucus chiefs of ruling majorities in the Senate").

[14] R. L. Peabody, Leadership in Congress: Stability, Succession, and Change 327 (1976). In a more detailed historical account:

Before 1828 especially, parties were weak . . . .

Between 1829 and . . . [1849] party leadership became more significant . . . . Within a few years, however, the fracturing of the prewar parties made the status of
(footnote continued)

Only near the end of the nineteenth century and the beginning of the twentieth did Senate party figures gain control. These figures, notably Senators Nelson W. Aldrich (R-R.I.), William B. Allison (R-Iowa), and Arthur P. Gorman (D-Md.), may have been "called floor leaders without formally bearing a title."[15]   Senator Aldrich and his brethren in nascent leadership based their authority on their personal skills and their control[16] of the party apparatus for committee assignment.   Pyramiding their power, they augmented their authority within the chamber

---

party control dubious . . . .

[A]s soon as the urgencies of [civil] war and reconstruction had passed, party discipline on questions of policy quickly vanished. Between 1869 and 1885 neither party was governed by consistently active and powerful leaders, and periods of activity alternated with periods of lethargy.

R. B. Ripley, Power in the Senate 27 (1969) (footnotes omitted).

[15]   Ripley at 26. By all accounts, the Republican Senators Aldrich ("probably the single most powerful senator in the history of the body," id. at 27), and Allison, and the Democratic Senator Gorman, held considerable power without formal position during this period. Id.; Peabody at 327; Rothman at 44; Munk at 27.

[16]   Their use of the Steering Committee foreshadowed the modern leadership role:

Control of the Steering Committee also confirmed the power of the Allison-Aldrich faction over the Senate business. Arranging the legislative schedule in detail week by week, the committee extended the party leaders' authority unimpaired from the caucus to the chamber. Senators knew that they had to consult the committee before attempting to raise even minor matters. For the first time one of its members managed the legislative proceedings, offering the required resolutions and directing the course of debate.

Rothman at 58; see id. at 48 (leaders' sources of power other than the Steering Committee).

through their external "close relationships with presidents from Benjamin Harrison to William Howard Taft . . . [which arose] because they were known to be the most powerful men in the Senate."[17]

In 1913, the Senate majority party formalized this development in formally choosing a "Majority Leader," namely Senator John W. Kern (D-Ind.), a political ally of newly elected President Woodrow Wilson, who successfully managed Wilson's legislative program.[18] Again in the 1930s and 1940s, first Senator Joseph Robinson (D-Ark.), and then Senator Alben Barkley (D-Ky.), took on highly visible roles as President Franklin D. Roosevelt's majority leaders.[19]

---

[17] Munk at 27.

[18] Munk at 27-28. Purists consider even this date premature, as not until 1920 (for the Democrats) and 1925 (for the Republicans) did the caucuses formally meet with the stated goals of electing party leaders. Majority and Minority Leaders of the Senate, at 4-5. Symbolically, the passage of leadership from the caucus (or conference) chairs to the Majority Leader was signified by who offered the organizational motions at the beginning of the Congress, such as the motion to inform the President that a quorum was present. That shift most clearly occurred in the 1920s. See Majority and Minority Leaders of the Senate, at 21-22 (table of offerors of organizational motions).

The Senate of the 1920s lacked visible Presidential leadership of Congress and corresponding visible legislative leadership. Nominally the Republican leadership controlled the chamber, but "party solidarity . . . no longer existed . . . [with] persistent deadlocks on major issues." Congressional Quarterly, Origins of Congress 224 (1976).

[19] In a famous 1944 incident, Majority Leader Barkley visibly broke with President Roosevelt over the latter's veto of a tax bill. As Allan Drury, then a journalist and later the famed author of Advise and Consent, described hearing Barkley's speech: "[Barkley] has repudiated the President, almost single-handedly guaranteed an override of the veto, greatly strengthened his own prestige, and probably made unhealable the breach between Roosevelt and Congress." A. Drury, A Senate Journal 90 (1963). The next (footnote continued)

As for the historic origins of the leaders' procedural authority, at first and preeminently it lay in the operation of party apparatus such as the steering committees.   However, the Senate augmented the majority leaders' procedural authority in the mid-twentieth century with several informal prerogatives.   First, the Senate firmly established,[20] most clearly by a ruling by the Vice President in 1937, the Majority Leader's prerogative of priority recognition by the Chair, further discussed below.[21]   Second, the Senate had historically proceeded with the use of unanimous consent agreements, also discussed in detail below.   "At some point prior to 1950, the complex unanimous consent agreement became the responsibility of party leadership."[22]   The Senate

---

day, Barkley resigned, and he was immediately reelected leader by the Senate Democratic party.   "[Senator] Elbert Thomas told me later, 'the impression was given [at Barkley's election as leader in 1937] and it has been the impression ever since, that [Barkley] spoke to us for the President.   Now that he has been unanimously elected, he speaks for us to the President.'"   Id. at 93.

[20]   The recognition prerogative may be connected with the leaders' prominent seats: "Since 1927 and 1937, the Democratic Leader and the Republican Leader, respectively, have continuously occupied the center aisle front row seats . . . which places them closest and most directly in the line of vision of the Presiding Officer."   Id. at 14. For Lyndon Johnson's use of the recognition power, see Huitt, infra, at 338.

[21]   The date usually given, as a formal matter, for the Majority Leader's recognition prerogative is Vice President John Nance Garner's key statement in 1937: "The Chair recognizes the Senator from Kentucky because he is the leader on the Democratic side of the Chamber.   He would recognize the Senator from Vermont (Mr. Austin), Acting Republican Leader, in the same way."   Majority and Minority Leaders of the Senate at 14.   See 125 Cong. Rec. 3025 (1979) (Majority Leader Byrd reminding of "the longstanding precedent that was announced, I believe, by Vice President Garner to the effect that the majority leader, if he seeks recognition, he shall be given recognition.").

[22]   Keith at 56.   A fuller discussion of unanimous consent (footnote continued)

incorporated neither these nor lesser leadership prerogatives into its rules, but as customs, the prerogatives seemed to grow firmer over time, just as the precedents were brought together in the authoritative volume on Senate Procedure by Floyd Riddick.

Modern Majority Leaders

Turning from historic to modern times, from the 1950s on a series of Majority Leaders developed the modern contours of the post. Standing apart as an almost legendary figure was Lyndon Johnson, an influential Minority Leader in 1953-54 and a unique Majority Leader in 1955-60. As a 1988 observer noted, Johnson succeeded in forging a complex relationship with President Eisenhower, largely accommodating the popular President while sometimes leading a "loyal" opposition.[23] Johnson's procedural legacy lay in how "efficiency was promoted through the use of

---

[23] Merry, The Prism of History: Johnson was King Among 20th-Century Senate Leaders, 46 Cong. Q. Week. Rep. 982 (1988). Also see chapter 6 of R. Evans & R. Novak, Lyndon B. Johnson: The Exercise of Power (1966); Huitt, Democratic Party Leadership in the Senate, 55 Am. Poli. Sci. Rev. 333, 337-41 (1961).

Johnson's use of leadership, with its media attention and political power, as his springboard for his campaign for President in 1960 raises interesting questions since Senator Kennedy won the nomination in 1960 and relegated Johnson to the Vice Presidency. A host of post-Roosevelt Senators who obtained national nominations -- Harry S. Truman (as Vice President), Richard M. Nixon (both as Vice President and as President), Barry Goldwater (R-Ariz.), Hubert H. Humphrey (D-Minn.) (both as Vice President and as President), George McGovern (D-S.D.), Dole (as Vice President), and Walter Mondale (D-Minn.) (both as Vice President and as President) -- all did so without a formal Senate leadership position. However, this has not stopped Senators who seek presidential nomination from obtaining Senate leadership posts as hoped-for stepping stones, such as Republican Leaders Baker and Dole, and Democratic Whip Alan Cranston (D-Calif.)
(footnote continued)

such devices as unanimous consent agreements, aborted quorum calls and night sessions."[24]   His "Johnson rule" gave important committee assignments to junior Senators, breaking the monopoly that had been a key component of centralized control by the "Inner Club."   His impatience with lengthy Senate debates helped usher in the modern style in which Senators come to the floor infrequently and only for votes and maneuvers, not to listen to each other.

Succeeding Johnson in 1961-76 was Mike Mansfield (D-Mont.).   Mansfield relaxed considerably the tight Johnson hold on the chamber, continuing the trend toward allowing freedom to junior Members,[25] and he consolidated a new procedural prerogative regarding the motion to proceed.[26]   Mansfield's successor as Majority

---

[24]   Congressional Quarterly, Origins and Development of Congress 242 (1976).

[25]   Part of the change came only with the arrival and maturation of the many Democratic freshmen in the class of 1958; these chafed even under the last two difficult years of Johnson's leadership, and began pressing to move up in the early 1960s.   For the classic comparison, see Stewart, "Two Strategies of Leadership: Johnson and Mansfield," in Congressional Behavior (N. W. Polsby ed. 1971), at 61. Although there were numerous aspects of Senator Mansfield's relaxation of control, perhaps the most enduring was the growth during his period of subcommittee chairs as positions of authority, and the allocation to junior Members of seats on key committees.   A more detailed history of his leadership differentiates the early 1960s, when Senate insiders such as Senator Robert Kerr (D-Okla.) maintained a version of the old control, particularly through their continuing control of committee assignments, from the later 1960s, when junior (typically liberal and northern) subcommittee chairs balanced off senior (typically conservative and southern) full committee chairs.   The transition from the old tighter control by senior Senators through the early 1960s, to the later period is treated in M. Foley, The New Senate (1980).

[26]   As discussed below, during his tenure it apparently became accepted that the responsibility of making the unanimous consent request (or motion) to proceed to (footnote continued)

Leader, Senator Byrd, created his own considerable procedural legacy.   Far more than any other Senator of the twentieth century, and perhaps in history, he took a deep personal interest in procedure, and became the master of the Senate's rules and precedents.   Without fanfare, and often without visibility at all, he guided the Senate through a number of modernizing rule changes -- the budget act in 1974 (when he was whip), the committee reorganization in 1977, the tightening of cloture in 1979, and even the beginning of televising in 1986 -- each a carefully crafted step which reformed the process while avoiding backlash such as that which blocked committee reorganizations in the House.[27]

Senator Byrd led the way to full use of complex unanimous consent agreements, which under him became the hallmark of Senate procedure.   He also established most firmly the role of the leader in accommodating the requests of individual Members, a key element in the current individualist climate.   As a contemporary observer notes:

> Robert C. Byrd . . . perform[ed] endless favors for Senate colleagues: keeping them up to date about when a vote was to take place, for example, or postponing the vote if they could not be there.   The "constituent service" that Byrd performed was largely responsible . . . for Byrd's ultimate accession as majority leader.   It has also imposed a burden of personal favors on all leaders in both parties since then.[28]

In 1981-86, the Republican Party became the majority party in the Senate, a major change in a

---

consideration of legislation belonged solely, as a prerogative, to the Majority Leader or his designee.

[27] Each of these is discussed elsewhere.   Senator Byrd also supervised the recodification of the Senate's rules.

[28] Senate of the '80s, at 2181-82.   Senator Mansfield had led the way in such service to individual Senators until he relinquished the task to Senator Byrd in his post first as Secretary to the Conference, and then as Majority Whip.

chamber that had last seen a change of party control in 1955.   The new Majority Leader, Senator Howard Baker (R-Tenn.), continued the dual role developed in the past: key political figure balancing the President, the party, and the media, and procedural helmsman with regard to scheduling legislation and accommodating individual Senators' requirements.[29]   "The wide distribution of power, a trend that began in the 1950s and came to full fruition in the 1960s and 1970s . . . remained intact.   Today's floor leadership is thus a complex and frustrating enterprise . . . ."[30]   At the same time, Senator Baker showed great skill in holding the floor to a semblance of order during times such as postcloture filibusters and endless amending processes for omnibus bills.   Senator Baker's successor as Majority Leader in 1985-86, Senator Robert Dole (R-Kans.), continued the leadership role defined by his predecessor, though with somewhat more partisan disputation at the leadership level.

When the Democrats regained the chamber, Senator Byrd became Majority Leader again in 1987-88.   In light of the Democratic control of both House and Senate, he led the Senate Democrats in setting their own national legislative agenda. Senator Mitchell's assumption of the majority leadership, starting in 1989, continued that pattern.   Rather than await President Bush's program, Mitchell announced upon assuming the leadership that he "would involve all 55 Democrats in agenda-setting exercises for the party and the Senate."[31]

---

[29]   Majority Leader Baker set the agenda in 1981 by which the Republican Party agreed to put the President's budget and tax program first, and leave social issues until later, a plan that secured a series of stunning legislative victories.

On the other hand, as one of Baker's chief aides said, "If somebody doesn't want a vote on a Monday, there's no vote on Monday . . .   Baker has 53 constituents, and he has to serve them."   Senate of the '80s at 2182.

[30]   Davidson at 235.

(footnote continued)

C.   OTHER LEADERSHIP POSTS: MINORITY LEADER, WHIPS, PARTY COMMITTEES

Minority Leader

The Senate accords a larger role than the House to its minority leadership, because the minority party has a greater role in the Senate than it does in the House.   At the least, the majority party accommodates the scheduling desires of the minority Senators, and consults on agenda setting.   In these matters, the Minority Leaders acts as their party's agent, obtaining consideration because of the minority's fallback mechanisms such as objecting to unanimous consent, raising non-germane amendments, and filibustering.[32]

Like the Majority Leader, the minority leader functions at both the political level -- balancing party, President, and media -- and at the procedural level.   Looking first to the political level, a sense of the Minority Leader's role can best be obtained from describing postwar leaders.   In the 1950s and 1960s the Republican Minority Leaders -- Robert Taft (R-Ohio), William Knowland (R-Calif.),[33] and Everett Dirksen (R-

---

[31]   Elving, Mitchell Will Try to Elevate Policy, Predictability, 46 Cong. Q. Week. Rep. 3423 (1988).   See Hook, The Byrd Years: Surviving in a Media Age Through Details and Diligence, 46 Cong. Q. Week. Rep. 976, 978 (1988).

[32]   Peabody, "Senate Party Leadership: From the 1950s to the 1980s," at 84-85.

[33]   Senator Taft, who functioned as the leading Senate Republican in the late 1940s and early 1950s (though not as the formal leader until the end), exercised a commanding influence on his side of the aisle.   Senator Knowland (Minority Leader 1953-59) and Senator Dirksen (Minority Leader 1959-69) "were the uncontested heads of their party in the Senate."   Malbin, The Senate Republican Leaders -- Life Without a President, National Journal, May 21, 1977, at 776, 777.   For a more detailed description, see Peabody, "Senate Party Leadership: From the 1950s to the 1980s," in (footnote continued)

Ill.) -- served as strong components of the
Senate's "inner club," and as key conduits to the
President.[34] From 1969-76, Senator Hugh Scott (R-
Penn.) served as the minority leader during the
terms of Presidents Nixon and Ford.   "He took
pains to support the Nixon administration . . . .
[and] stood up for Nixon during Watergate until
the White House tapes undercut the president's
credibility."[35]   Just as Majority Leader Mansfield
relaxed central control among the Democrats,
Minority Leader Scott did so among the
Republicans, providing an "open leadership" with a
"quiet and gentle" style.[36]   Senator Baker

Understanding Congressional Leadership (ed. F. H. Mackaman
1981), at 82.

[34]   As with the majority leaders, these Minority Leaders
oscillated between moving the President's program (or
working with an opposition President), and picking points of
resistance to a President of the other party (or creating
some political "distance" between themselves and a President
of their own party). For example, Senator Taft successfully
resisted virtually the entirety of President Truman's
domestic program.   In contrast, Minority Leader Knowland
worked closely with Majority Leader Johnson in accommodating
President Eisenhower.   Similarly, Minority Leader Dirksen
significantly accommodated President Johnson.   Not
accidentally, four out of five Republican leaders in 1953-80
-- Taft, Knowland, Hugh Scott (R-Penn.), and Baker -- sat on
the Senate Foreign Relations Committee, where they could
develop expertise in the issue that most visibly defines the
relationship with the President.   Peabody, "Senate Party
Leadership: From the 1950s to the 1980s", at 89.

In the leading historical example of accommodation,
Minority Leader Dirksen compromised with President Johnson
at the critical juncture that broke the filibuster on the
1964 civil rights bill -- a turning point in the history of
both civil rights and Senate procedure, as noted in the
chapter on filibuster and cloture.

[35]   Davidson at 235.

[36]   Davidson at 235.   Scott's contrast with his three
predecessors, Senators Taft of Ohio (leading Republican
1944-53, though only Minority Leader at the end), Knowland,
and Dirksen, resembled Mansfield's contrast with his
(footnote continued)

continued that relaxed style as Minority Leader, and varied his approach between working with, and opposing, President Carter.[37]

The Republican ascendancy to majority party status in 1981 stunned the new minority party. At first, Senator Byrd, as Minority Leader, avoided visible confrontations with the new majority.[38] However, as the "honeymoon" ended, he developed some of the effective techniques of previous Minority Leaders, varying his approach from issues on which to accommodate President Reagan to others on which to be the "loyal opposition."[39]

---

predecessor Senator Johnson.

[37] In an example much like that of Minority Leader Dirksen on the 1964 Civil Rights Act, Minority Leader Baker threw his support behind President Carter for ratification of the Panama Canal Treaty, a move that proved critical for ratification but that took a heavy cost in Baker's relationship with the rising right wing of his party.

[38] In 1981, while the minority raised particular proposed amendments to President Reagan's budget, on the final vote it gave him an overwhelming endorsement (completely unlike the House Democrats, who fought fiercely to the end).

[39] By 1982, Minority Leader Byrd was bargaining hard, and successfully, against majority loading of the reconciliation bill with extraneous provisions. By 1983, the Democrats became the architects of the budget passed by the Senate. The Minority Leader led and protected his party in a number of moves, constantly reminding the majority that he had the procedural powers and skills to block it if it ever attempted to run roughshod over minority rights.

For example, when Senator Gary Hart (D-Colo.) filibustered against approval of the MX missile, Majority Leader Baker responded by announcing a Saturday session. The Minority Leader commented that "if it is just myself who would be here on my side" -- in other words, if Senator Byrd were left by his party that Saturday to stand alone against the whole majority party -- even so, "the bill will not pass. I will have to protect my side." Senator Byrd noted that he personally supported the MX, and took the edge off his comment by adding that "[a] lot of what we are saying is in jest," but he reiterated the role of the Minority Leader: "Even though I might disagree with [the Democratic Members'] (footnote continued)

Conversely, when the Republicans became the minority party in 1987, Minority Leader Dole took on the role of defender of President Reagan and President Bush familiar to the Minority Leaders of 1969-76.

As to the Minority Leader's procedural role, it resembles the Majority Leader's insofar as it consists of working out the accommodation of individual Senators' scheduling desires with the overall schedule. As Professor Peabody observes:

> Cooperation between the majority and minority leaders takes place at four cross-cutting levels of communication: (1) through frequent telephone calls; (2) in private meetings between two or more leaders, held almost daily and usually in Byrd's leadership office; (3) through the exchange of rhetoric on the floor, most frequently at the opening of the Senate, but on other occasions at intervals through the day; and (4) through their leadership staffs and the majority and minority secretaries of the Senate. At all levels of communication, the constantly changing legislative agenda is the main preoccupation of the party leaders and the Senate secretarial and policy committee staffs.[40]

The Minority Leader possesses certain customary prerogatives. He plays the key role in working out time agreements with the Majority Leader; covers the floor at transitional points to assure party agreement on the movement; and enjoys priority recognition from the Chair (after the Majority Leader). He designates the control of time under time control agreements, making him, at least formally, the ultimate chooser of the minority managers on bills.

---

position, I would do everything I could to protect them." 129 Cong. Rec. S10059-60 (daily ed. July 15, 1983). The majority did not test that claim by any attempt to overpower Senator Hart; in the end, it negotiated away his filibuster.

[40] Peabody, "Senate Party Leadership: From the 1950s to the 1980s," at 74-75.

Whips

Like the House, the Senate possesses a party structure under the top leadership positions. However, at this time, its importance seems less than in the past: the trends toward individualism that have limited the leaders' control appear to have struck even harder below.

Each party has a whip, who may be considered the number two party figure after the leader. Like the leader, the whip as a formal post is a twentieth-century creation.[41]   As in the number two positions in the House (in the House's majority party, Majority Leader, who is number two after the Speaker; in the House's minority party, Minority Whip), the whip's authority depends in part on his chance of succession to the leader's post.   Although a whip is one of the main candidates for leader,[42] many whips do not become leaders.[43]   Many leaders of both parties, such as

---

[41]   Its history is traced in Majority and Minority Whips of the Senate, S. Doc. No. 86, 92d Cong., 2d Sess. (1972) (by W. J. Oleszek); 126 Cong. Rec. S5047 (daily ed. May 9, 1980) (Sen. Byrd).

[42]   Calmes, The Hill Leaders: Their Places on the Ladder, 45 Cong. Q. Week. Rep. 5, 10 (1987).   Regarding the Democratic side, in 1969 Professor Peabody could point out that "[s]ince 1947, all three Democrats who had that opportunity" -- the opportunity of the whip to seek the post of floor leader when a vacancy occurs -- "Scott Lucas in 1949, Lyndon B. Johnson in 1953, and Michael J. 'Mike' Mansfield in 1961 -- did, in fact become floor leaders."   Peabody (1969) at 331.   Moreover, after Peabody wrote, Senator Byrd succeeded in 1977 from the whip to the leader position.

[43]   During Mansfield's long reign, he worked with four different Democratic Whips, only the last of whom succeeded him: Hubert Humphrey (1961-64), Russell Long (1965-68) (D-La.), Edward Kennedy (1969-70) (D-Mass.), and Robert Byrd (1971-76).   Peabody, "Senate Party Leadership: From the 1950s to the 1980s," at 59.   Similarly, Senator Byrd's whip, Senator Cranston, did not succeed him.

"Senators often tend to see these positions [Leader and assistant leader] in terms of different positions to be (footnote continued)

Senators Mitchell, Baker, and Dole, did not serve as whips.[44]

A chief function of an active whip in the Senate can be floor coverage in the leader's absence.[45] The best-known function of the whip, as in the House, is to count votes; the key role of head counting in floor management is discussed below. Also as in the House, the whip may have deputy or assistant whips and a whip organization.[46] On the other hand, staff may

---

filled by different kinds of people," Norman J. Ornstein . . . said. "The characteristics you want in a whip -- on the floor a lot, counting votes, immersed in the process, juggling schedules for 99 other prima donnas -- are not necessarily the traits you want in a leader."

The Hill Leaders, supra, at 10.

[44] In 1969, Professor Peabody could say that "[t]hree of the last four Republican whips with that opportunity -- Kenneth Wherry in 1949, Everett Dirksen in 1959, and Hugh Scott in September, 1969 -- made similar advancements [to the leadership]." Peabody (1969) at 331. However, Senator Baker defeated Minority Whip Robert Griffin (R-Mich.) to succeed as leader in 1977, and Senator Dole defeated Minority Whip Ted Stevens (R-Alaska) to succeed as leader in 1985.

[45] On the Republican side, Senator Baker, both as Minority and as Majority Leader, frequently relied on the whip, Senator Stevens, to cover the floor. However, on the Democratic side, Senator Byrd "seldom delegates coverage of the floor" to his whip, Senator Cranston. Peabody, "Senate Party Leadership: From the 1950s to the 1980s," at 72.

[46] The election of Senator Alan J. Dixon (D-Ill.) as chief deputy whip is discussed in Elving, Cranston Beats Ford for Whip, Pryor Wins Secretary Position, 46 Cong. Q. Week. Rep. 3437 (1988).

In the Senate, the [Democratic] whip system has developed under Mr. Cranston to the point now that there is an active organization of deputy whips . . . . They meet each week . . . . Each deputy whip is assigned certain Members of the majority party to be contacted on issues that arise from time to time,

(footnote continued)

conduct counts.   One Senate Republican whip said:

> We usually delegate [polling] to [the
> Secretary to the Minority, a staff position]
> to do the actual contacting.   There are some
> [polls] where he can get a reading easier
> than we can.   There are others where we can
> get it better than he can -- it's just a
> personal situation . . .   You have to know
> each [Senator] personally -- how they
> react.[47]

Party Conferences and Party Committees

Each Senate party uses its conferences (a
term used in the Senate instead of "caucus"
because "caucus" used to connote that members were
bound by decisions) and party committees to
provide additional leadership.[48]   On paper, the
Senate Republican party historically chose a
decentralized party model.   Not the Republican
leader, but other Members, hold the posts of chair
and Secretary of the Conference and chair of the
various party committees -- the Committee on
Committees and the Republican Policy Committee.
In theory, these groups' chairs could provide

---

and that deputy whip will be responsible for reporting
on the positions of his assigned Members.

126 Cong. Rec. S4496 (daily ed. May 2, 1980) (Sen. Byrd).
The Republican assistant whip organization is described at
126 Cong. Rec. S5048 (daily ed. May 9, 1980) (Sen. Byrd).

[47] Peabody (1969) at 331.   That observation remains
accurate.   See 126 Cong. Rec. S4496 (daily ed. May 2,
1980)(role of secretaries to the majority and minority in
counts).

[48] For detailed descriptions of the party conferences and
committees, see Peabody, "Senate Party Leadership: From the
1950s to the 1980s," at 72-74 (Democratic party), 83-84
(Republican party); R. B. Ripley at 97-104 (description as
of 1969); F. Riddick, The U.S. Congress: Organization and
Procedure 104-07 (1949); 126 Cong. Rec. S10609 (Aug. 1,
1980) and S10654 (Aug. 4, 1980) (Sen. Byrd's histories of
the conferences and policy and steering committees).

rivals to the Republican leader.[49] However, this appearance is "deceptive," and "[m]ost Republican senators agree that in recent decades the floor leader is the premier leader and that the incumbents of other party positions have usually remained in the background."[50]

Besides the conference, the Senate Democratic party has two party committees: the Democratic Steering Committee, and the Democratic Policy Committee. Senator Byrd, both when Majority Leader and when Minority Leader, served ex officio as chair of each committee, following the party's tradition. However, when Senator Mitchell was chosen as Majority Leader in 1988, he allowed Senator Daniel K. Inouye (D-Haw.) to chair the Democratic Steering Committee and let Senator Thomas K. Daschle (D-S.D.) co-chair the Democratic Policy Committee. While the leader chairs the Democratic Conference, but the Conference also elects a Secretary -- the third-ranking officer of the party after the leader and whip.[51]

---

[49] Dole also has less power than Byrd within party circles, and that is true regardless of who heads the majority. A Democratic leader also chairs the party's conference, which is the Senate Democrats' caucus, its policy committee and the Steering Committee that makes committee assignments.

Dole must share those powers under Republicans' decentralized system. Separate leaders chair the conference ([John] Chafee) [(R-R.I.)], policy committee (William L. Armstrong of Colorado) and Committee on Committees (Paul S. Trible Jr. of Virginia).

The Hill Leaders, supra, at 9. These posts represent some authority inasmuch as real election contests may occur to fill them. For example, in 1988 "John H. Chafee of Rhode Island defeated challenger Frank H. Murkowski of Alaska to retain his title as chairman of the Senate Republican Conference." Republicans Re-elect Same Leaders, 46 Cong. Q. Week. Rep. 3437 (1988).

[50] Peabody, "Senate Party Leadership: From the 1950s to the 1980s," at 56, 83.

[51] See 126 Cong. Rec. S5524-5 (daily ed. May 16, 1980) (footnote continued)

The Democratic and Republican conferences meet in their most important session at the beginning of each Congress. At this time, they ratify (or overrule) committee assignments made by the steering committees, and decide contests over leadership posts or other party matters. Both parties' conferences have also tended to have frequent meetings during the session to discuss legislative business. The Republican Conference meets weekly during sessions to discuss political questions.[52] When the Democrats became the minority party in 1981, they also began weekly meetings.[53] Thus, both parties' conferences were meeting for Tuesday luncheons.[54]

(Sen. Byrd) (discussing post of Secretary to the Conference). In 1988, Senator David Pryor (D-Ark.) was elected to the post. Elving, Cranston Beats Ford for Whip; Pryor Wins Secretary Position, 46 Cong. Q. Week. Rep. 3437 (1988). For the distribution of party posts by Majority Leader Mitchell, see Elving, Mitchell Will Try to Elevate Policy, Predictability, 46 Cong. Q. Week. Rep. 3413 (1988).

[52]   126 Cong. Rec. S3921 (daily ed. April 18, 1980) (colloquy between Majority Leader Byrd and Sen. Thaddeus Cochran (R-Miss.)). The Republican conference had a tradition of "meet[ing] more often and discuss[ing] legislative questions," R. B. Ripley, Power in the Senate 37 (1969); see id. at 103.

[53]   "[T]hey could no longer rely on committee hearings or ample staffs to initiate their own plans or strategies. As a result, Byrd decided that they should spend more time with one another . . . [and so] Byrd organized luncheon caucuses nearly every Tuesday." Cohen, Byrd is Back -- SALT in the Wounds, National Journal, May 7, 1983, reprinted in 129 Cong. Rec. S6370 (daily ed. May 10, 1983).

Previously, the Democratic Conference did not meet as often. Then, under Majority Leader Byrd, the party averaged over ten conferences a year. 126 Cong. Rec. S3921 (daily ed. April 18, 1980) (Sen. Byrd); id. at S10612 (daily ed. Aug. 1, 1980).

[54]   See, e.g., 129 Cong. Rec. S7722 (daily ed. June 6, 1983) (Majority Leader Baker) (obtaining unanimous consent for a Tuesday recess from noon to 2 p.m., because "on Tuesday, Senators on both sides of the aisle caucus separately off (footnote continued)

Committee assignments are decided by the Republican Committee on Committees and the Democratic Steering Committee for their respective parties. Historically, these steering committees often enjoyed considerable power and made crucial decisions, and undoubtedly will exercise such power again.[55]   In 1981, for example, the Republican Committee on Committees took the opportunity in assigning a large number of open seats to stack the financial committees, particularly the Budget Committee, with freshmen conservatives, whose loyalty to President Reagan strongly bolstered the party strategy of implementing the President's legislative agenda through the budget. However, after 1981 the steering committees again left the limelight.[56] By law, each party has a Policy Committee with the theoretical prime purpose of the scheduling of legislation.[57]

---

the floor of the Senate.   Those caucuses are of a quasi-official nature, but they are important to the smooth functioning of the Senate.")

[55]   For example, the Democratic steering committee could face again the situation that made it key in the 1960s: southern Democrats might have the seniority in the party and thus the chairs of the standing committees, while less senior Senators coming from other regions might have the power of numbers in the conference.   A dispute over the distribution of assignments would thus bring into focus the membership and action of the steering committee.

[56]   The Republican committee's significance is limited by the party's strong adherence to the norm of seniority, see R. B. Ripley at 72.

In 1985, the Republicans responded to complaints about the excessive committee memberships and responsiblities of all the Senators by a limited contraction of committee seats, followed by a similar Democratic contraction.   This matter received very little public discussion; apparently the parties set the rules requiring relinquishment of seats, but individual Senators decided what they would relinquish, subject to rule waivers negotiated with the party leadership.   The Democratic committee had a number of slots to hand out in 1986, but did so with a minimum of publicity.

(footnote continued)

Each party also has a Senatorial Campaign Committee. Senator Mitchell, chair of the Democratic committee, received much credit for funding of the 1986 election races that won back control of the chamber. This proved to be a springboard for his ascending to Majority Leader.[58]

Given the small size and informal operations of the Senate, it is natural that authority within the party may reside in Members quite apart from any formal positions. On the Republican side, for example, Senator Paul Laxalt (R-Nev.) possessed major influence because of his close personal relationship with President Reagan.[59] On the Democratic side, Senator Richard Russell (D-Ga.) had been considered in the 1950s perhaps the party's key leader within the "inner club," quite apart from any formal position, just because the dominant southern bloc listened closely to him and, therefore, so too did others. Senator Edward Kennedy (D-Mass.) traditionally has a vital political role because of his ability to focus media and public attention on chosen issues, and because he -- like such diverse influential figures before him as Robert Taft, Hubert Humphrey, and Howard Baker -- had perennial prospects for a Presidential race. Likewise, informal groups may prove crucial. In both parties, the leaders meet periodically with their committee chairs as a group.[60]

---

[57] In the 1980s, the Democratic Policy Committee seldom convened, serving mainly to staff Senator Byrd's assistance to Members, such as his "whip notices" on upcoming legislation. The Republican Policy Committee also received little attention in this period.

[58] "While the Democratic senatorial campaign committee is mainly a conduit for fundraising and distribution, Republicans offer a range of public relations and campaign services in addition to campaign finance support." Peabody, "Senate Party Leadership: From the 1950s to the 1980s," at 90.

[59] Arieff, Sen. Paul Laxalt: Reagan's Man on the Hill, 38 Cong. Q. Week. Rep. 3396 (1980).

[60] See 126 Cong. Rec. S3921 (daily ed. April 18, 1980) (footnote continued)

D.   RULES AND THE CHAIR'S ROLE

Vice President and President Pro Tempore

The Constitution makes the Vice President presiding officer of the Senate. Article I, section 3, clause 4 provides that "The Vice President of the United States shall be President of the Senate, but shall have no Vote, unless they be equally divided." It is because of this clause that all Senators, when engaging in debate, address the chair by speaking to "Mr. President," as all House Members address the chair as "Mr. Speaker" (or, during proceedings in Committee of the Whole, as "Mr. Chairman") -- or, when a female Member is in these respective chairs, as "Madam President," "Madam Speaker," or "Madam Chairwoman."

Despite this clause, the Senate has refused to allow any extensive authority to the Vice President.[61] Since the Senate does not choose the Vice President, he normally lacks any natural base of support in the Senate -- unlike the Speaker, who must have a base of support to secure election by the House. Moreover, when the party that captures the Vice Presidency is not the one that wins a majority in the Senate, the Vice President

---

(Sen. Byrd) (regarding his establishment and convening of meetings of his committee of committee chairs). Majority Leader Baker held weekly meetings with his committee chairs, which came to be regarded as the place where key matters were worked out.

[61] In the nineteenth century, the Senate experimented with allowing authority like the Speaker's to its presiding officer, but the experiment failed. The Senate voted in 1823 that all committees "shall be appointed by the presiding officer of this House, unless otherwise ordered by the Senate." In 1824, John C. Calhoun was elected Vice President. Calhoun "appointed the committees with such obvious bias that the session was only four months old when, with hardly a dissenting vote, the Senate took the appointment of committees away" from the presiding officer. G. H. Haynes, The Senate of the United States: Its History and Practice 274 (1938).

becomes, at least potentially, a partisan opponent of the Senate majority party. Vice Presidents Nixon, Spiro Agnew, Nelson Rockefeller, George Bush (in 1987-88), and Dan Quayle presided over the Senate while another party was in the majority. The Senate majority would not allow such a chair to have power over it.

Accordingly, it is the rare Vice President who imagines, as Dan Quayle speculated in 1988, that he could be a power in the Senate.[62] The Vice President tends not even to attend the Senate most of the time, returning to preside mostly on just two types of occasions. One is when a close vote or a tie looms on an important matter. Article I, section 3 of the Constitution gives the Vice President one power, of voting to break ties, stating that "The Vice President of the United States shall be President of the Senate, but shall have no Vote, unless they be equally divided,"[63] and there are occasional dramatic uses of this power.[64]

The other reason the Vice President tends to return is for formal occasions, such as the opening day of the Congress and joint sessions with the House to hear the President or a foreign dignitary. A noteworthy example is that the Vice President occasionally returns to give rulings from the Chair on points of the highest moment.[65] In 1987, Vice President Bush took the

---

[62] Devroy, Quayle Weighs His Role: Activist Senate Presidency a Possibility, Washington Post, Dec. 3, 1988, at A1. The tradition remains powerful enough that even when the same party captures the Senate and the Presidency, as under Vice Presidents Johnson, Humphrey, and Bush (in 1981-86), the Senate has little desire to be led by the Vice President.

[63] See generally Riddick, "Vice President: Vote by Vice President," at 1124-26.

[64] For example, a tie-breaking vote by Vice President Bush for a budget proposal that cut back statutory increases in Social Security was raised as an issue in the presidential campaign debates of 1988.

[65] As Senator Russell Long commented, after Vice President (footnote continued)

chair for a ruling during "one of the first head-on tests of party strength in the 100th Congress"; when the Chair began ruling on procedural issues in heated dispute between the parties, Minority Leader "Dole, as the roll call began, was heard to say, 'Get the vice president,' [and] [t]he vice president rushed over to the Senate from the White House."[66]

Recognizing that the Vice President may be absent or unavailable (such as when he succeeds to the Presidency) the Constitution created a back-up post for a presiding officer, that of President pro tempore. Article I, section 3, clause 5, states that "The Senate shall chuse . . . a President pro tempore, in the Absence of the Vice President, or when he shall exercise the Office of President of the United States."[67] Senate Rule I

Mondale made a critical ruling regarding the cloture rule during the 1977 natural gas filibuster:

> Mr. President, I have been a Member of this body for 29 years, and I have had occasion to observe the conduct of several Vice Presidents . . . Alben Barkley, Lyndon Johnson, Hubert Humphrey, and Nelson Rockefeller. Without exception, Mr. President, when those men knew that a very significant ruling had to be made by that Chair and an historic ruling had to be made by that Chair they were here to make it. That is not the kind of ruling that should be made by a freshman Senator who is unfamiliar with the rules.

123 Cong. Rec. 31221 (1977). Probably the most famous examples are the Vice Presidents' rulings, during the contests over changing the cloture rules, regarding whether the Senate is a continuous body. These are discussed in the chapter on filibusters.

[66] Davis, Byrd and Bush Clash in Senate Power Struggle, 45 Cong. Q. Week. Rep. 221 (1987).

[67] Accordingly, Rule I of the Senate provides that: "In the absence of the Vice President, the Senate shall choose a President pro tempore, who shall hold the office and execute the duties thereof during the pleasure of the Senate and until another is elected or his term of office as a Senator expires." Before 1890, the Senate elected or reelected a President pro tempore each time the Vice President was (footnote continued)

allows any Senator to be elected President pro tempore, but in recent times there has developed "the practice of electing to the office of the President pro tempore the most senior member"[68] of the majority party. It is a post of honor (in fact, "one of the highest honors offered to a Senator by the Senate body,") rather than one of great authority.[69] A President pro tempore, like a Vice President, tends to use his time in ways other than presiding, given the limited nature of that role.

Accordingly, Senate Rule I provides for yet one further position, that of "Acting President pro tempore." Specifically, Rule I(3) states:

> The President pro tempore shall have the right to name in open Senate or, if absent, in writing, a Senator to perform the duties of the Chair, including the signing of duly enrolled bills and joint resolutions but such substitution shall not extend beyond an adjournment, except by unanimous consent.[70]

---

absent; since then, the Senate elects a President pro tempore once to serve during all of the Vice President's absences. G. H. Haynes, supra, at 249-51.

[68] 126 Cong. Rec. S5675 (daily ed. May 21, 1980) (Sen. Byrd).

[69] 126 Cong. Rec. S5674 (daily ed. May 21, 1980) (Sen. Byrd) (statement regarding "highest honors"). "[T]he President pro tempore has never been able to establish his authority as a party leader to the extent of the Majority Leader," owing to his "uncertain tenure over the years while serving in the absence of the Vice President." Id.

[70] See Riddick at 820-21. "Legislative days" are discussed below. Two details may be noted. First, the acting President pro tempore may himself "have the right to name in open session, or, if absent, in writing, a Senator to perform the duties of the Chair, but not to extend beyond an adjournment, except by unanimous consent." Thus, the President pro tempore may name Senator A to be acting; if Senator A needs to leave the Chair to make a speech on the floor, or to conduct business elsewhere, he may name Senator B to perform the duties of the Chair temporarily. The Congressional Record often notes new Senators assuming the (footnote continued)

Being the acting President pro tempore can be a
chore, so "for approximately the last thirty
years, the Senate has operated a system of
rotation of the Senators in the chair," and there
has been "a trend of appointing more and more
junior Senators to take the chair."[71]   Starting in
the 1970s,[72] only Members of the majority party
have been acting Presidents pro tempore.[73]

Chair during a day.   Second, Rule I(2) also provides for the
Secretary, or Assistant Secretary, to take the Chair if
vacant.   See Riddick, "Secretary of the Senate: Presides
Over Senate in Absence of Elected Presiding Officers," at
1001.

[71]   126 Cong. Rec. S5675 (daily ed. May 21, 1980) (Sen.
Byrd).

[72]   This probably dates from a dramatic 1975 incident in
which Senator Jesse Helms (R-N.C.) was in the Chair and
declined to accept the majority leader's recognition
prerogative.   The particular triggering incident for Senator
Byrd may have been the following:

> [O]n July 18, 1975, Majority Leader Mansfield sought
> recognition from Presiding Officer Jesse Helms
> (N.C.).   Instead, Helms recognized Senator James Allen
> (Ala.), which angered Senator Mansfield.   As the
> Majority Leader stated, "Mr. President, is it not true
> that the Senator from Alabama went to the Senator from
> North Carolina and asked that he be recognized at the
> conclusion of this vote?"   He further declared, "I was
> on my feet 20 minutes while the Senator from North
> Carolina and the Senator from Alabama were out in the
> hallway, after I had asked the Senator from North
> Carolina, sitting in that Chair, to recognize me, as
> the majority leader, which is the custom in this body,
> and the Senator from Alabama knows it."
>
> A few minutes after the exchange, the Senate recessed
> at 4:19 p.m. until 5:03 p.m.   When the Senate
> reassembled, there was a new Presiding Officer.

W. J. Oleszek, Dissent on the Senate Floor: Practices,
Procedures, and Customs 11 (Cong. Res. Serv. 1976).

[73]   I can recall a time when I was in my first term here
(footnote continued)

The presiding officer -- be he Vice
President, President pro tempore, or acting
President pro tempore -- has two sets of duties.
One set consists of the functions of presiding:
recognizing Senators in succession (to speak or to
make unanimous consent requests or motions),
putting the question on votes, maintaining
order,[74] and deciding points of order (and
answering parliamentary inquiries). The two
complex and important functions in presiding --
recognition and deciding points of order -- are
discussed next. The other set consists of a
variety of duties assigned to the chair as a
formal "head" of the Senate, apart from presiding
over the chamber, such as signing enrolled bills
or appointing conferees. These will be discussed
as appropriate in connection with the pertinent
area, such as conference procedure.[75]

Recognition -- Priority

As in the House, which Member receives
recognition -- that is, which Member obtains the
floor to speak or to make a motion or otherwise
act -- can matter greatly, as illustrated many
times below. In the House, a large measure of
discretion in recognition belongs to the Speaker,
and forms one of the pillars of his control over
the body. The Senate has not been willing to cede
control to its Vice President (or other presiding

---

that the presiding responsibilities were rotated
between Members of both parties. It was the decision
of Mr. Byrd, when he became majority leader, that that
practice should be discontinued and the Chair should be
occupied by the party that was in control of the
Senate.

129 Cong. Rec. S10160 (daily ed. July 16, 1983) (Sen. John
Tower (R-Tex.)).

[74] See Riddick, "Decorum," at 637-38.

[75] For a full listing of these functions, see T. H. Neale,
The President Pro Tempore of the U.S. Senate: The Historical
Development of the Office and a Synopsis of its Duties and
Responsibilities (Cong. Res. Serv. 1981).

officer), as previously discussed. Accordingly, the Senate has cabined the recognition power significantly, excluding discretion through its binding rules and precedents.

The Senate's rule regarding recognition, Rule XIX(1)(a), provides: "When a Senator desires to speak, he shall rise and address the Presiding Officer, and shall not proceed until he is recognized, and the Presiding Officer shall recognize the Senator who shall first address him." This mandatory rule -- that the Chair "shall" recognize the "first Senator" to seek recognition -- eliminates much of the potential discretion in recognition. There is no doubt about what it means to seek recognition: it means the Senator's rising and "address[ing] him," that is, addressing the Chair.[76] The Chair cannot refuse recognition, as the Speaker can, to a Senator who is the only one addressing him and asking for it. The Chair cannot condition recognition, as the Speaker can, by saying, "the gentlelady is recognized for the purpose of --;" the Chair cannot even temporarily withhold recognition until asking her, as the Speaker routinely does, "for what purpose does the gentlelady seek recognition?"[77]

---

[76] When a Senator desires to address a question to another Senator or desires to interrupt him, he should rise, and to obtain consent of the speaker, he shall address the Chair, and get permission through the Chair.

A Senator who does not rise when he addresses the Chair is not entitled to recognition.

Riddick, "Recognition: Chair Recognizes," at 880.

[77] A Senator responded angrily in 1983 to even the suggestion of recognition conditioned on a purpose:

The PRESIDING OFFICER: The Chair recognizes the Senator from Ohio for his amendment.

Mr. METZENBAUM: The Chair will recognize the Senator from Ohio period, not for his amendment.

(footnote continued)

The rule still leaves one large element of discretion, during the situations of procedural combat when Senators on opposing sides compete by seeking recognition at the same time. Since both (or more) stand and address the Chair as the prior action ends, neither is clearly first, and Rule XIX does not dictate which to recognize.[78]   At such times, several other principles of preferential recognition partially constrain the Chair. The first principle is that the Majority Leader and Majority Whip receive first preference, and the Minority Leader next preference, before other Senators.[79]   This principle has been established since a formal pronouncement of the Vice President in 1937 about the role of the Majority Leader discussed above. The tactical importance of this privilege cannot be overestimated. As Minority Leader Byrd commented, "[R]ecognition . . . is probably the most powerful weapon the majority leader has, with the exception of his also having the votes as well to back him up."[80]

The PRESIDING OFFICER: The Chair will recognize the Senator from Ohio. The Senator has the floor.

129 Cong. Rec. S10159 (daily ed. July 16, 1983).   Having been recognized, Senator Howard Metzenbaum (D-Ohio) used the opportunity to criticize the Chair at length for not following the rules, before talking about his amendment.

[78] "Of course, this [rule] gives the Chair discretion when several Senators simultanously address the Chair." Riddick at 878.

[79]   Riddick, "Recognition: Leaders -- Preferential Recognition," at 883.

Failure to recognize the Minority Leader, or someone standing in for the Minority Leader, can draw an angry complaint. In 1983, when Senator Bennett Johnston (D-La.), representing the minority leader, sought recognition but the Chair recognized his opponent, Senator Metzenbaum, because the latter "by a fraction of a second, did seek recognition first," Senator Johnston responded with a long and sharp critique, insisting that "the Chair can run this show any way he wishes. But that does not make it right." 129 Cong. Rec. S15313 (daily ed. Nov. 3, 1983).
(footnote continued)

Perhaps the most dramatic use of the priority recognition power came when Majority Leader Byrd ended one of the most searing Senate battles in history, the Metzenbaum-Abourezk filibuster of the natural gas deregulation bill in 1978.   When the chamber had reached the end of its tolerance of that filibuster, Vice President Mondale, following a plan devised with Majority Leader Byrd, began recognizing only the Majority Leader.   The Majority Leader kept calling up the amendments of Senators Metzenbaum and James Abourezk (D-S.D.) to be ruled out of order by the Chair (for correct reasons, such as for not being germane).   Over and over, the Chair did not recognize any Senator to take appeals from its rulings, but only recognized Majority Leader Byrd each time an amendment had been ruled out of order, for him to call up the next amendment (making any appeal of the prior ruling moot).   Ultimately, Senators Metzenbaum and Abourezk gave in.   This floor-monopolizing use of the recognition power broke the filibusterers' singular postcloture challenge to Senate operation.

A second, related principle of preference is that the managers -- majority and minority -- of any pending bill have priority in recognition over anyone else simultaneously seeking recognition (other than the leaders).[81]   This gives the managers a key resource in managing their bills. They have the right to the floor following a problematic speech or amendment so they can

---

[80]   129 Cong. Rec. S10362 (daily ed. July 19, 1983).   For example, in 1985, Majority Leader Dole wished to hold his fragile Republican coalition on the budget together.   His procedural approach relied upon his priority in recognition.   Senator Dole obtained priority recognition and offered dummy amendments, preventing Democratic amendments by monopolizing recognition until he had completed internal party bargaining.   Then he substituted amendments of other Republican Senators for the dummy ones he had offered.   This and other maneuvers brought him victory on the budget despite his razor-thin voting margin.

[81]   Riddick, "Recognition: Chair Recognizes," at 881 (tracing rule to 1933 and 1935); also "Recognition: Leaders -- Preferential Recognition," at 883.

immediately respond. The various options available to managers will form the central focus of the chapter below on floor management; the manager's priority in recognition is important for many of them.

As a third organizing principle for recognition, the floor managers of a bill will often prepare "lists" of Senators desiring the floor to speak or to offer amendments, as guides for the Chair's recognition. This lets Senators attend to business elsewhere with some assurance that they can have the floor at a prearranged point in the sequence. Such lists also give the floor manager tactical flexibility. However, the "list" approach, although accepted perhaps 99 percent of the time, gives way when Senators insist on Rule XIX being followed. As Senator Russell Long (D-La.) noted, lists are "a great advantage to the manager . . . . But there is nothing in the rules that gives [the manager] that right. The right is for any Senator to command recognition and to be recognized, the first one to address the Chair."[82] Finally, the Senators may establish by unanimous consent that a Member will obtain recognition at a particular time.[83]

These principles still leave a residuum of discretion. Notwithstanding these principles, the presiding officer "may go a long way in exercising his own discretion . . . . [H]e has not always

---

[82]   129 Cong. Rec. S10161 (daily ed. July 16, 1983).

While in practice the Presiding Officer, for convenience, frequently keeps at the desk a list of Senators desiring to speak, and recognizes them in the order in which they are so listed, the Senator who first addresses the Chair should be recognized upon a point of order being made, and the Chair on various occasions has held that the list at the desk has no parliamentary standing and gives way to the rule for recognition, which mandates that the Senator who shall first address the Chair shall be recognized.

Riddick, "Debate: List of Speakers," at 604-5.

[83]   Riddick, "Recognition: Unanimous Consent Suspends Rule on Recognition," at 886.

recognized the one rising first."[84]   This occasionally becomes a significant issue, as it did in 1983.[85] Senator Byrd noted, "the decisions of the Chair . . . cannot be appealed, and that means that the Chair can, if he so wishe[s] be somewhat arbitrary in the recognition of Senators."[86] Minority Leader Byrd then made one of his rare but unmistakable lightly-veiled threats:

> I would not want the situation to deteriorate to the point that the majority leader would not be able to get time agreements because of some wounded feeling on the part of a Member of the minority . . . . I know the majority leader does not want to see that happen [and will] . . . . talk with his colleagues to make sure they understood the rules better governing recognition.[87]

Majority Leader Baker responded on the floor, "the Senator first seeking recognition must be recognized regardless of his party affiliation and

---

[84] Riddick, The United States Congress, at 80. While floor watchers know such examples, they cannot be documented from the Congressional Record, as the preparers of the Record do not go to pains to dispute the Chair as to the sequence of events.

[85] After angry denunciations of Republican chairs by Democratic Senators, Minority Leader Byrd took the floor and, first, summarized the problem:

> There have been some cases in which Members on my side have sought recognition clearly, and in some cases repeatedly sought recognition, prior to recognition having been sought by a Member of the majority, and I have noted that the Chair has taken time to see if a Member of the majority wishes to be recognized before the Chair recognizes the Member of the minority.

129 Cong. Rec. S10362 (daily ed. July 19, 1983).

[86] Id.

[87] 129 Cong. Rec. S10363 (daily ed. July 19, 1983).

his location on the floor or his
seniority . . . . I will admonish Members on this
side to do this once more . . . ."[88]

Still, even when the rules are being
followed, when more than one Senator seeks
recognition at a conflict juncture, the Chair has
discretion who to consider to have sought
recognition "first,"[89] meaning, in practice, that
it depends on who is in the Chair. The President
pro tempore may take the Chair himself in
anticipation of such a juncture and recognize his
choice. Alternatively, he and the Majority Leader
may agree to select an acting President pro
tempore who will accept the Majority Leader's
choice. Dramatic choices sometimes occur --
giving one side or the other the floor and,
metaphorically, the "ball" -- in an atmosphere
akin to a "jump-off" in basketball, with Senators
all but jumping up and down to get the Chair's
attention.

Recognition and Yielding: Mechanics

Whoever the Chair recognizes, that decision
is final: "no point of order may be made nor [is
it a matter] from which an appeal will lie."[90]
Once Senators obtain recognition, they hold the
floor so long as they speak, but if they offer a
motion or amendment, "technically [they] lose[]
the floor."[91] As an ordinary custom, when the
offeror of an amendment loses the floor by
offering the amendment, the Chair rerecognizes the
offeror next to explain the amendment.

However, since the offeror technically loses

---

[88] Id.

[89] "[W]hen several Senators are demanding recognition, the
Chair has the privilege of choosing the one to recognize."
Riddick, "Recognition: Chair Recognizes," at 879.

[90] Riddick, "Recognition: Chair Recognizes," at 879.

[91] Riddick, "Amendments: Floor Relinquished on Calling Up
an Amendment," at 35-36, and "Amendments: Recognition to
Offer," at 38-39.

the floor, after an amendment is offered, other Senators can insist the Chair follow Rule XIX and the priorities in recognition. Thus, a leader or manager can cut right in, if so minded, after the offering of the amendment. The leader or manager can then move immediately to table the amendment, even before the offeror would be recognized to speak. Often this is perceived as not a polite step to take -- it summons up the term "railroading," much as House members will complain about "gag rules" that cut them off -- and leaders and managers tend to reserve this type of action for special situations.

Similarly, a Member who yields the floor technically loses it, even if his intention was to let some other Senator conduct some brief business and then to resume his speech.[92] The Senate recurrently uses the idiom that no Senator can "farm out" the floor,[93] meaning that no Senator can hold the floor, let Senator A speak, reclaim the floor at A's end, let Senator B speak, reclaim the floor, and so on. However, as an ordinary custom, a Member may yield to another on request, and then receive recognition again when the other has finished.[94]

Conversely, no Senator can interrupt another Senator who has the floor. If a Senator has the floor, and another Senator wants it, he asks for it by inquiring of the Chair if the Senator holding the floor will yield.[95] The Senator holding the floor then has the option of not

---

[92] Riddick, "Debate: Senator Forfeits Right to or Loses Floor Under Certain Conditions," at 630-31.

[93] Riddick, "Debate: Parceling Out Time Not in Order," at 630.

[94] To safeguard such yielding against technical demands that Rule XIX be followed instead of automatic rerecognition, a yielding Senator must obtain unanimous consent before yielding that he may yield without losing the floor. Riddick, "Debate: Senator May Retain Floor Under Unanimous Consent or When There is no Objection," at 632-33.

[95] Riddick, "Debate: Interruption of Senator Who Has the Floor is Not Allowed -- Except by His Consent," at 598-602.

yielding, yielding with unanimous consent that he
not lose the floor, or just yielding (and taking
his chances on rerecognition).   These rules take
on particular significance during filibusters.
Recognition and yielding also take on another
dimension when the Senate is under time control,
as discussed below in the chapter on floor
management.

E.   POINTS OF ORDER AND PARLIAMENTARY INQUIRIES

Obtaining a Ruling

As suggested above and further developed below,
the Senate's practical functioning relies much
less on the enforcement of rules through rulings
of the Chair than does House procedure.   To note
just two comparisons, in the House, the
germaneness rule guards the agenda, and the rule
for amending bills title by title structures the
amendment process.   Both rules are enforced by
rulings of the Chair.   By contrast, in the Senate,
only on certain limited occasions is there a
germaneness restriction or an enforced structure
for amendments.   More often, nonbinding informal
mechanisms provide what structure there is.[96]
Still, the Chair enforces a number of rules,
some of which generate a fair number of rulings,
such as in the various limited circumstances when
germaneness applies (including during
consideration of appropriation bills).[97]   The

---

[96]   These include the leadership prerogatives on motions to
proceed, willingness to follow managers on motions to table,
and managers' consensual sequencing activity. None of these
are enforced by rulings of the Chair.

[97]   This discussion does not purport to deal with the vast
range of matters on which the Chair rules or guides the
Senate, but only to name the areas in which formal rulings
on points of order, of the kind that may generate appeals,
are most common.   Also, the Chair rules on committee
jurisdiction, in referring bills to committees.   This
important matter is discussed separately, in the chapter on
committee jurisdiction.

rulings by the Chair, and appeals therefrom, matter greatly under cloture.[98] These add up to a respectable number of rulings and votes by the Senate thereon. In 1984, when there was no use of frivolous appeals for filibustering purposes, the Senate still held 14 roll-call votes on point of order matters -- votes on points of order, appeals, or motions to table these.[99]

Thus, in a variety of circumstances, the procedure matters for raising points of order to obtain rulings, and for taking appeals from such rulings. Senate Rule XX provides the procedure for raising points of order.[100] Pursuant to this rule, the Senate imposes no narrow "window" (as in the House) on when a point of order can be raised. A Senator can raise a point of order regarding an amendment "at any stage of the proceedings prior to its disposition, even if another amendment has been offered thereto . . . ."[101] Thus, an objecting Senator

---

[98] A number of strict rules operate under cloture, so that the Chair's rulings begin to impose a firm structure on proceedings. Conversely, under cloture the appeals from such rulings, on which filibusterers may demand time-killing roll-call votes, provide an important delaying tactic.

[99] Roll-call votes on point of order matters are recorded in the 1984 Congressional Quarterly Almanac as votes 87, 164, 236, 246, 247, 248, 255, 256, and 263 (points of order submitted to the Senate); 86 (motion to table point of order submitted to the Senate); 204 (appeal); and 239, 240, and 242 (motions to table appeals).

[100] The rule provides:

1. A question of order may be raised at any stage of the proceedings, except when the Senate is voting or ascertaining the presence of a quorum, and, unless submitted to the Senate, shall be decided by the Presiding Officer without debate, subject to an appeal to the Senate . . . .

2. The Presiding Officer may submit any question of order for the decision of the Senate.

[101] The one event that decisively closes the window to (footnote continued)

may withhold his objection until the offeror has a chance to explain his amendment, and only then object. In fact, the objecting Senator not only has the possibility of withholding an objection, but Senate rules may require doing so.[102]

A Senator must obtain recognition to make a point of order. This means that the Senator who has the floor has to be willing to yield before another Senator can make a point of order; "a Senator in possession of the floor may not be interrupted without his consent or be taken from the floor in the midst of his speech by a point of order."[103]   Again, typically, this allows the offeror of an amendment at least to explain it before the amendment is killed.[104]   However, if

---

points of order, at least temporarily, is the beginning of a roll call -- the calling of the first name -- since Rule XX prohibits points of order "when the Senate is voting or ascertaining the presence of a quorum . . . . After a response has been made to a rollcall, it is too late to raise a point of order . . . ." Riddick, "Points of Order: When Made Too Late," at 799. Otherwise, the ability to raise a point of order typically ends when the matter is adopted (or rejected) in some other fashion, such as by tabling or by adoption through voice vote. Riddick, "Points of Order: When in Order and When Not in Order," at 797.

[102]   Under unanimous consent agreements and other rules fixing a time for debating matters, points of order are not in order until the "time [for the amendment] has been exhausted or yielded back," Riddick, "Points of Order: When in Order and When Not in Order," at 798; "Amendments: Points of Order, When in Order," at 78. In that situation, there is a narrowed window for points of order, but it comes at the end of consideration; such points cannot be made until all time has expired, but they must be made then, before the roll-call on disposition begins or the matter is otherwise disposed of.

[103]   Riddick, "Points of Order: When in Order and When Not in Order," at 798-99.

[104]   Ordinarily the Chair will recognize offerors immediately after they offer amendments, for them to explain the amendments, and during that explanation the offerors cannot be interrupted with a point of order. Only afterwards may other Senators obtain recognition to make a (footnote continued)

the leadership or the managers feel determined to cut off amendments quickly -- as the expression goes, to "railroad" the bill through -- they may obtain recognition, through their priorities in recognition, immediately after the offering of an amendment, and make their point of order before the Chair would rerecognize the amendment's offeror for his explanation.

Once a Senator raises a point of order, technically Rule XX makes it nondebatable (unless submitted to the Senate), but "under recent precedents of the Senate, debate has been entertained in the discretion of the Presiding Officer . . . ."[105]   Thus the Chair often lets Senators provide a defense of their challenged amendments before ruling.   Although Rule XX lets the Chair submit any points of order to the Senate, there are only a few situations in which it is obligatory or customary for the Chair to do so.   The most solemn one is when a Senator makes the point of order that a matter is unconstitutional.   A common constitutional point of order concerns Senate origination of money bills,[106] such as in a 1983 instance in which such

point of order.

[105]   Riddick, "Debate: Points of Order, Debate of," at 612.   It is polite for the Chair to hear out a Senator who wishes to debate a point of order, and in the meantime, the Parliamentarian can study the matter.

[106]   This common constitutional point of order, historically speaking, is that a bill or amendment is unconstitutional because it involves revenues, and must originate in the House rather than the Senate.   Riddick, "Revenue," at 985-87.   Historically, the House has also insisted that not only revenue but appropriations must originate in the House. While the Senate has varied in its acceptance of this view, occasionally a Senator makes a point of order on this ground.   For example, in 1983, an amendment was offered to a Senate-originated defense authorization bill to change the appropriations for neutron bombs ("enhanced radiation" shells).   Senator Bennett Johnston (D-La.) made the point of order "that this is out of order as an appropriation on a Senate bill."   When the Chair asked, "Is the Senator making a point of order under the Constitution?" Senator Johnson replied, "Yes, in effect, I was."   The Chair then explained (footnote continued)

a point of order was raised but withdrawn.[107]

Notably, in 1984, the Senate gave the first formal consideration in the nation's history to whether Congress, by statute, could give the President a line-item veto over appropriations.[108] When a Senator objected to such a provision on grounds of constitutionality, the Chair submitted it to the Senate, which debated the point.[109] The Senate voted on the point of order and concluded that the provision was unconstitutional, sustaining the point of order by a vote of 56-35.

Another occasion, less solemn but more

---

that "under the Constitution, points of order are submitted to the Senate for decision. Is that what the Senator desires?"

[107] After Senator Johnston made his point of order, the manager, Senator John Tower (R-Tex.), explained the Senate view on the difference regarding the origination clause between revenue and appropriation measures: "an appropriations bill is not required by the Constitution to originate in the House. That is a matter of custom and usage. Only a revenue bill is required to originate in the House." For that and other reasons, Senator Johnson agreed to withdraw his point of order. 129 Cong. Rec. S9682-84 (daily ed. July 12, 1983).

[108] The debate is discussed in Fisher, Constitutional Interpretation by Members of Congress, 63 N. Caro. L. Rev. 707, 719-22 (1985).

[109] In that debate, many Senators argued as to whether the Senate should make for itself the constitutional judgment, rather than leaving the matter to the courts -- a debate that has also occurred among commentators. Compare Fisher, supra, with Mikva, How Well Does Congress Support and Defend the Constitution, 61 N. Caro. L. Rev. 587 (1983).

Majority Leader Baker expressed the historic view, that just as the Supreme Court could pass on the constitutionality of enacted statutes, "it is equally true, and the precedent is just as old, that the Senate of the United States must first exercise its own judgment as to whether a matter before it conforms with or violates the Constitution." 130 Cong. Rec. S5313 (daily ed. May 3, 1984).

common, when the Chair not only may, but must,
submits points of order to the Senate concerns
amendments to appropriation bills.[110] This
provision produces a major part of the Senate's
consideration each year of points of order.[111]
The Chair may also submit certain other questions
to the Senate to "duck" them.[112]

---

[110] Pursuant to Rule XVI, Senators can raise various points
of order against amendments to appropriation bills. The
chapters on the authorization-appropriation process and on
floor management discuss the substantive tests involved.
Here, it is noted that Rule XVI(4) prescribes a special
procedure for certain of these points of order: that "all
questions of relevancy of amendments under this rule, when
raised, shall be submitted to the Senate and be decided
without debate."

[111] Riddick notes several hundred rulings of the Chair or
Senate under Rule XVI. Riddick, "Appropriations:
Legislation to a General Appropriation Bill Not in Order,"
at 156-167. Of these several hundred, some of the numerous
votes that were submitted to the Senate (as opposed to
points of order that fall under Rule XVI but not Rule
XVI(4), which the Chair itself decides subject to appeal)
are at 160 n.201 and 161 n.203.

Of the 14 roll-call votes in 1984 on point of order
matters, nine consisted of points of order submitted to the
Senate. One was the constitutional point of order against
the line-item veto, but the other eight were points of order
submitted to the Senate under Rule XVI(4) concerning
amendments to appropriation bills. 1984 Congressional
Quarterly Almanac votes 164, 236, 246, 247, 248, 255, 256,
and 263 were points of order submitted to the Senate
pursuant to Rule XVI(4).

[112] From time to time the Parliamentarian may feel
compelled to avoid answering a question, particularly on
procedural questions where the politics are so controversial
that he, or the leadership, see only harm in making the
Chair the focus of the dispute. Then, in particular, the
Chair will draw on the doctrines that "[t]he Presiding
Officer has no authority to interpret legislation," or that
"[t]he Presiding Officer does not have the authority to
place any interpretation on amendments proposed to a
bill," Riddick, "Interpretation of Legislation," at 698;
(footnote continued)

Appeals

If the Chair does not submit a point of order to the Senate, then the Chair itself decides. Rule XX(1) provides that a point of order, "unless submitted to the Senate, shall be decided by the Presiding Officer without debate, subject to an appeal to the Senate." The Chair usually follows the Parliamentarian's recommendation. The Senate Parliamentarian performs roughly the same functions as the House Parliamentarian, as discussed in the chapter on the organization of the House. The Senate Parliamentarian, like the House Parliamentarian, has a historic record of relative independence and nonpartisanship in rulings.[113]

"Amendments: Interpretation of Amendments," at 52.

For example, in 1971, Senator Henry Jackson (D-Wash.) proposed an amendment to an appropriations bill to provide funds for the sale of jets to Israel, which the relevant committee chairs challenged as violating the requirement of an authorization for such a sale. As a commentator observed, "[r]ather than decide between the arguments, the chair ruled . . . 'that the point of order is addressed to an interpretation of the law. The Chair knows of no provision or precedent authorizing the Presiding Officer to interpret the law.'" The Senate overruled the point of order and adopted the amendment. T. Siff & A. Weil, Ruling Congress 59-60 (1975).

[113] The first Senate Parliamentarian, Charles Watkins, served from 1935 to 1965. Floyd Riddick technically served as Senate Parliamentarian from 1965 to 1975, and actually longer, as he filled a major role under his predecessor.

It must be noted that when the Republicans took control of the Senate in 1981, there was a change of Senate Parliamentarian, with Riddick's successor, Murray Zweben, leaving, and Zweben's chief assistant, Robert Dove, assuming the post. In 1987, there was again a change of Senate Parliamentarian, with Dove leaving and his chief assistant, Alan Frumin, assuming the post. An account of the House and Senate parliamentarians is in Hook, Parliamentarians: Procedure and Pyrotechnics, 45 Cong. Q. Week. Rep. 1951 (footnote continued)

Appeals from rulings of the Chair are debatable. Sometimes a very considerable amount of debate on appeals may occur for informative (not delay) purposes.[114] Instead of letting the appeal proceed to a vote, often a Senator will move to table the appeal. Rule XX(1) provides that "any appeal may be laid on the table without prejudice to the pending proposition, and thereupon shall be held as affirming the decision of the Presiding Officer."

As in other uses of the motion to table discussed in the chapter on floor management, the Senate may use tabling to cut off debate -- particularly when filibustering Senators take appeals for delay purposes. However, a Senator may allow full debate, and then use the motion to table to put the matter on a procedural basis, as little attuned as possible to the popularity of

---

(1987).

[114] Thus, for example, the Senate decided a significant appeal in 1983 concerning a point of order against an Appropriations Committee amendment to a supplemental appropriations bill. The committee amendment deferred FCC proceedings on a controversial broadcasting proposal; the issue had been heavily lobbied.

Senator Robert Packwood (R-Oreg.), chair of the Commerce Committee, the committee with legislative jurisdiction over the FCC, made the point of order under Rule XV that the Appropriations Committee amendment concerned a matter under another committee's (his) jurisdiction. (Rule XV(5) states: "It shall not be in order to consider any proposed committee amendment (other than a technical, clerical, or conforming amendment) which contains any significant matter not within the jurisdiction of the committee proposing such amendment." This simply requires that one committee's members who wish to tie to their bill a matter in another committee's jurisdiction can only offer that matter as a floor amendment. Of course, for a variety of tactical reasons, they may prefer to offer their matter as a committee amendment.)

When the Chair sustained the point of order, an appeal occurred, and many Senators took part in a full-length debate on the point of order. 129 Cong. Rec. S14742-44 (daily ed. Oct. 27, 1983). The Senate's vote sustaining the appeal established a key precedent for Rule XV.

the underlying substantive matter.[115] A motion to
table may also be made against a point of order
submitted to the Senate, for the same reasons --
either to cut off debate, or even after full
debate, in order to emphasize the procedural side
of the vote.[116]

When a motion to table fails, the question
recurs on the appeal from the Chair's ruling (or
the question submitted directly to the Senate)
itself.   Debate that stopped for the motion to
table may continue before the vote on the appeal,
although sometimes the Senate has fully discussed
the matter and just votes. Senate rules prevent
the piling of debatable appeals atop other
debatable appeals.[117]

---

[115] For example, in the appeal just discussed regarding the
FCC, at the end of the debate on the appeal, Senator
Packwood moved to table the appeal. Clearly he did not seek
to cut off debate, as he waited until debate was completed,
but sought only to emphasize the procedural side of the
issue. When Senator Packwood lost the motion to table, he
let the appeal be sustained (that is, the Chair's ruling
reversed) on a voice vote.

[116] The constitutional point of order described above
regarding the line-item veto illustrates this clearly.   A
motion to table that point of order lost only by the cliff-
hanging vote of 45-46.   Then, the vote on the actual
constitutional point of order sustained it by 56-34.
Considering the purely procedural distinction between voting
against the motion to table, and voting for the point of
order, this rather substantial shift shows how much
importance Senators may place on subtle tuning of messages.

[117] If debate occurs on an appeal (either before or after a
tabling motion), there is a potential for entanglements were
new points of order to arise or appeals from these occur --
a resistant faction could appeal, then appeal from a ruling
during the debate on that (first) appeal, then appeal from a
ruling during the debate on that (second) appeal, and so
on.   To forestall this, Rule XX(1) specifies a strict
procedure during appeals: "When an appeal is taken, any
subsequent question of order which may arise before the
decision of such appeal shall be decided by the presiding
officer without debate; and every appeal therefrom shall be
decided at once, and without debate."

As distinct from raising a point of order, a
Senator may make a "parliamentary inquiry." Such
an inquiry requests information from the Chair.
It may be something practical and unconnected with
rules, such as what the current amendment
situation is -- how many amendments are pending,
and in what order, or how much time is left under
a time agreement. On the other hand, it may ask
the same types of technical rule issues that a
point of order poses.[118]

Among the other reasons for formal
parliamentary inquiries on the floor is that they
create a record in the Congressional Record.[119]
Technically, "[u]nlike rulings of the Chair, the
responses to parliamentary inquiries do not create
precedents for the Senate," for "a Senator may not
take an appeal from the Chair on the response to a
parliamentary inquiry."[120] Still, once the Chair

---

[118]   As Riddick sums up their use:

> Parliamentary inquiries are addressed to the Chair by
> Senators who have questions on the procedure to be
> followed on a particular matter, how the Senate would
> go about transacting a particular piece of business,
> what would be the rules and procedure involving the
> disposition of a particular matter, or any question
> relating to the rules or procedure of the Senate.

Riddick, "Parliamentary Inquiry" (headnote), at 785.

[119]   They may provide an answer on a matter which requires
"immediate action," Riddick, "Parliamentary Inquiry"
(headnote), at 785; also, the mechanism of formal inquiry
can overcome some reluctance by the Parliamentarian to give
an answer off the floor. While "[t]he Chair may decline to
answer a parliamentary inquiry," the Parliamentarian has
greater reason to answer when receiving formally a floor
inquiry. As Riddick says, "unless such an inquiry involves
a decision on a very controversial matter, the Chair obliges
the Senate" in answering parliamentary inquiries. Id.

[120]   Id. This is not a rigid point. Even as a technical
matter, Dr. Riddick states that "if there are a series of
responses to parliamentary inquiries over a long period of
time on which nothing to the contrary has occurred, such
responses are used as guidelines for decisions." Id. In
(footnote continued)

has answered an inquiry regarding a particular matter, it will be reluctant to change positions on that particular matter.[121]

Votes on Procedure

As part of the Senate's trend after the 1950s toward decreasing central control, a decline has occurred in the protection the Senate gives to rulings of the Chair. As recently as 1975, a commentator could say that "rarely has a parliamentarian's decision been over[t]urned," and Robert Dove, then assistant parliamentarian (later Parliamentarian), could say that in his six years as assistant, "he ha[d] seen Riddick overruled only once."[122] In the House, that pattern still holds; there rarely are any appeals at all, and not once in the past 60 years has there been a successful appeal from the rulings of the Chair.

However, in the modern Senate quite a few points get appealed, and some appeals are successful. This in no way suggests any incorrect judgments by the Parliamentarian, for the appeals do not reflect any such error. In fact, during most appeals, no Senator even suggests that the Parliamentarian erred. Rather, the Senate simply does not treat certain rules as binding in the political sense that it would uniformly sustain the Chair when it enforces those rules. Rather, while the rule continues to require the Chair to uphold points of order, Senators feel free to vote on appeals without regarding so much those weak

---

other words, the Chair does give some weight to prior answers to parliamentary inquiries, for consistency if nothing else.

[121]   Thus, it is not unusual for Senators anticipating filibusters or other procedural battles to ask the Chair one or more parliamentary inquiries, in order to lock into place some firm guidance for when the crisis comes. For example, when Senator Jesse Helms (R-N.C.) anticipated the federal criminal code might come to the floor under a cloture rule, he asked the Chair a long string of parliamentary inquiries regarding the germaneness of amendments he might offer.

[122]   T. Siff & A. Weil, _supra_, at 55.

rules as with regard to the popularity of the underlying legislation.

The pattern for such treatment are the questions of order submitted to the Senate under Rule XVI(4), regarding germaneness of amendments to appropriation bills. Senators tend to vote freely on these appropriation points of order as they feel regarding the amendments' substance and politics, rather than with regard to whether, as a technical matter, the amendments violate the rule.[123] Similarly, appeals on Rule XVI's ban on legislation on appropriations reflect the political appeal of the amendments.[124]

---

[123] For example, in 1984, when Minority Leader Byrd offered his "Grove City" civil rights amendment to the continuing resolution, an amendment clearly non-germane by any technical standards, the Senate voted it germane by 51-48. Northern Democrats voted 30-1 that it was germane, nouthern Democrats 9-5, and Republicans 12-42, 1984 Congressional Quarterly Almanac 42-S, vote 236, refecting the measure's substantive appeal to the various groups.

Later, when Senator Daniel Moynihan (D-N.Y.) offered an amendment to the same continuing resolution to regulate armor-piercing (so-called "cop-killing") ammunition, the Senate voted 24-74 that it was non-germane. Every single Republican voted that it was non-germane, while the Democrats divided evenly, another vote far more reflective of political views than technical germaneness. Id. 45-S, vote 255.

[124] Rule XVI(4) does not require these questions to be submitted to the Senators, but when the Chair rules, the Senators tend to vote on appeals more as they feel regarding the amendment than regarding the technical correctness of the Parliamentarian's judgment. For example, in 1983, Senators offered various amendments to the continuing resolution, against which points of order were made and upheld by the Chair. In most of the appeals, concerning minority party amendments, the Senate sustained the Chair. 129 Cong Rec. S15884, S15919 (daily ed. Nov. 10, 1983) (Riegle and Melcher amendments; rulings of Chair sustained on appeal).

However, a ruling against an amendment of Senator Jeremiah Denton (R-Ala.), a member of the majority party, (footnote continued)

This trend of not sustaining the rules or the Chair extends beyond Rule XVI and appropriations.[125] In 1984, this trend threatened to destroy one of the central citadels of Senate procedure, during the "Grove City" civil rights bill debate.[126] Only as part of a complex solution were all the pending matters swept away, before the Senate could vote on the appeals.

Ultimately, the Senate could go the whole way toward majority rule without regard for rules.[127] Alternatively, the Senate could

---

was rejected by the Senate. 129 Cong. Rec. S15749 (daily ed. Nov. 9, 1983) (tie vote, which does not sustain the Chair).

[125] As noted above, in 1983 in the FCC incident, the Senate overruled the Chair on a point of order under Rule XV against a Commerce Committee subject that had been presented by an Appropriations Committee amendment. In effect, the Senate established an informal precedent regarding how it would treat that rule: that the Senate would not treat Rule XV as an inviolable rule protecting committee jurisdiction, but would override it as it overrides Rule XVI.

[126] In that debate, the Senate voted cloture on Minority Leader Byrd's amendment, imposing a germaneness rule. The Chair ruled two amendments on busing and gun control out of order, producing two appeals. At first, the Senate sustained the Chair by tabling the appeal on the busing amendment. However, the Senate then defeated a motion -- made by Majority Leader Baker himself -- to table the appeal on the gun control amendment.

That defeat meant that the Senate was ready to sustain the appeal and overrule the Chair's decision, which would have had a devastating effect. It "meant the Senate was primed to overturn its own rules restricting debate after cloture was invoked"; the Majority and Minority Leaders both "warned that senators were heading down a dangerous path that could cause legislative chaos," but "[f]or two days, Baker's pleas fell on deaf ears." 1984 Congressional Quarterly Almanac 242.

[127] It would do so by allowing any substantive proposition with majority political support, regardless of whether rulings of the Chair need to be overruled in the process. There is no assurance that the latter pattern is workable, (footnote continued)

continue just to override some rules some of the time, but not all rules all of the time.

F.   MECHANICS

Before addressing, in the next three chapters, the Senate's agenda setting, floor management, and cloture procedure, it is useful to address some basic mechanics of Senate operation: how it conducts speeches, routine business, its quorum calls, and its votes.

Decorum in Speeches

Rule XIX(1)(a) codifies the Senators' right to the floor, so long as decorum is maintained: "No Senator shall interrupt another Senator in debate without his consent . . . ." As Riddick explains, "[a] Senator who has been recognized holds the floor until relinquished, until called to order, or he proposes an action by the Senate by which he loses the floor . . . ."[128] A Senator can be called to order, and hence interrupted and stopped from speaking further, for violating the provisions of Rule XIX(2) and (3), specifying that "[n]o Senator in debate shall, directly or indirectly, by any form of words impute to another Senator or to other Senators any conduct or motive unworthy or unbecoming a Senator," or "refer offensively to any State of the Union."

A large body of precedents governs just how far Senators can go in their references to other Senators without violating the principles of decorum. There is a fine art to describing other Senators as being in error, rather than fools, or being at variance with the facts, rather than liars. Senators can easily fall into mistakes with this code, as Senator Ted Kennedy (D-Mass.) did when referring to some statements by Senator

---

as in the ultimate version it would mean that all issues would be pending on all bills.

[128]   Riddick, "Debate: Interruption of Senator Who Has the Floor is Not Allowed -- Except by his Consent," at 598.

Helms about the Martin Luther King holiday bill as "completely inaccurate and false."[129]   In the days gone by Senators were subtler.[130]

Because Senators can be very sensitive about losing the floor, Rule XIX has its own strict procedure: a Senator who does not have the floor may make the Rule XIX point of order, as Senator Helms did; if the Senator did speak out of order the Chair calls him to order, and that Senator "shall take his seat, and may not proceed without leave of the Senate, which, if granted, shall be upon motion that he be allowed to proceed in order, which motion shall be determined without debate."[131]

Theoretically, the "Pastore rule" Rule XIX(1)(b), could also provide a basis for points of order against speaking Senators.   That rule requires that for the first "three hours of actual session . . . all debate shall be germane and confined to the specific question then pending

---

[129] Senator Helms made a proper Rule XIX point of order against the forbidden accusation of falsehood, and the Majority Leader had to patch matters up by saying "'False' perhaps would imply a violation of rule XIX, and 'inaccurate' certainly would not.   However, the usage is so common in the Senate that I can fully understand how it is done.   I use it myself."   129 Cong. Rec. S14009-10 (daily ed. Oct. 18, 1983).   By unanimous consent, the word "false" was to be expunged.

[130] It was held not to violate Rule XIX for a Senator to say, "Let us have done with the sly innuendo, the intemperate inference . . . the thinly veiled implication, the vague hints in which some have indulged," Riddick, "Debate: Disorderly Language, Use of," in "Debate, and Restrictions on:" at 589.

[131] Just how sensitive some Senators used to be about this rule was suggested in 1863, when a Senator Saulsbury was called to order for impugning other Senators (for "blackguardism").   Senator Saulsbury ignored orders from the Vice President to stop talking, and when the Senate Sergeant at Arms was directed to take him in charge, "the enraged Senator had levelled a gun at the sergeant at arms and threatened to shoot him on the spot."   Burdette at 31.

before the Senate."[132]   However, that rule is
rarely invoked.

Routine Morning Business

As discussed in the chapters on House
procedure, certain automatic mechanisms have been
developed so that a vast volume of routine
business connected with bill introduction and
reporting can be conducted without tying up the
floor.   Bill   introduction   in   particular
illustrates   the   progress   of   automatic
mechanisms. As in the House, the enormous growth
of business following the Civil War necessitated
quick   methods.[133]   Accordingly,   the   Senate
simplified the process in the post-Civil War
recodifications of the rules.[134]

---

[132]   See Riddick, "Debate: Germaneness of Debate," at 592-
95; "Germaneness of Debate," at 684-85.

[133]   The close of the Civil War found the business of the
Senate so suddenly augmented, that what with the
precedence of appropriation bills and Executive
business, and what with the time consumed merely in the
introduction of petitions, bills, reports, and so
forth, not to mention unlimited debate, many important
committee measures failed for want of final
consideration and a vote. If a few of them did get
through, it was, in the language of Senator Edmunds,
"just by a kind of sporadic impulse."

L. G. McConachie, Congressional Committees 318 (1898).

[134]   Under the Senate procedure of the first half of the
nineteenth century, Senators had to give one day's notice of
a motion for leave to introduce a bill, before they could
introduce one. At first the Senate began allowing notice to
be "dispensed with, by unanimous consent." Around 1874,
"[v]arious means of avoiding the inconvenience and yet
maintaining the essential part of the rule were tried." C.
H. Kerr, The Origin and Development of the United States
Senate 54 (1895). By 1883, Senate rules omitted mention of
notice or motions altogether, and required a Senator to make
an objection in order to forestall immediate introduction.
See History of the Senate Committee on Rules and
(footnote continued)

The Senate's chief vehicle for streamlining
has been "routine morning business." Even in the
early eighteenth century, the Senate recognized
the value in letting Senators conduct routine
business, such as bill introduction and filing of
committee reports, at a rapid clip in one period,
rather than intermingling such business with the
longer processes of bill consideration.   To
separate out routine business, the Senate
developed a program for a "Morning Hour" -- often,
notwithstanding the name, a period in the
afternoon -- when it handled petitions, committee
reports,   and bill introduction, among other
matters,[135] though still requiring a floor
presence at that time.[136]

Administration, S. Doc. No. 27, 96th Cong., 1st Sess. (1979)
at 23 (Rule 25 in 1868: "one day's notice at least shall be
given of an intended motion for leave to bring in a bill or
joint resolution"); id. at 32 (Rule 22 in 1877: same as Rule
25 in 1868 "but in the introduction of bills or joint
resolution on leave, such notice may be dispensed with, by
unanimous consent"); id. at 44 (Rule XIV(1) in 1883: no more
notice requirement, only that "Whenever a bill or joint
resolution shall be offered, its introduction shall, if
objected to, be postponed for one day").

[135] A rule proposed by Benjamin Ruggles in 1828, and
evidently based upon the then prevailing practice,
prescribed as the daily order of business: 1,
Resolutions of State legislatures, petitions, and
memorials; 2, Reports of committees, and bills
introduced on leave; 3, Motions or resolutions of
individual Senators; 4, Orders of the day. This is the
framework for arrangements of to-day. The present
programme for the routine, so-called morning, business
dates from 1834.

L. G. McConachie, supra, at 317. See History of the Senate
Committee on Rules and Administration, S. Doc. No. 27, 96th
Cong., 1st Sess. 23 (Rule 24, in 1868, provides for that
sequence of business in the morning).

[136] The Senate continued the practice of having Senators
come to the floor, into the twentieth century, and even as
late as the 1960s, during morning hour to introduce bills
and file committee reports, and often to make short speeches
(akin to the House's "one minutes" today). F. Riddick, The
(footnote continued)

Ultimately, the Senate dropped the requirement of live attendance for conduct of routine business. Rather, at the beginning of each Congress, the Senate adopts a unanimous consent order that Senators can simply bring to the desk bills for introduction and committee reports.[137] Thereafter, during the days when the Senate is in session, bills for introduction and committee reports are brought to the desk at any convenient time. Periodically during the day, the leadership arranges by unanimous consent for a period for "routine morning business," which may be 15 or fewer minutes, or even one minute or less.[138] At that point in the Congressional Record will be printed, along with whatever business Senators conduct live on the floor (such as speeches or old-fashioned live introduction of bills), a listing of bills and reports brought to the desk during the day before then. The morning hour and morning business have sone special

---

United States Congress 348-51 (1949); Riddick, "Morning Business: Statement by Chair on Morning Business," at 733; D. R. Matthews, U.S. Senators and Their World 244 (1973 ed. of 1960 book); L. Froman, The Congressional Process 100, 111 (1967).

[137] For example, on the first day of the 99th Congress, the Senate agreed:

> that during the 99th Congress, Senators may be allowed to bring to the desk bills, joint resolutions, concurrent resolutions, and simple resolutions, for referral to appropriate committees,

and

> that during the 99th Congress it be in order for the proper members of the staff to receive reports at the desk when presented by a Senator at any time during the day of the session of the Senate.

131 Cong. Rec. S11, S12 (daily ed. Jan. 3, 1985).

[138] "Morning business need not take place in the morning, but can occur at any point during the day, and it is not uncommon for morning business to be ordered more than once on the same day." Gold, supra, at 6.

significance during filibusters with regard to the nondebatability of motions to proceed, which is discussed in the chapter on filibusters and cloture.

Quorum Calls: Uses

A quorum call is an attendance call of the Senate roll, not to ask the Senators to vote on a proposition, but simply for them to register their presence. Senators trigger a quorum call for a number of purposes: to obtain time out, to bring a majority of Senators to the floor, and to delay.

The main use is to obtain time out, for here is one of the devices by which the Senate accommodates the convenience of individual Senators. As a point of comparison, the House floor script requires that Members appear at an appointed time to proceed, and continue working until completion or recess, with all floor proceedings occurring "on the record" and making juggernaut-like progress. In contrast, the Senate adjusts to the burdens on its individual Members (and their greater retaliatory capacity were the Senate or its leadership to try to force individuals into obedience rather than accommodating them). When the Senate finishes for the moment with some matter, it needs to wait while the Senators needed for the next item are summoned or readied. Accordingly, a Senator will start a quorum call, by suggesting the absence of a quorum, and the clerk will slowly call the roll. When the needed Senators come and are ready, the quorum call is rescinded by unanimous consent.

Similarly, during floor deliberations, the Senators may wish to negotiate or to discuss something off the record. For example, the leadership may have a complex unanimous consent request, which only makes sense with a background explanation; or, the manager may be willing to make a deal with an amendment proponent, which requires lengthy or delicate discussion before it can be propounded on the floor. In the House, the tendency in to fight, to steamroller over any recalcitrant Member, and to keep the floor working on something while any negotiations occur.

In contrast, in the Senate, in such

situations, a Senator starts a quorum call. While
the clerk slowly calls the roll, explanations are
given, negotiations occur, or a deal is discussed
"off the record." Then, when the Senators desire
to go back on the record, the quorum call is
rescinded, and proceedings resume on the record.

For example, in 1977, Senator John Culver (D-
Iowa), as manager, faced the type situation
managers often do: he wanted Senator William Scott
(R-Va.), opposing his bill, to offer fewer
amendments in return for a negotiated deal. As a
journalist described the standard Senate sequence:

> Culver finds that they haven't got very far;
> Scott is insisting that either he be allowed
> to offer four amendments or he will
> ultimately offer twelve. Culver has asked
> for a quorum call -- a device used from time
> to time during a debate in order to gain time
> to get a senator to the floor, or to regroup,
> or to work out an amendment, or to negotiate
> -- and the clerk calls the roll
> slowly . . . .
>
>   Finally . . . Culver comes back to his
> desk and asks that the quorum call be
> ended. He has talked Scott into offering
> just one more amendment . . . .[139]

Senators also use quorum calls for summoning the
other Senators[140] or for delay, which will be

---

[139] E. Drew, Senator 176-77 (1979).

[140] Ordinarily, the leadership (or others) communicate
messages through direct contact, or through staff or
"hotlines," but since the Senate leadership requires much
consensual agreement, it needs a means to summon the
Senators on occasion and so a quorum call will be used to
summon the Senators. In 1983, there was a typical array of
examples. One time, on a major bill, none of the Senators
with amendments was calling up their amendments, and so
Majority Leader Baker used a quorum call to summon Senators
for this speech:

> It is now 2:15 in the afternoon and we have been on
>   this bill almost 2 hours without a single amendment
(footnote continued)

discussed in the chapter on filibustering.

Quorum Calls: Mechanics

For the Senate, as for the House, the Constitution prescribes that "a majority of each [House] shall constitute a Quorum to do Business."[141]   Accordingly, Senate Rule VI(1) prescribes that "A quorum shall consist of a majority of the Senators duly chosen and sworn." "The Senate operates on the presumption that a quorum is present at all times," until a Senator suggests otherwise or a roll-call vote shows that a quorum is not present.[142]

The point of order, or suggestion, that a quorum is not present triggers the procedure of Senate Rule VI(3).[143]   Pursuant to Rule VI(3),

---

having been called up.

> I apologize, Mr. President, for the necessity for this live quorum . . . but if we do not get this done, if we do not get underway, we are going to be here for a long, long time.

129 Cong. Rec. S2399 (daily ed. March 9, 1983). For a similar summoning, see 129 Cong. Rec. S15844 (daily ed. Nov. 10, 1983).

[141] U.S. Const., Art. I, sec. 5, cl. 1.

[142] Riddick, "Quorum: Assumption that Quorum is Present, Unless Question Raised," at 836. Even a division vote clearly showing that a majority was not present and voting, such as a 12-7 vote, does not raise the question of the presence of a quorum; only a roll call vote does. Riddick, "Quorum: Vote Less than Quorum not Valid," at 864.

[143] The rule provides that "If, at any time during the daily sessions of the Senate, a question shall be raised by any Senator as to the presence of a quorum, the presiding Officer shall forthwith direct the Secretary to call the roll and shall announce the result, and these proceedings shall be without debate." The Chair does not count a quorum without a roll call. Riddick, "Quorum: Counting of Quorum by Chair," at 845. The special way under cloture that the chair can dispense with a quorum call and just count (footnote continued)

when the Chair directs the clerk to call the roll,
Senators come to the chamber and answer their
names; they may then leave and still be counted
towards a quorum, though that means that only a
few Senators are present at the same time. In the
usual situation, when a quorum call has been
called just to fill time, it continues at a
leisurely pace, with almost no one coming to the
floor to be counted, until the need to fill time
is over, at which point the quorum call is ended
by unanimous consent.

If a quorum call has a real purpose -- either
the leadership's desire to summon Members, or an
individual Senator's insisting on a quorum call to
stall or to send a message -- then the quorum will
go "live."[144] A quorum call begins as soon as the
a Senator suggests the absence of a quorum and the
Chair directs the clerk to call the roll; it has
begun even before the Clerk calls the first name
or receives the first response, and once it has
begun, it cannot be stopped, except by unanimous
consent.[145]

Senators is discussed in the chapter on filibusters.

[144] This is announced to the Senate by the ringing of three
bells in the signal system (a quorum call that has not gone
live has only two rings), while the roll continues to be
called for an indefinite time until a majority appears, or
the Majority Leader takes one of his available actions.

[145] Riddick, "Quorum: Call of Quorum may not be
Interrupted," at 843. In a classic instance, Senator John
East (R-N.C.) lost a filibuster of the highway-gas tax
increase, when he mistakenly made the point of order that a
quorum is not present, immediately losing the floor and
beginning a quorum call, an error he could not retrieve
despite strenuous efforts prior to the first response on the
call. 128 Cong. Rec. S15478 (daily ed. Dec. 18, 1982).

Stopping a quorum call even by unanimous consent
presents a metaphysical problem, since while the roll is
being called, no Senator can obtain recognition to request
action. Minority Leader Byrd once questioned the Chair
about a similar paradox, regarding a Senator's obtaining
recognition during the reading of an amendment to ask
unanimous consent to end the reading:

(footnote continued)

The roll may be called for quite a while.
For example, the Monday after the Fourth of July
recess in 1983, it proved almost impossible to
obtain a quorum. When a quorum finally appeared,
the Majority Leader noted late in the afternoon
that "we have been on this quorum call -- one or
the other of two quorums -- since 2:25 this
afternoon. I anticipated a slow day, but I had
not anticipated it being this slow."[146]   "No
limitation can be set on the length of time of a
quorum call."[147]

On the other hand, the Majority Leader may be
impatient with the delay. In that case, taking
his cue from the Majority Leader, the clerk reads
the roll quickly to complete the "live quorum
call" and announces in short order that a quorum
is not present. The Constitution allows the
Senate to do only a few things with a quorum not
present.[148]   Chiefly, pursuant to Senate Rule
VI(4) a Senator -- almost invariably the Majority
Leader, who treats the motion as one of his
prerogatives -- moves that the Senate's Sergeant
at Arms request the attendance of absent Senators,
and the leader requests a roll-call vote on that
motion.[149]   Like any roll-call vote, this is

Mr. BYRD: But how is he to ask unanimous consent to
dispense with the reading of the amendment if he does
not have some kind of recognition?

The PRESIDING OFFICER: It is in the same manner that
the Senator can ask unanimous consent for suspension of
the quorum call. It is not a question of actually
having the floor.

129 Cong. Rec. S10363 (daily ed. July 19, 1983).

[146] 129 Cong. Rec. S9651 (daily ed. July 11, 1983).

[147] Riddick, "Quorum: Length of a Quorum Call," at 848.

[148] "[A] smaller Number [than a quorum] may adjourn from
day to day, and may be authorized to compel the Attendance
of absent Members, in such Manner, and under such Penalties
as each House may provide." U.S. Const., Art. I, sec. 5,
cl. 1.

[149] Rule VI(4) provides:
(footnote continued)

supposed to have a 15 minute time limit, and
Senators who care about their records of
attendance on roll-call votes appear rapidly, in
contrast to the languid response to a quorum
call. The arrival of a majority to vote on this
motion satisfies the quorum requirement and
vitiates the quorum call, allowing the Senate to
proceed with business.

G.   VOTING

Voice and Division

Ultimately, the legislative process consummates
with decisions that require votes. Of course, the
Senate takes many steps by unanimous consent, or
without objection. However, when the time comes
for a test of strength, the Senate employs three
voting methods: voice, division, and roll call
("yeas and nays"). If no Senator asks for any
other method, generally the Chair will put a
question and call for a voice vote. For this,
"the Chair usually calls for those in favor first,
and those opposed secondly,"[150] such as by asking
that "those in favor say aye," pausing to hear how
many Senators say "aye," then asking that "those
opposed say nay," and pausing to hear how many
Senators say "nay."
     On a noncontroversial matter, such as the
voice vote on an unopposed amendment, the Chair

Whenever upon such roll call it shall be ascertained
that a quorum is not present, a majority of the
Senators present may direct the Sergeant at Arms to
request, and, when necessary, to compel the attendance
of the absent Senators, which order shall be determined
without debate; and pending its execution, and until a
quorum shall be present, no debate nor motion, except
to adjourn, or to recess pursuant to a previous order
entered by unanimous consent, shall be in order.

For details of the procedure, see Riddick, "Attendance of
Senators," at 171-80.

[150]   Riddick: "Voting: Viva Voce Vote," at 1153.

may simply announce the result immediately upon hearing the vote. Alternatively, for a matter on which someone may have concerns, "the Presiding Officer announces that" the "'noes' or 'ayes' seem to have it."[151] Such a tentative announcement "is not conclusive, nor is it a final declaration of the result," and thus even after the tentative announcement, for a brief moment "it is in order to demand the yeas and nays"[152] or a division vote. As Majority Leader Byrd noted:

> it is always, I think, the understanding here that the Chair, in announcing the vote, will say, "the ayes appear to have it; the ayes have it." That gives any Senator, who may be distracted by thinking about something else for the moment, an opportunity to ask for a division or to ask for the yeas and nays.[153]

If no Senator asks for a division or a recorded vote, then "[f]ollowing the above announcement that the 'ayes or noes seem to have it,' the Chair announces that the ayes or noes, as the case might be, have it which is conclusive."[154] At that point, "[a]fter the result of a voice vote has been announced by the Presiding Officer, it is too late to ask for a division vote, or yeas and nays."[155]

Any Senator may ask for a vote by the second method, the division vote, or the Chair call for such a vote its own initiative.[156] Division

---

[151] Id. (emphasis supplied).

[152] Id.

[153] 123 Cong. Rec. 31747 (1977).

[154] Id. at 1154.

[155] Id.; also, "Voting: Division Vote," at 1133-34.

[156] "The Chair may request a division vote when he is in doubt of a result, or any Senator may request a division vote on any issue . . . ." Id. "There is no authority in the rules of the Senate for the method of voting by a division; the method is intended to advise the Presiding (footnote continued)

consists of the following procedure:

> The Chair requests that those in favor of the
> proposition raise their hands until counted,
> and then he requests that those opposed raise
> their hands until they are counted. Or, the
> Chair may state those in favor of the
> proposition will stand and be counted, and
> then those opposed will stand and be
> counted.[157]

A division produces a count without a record of
who voted which way.

Division votes on the Senate floor are
infrequent. Unlike the House, "[a] division vote,
while counted for the Chair by the Clerk, is never
recorded; the Record does not show how many voted
for and how many voted against -- it merely shows
the results; whether approved or not
approved."[158]   Thus, Senators may sometimes
tactically choose a division vote for the same
reason they choose a voice vote, to avoid being
embarrassed by a lopsided defeat. As two Senators
jested after a division vote:

> Mr. ARMSTRONG: Mr. President, I wanted to
> point out that in accordance with the
> precedents, the results of a division vote
> are not recorded in the Journal, and I am
> grateful for that because I did not do very
> well. I did not get very many votes. But I

Officer whether or not the majority of the Senators present
favor or oppose a given question." Riddick, "Voting:
Division Vote," at 1132. Although no Senate rule, and no
precedent cited in Riddick, accords Senators the right to
demand a division, it appears that any Senator can demand a
division.

[157] Riddick, "Voting," at 1127 (chapter headnote).

[158] Id. at 1132-33. Not only are the results never
recorded, they are rarely announced: "usually the number
voting for or against a proposition on a division vote,
under the practice of the Senate, is not stated by the
Presiding Officer; he merely declares the results," though
"on occasions the number voting on a division has been
announced." Id. at 1135.

thank the Members who voted with me on that
amendment.

Mr. SCHMITT: I am sure somewhere, someone
was standing in behalf of the Senator from
Colorado.

Mr. ARMSTRONG: . . . I will perhaps pick up
some steam on future amendments.

Mr. SCHMITT: Mr. President, if the Senator
loses any more ground, he would not even be
here.[159]

As with voice votes, "a division vote is not final
unless it has been announced by the Chair," so
Senators may call for the yeas and nays as they
see the division unfolding, but once the Chair has
announced the result in conclusive fashion, "then
it is too late to request the yeas and nays."[160]

Obtaining Yeas and Nays

Most familiar of all the three methods of
voting, and most important, is the third method:
the "yeas and nays."   The call for the "yeas and
nays" is itself a complex matter reflecting the
power of individual Senators.   The ready

---

[159]   128 Cong. Rec. S6034 (daily ed. May 25, 1982).

[160]   Riddick, "Voting," at 1133.   A further curiosity is
that a division vote in which less than a majority
participate (e.g., a vote of 15-8) "does not officially
disclose the absence of a quorum," id. at 1135. A point of
no quorum may be raised after the announcement of the vote,
but "[a]fter the result of a vote, on a division, has been
announced, it is too late to call for a quorum in order to
obtain the presence of Senators for the vote." Id. at
1134.   Hence, the result becomes final even though a count
of those voting revealed less than the "majority" required
by the Constitution for the Senate to "do business." It has
also occurred on occasion that "a quorum not having voted on
a division, the Chair announced the number voting, ordered a
call of the Senate to develop a quorum for a valid vote, or
for the yeas and nays." Id. at 1136.

availability of roll-call votes in the modern Senate has affected its entire operation; individual Senators can not only voice their own views by putting forth propositions, but can require all the other Senators to go on record by voting on those propositions. Hence, a maverick can make all the Senators go on record concerning some deal that they would prefer arranged quietly. A Senator with a strong ideological agenda can make all Senators go on record concerning issues such as abortion, busing, and school prayer, that many would have preferred not to face.

Article I, section 5 of the Constitution prescribes the obtaining of roll-call votes: "the Yeas and Nays of the Members of either House on any question shall, at the Desire of one fifth of those Present, be entered on the Journal." Once a Senator demands the yeas and nays, the Chair has to find out, in the words of the Constitution, whether having a roll-call vote is "the Desire of one fifth of those Present." The Chair asks after receiving such a demand, "Is there a sufficient second?" and those who support the demand raise their hands, which the Chair counts silently. "It is not customary for the Chair to announce the number of Senators who held up their hands to order the yeas and nays. Under the practices and precedents of the Senate, the judgment of the Chair as to whether or not the yeas and nays have been ordered is deemed sufficient."[161]

The nub is what is "one fifth of those Present" and whether the leadership helps Senators to reach that goal. As to what is one fifth, "[t]he Presiding Officer, in connection with a demand for the yeas and nays, has to assume that a quorum is present, and a request of four Senators only for the yeas and nays is not sufficient."[162] Instead, the "demand for the yeas and nays must be seconded by at least one-fifth of the presumptive quorum, a minimum of 11 with the present membership of 100."[163] In other words,

---

[161] Riddick, "Voting: Ordering of the Yeas and Nays," at 1144.

[162] Id. at 1142.
(footnote continued)

technically a Senator needs more than one-fifth of those present, when few are present; he needs at least 11.[164]   If a recent roll call has revealed the presence of more than a quorum, then the Senator needs one-fifth of that roll call.[165]

---

[163]   Id.   If a roll call has occurred recently, then the rule is followed that "the sufficiency of the number of Senators demanding a rollcall is based on the last preceding rollcall," id. at 1143; hence, if 80 Senators appeared at a recent roll call, 16 would be necessary for a sufficient second.   Absent a recent roll call, the Chair uses the presumptive quorum of 51 for the standard, and one fifth is considered to be 11.

[164]   A technical exception is that when there is no quorum, and one of the few allowed motions is made -- to adjourn or to recess, or to have the Sergeant at Arms request the attendance of absentees -- "there [only] needs to be one fifth of those Senators responding to order the yeas and nays," 123 Cong. Rec. 30814 (1977) (response of Chair on parliamentary inquiry), which can be very few, rather than one fifth of a presumptive quorum.

[165]   For example, the following discussion occurred during the 1977 natural gas filibuster:

Mr. ABOUREZK: I ask for the yeas and nays.

The PRESIDING OFFICER: Is there a sufficient second? There is not a sufficient second. The previous vote was 81.   That would require 17.   There were 16 hands raised . . . .   Is there a sufficient second?   We will count once more . . . .   There are 19 secondings.   The yeas and nays have been ordered . . . .

Mr. DANFORTH: After the yeas and nays are asked for, how long does a Senator have to muster a suffient number of seconds?

The PRESIDING OFFICER: There is no precedent on that.   A reasonable amount of time.   When Senators are still coming into the Chamber, it is the opinion of this Presiding Officer that that is reason enough to have a recount of Senators still entering the Chamber.

123 Cong. Rec. 31870 (1977) (omitting a number of (footnote continued)

The requirement of a minimum of 11 makes the availability of a second depend on whether the leadership helps on roll call requests. During the 1950s, the leadership and the senior Senators of the "Inner Club" were disinclined to second roll call demands from "outsiders," and junior Senators were not encouraged to second such demands. "In the 1950s, it was difficult for a senator to obtain a roll-call vote on any issue without the support of [Democratic leader Lyndon] Johnson or the Republican leadership,"[166] although there were certain methods available back then,[167]

---

intervening comments by the Chair and Senators).

[166] Senate of the '80s at 2180. As the study group of former Senators Jim Pearson (R-Kan.) and Abraham Ribicoff (D-Conn.) observed in supporting some restraint on roll call votes: "[W]hen Senators Robinson of Arkansas and McNary of Oregon [i.e., the 1930s and 1940s] were the Majority and Minority Leaders of the Senate, it was often noticeable when a roll call vote was requested, if the two Leaders did not favor the request, the request was not sufficiently seconded." See Congressional Research Service, "The Proposals of the Study Group on Senate Practices and Procedures With Selected Questions on Implications and Applications" (April 27, 1983, at 86, quoting the Pearson-Ribicoff report).

Senator Barry Goldwater (R-Ariz.) recalled, in a letter to the Pearson-Ribicoff team: "Possibly, you might want to go back to the days when the Majority or Minority leader had to hold up his hand before a roll call might be considered." 128 Cong. Rec. S7509 (daily ed. June 24, 1982) (reprinting letter). See also 125 Cong. Rec. 149 (1979) (Senator Robert Dole (R-Kan.)) ("there was a time in this body when . . . the minority leader and the majority leader would decide many times whether or not a rollcall vote was necessary").

[167] A Senator not bashful about being a nuisance could press for his second by suggesting the absence of a quorum, and then attempting to rally support from the Senators arriving for the quorum call, but that was not a course to endear a Senator to the leadership or his colleagues (who would be summoned twice, once for the quorum call, and then for the vote), and it could still be hard to obtain a second. For an account of the difficulty for a junior (footnote continued)

some of which remain available on the occasions
they are needed.[168]

More important than such methods, in the
1960s Majority Leader "Mansfield, as part of the
individual rights movement, decided to raise his
hand for a roll call regardless of the issue.
Within a few years, the leadership had essentially
lost any power to block a roll call even if only
one senator wanted it."[169] On the contrary, it is
now understood that as a courtesy, the leadership
almost invariably helps Senators to obtain a roll
call.[170]

Senator of assembling 11 supporters for a second when few
Senators would stay on the floor, see J. S. Clark, Congress:
The Sapless Branch 191-93 (1964).

[168] For example, during a filibuster, Senator Gordon
Humphrey (R-N.H.) moved to table a budget waiver motion,
obtained the yeas and nays, voted against his own motion
(which lost, 92-5), moved to reconsider that vote, and
another Senator moved to table reconsideration. When he was
told he did not have a sufficient second for a roll call on
tabling reconsideration, he suggested the absence of a
quorum. After the quorum call, he was told again that he
still did not have a sufficient second for a roll call on
reconsideration. So again he suggested the absence of a
quorum, and the Chair overruled a point of order that
asserted no business had transpired since the prior quorum
call, stating "[t]he denial of the yeas and nays is business
for the purpose of calling a quorum." 128 Cong. Rec. S14983
(daily ed. Dec. 16, 1982).

[169] Senate of the '80s at 2182.

[170] For an example of the leadership's attitude, in 1982
Senator S. I. Hayakawa (R-Calif.) had a minor amendment
concerning milk price supports. Senator Thadeus Cochran (R-
Miss.) moved to table it, and the Chair announced that the
motion had been agreed to. Senator Hayakawa complained,
after the announcement (and thus too late) that "[t]here is
no clear-cut majority of yeas and nays on it that I can
see," and the Chair could only suggest that he seek
recognition and asked if there was a sufficient second.
Majority Leader Baker generously said, "Mr. President, why
not let the Senator have his yeas and nays vote on the
motion to table?" The leader secured unanimous consent
agreement to adopt the motion to reconsider, then arranged
(footnote continued)

An observer of the Senate will often see that when a Senator demands the yeas and nays, typically the two leaders hold up their hands. Moreover, since the leaders could obviously summon a dozen other Senators to provide the second, the Chair will often not put the leadership to such a bootless labor, but will take the support of the leaders as itself sufficient for a second.[171]   In light of such a leadership view, one can read the Congressional Record for months without ever seeing a demand for a Senate record vote refused, in distinct contrast with the House, where such refusals occur frequently.   A major exception does occur in post-cloture filibuster situations, where the leaders will ask that the second be denied to stop the filibuster; this is discussed in the chapter on filibusters.   Critics of the current balance in the Senate for tilting too far toward power in individual Senators have called for fewer roll-call votes.[172]

Mechanics of Yeas and Nays

A successful demand for the yeas and nays need not, and frequently does not, mean that the roll call occurs immediately.   By unanimous consent, the yeas and nays can be ordered on a matter not yet pending.[173]   Once a matter, such as

---

to have the yeas and nays ordered on the motion to table. 128 Cong. Rec. S12397 (daily ed. Sept. 28, 1982).

[171]   The Pearson-Ribicoff report observed that "it is noticeable when requests for roll call votes are made, that often not more than seven or eight hands, if that many, are shown, and the Chair states that the request is sufficiently seconded." Congressional Research Service, supra, at 86.

[172]   The Pearson-Ribicoff Report suggested that "[t]he leadership of each party might see fit to prevail upon their respective membership to refuse to participate in seconding roll call votes unless the leadership feels that there should be a roll call vote on a particular subject . . . [in order] to eliminate an extraneous number of roll call votes." Congressional Research Service, supra, at 86.

[173]   Riddick, "Voting: Ordering of the Yeas and Nays," at (footnote continued)

an amendment, is pending, then ordering of the
yeas and nays does not require unanimous consent,
but following such an order, the Senate continues
freely with debate, second-degree amendments,
motions, switches to other business, and so
on.[174] The ordering of the yeas and nays merely
means that if and when the Senate eventually
votes, it will vote by roll call.[175] The Senate
can only rescind an order for the yeas and nays by
unanimous consent, although, of course, it can
avoid a vote (and thereby avoid a roll call) by
any number of ways, such as by following an order
for the yeas and nays on an amendment by a voice
vote to table.

When the time does come for the roll call,
"the Chair merely states upon presenting the
question for vote that the yeas and nays have been
ordered and the Clerk will call the roll."[176] A
Senator has his last chance to obtain recognition
right then, for "[a] Senator is entitled to
recognition after calling of the roll has started
and prior to a response thereto."[177] However,
after the first response, a roll call cannot be
interrupted -- not for debate, not for a point of
order (such as that the amendment being voted upon
is out of order), not even for a parliamentary
inquiry; at most, a Senator may ask what the
pending question is, and if no one objects, the
Chair may tell him.[178]

1146.

[174]   Riddick, "Amendments: Yeas and Nays Ordered on,
Amendments in Order," at 97-98; "Voting: Ordering of the
Yeas and Nays," at 1146-47.

[175]   There are certain collateral consequences discussed
elsewhere, such as that the offeror of an amendment can
ordinarily modify or withdraw his own amendment, but after
the yeas and nays have been ordered, can do so only by
unanimous consent.

[176]   Riddick, "Voting," at 1127 (chapter headnote).

[177]   Riddick, "Voting: Interruption of a Rollcall Vote Out
of Order," at 1139.

[178]   Apart from that, "[t]he Presiding Officer is precluded
(footnote continued)

Senate Rule XII prescribes the procedure for the roll call: "[w]hen the yeas and nays are ordered, the names of Senators shall be called alphabetically; and each Senator shall, without debate, declare his assent or dissent to the question, unless excused by the Senate." An internal informal Senate guide describes the ensuing process:

> The Clerk then begins to call the names of Senators alphabetically; the vote officially begins when the first Senator responds. At this time, the Clerk rings one bell and starts a clock that counts down the stipulated time for voting (usually 15 minutes). As the Clerk calls the names of Senators, those in the Chamber respond when their names are called, and their votes are tallied accordingly.
>
> After all Senators' names have been called, the Clerk stands and recapitulates the vote, reading first the names of the Senators who voted "in the affirmative" and then those who voted "in the negative." After the vote has been in progress for seven and half minutes (during a 15 minute vote) or two and a half minutes (during a 10 minute vote), the Clerk rings 5 bells to warn Senators in the Capitol and the Senate Office Buildings that seven and a half minutes remain to vote. A Senator coming into the Chamber after the Clerk has recapitulated the vote addresses the Chair and seeks recognition to vote. The Clerk then calls the Senator's name and the Senator responds with his or her vote. The Clerk repeats the Senator's vote to ensure that it has been recorded correctly.
>
> After the time for the vote has expired and the Clerk has completed the tally, the

from entertaining any request to suspend the rule [against interrupting the roll call vote for debate] even by unanimous consent." Id. at 1141; also, Riddick, "Debate: Rollcall Vote (Yeas and Nays), Debate Out of Order," at 619-20.

> Clerk gives the Chair the tally sheet with the tabulated results of the vote. Before announcing the vote, the Chair gavels for order and asks if any other Senator in the Chamber wishes to vote. Then the Chair announces the result of the vote, and the matter is decided.

A Senator "may change his vote at any time prior to the announcement of the result."[179] This simple principle produces a great deal of last-minute Senate maneuvering. Senators may hold back their vote until, or change their vote at, the last minute, sometimes with the leadership making the pitch for them to do so (or not). On controversial propositions, Senators may wish to vote on the side most popular with their constituents if at all possible, and may vote the other way, or change their vote, only when they see it as absolute necessary. Alternatively, Senators may vote for the more controversial side thinking it necessary for the securing of a close victory, but as that side loses, may change; a seemingly close defeat of such a proposition can thus quickly become, through rapid shifts, an overwhelming defeat.

Even after the announcement, Senate Rule XII provides that a Senator "may for sufficient reasons, with unanimous consent, change or withdraw his vote," and so by unanimous consent Senators sometimes do so.[180] However, the rule also sternly warns that "no Senator shall be permitted to vote after the decision shall have been announced by the Presiding Officer," and "[n]o motion to suspend this rule shall be in order, nor shall the Presiding Office entertain any request to suspend it by unanimous consent." Thus, Senators who miss the vote are out of luck: "[a]fter the result of a vote has been announced, it is against the rules, or it is too late for a Senator to vote or to have his vote recorded," and the Chair will not entertain a unanimous consent request for postannouncement voting or voting by

---

[179] Riddick, "Voting: Change of Vote," at 1129.

[180] Id.

absentees.[181]

To avoid penalizing Senators, before the Chair announces the vote and thereby cuts off further voting, the Chair asks for order and then asks whether any Senators present have not voted.[182]   Senators arriving too late do the only thing they can (apart from seeking reconsideration); they announce how they would have voted, had they arrived in time.[183]

Duration and Stacking

Votes may occur at times that are inconvenient for Senators, but as described above, if a Senator arrives too late, he is out of luck.   In the modern decentralized Senate, where few Senators stay on the floor and most follow high-pressured schedules, the requirement to show up on the floor to vote at odd times, on short notice, and on all kinds of unrelated and unorganized issues, creates an enormous tension. Three elaborate Senate practices deal with this tension, and influence the environment on almost every Senate vote: vote postponement and "stacking," lengthened duration of votes, and pairing.

The most important scheduling practice concerns vote postponement and "stacking," which follows old uses of unanimous consent agreements.[184]   In "postponement," the Senate

---

[181]   Riddick, "Voting: Absentee May Not Vote," at 1128; "Voting: Voting After Announcement Out of Order," at 1156.

[182]   Riddick, "Voting: Voting After Announcement Out of Order," at 1158 (announcement of Majority Leader Byrd).

[183]   Rule XII(3) also provides for a Senator to "decline to vote . . . when he believes that his voting on such a matter would be a conflict of interest"; declining to vote on other grounds theoretically requires either a Senate vote of consent, as prescribed by Rule XII(2), or unanimous consent.   Riddick, "Voting: Excused from Voting," at 1137-38.

[184]   The Senate has long used unanimous consent agreements (footnote continued)

agrees that roll-call votes on all matters, such
as amendments, motions, and other intermediate
steps, will be deferred until some later point.
In "stacking," the Senate not only agrees to
postpone votes, but also that when those votes do
occur, they will occur in a particular sequence
quickly and without stopping to debate, for
efficiency. The standing order in each Congress
that provides for a 15 minute limit on vote times
further provides that when votes occur immediately
in succession (as in "stacked" votes), the first
lasts 15 minutes, but the rest last only ten
minutes. Therefore, instead of Senators leaving
between votes or wasting time, they wait after the
first vote for abbreviated subsequent votes, and
finish all the votes in short order before
dispersing to their varied duties.

Majority Leader Baker and Minority Leader
Byrd noted in 1983 that it had "been the policy of
both Republican and Democratic leaders in the
Senate for a number of years" that "there will be
no rollcall votes on [a] Friday,"[185] absent
special circumstances. Thus, if the Senate
debated any bills on Fridays, it would agree to
postpone any roll-call votes until the following

---

for fixing times for voting, either explicitly (by
scheduling vote on final passage at a particular time) or
implicitly (by allocating a set time for debate on a matter,
which largely prevents a vote prior to the end of that
period). As discussed in the section on UCAs, an agreement
for an hour's debate on an amendment, for example, precludes
a premature vote on the amendment or offering of a second-
degree amendment or a tabling motion. A premature vote
could only occur if those controlling the time on the
amendment yield the time back. When it is understood that
Members relied on there not being a premature vote, yielding
back time to allow an early vote would be less courteous
than putting in a quorum call to kill unneeded debate time.

By the 1980s, the arranging of vote times reached the
level of a high art, due to Senator Byrd's sophisticated use
of unanimous consent agreements and Senator Baker's desire
to impose some regularity on voting that would allow
Senators to plan engagements away from the Senate and in
home states.

[185] 129 Cong. Rec. S688 (daily ed. Jan. 31, 1983).

week, and generally to stack those votes.   It
became regular, as Majority Leader Baker noted, to
go "about stacking votes as we have this week,
from Friday until Tuesday, or even from Monday
until Tuesday."[186]   Postponement and stacking may
also occur to prevent votes at certain times of
day, particularly lunch or dinner.[187]

However, the leadership has recognized
considerable dangers in the pressures by the
Senate membership for greater postponement and
stacking.[188]   Besides   possible   technical
problems,[188]   fundamentally, vote postponement and

----

[186]   129 Cong. Rec. S8222 (daily ed. June 10, 1983).

[187]   Majority Leader Baker noted that "it would be mutually
advantageous to allow a time, perhaps an hour, when Members
could feel free to go to dinner, or to fulfill commitments
at the dinner hour."   Id.   For example, a UCA on an
immigration bill provided "that any rollcall votes ordered
prior to the hour of 2 p.m. be postponed to occur at 2 p.m.
in sequence"; a UCA on a defense appropriation provided
"that any rollcall votes ordered prior to the hour of 2:45
p.m. on Monday, November 7, 1983, be stacked to occur
beginning at 2:45 p.m. in sequence, with the first vote to
be 15 minutes in length and any remaining amendments in
sequence be 10 minutes in length."   129 Cong. Rec. S6812,
S15473 (daily eds. May 17 and Nov. 4, 1983).

[188]   As Minority Leader Byrd pointed out, such UCAs opened
potentials for premature votes on final passage, or for the
offering of amendments either not germane or out of order.
"What bothers me is that when we say that we stack votes in
sequence, it could very well be that someone would walk on
the floor and ask for the yeas and nays on final passage of
the bill . . . And if that happens and we took that vote
[on final passage] in sequence, then that rules out any
votes on further amendments."   129 Cong. Rec. S8012 (daily
ed. June 8, 1983).   On another occasion, Majority Leader
Baker agreed: "the point raised by the minority leader, if I
understand it correctly, is that there is a jeopardy
involved in stacking votes to occur in sequence unless we
except out final passage."   129 Cong. Rec. S15519-20 (daily
ed. Nov. 7, 1983).

Senator Byrd elaborated that "someone could come on the
floor and call up a War Powers Resolution . . . and get the
(footnote continued)

stacking have diminished the Senate's work week, and contributed to the sense of the Senate being on a hair-trigger without collegial interaction. Without votes on Fridays or Mondays, Senators may leave town for short campaign trips home with a frequency formerly seen only in the House, without hurting their attendance record on roll call votes.[189] Several Senators testified before a committee on reform of Senate procedure that "[t]he Senate has grown accustomed to a three-day work week."[190]

Postponement and stacking radically segregate debate on propositions from voting. Debate and voting lack feedback; normally the defeat of one amendment suggests how to frame the next one, but stacking locks a set group of amendments on course before the voting even begins to show the will of the Senators. Only a handful of Senators attend to debate; then, later, comes a time of rapid-fire sequential votes on a mixed bag of propositions, for which Senators have no immediate exposure to the arguments, only cues. As significant interactive floor time drops, Senators' social contact with each other also drops, weakening the institutional ties and interchanges among Senators that at one time made it a close-knit collegial body. Vote postponement and stacking are simply

---

yeas and nays on it, and then we are locked in to vote on it, with stacked votes occurring before and after, and with no time for debate." Majority Leader Baker agreed that "I can think of a dozen situations like that that could happen." 129 Cong. Rec. S15520 (daily ed. Nov. 7, 1983).

[189] An example was Senator "Rudman, serving his first year in the Senate in 1981 [who] went home 38 weekends out of 52." Senate in the '80s at 2176.

[190] Report of the Temporary Select Committee to Study the Senate Committee System, S. Prt. No. 254, 98th Cong., 2d Sess. 49 (1984) (Sen. Daniel J. Evans (R-Wash.)); id. at 55 (Sen. Sam Nunn (D-Ga.)). By 1983, it had reached a point where Majority Leader Baker commented that "stacking votes to occur on another day . . . is what is getting us in trouble . . . where Members feel that the Senate has turned into a Tuesday-to-Thursday club. It has not. I can assure them that is not the intention of the leadership on either side." 129 Cong. Rec. S8222 (daily ed. June 10, 1983).

one of the many technical means discussed herein, by which the Senate evolves into "an institution whose members do not know each other very well," and "[m]any members believe this semi-stranger quality of Senate life has an unpleasant byproduct -- an increase in hostility and open confrontation on the floor."[191]

Another practice concerns the lengthening durations of votes, for obviously, the longer a vote lasts, the greater the chance of absent Senators reaching the floor in time to vote. At the beginning of each Congress, the Senate adopts a standing order limiting roll calls to 15 minutes, with shorter time for "stacked" votes as discussed below. However, vote time has tended to lengthen beyond this limit, as Senators ask the leadership, either ahead of time or during a vote (or the leadership, trying to corral votes, decides on its own), to extend a vote for an absentee. While there are no formal rules, the presiding officer decides when to announce the result of a vote, and generally looks to the leadership for guidance; impatient Senators pressure the leadership by cries for "regular order," which would be in this context the timely ending of a vote.

At one point in May, 1983, Majority Leader Baker announced that "we have not yet this year had our first 15-minute vote. I believe the shortest one was 18 minutes and the longest one was well over 30 minutes."[192] Accordingly, the

---

[191]   Senate in the '80s at 2176.

[192]   129 Cong. Rec. S6807 (daily ed. May 17, 1983). The problem tended to worsen, as timely Senators found themselves waiting for laggards, and drew the moral that they need not be so timely themselves. At one point, Senator J. James Exon (D-Nebr.) commented:

I simply rise to say once again I think it is about time that we break out of the mold running the U.S. Senate as if it were the Toonerville Trolley.

I would simply point out that we have just had two votes that consumed more than an hour of the time of the U.S. Senate.

(footnote continued)

Majority Leader began announcing that

> Senators should know that [a call for] regular order will produce regular order. This is, we will end the rollcalls. I urge Senators to stay on the floor, to be here and not wander away. If you do wander, there is a high degree of likelihood that you will miss the rollcall vote.[193]

The last practice relevant to Senators' scheduling problems is "pairing." Two Senators "pair" on opposite sides of a question when both refrain from voting; this allows both to be absent without affecting the outcome. In a special kind of pair, the "live pair," one Senator who is present refrains from voting, because he is paired with an absent Senator who would have voted opposite from him. Pairing is an ancient practice, familiar to Parliament in the 1700s and to both the House and Senate in the 1800s.[194] Pairing occurs outside the Senate rules: "[t]he Senate has no rule regarding the arrangement or governing the matter of pairs between Senators," "no official notice is taken of pairs at the desk, and the Presiding Officer has no jurisdiction over them, it being a personal matter of determination between Senators."[195]
As a practical matter, pairing works as follows:

> A Member who will be absent during a record

---

129 Cong. Rec. S10137 (daily ed. July 15, 1983).

[193] Id. at S6608. The problem was somewhat alleviated when a particular telephone, on which calls came in from laggard Senators requesting that pending votes be extended, was taken out. See 129 Cong. Rec. S8223 (daily ed. June 10, 1983).

[194] See S. Bach, "Pairing in Congressional Voting: Current Practice and Historical Development" (Cong. Res. Serv. Nov. 2, 1978), in which the House and Senate history are traced on pages 7-38.

[195] Riddick, "Pairs: Definition of," at 777-78.

vote and who wishes his position on the vote
to be recorded by means of a specific pair
informs his party's pair clerk, either
directly or through his staff. The pair
clerks then pair the absent Members who have
taken opposite positions on the question --
usually, but not invariably, pairing
Democrats with Republicans.[196]

Nothing audible need be said on the Senate
floor. For each record vote, an insert to the
Congressional Record, printed with the vote, is
given as a quote from the Majority and Minority
Leaders, or their assistants, who announce that
the various absent Senators are "absent on
official business," "absent due to illness," or
"necessarily absent"; for those who have indicated
their views, that "if present and voting, the
Senator from --, Senator --, would vote 'yea,'";
and when pairs have been arranged, the
announcement contains the pair.[197]

Pairing of two absent Senators does not
affect the result. It merely allows the absentees
to go on record, while suggesting that they have
not failed in promoting their position, because
their absence is matched with the absence of
someone on the other side. In contrast, live
pairs do affect the results on very close votes,
because the Senator who is present is withholding
his vote. For example, in 1983, an abortion
amendment to an appropriation bill was rejected by
a 44-43 vote. However, immediately thereafter, on
the routine motion to table the motion to
reconsider, amendment opponents failed, because
one Senator took a live pair with an absentee, and
therefore withheld his vote; the motion to table
reconsideration failed 43-43, preventing the
first-round result from being locked in.[198]

---

[196] Bach, supra, at 2.

[197] For example, "On this vote, the Senator from Washington
(Mr. EVANS) is paired with the Senators from Minnesota (Mr.
DURENBERGER). If present and voting, the Senator from
Washington would vote 'yea' and the Senator from Minnesota
would vote 'nay.'" 129 Cong. Rec. S15849 (daily ed. Nov.
10, 1983).
(footnote continued)

A Senator giving a live pair announces out loud that he is doing so. It can be a delicate solution to ambivalence.[199]   The Senator giving the live pair can tell persons on one side of the controversy, "I agreed with you, and said so, but just paired with an absentee as we routinely do in the Senate."   Then the Senator can tell persons on the other side, "I did you a favor by withholding my vote."

---

[198]   129 Cong. Rec. S15850 (daily ed. Nov. 10, 1983).

[199]   For a criticism of live pairing as one of "several cloud covers" for members "to remain less visible and less accountable to the electorate," see T. Siff & A. Weil, supra, at 156, 160-61.   In a close vote, one of the majority and minority leaders' last cards to play is to ask a party member voting against the party position to take a "live pair" instead.

8

Agenda Setting in the Senate[1]

Senate agenda setting, like House agenda setting,
matters enormously, as one of the most important
means by which the nation's government decides
what issues it will address and how it will
address them. The Senate leadership draws its
nationally recognized power in large measure from
its agenda setting power. However, agenda setting
in the Senate contrasts strongly with the House.
    While the House rules provide for complete
majority party control over the floor, and the
House tends to roll on, juggernaut-like, over any
individual opposition, "[i]n the Senate, by
contrast, majority control over the agenda is much
more tenuous."[2] Any Senator can withhold

---

[1] Sources cited frequently in this chapter include:
Enactment of a Law: Procedural Steps in the legislative
Process, S. Doc. No. 20, 97th Cong., 2d Sess. (1981)
("Enactment of a Law") (revised by the Senate
Parliamentarian); Keith, The Use of Unanimous Consent in the
Senate, in Commission on the Operation of the Senate, 94th
Cong., 2d Sess., Committees and Senate Procedures: A
Compilation of Papers (1976); F. L. Burdette, Filibustering
in the Senate (1940); L. A. Froman, The Congressional
Process: Strategies, Rules, and Procedures (1967); S. Bach,
Senator and Senate: Influence on the Legislative Agenda
(Cong. Res. Serv. 1983); M. Gold, Senate Procedure &
Practice 4 (1981).

(footnote continued)

unanimous consent or can filibuster, two potent
ways to resist majority scheduling; any Senator
can offer his proposals as non-germane amendments,
a potent way to put forth an agenda despite the
majority's wishes.

For all that, the Senate has to set some kind
of agenda, and its leadership guides it by
employing the procedures addressed in the
successive sections of this chapter. The Majority
Leader, usually acting in consultation with the
Minority Leader, has various prerogatives. These
start with control over whether the Senate
adjourns or recesses, which determines the
succession of "legislative" days (which differ
from "calendar" days)[3] and in turn regulates
layover requirements which set the basic agenda.

Also, the Majority Leader has the prerogative
of moving the Senate from item to item of
business, generally by unanimous consent, but if
consent is denied, then primarily by the motion to
proceed to consideration. The leadership also
runs an informal but effective "clearance"
mechanism for minor legislation. Finally, the
leadership negotiates the "unanimous consent
agreements" by which the Senate often governs its
consideration of legislation.

A further section in this chapter deals with
the mechanisms by which individual Senators may
force consideration of business without leadership
support (or by which Senators can circumvent
committees). Of far and away the most importance
is the non-germane amendment. The last section of
the chapter addresses the Senate's additional
responsibility besides legislation, namely, the
executive calendar for nominations and treaties.

---

[2]   Bach at 5.

[3]   As Riddick states, "[a] legislative day [is one] which
continues from the beginning of a day's session following an
adjournment until another adjournment." Riddick, "Day:
Legislative Day," at 566.

A.   BASIC DAILY CONTROL

Leadership Motions to Adjourn or Recess and New "Legislative Days"

Like the House's rules, the Senate's rules provide for a "daily procedure" which the chamber rarely, if ever, follows anymore. Senate Rule IV(1)(a), "Commencement of Daily Sessions," describes the start of each new day: "the Presiding Officer . . . take[s] the chair, following the prayer by the Chaplain."[4] However, that rule, and Rules VII and VIII, go on to describe a model procedure for the Senate that it rarely, if ever, follows anymore, involving approval of the Journal, "routine morning business," and a call of the Calendar.[5] The Senate has not called the Calendar since the early 1960s.[6]

---

[4]   This is usually accompanied by the announcement of the acting President pro tempore, unless, for some special reason, either the Vice President or the President pro tempore comes in to preside (as discussed above).

[5]   A more complete description of this procedure is as follows. "[A] quorum being present," the Senate approves the Journal of the preceding day, Rule IV(1)(a). Technically, the Senate does not "approve" the Journal. Rather, Rule IV(1)(a) states that "the Journal of the preceding day shall be read, and any mistake made in the entries corrected . . . ."   Thus, "the proper request, instead of asking for the approval of the Journal, is to ask that its reading be dispensed with."   Riddick, "Journal: Approval of the Journal," at 710-11.

The Senate then proceeds with "routine morning business," a special Senate term that, as previously discussed, includes introduction of bills and receipt of committee reports. Rule VII(1). "At the conclusion of the morning business at the beginning of a new legislative day . . . the Senate shall proceed to the consideration of the Calendar of Bills and Resolutions," Rule VIII(1).   That means a call of the Calendar, an orderly procedure for considering minor bills devised in the second half of the nineteenth century but no longer used.

(footnote continued)

Rather, the Senate avoids the procedures in Rules VII and VIII principally by the Majority Leader's control over new "legislative" days. Key matters require layovers for one or more "legislative" days. Rule XVII(4)(a) requires that "All reports of committees . . . shall lie over one day for consideration, unless by unanimous consent the Senate shall otherwise direct." "Day" in that rule means "legislative" day.[7] A similar delay applies to the readings of bills.[8] Thus, no matter how eager Senators may be to force a vote on a bill reported by a committee, or to introduce and move along a bill, they simply cannot do so from the moment of reporting or introduction until the Senate starts the next "legislative" day, absent unanimous consent.

The Senate only begins a new legislative day after a successful motion to adjourn; otherwise, when the Senate recesses at the end of a day without adjourning, it remains in the same "legislative" day when it reconvenes even though it is now the next "calendar" day. In other words, a legislative day often lasts more than one calendar day. As an extreme example, Riddick points out that in 1980, the Senate had a legislative day that lasted 162 calendar days: "[The Senate] convened on January 3, 1980, and recessed from day to day and did not adjourn until June 12."[9] For that 162-day period, the Senate remained in the same legislative day of January 3, 1980.[10]

---

[6] Even before then, it did so rarely for many decades, for the procedure would be time consuming, cumbersome, and inflexible. "Taking a recess from day to day obviates the requirement of the rule providing for the consideration of morning business." Riddick, "Recess: Purpose Of," at 875.

[7] Riddick, "Reports: Lie Over One Day, Reports Required To," at 961-62.

[8] Rule XIV(2) requires that "Every bill and joint resolution shall receive three readings previous to its passage which readings on demand of any Senator shall be on three different legislative days . . . ."

[9] Riddick, "Day: Legislative Day," at 567.

(footnote continued)

The Majority Leader decides whether to begin a new "legislative" day when he exercises his prerogative to choose at the end of a day between making a motion to adjourn, or just a motion to recess.[11]   This prerogative serves the Majority Leader as a tool against bills he refuses to schedule. For example, in 1981, the minority (the Democrats) wished to move a measure protecting Social Security from proposed budget cuts, which the majority (the Republicans) did not wish to schedule. To move the measure, Minority Leader Robert Byrd (D-W.Va.) had to satisfy the requirement of a one-day layover prior to consideration of the measure, by moving to adjourn the Senate and thereby advance the calendar one legislative day.

The Minority Leader knew full well that such a motion was a prerogative of the Majority Leader. Accordingly, he prefaced his motion "with an apology to the distinguished majority leader."[12]   As Senator Byrd anticipated, the

---

[10]   That date would have been listed as the legislative day on each bill introduced in that period, each committee report received, the Congressional Record, the daily Calendar of Business, and similar official documents. Ultimately, when the Senate "adjourns following a series of such recesses, the legislative day immediately catches up with the calendar day, skipping over all of the intervening calendar days." F. Riddick, The United States Congress 342 (1949). Thus, after the Senate finally adjourned on June 12 in 1980, the Senate's next legislative day caught up to June. That day, in turn, would persist (through day to day recesses) until the Senate's next adjournment.

[11]   "[T]he majority leader or someone acting for him almost invariably . . . offers motions to recess or adjourn from day to day . . . ." Majority and Minority Leaders of the Senate, at 23.

[12]   I know that I will fail [on this motion to adjourn]. I always maintained as majority leader that it is the majority leader who has the responsibility to make the motion to adjourn, but it is within the right of any Senator to make that motion, and during my tenure as majority leader . . . there were Senators from time to time on the other side who made the motion to adjourn. My argument always was that that is the
(footnote continued)

Senate followed traditional practice and rejected
the motion to adjourn offered by him on a party-
line vote,[13] precluding his minority party from
moving their measure at that time.   In contrast,
dissident Senators cannot use the one-day layover
rule effectively against bills on the Majority
Leader's agenda, because he will simply move a
brief adjournment.[14]   For example, in 1983
Majority Leader Baker obtained unanimous consent
"to adjourn for 1 minute in order to qualify the
debt limit bill . . . ."[15]

Actual Daily Sequence

Instead of the Senate following Rules VII and
VIII for its daily routine, it follows instead an

---

majority party's prerogative and the majority leader's
prerogative, but it is not necessarily a right that
reposes only in the majority leader.

127 Cong. Rec. S9078 (daily ed. July 31, 1981).

[13]   Id. at S9079.

[14]   Senator Howard Metzenbaum (D-Ohio) tried to block a
shipping deregulation bill by making the point of order
against the motion to proceed pursuant to the one-day
layover rule.   Majority Leader Howard Baker (R-Tenn.)
commented, "The point of order, of course, is well taken,"
but noted that since he would move that the Senate adjourn
to the next day, "The bill will qualify tomorrow."   129
Cong. Rec. S1493 (daily ed. Feb. 22, 1983).

[15]   129 Cong. Rec. S7489 (daily ed. May 25, 1983) (Sen.
Baker).   The Senate then adjourned from 2:37 p.m. to 2:38
p.m.   This is quite standard:

On various occasions when the Senate has been recessing
from day to day it has adjourned for very short periods
of time to get into a new legislative day in order that
legislation which had been previously reported, perhaps
for a number of days, would be in order for
consideration.   The Senate has adjourned to accomplish
such ends for as short a time as 2 seconds.

Riddick, "Adjournment: New Legislative Day," at 13.

informal routine.   Each day the Senate convenes at
a previously set hour, established by resolution
at the beginning of the Congress as noon.   The
leadership frequently adjusts the hour for
particular days, by motions made the day before,
as discussed below.   "When the Senate convenes,
the session opens with the Chaplain's prayer,
followed by the recognition of the Majority and
Minority Leaders for a period of time not to
exceed 10 minutes each,"[16] followed by "special
order" speeches of other Senators. [17]

Quite often, the Senate turns from these
opening speeches to a period of routine morning
business, as described in the previous chapter.
Then, "[f]ollowing the conclusion of these typical
housekeeping activities, the Senate turns to its
business, which normally includes a measure or
matter carrying over from the prior calendar day,
or which has been previously ordered for
consideration on the present day."[18]   During the
day, the leadership freely moves the Senate from
one item of pending business to another, with
intervals for unrelated speeches, routine morning
business, passage of cleared minor bills on the
calendar, and executive business (nominations and
treaties).

"At the day's end, proceedings are usually
concluded by unanimous consent action on non-

---

[16]   The leaders use this "leadership time" as they wish,
either to discuss the day's agenda, to comment on world or
national developments, or to provide some signal to their
party members.   Gold at 4.   For example, in the 99th
Congress, a unanimous consent agreement on the first day
provided "that the majority and minority leaders may daily,
as during the past Congresses, have up to 10 minutes each on
each calendar day following the prayer and the disposition
of the reading of, or the approval of, the Journal."   131
Cong. Rec. S12 (daily ed. Jan. 3, 1985).

[17]   "Thereafter, it is common for several Senators to be
recognized under 15 minute special orders entered by
unanimous consent on the previous calendar day.   Senators
desiring special orders to make speeches notify their
respective party cloakrooms."   Gold, supra, at 4.

[18]   Gold, supra, at 6.

controversial items on the legislative or
executive calendars, a morning business period
upon occasion, and arranging housekeeping details
for the forthcoming calendar day of session."[19]
Such end-of-day sweeps constantly move along the
minor business. The leaderships arrange the next
day's details by various unanimous consent
agreements, such as concerning the hour of
convening, the pending business upon reconvening,
and whether votes will be allowed to occur or will
be postponed and stacked. This furnishes the
structure within which Senators plan their own
activities.

"When there is no further business to be
transacted, the Majority Leader will move that the
Senate stand in recess pursuant to the order
previously entered."[20] The leader may simply move
to adjourn, or to recess, to a particular day, or
to a particular hour (termed adjourning or
recessing "to a day (or time) certain"), which may
be done in two steps.[21]   Different Majority

---

[19]   Gold, supra, at 6.

[20]   "At that point, an order is usually entered that when
the Senate completes its business on that day it stand in
recess until a particular hour on the following day of
session." Gold, supra, at 6.

[21]   First, the leadership has the Senate adopt by unanimous
consent, at some time during the day, an order providing
that at the conclusion of the day's business the Senate will
recess to a day or hour certain. This lets the majority of
Senators, sometimes including the leadership, go home while
a few Senators continue to make speeches, with the schedule
set beyond the possibility of mishap. From the time of
entry of such an order, no motion to adjourn is in order,
only a motion to recess. Riddick, "Recess: Absence of
Quorum" at 870.

Then, when the day's business is done, the last
Senators present, who may or may not include the leaders,
move to recess under the previous order to end the day
(almost invariably without a roll-call vote on the motion,
which would harass and embarass the Senators who left in
reliance on the schedule). That is, the end is not
automatic; but at least such a motion can be made without a
(footnote continued)

Leaders have different styles overall in setting
the weekly schedules and using the motions to
recess and adjourn.[22]

Other Aspects of Motion to Adjourn or Recess

The leadership can use the motion to adjourn
for other uses besides controlling "legislative"
and calendar days. As will be discussed later in
the chapter on filibusters, the motion to adjourn
defines what is "unfinished business," a category
that holds priority over efforts to start
something different. Also, the leadership can use
the motion to adjourn, or to recess, to stop bad
floor situations from degenerating further. This
use arises because motions to adjourn and recess
have the highest priority.[23] Even when another
motion is pending, such as an amendment or a

---

quorum being present. Thus, if only a few Senators stay
behind, and they were to be about some mischief, one Senator
standing guard alone simply suggests the absence of a
quorum. Either a quorum would appear, or nothing more could
happen (absent unanimous consent) other than a recess
pursuant to the previous order.

[22] Under Majority Leader Byrd, recesses were the rule;
adjournments occurred only rarely, allowing the leader
maximum flexibility in controlling the floor. Under
Majority Leader Baker, the Senate recessed each weekday, but
adjourned at the end of the week, starting the next week
with a new legislative day, but under unanimous consent
agreements that avoided most of the procedures normally
beginning such a new day. This was described as "the form
of late" at 129 Cong. Rec. S6667 (daily ed. May 16, 1983).
Examples of these adjournments include, in the same volume
and year, S2172 (March 3); S7609 (May 25); S9592 (July 11);
S10207 (July 15); S15513 (Nov. 4).

[23] Also, such motions are not subject to amendment,
tabling, or other delays. Simple motions to adjourn or
recess (to the regular convening time, or to a previously
ordered time) are not subject to amendment, though motions
to adjourn or recess to a day or time certain are. Riddick,
"Recess: Amend Motion to Recess," at 870; "Adjournment to
Day (Hour) Certain: Amendments to," at 8; "Adjournment:
Adjourn, Motion To -- Amendments Out of Order," at 2.

motion to table, a motion to adjourn may be made
which ends the action immediately (until
reconvening).[24] This motion thus serves as a
"Stop -- Time Out" move, allowing the Majority
Leader time to regroup his forces and arrange how
he will address the situation. The only limit on
using motions to adjourn and recess for time out
is that they cannot interrupt a quorum call or a
roll-call.[25]

On rare occasion, the Senate defeats its
leadership on an adjournment motion.[26] For
example, in 1983 Senator Robert W. Kasten, Jr.,
pushed the proposal, opposed by the leadership, to
repeal withholding of taxes on interest and
dividends. At one point, Acting Majority Leader
Stevens sought to put off a cloture vote on the
matter by adjourning. Although the adjournment
motion was a leadership prerogative, the Senate
refused to back the acting leader, and the motion
to adjourn was defeated.[27] It was a striking

---

[24] Rule XXII(1) gives the motions to adjourn and recess
precedence over all other motions. The only significant
"exception" is that a quorum call cannot be interrupted or
terminated by such motions. Riddick, "Adjournment:
Precedence of Motions," at 3, and "Recess: Motions,
Precedence of," at 874-75.

[25] Absent unanimous consent, once the absence of a quorum
has been suggested, the leadership must either produce a
quorum, or let the Chair announce that a quorum is not
present (hurting the attendance records of the Senators
absent on the call). Only after that announcement has been
made is a motion to adjourn or recess in order.

Also, the motion can only be to adjourn or recess to
the regular hour; "the Senate, in the absence of a quorum,
may not adjourn to an hour different from that fixed as the
regular hour of meeting of the Senate"; Riddick,
"Adjournment: Quorum, Absence of," at 5. Moreover, when
adjournment or recess occurs in the absence of a quorum, the
first order of business on convening is a quorum call.
Riddick, "Quorum: Adjournment in the Absence of a Quorum,"
at 835.

[26] This is somewhat comparable to when the House defeats
the previous question on a special rule.
(footnote continued)

demonstration that the leadership would not be able to restrain his proposal.[28]   Soon thereafter, the leadership relented and scheduled Senator Kasten's matter.

B.   MOTION, OR UNANIMOUS CONSENT, TO PROCEED

Majority Leader Prerogative

The Senate's Calendar of General Orders lists on a typical day a large number of matters available for Senate floor consideration, and there are typically many other matters "available" in thebroad sense for such consideration.[29]   On the floor, the Majority Leader steers among these by requesting unanimous consent, such as by his stating, for example, "I ask unanimous consent that the Senate consider S.1" or "I ask unanimous consent that there be a period of not more than 15 minutes for routine morning business."   When the matter has been cleared with both sides, no

---

[27]   As one Senator observed the next day, Senator Kasten had "prevailed against tremendous opposition . . . to the point of even winning by a substantial margin on defeating a motion to adjourn yesterday which traditionally, I think, would be viewed as simply a leadership prerogative."   129 Cong. Rec. S4977 (daily ed. April 20, 1983) (Sen. John Danforth (R-Mo.)); see id. at S4842 (actual 63-31 defeat of the motion to adjourn).

[28]   Similarly, in 1935, Majority Leader Robinson, supporting Southern filibusterers of an anti-lynching bill, attempted to adjourn "to sidetrack the pending measure.   But the party leader was defeated by 33 yeas against 34 nays;" the filibuster eventually succeeded.   F.L. Burdette, supra, at 180.

[29]   Matters not on the Calendar of General Orders, that may be available, include matters on the Executive Calendar; matters which are technically in committee, but that can be discharged from committee by unanimous consent and considered immediately; matters coming over from the House that are being held at the desk; and a host of other categories of typically minor business.

objection occurs, and the Senate so proceeds.

Since the 1800s each party has had either a steering or policy committee, or leadership officers, to decide the order in which to take up matters. As previously discussed, in the twentieth century the majority leader developed an increasing role in that decision making.[30]   This decision making must be distinguished from the implementation -- the actually making of the motion or request to proceed to consideration. Originally, any Senator would freely make such a motion or request, and committee chairs or other Members of the steering committee used to make the motion or request themselves.[31]   It might have been as late as the majority leadership of Mike Mansfield (D-Mont.) in the 1960s that making the motion to proceed became a widely known and accepted monopoly of the Majority Leader.[32]

---

[30]   By 1967, the majority leader's predominant role in scheduling appears to have been established. "What happens . . . depends upon what action the majority leader has scheduled for that day . . . [I]f objection is made, a motion to do what was asked by unanimous consent will almost certainly carry (or else the majority leader really is not the leader of the majority party)." Froman at 113.

[31]   "[D]own into the 1930's it was common practice for the chairmen of the standing committees" -- not the Majority Leader -- "to move to proceed to the consideration of . . . the proposed legislation reported by their respective committees." Majority and Minority Leaders of the Senate at 3.

[32]   In 1949, Riddick stated that "[t]he Senate is usually moved to action by Members of these 'two small groups,'" namely, the chairmen of the party committees and the standing committees. F. Riddick, The U.S. Congress: Organization and Procedure 107 (1949). Neither Froman nor Peabody, in their respective books in 1967 and 1969 extensively discussing Senate leadership, describes the motion to proceed as a prerogative of the majority leader, although they extensively discuss the majority leader's role in the decision making on scheduling. Peabody at 336-39. The first writing generally suggesting the prerogative appears to be Majority and Minority Leaders of the Senate, S. Doc. No. 42, 92nd Cong., 1st Sess. 18 (1971) (prepared by (footnote continued)

The Majority Leader's role in scheduling --
now both in decision-making, and in making the
implementing motion or unanimous consent request
-- has major importance for the Senate's
schedule. Since reported bills move only as the
Majority Leader wishes, the various committee
chairs and others seeking to move bills must come
to Majority Leaders to ask when they would bring
the bills up. Majority Leaders may bring reported
bills up immediately; may leave them on the
calendar for longer periods of time; and may, for
leave some there till they die at the end of the
session.

Examples of the Majority Leader's role in
this regard are legion. For example, in 1983,
Senator Max Baucus (D-Mont.) asked when the so-
called "sodbuster" bill would be brought to the
floor.[33]   Senator Thaddeus Cochran (R-Miss.)
commented that "I will join with [you] in urging
the majority leader to find some time on the
schedule to bring the bill to the
floor . . . ."[34]   Senator Baucus then asked
Majority Leader Baker, "what is the likelihood
that we could get the sodbusting bill scheduled
before the Senate before the August recess?" The
Majority Leader responded that he would "make
every effort" but:

Dr. Riddick), and even here it is described more as
something the leader does "almost invariably," rather than,
like the motions to recess or adjourn, as "virtually his
prerogative."

Now, the textual introduction to the discussion of the
question of consideration in Riddick reads: "Motions to
proceed to the consideration of bills . . . are usually made
by the Majority Leader or his designee, who, as spokesman of
his party and in consultation with his policy committee,
implements and directs the legislative schedule and
program." Riddick at 513.

[33] The "sodbuster" bill was to discourage plowing up easily
erodible land, and thus prevent dust bowls.   1984
Congressional Quarterly Almanac at 364.

[34] 129 Cong. Rec. S9455 (daily ed. June 29, 1983).   The
rest of the exchange is on the same page.

> [w]hether I can give [you] an outright
> promise to do it during those 3 1/2 weeks
> between July 11 and August 7 is something I
> will have to explore more closely, because I
> fear that time will be used primarily for two
> things: First, the Department of Defense
> authorization bill . . . and the remaining
> appropriation bills; and appropriations
> bills, of course, must take priority.[35]

Senator Baucus then pressed for assurances, and
the Majority Leader declined to give any that were
very specific, commenting, "There are 13
committees that have reporting jurisdiction,
regular standing committees. If I make that
commitment, I am afraid that I may make 1 friend
and 12 enemies."[36] Ultimately, the Senate did not
consider and pass the bill until November of that
year.

While the prerogative of making the motion
(or unanimous consent request) to proceed thus
gives the Majority Leader a central brokering
function for the Senate's floor time, the leader
has several marked constraints. First, in
contrast to the House Rules Committee -- which at
various historic times freely exercised a power to
kill bills it disliked -- there is no historic
sense that Majority Leaders are vested with
general power to kill bills, although they do make
tactical choices. As one observer put it,
"[t]here is no attempt by the leadership to detain
major legislation, nor would such attempts be
successful."[37] Majority Leaders persuade their
party to follow them by accommodating Senators.
It would be the antithesis of that role to
frustrate powerful committees by killing their
bills. Rather, Majority Leaders schedule by
pointing to competing demands and potential
filibusters. In effect the opponents, not the
leader, delay or kill such bills;[38] Majority

---

[35]   Id.

[36]   Id.

[37]   Froman at 109.

(footnote continued)

Leaders are usually not held accountable for refusing to bring doomed bills to the floor, unless they have made a commitment to do so.

"Holds"

The leadership consults with interested Senators on their views about proceeding to consider bills, especially when Senators express problems with a bill by "placing a hold" on the bill. Specifically, a "hold" is a notification, often by letter, to the Majority or Minority Leader from Senators stating that they have problems with a bill, and that they oppose proceeding with it, at least without giving them a chance to resist. An example is a letter reprinted in the Congressional Record:

September 28, 1982

Hon. Howard Baker,
Majority Leader,
U.S. Senate, Washington, D.C.

Dear Howard: Per our conversation, this will confirm the objection to any time agreement to the consideration of the National Peace Day amendment during Senate floor action on H.J. Res. 599, the Continuing Resolution. If any further time agreement is proposed, please notify the undersigned.

Sincerely,

John East,
Jeremiah Denton

---

[38] In fact, from time to time, Majority Leaders bring bills to the floor where they die from just such a filibuster; these bills' unhappy fate demonstrates the soundness of the leaders' sparing the Senate from other similar ones. For example, in 1983 Majority Leader Baker brought natural gas deregulation to the floor. It died there from filibuster, but Senator James McClure (R-Idaho), the chair who had tried to move it, thanked the majority and minority leaders "for having permitted us to be the pending business . . . because that was really the catalyst of the negotiations." 129 Cong. Rec. S16814 (daily ed. Nov. 18, 1983).

As the letter illustrates, Senators may place such holds against amendments being proposed for insertion in omnibus bills, as well as against freestanding bills. Some Senators make little use of holds; others make frequent use. For example, at the end of the 97th Congress in 1982, Senator Metzenbaum became renowned for resisting floor consideration of a number of bills. As the Washington Post reported,

> This   time   around,   the   legislative
> smorgasboard is heavy with goodies . . . .
> Metzenbaum has vowed to stop most of these by
> invoking his "hold," a device that can
> prevent a measure from being debated. "Every
> bill this senator has a hold on is a giveaway
> to a special interest," he said yesterday.[39]

Six years later, in 1988, the Wall Street Journal explained, in an article entitled "Senator No: Metzenbaum Amasses Power in the Senate by Blocking Action," that "In a body [like the Senate] where the rules allow a single lawmaker to bring everything to a standstill, [Senator Metzenbaum] repeatedly does just that to block legislation he doesn't like."[40]

The extent of deference granted by the leadership to a Senator's "hold" is a delicate and varying matter. A Congressional Research Service

---

[39]   Sinclair, "Metzenbaum Uses Hold to Choke Off Colleagues' Pre-Election Largess," Washington Post, Oct. 1, 1982, at A3. On the floor later in the year, Senator Metzenbaum continued his resistance by pointing out that he and other opponents of certain amendments had "the lung power to continue to discuss those matters for quite a period of time," and that he had "stayed until 2:30 last evening taking up some of the worst rinky-dinks [amendments] that I ever heard of, ideas that people came up with out of the blue that . . . in the middle of the night they concluded that these were great measures that the Nation needed so very badly." 128 Cong. Rec. S14993 (daily ed. Dec. 16, 1982).

[40]   Yank, Senator No: Metzenbaum Amasses Power in the Senate by Blocking Action, Wall St. J., June 19, 1988, at 1.

survey found that in the 1983-84 Congress, 98 percent of 247 matters laid before the Senate came up by unanimous consent, signifying that the Majority Leader had probably honored almost all holds on bills.[41]   However, holds do not mean every Senator has an absolute veto over all potential measures, but more that each Senator has some pre-floor-action bargaining leverage.   If a Majority Leader cannot obtain unanimous consent to proceed to a bill, he can move to proceed, requiring only a majority of Senators to support consideration (unless the motion to proceed is filibustered and the leader must invoke cloture).   In 1983, Majority Leader Baker became impatient with the spread of holds, and indicated that a "hold" would have limited effect:

> One sign of Baker's impatience was his decision to no longer treat a senator's "hold" on a bill as a sacrosanct order not to bring the bill to the floor, although that is the way Baker treated holds in the last two years.
>
> "The concept of a hold was misunderstood. It just means a senator needs to be notified that the bill will come up and he may come and object," [Assistant Majority Leader Ted] Stevens [(R-Alaska)] said.[42]

---

[41]   It was an unusual occasion, for example, when shortly after midnight on December 20, 1982, Assistant Majority Leader Stevens asked unanimous consent to proceed to an Alaska Railroad bill on which Senator Metzenbaum had placed a hold.   Immediately, Senator Long objected "because another Senator [i.e., Metzenbaum] who would object is not here at the moment."   128 Cong. Rec. S15749 (daily ed. Dec. 20, 1982).   Of course, holds from minority Senators do not have the same weight with the Majority Leader, but knowing the situation, the Acting Majority Leader apparently made his request to proceed only in jest.   Still, he did protest about "an objection from one person under antiquated rules that prevent [bills] from even being discussed."   129 Cong. Rec. S15750 (daily ed. Dec. 20, 1982).

[42]   Granat, Ruling Rambunctious Senate Proves to be Thorny Problem for Republican Leader Baker, 41 Cong. Q. Week. Rep. (footnote continued)

Even if a hold is less than an absolute veto,
it is more than a bare system of notification, for
the leadership tries by negotiation to avoid floor
fights. The extent to which a Majority Leader
will forbear before making the motion to proceed
in the face of a hold remains deliberately
flexible, reinforcing the nature of the hold as a
tool of negotiation and bargaining. Senator
Metzenbaum expressed the bargaining aspect in
stating that "every bill I have a hold on here, I
have indicated a willingness to talk about them .
. . . On some of them we found equitable
compromise and the bills have gone through."[43] As
Martin Gold stated:

1427 (1983).

This was not the first time leaders had trimmed back
the significance of "holds;" that seems to be periodically
required. In 1973, Assistant Majority Leader Byrd announced
the Senate Democratic Policy Committee's policy on holds:

> The leadership here is trying to get away from having
> to honor a "hold" on a bill, sometimes the "hold" being
> insisted upon for a week, 2 weeks, 3 weeks, a month, or
> 7 weeks; and in order to expedite the legislative
> process, it was thought by the policy committee, if we
> could have an understanding, that hereafter a "hold"
> placed by any individual or any group of Senators would
> not be recognized longer than 3 days, it would be
> helpful.

Congressional Research Service, Dissent on the Senate Floor:
Practices, Procedures, and Customs 28 (1976) (W. J. Oleszek)
(quoting Congressional Record).

[43] 128 Cong. Rec. S15751 (daily ed. Dec. 20, 1982).

In 1984, Senators Heflin and Melcher had holds on
consideration of agricultural target price legislation.
Ultimately, the Majority Leader decided to proceed to the
bill anyway. "Two attempts -- March 15 and March 20 -- to
start floor action on HR 4072 were blocked . . . . The
Senate finally passed the legislation March 22 after
concessions by the administration overcame most
obstacles." 1984 Congressional Quarterly Almanac 362.

When a Senator has particular concerns about
a measure, he may ask that a "hold" be placed
against it. It will be honored for so long
as the Majority Leadership can do so, but at
some point the Leadership may move the
legislation notwithstanding the hold which
has been placed against it.[44]

On the other hand, once the Majority Leader
makes a motion to proceed (notwithstanding any
holds), opponents have the choice of letting the
motion occur and simply fighting on the merits of
the bill, or of escalating the battle. A motion
to proceed is usually debatable, meaning opponents
willing to escalate can filibuster on that
motion.[45] As many as several filibusters a year

---

[44] Gold at 23.

By placing a "hold" on a measure, a Senator registers
an unofficial objection to any unanimous consent
request for the measure's consideration. The floor
leaders of both parties have tended to honor "holds"
for reasonable periods of time. And if the Majority
Leader eventually decides that the measure must be
considered anyway, the Senator who placed the "hold"
retains the right to object to taking up the bill by
unanimous consent as well as the right to filibuster
against a motion to consider it.

Bach at 6.

[45] Motions to proceed to privileged matters like conference
reports are not debatable and hence not subject to
filibuster, as discussed in the chapter on filibuster.

The motion to proceed itself offers few grips for
procedural maneuver. Opponents cannot amend the motion to
proceed, nor make another motion to proceed; they can move
to table it, postpone it, or adjourn before action on it
(which kills it), but these would be rare steps for the
opposition (though tabling is a natural response of the
Majority Leader to another's making such a motion).
Riddick, "Consideration, Question of: Amend Motion to
Consider, Out of Order," at 515; same, "Motions for
Consideration, Out of Order," at 528; same, "Motion --
Table, Postpone, or Adjourn Disposes of," at 529.

may occur on motions to proceed.[46]   The issue of
filibusters on such motions is discussed below in
the chapter on filibusters.

One other obstacle to consideration, the
layover rules, warrants attention.   Besides the
one "legislative" day layover for committee
reports discussed above, which the Majority Leader
can overcome by adjournment, there is also a
requirement for a layover of three calendar
days.[47]   This "three day" rule can block swift
action on bills with fresh reports.   Usually, the
Senate agrees to waive the rule by unanimous
consent, but a recalcitrant opposition may refuse
to do so, particularly just before an adjournment
when delay might kill the reported bill.[48]

One way around this is simply not to have a
printed report on a bill, for the rule only
requires the printed report, not the bill, to lay
over.   Thus, a chair foreseeing delay avoids the
layover by not printing any report, and just
inserting in the Congressional Record the
information that would have been in the report.
This is particularly common for appropriation

---

[46]   For example, in 1983 Senator John Melcher (D-Mont.)
objected to a unanimous consent request to proceed to
natural gas deregulation, the Majority Leader moved to
proceed, and Senator Melcher started to filibuster.   The
Senate voted cloture by an overwhelming margin, and two days
later the motion to proceed passed by voice vote.   129 Cong.
Rec. S15147 (daily ed. Nov. 1, 1983) (objection to unanimous
consent to proceed), S15311 (daily ed. Nov. 3, 1983) (voice
vote on motion to proceed).   In that same year, the motion
to proceed to the Radio Marti (broadcasting to Cuba) bill
required cloture.   129 Cong. Rec. S11428 (daily ed. August
3, 1983).

[47]   "Any measure or matter reported by any standing
committee shall not be considered in the Senate unless the
report of that committee upon that measure or matter has
been available to Members for at least three calendar days
(excluding Saturdays, Sundays, and legal holidays)."   Rule
XVII(5).

[48]   Rule XVII(5)(1) allows the layover to "be waived by
joint agreement of the majority leaer and the minority
leader of the Senate."

bills and continuing resolutions under time
pressure. When one Senator suggested he might
deny unanimous consent to waive the three-day rule
on a continuing resolution because of a particular
item that troubled him, Mark Hatfield (R-Oreg.),
chair of the Appropriations Committee, commented:

> If we cannot get the unanimous-consent
> agreement, I have to call an immediate
> meeting of the Appropriations Committee. We
> shall meet downstairs and what we shall then
> have to do is report this same [continuing
> resolution] back to the floor without a
> report. Then there is no 3-day rule that we
> have to waive . . . . [T]o get to that
> objective is just another hour's delay.[49]

The objecting Senator then withdrew his objection.

Pending and Unfinished Business

Once the Senate starts consideration of an
item, its rules provide for staying on that
item. Specifically, when the Senate proceeds to
consideration of a matter (i.e., once the Majority
Leader takes the Senate to that matter), that
matter becomes the Senate's "pending" business.
If the Senate adjourns while a matter is still
"pending," that matter becomes the "unfinished
business," to which the Senate will recur if
diverted absent unanimous consent.[50] The Senate

---

[49]   129 Cong. Rec. S15741 (daily ed. Nov. 9, 1983).

[50]   The Senate comes back automatically to the "pending"
business when it finishes another matter or after it
recesses and reconvenes (absent unanimous consent to go on
to something else). A matter becomes "unfinished business"
thusly:

> Unfinished business cannot be made by a resolution of
> the Senate, nor on motion, but is the business that is
> pending at the close of a day's session upon
> adjournment. When there is pending business and no
> unfinished business and the Senate adjourns briefly,
> following a recess from the previous day, that pending

(footnote continued)

can still juggle other bills, notwithstanding "pending" or "unfinished" business, if, but only if, the Majority Leader can obtain unanimous consent to go to juggle those other matters.

Thus, the status of "pending" (or "unfinished") business has significance once Senators withhold unanimous consent about scheduling. In that case, whenever the Senate meanders off to a matter other than such business, any Senator can bring the Senate back to "pending" business just by obtaining recognition and callingfor the "regular order."[51] In other words, once something becomes "pending" or "unfinished" business, the Senate does anything else on the sufferance of all Members.

While this rule serves orderly Senate procedure,[52] if too strictly kept, the rule would let individual Senators interfere at any time with the order of business. Accordingly, when the Majority Leader asks unanimous consent that the Senate consider something important other than the pending business, he may include in his request that a call for the regular order will not bring back the pending business.[53] This "safeguards"

---

business becomes the unfinished business.

Riddick, "Unfinished Business: Consideration and Definition of Unfinished Business," at 1107-8. The significance of "unfinished business" is discussed below in the chapter on filibusters.

[51]   Riddick, "Consideration: Question of: Displacement of Pending or Unfinished Business," at 525.

[52]   The Senate may have devoted a major effort to proceeding to consideration of an item (sometimes even breaking a filibuster on the motion to proceed), and the rule avoids redoing that work just to renew consideration.

[53]   In the face of resistance to such a request (which would be unusual), the Majority Leader may simply move (rather than ask unanimous consent) to proceed to consider something else. Adoption of such a motion displaces the pending business (unless it is privileged), which goes back to the Calendar. Riddick, "Consideration, Question of: Displacement of Pending or Unfinished Business," at 521-22. Bringing up an item by unanimous consent, rather than a (footnote continued)

the important other matter from losing its place
when a hostile Senator for the "regular order."
Historically, the "pending" business rules had
tactical uses,[54] and still have some complex
ramifications discussed below under filibuster
procedure.

C.   CLEARANCE FOR MINOR BILLS

Uses

The Senate depends heavily on a clearance system
run by its leadership for passing bills.   A few
statistics reflect this extent.   Out of the first
50 public laws passed by the 98th Congress, only
five had roll-call votes.[55]   Probably almost all
of the other 45 passed simply by the clearance

---

motion to proceed, does not so displace; it merely suspends
the pending business.   Similarly, proceeding to consider
privileged matters, such as conference reports, merely
suspends the pending business without displacing it.
Riddick, "Privileged Business," at 831.

[54]   Tactically, the "displacement" aspect of the rules
concerning pending business motivated bill opponents to try
to entice the Senate into considering something else.   For
example, in 1890-91, Democrats, who were opposing the so-
called "Force Bill" to enfranchise blacks, enticed western
Republicans to join them in moving to consider free-silver
legislation.   When the two sides joined in a motion to
consider, this displaced the civil rights bill, stalling
it.   Burdette at 53.

However, with the recognized prerogative of the
Majority Leader to control the motion for consideration,
that tactic is not seen much today.   Even when it was used,
the tactic of fighting bills by moving consideration of
something else usually failed.   For example, the attempt of
filibustering Senators to defeat an antilynching bill in
1938 by moving consideration of appropriations bills
failed.   Burdette at 197.

[55]   Congressional Research Service, Digest of Public General
Bills and Resolutions 1-21 (1984) (history of Pub. L. Nos.
98-1 - 98-50).

mechanism. Conversely, in all of 1984, there were only 42 roll-call votes on final passage for bills (out of 275 roll call votes in all). In sum, through the clearance mechanism, the Senate saves most of its voting for controversial propositions, such as amendments on major bills, and leaves passage of routine bills to clearance through the leadership.

Most of what the clearance mechanism passes is truly minor. Minor authorizations and extensions of statutory deadlines are grist for the clearance mechanism's mill. Large numbers of simple and concurrent resolutions for purposes such as budget waivers, authorizations for printing or for testifying or appearing in litigation or other kinds of housekeeping matters, and ceremonial, commemorative, and condoling pronouncements pass this way. Among those early 45 public laws of the 98th Congress that required no recorded vote were designations of various months, weeks, or days as honoring Lithuanian Independence, Mental Health Counselors, Amateur Baseball, and Alaska Statehood.

On the other hand, a fair number of items of some significance receive clearance in the Senate. It should be remembered that the House conducts more recorded votes than the Senate -- in 1986, 488 compared to 359.[56] This overall difference has its parallels in fewer votes on bills. For example, of those 45 public laws passed by the Senate without recorded votes, three received recorded votes in the House. Two amended the housing and securities laws, and one was an aid appropriation for Lebanon, which included a requirement that the President not expand American armed forces in Lebanon without statutory authorization -- a restriction which proved highly important in the war powers controversy when President Reagan subsequently did seek to expand the American armed role in Lebanon.[57] The House held a roll-call vote on this significant appropriation (276-76); the Senate merely cleared

---

[56]   1986 Congressional Quarterly Almanac at 57-S, 127-H.

[57]   Bill Digest, supra, at 16-17 (Pub. L. Nos. 98-35 (housing), 98-38 (securities), and 98-43 (Lebanon).

it.[58]

Senator Byrd, in discussing Senate procedure, summed up a number of characteristics of the clearance process:

> Bills and resolutions not subjected to objection are taken up in their order. Locomotive velocity may develop at this point, as bills come up and pass through with no objection. Thus, something of a record was established on December 30, 1924, whenthe Senate considered and passed in one afternoon 136 "unobjected to measures" involving appropriation of $14 million, a princely sum in those days. However, at any stage, objection may be raised to any measure . . . . [M]ore than once, this tool has been used as an instrument of mild retaliation by Senators who were irked by the prior actions of one or more of their colleagues.[59]

Majority Leader Baker noted the large scale of the process: "We deal every day in the course of a week on hundreds, maybe some weeks even on thousands of matters, and some of them very sensitive, and we have a clearance process set up on our respective staffs that functions magnificently."[60]

Mechanics

The mechanics of the clearance operation operate with a large portion outside of public view. Leadership staff keep a list of all matters on the Senate calendar, or otherwise available for clearance -- not merely bills and resolutions, but unanimous consent agreements on procedure, amendments, and anything else the Senate considers.[61] The staff track whether any Senators

---

[58] Bill Digest, supra, at 17.

[59] 127 Cong. Rec. S3618 (daily ed. April 8, 1981).

[60] 128 Cong. Rec. S15894 (daily ed. Dec. 21, 1982).
(footnote continued)

have written, or otherwise notified, the
leadership that they oppose clearance (a "hold"
notification).   As an affirmative matter, the
leadership staffs reach out to contact Senators
holding certain positions as a regular matter of
form, such as the chair and ranking minority
member of the committee of jurisdiction.

Finally, certain broadside notifications are
sent out to smoke out any objections, most
notably, the "hotlines." These are Republican and
Democratic automatic telephone systems which
deliver a recording to the office of each Senator
of that party, announcing that certain matters
will be considered cleared for action. Typically,
each Senator has a staff member who monitors the
hot line to alert that Senator -- and the
leadership -- if the Senator has a concern about a
matter being cleared.

Although these processes are usually not
public, from time to time floor comments, usually
by one of the leaders to the other, indicate how
the various clearance steps are proceeding. For
example, when Majority Leader Baker wished to
propound a unanimous consent agreement on the bill
regarding a holiday for Martin Luther King's
birthday, he said, "Why do I not just read it as I
have dictated it to our staff and as it is now
running our hotline procedure for clearance."[62]
When Appropriations Chairperson Hatfield asked
unanimous consent on agreement to some
noncontroversial committee amendments to an
appropriation bill, Minority Leader Byrd stated he
would not object because "we have had discussions
among ourselves here and we have run a hotline on
our side of the aisle."[63] Majority Leader Baker
paid tribute to the leadership staff in the course
of describing how he saw the clearance process:

---

[61]   Matters not on the calendar may be available for
clearance if the committee leadership indicates that the
matters should be discharged from committee by unanimous
consent, and then passed, rather than awaiting reporting by
the committee.

[62]   129 Cong. Rec. S13551 (daily ed. Oct. 4, 1983).

[63]   131 Cong. Rec. S14611 (daily ed. Oct. 26, 1983).

they, too, handle hundreds of items,
carefully collating and noting the desires
and wishes of Senators on both sides of the
aisle.

The two staffs working together
forthrightly and directly confer constantly
in the course of the day on the floor and off
the floor. We have set up a system here, the
minority leader and I, that works, and the
system is I never clear anything until I go
to my calendar staff and say, "Senator so and
so wants to do so and so. Is it cleared on
our side? If I get past that I say, "Would
you please see if the Democrats have cleared
it." If it is I go to Senator Byrd and I
say, "This is a matter I want to take up."
Sometimes he says, "no," but more often he
says, "Yes," because the calendar people have
already gone through it and worked out the
details.[64]

D.   COMPLEX UNANIMOUS CONSENT AGREEMENTS

Evolution

As indicated above, the Senate uses the complex
unanimous consent agreement as its chief tool for
structuring proceedings on particular bills. The
history of time agreements illuminates
considerably this subtle mechanism, for its
evolution reveals the layers of understandings
implicit in today's agreements. It has been
observed that "[s]imple requests for unanimous
consent are as old as the Senate itself"; the
Senate's original rules provided in 1789 for
simple unanimous consent to avoid layovers on
bills.[65] "The precise origin of the more formal
and complex unanimous consent agreements is
uncertain," though it goes well back into the

---

[64]   128 Cong. Rec. S15894 (daily ed. Dec. 21, 1982).

[65]   Keith at 142.

1800s.[66]

Since those early origins, the time agreement has evolved through what might roughly be divided into three steps.   First, by 1914, the Senate developed a standard form for such agreements, with regular contents and a standard procedure for adopting and recording.[67]   By a 1914 rule still in effect, the Senate changed the agreements' status from that of mere "gentlemen's agreements," unenforceable by the Chair and binding only on Senators' consciences, to making them an order of the Senate enforceable by the Chair.   The rule provided for a safeguard -- a quorum call -- prior

---

[66]   Keith at 148 (origin uncertain) "The custom of fixing a time for ending debate and taking the vote dates back at least to the 29th Congress (1845-1847), when an unsuccessful attempt was made to induce the minority to fix a day for taking a vote on the Oregon bill, which had been debated two months."   G. B. Galloway, The Legislative Process in Congress 553 (1953).   By 1871, one Senator noted that "half our business is done by unanimous consent."   Senator Trumbull, quoted in L. G. McConachie, Congressional Committees 302 (1898).

[67]   By 1913, the contents of time agreements had reached a standard state focusing on the time for voting on final passage.   "The purpose of such agreements was generally to set a specific date for votes on amendments to a bill and final passage of the bill itself.   Also, agreements frequently limited the time allowed for debate on amendments and final passage."   Keith at 149 (citations to Congressional Record omitted).

It was the custom for "the Senator in charge of the bill or the Senator interested in the bill" to make the request himself . . . .   At the time of the oral [request], usual practice required an explanation of the request, including a presentation of reasons pro and con.   Upon receipt of the request, the Secretary would read it aloud and the clerks would write it down in standard format.   Finally, the Legislative clerk would record the agreement on the cover of the Senate Calendar of Business for as many days as the agreement was pending or remained in effect.

Id.

to the making of time agreements setting a time
certain for votes on final passage, but the Senate
routinely waives that safeguard.[68]
    The impact of that rule should not be
overstated. Even today, Senators still retain a
sense that much of what makes a UCA is not the
mechanical process of request and nonobjection,
which the leadership may conduct in a virtually
empty chamber as a formality. Rather, unanimous
consent requires a "meeting of the minds" -- a
concordance, often after backroom discussions of
all the interested Senators, akin to the old
notion of the "gentlemen's agreement."

    A 1983 dispute illuminates this. Majority
Leader Baker sought a time agreement excluding
extraneous amendments from an appropriation.
Senator Melcher failed to object, even though such
an agreement would shut out an amendment he wanted
to offer, apparently because he had not heard the

---

[68]   Rule XII(4) provides:

> No request by a Senator for unanimous consent for the
> taking of a final vote on a specified date upon the
> passage of a bill or joint resolution shall be
> submitted to the Senate for agreement thereto until
> . . . a quorum of the Senate is present; and when a
> unanimous consent is thus given the same shall operate
> as the order of the Senate.

The rule's requirement for a quorum call and a quorum can
itself be waived by unanimous consent. Riddick, "Quorum:
Unanimous Consent Agreement to Fix Time for Vote on Bil --
When Quorum Call Required," at 861. Typically, the Chair
reminds the Majority Leader, in proposing such agreements,
to waive the quorum call. In one of Senator Baker's droll
exchanges:

> The PRESIDING OFFICER: Does the Senator also ask to
> waive paragraph 4 of rule XII?
>
> Mr. BAKER: I cannot remember whether it is paragraph
> 4, rule XII, or paragraph 12, rule IV. I cannot
> remember which one it is. I ask that it be waived.

129 Cong. Rec. S9096 (daily ed. June 27, 1983).

whole request.[69]   When the misunderstanding surfaced, Senator Russell Long (D-La.) argued on Senator Melcher's behalf that "there was no meeting of the minds.   There was no unanimous-consent agreement . . . . "[70]   However, when Senator Long made "a point of order that there was no agreement," the Chair responded that "The Journal of the Senate is conclusive, and the Journal shows that a unanimous consent was granted.   The point of order is not well taken."[71]

Senator Long then warned, "when this type thing happens it makes it difficult to get unanimous-consent agreements in the future . . . .   We did not have a meeting of the minds, and we should not do business that way."[72]   The debate reflected that today the UCA

---

[69]   Since Senator Melcher was present, his party leader, Minority Leader Byrd, was not required to protect Senator Melcher's rights by objecting.   The Minority Leader, who would have protected an absent Senator, did not object to protect Senator Melcher because he was on the floor and had had the matter explained to him.   As the minority leader noted, "when the majority leader put the request, I looked at the Senator [Senator Melcher], because I expected him to object; and when he did not, I thought he understood." 129 Cong. Rec. S8013 (daily ed. June 8, 1983) (Senator Byrd). "I thought, well, [Senator Melcher] is about to waive.   As it turned out, he had not been here for the entire request.   He was here only to hear the first part of the request, and he only heard part of the request." Id. S8060 (daily ed. June 9, 1983) (Senator Byrd).

[70]   129 Cong. Rec. S8014 (daily ed. June 8, 1983).

[71]   129 Cong. Rec. S8060 (daily ed. June 9, 1983).

[72]   129 Cong. Rec. S8060 (daily ed. June 9, 1983).   The two leaders recognized the point.   When Majority Leader Baker put the unanimous consent request to vitiate, and other Senators objected, Minority Leader Byrd made an eloquent statement about why both leaders would push to vitiate an agreement they liked when a Senator complained about it:

I have been around here 25 years, and I have found that the worm will turn, and that while a Senator may be disposed to object to the kind of offer the majority
(footnote continued)

is binding, but comity still forces all parties to try strongly to reinforce mere formal agreements with a genuine acceptance by all interested Senators.

Germaneness Rule and Leadership Role

Standardized binding unanimous consent agreements thus effectively predated the rise of Senate's formal majority and minority leadership. The last two key steps in evolution, a germaneness rule and elaboration of the time agreement's contents, occurred under the modern leadership. Starting in 1949, southern Democrats became concerned that liberals would move civil rights bills as non-germane floor amendments to avoid filibustering, a concern proved by events to be sound.[73]

---

leader has graciously made, the time may come when that Senator wants the same gracious attitude shown toward him.

I try to keep that in mind, and I have learned that Senators have long memories . . . . [W]e all at some point in time or other may have ourselves put in the same boat that Senator Melcher is in.

129 Cong. Rec. S8015 (daily ed. June 8, 1983). Nevertheless, other Senators objected to his unanimous consent request to vitiate the agreement.

[73] The 1949 filibuster that opened the door to an era of Senate combat over civil rights legislation is described in Shuman, Senate Rules and the Civil Rights Bill: A Case Study, Am. Poli. Sci. Rev. 955 (1957).

In 1960, Majority Leader Lyndon Johnson (D-Tex.), with Minority Leader Everett Dirksen's (R-Ill.) support, attached President Eisenhower's civil rights proposals as an amendment to a trivial bill authorizing Army leasing of an officer's club in Fort Crowder, Missouri. This tactic "infuriated the Southern Democrats," with Senator Richard Russell (D-Ga.) accusing Johnson of "lynching . . . orderly procedure in the Senate." D. M. Berman, A Bill Becomes a Law: Congress Enacts Civil Rights Legislation 57-58 (2d ed. 1966).

Accordingly,[74] the southern Democrats started insisting around 1950 that before they would accept time agreements, a new key element had to be included in the "usual form": a germaneness limit.[75]   The southern Democrats did not wish a general ban on non-germane amendments, as in the House, only a specific protection against unexpected civil rights amendments. Accordingly, the germaneness restriction in the time agreement evolved, not as a bar against all non-germane amendments, but just as a bar against surprise ones. This evolution producedd the current "usual form," by which any Senator who intends to offer a non-germane amendment simply informs the leadership in advance of the time agreement, and the leadership lists that amendment when stating the request for unanimous consent.   The Senate deems any amendment stated in the time agreement to be "germane" for purposes of that agreement.[76]

---

[74]   As dangerous as the filibusterers regarded any such amendment, their greatest concern was offering of a surprise amendment to a bill on which a time agreement had set the time for a final vote.   Such a vehicle could not be filibustered past that set time, and might pass with its non-germane civil rights amendment included.

[75]   As noted above, there had been, as early as 1913, a "standard format" (referred to today as the "usual form") for such agreements. The development is reflected in the contemporary text by George Galloway. "50 per cent of the agreements require motions and amendments to be germane to the business under consideration. The development of the requirement of germaneness in recent years is regarded as a safeguard against the attachment of civil rights riders." G. B. Galloway, supra, at 555. Galloway's own count shows only nine unanimous consent agreements in 1949, of which three required germaneness; in 1950, the number jumped to 35, with 19 requiring germaneness. Riddick's examples of time agreements with germaneness restrictions begin in 1950.   Riddick, "Unanimous Consent Agreements: Germaneness of Amendments Under Unanimous Consent Agreements," at 1085.

[76]   It had always been open for the time agreement specifically to waive that germaneness rule for particular non-germane amendments. "When operating under a unanimous consent agreement prohibiting nongermane amendments, any (footnote continued)

Another step in the evolution of time agreements has been the evolution of the Senate leadership's role. As the leading observer of time agreements notes, "[a]t some point prior to 1950, the complex unanimous consent agreement became the responsibility of party leadership. Typically, the majority leader or majority whip proposes the agreement."[77]

Explosive elaborations of time agreements came under Senator Byrd, starting in 1971 when he became Majority Whip and continuing after he became Majority Leader in 1977. Senator Byrd insisted on reaching time agreements before he would bring bills to the floor. "Rather than being a device used by the Senate primarily to extricate itself from entanglements on the floor, the complex agreement ha[d] become the means whereby the leadership charts the Senate's future course."[78]   Agreements increased in detail and

---

nongermane amendment is subject to a point of order unless the agreement grants the right to take up a specific nongermane amendment."   Riddick, "Unanimous Consent Agreements: Germaneness of Amendments Under Unanimous Consent Agreements," at 1086 (emphasis supplied).   Then, "[w]ithin the last few years, it has become generally understood that any amendments enumerated in the agreement will be considered germane." Keith at 161.

To be precise, the listed amendments are deemed germane only for purposes of the germaneness rule implied in the time agreement, not for purposes of any other germaneness rule.   Thus, listing amendments in a time agreement does not protect against a germaneness point of order if cloture is voted -- unless the time agreement expressly makes them qualified notwithstanding the cloture rule.   129 Cong. Rec. S1897 (daily ed. March 1, 1983).   Similarly, listing an amendment does not protect against a germaneness point of order for a budget resolution when the unanimous consent agreement specifies that the Budget Act's provisions remain in effect.   129 Cong. Rec. S5862 (daily ed. May 3, 1983).

[77]   Keith at 156.   During the 1950s, Majority Leader Lyndon Johnson (D-Tex.) made extensive use of time agreements to organize Senate floor proceedings.   Majority Leader Mike Mansfield (D-Mont.), his successor, continued.

[78]   Keith at 159.   Previously, the Senate had used time (footnote continued)

length, as they began to "script" many individual
proposed amendments.[79]

During the early 1980s, Majority Leaders
Baker and Dole placed less reliance on advance
arrangement of time agreements, in part because
the minority Democrats were unwilling to enter
into them because of fears of legislative
initiatives by the right wing of the majority
party. Accordingly, the majority leaders tended
to start consideration on bills with a very
unrestrictive time agreement or with no such
agreement at all. They devised UCAs later in
debate on a bill, when Senators were ready to name
all the amendments they wished to offer. It
became quite common for early, incomplete UCAs to
be amended by later ones.[80]

Modern Uses

Modern uses of UCAs follow the historic steps
outlined above. First, just as the Senate
developed the UCA to set the time for voting on
final passage, today the Senate uses such
agreements to set its schedule in a variety of
ways. Sometimes the Majority Leader cannot use a
UCA for scheduling because the Senate is not yet
ready for it. For example, when Majority Leader
Baker faced difficulties in arranging a time
certain for a vote on final passage of the budget
resolution,[81] devising the agreement gave him the

---

agreements primarily on matters already on the floor as the
pending business; the agreements scheduled votes on
amendments or final passage.

[79] "One striking example, albeit an extreme one, is an
agreement in May of 1975 which listed as germane 21
amendments to the military procurement authorization
bill." Keith at 159.

[80] In a sample of 38 UCAs in 1983-84, 12 were amended, some
more than once (for a total of 15 amendments). Survey by
Barry Fiedel, law student, Georgetown University Law Center
(on file with author).

[81] The Minority Leader responded to Majority Leader Baker's
effort that "there are those who are a little concerned at
(footnote continued)

context to push.[82]   When the Senate is ready, a
unanimous consent agreement locks the schedule
up.[83]

One of the all-time complex UCAs cemented a
1986 leadership deal in which the Democrats
secured the right to push through a South Africa
sanctions bill and the Republicans won the right
to push through aid to the Nicaraguan contras.
The UCA provided for cloture votes on both bills,
a very lengthy but finite list of amendments on
both bills, and provisions to ensure that the
Senate would complete both bills all the way to
going to conference.   That UCA arranged the
scheduling and procedure for an entire pre-

---

this stage that if we set a final time for a vote, they will
not have an opportunity to call up their amendments.   So I
think at this particular stage, we shall not be able to make
an agreement."   129 Cong. Rec. S5861 (daily ed. May 3,
1983).

[82]   Senator Baker stated that "absent an agreement, I do not
think we can do anything except plow ahead," but he
explained the scheduling consequences regarding disruption
of planned weekend visits to home states:

it is necessary sometimes to discommode the Senate
Members, their families, and schedules and plans that
are already laid and made, but that has to
happen . . . . We will be in much later tomorrow night
and Thursday night . . . . There will be votes on
Friday . . . . Members should assume that there will
be a session on Saturday.

129 Cong. Rec. S5861 (daily ed. May 3, 1983).

[83]   For example, when the Senate considered a resolution
condemning the Soviet Union for shooting down Korean
Airliner 007, since Senators desired to make an immediate
statement on the matter, the Majority Leader brought the
resolution up without a complete UCA.   When the Senate was
ready later in the week, he then devised a complete time
agreement.   The final UCA provided for 1 1/2 hours of
general debate, gave a list of ten amendments with specified
limited times for debate, and provided for a vote at the end
of that time, bringing the Senate directly to a conclusion
on the matter.   129 Cong. Rec. S12286-87 (daily ed. Sept.
15, 1983).

adjournment week of proceedings. As Congressional
Quarterly noted, the UCA "took nearly an hour for
the majority leader to read aloud to his
colleagues, and when printed in the *Congressional
Record* it consumed three pages."[84]

Secondly, just as the Senate historically
incorporated a germaneness rule into the standard
form, so today it uses time agreements to regulate
amendments. Sometimes the Senate agrees to the
equivalent of a closed rule -- a time agreement
allowing no amendments at all.[85] As a striking
example, the Senate agreed at one point to
consider a constitutional amendment on abortions
without any amendments.[86] In contrast, sometimes
dozens of Senators insist on their own
amendments. Supplemental appropriation bills
become magnets for amendments; a typical time
agreement for one (entered after much prior
consideration of the bill) listed five amendments
for consideration under the previous order and 28
more before final passage.[87]

The UCA on the 1988 omnibus drug bill
illustrated how flexibly UCAs can handle
amendments. With the bill coming up at the very
end of the Congress under severe time pressure and

---

[84]   Felton, *Senate's Climate of Partisanship Yields an
Agreement of Unusual Complexity*, 44 Cong. Q. Week. Rep. 1878
(1986).   The UCA's text is at 132 Cong. Rec. S10952-54
(daily ed. Aug. 9, 1986); the Senate agreed to it, with
final modifications, at id. S11075. The agreed upon cloture
votes occurred at id. S11490 (daily ed. Aug. 13, 1986)
(first cloture vote on contra aid); id. S11493 (cloture vote
on South Africa sanctions); id. S11497 (second cloture vote
on contra aid).

[85]   See, e.g., 129 Cong. Rec. S1287 (daily ed. Feb. 17,
1983) (broadcast deregulation bill) ("no amendments . . .
other than the committee amendment in the nature of a
substitute").

[86]   Apparently the opponents of the amendment agreed to the
UCA because they correctly anticipated the constitutional
amendment would fail. 129 Cong. Rec. S9096 (daily ed. June
27, 1983).

[87]   129 Cong. Rec. S2786-87 (daily ed. March 14, 1983).

with scores of amendments, the UCA organized the
process by dividing the amendments into three
categories: "a leadership package of noncontroversial amendments" which the Senate passed
by voice vote; amendments that would be reviewed
by four Senators, subject to being "appealed to
Byrd and Dole," and then either included in that
leadership package or killed; and the third
category of "controversial amendments that were to
be debated under time agreements," such as the
death penalty amendment.[88]

Bargaining over the UCA can make major
decisions about the content of legislation.
Throughout the early 1980s, Administration allies
urged adoption of controversial anticrime
measures. Finally, on the eve of Senate
consideration of a comprehensive crime control
bill in 1983, the closed-door bargaining sessions
produced a final agreement. The UCA provided that
no amendment dealing with the death penalty,
exclusionary rule, or habeas corpus would be in
order. Essentially the UCA, far more than floor
actions, defined the ultimate legislation.

Third, UCAs serve the leadership as a tool
for scripting proceedings. They provide for time
limits not only on final passage and amendments,
but on second-degree amendments, motions, points
of order, and appeals. They govern how that time
control will work, including who will control
time, a matter discussed in the next chapter
regarding floor management. They waive points of
order, particularly the several points of order in
the Budget Act, and quorum calls. They can
guarantee "up or down" votes (i.e., guarantee that
an amendment will not be killed by tabling), and
they can "stack" a series of votes (i.e., have
them follow each other without intervening break,
and be finished in a short time period). As
previously described, time agreements for
"stacked" votes took on increasing sophistication
as a means of arranging the Senate's program.

---

[88] The quotes are from Lawrence, Senate Breaks Deadlock,
Passes Anti-Drug Bill, 46 Cong. Q. Week. Rep. 2978 (1988).
The UCA is listed at 134 Cong. Rec. S15640-41 (daily ed.
Oct. 12, 1988) and 134 Cong. Rec. S15766 (daily ed. Oct. 13,
1988).

E. NON-GERMANE AMENDMENTS AND OTHER IRREGULAR
    PROCEDURES

Non-germane Amendments: Importance of Uses

The foregoing discussion may have left the impression that the Senate leadership controls the Senate agenda. Since the Senate leadership seems to have so many prerogatives -- control of the "legislative day," motions or request to proceed, manipulation of the "pending business," shaping of unanimous consent agreements, operation of the clearance mechanism -- it might appear to preclude dissident Senators from directing consideration.

Nothing could be further from the truth. Control over "days" and proceeding to consideration only allows the leadership to control what bills come up. Control over shaping unanimous consent agreements only insulates the agenda so long as the Senate is willing to give all bills restrictive UCAs, which has not been the case. So long as the leadership must bring bills to the floor not covered by restrictive UCAs, bills kept off the agenda by the leadership can be offered as floor amendments. The Senate's lack of a germaneness rule means that the answer to what can come to the floor usually is: anything.
A Senate study of current practices addressed the high importance of the lack of a germaneness rule:

> The opportunity to offer non-germane amendments lies at the heart of Senate procedure. It is an essential component of the principle of the protection of the minority. With this opportunity, the majority cannot foreclose debate and votes on issues that a minority wants brought to national attention. In addition, the opportunity to offer such amendments enables Senators to bring to the floor issues on which the committee of jurisdiction has not acted.[89]

Similarly, a Congressional Quarterly study of the

lack of power of the minority party in the House
drew this central contrast in the Senate:

> Senate rules permitting members to offer non-
> germane amendments to most legislation allow
> senators to bypass committee consideration
> and force a floor vote on pet proposals.
> Just last month, for example, Howard M.
> Metzenbaum, D-Ohio, won Senate approval of
> stiffer infant-formula standards as an
> amendment to another bill (HR 1848), although
> he had been unable to get even a hearing on
> his proposal in the Labor and Human Resources
> Committee.[90]

While non-germane amendments and their uses
do not fall into neat categories, they may be
discussed usefully in three groups with different
procedural consequences: "symbolic" votes,
omnibus vehicles, and individual serious items.
First, Senators may use the opportunity to offer
non-germane amendments as a means for obtaining
votes on propositions of symbolic value. Several
1984 examples may be given. When the Senate
considered S.1762, the Comprehensive Crime Control
Act, Senator Metzenbaum offered an amendment to
prohibit government officials from tape recording
their telephone conversations.
The amendment "was prompted by disclosures
that Charles Z. Wick, head of the United States
Information Agency, had recorded dozens of
telephone conversations without the other party's
consent."[91] By offering the amendment, Senator

---

[89] Report of the Temporary Select Comm. to Study the Senate
Committee System, S. Rept. No. 254, 98th Cong., 2d Sess. 15
(1984). "Without doubt, the right to offer non-germane
amendments is the most potent leverage that individual
Senators have to place matters on the floor
agenda . . . ." Bach at 17.

[90] Hook, Senate Rules, Closeness of GOP Margin . . . Keep
Democrats Influential in Minority, 44 Cong. Q. Week. Rep.
1394 (1986).

[91] 1984 Congressional Quarterly Almanac 222. The roll-call
on the motion to table this amendment is vote 5, id. at page
(footnote continued)

Metzenbaum immediately obtained an opportunity for public discussion of the practice currently in the news that he criticized. Ultimately he obtained a vote compelling Senators to line up, symbolically, for or against the offending practice.

Similarly, when the Senate considered bankruptcy court reform, Senator Jesse Helms (R-N.C.) offered an amendment to bar compulsory union dues for political purposes.[92] When the Senate considered the State-Justice-Commerce appropriations bill, Senator Don Nickles (R-Okla.) offered an amendment condemning Black Muslim leader Louis Farrakhan for anti-Semitic and racist statements.[93] When the Senate considered a supplemental appropriations bill, Senator Claiborne Pell (D-R.I.) offered an amendment regarding Taiwan policy, and Senator Baucus offered an amendment urging withdrawal of the recess appointment of Martha Seger to the Federal Reserve Board, prompting a two-hour debate.[94]

The Senators offering these non-germane amendments, and many others offering amendments each year for symbolic purposes, did not have to aim seriously at enactment of matters into law. In this regard, they pose no serious problem for Senate floor organization. If the symbolic amendment lacks support, it is defeated; otherwise, it dies in the House or in conference. The Senate's allowance of such amendments merely means that while Representatives without influential posts can only make speeches on current issues, Senators can force their colleagues to a vote. This use of amendments on symbolic issues transgresses somewhat the goals of the committee system, since the Senators vote without the committee of jurisdiction having

---

3-S.

[92]   1984 Congressional Quarterly Almanac 20-S, vote 108.

[93]   1984 Congressional Quarterly Almanac 30-S, vote no. 172. Because the amendment was framed as expressing the "sense of the Senate," it may not technically have been non-germane, but it had nothing to do with the legislation.

[94]   1984 Congressional Quarterly Almanac at 443 and at 36-S, votes 204 and 205.

control, hearings, or reports, but there is not as much transgression as if the amendment were headed toward enactment of a major law.

Non-germane Amendments to Omnibus Bills

Another group of amendments is offered to "omnibus vehicles." Typically these vehicles are items of financial legislation that must be enacted in some form by the Senate and House and signed into law by the President to avert financial problems or crises. Typical vehicles include debt limit increases, continuing resolutions, supplemental appropriations, and, to some extent, budget reconciliation bills.[95]

The 1983 debt limit bill illustrates the course of such an omnibus vehicle, with particular interest because it triggered extensive procedural discussions. Senator Dole, the manager, noted the scope of the non-germane amendments:

> nuclear freeze and press access and war powers and State severance taxes and military equipment for Jordan, line item veto, repatriation of Cubans, meat exports, nuclear builddown, need for spending cuts, study on the budget are nongermane amendments.[96]

Senator Dole concluded that the bill "is sort of a turkey shoot. Everybody has his own turkey and is going to put it in this bill." When the Minority Leader noted the consistent history of such omnibus vehicles -- "when we used to have the majority here . . . . Did we not see some handgrenades coming from the other side? [Laughter]" -- Senator Dole conceded that "I do

---

[95] The Budget Act imposes a strict germaneness rule on budget reconciliation bills, so there is no great tendency for non-germane floor amendments to be added on, but the committees may try to load extraneous provisions onto the bills. This problem of extraneous legislation on reconciliation bills is discussed separately in the chapter on the budget.

[96] 129 Cong. Rec. S15069 (daily ed. Oct. 31, 1983).

not suggest that there is not precedent for this. [Laughter]."[97]

In fact, the 1983 debt limit precipitated a debate over changing the procedures. Senator Long, the minority manager, proposed, and the Senate adopted, a sense of the Senate provision that "amendments in 1983 which will result in increased spending or which will lower revenues -- should not be offered to debt limit or reconciliation bills."[98] This amendment, which rushed to roll-call adoption by a vote of 66-11 without much consideration, received sharp rebuke from the Minority Leader when he returned to the floor. As he noted, such a restriction, if binding, would bar amendments "to restore those cuts in social security or medicare" on a reconciliation bill.[99] Later, Senator Dole filed notice that he would move to amend Senate Rule XV to add that "during the consideration of any bill . . . [regarding] the statutory limit on the public debt, no amendment not germane shall be received."[100] This evoked from Minority Leader Byrd one of his least veiled threats:

> I do not want to make an idle threat, and I am saying to Senators that there will not be a vote on this bill, or eve[n] on this amendment, tonight . . . . [I]f this amendment were not pulled down, there would not be a vote on this resolution for a week at least unless this amendment is pulled down. If anyone wants to know how I can make such a statement I will be glad to tell him.[101]

---

[97]   129 Cong. Rec. S14868 (daily ed. Oct. 28, 1983).

[98]   129 Cong. Rec. S14952 (daily ed. Oct. 29, 1983) (provision), S14954 (adoption).

[99]   Id.

[100]   This was a much stricter rule than any of the Senate's usual germaneness reform proposals. Moreover, the means for the proposal -- a suggested method of lightning-fast rewriting of the rules -- was alien to the Senate and much like the House's use of special rules.
(footnote continued)

With the issue framed, Senator Long --
although the author of the nonbinding provision
adopted by the Senate -- joined in strongly
opposing the proposed highly strict germaneness
rule.   Senator Long spoke in defense of how
omnibus vehicles gave other Senators the agenda
shaping privileges of committee chairs:

> The debt limit, to some extent, is something
> of an equalizer among a hundred Senators. If
> a Senator does not have prominence on a
> committee . . . he can offer [his proposal]
> on a debt limit bill . . . [alleviating] the
> frustration of junior Senators or Senators
> not on the appropriate committee . . . .

In addition, he noted how, in theory at least,
such a vehicle tested a proposal's support, and
could ultimately bring an amendment with
sufficient support to enactment:

> The Senator from Massachusetts had a proposal
> about a nuclear freeze. It may be that he
> did not have a majority. In fact, it turned
> out that he did not. But he had grave
> difficulty finding an opportunity to find
> some legislation headed toward the
> President's desk on which he could offer his
> proposal, something on which the House might
> be able to concur in the event he
> succeeded.[102]

Ultimately Senator Dole withdrew his proposal.
The debt limit became loaded with extraneous
provisions and failed at first, but then the
extraneous provisions were deleted and it passed.
    This category -- non-germane amendments
heaped, omnibus-fashion, on vital funding bills --
became the chief impetus for recurrent proposals
for a Senate germaneness rule.   Later in the
1980s, the Senate did adopt a rule against
extraneous amendments on reconciliation bills, the

---

[101]   129 Cong. Rec. S15069, 15071 (daily ed. Oct. 31, 1983).

[102]   129 Cong. Rec. S15070 (daily ed. Oct. 31, 1983).

"Byrd Rule" discussed in the budget chapter. More generally, Senators proposed germaneness requirements that would be triggered, like cloture, by a vote of a supermajority of Senators imposing the rule on any particular bill. Proposals in 1976, 1980, and repeatedly in the 1980s for such a rule all languished.[103]

In place of such a rule, leaders and managers developed a number of tactics discussed below which serve as the functional equivalent. The motion to table, discussed in the next chapter, constitutes the Senate's working tool for handling non-germane amendments, and when the leaders agree to move a bill, they may reach some understanding about the use of the motion to table.[104]

---

[103] The 1984 Senate committee to study rules changes summed up the proposal's history, drawing on work by Oleszek. Select Committee Report, supra, at 41-44. In 1976, the Senate Rules committee reported such a proposal, requiring a two-thirds vote to impose germaneness. The proposal drew strong opposition from Senators Ted Kennedy (D-Mass.) and Jacob Javits (R-N.Y.), among others; it "'does violence to individual senator's rights and allows an additional advantage to committees,' explained an aide to Senator Javits." Select Committee Report, supra, at 42 (quoting Oleszek study which, in turn, quoted a Congressional Quarterly Weekly Report quoting the Javits aide). The proposal did not pass.

In 1979, Majority Leader Byrd included in his rule reform package a proposal requiring a three-fifths motion to bar nongermane amendments. It was dropped in the deal by which the Senate enacted limits on postcloture filibusters. In 1980, Majority Leader Byrd reintroduced the proposal, responding to the Helms non-germane amendment on the death penalty discussed below. The proposal died in committee. Subsequent proposals for such a rule were made by the Pearson-Ribicoff study group, Majority Whip Stevens, Minority Leader Byrd, and the Quayle Committee. None made progress. These are summarized and compared in Congressional Research Service, Recommendations for Senate Reform: A Comparision of Selected Proposals 41-42 (1985).

[104] In consideration of the 1983 debt limit bill, the agreement reached was that "any tabling motions that are made will have to be agreed upon by both managers." 129 (footnote continued)

Bipartisan agreement on some form of use of
tabling can largely defuse the non-germane
amendments, for the bipartisan support makes
tabling a pure procedural tool for moving
legislation rather than a substantive statement on
each particular amendment.

Alternatively, at the completion of amending
the omnibus vehicle, the leadership may offer a
motion to recommit that strips all amendments
off.   This allows the amendment proponents to
obtain Senate votes on all the amendments.   Then,
after those votes have been provided, it offers a
purely procedural tool for moving the legislation
rather than a substantive statement on particular
amendments.

Non-germane Amendments: Enacting Legislation

Although, again, there are no neat
categories, a third type of non-germane amendment
can be distinguished from either symbolic votes or
omnibus vehicles.   This is the single non-germane
amendment offered to one bill, or more than one
bill, in a serious drive to enact it into law.
Some illustrations will assist in analyzing the
special focus of what may be called the serious
non-germane amendment.

Two bills illustrate this well: Senator
Robert W. Kasten, Jr.'s (R-Wis.) bill in 1983 to
repeal withholding of taxes on interest and
dividends, and the 1985 textile protection bill.
In planning a campaign for such a bill, Senators
start with the realization that either because of
committee or leadership opposition, an otherwise
strongly supported proposition will not reach the
floor through the usual route.   In the case of the
tax withholding bill, Senator Kasten knew that
strong opposition from the leadership of the
Finance Committee barred reporting the bill to the
floor.   Similarly, in the case of the textile
bill, Senator Ernest Hollings (D-S.C.), a
supporter of the bill, explained that "Senator
[John] Danforth [(R-Mo.)], who also serves as the
chairman of the Subcommittee on Trade of the

Cong. Rec. S14763 (Oct. 27, 1983) (unanimous consent request
element stated by Senator Byrd).

textile bill would never get out of the Senate Finance Committee."[105]

The sponsor of such a bill believes that he will get it enacted, not through some one-shot sudden move of offering it to "must" or omnibus legislation, but through the same extensive campaign as to move any major bill. Accordingly, he works with the strong lobbies that must stand behind such a bill, to round up cosponsors and to organize grass-roots support to persuade wavering Senators. Both the tax withholding and textile bills had powerful lobbying and the cosponsorship of a majority of the Senate.

The offeror then picks a vehicle on which to offer the legislation. Senator Hollings explained:

> In July, knowing that [the Finance Committee would never report the bill], I then searched around, not in a secretive way but trying to take what bills would appear, and I filed the textile bill as an amendment on the Micronesia Compact.
>
> I informed [Senator Danforth] . . . , and I also informed the distinguished majority leader, Senator Dole, I was trying to play the game on top of the table and not mislead anybody.[106]

Senator Kasten picked a series of vehicles for his bill, including agricultural payment in kind, supplemental appropriations, and social security.

These steps parry many of the thrusts available to leaders and managers fighting non-germane amendments. The most potent tool, the motion to table, will not work because a majority of Senators back the popular non-germane amendment. High-pressure leadership techniques used to enact "clean" amendments off of vital bills such as debt limit bills will not work because the amendment sponsor picks a vehicle that

---

[105]   131 Cong. Rec. S12444 (daily ed. Oct. 2, 1985) (Sen. Hollings).

[106]   131 Cong. Rec. S12444 (daily ed. Oct 2, 1985).

is not "must" legislation. Opposition can thus come down to filibustering.[107]

The ultimate target of those backing this kind of serious non-germane amendment is to reach the point at which the leadership's interest changes. A non-germane amendment with true support and staying power becomes a difficult problem for the leadership. It ties up the floor even without cloture, by returning repeatedly and engendering filibusters wherever it arises.

Once it begins to seem that cloture will be voted, it will tie up the floor even more firmly, for the cloture rule will make the clotured non-germane amendment the "pending" business, allowing nothing else to come up without unanimous consent. At this point, the leadership, which normally defends committee jurisdiction, begins to find it in its interest to get the non-germane amendment aboard some vehicle that will move it out of the way of the rest of the Senate's business. Once the leadership finds it in its interest to move the matter, the proponents of such a "serious" amendment have succeeded in taking control of the Senate's agenda and their proposal is well along toward enactment.

Rule XIV Placement on the Calendar

Another, more technical means of moving bills outside the normal channel of committee reporting is the use of Rule XIV. Rule XIV(3) provides in pertinent part:

> [E]very bill and joint resolution introduced
> on leave, and every bill and joint resolution
> of the House of Representatives which shall
> have received a first and second reading
> without being referred to a committee, shall,
> if objection be made to further proceeding

---

[107] Senator Kasten and Senator Strom Thurmond (R-S.C.) each were required to file a cloture petition on their legislation. 129 Cong. Rec. S4751 (daily ed. April 15, 1983) (Kasten cloture petition on withholding); 131 Cong. Rec. S12486 (daily ed. Oct. 2, 1985) (Thurmond cloture petition on textile protection).

>   if objection be made to further proceeding
>   thereon, be placed on the Calendar.

Pursuant to this rule, ordinarily when a Senator
introduces a bill or the House messages over a
bill it has passed, the Chair refers the bill to
committee.

However, Rule XIV allows any Senator to
invoke an alternative procedure. When the bill is
introduced, or messaged over, "if objection [is]
made to further proceeding thereon," the Chair
does not refer the bill to committee. Instead,
Rule XIV prescribes, in case of such an objection,
that the bill "be placed on the Calendar."[108]   If
the leadership supports the procedure, the bill
cannot be delayed long.[109] Once on the Calendar,
it still requires a motion or unanimous request to
proceed to the bill, before it comes before the
Senate.   Still, the bill has bypassed committee

---

[108]   For House bills, see Riddick, "References to
Committees: Bill Held at Desk Until Second Reading," at 930,
933; "References to Committees: House-Passed Bill,
References of," at   937.

[109] Rule XIV provides for the bill to receive two readings
on two legislative days. Minority Leader Byrd explained why
this did not allow very long resistance by the minority:

>   I can object at this point to [the bills receiving the
>   Rule XIV approach] being introduced on this legislative
>   day, but the majority leader has the votes and he can
>   adjourn for a half-minute and that cures the first
>   objection. Then the offering of the two measures could
>   be made, the request could also be made that there be a
>   first and second reading, and there could be an
>   objection to the second reading, which would mean that
>   the bill could not be placed on the calendar until the
>   Senate adjourns again.
>
>   The majority leader would have used his
>   adjournment weapon once on this legislative day. It
>   could not be used again until tomorrow, but he could
>   use it again tomorrow, after which rule XIV could be
>   used as a mechanism to automatically force the two
>   bills on the calendar.

128 Cong. Rec. S11403 (daily ed. Sept. 15, 1982).

referral, and thus avoided being bottled up permanently by a hostile committee.

Historically, the Rule XIV technique served as an important method for moving civil rights bills, which would otherwise have languished upon referral to a Judiciary Committee chaired by opponents of such bills like Chairman Eastland of Mississippi. "This is how both the Civil Rights Bill of 1957 and the Civil Rights Bill of 1964 were placed on the Senate Calendar."[110] The use of the technique in 1957, which required reversing a prior precedent,[111] pushed forward what turned out to be the Senate's first successful consideration of a civil rights bill since Reconstruction, albeit a weak bill.[112]

---

[110] Froman at 136.

[111] "There were only a few examples of a bill going to the calendar under Rule XIV prior to 1946," Shuman, Senate Rules and the Civil Rights Bill, Am. Poli. Sci. Rev. 955, 967 n.5 (1957), and only one from 1946 to 1948, id. In 1948, the Senate temporarily interpreted its committee jurisdiction rule, Rule XXV, to provide mandatorily for a reference to committee, precluding any Rule XIV end-run. However, "[i]n 1957, and on other occasions under a like situation . . . the Senate reversed its decision of 1948." Riddick, "References to Committees: Bills and Resolutions, Reference to Committees," at 933.

[112] By using Rule XIV, the bill supporters avoided the result that otherwise "the civil rights bill would no doubt have languished again in the Senate Judiciary Committee until the end of the Congress. This procedural move was a major and essential step towards the final passage of the bill." Shuman, supra, at 968. The maneuver, crucial to the progress of the 1957 civil rights bill pushed by then-Majority Leader Lyndon Johnson, foreshadowed the political revolution by which President Johnson later moved his own far more substantial civil rights and voting rights bills and his Great Society program:

> for the first important occasion since 1938, the coalition of Southern Democrats and conservative Republicans was shattered. The quid pro quo of that coalition has long been that Southern Democrats would provide enough votes to defeat liberal social and

(footnote continued)

Thereafter, the Rule XIV technique continued to be the route for other civil rights and voting rights bills.[113]

The Rule XIV approach has some advantages over simply offering a bill as a non-germane amendment. Compared to the latter approach, it was seen as "a more 'legitimate' procedure" since "[a]lthough this procedure still raises the question of by-passing committees, it is clearly provided for by the rules."[114] In fact, even committee chairs may use it on occasion, as a way of moving their bills more quickly.[115]

---

economic legislation while the conservative Republicans provided the votes to defeat civil rights moves. Now, for the first time, a coalition of Northern Republicans and liberal Northern Democrats had acted together on a procedural issue to further the progress of a civil rights bill.

Id. at 969.

[113] For example, in 1969, the House send an extension of the Voting Rights Act to the Senate. Supporters kept the bill on the Senate calendar using a Rule XIV objection to referral, until opponents agreed to accept a unanimous consent agreement for the bill to go to committee with a deadline requiring it be reported. 115 Cong. Rec. 39098, 39335 (1969). For a general treatment of Rule XIV, see 126 Cong. Rec. S7435-38 (daily ed. June 19, 1980) (Senator Orrin Hatch (R-Utah) on "Abuse of Rule XIV").

[114] Froman at 137. Moreover, even when used to by-pass the committee, the Rule XIV approach emphasized two points that supported such by-passing: it was used for House-passed bills, which held public attention and proven support; and it required leadership support, since bills could only be taken off the Calendar by the leadership. Hence, the technique put the burden on the recalcitrant committee chairs to justify why their will should stand against that of the House, the Senate leadership, and a presumptive majority of the Senate.

[115] For example, in 1982, Majority Leader Baker, acting on behalf of the chair of the Judiciary Committee, Senator Thurmond, used the Rule XIV approach for several items. The two leaders discussed the use of the device:

(footnote continued)

Because of these advantages, the Rule XIV technique began to be used not solely for major civil rights bills, but more generally, and even for minor bills.[116] However, in later times, the Senate leadership turned against the technique. In 1983, Majority Leader Baker and Minority Leader Byrd held a colloquy regarding the matter:

> Sen. Byrd: I think it is bad to allow more and more items to be held at the desk for further action without their going to committee.
>
> Sen. Baker: I agree . . . . If we are not careful, we are going to destroy the committee system by holding matters at the desk . . . .
>
> I have tried to convince a number of Senators who have come to me to propose a bill for the calendar under rule XIV that they should think about that and [not] attempt to do it routinely, because not only

---

Mr. BAKER: Mr. President, the distinguished President pro tempore, the Senator from South Carolina (Mr. THURMOND), has two items that he wishes to try to take to the calendar under the provisions of rule XIV . . . .

Mr. ROBERT C. BYRD: . . . there is no way -- no way -- that anybody on my side of the aisle can prevent the placing of the President's crime package and the bill which Mr. Thurmond introduced on insanity from going on the calendar . . . .

128 Cong. Rec. S11503 (daily ed. Sept. 14, 1982).

[116] See, e.g., T. R. Reid, Congressional Odyssey: The Saga of a Senate Bill 92 (1980) (use of Rule XIV technique to put barge waterway fee bill on the calendar instead of referring it to a hostile committee); 128 Cong. Rec. S11495 (colloquy between Majority Leader Baker and Senator Hatch, in which the latter drops a controversial abortion amendment in return for the Majority Leader's promise that "I will be happy to cooperate with him in seeing that he has full opportunity under rule XIV" to move a different legislative vehicle).

does it deprive the committee of
jurisdiction, but it also does something that
perhaps I should not say, but I am going to
say; it delivers that matter into the tender
mercy of the keeper of the calendar, and the
minority leader and I, really, as a practical
matter, are the keepers of the calendar.

In many cases, or in most cases,
perhaps, Members will do better to have it in
committee and have the reinforcing approval
of the committee reporting that measure than
they will just by putting it on the calendar
and then the leadership put to the test of
deciding whether they are going to take it up
or not.

I freely confess that I am not going to
take up matters unless I am convinced they
should be taken up because of a great
national importance or that I am convinced
that the committee would like to have them
taken up. So rule XIV is not a panacea.[117]

Miscellaneous Approaches

Three other procedures that are rarely used
deserve passing mention: discharge, suspension of
the rules, and consideration of resolutions "over
under the rule." A rarely used procedure allows
Senators to move to discharge a bill from a
committee that has been bottling it up. The
motion to discharge faces a severe obstacle
course. The motion must wait several legislative
days.[118] Even a successful discharge motion only

---

[117] 129 Cong. Rec. S12971 (daily ed. Sept. 27, 1983).

[118] It can only be introduced during the "morning hour,"
meaning only when the Senate adjourns (not recesses) and
then starts a new day with a formal "morning hour" procedure
-- something that rarely happens any more. Even then, the
motion lies over another legislative (not calendar) day,
pursuant to Rule XVII. This means it must await another
Senate adjournment (not recess).

(footnote continued)

brings the discharged bill to the calendar.[119]
There, it still requires a motion to proceed to
the bill, and then consideration of the bill,
before passage. This means that, in effect, a
discharge motion can lead to four successive
filibusters prior to passage, too many for anyone
to take on.[120] Accordingly, the Senate has only
discharged bills 14 times, and the last time was
in 1964.[121]

A second procedure is suspension of the
rules. Rule V provides: "No motion to suspend,
modify, or amend any rule, or any part thereof,
shall be in order, except on one day's notice in
writing." Besides the requirement of one day's
notice, a motion to suspend the rules has two far
more decisive restrictions. The motion requires a
two-thirds vote.[122] Moreover, the motion is

Then, at the start of that next legislative day, a
motion must be made to bring up the discharge motion, and
the Senate must finish that motion during the morning hour
that day; otherwise, at the end of the morning hour, the
discharge motion simply goes to the calendar. Riddick,
"Discharge of Committees: When in Order to Consider a Motion
to Discharge," at 643. It goes to the calendar under the
Rule XIV procedure known as "over under the rule," discussed
below. See Riddick, "Over Under the Rule: Resolutions
Required to go Over Under the Rule," at 774 (example 7: "To
discharge a committee from the consideration of a
nomination").

[119] Riddick, "Discharge of Committees: When Committee is
Discharged, the Proposition is Placed on the Calendar," at
642.

[120] Once on the Calendar the motion to discharge faces two
possible filibusters: one on the motion to consider the
discharge motion, and the second on passage of the
motion. And, of course, all of this activity is just
on the motion to discharge. If a bill is discharged
successfully, it then faces two more possible
filibusters: one on the motion to consider the bill
itself, and the other on passage of the bill.

Froman at 130-31.

[121] W. J. Oleszek, Congressional Procedure and the Policy
Process 196 (2d ed. 1984).
(footnote continued)

debatable,[123] so that it can be filibustered unless the Senate invokes cloture. Hence, the Senate rarely uses the procedure, except for one purpose: to make amendments in order to appropriation bills that would otherwise not be in order, such as amendments for unauthorized programs or legislation.[124]

Lastly, the Senate has a procedure with the curious name of "over under the rule." As discussed above, Rule XIV provides a special procedure by which bills may stay on the Senate Calendar instead of being referred. Rule XIV also provides this other special procedure, not for bills (which must pass both the Senate and House and be submitted to the President), but rather for simple resolutions, that is, resolutions which need only pass the Senate. The most important such resolutions would be ones to change the Senate's rules.

Rule XIV(6) provides for simple resolutions:

> When objection is heard to the immediate
> consideration of a resolution or motion when
> it is submitted, it shall be placed on the
> Calendar under the heading of "Resolutions
> and Motions over, under the Rule," to be laid
> before the Senate on the legislative day when
> there is no further morning business but
> before the close of morning business and
> before the termination of the morning hour.

---

[122] Riddick, "Suspension of Rules: Vote Required," at 1030.

[123] Riddick, "Debate: Suspension of the Rules, Debate of Motion for," at 627.

[124] "Almost all motions to suspend the rules in the Senate concern amendments to appropriation bills . . . . Such motions are quite common . . . ." Froman at 135. For examples, see Riddick, "Suspension of Rules: Amendments to Appropriation Bills, Suspension of Rules for," at 1026-28. However, currently the Senate tends instead to use other means, such as the "defense of germaneness," or the simple overruling of the Chair when it (correctly) rules some amendment to an appropriation bill out of order. These approaches are discussed in the chapter on appropriations.

While in theory this provides a way for such rule changes not to be buried in the Senate's Committee on Rules and Administration, in practice that way proves so cumbersome that no such proposals make progress.[125]

F.   PROCEDURE FOR EXECUTIVE BUSINESS

General

The Constitution vests in the Senate a category of business entirely distinct from legislation: nominations and treaties.   Article II, sec. 2, cl. 2 provides in pertinent part:

> [The President] shall have Power, by and with the Advice and Consent of the Senate, to make Treaties, provided two-thirds of the Senators present concur; and he shall nominate, and by and with the Advice and Consent of the Senate, shall appoint Ambassadors, other public Ministers and Consuls, Judges of the Supreme Court, and all other Officers of the United States, whose Appointments are not herein otherwise provided for, and which shall be established by law.

The business of giving "Advice and Consent" on treaties and appointments constitutes the "executive" business of the Senate, called that because the Senate acts in concert with the executive, which originates the appointments and treaties by submitting nominations and signed (but unratified) treaties.[126]   In contrast to enactment

---

[125] The procedure stalls any such resolution to change the rules.   Like a discharge motion, it must wait for new legislative days and formal "morning hours," and even then, absent completion of consideration, it goes to the Calendar from which it would have to be called up.   For an example of a rule change proposal that headed off down that course, see 129 Cong. Rec. S80 (daily ed. Jan. 26, 1983) (Sen. Byrd's proposal to change the rules, to eliminate the "defense of germaneness" technique for putting amendments on appropriations bills, goes "over under the rule").
(footnote continued)

of public laws, Senate action on these items of executive business does not require House approval. The Senate has separate procedures for disposing of its executive business, but before addressing those procedures, some background is in order.

Few subjects carry so heavy a weight of history and constitutional law, to say nothing of politics, as nominations and treaties. Whole books have been devoted to specific aspects of these, and there is no place here for duplicating those works. For procedural purposes, it suffices to say that ordinarily the Senate completes action on each item of executive business with only the most minimal formal attention through simplified procedures. Each year the Senate confirms thousands of nominations, and ratifies dozens of treaties, by streamlined procedures that require mere seconds or less for each nomination, and minutes for each treaty. This routine conduct of business does not minimize the Senate's role in choice of federal officers or in foreign policy; rather, the prevalence of routine treatment reflects that the Senators exercise their power mainly through consultations, in closed-door meetings and other informal contacts and in committees rather than in floor battles.

With regard to nominations, each Senator, and particularly each Senator of the same party as the President, has an ongoing consultative relationship with the Executive Branch concerning patronage. Majority party Senators have a recognized interest in nominations of several kinds: a large one in nominations concerning their own states, such as judges and United States Attorneys for the federal courts and federal prosecutive offices in their states; a significant one in nominations deemed to fall under their committee jurisdiction, such as regulatory commissioners for the Committee on Commerce, Science and Transportation; and one of some

---

[126] Congress' legislative powers are set forth predominantly in Article I of the Constitution, which begins by describing the legislative power. The Senate's powers regarding treaties and nominations are set forth in Article II, which begins by describing the executive power.

importance in other nominations, such as those ambassadorships that may be used to reward the party faithful. The Senate has a tradition of enforcing the necessity of consulting with Senators who have recognized interests, reflected today most clearly in the reluctance of committee chairs and the Majority Leader to proceed with nominations over intense resistance from such Senators.[127]

With regard to treaties, the Foreign Relations Committee has an ongoing consultative relationship with the State Department. Its power over treaty ratification is but one ingredient of the mix that includes confirmation of ambassadors and State Department officials, foreign aid and State Department authorization bills, measures to disapprove arms sales, other legislation either significant or symbolic, hearings and informal briefings, overseas trips and international contacts, and other elements of an elaborate legislative-diplomatic milieu. As with nominations, the influential Senators typically prefer to exercise their power connected with treaties through consultation behind closed doors, or publicity for their views in press conferences and public hearings, as much or more than through floor action.

---

[127] One result is that for Senators of the large states with sizable patronage, such as New York, sometimes their consultation regarding nominations is one of their most important political roles. Another is that for Senators with a pronounced agenda, such as Senator Jesse Helms (R-N.C.) in the 1980s, the holding up of nominations can constitute an important part of a struggle over national policy. See, e.g. Senate, After Delay, Confirms Envoy, 43 Cong. Q. Week. Rep. 2329 (1985):

Helms had delayed [the nominee for Ambasssador to China, Winston] Lord's nomination for several weeks as a tactic to pressure the Reagan administration into accepting his interpretation of a 1985 spending bill provision . . . [that] required ending all U.S. support for the United Nations Fund for Population Activities . . . . Helms said he received the assurances he wanted directly from President Reagan on Nov. 5, and so he allowed the Lord nomination to proceed.

Thus, the cases in which floor procedure matters in executive business are exceptional -- they are deviations from normal practice on the occasions when Senators make a floor issue of some particular nomination or treaty, either to defeat it, to change it (in the case of treaties), or to send a political message. Looking at their numbers alone, these exceptional cases would seem a small matter; in excess of 99 percent of nominations submitted by the President receive confirmation without incident. However, the exceptional cases carry significance far beyond their numbers.

To take some of the most famous examples, the defeat on the Senate floor of the Treaty of Versailles following World War I stamped United States foreign policy as isolationist in the period between the wars. Some consider the defeat of that treaty, and the isolationist policy that followed it, as one of the factors that ultimately led the Axis nations to believe they could discount both the League of Nations and the United States, and thus led to a pattern of aggression ending World War II. In 1979, the withdrawal of the SALT II treaty, in the face of a likely floor defeat in the Senate (particularly following the Soviet Union's invasion of Afghanistan), foreshadowed a major change in United States-Soviet Union relations from detente to years of chill.

As for nominations, the Senate's refusal to confirm President Nixon's first two nominees for the Supreme Court, Judges Clement Haynsworth and Harold Carswell, or two of President Reagan's nominees, Judges Robert Bork and Douglas H. Ginsburg, has significantly influenced the High Court for many years considering the slow rate of turnover on the Court. Conversely, the Senate's willingness in the 1980s to confirm a large majority of President Reagan's nominees of judges for district and circuit courts, even to the point of the Senate's breaking filibusters against those nominees by voting cloture, boosted the Administration's implementation of its judicial philosophy.

What matters most in these exceptional cases of floor fights, of course, is the numerical strength of supporters and opponents of the particular treaties or nominations against the

backdrop of issues and public opinion, rather than
procedure. Yet, procedure may play a significant
role in some cases.   This is more true for
treaties than for nominations, since treaty
ratification procedure allows some important
possibilities for maneuvering.   The example
discussed below, of the amendment process for the
Panama Canal Treaty, illustrates the major role of
tactical judgments about floor action.   The
procedure for nominations is much simpler and
allows no amendments, thus limiting the importance
of procedural tactics.

Executive Calendar

The Senate maintains a separate calendar for
all its executive business, both nominations and
treaties.   This is the Executive Calendar,
distinguished from the Calendar of General Orders
for legislative business.   No rule provides
expressly for this calendar, but as Rule IV(d)
alludes to obliquely, the Senate has kept separate
records for executive business from earliest
times.[128]
Although the Senate could have evolved a
rigid program in which it considered business on
the Executive Calendar on some particular days, as
the House considers its specialized calendars on
particular days, the Senate has not done so.

---

[128] Rule IV(d) provides: "The legislative, the executive,
the confidential legislative proceedings, and the
proceedings when sitting as a Court of Impeachment, shall
each be recorded in a separate book."   Pursuant to this
rule, the Senate keeps an Executive Journal distinct from
its Legislative Journal.   In the celebrated case of Marbury
v. Madison, 5 U.S. (1 Cranch) 137 (1803), William Marbury
wished to obtain evidence to prove that the Senate had
confirmed his judicial appointment, as part of his effort to
mandamus Secretary of State James Madison to provide him
with his commission.   Accordingly, Marbury petitioned the
Senate for an extract from its Executive Journal.   12 Annals
of Cong. 32 (1803).   An extensive debate ensued, in which
the Senate ultimately voted to deny the petition.   Id. at
34-50.   The historic case then proceeded without the Senate
records.

Instead, in line with its general organizational pattern, the Senate follows a flexible approach, typically handling legislative and executive business on the same days by going back and forth freely between the two calendars and from one matter to another on the same calendar. As in other scheduling matters, the Senate leaves the decisions in going back and forth to the Executive Calendar largely to the Majority Leader acting in consultation with the Minority Leader.[129]

The leadership may go to executive business by making the "motion to proceed to consideration of executive business" expressly recognized in Rule XXII(1). Just as the leadership ordinarily proceeds to consideration of legislative business by requesting unanimous consent, rather than by motion, so it ordinarily proceeds to consideration of executive business by unanimous consent, rather than by motion. The leadership bothers with a motion, rather than just obtaining unanimous consent, only when some Senators have insisted on requiring this.

Once Senators insist on a motion, the characteristics of the motion itself become significant. The motion to proceed to consideration of executive business cannot be tabled or amended,[130] but there is an unresolved procedural controversy over how susceptible that motion is to filibuster. The Majority Leader can make that motion either in a two-step form, which does allow filibuster, or in a one-step form, which arguably does not. The two-step form consists, first, of making a simple motion to go

---

[129] There has apparently not been any scholarly attention to whether there are recognized leadership prerogatives in this matter, comparable to the discussions of leadership prerogatives regarding recognition, making motions to adjourn and to recess, and the like, but the making of motions to proceed to executive business seems little different as a leadership prerogative from the making of motions to proceed to legislative business.

[130] Riddick, "Executive Business and Executive Session: Amend Motion to Proceed to Consideration of Executive Business, Out of Order," at 666; Riddick, "Executive Business and Executive Session: Table, Motion to," at 673.

into executive session, which in itself is not
debatable.[131] Once the Senate adopts that motion,
the Senate is in executive session. At that
point, if the Majority Leader does not want the
Senate to work on the nomination next on the
Executive Calendar in listed (chronological)
order, the Majority Leader may make a further
motion, as his second step: the motion to proceed
to a particular nomination on the calendar, much
like a motion (in legislative session) to proceed
to a particular bill. Like the motion to proceed
to a particular bill, this motion is debatable,[132]
and so it can be filibustered.

However, there is also a one-step form of
this whole procedure, starting when the Senate is
in legislative session. A motion may be made to
proceed to consideration of a particular
nomination on the Executive Calendar, which
combines the two steps of first going into
executive session, and second of proceeding to a
particular item.[133] Senator Byrd, as Majority
Leader, with agreement from the Chair, has stated
that such a motion is not debatable. However,
there have been some Senators who apparently
disagree, and they would deem the matter
unresolved even though the Chair has spoken.[134]
It is this unresolved tension that creates the
uncertainty over whether the motion to proceed may
be filibustered, as the motion to proceed to
consideration of a particular bill may be
filibustered.[135]

---

131 Riddick, "Executive Business and Executive Sesssion:
Debate of Motion to Consider Executive Business," at 669;
Riddick, "Debate: Executive Session, Debate of Motion for,"
at 592.

132 Riddick, "Nominations: Considered When Reached on Call
of Executive Calendar," at 752.

133 The precedents and discussion regarding this have
concerned nominations, but presumably would apply the same
to treaties.

134 Riddick, "Nominations: Considered When Reached on Call
of Executive Calendar," at 751-52.

(footnote continued)

Putting that issue aside, while the Senate moves frequently and easily from legislative to executive business and back, it does keep the two apart. Thus, the Senate may freely proceed (by motion or by unanimous consent) to a nomination, and then interrupt its deliberations to work on other nominations or treaties. However, it does not consider legislative business, like bills, unless it adopts a motion or a unanimous consent request to go back to legislative business.[136] Similarly, it does not consider executive business while it is in legislative session.[137]

---

[135] It should be recalled that with a bill, two filibusters are possible: on the motion to proceed, and on the bill itself. With a nomination, the Chair has indicated that the motion to proceed to a particular nomination is not debatable, so there would be only one filibuster, on the nomination itself, and this has been the pattern with past filibusters of nominations. However, under the view of some Senators that the motion to proceed to a particular nomination can be filibustered, two filibusters are possible: on the motion to proceed to a particular nomination, and then on the nomination itself.

[136] Riddick, "Executive Business and Executive Session: Legislative Business Out of Order in Executive Session," at 670. The motion to return to legislative business is not debatable. Riddick, "Executive Business and Executive Session: Legislation," at 669.

[137] Riddick, "Nominations: Legislative Session--Executive Business Out of Order," at 754; Riddick, "Executive Business and Executive Session: Legislative Session," at 670.

One exception is that the Senate prefers to avoid having to go into executive session just to handle the mechanics of referral of treaties and nominations. Accordingly, the Senate adopts a unanimous consent request at the beginning of each Congress that it be in order to make such referrals on the day when they are received from the President even when the Senate has no executive session that day. Riddick, "Executive Business and Executive Session: Receipt and Reference of Executive Business," at 672; Riddick, "Nominations: Unanimous Consent to Refer," at 761-62; Riddick, "Treaties: Reference to Committee," at 1057.

Nominations

Each Congress, the Senate receives thousands of nominations. A few of these are of the highest importance, such as for Justice of the Supreme Court, or major Cabinet positions. Conversely, the vast majority, by number, consist of routine commissions in the armed forces, the Public Health Service, or lesser foreign service posts. The Senate held 41 roll calls on nominations in the Senate in 1981-82, a better measure of Senate attention than the high numbers of nominations submitted.[138] Actually, this number of roll calls represented twice as many or more than in the years before 1979, perhaps suggesting a greater degree of ideological confrontation over nominees.[139]

Once the President submits the nomination, the Chair refers it to the committee of jurisdiction. As the Congressional Research Service has described:

> [S]ome committees process large numbers of nominations. These include Armed Services (military officers), Foreign Relations (Foreign Service officers), and Labor and Human Resources (Public Health Service officers).

> [From data on when nominations come in]

---

[138] Technically, the Senate receives not merely thousands, but hundreds of thousands of nominations, because of the huge number of commissioned officers in the armed services who receive confirmation: the total number of nominations sent to the Senate in 1981-82 numbered 186,264. However, the President submits the armed service nominations in batches, making submittals (individual or batch) a more meaningful unit; in 1981-82, there were 1,661 nomination submittals.

[139] The statistics are drawn from R. H. Davidson & M. E. Cook, Indicators of Senate Activity and Workload, (Cong. Res. Serv. 1984), at 16 (describing batch submittals), 56 (statistics on batch submittals), 63 (roll calls), and 64 (total number of nominations).

we can see the cycles of nominations over
time. Individual nominations are especially
numerous   at   the   beginning   of   a   new
Administration, tapering off in the later
stages. Group nominations are more evenly
distributed over the calendar, although these
represent   a   minimal   burden   upon   the
committees involved.[140]

The   post-Watergate   era   has   seen   greater
scrutiny of nominees, so committees more often now
have   rules   regarding   nominations,   which   may
require   nominees   to   fill   out   questionnaires
(particularly concerning disclosure of potential
financial conflicts of interest).   The committees
also tend more to hold public hearings on the
nominations, at subcommittee or full committee
level, and to print the hearings. When the full
committee votes to report out the nominations,
technically, the vote must be made by a quorum of
the committee physically present (that is, at a
committee meeting),[141] but polling out (without a
meeting) of nominations often occurs, particularly
when all committee members accept such a poll.
A written report is still relatively rare.
On occasion, the committee-level proceedings may
become protracted or major: the nominee may be of
the utmost importance, such as a Supreme Court
Justice,   or   controversial,   or   may   become   the
vehicle for a dispute over an issue or over
withholding by the executive of information, such
as when Attorney General Richard Kliendienst's
confirmation hearings became the vehicle for major
disputes   during   the   Watergate   era.   If   a
nomination hits extreme trouble, the President may
withdraw it, the committee may kill it by refusing
to report it out, or the committee may report it
out adversely, which (in contrast to a refusal to
report) allows the Senate to act on it even though
the   committee's   judgment   is   against
confirmation.[142]

---

140   Id. at 16.

141   Riddick, "Nominations: Reports -- Quorum Required to
Act on," at 759.

(footnote continued)

Once the committee reports the nomination, it goes on the Executive Calendar, until the Senate proceeds to consider it, as discussed above.[143] The Senate can vote to recommit a nomination to committee, either to allow follow-up proceedings such as hearings on new issues emerging since the committee reported, or as a slightly less humiliating means of killing a nomination than bluntly voting it down.

Also, the Senate can filibuster a nomination, simply by talking. For example, at the beginning of 1985, farm-state Senators filibustered the nomination of Edwin Meese as Attorney General, not from particular opposition to him personally, but to insist on legislative attention to farm problems. The Senators simply debated the nomination without end until reaching an agreement with the Majority Leader that farm relief legislation would receive consideration. In 1986, Senators filibustered the nomination of Sidney Fitzwater as district judge, asserting he had shown insensitivity to the rights of minorities; his nomination stalled on the Senate floor until the Senate ultimately voted 64-33 to impose cloture, and then 52-42 to confirm.[144]

Ultimately, when the Senate completes debate, it votes on the question set forth in Senate Rule XXXI(1): "Will the Senate advise and consent to

---

[142]   See Riddick, "Nominations: Reports-Adverse," at 758.

[143]   Rule XXXI(1) provides that the vote on confirmation "shall not be put . . . on the day on which [the nomination] may be reported by a committee, unless by unanimous consent."

From 1789 until 1929, the Senate considered nominations in closed session, but since 1929, the virtually invariant practice has been to consider the nomination in open session. Rule XXXI(2) provides that "[a]ll business in the Senate shall be transacted in open session, unless the Senate as provided in rule XXI by a majority vote shall determine that a particular nomination, treaty, or other matters shall be considered in closed executive session." See Riddick, "Nominations: Open Session," at 755.

[144]   Cohodas, Senate Confirms Texas Judge by Close Vote, 44 Cong. Q. Week. Rep. 670 (1986).

this nomination?"   A majority vote suffices.   A
close vote to confirm, although allowing the
nominee to take office, can send a message that
she lacks political support, or that there is
something else the Senate dislikes.[145]   Once the
Senate votes to confirm, it notifies the
President, who commissions the officer. Rule XXXI
allows for reconsideration of confirmation, so
that typically a Senator makes a pro forma motion
to reconsider and another moves to table that
motion, thereby forestalling any later
reconsideration.[146]

The Constitution provides a mechanism for the
President to make recess appointments, an end-run
around Senate confirmation that has presented
fruitful ground for constitutional confrontation
between the branches of government.[147]   Also,
Senate Rule XXXI(6) provides for returning to the
President nominations not acted upon when the
session ends or an extended recess occurs.
However, sometimes the Senate provides by
unanimous consent that it will hold onto the

---

[145]   For example, a sizable vote against Paul Warnke as
President Carter's head of the Arms Control and Disarmament
Agency, although it failed to defeat him, sent a warning
that the Senate would be wary of arms control initiatives in
the Carter Administration.

[146]   See Riddick, "Nominations: Reconsider," at 757. Senate
Rule XXXI(4) provides carefully that "Nominations confirmed
or rejected by the Senate shall not be returned by the
Secretary to the President until the expiration of the time
limit for making a motion to reconsider the same, or while a
motion to reconsider is pending unless otherwise ordered by
the Senate."   Caution is necessary in notifying the
President, for once notification has been sent,
reconsideration can only proceed with a request to the
President to return the notification. The Supreme Court has
upheld, as a matter of construing the Senate's rules, the
President's right not to return a nomination for
reconsideration, and thus to treat notification of
confirmation as final. United States v. Smith, 286 U.S. 6
(1932).

[147]   See L. Fisher, Constitutional Conflicts Between
Congress and the President 47-55 (1985).

unacted-upon nominations at such times.[148]

Treaties: In General

As a formal matter, Senate proceedings on treaties begin when the President submits a treaty.[149]   Pursuant to Senate Rule XXX, the President submits each treaty with an "injunction of secrecy," dating back to the earliest days of the Republic when President John Adams requested a secret mode of communication with the Senate on delicate diplomatic matters.   In modern practice, the Senate leadership almost invariably asks unanimous consent to remove the injunction of secrecy before referring the treaty to the Foreign Relations Committee.[150]

The Foreign Relations Committee then holds hearings and, if supportive, reports the treaty to the Senate with a resolution of ratification, which goes on the Executive Calendar. Technically, the Senate does not "ratify" the treaty itself.   Rather, the Senate adopts a resolution of ratification, which advises and consents to the ratification of the treaty; then the President ratifies the treaty.   The treaty itself floats along through the Senate, accompanied by its resolution of ratification, like a high-level diplomat accompanied in his journeys by an increasingly marked and creased

---

[148]   Riddick, "Nominations: President Submits Nominations Anew Each Session," at 755.

[149]   A President -- or a series of Presidents -- may devote years or even decades to the negotiation of major treaties such as arms control treaties or the Panama Canal Treaties.   Senators may well play an important role during that process, as the executive branch seeks their advice in anticipation of the ultimate requirement of Senate ratification.   See T. M. Franck & E. Weisband, Foreign Policy By Congress 138-41, 147-49 (1979)(role of Senators and staff during negotiations).   As noted above, consideration of treaties occurs as part of an elaborate consultative foreign policy milieu.

[150]   Riddick, "Treaties: Injunction of Secrecy," at 1054-55.

passport. (For simplicity, though, the customary expression that the Senate "ratifies" the treaty has been followed here.)

Other committees may also find ways of expressing an interest, as the Armed Services Committee expressed an interest in the SALT II treaty by holding hearings and issuing a negative report.   In any event, it may be a long wait before the Senate takes up ratification.   It was only in 1986, "[a]fter almost 37 years of intermittent debate, [that] the Senate . . . overcame opposition by conservatives and approved a treaty declaring genocide to be a crime."[151]

For most treaties, once floor action starts, the Senate acts very quickly.   Until the 1980s, the Senate had an elaborate procedure for treaty consideration involving use of the Committee of the Whole, a creature otherwise known only in House rather than Senate procedure.   For most treaties, the Senate bypassed that procedure by unanimous consent; in 1986, it finally changed its rules and abolished the procedure.[152]   On the typical noncontroversial treaty, no amendments are offered, except committee amendments if any.[153]

---

[151]   Cohodas, Decades-Old Genocide Treaty Finally Wins Senate Approval, 44 Cong. Q. Week. Rep. 458 (1986).

[152]   On only two treaties in the twentieth century, the Treaty of Versailles and the Panama Canal treaties, had the Senate engaged in the full procedure involving Committee of the Whole.   The change in 1986 came in S. Res. 28, 99th Cong., 2d Sess., adopted at 132 Cong. Rec. S1756 (daily ed. Feb. 27, 1986).   The proposal for change had originally been made by Minority Leader Byrd, in a package of changes submitted along with provisions for the Senate to be televised, presented at that time with the avowed justification that the Senate needed to update its procedures in light of televising.   The proposal regarding treaty procedures, a noncontroversial one, survived when other proposed changes were rejected.

[153]   Rule XXX(1)(b) simply provides: "When a treaty is reported from a committee with or without amendment, it shall, unless the Senate unanimously otherwise directs, lie over one day for consideration; after which it may be read a second time, after which amendments may be proposed."

simply votes on ratification.   Pursuant to the
Constitution, this vote requires a two-thirds vote
for approval.   There is no technical requirement
that the Senate hold a roll-call vote, but it has
a practice of doing so.[154]   There are exceptions:
in 1988, a major copyright treaty "which ha[d]
been under consideration, on and off, for 102
years, reached the floor in late afternoon with
only five senators on hand," who held the
ratification vote.[155]   Several treaties may be
ratified en bloc.[156]

---

[154]   The "practice of taking record votes was begun in 1953
after the news media the previous year gave publicity to the
fact that three noncontroversial consular conventions were
approved by the Senate at a time when two Senators were
present."   Senate Committee on Foreign Relations, 95th
Cong., 1st Sess., The Role of the Senate in Treaty
Ratification: A Staff Memorandum to the Sen. Comm. on
Foreign Relations 18 (Comm. Print 1977).

[155]   The quote is from Molotsky, Congress Passes a Series of
Bills in Rush to Leave, New York Times, Oct. 21, 1988, at
B6.   The division vote on the Berne Convention for the
Protection of Literary and Artistic Works is at 134 Cong.
Rec. S16940 (daily ed. Oct. 20, 1988).   For good measure the
Senate ratified eight other minor treaties en bloc with that
same division vote.   This seems characteristic of the ends
of sessions.   See 128 Cong. Rec. S15921 (daily ed. Dec. 21,
1982)   (ratifying treaty document no. 97-21, radio
regulations, without a roll call).

[156]   To speed up Senate approval of noncontroversial
treaties, "when a large number of similar treaties
(fisheries, double taxation conventions, customs treaties,
etc.) is on the executive calendar it has become a practice
to consider them either 'en bloc' -- that is one vote on
several resolution[s] of ratification -- or to have a single
vote, which, however, by unanimous consent is shown
separately in the Record for each treaty." Senate Committee
on Foreign Relations, supra, at 18.   This has the beneficial
side effect, doubtless unintended, of boosting Senators'
attendance record on roll calls.   Thus, for example, on June
18, 1984, the Senate held one roll call, a vote of 100-0,
which was deemed by unanimous consent to constitute 16 roll
calls agreeing to resolutions of ratification for 16
treaties covering everything from tax and extradition to
(footnote continued)

Treaties: Reservations

Senate procedure for treaties focuses above all on the consideration of amendments, which may be known generically as "reservations." The Supreme Court has long recognized the Senate's authority to condition ratification with reservations.[157] Reservations may simply preserve further a congressional role, such as by providing that a treaty will not be effective without implementing legislation.[158] However, they may be used for a range of other objectives, much like "killer" or "saving" amendments for legislation, to undermine or to bolster the likelihood of ratification of the treaty.

In the most famous case of "killer" reservations, that of the Treaty of Versailles, the Senate would apparently have ratified the treaty if presented with ratification as one simple question. However, a treaty opponent, Senator Henry Cabot Lodge, Sr. (R-Mass.), who chaired the Committee on Foreign Relations, devised a set of reservations that had great support within the chamber, but which were unacceptable to President Wilson. When President Wilson instructed his supporters not to ratify the treaty with those reservations, he doomed ratification.[159]

Canadian-United States waterways.   1984 Congressional Quarterly Almanac at 29-S.

[157] Fourteen Diamond Rings v. United States, 183 U.S. 176, 183 (1901) (concurring opinion); Haver v. Yaker, 76 U.S. (9 Wall. 32, 35 (1869); see generally L. Henkin, Foreign Affairs and the Constitution 379 (1972).

[158] See United States v. American Sugar Co., 202 U.S. 576 (1906) (applying Senate amendment tying effective date of treaty to legislative approval); Dorr v. United States, 195 U.S. 138, 143 (1905) (treaty provisions reserving civil rights of inhabitants of newly acquired territory for legislative decision).

[159] See generally Wright, Validity of the Proposed Reservations to the Peace Treaty, 20 Colum. L. Rev. 212 (footnote continued)

Reservations may serve as a focus of elaborate maneuvering and posturing for political advantage. When the Senate took up the Panama Canal treaties, on which a close vote was expected, Senator Dennis DeConcini (D-Ariz.), a freshman Senator, desired to strike a hard bargain for his vote. His "DeConcini reservation" provided that if "domestic problems were to cause the closing of the canal or interfered with is operation, the U.S. could use force 'in Panama' to reopen it and restore operations."[160] Ultimately, the Senator agreed to language which, unlike his original version, would not drive the Panamanians to the point of renouncing the treaties. The extended drama served as a graphic demonstration of the power of the reservation process.[161]

Finally, reservations may serve as a ground of compromise between supporters and opponents. Senator Helms had prevented ratification of the Genocide Treaty until 1986. Then, through "the effort by Senate Foreign Relations Chairman Richard G. Lugar, R-Ind., to assuage conservatives' concerns through 'reservations' within the treaty," the treaty finally secured ratification.[162]

(1920).

[160] That reservation provided protection for him against the wrath of constituents skeptical about the treaty, since he could depict his reservation as obtaining vital concessions for the United States. In fact, the opportunity to maneuver on the reservation yielded enormous publicity, as he ended up meeting personally with President Carter about the matter once and cancelling a second meeting.

[161] For a full account, see T. M. Franck & E. Weisband, supra, at 275-84.

[162] Cohodas, Decades-Old Genocide Treaty Finally Wins Senate Approval, 44 Cong. Q. Week. Rep. 458, 459 (1986). Specifically, Senator Helms allowed the treaty to come to a vote with several reservations, of which a key one was that the United States could exempt itself from compulsory jurisdiction in genocide treaty cases before the International Court of Justice. "Supporters of the treaty ha[d] strenuously opposed this provision," but "it was Lugar's willingness to deal with Helms in 1985 that broke (footnote continued)

Classification of reservations by type is a complex matter. In the traditional technical terms, there are a number of types of matters that may be adopted in connection with treaties. Senate Rule XXX(c) states that "the resolution of ratification when pending shall be open to amendment in the form of reservations, declarations, statements, or understandings." An "amendment" made a change in the language of the treaty itself; a "reservation" did not change the language of the treaty but modified or limited its legal effect; and an "understanding" or "interpretation" enunciated an interpretation of the treaty without modifying or limiting its legal effect.[163]

The Senate first considers the treaty itself, taking up amendments, and then the resolution of ratification, taking up other types of reservations. As two observers described the process in 1988:

> During the first stage of consideration,

Lugar's willingness to deal with Helms in 1985 that broke the committee logjam." Id.

[163] For this classification, how the Senate labels the statement (as reservation or as amendment) does not matter; rather, the substance of the statement determines its legal effect. This description draws on the fuller treatment in Senate Committee on Foreign Relations, 95th Cong., 1st Sess., supra, at 3-13.

To take a simplified set of examples for the case of an arms control treaty putting a ceiling of 100 on launchers, changing the treaty language so that it allowed 500 would be an amendment; adding language in a resolution of ratification that the ceiling would only apply when the Congress enacted a new defense authorization bill would be a reservation, as it limited treaty effect without changing treaty language; and adding language in a resolution of ratification that the term launchers was understood not to include spare parts for launchers even when these could be assembled over a period of days would be an understanding, as it could be considered not to modify the treaty. This analysis is offered tentatively; other considerations, such as the text and intent of a specific treaty, would be relevant to analyzing an actual example.

> Senators may offer amendments that propose to
> change the text of the treaty itself . . . .
> The second stage begins when the Senate takes
> up the resolution of ratification without
> ever voting on the treaty as a whole. This
> resolution, which incorporates any treaty
> amendments the Senate adopted, also is
> debatable and amendable.[164]

The nature of reservations affects when they may be offered:

> [At the second stage,] [a]dditional
> amendments to the text of the treaty no
> longer are in order, but Senators now may
> amend the resolution to include reservations,
> understandings, declarations, or provisos.
> Amendments to the treaty must be proposed [at
> the first stage] while the treaty itself is
> before the Senate, whereas reservations and
> other statements are in order during
> consideration of the resolution of
> ratification.[165]

The modern politics of the Senate's role has enlarged the importance of the reservation process. As a matter of traditional international law, the action following a nation's enunciation of reservations did not matter so much. Usually the same government negotiated the treaty, decided on any reservations, and then formally ratified by execution of protocals of exchange. Such execution of protocols of exchange had traditionally been a rather minor step, taken by functionaries well after the drama of signature of the treaty by high-level figures upon the conclusion of negotiations.

However, the complex politics of ratification for major treaties in a democratic society in which quite often a substantial fraction of the Senate differs on some major foreign policy

---

[164] Celada & Bach, <u>Treaty Making and the INF Treaty in the Senate</u>, Congressional Research Service Review, March 1988, 24, 25.

[165] <u>Id.</u> at 25.

questions from the President has made Senate consideration of reservations central. Accordingly, it became of importance what the President, and the foreign treaty partner, must do regarding Senate reservations. The choices range from whether the treaty partner must explicitly agree to each reservation, for example, or whether the treaty partner simply agree to the treaty, leaving its agreement to have only implied significance regarding the reservation.

For example, when Senator DeConcini first began proposing adjustments in the Panama Canal treaties, "he had at first drafted an amendment stipulating that, on the expiration of the U.S. base leases in Panama, either party could request negotiations for an extension." The content of this was not controversial, "[b]ut DeConcini wanted it added to the treaty as an amendment, which, by Panamanian Constitutional law, would have had to be subjected to approval by plebiscite," requiring a whole new process in Panama fraught with risks. Ultimately, "at an intense meeting . . . the Arizonan agreed to go with a reservation instead of an amendment."[166]

Thus, "[t]he practice of executing a protocol of exchange" between the President and his foreign treaty-partner, a process in which Senate reservations can be handled with varying degrees of explicit or implicit acceptance and insistence by the executing officials, "hitherto a relatively obscure stage in the process of treaty ratification, can be expected to gain greater prominence as attention focuses increasingly on the need for clarity and precision in treaty commitments."[167] Senate treaty procedure took on

---

[166] T. M. Franck & E. Weisband, supra, at 275-76.

[167] Glennon, The Senate Role in Treaty Ratification, 77 Am J. Int'l Law 257, 266 (1983). Professor Glennon was formerly Counsel to the Senate Foreign Relations Committee.

Accordingly, the Senate Foreign Relations Committee, in reporting SALT II, set forth three explicit categories of reservations, which may serve as a model in future complex reservation processes: "(1) those that need not be formally communicated to or agreed to by the Soviet Union; (2) those (footnote continued)

significance[168] in defining both the interaction
of the Senate and the President, and of this
nation and other nations.

---

to be formally communicated to the Soviet Union, but need
not necessarily be agreed to by it; and (3) those that would
require the explicit agreement of the Soviet Union." Id.,
citing S. Exec. Rep. No. 14, 96th Cong., 1st Sess. 72-78
(1979).

[168]   During the Panama Canal Treaty consideration, the
reservation process "amounted to a new trilateral round
involving Panama, the Executive, and various Senators."
This presents a problem compared to the simpler model of the
State Department handling all issues.   However, it accords
with other means, such as the War Powers Resolution and
oversight of covert actions, for providing democratic
participation through the Congress in the making of
controversial national commitments.   Like these other means,
the use of reservations also "creates a process for public
consultation, consensus-building, [and] credit sharing," T.
M. Franck & E. Wiesband, supra, at 286, providing popular
and political support, besides administration policy, to
signify an enduring national commitment.

9
Bills on the Senate Floor[1]

A. OVERVIEW OF FLOOR MANAGER'S ROLE

Importance

Once the leadership arranges a unanimous consent
agreement, if any, for a bill, and then obtains
consideration of a bill by motion or unanimous
consent, the leadership largely turns control over
to the floor manager. Floor management

> is   important   for   both   symbolic   and
> substantive   reasons.   Symbolically,   it
> represents control over the final stages of a
> bill's   journey   through   the   legislative
> process . . . .   For some bills, especially
> the more controversial ones, it also may mean
> the   difference   between   passage   unamended,
> significant   amendments,   or   defeat.
> Therefore, the skill of the bill manager may
> play   an   important   role   in   determining   the

---

[1]   Sources frequently cited in this chapter include: E.
Drew, Senator 145 (1979) (Drew); S. S. Smith & C. J.
Deering, Committees in Congress (1984) (Smith & Deering);
E. Redman, The Dance of Legislation (1973) (Redman); F.
Riddick, The United States Congress (1949) (Riddick, The
United States Congress; T. R. Reid, Congressional Odyssey
(1980) (Reid).

fate of a piece of legislation.[2]

The floor managers' many duties reflect their importance. Before floor consideration begins, the floor manager leads bill proponents in preparations: counting heads in anticipation of the floor fights, marshalling supporters, lobbying the undecided, making deals, and preparing speeches, counterarguments, and counter-amendments. Floor managers take a leading role in the shaping of the UCA that portends the course of floor action. Once floor consideration begins, symbolically, floor managers do not stay at their own personal desks in the chamber, but go to the front row aisle desk (normally belonging to the party leaders).[3] As discussed above, managers receive priority recognition by the Chair as party leaders do (though their priority is lower than the leaders). Floor managers explain the bill, sequence the floor speakers and amendments, and control time when it is controlled.

Floor management represents much more, politically, than just the smooth progress of bills; it represents committee power and the current Senate's complex response to individuation. The majority party usually chooses the chair of the committee or subcommittee of jurisdiction to manage a bill. Thus, the floor manager draws on committee power already developed at the prior stages of referral, hearings, markup, and reporting, and anticipated committee power at the conference stage. Moreover, as Senate individuation has flourished in recent years, part of the Senate's reaction has come in the sophisticated techniques of bill management. The heart of the recent power of individual Senators, apart from filibustering, has been the success of floor amendments, particularly non-germane ones.

---

[2] Smith & Deering at 194-95.

[3] See, e.g., Reid at 65: "The front-row desks on either side of this aisle are normally reserved for the two party leaders, but when a bill is up for debate, the leadership seats are taken by the chairpersons and ranking minority member of the committee or subcommittee that has jurisdiction over the legislation."

The heart of the Senate's response has been the array of tactics of bill managers discussed below for dealing with floor amendments.

Choice of Manager

Usually, the chair of the committee or subcommittee of jurisdiction becomes manager of those bills not simply cleared by the leadership. A survey of floor management in the 95th Congress (1977-79) found that the chairs of committees or subcommittees managed three-fifths of the bills not simply cleared by the leadership.[4]   Chairs bring their formal and informal powers to their floor management. They scheduled and chaired the hearings and markups; their staff worked the bill, and wrote the report.   Thus, they have dealt with the interest groups and the other Senators on a host of tactical and substantive decisions, making the deals, forming the alliances, and developing the pertinent record.   Expectation of the chairs' likely prominent role in conference, both in choosing the conferees and in leading the conference delegation, adds to their arsenal as floor managers.

For example, Senator Mark Hatfield (R-Oreg.), as chair of the Appropriations Committee, managed a supplemental appropriations bill in 1983. Senator Hatfield uttered what he recognized "may be harsh words" which proved effective in eliciting floor amendments from laggard offerors:

> I might say, I am going to make a judgment on
> the importance of those amendments as far as
> whether we should fight for them in the
> conference. If a Senator does not think that

---

[4]   Technically, the Majority Leader "managed" 45.2 percent of bills, but this survey included the routine bills for which the Majority Leader simply cleared the bill rather than performing floor management to any elaborate degree. Full committee chairs managed 13.6 percent, and subcommittee chairs managed 21.9 percent, adding up to three-fifths of the bills not simply cleared by the Majority Leader. Smith & Deering, supra, at 196.

> much about his amendment to be here on the
> floor to offer it within a reasonable period
> of time, it is obviously not terribly
> important. So why should we, even if it is
> adopted, make any efforts to hold it in the
> conference?[5]

Another floor manager expressed bluntly another
conference dimension of management. He accepted a
number of amendments that he disliked when offered
on the floor to his bill, explaining, "You can
take a couple of amendments you know you are going
to drop in a spittoon on the way to the
conference."[6]

There are no hard and fast rules for when
chairs manage bills, and when they let other
Senators such as bill sponsors manage bills.
Passage of one minor bill illustrates how the
Senate chooses its floor managers, sometimes very
deliberately, and sometimes quite haphazardly and
unpredictably. Eric Redman, a staffer for Senator
Warren Magnuson (D-Wash.), described the Senate's
strange choice of a floor manager for Magnuson's
bill to create a National Health Service Corps.

"As Chairman of the relevant committee,
[Senator Ralph] Yarborough [D-Tex.] would
ordinarily have been the bill's Floor Manager
during the Senate debate," but Senator Yarborough
was out of town. Senator Magnuson, as the bill's
sponsor, "might indeed have replaced him, but
ironically, Magnuson had not yet returned from a
weekend trip to Seattle."[7] Senator Henry Jackson
(D-Wash.), as an early senior cosponsor, was the
third logical choice, but when approached, "[h]e
winced . . . [and] explained he had a meeting and
could come to the Floor only to vote." The
remaining successive logical choices were
politically unattractive: "[t]he only Democrats on
the Floor from Yarborough's committees were the
type [Vice President] Spiro Agnew had just called

---

[5]   129 Cong. Rec. S8177 (daily ed. 10, 1983).

[6]   Drew at 175.

[7]   The quotes and description that follow are from Redman at
155-56.

'radic-libs' . . . . They could manage the bill,
but they might alienate potential votes from
conservatives . . . ."

When the key staffer for the bill (Redman
himself) explained the problem to the committee's
minority counsel, who also supported the bill,
that counsel suggested "with a smile" that the
manager be Senator Peter Dominick (R-Colo.), a
conservative Republican who was not the warmest
natural supporter of the liberal bill.   The
minority counsel explained, "Of course it's crazy
but why not? . . . .   He's the top Republican on
the Health Subcommittee, he's a cosponsor, and he
amended the bill in Committee -- so at least he
should know something about it."

The minority counsel then put the matter to
Senator Dominick, who "shrugged his shoulders and
smiled," and assumed the floor managership. As it
turned out, Senator Dominick's management turned
out to be a coup: his leading role assuaged
potential conservative opponents and virtually
eliminated any floor opposition.   The Senator
"managed S.4106 superbly," and accordingly the
bill "passed unanimously."[8]

One student of the matter singled out the
four   so-called   "elite"   committees   --
Appropriations, Armed Services, Finance, and
Foreign Relations, as committees for which the
chairs usually manage bills rather than letting
others do so.[9]   Other committees, with a mixture
of bills including more numerous and less crucial
ones, have a more varied pattern as to whether the
chairman or someone else manages.

For bills not managed by full or subcommittee
chairs, the Senate commonly lets the bill's

---

[8]   Id. at 160.

[9]   This is from a student paper in 1984, which sampled floor
management in 20 bills. These committees tend to report a
limited number of high-profile bills: the regular and
special appropriations, the defense and foreign aid
authorization bills, and major tax bills. Chairs would not
readily give these up to others to manage. Appropriations
subcommittee chairs typically manage their appropriations
bill, or the portion of a supplemental bill that falls
within their jurisdiction.

sponsor be the floor manager.[10]   An interesting
aspect of this is that sometimes minority Members,
when they have been key sponsors, have actually
takes the lead in floor management,[11] such as on
the 1974 War Powers Resolution,[12] much to the

---

[10]   An example of a famous nonchair manager was Senator
Hubert Humphrey's (D-Minn.) floor management of the 1964
Civil Rights Act, since the conservative chairman of the
Judiciary Committee, Senator James Eastland (D-Miss.),
opposed the bill emphatically.

> In addition to serving as lead-off speaker, the
> Minnesota senator also took over the functions of floor
> manager . . . .   This assignment normally goes to the
> chairman of the committee or subcommittee which has
> reported a bill.   The civil rights legislation,
> however, had not been reported by any committee, and in
> those circumstances it was natural for President
> Johnson and [Majority Leader] Mansfield to look to Mr.
> Humphrey . . . one of the most passionate advocates of
> civil rights in the Senate.   Since, in addition, he was
> a most skillful legislative technician, it was logical
> to put him in charge of the bill and allow him to make
> the crucial tactical decisions.

D. M. Berman, A Bill Becomes a Law 70 (1966 ed.).

[11]   Thus, commentators analyzing the 95th Congress observed:

> [V]irtually all Senate bills are managed by the bill's
> sponsor . . . .   In the 95th Congress, 75 different
> senators (including 19 minority party Republicans)
> managed at least one bill on the floor.   In contrast,
> almost all of the 122 bill managers in the House held a
> related formal position and virtually no minority party
> Republicans managed legislation.

Smith & Deering, supra, at 197.

[12]   A leading example of a minority sponsor-manager was
Senator Jacob Javits (R-N.Y.) regarding the War Powers
Resolution.   "No member of Congress has been so closely
identified with war powers legislation as Senator Jacob
Javits . . . ."   Although a minority Senator, Senator Javits
introduced the resolution, engaged in "very delicate and
difficult" negotiations to arrive at a consensus version,
(footnote continued)

incomprehension of the House.[13]

Preparations

The floor managers' work in advance of floor consideration involves vital political preparations. Above all, the manager does head counts in one form or another -- efforts to predict how Senators will vote on passage and on any crucial preliminary votes (such as major amendments or cloture). Thus, for example, a commentator describes the final days before Senator Peter Domenici's (R-N. Mex.) bill came to the floor in terms of the Senator's "carr[ying] with him on June 22 a small green card on which [his staffer] had scrawled about a dozen names -- the names of the Senators, according to the previous day's head count, who were still undecided on the user charge."[14]

---

served as lead floor manager, and devised the essential compromise in conference. House Committee on Foreign Affairs, 97th Cong., 2d Sess., The War Powers Resolution 52 (quote describing Senator Javits), 52 (introduces resolution), 81 (negotiations), 86 (manager), 146-47 (conference compromise).

[13] The two chambers perceived the status of Senator Javits as a minority sponsor-manager quite differently in terms of what matters in each chamber:

> The House conferees saw the Senate in a somewhat weakened position because the principal spokesman for the Senate position was a relatively junior minority member, opposed by his own chairman. Interview with Zablocki, May 20, 1981. On the other hand, Javits says he did not feel at a disadvantage because he believed he had "the Senate behind me." Interview, May 19, 1981.

Id. at 142 n.3. Senator Javits' successful efforts led to the Resolution's enactment over a veto by his own party's President Nixon.

[14] Reid at 59. As previously noted, the party whip and party staff may assist in performing counts, but involved managers take some responsibility for themselves.

The manager must prepare at two levels: at the lobbying level, to assist outside lobbyists, gather inside supporters, and persuade the undecided; and, at the technical level, to develop arguments for debate and language for amendments and motions, and strategy for the floor. Thus, Senator Bob Kasten (R-Wis.) described his moving, through the mechanism of a non-germane floor amendment, his bill to repeal withholding of taxes on interest and dividends, in terms of the duties his two staffers divided: "Elise [Paylan] was coordinating the outside groups, working vote counts and strategies . . . .   Dawn [Gifford-Martinez] and I were working the parliamentary procedure and getting amendments drawn up."[15] Perhaps the most useful short observation is the overwhelming importance of the internal contacts, drawing on personal ties, party and committee loyalties, and opportunities to compromise or logroll, of either the sponsor[16] or the opposition, particularly if they are masters of the art of Senate persuasion.[17]

---

[15]   129 Cong. Rec. S5626 (daily ed. April 28, 1983) (reprinting newspaper article quoting Sen. Kasten).

[16]   The two sides on Senator Domenici's barge fees bill both recognized this in their last minute preparations.   On Senator Domenici's side, his card listing the undecided Senators for him to contact personally,

> was a concession to the fact that, despite all the high-powered lobbyists, the constituent mail, and the briefs, brochures, and broadsides that might engulf Capitol Hill over a particularly controversial issue, the most important influence on an undecided Senator is usually the personal appeal of another Senator.

Reid at 60.

[17]   On the opposition side, Senator Long observed, to explain his "buttonholing [his] colleagues to ask for a vote against Domenici's bill":

> "You see," Long explained in his soft bayou drawl, "on one of these not-so-important bills -- I mean, something that's not really important to anybody who

(footnote continued)

B.   REGULAR PROCEDURE

Opening and Committee Amendments

When the preparations have ended, and the Senate (upon the Majority Leader's motion or request) proceeds to consideration of a bill, the clerk reports the bill's title. This simply identifies the bill; it is not one of the three formal "readings" of the bill.[18] "Unlike in the House, there is no period for general debate of a bill before the amending process begins,"[19] but speeches by the members most interested in the bill typically follow the report of it by title. Usually, the majority manager opens with a lengthy statement on the bill, often modeled on the committee report, which informs the members as to the bill's main features and serves as an important part of the legislative history.
    As one commentator described the opening Senate speech, it can be a bit dull:

> If the bill is both important and controversial, [the managers'] addresses are likely to be long, set speeches, delivered from a manuscript. Usually prepared, at least in part, by experts on committee staffs, in the executive departments, or employed by interested lobbying groups, these speeches tend to be dispassionate, technical,

---

> doesn't have a river in his state -- a lot of these Senators are not going to be thinking about this much. So if I can talk to them and get them thinking my way -- just by talking personally to some Senators, that's how you win these things around here."

Id.

[18] Pursuant to Rule XIV, the first and second readings precede referral to committee. There is no reading of the bill upon its reporting. Third reading occurs after the amending process.

[19] Riddick (1949) at 361.

> and factual.   A handful of the speaker's
> friends and supporters listen, largely as a
> matter of courtesy.   Sometimes they will ask
> the speaker to yield for a question.[20]

The minority manager may make an opening
statement which sets the tone for the minority
position.   This could vary from completely
supportive, or supportive but with hopes for
amendments on some points, to fiercely opposed.
As a commentator describes, such minority
speeches, like the majority opening speech, may be
dull.[21] Other Senators may join in with their own
opening remarks.

After these opening statements, the amendment
process begins.   During this process, if a time
limitation agreement (or cloture) take effect, the
managers usually control the time of the others
who seek to speak.   To speak on a bill being
considered under time control, Senators must
receive not only recognition from the Chair, but
also the yielding of some time by those
controlling the time.[22]   Under UCAs, the most
common situation, the majority and minority
managers each control half of debate time on the

---

[20] D. R. Matthews, U.S. Senators and Their World 244 (1973 ed.)

[21] When the opposition takes the floor, usually with an equally long and scholarly speech, there is heavy turnover in the Senate audience.   A few of the opposition speaker's friends and colleagues appear, while most adherents of the other side quietly slip away to the cloakrooms or their offices.   The "debate" remains, for the most part, an exchange of mutually agreeable remarks.

Id. at 245.

[22] "Under a unanimous consent agreement limiting debate with a division of the time on amendments and the bill and giving certain Senators control of that time, no Senator is entitled to be recognized unless yielded to by one of the Senators controlling the time."   Riddick, "Unanimous Consent Agreements; Debate of Proposals Under Unanimous Consent Agreements," at 1083.

bill itself. Once a Senator moves a floor amendment, normally the offerer and the majority manager (who presumably opposes the amendment) each control half the time.[23] If the majority manager supports the amendment, the offerer of the amendment controls half of the time, and the other half is controlled by the Minority Leader or his designee (often the minority manager).

Automatically, when opening remarks are completed and it is time to consider amendments,[24] the Senate first considers the committee amendments before taking up any floor amendments. Technically, a committee reports the original version of the bill as introduced, and reports the results of its mark-up in the form of proposed committee amendments to that original version. The committee may also later report additional committee amendments, even after it reports the bill.[25] If the Senate referred the bill to more than one committee (a multiple referral), both committees may report committee amendments.[26]

---

[23]   This can produce strange results in one unusual situation: where the offeror of an amendment opposes it.

[24]   After the initial speeches, the clerk automatically reports the committee amendments, as if an unseen Senator had inaudibly announced that he had just sent them to the desk and asked their immediate consideration.

[25]   When the committee proposes more committee amendments after it first reports the bill, such subsequent committee amendments "are to be treated as committee amendments and acted upon prior to amendments from the floor." Riddick, "Amendments: Committee Amendments, Offering and Disposition of," at 33; also, "Amendments: Modification of Committee Amendments, at 57."

Such subsequent committee amendments are supposed to receive committee approval, though it can occur that the committee simply clears the changes through the chair and ranking minority member and any other Senator signalling an interest. Subsequent committee amendments may range from technical corrections through the range of possible restriking of bargains prior to floor consideration.

(footnote continued)

Committees may report either a number of individual committee "cut and bite" amendments, or one comprehensive committee amendment that substitutes itself for the full text of the bill -- a committee "amendment in the nature of a substitute." For bills with individual committee "cut and bite" amendments, such as appropriation bills, Senators may offer second-degree floor amendments to each committee amendment before the next committee amendment receives consideration. Since consideration of committee amendments one by one tends to be slow going, "it is not uncommon for unanimous consent requests to be made to agree to all committee amendments to the bill en bloc,"[27] rather than one by one.

This swift uncontested consideration of committee amendments might run into certain technical problems.[28] However, managers avoid these problems by including in their request for unanimous consent to en bloc adoption of committee amendments a request that the bill as amended be considered as original text for the purpose of further amendments.[29] Senators who plan to oppose

---

[26] Riddick, "Amendments: Call Up for Senate Consideration: Committee Amendments, Offering and Disposition of," at 35; also, "References to Committee: Multiple References," at 941.

[27] Riddick, "Amendments: En Bloc Consideration and Adoption," at 47.

[28] Under the strict precedents, when particular numbers or text in a bill have been amended once (regardless of whether by floor or committee amendments), they cannot be re-amended. Hence, unanimous consent adoption of all the individual committee amendments would preclude floor amendments to the same numbers or text. Riddick, "Amendments: Call Up for Senate Consideration: Committee Amendments, Offering and Disposition of," at 31. Moreover, adoption of the committee amendments waives the points of order that might be made against them, such as when the Appropriations Committee reports legislative amendments to appropriation bills. Riddick, "Amendments: En Bloc Consideration and Adoption," at 49.

[29] Riddick, "Amendments: En Bloc Consideration and Adoption," at 48. This also protects points of order (footnote continued)

some committee amendment or to offer a floor amendment to that amendment may not go along with adoption of a committee amendment for fear it creates momentum for the committee version of the disputed matter.   In that case, the manager may request that only the noncontroversial committee amendments be adopted en bloc.[30]   When the committee reports a committee amendment in the nature of a substitute, these problems do not occur, as Senators offer all their floor amendments as amendments to the committee substitute.[31]

Floor Amendments: Printing and Cosponsorship

---

against the committee amendments. Id. at 49.   The committee amendments taken up en bloc may be the subject of a vote on that basis.   For example, when the Judiciary Committee reported a group of committee amendments to a shipping bill, a unanimous consent agreement provided for those amendments en bloc, except for one amendment separated out for distinct treatment, to be the subject of one vote.   129 Cong. Rec. S1773 (daily ed Feb. 28, 1983).

[30]   By separating the noncontroversial ones to be adopted en bloc, the manager encourages a potentially objecting Senator to accede to the (partial) en bloc request.   The insistence by a respected objector, such as Senator Howard Metzenbaum (D-Ohio), on excluding some committee amendment from en bloc treatment may itself constitute an important bargaining signal that the supporters of the excluded committee amendment had best deal with the objector's concerns by opening negotiations -- or preparing for combat.

[31]   To allow the full amendment tree, the manager may ask unanimous consent that the committee substitute be considered as original text for purposes of amendment. After the Senate finishes its floor amending, it then adopts the committee substitute "as amended."

A mess may sometimes occur if Senators offer amendments to the bill rather than the committee substitute, not deliberately, but simply because they have other things on their minds besides fine procedural distinctions; unanimous consent requests to fix matters can cure this, like so much else.

In the Senate, from the first moment of consideration, the entire bill is open for amendment at any point.[32] This contrasts directly with the House of Representives, which "reads" a bill for amendment part by part.[33] Thus, Senators freely hop from the first to the last titles and back in the process of amending. A Senator submitting an amendment for immediate consideration obtains recognition and intones the standard formula: "I send an amendment to the desk and ask for its immediate consideration".[34] If the Senator sends amendments to the clerk but does not ask immediate consideration, then the amendments are for later potential consideration. Each submitted amendment receives a number as an "unprinted" amendment if it is considered immediately or that same day (e.g., "Unprinted Amendment No. 1001.").[35] The Congressional Record refers to Unprinted Amendments by the short form "UP," and so one often reads that votes, second-degree amendments, and other matters refer to the corresponding amendment as "UP No. 3."

Unless the Senate conducts and completes action on an unprinted amendment the same day as it is submitted, overnight it is printed. Starting in 1983, the Senate began printing the submitted amendments in the Congressional Record rather than printing them separately to save on

---

[32] Riddick, "Amendments: Call Up for Senate Consideration: Amendments in Order," at 29.

[33] In the House of Representatives, the Chair of the Committee of the Whole announces for each part something like "Are there any other amendments for Title I? If not, the clerk will report Title II," and so forth.

[34] During the first day such an amendment is submitted, it is an "unprinted" amendment and receives an "unprinted" number (e.g., "Unprinted Amendment No. 1050"); if the amendment has not been resolved, from the next day on it receives a printed amendment number.

[35] Numbering began in 1976, and the sequence of numbering begins in each new Congress. Riddick, "Amendments: Numbering of Amendments for Identification Purposes," at 77.

printing bills.[36] Thus, what was submitted as
"Unprinted Amendment No. 1001" on Tuesday becomes
"Printed Amendment No. 2002" on Wednesday. Except
during cloture,[37] no particular procedural rights
accrue from prior printing, but printing does
inform other Senators and the public of the
amendment.   Advance   notification   makes   a
considerable tactical difference, as it trades
notice for surprise. One observer described part
of the process:

> Members sometimes introduce amendments weeks
> before a bill is considered on the floor,
> even when it is still in committee, in order
> to   publicize   their   position   and   garner
> support. Printed or unprinted amendments are
> sometimes   circulated   together   with   "Dear
> Colleague"   letters,   and   cosponsors   are
> sought, just as is done on behalf of many
> bills.[38]

---

[36] Until the 1980s, the old system had been for each such
submitted amendment to be separately printed on sheets of
paper.   However, once Senators began submitting large
numbers of amendments as threats for filibustering, the
printing bill became quite costly. According to a study by
then-Secretary of the Senate William Hildenbrand in 1983,
quoted by Majority Leader Howard Baker (R-Tenn.), "there
were over 5,600 amendments printed in the last Congress
. . . the total cost is estimated to be over $1,000,000."
129 Cong. Rec. S4930 (daily ed. April 20, 1983). Yet "of
the 5,611 printed amendments . . . only 230 or four percent
were ever called up for consideration." Id. Rather, the
vast majority were simply amendments submitted for potential
use, but never used, in a handful of filibusters: "Of the
total number printed, approximately 86 percent were
submitted to only six measures." Id.

[37] Under cloture, amendments must be filed in advance, as
discussed below.   Also, since in filibusters, and
particularly post-cloture filibusters, Senators may stall by
calling up large numbers of amendments, they can signal the
threat of such tactics by submitting large numbers of
amendments for printing.

[38] Russell, "Workings of Congress," in Effective Washington
Representation 239 (S. J. Marcuss ed. 1983).

On the other hand, the value of surprise is such that prior to floor consideration, the interested parties may engage in frenzies of lobbying and intelligence-gathering to deal with unknown possible amendments. Thus, whether to print involves a tactical judgment about the benefits and costs of advance notification. The same observer notes:

> Printed amendments, however, are just the tip of the iceberg.
>
> Most floor amendments in both the House and Senate are "unprinted," although not necessarily unexpected. Members of either body may wish to surprise the bill's managers and supporters with an amendment which . . . cannot be readily discredited in debate. If the bill managers and supporters . . . know in advance that an amendment will be offered and see its text, they will prepare counterarguments and substitutes for the amendment . . . [but, on the other hand,] offering a surprise amendment leave[s] little time to gather support and raises suspicions about the motivation and true objectives of those offering the amendment.[39]

The same observer describes the practice of cosponsorship of amendments as follows: "Printed or unprinted amendments are sometimes circulated together with "Dear Colleague" letters, and cosponsors are sought, just as is done on behalf

---

[39]   Id. at 239-40. If the Majority Leader sought a unanimous consent agreement for the bill, which bars non-germane amendments unless the UCA lists them, then Senators who want to offer non-germane amendments must tip their hands a bit by making sure the UCA lists their desire to offer amendments. However, Senators who want to offer germane amendments have no need to be listed in the UCA and thus no such requirement forcing them to tip their hands. Although concealed amendments are "a mild breach of etiquette," "surprises are common and seem to go unpunished, except where a junior member of a committee presents an unpleasant surprise to the committee chairman." Id. at 240.

of many bills."[40]   As in cosponsorship of bills,
so cosponsorship of amendments confers no formal
status on the amendment; it does not even bind a
cosponsoring Senator to vote in favor of the
amendment.   However, cosponsorship signifies
support, and while Senators can flip-flop if they
like, of course they prefer not to.   An
amendment's sponsor uses cosponsorship to line up
support, both to prepare to win a floor fight and
to strengthen his hand in negotiating with the
floor manager for acceptance of the amendment in
some form.

Floor Amendments: Offering

"After committee amendments have been
disposed of" -- which usually happens through
adoption by unanimous consent -- "the Senate
proceeds to the consideration of amendments
offered from the floor by individual
Senators."[41]   The procedure by which Senators
propose floor amendments has a deceptive
simplicity compared to the subtleties that may
ensue thereafter. To "call up" a floor amendment,
the Senator obtains recognition from the Chair,
states, "I offer (or propose) an amendment and ask
for its immediate consideration," and gives its
text to the Reading Clerk.[42]

Rule XV provides that the amendment "shall be
read before the same shall be debated."
Therefore, the Chair asks the clerk to "report"
the amendment, meaning to read it. Nearly always,
the Senator offering the amendment then asks
unanimous consent that the reading of the
amendment be dispensed with.[43]

---

[40] Id. at 239.

[41] Riddick (1949) at 362.

[42] Senate Rule XV prescribes that "All motions and
amendments shall be reduced to writing, if desired by the
Presiding Officer or by any Senator . . . ." Accordingly,
Senators virtually always submit their amendments in
writing.

(footnote continued)

Once the Clerk finishes reading the amendment (or reading is dispensed with), the Chair recognizes Senators to debate the amendment. Technically, the Senator offering the amendment relinquishes the floor by so offering, and another Senator may receive recognition. As a practical matter, the Chair will almost always[44] recognize the offeror immediately following the reading of the amendment. The offeror explains the amendment he has just offered -- whether it is major or minor, its procedural history, and, of course, its substantive merit.

Floor Amendments: Summary of Manager's Responses

The moment of truth in Senate floor management comes when a Senator has offered a floor amendment and the bill manager must decide how to respond. Floor managers work in two dimensions. They work strategically, to obtain passage of the bill in some form, which motivates them to oppose amendments that would kill or reshape the bill, but to accept amendments that move the bill towards passage in acceptable shape. Also, they work tactically, toward the elusive but vital goal of achieving and maintaining working control of the floor.

Working control comes from many sources: preproceeding expectations and agreements, rewards and punishments to give out, deals that are made, a commanding presence in action, and, at a

---

[43]   The Senator may also ask that the amendment be printed in full in the record, to avoid uncertainty later on about what he offered.

If no Senator objects -- and usually none does -- then the Clerk can stop reading. Occasionally, other Senators may object and thereby require reading of the amendment in full, either from some suspicion about the amendment's contents, to give time (like a quorum call) for off-the-record discussions, or as a tool of delay.

[44]   The exception is some kind of tense or filibuster situation in which a leader or manager with priority recognition jumps in to talk or to make a motion to table.

tactical level, the manager's skill in avoiding
fights over matters not worth contesting or not
winnable, and winning fights on the matters that
are worth it.   The informal aspects of control
stand out particularly in the Senate, as compared
with the House, because the Senate floor manager
has fewer formal procedural tools -- and less
potent ones -- than the powerful House tools of
the majority leadership, Rules Committee, and
floor manager. Lacking the House's structure such
as the germaneness rule, the terms of the special
rule, title-by-title reading, and motions to close
or limit debate, the Senate manager faces a
situation where, apart from UCAs, he must take on
any amendments that any Senator wishes to offer.

On the other hand, a Senate floor manager who
achieves control may be able to accomplish more in
the Senate than a manager in the House precisely
because the chamber's informal ways tend to create
a greater potential for informal acceptance of
deals.[45]   In essence, the busier and less formal
level from which Senators approach matters makes
them somewhat more interested in dealing with
managers, or accepting a floor verdict rendered
through one or a few decisive votes, rather than
scrapping over details.

Elizabeth Drew, asking a Senator for a
comment on the floor management of Endangered
Species Act amendments by Senator John Culver (D-
Iowa), received this description of floor control:

> Off the Senate floor, a Democratic senator
> talks to me about Culver. "He's doing a real
> good job of managing the bill," the senator
> says.   "It's a controversial issue; he's
> picking his way through the amendments, and
> working some out, and fighting and defeating
> others, and establishing his control over the
> floor.   That's very important: others will
> follow your lead if they feel that you're

---

[45]   The Senators' preoccupation with their own heavy
schedules and their general tendency on matters less than
critical to themselves to accept whatever deals the
interested parties work out, mean that Senate floor managers
may steer a bill without controversy if they maintain
control well enough.

being sensible and you have control."[46]

Drew recorded the floor manager's own concerns, in beating a key amendment early, and in wanting to close off an area where other amendments might succeed:

> "[Senator William] Scott [(R-Va.)] [the bill's principal opponent] has opened something up," Culver says after he comes off the Senate floor. "There could be lots of amendments on th[is] question . . . . I wish we could have kept the momentum going. There's a lot of momentum to these things. That's why it was important to defeat [the] Stennis [amendment] early. But it's harder to achieve momentum on this bill, because it's such a cross-quilt -- so many amendments, coming from every direction. That's why we're trying to work out as many as we can informally."[47]

Sometimes a bill manager can obtain too much control, from the perspective of bill opponents. In particular, in some circumstances, managers may "railroad" through their bill.[48] The various procedural tools available to a manager in maintaining control are discussed in detail in the later sections of this chapter.

In the course of a day, the bill manager may press forward with the bill for some intervals, while the leadership may break in with other business or go to other bills. Quite commonly the same bill remains on the Senate floor at various

---

[46] Drew at 175.

[47] Drew at 164.

[48] For example, the budget procedures, with their built-in procedures akin to cloture, vastly strengthen the manager's position, giving him a germaneness rule and a time limit on debate, on a bill where managers receive party-line support (or other forms of block support) on many votes. In such situations, the minority has little opportunity to make its voice heard, even if it offers meritorious amendments and stands ready to reach compromises.

times of several days. With some sort of sequence
-- usually worked out by the bill manager -- the
Senate works through the bill, until it finishes
all the amendments any Senator wishes to offer.

Third Reading and Final Passage

"When no Senator is seeking recognition to
offer an amendment, and no amendment is pending,
the Chair will order third reading of the bill.
Third reading closes off the amendment
process."[49]   Putting the bill in that form is
called "engrossment," the term for finalizing the
form of a bill as it has been amended by one
chamber, which contrasts with "enrollment,"
finalizing a bill as both chambers have passed it
before presenting it to the President.[50] However,

---

[49]   M. Gold, Senate Procedure and Practice: An Introductory
Manual 36 (1981). Rule XIV(7) provides that "When a bill or
joint resolution shall have been ordered to be read a third
time, it shall not be in order to propose amendments, unless
by unanimous consent . . . ." Historically, when bills were
handwritten or printed by cumbersome processes, the
formality of third reading marked an important practical
point: only when amending was all done could the bill could
be put in a final and authoritative form. Thomas Jefferson
discusses in detail how intolerable amendments or changes
after third reading would be: "[i]t is with great and almost
invincible reluctance that amendments are admitted at this
reading, which occasion erasures or interlineations," and
"[w]hen an essential provision has been omitted, rather than
erase the bill and render it suspicious, they add a clause
on a separate paper, engrossed and called a rider . . . ."
House Manual §§ 497, 495.

[50]   The eighteenth- and nineteenth-century Senate would hold
an important vote as to whether to go to third reading and
engrossment on a bill. House Manual § 498. For example, in
1846, when the Senate spent two months debating a resolution
concerning the dispute with Great Britain over Oregon, it
"passed the resolution to third reading by 40 yeas to 14
nays; immediately afterward, without a formal division, came
final passage." In other words, the test vote came on third
reading, not final passage. F. L. Burdette, Filibustering
in the Senate 25 (1940). Recorded votes on third reading
(footnote continued)

today third reading simply signifies the end of the amendment process, and that no more amendments will be in order; there is no actual pause for the work of engrossment.

In recent years, the lack of central control in the Senate has created difficulty in reaching third reading on some omnibus bills, such as supplemental appropriations, that attract large numbers of amendments. The problem is not filibustering -- the deliberate stalling of bills or amendments by their opponents -- but the slowness of the offerors of amendments to come forward with them.[51] As a response, the party leadership or bill managers have threatened to take bills to third reading when they reach the end of the amendments actually offered, thereby cutting off further amendments noticed but not offered.[52] Such threats often prove effective.

---

would still be in order, though it would be an antiquated procedure. See Riddick, "Bills: Third Reading," at 197 n.73a; "Engrossed Bills and Resolutions: Yeas and Nays Ordered on Engrossment," at 656.

[51] Offerors often hope that if they withhold a little longer, they can line up further support or negotiate a better deal. Therefore, they inform the leaders or managers that they intend to offer the amendment -- so that the leadership will protect them by not letting the bill go to third reading in their absence and cutting off their amendment -- but then withhold their amendment without coming forward to offer it in timely fashion.

[52] For example, on a 1983 supplemental appropriation, Majority Leader Baker reached a point where he explained that he

> want[ed] Members to know the level of frustration in being on this bill since 10:40 a.m. and absolutely nothing has happened with one exception . . . . We had seven amendments remaining [i.e., noticed but not yet offered] when we quit this bill on Friday . . . because no one was here and there were no amendments that could be offered. Now there are 14 [noticed amendments], but no one will offer them.

Accordingly, the Majority Leader called a live quorum, and told the assembled Senators that he was "going to ask (footnote continued)

Once the various clearance mechanisms report
that no more amendments remain, the floor manager
can indicate to the Chair to ask "Are there any
more amendments? If not, the question will be on
third reading and engrossment."[53]   After third
reading, Rule XIV(7) makes only one further
maneuver in order: a motion to recommit, which may
be made with instructions. The Senate uses this
motion much less often than the House, but it is
occasionally resorted to, as discussed below.

Rather, what happens most often at this point
is that the manager chooses the vehicle for the
vote on final passage: the Senate bill or, if one
is available, a House bill, depending on how this
will affect arranging of a conference and related
matters (as discussed in the chapter on
conferences).[54] Either way, immediately after the
Chair orders third reading, the Senate goes to
final passage on a bill (Senate or House). Final
passage may be by any of the voting methods --
voice, division, or roll call vote. The Senate
often (although less often than the House) uses
roll-call votes on final passage, to establish a

---

the managers of this bill on both sides to try to take this
bill to third reading regardless of whether there are
amendments that we know of that are still outstanding." The
Majority Leader concluded that "I am not a very good
fishwife . . . . I am not a very good slave driver. But I
am telling you that we are going to go to third reading on
this bill if Senators do not come to the Chamber and offer
their amendments . . . ." 129 Cong. Rec. S8404 (daily ed.
June 15, 1983). For a similar incident on an emergency jobs
appropriation, see 129 Cong. Rec. S2395 (daily ed. March 9,
1983).

[53] For minor bills rushed through quickly, the Chair may
not even ask the question aloud, but the Congressional
Record will include a notation of the question being put to
reflect an orderly process of enactment.

[54] In a nutshell, if the manager chooses to send a Senate
bill, he goes to final passage on the Senate's own bill; if
he chooses to send a House bill, with a few routine
unanimous consent requests he takes the House bill off the
calendar, amends it to substitute the contents of the Senate
bill at third reading, goes on to final passage on the House
bill, and later indefinitely postpones the Senate bill.

record for the media and others, and to send a signal to the House (and sometimes to the President) as to how much support there is for the bill.

For example, in 1984, the Senate held 42 recorded votes on final passage for measures. The Senate holds many votes on final passage that are unanimous or lopsided, which serve only symbolic purposes rather than to define Senators' precise positions or to test close propositions. In many of those cases a prior vote on some key amendment signified the real division in the Senate. For example, on a bill to extend a ban on credit card surcharges, the key vote occurred on an amendment to extend the ban permanently, which lost 22 to 66, Then, the bill, which only extended the ban three months, received a vote on final passage of 84 to 0.[55]

The vote on final passage, although common and significant for symbolic purposes, usually does not serve as a precise indicator of divisions in Senate opinion. In 1984, of the 42 votes on final passage, only two resulted in defeat for the measure: votes on a constitutional amendment for school prayer, and on an increase in the debt limit. Both represented very unique circumstances: the prayer amendment because of its supporters' rigidity, the debt limit only as a temporary defeat of a measure that was eventually enacted.[56] Of the other 40 recorded votes on

_____

[55] 1984 Congressional Quarterly Almanac, votes 19 and 20, at 6-S. Thus, all Senators took credit for the bill as a symbolic matter, although the amendment vote tested the closer proposition and showed that only a quarter of the Senators supported a long-term ban.

One commentator's description of passage of a bill makes a typical distinction. One vote on an amendment was key -- a relatively close 44-51 vote not to strip off the user charge provision from the barge bill. The commentator gave this vote extensive discussion. Then, "[w]ith the defeat of Stevenson's effort to kill the user charge, Senate passage of the Domenici bill became a foregone conclusion," and so final passage came up fairly promptly, "by a margin of 71 to 20," an event meriting, and receiving, only the briefest discussion. Reid at 69.
(footnote continued)

final passage, in only three did more than 25 Senators vote against final passage, although large numbers of the bills contained controversial provisions tested during the amendment process.[57] Thus, 37 out of 42 votes on final passage enacted the bill by lopsided margins; most were symbolic votes putting Senators on record as joining in a final outcome, while telling little or nothing of the Senate's real divisions on the issues of the bill.

C.   CONSENSUAL MANAGEMENT: SEQUENCING AND
     NEGOTIATING

Neutral Sequencing

The particular powers of the floor manager may now be given a detailed analysis. One of the more mundane roles of the floor manager is simply to arrange the sequence in which Senators offer amendments, deliver speeches, and conduct votes. The Senate's rules do not require or even provide for such sequencing, and it cannot occur without unanimous consent, but sheer convenience and logistics often encourage such organizing.   As Senator Dan Quayle (R-Ind.) noted in discussing Senate procedural reform in 1984, when the defense authorization bill came to the floor, the committee chair had "103 amendments to deal with

---

[56] The school prayer amendment went down to defeat because the supporters of the alternative that might well have passed, to allow silent prayer or meditation in the schools, voted down their own alternative in order to give President Reagan the vote he wanted on his stronger version. 1984 Congressional Quarterly Almanac at 246. The debt limit increase went down to defeat on its first vote regarding final passage, but the Majority Leader moved for reconsideration, and after a recess, lined up the support for a successful second vote for final passage. 1984 Congressional Quarterly Almanac at 166.

[57] 1984 Congressional Quarterly Almanac, votes 14, at 4-S; 57, at 12-S; and 275, at 48-S (capital punishment, budget reconciliation, and a debt limit increase).

over   a   10-day   period   of   time . . . ."
Accordingly,   "[t]he   chairman   of   the   committee
spent   more   time   organizing   and   dispatching
amendments than he did on substantive debate.   The
Senate appears to like it this way or we would
change our habits.,"   While he went on to add, "I
hope we change,"[58] the system he described had
been developing for years.
    The practical need for sequencing is apparent
on a bill where there are many amendments.   Most
amendments do not require the presence of all
Senators, but only of the offeror, the manager,
and at most a few other particularly interested
Senators. This small group creates the record for
and against the amendment, and usually debates or
bargains all the way to withdrawal of the
amendment or acceptance of it with or without
modifications, all without a record vote.   Even
when roll-call votes must occur, often they are
postponed and stacked at another day or time, so
that at the time of amendment offering and floor
discussion, only this small group needs to
attend.   After the manager handles one such
amendment, a group concerned with the next
amendment takes the floor.
    The   simplest   form   of   sequencing   was
illustrated by Chairperson Hatfield's management
of a continuing resolution in 1983.   Senator
Hatfield "asked for a list of names, and [said he]
would like to alternate on both sides of the
aisle, so that we can follow down a list, and
Senators will have an idea of when they are going
to be able to offer their amendment. That is the
plan   we   will   follow,   unless   there   is   an
objection."[59]   This standard plan of alternating
between amendment offerors from each party is
often referred to as "rotation."[60]   However, in

---

[58]   130 Cong. Rec. S10958 (daily ed. Sept. 12, 1984).

[59]   129 Cong. Rec. S15885 (daily ed. Nov. 10, 1983).

[60]   As the leadership may refer to such an arrangement:

      Mr. ROBERT C. BYRD: Could we have an understanding
      that there will be an alternation between the two sides
      on calling up amendments, as we have previously done on
(footnote continued)

some situations sequencing breaks down through
partisan suspicion.[61]

Rather than proceeding through informal
sequence lists on informal sufferance of all
Senators, the managers and leaders may provide for
sequencing by a unanimous consent agreement.[62]
Such agreements often include as a key feature a
provision for postponing and stacking votes, as
discussed above.

Tactical Role of Sequencing

The floor manager's sequencing activity

---

budget resolutions?

Mr. BAKER. Yes, Mr. President . . . I give the
minority leader my assurance that we shall do that
without exception . . . absent extraordinary
circumstances such as the absence of Senators from the
floor . . . .

128 Cong. Rec. S5409 (May 18, 1982).

[61] In the case of the 1983 continuing resolution mentioned
above, such a breakdown occurred, and minority Senators then
raised the point that there had been no "order agreed to by
the Senat[e] that Senators will be recognized only on the
basis of when they appear on the list." The Minority Leader
objected that he was "against pursuing calling up of
amendments by virtue of a list that has been drawn. I
prefer to go by the rules and treat everyone alike."
Accordingly, he insisted "that the Chair follow the Rules of
the Senate in the recognition of Senators," 129 Cong. Rec.
S15889 (daily ed. Nov. 10, 1983), meaning recognition by the
Chair of whatever Senator stands up and seeks recognition
first when the prior speaker finishes.

[62] For example, in 1983 the Majority Leader arranged a
unanimous consent agreement on the immigration bill that
established time limits on 11 amendments. 129 Cong. Rec.
S6812 (daily ed. May 17, 1983). As another example, the
leadership arranged a unanimous consent agreement for the
defense appropriation in 1983 that established the time
limits on 27 amendments, with debate times ranging from 20
minutes to two hours. 129 Cong. Rec. S15473 (daily ed. Nov.
4, 1983).

serves more than a neutral function of convenience for other Senators. It plays an important part in his efforts to maintain control of the floor, allowing him some leeway to schedule some amendments early when their debate or defeat will help control other amendments later. Thus, for example, in Senator Culver's floor management of the Endangered Species Act amendments discussed earlier, Culver focused on sequencing: "[I]n the discussion [Culver] and his staff had earlier this morning it was generally concluded that the best approach would be to have the Stennis amendment brought up first, and [Culver would] informally ask the chair to recognize him first." Culver sequenced the amendments that way because dealing with an amendment from one side first would help him deal with an amendment from the other side later.[63] He explained subsequently that he had arranged the sequence

> because so many of the arguments I will use against [Senator Gaylord A.] Nelson [(D-Wis.)] about how our amendment will strengthen the Endangered Species Act could then used by [Senator John] Stennis [(D-Miss.)] and company to show why our proposal should be weakened. So if I make a major argument against Stennis and defeat him, then I can take on Nelson and make the other arguments at that point.[64]

Later in debate on the same bill, Culver sequenced a key amendment because he preferred to fight it in the morning rather than in the afternoon:

> Scott was not enthusiastic about offering the amendment at this point, but Culver has

---

[63]   The strategy worked: Culver defeated the Stennis amendment, then argued Nelson into withdrawing his amendment. Afterwards, at a dinner at Senator Nelson's house that evening, the two participants recognized the strategy. "`You son of a bitch,' Nelson sa[id]. `You used my arguments.' Nelson and Culver laugh[ed]." Drew at 166.

[64]   Drew at 145.

talked him into it. The theory behind having
Scott bring up the amendment now is that it
is better to have such a proposal come up in
the morning -- a time when many senators are
in committee meetings or in their offices and
are   more   distracted   than   usual   form   the
business that is taking place on the floor.
Also, Culver figures that most of his
colleagues   will   assume   that   at   this
point . . . only   routine,   'houskeeping'
amendments are being considered, and that
they will pay less attention to the issue, be
less eager to join the fray, than they might
be later on.

These are the sorts of calculations that
managers of bills must make.[65]

Sequence Control Through Committee Amendments

In the 1980's, Senate managers began using
occasionally a new technique for floor control
through   the   use   of   committee   amendments.[66]
"Committee amendments, or amendments thereto, are
acted upon first after a bill is brought up for
consideration, as opposed to amendments from the
floor.   Amendments from the floor, as opposed to
committee amendments, are not in order until all
committee   amendments   have   been   disposed   of."[67]

---

[65]   Id. at 173-74.

[66]   Senator Metzenbaum raised the visibility of this
technique by a complaint in 1983:

I have a particular interest in a procedure that has
started to develop and has actually developed in the
Senate concerning the matter of the manager of a bill
laying down technical amendments, calling them up, and
then being in total control of those amendments that
may be offered on the floor.

129 Cong. Rec. S14611 (daily ed. Oct. 26, 1983).

[67]   Riddick, "Amendments: Committee Amendments, Offering and
Disposition of," at 31.

Bill managers can hold some committee amendments back -- "except" them from the adoption of the rest -- rather than dispose of them all at the outset, and by unanimous consent[68] allow floor amending to begin.   Then, if a floor amendment is offered that the manager does not want to deal with, the manager calls for the regular order, which displaces that floor amendment and the Senate goes back to the "excepted" committee amendments (the ones held back).[69]

This approach provides protection for the floor manager who has no comprehensive UCA for his bill.   Rather than be exposed to ambush by non-germane amendment, the manager can bring the bill up and deal with ambushes by a call for the regular order.   This does not get the bill

---

[68] A variation is to obtain a unanimous consent agreement at the outset that holding back excepted committee amendments, and allowing floor amendments, will not require unanimous consent, but only the agreement of the majority and minority managers. "It is a matter of the two managers setting aside [excepted committee amendments], as we have traditionally done" 128 Cong. Rec. S15012 (daily ed. Dec. 15, 1982) (Chairperson Hatfield of Appropriations Committee) (during consideration of continuing resolution).

[69] Minority Leader Byrd had explained the technique to Senator Metzenbaum on the floor in 1982:

Mr. ROBERT C. BYRD: . . . The chairman [in that case, Chairman Hatfield of the Appropriations Committee] is proceeding in an orderly manner. He has proceeded to get consent en bloc for most of the committee amendments. Certain committee amendments were excepted from that en bloc agreement. Now before the Senate are those excepted committee amendments. Amendments from the floor are not in order until the committee amendments have been adopted or disposed of. So there are four or five committee amendments that have been excepted . . . . They must be disposed of before amendments from the floor may be offered unless the amendments from the floor are to those amendments or unless unanimous consent is given to set those aside to allow amendments from the floor . . . .

128 Cong. Rec. S12453 (daily ed. Sept. 29, 1982).

enacted, or even prevent roll-call votes on non-germane amendments, but at least it prevents managers' prime nightmare: finding their precious bill instantly and irrevocably chained to some other Senator's irrelevant hot potato.

An example of this technique occurred in 1985. Senator James A. McClure (R-Wyo.) called up the "compact of free association" with Micronesia, a charter for United States relations with certain Pacific islands.[70] At his request, the Senate adopted the committee amendments from his committee, but held off on the committee amendment from the Finance Committee (which shared jurisdiction over the compact).[71] During consideration of the compact, Senator Strom Thurmond (R-S.C.) offered a completely unrelated non-germane amendment, a bill to protect the textile industry from imports representing the high-powered trade issue dogging the Senate.[72]

After some debate, another Senator "call[ed] for regular order . . . ." The Chair noted that "[o]ne committee amendment was excluded from the en bloc agreement [under which the others were adopted] . . . . Under the Senate's precedents, a call for the regular order returns the Senate to the amendment that was set aside by unanimous consent."[73] The recurrence of the committee amendment pushed the trade amendment aside. In this case, that setback did not keep Senator

---

[70] Senator McClure managed the compact because he chairs the Committee on Energy and Natural Resources, which as the heir of the old Interior Committee, has jurisdiction over United States territories and possessions. Micronesia was a United States trust territory following World War II.

[71] 131 Cong. Rec. S12436 (daily ed. Oct. 2, 1985).

[72] As Senator Ernest Hollings (D-S.C.), his cosponsor, explained, having been told that "this textile bill would never get out of the Senate Finance Committee," Senator Hollings had looked for "what bills would appear" on which the textile bill could be offered as a non-germane amendment, and chose the compact. 131 Cong. Rec. S12444 (daily ed. Oct. 2, 1985).

[73] 131 Cong. Rec. S12459 (daily ed. Oct. 2, 1985).

Thurmond's amendment off the floor completely, as he was willing to file a petition for cloture to overcome a threatened filibuster.[74]

In short, the reserved committee amendment and the call for the regular order allowed the quick emplacement of elaborate obstacles to a non-germane amendment. It remains to be seen whether this approach becomes one of the enduring aspects of Senate procedure. More fundamentally, the example illustrates how bill managers can use their initiative to overcome their lack of formal power to exclude floor amendments.

Negotiation: Acceptance, Modification, and Withdrawal

A bargaining process over potential amendments, which begins even before floor consideration with the circulation and printing of amendments, climaxes on the floor. In the House, Members can only modify or withdraw their

---

[74] To be precise, first Senator Bill Bradley (D-N.J.) who had called for the regular order, offered his own amendment as a second-degree amendment to the committee amendment. After his was tabled, Senator Thurmond re-offered his original amendment, and Senator Hollings noted that "this is on the Finance Committee amendment in the second degree." 131 Cong. Rec. S12467 (daily ed. Oct. 2, 1985).

A short time after Senator Thurmond filed his cloture petition, he withdrew it when the Majority Leader indicated that he would not support cloture and was willing to work something else out. 131 Cong. Rec. S12487 (daily ed. Oct. 2, 1985). Senator Thurmond's amendment's status as a second-degree amendment clearly set him back considerably in attempting to force it onto the bill. As discussed in the chapter on cloture, when a second-degree amendment is not germane, to get it onto the bill over a filibuster the mover must first obtain cloture on the second-degree amendment, have the second-degree amendment adopted, then obtain cloture on the first-degree amendment as amended, have it adopted, and then obtain cloture on the bill, and have the bill adopted. A Senator faced with such obstacles will likely make a reasonable deal even when he has strong support backing his amendment.

amendments by unanimous consent (though such
consent is often granted). In the Senate, Rule XV
provides as a matter of right -- not unanimous
consent -- that "[a]ny motion, amendment, or
resolution may be withdrawn or modified by the
mover at any time before a decision, amendment, or
ordering of the yeas and nays . . . ."[75]   This
leads bargaining that might be called "trading in"
amendments. Members may offer amendments, then
withdraw them at the request of the floor manager
in return for any of a variety of deals.
Sometimes the managers provide as little as an
expression that they, too, care about the problem
addressed in the amendment; sometimes the managers
promise that as chair of the committee or
subcommittee, they will schedule hearings on the
amendment's subject; sometimes the managers as
much as offer (most useful if joined by the
leadership) to find an alternative floor vehicle
for the amendment.

The same process may occur in behind-the-
scenes negotiations, without visible floor
movement of an amendment at all, though the
Senators may still prefer to record the deal in
the Congressional Record. For example, in 1983,
during consideration of the bill to repeal
withholding of taxes on interest and dividends,
Senator Carl Levin (D-Mich.) noted that he "had
intended to offer an amendment . . . dealing with
the IRS's use of the powers of lien, levy and
seizure . . . based on S. 1032, the Taxpayer's
Bill of Rights."[76]   Senator Charles Grassley (R-
Iowa), chair of the subcommittee of jurisdiction,
responded that he "share[d] [Levin's] keen
interest in the subject . . . .   I assure the
Senator of . . . my desire to pursue this issue
farther. When the subcommittee convenes hearings
on this topic, the Senator from Michigan can be
sure that S.1032 will be among the legislative
proposals that we consider."[77]   Accordingly,

---

[75]   For discussion, see Riddick, "Amendments: Withdrawal of
Amendments," at 94-97.

[76]   129 Cong. Rec. S8574 (daily ed. June 16, 1983).

[77]   Id.

Senator Levin said he was "willing to withdraw the amendment . . . ."[78]

Of course, obtaining a hearing is not a guarantee of further action. As Senator Robert Dole (R-Kans.) commented on another occasion, he would withdraw an amendment upon receiving "the assurance we are going to have hearings. [But] I know what generally happens. We have the hearing and we w[a]ve goodby to the witness,"[79] i.e., nothing further may happen.

The Senator's right to modify his amendment, instead of completely withdrawing it,[80] provides further room for trading. A Senator can offer an amendment, learn that the manager cannot accept it because of some particular concern, but modify it to meet that concern. Both the majority and minority managers may have concerns, leading to multiple modifications. The amendment-offeror, like a submanager, may deal with other amendment-offerors, modifying her amendment to incorporate theirs (in return for support).[81]

More complex approaches involve initially putting one form of an amendment on the table,

---

[78]   Id.

[79]   129 Cong. Rec. S15071 (daily ed. Oct. 31, 1983).

[80]   Riddick, "Amendments: Modification of," at 52.

[81]   For example, when Senator Hatfield moved an amendment to bail out Oregon timber contracts, he modified it to incorporate a similar bailout amendment offered by Senator Ted Stevens (R-Alaska) for Alaskan timber contracts. 129 Cong. Rec. S15918 (daily ed. Nov. 10, 1983).

For a simple example, Senator Tsongas asked for an early report by the President on the impact of the strategic defense programs on arms control. Senator Stevens, the manager, did not fight the amendment, but said "I really am concerned about the timeframe. I have suggested July 1 . . . [W]hat would [you] say to May 15?" 129 Cong. Rec. S15445 (daily ed. Nov. 4, 1985). Initially Senator Paul Tsongas (D-Mass.) thought he had to "ask unanimous consent" to modify, and the Chair corrected, "The Senator has a right to modify his amendment." Id. Senator Tsongas modified the amendment, and it was adopted.

with the full expectation of eventually agreeing to another. As one commentator said:

> A strategy often used is to introduce a printed amendment which, if adopted, would achieve even more than the amendment's sponsors believe is really necessary . . . which stakes out a bargaining position. If bargaining between the bill's sponsors and the amendment's sponsors does not yield a satisfactory compromise before the bill is considered on the floor, the sponsors of the printed amendment may offer an unprinted amendment which can be described as a compromise offer but which in fact would achieve all the essential objectives originally sought. The bill managers may feel constrained to offer a alternative compromise . . . . The result can be a bargaining process . . . in the form of amendments and counteramendments . . . .[82]

After virtually any action on amendments, Senators loses their right to modify or withdraw the amendment; thereafter, withdrawal or modification requires unanimous consent. Once the amendment has been amended by another Senator, no matter how trivially, or even has had the yeas and nays ordered on it, it can no longer be unilaterally withdrawn or modified.[83] Hence, if Senator A has an interest in Senator B's amendment, he may ask for the yeas and nays on it, freezing Senator B's amendment in its offered form (absent unanimous consent to modify). Then, later, the yeas and nays can be vitiated by unanimous consent to avoid a needless roll call.

As Rule XV states, it is the mover of the amendment who can withdraw or modify it; other Senators could only do so with unanimous consent. Committee amendments may be modified or

---

[82] Id. at 240.

[83] The detailed precedents regarding what does and what does not foreclose modification or withdrawal are discussed in Riddick, "Amendments: Modification of," at 53-56; "Amendments, Withdrawal of," 95-97.

withdrawn only with the authorization of the
committee. However, the committee can authorize
by an informal means, such as a poll; the
committee need not meet.[84]

D.   MOTION TO TABLE

Historic Rise

The motion to table has become the "workhorse" of
Senate procedure -- the most frequently used tool
of bill managers and leaders for controlling floor
situations. This key role for the motion appears
to be a relatively recent phenomenon.[85] While the
Senate made the motion to table nondebatable in
1820, the motion still played no prominent role as
late as 1969.[86] By the 1970s, the motion began to

---

[84]   128 Cong. Rec. S14650 (daily ed. Dec. 14, 1982) (Chair:
"A meeting is not necessary. It is necessary, however, that
a majority of the members of the Committee on Finance agree
to the withdrawal of the amendment").

[85]   The motion "to lay on the table" dates back to the
earliest Senate procedure, when it had a different purpose
than at present. At that time, when the Senate "ha[d]
something else which claims its present attention, but would
be willing to reserve in their power to take up a
proposition whenever it shall suit them, they order it to
lie on their table. It may then be called for at any
time." House Manual § 445 (section XXXIII(4) of Jefferson's
Manual, describing the motion "To lie on the table" as one
of the privileged questions).

[86]   L. G. McConachie, Congressional Committees 316
(1898)(1820 change). McConachie termed the rule change
making tabling nondebatable one of the "prohibitions of
debate upon secondary and subsidiary motions," signalling
the low importance of the motion in the nineteenth century.

    Riddick noted in 1949 that "[w]hile the motion is
applicable to pending business, it is not commonly used for
the disposition of legislation -- bills and amendments
thereto are generally either voted up or down." Rather, it
was "used generally to reach a final disposition on motions
(footnote continued)

grow in importance.   While several factors contributed, probably the key was the Senators' increasing demands for obtain roll-call votes on amendments.[87]   As the prior custom disfavoring roll-call votes broke down, the Senators needed a new means to keep at least limited control of how they were required to vote.   Majority Leader Byrd explained:

> A motion to table is a procedural motion.   It obfuscates the issue, and it makes possible an explanation by a Senator to his constituents, if he wishes to do so, that his vote was not on the merits of the issue.   He can claim that he might have voted this way or he might have voted that way, if the Senate had voted up or down on the issue itself.   But on a procedural motion, he can state he voted to table the amendment, and he can assign any number of reasons therefore, one of which would be that he did so in order that the Senate would get on with its work or about its business.[88]

---

to reconsider or appeals from the decision of the chair." F. Riddick (1949).   The motion receives no mention in Galloway's 1955 study, further suggesting its limited use at the time.   Even as late as 1969, in a whole year only six motions to table occurred with recorded votes.

[87]   As an observer comments:

> In the 1950s, it was difficult for a senator to obtain a roll-call vote on any issue without the support of [then Majority Leader] Johnson or the Republican leadership.   [In the 1960s, Majority Leader] Mansfield, as part of the individual rights movement, decided to raise his hand for a roll call regardless of the issue.   Within a few years, the leadership had essentially lost any power to block a roll call even if only one senator wanted it.

Ehrenhalt, In the Senate of the '80s, Team Spirit has Given Way to the Rule of Individuals, 40 Cong. Q. Week. Rep. 2180-81 (1982).

[88]   121 Cong. Rec. 29814 (1975), quoted in W. J. Oleszek, Congressional Procedures and the Policy Process 216-17 (3d (footnote continued)

The Congressional Research Service found approximately 140 successful motions to table in the Senate per Congress in the period 1979-84. Of these, about 98 percent occurred with roll-call votes.[89] To put it differently, out of 275 Senate roll calls in 1984, 84 were for motions to table amendments; six were for motions to table other matters (e.g., appeals from rulings of the Chair). Thus over 30 percent of all roll-call votes occurred on motions to table.[90] With regard to disposing of amendments by roll-call votes, motions to table thus equal in importance, if not exceed, straight voting up or down.[91]

Party Loyalty and Procedural Nature

The salient rules and practices for the motion to table may be summed up thusly: it evokes a considerable degree of majority party loyalty, and it is procedural, privileged, and nondebatable. First, it serves in practice as a majority party tool. That is not a matter of prerogative, at least not at the present, like the majority leader's prerogative over motions to adjourn, to recess, or to proceed to a bill: no one accuses a minority Senator of infringing any prerogative of the manager or Majority Leader if he moves to table. Rather, minority Senators do not offer motions to table because they are sure losers. Minority Leader Byrd contended in 1983 that "if I move to table an amendment that comes from the majority side, I will not have the support of Senators on that side . . . . If the

---

[89] Ilona B. Nickels, Unanimous Consent: A Study of Its Use in House and Senate Practice from 1979-1984 20, 34 (Cong. Res. Serv. 1984).

[90] Votes adopting or rejecting amendments constituted a bit over 30 percent, and the remainder consists largely of votes on final passage, cloture, and miscellaneous procedural votes.

[91] The 275 roll calls are from 1984 Congressional Quarterly Almanac at pages 2S to 48S.

Democrats move to table a Republican-sponsored amendment, the Republicans, almost to the man, vote against that tabling motion."[92]

Thus, although no prerogative excludes minority Senators from moving to table, the pattern could not be clearer. Out of the 90 motions to table that produced roll-call votes in 1984, majority (Republican) Senators made 89. In contrast, minority (Democratic) Senators made only a single motion to table out of the ninety.[93]

---

[92] 129 Cong. Rec. S14761 (daily ed Oct. 27, 1983). Majority Leader Baker hardly disagreed, stating as to the pattern of party-line voting on tabling that "I confess and plead guilty to the charge that I originated that policy on this side when I was minority leader, and I have regretted it ever since I became majority leader." 129 Cong. Rec. S14761 (daily ed Oct. 27, 1983). In another of his amusing asides, Senator Baker described his policy as to "motions to table Republican measures, which I had refused to do steadfastly before," as "one of my long and growing list of things I should never have done." 129 Cong. Rec. S14761 (daily ed Oct. 27, 1983).

[93] Typically the bill manager, the Majority Leader, or their designees made the motion, although there were many exceptions when majority Senators not in these formal roles moved to table amendments.

The single minority motion to table occurred during a unique battle, as one of several unorthodox tactics used by Western Senators of both parties, defending their region, to crush Senator Metzenbaum's attempt to raise the price of low-cost power from Hoover Dam. Senator Alan Cranston (D-Calif.), the Democratic Whip, made this single Democratic motion to table of 1984. 1984 Congressional Quarterly Almanac 32-S (vote no. 183). Other tactics of that fight included a cloture petition after only four hours of debate, and leadership stalling during the roll call on that cloture petition until additional pro-cloture votes could be rounded up. Senator Metzenbaum commented the next day that "Yesterday, our integrity -- and our reputation as the world's greatest deliberative body -- took repeated body blows," while Senator Dale Bumpers (D-Ark.), who actually disagreed with Senator Metzenbaum on the merits, nevertheless said that he "thought the conduct of the Senate yesterday was deplorable." 1984 Congressional Quarterly

(footnote continued)

While only majority Senators tend to move to table amendments, they do not do so solely as a partisan weapon; they make the motion against amendments of majority and minority Senators alike.[94]   However, the motion succeeds much more often when employed against minority amendments,[95] generaly succeeding except in odd situations[96] like efforts to table popular or bipartisan initiatives.[97]   For example, during consideration

---

Almanac at 327.

[94]   For example, during consideration of the Deficit Reduction Act of 1984, 43 roll-call votes occurred, including 18 on motions to table. Thirteen motions to table were made against amendments offered by Democrats, one against a point of order by a Democrat, and four against amendments by Republicans. The greater number of motions to table against minority Senators may result simply from the greater frequency with which the minority necessarily resorts to amendments, particularly non-germane amendments, to raise its issues, simply because the minority lacks the control over the agenda of the majority.

[95]   Looking overall at the 90 motions to table in 1984, 18 failed, of which 11 were against Republican propositions. Although a large majority of the motions to table were against minority propositions, only seven failed against minority propositions.

[96]   Of those seven that failed against minority propositions, two were short-term aspects of a last-minute drama. In order to accede to House requests for a clean debt limit bill, Majority Leader Baker moved to table two non-germane propositions being tied to the debt increase, both very popular in the Senate: one a budget freeze, the other a limit on the politically unpalatable taxing of imputed interest in real estate sales. For these two, after the Senate signaled its support by refusing to table, the sponsors agreed to put the amendments on another vehicle. 1984 Congressional Quarterly Almanac at 166-67; vote nos. 267 and 268, at 46-S.

[97]   One motion failed to table Senator Dennis DeConcini's (D-Ariz.) amendment to cut appropriations by reducing expenditures on travel, public relations, and consultants. Id., vote no. 81, at 16-S. Another failed to table a resolution condemning the nomination of Anne Burford to an (footnote continued)

of the Deficit Reduction Act of 1984, 12 out of 14
motions to table against Democratic propositions
succeeded, while only two out of four motions to
table against Republican propositions succeeded.[98]
     A key factor is simply that when the majority
manager makes a motion to table against a minority
proposition, he draws on party loyalty.   As
Minority Leader Byrd noted in 1982:

> we have seen in the last session of this
> Congress and in this session an almost
> consistent pattern of simply moving to table
> or of voting an amendment down if that
> amendment is offered by a Democratic
> Senator. It is done without serious debate
> from the other side of the aisle.[99]

Senator Barry Goldwater (R-Ariz.) responded:

> the recitation [Minority Leader Byrd] just
> made was reflected almost exactly in
> arguments that I used to make with him when
> he motioned to table bill after bill and
> amendment after amendment.

---

advisory post.   Id. 346, vote no. 176, at 31-S.   Another
failed to table an amendment relaxing noise controls on
Florida and Maine airports.   While offered by a Democrat
(Senator Lawton Chiles (D-Fla.)), the amendment was really
the bipartisan child of two other Republican Senators as
well, Senator Paula Hawkins (R-Fla.) and Senator William S.
Cohen (R-Maine).   Id. at 15, vote no. 260, at 45-S.

[98]   The 13 motions to table are in 1984 Congressional
Quarterly Almanac 13-S - 19-S; the motions to table
Republican propositions are vote nos. 61, 66 (motion
failed), 69 (motion failed), 93; to table Democratic
propositions, vote nos. 65, 68, 70, 71, 72, 73, 75, 76, 81
(motion defeated), 86 (motion to table point of order
defeated), 89, 90, 91, and 98.

[99]   128 Cong. Rec. S5788 (daily ed. May 21, 1982).   In 1983,
the Minority Leader noted again: "[I]f the majority leader
moves to table an amendment offered by Democrats, he has the
Republican votes to table.   I have watched the other side of
the aisle over the years."   129 Cong. Rec. S14761 (daily ed.
Oct. 27, 1983).

> You are living through, I must say,
> exactly what we lived through [when
> Republicans were in the minority]. I
> remember the days when I begged you not to
> move to table.[100]

Party loyalty on motions to table should not be overestimated. It is strongest when the vote is on a procedural point, so that the majority members can consider their vote not to be substantive. A combination of party loyalty and procedural ducking usually proves decisive. On the other hand, on substantive amendments, Senators to some degree must vote in line with their consistent individual substantive positions, or the Senate's institutional position, rather than the party position.[101] In contrast to the effectiveness of motions to table against minority propositions, motions to table against majority Members' amendments cannot draw so well on party loyalty. Such motions to table may often fail, on major amendments[102] and even on minor

---

[100] 128 Cong. Rec. S5791 (daily ed. May 21, 1982).

[101] Two minority initiatives in 1984 that survived motions to table reflect this. One stated the Senate's sense that President Reagan should seek Senate approval of treaties banning underground nuclear explosions. 1984 Congressional Quarterly Almanac at 51; vote no. 146, at 26-S.

The other was a historic point of order against the statutory line-item veto as unconstitutional. After refusing to table the point of order on a 45-46 vote, the Senate then upheld the point of order 56-34; the tabling aspect may be said to have been worth five votes extra for the majority manager. 1984 Congressional Quarterly Almanac 154; vote no. 86, at 17-S.

Both of these issues not only matters of high principle, but also the Senate's own institutional prerogatives (on advice and consent to treaties, and on appropriations); the majority Senators overcame party loyalty to send those signals, not so much against their party position in the Senate as against the White House on matters of Senate prerogative.

(footnote continued)

amendments.[103]

The motion to table possesses two other characteristics basic to its importance besides its party loyalty signal. First, it takes precedence over most matters. Under Senate Rule XXII(1), motions have precedence "as they stand arranged," i.e., in the order they are stated in the rule, and so the motion "To lay on the table" has precedence over the motions to postpone (indefinitely or to a date certain), to commit (including to recommit), and to amend. Thus, after these other motions, Senators can move to table, and the motion to table will have precedence over the motion being tabled; this is why, even though a Senator moves first to amend, and another moves later to table, the Senate votes first on the motion to table. Motions to table

---

[102] In a dramatic example, during the debate on the Grove City civil rights proposal, Majority Leader Baker attempted to support the Chair in its ruling that amendments for gun control and busing proposed by majority Senators were non-germane. The motions to table failed, despite the combination of the Chair's undoubtedly correct ruling as a technical matter on the procedural point, the status of the Majority Leader, and the hitherto sacrosanct rule of germaneness under cloture. 1984 Congressional Quarterly Almanac at 242; vote nos. 240 and 242, at 43-S.

The motion to table also failed to kill a majority Senator's amendment for requiring arms control negotiations about antisatellite missiles, or to kill the Deficit Reduction Act conference report. Vote no. 120, 23-S (antisatellite talks), and no. 160, 28-S (conference report), in 1984 Congressional Quarterly Almanac.

[103] At a more mundane level, various managers proved unable to table majority Senators' amendments regarding Federal Reserve Board nominees, "GI Bill" benefits, and condemnation of Bulgaria's role in terrorism. The votes on these motions are in 1984 Congressional Quarterly Almanac at 7-S (vote no. 28, on Federal Reserve nominees); 23-S (vote no. 123, "GI Bill" benefits); 30-S (vote no. 170, Bulgaria). The remaining majority Senators' propositions for which motions to table failed are vote no. 40, at 10-S (second-degree amendment by Majority Leader); 66, at 14-S (role of tax-exempt income in retiree taxation); 69, at 14-S (energy credit); and 202, at 35-S (anti-abortion).

may also be used against motions to proceed, against appeals, and against motions to reconsider.[104]

In contrast, only three motions have higher precedence that the motion to table -- to adjourn (including to a date certain), to take a recess, or to proceed to executive business. These higher-priority motions all serve as scheduling tools of the Majority Leader, and their precedence preserves his scheduling moves from interference.[105]

The second key procedural characteristic that Rule XXII(1) provides is that the motion to table "shall be decided without debate."[106] Standard unanimous consent agreements preserve the motion to table itself as nondebatable,[107] but paradoxically they prevent the motion from being used to cut off all debate on amendments. When the Senate enters a unanimous consent agreement, that UCA typically allocates a certain limited amount of time for debate on each amendment. The Senate deems such a UCA to guarantee the availability of that debate time. Thus, while the motion to table an amendment is itself not debatable, it is not in order to make such a

---

[104] Riddick, "Table: Motions to Table -- in Order," at 1037.

[105] Besides these, only the motions to obtain a quorum cannot be tabled, for a different reason than precedence: because the constitutional provision stating what the House and Senate can do without a quorum does not include motions to table, so once the lack of a quorum has been revealed, the motion to table cannot be made until a quorum appears. Art. I, sec. 5 of the Constitution; see Riddick, "Attendance of Senators: Table -- Motion to Get Attendance -- Not in Order," at 178.

[106] Riddick, "Debate: Table, Motion to, Not Debatable," at 627. This also means that "[a]fter a motion to table has been made, all points of order, motions or actions, until the vote on the motion to table has been taken and announced, must be transacted without debate," id.

[107] Standard-form UCAs provide debate time only for "debatable motions," which excludes the motion to table.

motion until the end of the time period provided in the UCA to debate the amendment or until all time on the amendment is yielded back.[108]

Use Against Non-germane Amendments

Broadly speaking, the motion to table may be used against three types of propositions. First, it may be used against non-germane amendments, to preserve a bill debate's focus on germane matters. Second, it may be used against germane amendments, simply to deny them plenary consideration. Finally, it may be used against matters other than amendments, as a key weapon in procedural fights.

Starting with the motion's use against non-germane amendments, this is the single strongest counterbalance to the Senate's lack of a germaneness rule. Professor Lewis Froman noted in 1967 that the motion was used effectively to eliminate the "non-germane amendment [that] does not have the support of at least a relatively large minority of the Senate."[109] He also explained how the motion eliminated those non-germane amendments that did have such support -- but were opposed by the leadership:

> [A] non-germane amendment . . . may be tabled immediately . . . . [This] means that if a bill does not have the support of the leadership it is usually tabled. The majority leader is essentially in charge of

---

[108] Riddick, "Unanimous Consent Agreements: Table, Motions Under Unanimous Consent Agreements," at 1100; "Table: When Motion to Table is Not in Order," at 1044.

It may seem odd that a UCA intended to limit debate time has the effect of extending time by precluding tabling motions from cutting the amendment off early, but apparently this form of the UCA gives Senators intending to offer amendments the assurance and incentive they want to enter into such UCAs, and thus advances Senate business.

[109] L. A. Froman, The Congressional Process: Strategies, Rules, and Procedures 133 (1967).

the schedule for the Senate . . . . Moving a
non-germane amendment is, of course, taking
the control of scheduling away from the
majority leader, unless the majority leader
himself supports such an action.[110]

While many bills become targets for non-
germane amendments,[111] sometimes a particular bill
will attract a string of non-germane amendments,
eliciting a string of motions to table. For
example, in 1984, the Senate took up a long-term
renewal of the Export Administration Act. This
drew non-germane amendments regarding wheat price
supports, which Majority Leader Baker himself
moved to table, and non-germane amendments
regarding oil company mergers, oil leases, and
Federal Reserve Board nominees, which the manager
moved to table.[112]
    The Senate's actual use of tabling on non-
germane amendments only hints at the deterrent
effect of the motion's availability. Absent any
such tool, Senators with non-germane propositions
to raise might decline to enter into any UCA on a
bill, preferring surprise and unlimited debate

---

110 Id.

111 Non-germane amendments subjected to motions to table in
1984 included, on a bankruptcy court act, an amendment to
the election laws regarding political use of union dues; on
a deficit reduction bill, an amendment to cancel inflation
indexing of tax brackets (the bill had nothing comparable);
and on an appropriation bill, an amendment asking the
President to withdraw an appointment to an advisory
commission. These were, respectively, 1984 Congressional
Quarterly Almanac at 20-S, vote no. 108; at 13-S, vote no.
61; at 31-S, vote no. 176. The amendment urging the
withdrawal of the nomination may have technically been
germane because "sense of the Senate" provisions are seen as
per se germane even when they discuss an unrelated subject
(such amendments are seen, though, as dilatory under
cloture).

112 1984 Congressional Quarterly Almanac at 6-S - 7-S, vote
nos. 26 (Baker motion to table Melcher wheat amendment), 23
(oil mergers), 24 (oil leases) and 28 (Federal Reserve
nominees).

time. However, potential proponents of amendments
know that managers can simply move to table, both
cutting off debate on their amendment and denying
them an up or down vote. This prospect deters
some non-germane amendments, and gives some
proponents of non-germane amendments an incentive
to bargain and ultimately enter into a UCA to
secure organized and predictable debate time and
perhaps an up-or-down vote. The motion thus gives
amendment offerors something to bargain over with
managers.

Use to Deny Plenary Consideration and Control Procedure

Notwithstanding the importance of this first
use of the motion to table, the second use, to
deny plenary consideration to germane amendments,
appears to predominate in terms of the frequency
of motions to table. Senators often refer to some
bill going through as a "railroad," meaning that
its manager will not brook any delay and will
attempt to defeat all amendments; the locomotive
that drives the "railroad" over all amendments in
its path is the motion to table. An old example
of a "railroad" was the Civil Rights bill of
1960. Then-Majority Leader Johnson had determined
to pass a very limited bill, which he could show
on the campaign trail as a legislative
accomplishment, without it being so strong as to
trigger either a southern filibuster in the Senate
or a backlash once passed.

As a commentator observed, "the tactic that
the leadership was using to carve out a bill that
would be 'acceptable' to the Senate" was that
"[e]ach time a strengthening amendment was
offered, a motion to table it would be made." To
signal the leadership's intention, "[of]ften it
was Johnson himself, or Dirksen, who offered the
motion to table; at other times the motion was
made by a member who was close to the
leadership." Upon such a motion, either the
amendment died, or if tabling had failed, "the
southerners would, as usual, have the right to
filibuster."[113]

In 1984, with defense issues heading the
legislative agenda, the annual Defense Department
authorization managed by Senator John Tower (R-

Tex.) drew 40 roll-call votes. Apart from three miscellaneous roll-calls, these consisted of 19 roll calls deciding to adopt amendments and only one deciding not to adopt, and 14 deciding to table amendments with only three not to table. Thus, Senator Tower essentially took every amendment that he could defeat and tabled it (except one amendment which was defeated on an up-or-down vote). In other words, he allowed up-or-down roll calls only on those amendments that could pass; his skill in judging the strength of each amendment is reflected in how consistently he won his tabling motions.

Such an approach has nothing to do with germaneness. All but one of the tabled amendments were germane in a general sense, and most would satisfy even the strictest test of germaneness. The tabled amendments on that defense bill concerned U.S. military expenditures in Europe vis-a-vis NATO's, "GI Bill" benefits, the Strategic Defense Initiative, an overall expenditure cut, two amendments for MX missiles, military pay raises, Pentagon chauffeurs, use of combat troops in Central America, aid to Nicaraguan contras, military spousal benefits, another NATO amendment, and a military truck purchase restriction.[114] Rather, Senator Tower, well known in the Senate as a tough fighter, chose this approach as manager to establish a strong position on the floor. Each of his motions to table signaled his conviction that the amendment would lose, and that he intended to deny an up-or-down vote to those proposing non-meritious amendments and, in some cases, to deny them debate time.[115]

Finally, motions to table serve during

---

[113]   D. M. Berman, A Bill Becomes a Law 82-83 (2d ed. 1966).

[114]   Respectively 1984 Congressional Quarterly Almanac at 22-S - 27-S, vote nos. 115, 125, 127, 130, 131, 132, 133, 134, 140, 141, 145, 149, and 151. The only clearly non-germane amendment that was tabled concerned oil exports. Id. at 25-S, vote no. 139.

[115]   The roll calls are in 1984 Congressional Quarterly Almanac at 22-S - 27-S, nos. 113-152.

procedural fights as a key means for maintaining control. This is not the common use of the motion -- whole years may pass without a postcloture battle or other reason for much use of the motion to table this way -- but when it does occur, the motion to table serves important purposes.   As discussed above, when the Chair rules on a point of order and a Senator appeals, the appeal can be tabled; the appeal may be debatable, but the motion to table is not.   Hence, points of orders and appeals either intended as delaying tactics, or raising sticky issues, can meet a quick kill in a motion to table.   The motion to table has another subtle advantage in these situations.   If the leadership makes a motion to table an appeal and loses, that does not yet decide the appeal. Hence, the leadership can still regroup and adopt a new approach, without losing control or establishing a bad precedent.[116]

E.   OTHER TACTICS

Amendment Tree

More than one amendment can be offered at one time, though not an unlimited number.   The structure of several pending amendments is depicted typically by a diagram with the bill as a base and each amendment as a branch, called the "amendment tree," a name given to this subject in general.   Before addressing in detail the rules of the Senate "amendment tree," it may help to illustrate its major tactical importance.

The Senate provided a stiking illustration in the series of maneuvers that ultimately defeated

---

[116]   For example, in the case of the extraordinarily threatening Grove City filibuster, when Majority Leader Baker's motion to table the appeal from a germaneness ruling failed, that did not yet establish a precedent that would destroy the germaneness rule under cloture.   Instead, it simply warned that the Senate was on the brink of the abyss; the Majority Leader then regrouped, negotiated a dropping of the whole Grove City matter, and this time his second motion to table passed (by voice vote).

the Grove City bill, a key civil rights initiative intended to deal with a restrictive Supreme Court ruling.[117] The House had passed a Grove City bill, but Senator Orrin Hatch (R-Utah), chair of the Senate subcommittee of jurisdiction, refused to bring the bill to the Senate floor. Accordingly, Minority Leader Byrd offered the Grove City proposal as a (non-germane) amendment to the 1985 Continuing Resolution, the government's funding mechanism.[118]

Senator Byrd followed up the Grove City amendment by offering a second version of it as a substitute amendment to the first. This unusual maneuver was subtler than most amendment tree efforts; it allowed other amendments but guaranteed a vote on Senator Byrd's version.[119] Opponents then chose the gambit of offering their own three other amendments, on tuition tax credits, gun control, and busing. This precluded any further amending as the "tree" was full, and countered the Grove City measure, with its wide

---

[117] For a description of those aspects of the matter not in the citations below to the Congressional Record, see 1984 Congressional Quarterly Almanac 241-43.

[118] Technically, he offered it to a first committee amendment to the resolution, but the Senate was treating that committee amendment as though it were original text, and the tree is complex enough without referring constantly to an unimportant layer of branching.

In the ensuing maneuvers, "[e]ach side had its procedural wizard. For the civil rights advocates, it was . . . [Minority Leader] Byrd . . . a widely acknowledged parliamentary master. For the opposition, it was . . . Chairman Hatch . . . . In the middle was [Majority Leader] Baker, relying on advice from Senate Parliamentarian Robert B. Dove." 1984 Congressional Quarterly Almanac 242.

[119] The rules regarding amendments would allow further amendments to the underlying bill, or to Senator Byrd's first amendment. Yet no matter whether the Senate adopted any such amendments, Senator Byrd's second amendment, which could not be amended, would be voted upon as an amendment to whatever else the Senate adopted.

support (but the prospect of a filibuster by conservatives), with three other measures with wide support (but also with the prospect of a filibuster, this time by liberals). The filibuster and cloture aspects of this are discussed elsewhere. For amendment-tree purposes, it may simply be noted that while Minority Leader Byrd's gambit was as skillful as could be, the opposing gambit ultimately carried the day, and when the Senate proved unable to defeat any one of the popular proposals, it put aside all of them, including the Grove City amendment.

With this illustration of importance of the Senate amendment tree in high-level maneuvering, its principles can be described using some humbler and simpler illustrations. The Senate allows amendments in two degrees, but no more, and amendments may strike language,[120] insert language, or strike and insert. Thus, to a resolution, "Resolved, that blueberry pie is the official American dessert," Senator First can offer an amendment to strike blueberry pie and insert blueberry cobbler. Senator Second may offer a second-degree amendment to strike blueberry from First's amendment or a second-degree amendment to insert with whipped cream after cobbler in First's amendment. However, if Senator Third came along, and proposed, with respect to Second's second-degree amendment to add with whipped cream, to offer a third-degree amendment proposing to add and nuts, and raisins, or any other third-degree addition to the confection, he would be out of order.

The Senate uses its own definitions of types of amendments and rules regarding the types, which differ from the House's even when the same words are used, and no use should be made of the House tree in understanding the Senate.[121] The Senate

---

[120] A request just to strike language, although akin to an amendment, is usually called a "motion to strike" rather than an amendment.

[121] In particular, the House speaks of a substitute amendment "for" an amendment, such a substitute not being considered as a higher degree than the amendment for which it substitutes. Thus, a substitute for an amendment can (footnote continued)

only calls one kind of amendment a "substituting amendment"; that is an amendment that strikes out either the whole underlying matter or some whole portion of it (such as a whole title), and inserts language in its place.   Any other amendment -- either one that inserts without striking, or one that strikes only a part or a partial portion before inserting -- the Senate calls a "perfecting amendment."

For example, the Senate might take up a resolution which "Resolved, that blueberry pie shall be the official American dessert." Amendments to insert <u>a la mode</u> after pie, or to strike <u>blueberry</u> and insert <u>apple</u>, would be perfecting.   An amendment to strike everything after "Resolved," and insert "that apple pie shall be the official American dessert," would be a substitute.   Thus, the identically worded end result, a resolution sanctifying apple pie, can be achieved either by a perfecting amendment changing the one different word, or by a substitute amendment replacing the whole text with another whole text (different by only one word), depending purely on the moving Senator's choice of form. That choice of form would result in distinct tactical differences.

The forms of first-degree amendment affect what can be offered as a second-degree amendment.   To a first degree perfecting amendment, there can only be a single second-degree amendment (of whatever kind).   However, to a first degree substitute amendment, there can be two second-degree amendments: one substitute, one perfecting.   For example, if Senator First

----

itself be amended in the second degree.   Adoption of such a substitute amendment completely replaces the amendment with the substitute.

In contrast, the Senate speaks of a substitute amendment "to" an amendment, such an amendment being considered as a higher degree than the amendment to which it is a substitute; thus, in the Senate a substitute to an amendment cannot be further amended.   Moreover, the substitute amendment need not be one that would completely replace all the amendment; to be a substitute amendment, it need only completely replace some discrete portion, such as one title of a multititled amendment.

proposes a perfecting amendment to strike
blueberry pie and insert apple pie, then only one
other Senator can offer a second-degree amendment
-- which could be either a substitute (strike
apple pie, the full length of First's amendment,
and insert diet sherbet) or a perfecting amendment
(insert no-cal before apple). However, if Senator
First proposes a substitute amendment to strike
everything after "Resolved," and insert that apple
pie shall be the official American dessert, then
two Senators can offer second-degree amendments;
Senator Substitute can propose to strike the whole
amendment, and insert that ice cream shall be the
official American dessert, and Senator Perfecting
can propose to add crumb between apple and pie.

Finally, Senate rules determine the order of
offering and voting on multiple pending
amendments. Amendments with "precedence," and
only such amendments, can be offered after ones
with less precedence; then, when the Senate is
ready to vote, it votes on amendments with
precedence first. As Martin Gold summarized the
rules of precedence:

> (a) A second degree amendment [can be
> offered after, and] is voted upon before a
> first degree amendment.
>
> (b) A perfecting amendment to the language
> proposed to be stricken out by a substiute
> [can be offered after the substitute, and] is
> voted on before a vote occurs on the
> substitute itself.[122]

The Senate respects four increasingly complex
forms of amendment trees that may be set up,

---

[122] M. Gold, Senate Procedure and Practice: An Introductory
Manual 22 (1981). The language inserted in the quote
reflects the twin nature of the precedence principle --
opportunity to offer, and order of voting.

There are two other rules of precedence, that concern
motions to strike: a perfecting amendment is voted upon
before a motion to strike, and a motion to strike is voted
upon before a motion to strike and insert, when these all
concern the same underlying language. Id.

recorded in four diagrams in Senate Procedures.

Principal Tactical Uses of Amendment Tree

Three principal tactical uses of complex Senate amendment trees may be noted: to obtain priority, to protect an amendment from further amending, and to prevent any further amending at all. First comes the simplest desire of all, the desire to obtain priority. Frequently two Senate factions compete over versions of legislation, each with fairly reasonable propositions that might win Senate approval, the question being which one the Senate will take. As Stanley Bach said of several Senators' seemingly over-complex amendment-tree maneuvers, the explanation "may lie in a belief shared by all four Senators that a strategic advantage belonged to the proposition on which the Senate would vote first . . . . [A] majority [of the Senate] might be inclined to support the first reasonable approach presented for a vote . . . ."[123]

To tap the advantage given to the amendments voted on first, Senators seek priority by offering their amendments as second-degree amendments rather than first, because a second-degree amendment has precedence -- is voted on first -- over a first degree amendment.[124]   Similarly,

---

[123]   Bach, Parliamentary Strategy & the Amendment Process: Rules & Case Studies of Congressional Action, Polity, Summer 1983, at 573, 589.

The "strategic advantage" of the "first reasonable approach" may lie in Senators' fears that interest groups or campaign opponents would cite a negative vote on that first reasonable proposition as signifying opposition to it (rather than simply preference for what is expected later). Also, Senators often simply do not know for certain what will come after that first reasonable proposition. Having voted "yes" on the first reasonable amendment, they may vote "no" against attempts to substitute competing formulations, preferring to appear consistent in their support and to take no further risks, since they no longer need to fear that their vote will be seen as purely negative when it is mere preference among various formulations. (footnote continued)

priority-seeking Senators offer a second-degree
amendment in a perfecting rather than a substitute
form, again so that the Senate will vote on their
amendments first.   In the complex maneuver
analyzed by Bach, Senators even offered amendments
doomed, by their particular position in the tree,
to be wiped out later, because by offering them at
that particular position, the offering Senators
secured the first vote.[125]   Such Senators assumed,
fairly reasonably, that if they win that first
vote, their amendment will have the Senate's
blessing, and they can later re-offer the
amendment at a secure position elsewhere on the
tree.

   A second goal of amendment tree maneuvers is
to protect an amendment from further amending.   As
described above, Minority Leader Byrd sought to
offer his Grove City amendment in such a fashion
that no other Senator could amend it.   This
maneuver has obvious value.   Opponents or
competitors can achieve all kinds of undesirable
effects by amending one's own amendment.   They can
offer "killer" amendments.[126]   Alternatively,

---

[124]   If no one offers a real first-degree amendment, a
Senator may offer a "dummy" one, just to be able to offer
the real amendment as a second-degree amendment (in case the
competition is lying back in ambush, waiting to offer its
own amendment as a second-degree amendment).

[125]   Specifically, when the Senate took up a veteran's
health care bill, with a committee amendment in the nature
of a substitute, Senators Larry Pressler (R-S.D.) and John
Heinz (R-Pa.) offered first- and second-degree amendments to
that committee substitute.   In order to secure the first
vote, Senators Spark Matsunaga (D-Hawaii) and Cranston
offered their amendments directly to the underlying bill
rather than to the committee substitute.   In that position,
the Matsunaga-Cranston language, even if adopted, was
certain to be wiped out later when the Senate adopted the
committee substitute; but the amendments to the underlying
bill would receive the first vote, which was what was
sought.   See Bach, _supra_, based on Congressional Record, May
16, 1979.

[126]   These are propositions attractive enough to pass, yet
carrying with them seeds of destruction for the underlying
(footnote continued)

opponents can offer weakening amendments -- propositions attactive enough to pass that reduce the value of the underlying proposition.

As Minority Leader Byrd illustrated, the Senator seeking to protect his amendment from amending offers a dummy first-degree amendment as a substitute, and then offers his amendment as a second-degree substitute. The second-degree substitute cannot itself be amended because of the bar against third-degree amendments. Once it is adopted, and the first-degree amendment, as thus amended, is in turn adopted, no further amendments can be made, because of the "lock-out" rule that text completely amended by a substitute cannot be amended again.

Finally, perhaps the most common amendment tree maneuver of all is to attempt to prevent any further amending at all. This freezes out the opposition from employing any further tactics, preserves intact any deal that has been cut, and allows one's own amendments to dominate the discussion.[127] The Senator who wishes to prevent any further amending fills up all the positions in the tree. In the simplest case, when no other amendments have been offered, he offers a first-degree perfecting amendment and then a second-degree perfecting amendment.

In a prominent example, in 1983 Senator McClure brought to the floor a bill to provide for a "phased deregulation" of natural gas prices. Senator Metzenbaum indicated he would filibuster, and so Senator McClure evidently planned to dominate the discussion and not allow his opposition to put its amendments into play. His play was to offer a first-degree perfecting amendment, and have Senator Bennett Johnston (D-La.), the minority manager who supported him,

---

proposition. The classic is the strengthening amendment, which "extremists" at both ends of the specturm unite to adopt, but allows the extremists in opposition to unite with moderates to kill the whole matter.

[127] Particularly when Senators have threatened filibusters, each side wants its own amendments to be the ones dominating the discussion, because those amendments may be in front of the Senate during a long time and a lot of lobbying and bargaining.

offer a second-degree perfecting amendment.[128] Senator Johnson expected recognition "as a representative of the minority leader," who has priority in recognition.[129] However, the Chair recognized Senator Metzenbaum instead, disrupting the managers' planned strategy. Senator Metzenbaum offered his own amendment, framing the issue as whether to allow "decontrol of old gas," and after some filibustering, Senator McClure gave up and pulled the bill.

Recommittal and Reconsideration

A further complex tactical opportunity comes with the use of the motion to recommit with instructions. The Senate's use of this motion differs sharply from the House's: in the House, it is a prerogative of the minority; in the Senate, it has emerged recently as a tool for the majority leader to present a comprehensive proposal to the Senate. While the majority leader could do this by offering an amendment instead of a motion to recommit, that motion has certain advantages discussed below.

The majority leader has varying goals in offering comprehensive proposals. Sometimes he aims simply to strip off all amendments that have been encrusted on some important bill. As previously discussed, a key thrust of 1980s Senate procedure has been the use of "must" bills as "vehicles" to attempt attachment of large numbers of extraneous amendments. In the end, these often bog the vehicle down in dispute and filibuster. To pass the "must" bill, a motion to recommit may be used. Thus, for example, in 1982, Majority Leader Baker noted regarding a debt limit increase

---

[128] Senator Metzenbaum noted subsequently that he had "underst[ood] the procedure that was contemplated . . . that the managers of the bill would send an amendment to the desk and then a second-degree amendment; and, as a consequence, the rest of us would not have an opportunity . . . [to] crystallize the issue," by offering amendments of their own. Id. at S15312.

[129] 129 Cong. Rec. S15313 (daily ed. Nov. 3, 1983).

bogging down in extraneous amendments:

> we must pass this bill . . . .   This may
> entail, if we cannot finish the bill
> otherwise, a motion to recommit the bill with
> instructions to report back forthwith a clean
> bill as passed by the House of
> Representatives . . . .
>
> Mr. President, no one should be taken by
> surprise. I have said a number of times that
> at some point, if necessary, I would be
> willing to file a motion to recommit with
> instructions.[130]

Then-Chairperson Robert Dole (R-Kans.) made a
humorous point about the political advantages for
both the Senators and the leadership in this
approach of first adopting amendments, then wiping
them off by recommittal. As Congressional
Quarterly described, Senator Dole

> suggest[ed] facetiously that the Senate
> should simply accept all 1,400-plus
> amendments [which had been submitted on the
> debt limit increase] in a bloc, then proceed
> with Baker's plan to excise all amendments.
> "Everybody could write home and say,'They
> have accepted my amendment, but because of
> some procedural thing they took it off,'"
> Dole said.   "It would make great copy for a
> newsletter."[131]

Sometimes the leadership makes more ambitious
use of the motion to control floor proceedings and
pass a comprehensive part position. In 1982,
Senator Dole may have made light of the use of the
motion to recommit, but when he became Majority
Leader in 1985, he made skillful use of that same
motion in passing a budget resolution, his major
challenge for the year. He blocked floor
amendments to the resolution by filling up the
whole amendment tree himself (using his leadership

---

[130]   128 Cong Rec. S11938 (daily ed. Sept. 22, 1986).

[131]   1982 Congressional Quarterly Almanac at 44.

priority in recognition to monopolize the Chair's attention while offering the amendments).[132]   By offering a motion to recommit and a series of amendments thereto, he set up a situation where he could control the floor and preclude amendments by the minority, and used the time to develop and refine an initial compromise proposal that obtained a symbolically important first victory by 50-49.[133]

Then, the Majority Leader relaxed discipline, standing aside while the Senate amended that motion to recommit with all kinds of other symbolic and substantive amendments.[134]   During this time of amendments, he and the Budget Committee chair "indicated that when the amending was over -- perhaps by the end of the week of May 6 -- they would offer a comprehensive substitute to replace the amended resolution.   This procedure . . . could be used to cancel or revise previously adopted amendments."[135]

---

[132]   Immediately upon adoption of the motion to proceed to the consideration of the budget resolution, Majority Leader Dole began offering his amendments.   131 Cong. Rec. S4804 (daily ed. April 25, 1985).   After explanations by Minority Leader Byrd, Senator Metzenbaum concluded, "As I understand the procedure . . . the purpose of going through the seven steps [i.e., filling up the amendment tree] is to bring the issue to a void without any amendments [by the minority] being offered?"   Id. at S4805.

[133]   Minority Leader Byrd noted that as a key point: taking the floor immediately after the reading of the amendment, he explained that "it completes the tree of amendments on a motion to recommit with instructions.   The distingished majority leader's amendment is not amendable at this point."   131 Cong. Rec. S4991 (daily ed. April 30, 1985). The amendment's adoption is at 131 Cong. Rec. S45048 (daily ed. April 30, 1986).

[134]   The majority package had curbed the Social Security increase.   To obtain the required votes, the Majority Leader had to promise the credit for deleting that increase to Senators Paula Hawkins (R-Fla.) and Alphonse D'Amato (R-N.Y.), in whose name he offered an amendment to delete it. 131 Cong. Rec. S5086 (daily ed. May 1, 1985).   The floor was then opened to amendments from all sides.
(footnote continued)

Ultimately, when the Majority Leader had his compromise devised, he put it forth as another second-degree amendment to the instructions on the motion to recommit. The Senate voted by 50-49 to adopt that amendment, in a moment of high drama as Senator Pete Wilson (R-Calif.) was brought from a hospital trailing intravenous connections to provide the needed last vote.[136] The Senate adopted the budget resolution as modified by the motion to recommit.[137]

Technically, the motion to recommit is fairly straightforward. Senate Rule XXII(1) provides for a motion "to commit," and Senate Rule XIV(7) provides that "it shall be in order at any time before the passage of any bill or resolution to move [the bill's] commitment." To "recommit" is simply to "commit" (i.e., refer) a bill to committee. Such a motion, according to Rule

---

[135] Senator Dole promised "reporters that 'We'll put it all back together like Humpty-Dumpty.'" Wehr, Republican Budget Package Picked Apart on Senate Floor, 43 Cong. Q. Week. Rep. 815-16 (1985).

[136] Wehr, Budget Squeaks Through Senate Floor Vote, 43 Cong. Q. Week. Rep. 871 (1985). That vote -- on a second-degree amendment to a motion to recommit -- was decisive, and after it, the Majority Leader tabled all other proposals, proving the matter was over. The procedure had effects described thusly:

> Dole also shrewdly deployed parliamentary maneuvers to control action on the floor to his advantage. For instance, under an unusual procedure for which he had laid the groundwork the previous week, attempts to amend the much-negotiated "final" GOP budget resolution were not in order until after its adoption on the 50-49 vote.

Id. at 873.

[137] The Senate finally recessed its night session at 3:44 a.m. 131 Cong. Rec. S5905 (daily ed. May 9, 1985) (although the events took place after midnight, and thus on May 10) (tabling of last amendment, followed by remaining steps short of passage of the budget resolution); id. S5916 (passage of the resolution); id. S6006 (3:44 a.m. recess).

XVII(2) "shall not be open to amendment, except to
add instructions."   A motion to recommit with
instructions may include the instruction to report
back forthwith.   Upon adoption of such a motion,
the committee chair reports the matter back at
once, without a meeting of the committee, and the
bill is modified per the instructions.   "The
adoption of a motion to recommit a bill nullifies
any action the Senate has taken on amendments
thereto."[138]   Typically, the instructions are to
include amendments.   Instructions can be amended
in two degrees,[139] so there is an amendment tree
for instructions in motions to recommit, but it is
a very simple one, at most a single first-degree
amendment and two second-degree amendments (one of
them perfecting).   If one motion to recommit
fails, the leadership (or others) can try
another.[140]
    Rule XIV(7) gives the motion its particular
attractions by conferring precedence on it.   The
rule gives the motion to commit a higher
precedence than the motion to amend, guaranteeing
the offeror the first vote on an issue.   Thus, the
majority leader can offer it without fearing
preemption by a minority amendment-offeror.
Moreover, the rule provides that after a bill
receives third reading, "it shall not be in order
to propose amendments" except for a motion to
commit (including a motion to recommit with
instructions to report back forthwith).   Thus, it
can be used at the end of the process, as well as
at the beginning.[141]

---

[138]   Riddick, "Recommit: Amendments to a Recommitted Bill,"
at 890.

[139]   Riddick, "Recommit: Amendments to a Motion to
Recommit," at 889.

[140]   "There is no provision in the Senate rules which
forbids the repetition of a motion to recommit, and,
therefore, the number of motions to recommit a matter is not
limited under the rules . . . .   A further motion to
recommit a bill may be made after a reasonable length of
time has intervened, and changes have been made in the
bill."   Riddick, "Recommit: Motions to Recommit and their
Consideration," at 895.
(footnote continued)

The motion for reconsideration has a limited role.   Rule XIII(1) provides in part: "When a question has been decided by the Senate, any Senator voting with the prevailing side or who has not voted may, on the same day or on either of the next two days of actual session thereafter, move a reconsideration." The motion can only be used by a Senator who voted "with the prevailing side" (or "who has not voted") since the only way a vote outcome could change would be if Senators on the winning side changed.   Since the motion can be used to reopen matters, the Senate custom after most votes, in order to finalize the matter, is for one Senator to move to reconsider, and for another to move to table the motion to reconsider.[142]   By tabling the motion to reconsider, the Senate gives that motion that "final disposition," and thereby finalizes the underlying vote as well. An occasional gambit is to "enter" a motion to reconsider,[143] or to move

_____

[141]   If the leadership makes a motion to recommit after third reading, then the Senate can adopt that motion for the bill to be reported back as per the instructions, but no further amendments can occur.   Riddick, "Recommit: Instructions to Report Forthwith, Recommit With" at 893.

    The precedents warn that the instructions on a motion to recommit are not in order if "the Senate would be trying to accomplish indirectly what it could not do directly"; Riddick, "Recommit: Instructions to Report Forthwith, Recommit With," at 893.   However, the precedents also suggest otherwise; for example, that a motion to recommit an appropriation may contain nongermane matter, which an amendment could not. Riddick, "Appropriations: Recommit," at 138-39.

[142]   Rule XIII(1) provides: "Every motion to reconsider shall be decided by a majority vote, and may be laid on the table without affecting the question in reference to which the same is made, which shall be a final disposition of the motion."

[143]   The effect of entering a motion to reconsider is as follows:

    The entering of a motion to reconsider the action of (footnote continued)

to reconsider, but not vote on or table the motion for awhile. This is a way for the losing side to keep open some vote in the hope of change.[144]

Germaneness

The tests of germaneness have far less importance in the Senate than in the House. In the House, germaneness governs all bills, serving a prime purpose in agenda control. In contrast, in the Senate, germaneness only applies in certain limited circumstances, serving merely to preserve the integrity of four special procedures -- UCAs,

---

the Senate in sending a bill to conference or the vote on the passage of a measure prevents the transmittal of the papers thereon to the House of Representatives until the motion to reconsider has been disposed of. In fact, the entering of such motion holds up further action on a bill until the motion is disposed of.

Riddick, "Reconsideration: Entering of Motion to Reconsider," at 912. For example, after a vote of 50-42 failed to ratify the Montreal Aviation accords, Majority Leader Baker immediately stated "Mr. President, I enter a motion to reconsider the vote by which the resolution of ratification regarding Executive B, 95-1 Montreal Protocols Nos. 3 and 4 was defeated." 129 Cong. Rec. S2279 (daily ed. March 8, 1983). Because the motion to reconsider had been entered rather than actually made, it could not be tabled (as the Chair informed a Senator attempting tabling, id.), and served to keep open indefinitely the possibility of future reconsideration.

[144] In a major 1986 party battle over the judicial nomination of Clarence Manion, the majority appeared on June 26 to have an initial victory, as a 47-47 tie was going to be broken by Vice President George Bush in the majority party's favor. Minority Leader Byrd kept the matter open, by switching sides (so that he would be on the "prevailing side" and thus able to make the motion) and moving to reconsider. The majority prevented a vote on the motion until July 23, when the Senate voted again for Manion, defeating the motion to reconsider by 49-50 (with Vice President Bush providing the 50th vote). Cohodas, Senate Makes it Official: Manion is Confirmed, 44 Cong. Q. Week. Rep. 1685 (1986).

cloture, budget act, and appropriations.   Even
this significance is further limited, for three of
the four procedures have exceptions to allow non-
germane amendments.[145]
     Still, these caveats notwithstanding, the
germaneness rule has significance in many
instances, particularly when Senators do not have
the votes for the procedures to circumvent the
rule.   Proponents of amendments to budget
reconciliation bills, to bills under cloture, and
to appropriations, who lack votes to circumvent
the rule, cannot obtain consideration of
amendments except germane ones.   Senators who
would like to offer amendments by surprise, and
therefore do not wish to list their amendments in
UCAs, similarly can offer only germane ones.
     Much less is known about the Senate's
germaneness rule than the House's.   There are
fewer Senate precedents, reflecting not only the
more limited use of the germaneness rule in the
Senate and its more porous application (as
discussed above), but also its relative youth.
The House has always lived under germaneness, and
so Hinds' Precedents (down to 1907) or Cannon's
(down to 1937) are full of germaneness
precedents.   In contrast, in the Senate, generally
speaking until the 1950s there were no UCAs "in
the usual form" imposing germaneness, until the
1960s almost no successful cloture votes, and
until the 1980s no budget reconciliation bills.
     The Senate does have some formulae, such as
that the germaneness rule blocks "new subject
matter" or "language unrelated to the subject
matter."[146]   However, subject matter tests alone,

---

[145]   On UCAs, before the Senate adopts one, Senators can
insist on listing their (non-germane) amendments in the UCA
and hence excepting them from the germaneness rule.   On
appropriations bills, the Chair's germaneness rulings are
frequently circumvented by various techniques -- if all else
fails, by appealing from the Chair's ruling, the particular
type of appeal most often indulged by the Senate.   On budget
bills, principally reconciliation bills, the germaneness
rule can be waived like other budget rules.   Only under
cloture has the Senate strictly kept the germaneness rule,
recognizing that the loss of that barrier would lead to a
crisis in Senate self-governance.
(footnote continued)

though they can knock out an amendment as non-germane,[147] can be misleading. As the Chair explained in 1982, "[t]he germaneness test has never been interpreted as a subject matter test. It is basically a technical amendment test."[148]

The Chair appears to apply some highly technical, and very stringent, rules to determine germaneness, emphasizing above all that the amendment must "restrict" rather than "broaden" the bill. As the Chair explained, "even expanding the bill dealing with the same subject matter has been ruled nongermane."[149]   Thus, while the House considers germane an amendment adding one more item to several similar items, the Senate considers such an amendment non-germane as broadening the scope of the bill.[150]

As for what "restricts" a bill, there are some guidelines. When the Chair analyzed a criminal code reform bill, it noted that amendments that strike language are deemed germane per se.[151]   Amendments that "strike a figure and

---

146   Riddick, "Unanimous Consent Agreements: Germaneness of Amendments Under Unanimous Consent Agreements," at 1087.

147   See, e.g., 128 Cong. Rec. S8887 (daily ed. July 22, 1982) (ruling of the Chair) ("The amendment of the Senator from South Carolina contains a new subject matter not contained in the bill nor in any of the amendments reported by the Finance Committee. So, for that reason, it is nongermane.")

148   128 Cong. Rec. S3880 (daily ed. April 22, 1982).   On this occasion, the Chair answered parliamentary inquiries concerning a large number of amendments Senators McClure and Jesse Helms (R-N.C.) were considering offering to the Criminal Code Reform Act.   It is an unusually full discussion by the Chair of Senate germaneness rules.

149   Id.

150   Hence, when a bill dealt in programs for wheat, grain, barley, and corn, an attempt to add an amendment dealing with potatoes was not germane.   124 Cong. Rec. S4230 (daily ed. March 21, 1978).

151   Id. at 3879 (the Chair) ("No amendment to strike, (footnote continued)

substitute   in   lieu   thereof   another
figure . . . therefore   would   be   germane."[152]
Amendments adding a word that changes an "original
meaning [that] included both a conduct and a
result test," into a "new meaning [that] only
includes a result test," would be germane.[153]
However, amendments would be non-germane when they
"add a new crime" or otherwise "expand the bill";
in fact, an amendment would not be germane that
struck language in one part of the bill and
inserted more restrictive language elsewhere in
the bill (such as replacing a proposed new broad
crime, with the current law's version), assuming
the amendment were divided, because "[o]nce
language has been stricken, it no longer sets the
parameters for germaneness."[154]

Thus, the Senate's germaneness tests curb
amendments   very   strictly.   For   example,   an
amendment proposing school lunch programs abroad
to a bill to amend further the foreign aid law was
considered   non-germane,   even   though   aid   could
reasonably be used for such proposes, because
there   was   nothing   specifically   in   the   bill
involving school lunches.[155]   As an anomaly,
amendments that merely express the sense of the
Senate are germane, even though what they express
may be unrelated to the bill, because they do not
change the "effect" of the bill (its legally
binding impact).[156]   Hence, while on the foreign
aid bill cited above, even a school lunch program
was non-germane, a provision that the sense-of-
the-Senate was to auction the whole Agriculture
Department to the private sector would have been
germane.

The Senate's germaneness tests also include a

---

regardless of its effect, can be ruled nongermane").

[152]   Id.

[153]   Id.

[154]   Id. at 3879-80.

[155]   Id. at 1088.

[156]   During cloture, such amendments may be ruled out as
dilatory even though germane.

subtle distinction regarding committee amendments. Even before committee amendments have been adopted (in fact, even when those amendments would be subject to a point of order), germaneness of a floor amendment is tested against the bill and the committee amendments. This creates opportunities for maneuvers for getting non-germane matter into a bill with the agreement of the committee of jurisdiction.[157] As for the committee amendments themselves, how germane they are depends on whether the basis for applying germaneness is a UCA, or the budget and cloture rules.

Pursuant to UCAs in the usual form, committee amendments are germane _per se_, like amendments explicitly listed in the UCA. On the other hand, pursuant to the cloture rule and the budget rules, committee amendments need not be germane. Hence, managers facing intense filibusters who have non-germane committee amendments, or other non-germane amendments they wish to add, have to follow a difficult route: they must get cloture on the (non-germane) amendments, have them adopted, and only then get cloture on the bill, lest their

---

[157] In a procedural maneuver that can only be described as extraordinary, during 1982 consideration of reconciliation legislation, Senator Robert Packwood (R-Oreg.), chair of the Commerce Committee, persuaded the Finance Committee to report out his airport development bill as its second committee amendment. The amendment itself, as the Chair noted on a parliamentary inquiry, was not in order, because it "contains significant matter within the jurisdiction of another committee and, therefore, would violate rule XV, paragraph 5." 128 Cong. Rec. S8703 (daily ed. July 20, 1982).

However, before that point of order could be made, Senator Packwood offered his bill as a second-degree floor amendment to the _first_ committee amendment. At that point, since the second committee amendment had not been knocked out, it served as part of the standard for germaneness. Hence, the Chair was constrained to rule that Senator Packwood's second-degree floor amendment was germane: it "is germane to the bill and to the amendments offered by the Finance Committee." _Id._ at S8702. On appeal, the Senate upheld that ruling. _Id._ at S8704.

cloture knock out their own amendments.

10
Filibuster and Cloture[1]

A. OVERVIEW AND HISTORY

Importance and Basics

Someone is said to have asked, "Who is this Senator Filibuster that I always hear talking so much?" No other congressional procedure is so famous, and yet so enmeshed in obscure subtleties, gambits and countergambits, unresolved issues, and complex calculations. The most seemingly arcane procedural points can be the most important. Filibusters and cloture are a looking-glass world in which the stakes are high, technicalities are sometimes exalted, and all-out combat between masters of obstruction and of overcoming obstruction strain the chamber's operation to the limit.

The essential rules of modern filibuster and cloture can be stated briefly before the detailed discussion that follows. Ordinarily, the Senate operates on the rule of unlimited debate:

---

[1] Sources cited frequently in this chapter include Senate Committee on Rules and Administration, 96th Cong., 1st Sess., Senate Cloture Rule (1979) (Senate Cloture Rule); F. L. Burdette, Filibustering in the Senate (1940) (Burdette); S. Prt. No. 254, 98th Cong., 2d Sess. 15 (1984) (S. Prt. No. 98-254).

amendments and bills do not pass until all
Senators have spoken as much as they want and
offered any amendments they wish (absent unanimous
consent limitations). Hence, Senators can take up
unlimited time by filibustering -- offering
extended debate and unconstrained numbers of
amendments. Senators from the South during the
era of segregation, who opposed national civil
rights laws, and Senators from small (low-
population) states, have traditionally seen the
filibuster as their ultimate protection against
the imposition by weight of the population in the
rest of the country of distateful central
government controls.[2]

To respond to a filibuster, Senators seeking
to move a matter along file a motion for
cloture. Two days later, the Senate votes on
cloture, which requires 60 votes to approve. If
it votes cloture, various limits come into play:
the matter at issue becomes and remains the
pending question until disposed of, only germane
amendments can be offered, each Senator gets no
more that one hour for debate, and debate as a
whole ends in 30 hours. Filibusterers can respond
to these constraints with what are known as
"postcloture" tactics, namely, stalling by large
numbers of quorum calls, and by roll-call votes on
amendments, motions, and appeals from rulings of
the Chair. In turn, the Senate has used a variety
of means to break postcloture filibusters.

Senate filibuster practice can best be
understood by starting with its origins and then
continuing with developments after 1975. The
current pattern, in which both filibusters and
votes to impose cloture occur frequently, arises
from, and is shaped by, the breakdown of a prior
pattern from 1938 to 1962; the postcloture
filibuster is shaped by the events of 1962 to
1975. After this section and the next discuss the
history until the 1970s, and then the period after
1975, the subsequent sections will turn to the
rules of cloture and filibuster, and then the

---

[2]   For example, in 1987, Senator Harry Reid (D-Nev.)
filibustered against national legislation to force Nevada to
accept a nuclear waste repository. 1987 Congressional
Quarterly Almanac 16, 309.

advanced and specialized aspects.

Origins of Modern Practice

The antecedent of the filibuster, simple talking for purposes of delay, dates back to the Senate's origins,[3] but filibusters lasting a considerable period were relatively few at first.[4] There was a lack of sharp limitations on debate, allowing filibusters to occur.[5] However, until late in the century, the Senate kept down the number of effective filibusters, primarily through its great ability, in the absence of time

---

[3]   In 1790, Senator William Maclay (D-Pa.) observed an abbreviated version of the tactic in the First Senate, noting in his diary that when the Senate considered a new building for itself, "the design of the Virginians and the Carolina gentlemen was to talk away the time, so that we could not get the bill passed." Burdette at 14, quoting Journal of William Maclay 158 (1790).

[4]   See Congressional Quarterly, Origins and Development of Congress 194-95 (1976). Early filibusters were not intense. The first in 1841 "was a mild demonstration," Burdette at 22. In 1846, the Senate simply let filibusterers on Oregon policy, an issue of national importance, talk themselves out for two months. Id. at 25. That "filibusterous delay had not been fatal even if it had been provoking." Burdette at 24. A month of debate in 1847 did prevent antislavery conditions on the appropriations for purchase of the Mexican Cession, id. at 27, but even so, "the unsuccessful filibuster of 1863 is the first in Senate annals which can be said without shadow of doubt to have been truly intense." Burdette at 34. "[S]ixteen years were to elapse after the stirring events of 1863 before the Senate witnessed a filibuster of equal magnitude." Burdette at 35.

[5]   Some have argued that the filibuster was all-powerful in the nineteenth century, since there was no cloture rule. "From 1806 to 1917, then, debate was absolutely free and unlimited except during the interregnum of the War Between the States." W. S. White, Citadel: The Story of the U.S. Senate 60 (1956); see Calmes, Dilatory Debate: A Tactic as Old as the Senate, 45 Cong. Q. Weekly Rep. 2119 (1987).

pressures comparable to today's, to outwait even a longwinded minority.[6]

Thus, until the latter part of the nineteenth century,[7] and perhaps even "until the Force Bill of the winter of 1890-91, there was no spectacular and successful filibuster."[8]   Only on that occasion did traditional restraints falter before a filibuster which "shook not only the Senate but also the country as few parliamentary battles have done."[9]   The "Force Bill" filibuster inaugurated

---

[6]   An examination of the actual practice shows that the Senate restrained filibusters by several means. First, the Senate had some debate-limiting rules. See G. H. Haynes, The Senate of the United States 395 (1938); L. G. McConachie, Congressional Committees 313, 316-21 (1898); Senate Cloture Rule at 7-11.

Second, the ambiguities in the rules, the threat of rules changes and occasional arbitrary actions, also served as restraints. Until 1806, the Senate had a motion for the previous question among its rules to curb filibusters. Thereafter, the issue remained open until 1848 whether the Chair, or the Senate, could call a Senator to order for speaking beyond the point. Beeman, Unlimited Debate in the Senate: The First Phase, LXXXIII Poli. Sci Q. 419, 428, 430 (1968).   For threatened changes in the rules to curb speakers, see id. at 426 (Henry Clay (Ky.)) (1841), and 432 (Rules Committee, 1856). In 1863, the Republican majority ruthlessly and arbitrarily crushed a filibuster. Burdette at 32-33.

[7]   Filibusters occurred in 1879 and 1881, but the Senate responded by considering (although rejecting) a Rules Committee proposal in 1883 to reintroduce the motion for the previous question. Id. at 35-51 (1879, 1881 filibusters); L. Rogers, The American Senate 167-68 (1926) (1883 proposal).   For a chronology of the threatened rules changes, see Senate Cloture Rule at 7-11; 127 Cong. Rec. S1929 (daily ed. March 10, 1981) (address by Sen. Robert Byrd (D-W.Va.)).

[8]   L. Rogers, supra, at 167. For a similar account of the growth in filibustering at the end of the nineteenth century, see C. H. Kerr, The Origin and Development of the United States Senate 64-67 (1895).

(footnote continued)

a regime that proved stable for over three-quarters of a century, in which southern Democrats stood firm behind the filibuster to hold off civil rights legislation.[10]

In 1917, another battle of national proportions broke out on the eve of American entry into World War I, as antiwar Senators filibustered a bill to arm merchant ships against German submarine warfare. President Wilson responded by convening the Senate in special session with his famous philippic against the filibuster:

> The Senate of the United States is the only legislative body in the world which cannot act when its majority is ready for action. A little group of willful men, representing no opinion but their own, have rendered the great Government of the United States helpless and contemptible.
>
> The remedy? There is but one remedy. The only remedy is that the rules of the Senate shall be so altered that it can act.[11]

---

[9] Id. The Force Bill proposed "federal supervision of Congressional elections, a measure aimed especially against Negro disqualification and intimidation in the South," Burdette at 52, on the rise with the expansion of the Jim Crow system.

[10] Faced with extreme obstruction, the Republicans planned to force through a cloture rule, to carry out the implied threat that had previously kept the filibuster within limits. However, forcing through such a rules change required tough favorable rulings from the Chair; when the Vice President would not make the necessary rulings, both the proposal for a cloture procedure and the bill itself died. L. Rogers, supra, at 168.

That bill also inaugurated a period of extensive filibustering on a range of issues. "For the next quarter of a century the Senate was the scene of filibusters but gave no serious consideration to devices for making them impossible"; at most, rulings of the Chair placed some checks on a few filibuster tactics, such as repetitive quorum calls, a tool of lone-wolf filibusterers. Id. (quote); Burdette at 59-121 (history from 1891 to 1917); Senate Cloture Rule at 11-13.
(footnote continued)

On the third day of the special session the Senate adopted a cloture rule by 76-3.   The rule only went so far as to allow cloture by a two-thirds vote.[12]

1927-75: Rise and Fall of the Model of Rare Cloture

Although the Senate voted for cloture four times in the decade immediately following the 1917 rules change, thereafter it settled down to a cloture-free era: 35 years passed before the Senate voted cloture again.   A conservative coalition consolidated its power in both Houses of Congress starting in the 1930s, with filibusters as its key tool in the Senate through a stable two-part pattern.   On the one hand, the conservative coalition exercised a degree of self-restraint unknown later, by reserving filibusters primarily for civil rights legislation.   Of the 15 cloture petitions voted on by the Senate from 1938 until May, 1962, and all rejected, 11 concerned civil rights bills.[13]   Conservatives did not

---

[11]   Burdette at 121.

[12]   "Few Senators believed that so mild an arrangement would end obstruction in the chamber, or even that it could often be applied."   Burdette at 128.

[13]   Two were on antilynching in 1938, three on antipoll tax in 1942, 1944, and 1946, three on employment discrimination in 1946 and 1950, one on an omnibus civil rights act in 1960, and two on literacy tests for voters in 1962.   One other, concerning amending the cloture rule in 1961, was a strategic necessity for that primary use.   Only three cloture votes in those 25 years concerned issues other than civil rights -- two during the brief Republican ascendancy in 1946, and a unique filibuster by liberals in 1954 against the Eisenhower Administration's atomic energy bill.   S. Prt. No. 98-254, at 44.

As Congressional Quarterly observed retrospectively, "[t]hroughout the 1960s the filibuster was basically a weapon of southern state senators to block civil rights (footnote continued)

filibuster other bills even when they found such bills very distasteful.[14]

On the other hand, southerners maintained iron-clad discipline against voting cloture. As Congressional Quarterly explained in 1968: "The view of the Southerners was expressed by their leader, Sen. Richard B. Russell (D. Ga.), in 1962 when he told a reporter: "I'll vote to gag the Senate when the shrimp start to whistling 'Dixie.'" Of the 26 Senators from southern states who in 1968, 14 never in their careers voted for cloture.[15]

The conservative coalition gave little ground, and gave it up very slowly, during decades of combat. Until 1949, the cloture rule was by

---

legislation. Monumental battles were fought over this issue, with the filibuster and cloture the central weapons of the opposing Senate sides." Congressional Quarterly, Congress and the Nation, Volume IV: 1973-76 774.

[14]   For example, in 1937, southern Democrats fiercely opposed national minimum-wage legislation as antithetical to their regional low-wage economy and as regionally discriminatory, yet they let it pass without a filibuster. See J. T. Patterson, Congressional Conservatism and the New Deal 152-53 (1967). In contrast, in 1937 and 1938 southern Democrats successfully filibustered an antilynching bill -- the latter year, for six weeks straight -- defeating two cloture petitions. Id. at 156-57 (description); S. Prt. 98-254, at 44 (two cloture votes).

[15]   Congressional Quarterly, Congress and the Nation, Vol. II: 1965-69 381. Additional votes against cloture came from conservative Republicans, and from Senators representing states with small populations, who sympathized with the tactic that exalted their states' power through equal representation in the Senate. Some "Senators took the historic position that a filibuster was the ultimate protection for the small states against the superior voting strength of the large." Id.

Observers justified the anticloture position by John Calhoun's (D-S.C.) philosophy that the government should not exercise majority will on issues strongly affecting particular regions, of which civil rights bills affecting treatment of Southern blacks were the prime example. See W. S. White, supra, at 20-21, 24.

its terms almost useless.[16]   Even after 1949, well-organized filibusterers defeated attempts to force through bills by all-night sessions.[17]

Ultimately, in the mid-1960s, President Johnson led the Senate in breaking the pattern. In 1964, "after fifty-seven days of Senate debate, beginning March 26 and ending June 10, the longest filibuster in Senate history was ended by a 71-29 vote for cloture, marking the first time the Senate had ever forcibly closed debate on a civil rights question."[18]   Other cloture votes on civil rights measures followed.[19]

----

[16]   The rule spoke only of cloture on pending "measures," and thus could not be used to end a filibuster on a motion to proceed to a bill.   That 1949 compromise curing this defect passed only after a bitter struggle, and further efforts to strengthen the rule to any significant degree foundered.   For details of the pre-1949 rule and the 1949 struggle, see G. B. Galloway, The Legislative Process in Congress 561-64 (1953); Senate Cloture Rule at 16-17 (1979); Congressional Quarterly, Congress and the Nation: 1945-63 1426.   Part of the 1949 compromise was that the votes needed for cloture were tightened from two-thirds of those present and voting (the 1917 standard) to two-thirds of the whole Senate (then 64 of 96 Senators).   In 1959, the filibusterers gave back that ground, and thereafter the rule remained unchanged until 1975.   The efforts to change it are discussed in a later section.

[17]   Particularly effective resistance was led by Senator Russell: "Richard Russell . . . organized his Southern Senators in platoons [in 1964], just as he had done in the 1960 civil rights fight, in a 1962 fight over state literacy tests which effectively dis[en]franchised Negroes, and in the 1961 and 1963 struggles over Rule XXII."   R. Evans & R. Novak, Lyndon B. Johnson: The Exercise of Power 400 (1966).   Those tactics are discussed in a later section on basic cloture procedure.

[18]   R. Evans & R. Novak, supra, at 400.   The key break in the conservative coalition came when Minority Leader Everett Dirksen (R-Ill.) agreed to support cloture on the omnibus civil rights bill, explaining to the Senate: "[s]tronger than all the armies is an idea whose time has come."   D. M. Berman, A Bill Becomes a Law 79 (2d ed. 1966).

(footnote continued)

This opened the way for three major changes in the 1960s and early 1970s in patterns of filibustering and in the cloture rule. First, liberals began using the filibuster.[20] Passage of the main civil rights agenda in the 1960s, and the coming to office of the Nixon administration in 1969, caused liberals to engage "in 1970 [in what] appeared to be the first widespread re-evaluation of their position on Rule 22"; the "change of heart by many Senate liberals of their position on the filibuster occurred in December 1970 when opponents of the supersonic transport (SST) aircraft succeeded in killing a bill containing [its] funds . . . ."[21] Liberals and moderates led some of the key filibusters of the late 1970s and 1980s described below against natural gas price deregulation, draft registration, and curbs on busing.[22]

---

[19] Cloture followed on a voting rights bill in 1965 and on a housing discrimination bill in 1968. S. Prt. 98-254 at 44.

[20] There had been occasional liberal filibusters before the 1970s. See 1962 Congressional Quarterly Almanac 378 (filibuster of COMSAT bill for antitrust reasons). However, liberals had largely scorned filibustering "since the 1930s and 1940s when the filibuster came to be identified with the effort by southerners to block civil rights legislation." Congressional Quarterly, Congress and the Nation, Vol. III: 1969-73 371.

[21] Id.

[22] After the SST filibuster, the dam against liberal filibusters broke, "largely because these senators became increasingly concerned about certain [conservative] civil liberties, economic and social welfare proposals which they feared a conservative Republican administration headed by Presidents Nixon and Ford and its congressional allies could enact." Congressional Quarterly, Congress and the Nation, Vol. IV: 1973-76 774. In 1971, liberals

filibustered against extension of the military draft, a proposed loan to the Lockheed Aircraft Corp., President Nixon's nomination of William H. Rehnquist to the Supreme Court, funding of the Vietnam War and funding for various weapons programs. The trend continued in
(footnote continued)

Second, southern Democrats began voting to break filibusters by cloture, ending their prior taboo against such votes.[23] The passage of the principal civil rights agenda reduced the southern Democratic motivation to preserve cloture at all costs, and the spate of liberal filibusters frontally threatened their own interests.[24] A lesser taboo replaced the older one for a time:

1972 as Senate liberals successfully filibustered an anti-busing bill.

Id.

[23] Until the 1970s, southern Democrats had been able to maintain their iron taboo against voting for cloture because filibusters on conservative legislation by liberals were rare; when they did occur, as in a 1962 filibuster regarding COMSAT, the southern Democrats avoided voting for cloture, 1962 Congressional Quarterly Almanac 378 (seven key anticloture southern Democrats simply stayed absent when cloture was voted with only three votes to spare by 63-27). In 1954, liberals filibustered a Republican atomic energy bill. To avoid "the chance that frustrated Midwestern Republicans would . . . liberalize Rule XXII . . . . [which,] of course, would affect Southern veto power over civil rights," R. Evans & R. Novak, supra, at 92, southern Democrats pressured Minority Leader Lyndon Johnson (D-Tex.) into helping crush the filibuster without a cloture vote.

[24] The change occurred in the Senate's 1971 vote for cloture on a draft registration bill to cut off an anti-Vietnam War debate. It was the first time the Senate voted in favor of cloture since 1927, other than the votes over COMSAT and the three key civil rights bills of the 1960s, and this vote tore down the barriers against southern Democratic support for cloture:

Cloture was largely attributable to the support of Senators who had never before voted to restrict debate -- Alan Bible [(D-Nev.)], Sam Ervin [(D-N.C.)], Clifford Hansen [(R-Wyo.)], Ernest Hollings [(D-S.C.)], B. Everett Jordan [(D-N.C.)], John Stennis [(D-Miss.)], Herman Talmadge [(D-Ga.)], and Strom Thurmond [(R-S.C.)].

Senate Cloture Rule, supra, at 42.

now a number of Senators would vote for cloture, but not early in a debate or on the first cloture vote.[25] Thus, the Senate developed a new pattern of successful invocation of cloture after votes on multiple cloture petitions.[26]

Finally, conservatives began using filibusters on a broad range of issues. They were led by Senator James Allen (D-Ala.), a courtly southern Democrat with unsurpassed procedural skill, and by Senator Jesse Helms (R-N.C.), advance guard and leader of the New Right.[27] Eventually, Senators of all ideologies began making broad use of filibusters. As Congressional Quarterly noted in 1987, after a session filled with filibusters and cloture votes, "[c]ritics say that frequent resort to the filibuster, even over what Iowa Republican Charles E. Grassley calls 'piddly little issues,' has diminished its value."[28]

The upshot of these three trends was use of filibustering and cloture with a frequency never seen before. In five days alone from December 13 through December 17, 1974, as the Senate attempted to complete its business for the year, it voted cloture four times, as many times as in the entire decade of the 1960s. Filibusters thereafter occurred with a high frequency. As Congressional

---

[25] 121 Cong. Rec. 5260 (1975) (reprinting news article).

[26] The Senate voted for cloture twice in 1972, twice in 1973, and seven times in 1974, almost invariably after several unsuccessful petitions on the same bills. S. Prt 98-254, at 45.

[27] With the civil rights agenda largely enacted, conservatives had less reason to hoard their filibuster weapon. In 1973-74, with the weakening of the Republican administration by Watergate, Senate liberals had the power to push through their own agenda unless filibustered. Filibusters by conservatives requiring votes of cloture started occurring on such lesser matters as a government pay raise, a supplemental appropriation, and a legal services bill.

[28] Calmes, "Trivialized" Filibuster is Still a Potent Tool, 45 Cong. Q. Week. Rep. 2115, 2116 (1987).

Quarterly observed in 1987, "Of the 245 cloture votes in the past 70 years, 58 percent have been in just the dozen years since the 1975 rules change,"[29] the change now to be discussed.

Reducing the Cloture Requirement to Three-Fifths

As discussed above, the modern filibuster dated from the Southern Democrats' defeat of the Force Bill in 1890-91. That debate revealed quite clearly what it would take to curb the filibuster: a Senate majority determined to change the rules, aided by a Vice President in the Chair willing to bring the Senate to an immediate vote on the path to a rules change, overcoming all resistance in the process.[30]

The modern effort to adopt a rule for easier cloture effectively began with a limited change in the rule in 1949.[31]   In 1953, liberals resumed their effort, with the thesis that "each new Congress brings with it a new Senate, entitled to consider and adopt its own rules"; thus, on the first day of a new Congress, the Senate could cut short debate, and make a rules change, by majority vote, without regard to the two-thirds requirement for cutting short debate under the rules of the previous Congress.[32]

In 1953, on the first day of the Congress, the Majority Leader tabled the liberal motion to

---

[29]   Id. at 2116.

[30]   See Burdette at 56 (basic filibuster-breaking strategy formulated by Senator Nelson Aldrich (R-R.I.)).

[31]   That year, after a bitter struggle, the liberals compromised in rewriting the cloture rule to make cloture possible on motions to proceed. See note 13 supra.

[32]   Senate Cloture Rule at 19.   The conservative response was that the Senate was a continuing body, with rules continuing in force from one Congress to the next until changed, and thus that changes could only be made pursuant to the cloture rule in force, which required a two-thirds vote.

consider new rules.   In 1957, liberals repeated
the 1953 motion, and again it was tabled.[33]   In
1959, 1961, 1963, and 1967, liberals failed in
efforts to change the rule.[34]   In 1969, liberals

---

[33] Tabling occurred only after Vice President Richard Nixon
gave a complex advisory opinion supporting the liberals.
"During the debate preceding [the tabling] vote, Vice
President Nixon said he believed the Senate could adopt new
rules 'under whatever procedures the majority of the Senate
approves.'"   Senate Cloture Rule at 20.   He stated that "he
regarded as unconstitutional the section of Rule XXII
banning any limitation of debate on proposals to change the
rules, but added that the question of the constitutionality
of the rule could be decided only by the Senate itself."
Id.   For a description of the 1957 debate in its larger
context, see Shuman, Senate Rules and the Civil Rights Bill:
A Case Study, Am. Poli. Sci. Rev. 955, 959-60 (1957).

[34] The failure was partly because of Lyndon Johnson's lack
of interest in leading the effort (in his successive key
roles as Majority Leader, Vice President, and President).

In 1959, Majority Leader Johnson sidetracked the issue,
by securing adoption of a compromise change in Rule XXII: he
reduced the requirement for cloture from two-thirds of the
Senate as a whole (imposed in 1949) to two-thirds of the
Senators present and voting.   At the same time, he
incorporated a special provision in Rule XXII that "The
rules of the Senate shall continue from one Congress to the
next Congress unless they are changed as provided in these
rules," intended to undercut the liberal argument of 1953
and 1957 for first-day rule changes by majority vote.
Senate Cloture Rule, at 21; R. Evans & R. Novak, supra, at
216.

In 1961 and 1963, liberal efforts crumbled before
bipartisan leadership resistance and southern Democratic
filibusters; southerners controlling committee assignments
punished the liberal insurgents.   Senate Cloture Rule at 21-
22; Clark, Congress: The Sapless Branch 126 (rev. ed. 1964).

In 1967, as previously, a liberal Senator (Senator
George McGovern (D-S.D.)) moved at the start of the Congress
to end debate on a resolution to change the cloture rule.
This time, Vice President Humphrey submitted a point of
order made against the motion to the Senate, and the
(footnote continued)

again renewed their effort, obtaining a landmark ruling from Vice President Hubert Humphrey.[35]

Finally, in 1975, 26 years of effort finally bore fruit.   By then, the new voting patterns, particularly the frequent conservative filibusters, produced a reaction against filibustering.   Then, too, in 1975 Vice President Nelson Rockefeller, a figure of unique forcefulness, sat in the Chair.   The year began with a motion to change the rules, followed by weeks of delaying tactics by Senator Allen such as roll-call votes on other motions and numerous quorum calls.   Ultimately, Majority Leader Mike Mansfield (D-Mont.) made a point of order against the motion.[36]

---

liberals moved to table the point of order to get an immediate vote, but the Senate voted to uphold the point of order.   Senate Cloture Rule at 23.

[35]   "The Chair informs the Senate that in order to give substance to the right of the Senate to determine or change its rules . . . if a majority of the Senators . . . vote in favor of the pending motion for cloture, the Chair will announce that . . . debate will proceed under the cloture provisions of that rule." Senate Cloture Rule at 24-25.   On appeal, the Senate reversed this ruling on a 45-53 roll call, but this additional Vice Presidential opinion, added to the prior Nixon one, and the close vote, gave a boost to the strategy for changing the rule.

In 1971, Vice President Agnew would not help the assailants of the cloture rule, and conservatives conducted a successful six-week battle against change. Senate Cloture Rule at 25-26.

[36]   He made the point of order, not because he wanted to win on that point of order, but hoping to have the point of order defeated, setting the stage for proceeding with revision of the rules.   On February 24, 1975, with the Senate still in the first legislative "day" of session (the Senate having recessed from day to day without adjourning), the motion was renewed.   Majority Leader Mansfield made his point of order, and for the next two days, Senator Allen again made a series of sidetracking motions.   The motion was that "debate upon the pending motion to proceed to the consideration of Senate Resolution 4 [to institute majority cloture] be brought to a close by the Chair by immediately (footnote continued)

There ensued the key steps that broke the
barrier to the rules change. Senator Edward
Brooke (R-Mass.) moved to table the Mansfield
point of order, a nondebatable motion intended to
produce a decisive vote.[37] The Senate voted 46-43
to table the point of order.   Vice President
Rockefeller then announced, "the motion now is to
be put to the Senate for an immediate vote."[38]
     Opponents of the rules change railed against
the Vice President for having put a question when
Senator Allen was seeking recognition, and thus
having prevented him from obstructing further.
The Vice President apologized to Senator Allen,[39]
but by the putting of the question, the decisive
step had occurred and the die was cast. At this
point, rather than go on to have a rules change
forced   through,   Senator   Russell   Long   (D-La.)
brought forth a compromise for a "constitutional"
three-fifths cloture, that is, cloture requiring a
vote of 60, which the Majority Leader accepted.[40].
     Although   there   had   been   a   face-saving
solution,[41] the Rubicon had been crossed.   Even

---

putting this motion to end debate, without debate,"   121
Cong. Rec. 4108 (1975).

     As Senator Charles Mathias (R-Md.) noted at one point,
"on   no   less   than   27   occasions   the   Senate   has   been
effectively prevented from voting on the Mondale motion
through   the   use   of   quorum   calls,   motions,   and   similar
parliamentary practices."   Id. at 4369.

[37]   As   Vice   President   Rockefeller   prepared   to   put   the
question,   Senator   Allen   asked   to   put   "a   parliamentary
inquiry," an evident prelude to further delay. Overriding
Senator Allen's request, the Vice President instructed the
clerk to call the roll.

[38]   Id. at 4370.

[39]   Id. at 4372.

[40]   Id. at 4371 (Majority Leader Mansfield, describing Long
proposal). On March 7, the Senate voted 73-21 to impose
cloture   on   adoption   of   the   Long-Mansfield   three-fifths
proposal, and after a few more delaying moves, adopted the
change Id. at 5612 (cloture vote); 5652 (adoption).

(footnote continued)

skeptics of the liberals' justification for changing rules had seen the approach work.[42] Also, Senator Allen's January through March filibuster of the rules change had not relied on the traditional methods of long speeches, but on an array of delaying tactics such as motions, appeals, and quorum calls.   Thus began the postcloture filibuster.   Before turning to that phenomenon, the basic filibuster and cloture procedure should be described.

B.   OBTAINING CLOTURE AND BASIC CLOTURE PROCEDURE

Filibustering Prior to Cloture -- Holding the Floor

As the previous section showed, the 1970s shifted the filibuster away from the past predominance of southern Democrats filibustering a few civil rights bills in long continuous sessions, to a more complex procedural interaction.   More

---

[41] As part of the compromise, the Senate reconsidered and, this time, rejected the motion to table the Mansfield point of order, thereby allowing opponents to say the Senate had never yet established a precedent allowing nondebatable rules changes on the first day by majority vote.   Id. at 4972.

[42] As Majority Whip Byrd commented:

Mr. President, I again say that Senators can argue these precedents any way they wish . . . .   But at any time that 51 Members of the Senate are determined to change the rule and if they have a friendly Presiding Officer, and if the leadership of the Senate joins them -- especially if it is the joint leadership -- that rule will be changed, and Senators can be faced with majority cloture.

The Majority Whip added: "I again call attention to the position taken by the Vice President in 1969 . . . .   I have never thought too much of the fiction that a continuing body does not have continuing rules.   But there are many fictions -- many fictions that are recognized in law . . . ."   Id. at 5249, 5531.

Senators filibustered thereafter over lesser matters, and more Senators vote for cloture, which requires fewer votes to obtain than before. This shifting pattern still leaves some importance in the basic "talkathon" filibuster, for several reasons. Most important, all filibusterers must be able to mount the basic talkathon before they can raise the stakes to any of the more complex patterns. Otherwise, those who wish to end the filibuster (termed here "managers" for simplicity)[43] could simply bring a bill out and wait, instead of trying to corral 60 votes for cloture, as the would-be filibusterers give up or fumble.[44]

For the filibusterers, the basic talkathon is easiest when they can regain the floor at any time, have no concern about losing the floor, and only wish to prevent final Senate action. In such a situation, filibusterers can do many things besides talk. They can demand quorum calls, which take much time. They can offer amendments and object to dispensing with their reading. In a classic example in 1902, a filibustering Senator "began obstruction by starting the clerks reading an amendment . . . forty-six printed pages in length."[45] As Minority Leader Byrd warned in

---

[43] Strictly speaking, bill managers may not be the ones trying to break the filibuster. Often, they will step aside and let the leadership run the show. Occasionally, they will even support the filibuster, if, for example, it is aimed at some controversial matter attached to their bill by a non-germane floor amendment. However, for terminological simplicity, those opposing the filibuster will be described here as the "managers."

[44] Also, filibusterers may have to mount a basic filibuster to stall while the two sides attempt to line up votes on the cloture motion. Finally, as discussed below, there are all kinds of situations in which a talkathon occurs either before or after a cloture vote. For example, in 1982, Senator Lowell Weicker (R-Conn.) delivered an eight-hour speech reminiscent of an old-fashioned filibuster, talking to stave off temporarily a tabling motion against an amendment of his in order to dramatize his position.

[45] Burdette at 75 (1902 filibuster of statehood bill for (footnote continued)

1981, in successfully threatening against overloading a budget reconciliation bill with extraneous matters:

> there are various ways in which a minority can filibuster the reconciliation bill . . . . All I have to do is send this book to the desk as an amendment and object to dispensing with its reading. The amendment would have to be read and will be read, except by unanimous consent. I could sent it to the desk, offer it as an amendment, and it would be read . . . .
>
> So I can keep us all in over the weekend, but there would be no action except the reading of this amendment.[46]

Filibusterers in this easy situation worry about two problems. They must have a Senator watching the floor at all times, even when they are not talking, lest the managers by unanimous consent call off reading or quorum calls and forge ahead. Depending on the filibuster, their party leadership may or may not be willing to perform such protective floor watching. Second, they must beware the two-speech rule. The rule dates back all the way to 1789,[47] when it promoted the opportunity of all the Senators to speak without too many speeches by any one individual. "[T]he rule is not self enforcing,"[48] and it

---

Arizona, New Mexico, and Oklahoma). The filibuster was dropped when it became clear the pertinent bill would not pass. Id.

[46] 127 Cong. Rec. S6977 (daily ed. June 25, 1981).

[47] Rule XIX(1)(a) provides in part: "no Senator shall speak more than twice upon any one question in debate on the same legislative day without leave of the Senate, which shall be determined without debate." Rule IV of the first Senate's rules provided that "No member shall speak more than twice in any one debate on the same day, without leave of the Senate." S. Doc. No. 27, 96th Cong., 1st Sess. 5 (1980).

[48] Riddick, "Debate: Speeches Allowed in Same Legislative Day," at 624.

is generally not invoked except in filibuster situations, where, potentially, it could disable a filibuster that was run carelessly. Pursuant to the rule, any time a speaking Senator loses the floor, that ends one of the two speeches. A Senator loses the floor when he leaves the chamber, offers an amendment, or even yields to another Senator (other than for a question), with a resumption counted as a second speech. A tired talker who allows an interruption thus uses up a whole speech. Moreover, the rule limits speeches "on the same legislative day," and by recessing rather than adjourning the Senate, the Majority Leader can make the legislative day last an indefinite number of calendar days.

Seemingly, managers could break talkathons just by letting filibusterers use up their two speeches. However, the two-speech rule only imposes limits on speeches "upon any one question." A Senator can generate different questions, and thus the right to give more speeches, simply by offering an amendment before she resumes talking.[49] Only in some situations is that way of avoiding the rule unavailable, namely when the pending question being stalled is unamendable, such as a conference report.[50]

For the filibusterer, the harder situation occurs when she must not only kill time, but must avoid letting the opposition obtain recognition. This may be to husband speeches against the two-speech rule. More often, the situations when Senators must monopolize the floor are when they must prevent a manager from making some nondebatable motion such as tabling of a prized amendment, or when a manager's call for the

---

[49] "If a Senator has spoken twice on an amendment in the same day, he is entitled to make two additional speeches on an amendment proposed to that amendment, or any different question brought before the Senate, as a motion to recommit." Riddick, "Debate: Speeches Allowed in Same Legislative Day," at 625.

[50] In those situations, filibustering Senators must insist, before allowing interruptions, on unanimous consent that the interruption will not be counted against the two-speech rule, or else they could run out of speeches.

regular order would bring back some undesired business. In these situations, the Senator holding the floor must avoid taking any action that loses the floor, such as calling for a quorum, making a motion or amendment, asking for a vote, or yielding to another Senator for anything but a question.[51]

Basic talkathons press Senators to their physical limits in speaking as long as possible. The record for filibuster length is held by Senator Strom Thurmond (R-S.C.), for a 1957 speech 24 hours and 18 minutes long.[52] Long-term talkers worry not about nourishment, but about exhaustion, since Rule XIX(1)(A) requires a Senator to "rise" (stand) while speaking absent unanimous consent, and the need for an occasional break to answer the call of nature.[53]

A Senator can usually obtain a brief break by yielding to a supportive Senator for a question.[54] In practice such questions are often

---

[51] Riddick, "Debate: Senator Loses Floor," at 621-22," and "Debate: Yielding: Senator forfeits Right to or Loses Floor Under Certain Conditions," at 630-32.

[52] One of the prior record-holders, who talked 18 hours, had faced a particularly difficult time:

> with the temperature over 90 degrees in the chamber, [Robert] La Follette [(R-Wis.)] talked on into the night, fortifying himself with turkey sandwiches and egg nog from the Senate Restaurant. At one point, he took a sip of egg nog and immediately cast it away, exclaiming that it had been drugged. (Subsequent chemical analysis revealed that the amount of ptomaine in the glass would certainly have killed the Wisconsin Senator, but the culprit was never identified.)

127 Cong. Rec. S1929 (daily ed. March 10, 1981).

[53] Riddick, "Debate: Speeches," at 623 (must stand). "Senate rules do not prohibit a Senator from sipping milk during his speech," Riddick, "Debate: Milk While Speaking," at 606, or presumably taking other nourishment.

[54] When a Senator yields for a question, technically he never loses the floor; he needs no unanimous consent to (footnote continued)

cutely framed speeches; when a Senator needs a
break, another begins asking a "question" by
saying something like, "will not the distinguished
Senator agree with me that this bill deserves
defeat because of a, b, c, and so on . . ," and
the filibusterer leaves, returning when the
"questioning" Senator is adding "and x, y, and z,"
at which point the Senator who in theory has held
his right to the floor during this "question"
reclaims the floor and thanks the questioning
Senator for his "thoughtful question" before
resuming.[55]   Yielding for a question does not
constitute a new speech under the two-speech rule,
and the speaking Senator retains her right to the
floor while obtaining a pause.   Under a strict
view of the rules, the Senator holding the floor
cannot leave the chamber during a question,[56] but
that is often overlooked.

One of the most dramatic aspects of
filibusters is the rare night session. In either
precloture or postcloture situations, the

---

retain it.   Riddick, "Debate: Yield for Question Only," at
634-37.   This was firmly established in a 1916 sequence.
Breaking with the historic rule in order to constrain an
active filibuster, the Chair ruled, and the Senate at first
sustained the ruling, that yielding for a question required
unanimous consent.   However, upon reflection, "[s]o stern a
ruling, which might also cut off much of the important
cross-fire of debate, troubled the conservative Senate."
Burdette at 98.   "'[I]f enforced it would reduce the whole
procedure to a series of soliloquies . . . . a funereal
proceeding.'"   Id. (quoting Senator Frank B. Brandegee
(Conn.).   Accordingly, "when many Senators had become
convinced that the value of debate would be seriously
limited if a single objection could prohibit a speaker from
yielding even for a question . . . . the august body
reversed itself, 15 voting for the new interpretation and 35
against it."   Id. at 99.

However, if the filibuster is not polite, upon demands
for the regular order, the Chair will require that the
Senator holding the floor reclaim his time once the
"questioner" actually starts a speech instead of a question.

[55]   Riddick, "Debate: Yield for Question Only," at 634.

[56]   Riddick, "Debate: Yield for Question Only," at 637.

leadership may keep the Senate in late at night without recessing or adjourning. This could be a major effort to break the filibuster by exhausting the filibusterers, or a more focused tactical effort.   At one time, managers succeeded in breaking filibusters through such drawn-out sessions.   For example, in 1954, as liberals filibustered an atomic energy bill:

> [f]or the first time in decades, the Senate [was] held in continuous session -- all day and all night -- in an effort . . . to break [the] filibuster . . . .   For eleven days liberals held the floor in continuous speechmaking. Senate corridors had the look of an overcrowded hospital, with cots and bedding scattered about . . . .
>
> [T]he all-night sessions [took] their toll . . . .[57]

However, the Senate has difficulty breaking a well-organized filibuster by such means, as when night sessions failed to break a filibuster against a civil rights bill in 1960:

> [D]isciplined, determined Southerners under Russell's expert generalship in 1960 were not the scattered, leaderless liberals of 1954.   Working in teams, the Southerners tied the Senate in a knot. They got away with a minimum of talk themselves by demanding quorum calls whenever the Northerners strayed away from the Senate floor for a bit of shut-eye. It often took hours to rout enough sleepy-eyed Northerners out of their beds to make a quorum and resume the debate.   Ironically, it was the filibustering Southerners, dividing the labors in their three-platoon setup, who seemed sleek and rested and the Northerners who were harassed and fatigued.[58]

---

[57]   R. Evans & R. Novak, *supra*, at 90-91.

[58]   Id. at 237.   The Russell system relied upon deploying one "platoon" of filibustering Senators on the floor while (footnote continued)

Since 1960, the Senate has had little stomach for night sessions simply to try to wear out filibusterers, using them primarily during postcloture filibusters such as those described below: the 1976 antitrust, 1977 gas deregulation, 1980 draft registration, 1981-82 antibusing, and 1982 highway gas tax filibusters. The leadership can use night sessions to dramatize that a filibuster is a war in which the rest and time of neutral Senators is the first casualty, warning such Senators they will suffer until the filibuster ends. Nights lay the necessary symbolic and emotional foundation for the leadership to resort to rougher filibuster-breaking tactics -- denials of seconding on yeas and nays, expansive rejection by the Chair of "dilatory" motions and quorum calls, and ultimately some sort of steamroller. A night session simply to run out the clock is possible without exhausting the Senate by scheduling a series of speeches.[59]

However, usually the purpose of the filibuster necessitates that either the filibusterers or managers threaten roll calls or quorum calls during the night, so that the Senators cannot go home. Majority Leader Byrd painted a graphic picture of the preparations for

---

others stayed away and rested. For details of that system, see Berman, supra, at 66. Ultimately, the Senate passed a civil rights bill in 1960, but the successful filibuster forced it to be watered down into meaninglessness.

[59] During the 1980 filibuster by Senator Mark Hatfield (R-Oreg.) of draft registration, the Senate held an all-night session to run out the 100-hour clock under cloture. A small group of Senators on both sides of the issue made successive one-hour speeches all night concerning registration; the Senate stayed in session 33 hours while most Senators went home to sleep. Senator Hatfield accepted the point and graciously conceded, noting in contrast to other filibusters using pure time-wasting tactics, that the night of edifying addresses meant that "the Senate has conducted this debate in a dignified manner, to the credit of the institution of the Senate." 126 Cong. Rec. 14215 (1980). The all-night speeches are at 126 Cong. Rec. 14053-14102 (1980).

such a night session during the 1977 Metzenbaum-Abourezk filibuster:

> Mr. President, apparently there is some doubt or some question on the part of some Members as to whether or not the Senate will be in all night.

> So that there will be no doubt, let me say this: This afternoon . . . I asked the Sergeant at Arms to proceed to make preparations for an all-night session . . . .

> Cots have been set up in room S-207; cots are set up in the Vice President's Ceremonial Room; cots are in the Marble Room; cots are in the lobby or will be soon; there are cots in the Senate gym which, incidentally, is another good use of the Senate gym.

> The gym will be open all night, and blankets and pillows have been supplied by the Army and the Air Force. I hope that there is no Doubting Thomas left among us.

> I look upon an all-night session with about as much joy and comfort as does any other Senator here.[60]

There was even less confidence in attempts to forcefully break filibusters after that 1977 filibuster than before. Robert "Dove, an assistant parliamentarian at the time, says Metzenbaum and Abourezk were successful enough that leaders really have not forced confrontations of the classic sort since."[61]

Procedure for Cloture Petition

Since talkathons cannot be readily broken by

---

[60]   123 Cong. Rec. 31233 (1977).

[61]   Calmes, "Trivialized" Filibuster is Still a Potent Tool, 45 Cong. Q. Week. Rep. 2115, 2117 (1987).

waiting or trying to exhaust the filibusterers, managers must turn to cloture. The cloture process begins with the filing of a written motion, which may be referred to as the cloture petition. Rule XXII(2) provides in part:

> . . . . at any time a motion signed by sixteen Senators, to bring to a close the debate upon any measure, motion, other matter pending before the Senate, or the unfinished business, is presented to the Senate, the Presiding Officer, or clerk at the direction of the Presiding Officer, shall at once state the motion to the Senate . . . .

The motion's noteworthy characteristic is that it "may be presented at any time, and a Senator who has the floor may be interrupted for such purpose."[62] It is one of the very few means by which a Senator monopolizing the floor can be interrupted without his consent, and the interruption for the filing of the cloture petition, although brief, symbolizes the test about to occur of the right of unlimited debate.

Any Senator can present a cloture petition, although Majority Leader Byrd, by making a point of presenting them himself, took the record for filing such petitions.[63] Rule XXII imposes two requirements to present a cloture motion. It requires sufficient signatures ("a motion signed by sixteen Senators"), and a "pending" matter (the motion is "to bring to a close the debate upon any measure, motion, other matter pending before the Senate, or the unfinished business") (emphasis supplied). In demanding 16 signatures, the rule does not impose a high threshhold, considering that the cloture petitioner will have to find 60 votes to obtain cloture.

---

[62]   Riddick, "Cloture Procedure: Motions -- Signing and Presentation of:" at 253.

[63]   "By 1987, Byrd bragged of his records for sponsoring cloture motions. As a party leader since 1971, first as whip and then as leader, Byrd had offered 67 of the 253 cloture motions voted on -- just over one-fourth of the total." 1987 Congressional Quarterly Almanac 51.

Managers often choose to make the petition a political statement, hoping to influence the vote on cloture, not by its wording -- it is invariably a one-paragraph statement tracking Rule XXII's language -- but by the choice of cosigners, much like the choice of cosponsors of a bill. The manager can sign up many cosignors, rather than just 16, and can look for bipartisan, eminent, and above all leadership support.[64] Of course, the leadership cannot necessarily deliver cloture. In 1984, Majority Leader Howard Baker could only muster 37 votes for cloture in his effort to open the Senate to televising, while opponents presented 44 in opposition.[65]

A subtler requirement is that the question must be "pending." When time is short, filibusterers may filibuster on some extraneous matter, or otherwise prevent the real bill or amendment of interest from becoming the pending question.[66] This is one of those situations where the filibusterer must monopolize the floor without yielding, for as soon as the filibusterer loses the floor, and the manager obtains recognition, the manager can move to proceed to the matter on which to file a cloture petition.[67]

---

[64] The petition for the 1964 civil rights bill that was the first time the Senate ever voted cloture on a civil rights bill used all these approaches: "[t]he actual petition for cloture, [was] signed by a bipartisan group of 39 members, [and] was filed by [Majority Leader] Mansfield and [Minority Leader] Dirksen . . . ." D. M. Berman, supra, at 80.

[65] S. Prt. 98-254, at 47.

[66] A prime example of such a stall was Senator John East's (R-N.C.) filibuster in 1982 of a continuing resolution, to prevent the Senate from completing it and getting back to the real target of his filibuster, the highway gas tax bill. 1982 Congressional Quarterly Almanac 327-28.

Of course, the managers could first obtain cloture on the subject of that premature talkathon, dispose of that subject, and then move toward the subject of interest, but that is quite a long way around.

[67] For example, on August 27, 1976, Senator Allen sought (footnote continued)

In drafting the cloture motion, the manager may have a tactical choice about what to make the "pending question," for when a bill and amendments are pending, the cloture motion could name as the pending question either the bill, or one of the amendments.   This tactical choice can matter a great deal.   For example, during the Weicker filibuster against antibusing legislation in 1981, the Senate rejected Senator Jesse Helm's (R-N.C.) first cloture motion by the overwhelming vote of 48 against cloture and only 38 for.   Senator Helms had filed a cloture motion naming the bill as the pending question.   In contrast to the overwhelming vote against the Helms cloture motion, the next cloture motion voted on July 13 named the Johnston amendment as the pending question, and it received a vote of only 32 against and 54 for.[68]

Once the cloture motion has been filed and stated to the Senate, Rule XXII(2) lays down a strict timetable:

---

recognition to demand the reading of a Senate antitrust bill that had returned from the House with a House amendment. However, with a filibuster in the offing, Majority Whip Byrd wanted the pending question to be, not the House amendment, but a Senate substitute.   The Majority Whip obtained recognition to offer the substitute, and immediately Majority Leader Mansfield filed a cloture petition on the (pending) substitute;   only then was Senator Allen recognized.   "Allen, Roman L. Hruska (R Neb.) and other opponents of the bill, protest[ed] that their rights had been violated by this procedure," 1976 Congressional Quarterly Almanac 437, but it was too late.

[68]   Cohodas, DOJ Measure Laid Aside After Senate Fails to End a Month-Old Filibuster, 40 Cong. Q. Week. Rep. 1290 (1981).   Senator Bennett Johnston (D-La.) had offered his very strong antibusing amendment (the "Neighborhood Schools Act") as an amendment in the second degree and so "[t]he [Helms] cloture motion was opposed both by liberals supporting Weicker and by senators who favor Johnston's stiffer proposal.   The latter feared adoption of this particular cloture motion would bar further consideration of the Louisiana Democrat's amendment, which the Senate parliamentarian was expected to rule non-germane to [the bill]." Senate Fails to Halt Anti-Busing Filibuster, 40 Cong. Q. Week. Rep. 1254 (1981).

> one hour after the Senate meets on the
> following calendar day but one, [the
> presiding officer] shall lay the motion
> before the Senate and direct that the clerk
> call the roll, and upon the ascertainment
> that a quorum is present, the Presiding
> Officer shall, without debate, submit to the
> Senate by a yea-and-nay vote the question:

> "Is it the sense of the Senate that the
> debate shall be brought to a close?"

This two-day timetable counts calendar days, not legislative days, so a cloture petition comes to a vote quickly.[69]   In fact, some time on the day after the filing of the cloture petition, a Majority Leader in a rush can recess the Senate to reconvene for a "new" day around 1:00 a.m. that night, and then have a cloture vote immediately thereafter, because technically 1:00 a.m. can be the start of a new calendar day.[70]

During the two days after filing of the motion, Senators have much to do. Rule XXII requires that they submit any amendments during that time that they will offer after cloture is voted:

> Except by unanimous consent, no amendments
> shall be proposed after the vote to bring the
> debate to a close, unless it had been
> submitted in writing to the Journal Clerk by
> 1 o'clock p.m. on the day following the

---

[69]   If the Senate stays in session after midnight, it is still reckoned to be in the original calendar day for purposes of this rule; when a Wednesday session runs past midnight, cloture filed after midnight (such as at 2:00 a.m. Thursday) still gets voted on Friday.

[70]   For example, if the petition is filed Monday, on Tuesday night the Majority Leader can keep the Senate in until 11:00 p.m., recess it for two hours, reconvene at 1:00 a.m. Wednesday morning, and have a cloture vote at 2:00 a.m. -- not a fun schedule, but one that starts the clock for cloture running early. The Senate must recess before reconvening; if it does not recess, technically it stays in same calendar day even after midnight.

> filing of the cloture motion if an amendment
> in the first degree, and unless it had been
> so submitted at least one hour prior to the
> beginning of the cloture vote if an amendment
> in the second degree.

Thus, Senators planning serious amendments must finish drafting the amendments and submit them on that schedule. If Senators plan a postcloture filibuster, they may submit hundreds of amendments at this time, and the drafting of these amendments requires care, as discussed below.

Quite commonly, after the filing of the cloture petition on the then-pending question, the Senate turns to other questions until the vote on that petition. The Senate need not take any steps to get back to that previously pending question; Rule XXII makes it recur automatically at the appointed hour. Sometimes high drama will occur during the one hour preceding the quorum call and the cloture vote, as the protagonists in the filibuster make their plea to the Senate, often pursuant to a time agreement formally dividing the hour. Alternatively, the hour can be used for ordinary business, or that hour and the quorum call can be rearranged or foregone by unanimous consent, since the frequency of cloture votes after the 1960s makes many of them rather mundane.

More than one cloture petition may be pending at the same time, as in the Grove City filibuster, when the Senate scheduled six cloture votes in two days. Managers sometimes file cloture motions on more than one matter, requiring complex scheduling.[72] Also, managers may have to file

---

[71] Riddick, "Cloture: Hour Preceding Time for Vote on Cloture Motion," at 252.

[72] If two cloture motions are filed the same day on different matters, both are due for a vote an hour after the Senate convenes two days later. The procedure then is for the Senate to vote first on the first-filed motion. If the Senate adopts the first-filed motion, it puts the second-filed motion off until disposing of the question pending under the first-filed one; if the Senate rejects the first-filed motion, it votes immediately on the second-filed motion. 129 Cong. Rec. S10354 (daily ed. 1983).

several extra cloture petitions on the same matter
before they obtain cloture. Often they file extra
ones even before the vote on the first one, to
avoid waiting two days after a first vote for a
second one.[73] Use of multiple cloture petitions,
whether simultaneous or separated in time,
represents a practice starting in the 1970s. As
Senate Parliamentarian Emeritus Floyd M. Riddick
explained, under Majority Leader Mansfield the
practice began "that you would keep on trying, as
long as you felt there was a chance, or as long as
you felt it was necessary to convince the country
that you were trying to bring the issue before the
Senate so as to get a vote."[74] In 1987, Senate
Democrats set a record of "seven efforts to invoke
cloture -- the most ever attempted on a single
question," without ending the Republican
filibuster on campaign finance legislation.[75]

Rule XXII specifies the vote requirement for
cloture: "that question [of cloture] [must] be
decided in the affirmative by three-fifths of the
Senators duly chosen and sworn -- except on a
measure or motion to amend the Senate rules, in
which case the necessary affirmative vote shall be
two-thirds of the Senators present and voting
. . . ." The historic dynamics that have led to
the pattern of relatively frequent filibusters and
cloture votes has made it relatively easy to
obtain the 60 needed votes, at least compared to
the pre-1975 and especially the pre-1970 period.
Reluctant Senators still prefer to wait until
after some debate on an issue, or the second or
later petition, before voting for cloture.

However, often even the Senators who oppose
an amendment or bill on its substantive merits
will vote for cloture on it after some debate, in
recognition of the need for the Senate to finish

---

[73]   Alternatively, the Senate can reconsider a vote that
rejects cloture, and upon reconsideration vote in favor of
the motion, as a simple way to get a second vote. 126 Cong.
Rec. S15666 (daily ed. December 5, 1980).

[74]   Riddick is quoted in Calmes, "Trivialized" Filibuster is
Still a Potent Tool, 45 Cong. Q. Week. Rep. 2120 (1987).

[75]   1987 Congressional Quarterly Almanac 13.

its business. This is illustrated by such cloture votes as 70-17 for cloture during the Metzenbaum-Abourezk natural gas filibuster, or 87-8 for cloture during the Helms-East highway gas tax filibuster.   In both cases, far more Senators voted for cloture than later voted for the underlying substantive propositions.

Cloture: Pending Question and Time Limits

Cloture does not impose a simple or drastic end of debate like the House's motion for the pending question. Rather, it applies a set of limits, each with its complex aspects, intended not to cut off debate immediately, but to control it, focus it, and move it toward an end. Cloture imposes three main types of limits: fixing the pending question, time limits, and restraints on amendments and motions. Each will be discussed separately.

Starting with the first, Rule XXII prescribes that once the Senate votes cloture on a pending measure, "then said measure . . . pending before the Senate, or the unfinished business, shall be the unfinished business to the exclusion of all other business until disposed of." This contrasts sharply with the normal agenda-governing Senate practice prior to (and absent) cloture, under which opponents could stall one matter by making something else the pending business.[76]   The

---

[76] Normally, although the Senate continues on the pending or unfinished business after every recess or adjournment, at any time a majority vote to proceed to another bill can displace the pending business, sending it back to the Calendar. Thus, normally, opponents can try to fight a bill by moving to proceed to some other bill instead, for by such a motion, opponents can form a coalition with the supporters of that other bill and obtain a majority in that fashion. This was one of the southern Democrats' successful moves in the great 1890-91 "Force Bill" filibuster: after the bill came up, they formed a coalition with populist pro-silver western Republicans to move to proceed to a bill for free coinage of silver.   The motion carried, and silver deliberations diverted the Senate from January 5 to January 14, before it came back to the Force Bill. See Burdette at (footnote continued)

cloture rule prevents such displacement, as the Senate can leave the clotured business (to do something else) only by unanimous consent.[77]

This aspect of cloture complicates the regular agenda-handling routines of the Senate leadership, who can normally glide smoothly from one matter to another by motion to proceed even absent unanimous consent. In fact, cloture on one bill can be used as a weapon against another, particularly in the last days of a session. For example, in 1981, on the eve of adjournment, cloture on the Helms-Johnston busing amendment prevented the Senate from getting on with congressional veto of the Federal Trade Commission's used car rule.[78] This creates pressure for the Senate to complete the clotured matter.[79] Otherwise, to get other business done,

---

53-54; D. J. Rothman, Politics and Power: The United States Senate 1869-1901 100-101 (1966).

[77] As the Chair noted after cloture had been voted in 1982 on the highway gas tax: "The Senate is operating under cloture at the present time. Under those circumstances it requires unanimous consent to consider any other measure." 128 Cong. Rec. S15753 (Dec. 20, 1982).

[78] As Majority Leader Baker explained: "By reason of a unanimous consent agreement that was entered into a few days ago, the provisions of rule XXII, postcloture in respect to any bill, would not prevent us from proceeding to certain listed items, and the legislative veto item on used car dealers is not one of that listed group." 127 Cong. Rec. S15066 (daily ed. Dec. 11, 1981). In an early example, cloture on a 1920s bill to enforce Prohibition blocked another filibustered matter, a partisan investigation of campaign practices. Burdette at 154-55.

[79] For example, in 1982, Senators pressured Senator Helms to finish his filibuster of the highway gas tax by denying the necessary unanimous consent to bring up another bill, the PIK (payment-in-kind) bill, a bill doubly vital to Senator Helms as chair of the Agriculture Committee and as a farm-state Senator. See 128 Cong. Rec. S15753 (daily ed. Dec. 20, 1982) (Senator Paul Tsongas (D-Mass.) ("I shall state, as someone who has been here unnecessarily for 4 days, that . . . . I will stay to object [to going by unanimous consent to PIK] as long as is necessary").

the leadership must arrange UCAs as it did during the 1988 cloture on the death penalty bill for drug-related killings.[80]

Rule XXII imposes time limits of two kinds, which are its most important limits. First, it imposes a limit of one hour on how long individual Senators can debate. The rule provides that after the Senate votes cloture,

> no Senator shall be entitled to speak in all more than one hour on the measure, motion, or other matter pending before the Senate, or the unfinished business, the amendments thereto, and motions affecting the same, and it shall be the duty of the Presiding Officer to keep the time of each Senator who speaks.[81]

That one-hour limit applies no matter what subject the filibustering Senators talk about, and "all time is charged to the Senator having the floor, even if he yields for an interruption," and even if he yields for a question.[82] On the other

---

[80] One UCA laid the death penalty bill temporarily aside for a conference reports on polygraphing and on rail safety and on an El Salvador resolution. See 134 Cong. Rec. S7502 (daily ed. 1988).

[81] The single exception by which a Senator gets more than one hour is a provision allowing Senators to yield time to the leaders or managers, who can yield time to others. Rule XXII states:

> Notwithstanding other provisions of this rule, a Senator may yield all or part of his one hour to the majority or minority floor managers of the measure, motion, or matter or to the Majority or Minority Leader, but each Senator specified shall not have more than two hours so yielded to him and may in turn yield such time to other Senators.

Only leaders and managers can yield time to others (except by unanimous consent). 130 Cong. Rec. S11130 (daily ed. Sept. 13, 1984). This prevents Senators sympathetic to the filibuster from strengthening its hand by yielding their hour to the filibusterer.
(footnote continued)

hand, it does not apply to time used in calling up an amendment for a roll-call vote or demanding a quorum call.[83]   Thus, the heart of postcloture tactics consists of taking actions, such as demanding roll-call votes and quorum calls, that do not take time out of the brief hour of each filibustering Senator.

Besides the one-hour limit on each Senator, the Senate has an overall time limit on proceedings.   The cap began in 1979, when the Senate set it at 100 hours; in 1986, the Senate shortened it to 30 hours.   Rule XXII provides: "After no more than thirty hours of consideration of the measure, motion, or other matter on which cloture has been invoked, the Senate shall proceed, without any further debate on any question, to vote on the final disposition thereof . . . ."   Unlike the one-hour limit, this cap includes all actions that take up time: "the time used for quorum calls, rollcall votes, reading of amendments, parliamentary inquiries, points of order, and the like is charged against the [overall cap]."[84]

During the period when the Senate set the cap

---

[82]   Riddick, "Cloture Procedure: Debate," at 244, and "Cloture Procedure: Debate and Yielding," at 246.   Thus, the filibustering Senator rations his debate time sparingly, insisting when he yields for a question or otherwise that by unanimous consent the time be charged to the other Senator.

[83]   Riddick, "Cloture Procedure: Amendments After Cloture: Senators Time Exhausted -- Call Up Amendment," at 240; "Cloture Procedure: Debate," at 245.

[84]   Riddick, "Cloture Procedure: Debate," at 244.

The two caps stay quite separate.   Individuals Senators cannot shorten the overall cap by yielding back their own individual hours, and time may be charged against the overall cap while not being charged against any particular Senator's hour.   The leadership often provides for such charging, by unanimous consent, for such matters as procedural debates of significance, or short recesses, so as to keep the clock running on the overall cap while not depleting the hour of individual Senators whose cooperation they seek on these matters.

at 100 hours, it never once ran out the full 100 hours, so while Rule XXII provides an elaborate end-game for what happens when the clock runs out, that has never actually occurred.[85]   With a 30-hour cap, running the clock became more feasible.   A significant consideration became how many successive 30-hour cloture periods might be needed to end of filibuster.   Separate filibusters may be required on the motion to proceed to the bill; on the bill (and on any non-germane amendments that must be added); on the motions leading up to conference; and on the conference report.   These separate cloture periods provide more complex postcloture scenarios, as discussed below.[86]

---

[85]   Rule XXII provides that when the time runs out, the Senate proceeds to final disposition:

> to the exclusion of all amendments not then actually pending before the Senate at that time and to the exclusion of all motions, except a motion to table, or to reconsider and one quorum call on demand to establish the presence of a quorum (and motions required to establish a quorum) immediately before the final vote begins.

Rule XXII also covers the possiblity that some Senators will use up the overall cap before each Senator has a chance to speak even briefly, by guaranteeing such a brief time: "Notwithstanding any other provision of this rule, any Senator who has not used or yielded at least ten minutes, is, if he seeks recognition, guaranteed up to ten minutes, inclusive, to speak only."

[86]   Conversely, Rule XXII allows a motion to extend the cap.   Rule XXII provides:

> The thirty hours may be increased by the adoption of a motion, decided without debate, by a three-fifths affirmative vote of the Senators duly chosen and sworn, and any such time thus agreed upon shall be equally divided between and controlled by the Majority and Minority Leaders or their designees. However, only one motion to extend time, specified above, may be made in any calendar day.

(footnote continued)

Germaneness of Amendments

As its third limit besides the pending question and time limits, the cloture rule imposes germaneness on amendments. Rule XXII states that "[n]o . . . amendment not germane shall be in order." That rule is strictly kept. Even committee amendments will be ruled out of order if non-germane. Even prior listing of an amendment in a unanimous consent agreement, which satisfies the germaneness restriction imposed by the UCA itself, does not make a non-germane amendment in order under cloture.[87]

The Grove City filibuster in 1984 taught the enormous significance of this rule. When the Senate appeared on the verge of voting to reverse the Chair's ruling that the anti-gun control amendment was out of order as non-germane, Senator John Chafee (R-R.I.) commented that "we are quite simply adopting 'cloture by 51 percent.'"[88] Cloture by 51 percent would occur because as soon as the Senate adopted cloture on any measure, 51 percent of the Senate could subject any other measure to cloture by offering that other measure as a non-germane amendment to the clotured measure, thereby bringing it within cloture.[89]

No such motion has ever been adopted, but with the basic cap so short, occasional extension by motion or unanimous consent agreement becomes a possibility, much as the Senate has extended the statutory cap on consideration of some budget matters.

[87]   129 Cong. Rec. S1807 (daily ed. March 1, 1983).

[88]   130 Cong. Rec. S12512 (daily ed. Oct. 1, 1984).

[89]   Senator Chafee described:

When we are in a situation when cloture is invoked, and someone comes along with a totally nongermane amendment, the Chair rules it is nongermane, the appeal is taken to the ruling of the Chair, 51 Senators vote that it is germane, the matter then comes up for consideration, and because cloture has been invoked, the matter no longer can be debated beyond the

(footnote continued)

Actually, the Senate has casually[90] bent that rule

> postcloture limit of 100 hours and 51 Senators can go
> on and approve it.
>
> .... If that is indeed the situation why would any
> Senator ever again vote for cloture[?] .... I for
> one, if this is the way it is going to be, would find
> it extraordinary were I ever to vote for cloture again.
> ...

Id. Minority Leader Byrd echoed that if

> these new precedents are nailed down, then, Mr.
> President, it can rightly be said that the most
> destructive procedural votes that have occurred in my
> 26 years in the Senate, with respect to clotured
> matters and postcloture filibusters, will have taken
> place. . . . We shall have made a shell out of rule
> XXII. . . . So the heck with rule XXII.

Id. at S12513. Since unanimous consent agreements also
impose time limits and a germaneness rule, the Minority
Leader later added that if the new precedent was
established, "[t]hose time agreements will not be worth, as
I say from time to time, a hill of beans." Id. at S12520
(daily ed. Oct. 1, 1984).

[90] The casual occasions were during the 1980 Hatfield
filibuster of the draft registration bill. Twice, the
Senate simply reversed rulings by the Chair rulings that
certain amendments were non-germane, despite Majority Leader
Byrd's warnings. This action does not seem to have been
regarded as a precedent for any general weakening of the
germaneness rule for cloture, but an ad hoc adaptation to
particular amendments that seemed relevant although
technically non-germane. 126 Cong. Rec. 13868 (1980) (Byrd
warnings); id. 13869 (vote to overrule the Chair); id. 13877
(vote to overrule the Chair on another amendment). In
particular, the second amendment, Senator Nancy Kassebaum's
(R-Kans.) amendment for registration of women, seemed
relevant although technically non-germane.

Interestingly, although the Senate allowed that
amendment to be offered despite its non-germaneness, it
rejected the amendment, id. 13898, showing that whatever it
was doing, it was not breaking the germaneness rule just to
enact some favored proposition. The Senate also overruled a
(footnote continued)

on occasion, and even did so deliberately once in 1982.[91]

Since the Senate lacks a general rule of germaneness, or any method other than cloture for imposing germaneness apart from unanimous consent, it occasionally uses the cloture rule just to impose germaneness selectively on a measure, as in a 1978 tax bill, and a 1980 antitrust exemption bill.[92]   Senator Byrd has proposed the creation of

---

ruling of the Chair on germaneness under cloture in 1968. Riddick, "Cloture Procedure: Germaneness of Amendments under Cloture," at 237.

[91]   During consideration under cloture of a supplemental appropriation bill, when Senator Richard Lugar (R-Ind.) offered a non-germane amendment subsidizing mortgage interest rates. The leadership worried that the amendment's adoption:

> would set a bad precedent by weakening the cloture rule against extraneous amendments.
>
> Instead, Lugar moved to suspend the germaneness rule, a procedure requiring a two-thirds majority. His motion -- the key procedural vote -- was agreed to, 63-27 . . . .
>
> In agreeing to Lugar's motion, the Senate made parliamentary history. It was the first time since the cloture rule was adopted in 1917 that the Senate had voted to suspend the rule prohibiting non-germane amendments after cloture had been invoked.

1982 Congressional Quarterly Almanac 209. Using suspension of the rules resembled the time-honored technique of using suspension of the rules to allow non-germane amendments on appropriation bills (which also, like clotured bills, have a requirement of germaneness for amendments).   Riddick, "Suspension of Rules: Amendments to Appropriations Bills, Suspension of Rules for:" at 1026-28.

[92]   "[T]he miscellaneous amendments [to the tax bill] were abruptly cleared away, Oct. 29, when the Senate approved, 62-28, a motion by Majority Leader Robert C. Byrd, D-W. Va., invoking cloture. Under cloture, which required the votes of 60 senators, 'non-germane' amendments can't be considered." 1978 Congressional Quarterly Almanac 240; 1980 (footnote continued)

a motion by which the Senate would specifically impose germaneness on a measure by three-fifths vote without the other aspects of cloture.[93]

C.   AFTER 1976: ANATOMY OF FIVE KEY FILIBUSTERS

The more complex procedural developments since the 1975 rules change -- particularly the rise of the postcloture filibuster -- can best be depicted by describing the five key filibusters of the following decade.

1976-77: Birth of the Postcloture Filibuster

In 1976, Senator Allen inaugurated the post-cloture filibuster, either in reaction to the 1975 reduction in the cloture requirement, or to political changes. On May 27, 1976, consideration of an antitrust bill, the Hart-Scott-Rodino bill, began, and on June 3, the Senate voted cloture by 67-22.[94] As Congressional Quarterly described the ensuing proceedings:

> Opponents proceeded to offer amendments, demanding roll-call votes and frequently using the parliamentary tactic of voting with the majority in order to be eligible to demand reconsideration of a vote. Many of the 70 roll-call votes on the bill came on

---

Congressional Quarterly Almanac 381 (antitrust exemption bill protected from non-germane amendment to expand consumer antitrust rights).

[93] In 1984, a select committee headed by Senator Dan Quayle (R-Ind.) endorsed Minority Leader Byrd's proposal: "One way to preserve the protection that non-germane amendments give, while protecting the ability of the Senate to conduct its business, is to provide for a special germaneness rule, invoked by 60% of those present and voting." S. Prt. No. 98-254 at 15. The committee print describes the history of Senator Byrd's proposal. Id. at 41-44 (reprinting study by Walter Oleszek of the Congressional Research Service).

[94] 122 Cong. Rec. 16472 (1976).

motions to table motions to reconsider votes,
motions to table amendments and motions to
round up absent senators after a quorum call
had failed.[95]

Senator Allen also made motions to adjourn and to
recess, and required roll-call votes on the
leadership's motions to recess and on tabling
appeals from the Chair's rulings.[96]
On June 10, this phase of the filibuster
ended, with agreement on a compromise on the bill
between supporters and opponents.[97]   A second
filibuster phase also ended when Majority Whip
Byrd made a sharp threat to have the remaining
motions and amendments ruled out of order as
dilatory,[98] a precedent Senator Allen did not want

---

[95]   1976 Congressional Quarterly Almanac 434.

[96]   122 Cong. Rec. 16707 (1976) (June 4; motion to adjourn,
no roll call); id. at 16820 (June 7 motion to recess, roll
call); id. at 16844 (June 7 motion to recess, roll call);
id. at 17274 (June 9 roll call on tabling appeal).

After some time of this, Majority Leader Mansfield
summed up proceedings thusly:

> Mr. President, we have been considering the antitrust
> bill for 9 days . . . . We have had 54 votes on this
> bill. We have voted on 12 amendments, 18 motions to
> table amendments, 8 motions to table motions to
> reconsider previous votes, 2 motions to reconsider
> previous votes, 1 motion to table an appeal of a ruling
> of the Chair, 7 motions to instruct the Sergeant at
> Arms to request the attendance of absent Senators, 4
> motions to recess or adjourn, and 1 cloture motion.

122 Cong. Rec. 17275 (1976).

[97]   1976 Congressional Quarterly Almanac 434-35.

[98]   When the bill came back from the House on August 27 with
a request for a conference, which the Senate ordinarily
agrees to immediately by unanimous consent, Senator Allen
and others "filed more than 100 amendments that they
intended to offer after cloture was invoked."   1976
Congressional Quarterly Almanac 437.   On August 31, the
(footnote continued)

to see established.

The next postcloture filibuster was not long in coming. When the Senate took up President Carter's comprehensive energy program, supporters of natural gas price regulation, led by Senators Howard Metzenbaum (D-Ohio) and James Abourezk (D-S.D.), filibustered against deregulation. The Senate voted for cloture on its first cloture vote, by 77-17, and Senators Abourezk and Metzenbaum then resorted to post-cloture tactics. As Congressional Quarterly described:

> Metzenbaum and Abourezk began calling up an arsenal of amendments they had filed before the cloture vote, demanding time consuming roll-call votes on each one. They also insisted at every opportunity that a quorum was not present, forcing a halt to action until 51 senators could be rounded up.
>
> They objected to virtually every routine unanimous consent request . . . .
>
> They sometimes forced two roll calls on a single amendment . . . . [by] often insist[ing] that motions to reconsider votes had to be decided themselves by roll-call votes.[99]

Majority Leader Byrd noted that "I am informed that there are more than 500 amendments at the desk . . . . I hope that Senators understand that we are in a very difficult situation."[100] Other Senators joined in

---

Senate voted cloture 63-27, and the postcloture filibuster began again, with insistence on reading of amendments and 13 postcloture roll calls late into the evening. Id. The Byrd threat is at 122 Cong. Rec. 28597 (1976).

[99] 1977 Congressional Quarterly Almanac at 735.

[100] 123 Cong. Rec. 30810 (1977). The session continued with roll-call votes until late in the evening. On the second day of cloture, September 27, Majority Leader Byrd could state:

(footnote continued)

expressions of amazement or horror at the tactics.[101] Senator Abourezk responded:

> [T]he Senate rules were devised to allow
> Senators to object. If there is only one man
> who wants to object, the rule allows him to
> object as long as he is physically able to do
> so . . . .
>
> All kinds of peer pressure is put on
> one . . . . But I hope [the Senators]
> understand that some day . . . they will have
> an issue that strikes them, that grabs them
> so hard, about which they will feel so
> strongly, that they might want to do the same
> thing.[102]

The Majority Leader tried an all-night session, the first since the early 1960s. As Minority Leader Howard Baker afterwards described the "torture" of that night session: "we have gone through a torture that the Senate has seldom encountered, including not just an all-night session, but an all-night session that was unique and different from others, as we all painfully know, because the rollcalls and quorum calls came at 15, 30, and 45-minute intervals."[103] Daytime

---

> Today is our eighth day of deliberations . . . .
> Yesterday, there were 18 rollcall votes, not counting
> the vote on the treaties. That is a total of 270
> minutes spent on rollcall votes alone . . . . .
>
> I have heard it said that every amendment will be
> called up, and I have heard it said that the Senate
> will go on for weeks. I have heard it said that we may
> go on for 3 months.

123 Cong. Rec. 31151-52 (1977) (some paragraphing omitted).

[101] Senator Warren Magnuson (D-Wash.), dean of the Senate, commented that Minority Leader Baker had "said he had been here 11 years and he has never seen a situation like this before. I have been in the Senate 31 years and I have not seen it." 123 Cong. Rec. 31153 (1977).

[102] 123 Cong. Rec. 31154 (1977).

(footnote continued)

postcloture filibustering continued on September 27, 28, 29, 30, and Saturday, October 1.   The Senate set many precedents against postcloture filibusterers, holding to be out of order as dilatory certain kinds of quorum calls, amendments, motions, and even appeals from the Chair's rulings, but it did not rule these out of order wholesale and so the filibuster continued.[104]

Ultimately, leadership discussions prepared for a dramatic move on Monday, October 3.   With Vice President Walter Mondale in the chair, the Majority Leader established the precedent that, instead of Members having to make points of order from the floor for each amendment not in order, the Chair would announce amendments out of order as soon as they were called up.[105]   Then:

---

[103]   123 Cong. Rec. 31466 (1977).   Senators could get no sleep, or only sleep repeatedly interrupted, because they were awakened for votes and quorum calls, rather than just sleeping through night speeches.

[104]   See 123 Cong. Rec. 30818 (1977) (request for a quorum call held to be dilatory); id. 30824-25 (Chair ruled an amendment out of order; its ruling was sustained on appeal; a motion to reconsider the vote on the appeal was ruled by the Chair to be dilatory; an appeal from that ruling was ruled by the Chair also to be dilatory); id. 31238 (Majority Leader Byrd brings out old precedents supporting the Chair counting quorums); id. 31242 (points of order can be made against amendments before their reading is done); id. 31244 (amendments can be out of order as amending the bill in more than one place, simply for stating that upon insertion of the proposed language as a new section, the other sections of the bill should be renumbered accordingly); id. 31587 (point of order that a quorum is not present is held dilatory, even though there had been intervening business since the prior ascertainment of a quorum); id. 31590 (again, quorum call held dilatory).

[105]   The point of order was that "when the Senate is operating under cloture the Chair is required to take the initiative under rule XXII to rule out of order all amendments which are dilatory or which on their face are out of order." 123 Cong. Rec. 31916 (1977).   Vice President Mondale upheld the Majority Leader's point of order, and the Senate tabled an appeal from the ruling. Id.

[i]n mid-afternoon, the new powers to shut off delays were employed with devastating effectiveness.

Mondale, responding to points of order from Byrd and Majority Whip Alan Cranston (D Calif.), overrode Abourezk's requests for quorum calls and a division vote. As Abourezk sought to make a point of order, Byrd called up an amendment:

"Mr. President, I call up amendment number eight-nine-oh," Byrd yelled, rapid-fire.

"The amendment is not in order . . . ." Mondale answered immediately.

"Mr. President, I call up amendment number eight-nine-eight," Byrd shouted. "The amendment is not in order . . . ." Mondale answered back.

Abourezk tried repeatedly to cut in, but was ignored. Byrd, yelling, rattled off each amendment like an auctioneer unleashing a machine-gun spiel, and as each was called, Mondale pronounced the amendment's death.

"Mr. President, I make the point of order that this is a steamroller," Abourezk bellowed, and, ignored, turned his back to return to his seat.

Other senators were on their feet, obviously shocked . . . .

But Mondale recognized only Byrd, over and over again. The "steamroller" lasted less than 10 minutes, but 33 amendments were killed.

At length, Sarbanes managed to gain recognition. He asked why there had been no appeals allowed. Mondale explained he was following Senate custom which requires the presiding officer to recognize party leaders when they are among several senators contesting for recognition.[106]

There ensued one of the fiercest procedural debates in the modern Senate. Opponents of the Majority Leader's move charged it was "fraught with danger," "a change in the rules," "an outrageous act," and "in effect, to establish a dictatorship in the Senate."[107] They contended that by monopolizing recognition, the Majority Leader effectively denied the sacred right of Senators to appeal the Chair's rulings.[108] Shocked Senators threatened to make a point of order directly impugning the correctness of the Majority Leader's actions.[109] Majority Leader Byrd responded with an uncharacteristically intense speech:

> We have heard talk about the abuse by the leadership of its prerogatives . . . . I have tried in every possible way available to me to get the Senate to come down to a resolution of the issue, and my words and pleadings have fallen upon deaf ears.

> Now it came to the point that we saw we could not reason with a handful of filibusterers . . . . Time and time and time and time again, over the years, I have been the spear carrier, in fighting this able and honorable man, [Senator Allen] . . . . for those who are seeking to get the Senate to

---

[106]   1977 *Congressional Quarterly Almanac* 737. The Byrd-Mondale actions are at 123 Cong. Rec. 31927-28 (1977).

[107]   123 Cong. Rec. 31919 (1977).

[108]   The Senate had recently explicitly ruled, by 71-9, that appeals were not dilatory. In fact, the Majority Leader had stated when making his earlier points of order that they would not deny Senators an appeal. In the debate on his point of order concerning the Chair ruling amendments out of order on its own initiative, Senator Byrd had affimed that "the right to appeal . . . is not touched in this point of order, Senators may still appeal . . . . An appeal can be taken. I am leaving open the appeal."

[109]   *Id.* 31917.

take action now to denigrate me.

. . . . I carried the scars, and I
still carry those scars.

. . . . I, in this instance, took
extraordinary advantage of my prerogative as
leader to be recognized. One has to fight
fire with fire when all else fails.

[Applause, Senators rising.][110]

Shortly thereafter, Senators Metzenbaum and
Abourezk abandoned their filibuster, but while
that specific postcloture filibuster had been
broken, the leadership's tactics could not be
repeated except in extraordinary situations.
Conservatives showed thereafter that they could
delay bills and win compromises by introducing
hundreds of amendments and implying each would be
called up even if cloture were invoked, a
significant brake for several years on the whole
course of national government.[111]

By 1979, the Senate majority backed a rules
change. On the first day of the 96th Congress,
Majority Leader Byrd filed a resolution proposing
a 100-hour cap on proceedings under cloture, plus
some other changes in cloture and noncloture
rules, starting off lengthy negotiations.[112]

---

[110] 123 Cong. Rec. 31930-31 (1977). As Congressional
Quarterly observed -- and its version is stronger even than
the Congressional Record's, such as quoting Byrd as saying
"My words have fallen upon deaf ears! Deaf ears!" The
magazine noted: "There was more, but at length, Byrd's
oration was over. It was all the more stunning because it
was wrenched from a man who normally is a study in self-
control, a master of calculation who -- usually -- weighs
every word before its utterance." 1977 Congressional
Quarterly Almanac 738.

[111] See Cooper, The Senate and the Filibuster: War of
Nerves -- and Hardball, 36 Cong. Q. Week. Rep. 2307 (1978);
1979 Congressional Quarterly Almanac 594.

[112] See 125 Cong. Rec. 145-46, 2033 (1979); 1979
Congressional Quarterly Almanac 593-95. To press the
minority not to filibuster the changes, the Majority Leader
(footnote continued)

Ultimately, the Republicans agreed to the 100-hour cap and to some other technical changes.[113]   The 1979 rules strengthened the leadership somewhat, but not enought to prevent combat from continuing over postcloture tactics and multiple cloture petitions.[114]

---

minority not to filibuster the changes, the Majority Leader reminded the Senate of "rulings of Vice Presidents of both parties and by votes of the Senate in essence upholding the power and right of a majority of the Senate to change the rules of the Senate at the beginning of a new Congress." 125 Cong. Rec. 144 (1979). The Majority Leader recessed the Senate from day to day, but did not adjourn, keeping it on its first legislative day; he demonstrated his strong position by party-line procedural votes.

[113]   The technical changes that were made concerned reprinting of amendments, opportunities for Senators to offer at least two amendments and present at least ten minutes' debate notwithstanding the cap, dispensing with reading of amendments and approval of the Journal, and submission of second-degree amendments.   125 Cong. Rec. 3037-38 (1979); see also id. at 3194 (section-by-section analysis of S. Res. 61 as adopted).

[114]   In that Congress, the one high-powered postcloture filibuster, Senator Hatfield's 1980 filibuster of draft registration, ended after the running of most of the new 100-hour clock through all-night speeches.   Senator Gravel stalled an Alaska lands bill but gave up after alienating the Senate by abrasive tactics and losing a cloture vote. Multiple petitions for cloture became common, signifying the position of a bloc of Senators who would not vote for cloture on an initial petition but would come around if delay persisted.   In 1979, the Senate voted on four petitions on the windfall profits tax, and in 1980, on four for a bill on the rights of the institutionalized, and five on two different nominations, before obtaining cloture in each instance.   Report of the Temporary Select Committee to Study the Senate Committee System, supra, at 46-47 (table).   Moreover, filibusters killed a fair-housing bill, for which the Senate voted cloture on the motion to proceed but not on the bill itself.   1980 Congressional Quarterly Almanac at 373.

1981-84 Postcloture Filibusters

With a Republican majority in control of the Senate in 1981, the shoe switched to the other foot: now conservative Republicans tried to pass "social agenda" legislation on busing, abortion, and school prayer, while liberals became the filibusterers. The key test came in a filibuster of exceptional duration on a Justice Department bill, when Senator Helms offered two antibusing amendments that Senator Lowell Weicker (R-Conn.) filibustered. It was not until after taking five votes on cloture petitions in 1981 from July to September that the Senate voted cloture on, and adopted, the second-degree busing amendment; not until December 10 that it voted cloture on the first-degree amendment;[115] and not until February, 1982, that it adopted the amendment and voted cloture on the bill.[116]

Then, ineluctably, the Senate faced the postcloture filibuster, signaled by the announcement that "[e]ven if cloture is invoked, Weicker said he had some 300 amendments pending at

---

[115] Senator Helms had offered a first-degree amendment, and a second-degree amendment subsequently modified to incorporate Senator Bennett Johnston's (D-La.) whole "Neighborhood Schools Act of 1981." The cloture votes are at 128 Cong. Rec. S7468, S7523, S8746, S9397, S9719 (1981). Because the second-degree amendment was not germane even to the first, let alone to the bill, cloture on the bill would have wiped it out, necessitating cloture on the second-degree amendment, then the first-degree, and only then on the bill.

[116] 128 Cong. Rec. S15069 (daily ed. Dec. 10, 1981) (acceptance of unanimous consent agreement for vote on amendment); 129 Cong. Rec. S414 (daily ed. Feb. 4, 1982) (amendment adopted); 129 Cong. Rec. S703 (daily ed. Feb. 9, 1982) (cloture voted on the bill). The months of delay reflected not only the opposition to the measures and to cloture, but also the Majority Leader's scheduling, which traded tolerance of delay on his part for noninterference by the filibusterers in the conduct of regular business. See articles in 39 Cong. Q. Week. Rep. 1152 (June 27), 1254 (July 11), 1290 (July 18), 1421 (Aug. 1), 1755 (Sept. 12), and 1789 (Sept. 19).

the Senate desk and vowed to keep fighting against the bill."[117]   To end the matter, Majority Leader "Baker kept the Senate in session from 10 a.m. Feb. 24 until 1:21 a.m. Feb. 25."[118]   Near the end, the Majority Leader depended on a short dramatic speech seeking consensus from a packed and attentive (albeit weary) Senate, rather than force:

> Mr. President, in just a moment I intend to call up another amendment. It is now 1:15 a.m. in the morning and we have completed, I believe, 21 votes today . . . .
>
> I have made no effort to try to circumvent or short-circuit the appeal process. I think the Senate has been very patient and fair in this respect. But I think that now when three of those amendments remain, it is time to get to the business at hand.[119]

The Senate acceded to the Majority Leader's request for cooperation in closing the filibuster down.   A quorum stayed in place for the Chair to count, so quorum calls were ruled out of order as dilatory, and the Senate denied a sufficient second for roll calls on appeals.[120]   The next day Senator Weicker conceded on the filibuster, and

---

[117]   40 Cong. Q. Week. Rep. 210 (1982).   By the deadline, Senator Weicker had filed 604 amendments. Cohodas, Weicker Halts Filibuster on Tough Anti-Busing Rider to Justice Authorization," 40 Cong. Q. Week. Rep. 464 (1982).   On February 10 and 23-24, 1981, the Senate slogged through large numbers of votes on amendments, appeals from rulings by the Chair, and quorum calls, reminiscent of the previous postcloture filibusters.

[118]   Id.   That evening, he called up, one by one, a large number of amendments which the Chair ruled out of order as dilatory or non-germane, while Senator Weicker had roll-call appeals of a few of the rulings.

[119]   128 Cong. Rec. S1138 (daily ed. Feb. 24, 1982).

[120]   128 Cong. Rec. S1138 (daily ed. Feb. 24, 1982).

the bill passed the Senate, going to a burial in
the House Judiciary Committee while both sides in
the Senate filibuster claimed victory. Again, the
chief lesson was the enormous power of delay
tactics.

In fact, numerous filibusters marked the rest
of 1982, and the core of Senate civility came
close to a breakdown. On December 10, opponents
began filibustering the motion to proceed to a
bill for a highway construction program financed
by a gasoline tax, in a series of gambits that
reflect the intricate nature of end-of-session
filibusters.[121] On December 19, the Senate voted
cloture on the leader's substitute amendment by
89-5, and on December 20 it voted cloture on the
bill by 87-8, a pair of record-shattering cloture
votes signifying the now-total willingness of
Senators to vote for cloture.[122] On December 23
it voted cloture on the conference report by 81-5
-- the fourth successive cloture vote needed to
move the bill.[123]

Such futile delaying elicited furor from
Senators forfeiting their prized Christmas
vacation.[124] Senator Alan Simpson (R-Wyo.) argued

---

[121] On December 13, the Senate voted for cloture on the
motion to proceed. Delays at this critical end-of-year
point forced the Majority Leader to seek to lay the bill
aside to clear a continuing resolution in a Saturday
session. Senator East filibustered that, too, until he
forfeited the floor by an erroneous request for a quorum
call. 128 Cong. Rec. S15478 (daily ed. Dec. 18, 1982);
Sarasohn, Filibuster Slows Action on Gas Tax Hike, 40 Cong.
Q. Week. Rep. 3047-48 (1982); Sarasohn, Battle-Weary Senate
Clears Highway-Public Transit Bill Raising Fuel and Truck
Taxes, 40 Cong. Q. Week. Rep. 3088 (1982). The Senate then
quickly passed the continuing resolution.

[122] Not a single southern Democrat, hitherto a group of
stalwart defenders of the right to filibuster, voted against
cloture either time. 128 Cong. Rec. S15721 (daily ed. Dec.
20, 1982) (cloture on the bill).

[123] 40 Cong. Q. Week. Rep. at 3089.

[124] As Congressional Quarterly noted:

(footnote continued)

that "those rules [permitting delays] were never drafted . . . to protect a minority within a minority within a minority within a minority -- like three.   They were created to protect a minority of 20, 30, or 25 . . . ."[125]   Senator Helms responded in defense of his tactics that "I say, Senator, you are dead wrong.   Those rules were designed for [delay by] one Senator."[126]

The last filibuster of the five addressed here, against a bill to overrule the Supreme Court's _Grove City_ decision (limiting the applicability of civil rights laws), shook the foundations of Senate order.   On September 27, 1984, the Senate took up a continuing resolution. Minority Leader Byrd offered versions of a Grove City bill as first-degree and second-degree amendments.[127]   As a counterstrategy,

---

Senators left in a particularly foul mood . . . .
The bill eventually passed, but not before the mannerly Senate dissolved into chaos . . . .

Marathon sessions were required to break the logjam, the longest such "all-nighters" in more than 20 years. At one point the Senate was in session for just shy of 38 straight hours.

Plattner, _Tired Congress Finally Heads Home_ Dec. 23, 40 Cong. Q. Week. Rep. 3087 (1982). Senator S. I. Hayakawa (R-Calif.) said: "Does the Senator from North Carolina believe that his own wisdom is so great that no opinions . . . on this floor matter but his own? . . . Why does he demean himself by associating himself with clods and peasants and idiots like us?" 128 Cong. Rec. S15465 (daily ed. Dec. 18, 1982).

[125] 128 Cong. Rec. S15972 (daily ed. Dec. 21, 1982). He added: "Seldom have I seen in my legislative experience of 17 years or more, a more obdurate and obnoxious performance." _Id._

[126] 128 Cong. Rec. S15983 (daily ed. Dec. 21, 1982).

[127] He immediately filed two cloture petitions on the amendments, and later filed two more. 130 Cong. Rec. S12135-36 (daily ed. Sept. 27, 1984)(first two cloture petitions). The Chair submitted to the Senate the question of whether the Grove City amendment was non-germane (and (footnote continued)

filibustering opponents, Senators Orrin Hatch (R-Utah) and James A. McClure (R-Idaho), offered their own controversial amendments -- amendments against gun control, against busing, and for tuition tax credits. They filed two cloture petitions on these amendments.[128]

On the Grove City amendment, the Senate voted cloture overwhelmingly by 91-4. Under cloture, the Chair ruled the anti-gun control amendment out of order as non-germane, and an appeal was taken. The filibuster took its menacing turn when the Senate rejected the motion to table that appeal, making it next in order to vote on the appeal and likely sustain it. Such a vote, allowing a non-germane amendment to be pushed onto a clotured matter, would have vastly undermined the germaneness rule in cloture, and with it the cloture rule itself.

Rather than thereby bust the heart of Senate procedure, the Republican cosponsor of the Grove City amendment, Senator Robert Packwood (R-Oreg.), agreed to table the amendment, which the Senate did.[129] The Senate then agreed to table the anti-

---

hence out of order on a continuing resolution, pursuant to the germaneness rule for appropriation bills). The Senate voted the amendment germane, id. at 12167. The second two cloture petitions were filed the next day. 130 Cong. Rec. S12279 (daily ed. Sept. 28, 1984).

[128] Id. at S12167-73 (amendments); id. at S12175 (first cloture petition); id. at S12279 (daily ed. Sept. 28, 1984) (second cloture petition). Majority Leader Baker commented: "Mr. President, that would be six cloture votes in 2 legislative days. For whatever it is worth, it took us 7 years before the Senate voted five times on cloture after the rule was first enacted. I just thought I might show you how far we have come in our progress toward Valhalla." Senator J. James Exon (D-Nebr.) agreed that "[i]t seems to me that we can best be described as not the most deliberative body in the world, but as the most cloture-minded body in the world." The exchange is at id. S12280.

[129] Id. at S12643 (daily ed. Oct 2, 1984). Previously, Majority Leader Baker executed a complicated maneuver. At an earlier point, the Senate had tabled an appeal from the Chair's ruling that the busing amendment was out of order as (footnote continued)

gun control amendment by voice vote, taking with
it the point of order that had threatened the
cloture rule.[130]   This course meant the
filibusterers had won even after 91 Senators voted
for cloture, an incredible statement on the Senate
majority's inability to work its will.

Observers pointed to these postcloture
filibusters of 1982 and 1984 as indicating a
general breakdown of control in the Senate. Once
more, Minority Leader Byrd led the response, as he
had in rules changes in 1974 (budget act), 1977
(committee jurisdiction), and 1979 (postcloture
filibuster). His reduction of the cap from 100 to
30 hours accompanied the Senate's 1986 resolution
to televise its proceedings, and was justified as
necessary to give the Senate a better television
image.[131]

D.   SPECIAL TACTICS AND SITUATIONS UNDER
     CLOTURE

Beyond the basic procedures and patterns for the
general use of filibusters and cloture lie
strategy and tactics for particular filibusters

---

nongermane. Several Republican Senators wished, after the
action on the anti-gun control amendment, to undo their vote
for that tabling motion, as it suggested some substantive
lack of sympathy for the antibusing amendment. Accordingly,
the Majority Leader had the Senate vote to reconsider the
tabling, and then to vote against tabling that appeal. Id.
at S12521, S12523 (daily ed. Oct. 1, 1984).

[130]   Id. at S12643.

[131]   Other proposals, such as to preclude filibusters on
motions to proceed, were dropped. The 30 hour cap seemed to
promise that pure delaying tactics would not be effective
when the clock could run, such as on bills reaching the
floor well before adjournment. On the other hand, the cap
did not deal with a variety of special tactics, such as
separate filibusters at different stages of a bill (like the
1982 gas tax filibusters) or the offer of popular non-
germane amendments after cloture, as had killed the Grove
City amendment.

more complex and subtle than in any other area of
congressional procedure, reflecting the Senate's
great tension.   Senators desire to restrain the
postcloture   delaying   tactics   such   as   endless
amendments, quorum calls, appeals, and others -- a
desire   that   becomes   excruciating   in   end-of-
session,   all-night,   and   deadline-confronting
situations.   However, they also strongly desire
not to destroy the essential fabric of individual
rights that are each Senator's pride and power.
The   Senate's   resolution   of   that   tension   has
produced a highly reticulated set of tactical and
precedential   constraints   and   opportunities.
Moreover, filibusters occur in a number of special
situations, such as on motions to proceed, motions
leading to conference, conference reports, and
nominations.   Each   has   its   own   unique
circumstances and strategies.

Drafting of Amendments

The   procedure   for   treatment   of   amendments
under cloture reflects the tension between curbing
dilatory tactics, and not imposing a closed or
"gag   rule."   Rule   XXII   provides   that
"[n]o . . . . dilatory amendment, or amendment not
germane shall be in order," but it does not define
dilatoriness.   The cloture rule changes adopted in
1979 barred the reading of amendments after
invocation of cloture, curbing one of the most
obvious dilatory tactics.[132]   Also, the cloture
rule only allows the offering of amendments that
have been submitted in writing prior to the vote
on cloture.[133]

---

[132]   Rule XXII now provides: "After cloture is invoked, the
reading of any amendment, including House amendments, shall
be dispensed with when the proposed amendment has been
identified and has been available in printed form at the
desk of the Members for not less than twenty-four hours."

[133]   Rule XXII provides:

Except by unanimous consent, no amendment shall be
proposed after the vote to bring the debate to a close,
unless it had been submitted in writing to the Journal
(footnote continued)

Filibusterers respond to that limit by filing
hundreds of amendments prior to the vote on
cloture, but this sets off an intricate game of
disqualifying such amendments.   Under the
precedents established by Majority Leader Byrd in
1977, amendments that are out of order will be
ruled out of order by the Chair as soon as they
are called up, before the Clerk even states them
or a point of order is made.   This allows the
Chair to rule out a large number of amendments
very swiftly.[134]   Moreover, when the Senate votes
cloture, Senators lose their normal right to
modify their amendments at will.[135]

Hence, if a Senator's amendments filed
precloture are out of order on some technical
ground, or can be rendered out of order after
cloture, the Chair can dispose of them quickly.
It is too late for the Senator either to modify
them to cure the problem or to file new
amendments.   Moreover, the Senate can become quite
finicky about the drafting of amendments after it
votes cloture.[136]

Clerk by 1 o'clock p.m. on the day following the filing
of the cloture motion if an amendment in the first
degree, and unless it had been so submitted at least
one hour prior to the beginning of the cloture vote if
an amendment in the second degree.

[134] A filibusterer who wishes to appear as little dilatory
as possible, such as Senator Weicker in 1981-82, accepts the
rulings of the Chair rather than taking large numbers of
futile appeals.   A Senator who does not mind the appearance
of dilatoriness can take many appeals, but appeals of that
kind can trigger a range of rougher counter-tactics, as
discussed below.

[135] Riddick, "Cloture Procedure: Amendments After Cloture:
Modification Out of Order," at 238.

[136] In a classic demonstration, during the 1977 natural gas
filibuster, the Chair concluded about a large number of
amendments that they amended the bill in more than one
place.   The amendments all proposed something that changed
the number of sections in the bill, typically by adding a
new section, and then provided for consistency that the
other sections would be renumbered accordingly.
Technically, because such amendments changed the other
(footnote continued)

In drafting floor amendments for postcloture use, the most difficult problem becomes what to anticipate as the text to which the floor amendments will be offered. The drafter needs to know the text to comply with the strict germaneness rule.[137] However, the anticipated text can change, since committee amendments (which are part of it) can, like other amendments, can be recalled after cloture.[138] As an even more aggressive counterfilibuster tactic, the manager can prepare in advance to amend the bill after cloture deliberately in order to make prefiled amendments unofferable to the bill as amended.[139]

---

section numbers, they amended the bill in more than one place, something forbidden by the Senate rules (but ordinarily not questioned in practice). This technical ground served as a basis for ruling large numbers of amendments out of order. Riddick, "Cloture Procedure: Amendments After Cloture: Amends Measure in Two or More Places," at 232-33. Technically, amendments should simply add or subtract sections, and after passage, the Senate will direct its Secretary to make technical corrections.

[137] For example, germaneness makes the safest amendment a motion to strike some provision or to change some number, which are *per se* germane, but offering such amendments requires knowing what there will be to strike or change.

[138] For example, often a committee reports a bill along with a committee amendment in the nature of a substitute, and everyone anticipates that after that committee amendment has been itself amended on the floor, it will be adopted and will be the bill ultimately passed.

A "Senator has 'the right to recall his own amendment' in post cloture which was otherwise qualified and [to] have [his amendments] removed from the desk prior to having them called up." Riddick, "Cloture Procedure: Amendments After Cloture: Withdrawal of Amendments," at 241.

[139] The 1979 rules change did protect Senators from amendments that change only the bill's pagination or lineation (such as by adding a section early on), but that protects only against purely formal, not against deliberately devised, changes. Rule XXII provides:

If, for any reason, a measure or matter is reprinted (footnote continued)

Ultimately, Rule XXII explicitly arms the Senate against amendments when it states that "[n]o . . . dilatory amendment . . . shall be in order." The Senate has rarely ruled amendments out of order as dilatory when they suffered from some independent problem, such as imperfect drafting, unofferability to a changed text, or non-germaneness.[140] However, the rule arms the Senate to make such rulings if need be,[141] particularly when some special reason can be pointed to for considering the amendments frivolous.[142]

---

after cloture has been invoked, amendments which were in order prior to the reprinting of the measure or matter will continue to be in order and may be conformed and reprinted at the request of the amendment's sponsor. The conforming changes must be limited to lineation and pagination.

For example, in a wily move after cloture was voted in 1982 on antibusing provisions, they were amended to make a large number of Senator Weicker's amendments unofferable, too late for Senator Weicker to file new floor amendments or modify his old ones. 40 Cong. Q. Weekly Rep. 464 (1982); 129 Cong. Rec. S955 (daily ed. Feb 23, 1982).

[140] Riddick, "Cloture Procedure: Amendments Ruled Out as Dilatory," at 247.

[141] Majority Whip Byrd threatened to seek such a ruling during the very first postcloture filibuster of a bill, Senator Allen's against the Hart-Scott-Rodino antitrust bill. Senator Byrd warned:

According to the clerk, 79 amendments are yet at the desk. Thirty-four motions are yet at the desk . . . .
Paragraph 2 of Rule XXII states in part, once cloture is invoked:
No dilatory motion, or dilatory amendment . . . . shall be in order . . . .
Mr. President, I take the floor at this time simply to state that as of 2 hours from now it will be my purpose, upon getting recognition, to make a point of order that all remaining amendments and motions at the desk are dilatory and, therefore, are not in order.

122 Cong. Rec. 28597 (1976).
(footnote continued)

Miscellaneous Dilatory Tactics and Appeals

To supplement mere offering of amendments, the filibusterer can ask for reconsideration of each vote as it occurs, and obtain a vote either on the motion to reconsider or on tabling that motion. Whether and when reconsideration is dilatory is a controversial issue. Under cloture, the Chair has ruled the motion to reconsider out of order as dilatory a number of times, as Riddick describes:

> Under post cloture proceedings, a motion to reconsider has been ruled dilatory and out of order under different circumstances as follows: (1) on a vote of 64 yeas to 24 nays on tabling an appeal, (2) on a vote of 60 yeas to 31 nays sustaining a ruling of the Chair, (3) on a vote of 78 yeas to 8 nays to table a motion to postpone indefinitely, (4) and on a vote of 15 yeas to 69 mays to table an amendment.[143]

Still, the issue is far from foreclosed.[144] The

---

[142] The particular justification available to the leadership in the instance just cited of the Hart-Scott-Rodino bill filibuster was that the Senate had already acted on the bill, and wished to get it to conference, so the Senate had fully spoken previously on the bill and further amendments were dilatory. This threat caused Senator Allen to agree to end that filibuster. It may be imagined that in any strained postcloture situation, such as when the Senate had already passed and rejected ten or 20 amendments from the same sponsors, a similar justification might be available.

[143] Riddick, "Cloture Procedure: Dilatory Procedure: Reconsideration," at 249.

[144] On the vote cited by Riddick of 78 yeas to eight nays to table the motion to postpone indefinitely that occurred on June 10, 1980, the Chair did at first accept the Majority Leader's contention and state that "the Chair would have to hold that the motion is dilatory." However, Minority Leader (footnote continued)

filibusterer can also make motions concerning the
Senate's schedule and agenda, including motions to
recess or adjourn. Ordinarily, most such motions
are the prerogative of the leadership, which
reacts jealously to usurpation, but the hardened
filibusterer may feel ready to alienate the
leadership that extra bit on top of everything
else.   The Chair's attitude toward the
dilatoriness of motions to reconsider, recess, or
adjourn, remains discretionary, perhaps turning on
how the particular Senator in the Chair feels
about the filibusterer's approach.[145]
     A most important issue concerns appeals.
Rule XXII makes special provision for preventing
delay by debate of appeals, specifying that
"[p]oints of order, including questions of
relevancy, and appeals from the decision of the
Presiding Officer, shall be decided without
debate." This does not mean debate never occurs,
but it occurs only by unanimous consent on
particular appeals raising questions that all
agree warrant airing.   Still, the provision
barring debate does not deal with the more
difficult issue posed by the opportunity for a
time-wasting roll-call vote on the appeal.
     This confronts the Senate with one of its
ultimate questions, as to when the Chair can rule
not only motions on the floor, but appeals from
its own rulings, out of order. Cloture depends on
an active Chair cutting off delay by ruling out

Baker made a strong pitch that he "kn[e]w of no precedents
of the Senate heretofore, and I would inquire of the Chair,
is there any previous precedent that would support a
ruling by the Chair that a motion is dilatory under the
provisions of rule XXII simply because, as I understood the
Chair to rule, the vote was lopsided, one way or the
other?" After reflection, the Chair stated "[t]he Chair
reverses itself.   The motion is in order," and after a
dispute over another matter, the Senate voted on the motion
to reconsider (rejecting it 71-14).   126 Cong. Rec. 13903-5
(1980).

[145] See Riddick, "Cloture Procedure: Dilatory Procedure:
Adjourn," at 247; "Cloture Procedure: Dilatory Procedure:
Recess," at 249; "Cloture Procedure: Dilatory Procedure:
Postpone Indefinitely," at 249; and "Cloture Procedure:
Recess," at 254.

motions and amendments as dilatory or non-germane. In theory, if the filibusterer can appeal all adverse rulings and obtain a vote that way on the appeal or on the motion to table the appeal, such rulings would never succeed in avoiding a filibusterer's delay.[146]

On the other hand, Senators consider their right to appeal to be sacred, signifying their membership in a chamber of equals as representatives of sovereign states, governed procedurally only by their collective peers, not a single overlord in the Chair. Moreover, the denial of appeals could be the prelude to the abridgment of all other rights, a threat made doubly dangerous by the peculiar nature of the Senate Chair, who is often a Vice President of a party opposite to the majority.[147] While the Senate has precedents that the Chair can hold appeals dilatory, it also has expressed itself

---

[146] In other words, a never-ending stream of frivolous appeals during postcloture filibuster would simply prevent any other rule from effectively foreclosing dilatory tactics, by making each ruling that a motion was dilatory just another occasion for delay. Accordingly, on a number of occasions during the Metzenbaum-Abourezk filibuster of 1977, the Chair did hold appeals out of order as dilatory. Riddick, "Cloture Procedure: Dilatory Procedure: Appeals," at 247-48.

[147] Senator Edward Muskie (D-Maine) protested that

> if the present occupant of the chair rules that the appeal is dilatory, we are powerless -- all 100 of us -- to change that unilateral, individual ruling by someone who temporarily presides over the chair . . . . Once the Chair asserts the right to deny any Senator [an] appeal from his ruling, that precedent can be built upon to deny appeals for any reason.

123 Cong. Rec. 31867 (1977). Senator Harry F. Byrd, Jr. (Ind-Va.) agreed that while he "ha[d] consistently voted to uphold the rulings of the Chair," "[i]f the Chair can make rulings and the Senate itself does not have an opportunity to override the decision of the Chair, then the Senate is putting itself totally in the hands of the Presiding Officer and the Parliamentarian." 123 Cong. Rec. 31862 (1977).

strongly against such a procedure.[148]   This
remains one of the ultimate points on which the
procedure in the Senate remains to be defined.

Quorum Calls and Roll-Call Votes

Considering the array of amendments, motions,
and appeals available for the postcloture
filibuster, filibusters do not tend to run short

---

[148]   To concretize these protests, during the Metzenbaum-
Abourezk filibuster, Senators John C. Danforth (R-Mo.) and
Muskie produced a test, with a point of order against
another appeal as dilatory. Senator Muskie warned that

> what we are talking about is a precedent that has the
> potential for putting arbitrary power in the hands of
> the temporary occupant of the Chair, power from which
> the whole Senate could not appeal if this precedent is
> established and sustained . . . .   I sought to have a
> test case made so that the Senate as a whole could
> decide whether that should be the precedent.

126 Cong. Rec. 31869 (1977). Senator Danforth argued back:

> So, really, the question is, when it is absolutely
> clear on its face that the amendment is clearly not in
> order, it would seem to me, then, tha[t] an appeal from
> the decision of the Chair that it is not in order is
> itself simply a dilatory delaying tactic, and that such
> appeal should not be permitted.

Id.   The Chair submitted the question to the Senate as
"whether a point of order that an appeal taken from a ruling
of the Chair that an amendment is out of order on its face
is dilatory is well taken." Id.

The Senate voted 71-9 against the point of order,
upholding the right to appeal as not dilatory. This was a
strong statement, considering that by then the Senate was
thoroughly and completely disenchanted with the Metzenbaum-
Abourezk filibuster and that the Senate turned around and
sustained the particular ruling of the Chair from which the
appeal had been taken (that the amendment was out of order)
by no less a vote than 77-3. Appeals voted frivolous by a
more overwhelming margin than that come along rarely.

of the raw material for roll calls. Their limit
has been the means for translating mere Senate
decisions into time-wasting calls of the roll.
This depends on the different rules for roll-call
votes and quorum calls.

     As described elsewhere, obtaining a roll-call
vote pursuant to the strict procedures requires a
sufficient   second   ranging   from   11   to   20
Senators.[149]   Ordinarily, since the early 1960s
the leadership has cooperated with requests for
roll-call votes, even during filibusters, and even
during the early phases of orderly postcloture
filibusters.   Senators   consider   themselves
entitled to those roll-call votes, and can
reproach the leadership bitterly for attempting to
deny that right. In fact, the Senate come so far
from the tightly controlled condition of the 1950s
that there is considerable uncertainty in the
realm of unwritten Senate custom about the moral
rightfulness of withholding that second.

     However, in extended postcloture filibusters,
several times a point has come that the leadership
states that the Senate's patience has been
exhausted. The leadership then asks that Senators
withhold   a   sufficient   second   from   the
filibusterer. Majority Leader Baker did this on
the Weicker filibuster in 1982, when he ultimately
asked, "I hope the yeas and nays will not be given
and that we can dispense with the remainder of the
amendments . . . ."[150]

---

[149]   A sufficient second is one-fifth of the Senators
present. When only a presumptive quorum is present, one-
fifth is 11 (a fifth of 51, rounded up). During the period
immediately after a roll call or other indication of the
presence of some actual large number of Senators, one-fifth
ranges up to the maximum which is 20 (one-fifth of 100).

[150]   128 Cong. Rec. S1138 (daily ed. Feb. 24, 1982).
Senator Weicker's supporters knew that if they thwarted the
leadership, the leadership had rougher means available, such
as those used by Majority Leader Byrd to end the Metzenbaum-
Abourezk filibuster in 1977. Although Senator Weicker asked
for more roll-call votes, his supporters largely accepted
the leadership judgment, and agreed with the request not to
give a sufficient second, leading in short order to an end
of the filibuster.

In effect, this establishes a kind of higher-level test than the vote for cloture. Sixty Senators can vote cloture, but that does not close down a postcloture filibuster; it only starts the clock rolling and increases the burdens on the filibusterer and the Senate from any further stalling. It takes a larger consensus to deny a postcloture filibusterer his yeas and nays. While the Senate will vote cloture much more readily than in the past, it must reach an extreme point before that larger consensus will take the more drastic cutting-off step.

Quorum calls pose a special problem. The Constitution's Quorum Clause, Art. I, sec. 5, cl. 1, specifies that for each House, "a Majority of each shall constitute a Quorum to do Business." Hence, the Constitution itself guarantees the filibusterer the right to demand a determination of whether a quorum is present before the Senate can continue doing business. The filibusterer does not need support from anyone else, only recognition by the Chair. One way to limit quorum calls is the way the House chose in 1890 of allowing the Speaker to count a quorum. In the Senate, it remains today the rule that "[t]he Chair has no authority to count a quorum."[151]

However, the Senate has worked out ways around that rule.[152] In 1977, as the Metzenbaum-

---

[151] Riddick, "Quorum: Counting of Quorum by Chair," at 845.

[152] The Senate broke a 1908 filibuster by Senator Robert La Follette (R-Wis.) in the following fashion:

Thomas P. Gore of Oklahoma immediately raised the point that the division had revealed one short of a quorum. How had the issue been settled in the absence of a quorum? The Vice President replied that one Senator not voting had been present to make a quorum; and to sustain his position he read a precedent on June 19, 1879, when Allen G. Thurman of Ohio was in the chair. But the Vice President had now taken an important step beyond the Thurman ruling. The latter had merely counted a quorum to determine whether enough Senators were present to do business; [Vice President] Fairbanks had counted a quorum, as had Speaker Thomas B. Reed in the House in 1890, to declare that action on
(footnote continued)

Abourezk natural gas deregulation filibuster ground on, the Chair began to reject demands for quorum calls when it saw that a quorum was present, and after a tentative start,[153] soon announced that as a rule.[154]

---

a vote had been taken.

Under such a ruling the regular practice of breaking a quorum on roll-call votes by sitting silent in the chamber was ended. Filibusterism had received the first significant blow.

Burdette at 85.

[153] The issue was much disputed in 1977. On the first day of the natural gas filibuster, the Senate ruled a quorum call dilatory, but the circumstances were not clear and the issue was not well developed. 123 Cong. Rec. 30818 (1977). Subsequently, Majority Leader Byrd acknowledged that "[t]he prevailing precedents are that the Chair may not count to see whether or not there is a quorum present," id. at 31235, but his research turned up the contrary historical deviations, including that of 1908, id. at 31238. As the quorum calls continued, the point came in for further debate, and after several days the following inquiry occurred:

> Mr. HARRY F. BYRD, JR. It is not correct that throughout this debate, under cloture, the Chair has ruled consistently that the Chair, itself, on its own initiative, could not determine whether or not a quorum was present?

> The VICE PRESIDENT. The Chair has ruled, according to the Parlimentarian, not consistently.

Id. at 31925.

[154] Ultimately the Chair had this to say:

> Mr. METZENBAUM. Am I correct, that the rules and precedents of the Senate specifically provide in unequivocal language that the Chair may not count the Members of the Senate in order to determine whether a quorum is present?

> The VICE PRESIDENT. The point of order has been

(footnote continued)

Although conceptually the Chair was treading a fine line, its approach became a firm precedent.[155] During the 1980 Hatfield filibuster of draft registration, the Senate sustained a clear ruling that during cloture, the Chair can rule a demand for a quorum call out of order as dilatory based on its count.[156]

Even so, the Chair's count only eliminates quorum calls when a quorum stays on the floor to be counted. Often, during cloture, Senators eager to end the filibuster will plead with other Senators to stay on the floor to be counted, but Senators do not like to stand around hour after hour on the floor, idly watching a filibuster. Rather, they leave the floor, returning only briefly to answer quorum calls or votes.

Thus, delay becomes a question of how frequently filibusterers may demand quorum calls. Senators cannot simply demand one quorum call after another.[157] As to what constitutes sufficient "intervening business" to justify the next quorum call, some things clearly are always "business": adoption of an amendment, engrossment and third reading, and recess or adjournment.[158]

---

sustained. The Chair possesses the authority to determine the existence of a quorum under cloture.

Id. at 31934.

[155] Technically, the Chair did not count the quorum itself, but rather, counted the number of Senators present to determine that a demand for a quorum call was out of order as dilatory, and therefore rejected the demand for the quorum call.

[156] 126 Cong. Rec. 13904 (1980); Riddick, "Cloture Procedure: Quorum Calls," at 249-50.

[157] Rather, "[b]usiness must intervene before a second quorum call or between calls, or a quorum call is not in order when there has been no business transacted since the previous call which was completed . . . ." Riddick, "Quorum: Business Between Calls -- Definition of What Constitutes Business Since the Previous Quorum Call for the Purpose of Calling Another Quorum," at 837.

[158] Id. at 838-39. Of course, if the Senate adopts an (footnote continued)

Some things clearly are never "business": pure debate, parliamentary inquiries, or unanimous consent requests not acted upon.[159] Some things are not business during cloture (even if they might be otherwise) for purposes of determining whether a new quorum call is dilatory -- for example, that the offering of dilatory amendments was not business.[160]

Still, filibusterers can demand quorum calls so long as the Chair has not resorted to ruling their motions or amendments out of order as dilatory, even if the leadership has been tabling them without a roll-call vote.[161] Accordingly,

---

amendment by roll-call vote, that vote itself discloses the presence of a quorum, so that no new quorum call can be demanded immediately. "It has been held not in order for a Senator to demand a quorum call immediately following a yea and nay vote which discloses the presence of a quorum." Riddick, "Quorum Call: Suggestion of the Absence of a Quorum When in Order," at 856. If the Senate adopts the amendment by voice vote, that serves as "business" warranting a new quorum call.

[159] Id. at 839-40.

[160] During the Metzenbaum-Abourezk filibuster, Minority Leader Baker established a decisive precedent in that regard that failed actions of filibusterers such as offering of dilatory amendments did not constitute "business" sufficient to justify a new quorum call. The Baker point of order was:

> when the Senate is operating under cloture, a request by a Senator to conduct business which the Senate declines to conduct, for instance, the making of a motion which is ruled dilatory, the offering of an amendment which is ruled out of order or dilatory, a request for the yeas and nays which is refused, is not the transaction of business for the purpose of calling another quorum.

123 Cong. Rec. 31926 (1977).

[161] For example, Senator Weicker obtained numerous quorum calls by demanding one after the tabling of each of his amendments during his filibuster of the Helms-Johnston antibusing proposal. 128 Cong. Rec. S1158 (daily ed. Feb. 25, 1982). The Baker precedent from 1977 denies the status (footnote continued)

managers' primary recourse against a quorum call strategy backed by amendments remains to persuade Senators to stay on the floor to be counted. Beyond that, the Chair would have to take those ultimate steps that the Senate has remained loath to condone because of their impact on individual Senators' rights and status: declaring amendments, motions, and appeals dilatory on a wholesale basis.

Filibusters on Motion to Proceed

Besides the general type of filibuster on bills and amendments, there are specialized kinds of filibuster presenting particular strategic and procedural issues. The most common and available is the filibuster on the motion to proceed. Because the Senate uses the motion to proceed to bring legislation to the floor (absent unanimous consent), opponents of legislation can start opposition to any bill by filibustering the motion to proceed. Since 1949 the Senate has been able to respond by voting cloture on that motion. For example, in 1984, the Senate voted cloture on three different motions to proceed: on a banking deregulation bill, on the resolution to televise Senate proceedings, and on a highway construction bill.[162]

Numerous filibuster threats each Congress persuade against making particular motions to proceed. In 1982, Senator Hatch relented from attempting to bring up his constitutional amendment regarding abortion, when he saw "that there will be a filibuster not only on the constitutional amendment itself but also on the motion to proceed. There will not be a genuine debate on this issue."[163]

Filibusterers face an important decision on whether to filibuster the motion to proceed. On the one hand, it offers a tempting target,

---

of "business" to declaring dilatory amendments out of order, not to tabling of non-dilatory amendments.

[162]   S. Prt. No. 98-254 at 47.

[163]   128 Cong. Rec. S11494 (daily ed. Sept. 15, 1982).

allowing a double filibuster on the motion to proceed and on the bill itself, with separate opportunities for precloture filibuster, separate opportunities to defeat the cloture vote, and separate clotured time limits after the vote. Even a loss on the filibuster on the motion to proceed may presage victory against the bill itself, for Senators may signal ambivalence by voting for cloture only the first time, not the second. In fact, this may allow a swing group to give something to both sides without the bill going through.[164]

On the other hand, many filibusterers forego a filibuster on the motion to proceed. Such filibusters are quite likely to fail. Once the Senate votes cloture, there is no ready means for a postcloture filibuster on the motion to proceed.[165] Moreover, Senators regard the motion to proceed as a leadership prerogative. Senators of the majority party may consider themselves bound to support the motion, minority Senators may concede the motion, would-be offerors of amendments may let the bill come up so they can amend it, and even strong critics of the bill may not want to position themselves as so obstructionist as to object even to discussing it. In light of the likelihood of failure in a filibuster on the motion to proceed, filibusterers may fear drawing the issue prematurely on a weak

---

[164] For example, in 1980, the Senate voted for cloture on the motion to proceed to the fair housing bill, but not on the bill itself, as in 1984 the Senate voted for cloture on the motion to proceed to the resolution for televising the Senate, id. at 46-47, but not on the resolution itself. In the television case, a swing group of reluctant Senators showed by voting cloture only on the motion to proceed that they "were willing to at least discuss the proposal"; "there was considerable support for limited television coverage of the Senate, but not gavel-to-gavel broadcasts." 1984 Congressional Quarterly Almanac at 209.

[165] The motion cannot be amended. Riddick, "Consideration, Question of: Amend Motion to Consider, Out of Order," at 515. A few other motions could be made, such as to table and to reconsider, but not much delay could be obtained this way.

ground, and may prefer to hold their fire until the decisive issue of cloture on the bill itself.[166]

To avoid redundant filibusters, the Senate has considered proposals to make the motion to proceed nondebatable.[167] Actually, a mechanism already exists for nondebatable motions to proceed. The Senate begins each new legislative day with a two hour period, the "Morning Hour, and Rule VIII(2) provides: "All motions made during the first two hours of a new legislative day [i.e., during "Morning Hour"] to proceed to the consideration of any matter shall be determined without debate . . . ."[168] During the first hour, "Morning business," previously discussed,[169] is privileged, but after that hour, morning business

---

[166] For example, filibusterers of a 1982 bill releasing antitrust defendants from duties of contribution faced the problem that many Senators opposed only the measure's retroactive feature, not the basic idea, and were willing to proceed to the bill. Accordingly, the filibusterers decided to let the Senate proceed to the bill, and not to filibuster the motion to proceed. The strategy proved sound. Once the Senate had the bill before it, it voted overwhelmingly not to invoke cloture on the committee retroactivity amendment, and the manager then acceded to withdrawing the bill. 128 Cong. Rec. S13768 (daily ed. Dec. 2, 1982) (vote of only 38 for cloture, and 58 against); id. at S13771 (manager accedes to sending bill back to the calendar).

[167] For example, the 1984 Quayle Committee recommended "providing for a two hour time limit on the motion to proceed," S. Prt. No. 98-254 at 16.

[168] See Riddick, "Morning Hour," at 739-45. The rule excepts from nondebatability "motions to proceed to the consideration of any motion, resolution, or proposal to change any of the Standing Rules of the Senate [which] shall be debatable."

[169] "Routine morning business" was previously discussed as the period for mechanical matters such as introduction of bills and committee reports. Usually, the Senate avoids "Morning Hour" by unanimous consent, and simply has periods for routine morning business at convenient times during the day, also by unanimous consent.

does not stand in the way of motions to proceed.[170]

Besides its other complexities,[171] the chief problem with that mechanism used to be delay on the Journal.[172] The 1986 rules change to televise

---

[170] Rule VII(2) provides in pertinent part that "[u]ntil the morning business shall have been concluded, and so announced from the Chair, or until one hour after the Senate convenes at the beginning of a new legislative day, no motion to proceed to the consideration of any bill . . . shall be entertained . . . ." Thus, "[a]fter the morning business has been concluded, even prior to the expiration of 1 hour, under paragraph 2 of Rule VII, a motion to proceed to the consideration of a specific bill or resolution . . . is in order . . . ." Riddick, "Morning Hour: Procedure in the Morning Hour," at 743; Riddick, "Morning Business" (chapter introduction), at 731.

[171] Two caveats are that unfinished business from the previous day displaces bills proceeded to during Morning Hour. Riddick, "Unfinished Business: Consideration and Definition of Unfinished Business," at 1105-7.) Also, on Mondays the rules provide for a special calendar procedure. Riddick, "Calendar: Call on Mondays," at 210-11.

[172] For example, during efforts to bring up the 1964 civil rights bill, Majority Leader Mansfield aimed to make a nondebatable motion to proceed during the Morning Hour, and then continue with the bill after the "Morning Hour":

> Senator Mansfield badly wanted to make his motion [to proceed] and have it voted on in the course of the "morning hour," a period reserved for such normally routine matters. For during the two hours that the "morning hour" lasts, there can be no debate on a motion of the type that he intended to offer. Thus the motion could be made and approved without any possibility of a filibuster.

D. Berman, supra at 68.

> [The filibusterers] managed to kill almost half of the two hours just by insisting upon reading the previous day's Journal. Normally, this reading is dispensed with; but there must be unanimous consent for that to be done, and Senator Russell quickly

(footnote continued)

the Senate appeared to eliminate that problem by
amending Rule IV to specify that the Journal shall
be read "unless by nondebatable motion the reading
shall be waived, the question being, 'Shall the
Journal stand approved to date?'"   An initial
attempt   in   1987   to   use   the   newly-improved
procedure for avoiding a filibuster on a motion to
proceed became tangled in a rough partisan battle,
but a later attempt worked.[173]

Filibusters on Conference and Nomination

Even after a manager moves to proceed to a
bill and gets the Senate to pass it, the battle
may still be far from over.   A filibuster can
occur on motions to take a bill to conference or
to adopt the conference report.   In the Helms-East
filibuster in 1982 of the highway gas tax, Senator
Helms   continued   filibustering   at   the   late
stages.   When   the   bill   reached   third   reading,
Senator Helms objected that the rules required
waiting another legislative day, so the Majority
Leader moved "that the Senate stand in adjournment
for   1   minute," and   started   a   new   legislative
day,[174] allowing   the   bill   to   immediately   go   to

---

interposed an objection.   The reading of the Journal
. . . consumed 44 minutes.   Then Russell earned the
right to speak for the remainder of the time by
moving that the journal be amended to include
additional matter.   That motion was debatable, and of
course its author chose to discuss it at great
length.   By the time he yielded the floor, the
"morning hour" was over and Senator Mansfield had no
alternative but to make his motion in a parliamentary
context permitting full debate.

Id.

[173] Davis, Byrd and Bush Clash in Senate Power Struggle, 45
Cong. Q. Week. Rep. 221 (1987); 1987 Congressional Quarterly
Almanac 43, 206, 243.

[174] 128 Cong. Rec. S15736 (daily ed. Dec. 20, 1982).   To be
precise, Senator Helms complained that third reading had
occurred without the delay of a day.   The Majority Leader
went so far as by unanimous consent to vitiate third
(footnote continued)

third reading and engrossment and a vote on final passage. The filibusterers did not stall on the motion for going to conference, but they did require a vote of cloture on the conference report, on December 23, 1982, by 81-5 -- the fourth successful cloture vote and the last one needed to move the bill.[175] The Senate overcame that filibuster without using the historic weapon available against stalling on unamendable conference reports, namely, the two-speech rule.[176]

The fact that the Senate readily overcame that filibuster did not mean that filibusters are always doomed at these final stages. A number of

---

reading, to prove to Senator Helms, who at this point in the Christmas Eve filibuster was not popular in the chamber, that no one "has tried to play hardball with him," id.

Pursuant to Rule IV, "[w]henever the Senate is proceeding under paragraph 2 of rule XXII [i.e., under cloture], the reading of the Journal shall be dispensed with and shall be considered approved to date." Senator Baker noted that despite the adjournment, "[t]here is no reading of the Journal, nothing comes over under the rule, nothing of the procedure that follows after adjournment is actuated, and we are right back where we started." Id.

[175] 40 Cong. Q. Week. Rep. at 3089.

[176] In 1908, Senator Robert La Follette (R-Wis.) attempted to filibuster the conference report on a currency bill. The filibuster "was aimed at an unamendable conference report. When Senators had spoken twice, under strict enforcement of the [two-speech] rule, and with the Senate technicallly held (through recesses) in one legislative day, the filibuster could be throttled with relative ease." Burdette at 86. To avoid using up his ration of speeches, La Follette had to deliver his record-setting oration -- the one almost interrupted by ptomaine poisoning -- but the filibuster could not be sustained indefinitely by a small crew limited to two speeches apiece, and it soon died. Id. at 86-91.

This tactic would not work for the conference report on an appropriation bill, which usually has amendments in technical disagreement. Not only could there be separate speeches on these amendments, but unlike the conference report, such amendments are themselves amendable.

successful stalls have occurred at the last minute. One of the first key modern filibusters by liberals, on the supersonic transport in 1971, occurred on the conference report.[177] A heavy barrier both against filibustering on conference reports, and against fighting filibusters, is that conference reports come to the floor in unamendable form. Once the conference report comes to the floor, neither supporters nor opponents have procedural opportunity to negotiate compromises without some very complex backtracking. Accordingly, a filibuster threat more often occurs earlier, when concessions can be made in the content of the conference report.

In general, the availability of filibustering on motions going to conference, and on the conference report, tends to influence bargaining rather than leading to actual filibusters. Among other reasons, the relative strengths and interests on both sides, including the likely House actions,[178] are clear enough by that late

---

[177] On the Senate floor, the supersonic transport had proved unpopular, but the conferees on the bill, coming from a committee supporting the SST, had struck a compromise in conference with like-minded House conferees that was considered "so patently a surrender of the Senate position, that the Senate stuck by its guns and refused to agree to the conference report," due to the filibuster. Gore, "The Conference Committee: Congress' Final Filter," Washington Monthly, June 1971, at 43, 46. Two attempts to vote cloture, on December 19 and 21, 1970, both failed by a wide margin, "killing a bill continuing funds to continue development of the plane. This led in 1971 to a cancellation of the entire project." Congressional Quarterly, Congress and the Nation: Vol. III, 1970-73, at 371.

[178] In the Weicker filibuster of the Helms-Johnston antibusing amendment, an interesting, if academic, question is whether the antibusing sponsors could have forced a conference had they been willing to pay the price in Senate filibustering. The House would not have deemed the bill to be at the stage of disagreement, since there had been no prior disagreement or insistence by the House. House Manual § 528. Thus a motion in the House to disagree to the Senate amendments and to agree to the request for conference would (footnote continued)

stage in the legislative process for sound negotiation.[179] Thus, bill proponents may quietly accept some preconference version of a bill, or strike a deal with opponents over that version, so that the bill can be enacted without facing a Senate filibuster on the conference report.

Filibusters on executive business pose a question of particular interest. The issue does not occur much regarding treaties, where the requirement of two-thirds to ratify assures any successful treaty could overcome obstruction anyway; the threat to treaties is killer reservations, not sheer stalling.[180] However, filibusters on nominations do occur in a very visible way, such as the successful filibuster of the nomination of Justice Abe Fortas for the post

---

not have been privileged. Absent unanimous consent, suspension of the rules, or a special rule, such a motion in the House would not be in order. Thus, with House leadership opposition, a likely course would still have been referral of the bill to committee and burial.

[179] With the 1982 Weicker filibuster, for example, if the sponsors of the Helms-Johnston antibusing amendment had felt strong and determined enough, they could have moved the bill to conference. "The Senate under its practice, at the time of the passage of a House bill with amendments, may insist upon its amendments and ask for a conference." Riddick, "Confferences and Conference Reports: Conferences: A Bill is Sent to Conference," at 388. Hence, the Senate could have asked the House for a conference. However, Senator Weicker would have had at least two more filibusters, on the motion to insist on the Senate amendments and request a conference, and on the motion to appoint conferees. These are debatable. See Riddick, "Debate: Debatable Matters," at 586 (example 9: "A motion that the Senate disagree to a House amendment, agree to a conference asked by the House, and that the conferees be named by the Senate" is debatable). The bill sponsors, rather than carry on the fight longer, preferred to pass the bill through the Senate, even if the House could be expected to bury it in committee.

[180] The Senate's first cloture vote did come on the Treaty of Versailles. S. Prt. No. 254, supra, at 44. As a recent example, Senator Helms proved able to obtain reservations to the Genocide Treaty, but that ability cannot be parsed readily into procedural and political components.

of Chief Justice.[181] Fortas became highly controversial, the Senate rejected cloture by 45-43, and the nomination was withdrawn.[182] That first filibuster was by conservatives, but in 1971 liberals filibustered against the nomination for Justice of William Rehnquist, in 1980 filibusters were occurring even against lesser nominations to the National Labor Relations Board, and in 1986 Justice Rehnquist was again being filibustered, this time on his nomination for Chief Justice.[183]

Until now, there have not been complex procedural aspects to filibustering a nomination, although some issues and tactics could surface at any time.[184] Rather, the filibuster simply provides a means for the opponents of the nomination to make a public issue of the nominee's ethical or ideological drawbacks, or over some controversy the opponents wish to tie to the nomination. The ultimate question is whether opponents can use filibustering to block nominees reflecting a particular ideological viewpoint. For example, Senator Helms "frequently ha[s] opposed nominees whose positions did not square with his own conservative views."[185] Conversely,

---

[181] Burdette does not record any filibusters of nominations. The Congressional Research Service's study concluded about the Fortas filibuster that "[t]he effort to block a confirmation by means of a filibuster was without precedent in the history of the Senate." Senate Cloture Rule at 38.

[182] Senate Cloture Rule, supra, at 38.

[183] The cloture votes are noted in S. Prt. No. 254, at 45, 46.

[184] As discussed in the section on executive procedure, there could be a dispute over the debatability of the motion to go into executive session and to proceed to a particular nomination, but it has not yet occurred. An effort could be made to break a filibuster by invocation of the two-speech rule because a nomination is not amendable, but none has yet occurred.

[185] 1985 Congressional Quarterly Almanac 419.

Senate   Democrats   opposed   various   Reagan
administration   judicial   nominations.
Filibustering raises the issue of whether the
votes   needed   to   move   an   ideologically
controversial nomination will be the 51 majority
needed for confirmation, or the 60 needed for
cloture.   If the latter, then this could pose some
significant limits on the President's powers in
the appointment process when pitted against the
resistance powers of a unified Senate minority.

11
Conference Procedure[1]

A. OVERVIEW AND HISTORY

Overview

The "Great Compromise" underlying Article I of the
Constitution -- creation of a bicameral
legislature, with the two chambers built on
different political bases -- necessitates a means
for reconciling differences between the chambers
in order to enact legislation. Congress' chief
means is the system of conference committees.
    Seemingly, that system often faces a
difficult task. Each chamber often approves a
very different version of a bill than the other
chamber's version. Conferees must often get their

---

[1] Sources cited frequently in this chapter include A.
McCown, The Congressional Conference Committee (1927)
(McCown); L. A. Froman, The Congressional Process:
Strategies, Rules, and Procedures (1967) (Froman); Reform
Penetrates Conference Committee, 33 Cong. Q. Week. Rep. 290
(1975) (Reform Penetrates Conference Committee); D. Vogler,
The Third House: Conference Committee in the United States
Congress (1971) (Vogler); T. Siff & A. Weil, Ruling Congress
(1975) (Ruling Congress); and Hook, In Conference: New
Hurdles, Hard Bargaining, 45 Cong. Q. Week. Rep. 2080 (1986)
(Hook).

chamber to give up items dear to its hearts, and to approve items in the other chamber's version that are highly distasteful, in order to devise a compromise.   Moreover, as their fee, conferees routinely shape the compromise, not as either chamber might like, but to suit their own preferences.   Thus, conferees bring versions back to their chambers for approval that would appear quite likely to raise opposition.

Yet despite this seeming difficulty, Congress has an extraordinary record of approving the outcomes of conferences.   In 1981-82, both Houses ultimately approved every single bill after it went off to conference; all became law except the ones vetoed by the President.   This record exceeded that of most years, but not by very much.   For example, in 1963-64, 89 bills were sent to conference and of these 85 finally became law.[2]   This makes conference procedure a study in the enormous momentum of the conference process, and of who Congress vests with the resulting power and what curbs it puts on that power.

In some respects, conference procedure involves the most formal, complex, and technical of all procedural rules.   Each chamber has formal methods for getting to conference, formal methods for approving conference reports that stay within the allotted range of discretion, and complex postconference methods for approving reports straying beyond that range.   On the other hand, conference involves some of the most informal, discretionary, non-rule-bound aspects of all congressional procedure.   In the conference committee itself, there are virtually no rules at all, except for sunshine rules.   The conference committee runs itself just as it likes, without procedural restraints.

This chapter's first section starts with what might be called the "primitive" form of reconciling differences between the chambers, the method of "amendments between Houses."   In that method, no conference is used; the chambers shuttle back and forth their different versions of a bill until they agree on a version.   This section lays the groundwork for conference

---

2   Froman at 158-59.

procedure, since the conference method uses certain aspects of the more primitive method.

The following two sections treat how the two chambers get to conference, and the most important aspect of that, how they select their conferees. Traditionally, conferees come from the committee of jurisdiction for the bill and are selected by the chair and ranking minority member of that committee, who themselves serve on the conference committee.

A separate section treats how the conference committee conducts itself. In light of the vast discretion vested in the conference committee, this section largely consists of a description of the range of methods currently employed rather than any limits on such methods. Finally, the last two sections address the handling of conference reports on the floor. One deals with the ordinary handling of such reports, focusing on why it is that the two chambers overwhelmingly approve conference reports. The other of the two final sections deals with the complex postconference methods used when conferees go beyond their allotted range of discretion. New mechanisms created since 1970 have completely altered this area of procedure.

History

The conference system results from a long historic evolution, going back to the middle ages and yet with major adjustments in the 1970s and 1980s. Particularly in the last century, that history largely concerns the balance of giving the conferees enough leeway to compromise differences without reducing the role of the chamber itself to a meaningless ritual.

In Parliament, conferences occurred as early as 1378. Then, as now, the conference system played a key role in taxes proposed by the Executive Branch, and the procedure six centuries ago is not unrecognizable: "It came to be a custom for a number of the Lords, selected either by their own House or by the House of Commons, to be assigned to confer with the whole body of Commons on the answer to be given to the king's request for money."[3]   In the bicameral colonial legislatures, there were conferences as early as

1645.[4] By setting up a bicameral Congress, the
Framers of the Constitution made use of the
conference mechanism inevitable, and the First
Congress immediately resorted to that old process,
making important use of conferences such as the
one that resolved differences over the Bill of
Rights.[5]

Despite the long history, it took another
three quarters of a century for the conference
committee system to take on a modern form. First,
the chambers had to develop their system of
standing committees and relate conferences to
it.[6]   Then, the two chambers had to develop
procedures bestowing special status on conference
reports: acceptance of the report as a whole
without amendment; the privilege for reports to be
taken up at any time; and the tendency for reports
to come up at the end of sessions when the chamber
had little choice but to swallow them. With these
pieces significantly in place, "[t]he
Congressional Conference Committee System was in
existence by 1850 and its power was beginning to
be felt."[7]

Toward the end of the 19th century, the
seniority principle hardened so that only the most
senior members of the committee of jurisdiction
served on conference committees. The two chambers
took key steps towards some restraint on
conferees' power. There had long been hostility
to conferees' enjoying the enormous power to add
new original provisions to bills, technically
referred to as making changes in bills beyond the
"scope of the differences" between the chambers.
By the 1870's, the Speaker was willing to

---

[3] McCown at 23.

[4] Id. at 33.

[5] Id. at 46.

[6] Initially "in many cases the managers chosen" -- that is,
each House's chosen conferees -- "did not even belong to the
committees that had reported the bill in either house." Id.
at 62.

[7] Id. at 73.

entertain points of order against reports with new
matter, and in 1918 the Senate adopted a rule for
its presiding officer to do the same. In 1920,
the   House   attempted   to   control   the   great
discretion   of   its   Appropriations   Committee   to
revise spending bills in conference by creating
the first of the modern postconference mechanisms
for allowing separate floor votes on items brought
back by conferees.

The   1970s   and   1980s   have   seen   some   major
steps towards restraint on the conference system,
although   leaving   it   enormous   power   and
discretion.   There has been a slow but steady
tendency to allow more junior Members to serve as
conferees, opening up what had previously been the
senior Members' monopoly.[8] In 1975, the chambers
adopted a sunshine rule for conference committees,
opening   up   conferences   to   a   degree   of
accountability.   Finally, in the 1970s the House
forged   ahead   with   a   second   postconference
mechanism designed to limit the use of conferences
on Senate non-germane amendments to bypass the
House's own committees and floor.

Amendments Between Houses: Mechanics

Congress   uses   two   methods   to   resolve
differences between the Houses: the conference
committee method, and the more frequently used
(for minor bills), if somewhat primitive, method
of "amendments between Houses." Congress uses the
conference   committee   system   for   most   of   its
important bills, but it does enact large numbers
of measures through amendments between Houses --
far   more   in   number,   than   by   conference
committee.[9]   While   most   are   minor,   some   major

---

[8]   Also, in 1965, the House created a new motion to end the
Rules Committee's ability to kill bills on the way to
conference by denying them special rules.   The Senate's
liberalization of its cloture rule in 1975 also diminished
the previous ability of a minority of Senators to kill a
conference report. The appointments of junior Members, and
these two rules changes, considerably restrained aspects of
the conference system that had given the conservative
coalition great power in its heyday.
(footnote continued)

bills do get passed that way for tactical
reasons.   For example, in 1988, Congress
overhauled the insurance law for the nuclear
industry: "[r]ather than appoint a House-Senate
conference, the bill's managers chose to negotiate
informally and work out their differences in
amendments to the bill,"[10] meaning that they used
the method of amendments between Houses.   The
chambers use this route, among other reasons, to
avoid filibusters on conference reports[11] or when
the chambers distrust those who would be
conferees.[12]   Circumvention of conference may, in
turn, arouse the ire of those who would have
participated in conference.[13]

---

[9]   "[O]f the 1,026 public and private bills which were
passed in the Eighty-eighth Congress (1963-64), 89 bills
were sent to conference." Froman at 158.   Besides all these
public laws that do not go through conference, there are
also private laws and concurrent resolutions, which are
almost always adopted without conference committee action
(except for the annual concurrent resolution on the budget).

[10]   Davis, Congress Clears Nuclear-Insurance Measure, 46
Cong. Q. Week. Rep. 2196 (1988).

[11]   In 1981-82, for example, Congress enacted the Voting
Rights Act extension, the nuclear waste bill, the debt limit
extension, and several continuing resolutions by amendments
between Houses.

    Traditionally, concerns about filibuster were a major
reason that civil rights bills like the Voting Rights
extension avoided conference.   Froman at 160-61.

[12]   For example, in the historic procedural battle over the
tariff of 1883, low-tariff supporters fought desperately
(but unsuccessfully) for the House to accept a Senate bill
without a conference, fearing (correctly) that conferees
would come up with a tariff higher than desired by either
the Senate or the House.   McCown at 112.

[13]   A 1982 example concerns the anticrime bill discussed in
the next footnote.   Representative John Conyers (D-Mich.),
chair of one of the key House subcommittees with
jurisdiction over elements of the bill, complained that the
bill came
(footnote continued)

Moreover, the mechanics of amendments between Houses illuminate how the conference committee system works. All bills going to conference must shuttle back and forth between the House and the Senate at least three times, following a path akin to bills passed by amendments between Houses. The postconference mechanisms depend heavily on amendments between Houses.[14]

To enact a bill through amendments between Houses, the House and Senate must take two steps: they must pick a common vehicle; and they must send the vehicle back and forth, amending it until they agree on a version. Picking a common vehicle is an absolute requirement. It is not enough for the Senate to enact a Senate bill and for the House to then enact a House bill identical to the Senate bill; either the House must enact the Senate bill, or the Senate must enact the House bill.

Mechanically, when the first chamber to act

---

before the House through probably the most disgraceful procedure that has ever been utilized with regard to the Federal Criminal Code . . . . [T]his bill was unilaterally removed from conference last Saturday evening. My staff reported to me that our Parliamentarian's Office told them that it was unable to find any precedent for removing a bill unilaterally from conference in this manner.

129 Cong. Rec. H10506 (daily ed. Dec. 20, 1983). The bill never became law, because President Reagan pocket vetoed it.

[14] For example, in 1982 the House and Senate appointed conferees for an omnibus anticrime bill, H.R. 3963, in the final month of the Congress, but soon the Senate "decided that there was not sufficient movement and dismissed their conferees." 129 Cong. Rec. H10504 (daily ed. Dec. 20, 1982) (Rep. Peter Rodino (D-N.J.)).

In the final days of the session, there was no way to handle the matter except by swift resort to amendments between Houses. The Senate went back to the method of amendments between Houses on Saturday, December 18; by Monday, December 20, the House completed informal negotiations and passed its version; the Senate accepted that version on December 21.

on a bill enacts it, that chamber sends it with a
message, or "messages" it, to the second
chamber.[15] A simple method of action is for the
second chamber to refer the bill to committee, for
that committee to report out the bill, and for the
second chamber then to enact the bill.   There is
no problem with the House acting on a Senate bill,
or the Senate acting on a House bill; each
chamber's rules largely treats the other's bills
as equivalent legislative vehicles to its own.[16]
However, in practice each chamber prefers somewhat
to work on its own bills, and to deal with the
other chamber's bills only at the final stage.

   Accordingly, when the House enacts a House
bill and sends it over to the Senate, the Senate
will refer that House bill to committee, but often
the Senate committee will still mark up and report
its own Senate bill.   When the Senate committee
reports the amended Senate bill to the floor, it
sends along the "companion" House bill almost as
an afterthought. The Senate floor then amends the
Senate bill, ignoring the companion House bill,
until stopping just short of final passage. Then,
with some boilerplate phrases, the Senate will

---

[15] Physically, one of the House or Senate clerks walks over
to the other chamber with the bill, where he is announced
with a brief ceremony, and gives the bill and messages to
the other chamber's presiding officer, whose clerks make
appropriate entries in the journal and Congressional
Record.   Usually this passes virtually unnoticed.   On
occasion, arrival of the messenger may be important, such as
when the deadline is nearing on a continuing resolution, or
adjournment awaits action on a last bill from the other
chamber.

[16] An exception is a bill in one of the areas for which the
House monopolizes origination, namely revenue and
appropriation bills; the House will not act on a Senate bill
in such an area, other than to send a protest to the Senate.

   House Rule XXIV(2) prescribes that Senate bills on the
Speaker's Table "may be referred to the appropriate
committees in the same manner and with the same right of
correction as public bills presented by Members." Senate
Rules VII(1) and XIV(3) and (4) prescribe handling of House
bills similar to that for Senate bills.

take up consideration of the companion House bill,
strike all of its contents, insert the contents of
the Senate bill as amended, and enact the House
bill as amended. It then "indefinitely postpones"
its own Senate bill. In this way, both the Senate
committee and the Senate floor do all the work on
their own Senate bill, and then put its provisions
aboard a House vehicle.

The House follows a procedure roughly the
same, except the House processes its own House
bills all the way to enactment. That is, the
House committee may report out a House bill and a
companion Senate bill, and then the House floor
will amend the House bill and actually enact it.
Then, the House takes up consideration of the
companion Senate bill, strikes all of the contents
of the Senate bill, inserts the contents of the
House bill as amended, and then enacts the Senate
bill as amended. The House then tables, rather
than indefinitely postpones, the House bill
previously enacted. The formal difference in
Senate and House methods is that the Senate passes
one bill, while the House passes two bills.
However, both chambers work on their own bill and
then insert its contents into the other chamber's
bill when that is to be the vehicle.

Both the House and Senate devise an
additional procedure, "holding at the desk," to
streamline this process in many cases. Quite
often, by the time one chamber enacts a bill, the
other chamber already has completed committee
action on its companion bill. To streamline
enactment, each chamber "holds at the desk"
incoming bills from the other chamber for which it
has completed committee action and has its own
bill on the calendar. This avoids the need for
referring the other chamber's bill to committee
and then reporting or discharging it out. Each
House has its own term for where matters go when
they are "held at the desk."[17] When the House or

---

[17] In the House, incoming Senate bills for which there is a
companion House bill already on a calendar go to the
"Speaker's Table"; in the Senate, incoming House bills for
which there is a companion Senate bill already on the
calendar are "placed on the Calendar" to await Senate action
on the Senate bill.
(footnote continued)

Senate completes action on a bill for which a companion has been "held at the desk," it takes the other chamber's bill from the Speaker's Table or the Senate Calendar where that bill has been held, inserts the contents of its own bill, and sends it back to the first chamber.

Once the first chamber has passed a bill, and the second chamber has passed it and sent it back with an amendment through the process described above, the Houses begin a process that can be short or long. In 1981-82, of 472 public laws, 72 involved conference committee action. Of the 401 remaining, 285 were passed by the two Houses in identical form, without the necessity for the third step of sending the bill back to the first chamber for consideration of the second chamber's amendments. Seventy-seven bills required three steps, being passed by the first chamber, amended by the second, and accepted as amended by the first chamber. Thirty-one bills required four steps, six required five steps, and one required six steps. The champion badminton birdie of the Congress, the Federal Oil and Gas Royalty Management Act of 1982, was swatted back and forth between the Houses seven times before enactment.[18]

The House has no express rule for this, but since House Rule XXIV provides only that the Speaker "may" refer Senate bills to committee, it implies discretion not to refer, so technically what is happening when a Senate bill is held at the desk is simply that the Speaker is exercising his discretion not to immediately refer it. Similarly, the Senate has no express rule for this. Senate Rule XIV provides for House bills to go to the Senate calendar "if objection be made to further proceeding thereon," but this does not depend on whether there is a companion Senate bill on the Senate calendar. It serves quite a different function. Like so much else in the Senate, bills are held at the desk by unanimous consent.

[18]   The House passed it on September 29, 1982. The Senate amended it on December 6. The two versions differed over a House proposal for raising the royalty rate paid to the government for oil and gas produced on federal lands. The Senate rejected the House's proposal to raise the rate, but "the bill's House managers insisted on keeping it, and that set off a struggle between the House and Senate. The (footnote continued)

Agreeing and Disagreeing Motions

A specialized vocabulary describes the actions of the House and Senate on each others' bills and amendments thereto -- the agreeing and disagreeing actions.[19] First, one chamber enacts a bill: for example, the House. Second, the other chamber (the Senate) then "agrees" to the bill -- either with, or without, an amendment -- by the adoption of a motion to agree. Those two steps, with the second being agreement with amendments, produce a "House bill with Senate amendments." (If the Senate had been the chamber initially enacting the bill, the result would now be a "Senate bill with House amendments.")

Third, as the product of the Senate goes back to the House, the House might take one of the "agreeing" actions. It may "concur" with the Senate's amendments -- either with, or without, an amendment -- by adoption of a motion to concur. As a third step, such concurrence with amendments produces "House amendments to Senate amendments to a House bill." (If the Senate had been the chamber initially enacting the bill, the result would now be "Senate amendments to House amendments to a Senate bill.")

If the House previously took a disagreeing action (as discussed below) and at this third stage now wants to take an agreeing action, it "recedes" from the disagreeing action and does something else. For example, the House could

---

measure went back and forth between the chambers three times before the House finally gave in and dropped the provision." 1982 Congressional Quarterly Almanac 446-47. To be precise, the House amended the bill on December 13. The Senate amended it on December 16. The House amended it on December 18. The Senate rejected that last House amendment on December 21. Later on December 21, the House gave in and adopted the version that had come back from the Senate.

[19] It should be noted that the terms "disagreeing" and "agreeing" are purely technical; both types of actions are the ordinary, amicable method by which the chambers resolve differences.

recede from previous disagreement to the Senate's amendments, and concur in those amendments with an amendment; this could occur by a motion to recede and concur with an amendment. As a third step, such House receding and concurring with an amendment would produce House amendments to Senate amendments to a House bill.

A separate line of consideration concerns the "disagreeing" actions. Each chamber has three disagreeing actions it can take instead of the afore-described "agreeing" actions: it can "insist" on its prior amendments; it can "disagree" to the other chamber's amendments; or, having insisted yet received renewed requests for change from the other chamber, it can "adhere" to its amendments, an uncompromising stance, rarely reached, which signifies an unwillingness to bend. These actions occur, not surprisingly, by the motion to insist, the motion to disagree, and the motion to adhere. For example, the House can enact a bill, the Senate can agree to the bill with an amendment (a "Senate amendment to a House bill"), and the House could disagree to that Senate amendment. The Senate could then insist on the Senate amendment. That would mean each chamber had taken "disagreeing" actions.

These actions can be taken in combinations. If the House passed a bill, and the Senate agreed with amendments, then the House could concur in some of the Senate amendments with House amendments, and disagree with the other Senate amendments. The Senate could insist on the Senate amendments disagreed to, and concur in some of the House amendments with more Senate amendments. Then the House could respond with a four-part combo: the House could recede from its disagreement with some of the Senate amendments and concur in those with more House amendments; the House could concur in some of the Senate amendments; the House could concur in other of the Senate's amendments with more House amendments; and the House could disagreeing to yet other of the Senate's amendment.[20] As the next

---

[20]   In theory, there is a limit of two degrees of amendments, counted in a peculiar way that starts only after each chamber has acted. Thus, the theoretical limit would (footnote continued)

section will discuss, these varying actions have significance in the context of conference.

Usually, after the second chamber has acted, the successive steps occur without referral to committee or roll-call votes. A returning bill is held at the desk, called up by unanimous consent, and the appropriate agreeing or disagreeing action, with or without amendment, occurs by unanimous consent on request of the bill manager. More elaborate procedures occur only for rare fancy maneuvers. For example, the Senate may seize a minor bill shuttling back and forth, and use it as the vehicle for some irrelevant major matter tacked on as a non-germane amendment, requiring the House to use an elaborate procedure on its next step.[21] Apart from such situations, it is unusual, and perhaps a bit discourteous (absent some reason) to withhold unanimous consent from the steps necessary to send back and forth a bill that has received full consideration on the floor already.[22] In this respect, the method of

---

be when Chamber A's bill has been amended by B, then amended again by A (first counted degree), then amended by B (second counted degree). Actually, this limit is rarely reached, and when it is, points of order may be foregone, as in the royalty bill described above, which went a degree too far.

[21] In the example mentioned above of the 1982 omnibus anticrime bill, when the Senate resorted to amendments between Houses, the House could not simply handle something so controversial by unanimous consent. In order to take up the House bill with the Senate amendment and amend it, the House sponsor used suspension of the rules to do what was necessary -- "take from the Speaker's table the bill . . . recede from disagreement to the Senate amendment and concur to the Senate amendment with an amendment." 129 Cong. Rec. H10491 (daily ed. Dec. 20, 1982) (Rep. William J. Hughes (D-N.J.)). The motion required a two-thirds vote, which it received on a roll call.

[22] There is one important occasion when bills are privileged in the House because they have previously reached the stage of disagreement: when bills go to a conference but subsequently falter (such as by defeat of the conference report, a point of order on the conference report, failure to reach agreement in conference, or resort to the complex postconference mechanisms for achievement of results that (footnote continued)

amendments between Houses is one example of how even the House relies for its smooth routine functioning on unanimous consent among Members.

B.   GOING TO CONFERENCE

In most instances, the Senate and House employ simple, routine steps to send a bill to conference.   On occasio, going to conference presents possibilities for tactics such as instructions, manipulation of which chamber will acts first, and surprise kills or delays.

Stage of Disagreement

A bill goes to conference by a variation on the procedure for amendments between Houses discussed in the previous section.   As in that procedure, the bill shuttles back and forth between the chambers, being successively amended by each.   Two extra steps take a bill out of that procedure and send it to conference: reaching what is technically referred to as the "stage of disagreement" in both Houses, and the adoption by both Houses of necessary motions to request (in one chamber) and to agree (in the other) to conference, and to appoint conferees.

The progress of an ordinary bill, the Communications Amendments Act of 1982, illustrates these two extra steps for going to conference.   On June 9, 1981, the House passed the bill, H.R. 3239, and sent it to the Senate.[23]   The Senate

---

cannot be achieved through conference.)   Since the bill reached the "stage of disagreement" before it went to conference, after the conference falls through, the bill reverts to that stage, and the House can take it up as a privileged matter.

If unanimous consent is withheld in the House, then the bill being shuttled back and forth may or may not be privileged for the requisite floor motions to keep shuttling it, depending whether the "stage of disagreement" has been reached, as discussed in the next section.

(footnote continued)

took up consideration of, amended, and passed H.R.
3239 on August 18.   The Senate was not seeking a
conference immediately, so it "agreed" to the
House bill "with an amendment";[24] "agreeing" does
not produce the "stage of disagreement" needed for
conference.   The Senate messaged the bill, with
its Senate amendments, to the House the same day,
where, like all incoming bills (i.e., Senate
bills, and House bills with Senate amendments) it
went to the Speaker's Table.

By unanimous consent, the House took up the
bill, and the majority manager, Representative Tim
Wirth (D-Colo.), asked that the House "disagree to
the Senate amendments . . . ."[25]   "Disagreeing,"
like "insisting" and "adhering," placed the House
in the "stage of disagreement," thus able to seek
a conference.   Thus, in the same breath,
Representative Wirth asked the House to "request a
conference with the Senate thereon."[26]

When there was no objection to Representative
Wirth's requests, the Speaker pronounced that they
were so ordered, and the Speaker then appointed
conferees.   The bill was then messaged back, and
laid before the Senate the next morning, December
19.   Senator Ted Stevens (R-Alaska), the Assistant
Majority Leader, moved "that the Senate insist on
its amendments . . . ."[27]   Such insistence being a
disagreeing action, like disagreement to the other
chamber's amendments, this placed the Senate, like
the House, in the stage of disagreement ready for
conference.   So, in the same breath, Senator
Stevens moved that the Senate "agree to a
conference as requested by the House of
Representatives," and that "the Chair be
authorized to appoint conferees on the part of the

---

[23]   Because there was already a companion measure on the
Senate calendar, S. 821, reported by the Senate Committee on
Commerce, Science and Transportation on May 15, the House
bill was held at the desk in the Senate.

[24]   128 Cong. Rec. S10730 (daily ed. Aug. 18, 1982).

[25]   128 Cong. Rec. H6443 (daily ed. Aug. 18, 1982).

[26]   Id.

[27]   128 Cong. Rec. S10829 (daily ed. Aug. 19, 1982).

Senate."[28]   Upon adoption of that motion, the
Chair appointed conferees.   The bill had gone to
conference.

In this instance, after the House and Senate
had acted on the bill it took two more shuttle
trips -- House disagreement to Senate amendment,
and Senate insistence on Senate amendment -- to
get to conference.   In the faster method that
takes only one more shuttle-trip, the second
chamber to act on the bill "insists" on its
amendments at the same time that it makes them,
before the first chamber has even seen them.
Insistence, as a disagreeing action, puts the
second chamber instantly into the stage of
disagreement, so it takes only the disagreeing
action of the first chamber to precipitate a
conference, saving a trip.[29]   Today, Congress
passes virtually all appropriations bills this
way; about two-thirds of all the bills that went
to conference in 1981-82 went this way.[30]

---

[28]   Id.   To be technical, it is one single motion, not two,
to disagree and ask for (or agree to) a conference, or to
insist and ask for (or agree to) a conference.   It then
takes a second motion, in the Senate, to authorize the
presiding officer to appoint conferees.   This matters only
for filibusterers wishing to multiply the debatable motions.

[29]   The development of this practice is described in McCown
at 82-83.   A century ago, it always took at least these two
additional trips.   Then, in or just before the 1870s, the
shorter practice developed.   In 1879, when the shortened
procedure was suggested in the Senate for action on a
pending appropriation bill, "Senator [James G.] Blaine [(R-
Maine)], who had long been Speaker of the House, said that
this had been done before, he thought about three or four
times during the last fifteen years."   Id. at 83.

[30]   For example, in 1982 the House adopted the District of
Columbia Appropriation Act of 1983, H.R. 7144, on September
30, 1982.   The Senate amended and passed it on December 7,
and at the same time "insisted" on its amendments and asked
for a conference.   On December 13, the House disagreed to
the Senate's amendments and agreed to a conference.

Of the 72 bills that went to conference in 1981-82, 14
required two extra passes after each chamber's first look,
(footnote continued)

This minuet has tactical importance. The bill managers in the second chamber choose whether to become the "requesting" chamber or the "agreeing" chamber by using either the short method of insisting right away on amendments or the longer method of awaiting the other chamber's disagreement.[31] Since generally the chamber that requests a conference, acts last on the conference report, the managers thereby steer controversial conference reports first to one chamber or the other.[32] The minuet of the stage of disagreement also occasionally matters when a bill en route for conference either has postconference proceedings or does not pass by the usual conference system.[33]

---

and a half-dozen required additional or more complicated steps. This count is based on the listings in the Congressional Research Service's Bill Digest.

[31] The number of steps can also be manipulated by the choice of vehicle: the second chamber can use the first chamber's bill and insist and ask for conference, or ignore the first chamber's bill and send its own over, setting up the first chamber to ask for conference. However, other considerations, such as comity between chambers and judicious allocation of the prestige and credit to the Member who wants "his" bill to be the vehicle, may constrain tactical manipulation of the choice of vehicle.

[32] The formal process is that the chamber that agrees to conference sends the papers -- the bill, amendments, and messages -- back to the requesting chamber. The requesting chamber's conferees bring the papers to conference, and at the end, in signification of the success of conference, give the papers to the other (agreeing) chamber's conferees. Only the chamber in possession of the papers can act on the conference report, and so the agreeing chamber, having received the papers, acts first on the conference report.

[33] For example, the Senate may pass a House bill with amendments, insist on its amendments, and ask for conference, but the House may then disagree to the Senate's amendments and not agree to conference, going back to the route on amendments between Houses. Because the complexities come up most often in certain postconference procedures, they will be discussed in this chapter's last section.

Instructions

Each chamber has an additional option in going to conference: it may "instruct" its conferees. This is an option the House uses only occasionally, and the Senate even less often.[34] After the chamber has requested or agreed to conference, and before the appointment of conferees, a Member can offer a motion to instruct the conferees to take a particular position in conference. For example, in 1981, the House passed, and the Senate passed with amendments, the Department of Defense Appropriation, H.R. 4995. The Senate insisted on its amendments and asked for a conference, and the House disagreed to the Senate amendments and agreed to a conference. At this point, Representative Margaret S. Roukema (R-N.J.) moved

> that the managers on the part of the House . . . be instructed to insist upon the total amount appropriated (for "procurement") under the provisions contained in title IV of the House bill, and upon the total amount appropriated (for "research, development, test and evaluation") under the provisions contained in title V of the House bill.

---

[34]   The House, in 1981-82, adopted instructions about a half-dozen times.

The Senate is different. "Only in rare instances has the Senate instructed." House Manual § 541. In fact, in one extensive nineteenth-century debate the Senate overruled a decision of the Chair and, in effect, held that instructions were not in order. McCown at 93-94; V Hinds § 6397. Senate examples are collected and the procedure described in Riddick, "Conferences and Conference Reports: Instruction of Conferees," at 401-4. In 1981-82, apparently the Senate adopted instructions to conferees only once, regarding the authorization for Head Start in the 1981 omnibus budget reconciliation bill. The instructions were noncontroversial, as they responded to an "oversight" by which the House version failed to include that authorization level. See 127 Cong. Rec. S7575-77 (daily ed. July 14, 1981).

Representative Roukema explained that she wished
to avoid "the usual practice of meeting halfway on
these appropriations," because "the funding levels
appropriated by the other body . . . within these
two titles [are] an open invitation to
inefficiency and poor management."[35]   The House
adopted the motion by voice vote.

Instructions serve only a limited purpose.
They are not binding, and there is neither a point
of order nor any other particular sanction applied
when a conference report comes back that does not
follow the instructions.[36]   Moreover, instructions
are subject to certain procedural limitations.
Conferees can only be instructed to do things that
would be in order without the instruction; thus,
for example, they cannot be instructed to insert
new matter not already present in either chamber's
version.   After conferees have been appointed,
only the House, not the Senate, allows
instructions, and then only after 20 calendar
days; such instructions occur infrequently. [37]

---

[35]   127 Cong. Rec. H9440 (daily ed. Dec. 14, 1981).

[36]   In the case of Representative Roukema's defense
appropriation instruction, the House conferees brought back
a report that did not follow the instructions to stay within
the House amounts for titles IV and V.   The conference
version was closer to the House version than to the Senate
version, but still gave the Senate over one-third of the
difference between the two versions.   1981 Congressional
Quarterly Almanac 312.

[37]   See Riddick, "Conferences and Conference Reports," at
402 (Senate instructions only before appointment of
conferees); Deschler at 33 § 11; House Rule XXVIII(1)(b).
One recent example was the Cash Discount Act, H.R. 31, to
which the Senate tacked a nongermane amendment to eliminate
an age restriction that was preventing Dr. C. Everett Koop
from being appointed Surgeon General.   Six weeks after the
House appointed conferees, and three weeks after the Senate
appointed conferees, the conference had "unsuccessfully
attempted to meet on two occasions," with a "worthwhile
piece of legislation . . . blocked due to nongermane
language."   127 Cong. Rec. H2344 (daily ed. May 20,
1981)(Rep. Edward Madigan (R-Ill.)).   The House conferees
(footnote continued)

Although limited in these ways, instructions
can be useful. In the House, they are one of the
few motions, like the motion to recommit, which is
the prerogative of the minority, i.e., which a
minority Member will be recognized to offer before
any majority Members. Whichever side offers them
can push the chamber into expressing its political
will on a proposition shaped just as the moving
Member wishes.[38] If the expression does not bind
the conferees, it exerts some pressure on them.
On the other hand, both chambers, and especially
the Senate, have somewhat a prejudice against
instructions, because conferees do not like being
instructed, needing freedom to accommodate the two
chambers' differences.[39]

---

were instructed to agree to the Senate's amendment
eliminating the age restriction, id. at H2350, and they
did. That was apparently the only set of instructions in
1981-82 after conferees were appointed; the rest were for
conferees before appointment. This contrasts with the older
pattern noted by the commentators, in which instructions
before appointment of conferees were rarer than after.

[38] In theory, instructions can be amended. However, since
the motions to instruct are offered in the House, not in
Committee of the Whole, they are governed by the hour rule,
and debate and amendment can be cut off by the motion for
the previous question. Hence, in practice, "amendments are
not easily offered." House Republican Manual, "When the
Houses Differ: Procedure After a Conference is Requested:
Instructing the Conferees," at 326.

[39] As an example of a successful fight against
instructions, in 1983 Representative Byron Dorgan (D-N.D.)
successfully fought an effort by Representative Silvio Conte
(R-Mass.), ranking minority member on the Appropriations
Committee, to instruct conferees on a continuing resolution
to kill funds for a North Dakota water project:

Dorgan's strategy also depended on the fact that the
challenge came on a "procedural" vote. This allowed
Conte's opponents to say they were voting against the
instruction procedure rather than casting a substantive
vote for the project or against the environment. They
could argue that it was a mistake to tie the conferees'
hands as a general practice on any single issue, since
it could reduce their ability to negotiate successfully
(footnote continued)

House and Senate Routes to Conference

Normally, the steps for going to conference occur quickly and easily in the House. The bill's manager does face the problem that motions to send a bill to conference are not privileged,[40] even when the House has previously adopted the bill, when (as per usual) "the stage of disagreement"[41] has not yet been reached. The House takes up such bills and sends them to conference by unanimous consent "in the vast majority of cases."[42]

---

on a whole range of House-Senate differences.

The Garrison Diversion in North Dakota -- A Case Study in Water Project Politics, 40 Cong. Q. Week. Rep. 1554, 1555 (1983).

[40] When Senate amendments are before the House for the first time, or when the Senate has returned a bill with House amendments to which it has disagreed . . . no privileged motion is in order . . . . [M]otions to dispose of amendments between the Houses are not privileged until the stage of disagreement has been reached on a bill with amendments of the other House.

House Manual § 528; see Deschler 32 § 7.2.

[41] The "stage of disagreement" is defined thusly:

The House has reached the stage of disagreement on a bill when it is again in possession of the papers thereon, having previously disagreed to Senate amendments or insisted on House amendments (with or without requesting or agreeing to a conference). Only previous insistence or disagreement by the House itself places the House in disagreement (and not merely disagreement, insistence, or amendment by the Senate) . . . . Once the stage of disagreement has been reached on a bill with amendments, the House remains in the stage of disagreement until the matter is finally disposed of and motions for its disposition are privileged whenever the House is in possession of the papers.

House Manual § 528.
(footnote continued)

Although Members know that a single objection will block that route, few object, because they know the alternative routes available.[43]
    Until 1965,[44] there were two ways for the House to get to conference when some Member objects to going by unanimous consent, both of which are still available: suspension of the rules, which requires a two-thirds vote, or a special rule from the Rules Committee.[45]   The

---

[42]   House Republican Manual, "When the Houses Differ: The Stage of Formal Disagreement," at 315.   Absent such unanimous consent, the House has to use one of the methods for conferring privilege on a bill -- suspension of the rules, a special rule, or Rule XX as discussed below.

[43]   A colloquy on the House's next-to-last day in 1982 illustrates why Members will give unanimous consent even for controversial bills to go to conference.   Chairperson Dan Rostenkowski (D-Ill.) of Ways and Means asked unanimous consent, and obtained it, to take up the surface transportation bill, H.R. 6211.   Minority Leader Robert Michel (R-Ill.) asked: "And if the gentleman does not get unanimous consent, would it be the gentleman's intention to get a rule?"   Representative Rostenkowski answered: "The chairman of the Committee on Ways and Means or the conference would be constrained to get a rule, yes." 128 Cong. Rec. H10516 (daily ed. Dec. 20, 1982).

[44]   The conservative coalition controlling the Rules Committee was willing at times to withhold such a special rule, thereby killing legislation even after both Houses had passed it.   Froman at 144-53.   In a famous 1960 instance, the Rules Committee denied a special rule for going to conference for a bill granting federal aid to education that was one of the Democratic Party's top priorities, killing the bill in an embarrassment on the eve of the 1960 election.

[45]   For example, in 1982, Representative Samuel Stratton (D-N.Y.), an opponent of the nuclear waste bill, H.R. 3809, noted that "Somebody found out that [I] was going to refuse unanimous consent, so suddenly we get the Rules Committee to come out with a rule," and he acknowledged, even as he fought the special rule (unsuccessfully), that "probably nothing is more futile than to try to take on the distinguished Committee on Rules."   128 Cong. Rec. H10518 (footnote continued)

Rules Committee can use elaborate special rules at
this point, such as ones coupling nongermane
propositions to go to conference together, and
allowing only a single vote that both adopts the
special rule and accomplishes the coupling and
sending to conference. As a third method for
getting to conference, in 1965 the House adopted
House Rule XX(1), creating a motion which allows
the House to take up a bill and send it to
conference without a special rule.[46]

There remain theoretical possibilities for
how the House could still kill a bill on the way
to conference even though it had majority
support.[48] However, the more likely reasons for a

_____

(daily ed. Dec. 20, 1982).

[46] The 1965 creation of Rule XX was a reaction to the 1960
education bill incident. The House adopted the new rule on
the eve of submission by President Johnson of his Great
Society program, in order to safeguard that program. Rule
XX provides in part: "a motion to disagree with the
amendments of the Senate to a House bill or resolution and
request or agree to a conference with the Senate, or a
motion to insist on the House amendments to a Senate bill or
resolution and request or agree to a conference with the
Senate, shall always be in order . . . ." The rule imposes
the requirements that the motion is in order only "if the
Speaker, in his discretion, recognizes for that purpose and
if the motion is made by direction of the committee having
jurisdiction of the subject matter of the bill or
resolution."

[48] Rule XX(1) still leaves one opportunity in the House for
killing a bill on the way to conference despite majority
support. A majority of members out of sympathy with the
leadership -- for example, a conservative coalition of
Republicans and southern Democrats -- may push a bill
through the House against the desire of the leadership, such
as by discharge. This type of majority could fail to get to
conference because either the committee majority or the
Speaker would refuse to allow use a Rule XX(1) motion, and
the Rules Committee would deny a special rule.

This maneuver has not occurred much if at all, given
the many other obstacles House procedure lets the leadership
put in the way of such a majority. Also, ultimately, there
remains the power of such a disgruntled majority to
(footnote continued)

bill to die on the way to conference are lack of
time at the end of a session, or one chamber's
belief that the gap between the versions is too
big to bridge in conference.[49]
     In the Senate, the rules help bring onto the
floor the bills that have passed both chambers, by
making   House   amendments   to   a   Senate   bill
privileged (i.e., making the motion to consider
them nondebatable).[47]   However, opponents of a
bill can still delay or kill it after the Senate
takes   up   the   version   from   the   House   --   by
filibustering, or threatening to filibuster, the
motions to send it to conference. At that point,
the motion to reach the stage of disagreement and
the   motion   to   authorize   the   Chair   to   appoint
conferees are debatable, and there may be other
filibuster opportunities.[50]

---

discharge the Rules Committee from a special rule to send
such a bill to conference.

[49]   For example, in 1982 the House passed a broad version of
a bill to extend the Economic Development Administration;
the Senate passed a much thinner version.   It was "a
question of who w[ould] blink first," i.e., whether the
Senate would go to conference on the House version or the
House would relent and pass a "thin" version acceptable to
the Senate.   In the end, "the Senate did not agree to a
conference,   and   the   legislation   died   when   Congress
adjourned." 1982 Congressional Quarterly Almanac 63.

[47]   Rule   VII(3);   Riddick,   "Amendments   Between   Houses:
Consideration of Amendments Between Houses: Laid Before the
Senate at Any Time," at 106.

[50]   The motion to reach the stage of disagreement would be
the motion to disagree to the House amendments, or insist on
the Senate amendments, and to ask for a conference, or to
agree to one.

     As for additional filibuster opportunities, if the
vehicle for conference would be a House bill, but the Senate
has, as usual, debated its own Senate bill, then the
managers must move to proceed to the House bill (a debatable
motion) and then move to strike out its contents and insert
the   contents   of   the   Senate   bill   (another   debatable
motion).   Only then can they make the motions to go to
conference.

Those opportunities to filibuster killed quietly one of the most controversial bills of the 97th Congress, the Department of Justice authorization with its busing amendment.[51] To go to conference required passing the House version of the bill, which, in turn, would have created additional opportunities for Senator Weicker to filibuster. Rather than face that,[52] the bill managers negotiated a final passage of the Senate bill, which scored a visible victory but sent their bill to its unconferenced death.[53]

C.   SELECTION OF CONFEREES

In all the conference process, the selection of conferees is probably the step least visible -- and most important. Considering the conferees' enormous discretion in resolving differences, and the overwhelming likelihood that both chambers will adopt a conference report just as the conferees write it, appointment as a conferee is as near an absolute license for a member to write major legislation to one's taste as the Congress ever grants. Beyond question, the authority to

---

[51]   The chapter on filibuster discusses Senator Lowell Weicker's (R-Conn.) filibuster from June, 1981 to March, 1982, against the Helms-Johnston busing amendment. The Senate voted cloture against five different stages of Senator Weicker's filibuster and broke his postcloture filibuster before it approached passing the Senate bill.

[52]   "Although Senate backers of S. 951 could seek a conference with the House on the authorizations, [Sen. Bennett] Johnston [D-La.] said Feb. 25 he did not think the Senate would take this route. Johnston said he expected that Weicker would filibuster an attempt to bring up the House bill in the Senate and then filibuster any effort to substitute Senate language under the House number." 40 Cong. Q. Week. Rep. 464 (1982).

[53]   When the bill arrived in the House, there was no way for its supporters to fight for an immediate conference. Instead, the Speaker referred it to the hostile House Judiciary Committee from whence it never emerged.

name conferees is one of the greatest of the committee chair's powers.

As a formal matter, both the House and Senate vest the power to choose conferees in their presiding officers. In the House, the Speaker continues to appoint conferees; this is a surviving vestige of the power he had until 1911 to appoint all committees.[54] In the Senate, technically the body as a whole holds the power, and can directly elect conferees if it is so inclined,[55] but whenever conferences are agreed to, the Senate invariably agrees by unanimous consent to vest in the Chair the authority to appoint conferees.

Notwithstanding this formal authority of the presiding officers, actually in both chambers the chair of the committee with jurisdiction over the bill usually makes recommendations which determine who will be the conferees, although the House's Speaker has some significant powers.[56]   Since

---

[54] House Rule X(6)(f) provides: "The Speaker shall appoint all select and conference committees . . . . " See McCown at 154.

[55] For the precedents regarding appointment of Senate conferees, see Riddick, "Conferences and Conference Reports: Action for Appointing Conferees," at 376-78. Technically, Rule XXIV(1), which provides for the appointment of all committees (and thus would control conference committees) specifies that "the Senate, unless otherwise ordered, shall by resolution appoint the chairman of each such committee and the other members thereof."

[56] In the 1970s, it was be said that the last time a House Speaker picked conferees over a chair's wishes was 1947. Siff and Weil, at 172 n.*. However, Speaker O'Neill left a stronger legacy:

> Usually the Speaker . . . appoint[s] conferees selected by the relevant committee chairmen   But . . . . Speaker Thomas P. O'Neill Jr., D-Mass., made critical decisions about whom to appoint as negotiators on the Gramm-Rudman-Hollings measure, because that proposal had never been considered by any House committee. Instead, it was attached by the Senate as an amendment to a bill raising the debt ceiling.

(footnote continued)

there is no fixed size for conference delegations, that committee chair picks the size, and provides a list to the presiding officer for following in naming conferees. On that list, usually committee chairs put only members of their committees (barring a multiple committee situation, discussed below).[57] Committee chairs generally pick the proportion of minority party conferees based on their ratio in the chamber[58]; during some historic periods when House committee ratios did not match the ratio in the chamber, minority party conferees have been picked based on their ratio on the committee.[59] For selecting the particular

---

And before Rostenkowski chose conferees on the tax overhaul bill, sources said, O'Neill made it clear he wanted one of them to be Rep. Richard A. Gephardt, D-Mo., an early Democratic proponent of tax reform.

Hook at 2081. The choice of Representative Gephardt is described in Birnbaum and Murray, supra, at 257.

[57] Vogler at 5; Reform Penetrates Conference Committees at 291.

[58] In the Senate, the party ratio of conferees reflects the party ratio in the chamber. For example, in the continuing resolution conference described in the last footnote, the 27 Senate conferees were divided 14:13, reflecting the party ratio in the Senate.

[59] In the House, the party ratio of conferees has reflected the party ratio on the committee of jurisdiction (a ratio that, particularly during the late 1970s and early 1980s, was more favorable to the majority). House Democratic Caucus Rule 41 provides that "[t]he Democratic Party representation on conference committees also shall be no less favorable to the Democratic Party than the ratio for the full House committee."

To illustrate, in 1982 the party ratio in the House was 243:192, so that the Republicans had 40 percent of the committee seats. On the conference on the all-important omnibus continuing resolution, H.J. Res. 631, which was really several appropriation bills rolled into a continuing resolution, the ratio of House conferees was 14:8, so that the Republicans had only 36 percent of the conference (footnote continued)

minority   conferees,   they   rely   on   the
recommendation of the ranking minority member.[60]

Regarding the choice of the majority members,
at one time the committee chairs picked largely by
fixed adherence to committee seniority.[61]   The
seniority system began hardening late in the 19th
century, but did not achieve strict control,
particularly in the Senate, until well into the
twentieth century.[62] Once it became dominant, the
seniority system concentrated tremendous power in

---

appointments.   If the 22 conferees had been divided to
reflect the House party ratio, the party split would have
been 12:10, which would have given the Republicans 45
percent.   Thus, by the ratio in the full House, the majority
would have had only two more conferees than the minority; in
actuality, it had six, providing considerably more leverage.

[60] Sometimes a chair may not back fully his ranking
minority member.   A long-term study of the House
Appropriations Committee's conferees illustrates how this
may vary:

> The presence of the ranking minority Committee member
> on every conference team began about 1951 when Chairman
> [Clarence] Cannon [(D-Mo.)] agreed to make John Taber
> [(R-N.Y.)] an ex officio member of each subcommittee.
> The arrangement continued until 1963, when Cannon
> declined to extend ex officio prerogatives to Taber's
> successor, Ben Jensen.   Chairman George Mahon [(D-
> Tex.)] reverted to the former practice with Frank Bow,
> Jensen's successor.

R. F. Fenno, The Power of the Purse: Appropriations
Politics in Congress 643 (1966).

[61] "The conference committee is the ultimate flowering of
the power of seniority." Member of the House: Letters of a
Congressman 114 (ed. J. W. Baker 1962) (reprinting a
Congressman's letter).

[62] McCown at 149-64.   Part of the force holding back the
seniority principle was the established principle, dating
back to Jefferson's Manual, that conferees were to be
appointed who were sympathetic to a measure. Junior or off-
committee Members who succeeded in passing a bill over the
opposition of the committee chair had demonstrably more
sympathy to their measure.

the senior Members, and bolstered committee chairs by allowing them to take a tight clique of loyal, like-minded senior Members to all the conferences, while virtually disenfranchising the junior Members.[63]

Junior and Multiple Committee Conferees

In recent decades, some flexibility in making appointments was being achieved again. A principal source of flexibility was that committees handled much legislation in subcommittee, and so conference appointments could be made based on subcommittee seniority, which favored junior Members.[64]   As Congressional Quarterly observed in 1986: "[I]ncreasingly in recent years, more junior lawmakers have been named if they are members of the relevant subcommittee, sponsors of important amendments or have special expertise."[65]   The House prescribed such choice by House Rule and committee rules.[66]

---

[63]   For example, in 1959 Senator William Proxmire (D-Wis.) noted that of the 49 positions on the various conferences then meeting, 33 were held by just 11 Senators, a concentration of power in the hands of a mere ninth of the Senate. All of the 11 were of high seniority and seven were from southern states. Ruling Congress at 172.

For another perspective, Representative Lester L. Wolff (D-N.Y.) noted in 1973 that he had served in the House for nearly ten years before he was asked to be a conferee. Reform Penetrates Conference Committee at 292.

[64]   Subcommittee appointments favor junior Members because senior Members tend to distribute themselves among the different subcommittees to get the chairmanships of those subcommittees. If subcommittee seniority is used as the criterion, only the senior Members on the particular subcommittee can serve as conferees, making room for junior Members to be conferees. In contrast, if committee seniority is used as the criterion, senior Members who sit on different subcommittees can be pulled together for the conference, excluding junior Members.

[65]   Hook at 2080.
(footnote continued)

Over the years, there has been much debate about the broader question of the extent to which conferees are -- or should be -- appointed on the basis of sympathy to legislation. The question most forcefully arises when a chamber adopts a bill or a major floor amendment offered by a Member not on the committee of jurisdiction, particularly when the committee chair opposes the bill or amendment. As one observer commented,[67]

> one might whimsically claim that any similarity between the views of the House or the Senate and those of the conferees representing the House or the Senate is purely coincidental. Many members come to conference committee eager to defend the views represented in the bill passed by the other house or to strike out provisions inserted in their own house.[68]

---

[66]   House Rule X(6)(f) provides: "In appointing members to conference committee the Speaker . . . shall name Members who are primarily responsible for the legislation . . . ." As for committees, House Ways and Means, for example, adopted a rule prescribing conferee appointment by subcommittee seniority. House Ways and Means Rule 16 provides:

Recommendation for Appointment of Conferees

Whenever in the legislative process it becomes necessary to appoint conferees, the Chairman shall recommend to the Speaker as conferees the names of those members of the subcommittee (or subcommittee) which handled the substantive legislation in the order of their subcommittee seniority and such other committee members as the Chairman may designate. In making recommendations of minority members as conferees the Chairman shall consult with the ranking minority member of the Committee.

[67]   B. Gross, The Legislative Struggle 321 (1953).

[68]   For example, in 1970, when a principal issue regarding an appropriation bill was funding for the supersonic transport, Senator Proxmire complained that even though the Senate had voted against the transport, four of the seven

(footnote continued)

In the 1970's, the House went so far as to adopt
an express rule, House Rule X(6)(f), directing the
Speaker to appoint supporters and proponents of a
bill's provisions as conferees.

As a practical matter, committee chairs still
enjoy great power in choosing conferees.   They
have double discretion: to deviate somewhat from
seniority in choosing, and to determine how far
down the seniority list to go by deciding how many
conferees to appoint.[69]   Committee chairs balance
many factors relating to the particular bill in
making appointments -- which subcommittee handled
the bill, which Members were most active on the
bill, or will be able to win support of a
necessary voting bloc when the conference
committee reports back, or will represent the
interests at stake in the bill.

Committee chairs also balance many factors
beyond the particular bill: who has backed the
committee chair on other matters, or has been
neglected in previous conference selections, or
has other "chips" to offer or strings to pull,
from leadership ties to campaign contributions.
Perhaps most important, a committee chair can pick
conferees most loyal to him.   For example, the
chairs of the tax-writing committees,
Representative Rostenkowski and Senator Robert
Packwood (R-Oreg.), picked loyal committee members

---

conferees were supporters of it: "There is no secret that
the conferees were appointed who would vote for the SST,
which is a direct and express violation of the rules of the
Senate."   Quoted in Oleszek, House-Senate Relationships:
Comity and Conflict, 441 Annals Am. Academy Poli. and Soc.
Sci. 75, 77 (1974).

In that instance, the bias of the conferees was
considered so blatant that the Senate defeated the
conference report.   Gore, The Conference Committee:
Congress' Final Filter, The Washington Monthly, June 1971,
at 43, 46.

[69]   "[B]y having the option of allowing committee or
subcommittee seniority in appointing managers, [chairmen
were] able to exercise a control over conference
representation which would be precluded by a single
seniority system." Vogler at 38.

for the conference on the tax reform bill of 1986,
thereby ensuring their own control of that
supremely important conference which all but
rewrote the whole tax code.[70]
    Besides the trend toward junior Members as
conferee choices, the most notable trend in recent
years has been toward "multiple committee"
conferees. Traditionally, all conferees for a
bill had come from the single committee with
jurisdiction over a bill. While there were
historic examples of conference delegations drawn
from more than one committee, they were relatively
few.[71]
    However, with the rise of multiple referrals
and omnibus bills, multiple-committee conference
delegations have become increasingly important.
At one extreme, the most dramatic examples have
been the conference committees on the omnibus
budget reconciliation bills. In 1981, the
conference on that bill had 208 House conferees
and 72 Senate conferees. The House conferees were
drawn from 17 committees, the Senate conferees
from 14.[72] In 1987-88, a trade bill went to a
conference committee which "included 44 senators
and 155 House members from the nine Senate and 14

---

[70]   Hook at 2082; Birnbaum and Murray, _supra_, at 256-58.

[71]   Examples from before the 1975 rule authorizing the
Speaker to make multiple referrals are provided in Deschler
33 §§ 5.5 - 5.9. For example, in 1961 conferees on a
federal highway bill were appointed from the two committees
that have historically divided jurisdiction over the
program, Public Works, and Ways and Means. _Id_. § 5.7.
"Former Rep. John N. Erlenborn . . . said it was considered
extraordinary in 1974 when a conference on pension
legislation drew negotiators from four committees." Hook at
2082.

[72]   In 1980, it could be said with wonder that "[t]he
largest conference in the history of Congress convened Sept.
18 [1980], with more than 100 representatives and
senators." 1980 _Congressional Quarterly Almanac_ 130. In
1986, it could be said that "[t]he second largest conference
[after the 1981 reconciliation conference], which brought
together 242 conferees in 31 subgroups, met on the fiscal
1986 reconciliation bill (PL 99-272)." Hook at 2082.

House committees that had a hand in crafting the bill."[73]

Multiple-committee conferences are not restricted to such gargantuan omnibus bills. Of 51 nonappropriation bills that completed conference in 1981-82, 20, or almost 40 percent, had conference delegations from more than one committee.[74] Sometimes, only one chamber's delegation came from more than one committee.[75] Often, both the Senate and House delegations came from more than one committee.[76]

---

[73] 1987 Congressional Quarterly Almanac 25.

[74] Of the 20 bills, ten had multiple-committee representation on both House and Senate conference delegations, nine bills had such representation only for the House conference delegation, and one had multiple-committee representation only from the Senate. For a discussion of massive conferences, see Granat, The Big Conference: Getting to Be Old Hat, 43 Cong. Q. Week. Rep. 1298 (1984).

[75] The House uses such multiple-committee conferences more than the Senate, just as it makes more use of multiple referrals in general. Of the 20 conferences being discussed, nine had multiple-committee representation only on the House side were: H.R. 6530, the Mt. St. Helens Act; H.R. 6133, the Endangered Species Act Extension; H.R. 5890, the NASA Authorization; H.R. 2330, the Nuclear Regulatory Commission Authorization; H.R. 5447, the Commodities Futures Act; S. 815, the Department of Defense Authorization of 1981; S. 2322, the Energy Emergency Act; S. 734, the Export Trading Company Act; and S. 1018, the Coast Barriers Act. One had multiple-committee representation only on the Senate side: S. 1196, the State Department Authorization for fiscal 1982-83.

[76] Of the 20 conferences with multiple-committee representation being discussed, ten conferences had such multiple committee representation from both chambers: H.R. 31, the Cash Discount Act; H.R. 3982, the 1981 Omnibus Budget Reconciliation Act; H.R. 3454, the 1981 Intelligence Authorization; H.R. 4961, the Tax Equity and Fiscal Responsibility Act; H.R. 6955, the 1982 Reconciliation Act; H.R. 6068, the 1982 Intelligence Authorization; H.R. 6211, the Surface Transportation Act; S. 884, the Agriculture and Food Act of 1981; S. 1193, the Foreign Aid Authorization; (footnote continued)

Sometimes one committee clearly dominated in concern, and the other committee participated only because of some particular provision.[77] Since the conferees from different committees may have interests only in particular parts of the bill, the chambers may appoint them as conferees only for limited parts.[78] In the extreme example, the 1981 omnibus budget reconciliation bill, the conference split into 58 subconferences. House Education and Labor alone sent nine distinct sets on conferees, each concerned with particular provisions.

Conferees with limited jurisdiction may sign only that part of the conference report dealing with their particular area.[79] The importance of participation in conference provides much of the incentive for the battles for committee "turf" at prior stages of the legislative process, such as referral and House Rules Committee consideration.

---

and S. 2248, the Defense Department Authorization.

[77] For example, a conference on the Cash Discount Act of 1981, H.R. 31, which amended the Truth in Lending Act, largely concerned the banking committees. Since the Senate had tacked on, as a non-germane amendment, a provision to eliminate an age restriction on appointment of the Surgeon General, conferees were also appointed from House Energy and Commerce and Senate Labor and Human Resources.

[78] See Deschler 33 §§ 5.14 - 5.18.

[79] Deschler 33 §§ 14.4 - 14.5. Complex arrangements for participation are possible; on the omnibus budget reconciliation bill of 1981, all the particular committees with substantive jurisdiction participated only with respect to their own area, while the budget committee conferees had the right to participate in all the subconferences. On the omnibus trade bill of 1988, "all but two of the Senate conferees ha[d] jurisdiction over the entire measure. But note of the House conferees, not even [Dan] Rostenkowski [D-Ill., chair of the House delegation] has similar rights to review the entire bill. House conferees were appointed only for issues under the jurisdiction of their respective committees." Wehr, Dispute Over Final Trade Bill Narrows to a Few Tough Issues, 46 Cong. Q. Week. Rep. 936, 937 (1988).

D.   PRACTICES IN CONFERENCE AND CONFEREES' SCOPE

Congress imposes few procedural rules on conferences, which largely determine their own practices regarding such matters as the choice of conference chair, pattern of meetings, and bargaining tactics, although certain standard choices may be noted. As to substantive authority, in theory Congress limits conferees' authority to resolving the differences between House and Senate versions of the bill.

Few Rules

The few procedural rules for conference committees, on voting and sunshine, are fairly straightforward. Regarding voting, conferees must return their verdict in one particular way: the conference report must be approved by a majority of the House conferees and a majority of the Senate conferees, voting separately.[80] Because of this voting method, it does not matter whether one chamber sends many more conferees than the other, since the votes of each chamber's conferees do not count in the counting of the votes of the other chamber's conferees. Conferees can only approve the conference committee's conclusions -- its report -- as a whole, not just the parts they prefer. There is no provision for additional, separate, or dissenting views for conference reports (although of course a conferee could just voice views on the floor as a general-purpose

---

[80] In 1900, a Senate clerk, Thomas P. Cleaves, compiled a set of precedents that is the classic statement of the rules in this area, Cleaves' Manual of the Law and Practice in Regard to Conferences and Conference Reports, which the Senate reprints in the Senate Manual. Section 17 of Cleaves' Manual states:

The managers of the two Houses while in conference vote separately, the majority determining the attitude to be taken toward the propositions of the other House. When the report is made the signatures of a majority of each board of managers are sufficient.

speeches), so "a conferee cannot formally demand
the attention of his fellow members the way one
can raise objections in a standing committee's
minority report."[81]

The rise of multiple committee conferees,
discussed in the previous section, slightly
modified the requirement that conferees approve
the conference report as a whole. Conferees
appointed only for their committee's particular
parts of the bill only vote on their parts.
Still, in approving their part, such limited
conferees must approve that part either completely
or not at all, with no opportunity to express
reservations in the conference report about some
particular item.

In the last decade, Congress also imposed a
sunshine rule on conferees. Historically,
conferences shielded themselves completely from
outside scrutiny: until the 1970s, there had been
only two open conferences in history: one in 1789,
the other in 1911.[82] Intense suspicion surrounded
conference secrecy, and eventually, in 1975, first
the House and then the Senate voted to open the
conference committee meetings.[83] House rules
require a recorded House vote to authorize a

---

[81]   Ruling Congress at 189.

[82]   See McCown at 41-43 (1789 conference), 177-78 (1911
conference). Indeed, there had been a tradition about the
"sacredness" of the conference precluding outsiders from
intruding to lobby and participants from retelling what
transpired. Notwithstanding such a tradition, Members would
often tell the press and lobbyists about the events in
conference. See G. Y. Steiner, The Congressional Conference
Committee: Seventieth to Eightieth Congresses 35 n.14
(1951).

[83]   Senate Rule XXVIII(6) provides that "[e]ach conference
committee . . . shall be open . . . except when managers of
either the Senate or the House . . . determine by a rollcall
vote . . . that all or part . . . shall be closed to the
public." House Rule XXVIII(6)(a) provides that "[e]ach
conference committee . . . shall be open . . . except when
the House, in open session, has determined by a rollcall
vote . . . that all or part . . . shall be closed to the
public."

closed   conference,   and   the   House   typically
authorized closed conferences only on defense and
intelligence bills.

This is not to say that conference decision
making is always public.   It is always possible
for   some   conferees   to   meet   privately   and
informally, excluding not only the public but even
the junior conferees, and then to ratify their
deals   in   pro   forma   committee   meetings.[84]
Occasionally,   excluded   Members   ask   the   House   to
invoke   its   sunshine   rule   when   such   private
meetings particularly enrage them.[85]

However,   even   reform   enthusiasts   defend   the
need   for   some   privacy   in   deal-making,   as
Congressinal Quarterly noted:

> "Sunshine laws kid the public," said Richard
> Bolling   [(D-Mo.)] . . . .   Bolling   said
> openness was healthy but cautioned that some
> compromises and accommodations would have to
> be made in secret if the legislation was to

---

[84]   Senator   Albert   Gore,   Sr.   (D-Tenn.)   contributed   an
account   of   a   tax   bill   conference   in   1969   where   he   was   a
conferee excluded from the key informal private meeting:

> As I began to depart I noted a whispered conference
> between Senator Wallace Bennett, a ranking Republican
> on the Senate Finance Committee, and the Assistant
> Secretary of the Treasury.   Unavoidably, I overheard
> Senator Bennett say, "Let's meet in my office."
>
>   . . . Sure   enough,   on   the   reconvening   of   the
> conference committee . . . Chairman [Wilbur] Mills [(D-
> Ark.)]   quickly   reopened   the   [key]   question . . . .
> This was a clear breach of our earlier agreement but it
> availed me nothing to make this charge, which I did
> angrily, for I was hopelessly outnumbered.

See Gore, supra, at 45-46.

[85]   For   example,   when   conferees   on   a   natural   gas
deregulation bill in 1978 met in private, Representative
Toby Moffett (D-Conn.) offered a motion to close the
conference, and asked for its defeat, as a way to suggest
that the meeting should be open.   On April 13, 1978, the
motion was rejected (as he had asked) by 6-371.

succeed.   In those cases, he added, "if we
have to meet in our wives' boudoirs -- if
they still have such things -- we will."[86]

For example, in the 1986 conference on the flat
tax bill, the

opening   shots   were   mostly   for   public
display.   After   the   first   two   days   of
meetings, the conferees secluded themselves
behind closed doors and did not meet again in
public   until   the   final   night   of   the
conference, three weeks later.   Packwood and
Rostenkowski both believed that they had to
shield the conference from lobbyists, the
press,   and   the   public   in   order   to   make
progress.[87]

Practices

Apart from these few rules for voting and
sunshine, conference committees determine their
own practices on such key matters at choice of
chairs,   role   of   meetings,   and   bargaining
tactics.   Regarding   chairs,   each   chamber's
delegation has its own leader.   Technically, the
presiding officer, in appointing the conferees,
chooses delegation heads by listing them first
when   naming   the   conferees.   Not   surprisingly,
since   committee   chairs   actually   pick   their
delegations, they typically name themselves, or
name the subcommittee chair who managed the bill,
as head of the conference delegation.
One chamber's delegation head becomes chair
of   the   conference   committee;   the   other   can   be
called   vice-chair.   As   to   which   chamber's
delegation   head   becomes   conference   committee
chair, each conference committee decides this by
any method it pleases.   For example, there is a
tradition   that   "the   chairmanship   of   tax
conferences alternates between the chairman of the
Ways and Means Committee and the chairman of the
Finance Committee."[88]   This became the subject of

---

[86]   Reform Penetrates Conference Committees at 291.

[87]   Birnbaum and Murray, supra, at 260
(footnote continued)

maneuvering in 1986, as Senator Packwood tried unsuccessfully, by declining the chair of a minor conference, to obtain the chair of the conference on the next all-important bill, the "flat tax" (tax reform) bill.

Of course, a conference committee chair does not control the two chamber's halves of a conference committee the way a standing committee chair controls a committee in one chamber. Although conference committee chairs are the heads of their own chamber's delegation, "[u]nder no circumstances is the conference chairman expected to play a leadership role with regard to the managers of the other house."[89] While the chair can threaten to break off negotiations and fail to report back a compromise bill, in general conference chairs do not bottle up or kill bills as committee chairs may kill bills in committee in their own chamber.[90] The House even has a special motion to deal with a chair who tries this.[91] A

---

[88]   Birnbaum and Murray suprpa, at 256.   For another example, until 1962 Senators chaired all appropriations conferences.   In that year, a famous battle between the chambers occurred, and as a result, appropriations conferences began choosing their chairs by a variety of methods: "When the first conference was held, the chairmanship was decided by a flip of the coin.   Some conferences have followed this procedure, others have rotated, and still others have permitted the Senate subcommittee chairmen to preside."   See J. L. Pressman, House vs. Senate 2-3 (1966).

[89]   R. F. Fenno, supra, at 647.

[90]   As noted above, the vast majority of bills that go to conference come back from conference and pass both Houses. There certainly have been conference chairs, and conferees in general, opposed to parts of the bills they took to conference, but the chambers have ways of dealing with such conferees.

[91]   As the ultimate weapon against recalcitrant conferees, House Rule XXVIII(1)(b) provides that after conferees have been appointed for 20 days there is "a motion of the highest privilege to move to discharge said conferees and to appoint new conferees, or to instruct" them.   During the last six (footnote continued)

Senate chair has a bit more leeway in this regard
than a House chair.[92]
     Nevertheless,   conference   chairs   have
substantial powers.   First, they come with their
existing power as committee or subcommittee chair,
particularly since they have usually just picked
the delegation on her side.   In addition, chairs
have important procedural authority in conference:

> Despite the informal selection process, the
> chairman plays an important role in the
> conference procedure, arranging the time and
> place of meetings, the agenda of each
> session, and the order in which issues are
> discussed.   The chairman sets the pace of
> conference   bargaining,   and   recommends
> tentative agreements.

Accordingly, observers find that the delegation
heads can steer conferences.[93]

----

days of any session, that motion is privileged "after House
conferees shall have been appointed thirty-six hours without
having made a report."   For example, in 1972 the House and
Senate   Appropriations   Committees   deadlocked   over   a
supplemental appropriation bill, as hawkish House conferees
refused   to   move   on   the   Senate's   anti-Vietnam   War
amendments.   Ultimately the House disavowed its own
conferees and receded from its disagreement with the Senate
in a move that was "highly unusual, even historic -- not
only in the substance of what Congress was now doing but
also the procedure by which it was accomplished."   T. M.
Franck & E. Weisband, Foreign Policy by Congress 20
(1979).   Thus, the House can deal with obstructive House
conferees.

[92]   The Senate has the same means for dealing with
obstructive Senate conferees that it has for circumventing
committees generally, such as working out informally with
the House a version it will accept and then enacting that as
a non-germane amendment to some bill not going through
conference. Still, "if the Senate conferees are the problem
and if the Senate fails to remedy that, there is little that
can be done."   House Republican Manual, "When the Houses
Differ: Procedure in Conference: Instructing and Discharging
Conferees," at 328, 330-31.

[93]   A dated account shows how powerful chairs were in the
(footnote continued)

Conferences also determine their own practices regarding the role of meetings of Members and staff. Sometimes the conference committee will handle all matters in formal meetings, as in one description:

> The conference is the most interesting thing that happens on Capitol Hill. The managers on the part of the two houses sit at the head of the table, and the others straggle on down the sides. Most of the conversation goes on between these two -- the chairman and the vice chairman of the conference. There's a lot of jockeying around -- "I'll give you this if you'll give me that."

Often, even if conferences resolve the major issues in the formal meetings, preliminary contacts of committee leaders or staff clear away minor issues. Also, after a formal meeting resolves major issues, subsequent contacts of committee leaders or staff may work out the details and draft precise language. In the case of the 1986 "flat tax" reform bill, the conferees from both chambers dealt with a tough impasse by accepting Senator Russell Long's (D-La.) suggestion that "We senators have a lot of confidence in Mr. Packwood, and I suspect you folks do in Mr. Rostenkowski. So I don't see why those chairmen don't get together by themselves and come up with a proposal that we all can then consider."[94]

---

past:

> Conferees ritualistically stick behind the powerful chairmen who appointed them. Representative Otis Pike (D., N.Y.) described his first conference on the Armed Services Committee . . . . [T]he Senate and House conference chairmen did most of the battle with onlookers getting more and more bored by the minute . . . . . "'A conference is two gentlemen from Georgia talking, arguing, laughing, and whispering in each other's ears.'"

Ruling Congress at 181.

[94] Birnbaum and Murray, supra, at 268. Similarly, a (footnote continued)

Sometimes all or virtually all the conference committee's work will be done by such informal contacts, with the actual conference meetings either being symbolic or, in the extreme case, never occurring. For example, the conference committee on the 1982 bill to protect intelligence agents' identities, H.R. 4, resolved its differences by "nearly two months of private negotiations," a course that evoked vocal complaints: "Reps. C. W. Bill Young, R-Fla. . . . and Henry J. Hyde, R-Ill., refused to sign [the conference report], Hyde said, because no formal meeting of conferees was called, and they were dissatisfied with the conference report negotiated by staff members . . . ."[95]

In fact, one observer provided a detailed study of what he termed a "phantom conference," concerning the 1977 GI Education Bill. After both Houses passed the bill in very different form, "Conferees never were appointed and the leading members met only once over an informal breakfast . . . . Key staff people simply sat down for three days in late October and early November and resolved the differences between the two bills."[96] In 1982, the House sustained a

---

stalemate threatened on the key health issue in the 1987 reconciliation bill, but "a nasty fight over how to divvy up inflation increases for Medicare payments to hospitals was settled Dec. 19 in a private meeting between [Senator Lloyd] Bentsen [D-Tex.] and ways and Means Chairman Rostenkowski." 1987 Congressional Quarterly Almanac 567.

[95] 1982 Congressional Quarterly Almanac 131-32. For another example, the conference committee on the Congressional Budget and Impoundment Control Act met only twice, once at the beginning, and once at the end, with neither meeting being an occasion for resolving substantive differences. The real work was done inbetween, in informal sessions of a few key staff working under the direction of the House and Senate chairs, Representative Bolling and Senator Sam Ervin (D-N.C.). In a typical situation, the 1987 State Department authorization bill, "[g]oing into the House-Senate conference . . . roughly 170 items were in dispute. Staffers settled most, leaving about 30 topics for conferees to resolve." 1987 Congressional Quarterly Almanac 145.

(footnote continued)

point of order against a conference report from a
conference that had never formally met after
appointment of the conferees, on the ground that
the conference had violated the sunshine rule.[97]
    Concerning the variety of conference
bargaining tactics, whole books could be (and have
been) written. The two goal expectations shaping
the conference are obvious: "the task of each
group of conferees is to fight and win," but there
is a "practical impossibility of total victory and
the necessity of compromise if there is to be a
bill."[98]   Conference bargaining partly follows
principles applicable to all bargaining, and
partly follows principles peculiar to the
political arena and the legislative context.
Members may draw strength for their position from
instructions, roll calls, pledges, the necessity
for bargaining to recur again in the future, and
chamber rules restricting the agenda.[99]
    Executive and interest group lobbyists always
influenced conferees,[100] and do so particularly
closely now that conferences are open and
lobbyists can often follow their progress
closely. One pair of journalists who described in
detail the 1986 "flat tax" conference reported:

>   The interplay of personality -- always an
>   important element in the workings on Capitol
>   Hill -- takes on magnified significance in

---

[96]   M. J. Malbin, Unelected Representatives: Congressional
Staff and the Future of Representative Government 76 (1983).

[97]   128 Cong. Rec. H10468 (daily ed. Dec. 20, 1982).

[98]   R.F. Fenno, supra, at 617, 619.

[99]   General bargaining principles were elaborated in T. C.
Schelling, The Strategy of Conflict (1963), and the
application of Schelling's discussion to conferences in
particular is discussed in Vogler at 79-105. See also G. Y.
Steiner, supra.

[100]   "As forms of lobbying, the president or his spokesman
write letters to conferees; some administration personnel
show up at conference meetings; and the president freely
threatens to use his veto unless conferees compromise."
Ruling Congress at 184.

conference.   Conference meetings are like
labor-management bargaining sessions, and the
skill and stamina of the lead negotiators can
be critical.[101]

Owing to the greater number of conflicting
commitments of Senators and the specialization of
Representatives, "the tighter organization of
House committees is reflected in preconference
strategy sessions, smaller and more hierarchically
structured bands of conferees, better conference
attendance records, and 'tougher' bargaining
stances by the House conferees."[102]   In contrast,
only a few Senators may stay through a whole
conference and know the issues.[103]
    A perennial question for political scientists
has been which chamber (if either) does better in
conference.   Sometimes this question seems subject
to a ready answer, as when bills with numerical
House-Senate   differences,   like   appropriation
bills, go to conference and the final figure comes
closer either to the House or the Senate figure.
"Almost all evidence shows that the Senate wins

---

[101]   Birnbaum and Murray, supra, at 254-55.

[102]   Strom & Rundquist, A Revised Theory of Winning in
House-Senate Conferences, LXXI Am. Poli. Sci. Rev. 448, 449
(1977).

[103]   One Representative recalled a conference where a
particular Senator "was the only member sitting in from the
Senate most of the time, holding all their proxies." C. L.
Clapp, The Congressman: His Work as He Sees It 250
(1963).   Regarding appropriations conferences, two Senate
staff members noted:

"We never get together prior to a conference," said
one. Senators don't have the opportunity. They are
too busy . . . . A second clerk lamented, "The House
conferees hold a meeting and decide which way they are
going to jump on every item. . . . [The Senators] may
start the conference with 8 men and they may stay for
an hour. Then you're down to 4 and by the time it's
over, nearly everyone is gone . . . .

R. F. Fenno at 645.

more often than does the House."[104]

Many theories for this have been offered. One is that whichever chamber acts first on a bill "loses" in conference, but actually wins on the bill, because the chamber that acts first sets the basic parameters for the bill; by taking the first chamber's bill and amending it, the second chamber proposes marginal changes that are accepted in conference to gain support for those basic parameters.[105] For example, the House determines most of the numbers in an appropriation bill just by passing it first; the Senate then makes marginal changes, most of which are accepted in conference, allowing the Senate to appear to "win" in conference even though the House's influence predominates regarding the bill. Since the House originates tax and appropriation legislation, it acts first on more legislation that the Senate does, explaining why the Senate appears to win more often in conference.

Scope

Since, as noted above, Congress approves the vast majority of conference reports, the conferees' scope of authority becomes important, since it defines the boundaries of their ability to legislate. In theory, Congress limits that authority to the differences between the House and Senate versions of the bill, the "scope of the differences", by allowing points of order on both the House and Senate floors against conference reports that exceed that scope.[106] Thus, for example, Senate conferees on the 1986 "flat tax" bill needed to fill a giant revenue shortage, by

compiling a hodgepodge of ideas to pick up

---

[104] Strom & Rundquist, supra, LXXI Am. Poli. Sci. Rev. at 448.

[105] Id.

[106] House Manual § 546 (describing principles of scope); House Rule § 913a (principles of scope regarding amendments in the nature of a substitute); Senate Rule XXIII.

the revenue [and then winnowing some out;
however, when the] Senate's proposals were
sent to the House . . . they were received
coldly . . . . [Representatives] complained
that roughly half of the sixteen proposals
went 'outside the scope of the conference.
Conferees are only supposed to deal with
issues on which the two bills are in
disagreement, but the [Senate conferees']
money-raising list contained many proposals
that were not in either bill.[107]

In practice, conferees, particularly Senate
conferees, have a vast amount of discretion, which
starts with an all-important technicality involved
in how much discretion conferees receive. It
distinguishes between two methods of amendment.
Each chamber can amend the other's bill in one of
two ways. It can make a number of particular
amendments changing particular provisions ("cut-
and-bite" amendments). Alternatively, it can make
one amendment in the nature of a substitute,
putting in place a complete substitute text. The
two approaches cannot be distinguished in terms of
what they produce, only how they do it.[108]

While the products may be identical, for
purposes of determining the conferee's scope, the
two methods of amendment are treated quite
differently. When a number of "cut and bite"
amendments are made, Senate rules and House
precedents only authorize the conferees to act
within the scope of the differences.[109] Conferees
cannot remove language both chambers agree on, or

---

[107] Birnbaum and Murray _supra_, at 264-65.

[108] For example, to change section 101 of a bill, a chamber
can either amend section 101, or it can put in place an
amendment in the nature of a substitute that is identical
with the underlying text except for the change in section
101. As a general matter, appropriation conferences tend to
concern "cut-and-bite" amendments, but for most
nonappropriation bills, the conferees take to conference an
amendment in the nature of a substitute.

[109] See House Manual § 546; Deschler 33 § 15; Senate Rule
XXVIII(3).

insert new provisions not in either chamber's version. On provisions where the two chambers disagree, the conferees must report numbers or provisions inbetween the two versions.

If, for example, a House bill authorizes Programs I and II at $10 million apiece, and the Senate version also authorizes Program I at $10 million and authorizes Program II at $20 million, the rule concerning "scope of the difference" requires the conferees not to tamper with Program I, and to achieve a figure for Program II between the House and Senate figures of $10 million and $20 million. In contrast, when one chamber adopts an amendment in the nature of a substitute, the conferees are not bound by the scope of the differences, but can offer a "germane modification."

Just what that means differs somewhat in the Senate compared to the House, as history fleshes out. In 1917, there occurred a "sensational case of new matter being included in a conference report," and the following year the Senate responded by adopting a rule allowing a point of order against scope violations by conferees.[110] However, in 1940, the Senate decided that conferees dealing with an amendment in the nature of a substitute had "the widest possible latitude," including "authority to write a new bill eliminating provisions previously agreed upon by both houses, and authority to insert material not committee to conference by either house."[111]

---

[110] A conference committee on an excess profits tax added, as new matter, tax exemptions for the salaries of Senators, Representatives, and other government employees. The country reacted with fierce criticism about special treatment by Congress of Congress. McCown at 204-6.

Under the system that prevailed until 1917, the Senate chair did not rule at all on scope violation. "[T]he Senate was long indifferent, presiding officers ruling that it was for the Senate itself to decide whether it would accept or reject" conference reports outside the scope of the differences. R. Luce, Legislative Procedure: Parliamentary Practices and the Course of Business in the Framing of Statutes 405 (1922).

(footnote continued)

Thus, the Senate allows extremely broad scope for conferees dealing with an amendment in the nature of a substitute.[112] For example, when the tax reconciliation bill came back from conference in 1982, it included a provision for reporting of restaurant employee tip income that neither chamber had approved.[113] A Senator opposing the bill raised a point of order, but the presiding officer overruled it, commenting: "The conferees went to conference with a complete substitute, which gives them the maximum latitude allowable to conferees. The standard is that matter entirely irrelevant to the subject matter is not in order. That standard has not been breached."[114].

In the House, the Speaker's authority to decide points of order against conference reports, and the larger scope allowed for amendments in the nature of substitutes, date back principally to the mid-1800s.[115] In the Legislative

---

[111]   G. Y. Steiner, supra, at 106. The Senate's presiding officer submitted the question to the Senate itself to decide because the precedents were in such hopeless conflict.

[112]   See Senate Rule XXVIII(2,3); Riddick, "Conferences and Conference Reports: Substitute Versions," at 386-88. The Senate is generally not so jealous about its committee structure, reflected in its tolerance for nongermane floor amendments. Moreover, the Senate must have a loose rule about conferences because it does not have (apart from unanimous consent) the machinery -- special rules, and suspension of the rules -- which allows the House to waive its stricter rules. For the Senate, the alternative to a loose rule would be to frequently overrule its Chair's rulings on conference reports with scope transgressions (the way it overrules its Chair's rulings on germaneness for appropriations), a messy way to do business.

[113]   Indeed, the Senate specifically rejected the provision on a 70-25 roll call. 1982 Congressional Quarterly Almanac 35.

[114]   128 Cong. Rec. S10899 (daily ed. Aug. 19, 1982). An appeal from the ruling lost overwhelmingly.

[115]   Isolated rulings on such point of order date back to 1812 and 1834, McCown at 70, but the first definite ruling (footnote continued)

Reorganization Act of 1970 the House amended its
rules to limit somewhat the power of conferees
even over a complete substitute.[116]   While House
Rule XXVIII(3) continues to say that conferees
working on a complete substitute can "propose a
substitute which is a germane modification," it
adds that "the introduction of any language in
that substitute presenting a specific additional
topic, question, issue, or proposition not
committed to the conference committee shall not
constitute a germane modification . . . ."[117]
Accordingly, House conferees must often check back
with their Parliamentarian about whether
conference proposals fit within their scope of
discretion.[118]

The use of the amendment in the nature of a
substitute allows most conferees great discretion
even within the rules.   However, when conferees go
outside the rules, there are still a number of
ways for them to get their product approved.
Among the methods by which conferences can beat
points of order on scope, discussed in detail in
the next two sections, are: (1) in the House, by

---

that managers who had a complete substitute could report any
bill that was germane did not occur until 1862, id. at 78-
79.

[116]   The House had had a generous rule on conferees'
discretion, identical to the Senate's since both derived
from the Legislative Reorganization Act of 1946.   By 1970,
House Members appear to have been particularly incensed by
then-recent conferences that had included new legislation in
the conference report.   In one conference on an airline tax,
the conferees had dreamed up new language not in either
chamber's version requiring that airline tickets not
separately itemize the tax, thereby concealing it.   The 1970
change in the rules passed without much debate on a voice
vote.   116 Cong. Rec. 31834-36 (1970).

[117]   See House Manual at § 913a.   The rule not only
precludes specific new language, but modifications "beyond
the scope" of the propositions committed to the conference.

[118]   Ruling Congress at 182.   The House's restraint of
conferees pattern may result from the House's jealousy about
its committee structure, as reflected in its germaneness
rule.

special rules and suspension of the rules; (2) in the Senate, by unanimous consent, by taking advantage of the Senate's special laxity discussed above, or by having the Senate overrule a decision of the Chair upholding a point of order;[119] and (3) in either House, by reverting to amendments between Houses either instead of, or after, consideration of a conference report. Because this last method is extensively used for appropriation bills, it will be discussed fully in the last section in this chapter.

Both chambers place some procedural requirements on the form and timing of conference reports as well as on their content's scope. Both chambers require that the report be printed, although they may let the other chamber's printing suffice.[120] Sometimes, the most difficult part of presenting a conference report may be hunting down the members to sign it, in the common situation that they do not meet formally for signing as in the ideal model.[121] The Legislative

---

[119] These methods do not always succeed. For example, in 1982, the Senate upheld a point of order against conferees on an aviation insurance bill's provisions for labor protection in airline acquisitions. The conferees had provided more protection than either the House or the Senate. After a Senate debate in which both procedural and substantive arguments were made, the conference report was recommitted and the conference committee was forced to trim back to the protection provided by the Senate version. 1982 Congressional Quarterly Almanac 332.

[120] The Senate sometimes provides by unanimous consent that for an entire session, conference reports and explanatory statements will not be printed as Senate reports if they have been previously printed and agreed to by the House; alternatively, a particular unanimous consent request may be made for a particular report and statement already printed by the House. Riddick, "Conferences and Conference Reports: Statement to Accompany," at 412-13.

[121] To look at the reality:

> The requisite signatures are apparently conclusive proof that a quorum was present although it is not uncommon for staff to procure signatures in

(footnote continued)

Reorganization Act of 1970 prescribed that
conference reports must be accompanied by an
explanatory statement of the conferees.[122] While
that helps, it remains true that "Members must
often struggle to unravel what the conferees have
done to their bills."[123]

E.   ACTION ON CONFERENCE REPORTS

As described below, Congress has an amazing record
of adopting conference reports. This section will
describe the adoption process, focusing first on
three reasons for that record: the "all or
nothing" rule, the ability of bill proponents to
control which chamber acts first on the conference
report, and the end-of-session crush. It will
then look at the details of how the House and
Senate take up conference reports, and how in
either chamber they may (occasionally) be

---

restaurants, elevators, hallways, and offices
throughout the Capitol. As a practical matter, it is
often impossible for all of the staff persons compiling
the report to have the original documents with them
when obtaining signatures. A staff person caught in
this predicament must recognize his responsibility in
fully and fairly explaining to absent Members the
import of the conference agreement before signatures
are procured. While the Parliamentarian's Office will
not reject out of hand a report on which original
signatures have been pasted, a staff person must be
doubly cautious that there are no misunderstandings
lest he become embarrassed if others call this practice
into question.

House Republican Manual, "When the Houses Differ: Conference
Report," at 331.

[122] Senate Rule XXVIII(4); House Rule XXVIII(c). Observers
often refer to both the report and the explanatory statement
as the "report," since usually they are printed together as
one document, but technically the "report" is the bill
language agreed to by the conferees, while the "explanatory
statement" is the explanation of how the conferees decided
on that language.

[123] Ruling Congress at 190.

defeated.

All-or-Nothing Rule, Who's on First, and End-of-Session Crush

Perhaps the chief reason conference reports pass is the basic rule that such reports must be adopted or rejected as a whole.[124] No matter how distasteful any particular provision is, or how desirable some amendment would be, generally there is no way to amend a conference report; it can only be accepted or rejected as a whole. Thus, the question for Members is not how they feel about any particular provision, but how they feel about the bill as a whole, and they can always justify a vote for a conference report on the ground that they accepted the distasteful parts only to save the good ones. For example, in the 1982 tax reconciliation bill, Members intensely disliked the provision for withholding of taxes on interest and dividends,[125] but voted for the conference report because of its numerous other tax and spending cut reforms.

The first chamber to act on a conference

---

[124]   There is no written rule on this fundamental point. The precedent goes back to Jefferson's Manual. See House Manual §§ 542, 549; Deschler 33 § 24.2. Actually, despite Jefferson's early view, it took some time to settle the point, with the definitive ruling not coming in the House until 1850. See McCown at 50-54.

[125]   That conference report passed with provisions for withholding of taxes on interest and dividends. Congress disliked those provisions so much that the following year, it pushed through legislation to repeal them despite a presidential veto threat, a filibuster threat by the Senate Finance Committee chair, and strong resistance to passage in the committees of jurisdiction in both chambers. Indeed, those provisions were so disliked that a discharge petition in the House for the repeal bill, ordinarily a very difficult matter, obtained the necessary signatures almost immediately after it started. In short, withholding of taxes on interest and dividends was about as popular as the plague, yet even that had gotten through Congress in a conference report.

report does have one option besides accepting or rejecting it: recommittal. That chamber can adopt a motion to recommit the report to the conference committee, which leads either to rewriting the conference report, or to killing the bill if there is not time or will to redo it in conference. To take two examples, on August 17, 1982, the House recommitted the conference report on the omnibus budget reconciliation bill.   Members had discovered in the conference report a provision allowing a large congressional pay increase.[126] The conference committee reconvened the same day, dropped the pay raise potential, and reported back.   On August 18, the next day, the House approved that version.

In contrast, in 1979 the House and Senate passed initial versions of legislation to create an Energy Mobilization Board.   The conference stalemated for months, and the ultimate compromise proved unpalatable in the House.   By a stunning 232-131 majority, the House recommitted the report to conference, "to be rewritten with the threats to state and local laws deleted.   But that was its last gasp in the 96th Congress."[127]

To make a sharper point, opponents of a conference report can accompany their motion to recommit with a set of instructions to the conferees.   Like other instructions to conferees, these are not binding,[128] but they send a clear message.   In the House, the minority has preference in offering the motion to recommit a conference report, as in offering the motion to recommit a bill, allowing it to structure minority alternatives.[129]

---

[126]   1982 Congressional Quarterly Almanac 204.

[127]   1980 Congressional Quarterly Almanac 483.

[128]   See Deschler 33 § 26; Riddick, "Conferences and Conference Reports: Recommit: With or Without Instructions," at 408-9; "Recommit: Conference Reports, Recommittal of," at 891.

[129]   For a discussion of the precedents regarding the details of the motion to recommit a conference report in the House, see Deschler 33 § 26.   Among the points of (footnote continued)

However, only the first chamber to act on the conference report may consider a motion to recommit. Once the first chamber approves the report, the conference committee is considered discharged, so there is no committee to which to recommit. Because there is no motion to recommit in the second chamber, that second chamber appears to face no choice but to accept or to reject. The House Republican Manual argues that this "ultimatum" is "more psychological than parliamentary" because the second chamber can couple a defeat for the conference report with a request for a second conference, which can be held as soon as the first chamber agrees.[130]

In the nineteenth century, multiple conferences on bills were quite common, there sometimes being as many as half a dozen successive conferences on a major appropriation bill.[131] Today, there is still no parliamentary rule against successive conferences, only the practical problems such as the lack of time at the end of sessions. Nonetheless, such conferences are highly infrequent.[132] Thus, the "all or nothing"

---

interest: (1) the motion is made after the previous question is ordered on the conference report, Deschler 33 § 26.6; (2) while ordinarily instructions are in order, a special rule may preclude them -- the rule for the tax reconciliation bill allowed only a straight motion to recommit, without instructions -- or they may be blocked by the offering of one motion to recommit (with or without instructions), followed by moving the previous question on that motion to recommit, thereby precluding attempts to amend it with different instructions, Deschler 33 § 26.10.

[130] House Republican Manual, "When the Houses Disagree: On Going to Conference Twice," at 279 and "Acting on a Conference Report: Which House Acts First," at 292.

[131] L. G. McConachie, Congressional Committees 248 (1911). Riddick discusses further conferences. Riddick, "Conferences and Conference Reports: Action for Appointing Conferees: Second Conference," at 380, and "Authority and Jurisdiction of Conferees: Amendments in Disagreement Sent to a Second Conference," at 385. See Deschler at 33 § 25.6; House Manual at § 537.

[132] In 1981-82, there were no true second conferences, (footnote continued)

"ultimatum" has real weight to members.

The rule that the first chamber's options are broader than the second chamber's options points to the second reason conference reports pass: bill proponents can exercise tactical control over which chamber will be the first to take up the report. Ordinarily (for reasons having to do with the formal conference documents or "papers"),[133] the rule is that the chamber that asks for a conference first, acts on it last.[134] Thus, ordinarily, when bill proponents first pass their bills before conference, they may decide which

---

i.e., no occasions on which one chamber had to ask for, and the other chamber to agree to, a second conference after the first failed.   On three occasions the first conference reconvened, one after a motion to recommit (the 1982 omnibus budget reconciliation bill) and two after points of order against conference reports (both of which are discussed here -- the aviation war risk and fishery conservation bills).

[133] As a formal matter, the reason for the rule regarding conference sequencing is that only the chamber in possession of the "papers" has the formal authority to consider the conference report, and the chamber that agrees to conference gets the "papers" after conference.   The papers consist of the bill, amendments, and messages.   During the process of amendments between Houses, the papers go back and forth.

[134] When one chamber, the asking chamber, asks for a conference, it messages the papers to the other chamber. When that other chamber, the agreeing chamber, agrees to a conference, it messages the papers back to the asking chamber.   The asking chamber's conferees bring the papers to conference.   If the conference fails, they bring the papers back with them.   If it succeeds, as usually occurs, they give the papers to the other (agreeing) chamber's conferees as a token of the success.   Thus, after a successful conference, the agreeing chamber gets the papers.

Only the chamber in possession of the papers can act on the conference report.   Thus, since the chamber that agreed to the conference gets the papers after conference, it acts first.   If it accepts the conference report, it messages the papers to the asking chamber, and then the asking chamber can take up the conference report.   See Riddick, "Conferences and Conference Reports," at 375; House Manual § 555; Deschler 33 § 18.

chamber will ask for conference, based on which chamber they want to act last on the conference report.[135]

Typically, bill proponents want the more reluctant chamber to ask first, so that it will act last. That means the chamber more favorable to the bill will act first on the conference report. The more favorable chamber's approval will give momentum to the conference report in the more reluctant chamber, and will also foreclose the option of recommittal.

Even when the chamber which asks first does not automatically act on it last,[136] bill proponents have ways to bring about their preferred sequence. Despite the ordinary rule that the chamber which asks first, acts last, the conferees may swap papers and reverse the order of action on the conference report.[137] This was done on ten conference reports in 1981-82.[138] A 1982

---

[135] It must be remembered that ordinarily, either chamber can ask regardless of which chamber acts on the bill second. The second chamber can insist on its amendments, and ask for conference, or not insist, letting the first chamber disagree and ask.

[136] Certain special procedures discussed in the next section would flip the order of consideration. These special procedures require that the conferees report back in technical disagreement, even though they actually are in agreement. When conferees report back in disagreement, the papers remain with the asking chamber's conferees. Thus, while the asking chamber acts last on conference reports, it acts first on reports in technical disagreement. This means that these special procedures flip the order of consideration.

However, in such situations, the papers may be switched to the agreeing house to permit it to act first. See Deschler 33 § 18.4, 18.5.

[137] See Deschler 33 § 18.1.

[138] Conferees may reverse the order for a prosaic reason. At the very end of the session, one chamber may adjourn a bit earlier than the other, necessitating that the late conference reports go first to the chamber that will be (footnote continued)

bill illustrates the reasons such manipulation of the order of action, and how it occurs. In March, the Senate asked for a conference on the Nuclear Regulatory Commission authorization for fiscal 1982 and 1983, and in April, the House agreed to a conference.[139]

The prospects for adoption of the conference report apparently looked a lot better in the Senate in the House, so although the Senate had asked for conference, the conference committee swapped the papers. This let the Senate act first on the conference report, and it approved the report by voice vote on October 1. Even with Senate approval, and no option to recommit, the House revolted against the conference report, defeating it on December 2.[140]

A third reason for the overall high success rate of conference reports is the control of bill proponents over timing, and their tendency to move the conference reports at the end of the session. An end-of-session crush, with predictable effects, is an old, old tradition in Congress. Ada McCown noted in 1927 that "[t]he congestion at the end of the session has been repeated in Congress after Congress." She observed that the same Members who control the timing that legislation is taken up also control

---

departing early lest they get there too late. Of the ten bills taken up in reverse order in 1981-82, four bills -- H.R. 5002, H.R. 6065, H.R. 4566, and H.R. 6094 -- which would normally have been taken up in the Senate first, were taken up in the House first on December 20 and 21. The House adjourned December 21; the Senate, not until December 23. These four were apparently switched in order that they go first to the chamber about to adjourn.

[139] "For several years, authorization bills for the NRC had become tied up in controversy because of nuclear-related provisions," and bill "was dogged by controversy throughout the 97th Congress." 1982 Congressional Quarterly Almanac 311.

[140] The defeat was part of the special procedural mechanism, discussed below, necessary to excise a non-germane provision that offended the antiprotectionist Ways and Means Committee. 1982 Congressional Quarterly Almanac 313. Ultimately the bill became law.

the timing of conference reports, and commented drily that "[i]t would be strange if [those Members] did not many times plan to take advantage of the relaxed rules and sometimes relaxed attention of the last days of the session."[141]

Nothing had changed a half-century later. In the 1970s, the Ralph Nader Congress Project commented that "true debate on the conference reports rarely takes place. Without much discussion or analysis, conference reports get ramrodded through Congress, especially in the closing days of a session, and get signed into law."[142]

The schedule in 1981-82 amply confirmed these past observations.[143] In 1981, roughly speaking, a third of the conference reports was adopted in the first nine months of the session, a third in the last month, and a third in the last two days.[144] If anything, 1982 was even more of a crush, with almost all the conference reports adopted on the eve of one recess or another. Again speaking roughly, in 1982 Congress enacted the overwhelming majority of its conference reports in the last week or so before each of its three pertinent recesses. On October 1 and December 21 alone, the chambers individually adopted 20 conference reports, or five reports per chamber per day. It was not a pace to suggest

---

141 McCown at 169, 171.

142 Ruling Congress at 194.

143 For purposes of this schedule, a few instances are counted as adoptions that used special procedures and thus, technically, were not adoption of the conference report, but adoption of an amendment (when one of the Houses chose to adjust the conference report by resorting to amendments between Houses).

144 Of 30 public laws enacted based on conference reports in 1981, ten had their conference reports approved from January to mid-November, with the other 20 in the last month before adjournment. Counting adoptions in each chamber separately, the last two days alone, December 15 and 16, saw adoption of 20 conference reports, or the equivalent of ten public laws.

elaborate deliberation.[145]

House Floor Procedure

An examination of the House and Senate floor procedure for conference reports will show the few ways they may be defeated. As described in the previous section, at the end of conference the committee prepares and signs a report.   In the House, the head of the conference delegation presents the report, and asks that it be printed and files it,[146] and then usually lets it wait for

---

[145]   There were really three "ends" of the second session in 1983:   August 20, the beginning of the long Labor Day recess; October 2, the end of the regular session; and December 23, the end of the lame-duck session. Of 45 public laws enacted based on conference reports in 1982, only four were enacted from January through August 12.   Seven were enacted in the week before the August 20 recess.   Two more were enacted in the first part of September, and the remaining chamber's approval of those, plus both chambers' approvals of 14 more, came in the last week before the recess on October 2.   (To be precise, of the 38 adoptions, one had been on August 20, six were from September 8 to September 24, and the remaining 31 were from September 27 through October 2.)

The lame-duck session passed 15 more public laws based on conference reports.   One chamber adopted one conference report before December 15; the second chamber adoption of that report, and both chambers' adoption of 14 more, occurred in the last nine days of the session.

[146]   Presentation of the report, under House Rule XXVIII(1)(a), is one of the most highly privileged actions in House procedure.   A Member who comes brandishing a conference report to present can interrupt virtually everything, including another Member's speech, except a roll call. See House Manual § 909.

Routinely, unanimous consent will be asked to defer filing until midnight. This starts the clock running on the layover, while accommodating the time necessary for the conference report to be prepared, which may be a frenzied matter of hasty staff composition and signature hunting.

its layover.

House Rule XXVIII(2)(a) requires that, except during the last six days of the session, conference reports not be taken up until the third day after the report has been filed. Because the report may well not yet be printed when it is filed, filing does not ensure that the Members will be able to read the report. Accordingly, the House rule additionally guarantees that a report has to be available to the members for two hours before it can be taken up. If the conference report must be taken up before the layover is finished, the manager can have the layover waived.[147]

Since conference reports are privileged, no rule is needed for their consideration, except to waive points of order, once the layover has occurred.[148] Points of order against the report must be made immediately, before debate begins.[149] After disposing of the points of

---

[147] To waive the layover, the manager either obtains unanimous consent, obtains a special rule from the Rules Committee waiving the layover, or has the conference report taken up under suspension of the rules or by unanimous consent. See Deschler 33 §§ 21.3 - 21.9.

[148] No vote is required to call up a conference report. If opponents want to, they can obtain a vote by raising the question of consideration, see House Manual §§ 780, 879, but this is rarely done, as it is the recognized prerogative of the majority party to control the order of consideration.

The report does not have to be read. Rather, the majority manager calls it up, and the Clerk just reads it by title. House Rule XXVIII(2)(c). Sometimes the manager first obtains unanimous consent to have the joint explanatory statement read in lieu of the conference report, then obtains unanimous consent to have the joint explanatory statement considered as having been read.

[149] Deschler 33 § 19.1. There used to be confusion, because points of order had to be raised after the conference report is read but before the joint explanatory statement of the managers is read, but now the Speaker just indicates that under Rule XXVIIII(2)(c) the reading has been dispensed with, and that is the signal for raising points of
(footnote continued)

order, the Speaker then proceeds under the hour
rule to recognize the majority manager of the
conference report and allow him half of one hour
for debate, and to allow the minority manager the
other half-hour.   House Rule XXVIII(2)(a)
prescribes that if the two managers "are both
supporters of the conference report, one third of
such debate time shall be allotted to a Member who
is opposed to said conference report."[150]

When the debate is done, the conference
manager moves the previous question on the
conference report.[151]   If the House is the first
chamber to act on the conference report, a motion
to recommit may be made at this point.   When the
motion to recommit is not made, or when it fails,
the House then votes on adoption of the conference
report.   If the House adopts the conference
report, that ends the matter, unless it is
reopened by adverse Senate action or presidential
veto.

As indicated, there are several different
points at which the conference report may be
defeated, and there are several possible routes
for further action, depending largely on whether
the report is defeated on a technical point or on
a matter of substance.   The conference report may
be defeated on a technical point of order, such as

---

order.   House Republican Manual 297-98.

[150]   The hour of debate often consists of standard
statements: the conference managers congratulate each
other.   They say that this is the best deal that could be
made, that they got more than the Senate did, or that the
budget has been complied with.   They explain the conference
report's contents, not infrequently confusing the
legislative history by suggesting that what the Senate got
in conference it did not really get.   Opponents, if there
are any, then say that the conference managers only looked
after their own preferences and not what the House did to
the bill on the floor, that the Senate won, that tricks are
being used to fake compliance with the budget, and that if
only the report will be recommitted or defeated a much
better deal will be arranged quickly.

[151]   Since the conference report cannot be amended, the
previous question simply cuts off further debate, and is not
controversial.

that the conferees violated the sunshine rule, or
the rule about the scope of their authority, or
the layover rule, or the budget ceiling. Whether
the House is first or last to act on the
conference report, a technical point of order may
be waived by going to the Rules Committee for a
special rule waiving the point of order, or by
having the conference report taken up under
suspension of the rules.[152]

Often, the conference manager may anticipate
such a point of order, and obtain (or try to
obtain)[153] such a special rule, or use suspension
of the rules, to prevent it.[154] In 1981-82, the
Rules Committee granted special rules for seven
conference reports, and two conference reports
were taken up under suspension of the rules.[155]

---

[152]   See Deschler 33 § 24.8.

[153]   In one particularly controversial instance, concerning
airbags for automobiles, a conference report subject to a
point of order was first brought up under suspension of the
rules, where it was defeated. Then a special rule was
reported waiving the point of order, but the House defeated
the rule, an unusual occurrence. See State Farm Mut. Auto
Ins. Co. v. Department of Transportation, 680 F.2d 206, 227
(D.C. Cir. 1982).

[154]   For example, the House adopted the conference report
on the tax reconciliation bill discussed above under a
special rule waiving points of order. 128 Cong. Rec. H6547,
H6554 (daily ed. Aug. 19, 1982). An opponent of the rule
waiving points of order on the conference report said "[t]he
conference committee went beyond the scope of the bill in
conference, at least some eight times on substantive
provisions, according to staff, and many more times on more
minor provisions." 128 Cong. Rec. H6548 (daily ed. Aug. 19,
1982) (Rep. Moore).

For a less controversial bill, the manager may ask
unanimous consent when presenting the conference report for
points of order to be waived; if an objection is made, he
knows he must obtain a special rule waiving the point of
order or else must proceed under suspension of the rules.

[155]   One of the conference reports taken up under suspension
of the rules was for the massive tax cut bill of 1981, H.R.
(footnote continued)

The usual principles and maneuvers for special rules and suspension of the rules apply when these are used for conference reports, such as that bill opponents must defeat the previous question to alter a special rule.[156]

If the House fails to waive a point of order, and it is the first chamber to act on the report, defeat on a point of order recommits the conference report to the conference committee. Alternatively, recommittal may occur on motion. Either way, the manager may deal with the problem by reconvening the conference committee.[157] However, if the House is last to act, defeat on a point of order rejects the conference report, just like a vote to reject the report.

Either of these ways, a rejected report does not go back to conference committee. Rather, the bill reverts to its status before conference.[158]

4242:

> Ways and Means Democrat James M. Shannon, Mass., attempted to prevent a final vote on the bill until oil tax breaks could be trimmed back. But his plan to raise a point of order against the conference report was blocked by [Ways and Means Chairman] Rostenkowski, who won approval of the measure under suspension of the rules, a procedure that requires a two-thirds vote.

1981 Congressional Quarterly Almanac 104.

[156] For example, the managers of the 1982 tax reconciliation bill obtained a special rule waiving all points of order on the conference report. When the House took up the special rule, and the special rule's manager moved the previous question, bill opponents attempted to defeat the previous question, to adopt a substitute special rule allowing separate votes on individual propositions reported by the conference, especially on the intensely disliked provision for withholding of taxes on interest and dividends. The motion for the previous question on the rule squeaked by, 220-210. 1982 Congressional Quarterly Almanac 39.

[157] For example, the point of order against the fisheries bill under the sunshine rule was cured by recommitting the report, reconvening the committee in compliance with the rule, and then taking up the conference report.
(footnote continued)

Members who can get recognition[159] can move that
the House ask for a conference again (a second
conference). They can also use the procedure for
amendments between Houses.[160]

Senate Floor Procedure

In the Senate, the option of a filibuster can
make the endgame tricky. As in the House, the
head of the conference delegation presents the
report. There is no layover requirement.[161]

---

[158] Specifically, the bill is in the stage of disagreement
over the last amendment, which typically means the House has
disagreed to the Senate amendment.

[159] If a conference report is defeated on a point of order,
the right of prior recognition (and thus the right to
formulate the dispositive motion) stays with the majority
manager; if the conference report is defeated on a vote, the
right of prior recognition shifts to the opponents. See
Cannon at 133. However, that does not tell the whole
story. The opposition to the side that has prior
recognition is not helpless; it has certain complex
countergambits at this point for propounding its preferred
dispositive motion, as in other cases when the House uses
dispositive motions, as discussed below.

[160] To do that, they would move that the House amend the
bill and send it to the Senate in whatever form the House
will accept. See Deschler 33 § 25. Whoever has the right
of prior recognition decides whether (1) to move for a
second conference, or (2) to offer a dispositive motion of
the type seen in amendments between Houses -- typically,
that the House recede from its disagreement, and accept the
Senate amendment with a further House amendment. In the
latter case, the Member making the motion formulates the
"further House amendment," which will presumably be a
compromise between what the House has just indicated it
wants and what the moving Member wants. Clearly, although
such situations do not arise often, what bill Congress will
pass can depend at this point on who can put the dispositive
motion.

[161] Senate Rule XXVIII(1) provides that "[t]he presentation
of reports of committees of conference shall always be in
(footnote continued)

However, the conference report must be read unless
the reading is waived by unanimous consent, there
being no Senate rule like the House one for
avoiding the reading.[162]   In 1976, Senate
opponents of amendments of the Clean Air Act
killed it by insisting on a reading of the
conference report, which would have caused a delay
the Senate could not afford in its waning hours.

The conference report manager then obtains
consideration of the report, either by unanimous
consent or on motion.[163] A conference report is a
privileged matter, and the motion to proceed to it
is not debatable.[164]   Once the Senate votes to

---

order," with minimal exceptions, and that "when received,
the question of proceeding to the consideration of the
report, if raised, shall be immediately put . . . ." This
lack of a layover removes an opposition weapon; the
opposition cannot force the majority leader to move the
calendar one legislative day by adjourning, with that
action's side potential for delay, as the opposition can for
reporting of regular bills.

[162] Riddick, "Conferences and Conference Reports: Reading
of Report," at 399, and "Debate: Conference Reports, Debate
of: Reading of, Not Interrupted by Debate," at 582.   The
report must also be printed.   Riddick, "Conferences and
Conference Reports: Printing of Report," at 407.   One
assumes that in the last eventuality an obstructor insisting
on the reading of a conference report would merely force the
Senate to use its ability by motion under Rule V to suspend
the rules by a two-thirds vote, after Rule V's one-day
delay, assuming that the Senate did not simply reverse its
precedents and decide that no reading was necessary.

[163] It is interesting that the Majority Leader himself does
not customarily do this.   This resembles the pattern in the
last century, when committee chairs, not the leader, moved
to proceed to committee reports.

[164] Senate Rule XXVIII provides that "the question of
proceeding . . . shall be immediately put, and shall be
determined without debate."   See Riddick, "Conferences and
Conference Reports: Consideration of Conference Reports
Privileged Business and Immediate Consideration," at 395;
"Debate: Conference Reports, Debate of: Consideration of:
Motion to Consider not Debatable," at 581.   The privileged
status of the conference report also means that its
(footnote continued)

proceed, or agrees to proceed, to the report, the report is debatable.[165] Points of order can be made at any time.[166] At any time, opponents of the report have ready options, either to move to recommit (if the Senate is acting first on the report) or to move to table.

If a filibuster occurs, proponents of the conference report must invoke cloture, and even with cloture, they may have a hard time. At the end of 1982, Senator Jesse Helms (R-N.C.) delayed adjournment by insisting on a layover for a conference report, which he could readily obtain because a vote on a cloture petition to shut him off would have required a delay of a day anyway.[167] The filibuster option adds a special twist, because, as described above, conference reports tend to come at the end of the session or just before a recess, when the filibuster threat is most potent.[168] Proponents of a bill have to

---

consideration does not displace the pending business. See Riddick, "Conferences and Conference Reports: Consideration of Conference Reports Privileged Business and Immediate Consideration: Suspends Other Business but does not Displace," at 397.

[165] Riddick, "Debate: Conference Reports, Debate of: Consideration of: to Adopt, Debatable," at 581. In other words, while there are two filibusters possible on bills (on the motion to proceed and on the bill), on a conference report there is only one.

[166] Riddick at 406 (anytime after the report is read).

[167] Senator Helms explained that he "still want[ed] a copy of this conference report," and "hope[d] to spend tomorrow looking at it," and at his insistence the vote on cloture was put off until December 23. When Senator George Mitchell (D-Maine) asked: "What conceivable purpose would be served by compelling the Members of the Senate to remain here overnight on Wednesday until Thursday and then get home, in some cases, less than 24 hours before Christmas?" Senator Helms responded: "Do you know what is in the conference report?" 128 Cong. Rec. S15985 (daily ed. Dec. 21, 1983).

[168] Even in the 1980s, there had not yet been a postcloture filibuster on a conference report. For example, when cloture was overwhelmingly voted in 1982 on the surface (footnote continued)

summon 60 votes for cloture on the bill as
compromised with the House.   The result, as
mentioned above, is that the House has accepted
the Senate versions of bills, such as civil rights
bills, just to avoid conference with the threat of
a Senate filibuster on the conference report.

Otherwise, the final moves in the Senate
resemble those in the House.   If the Senate acts
first, it may move to recommit, or a point of
order will recommit the report.[169]   If it acts
last, or if it votes to reject the report,
proponents may either move for a second conference
or resort to amendments between Houses.   Under
normal recognition principles, the majority
manager would obtain recognition to decide which
way to proceed.

F.   SPECIAL POSTCONFERENCE PROCEDURES

Besides the mechanisms previously devised, the two
chambers, and primarily the House, have developed
more complex postconference mechanisms.   These
complex mechanisms merit study, for almost all
appropriation bills use these mechanisms, as do a
number of the more controversial nonappropriation
bills.   Two postconference mechanisms exist: one

---

transportation conference report, no opposition was raised
to an immediate vote on the report.   It may be that there
could not be such a filibuster.

If the Senate were the first chamber to act, a motion
to recommit with instructions might be offered, and the
instructions are subject to amendment.   That might offer
postcloture filibuster possibilities.   The same does not
appear immediately to be the case when the Senate is the
last chamber to act, but one hesitates to suggest that there
is any Senate situation without a potential for endless
delaying tactics.

[169]   For example, on August 12, 1982, the Senate upheld a
point of order against an aviation insurance bill for a
provision concerning labor protection that exceeded the
conference scope.   By upholding the point of order, the
Senate recommitted the conference report.   A second report
was filed September 23 and adopted by the Senate and House
on September 30.   1982 Congressional Quarterly Almanac 332.

primarily for appropriation bills, that deals with bills for which the conferees exceed their scope; the other for House bills on which the Senate has tacked non-germane amendments. These mechanisms make an exception to the "all or nothing rule" and allow the chambers to adopt these bills, with a separate vote on the sensitive points -- the appropriations outside the conferees' scope or the non-germane Senate amendments.

Appropriations Outside Scope

In 1920, as part of a major reform of budget procedure, the two chambers reconsolidated all power over appropriations in single Appropriations Committees, raising the specter of excessive power through those committees' control of conference reports.[170]   To avoid this, in 1920 the House adopted a rule aimed at "restricting the old practice of the Senate of loading appropriation bills with legislative amendments and the old practice of House managers of agreeing to these amendments."[171]   House Rule XX(2) provided, and still provides today: "No amendment of the Senate to a general appropriation bill which would be in violation of the provisions of clause 2 of Rule XXI, if said amendment originated in the House . . . shall be agreed to by the managers on the part of the House . . . ."[172]

---

[170] Since the House Appropriations Committee now controlled conferences on all appropriation bills, the specter was raised that the committee members could enact anything they wanted, notwithstanding the opposition of the rest of the House. They could do so by putting anything they wanted in a conference report on one of the appropriation bills (where it could only be defeated with great difficulty by defeating the whole conference report). The threat was greatest in appropriation bills because they were must-pass bills that collectively covered the whole government.

[171] McCown at 192-93.

[172] Rule XXI(2) prohibits legislation on appropriations and unauthorized appropriations. See House Manual § 834 et seq. Rule XX(2) provides that the House, "by a separate (footnote continued)

In theory, Rule XX(2) sharply narrows the scope for House appropriation conferees. It makes matter agreed to by House conferees out of order, even though within the scope of differences. More important, it makes out of order any of the Senate's unauthorized appropriations and legislation on appropriations.[173] As a practical matter, Rule XX(2) does not constrain House Appropriations conferees, but only forces them (since they usually do not use special rules to waive this House Rule)[174] to use a special procedure that was quickly developed to deal with the 1920 rule: the first postconference procedure of presenting a report in technical partial disagreement.[175]

---

vote on every such amendment," can authorize the managers to agree to such Senate amendments, but House Appropriations managers do not seek such authority.

[173] Note that normally, conferees could not be criticized as exceeding the scope of the difference for accepting such Senate amendments, since such amendments are within the scope of the conference once the Senate has enacted them. The House could, and does, declare Senate amendments that make unauthorized appropriations, or that put legislation on an appropriation bill, out or order. However, it could only enforce such a principle to the limit if the Senate were willing to accept a complete loss of its right to offer unauthorized appropriations and legislation and thus take a distinctly secondary role in appropriation bills. The Senate's longstanding loose rules in the regard are discussed more fully in the chapter on appropriations.

[174] The House Appropriations Committee has chosen to solve the problems raised by the 1920 rule in its own way, rather than as most House committees would have, by obtaining special rules waiving the 1920 rule. The Appropriations Committee occasionally uses such special rules, but historically "[t]he practice of reporting special resolutions from the Committee on Rules in connection with conferences on appropriation bills has not become a general one." McCown at 192. After all, the Appropriations Committee never developed the dependence on special rules of other committees, because its bills were privileged for floor consideration without a special rule.

[175] The practice that developed in 1921 is described in (footnote continued)

Congress now uses this mechanism of partial disagreement virtually universally for appropriations,[176] warranting careful study of the following general principles regarding "disagreement." When conferees on any bill can reach no agreement, they can report back in total disagreement, at which point their chambers may go to a second conference, or switch to amendments between Houses, or just give up. When conferees can reach agreement on some parts of a bill but not others, they can report back in partial disagreement.[177]

Imagine an appropriation with only two items, for salaries and battleships, with conferees agreeing on salaries but not battleships. Suppose the House is the first chamber to take up the conference report.[178] The House disposes of the

---

McCown at 186-91. It should be noted that the use of the procedure of reporting amendments in partial disagreement was in use for appropriations before then, Riddick, "Amendments Between Houses: Amendments Reported in Disagreement by Conferees," at 105 n.49, particularly because of the tendency in that area, unlike today, to take successive conferences in stride.

[176] In 1981, reports in partial disagreement were made for every conference report on an appropriation -- nine regular appropriations, one supplemental, two continuing resolutions (one of them vetoed), and the first budget resolution. In 1982, reports in partial or total disagreement were made for almost every conference report on an appropriation -- six regular appropriations, two supplementals (one vetoed), and one continuing resolution, and also the first budget resolution. However, the omnibus continuing resolution that folded in six appropriation bills, H.J. Res. 631, was not reported in disagreement.

[177] House Manual § 544; Deschler 33 § 23; Riddick, "Amendments Between Houses: Amendments Reported in Disagreement by Conferees," at 104-5; "Conferences and Conference Reports: Amendments Reported in Disagreement," at 382-83; "Conferences and Conference Reports: Consideration of Conference Report: Amendments Reported in Disagreement," at 392-93.

[178] This postconference mechanism works the same way, with slight deviations discussed below, whether the House or (footnote continued)

conference report containing the agreed-upon salaries as with any conference report, and then the House takes up the amendment reported back in disagreement (the "amendment in disagreement") concerning battleships. Regarding an amendment in disagreement, House conferees can present any of three options[179] for their chamber: to recede and concur in the Senate amendment, to disagree to the Senate amendment, or to compromise by moving to recede and concur with a new House amendment (in this example, an intermediate figure for battleships).[180]

This mechanism serves admirably as a response to the 1920 rule. Points of order available against a conference report are not available against amendments in disagreement,[181] because the

---

Senate acts first. In general, the House acts first, because this mechanism is used primarily for appropriations bills. The House originates appropriations, and typically the Senate, acting on the House bill, asks for a conference; the chamber that asks first, acts last on the conference report.

[179] It is irrelevant that, as a practical matter, the managers do agree on how they will resolve the amendments in disagreement. What counts is that, technically, they report back that they have not agreed, leading to a separate vote from the vote on the conference report. The managers' profession of disagreement is a pure example of a legal fiction, an accepted and understood fabrication for purposes of avoiding a disagreeable technical requirement.

[180] Regarding the chamber's own amendments, the chamber may insist on them, or recede from them. (The one fluke is that a chamber cannot take a compromise position on its own amendment -- it cannot recede from its insistence on its own amendment, with an amendment. However, even here, the chamber may recede from an amendment to the other chamber's amendment, and concur in the other chamber's amendment, with an amendment. See House Manual § 526.)

[181] Riddick, "Conferences and Conference Reports: Amendments Reported in Disagreement," at 383 n.55; Deschler 33 § 23.8. For example, suppose the conferees on the appropriations bill not only want more money for battleships than either chamber voted, but also want to accept a Senate item of legislation (e.g., that all battleship captains must (footnote continued)

chamber is not being forced to swallow whole the amendments in disagreement as it must swallow conference reports whole.   It has a separate choice.[182]

When the House is done, its version goes to the Senate.   The Senate first votes on the conference report.   Then, the amendment in disagreement concerning the battleship money is dealt with by motions to recede and concur, with or without amendments, as in the House.[183] Usually the Senate will accept the version as the House finished with it, but the Senate may resolve differently any of the points in disagreement.   In that case, the points in disagreement shuttle back to the House (with the agreed-upon points just coming along without any new votes) as in the method of amendments between Houses.

Ordinarily, the chambers adopt the conference chairs' motions for resolving the points in disagreement, with perhaps a single simple opposing motion that loses, in which case the process can be swift and simple.[184]   When some

---

be under 60).   Under House Rule XX(2), neither of those items would be in order in a conference report.   (The battleship money exceeds the conference's scope, and the Senate legislation is prohibited by Rule XX(2).)   However, when the appropriation conferees report back in partial disagreement on those items, the motions then offered to resolve the amendments in disagreement were not "agreed to by the managers on the part of the House" (Rule XX(2)).

[182]   In this example, after the House accepts the partial conference report, the House Appropriations chair asks his chamber separately to recede and concur in the Senate amendment concerning battleship money with a (House) amendment boosting the amount of that money.   Unlike the normal "all or nothing" situation, the House decides each of these motions to recede and concur separately, as amendments in disagreement, not as agreed-upon matter in a conference report.

[183]   The House usually trudges through the amendments in disagreement one by one.   The Senate customarily considers all of them, or at least all of them except any controversial ones, en bloc.

[184]   For example, the conferees on the District of Columbia (footnote continued)

opponent wishes not merely to oppose, but to take
the tempting opportunity to offer an alternative
proposal,[185] the procedure can become technical
and complex -- very complex. In the House, debate
proceeds on the committee chair's motion, or on
the countermotion of an opponent, under the hour
rule; in the Senate, these are debatable
motions.[186]

---

appropriation in 1982, H.R. 7144, reported in partial
disagreement. On December 17, the House adopted the partial
conference report, and the conference chair then offered
various motions to dispose of the Senate amendments in
disagreement. On amendment 39, which concerned a government
employee's salary, the conference chair offered a motion to
concur with an amendment. Representative Walker offered an
opposing motion, which he lost.   128 Cong. Rec. H10174
(daily ed. Dec. 17, 1982).

   The next day, the Senate adopted the partial conference
report.   Then, the chair for the Senate conferees, Senator
Alphonse D'Amato (R-N.Y.), obtained unanimous consent for
the amendments in disagreement to be considered en bloc, and
moved successfully to recede and concur in ten amendments,
including amendment 39. Id. at S15345 (daily ed. Dec. 18,
1982).

[185] Opposition groups try to seize such opportunities both
because the target is broad and because the timing makes
victory particularly desirable. Appropriations bills pay
for the whole government and offer a broad target for
germane amendments. If the opposition wins, its timing puts
it much closer to success than is usual with floor
amendments, because the bill is not only too far along to
get bottled up in committee, it is too far along to get
watered down or eliminated in conference. A victory at this
point is almost certainly locked into enactment.

[186] There is no Senate filibuster on proceeding to these
amendments: it will be recalled that the motion to proceed
to a conference report is not debatable, and "[a]fter a
conference report has been agreed to, if there are any
amendments reported by the conferees in disagreement, the
Chair lays them before the Senate for action."   Riddick,
"Conferences and Conference Reports: Amendments Reported in
Disagreement," at 382. However, the motions themselves, as
motions on amendments between Houses, are debatable.
Riddick, "Amendments Between Houses: Debate of," at 108.

This area requires elaborating some key points in the general procedure for amendments between Houses. A House Member's ability to put forward alternative amendments during the phase of amendments between Houses depends on whether the House is in the "stage of disagreement" on the bill.[187] Reports in partial disagreement occur, by definition, in the stage of disagreement.[188] In that stage, the House conference chair's manager's motion simply to accept the other chamber's amendment -- a motion to recede (from being in the state of disagreement) and concur (in the other chamber's amendment) -- takes precedence over efforts to put forth an alternative.

Thus, the House conference chair starts out able to block the opposition's alternative amendment by using the motion for the previous question.[189] For the opposition to get precedence

---

[187] Each chamber has one order of precedence for dispositive motions -- motions to concur, concur with an amendment, etc. -- before the stage of disagreement, and a second order after the stage of disagreement. For the listing of the precedence of motions, see House Manual § 528; Riddick, "Amendments Between Houses: Acted on by Adoption of Motions," at 100-102. The guiding principle underlying that order of precedence is summed up thus: "before the stage of formal disagreement has been reached, the order of priority favors exploration of the legislative possibilities, whereas in disagreement, the expeditious resolution of differences is preferred." House Republican Manual, "When the Houses Differ: The Stage of Formal Disagreement," at 316.

[188] The chambers went to conference by getting into the stage of disagreement and that is where they still are.

[189] If the manager offers a motion to recede and concur, then whether the opposition can offer a motion to recede and concur with an amendment depends on precedence considerations discussed below. If the manager offers a motion to recede and concur with an amendment, when he is done with debate on that amendment he will move the previous question, cutting off amending. For the opposition to offer its amendment, it must defeat the motion for the previous question, Deschler 32 § 8.12, or defeat the manager's motion, Deschler 32 § 8.2, either of which shifts control of (footnote continued)

for itself in this situation requires a special maneuver.   When the conference chair makes a motion to recede and concur, the opposition asks for a division of the question, producing two motions, one to recede, the other to concur, and then the opposition jumps in between the two.[190]

For example, when House conferees brought back the first continuing resolution for fiscal year 1983 on October 1, 1982, a motion was made to recede and concur in a Senate amendment, number 83, to give a raise to the strikebreaking air traffic controllers.[191]   As soon as the motion to recede and concur in Senate amendment 83 was made, Representative William Ford (D-Mich.) asked for a division of the question.[192]   He then rose to "offer a preferential motion" to "concur in Senate amendment numbered 83 with an amendment as follows . . . ," thereby having a precious opportunity to offer his amendment.[193]   In an era when Congress

---

time to the opposition.   The manager may, of course, voluntarily yield for an amendment instead of cutting off such amendments by making a motion for the previous question.   Deschler 32 § 8.14.

[190] The motion to recede and concur is divisible.   Deschler 32 § 7.8; House Manual § 525.   The House can adopt the motion to recede, which takes the House back before the stage of disagreement.   When the motion to recede carries, the House has receded from the stage of disagreement, and prior to the stage of disagreement, the minority's motion to concur with an amendment has precedence over the majority's motion to concur.   Deschler 32 §§ 7.9 - 7.11; House Manual §§ 482, 528.

[191] Representative Ford, the opposition on this matter, wanted to offer an amendment to let the administration rehire the fired striking controllers.   Representative Ford chaired the House Post Office and Civil Service Committee.   He was the "opposition" because most of the House was unsympathetic on this point to the striking air traffic controllers.

[192] That divided the motion into a motion to recede and a motion to concur.   The House immediately agreed to recede.

[193] After Representative Ford's amendment was read, under the hour rule, he was recognized for 30 minutes, and the (footnote continued)

uses appropriations as all-purpose vehicles for action and with partial disagreement as a universal procedure for appropriations, this postconference window for amendments, complicated as it is, took on significant importance.[194]

Senate Non-germane Amendments

The other postconference procedure deals with non-germane Senate amendments to House bills. Historically, the Senate's lack of a general germaneness rule created what was, in effect, a potent tool for bypassing House obstacles to legislation. As Professor Froman describes the process:

> One way of avoiding a whole series of pitfalls in the House of Representatives is for the proponents to use some noncontroversial bill already passed by the House, and, because the rule of germaneness does not apply in the Senate (except for general appropriations bills), attach another bill to it.[195]

When the House bill, with its unrelated Senate amendment, arrives back at the House, it can be taken up directly on the floor and thereby sent to conference in any of a number of ways: by unanimous consent, by suspension of the rules, under a special rule, or by the motion developed in 1965.

The House majority thereby bypasses a number

---

administration's backer (Representative Lawrence Coughlin (R-Pa.) who had offered the motion to recede and concur) was recognized for 30 minutes. 128 Cong. Rec. H8377 (daily ed. Oct. 1, 1982). After debate, the previous question was ordered, and then the record vote occurred. Id. at H8387. The amendment was defeated, 128-267.

[194] The House Republican Manual devoted much attention to it, including sophisticated analysis of further details not treated here. House Republican Manual, "When the Houses Disagree: The Stage of Formal Disagreement," at 313-17.

[195] Froman at 149.

of its own chamber's barriers to legislation, as
one observer noted: "First, committee and
subcommittee hearings, consideration, and votes
have been avoided; then a request for a rule from
the Committee on Rules has been by-passed; and, of
course, the strategy avoids an initial floor
fight."[196] The House majority could just send the
bill to conference, or, even if it struck off the
Senate non-germane amendment, the conference might
agree to some compromise of that amendment,
thereby enacting some provision that might never
have come out to the House floor, or passed
through it, any other way.

Sometimes major legislation passed this way,
despite the affront to the House committee
system. For example, in 1970 the Senate took the
House bill extending the Voting Rights Act, and
attached an amendment extending the franchise to
voters between the ages of 18 and 21. By so
doing, the Senate evaded the House Judiciary
Committee, whose 80-year-old chair, Representative
Emanuel Celler (D-N.Y.) strongly supported civil
rights (including the voting rights act) but
bottled up any proposals for what he called "teen
age voting."[197] When the House received the bill,
it took the bill up under a rule allowing no
amendments, went to conference, and later adopted
the conference report, enacting the "teen age
vote".[198]

Although this procedure still required a
House majority to enact the measure as a whole,
the House experienced strong indignation at
procedures by which all its rules were bypassed,

---

[196] Id. Froman offers several examples of the strategy in
operation at 146-53 by which, in effect, a strategy could be
"devised to attempt to 'skip' the House of
Representatives," Id. at 147.

[197] 28 Cong. Q. Week. Rep. 775, 779 (1970). This example
was developed by a student in the author's seminar, Richard
Heinle.

[198] Pub. L. No. 91-285. The act's provisions reducing the
voting age for state elections were struck down as
unconstitutional in Oregon v. Mitchell, 400 U.S. 112 (1970),
whereupon Congress enacted the 26th Amendment.

particularly   at   the   instigation   of   the
Senate.[199]   Accordingly, in 1970, 1972, and 1974
the House adopted and amended Rule XXVIII(4) and
(5).[200]   As amended, the rule set up a two-step
procedure for House bills with non-germane Senate
amendments.[201]   This procedure will be illustrated
by the House's handling in 1988 of a controversial
provision to prohibit "dial-a-porn" -- indecent
telephone messages available by purchase.

In the first step, the Senate took a school
improvement bill, and added a prohibition on dial-
a-porn as a non-germane amendment.   The House
Rules Committee proposed a special rule to fend
off the issue, but the opposition defeated the
previous question on the special rule,[202] and

---

[199] One Congressman said that by accepting the Senate's use
of non-germane amendments, his colleagues "have sacrificed
our dignity, we have acknowledged our inferiority, [and] we
have refused to recognize the inequity of the situation
. . . ."   Ruling Congress at 167-68 note * (quoting Rep.
Paul C. Jones (D-Mo.).

[200]   Rule XXVIII(4) deals with non-germane matter in
conference reports.   Rule XXVIII(5) deals with non-germane
matter taken up in amendments between Houses.   To simplify
the discussion, only the former rule will be discussed, as
the latter parallels it.

The rule was known as the "Colmer rule" after the Chair
of the House Rules Committee, Representative William Colmer
(D-Miss.), S. Bach, House Consideration of Nongermane Senate
Amendments 14 (Cong. Res. Serv. 1976), whose committee had
reported the bill changing the rule and who so disliked the
liberal legislation being enacted through the use of non-
germane Senate amendments.

[201]   The rule had to be amended after the House
Parliamentarian ruled that a point of order under the rule
would kill a conference report -- not just deal with the
non-germane amendment -- if, as usual, the conference report
was for a bill for which there had been an amendment in the
nature of a substitute.   See Ruling Congress at 38-45, 169.

[202]   134 Cong. Rec. H1715-16 (daily ed. April 19, 1988)
(previous amendment defeated, and special rule amended and
adopted).

obtained the regular procedure. Accordingly, the
conference   manager,   Representative   Augustus
Hawkins (D-Calif.), called up the conference
report on the House floor. The opposition leader,
Representative Thomas J. Bliley, Jr. (R-Va.) made
a point of order under Rule XXVIII(4)[203] against
section   6101   of   the   conference   report   (the
Senate's compromise provision on dial-a-porn) as
non-germane.[204]   The Speaker sustained the point
of order.

In the second step follows, Representative
Bliley moved to reject the non-germane section
6101, so that he could bring his own proposal
up. This motion is "of high privilege," and is
subject to debate for 40 minutes, with one-half of
the   time   to   each   side   pursuant   to   Rule
XXVIII(4)(b). At this point there is a fork in
the road. If the House defeats the motion to
reject, it says, in effect, that it accepts the
Senate   non-germane   amendment.   The   House   has
accepted this particular affront to its rules, and
proceeds to consider the rest of the conference
report.

However, if the House agrees to the motion to
reject, it says, in effect, that it does not
accept the Senate non-germane amendment. In that

---

[203] The rule allows a point of order against non-germane
matter ("any matter which would be in violation of the
provisions of clause 7 of Rule XVI if such matter had been
offered as an amendment in the House") contained either in
"any Senate amendment to that measure . . . agreed to by the
conference committee . . . or contained in any substitute
agreed to by the conference committee."

[204] An illustration is the House's handling in 1982 of a
controversial   provision   for   a   moratorium   on   uranium
imports. The Senate had adopted that provision "at the
insistence of Sen. Pete V. Domenici, R-N.M., whose state was
the   center   of   the   financially   ailing   U.S.   uranium
industry." 1982 Congressional Quarterly Almanac 311. When
the conference manager, Rep. Morris Udall (D-Ariz.) called
up the conference report on the House floor, Rep. William
Frenzel (R-Minn.) made a point of order under Rule XXVIII(4)
against section 23 of the conference report. Rep. Udall
conceded the point of order, and the Chair sustained it.
128 Cong. Rec. H8802 (daily ed. Dec. 2, 1982).

case, once the House finishes consideration of other matters,[205] Rule XXVIII(4)(d) provides that "the conference report shall be considered as rejected and the question then pending before the House" shall be whether to adopt and send to the Senate a measure "which shall consist of that portion of the conference report not rejected."[206] This means, essentially, that the House refuses the product of the conference and falls back on amendments between Houses, sending to the Senate an amended version of the original bill.

In this 1988 example, the House agreed to the motion to reject the Senate amendment (section 6101), and the conference report was considered as rejected. The Speaker recognized Representative Bliley to offer a privileged motion, consisting of the portion of the conference report not rejected, together with his own strong version of the dial-a-porn prohibition. The House receded and concurred with a provision as he requested.[207]

---

[205]   There may be more than one non-germane Senate amendment, and all must be dealt with before going to the next stage of voting on a motion to adopt the (germane) remnant. For example, in the 1982 uranium example, the Senate had added such an amendment to bar the government from using spent fuel from civilian reactors to make plutonium for nuclear weapons, considered a threat to international nonproliferation efforts. Representative Stratton made a point of order against the Senate amendment, which was sustained, 128 Cong. Rec. H8809 (daily ed. Dec. 2, 1982), but after a debate Representative Samuel Stratton's (D-N.Y.) motion to reject the non-germane amendment was defeated, id. at H8817.

[206]   Often there is more than one Senate non-germane amendment to deal with. Rule XXVIII(4)(c) expressly provides for "further points of order" against non-germane provisions, even after the first point of order has been sustained. However, the rule does not provide for further points of order on grounds other than non-germane provisions, such as on the ground the conference report exceeds the scope of the conference. Such points of order must be made earlier than the first point of order against a non-germane provision to be properly preserved. See Deschler 33 § 19.11 - § 19.12.
(footnote continued)

The rule is a complex one, with many technical aspects.[208] An interesting question is the extent to which it has dampened the Senate's enthusiasm for non-germane amendments. Undoubtedly it has to some extent, and the old tactic for end-running House committees has lost some of its force; but the question is how much. The Senate can still get non-germane amendments through the House in several ways. Of course, the House itself may want something accomplished with a non-germane amendment, such as proved true for the tougher dial-a-porn provision in 1988. Alternatively, if the "nongermane Senate provisions" are "strongly supported by the Senate and House conferees,"[209] the provisions' backers may fight on the House floor. Perhaps most important under the logic of current House procedure, the Rules Committee[210] may grant a rule

---

[207] 134 Cong. Rec. H1717 (daily ed. April 19, 1988) (Bliley offers motion), H1836 (vote adopting Bliley motion).

In the 1982 uranium example, after the Speaker pro tempore sustained the point of order, he announced that the Nuclear Regulatory Commission bill "conference report is considered as rejected," and then recognized Representative Udall "to offer an amendment consisting of the remainder of the conference report." 128 Cong. Rec. H8817 (daily ed. Dec. 2, 1982), which was adopted by voice vote. Subsequently, Chairs Udall and Peter Domenici (R-N.Mex.) worked out a compromise by which the Senate adopted a concurrent resolution with some supplementary understandings, a resolution passed by the House on December 20 at virtually the end of the session. 1982 Congressional Quarterly Almanac 313.

[208] See House Republican Manual, "When the Houses Disagree: Nongermane Senate Provisions," at 341-46; House Manual §§ 913b - 913c.

[209] R. W. Russell, Working of Congress, in Effective Washington Representation (ed. S. J. Marcuss 1983), at 245.

[210] See Deschler 33 § 20, especially 33 § 20.8. This brings House procedure full circle: the House rules change of 1965, curbing the Rules Committee, created such problems with excess Senate non-germane amendments that Rule XXVIII was (footnote continued)

waiving the separate votes required by Rule XXVIII
-- or may even grant a targeted complex rule
allowing separate votes under Rule XXVIII on some
matters but not others.

---

needed; the problems from Rule XXVIII are so difficult that
the House deals with them through the Rules Committee.

12
The Budget Process[1]

In the 1980s, Congress became intensely -- some would say obsessively -- preoccupied with the budget and the budget process. That process provides a major arena for national policy contests, it structures the consideration of the most important legislation, and it takes up vast amounts of media coverage, floor time, and attention from the administration and congressional leadership. Yet, the budget procedure involves so many aspects and complexities that only a handful of participants or observers understand all its workings. It uses its own concepts, vocabulary, committees, schedule, legislative vehicles, points of order, and waiver mechanisms. Congress has had to struggle time and again to relearn that process:

---

[1] Sources cited frequently in this chapter include: A. Schick, Congress and Money: Budgeting, Spending and Taxing (1980) (Schick); R. G. Penner and A. J. Abramson, Broken Purse Strings: Congressional Budgeting, 1974-88 (1988) (Penner and Abramson); Congressional Budgeting: Politics, Process, and Power (eds. W. T. Wander, F. T. Hebert, and G. W. Copeland 1984) (Congressional Budgeting); Stith, Rewriting the Fiscal Constitution: The Case of Gramm-Rudman-Hollings, 76 Calif. L. Rev. 593 (1988) (Stith); Report of the House Committee on Rules on the Congressional Budget Act Amendments of 1984, H.R. Rept. No. 1152, 98th Cong., 2d Sess. 1984 (Beilenson Report) (this is the authoritative report of the full committee, not the Beilenson task force).

first when it was enacted in 1974, later when major changes occurred in ad hoc fashion starting in 1980 and 1981, and again when it was revised thoroughly by the "Gramm-Rudman" act in 1985 and by "Gramm-Rudman II" in 1986.

This section provides two overall approaches to the budget process: through its timetable and basic concepts, and through its history. Subsequent sections then turn to the details of the formulation and contents of the budget resolution, to reconciliation and revenue legislation, and to points of order and waiver mechanisms. Spending allocations will be discussed in the chapter concerning appropriations.

A. OVERVIEW AND HISTORY

Overview

The budget process aims to lay down, in an annual budget resolution devised each spring, a master budgetary program, with execution of the plan the rest of the year largely through three processes: reconciliation, revenue targets, and committee allocations. In formulating and executing that budget plan, Congress distinguishes sharply between two main types of budget authority: appropriations and entitlements.[2] Congress votes appropriations annually, and therefore the budget process can shape appropriations simply by "allocating" the funds for the annual appropriation bills. In contrast, Congress enacts entitlements on a permanent or long-term basis. Entitlements are legislation entitling individuals to benefits, such as Social Security, Medicare, Medicaid, and federal retirement pay.[3]   Since

---

[2]   There are other forms of budget authority, such as contract and borrowing authority. However, these have been somewhat curbed, and are much smaller in scale than entitlements.

[3]   An "appropriated entitlement" (see Beilenson Report at 27) or "quasi-entitlement," like food stamps, may (footnote continued)

entitlements consist of permanent legislation, to shape them the budget process must go beyond allocating annual spending, and must push the enactment of special spending-cut legislation. That is the "reconciliation" process.

Congress' annual drama of enacting a budget resolution follows a timetable established by Gramm-Rudman, and set forth in section 300 of the budget act.   It begins with the President submitting his proposed budget on the first Monday after January 3 (a deadline almost certain not to be achieved). Although the President's budget is technically a mere proposal not binding in any way on Congress, it exerts great influence.   The description here will follow the timetable as revised by the Gramm-Rudman acts, but will use examples from the most impressive budget year, 1981: Legal Services for an appropriation example, and Medicaid for an entitlement.   In 1981, President Reagan's budget proposed denying funds completely to Legal Services (in the budget lexicon, "zeroing it out") and proposed "capping" Medicaid.

Next, the congressional committees weigh in.   Each congressional committee prepares its views on the budget by February 25.[4] In 1981, the House and Senate authorization committees expressed opposing views on funding for Legal Services[5] and Medicaid.[6]   More important, the

---

technically require appropriations, but as a practical matter discretion is not exercised in shaping the appropriations.   The permanent law specifies the payment formula. The appropriations must fund the amount needed to pay for the law as written, unless the federal government intends to default on its stated obligations.

[4]   These "301(d) views" (named after the budget act section requiring them, formerly section 301(c)) occasionally serve as an important channel of expression, as in 1981, but that year was atypical; more often the committee views do not matter greatly. Until the Gramm-Rudman Act, committees had to submit them by a March 15 deadline.

[5]   Senate Labor and Human Resources agreed with the President on cutting Legal Services, and House Judiciary sharply disagreeing and urging full funding. The House and Senate appropriations committees, which can express views (footnote continued)

House and Senate budget committees report proposed budget resolutions.   The Gramm-Rudman timetable calls for the Senate Budget Committee to report a resolution by April 1.[7]   When the budget committees report out their resolutions, these resolutions set forth budget targets on three levels: aggregates, functions, and (in its legislative history) underlying assumptions.   The aggregates are grand totals, the functions are categories, and the underlying assumptions are program-level details.   Thus, in 1981, the House and Senate budget resolutions stated various aggregates for total spending, and stated the gross figures for the functions that contain Legal Services and Medicaid.[8]

---

about programs funded through appropriations, expressed ambiguous views about Legal Services. House Appropriations' and Judiciary's views can be found in House Committee on the Budget, Views and Estimates of Committees of the House on the Congressional Budget for Fiscal Year 1982 (Comm. Print 1981).   Senate committee views are in committee prints of the individual committees on file with the Senate Budget Committee's Office of Publications. See also Lawyers Begin Effort to Save Legal Services, 39 Cong. Q. Week. Rep. 529 (1981).

[6]   Senate Finance agreed with the President's cap, and House Energy and Commerce rejected the "cap" in favor of other Medicaid cuts. New Federalism No Panacea for State, Local Governments, 39 Cong. Q. Week. Rep. 708, 710 (1981). Since Medicaid is an entitlement, the appropriations committees were not involved.

[7]   The timetable is section 300 of the Budget Act, 2 U.S.C. § 631.   Gramm-Rudman does not set a date for the House Budget Committee to report.

[8]   Pursuant to section 301(e), the budget committee reports discuss the "assumptions" of how, in the committees' view, Congress could achieve those aggregates and functions, namely, how much might go to particular programs or how the programs could be reshaped.   In 1981, for Legal Services, the House Budget Committee's report assumed $200 million, while the Senate Committee's report assumed $100 million.

For Medicaid, the Senate Budget Committee's report assumed the concept of a "cap" as the President had (footnote continued)

Once the budget committees report their budget resolutions, the House and Senate amend and adopt those resolutions, and ultimately settle a resolution in conference. Gramm-Rudman moved the date on which Congress is supposed to complete all this action on the budget resolution to April 15 (formerly May 15). In 1981, on the floor, the Senate considered an amendment to cut Function 750, Administration of Justice, by $100 million, which was assumed to "zero out" Legal Services, but the floor vote rejected that amendment, leaving in place the committee figure for Function 750 with its assumption of $100 million for Legal Services.[9] The House in 1981 revolted against its own budget committee's proposal, thereby overthrowing its majority party's position and instead choosing a conservative proposal embodying the President's spending cuts, including those for Medicaid.[10] This revolt signalled the initial success for the President's use of the budget process to enact his program.

Besides aggregates and functions, the budget resolution includes reconciliation instructions, which may direct cuts in existing entitlements,[11] and which may also direct revenue increases. Each reconciliation instruction directs a named committee to report, by a specified deadline, changes in law to achieve a spending or revenue goal. Gramm-Rudman's timetable specifies that reconciliation shall be completed by June 15, far earlier than has generally been, or is likely to

---

proposed, while the House committee's report did not. Medicaid assumptions did not make their figures diverge, even though the Senate Budget Committee assumed part of Medicaid savings would come from a cap while the House Budget assumed no cap, because the House committee assumed savings other than the cap.

[9] 127 Cong. Rec. S4542 (daily ed. May 7, 1981) (Legal Services amendment rejected), S4871 (daily ed. May 12, 1981) (resolution adopted).

[10] 127 Cong. Rec. H2055 (daily ed. May 7, 1981).

[11] In 1981, reconciliation instructions also directed cuts in authorizations to force lower appropriations, but this was aberrational and will not be discussed.

be, congressional practice.

In reconciliation, the authorizing committees, as instructed, recommend legislation making cuts in existing entitlements. Then, the budget committees package the various committees' recommendations into omnibus bills. Through the reconciliation bill in 1981, Congress cut Medicaid but without a "cap."[12] Thus, when the budget process had run its course, the assumptions underlying the budget resolution held true about where the cuts would be, i.e., in Medicaid, though not about how the cuts would be made.

As for appropriations, the budget committee conferees devise committee allocations, which break down the spending aggregates into figures for each committee.[13] The appropriations committees take their allocations and "suballocate" them among subcommittees. This chain of allocating and suballocating aims to hold each spending bill within a specific slice of a carefully allocated pie.

_____

[12]   The Senate Finance Committeee complied with the reconciliation instruction by proposing cuts for Medicaid, though not the cap sought by the President and assumed by the legislative history of the budget resolution. House Energy and Commerce deadlocked over reconciliation, and the issue went to the House floor and ultimately to the conference on the reconciliation bill. 1981 Congressional Quarterly Almanac 479-80.

The first budget resolution of 1981 included reconciliation instructions mandating cuts in authorizations, which assumed the reduction of Legal Services to $100 million. The Senate included a $100 million authorization for Legal Services in the reconciliation bill, but it was not in the House bill. House conferees insisted Legal Services not be addressed.

[13]   In 1981, the conferees allocated $465 billion to the House Appropriations Committee for fiscal year 1982. Theoretically, this reflected the assumption of $100 million for Legal Services. Practically, as the difference in scale reflects, allocations have little control over specific items 1/40th of one percent of their size. Allocations matter principally as ceilings on appropriations, and will be discussed mainly in the next chapter on appropriations.

In 1981, of the $465 billion allocated to the House Appropriations Committee, $8.8 billion was suballocated to the subcommittee for the State-Justice-Commerce appropriation, which reports the bill that includes funds for Legal Services.[14] Both House and Senate appropriations committees reported State-Justice-Commerce bills with $241 million for Legal Services, and the House and Senate rejected amendments on the floor to cut Legal Services.[15]   Thus, the assumptions underlying the budget resolution did not end up controlling the outcome on Legal Services.

For taxes, the resolution includes an aggregate stating the recommended level of revenues, and the amount by which revenue should be raised or lowered. The resolution may also include a reconciliation instruction. In 1981, the budget resolution's revenue aggregate anticipated a large tax cut. Congress enacted just such a cut in the Economic Recovery Tax Act.

In sum, the budget process allows the Congress, influenced by the President and using the budget committees as its drafters, to devise and to follow an annual national spending plan. At its most potent, the budget process can serve as the tool for major redirection of spending and taxing. However, that process, with the subtle interplay of aggregates, functions, assumptions, and actual enforcement, and its varying enforcement regarding allocation and reconciliation, also allows Congress and its committees many ways to resist or impede any such drastic redirections.

History

---

[14] As a practical matter, that suballocation no more constrained the figure for Legal Services than did the function number or the allocation, all of which were too big in relation to that particular line item to keep it to the $100 million assumed in the resolution.

[15] Those bills were delayed, and Legal Services was funded by continuing resolution. See 1981 Congressional Quarterly Almanac 364-68.

The historic development of the budget process sheds much light on how it came to take its complex and delicately balanced form. That history starts with the 1974 act, continues with evolution in 1975-85, and reached a new key point in enactment of Gramm-Rudman in 1985.

Initially, the Congressional Budget Act of 1974 took shape in reaction to both budget trends and changes in congressional operations.[16] Prior to the late 1960s, executive leadership and informal congressional mechanisms, particularly the antispending biases of the House Appropriations Committee, had controlled spending and deficits.[17] However, Vietnam War inflation, increasing "backdoor" spending measures (particularly entitlements), and weakening of the House Appropriations Committee's controls on spending, led to loss of control over spending.

After 1966, Congress and the President began what Allen Schick, the leading commentator, describes as the "seven-year budget war."[18] Attempts were made at ad hoc spending ceilings, or across-the-board cutbacks, linked with tax increases.[19] When these failed, President Nixon retaliated with impoundments: unilateral Executive decisions not to spend appropriated funds. Congress determined to fight back both by asserting congressional control over impoundments and by improving its budgeting ability.

Drafting of a budget act began with a Joint Study Committee on Budget Control.[20] It proposed

---

[16] The background is explored thoroughly in Schick. For another account of this period, see Wander, The Politics of Congressional Budget Reform, Congressional Budgeting at 7-16.

[17] The background is discussed in the appropriations chapter.

[18] Schick at 17.

[19] Schick at 32-42.

[20] The Joint Study Committee was a creature of the House and Senate appropriations and tax committees, which furnished 28 of its 32 members. The committee's "primary (footnote continued)

an annual budget resolution allocating budget
authority among committees.   Spending would be
held down by a tight system of points of
order.[21]   The House replaced the rigidly binding
single resolution proposed by the Joint Study
Committee with two annual resolutions and a fall
"reconciliation" process for adapting previously
enacted spending and taxing legislation to fit the
second resolution.[22]

Two Senate committees worked on the budget
act.   One proposed a complex system relying on a
single budget resolution.[23]   The other, guided by
then-Majority Whip Robert Byrd (D-W.Va.),[24]

---

mission was to devise a coordinating process acceptable to
both the spending and revenue committees . . . . by dividing
budgetary power between them."   Schick at 56.

[21]   The resolution would be devised by House and Senate
budget committees with memberships to be drawn largely from
the appropriations and tax committees.   For accounts of the
Joint Study Committee, see Schick at 55-60; Wander, supra,
Congressional Budgeting at 17-19.

[22]   In the House, the Speaker referred legislation embodying
the proposal to the Rules Committee, where Representative
Richard Bolling (D-Mo.) took charge of it.   In a brilliant
strategic move, Representative Bolling coupled the budget
process to impoundment control legislation, and allowed the
appropriation and tax committees only 45 percent, not two-
thirds, of the House Budget Committee's membership.   Schick
at 60-65; Wander, Congressional Budgeting at 19-23.

[23]   In the Senate, legislation embodying the Joint Study
Committee proposal first went to the Government Operations
Committee, chaired by Senator Sam Ervin (D-N.C.), also then
chair of the Watergate Committee, which proposed a budget
process in which the annual budget resolution would be a
hybrid of ceiling and target.   S. Rep. No. 579, 93d Cong.,
1st Sess. 21-23 (1973).   The process also envisaged major
control on tax expenditures.   Id. at 23-24.

[24]   The bill, after being reported by the Governmental
Affairs Committee, was sequentially referred to the Rules
and Administration Committee, which sent it to a three-
member subcommittee chaired by Senator Byrd.   The
subcommittee convened an extraordinary working group of 45
staffers "from ten standing committees of the Senate, four
(footnote continued)

simplified the proposal, particularly by creating a process that depended less on points of order.[25]   As enacted, the act depended more on guidance from broad-based budget committees and timely budget information than on tight procedural constraints.[26]

During the first five years of the budget process in 1975-79, the budget process exerted only gentle guidance of Congressional fiscal activity.   In the Senate, Senators Edmund Muskie (D-Maine) and Henry Bellmon (R-Okla.) developed a bipartisan style in the Senate Budget Committee, winning general acceptance of their consensus budgets.[27]   In the House, a much more partisan

---

joint committees, the House Appropriations Committee, the Congressional Research Service, and the Office of Senate Legislative Counsel."   S. Rept. No. 6788, 93d Cong., 2d Sess. 2-3 (1974).

[25]   This extraordinary group, whose product was extensively edited by Senator Byrd himself, reworked the bill into a form that harmonized the Senate's historic reluctance to bind itself procedurally, with mechanisms for the Senate to work its will on the budget if so minded.   "[T]he 25 new point-of-order situations [in the Government Operations bill] were reduced to ten and these may be waived by majority vote, thus giving a maximum of flexibility to the procedures."   S. Rept. No. 688, 93d Cong., 2d Sess. 25 (1974).

For accounts of the Senate consideration, see Schick at 65-70; Wander, Congressional Budgeting at 23-26.

[26]   As the Senate Rules Committee report stated, "[t]he constant objective of budget reform should be to make Congress informed about and responsible for its budget decisions, not to take away its power to act."   A conference committee reconciled the different House and Senate proposals for controlling impoundments, the conference report swept the House by 401-6 and the Senate by 75-0, and President Nixon signed the bill into law barely a week before he resigned.

[27]   Schick discusses the Muskie-Bellmon collaboration throughout, and particularly at 282-84.   Another account is in LeLoup, The Impact of Budget Reform on the Senate, in Congressional Budgeting 78, 79-85.

pattern emerged, with Democratic proposals passing almost completely bereft of Republican support.[28]   The party differences put "house leaders of both parties . . . . much more clearly in the role of national policy leaders than they have been in the past,"[29] although the budget process lacked much enforcement muscle.[30]

Sharp changes began in 1980 and 1981.   In 1980, the House passed the budget resolutions under complex special rules.   For the first time, Congress used reconciliation, with reconciliation instructions in the first budget resolution (not in the second resolution as the 1974 act had envisioned).[31]   In 1981, when the Republican Party took control of the White House and the Senate, David Stockman, Director of the Office of

---

[28]   Schick at 235-56; Copeland, Changes in the House of Representatives after the Passage of the Budget Act of 1974, in Congressional Budgeting 51, 69-72.

[29]   Copeland, Changes in the House of Representatives after the Passage of the Budget Act of 1974, in Congressional Budgeting at 74.   While spending stayed generally within budget resolution targets, it did so largely because the two annual budget resolutions ratified what the committees volunteered to do, without meaningful use of reconciliation procedures.

[30]   In the 1970s, Congress used a two-resolution budget process lacking in procedural enforcement tools (apart from the section 311 ceiling).   In the spring, Congress enacted first budget resolutions with nonbinding target figures that provided some guidance for appropriations and new entitlements.   In the fall, Congress enacted a second budget resolution, which largely totalled up the legislative outcomes and simply ratified them.   Reconciliation was virtually unknown.   For a description of the "accommodating budgetary process" of the 1970s, see Penner and Abramson at 23-36.

[31]   The history of the rise of reconciliation is discussed below in the section on reconciliation.   The 1980 reconciliation bill required what was then a record conference of more than 100 Representatives and Senators. For the 1980 process as "prelude" to the subsequent years, see Penner and Abramson at 36-37.

Management and Budget, pushed through much of the President's legislative program by use of reconciliation.

As Speaker Thomas P. "Tip" O'Neill described that coup in his 1987 memoirs, "I still wasn't prepared for what happened in 1981. As part of the Gramm-Latta budget, the administration put all its proposals into one huge package, an eight-hundred-page bill that passed the House so quickly that many members didn't even know what they were voting for."[32] Also in 1981, the budget process started proceeding with only one meaningful budget resolution per year (unlike the earlier pattern of two resolutions a year).[33]

Post-1981 events followed a less dramatic but evolutionary course.   In 1982, the House leadership reasserted Congressional independence, taking a decisive negotiating role through "Gang of 17" talks with the White House and controlling the floor procedure for a tax bill and reconciliation bills.[34] In 1983, Congress passed a bipartisan reform plan for Social Security, but failed to enact a reconciliation bill, only doing so in 1984 after the "Rose Garden plan" was worked out with the White House.[35]

In 1985, President Reagan was at odds with his own party in the Senate after it voted to freeze Social Security cost-of-living inscreases, and Congress could not even pass a reconciliation

---

[32]   T. O'Neill, Man of the House 413 (1987).

[33]   Adverse economic developments during the year made second resolutions a painful, unproductive exercise.   The 1981 second resolution was pro forma. In later years, there was no second resolution at all.

[34]   1982 Congressional Quarterly Almanac 203 (reconciliation), 201 (tax bill); Penner and Abramson at 66-67.

[35]   1983 Congressional Quarterly Almanac 231 (failure to implement reconciliation), 435 (overall budget process); 1984 Congressional Quarterly Almanac 160 (eventual enactment of reconciliation bill); Penner and Abramson at 67-68. In 1984, Congress reversed normal procedure, first passing its budget reconciliation, and only then its budget resolution. 1984 Congressional Quarterly Almanac 143-44.

bill (it finally enacted one the next year).[36]   To
pass the bill raising the ceiling on the national
debt over $2 trillion, the Senate attached the
proposal of Senators Phil Gramm (R-Tex.), Warren
Rudman (R-N.H.), and Ernest Hollings (D-S.C.) for
automatic   across-the-board   cuts   ("automatic
sequestrations")   to   force   reductions   in   the
deficit in following years, from $144 billion in
FY 1986 down to zero in FY 1990 -- the "Gramm-
Rudman" bill.   The House countered with a own
version containing the budget reform proposals of
the 1982-84 Beilenson Task Force of the House
Rules Committee,[37] many of which survived to the
final enacted version.[38]

Gramm-Rudman scheduled tight budget deadlines
to combat the delays in enacting appropriations in
prior years, which had led to a dependence upon
continuing resolutions.[39]   The new act's fast

---

[36]   1985 _Congressional Quarterly Almanac_ 441 (budget
resolution), 498 (reconciliation bill); Penner and Abramson
at 68-70.

[37]   The committee established the task force in 1982, and
the task force and its parent Rules Committee reported a
reform proposal in 1984.   For a description of its
proceedings, see _Beilenson Report_ 11-20.

[38]   See _Increasing the Statutory Limit on the Public Dept_,
H.R. Rep. No. 433, 99th Cong., 1st Sess. (1985) (conference
report on Gramm-Rudman):

> Specifically,   the   legislation   provides   for   an
> accelerated   congressional   and   executive   branch
> timetable, expands the application of the Budget Act to
> cover credit authority, includes off-budget programs in
> the   congressional   and   executive   budgets,   and
> streamlines   the   congressional   budget   process   by
> providing   for   an   annual   budget   resolution   and   by
> removing unnecessary obstacles to the consideration of
> authorization and appropriation bills.

_Id._ at 100-101.   For a comprehensive treatment of Gramm-
Rudman, see Stith, _Rewriting the Fiscal Constitution: The
Case of Gramm-Rudman-Hollings_, 76 Calif. L. Rev. 593 (1988).

[39]   In the election years of 1980, 1982, and 1984, Congress
(footnote continued)

schedule required a budget resolution by April 15, and allowed the House to start consideration of appropriations after May 15 if the budget resolution had not been adopted. Gramm-Rudman required the House Appropriations Committee to report all appropriations by June 10, and the House to complete action on all appropriations by June 30.[40] Gramm-Rudman also streamlined the budget process by dropping aspects that had proven to be hindrances.[41]

After the Supreme Court struck down the General Accounting Office's binding role in Gramm-Rudman sequestrations, Congress substituted the binding power to the Office of Management and

---

had to fund respectively five, seven, and nine of the 13 regular appropriations through the continuing resolution. 1980 Congressional Quarterly Almanac 218; 1982 Congressional Quarterly Almanac 172-73 (chart and discussion) (counting legislative branch appropriation, enacted as full-year funding in first continuing resolution, as not free-standing); 1984 Congressional Quarterly Almanac 367. Such delay figured prominently in the Beilenson Report, at 43-44. In 1985, six of the 13 regular bills, including the biggest appropriation of all, the defense appropriation, had to be funded through the continuing resolution. 1985 Congressional Quarterly Almanac 315.

[40] Section 300 (overall timetable); section 301(a) (budget resolution by April 15); section 303(b) (appropriations may be considered after May 15); section 307 (appropriations reported by June 10); section 310(f) (appropriations action completed by June 30). The new act adopted the Beilenson proposal for a point of order that Congress could not adjourn during July unless the House completed action on appropriations, section 309 (see Beilenson Report at 45), but the House tended to simply waive that by unanimous consent.

[41] Gramm-Rudman followed the Beilenson task force report in eliminating some requirements of the 1974 act and seeking thereby to streamline the process. It dropped the previous section 402 deadline for reporting authorizations by May 15, and it dropped the previous section 307 requirement that the House Appropriations Committee complete and consider all its appropriations before reporting any. See Beilenson Report at 32-34, 39-42 (regarding authorization deadline); id. at 44 (section 307).

Budget, and made further procedure changes
("Gramm-Rudman II").[42]   An initial round of
automatic sequestrations occurred in 1986. Delays
that year forced all the appropriations into one
huge continuing resolution. Following the stock
market crash of October 19, 1987, President Reagan
and Congress reached a "summit agreement" which
facilitated reconciliation and appropriation bills
for both years for 1987 and 1988.[43]

     To summarize the pattern after 1981, deficit
control dominated the political agenda.   The
budget process became the chief arena for annual
national policy contests over deficits, tax
increases, and defense spending increases; often
the process seemed on the verge of stalemate or
collapse, and just as often it revived.[44]
Reconciliation remained a central concern of
budgeting.   Complex special rules (discussed in
the chapter on scheduling in the House) continued
to dominate House proceedings. The Congressional
leadership took on critical importance as
developers of party positions, negotiating
partners of the President, and implementers of
majority party or negotiated deals.[45]

B. FORMULATION OF THE BUDGET RESOLUTION

President's Budget and Committee
Consideration

Formulation of the first budget resolution begins

---

[42]   1987 Congressional Quarterly Almanac 604-09 (enactment
of Gramm-Rudman II).

[43]   Penner and Abramson at 71-73.

[44]   In 1981 the second resolution (pro forma though it was)
came near defeat, in 1982 the House defeated the first
resolution its first time on the floor, and in 1983 the
Senate gave painful birth to a first resolution by a one-
vote margin. The tribulations of reconciliation bills have
been discussed above.

[45]   Penner and Abramson at 79.

with the President's budget, required by Gramm-
Rudman to be submitted by the first Monday after
January 3.[46]   That presidential budget emerges
from its own elaborate process more than a year
long,[47] backed by the President's own political
resources, and the extensive planning resources of
the departments and OMB.   In some years, like
1981, the President's budget may serve virtually
as a blueprint for congressional action, or may
influence   Congress   very   strongly   through
negotiated agreements between the President and
the leaderships.   Even when Congress writes its
own budget without agreement with the President,
the President's budget greatly influences line
item decisions.[48]

With the President's budget in hand, the
standing committees submit their views and
recommendations to the budget committees by
February 25 under section 301(d) of the budget

---

[46]   Previously, the President was supposed to submit it 15
days after Congress convenes, i.e., by late January, but
submissions were delayed, particularly when administrations
changed.   See Review of the Congressional Budget and
Impoundment Control Act of 1974: Hearings Before the Senate
Comm. on Governmental Affairs, 97th Cong., 1st Sess. 63
(1981) ("1981 Review Hearings") (1981 late submission).   In
1982, a typical year, the President submitted his budget
February 8.

[47]   Individual units in the various departments make
proposals, which are refined by the heads of departments and
then by the Office of Management and Budget, with ultimate
appeals on the most sharply contested points (if
departmental heads care to challenge OMB) to top White House
aides or to the President.   The classic description of this
process is A. Wildavsky, The Politics of the Budgetary
Process (4th ed. 1984).

[48]   As a commentator notes: "virtually all congressional
budget activities that take place over the rest of the
process will, either formally or informally, use the
president's budget as a starting point for debate.   More
importantly, the large majority of minute decisions made in
compiling the president's budget will not be reviewed by
Congress because of a lack of interest, staff, and time." S.
Collender, The Federal Budget Process 24 (1983 ed.).

act, some with details,[49] others very briefly to
express independence of the process.[50] Pursuant
to section 301(e) of the Act, the budget
committees hold highly publicized hearings on
national economics and fiscal policy.
     At a technical level, the Congressional
Budget Office (CBO) develops projections about the
economy, such as projected rates of inflation,
unemployment, and change in the Gross National
Product. The budget committees may use CBO's,
OMB's, or their own projections of these
rates.[51]   Based upon their projections,

---

[49]   Some committees hold hearings to consider, and markups
to decide, what they will state as their views.   Other
committees simply let their chair, or staff, submit a
statement to the budget committee with minimal committee
action.   Some committees write lengthy and elaborate
statements of their plans. In 1983 the House Energy and
Commerce Committee submitted a 242-page report detailing
spending by subfunction and appropriation account. House
Committee on the Budget, 98th Cong., 1st Sess., Views and
Estimates of Committees of the House 205-447 (Comm. Print
1983).

[50]   For example, in the 1970s the Senate Finance Committee
expressed a haughty independence of the budget committee by
submitting only a short letter stating total figures, and no
details, about its revenue plans. Interestingly, it took
great pains before making that slender submission:

     The Senate Finance Committee has conducted more formal
     and extensive markups of its March 15 reports than most
     Senate committees have, but Finance has provided little
     more than summary information in its annual "letter"
     (the format it uses for the report) to [the Senate
     Budget Committee].   For example, Finance's staff
     prepared an 80-page print for its markup of the fiscal
     1978 budget, while its letter to [the Senate Budget
     Committee] totaled 12 pages, with only 2 pages devoted
     to revenues. By complying with the bare minimum of the
     Budget Act, Finance has signaled [the Senate Budget
     Committee] that it should not stray into the details of
     revenues or other matters within Finance's
     jurisdiction.

Schick at 558.
(footnote continued)

"baselines" can be calculated of the level of
spending and revenue that would occur based on
current law.[52]   The budget committees, and the
floor proceedings, determine what changes in the
laws must occur from those baselines.   When the
budget committees begin marking up the resolution,
they have a range of approaches, from the
bipartisan style of the 1970s Senate Budget
Committee style under Senator Muskie, to the
sharply partisan House style.[53]

Gramm-Rudman establishes a specific set of
targets for the deficit[54] which the reported

---

[51]   Often, the conference on the budget "allow[s]
programmatic bargains to determine economic assumptions
. . . .   Although analytically poor, this approach does
have the virtue of helping the two sides reach an
agreement.   Thus, it is not unusual for the economic
assumptions to be set after the compromises for the other
numbers have been reached."   Ellwood, Budget Reforms and
Interchamber Relations, in Congressional Budgeting 100,
117.   The conference report on the first budget resolution
explains what economic assumptions are used.   In 1980 and
1983, CBO's were used.   H.R. Rept. No. 792, 96th Cong., 2d
Sess. 17 (1980); S. Rept. No. 155, 98th Cong., lst Sess. 31
(1983).   In 1981, the administration's were used, and in
1982, a negotiated set of CBO-OMB assumptions were used.   S.
Rept. No. 86, 97th Cong., lst Sess. 38 (1981); H.R. Rept.
No. 614, 97th Cong., 2d Sess. 20 (1982).   The persistent
problems with economic assumptions are described in Penner
and Abramson at 98-103.

[52]   These are discussed further below in connection with
crosswalking.

[53]   Part of the difference between the approaches is that
the budget act bequeathed the House Budget Committee
structural weaknesses when it provided for rotating
memberships and a rotating chairmanship.   Less continuity
and seniority gives the committee less clout on the floor,
making it hard to imagine the committee carrying an internal
consensus to a floor victory.   In contrast, the Senate
Budget Committee, like almost all congressional committees,
drew strength from the steady retention of the same members
and chair from Congress to Congress, encouraging the members
to be loyal to the committee and accruing for them the
respect and power generally accompanying seniority.
(footnote continued)

budget resolution (and the floor amendments and conference report on ther resolution as well) must achieve or face a point of order.[55]   In the Senate, the fact that Gramm-Rudman provides the point of order can only be waived by a three-fifths vote is special but not extraordinary; in the House, it stands out as one of the very few points of order anywhere in the chamber's procedure that can only be waived by a supermajority (three-fifths).[56]

House and Senate Floor

House and Senate floor procedures on the budget resolution diverge starkly.[57]   In the House, the Rules Committee has a double role. After the House Budget Committee reports a budget resolution, the Speaker usually refers that concurrent resolution to the Rules Committee for

---

[54]   The deficit targets, defined as "maximum deficit amounts" in section 3(7), decreased from $171.9 billion for fiscal year 1986 to zero in fiscal year 1991 (a deadline subsequently extended).

[55]   Section 301(i) provides:

Except as provided in [the section on waivers], it shall not be in order in either the House of Representatives or the Senate to consider any concurrent resolution on the budget . . . or to consider any amendment . . . [or] conference report on such a concurrent resolution, if the level of total budget outlays . . . exceeds the recommended level of Federal revenues . . . by an amount that is greater than the maximum deficit amount . . . as determined under section 3(7) . . . .

[56]   Section 301(i)(2).

[57]   As Representative Leon Panetta (D-Calif.) of the House Budget Committee commented, "[i]n the Senate it is a little different because you do have an open process. We in the House with a rule in place can essentially avoid a lot of individual votes on major issues." 1981 Review Hearings at 164-65.

review of its procedural contents,[58] as provided
by section 301(c).[59]   More important, the Rules
Committee reports a complex special rule for floor
consideration of the budget resolution, one of the
most dramatic developments in budget procedure.
These rules, usually semiclosed, started in
reaction to dissatisfaction with the 1979 floor
action: the first resolution was on the floor for
nine days, an amazingly long time, with about 40
amendments considered and dozens of recorded
votes.[60]   A special rule was used for the second

---

[58]   The 1974 act included an elastic clause allowing the
budget committees to include provisions in the budget
resolution to "require such other procedures, relating to
the budget, as may be appropriate to carry out the purposes
of this Act."   Former section 301(b)(2), now section
301(b)(4).   As the House Budget Committee began using this
to make major changes in budget procedure, above all
reconciliation on the first budget resolution, but also
matters such as deferred enrollment and a credit budget, the
House Rules committee insisted on a sequential referral to
look into these procedure-shaping aspects.

[59]   Gramm-Rudman codified the prior practice in section
301(c):

> If the Committee on the Budget of the House of
> Representatives reports any concurrent resolution on
> the budget which includes any procedure or matter which
> has the effect of changing any rule . . . [it] shall
> then be referred to the Committee on Rules with
> instructions to report it within five calendar days
> . . . .

For a discussion, see Beilenson Report at 79-83. Possibly,
if the House Budget Committee kept procedural matters out of
the resolution, it could circumvent the Rules Committee.
Also, Gramm-Rudman did not include a Beilenson Report
proposal for a separate vote in the House on any budget
procedures inserted in the budget resolution in
conference. Id. at 83, 99.

[60]   The budget act includes in section 305(a) an elaborate
House procedure for budget resolutions that was followed
until 1979.   The weary 1979 chronicle is worth summarizing
from the Daily Digest of 125 Cong. Rec.: D498 (April 30)
(footnote continued)

resolution.[61]

By 1980, both party leaderships favored a complex special rule to let each party put forward a comprehensive position, instead of having minor distracting amendments and fractured factions. The Rules Committee reported a rule allowing only eight amendments, principally three alternatives.[62] That rule's adoption established

---

(general debate), D511 (May 1) (two amendments agreed to, one rejected, two recorded votes), D524 (May 2) (two agreed to, five rejected, seven votes), D535 (May 3) (four agreed to, four rejected, four votes), D552 (May 7) (four rejected, three votes), D562 (May 8) (one accepted, five rejected, five votes), D573 (May 9) (five rejected, five votes), D584 (May 14) (two rejected, two votes). This omits numerous votes on procedural motions. That was 28 recorded votes for this one nonbinding resolution. See B. Sinclair, Majority Leadership in the U.S. House 178-80 (1983).

[61] The second 1979 resolution failed to be passed on its first try, necessitating a complex rule for passage on a second go-around. Modern House procedure for the budget resolution may be said to date from that strange rule. It provided only "That upon the adoption of this resolution it shall be in order to consider the concurrent resolution [on the budget] in the House." This made the resolution subject to the hour rule. It was agreed that the budget committee chair would be recognized for one hour and would move the previous question on his version, thus precluding the offering of amendments unless the motion failed. If it failed, the ranking minority Member would be recognized for one hour and would move the previous question on his version. See 125 Cong. Rec. H8577 (daily ed. Sept 27, 1979).

[62] The move to a complex rule in 1980 is discussed in B. Sinclair, supra, at 183. In the spirited floor debate in 1983, Representative Robert Bauman (R-Md.), who did not agree with his party leadership's acceptance of the closed rules for the budget, challenged their use, and Rules Chairperson Bolling defended his proposal:

> we felt that a majority of the Members of the institution wish to vote on the broad issues . . . . rather than the specifics . . . . [Thus,] virtually everything [allowed as an amendment by the rule] is a real substitute. The line that we drew on the rule is

(footnote continued)

the pattern for later years.[63]   Interestingly, these special rules have often not aroused major partisan controversy.   Sometimes they are accepted when they do not exclude the minority, but allow it to offer its own comprehensive alternative.[64]

For the Senate, the Congressional Budget Act provides the equivalent of a unanimous consent agreement limiting debate time.   Section 305(b) limits debate on the first resolution to 50 hours, with debate on first-degree and second-degree amendments limited, respectively, to two hours and one hour apiece.   It imposes a tight germaneness rule.   At some time during the proceedings, the Majority Leader may arrange a unanimous consent agreement listing and ordering the amendments not yet resolved, stacking the votes for a convenient time, and specifying when the vote will occur on final passage.[65]   This does not tie things up as

---

at the individual particular interests; and very frankly, they are not given an opportunity for a single shot.

126 Cong. Rec. H2804 (daily ed. April 23, 1980).

[63]   The rule for the 1980 second resolution allowed only two main alternatives.   The rule for the 1981 first resolution allowed only four amendments, and involved "nothing new," Rep. Bolling explained, because it did "precisely what was done the last occasion, I believe, that we dealt with the budget."   127 Cong. Rec. H1588 (daily ed. April 30, 1981). The first rule for the 1982 first resolution allowed many alternatives, but the budget resolution went down to defeat, and it took a second rule with much more constrained alternatives to get the resolution successfully passed. 1982 Congressional Quarterly Almanac 192-95.

[64]   As Congressional Quarterly noted in 1982, when the resolution was defeated because of killer amendments offered pursuant to a relatively open rule, "[a]fter the debacle of May 27-28, when the House turned down eight budget options -- including major plans advanced by each party -- many members wanted to pass a budget just to get it over with." 1982 Congressional Quarterly Almanac 195.

[65]   125 Cong. Rec. S4553-54 (daily ed. April 24, 1979); 126 Cong. Rec. S5077-81 (daily ed. May 9, 1980); 127 Cong. Rec. S4729 (daily ed. May 11, 1981).

tight as the House complex rules, but does structure them considerably.

Senate floor amendments come in all types, from comprehensive alternatives to "nickle-and-dime" amendments to add small amounts to particular functions. However, the Majority Leader or floor manager may constrain the floor, either by filling up the amendment tree, as Majority Leader Robert Dole (R-Kans.) did in 1985 and Majority Leader Byrd did in 1987, or by moving to table all amendments.[66]

Conference proceedings on the budget resolution can be difficult politically when the House and Senate differ sharply. The chambers assemble a small conference committee just from budget committee members.[67] Negotiations occur in an atmosphere of much media attention and sometimes much tension, when close votes sending the resolutions into conference augur peril for the resolution that comes out of conference. Formally, the conference often reports a resolution in the form of amendments in technical disagreement.[68] A side effect of this practice is that even after conference, amendments may be offered on the floor to the conference compromise for symbolic purposes, such as Senator Dole's 1983 amendment to align the conference compromise with his and President Reagan's preferences.

---

[66] Tabling does not prevent debate, since section 305(b) guarantees time for debate on each amendment and a tabling motion is not in order until time has expired or been yielded back. However, the tabling motion does prevent the amendment proponents from getting a clear "up-and-down" vote, somewhat discouraging the offering of amendments.

[67] The conferences are described in Ellwood, Congressional Budgeting at 110-130.

[68] This is because the conference report is often technically outside the scope of disagreement, which can easily happen considering that the combinations of spending, revenue, and deficits may result in two sets of numbers within the scope of disagreement adding up to a third that is outside. This is discussed in the chapter on conference procedure.

C. THE BUDGET RESOLUTION: CONTENTS

With the process for formulation of the first resolution in mind, it is useful to address its targets in three areas -- spending aggregates and functions, revenue aggregates, and borrowing aggregates -- and other features of interest in the budget resolution such as committee allocations, the credit budget, and multiyear numbers. Reconciliation instructions will be addressed in the next section.

Targets: Aggregates and Functions

All the budget resolution's spending targets make a fundamental distinction between two very different measures of spending: budget authority and outlays. Congress enacts budget authority when it creates authority to spend, or more precisely, authority to enter into obligations (binding commitments to pay).[69] Appropriations and entitlements, in their different ways, both

---

[69] A more technical definition of budget authority is:

Authority provided by law to enter into obligations that will result in immediate or future outlays involving Federal Government funds, except that budget authority does not include authority to insure or guarantee the repayment of indebtedness incurred by another person or government. . . . Budget authority may be classified by the period of availability (1-year, multiple-year, no-year), by the timing of congressional action (current or permanent), or by the manner of determining the amount available (definite or indefinite).

General Accounting Office, A Glossary of Terms Used in the Federal Budget Process 41 (3d ed. 1981) (hereafter called "GAO Glossary"). There is also a "negative" form of spending, the "offsetting receipts," which are payments to the government for business-like transactions, such as sales of government property and royalties on mineral leases on government lands.

create budget authority.[70]

In contrast, outlays occur later. After Congress enacts budget authority, and after the agencies then "obligate" that authority, then later the agencies liquidate those obligations by outlays.[71] Outlays measure the actual payments, or, more precisely, the liquidation of obligations (generally by payment through checks or cash).[72]

---

[70] Other kinds of budget authority include authority to borrow, and contract authority. These two kinds of "backdoor" spending (budget authority other than appropriations) grew in significance prior to the 1974 act, which somewhat curtailed their use. For discussions of contract authority, see L. Fisher, Presidential Spending Power 136-38 (1975); for backdoor spending generally, Stith, Congress' Power of the Purse, 97 Yale L.J. 1343, 1379-80 (1988); Stith, 76 Calif. L. Rev. at 606-07.

[71] To label the intermediate stages, when Congress has voted budget authority, that authority is, for the time being, an unobligated balance. Once the agency obligates it, it is an obligated balance. If the agency does not obligate such authority before the term of the authority runs out, the authority expires. Some aspects of this are discussed in General Accounting Office, Principles of Federal Appropriation Law 4-33 - 4-31 (1982).

This discussion omits the many intermediate stages at the administrative end supervised by OMB and agency financial officers, such as apportionment, issuance of warrants, and allotment. These largely do not enter into congressional procedure.

[72] A more technical definition of outlays is:

Obligations are generally liquidated when checks are issued or cash disbursed. Such payments are called outlays . . . .

Outlays during a fiscal year may be for payment of obligations incurred in prior years (prior-year outlays) or in the same year. Outlays, therefore, flow in part from unexpended balances of prior-year budget authority and in party from budget authority provided for the year in which the money is spent . . . .

(footnote continued)

The deficits consist of the excess of outlays over revenues. Thus, knowing how spending legislation (budget authority) will affect the next year's deficits requires knowing the "outlay rate" -- the rate at which the budget authority will become outlays,[73] which is particularly hard to know for entitlements.[74]

Section 301(a)(1) requires that the budget resolution state, as the spending aggregates, the "totals of new budget authority [and] budget outlays." For example, the 1981 first budget resolution, as ultimately adopted, projected (for fiscal year 1982) aggregate outlays of $696 billion, aggregate revenue of $658 billion, and therefore a $38 billion deficit. Then, section 301(a)(4) requires a breakdown of the spending

---

The terms expenditure and net disbursement are frequently used interchangeably with the term outlays.

GAO Glossary at 69 (emphasis supplied). See Stith at 604.

[73] For a reflection of the problems of knowing outlay rates, see the conference report on the Gramm-Rudman act, H.R. Rep. No. 433, 99th Cong., 1st Sess. 79-80 (1985). Earlier, as the Beilenson Report explained, the House had rejected constraining itself by outlays: "Congress does not directly control outlays. When Congress appropriates, it provides budget authority . . . . Estimates of outlays expected to result from the budget authority provided in a measure are based on historical spendout rates and predictions abo[ut] relevant external factors ranging from demographic trends to the weather." Beilenson Report at 93-94.

[74] For many entitlements, there is no meaningful relationship between budget authority and outlays. For those which have a meaningful relationship, the outlay rate varies from rapid spend-out budget authority to slow spend-out budget authority. Entitlements for individuals (like Medicare), and appropriations in personnel accounts (like employees' pay) may spend out rapidly, so that cuts in their budget authority produce equivalent cuts in current outlays and hence equivalent reductions in current deficits. On the other hand, military procurement may spend out more slowly, so that disproportionate cuts must be made in budget authority to produce significant reductions in current outlays and current deficits.

aggregates into "functional categor[ies]."[75]   In the 1980s, there were 21 functions, more or less.

Functions vary greatly in size, from $5.8 billion for Function 750, Administration of Justice (in the 1983 budget resolution, for FY 1984), to $268.6 billion for Function 050, National Defense.[76]   They also vary greatly in complexity, from Function 900, Net Interest, which essentially covers only the single item of interest on the national debt, to Functions 800 and 500, General Government and Education, Training, Employment and Social Services, which cover a enormous variety of items. Moreover, the functional scheme is changed from time to time, sometimes making comparisons more difficult.

Functions have been called the "orphans" of the budget process, for they do not constrain committees to do or not to do anything, in contrast to figures like reconciliation instructions and committee allocations.   Yet through functions, Congress makes the decisions on national priorities. For example, through setting the budget function levels for national defense, Members express their weighing of defense against other needs.   Then, such tools as committee allocations and reconciliation instructions implement the decisions implicit in the function levels.   Later, the armed services committees and defense appropriations subcommittees lead Congress in enacting authorization and appropriation bills for national defense, such as the appropriations (in separate bills) for defense, for military construction, and for the nuclear weapons program.   In theory, at least, Congress decides the overall priorities through functions, separating this from the specific line-item decisions in such later detailed legislation.

---

[75]   Section 301(a)(4), prescribing the contents of the budget resolution, requires that it include "new budget authority, budget outlays, direct loan obligations, and primary guarantee commitments for each major functional category, based on allocations of the total levels set forth pursuant to [section 301(a)(4)]."

[76]   Figures are from H. Con. Res. 91 concerning budget authority for fiscal year 1984.

Unlike spending, the revenue aggregates prescribed by section 301(a)(2) are neither divided by function, nor allocated by committee. Thus, the revenue aggregate constitutes the whole statement of the budget resolution about taxes, (apart from reconciliation instructions). The directions in the aggregates may swing wildly from year to year: in 1980, they called for raising revenues by $4.2 billion for the next fiscal year; in 1981, for lowering revenues by $51.3 billion; in 1982, for raising revenues by $20.9 billion. Their precise significance is discussed below in the section on taxes.

Section 301(a)(3) provides for two debt aggregates, "the surplus or deficit in the budget," and the size of "the public debt." To foreign and domestic audiences interested in the size of the American budget deficit, they express Congress' intentions, however imperfectly carried out, regarding the size of the deficit. Gramm-Rudman directs Congress, in its amendment of section 301(i) of the 1974 act, to achieve set targets for reducing the deficit aggregate. In addition, because the House finds it painful to vote periodically to raise the national debt ceiling, House Rule XLIX, adopted in 1979, provides for an automatic House "enactment" of a joint resolution increasing the public debt limit by the amount set forth in the budget resolution.[77] Since the Senate has no comparable rule, the automatic House-generated debt resolution still comes to the Senate for enactment.[78] When the Senate sends back an amended debt resolution, then the House must vote on it; this limits the significance of the automatic mechanism.

---

[77] Technically, the House Enrolling Clerk takes the debt figure from an adopted budget resolution, enrolls a joint resolution with that amount, and messages it to the Senate.

[78] For example, in 1982 Senator Jesse Helms (R-N.C.) sought to attach school prayer and abortion riders to the debt ceiling, provoking fierce filibusters with 1,400 amendments waiting to be offered to the joint resolution. 1982 Congressional Quarterly Almanac 44. In 1985, Gramm-Rudman was attached to the debt resolution.

As noted above, the deficit aggregate equals the amount by which the revenue aggregate exceeds the spending (outlays) aggregate. In a simple world, the deficit would also equal the increase in the national debt, producing a close-knit pattern among the debt aggregates. However, the government borrows a great deal "off-budget" to finance lending activity, so the debt grows by amounts bigger than the deficit. While Congress could bring the "off-budget" debt onto the budget, to date it has shown an understandable reluctance thereby to make the deficit seem any larger.

Committee Allocations

Committee allocations translate the spending aggregates and functions in the budget resolutions into spending amounts for each committee. This section will introduce the committee allocations process. The chapter on appropriations takes the process further, to show what is done with the allocations, namely, the impact of suballocation and the mechanics of policing through the section 302(d) point of order.

Section 302(a) prescribes that the conference report on the budget resolution "shall include an estimated allocation . . . of total budget outlays [and] total new budget authority . . . among each committee . . . ."[79]   In other words, the conference committee on the budget resolution (consisting of members from the House and Senate budget committees) must include in the conference report an allocation to each congressional committee of the spending under that committee's jurisdiction.

Making that allocation is called preparing a "crosswalk." The budget committee staffs and CBO use computers to track figures for each of the thousand or so accounts in the budget throughout the budget cycle.[80]   Such tracking begins each

---

[79]   This language appears separately in subsections 302(a)(1) and 302(a)(2), which contain the variations discussed below.

[80]   Of the thousand or so individual elements (accounts) (footnote continued)

year with a set of economic projections from CBO. Based on these, CBO makes a budget projection of what would be spent in each account under current law assuming no change (the "current services" level).[81]

Thereafter, CBO and the budget committee staffs figure out what the changes mean for each individual account when the budget committees mark up proposed budget resolutions, and later when the floor and the budget conference committee make their own changes in the resolutions.[82]   In

---

that make up the budget, some are funded by appropriations, some by receipts, and some by the various backdoor spending methods such as entitlements.

[81]   At the beginning of the year, CBO starts with a "current law" baseline for each account.   Section 202(f) of the budget act provides that "each year, the Director [of CBO] shall submit . . . a report . . . with respect to fiscal policy, including (A) alternative levels of total revenues, total new budget authority, and total outlays . . . under existing law, taking into account projected economic factors . . . ."   This consists either of what current law provides (for receipts and permanent spending) or what appropriations would be projected to provide (by taking the previous year's figure and adjusting for inflation and other economic projections).

[82]   In marking up a budget resolution, the House and Senate Budget Committees change the aggregates by adding or subtracting amounts from each function.   Similarly, when the House and Senate amend the reported budget resolutions on the floor, each amendment adds or subtracts amounts from aggregates and functions.   CBO develops corresponding figures for what the changes mean to individual accounts, as Members push their proposals to change the functions, taking its cue from what the proponents of each change in a function number describe as their assumption about the change.

In the simplest case, a sponsor in the budget committee, or on the floor, of a cut in Function 750, Administration of Justice, by $100 million, may explain that he intends that the cut should come from Legal Services.   If the amendment carries, CBO knows to adjust its assumed figure for Legal Services' account by $100 million.   More complex adjustments sometimes require sophisticated analysis (footnote continued)

practice, they translate the functional category figures into estimates for each budget account. "Crosswalking" consists of taking the estimates for the individual accounts and adding them up again by the committee of jurisdiction, coming up with each committee's share of the total pie. Needless to say, crosswalking can be a technically complex calculation.[83]

Allocations concern only "spending authority" -- primarily appropriations and entitlements -- not authorizations. Thus, the lion's share of committee allocations goes to the Appropriations Committee.[84] Committees other than Appropriations receive allocations mainly for their entitlement programs. Once the committees receive their section 302(a) allocations, they are then supposed "[a]s soon as practicable" to divide those allocations up among their subcommittees, or programs, pursuant to section 302(b).[85] This is

---

by budget committee staff and CBO.

[83] The complexity comes because functions usually involve spending under the control of several committees, and conversely, each committee may be able to spend on programs falling within different functions.

For example, Congress decided in the 1981 first budget resolution that it would target $263 billion for Function 600 (Income Security) in fiscal year 1982. That did not mean that one particular committee was supposed to hold its spending to $263 billion. Rather, that amount had to be allocated in the House among all the committees which have spending programs in that function, namely Appropriations, Banking, Education and Labor, Energy and Commerce, Foreign Affairs, Judiciary, Post Office and Civil Service, and Ways and Means. Conversely, figuring out how much of the Function 600 money to allocate to each of these committees did not tell the size of the committee allocation. Each committee got a share of several functions; indeed, Appropriations gets a share of virtually all functions.

[84] For example, the Appropriations Committees receive the lion's share of the allocation from Function 050 (National Defense), while the Armed Services Committees receive miniscule allocations, because defense spending occurs mainly by appropriations, not entitlements.

(footnote continued)

called the "suballocation" process.

The end result of the allocation and suballocation process is a remarkable set of target figures.   In the budget resolution, Congress each year sets its targets by the general functions of the budget.   Individual Members can hardly keep sight of that budget when the various appropriations bills (or other spending bills) come to the floor, with all their separate complex baggage of authorizations, legislation and limitation amendments, differences from the President's budget, contests over particular projects, and the host of other appropriations issues and comparisons.   However,   the suballocation process allows such Members to know whether, all other complications apart, a spending bill fits within the congressional budget. Moreover, once Gramm-Rudman imposed strict points of order, to a certain degree the allocation and suballocation process carried its own teeth for any appropriation bill that would bust the budget.   How this shapes the appropriations process is discussed in the chapter on appropriations.

Credit Budget

During the 1970s, the budget resolutions addressed spending, not credit programs like loans to students, farms, and small businesses or FHA and VA mortgage loan guarantees.   During this period, government credit activity mushroomed.   As Professor Kate Stith observed retrospectively in 1988,   "Congress [in the 1970s] found credit programs, such as guaranteed loans, particularly alluring; they involved little or no initial outlay,   and the contingent liabilities they represented were not reflected in the budget, which employed cash accounting."[86]   However, such

---

[85]   Gramm-Rudman creates a point of order, in section 302(c), against spending bills from committees that fail to suballocate.

[86]   Stith, Rewriting the Fiscal Constitution: The Case of Gramm-Rudman-Hollings, 76 Calif. L. Rev. 593, 619 (1988). As the Beilenson Report noted: "Annual credit activity (footnote continued)

credit activity affected the economy much like spending, by rationing the money available in different sectors of the economy and arguably affecting interest rates.[87]

Accordingly, starting in 1980, budget resolutions included credit budgets. Over time, the resolutions elaborated lending into loan obligations, primary loan guarantees, and secondary guarantees, and subdivided credit figures into the same functions that subdivide spending.[88] Following the Beilenson Report,[89] Gramm-Rudman created an elaborate structure incorporating credit budgeting into the budget resolution and its implementation. Section 301(a)(4) requires that the budget resolution include credit figures for both aggregates and functions. Section 302(a) requires that these

---

. . . grew 277 percent from $36.8 billion in fiscal year 1974 to $138.6 billion in fiscal year 1983 . . . . The federal participation rate (ratio of federal net lending to total funds advanced in U.S. credit markets) increased from 8 percent to 13 percent between 1974 and 1981." Beilenson Report at 70.

[87] Observers had pushed for the kinds of enforcement tools for credit that the budget has for spending, contending that both have similar impact on the economy. Ms. Rivlin testified in 1981 that proposals for more inclusive treatment of credit would "focus the attention of the Congress on the magnitude of Federal lending and Federal borrowing . . . . If . . . Congress were to reduce the magnitude of federal involvement in the credit markets . . . it would take some pressure off interest rates and help bring them down." 1981 Review Hearings at 129.

[88] The first year, the resolution simply provided an aggregate: the total "new direct loan obligations" which the government lends, and the total "new primary loan guarantee commitments" which the private sector lends and the government guarantees. Later budgets kept these aggregates: for example, the 1983 budget resolution provided for $46.7 billion in new direct loan obligations for fiscal year 1984, $99.6 billion in primary loan guarantees, and $68.2 billion in secondary loan guarantees. Those later budgets added more detailed breakdowns into functions.

[89] Beilenson Report at 25, 70-71.

credit figures be allocated by committee, and section 302(b) requires that they be suballocated. Section 302(f) creates a point of order for legislation from committees exceeding their credit allocations, while section 310(a)(1)(D) allows reconciliation instructions for credit.

The credit budget tends to affect mainly a few budget functions covering most of government loan activity. In a typical year, each of three functions has a little over a quarter of loan obligations: Function 350 for Agriculture (farm loans), Function 150 for International Affairs (international loans), and Function 370 for Commerce and Housing Credit (housing loans). More than half of the primary loan guarantees, and all of the secondary loan guarantees are in Function 370 for housing mortgage guarantees.

Multiyear Budgeting

Another transformation in the 1980s of the budget resolution has been its inclusion of long-term directions. Starting in 1980, budget resolutions began including aggregates, and in 1981, functions as well, for the two "outyears" -- the two fiscal years after the next one.[90] Soon, the resolution provided outyear figures for virtually everything.[91] Gramm-Rudman inscribed this in law. Section 301 prescribes budget aggregates and functions of the various kinds at "appropriate levels for the fiscal year beginning on October 1 of such year, and planning levels for each of the two ensuing fiscal years . . . ." Section 310 provides for reconciliation of these outyears.[92]

---

[90] The early history is recounted in Beilenson Report at 28-29.

[91] However, committee allocations are only provided for the current and next fiscal year, not the outyears. This reflects the primary focus of committee allocations on appropriations, which are made primarily for the current and next fiscal year, not outyears.

[92] Originally, the House proposed providing allocations and (footnote continued)

It is one thing to make outyear projections, and quite another to be accurate. To some extent, outyear projections lack even the minimal rigor of next-year projections. As David Stockman commented in another context, "[t]here is no point arguing about an interest rate 3 years out nobody can predict anyway."[93]   In 1981, OMB projected a growing economy instead of the severe 1982 recession, so it projected a balanced budget in a few years, instead of what actually occurred -- the greatest deficits in United States history. The former head of the Congressional Budget Office, Rudolf Penner, concluded in 1988 that despite all the advantages of advance planning, the imponderables of projection mean "it is not desirable to prescribe a rigid, comprehensive two-year budget process."[94]

Notwithstanding the imperfection of prediction, outyear figures serve vital functions. Reconciliation instructions for outyears provide very different directions from those for current years: they allow and in fact require long-term cuts, like slowing down cost-of-living increases in entitlements and long-term tax increases. In 1985-86, Congress passed large-scale long-term spending cuts pursuant to multiyear reconciliation instructions.

---

reconciliation instructions lumping together current years and outyears. Beilenson Report at 60-61, 94. This language was dropped from Gramm-Rudman. Accordingly, the budget resolution in 1986 provided separate reconciliation instructions for the 1987 year and for the two outyears.

[93]   1981 Review Hearings at 55.

[94]   Penner and Abramson at 116. As Louis Fisher observes: "The second budget resolution for FY 1982 (which reaffirmed the first) projected a $37.65 billion deficit, [and] a $19.05 billion deficit for FY 1983 . . . . So much for projections in budget resolutions. The actual deficit for FY 1982 reached $110.6 billion, [and] the deficit for FY 1983 topped $200 billion . . . ." Fisher, "The Budget Act: Further Loss of Spending Control," at 187, in Congressional Budgeting.

D. RECONCILIATION

Few aspects of Congressional procedure have had so dramatic an impact as reconciliation.   It is the centerpiece of the new budget process of the 1980s, a focus for leadership-strategizing and a major determinant of the balance of power in the Congress. This section will first discuss briefly the history of reconciliation, then its four steps: instructions, compliance, packaging, and floor proceedings.

History

Congress has transformed reconciliation radically from the original conception of the 1974 Act.   That act intended that Congress use reconciliation at the very end of the budget process.[95]   Congress never followed that scheme. Instead, throughout the 1970s, the budget committees' reports politely asked the standing committees to report the bills needed to make "legislative savings."   The other committees virtually ignored those nonbinding suggestions.[96]

---

[95]   Section 307 of the Act provided that "Congress shall complete action on all bills and resolutions -- (1) providing new budget authority" -- that is, appropriations and new spending authority, chiefly new entitlements -- "not later than the seventh day after Labor Day."   Section 301(b)'s deferred enrollment provision allowed Congress to keep those appropriations and new spending bills from being enrolled until reconciliation. Section 310(b) provided that Congress shall complete action on the second concurrent budget resolution about a week later, by September 15. Section 310(a) allowed the second budget resolution to include reconciliation instructions requiring the standing committees to make recommendations for budget cuts and tax increases.   Section 310(d) required Congress to complete action on the packaged recommendations by September 25, in time for the beginning of the new fiscal year on October 1.

[96]   At year's end, the budget committees reported second resolutions without reconciliation instructions, which merely ratified what the other committees had done.

Reconciliation first took on a binding and significant character in 1980 and 1981.[97]   In 1980, an election year, interest and inflation rates were zooming, and the President and Democratic Members desired to campaign on having balanced the federal budget, which meant making cuts.   Accordingly, the Democratic leadership decided to force such cuts by adding reconciliation instructions to the first budget resolution.[98]   That reconciliation bill introduced key themes: fights in the House over complex special rules; disputes over inclusion of assertedly "extraneous" nonbudget legislation in the reconciliation bills; and a huge reconciliation conference committee.[99]

In 1981, OMB Director Stockman made reconciliation the chief means for enacting President Reagan's economic program.   To prevent mere temporary changes in the laws, the 1981 reconciliation instructions were multiyear.[100]   As in 1980, key elements included complex special rules, extraneous legislation, and an even bigger conference committee.   The result of reconciliation   --   the   Omnibus   Budget Reconciliation Act of 1981 -- was achieved through

---

[97]   In 1979, the Senate went so far as to enact a second budget resolution with reconciliation instructions, but the House refused, and the conference committee eliminated the instructions.   1979 Congressional Quarterly Almanac 181.

[98]   House committee chairs made a vigorous effort to knock the reconciliation instructions off the first budget resolution, but their amendment went down to defeat.   126 Cong. Rec. H3316-51 (daily ed. May 7, 1980).

[99]   1980 Congressional Quarterly Almanac 129-30.   The committees obeyed the 1980 reconciliation instructions, but with temporary, rather than permanent, changes in the laws.   1980 Congressional Quarterly Almanac 126.

[100]   Also, a unique step, not subsequently repeated, was taken: the reconciliation instructions directed cuts both in direct spending, and in authorizations, which swelled the figures for the claimed size of the cuts (with the justification that low authorizations would compel low appropriations).

a drastic foreshortening of the normal legislative process.[101]

In 1982, reconciliation again played a major role. Congress passed a $98 billion tax increase responsive to reconciliation instructions, as well as spending cuts.[102]   While there was a degree of reaction against the enormous tension created by the foreshortened 1981 process,[103] reconciliation remained a yearly feature of the budget process, though never on the scale of 1981. The basic features in 1980-81 -- House complex special rules, disputes over inclusion of extraneous legislation, and giant conferences -- repeatedly recurred throughout the 1980s.[104] In 1985, Gramm-Rudman largely codified the reconciliation process as it had evolved previously, with some further tightening of Senate procedures.

Instructions

Section 310(a) of the budget act provides that the reconciliation instructions contained in the budget resolution shall "specify the total

---

[101] Even in the Senate, there were expedited markups and few hearings, and in the House, the reconciliation bill's contents came from a single thousand-page floor amendment not even available to the members in time to read.

[102] 1982 Congressional Quarterly Almanac 32-39, 201 (tax reconciliation), 202-4 (spending reconciliation).

[103] The first resolution limited its reconciliation instructions to cuts in direct spending and revenue increases, not authorization cuts. Even so, several House committees snubbed the instructions. 1982 Congressional Quarterly Almanac 203. On the spending cuts, the Democratic leadership took back control of packaging and won the procedural fights over the special rules for the reconciliation bills.

[104] For a number of measures of reconciliation after 1981, see House Committee on the Budget, The Whole and The Parts: Piecemeal and Integrated Approaches to Congressional Budgeting 28-32 (Comm. Print 1987) (report prepared for the Task Force on the Budget Process by Allen Schick).

amount by which" the various kinds of spending authority "contained in laws, bills, and resolutions within the jurisdiction of a committee, is to be changed and direct that committee to determine and recommend changes to accomplish a change of such total amount."[105] Each reconciliation instruction states, for a single committee: (1) the amounts of money it must save, expressed in budget authority and in outlays; (2) the type of legislation in which to make the savings (new or old entitlements), and (3) a deadline for recommending the legislation.

Separate figures in the reconciliation instructions cover each of the next three years. Typically, the budget committees in their reports, and the proposers of floor amendments, indicate their underlying assumptions as to what programs should be cut and how. However, the instructions themselves, with rare exceptions, do not specify what programs must be cut. Instead, instructions leave the committees discretion to recommend whatever legislation they choose, so long as it meets the specified amount.

To use the 1981 example discussed above, that year's first budget resolution included reconciliation instructions to the House Energy and Commerce and the Senate Finance committees, the committees with jurisdiction over Medicaid, requiring major cuts. The instructions directed that "the House Committee on Energy and Commerce shall report changes in laws within the jurisdiction of that committee which provide spending authority . . . sufficient to reduce budget authority by $787,000,000 and outlays by $1,103,000,000 in fiscal year 1982 . . . ."[106]

---

[105] Section 310(a)(1) provides for reconciliation for "new budget authority for such fiscal year," "budget authority initially provided for prior fiscal years," "new entitlement authority which is to become effective during such fiscal year," and credit authority. Section 310(a)(2), providing for tax reconciliation, will be discussed below in the section on tax.

[106] Section 301(6)(A) of H. Con Res. 115, 97th Cong., 1st Sess. The Senate Finance Committee received a similar instruction to cut budget authority by $4,394,000,000 in (footnote continued)

Nowhere in the instruction were the committees expressly told to make their cuts by imposing a Medicaid cap; that was merely an assumption. Since both committees ultimately preferred other alternatives, they reported recommendations for other Medicaid cuts, and in conference did not adopt a cap. Although reconciliation instructions include a deadline, that deadline has often slipped.[107] Committees may dispute the "scoring" of cuts "credited" to the committee,[108] and whether they can do something besides cuts, such as levy user fees.[109]

---

fiscal 1982. Section 302(7)(A) of H. Con. Res. 115, 97th Cong., 1st Sess.

[107]   The 1981 instructions worded the deadline thusly: section 304 of the resolution provided that "[n]ot later than June 12, 1981, the committees named in section 301 and 302 shall submit their recommendations to the Committees on the Budget of their respective Houses. Those recommendations shall be sufficient to accomplish the reductions required by such sections."

[108]   For example, in 1982 the House and Senate agriculture committees received identical instructions, but the Senate committee made $2.1 billion in cuts in food stamps over three years while the House committee made only $1.3 billion. The Senate committee accepted administration projections as to how its cuts would work, while the House committee used more optimistic CBO projections. See 108 Cong. Rec. H5488 (daily ed. Aug. 10, 1982); 1982 Congressional Quarterly Almanac 483. In conference the conferees split the difference.

[109]   Although Gramm-Rudman did not change the basic wording of reconciliation instructions, it did provide, in section 310(c), that a committee could substitute revenue increases for 20 percent of mandated spending cuts. This has great significance for House Ways and Means and Senate Finance, which traditionally receive instructions to make a large share of the spending cuts (primarily because of their Medicare and Medicaid jurisdiction). Since they have tax jurisdiction, they can substitute revenue increases for cuts in those programs. "Ways and Means has consistently had to make major adjustments under reconciliation -- about one-fourth to one-half of all spending cuts have been under its jurisdiction, along with essentially all revenue (footnote continued)

Committee Compliance

Once the budget resolution provides its instructions, the next question is compliance. The budget act does not specify what happens to a committee which fails to propose sufficient cuts. It does not state the "teeth" of the budget process.[110]   In essence, two types of sanctions may apply. One sanction is informal political pressure from the leadership, the budget committee, the media, the President, or the business community.[111]

---

adjustments."   Copeland, Changes in the House of Representatives after the Passage of the Budget Act of 1974, in Congressional Budgeting at 61.

[110] In 1980, when offering his losing amendment to strike the reconciliation instructions, Representative Morris Udall (D-Ariz.) told the following story about lack of teeth on Judgment Day:

> Mr. Chairman, there is an old story about the minister who was giving his semiannual hell, fire, damnation Judgment Day sermon to the congregation, and he said, "Brothers and sisters, Judgment Day is coming." He said, "On that great Judgment Day, there will be lightning and rain . . . . [and] there will be earthquakes, and on the Judgment Day," he said, "there is going to be weeping and wailing, and you are all going to gnash your teeth." The lady in the front row said, "But Reverend, I ain't got no teeth." And he said, "Madam, on that terrible Judgment Day, teeth will be provided."

126 Cong. Rec. H3317 (daily ed. May 7, 1980).

[111] For example, in 1981 the House Education and Labor Committee strongly disliked the first budget resolution's reconciliation instructions, which forced it to make massive cuts in prized programs. The committee "initially considered refusing to recommend any cuts but finally approved over $12 billion of reductions" as part of the Democratic leadership's first strategy, which was to report cuts and then to seek to restore them on the floor. Smith, Budget Battles of 1981: The Role of the Majority Party (footnote continued)

The other and more procedural sanction is the alternative floor amendment. When the reconciliation bill is under consideration, the budget committee, or the minority party, may fill the vacuum created by a noncomplying committee by offering an amendment to the reconciliation bill to make the requisite savings in the area of that committee's jurisdiction. In the House, the Rules Committee, which protects the reconciliation bill's provisions from amendment through complex special rules, may make that amendment in order.[112]

In many years, there are major floor battles over compliance. Sometimes the noncomplying committees win, making only partway gestures[113] or even completely refusing to comply.[114] However,

---

Leadership, in American Politics and Public Policy: Seven Case Studies 43, 62 (A. P. Sindler ed. 1982).

[112]   Gramm-Rudman codified this procedure in section 310(d)(5):   "The Committee on Rules of the House of Representatives may make in order amendments to achieve changes specified by reconciliation directives contained in a concurrent resolution on the budget if a committee or committees of the House fail to submit recommended changes to its Committee on the budget pursuant to its instruction."

[113]   In 1980, the Senate Governmental Affairs Committee complied with a reconciliation instruction by making only a temporary cut in the cost-of-living adjustment for federal retirees, while the Senate Budget Committee believed that a permanent cut was required.   One Senator asked the Chair what the Senate Parliamentarian thought, and received the cold answer: "The Chair states, compliance is not for the Chair to resolve, but for the Senate to resolve." 126 Cong. Rec. S8949 (daily ed. June 30, 1980).   The Budget Committee offered a substitute amendment for what Governmental Affairs had done, but it was beaten badly.

[114]   In 1982, the House Postal Operations and Civil Service Committee flatly refused to report out the size savings called for in its instructions. The Rules Committee made in order a floor amendment to make sufficient cuts, and Democrats insisted that Republicans could, and should, offer that amendment.   However, despite Democratic taunts, the Republicans declined even to offer the amendment, facing certain defeat after they lost on an effort to defeat the (footnote continued)

in 1981, the conservative coalition believed that half the House committees had complied inadequately, and accordingly offered a complete substitute for the reconciliation bill. This "Gramm-Latta II" substitute won on the House floor, enacting an enormous body of legislation distasteful to those committees, and teaching a transcendant lesson as to the risks of a posture inviting such substitutes. Between clear compliance and clear defiance lies an uncertain middle ground, where the Budget Committees may push for what they consider true compliance, and the standing committees may hold out for the least painful measure with which they can get by without facing undue leadership pressure or floor amendments.[115]

Besides refusal to make savings or making dubious savings, the other major issue of committee compliance concerns the inclusion of "extraneous" nonbudgetary provisions. Committees face a great temptation to slip legislative proposals having little or nothing to do with making spending cuts into their recommendations. As Senator Byrd, then Minority Leader, observed during his struggle in 1981 against extraneous provisions in the reconciliation bill, such provisions can "bypass the normal legislative process . . . . [They are] insulated from troublesome amendments, from the possibility of lengthy debate or a filibuster . . . ."[116]

It took years of floor combat before the Senate adopted a rule to deal with extraneous provisions. In 1981, both the Senate Commerce and Senate Banking committees loaded the 1981 reconciliation bill with extraneous provisions.[117] An intense struggle resulted

---

rule. 1982 Congressional Quarterly Almanac 203, 515.

[115] See The Whole and the Parts, supra, at 28 (discussing several such fights).

[116] 127 Cong. Rec. S6665 (daily ed. June 22, 1981).

[117] The Senate Commerce Committee loaded seven extraneous provisions, from radio deregulation to establishment of an international telecommunications and information task force, onto their recommendations. The Senate Banking, Housing and (footnote continued)

between the majority and minority on the Senate floor,[118] with Minority Leader Byrd threatening a major filibuster.[119]

In the end, a delicate compromise was struck, in which the majority agreed to strip off extraneous provisions but kept and used the right to re-offer them, and although some were stripped in conference, many were enacted into law.[120]

Urban Affairs Committee loaded on everything from a cutoff of new construction funds for cities that use rent control to an exemption from reserve requirements on checking accounts for Hawaiian savings and loans. 127 Cong. Rec. S6887-88 (daily ed. June 24, 1983)(Sen. Byrd).

[118]   Initially, Majority Leader Howard Baker (R-Tenn.) agreed to delete a few extraneous provisions, but opposed Minority Leader Byrd's amendment to strip them all off. 127 Cong. Rec. S6664-67 (daily ed. June 22, 1983); id. S6887-91 (daily ed. June 24, 1981). Minority Leader Byrd observed that the party that was the majority today might be the minority tomorrow and would then rue the precedent, and drew on bipartisan support for the Senate's cloture rule that was being circumvented by adding provisions to a reconciliation bill with limited debate time.

[119]   He alluded to the availability of postcloture filibuster tactics notwithstanding the time limits in the 1974 act:

> All I have to do is send this book to the desk as an amendment and object to dispensing with its reading . . . . The time that would be consumed in reading that amendment cannot be charged against the 20 hours, because the 20 hours cover debate, and reading an amendment is not debate . . . . So I can keep us all in over the weekend, but there would be no action except the reading of this amendment . . . . There can be a filibuster by a minority at the end of the 20 hours simply by calling up amendment after amendment, having no debate, and demanding roll calls.

127 Cong. Rec. S6977 (daily ed. June 25, 1981).

[120]   The unanimous consent agreement striking the provisions is discussed at 127 Cong. Rec. S7002-5 (daily ed. June 25, 1981). While full radio deregulation was not enacted, the conference agreement included a provision extending the life (footnote continued)

Again in 1982, a comparable struggle also ended
with inclusion of extraneous provisions.[121]   Yet
another floor struggle over extraneous provisions
occurred in 1985, with a vote intimating they
would not be allowed in the future.[122]
   The   outcome   of   those   struggles   became
enshrined   in   budget   procedure   as   the   "Byrd
Rule."[123]   This rule applies to the reconciliation
bill itself, to any amendments offered to it, and
to the conference report for it.   Any Member can
raise   the   point   of   order   that   these   contain
material   "extraneous   to   the   instructions   to   a
committee," a point of order that not only leads,
if sustained, to striking the "extraneous matter,"
but   also   to   precluding   the   offering   of   the
material   from   the   floor.[124]   The   Senate

---

of   radio   licenses   from   three   to   seven   years.   1981
Congressional Quarterly Almanac 266.

[121]   In   a   procedurally   complex   battle,   Senator   Robert
Packwood, Chair of the Commerce Committee, attached airport
development legislation to the tax reconciliation bill.   He
overrode protests from the minority that the legislation had
not   received   consideration   in   the   Commerce   Committee.
Senator Byrd struggled against Senator Packwood's move by a
motion to recommit the bill with instructions to delete the
extraneous provision, but this motion was defeated.   See
1982 Congressional Quarterly Almanac 334.   This is discussed
below in the section concerning points of order.

[122]   The   dispute   ended   with   adoption   of   an   amendment   by
Minority   Leader   Byrd   "to   restrict   amendments   to
reconciliation bills in the future . . . [by] requir[ing] a
three-fifths vote, rather than a majority vote, to overturn
a ruling that an amendment to a reconciliation bill was
extraneous or not germane."   1985 Congressional Quarterly
Almanac 510.

[123]   It   is   cited   as   section   20001   of   the   Consolidated
Omnibus Budget Reconciliation Act (as amended by Pub. L. No.
99-509 and Pub. L. No. 100-119), and S. Res. 286, as amended
by S. Res. 509, 99th Cong.

[124]   In the case of a floor amendment, the amendment cannot
be offered; in the case of a conference report or a House
amendment, the extraneous matter is stricken, but the Senate
can consider the remainder.

Parliamentarian looks for guidance on what is "extraneous" to the Senate Budget Committee.[125]

Floor and Conference Procedure

Once committees provide their recommendations for legislation in compliance with reconciliation instructions, the stage of packaging is reached. Section 310(c) of the Act provides that if there are instructions for more than one committee, the committees provide their recommendations to the budget committee, "which, upon receiving all such recommendations, shall report to its House a reconciliation bill . . . carrying out all such recommendations without any substantive revision."[126]

This budget act language suggests that packaging is ministerial. In fact, the highest level of political strategy can come into play regarding packaging. To be sure, sometimes all reconciliation recommendations will be packaged in one bill.[127] However, more often, there are two packages: one from the tax committee, with tax increases and sometimes entitlement spending cuts (principally in Medicare); and a second "omnibus" package consisting of the cuts from all the other committees.[128]

---

[125]   The Budget Reconciliation Process: The Inclusion of Unrelated Matters: Hearings Before the Subcomm. on the Legislative Process of the House Comm. on Rules, 99th Cong., 2d Sess. 45 (1986).

[126]   If there are only reconciliation instructions for one committee, that committee itself reports its recommendations to the floor as a reconciliation bill.

[127]   This occurred in both chambers in 1981, by far the most important reconciliation action, and occured in the House in 1980, and the Senate in 1984 and 1985. 1981 Congressional Quarterly Almanac 262-65; 1980 Congressional Quarterly Almanac 129; 1984 Congressional Quarterly Almanac 150-52, 154; 1985 Congressional Quarterly Almanac 509-11.

[128]   For example, that is how the Senate handled reconciliation in 1980, 1982, and 1983 (in a sense). 1980 (footnote continued)

Often tax and spending cuts have entirely different political appeal, and by packaging them separately, they can avoid encumbering each other. The tax committees tend to move their own bills, even reconciliation bills, while the budget committees take the lead in moving omnibus spending reconciliation bills. The most radical deviation from one-bill packaging came in the House in 1982, when the Democratic leadership brought to the floor the spending cuts from four committees in four separate packages.[129]

Once the reconciliation recommendations are packaged, the House and Senate take them up, under differing procedures. For the House, each year the Rules Committee reports out a complex special rule to govern consideration that particular year.[130]   The 1980 rule that established the

---

Congressional Quarterly Almanac 126-29; 1982 Congressional Quarterly Almanac 201-2.   (In 1983, the Senate passed neither bill, but it did pass its "1983" omnibus (non-Finance Committee) reconciliation bill in early 1984, 1984 Congressional Quarterly Almanac 160, and passed a separate 1984 tax reconciliation bill.   1984 Congressional Quarterly Almanac 150-51.)

That is also how the House handled reconciliation in 1983, 1984, and 1985.   1983 Congressional Quarterly Almanac 233-36; 1984 Congressional Quarterly Almanac 150-52; 1985 Congressional Quarterly Almanac 505-07.

[129]   The Republicans protested this decision bitterly as "part of a Democratic strategy to force Republicans into a series of potentially embarrassing election-year votes on budget cuts." 1982 Congressional Quarterly Almanac 203.   It exposed the minority to separate votes on a committee-by-committee, almost program-by-program basis for any alternative deeper cuts, instead of being able to wrap all their proposals in one presidentially supported package as they had in 1981.

[130]   Taken together, House floor procedure for reconciliation bills in 1980-85 established a pattern that may come to appear, in time, as important as the old House floor pattern of closed rules on tax measures.   Just as the closed tax rule means the House largely writes its tax measures in committee, so the restrictive complex reconciliation rules mean the House largely writes its (footnote continued)

pattern allowed only Budget Committee amendments and three other amendments to the reconciliation bill.   In   1981,   the   procedures   for   the reconciliation process became the focus of the most   important   single   vote   on   the   floor   of Congress of that year and arguably of the half-decade   before   or   after.[131]   The   Democratic proposal for the procedure, set forth in the rule reported by the Rules Committee, did allow the minority to offer their alternative spending cuts.

However, that Democratic rule required that minority cuts be offered in six separate pieces -- exposing   each   separate   unpleasant   vote   to   cut programs   --   and   deleted   from   those   pieces   the "sweeteners" meant to entice southern Democrats. The Republican-southern Democratic coalition won, defeating the previous question on the rule by 210-217.[132]   It   then   adopted   its   own   rule providing for a single up-or-down vote on two alternatives   --   the   committee   proposals   for reconciliation, and the conservatives' alternative -- and the next day passed the latter.[133]

In 1982, the majority leadership took back control, and of the four separate packages, one minor package came up under suspension of the rules, and the others under separate restrictive rules.[134]   After   1982,   the   House   majority

---

reconciliation measures in committee and with guidance from the majority leadership.

[131] For the preparations, see Smith, *supra*, at 60-66.

[132] 127 Cong. Rec. H3382 (daily ed. June 25, 1981)

[133] Certain complications regarding the Energy and Commerce committee budget proposal and the motion to recommit are omitted from this description.

[134] H.R. 6782, from the Veterans Affairs Committee, came up under suspension of the rules. H.R. 6862, from the Post Office and Civil Service Committee, came up under a rule allowing no amendments except one amendment for a four-percent limit on cost of living adjustments, which was stated *in haec verba* in the rule itself. 126 Cong. Rec. H4708 (daily ed. July 28, 1982). H.R. 6892, from the Agriculture Committee, came up under a rule allowing only the committee amendments and two other amendments. *Id.* at (footnote continued)

leadership maintained the pattern of complex and highly restrictive rules on reconciliation bills.[135]

By contrast with this House pattern, in the Senate, section 310(e) of the budget act itself specifies the floor procedure for reconciliation bills.   Section 310(e) allows only germane amendments, limits debate time on each amendment to two hours, and limits time on the whole bill to a mere 20 hours.   These provisions, as strict as cloture though not as proof against delays,[136] cramp those who would offer alternatives and put

---

H5484 (daily ed. Aug. 10, 1982).   H.R. 6812, from the Banking Committee, came up under a rule allowing only the committee substitute and one amendment.   Id. at H5206 (daily ed. Aug. 5, 1982).   The banking and agriculture rules allowed motions to recommit with instructions; the civil service rule did not even allow that, only a simple motion to recommit.

After all four bills had passed, they were put together in a single vehicle for conference with the Senate.   Id. at H5539, H5551 (daily ed. Aug 10, 1982).

[135] The 1983 special rule was closed, barring a liberal Democratic alternative.   1983 Congressional Quarterly Almanac 233.   The 1984 special rule was closed to bar amendments to strip some spending increases that had been included and some Medicare billing provisions.   Republicans voted unanimously (161-0 and 160-0) against the motion for the previous question and against adoption of the rule, but it passed.   1984 Congressional Quarterly Almanac 152 (floor debate), 26-H (vote tallies).   The 1985 special rule only allowed three amendments, and passed by a bare 230-190 "with mixed support from Republicans," 1985 Congressional Quarterly Almanac 507, because the rule resolved a jurisdictional struggle between the Public Works and Appropriations committees.

[136] Section 305(b) was drafted in 1974 to impose debate limits prior to the era of postcloture filibusters.   It does not even include the restrictions of the cloture rule of that time (there is, for example, no prohibition against dilatory motions), let alone those devised in 1979.   Hence, as Minority Leader Byrd elaborated in 1981, it is vulnerable procedurally, although perhaps less so politically, to postcloture tactics.

reconciliation bills on a "fast track." Senators cannot even offer alternative approaches to making equivalent savings, because unless the alternatives concern the same subjects as the committee recommendations, they are out of order as non-germane. It is this strictness that has prompted the many years of struggle, described above, by Minority Leader Byrd against extraneous provisions on reconciliation bills.[137] Although no closed rule barred germane amendments, the Senate majority has achieved a similar result by holding ranks against amendments.[138]

Gramm-Rudman tightened up floor procedure on reconciliation bills even further. Section 310(d) prohibits amendments that would either "decreas[e] any specific budget outlay reductions" or "reduc[e] Federal revenue increases" below "the level . . . provided . . . in the reconciliation instructions." In other words, any amendment to meliorate the spending cuts or revenue increases must make up what it loses. Considering the strict way the germaneness rule restricts alternatives, this amounts to the closest the Senate has ever come to a closed rule under which the Senate gets an up-or-down vote, and no amending, of reconciliation.

After the House and Senate act, mammoth conferences resolve the differences over reconciliation bills. In 1980 and 1982 about 100 conferees met; in 1981 and 1985, well over 200

---

[137]   In 1981, with the enormously lengthy omnibus budget reconciliation bill going through, the time limit forced the Senate to extreme steps. Because of all the amendments sought to be offered, the Senate started out in 1981 by a unanimous consent agreement limiting time on first degree amendments to one hour, and then, as debate went beyond the 20-hour limit, to a bare ten minutes per amendment. 127 Cong. Rec. S6664 (daily ed. June 22, 1981) (one hour per amendment); id. S7035-6 (daily ed. June 25, 1981) (ten minutes per amendment).

[138]   "While the Senate made some minor revisions in its $39.6 billion reconciliation package, the significant elements remained the same as the measure drafted by the Senate authorizing committees and put together by the Budget Committee." 1981 Congressional Quarterly Almanac 264.

met.   Such huge conferences are necessary because
so   many   committees   are   involved   in   the
legislation.   The   conferences   break   up   into
subconferences,   in   which   the   Members   from
particular committees meet to deal with their own
portions   of   the   bill,   with   Budget   Committee
members joining in any subconference.

When the conference committee brings back its
report, section 310 prescribes a floor procedure
in the Senate in which debate is limited to ten
hours.   Conferences,   and   the   enactment   of
conference reports, sometimes occurs quickly.[139]
However, when faced with difficult issues, they
may take months.[140]   In fact, it may be a year
before the chambers finally enact a reconciliation
bill.[141]

In sum, the House and Senate floor and
conference procedures for reconciliation provide

---

[139]   Considering   the   enormous   scale   of   the   1981
reconciliation bill, the 1981 conference took surprisingly
little time, only the second half of July, as "conferees
struggled to complete action on reconciliation before
Congress' August recess."   1981 Congressional Quarterly
Almanac 265.

[140] In 1980, "it took conferees two months to resolve major
differences   in   controversial   revenue-raising   measures,
Medicare-Medicaid   changes   and   other   issues,"   1980
Congressional Quarterly Almanac 130, although that was
partly due to reconciliation stretching over the election
recess.

[141] In 1983 and 1985, Congress failed to enact the year's
reconciliation legislation until the following year.   1983
Congressional Quarterly Almanac 231 (failure to implement
reconciliation),   435   (overall   budget   process);   1984
Congressional Quarterly Almanac 160 (eventual enactment of
reconciliation bill).   1985 Congressional Quarterly Almanac
441 (budget resolution), 498 (reconciliation bill).

In 1981, the House Democratic leadership did use this
stage. The conference report required a rule waiving points
of order, and the Rules Committee used that leverage to get
a separate vote on the elimination of a Social Security
benefit, a point of much political significance.   See 1981
Congressional Quarterly Almanac 266.

both momentum and incentives.   The force comes
from closed floor procedures in the House (through
restrictive rules) and the Senate (through the
germaneness rule and limits on debate).   Compliant
"committees" enjoy two key "carrots": their
proposals can be largely shielded from change on
the floor, and they can then participate in a
conference where the final provisions are
crafted.   Hence, the committees have their great
incentive to include "extraneous" provisions in
reconciliation bills.

Taxes: Resolution Contents

Congress makes much of its fiscal policy
through its tax decisions, stimulating or curbing
the economy and raising or lowering the deficit
through tax cuts and increases.   Moreover,
Congress makes a great deal of policy regarding
particular substantive goals through the tax
code.[142]   As the Beilenson Report noted, "the sum
total of tax expenditures grew more than 600% from
fiscal years 1968 to 1983, from $36.6 billion to
$290.3 billion."[143]   The 1986 "flat tax" bill made
some, but still only limited, reductions in such
tax expenditures.   Potentially, the budget process
could have played a role for tax legislation
comparable to its role for spending legislation,
and made systematic trade-offs between tax

---

[142]   A 1982 Congressional Budget Office study concluded that
"[i]n many areas, the federal government exerts more
influence through tax expenditures than it does through
direct spending . . . . [for example,] tax expenditures for
housing exceed outlays by more than four to one."
Congressional Budget Office, Tax Expenditures: Budget
Control Options and Five Year Budget Projections for Fiscal
Years 1983-1987 13 (1982).   Tax expenditures for housing
include the deductibility of mortgage interest on owner-
occupied houses, which for fiscal year 1983 cost over $25
billion; deductibility of property tax on owner-occupied
homes, costing over $10 billion; and deductibility of
nonmortgage interest in excess of investment income, costing
over $7 billion. Id. at 74.

[143]   Beilenson Report at 73.

expenditures and spending.

In practice, the budget process has had only limited effect on tax legislating. Tax bills receive consideration at irregular intervals under ad hoc procedures, and there is extensive opposition, from "flat tax" and "supply side" proponents, to focused tax increases as policy tools. Moreover, the Senate Finance and House Ways and Means Committees have resisted the budget committees nimbly and effectively.[144] For various reasons, the 1974 budget act lacked the tools regarding taxes that it had for spending, the Senate Finance Committee fought off attempts of the budget committee in the 1970s to impose budget control, and Gramm-Rudman did not include the proposals that had been mooted to subject the tax committees to greater external control.[145]

---

[144]   As one commentator observed:

> Why has the budget process had more impact on the spending side of the budget than on the revenue side? The budget committees argue that the 1974 Congressional Budget Act provides more controls on spending than on revenue. The authors of the act reply that the act is unbiased but the budget committees have failed to take as great an interest in the spending side of the budget as the revenue side. The truth is probably a little of each.

Havemann, The Congressional Budget Process and Tax Legislation, in The Congressional Budget Process After Five Years 174, 175 (ed. R. G. Penner 1981).

[145]   Referring back to the legislative history of the 1974 act discussed in the first section, tools to control tax legislation were not proposed by the Joint Study Committee; they were proposed by the Senate Governmental Affairs Committee, but were dropped in the Senate Rules Committee. For the 1970s combat between the Senate Budget Committee and the Senate Finance Committee, see Schick at 533-36.

The Beilenson Report, at 28, 72-76 and 88, recommended a tax expanditure aggregate target. A second, more radical alternative was to allocate tax expenditures jointly to tax committees and to spending committees of pertinent jurisdiction. Under the proposal of CBO Director Alice (footnote continued)

For tax legislation, as for spending legislation, the budget proceeds through the President's proposals and the views of the committees,[146] the Budget Committee reports, and the first budget resolution. However, the content of these steps for taxes differs from the content for spending. The budget resolution contains two items of key importance for tax legislation. First, the resolution has a pair of aggregate revenue figures: under section 301(a)(2) of the Congressional Budget Act, these consist of "total Federal revenues and the amount, if any, by which the aggregate level of Federal revenues should be increased or decreased by bills and resolutions to be reported by the appropriate committees." Through these aggregate figures -- the revenue total, and the amount of increase or decrease in revenue -- each year Congress establishes its target for raising or lowering taxes by a specific

---

Rivlin, "[a] committee's actions on tax expenditures could be credited to its spending allocations, thereby encouraging trade-offs between the two." Proposed Improvements at 131 (testimony of CBO Director Alice Rivlin).

[146]   The tax committees often prepare carefully before expressing their views to the budget committees, by preparing elaborate backup material and holding markup sessions, but rarely commit themselves in those views. "The Senate Finance Committee has one of the most elaborate processes in Congress for putting together its views and estimates, but little of the process appears in its official report."   Schick at 213.   For examples of the elaborate backup materials of the tax committees, see Data and Materials for the Fiscal Year 1984 Finance Committee Report Under the Congressional Budget Act, S. Prt. No. 13, 98th Cong., 1st Sess. (1983);   House Ways and Means Committee, Background Material and Data on Major Programs Within the Jurisdiction of the Committee on Ways and Means, (Comm. Print 1982).

As an example of the noncommittal nature of the views, in 1983 the Senate Finance Committee's March 15 report just described the President's tax proposals and "voted to forward these proposals to the Budget Committee, without endorsement of any specific proposal or the overall revenue total."   S. Prt. No. 13, 98th Cong., 1st Sess. 99 (1983) (reprinting previous year's views).

amount.

Second, Congress may include reconciliation instructions in the budget resolution directing the House Ways and Means and Senate Finance committees to report out recommendations for legislation to increase revenues by specified amounts. Real use was not made of this authority until the 1980s,[147] but then Congress included such reconciliation instructions and passed important tax reconciliation bills pursuant thereto. The aggregate revenue figures are merely targets; the reconciliation instructions are supposed to be binding commands.

What the resolution does not contain concerning taxes is as important as what it does contain.   The budget act does not contain committee allocations for revenues, since Congress largely vests revenue-raising authority in one pair of committees.   The act does not specify functional breakdowns for revenues or for tax expenditures,[148] although CBO provides some figures.[149] Apart from reconciliation, the Budget

---

[147] A 1976 tax bill was enacted under reconciliation instructions, but this was an isolated matter.

[148] Section 301(d)(6) of the Congressional Budget Act requires the budget committees to report projections of "the estimated levels to tax expenditures (the tax expenditures budget) by major functional categories," and "an allocation of the level of Federal revenues . . . among the major sources of such revenues." With much effort over the years, the budget committees and the Congressional Budget Office have listed and analyzed the scores of individual tax expenditures, projected their costs in terms of lost revenue, and determined which of the functional spending categories they would fit in if they were direct spending programs.

[149] CBO and the budget committees they have projected the revenue costs of two tax expenditures relating to National Defense (Function 050): the exclusion from taxation of benefits and allowances to Armed Forces personnel, and the exclusion from taxation of military disability pensions. A description of the individual tax expenditures is contained in Senate Committee on the Budget, 97th Cong., 2d Sess., Tax Expenditures: Relationships to Spending Programs and

(footnote continued)

Act only includes one provision for guiding revenues after adoption of the budget resolutions, the section 311 floor under aggregate revenues comparable to the ceiling on expenditures, discussed in the section below regarding points of order.

Taxes: Impact on Various Bills

The budget process significantly directs the overall changes in revenues made by new legislation, but has little consistent impact on the details of those revenue changes.[150] Looking at the overall figures, Congress tends to follow the aggregate revenue figures it sets for itself in the budget resolution, apart from the inevitable shifts in economic conditions after the resolution. Following of the budget resolution has been particularly noticeable when Congress used revenue reconciliation instructions, such as in 1980, 1982, 1985, and 1986.[151] Even without

---

Background Material on Individual Provisions (Comm. Print 1982).

[150] Schick divided tax bills in the 1970s into three categories: changes in total federal revenues, special tax legislation (e.g., energy or social security taxes), and changes in tax distribution (e.g., tax reform bills). He concluded that the budget committees and the budget process had maximum influence over the first category, changes in total federal revenues. "The budget process appears to have been somewhat more relevant to tax reductions than to special revenue legislation." Schick at 525.

Any more ambitious predictions run into the wild variation from year to year in tax legislation noted by the Congressional Budget Office when it commented drily, "[e]xperience over longer periods suggests [that] extrapolations based on one-year trends in tax policy may not be wholly reliable." Tax Expenditures, at xv.

[151] In 1980, the reconciliation instructions called for increases in fiscal 1981 revenues of $ 4.2 billion; the reconciliation bill included $ 3.6 billion in revenue-raising provisions. 1980 Congressional Quarterly Almanac 124-25. In 1982, the instructions called for increases in (footnote continued)

reconciliation instructions, Congress has usually followed revenue aggregates, both in the tax cuts of the 1970s and the mammoth tax cut of 1981.[152] In contrast, the reconciliation instructions in 1983 were virtually a dead letter,[153] and in 1984 Congress followed the peculiar "Rose Garden" scenario in which it first enacted its revenue increases, and then adopted a budget resolution in effect telling it to do what it had already done.[154]

The budget process has had little effect on the details either of the major revenue bills, or of the contents of the special bills.[155]   The

---

revenues by $20.9 billion in fiscal 1983, and $98.3 billion overall in fiscal years 1983-85; the reconciliation bill raised revenues by $17.9 billion in fiscal 1983, and the precise figure of the instructions -- $ 98.3 billion--in fiscal years 1983-85.   1982 Congressional Quarterly Almanac 30.   In 1985, the instructions called for increases in revenues of $8.4 billion; the reconciliation bill (which did not pass until the next year) raised revenues by $6.1 billion.   1985 Congressional Quarterly Almanac 500; 1986 Congressional Quarterly Almanac 556.   In 1986, the instructions called for $8.5 billion in increases in revenues; the first year increased revenues of $11 billion from the "flat tax" bill was credited for reconciliation purposes.   1986 Congressional Quarterly Almanac 559, 570.

[152]   In that year, the budget resolution stated that "the net amount by which the aggregate level of Federal revenues should be decreased is $51,300,000,000." Section 201(1) of H. Con. Res. 115, 97th Cong., 1st Sess. (1981).   That figure did not turn out to be precise, but it showed that Congress would make a major tax cut, and Congress subsequently enacted the Economic Recovery Tax Act (ERTA) with a $37.7 billion tax cut for the next fiscal year.   1981 Congressional Quarterly Almanac 91.

[153]   In 1983, the reconciliation instructions called for increases in revenues over three years of $73 billion; when House Ways and Means reported out a reconciliation bill to raise a mere $8 billion in that period, the rule for the bill met disaster on the floor, and the Senate did not even try.   1983 Congressional Quarterly Almanac 446, 233-36.

[154]   1984 Congressional Quarterly Almanac 155.

(footnote continued)

shaping of details (as opposed to aggregates) in the 1970s of special energy and social security tax bills,[156] and in the 1980s of special tax bills such as windfall oil profits, social security, highway gasoline and construction, windfall oil profits, and the "flat tax" of 1986, involved little role for the budget committees or the budget process. The same was true of the details of the major tax-raising reconciliation bills of 1980, 1982, and 1984, and of the large tax cut of 1981.

For example, in the mammoth 1981 tax cut, House Democrats and Republicans squared off with different proposals. The Republican proposal emphasized a 33-month, 25 percent across-the-board cut in individual taxes, and very large cuts in corporate taxes. The Democratic proposal also cut individual taxes, but skewed the cuts toward those earning under $50,000, and oriented the business tax cuts more toward small business.[157]   Each side's alternative would have fit the revenue aggregates in the budget resolution. Not the budget resolution, but a separate and distinct floor fight, gave the victory on that to the Republicans.

The budget process has one major procedural effect on tax legislation: in the Senate, it gives the Finance Committee several tools for restraining the otherwise unruly floor. As described in the section on reconciliation, the budget act imposes germaneness and a limit on debate time on Senate consideration of reconciliation bills, include tax reconciliation bills. The germaneness rule means that once the Finance Committee chooses the areas for raising

---

[155]   As Schick concluded about the 1970s: "The 1978 events point to a jurisdictional demarcation between the tax and the Budget Committees, with the latter concentrating on the revenue aggregates, the former on the particulars of tax laws."   Schick at 543.

[156]   Schick at 508-18. "In the two energy bills and in the Social Security legislation, the Budget Committees (and their resolutions) hedged or kept silent, and were largely disregarded in the final outcomes." Id. at 517.

[157]   1981 Congressional Quarterly Almanac 97-100.

revenue, those are the only areas on the table. For example, in 1982, Senator Wendell Ford (D-Ky.) wanted to offer alternatives to a proposed cigarette tax increase but refrained from doing so because of the restrictive germaneness rule.[158] Senator Strom Thurmond (R-S.C.) actually offered an alternative which was held out of order as non-germane, and lost an appeal on that ruling.[159] Gramm-Rudman added a new budgetary point of order, section 310(d) preventing revenue-losing amendments on reconciliation bills, which has an even more constraining effect. Even germane amendments are not in order unless they are at least revenue-neutral.[160]

Amendments with sufficient support, particularly support from a committee with pertinent jurisdiction,[161] can circumvent these

---

[158]   128 Cong. Rec. S8813 (daily ed. July 21, 1982).

[159]   Id. at S8886.

[160]   To some extent, there is another point of order against revenue-losing amendments: the section 311 revenue floor discussed below in the section on points of order.

[161]   In 1982, Senator Packwood, chair of the Commerce Committee, used a unique maneuver to tack a non-germane airport development title onto the reconciliation bill. The Finance Committee was reporting out an increase in the earmarked tax that pays for airport development. Senator Packwood persuaded the Finance Committee to report his non-germane amendment as its second committee amendment. On the floor, Senator Packwood offered his amendment again, as a floor amendment to the first committee amendment. 128 Cong. Rec. S8687 (daily ed. July 20, 1982). The Chair could, and did, hold that Senator Packwood's amendment was germane to the bill and to the committee amendments (since of course it was germane to the second committee amendment). Id. at S8702 (overruling Senator Cannon's point of order). The Senate sustained the Chair on almost a party-line vote. Id. at S8704.

When the second committee amendment came up, it would have been subject to a point of order against committee amendments in other committees' jurisdiction, 128 Cong. Rec. S9045 (daily ed. July 22, 1982), but such a point of order (footnote continued)

restrictions. The rules can be waived or a ruling
of the Chair overruled, although Gramm-Rudman and
subsequent legislation raised the threshold for
either maneuver to a three-fifths vote.[162]   The
budget act's limit of 20 hours of Senate floor
time for a reconciliation bill can seem drastic
for major tax legislatiion.   Senator Long
commented in 1982 that with a $98 billion tax bill
on the floor, the limit meant "you might say that
on the average, we are allowing the Senate a total
of only 12 minutes to consider each billion
dollars of increased taxes . . . ."[163]   In the
end, the Senate exceeded the time limit, debating
the bill for just short of 35 hours,[164] but that
included extensive consideration of spending cut
provisions in the bill as well as revenue
provisions. That bill was on a very fast track.

E.   POINTS OF ORDER AND WAIVERS UNDER THE BUDGET
     ACT

Basic Points of Order

The 1974 budget act provided several points of
order to safeguard budget procedures, and Gramm-
Rudman augmented and strengthened the original
points of order.   Originally, the few points of
order sought just to assure the spending and

---

was too late; the Packwood amendment had been attached.
Senator Byrd moved to recommit with instructions to strip
off the offending provisions, but the motion failed. Id. at
S8705-9.

[162] In 1980, backers of a non-germane amendment to cut back
on the windfall profits tax made a motion to waive the
germaneneness rule, and the amendment carried.   1980
Congressional Quarterly Almanac 36.   In 1985, the Senate
overruled a point of order for germaneness against attaching
an amendment restricting textile imports to the
reconciliation bill.   1985 Congressional Quarterly Almanac
510.

[163] 128 Cong. Rec. S8650 (daily ed. July 19, 1982).

[164] 128 Cong. Rec. S9046 (daily ed. July 22, 1982).

revenue bills would be considered in the context of the budget resolution, not to enforce particular substantive budget outcomes. By 1985, Gramm-Rudman reflected a greater willingness to try compelling deficit reduction through points of order. As amended, the budget act imposed a series of points of order throughout the budget process, each of which is discussed below: section 303(a) prior to the annual enactment of a budget resolution, section 301(i) for the budget resolution, section 302(f) for allocations, section 310(d) for reconciliation, and section 311(a) to provide an overall spending ceiling and revenue floor. Section 305 provides the general floor procedures for the budget resolution and (as modified in section 310(e)) for Senate reconciliation bills, as previously discussed, and there are also various other points of order mostly attempting to drive the schedule faster.[165]

At the start of the year, section 303 prevents Congress from considering legislation affecting the budget until after a budget resolution is passed.[166] The Beilenson Report explained that "[t]he purpose of the prohibition is to ensure that Congress adopts an overall plan

---

[165] Section 304(b) provides that in any revised budget resolutions, the maximum Gramm-Rudman deficit amount may not be exceeded. Section 306 protects the jurisdiction of the budget committees. Section 307 requires the House Appropriations Committee to report the annual bills by June 10. Section 308 requires CBO estimates in reports on all legislation. Sections 309 and 310(f)(2) require House approval of appropriations bills before any July recess. Section 310(g) prohibits Social Security changes in reconciliation.

[166] For selected spending and revenue matters, section 303(a) specifies: "[i]t shall not be in order in either the House of Representatives or the Senate to consider any bill or resolution (or amendment thereto) . . . until the concurrent resolution on the budget for such fiscal year has been agreed to pursuant to section 301." Those matters include bill or amendments providing new budget authority, new entitlement authority, new credit authority, or an increase or decrease in either the public debt limit or in revenues.

before it considers the bills and resolutions that implement it."[167]   Obviously, Congress must, and will, consider some bills in the spring and summer notwithstanding the lack of a budget resolution to measure their budgetary significance. Frequently section 303 is waived, by special rule in the House and by the various waiver methods in the Senate. Section 303 has an exception (the "Fazio exception") to allow consideration in the House of Representatives of appropriation bills prior to the budget resolution in years when the budget resolution is late in formulation.[168]

The budget act makes generic exceptions for two other types of spending or revenue legislation that may come up at any time in the fiscal year and transgress section 303: revenue or spending bills for future years after the next. First, section 303(b) allows long-term revenue changes.[169] Ideally, Congress only specifies such changes so that "[r]evenue changes are phased in over several years . . . ."[170] In reality, the Senate Finance Committee showed in the 1970s that this section could be used to evade section 303 for most revenue bills and amendments, simply by specifying far-off start-up dates.[171] Section

---

[167]   Beilenson Report at 53.

[168]   This part of section 303 is discussed in the chapter on appropriations.

[169]   Section 303(b)(2) allows bills "increasing or decreasing revenues which first become effective in a fiscal year following the fiscal year to which the concurrent resolution applies."

[170]   Beilenson Report at 54, which further explains that such changes are phased in "to permit taxpayers to plan for the new provisions in the tax code or to provide an opportunity for states and local govenments to adjust their tax provisions which are linked to the Federal tax code."

[171]   "[T]he tax committees have been adept at leap-frogging the budget year with revenue provisions that become effective in future years." Schick at 551. The appeal to the Senate which established this point is discussed in Schick at 552 and at Riddick, "Congressional Budget: Revenue (footnote continued)

303(b) also allows long-term advance appropriations,[172] but most advance appropriations have limited significance because the Appropriations Committees jealously protect their own annual functioning.[173]

Once the budget resolution comes to the floor, section 305 specifies floor procedures for enactment of the budget resolution and particularly the time constraints and germaneness rule in the Senate.[174] Originally, no points of order constrained the results of the process, but Gramm-Rudman added a point of order in section 301(i) requiring that the budget resolution not set forth a larger deficit that the maximum deficit amount on the Gramm-Rudman schedule.[175]

Bills and Amendments Thereto Under the Budget Act," at 462-63.

[172]   Section 303(b)(1) specifies an exception for bills "providing new budget authority which first becomes available in a fiscal year following the fiscal year to which the concurrent resolution applies." Congress uses these "to allow agencies or state and local governments administering these programs to make the necessary plans for carrying out the funded activities." Beilenson Report at 54.

[173]   The Beilenson Report listed these:

Programs authorized to receive advance appropriations in fiscal year 1985 appropriation bills include: Corporation for Public Broadcasting; grants to states for medicaid; AFDC; child nutrition programs; food program administration; [f]ood donations programs; Department of Education (including bilingual education, compensatory eduction for the disadvantaged, impact aid, Indian education, student financial assistance, vocational and adult education); and the urban mass transportation fund.

Id. at 53-54.

[174]   As discussed above, the House now relies on special rules for its budget resolutions rather than on the procedure in section 305(a).

[175]   Gramm-Rudman provided in section 301(i)(1)(B) that this (footnote continued)

After Congress adopts a budget resolution, it proceeds with two types of implementation: allocations and reconciliation. Regarding allocations, Gramm-Rudman strengthened the requirement that committees expeditiously suballocate funds among their subcommittees or programs, by creating a point of order in section 302(c) against committees that have failed to do so. Then, section 302(f) created a powerful point of order to implement suballocations, by precluding bills or amendments that exceed suballocations for budget authority in the House, and for either budget authority or outlays in the Senate. As for reconciliation, section 310(d) created a point of order against amendments to increase outlays or reduce revenues compared to the bill as reported. Taken together, the two points of order strengthen the implementation procedures; their particular impacts are discussed in the section on reconciliation and the chapter on appropriations.

Finally, the "Byrd Rule" in the Senate creates a point of order against extraneous material in reconciliation bills, whether in the reconciliation bill as reported, in floor amendments, in the conference report, or in House amendments. It requires a three-fifths Senate vote to waive either this point of order (or appeal it successsfully), or the germaneness rule for reconciliation bills.[176]

In an ideal world, that would be the end of the points of order. However, despite the budget resolution's guidance and its implementation devices, Congress anticipates that its spending may exceed the resolution's ceiling and its revenue may hit the resolution's floor. Once spending and revenues hit those limits, section 311 creates a point of order against bills or amendments to add spending or cut revenues.[177] At

---

point of order could only be waived, at the conference report stage, "by a vote of three-fifths of the Members present and voting," one of the rare supermajority procedural requirements in the House.

[176] For an example of the Byrd rule in operation, see 132 Cong. Rec. S13047 (daily ed. Sept. 19, 1986).

(footnote continued)

some point, unless spending is being kept down
(not the case in the 1980s), the sum of spending
under enacted laws will hit the aggregate total in
the prior budget resolution. From that point on,
any spending bill is subject to a point of order
until a new budget resolution is adopted with a
different aggregate spending figure.

The spending ceiling is about as crude a tool
as one could devise, with two major problems. The
aggregate spending figure in the resolution tends
to get obsolete as revenues fall below projections
and entitlements exceed projections. This means
that even if appropriations are kept down,
Congress hits the spending ceiling early, which
"creates an interval during which virtually no
legislation with a budgetary impact can be
considered without a waiver of Section 311(a).
Although such periods normally occur only for a
few months in the spring,"[178] the periods may get
longer in bad economic times, when revenues drop
sharply and the "safety net" entitlements, like
unemployment compensation and food stamps, go up
rapidly. A new budget resolution could be adopted
raising the ceiling, as the framers of the 1974
act envisaged, but that often involves too great
an effort.

Moreover, the point of order falls without
discrimination on "lean" and "fat" bills,
depending on their timing. All that matters is
whether the ceiling is in place when the bill is
under consideration, so essentially it catches all
the late bills and none of the early ones. A
"fat" bill -- an appropriation bill exceeding its

------

[177] In operation, the budget committees keep score each
session of the amount of spending required by existing law
(primarily entitlements on the books), plus each new
appropriation bill and other spending bill as it is
enacted. From time to time "the House and Senate Budget
Committees prepare 'status reports' that inform the
presiding officers of the respective chambers of the
'current level' of spending and revenues." Keith,
Enforcement of Spending Ceilings and Revenue Floors in
Budget Resolutions, CRS Review, July/August 1983, at 18.
These status reports may be reprinted in the Congressional
Record.

[178] Id. at 19.

section 302 suballocation -- does not violate
section 311(a) if consideration occurs before the
spending ceiling is hit. A "lean" bill, within
its 302 suballocation, does violate section 311 if
it comes up after the spending ceiling is hit.
This is politely termed the "Last Horse Out of the
Barn"[179] problem, or sometimes the "last pig at
the trough" problem.

Gramm-Rudman provided a partial remedy, in
section 311(b), by exempting House bills and
amendments for a committee within its section
302(a) allocation.[180] However, the "last pig at
the trough" penalty still remains applicable to
all Senate bills. It also remains applicable in
the House to bills from any committee that has
filled its section 302(a) allocation, however lean
the particular bill.

Given the "last pig at the trough" problem,
the section 311 point of order is sometimes
waived. "The House tends to use special rules and
the suspension procedure to waive Section 311(a),
while the Senate generally uses motions under
Section 904 of the Budget Act or unanimous
consent."[181] Virtually every supplemental
appropriation goes through with such waivers.
Sometimes, a Member will protest. When a
conference report on a supplemental appropriation
came to the House floor in 1983, one
representative commented in typical fashion, "I
have not checked the Guin[n]ess book, but that
must be close to a new record for the Rules
Committee . . . . [Its rule for the bill] waived
the entire Budget Act for the whole bill."[182]
That bill went through, notwithstanding the
protest.

---

[179]   Id. at 19.

[180]   It had been customary before Gramm-Rudman to include
such an exemption in the budget resolutions.

[181]   Keith, Enforcement of Spending Ceilings, supra, at 20.

[182]   129 Cong. Rec. H5987 (daily ed. July 29, 1983) (Rep.
William Frenzel (R-Minn.)).

Basic Waiver Mechanisms

The House has two basic methods to waive budget act points of order. It can take up a bill under suspension of the rules, which overcomes all budget points of order. Alternatively, for the majority of bills (which come to the floor pursuant to special rules), it can include a waiver of budget points of order in the special rule. Such waivers have been very common. The Rules Committee gave 98 waivers of Budget Act requirements in the 97th Congress, and 132 such waivers in the 98th Congress.[183]

In granting or withholding budget waivers, the Rules Committee generally follows the decisions of the House Budget Committee. As the Rules Committee explained its procedure: "Prior to the granting of most of these waivers the committee consulted with the Committee on the Budget. These consultations were instituted by the Committee on Rules to ensure a coordinated response to the various violations of the budget process."[184] The House Budget Committee may routinely poll out requests for waivers, though

---

[183] Survey of Activities of the House Committee on Rules, 97th Congress, H.R. Rep. No. 1007, 97th Cong., 2d Sess. 15 (1983); Survey of Activities of the House Committee on Rules, 98th Congress, H.R. Rep. No. 1192, 98th Cong., 2d Sess. 31 (1985). The committee counts waivers for a bill and for each amendment separately, so that the number of bills or special rules involved is much lower than this total number of waivers.

Almost half of the waivers concerned a technical point of order abolished in 1985 by Gramm-Rudman. Fifty-four of the waivers in the 98th Congress concerned the section 402(a) point of order against authorizations reported after May 15, Survey of Activities of the House Committee on Rules, 98th Congress, supra, at 34, abolished by Gramm-Rudman. Accordingly subsequent years may include smaller numbers of waivers.

[184] Survey of Activities of the House Committee on Rules, 97th Congress, supra, at 14. For a discussion of the relationship between the House Rules and House Budget committees regarding waivers, see Schick at 378.

the committee takes procedural regularity as one of its specialities.[185]

For the Senate, section 303(a), forbidding spending or revenue legislation prior to adoption of a budget resolution, provides that the committee reporting such legislation can report a Senate resolution waiving the point of order. More generally, the 1974 budget act provides its own waiver motion in section 904(b): "[a]ny provision of title III or IV may be waived or suspended in the Senate by a majority vote of the Members voting, a quorum being present, or by the unanimous consent of the Senate." Gramm-Rudman tightened this up, by specifying that certain points of order "may be waived or suspended in the Senate only by the affirmative vote of three-fifths of the Members, duly chosen and sworn." The chief points of order requiring a three-fifths vote concern allocations (bills and amendments exceeding committee suballocations), reconciliation (amendments to reconciliation bills increasing spending or cutting revenues), the spending ceiling,[186] and germaneness on budget resolutions and reconciliation bills.[187]

---

[185] Regarding the committee's seriousness, see Schick at 370-71. The committee's procedure for polling out decisions on requests for budget waivers is described in Reform of the Federal Budget Process: Hearings Before a Subc. of the House Comm. on Government Operations, 100th Cong., 1st Sess. 282 (1987)(Rep. Gray).

[186] Respectively section 302(f) (allocations), section 310(d) (reconciliation), and section 311(a) (spending ceiling and revenue floor). Section 271(b) of Gramm-Rudman lists the "three-fifths" points of order as "[s]ections 301(i), 302(f), 304(b), 310(d), 310(g), and 311(a) of the Congressional Budget Act of 1974." Besides the ones noted in text, the other section 271(b) points of order waivable only by three-fifths require that budget resolutions not exceed the Gramm-Rudman deficit ceilings, section 301(i) (regular annual resolutions) and section 304(b) (revised resolutions), and that reconciliation not change Social Security, section 310(g).

[187] Section 271(a) of Gramm-Rudman added a new subsection 904(c) to the budget act, providing that "[s]ections (footnote continued)

In the vast majority of cases, the Senate simply waives budget points of order by unanimous consent or by adopting a 904(b) waiver or a 303(c) waiver resolution by voice vote, or just ignores the potential points of order. For example, after the Senate hits its section 311(a) spending ceiling, the chairman of the Appropriations Committee, when bringing up appropriation bills, will routinely move to waive the section 311(a) point of order, usually without opposition.[188] Whether this results from completely ignoring points of order, or from behind-the-scenes bargaining, depends on the circumstances.

In the 1970s and early 1980s, there was

305(b)(2) and 306 of this Act may be waived or suspended in the Senate only by the affirmative vote of three-fifths of the members, duly chosen and sworn." This adds another pair of points of order to the three-fifths group: the point of order for germaneness on budget resolutions and reconciliation bills, section 305(b)(2), and the point of order for the jurisdiction of the budget committee, section 306.

[188] As Chairperson Mark Hatfield (R-Oreg.) stated in making the motion to waive, in order to allow bringing up a supplemental appropriation:

Congress did not revise its first budget resolution . . . and so the budgetary ceilings now in place are nearly a year old, and badly out of date . . . . [which] has left us with meaningless budget ceilings which were breached months ago and for which therefore, technically, make any spending or revenue bill subject to a point of order under section 311, of the Budget Act . . . .

This matter has been cleared on both sides of the aisle and with the chairman of the Budget Committee, Senator Domenici.

129 Cong. Rec. S2395 (daily ed. March 9, 1983); see 129 Cong Rec S8031 (daily ed. June 9, 1983) (similar waiver on another supplemental); 129 Cong. Rec. S8879 (daily ed. June 11, 1983) (similar waiver on Energy and Water Appropriation). The same has to be done on conference reports. 129 Cong. Rec. S3629 (daily ed. March 22, 1983). None of these waivers required a recorded vote.

little open combat in the Senate over points of
order.   In all of 1985, only two recorded votes
occurred for motions waiving budget points of
order.[189]   Recorded votes may also occur on Senate
resolutions to waive budget resolutions, but not
very often.[190]   After Gramm-Rudman and Gramm-
Rudman II tightened up the points of order and
imposed three-fifths supermajority requirements
for waivers, combat over waivers occurred more
often.[191]

Senators may well complain on the occasions
when others publicly insist on budget points of
order.   Senator John Melcher (D-Mont.) complained
thusly in 1983, when the Senate tabled his attempt
to waive a budget point of order on an amendment:

> Those waivers are generally granted by
> unanimous consent and indeed, sometimes not
> even unanimous consent is asked on a budget
> waiver   . . . .   [T]he budget waiver
> requirement is ignored.
>
> There are perhaps six -- I am advised several
> -- probably six amendments already accepted
> to this bill that impact the budget and would
> be subject to a point of order, requiring a
> waiver of the budget rules.[192]

---

[189]   One was on an obscure revenue-losing amendment (in
which the Senate tabled a motion to waive the point of order
against the amendment), and the other to waive germaneness
on the reconciliation bill for an amendment limiting textile
imports.   The two recorded votes are in 1985 Congressional
Quarterly Almanac at 28-S (vote number 138) and 46-S (vote
number 252).

[190]   In 1983, out of 33 such resolutions reported to the
Senate (some of which never received floor consideration,
such as when the associated bill never reached floor
consideration), three received roll-call votes: S. Res. 146
(IMF funding), 160 (Radio Marti), and 165 (rubber research
and development), all 98th Cong., 1st Sess. (1983).   That
was before Gramm-Rudman abolished the section 402(a) point
of order against authorizations after May 15, a chief source
of points of order.

[191]   1987 Congressional Quarterly Almanac 45, 408, 690.
(footnote continued)

When fights occur over budget waivers, most often
the waiver opponents object to the substance of
the bill or amendment, not the budget violation,
and simply use the budget waiver as an occasion to
resist.   For example, in 1982, Senator Edward
Zorinsky (D-Nebr.) successfully filibustered a
routine budget waiver in order to kill a bill to
create Radio Marti, an anti-Castro station to
broadcast to Cuba.[193]

---

[192]   129 Cong. Rec. S3587 (daily ed. March 22, 1983.)
Senator Melcher's motion was to waive the section 311
revenue floor so that he could offer his amendment to repeal
withholding of taxes on interest and dividends.

[193]   For a description of the filibuster, see 1982
Congressional Quarterly Almanac 151.   The budget point of
order concerned the requirement, later repealed by Gramm-
Rudman, that authorization bills be reported no later than
May 15.

13
Appropriations[1]

A.   HISTORY AND OVERVIEW

Importance

Congress passes no more important bills than
appropriations -- and none with a procedure so
distinctive. Appropriations' number one aspect is
their enormous scale. By the late 1980s, one
regular annual appropriation bill, the defense
bill, appropriated $300 billion, and the omnibus
appropriation bill appropriated $600 billion.[2]
The appropriations bills, together with major tax
and budget reconciliation bills, legislate the
fiscal policy of the United States. Moreover,
appropriations recur on this enormous scale year

---

[1]   Sources cited frequently in this chapter include: Fisher,
The Authorization-Appropriation Process in Congress: Formal
Rules and Informal Practices, 29 Cath. U. L. Rev. 51 (1979)
(Fisher); Granat, House Appropriations Panel Doles Out Cold
Federal Cash, Chafes at Budget Procedures, 41 Cong. Q. Week.
Rep. 1209 (1983) (Granat); R. F. Fenno, The Power of the
Purse: Appropriations Politics in Congress (1966) (Fenno);
A. Schick, Congress and Money: Budgeting, Spending and
Taxing (1980) (Schick).

[2]   1987 Congressional Quarterly Almanac 401 (omnibus fiscal
1988 appropriation).

in and year out.

The comprehensiveness and policy importance of appropriations match their scale. Virtually every department and agency receives its funding from one of the 13 regular appropriations bills, from the White House (in the Treasury-Postal Service bill) down to the most remote, forgotten agricultural extension office (in the Agriculture bill). Accordingly, the fiscal 1988 omnibus appropriation bill ran so long -- a ten pound package over 1,000 pages in length -- it had to be "lugged in boxes" to the House and Senate floor.[3]

Appropriations not only determine spending, but also serve as the vehicle for decisions on many of the government's policies. As Professor Kate Stith noted in 1988, "[d]uring the Vietnam War, Congress cut off funds for Cambodian operations," while "a decade later," it similarly used the the Boland amendments "to constrain United states involvement in support of the armed Nicaraguan opposition, or contras." On domestic matters, Congress uses limitations on appropriations to debate and resolve issues ranging from abortions to televising the House's own proceedings.

Historically, the constitutional and political importance of appropriations -- the "supply" or "money" bills -- evolved as a bulwark of Anglo-Saxon democracy. After centuries of struggle between Parliament and the British monarchy, Parliament cemented democratic rule by obtaining control over raising taxes, and then over spending the money thereby raised, controlling the monarchy through appropriations.[4] The colonial legislatures gained similar

---

[3] 1987 Congressional Quarterly Almanac 480-81, 485, 488.

A very few agencies, such as the Federal Reserve Board, have found ways to fund themselves without going through the appropriations process; the FRB retains a portion of the earnings from its banking operations to finance its work.

[4] Parliament sealed its victory in the Act of Settlement in 1701, which provided that parliamentary appropriations were to be applied "to the several Uses and purposes by this act directed and intended as aforesaid, and to no other Use, Intent or Purpose." 12 & 13 Will. 3, c. 11, § 26, 3 (footnote continued)

predominance over royal governors by control of spending. When the Constitution established a strong central government, James Madison emphasized, in the Virginia ratifying convention, the division of powers long deemed essential to popular self-government:

> [T]he sword and purse are not to be given to the same member. Apply it to the British government, which has been mentioned. The sword is in the hands of the British king. The purse [is] in the hands of the parliament. It is so in America, as far as any analogy can exist . . . . The purse is in the hands of the representatives of the people. They have the appropriation of all monies.[5]

In fact, the Framers considered a regular legislative appropriations process so important for democratic control of the (executive-directed) military that the Constitution explicitly forbids army appropriations "for a longer Term than two Years."[6]

Statutes at Large 367 (1758), cited in R. Berger, Executive Privilege: A Constitutional Myth 113 n.174 (1974).

[5] 3 J. Elliott, Debates on the Adoption of the Constitution 367 (1836).

[6] Art. I, sec. 8, cl. 12, provides that Congress shall have the power "To raise and support Armies, but no Appropriation of Money to That use shall be for a longer term than two Years." Art. I, sec. 8, cl. 13, also provides that Congress shall have the power "To provide and maintain a Navy." As Justice Jackson of the Supreme Court noted:

> The Constitution expressly places in Congress power "to raise and support Armies" and "to provide and maintain a Navy." (Emphasis supplied.) This certainly lays upon Congress primary responsibility for supplying the armed forces. Congress alone controls the raising of revenues and their appropriation and may determine in what manner and by what means they shall be spent for military and naval procurement.

Youngstown Sheet & Tube Co. v. Sawyer, 343 U.S. 579, 643

(footnote continued)

The Framers also included in the Constitution a provision that bills to "raise revenues" would originate in the House, although the Senate would have the right to amend them. Whatever the original intent of this provision, Congress has developed and nursed a tradition that appropriation bills originate in the House.[7]   On occasion, if the Senate grows impatient over slow passage of appropriations bills in the House, it may originate its own bill to give its Appropriation Committee a vehicle for markup, but it rarely goes so far as to enact such a bill and send it to the House. When it does, the House invariably returns the bill with what is known as a "blue slip," a form rejecting the bill as violating the House's privileges.[8]

In this chapter, the following sections lay the foundation for appropriations procedure: the historic evolution of the basic rules, the significant breakdowns of those rules in the 1970s, and the swing back of the pendulum in the 1980s.   Then, the next chapters treat the three main procedural components of the process: the budget process and spending decisions, authorizations, and legislative riders on appropriations. Finally, the last chapter treats continuing appropriations and supplementals, the most irregular and increasingly important components of the system.

Basic Rules

Congress evolved basic rules for consideration of appropriations over two centuries, which can be summed up in what Louis Fisher describes as the "customary" model, a "simple, two-step procedure": "authorization of

---

(1952) (concurring opinion).

[7]   See, e.g., Fisher at 89-91; J. Pressman, House vs. Senate: Conflict in the Appropriation Process (1966).

[8]   For a discussion of the "blue slip" procedure and related issues, see T. R. Reid, Congressional Odyssey 70-71 (1980); House Manual § 102; Deschler 13 § 3.

programs as recommended by substantive (legislative) committees, followed by the financing of those programs through measures reported by the funding (appropriations) committees. As a general rule, authorization bills should not contain appropriations, nor should appropriation bills contain authorizations."[9] The procedure follows three basic rules: appropriations only on appropriation bills (i.e., only under the appropriations committees); no unauthorized appropriations; and no legislation on appropriations.

Under the basic model, first, Congress does not mingle appropriations with other bills, as so often occurs in other contexts through the multiple referrals or nongermane amendments. Historically, Congress made a series of decisions to grant the appropriations committees and the appropriations bills a monopoly on appropriations. In the early 1800s, one pair of committees, House Ways and Means, and Senate Finance, held responsibility both for revenue bills and for appropriations. After the Civil War, Congress split these money committees into two separate pairs, one for revenue (House Ways and Means, and Senate Finance), and one for appropriations.[10]

To further subdivide, while at first Congress had used only one annual appropriation bill for the whole government, starting in 1794 it split off a separate army appropriation bill. Thereafter it divided appropriations among a growing set of bills. By 1880 the division reached 13 regular annual bills, which has remained roughly the number down to today,

---

[9]   Fisher at 52.

[10]   More precisely, the Senate only developed its standing committee system in 1816, and even then at first it let appropriations be reported by committees other than Finance, until Finance took over that whole jurisdiction in the 1820s and 1830s. Fisher at 54. The probable reason Appropriations split from Finance after the Civil War was as an economy move in light of the huge Civil War deficits. Committee on Appropriations: 100th Anniversary, 1867-1967, S. Doc. No. 21, 90th Cong., 1st Sess. 5 (1967).

although the respective contents of the regular appropriation bills have changed frequently.[11] The appropriations committees have one subcommittee for each regular appropriation, and this set of 13 appropriations subcommittees in the House, and 13 in the Senate, run the appropriations process today.

These 13 regular appropriation bills range from the smallest, the legislative branch appropriation for Congress' own operations, to the largest, the massive defense appropriation bill. Each bill funds its area for one fiscal year, beginning on October 1 (unless enacted late) and ending September 30. Besides these 13 regular bills, Congress generally enacts at least two supplemental appropriation bills later in the fiscal year, carrying items for which it does not wish to wait until the next year's regular bills. Also, when Congress fails to meet the October 1 target, it enacts one or more continuing resolutions. Traditionally, these fund agencies during temporary periods at the beginning of the fiscal year when some regular bills are not yet enacted. Starting in the 1970s, continuing resolutions also served increasingly as omnibus appropriations, supplanting regular bills for an entire year.

From 1877 to 1920, other jealous committees seized from the appropriations committees the right to report some of the regular appropriation bills.[12] However, dividing up responsibility for

---

[11]   McConachie provides a table of the origin of the appropriation bills during that era.   L. G. McConachie, Congressional Committees 176 (1911).   In some historic periods a "deficiency" bill (as discussed below, akin to supplementals) has been counted as a regular bill, there being a particular appropriations committee subcommittee for the deficiencies, bringing the number of "regular" bills to 14.

[12]   For the fullest account of the breakdown, which commenced in 1887-85 in the House, see DeA. S. Alexander, History and Procedure of the House of Representatives 236-50 (1916).   The corresponding breakdown in the Senate largely did not occur until 1899.   L. Fisher, Presidential Spending Power 23-24 (1975); Committee on Appropriations: 100th (footnote continued)

appropriations among different committees meant that Congress "lost an overall coordinated view of income and outgo, and the several appropriation committees tended to become protagonists rather than critics of the fiscal needs of their departmental clientele."[13] Criticism of this divided responsibility as causing wasteful and excessive spending led the House in 1920, and the Senate in 1922, as part of the budget reform after World War I, to reconcentrate jurisdiction over all the regular appropriations in the Appropriations Committees.[14]

House Rule XXI(5)(a), adopted in 1920 and unchanged to this day, established this monopoly by comprehensive proscriptions, both against other committees reporting bills, and against floor amendments: "No bill or joint resolution carrying appropriations shall be reported by any committee not having jurisdiction to report appropriations, nor shall an amendment proposing an appropriation be in order during the consideration of a bill or joint resolution reported by a committee not having that jurisdiction." House Rule XXI(5)(a) provides a procedural bulwark insofar as "[a] question of order on an appropriation in any such bill, joint resolution, or amendment thereto may be raised at any time." The resolution of technical issues under this rule generally reflects the broad scope of appropriations.[15]

Anniversary, 1867-1967, S. Doc. No. 21, 90th Cong., 1st Sess. 7-8 (1967).

[13] G. Galloway, History of the House of Representatives 213 (1976).

[14] L. Fisher, Presidential Spending Power 36-37 (1975) (describing reconcentration). "These steps toward a more systematic approach to federal expenditures" figured in an economy drive by which "the public debt was reduced from $25 billion in 1919 to $16 billion in 1930." Congressional Quarterly, Origins and Development of Congress 192 (1976).

[15] See Deschler 25 § 3. An issue reflecting the broad scope of appropriations is that even a provision on a legislative bill, not to appropriate money, but simply to lift a limitation in a prior appropriation bill, may be deemed a forbidden appropriation, unless it makes a (footnote continued)

In two other somewhat related rules, Congress forbids either "unauthorized" appropriations, or "legislation" on appropriations. The rule regarding authorizations requires the enactment of authorizing legislation for new projects, programs, officers' salaries, and the like, before an appropriation would be in order. Such authorizing legislation may put a ceiling, which the appropriation may not exceed, on the amounts it authorizes for these purposes. The rule against legislation prohibits provisions in appropriations bills from containing changes in the existing law established by those authorizations. Thus, in the "customary" model established by these basic rules, the appropriations committees do not enact substantive law, or create whole programs, through their power to fund. Their bills only decide how much funding a program will receive after the authorizing committees create the program, enact its substantive law, and fix a ceiling.

The Supreme Court described the distinction between authorizations and appropriations thusly:

> Authorizing legislation is defined [as] . . .:
>
> "[b]asic substantive legislation enacted by Congress which sets up or continues the legal operation of a Federal program or agency . . . . Such legislation is normally a prerequisite for subsequent appropriations . . . ."
>
> Appropriation, on the other hand, is defined as:
>
> "An authorization by an act of the Congress that permits Federal agencies to incur obligations and to make payments out of the Treasury for specified purposes. An appropriation usually follows enactment of authorizing legislation . . . ."[16]

---

permanent change in the law. Id. 25 §§ 3.25, 3.27.

[16] Andrus v. Sierra Club, 442 U.S. 347, 359 n.18 (1979) (quoting definitions by the Comptroller General).

These basic rules generate an intricate body
of parliamentary procedure, but their purposes are
straightforward: to limit controversy and to
divide power.   Each year, Congress must pass
appropriations (leaving aside the special question
of continuing resolutions) or the relevant
departments of government, lacking the right to
draw money from the Treasury, will shut down.
These necessary bills must not bog down in side
disputes within each chamber, blackmailing by each
chamber of the other and by both of the President,
or other disastrous impasses. 'Moreover, the other
committees will not stand to see the great power
of appropriating committees, which necessarily
encompasses oversight of all activities of
government, encroach on their own jurisdiction.

As early as 1818, a House conference report
on an appropriation explained the necessity that
"appropriations, in regard to the propriety or
extent of which the two Houses find, after
deliberation that they still differ, should be
separated from those which both consider
necessary" to the public service: "If either
branch of the legislature determine that it will
not make the great mass of necessary
appropriations while there remains one unprovided
for . . . it throws upon the other branch the
necessity of concurring . . . or of endangering
all the appropriations of the Government."[17]

Accordingly, to get appropriations through,
rules evolved, through a long and tortuous
process, to protect the appropriation bills
against (and to reserve from the appropriations
committees) extraneous issues, such as changes in
legislation or the creation of new programs or
agencies.   Congress began observing the policies
against legislation on appropriations in the
1810s.[18]   Impasses in the 1830s and the heavy

---

[17]   IV Hinds § 3905, at 608-9.

[18]   The Senate conferees indicated in their own report on
the 1818 military pay dispute that "generally it would not
be the most correct course to amend a law establishing
salaries or authorizing an expenditure by a provision in a
general appropriation law, though they believed that there
(footnote continued)

expenditures of the Mexican War (1846-48) led to formal written rules against unauthorized appropriations and legislation on appropriations developing in 1837-54.[19]

In the House, enactment of popular legislative provisions by attaching them to appropriations led in 1876 to an exception known as the "Holman Rule," which allowed legislative provisions on appropriations as long as they "retrenched" (reduced) spending. This exception was repealed and reenacted, interpreted broadly sometimes and narrowly at other times, and thus served as a weather-vane for the competing desires.[20] The 1877-1920 breakdown in the appropriations' committees' monopoly appears partly to have been a reaction to jealousy of the power expanded by the Holman Rule.[21] During the twentieth century, that exception has largely dwindled in significance. Instead, waivers in special rules serve the function of allowing some legislative riders but not others, depending on

---

was no constitutional or legal objection to it." IV A. Hinds § 3905, at 609 (the quoted language is Hinds', not the Senate committee's). L. G. McConachie, supra at 178, comments that in the House, "Riders were first forbidden by rule in 1814."

[19] See Fisher at 54-56. In the Senate, the main drive against unauthorized appropriations apparently resulted from an economy move after the heavy spending of the Mexican War. Senate Committee on Appropriations, Committee on Appropriations: 100th Anniversary, 1867-1967, S. Doc. No. 21, 90th Cong., 1st Sess. 3-4 (1967).

[20] IV A. Hinds § 3578, at 382-85; Fisher at 54-56. The original purpose appears to be that Democrats were in the majority in the House under Republican Presidents, and "in their attempts to repeal certain Reconstruction laws, the Democrats revived the practice of adding legislative riders to appropriation bills in the hope of forcing the President to accept them." Congressional Quarterly, Origins and Development of Congress 102 (1976).

[21] Fisher at 57. It was also a reaction to the appropriation "committee's excessive concern for economy." Congressional Quarterly, Origins and Development of Congress 103 (1976).

the will of the leadership and the chamber.

In the Senate, widely varying votes on points of order[22] regarding the rules against unauthorized appropriations long served that same weather vane function. The Senate did not add a rule against legislation on appropriations until the 1922 reconcentration of jurisdiction in the Appropriations Committee.[23] Not only widely varying votes on points of order, but some particularly fancy procedures, exist in the Senate specifically to allow floor votes to end run these strictures.

As discussed below, certain political structures clearly evident in the second half of the twentieth century supplemented these basic rules for structuring the appropriations process. Notably, assignment practices for the House Committee on Appropriations made it a bastion of antispending feeling. The committee's power, joined with procedures strengthening the hand of chairmen against floor amendments, gave the committee supremacy on the floor. Meanwhile, the Senate Appropriations Committee was content to take a back seat, serving an "appellate" function of restoring some items sought by agencies but cut in the House.[24]

1970s Breakdown

The basic appropriations structure faced novel challenges in the 1970s on all its three basic rules, which set the stage for the current

---

[22] G.H. Haynes, The United States Senate 464-68 (1938). As Haynes notes regarding Gilfry's 1909 compilation of prior Senate precedents, "[o]f the nearly 1000 pages devoted to setting forth Precedents of the United States Senate, the compiler, Henry H. Gilfry, has devoted more than one-fifth to 'Amendments to General Appropriation Bills.'" Id. at 464 n.3.

[23] The 1922 rule change is discussed in G. H. Haynes, The Senate of the United States 460 (1938).

[24] These matters are discussed below. The fullest treatment of the classic system is in Fenno.

situation.   First,   notwithstanding   the   rule
restricting   appropriations   to   appropriations
bills, Congress funded major expenditures through
"entitlement"   legislation   rather   than   through
discretionary appropriations.[25]   During the 1960s
and 1970s, authorizing committees reported major
entitlements legislation or changes and increases
in existing ones, often with further built-in
cost-of-living   increases: Social   Security,
Medicare, Medicaid, Civil Service and Military
Retirement, SSI and various disability programs,
unemployment   compensation,   AFDC,   railroad
retirement and pensions, and revenue sharing. The
mushrooming of these entitlements reduced the role
of   the   annual   appropriations   process   to   a
relatively   limited   portion   of   non-defense
spending.[26]

Second,   authorization   committees   used   the
rule against unauthorized appropriations for a
major thrust for power in the form of a drive for
periodic   authorizations.   In   the   1960s   and
1970s,[27] the authorizing committees enacted many
laws   providing   that   particular   agencies   and
programs would receive periodic, and often annual,
authorizations, prior to the annual appropriations
for   the   program   or   agency.   Such   annual

---

[25] As discussed in the budget chapter, entitlements create
budget   authority   either   without   a   need   for   any
appropriations at all, such as interest on the national debt
(with its permanent appropriation) and Social Security and
Medicare (which do not get appropriations); or with a
technical   need   for   appropriations,   but   without   any
discretion in the appropriations process, which must provide
the budget authority as an obligatory matter, as with food
stamps.

[26] "As a consequence of this growth in entitlements and
transfer   payments,   the   portion   of   the   budget   that   is
'uncontrollable' climbed from 60 percent in fiscal 1968 to
72 percent in the 1974 budget." Schick at 27.

[27] Prior to 1960, when Congress established new civilian
agencies and programs, it tended to give them an indefinite
(i.e., permanent) authorization, ending the authorizing
committee's role until it engaged in a new legislative
initiative.

authorizations could contain new legislative provisions and controls, as well as providing an occasions for influential committee reports and hearings. Periodic authorizations allowed the authorizing committee its own control or encouragement, and (when the authorizations were not enacted in timely fashion) subjected appropriations bills to points of order for unauthorized appropriations or squeezed their schedule.[28] In short, periodic authorizations intruded on appropriations' former monopoly on annual review and expression of congressional views.

Third, Members made extensive use of the major end-run around the rule against legislation on appropriations, the allowability of "limitation" riders on appropriation bills. Limitation riders are provisions such as that "none of the funds appropriated herein shall be used for abortions."[29] As the numbers, importance, and success rate of limitation amendments rose in the 1970s, "some members of Congress argue[d] that appropriations bills loaded with riders [were] becoming the major vehicles for congressional policy making."[30]

Also in the 1970s came assignment reforms that took much of the power previously held by conservative Appropriations Committee and Subcommittee chairs. Moreover, the decade saw the rise of the budget process, in part as a commentary on the breakdown of appropriations discipline, although in its early years the budget process did not seriously constrain appropriations and in some respects served the Appropriations

---

[28] For a comprehensive treatment of the subject, see Fisher, Annual Authorizations: Durable Roadblocks to Biennial Budgeting, Public Budgeting & Finance, Spring 1983, at 23.

[29] Congress deems them not to be legislation when drafted to technical standards regarding their restricting spending on the particular bills rather than changing the permanent law.

[30] Murray, House Funding Bill Riders Become Potent Policy Force, 38 Cong. Q. Week. Rep. 3251 (1980).

Committees' interests.[31]

All these changes tended to eclipse the authority of the appropriations committees, to threaten the power of the appropriations process, and even to impair their schedule. Appropriations had been failing to meet their deadline of the start of the fiscal year, until the 1974 budget act started the fiscal year three months later (shifting its beginning from July 1 to October 1). Then, in the latter part of the 1970s, appropriations began again to experience scheduling breakdowns, due to budget and rider controversies. By the early 1980s, most appropriations did not get enacted even several months into the new fiscal year.

1980s Reaction

As in other areas of procedure, the 1980s saw something of a swing back of the pendulum from the 1970s revolt against old power centers. In this case, that reaction took the form of a partial restoration of the centrality and authority of the appropriations process and particularly the appropriations committees, through a host of developments. An overview will show the significance of matters discussed below in greater detail.

First, power shifted back from the authorizing to the appropriating committees. The budgetary shifts of the 1980s controlled entitlements, restoring centrality in some respects to appropriations. Large deficits, more conservative attitudes on the floor and in the White House, and discipline through the budget procedure made it all but impossible to enact new entitlement programs or to enlarge old ones.[32]

---

[31]   The act included restraints on backdoor spending, somewhat constrained the creation of new entitlements, and tended to give the chair of the full Appropriations Committee some additional control over subcommittees. In the 1970s, appropriations committees did not tend to clash with budget committees the way that Senate Finance clashed with Senate Budget. Schick at 445-81.

(footnote continued)

From 1980 on, the authorizing committees found themselves partially preoccupied with trimming old entitlements pursuant to reconciliation instructions. Through the budget process, Congress procedurally tightened up enactment of backdoor spending, by creating points of order requiring that new entitlements and other forms of backdoor spending go through the annual appropriations process.[33]

The trend toward periodic authorizations waned in the 1980s, as political stalemates on reauthorizations necessitated increasing allowance of appropriations in the absence of the periodic authorizations. Meanwhile, a massive defense buildup gave great power to appropriations, since appropriations, not entitlements, fund defense. Even with the major role of the armed services committees through their annual authorizations, defense and military construction appropriations played a surpassingly important role in distributing this major government largesse.

Second, paradoxically, the very breakdown in scheduling of appropriations ended up contributing to the autonomy of the appropriations

---

[32] The mood changed most after California's enactment of the budget-cutting Proposition 13 in 1978, and emerged in Congress most clearly with the 1980 budget, which first used reconciliation, and then in maxiumum force with the budgets of the Reagan years.

[33] Section 401(a) of the 1974 act had required appropriations for bills or amendments providing new contract or borrowing authority, and section 401(b) of that act had required new entitlements be referred to the appropriations committees. These rules provided the basis for some hard bargaining that restrained new entitlements. Schick at 395-401. As an additional interim step, Congress included provisions on budget resolutions providing that loans had to be appropriated, such as Section 3 of S. Con. Res. 92 in 1982. Gramm-Rudman revised section 401, extending it to conference reports and expanding the definitions of backdoor spending. In addition, it added a new section 402 requiring appropriations for new credit authority. This was part of the new credit budget proposed by the Beilenson Report (Report of the House Committee on Rules on the Congressional Budget Act Amendments of 1984, H.R. Rept. No. 1152, 98th Cong., 2d Sess. 1984) at 71.

committees.   In response to the scheduling breakdown, Congress crowned a device of previously limited significance, the continuing resolution. That device metamorphosed from a simple interim holding-pattern to an enormous, year-long omnibus conglomeration of appropriations bills. Continuing resolutions developed a procedure all their own that maximized the speed of floor consideration, and in the House, used complex rules to preclude points of order, and to bar all but a few amendments, and thus largely insulate the committee against floor-reworking.   In the extreme case of the foreign aid appropriation, for many years no such appropriations came as independent bills to either the House or Senate floors.   Year after year, the appropriations subcommittees simply marked up their versions and put them in the continuing resolutions.

Also, the House adopted a specific rule in 1983 to allow curbing of limitation riders.   In 1985, the Gramm-Rudman bill considerably strengthened the discipline of the budget process over appropriations, but without simplifying the fundamental components of the system.

All this contributed less to a sense of stability in the appropriations procedure of the 1980s than to some swing back from the 1970s, but also a sense of unresolved and conflicting tensions.   Many Members, particularly in the Senate, expressed disdain for a budget system in which the same issues could be fought over three or four times a year on budget resolutions, authorizations, regular appropriations, and continuing resolutions.

B.   SPENDING DECISIONS AND THE BUDGET PROCESS

Appropriations draw numerous and powerful political players into a major process. In each chamber, the Appropriations Committee is the largest of the legislative committees, with 57 Members on the House committee, and 29 on the Senate committee -- almost one-third of the entire Senate.[34]   Appropriations is a choice assignment,

---

[34] The figures are for 1985-86. The House Select Committee (footnote continued)

and each of those Members, even the junior House
Members in the minority, derives considerable
cachet from his voice in appropriations.   The
appropriations process -- hearings, markups, floor
debate -- extends in time and attention far beyond
any other legislating process within the
Congress.   As a reflection of the weight of that
process, appropriations make up a significant
fraction of the annual conferences -- a sign of
the most important congressional bills.   For
example, of the 33 bills that went through
conference committees in 1983, 16 were
appropriations -- 11 regular appropriations, three
supplementals, and two continuing resolutions.[35]

Prologue: Crosswalking and Suballocation

To review briefly the discussion in the
budget chapter, the annual budget resolution
specifies spending figures in aggregate and
function amounts.   In the conference report on the
resolution, the budget conferees allocate the
spending figures by committee pursuant to section
302(a) of the Budget Act.   By far the largest
committee allocation goes to the Appropriations
Committee, with the rest going for entitlements.
For example, defense spending occurs mainly
by appropriations, not entitlements, and the
allocation concerns budget authority (in
Appropriations), not mere authorization
jurisdiction (in Armed Services).   Accordingly,
the Appropriations Committees receive the lion's
share of the allocation from Function 050
(National Defense), while the Armed Services

---

on Aging is bigger than House Appropriations, but its
importance, although symbolic, is not commensurate with its
size; it does not have jurisdiction to report bills and is a
secondary assignment for its members.

[35] 1983 House Calendar. This was a higher fraction than in
most years, partly because so many regular appropriations
went through, and partly because odd-numbered years are the
first years of each two-year session, and while
appropriations go through in such years, many other bills do
not approach the finish line of their long course until the
second year of the session.

Committees receive miniscule allocations.

In the two chambers, there is a somewhat different relationship between the budget and appropriations committee, formally expressed in how committee allocations are presented. Philosophically, the Senate Budget Committee deals more in broad concepts, while the House Budget Committee deals in more precise delineations. Gramm-Rudman amended the committee allocation process to reflect these somewhat different approaches.[36]   Section 302(a)(2) requires, for the Senate, mere lists of the amounts of budget authority, outlays, and new credit authority allocated to each committee.[37]   In contrast, section 302 requires elaborately analyzed allocations for the House.   The House budget conferees break down the allocation to each House committee between "mandatory" and "discretionary" spending,[38] and further break down the allocation

---

[36]   When Gramm-Rudman provided for a "mandatory"-"discretionary" breakdown, it merely codified past House Budget Committee practice under the 1974 act.

[37]   Section 302(a)(2), as amended by Gramm-Rudman, requires for the Senate "an estimated allocation . . . of the appropriate levels of total budget outlays, total new budget authority and new credit authority among each committee of the House of Representatives and the Senate . . . ."   Thus, the Senate table provides figures for House committees as well as Senate committees.

[38]   Section 302(a)(1), as amended by Gramm-Rudman, requires for the House "an estimated allocation . . . of the appropriate levels of total budget outlays, total new budget authority, total entitlement authority, and total credit authority among each committee of the House of Representatives . . . ."   Thus the House table only includes House committees, and covers total entitlement authority and total credit authority as well as the other figures.   The section goes down to describe the futher breakdown of the figures:

The allocation shall, for each committee, divide new budget authority, entitlement authority, and credit authority between amounts provided or required by law on the date of such conference report (mandatory or
(footnote continued)

by function.[39]

Once the appropriations committees receive their section 302(a) allocations, section 302(b) requires them "[a]s soon as practicable" to divide those allocations up among their subcommittees.[40] This is called the "suballocation" process, and it has greater importance than outsiders realize. Suballocation translates the budget resolution into specific ceilings for each subcommittee and thus each regular appropriation bill. While Congress sets targets in the budget resolution's figures for the various budget functions, the Budget Act does not require the Appropriations Committees to follow those priorities in making this suballocation. The Appropriations Committees can -- and do -- suballocate different funding to each subcommittee than indicated by the budget resolution's functions.[41] Since Gramm-Rudman keys its points

---

uncontrollable amounts), and amounts not so provided or required (discretionary or controllable amounts), and shall make the same division for estimated outlays that would result from such new budget authority.

[39] For example, the conference report for the 1981 first budget resolution listed, for fiscal year 1982, an allocation for the House Appropriations Committee of $465 billion. This was further subdivided among seventeen functions, ranging from $4.4 billion for Appropriations' share of Function 750 (Administration of Justice) to $182 billion for its share of Function 050 (National Defense). Gramm-Rudman does not mandate this; it is the established practice of the House Budget Committee.

[40] Section 302(c) creates a point of order against bills (or amendments) with new budget, spending, or credit authority within the jurisdiction of any committee that receives a 302(a) allocation "unless and until such committee makes the allocation or subdivisions required by subsection (b) . . . ."

[41] To take an exaggerated hypothetical, Congress in enacting the annual budget resolution may put $250 billion in the national defense function, and $15 billion in the international affairs function, and may allocate all of that to the appropriations committees. The report of the House conferees will specify that Appropriations received $250 (footnote continued)

of order to the section 302(b) suballocation
ceilings, not to the functions in the resolution,
in the end the Appropriations Committee must only
obey its own suballocation, not the functions.

Thus, by the suballocation process, the
Appropriations Committees set their own priorities
rearranging those of the budget resolution.
Suballocation is largely negotiated internally
among the Appropriations Committee chair and his
subcommittee chairs in each chamber,[42] reflecting
their priorities and political calculations[43] as

---

billion in the national defense function and $15 billion in
the international affairs function (as described above, the
Senate report does not mention any breakdowns by
function). Yet, either Appropriations Committee may decide
that its defense appropriations subcommittee should get
less, and its foreign aid subcommittee should get more, and
may take this allocation of $265 billion and suballocate
$240 billion to the defense subcommittee and $25 billion to
the foreign aid subcommittee.

Shifting of funds by suballocation away from the
priorities in the budget resolution has been noted by a
number of well-placed observers. See Proposed Improvements
In the Congressional Budget Act of 1974: Hearings Before the
Sen. Comm. on the Budget, 97th Cong., 2d Sess. (Proposed
Improvement Hearings) at 128 (Alice Rivlin), 361 (Rep.
Delbert Latta (R-Ohio)).

[42] An additional factor is that the appropriations
committees of the House and Senate consult on, but do not
have to agree on, their suballocations. In the hypothetical
example just stated, the House Appropriations Committee
might decide to give defense $245 billion and foreign aid
$20 billion, while Senate Appropriations might decide to
give them, respectively, $255 billion and $10 billion.
David Stockman, Director of the Office of Management and
Budget, commented about such "variant" shifting that "[i]n
such an environment, judging an appropriations bill on the
grounds of its consistency or inconsistency with the
[budget] resolution . . . is probably impossible." Proposed
Improvements Hearings, supra, at 338.

[43] One observer on the House Budget Committee staff
explained the matter thusly, referring to 302(b)
suballocations in the 1980s:

(footnote continued)

they change over time.[44]   In sum, the upshot of
the allocation and suballocation process each year
is that each appropriation subcommittee receives a
ceiling consisting of that subcommittee's
suballocation.

Appropriation Subcommittees and Committees

In the 1970s and 1980s, changes in assignment
practices had a major effect on the House
Appropriations committee, although the working
practices of the committee did not change
radically. Prior to the 1970s, House
Appropriations had a number of assignment
practices that held down spending.[45] The House

---

those of us on the Budget Committee staff knew to watch
for the unchangeable verities in life. The Defense
Subcommittee [sub]allocation would be reduced [from the
priorities of the budget resolution], as would Military
Construction and Foreign Assistance. Subcommittees
containing domestic programs important to Democratic
constituencies would be increased . . . .

FY 1983 was a good example of these forces at work
in the appropriations process . . . . The Defense
Subcommittee was reduced by over $1.5 billion, Military
Construction by over $700 million and Foreign
Assistance by $800 million, for a total of some $3.0
billion. This "found money" was redistributed to
Agriculture ($300 million), Commerce-State-Justice
($500 million) and Treasury-Postal ($400 million); and
$1.6 billion went to offset a reduction assumed in the
Budget Resolution which had not been distributed by
subcommittee.

(Quoted from an unpublished paper on file with the author).

[44] In the 1970s, it is said that when Senator Warren
Magnuson (D-Wash.) chaired Senate Appropriations, he shifted
billions of dollars from defense to health spending by
suballocation. His successor, Senator Mark Hatfield (R-
Oreg.), was also known as a supporter of lower defense
spending, as was the House chair of the Defense
Appropriations Subcommittee (until his death in 1986),
Representative Joseph P. Addabbo (D-N.Y.).

(footnote continued)

assigned   antispending   Members   to   the
committee.[46]   More   important,   within   the
committee,   appropriations   chairs   assigned   to
particular subcommittees those Members lacking a
local interest in those subcommittees' spending,
and these disinterested Members provided spending
restraint.[47]   Also, conservative, antispending
subcommittee chairmen gained their position solely
from seniority, not being particularly accountable
to   spending   pressure   from   junior   committee
members, let alone from off-committee members.[48]

As   a   result,   the   House   Appropriations
Committee was renowned for anti-spending attitudes
shown by the committee's vocabulary:

> It is a mark of the intensity and the self-
> consciousness with which the consensus on
> budget-cutting is held that it is couched in
> a   distinctive   occupational   vocabulary
> . . . .   The action verbs most commonly used
> are   "cut,"   "carve,"   "slice,"   "prune,"

---

[45]   These are summed up in Shepsle, "The Congressional
Budget Process: Diagnosis, Prescription, Prognosis," in
Congressional Budgeting: Politics, Process, and Power 211
(ed. by W. T. Wander, F. T. Hebert, and G. W. Copeland 1984)
(summarizing Fenno).

[46]   As Allen Schick describes the pattern: "The House
Appropriations Committee carefully selected its members from
relatively "safe" districts.   Because their reelection
prospects were good, these members could afford to resist
pressure from interest groups.   Turnover on the committee
was low, and new members went through a prolonged
apprenticeship before they gained positions of authority."
Schick, The Three-Ring Budget Process: The Appropriations,
Tax, and Budget Committees in Congress, in The New Congress
297 (ed. by T. E. Mann and N. J. Ornstein 1981) (Schick, The
Three-Ring Budget Process).

[47]   As early as 1928, on the Naval Appropriations
Subcommittee there was "[n]ot a seacoast man . . . .   The
object, of course, is not to have men on that committee who
have local interests to consider." VII Cannon § 1117.   The
pattern lasted through the 1960s.   Fenno at 141-43 (citing
numerous quotes and careful surveys).

[48]   Schick, The Three-Ring Budget Process, supra, at 297-99.

> "whittle," "squeeze," "wring," "trim," "lop
> off," "chop," "slash," "pare," "shave,"
> "fry," and "whack" . . . . The tools of the
> trade are appropriately referred to as
> "knife," "blade," "meat axe," "scalpel,"
> "meat cleaver," "hatchet," "shears,"
> "wringer," and "fine-tooth comb."[49]

In the 1970s, procedural reforms undid the prior assignment structure and the attitudes it fostered. Many pro-spending Members were assigned to the committee.[50] Once on the committee, "members were allowed to pick their subcommittees," and they picked subcommittees hoping to vote increases for local interests; as one staff member noted, "[w]hat we find is that inner-city guys are all on Labor-HEW, [and] all of the hawkish guys go to Defense."[51] Most formally, in 1975, the Democratic Caucus adopted Caucus Rule 27(B), which provided that "[t]he full Democratic Caucus shall vote on each Member nominated to serve as chairman of an Appropriations subcommittee following the same procedure set forth in Caucus Rule 20 for the election of standing committee chairmen." Thus, while seniority still serves as the means that puts Members forward to become chairs of subcommittees, the chairs know the Democratic Caucus may, if it so chooses, reject them, just as the caucus has deposed full committee chairs.[52]

---

[49] Fenno at 105.

[50] Schick, The Three-Ring Budget Process, supra, at 302.

[51] Id. at 300; Clark, Appropriations Committees Losing Their Grip on Spending, National Journal, July 22, 1978, at 1169, 1174. Representative David Obey (D-Wis.) gave a similar analysis. Granat at 1210.

[52] The explicit justification for a rule applicable only to Appropriations subcommittees was that "Appropriations subcommittees are virtually autonomous and function almost as if they were full committees," but the "unstated motive" was that the Caucus, which was deposing three committee chairs in 1975, "was putting the conservatives on notice that they would risk losing their posts [as Appropriations (footnote continued)

The results could be seen most clearly in the subsequent reaction of the Appropriations committees to Republican presidential requests. For the first time in 40 years, the pattern that "the aggregate appropriations enacted by Congress have been below the president's spending request" was broken[53] in 1976 (President Ford) and for 1981 and 1982 (the first years of President Reagan) -- despite a countervailing shift against spending on the Senate side after 1980.[54]

Notwithstanding the political changes resulting from these assignment shifts, the working practices of the appropriations committees remained roughly the same.[55] In the House, the Appropriations Committee tends toward bipartisanship; "Appropriations Republicans seem to get a nearly equal say in spending money for pet projects."[56] Each subcommittee chair has very great informal influence, backed up by the following "impressive formal decision-making prerogatives":

---

subcommittee chairs] if their subcommittees blocked liberal spending proposals." Schick, The Three-Ring Budget Process, supra, at 299; Representative Obey made the same point, in Granat at 1210.

[53] Granat at 1210.

[54] In the Senate committee, "in 1977, more than half of the Republicans could be classified as liberals," Schick, The Three-Ring Budget Process, supra, at 303, but after the 1980 election, a half-dozen more conservative Republican first-term Members with relatively antispending attitudes joined the committee. S. S. Smith & C. J. Deering, Committees in Congress 95, 117 (1984).

[55] "In many respects, the House Appropriations Committee in the early 1980s was much the same institution that it had been in the 1960s and 1970s." Bach, Representatives and Committees on the Floor: Amendments to Appropriations Bills in the House of Representatives, 13 Congress & The Presidency 41, 44 (1986).

[56] Granat, at 1213. Historically, close working relationships between subcommittee chairs and ranking minority members at Appropriations had been the goal. Fenno at 174.

> He is expected to allocate tasks to
> subcommittee members, set the timetable for
> subcommittee hearings, preside over the
> hearings, preside over subcommittee markup
> sessions, initiate action in those sessions,
> write (or oversee the writing of) the
> subcommittee report, present the
> subcommittee's recommendations to the full
> Committee, manage the floor debate on his
> subcommittee's bill, lead the House conferees
> in conference on the bill, and speak for the
> subcommittee to the agencies of the executive
> branch.[57]

These powers, and a tendency toward secrecy,
earned the House appropriations subcommittee
chairs the nickname of the "College of Cardinals."
     In the Senate, the pattern of chair
domination is even clearer. "Because senators
face more time constraints, 'the subcommittee
chairmen totally dominate in the Senate,'"
according to a former staff member who became a
Member of the House.[58] Senators on Appropriations

------

[57] Fenno at 168.

[58] Granat at 1214. Significantly, in the House, Members
serving on the Appropriations Committee do not serve on
other committees, except for the slots on the Budget
Committee reserved for Appropriations Members. In the
Senate, they do. In fact, it is not uncommon for the chair
of a Senate appropriations subcommittee to chair the
corresponding authorizing committee, an overlap that gives
that chair a lock on policy in that area. For example, in
1986, Senator Jake Garn (R-Utah) chaired the Committee on
Banking, Housing, and Urban Affairs, and the HUD
appropriations subcommittee; Senator James A. McClure (R-
Idaho) chaired the Committee on Energy and Natural Resources
and the Interior Appropriations subcommittee. Many other
chairs at least sit on the corresponding authorizing
committee, such as Senator Paul Laxalt (R-Nev.), who sat on
the Committee on the Judiciary and chaired the State-
Justice-Commerce appropriations subcommittee. In fact, the
Senate used to provide by rule that authorizing committee
members would sit ex officio on the appropriations
committee. In short, the Senate views multiple duties and
especially overlapping assignments as coordinating devices,
(footnote continued)

serve on several subcommittees, but almost all (except the most junior) serve as either chair or ranking minority member of their own subcommittee.[59]   Considering the time constraints and the norms of reciprocity, Senators leave the running of subcommittees to the chairs.[60]

The appropriations subcommittees in both chambers start with detailed justifications from the executive departments for the administration's budget proposals, on which the subcommittees hold extensive hearings in the spring.   As the House Appropriations Committee proclaimed proudly in 1985, "[d]uring the 98th Congress, the thirteen subcommittees conducted 600 days of hearings, receiving testimony from 10,270 witnesses . . . .   In the process, 200 volumes of hearings were generated, comprising more than 180,000 printed pages."[61]

By late spring, the House subcommittees mark up their proposed bills.   In response to 1970s rules changes, for a time the meetings were open, but then in the 1980s, closed markups returned, as a refuge from spending pressures.[62]   Once the

---

not distractions.

[59]   In 1986, there were 13 subcommittees, and 29 members -- 15 Republicans and 14 Democrats.   All but two Republicans chaired a subcommittee, and all but one Democrat served as a ranking minority member.

[60]   Also, because Senators sit on several subcommittees, departure of a single Senator precipitates a significant game of musical chairs.   For example, when Senator Harrison Schmitt (R-N. Mex.) was defeated in 1982, he left his Labor-HHS subcommittee chair to Senator Lowell Weicker (R-Conn.), who, in turn, left his State-Justice-Commerce chair to Senator Laxalt, who, in turn, left his Military Construction chair to Senator Mike Mattingly (R-Ga.), who, in turn, left his Legislative Branch chair to Senator Alphonse D'Amato (R-N.Y.), who, in turn, left his District of Columbia chair to Senator Arlen Specter (R-Pa.).   Senator Specter, as the most junior majority member, had been one of the only two without chairs; then Senator Pete Domenici (R-N. Mex.) joined the committee without a subcommittee chair for the time being.

[61]   Report of Committee Activities -- 98th Congress, H.R. Rep. No. 1194, 98th Cong., 2d Sess. 1-2 (1985).
(footnote continued)

House subcommittee marks up and reports its bill,[63] the full committee takes it up, usually not altering it: "the subcommittees often have philosophic tilts . . . . These leanings are rarely adjusted by the full committee, where Members are reluctant to tamper with programs outside their jurisdiction."[64]

In deference to the House's claim to originate appropriation bills, the Senate Appropriations Committee usually tends not to take up original Senate bills,[65] or at least not to

---

[62]   Compare Clark, supra, at 1174 (in the 1970s, "if the Appropriations Committees [were] becoming less fiscally conservative, it is in part because most of the meetings [were] no longer closed, and members hesitate[d] to speak out for spending reductions when lobbyists for the programs are sitting in the same room") with Granat at 1211 (in the 1980s, meetings closed).

[63]   The committee chair and ranking minority member vote on subcommittees as ex officio members. Granat at 1220. That had been the historic pattern, although on occasion chairs had declined to allow ranking Members this role. Fenno at 255 (Chairperson Clarence Cannon (D-Mo.) denies ex officio status to his ranking minority member), 259 (Chairperson George Mahon (D-Tex.) allows ex officio status to Representative Frank Bow (R-Ohio)).

[64]   Granat at 1211.

[65]   The Senate made one major exception in the 1980s to waiting for House origination: the foreign aid appropriation. From 1979 until 1985, Congress only once succeeded in enacting a freestanding foreign aid appropriation, funding the other six years through continuing resolutions. Repeatedly, House Appropriations would not even bring the bill to the floor, particularly in election years, because of the controversiality and unpopularity of voting for foreign aid, as well as sharp policy disputes with the administration. To have an opportunity for the Senate to develop its own position without waiting indefinitely for the House bill, in 1981 the Senate went so far as to enact a foreign aid appropriation bill, and "[s]ome House members were angered by the Senate action, regarding it as an attempt to usurp a traditional House prerogative to initiate all appropriations bills." (footnote continued)

have the Senate enact them.[66]   Instead, it holds its hearings, but does not conduct formal markup until the House passes an appropriation bill, which is then referred to the Senate committee. As the committee some years ago described its process at this point:

> At the conclusion of the hearings, the bill is "marked up" by the subcommittee. It is at this session that the members of the subcommittee sit in executive session and decide the amounts to be provided in the bill for each segment on the particular executive agency under consideration. This may be accomplished in 1 day, although subcommittee action frequently takes much longer. "Committee prints" of the bill and report are developed by the staff under the supervision of the subcommittee."[67]

The full Senate Appropriations Committee generally upholds the subcommittee versions, but occasionally overrules them. For example, in 1987, "[h]ungry for more funding for space, science, house and urban renewal programes, the Senate Apropriations Committee rebelled" against the tight version reported by the subcommittee chaired by renowned penny-pincher William Proxmire (D-Wis).[68]

1981 Congressional Quarterly Almanac 344.

[66]   In contrast to the 1981 situation described in the preceding footnote, the Senate committee in 1982, 1983, 1984, and 1985 reported a Senate-originated foreign aid appropriation bill to the floor but did not have the Senate enact that bill. Rather, it used the bill as reported as a base for negotiation in the conference on the continuing resolution. 1982 Congressional Quarterly Almanac 242; 1983 Congressional Quarterly Almanac 521; 1984 Congressional Quarterly Almanac 390; 1985 Congressional Quarterly Almanac 376.

[67]   Committee on Appropriations: 100th Anniversary, 1867-1967, S. Doc. No. 21, 90th Cong., 1st Sess. 22 (1967).

[68]   1987 Congressional Quarterly Almanac 436.

Floor Action

Once the appropriation bill proceeds to the
floor, the budget process uses various tools to
constrain the bill and amendments. As its first
tool, the budget process uses information and
persuasion. The Congressional Budget Office (CBO)
keeps track of how Congress adheres to the budget,
an activity called "scorekeeping."[68] Pursuant to
the budget act, when committees report bills, CBO
tells the committees, and they state in their
reports, whether the bills have stayed within
their allocations and suballocations.[69] The House
and Senate Budget Committees announce whether
upcoming bills obey consistent, negotiate behind
the scenes, and take part in floor debates.[70]

---

[68]   Scorekeeping . . . provides information on the status
of congressional budget decisions. The Congressional
Budget Office (CBO) maintains a data base of
information on budget authority and outlays for each
congressional committee. The data base contains data
on (a) the crosswalk allocation to each committee, (b)
the amounts spend by past actions, and (c) the amounts
spent by current legislation.

Congressional Research Service, Manual on the Federal Budget
Process 75 (1982) (prepared by R. Keith and A. Schick).

[69]   As amended by Gramm-Rudman, section 308(a)(1) provides:

Whenever a committee of either House reports to its
House a bill . . . providing new budget
authority . . . the report accompanying that
bill . . . shall contain a statement . . . --

(A) comparing the levels in such measure to the
appropriate allocations in the reports submitted under
section 302(b) for the most recently agreed to
concurrent resolution on the budget for such fiscal
year; . . . .

(C) containing a projection by the Congressional
Budget Office of how such measure will affect the
levels of such budget authority . . . . for such fiscal
year and each of the four ensuing fiscal years . . . .
(footnote continued)

Beyond mere persuasion, Gramm-Rudman retained, with modifications, the prior points of order and optional enforcement tools for inclusion in budget resolutions. Until the enactment of the annual budget resolution, section 303 of the budget act creates a point of order against any new budget authority. Ordinarily, consistent with section 303, the appropriations committee waits for a budget resolution to know its targets, unless Congress falls far behind schedule in enacting a budget resolution.[71] An exception to section 303, known as the "Fazio exception" after Representative Vic Fazio (D-Calif.), allows consideration of appropriation bills in the House after May 15.

Another point of order comes later in the year, when Congress has spent all the way up to the budget resolution "ceiling" on spending. At that point, section 311(a) creates a point of order against any further spending. Section 311(b) waives the point of order in the House for bills under their suballocation; the Senate has its own waiver mechanisms. Besides these permanent points of order, Congress may include in the budget resolution a provision that defers the enrollment of bills.[72] Deferred enrollment did

---

[70]   See S. Callendar, The Guide to the Federal Budget 47 (1983). The format used in past years for such information, in the House, was the "Early Warning Report." Later, only information memoranda were used, not such Early Warning Reports. With or without such reports, the budget committees may distribute budget information through computerized information systems available to members, "Dear Colleague" letters, Congressional Record inserts, distributions to a mailing list, or the other informal communications networks.

[71]   When Congress falls behind, such as in 1984, the House Appropriations Committee will use the House-passed version of the resolution (or any later version) to provide targets, and the Rules Committee will waive section 303 in a special rule.

[72]   "Deferring" enrollment of a spending bill means that Congress completes all action on the bill -- passage by House and Senate, a conference, and adoption of the (footnote continued)

not prove to be a particularly significant tool when used in 1980-83[73] and was not used in subsequent years.[74]

Gramm-Rudman created a potent point of order supplementing the prior mechanisms. As Professor Kate Stith described this in 1988, "[p]erhaps the most significant [budget process] control mechanism is [Gramm-Rudman's] 'deficit neutrality' rule, which prohibits any floor amendment that

---

conference report -- but then holds onto the bill instead of presenting it to the President. Unlike a point of order, which kills the bill, deferring enrollment merely keeps the bill on hold for possible later reconsideration. Section 301(b)(3) provides that the resolution can: "require a procedure under which all or certain bills or resolutions providing new budget authority or new entitlement authority for such fiscal year shall not be enrolled until the Congress has completed action on any reconciliation bill . . . ."

[73] Deferred enrollment provisions were: section 305 of H. Con. Res. 115, 97th Cong., 1st Sess. (1981); section 4(a) of S. Con. Res. 92, 97th Cong., 2d Sess. (1982); section 4 of H. Con. Res. 91, 98th Cong., 1st Sess. (1983). These were not always noncontroversial; House Members still seething over the shock impact of the 1981 budget process revolted in 1982 and struck the deferred enrollment provision from the first budget resolution, but it was restored in conference.

[74] Deferred enrollment is discussed in Beilenson Report at 57. In 1979, the House Budget Committee first reported a budget resolution with a deferred enrollment provision, but the provision was stripped off the resolution on the House floor on a motion by Appropriations Chair Jamie Whitten (D-Miss.). Representative Whitten said such a provision would leave "no reason for us to proceed with this rigorous schedule in the Appropriations Committee if bills cannot be finalized," and would leave Congress "in a disadvantageous, if not altogether unworkable position -- particularly if Congress adjourned immediately after passing the budget resolution and was placed in a pocket veto situation." 125 Cong. Rec. H2653-54 (daily ed. May 3, 1979). The 1980 provision did not defer every spending bill, like the 1979 provision proposed in the House, but only deferred bills that exceeded the section 302 allocations or suballocations. Section 9(a) of H. Con. Res. 307, 96th Cong., 2d Sess. (1980).

would, in net effect, increase the projected
deficit by exceeding the allocations in the budget
resolution."[75] A point of order in both chambers
bars bills, amendments, and conference reports
that result in exceeding of section 302(b)
suballocations, based on the estimates by the
budget committees. Thus, as Professor Sith notes,
"an amendment to increase funding for a program
. . . simultaneously must reduce funding elsewhere
in the budget or propose some equivalent revenue
gain."[76] In the House, this point of order
applies only to budget authority.[77] However, in

---

[75]   Stith, Rewriting the Fiscal Constitution: The Case of
Gramm-Rudman-Hollings, 76 Calif. L. Rev. 593, 626 (1988).
The conference committee on Gramm-Rudman put in that point
of order against outlays after a highly visible campaign by
Senators Pete Domenici (R-N. Mex.) and Lawton Chiles (D-
Fla.) (chair and ranking minority member on the budget
committee). As Congressional Quarterly described, "The
issue surfaced Sept. 24, when Domenici and Chiles won Senate
approval of an amendment paring 2 percent, about $139
million, from the Treasury funding bill so that it would
comply with the budget resolution's outlay targets." 1985
Congressional Quarterly Almanac 315. The Senate backed
Domenici-Chiles across-the-board cuts to meet outlay targets
on Treasury-Postal Service, transportation, and housing
appropriations, and the Appropriations Committee itself then
cut its State-Justice-Commerce bill to meet the outlay
targets. 1985 Congressional Quarterly Almanac 315, 349.

[76]   Stith, Rewriting the Fiscal Constitution, 76 Calif. L.
Rev. at 626. The point of order is in section 302(g).
Because the point of order applies to conference reports, it
may prevent conference committees from compromising on
appropriations by combining each chamber's high numbers on
particular accounts and bringing back a report over the
suballocation levels.

[77]   Section 302(f)(1) provides in part:

    it shall not be in order in the House of
    Representatives to consider any bill, resolution, or
    amendment providing new budget authority for such
    fiscal year, new entitlement authority effecting during
    such fiscal year, or new credit authority for such
    fiscal year, or any conference report on any such bill

(footnote continued)

the Senate, it also applies to outlays, which may present major problems, for outlays can be a much harder constraint, and waivers in the Senate under Gramm-Rudman require a three-fifths vote.[78]

Traditionally, House Appropriations' reported bills voluntarily stayed within the overall section 302(a) allocation, and most stayed within the 302(b) suballocation, at least for budget authority.[79] Senate Appropriations has also tried to show such discipline in reported bills in the 1980s.[80] However, if self-restraint does not

_____

or resolution, if -- . . . . [it] would cause the appropriate allocation made pursuant to subsection (b) for such fiscal year of new discretionary budget authority, new entitlement authority, or new credit authority to be exceeded.

See Beilenson Report at 59-60 (justifying not having a point of order regarding outlays).

[78] Section 302(f)(2) provides in part: "it shall not be in order in the Senate to consider any bill or resolution (including a conference report thereon), or any amendment to a bill or resolution, that provides for budget outlays or new budget authority in excess of the appropriate allocation of such outlays or authority reported under subsection (b) . . . ." For example, until Gramm-Rudman, the defense appropriations subcommittee could meet a ceiling on budget authority simply by taking unobligated past balances (usually high in the defense department) and reappropriating them for new uses, but while that does not count as new budget authority, it does count as a projected outlay.

[79] Representative Leon Panetta (D-Calif.), then a member of the House Budget Committee, noted in 1982 that "appropriations has never exceeded, since 1974, their 302 targets. Appropriations has stayed within their overall targets established by the budget resolution." Congressional Budget Process Hearings, supra, at 15.

[80] In 1982, Senator Mark Hatfield (R-Oreg.), who chaired Senate Appropriations, "indicated early in the appropriations process that bills would not be reported to the full Senate that exceeded the subcommittee allocation, and every one of the bills reported was under the allocation to the Subcommittee." Year End Report of the 2d Session of the 97th Congress, S. Doc. No. 38, 97th Cong., 2d Sess. 22 (footnote continued)

suffice, the response is usually not outright defeats of appropriations bills on the floor, which are rare for any reason.[81]

Rather, floor sentiment about budgeting pressures expresses itself most readily through across-the-board cuts. The Senate example of the 1985 Domenici-Chiles across-the-board cuts to meet outlay targets is discussed in note 75. In the House, the history of this type of amendment can be traced through the work of Representative Clarence Miller (R-Ohio), who

> has made a career out of one simple amendment -- the one that has led his colleagues to nickname him 'Five Percent Clarence.' Year after year, on bill after bill, he has taken the floor to propose that appropriations be reduced by 5 percent across-the-board, or, if that seems politically impossible, 2 percent, or 5 percent with a few exemptions.[82]

The ranking minority member on House Appropriations had offered across-the-board cut amendments in the 1960s; Representative Miller inherited the tool and offered the amendments in the 1970s and 1980s.[83] Often, the across-the-

---

(1982).

[81] In 1983, the House defeated an appropriations bill on the floor for the first time since 1979, the Treasury-Postal Service appropriation, but even that occurred only by what some might consider a fluke combination of a controversial rider and other controversy over funding. Congressional Quarterly described the defeat as the work of "an odd, informal coalition of House conservatives convinced that the bill was too expensive and 'pro-choice' liberals angered by [an] anti-abortion rider . . . ." 1983 Congressional Quarterly Almanac 533.

[82] Politics in America -- 1986 1211 (A. Ehrenhalt ed. 1985).

[83] In 1976, Miller "offered it to 10 separate bills that year, and never got it passed," and had some ups and downs in the late 1970s. "Only the enormous deficits of the 98th Congress and the difficulty of reducing them any other way brought the Miller method back into fashion." Id. at (footnote continued)

board cut uses various procedural devices of partisan floor combat.[84]

A peak use of the device came in 1981, when President Reagan used his veto to insist on cutting the omnibus continuing resolution, obtaining a complex four per cent across-the-board cut with a number of exceptions and provisions for flexibility.[85] By 1986, the House Democratic leadership had accepted the device: when "[t]he House Democratic leadership ha[d] decided the chamber should observe outlay limits," it used a 1.25 percent across-the-board cut in the omnibus continuing resolution "to bring the overall discretionary spending total down to the so-called '302 allocation.'"[86]

C. AUTHORIZATIONS

Judicial and Congressional Views

The distinction between authorizations and appropriations generates a body of experience and attitudes both outside and inside Congress. Outside Congress, courts and agencies face authorizations and appropriations as a subtle problem in interpretation, as two sets of laws,

---

1212. The same was true of subsequent high-deficit Congresses. 132 Cong. Rec. H4646 (daily ed. July 17, 1986) (across-the-board cut in State-Justice-Commerce appropriation).

[84] For examples, see 1980 Congressional Quarterly Almanac 156 (Miller motion to recommit with instructions the transportation appropriation, for two percent cut); 1983 Congressional Quarterly Almanac 465 (across-the-board cut amendment adopted 211-209 in Committee of the Whole; majority party obtains second vote on amendment in the House, and defeats it 206-213); 1984 Congressional Quarterly Almanac 376 (recommit motion with instructions on State-Justice-Commerce appropriation, for four percent cut).

[85] 1981 Congressional Quarterly Almanac 330-31.

[86] Wehr, House Panel OKs $566.9 Billion Spending Bill, 44 Cong. Q. Week. Rep. 2181, 2182 (1986).

both expressing the "intent of Congress" about the
same programs and agencies, but in different
ways. As a general rule, the courts and agencies
take their basic substantive law from the
authorizing statutes -- the organic statutes for
agencies and programs, plus any temporary
authorizations. Long ago, the courts established,
as a basic rule of interpretation, a presumption
that appropriation bills do not change the
substantive law, absent express language in the
appropriation bill showing the contrary.[87]

Most recently, the Supreme Court confirmed
that rule of interpretation in 1978 in TVA v.
Hill.[88] In that case, the Endangered Species Act,
a piece of permanent substantive legislation,
appeared to bar the Tellico Dam, for the dam
jeopardized the endangered "snail darter," but
Congress had appropriated funds that (according to
appropriations committee reports) included the
dam. Justice Powell, in dissent, took the
appropriations as Congress' sign not to stop the
dam.[89] However, the Court rejected the argument
that the appropriations had overridden the
Endangered Species Act. Instead, the Court relied
upon the congressional rules against

---

[87] In a classic early case in 1886, United States v.
Langston, 118 U.S. 389 (1886), the relevant permanent
authorizing statute for the diplomatic corps provided that
there be an American Minister to Haiti, receiving a salary
of $7,500 per year. However, the appropriation bills for
Fiscal Year 1883, 1884, and 1885 provided only $5,000 per
year, and the minister sued for the difference. The Supreme
Court decided that the appropriation bill lacked "express
words of repeal," 118 U.S. at 394, or otherwise effective
expressions of change in the prior authorizing law, and so
it held for the minister.

[88] 437 U.S. 153 (1978).

[89] He pointed to the understanding in the appropriations
committee reports that the snail darter would not block the
Tellico Dam, and contended, "[w]e cannot assume -- as the
Court suggests -- that Congress, when it continued each year
to approve the recommended appropriations, was unaware of
the contents of the supporting Committee Reports." Id. at
210.

appropriations bills making changes in the law, as confirming the presumption against such overriding (absent express language):

> There is nothing in the appropriations measures, as passed, which states that the Tellico Project was to be completed irrespective of the requirements of the Endangered Species Act . . . . We recognize that both substantive enactments and appropriations measures are "Acts of Congress," but the latter have the limited and specific purpose of providing funds for authorized programs . . . . [R]epealing by implication [from appropriations] any prior statute which might prohibit the expenditure . . . would flout the very rules the Congress carefully adopted to avoid this need.[90]

Although the courts and agencies presume an appropriation does not change the law, they allow that presumption to be rebutted, and in some circumstances find in an appropriation of money a "ratification" by Congress.[91]

The presumption against interpreting appropriations as providing authority or overriding law can produce dramatic clashes, for the Executive Branch may justify unauthorized actions by citing appropriations. For example, legal critics of the Vietnam War contended that the Nixon administration exceeded its authority by

---

[90] 437 U.S. at 190-91.

[91] For example, in a case challenging the imposition of grazing fees for public lands, the Supreme Court found "[t]he repeated appropriation of the proceeds of the fees . . . . constitutes a ratification of the action of the Secretary [of Interior] as the agent of Congress . . . ." in setting them. Brooks v. Dewar, 313 U.S. 354, 361 (1941). Similarly, in a case challenging the operation (pursuant to an executive order) of an office of temporary price controls, the Court found the appropriation for salaries and expenses of the office to be "an acceptance or ratification by Congress of the President's action in [the] Executive Order." Fleming v. Mohawk Wrecking & Lumber Co., 331 U.S. 111, 119 (1947).

maintaining and expanding the war, in the absence
of a declaration of war or equivalent enactment,
particularly after Congress repealed the Tonkin
Gulf Resolution. To show legal authority for the
war, the President's supporters cited not only his
inherent powers, but also the Congress' enactment,
year after year, of the appropriations to maintain
the war. The courts heard cases on the issue, but
stayed out of it, largely in regard for their own
limited role in war matters.[92]   Ultimately, the
War Powers Resolution sought to resolve the issue
for future wars by prescribing that appropriations
not be interpreted as war authority, absent very
specific language.[93]

On the other hand, if Congress puts explicit
legislative language in an appropriation bill,
then that is as valid as any language in an
authorization law. The typical appropriation bill
provides a large number of policy directives in
limitation language, such as the Hyde Amendment to
the Labor-HHS appropriation that "none of the
funds provided by this act shall be used to
perform abortions" (with various exceptions, such
as in cases of rape or incest).   In 1980, the
Supreme Court upheld the Hyde Amendment against
constitutional challenge.[94]

---

[92]   Of course, the issue was bound up with larger questions
of the respective war powers of Congress and the
President. The issue and the litigation are discussed in A.
M. Schlesinger, Jr., The Imperial Presidency 280-84 (1973).

[93]   Section 8(a)(1) of the War Powers Resolution provides:
"Authority to introduce United States Armed Forces into
hostilities . . . shall   not   be   inferred   from
any . . . provision contained in any appropriation Act,
unless such provision specifically . . . states that it is
intended to constitute specific statutory authorization
within the meaning of this joint resolution . . . ."

[94]   Harris v. McRae, 448 U.S. 297 (1980). The Court treated
Medicaid, and the Labor-HHS Appropriation, as a classic
authorization-appropriation pair; Medicaid authorized the
funding of operations for the indigent, but did not require
it, and the later appropriation limitation settled the
question whether the particular appropriation funded
particular operations. The Court declined to find that the
(footnote continued)

These legal understandings outside Congress of the division between authorizations and appropriations set the stage for the balance of power within Congress.   The foreign aid appropriations and authorization provide an example of the balance between authorization and appropriation processes, and particularly between the authorization committees and appropriations subcommittees with jurisdiction regarding the same agencies and programs.

In 1981, Congress passed both a foreign aid authorization and a foreign aid appropriation, with the two bills largely playing accustomed roles.   The authorization bill established policy in many aspects on a nation by nation basis, such as requiring presidential certifications of human rights progress as a condition for aid to El Salvador.   It provided an overall authorization for amount of foreign aid and a number of earmarkings of funds for particular countries and programs.[95]   The appropriation bill stated amounts of money, country by country and program by program, with some limitation provisions (for example, prohibiting the use of funds for the United Nations Decade for Women).[96]

In that situation, the appropriation subcommittee functioned to a significant degree as the junior partner to the authorizing committee, the Foreign Affairs committee, which made the substantive law.   However, in 1982, 1983, and 1984, Congress did not pass foreign aid authorization bills, because of lack of administration support and because "leaders of both parties showed no enthusiasm for devoting days of floor time to the politically difficult issues posed by foreign aid."[97]   Inability to move

---

Medicaid authorization law required states to fund abortions on their own even with the federal funding restriction.   It interpreted the Medicaid law as only requiring states to fund operations when the federal government cooperated in the funding, and the limitation rider meant the federal government had declined to cooperate regarding abortions. 448 U.S. at 308-11.

[95]   1981 Congressional Quarterly Almanac 161.

[96]   1981 Congressional Quarterly Almanac 340. (footnote continued)

authorization bills not only relaxed congressional
control over the administration, it shifted power
from   the   authorizing   committee   to   the
appropriations subcommittee.[98]   "In the Senate,
Foreign Operations Subcommittee Chairperson Bob
Kasten (R-Wis.) seemed to relish the power,
reportedly telling Reagan officials and lobbyists
for foreign governments that he held the purse
strings for foreign aid."[99]   Then, in 1985,
Congress again enacted a foreign aid authorization
as it had in 1981, shifting the power back.[100]

Thus, just as courts and agencies presume
appropriations have a limited role but may
sometimes accord them a greater role in

---

[97]   1983 Congressional Quarterly Almanac 140 (noting
observation of Chairperson Clem Zablocki (D-Wis.) of House
Foreign Affairs Committee about the failure to enact in
1983). The 1981 foreign aid authorization had been for two
years, so in 1982 the Foreign Affairs Committees only wanted
to pass a "supplemental" authorization a fraction of the
size of the annual bill, but even that did not receive floor
consideration in either chamber.   1982 Congressional
Quarterly Almanac at 156. In 1983 neither chamber passed
the authorization, 1983 Congressional Quarterly Almanac
140. In 1984 the House passed an authorization, but the
Senate did not, "facing protracted debate and a losing race
against the election-year calendar."   1984 Congressional
Quarterly Almanac 84.

[98]   As Congressional Quarterly described:

Foreign Relations was responsible for authorizing
legislation, which set overall policy guidelines for
appropriations bills. But from 1982 through 1984, the
House and Senate Appropriations committees, and their
respective Foreign Operations subcommittees, had
wielded most of the congressional power over foreign
aid.   That was because Congress failed to enact
authorization bills but did enact appropriations as
part of omnibus continuing resolutions.

1985 Congressional Quarterly Almanac 376.

[99]   1985 Congressional Quarterly Almanac 376.

[100]   1985 Congressional Quarterly Almanac 376.

ratification, limitation, or explicit change in the law, so within Congress, appropriations start with limited policymaking power but may sometimes increase their power.   Much depends on floor action, particularly the extent to which authorizing committees move their bills, appropriation bills contain provisions taking power, or other players -- the administration, Members not on the committees, or interest groups -- choose either type of bill as their vehicle for floor amendments.

Periodic Authorizations

As suggested above, "[a]nnual authorizations, once rare, are now commonplace . . . .   In the last three decades, many permanent and multiyear authorizations were transformed into annual authorizations."[101]   This key development in appropriations warrants close examination.   The trend developed with greatest continuity in the realm of national security.   In 1948, Congress implemented the Marshall Plan for foreign aid to Europe, but subjected it to annual authorizations to provide flexibility and control.[102]   In 1959, after Congress learned of costly duplication in Army and Air Force procurement, it subjected military procurement to annual authorization; in 1962, it subjected military research and development to such authorization; and in 1980, it extended that authorization to operation and maintenance.[103]   The 1959, 1962, and 1980 changes consisted of the Armed Services Committees enacting into law a requirement for annual authorization that gave those same committees a new annual role.   Those enactments responded either to military problems warranting oversight or to jockeying with the appropriations committees.

In the civilian area, Congress in the 1950s,

---

101   Beilenson Report at 39.

102   Fisher, Annual Authorizations, at 31.

103   Fisher, Annual Authorization, at 33.

1960s, and 1970s created new agencies subjected to annual authorization, such as the National Aeronautics and Space Administration, the Peace Corps, the Federal Election Commission, the Department of Energy, and the Panama Canal Commission.[104] In the era of Watergate, Congress developed new serious concerns about parts of the Executive being out of control, and about the President setting too much policy, and it began extending annual authorization to established agencies.[105]

For each of these agencies, Congress expected to enact an annual authorization bill as a prelude to the annual appropriation. This provided a focus for oversight, a vehicle for policy direction and specific conditions, and a ceiling under which appropriations would set the actual level of spending.[106] A subcommittee chair on the Foreign Affairs Committee, Representative Steve Solarz (D-N.Y.), explained the political significance of the periodic foreign aid authorization:

> oversight detached from legislation relating

---

[104]   Id. at 34.

[105]   Until [1972], the Department of State was covered by a permanent authorization. A series of executive-legislative clashes, particularly the withholding of information from Congress, led to annual authorization . . . .

The obvious failure of the Appropriations and Armed Services Committees to oversee the Central Intelligence Agency resulted in the creation of legislative committees and the imposition of annual authorization. The Justice Department came under annual authorization in 1976 after Congress uncovered systematic abuses of agency authority, especially by the Federal Bureau of Investigation.

Fisher, Annual Authorizations, at 35.

[106]   House Comm. on the Budget, 95th Cong., 1st Sess., Congressional Control of Expenditures 24-25 (Comm. Print 1977).

>to money is oversight which is not likely to
>have a very great impact.   It is precisely
>our capacity -- to a large extent exclusively
>our capacity -- to affect the levels of
>foreign aid on a country-by-country, or
>region-by-region, or program-by-program basis
>[that gives strength to oversight].   This
>legislation annually is the only vehicle that
>presents itself for expression of the views
>of the House on foreign policy matters.[107]

Naturally the appropriations committees may see
the   authorizations   process   as   taking   away
authority or as upsetting their schedule.[108]
     In the 1980s, the trend towards a potent
authorization process waned somewhat.   Stalemates
occurred very commonly on annual reauthorization
bills.   The   authorizing   committees   in   the
Democratic House and the Republican Senate (during
1981-86)   often   did   not   share   each   other's
enthusiasms, such as, respectively, for critical
oversight rolling back administration initiatives,
and   for   supportive   oversight   enacting   those
initiatives into permanent law.   The result was a
diminution -- whether desirable or not -- in the
availability   of   periodic   authorizations   as   a
policymaking   vehicle.[109]   For   authorizing

---

[107] Congressional Budget Act Amendments of 1984: H.R. Rept.
No. 1152, 98th Cong., 2d Sess. 40 (1984) (quoting 1981
hearing).

[108] As the House Appropriations Committee complained about
the 1979-80 period:

>The   apparent   inability   of   the   Congress   to   enact
>authorizing legislation prior to the consideration of
>appropriations bills is severely distorting the whole
>appropriation process.   The Committee must, on a
>routine basis, either waive the House rule requiring
>authorization or else have significant parts of the
>[appropriations] bill eliminated due to a lack of
>authorizing legislation.

Report of Committee Activities -- 96th Congress, H.R. Rep.
No. 1562, 96th Cong., 2d Sess. 3 (1981).

(footnote continued)

committees to make binding law, they had to resort
to two alternatives in the absence of a fully
functioning authorization process: riders on
appropriations, or provisions on omnibus vehicles
such as reconciliation bills.

Apart from regular annual or periodic
authorizations, a different set of battles occurs
between the authorizations and appropriating
committees. These battles concern issues which
each committee believes its own vehicle should
resolve. The authorizing committee may want to
set either detailed maximums, or earmarked
minimums, for spending. Meanwhile, the
appropriations subcommittee contends that the
authorizing committee should only adopt broad
ceilings, stick to legislating, and leave it to
appropriations to decide in detail where funds
should go.

Several examples of such disputes illustrate
the varied ways Congress responds to them, by
negotiation, pressure, leadership arbitration, or
simply by enduring a deadlock.[110] Major turf
battles in the 1980s pitted each chamber's Armed
Services Committee against its Defense
Appropriations Subcommittee. As Congressional
Quarterly described the Senate's "long-running
jurisdictional fight over spending levels" in
1985: "At stake this time was some $7.6 billion,
spread across nearly 100 defense programs. In
each case, the Senate Appropriations Subcommittee
on Defense had approved more than had been allowed
by the Senate Armed Services Committee."[111] A
"compromise was adopted by voice vote . . . in an
amendment to the continuing resolution," which
"made the Armed Services ceilings binding for
broad categories of programs . . . but not for

---

[109] Legislating committees did not simply give up: for
example, the House Judiciary Committee conscientiously
marked up and reported, each year, an annual authorization
bill, which the full House generally passed. That bill gave
considerable guidance to the House Appropriations Committee,
even if it was not binding law.

[110] For other examples and further analysis, see Fisher at
60-67.

[111] 1985 Congressional Quarterly Almanac 391.

specific projects."[112]

A similar battle in the House in 1988 put the Armed Services Committee and the Defense Appropriations Subcommittee "at loggerheads over $4.3 billion in defense funding add-ons" inserted by the latter, without authorization, in the continuing resolution.[113] This issue was resolved by an agreement, which made spending subject to later authorization, decided at a meeting with Speaker Jim Wright (D-Tex.).

Another classic turf battle occurred in the House in 1984 over mass transit funds between the authorizing committee, Public Works and Transportation, and the Transportation Appropriations Subcommittee, when "[e]ach committee claimed authority to earmark funds and impose caps on obligations."[114] When no solution could be worked out, Public Works urged defeat of the special rule providing waivers for the unauthorized appropriations, "[t]he House leadership was not able to arbitrate the dispute, and it became necessary to include funding for transportation programs in the continuing resolution."[115]

One final example follows from the previous discussion of the balance between the foreign aid appropriations subcommittee, and the foreign affairs committees. When the foreign affairs

---

112   Any funds appropriated for the categories -- or "accounts" -- above the level set by the authorization bill (S 1160) could not be spent until Congress enacted separate legislation authorizing the funds . . . .

[B]ecause the authorizations were made binding for accounts rather than specific projects, only about $3.2 billion of the $7.6 billion would require separate authorization.

1985 Congressional Quarterly Almanac 391.

113   Mills, Authorizers, Appropriators Declare a Truce, 46 Cong. Q. Week. Rep. 1142 (1988).

114   1984 Congressional Quarterly Almanac 413.

115   1984 Congressional Quarterly Almanac 411.

committees enacted an authorization in 1985, the appropriations subcommittee tried to retain the authority secured by default in prior years by "add[ing] to the appropriations bill an obscure item, section 523, that would have had the effect of repealing many of the most important provisions of the authorization bill: the "earmarks" and prohibitions that set minimum or maximum amounts of aid for individual countries and groups.[116] The appropriations subcommittee chair ultimately backed down in the face of strong bipartisan opposition from the Senate Foreign Relations Committee.[117]

As these examples show, such disputes arise rather naturally from the uncertain division of power, as authorizing committees attempt to dictate funding by earmarking, and appropriating subcommittees attempt to make policy by legislative provisions or appropriations above authorizations. If the disputing committees do not settle the matter by negotiation, sometimes the leadership (including, in the House, the Rules Committee) can resolve it. However, the ultimate resolution may come on the floor, in a vote by the chamber on amendments to the authorization or appropriation bill.

House Rules and Waivers on Unauthorized Appropriations

In light of these considerations, the details of the rules and waivers in the House can be usefully described. The House establishes its authorization requirement in Rule XXI(2)(a): "No appropriation shall be reported in any general appropriation bill, or shall be in order as an amendment thereto, for any expenditure not previously authorized by law, except to continue appropriations for public works and objects which are already in progress." The rule applies only to the "general appropriation bill," which includes regular and supplemental appropriations,

---

[116]   1985 Congressional Quarterly Almanac 377.

[117]   1985 Congressional Quarterly Almanac 377.

but not continuing resolutions or the occasional very narrow ("special") appropriations.[118]

Congress authorizes clearly when it includes explicit provisions either in organic acts creating departments, or in periodic authorizations. Disputes may occasionally occur as to whether general language in those authorizing acts provides specific enough authorization for some program. For example, the Chair ruled out of order early attempts to appropriate for an employment service in the Department of Labor. The Department's organic act pronounced generally the duty of the Department "to advance [the] opportunities" of "the wage earners of the United States" for "profitable employment." However, the Chair considered that if such purely precatory and "very peculiar language as contained in this organic act," "like the whereas of a resolution," authorized such expenditures, "there is absolutely no limitation that you could put upon your Committee on Appropriation."[119] On the other hand, the organic authority for a department does authorize necessarily incidental expenditures even when not explicitly mentioned, like law books for the Army, or shore patrol expenses for the Navy.[120]

The rule's language requiring appropriations be "previously authorized by law" has one powerful effect. It is not enough to satisfy the rule that the House has passed an authorizing bill; the authorization must pass both the House and the

---

[118]   House Manual § 835.   Special appropriations concern limited purposes, such as a narrow supplemental bill only for certain public works.   VII Cannon § 1122.

[119]   VII Cannon § 1264.

[120]   VII Cannon §§ 1234, 1273.   In upholding the shore patrol appropriation as authorized, the Chair commented, "In the view of the Chair the question seems to come down to whether this duty is such an incident of the operation of the Navy Department which is to be performed by officers acting under orders as to make it a necessary part of the conduct of the navy for which an expenditure can be incurred without specific detailed authority in a legislative act." VII Cannon § 1234, at 292.

Senate, be presented to the President, and thereby become "law."[121]   Also, appropriations cannot exceed the specific amount authorized.   For example, when existing law authorized $7,500 for the National Board for the Promotion of Rifle Practice, an appropriation for $10,000 was out of order as unauthorized.[122] More abstruse questions occasionally arise as to whether appropriations are authorized by "law" when authorized by executive orders (no), treaties (yes), or asserted general constitutional duties of the President (usually no).[123]

Regarding the mechanics of points of order, first, the House either takes up an appropriation bill without a special rule, or takes up a special rule containing waivers of points of order.   When the House takes up the appropriation bill itself, potential objectors must reserve points of order concerning the bill (not waived by the special rule) when the House refers the bill to the Committee of the Whole.[124] The Committee of the Whole reads appropriation bills for amendment paragraph by paragraph, and the "window" for making a point of order is after the pertinent paragraph is read, but before any amendments are

---

[121] Deschler 25 § 5.3. Because the appropriation must be "previously authorized by law," technically the House cannot appropriate, even if it adds a proviso that the money will become available subsequently only upon enactment of authorizing legislation.

[122] Deschler 25 § 8.2.

[123] For executive orders, see Deschler 25 §§ 7.1, 7.20, 8.22; for treaties, VII Cannon § 1137. Regarding the President's constitutional duties, compare VII Cannon §§ 1144, 1197 (duty to report to Congress regarding proposed legislation does not, in itself, authorize an appropriation) with VII Cannon § 1248 (duty to recognize governments and nominate ambassadors authorizes salaries for those ambassadors).

[124] House Manual § 835; Deschler 25 § 21.28. Typically, some Member, such as the ranking minority member on the subcommittee, announces to the House when the bill is being reported that points of order are being reserved.

offered or the next paragraph is read.[125]

   At the time of a point of order, it is the
proponent of the appropriation -- either the
Committee on Appropriations for an appropriation
in the bill, or the proponent of a floor amendment
-- who has the burden of demonstrating, in the
face of any objection, that the appropriation is
authorized. These can often be difficult points
of order to resolve, as they involve construing
not only House rules and precedents, but the
various authorizing law schemes for each of the
myriad of agencies and programs. It is thus not a
bit surprising that Members may use memoranda of
law to bolster their case, and that the Chair may
rule out some appropriation as unauthorized and
then later reverse its ruling when the proponents
finally locate some obscure authority for the
appropriation.[126]

   The key question often becomes whether there
will be a special rule with waivers, and if so,
which waivers. Particularly when the House has
enacted an authorization bill, and only the Senate
has balked, proponents have a strong case to
obtain a waiver for the "unauthorized"
appropriation since the appropriation subcommittee
has not usurped the role of the House authorizing
committee. Proponents may also have a strong case
when the Rules Committee has reason to look with
favor on the appropriation.[127] For example, in
1988, the Rules Committee provided waivers on the
Transportation Appropriation for some, but not
all, water projects being sought. A Rules

---

[125] House Manual § 835; Deschler 25 §§ 21, 22.

[126] Deschler 25 § 6.4 (Department of Justice legal
opinion); House Manual § 835 (Chair's reversal).

[127] Congressional Quarterly reported, regarding a
supplemental appropriation for water projects: "When the
Public Works and Transportation Committee objected to
Appropriations' inclusion of unauthorized projects in the
spending package, Rules issued a rule that left a number of
them vulnerable to a point of order when the bill reached
the floor. But the rule protected most of the projects
sought by Rules members . . . ." Plattner, Rules Members
Gain By Helping Others, 43 Cong. Q. Week. Rep. 1673 (1985).

Committee member, Representative David Bonior (D-Mich.), explained as follows:

> Bonior, whose project received a waiver, said
> that in reviewing requests for waivers, Rules
> typically considers merit, the personal ties
> between the sponsor of a provision and
> members of the Rules committee, diligence
> with which a sponsor lobbies Rules for a
> waiver, and the members' record on voting
> against rules reported by the panel.[128]

On the other hand, opponents of controversial programs may threaten, sometimes successfully, to defeat a rule waiving points of order, arguing that such waivers take the force out of a drive to enact a new authorization with substantive restrictions (or even to eliminate the program). An illustration is the State-Justice-Commerce appropriation, about which the subcommittee chair, Representative Neil Smith (D-Iowa), commented dryly "I do not know why it is that our little old bills always get into somebody else's arguments."[129]
Those "little old bills" fund legal services and the Federal Trade Commission, among many other bones of contention, which had been the targets of efforts to completely defund or to sharply restrict. In 1982, when the Rules Committee reported its first rule for the State-Justice-Commerce Appropriation to the floor, the House defeated the previous question, and the Rules Committee withdrew it from the floor by a motion to refer it back to committee. The Rules Committee reported a second rule that did not waive points of order for the FTC, and this time the rule passed. On a point of order during consideration of the appropriation bill, the Chair ruled funding for the FTC out of order as unauthorized.[130] In 1983 and 1984, Chairperson

---

[128]   Starobin, $10.6 Billion OK'd for Transportation Programs, 46 Cong. Q. Week. Rep. 1758, 1759 (1988).

[129]   128 Cong. Rec. H9240 (daily ed. Dec. 9, 1982).

[130]   128 Cong. Rec. H9225 (daily ed. Dec. 9, 1982).

Smith refused even to obtain a special rule with waivers, and accordingly, large parts of his appropriation were struck on the floor as unauthorized.[131] In 1985, Chairperson Smith went back to the Rules Committee, and obtained a special rule which "allowed funding of some 32 agencies and programs in the Commerce-Justice-State bill that had not yet been authorized for fiscal year 1986."[132]

Thus, the Appropriations Committee has an uneasy relationship with the Rules Committee: protective rules help smooth the path of appropriations, but the Appropriations Committee considers it a favor to others more than to it for such rules to be adopted. To recount one dramatic historic incident:

> When, on a supplemental bill in 1955, the Committee on Rules refused to grant a rule waiving points of order, Chairman Cannon [of the Appropriations Committee] decided to pound this point home to the House. He and another Committee leader stood on the floor and offered objections to every item carrying legislation, and every one to which they objected was thrown out on a point of order. The bill which was reported to the

---

[131] 1984 Congressional Quarterly Almanac 376; 1983 Congressional Quarterly Almanac 475. As Congressional Quarterly described in 1983:

> As reported by the Appropriations Committee, the bill had provided $10.69 billion. But by the time the House finished with it, the total had been trimmed to $6.71 billion. The cuts were the result of points of order lodged against funding for programs that had not yet been authorized . . . .

1983 Congressional Quarterly Almanac 475. These incidents did not lead to elimination of the FTC or Legal Services, but to their being funded at later stages of the enactment process, as described below.

[132] 1985 Congressional Quarterly Almanac 348. The rule passed by only 234-188, reflecting the traditional controversy.

House carrying $1.2 billion on July 12
carried only $224 million when it was passed
two days later. The anguish and
consternation of House members were
prodigious. But the lesson was clear.
Waiver rules help the Appropriations
Committee; but they may help House members as
well.[133]

Senate Rules on Unauthorized Appropriations

The Senate takes a much more relaxed stance
towards unauthorized appropriations. The Senate
starts with its Rule VI, which, like the House's
similar rule, forbids unauthorized appropriations,
whether they "increase an appropriation" or "add a
new item": "On a point of order made by any
Senator, no amendments shall be received to any
general appropriation bill the effect of which
will be to increase an appropriation already
contained in the bill, or to add a new item of
appropriation, unless it be made to carry out the
provisions of some existing law . . . ." The rule
concerns amendments, not the bill itself, because
typically the bill originated and was passed by
the House, and the Senate does not raise points of
order against the House's decisions to included
unauthorized appropriations.

Rather, the Senate rule sets forth a series
of exceptions. Appropriations can be authorized,
not only by existing law, but also by "act or
resolution previously passed by the Senate during
that session." This contrasts with the House,
which requires enactment of authorization into law
(i.e., by the Senate and House, with presentation
to the President) rather than mere passage by the
chamber alone.[134] Also, the rule accepts an
unauthorized appropriation if moved either by the

---

[133]   Fenno at 424.

[134]   In practice, though, the House looks much more
favorably, in giving waivers through special rules, on
appropriations for which authorizations have at least passed
the House, and so the House and Senate do not differ so much
on this.

Committee on Appropriations or the "committee of
the Senate having legislative jurisdiction of the
subject matter."[135]   These committees can move
such appropriations "in excess of authorizations
or even in the absence of any legislative
authority as long as the proposed amendment does
not contain legislation."[136]   The rule thus does
not guard against the Appropriations Committee
funding unauthorized programs; it only prevents
individual Senators from doing so on the floor
without committee sanction.[137]

The Senate constrains these exceptions a bit
by not providing similar shielding against points
of order under the related prohibition, discussed
below, against "legislation" on appropriations.[138]   Rule XVI(2) specifically forbids the
Committee on Appropriations to report legislation

---

[135]   Senate Rule XVI. The Senate rule does prevent surprise
unauthorized amendments by legislative committees, since an
additional provision requires a referral to the
Appropriations Committee before a legislative committee can
move an unauthorized appropriation on the floor.   Rule
XVI(3) provides:

> All amendments to general appropriations bills moved by
> direction of a committee having legislative
> jurisdiction of the subject matter proposing to
> increase an appropriation already contained in the
> bill, or to add new items of appropriation, shall, at
> least one day before they are considered, be referred
> to the Committee on Appropriations, and when actually
> proposed to the bill no amendment proposing to increase
> the amount stated in such amendment shall be received
> on a point of order made by any Senator.

[136]   Riddick, "Appropriations: Amendments to General
Appropriations Bills -- When in Order: Reported by
Appropriations Committee, an Increase of New Item," at 150.

[137]   For example, El Salvador aid in 1984, discussed below,
was in order in the Senate even though unauthorized as an
Appropriations Committee proposal.

[138]   Riddick, "Appropriations: Amendments to General
Appropriations Bills -- When in Order: Legislation to a
General Appropriation Bill Not in Order," at 157.

on appropriations, even while Rule XVI(1) lets the committee report unauthorized appropriations.[139] There remains the political barrier, that an authorizing committee might contest an unauthorized appropriation as encroaching on its turf, which does happen. A common compromise is to allow the appropriation, contingent on a subsequent authorization.[140]

Even apart from the looseness of the stated exceptions,[141] the Senate often ignores the rule requiring authorizations. Often, points of order will not be made, particularly when the Senate has previously endorsed a program, such as by a vote on a budget resolution or a vote in previous years.[142] When the law must be interpreted to

---

[139] For example, in 1984, Legal Services lacked its authorization. Rule XVI(1) let the Appropriations Committee report funding for it anyway. However, when the committee included the restrictions on Legal Services' activities that would be in an authorization, Senator Helms made a point of order, which the Chair sustained, that the restrictions were legislation on an appropriation. 130 Cong. Rec. S8586 (daily ed. June 28, 1984).

[140] Water projects have furnished examples of the tensions, as the Appropriations Committee wants to go ahead with funding for projects when the authorizing committee has not yet resolved the political deadlock over their authorization. 128 Cong. Rec. S8887 (daily ed. June 22, 1983). The solution is sometimes contingent appropriation. See, e.g., 128 Cong. Rec. S8420 (daily ed. June 15, 1983) (health insurance program contingent upon subsequent authorization).

[141] Also, the rule accepts appropriations authorized by "an estimate submitted in accordance with law," a courtly phrasing of the President's budget submissions (which, before 1921, were departmental estimates). However, these cannot include items in the President's budget "in excess of a specified authorization . . . particularly when the budget acknowledges the need for additional legislative authorization." Riddick, "Appropriations: Amendments to General Appropriations Bills -- When in Order: Budget Estimates Pursuant to Law," at 143.

[142] See, e.g., 128 Cong. Rec. S8420 (daily ed. June (footnote continued)

determine whether it authorizes an appropriation, the Chair submits the question to the Senate for a decision under Rule XX, leaving the Senators to vote as they wish.[143] More generally, even when the Chair rules, the Senate can, and on occasion does, vote on appeal to overrule it.[144] Other safety valves for unauthorized appropriations besides the Senate's loose practice include the addition of such appropriations by the conference committee[145] or their inclusion in a continuing resolution.

To illustrate how the two chambers treat

15,1983) (allowing amendment to fund health care benefits for the unemployed, subject to a subsequent authorization being passed; the lack of authorization is excused because the Senate had voted 90-9 during the budget resolution's consideration in favor of this program); 128 Cong. Rec. S15446 (daily ed. Nov. 4, 1983) (allowing amendment denying funds to countries failing to control drugs notwithstanding possible points of order; Senator John C. Stennis (D-Miss.) notes "[t]he fact that Senator has offered this amendment on several occasions and it has never been defeated . . . . [s]hows the great strength the Senator has for his proposal . . . .").

[143]   Riddick, "Appropriations: Amendments to General Appropriations Bills -- When in Order: Authorization -- Interpretation of Law Decided by Senate," at 142.   In contrast, in the House the Chair will rule without submitting the point of order to the chamber.

[144]   Thus, for example, in the 1984 case of Senator Helms' point of order on Legal Services, the Chair's ruling was appealed and overruled by the overwhelming vote of 72-17. The argument for overruling made no attempt to justify the appropriation as complying in any way with the technical requirements of the authorization rule, being couched solely in practical terms that "[t]he problem we have with Legal Services Corporation is for 4 years we have not had an authorization bill."   130 Cong. Rec. S8586 (daily ed. June 28, 1984).

[145]   House Rule XX(2) specifically bars House conferees from accepting Senate unauthorized appropriations or legislation on appropriations, but this has been circumvented by the use of amendments in technical disagreement, as discussed in the chapter on conference reports.

unauthorized appropriations, in 1984 the administration sought funding for aid to Central America, particularly to El Salvador, as an unauthorized appropriation on a supplemental appropriation bill. In the House, the Chair struck the proposal as out of order. As Congressional Quarterly noted, "Jack Brooks, D-Texas, who was presiding over the House [technically, the Committee of the Whole] during the debate, wasted no time in sustaining [Clarence] Long's [(D-Md.)] objection. "It's not authorized and everybody knows it," said Brooks.[146]   In the Senate, however, the Appropriations Committee reported the funding, so the unauthorized appropriations were not subject to a point of order. Accordingly, Senator Christopher Dodd (D-Conn.) offered an amendment

> to prohibit Congress from spending more than was authorized in existing legislation.
>
> "I'm saying you shouldn't spend taxpayers' money on something that you haven't authorized," said Dodd.
>
> [Appropriations subcommittee chair] Kasten acknowledged that Congress had not authorized the increased money . . . . But he said that the need for the money in the troubled region outweighed Dodd's procedural objections.
>
> "It's not the right way to do it but it's the only way to do it," said Kasten. Dodd's amendment was rejected 37-62.[147]

The dispute over the unauthorized appropriation deadlocked the conference committee, until the

---

[146]   1984 Congressional Quarterly Almanac 442.   "Brooks' blunt language was reported more diplomatically in that day's Congressional Record. 'Failing any citations to laws authorizing the appropriations contained in the amendment, the chair sustains the point of order,' the Record quoted Brooks in a polite alteration of what he actually said." Id.

[147]   1984 Congressional Quarterly Almanac 442-43.

House conferees came back to the House floor for a
specific vote to accept a high level of
unauthorized funding for El Salvador.[148]

D.   LEGISLATION AND LIMITATION RIDERS

Although House and Senate rules prohibit
legislation on appropriation bills, Congress makes
extensive use of such "legislative riders." Since
Congress must pass (and usually the President must
sign) appropriations bills for the government to
function, those bills' comprehensiveness and
likelihood of passage makes them irresistible
vehicles. "Riders" already had such importance in
the nineteenth century that an 1895 treatise on
political science devoted three pages of small
print to the topic "Riders (in U.S.
History)."[149] Congress has dealt with numerous
major controversial issues through riders on
appropriations, from slavery in the territories,
and Congress's Reconstruction struggle with
President Andrew Johnson, to the ending of
American involvement in the Indochina War.[150]
    For a number of reasons, riders on
appropriation bills rose to new and incredible
heights of significance in the 1970s.[151] In 1970,
only 13 limitation riders had been offered on the
House floor, and the House had adopted only
one;[152] a decade later, for the appropriation

---

[148] Id. 439.

[149] III Cyclopaedia of Political Science, Political
Economy, and of the Political History of the United States
642-645 (J. J. Lalor ed. 1895) ("Lalor").

[150] Lalor at 643 (slavery and Reconstruction); T. M. Franck
& E. Weisband, Foreign Policy By Congress 20 (1979)
(Indochina).

[151] The Appropriations Committee themselves used large
numbers of riders, and floods of them came on the floor as a
major response to the new availability of recorded votes on
amendments in the House and the general slippage of previous
control by committee chairs.
(footnote continued)

bills for fiscal 1981, 74 limitation riders were offered on the House floor, and the House adopted 57.[153]   By that time, riders nosed out regular spending amendments in significance, as on the 1980 Treasury-Postal Service bill: "Of the two days of House debate devoted this year to the [bill], for example, scarcely an hour was given to discussion of money matters.   The rest revolved around a string of controversial riders . . . . Of the 19 amendments adopted, only one altered the funds appropriated in the bill."[154]

In the 1980s, conservative Members used riders for major parts of their social agenda, notably abortion and school prayer.   However, the overall numbers of riders adopted on the floor declined in the 1980s, due to a general decline in the number of floor amendments and recorded votes and the adoption of the House rule designed to curb limitation riders.

House Rules: Legislation and Rules Waivers

Starting with the House and then the Senate, this section discusses the rules concerning legislation on appropriations, and then the issue of limitations.   For legislation, House Rule XXI(2)(a) sets forth two separate restrictions. One aims at bills reported by the Appropriations Committee: "No provision changing existing law shall be reported in any general appropriation billl . . . ."   The precedents regarding this rule constitute a whole universe in themselves. Precedents since 1937 regarding legislation on appropriations take up most of a 1300-page volume of Deschler's Precedents.[155]

---

[152]   Murray, House Funding Bill Riders Become Potent Policy Force, 38 Cong. Q. Week. Rep. 3251, 3252 (1980).

[153]   Richard B. Sachs, Limitation and Other House Amendments to General Appropriation Bills: Fiscal Years 1979-1983 9 (1982) (Congressional Research Service).

[154]   Murray, supra, at 3251.

[155]   Volume 8 of Deschler's Precedents covers both (footnote continued)

Three of the key principles warrant special mention. This rule precludes a number of possible gambits for appropriations language to change existing law, such as making funds available beyond the next fiscal year,[156] or "mandat[ing] a distribution of funds in contravention of an allocation in existing law."[157] Accordingly, this rule makes programs like food stamps a quasi-entitlement: once the authorization bill specifies the formula or allocation for funds, an attempt on the appropriation to substitute a different formula would be legislation.[158] Rule XXI(2)(a) also includes an express exception, the so-called

---

unauthorized appropriations and legislation on appropriation bills. The volume is 1322 pages long.

[156] The rule forbids provisions "permitting funds to remain available until expended or beyond the fiscal year covered by the bill . . . or [by] merely permit[ting] availability to the extent provided in advance in appropriation Acts but not explicitly beyond the fiscal year in question." House Manual § 842a.

Formerly, an appropriations bill could not transfer or condition funds in any other act. Deschler 26 § 3, 7. However, in 1974, the House Select Committee on Committee gave the Appropriations Committee jurisdiction over "[t]ransfers of unexpended balances," House Rule X(1)(b)(3), and so an appropriations bill can include such transfers of old money in prior acts to new purposes. House Rule X(1)(b) requires that such transfers be stated under a "separate heading[]" in the appropriations bill and that there be a "separate section with respect to such . . . transfers in the accompanying committee report." The change is discussed in Fisher at 68.

[157] House Manual § 842e. For precedents regarding changes in existing laws, see 8 Deschler's, Chapter 26, Part C ("Provisions as 'Changing Existing Law,' Generally").

[158] Categories of funding authorized in the law could be cut off by limitations, consistent with the tests specified below, the way the Hyde Amendment cuts off abortion funding. However, as the discussion below shows, the drafting requirements for limitations make them singularly ill-suited for complex and delicate matters such as alteration of eligibility formulae.

"Holman Rule."[159] Adopted in 1876 on the proposal of Representative William S. Holman, the Holman Rule had a controversial history of great nineteenth- and early twentieth-century importance, but has had limited significance thereafter.[160]

The other two most important tests distinguishing legislation from appropriations concern new directions and duties for executive officers, and contingencies.[161] "Propositions to

---

[159] After stating that "[n]o provision changing existing law shall be reported in any general appropriation bill," the rule adds, "except germane provisions which retrench expenditures by the reduction of amounts of money covered by the bill . . . ." A 1983 amendment of the Holman Rule restricted it only to explicit "reduction of amounts of money," requiring the savings be very concrete, and added that such germane retrenchment provisions "may include those recommended to the Committee on Appropriations by direction of any legislative committee having jurisdiction over the subject matter thereof." This language suggests that authorizing committees submit proposed Holman Rule riders to the Appropriations Committee, and the Appropriations Committee can then report them with the bill.

[160] It was amended, repealed, reinserted, repealed, and reinserted. Its history is recited in House Manual § 834. At times it was construed broadly, allowing the Appropriations Committee the enormous power to put on appropriations bills virtually any legislation it wanted that arguably might save money ("retrench expenditures"). This brought a fierce reaction from other committees, namely the 1877-1920 interlude when other committees seized the power to report their own appropriations.

In the twentieth century, the Holman Rule has been interpreted restrictively as applying only when the savings can be specified as an actual reduction of amounts in the bill. House Manual § 844a. The 1983 amendment to Rule XXI(2), which allowed the cutting off of limitation riders by a motion to rise, thereafter allowed Holman Rule amendments from the floor, but only after the opportunity for that motion to rise. See House Rule XXI(2)(d) (governing the offering of "germane amendments which retrench expenditures").

(footnote continued)

establish affirmative directions for executive
officers . . . even in cases where they may have
discretion under the law so to do . . . or to
affirmatively take away an authority or discretion
conferred by law . . . are subject to the point of
order."[162]   Contingencies pose a particularly
difficult question.   Appropriations with
contingencies can be used as a carrot-and-stick to
change administration policies, push legislation
toward passage, and change outside domestic and
even foreign conduct.[163]   However, such
contingencies usually are legislation requiring
executive officers to make policy determinations
beyond existing law, or are non-germane where the
contingency is unrelated to the appropriation.[164]

Despite the rule, the Appropriations
Committee reports large numbers of legislative
provisions.   In 1980, Congressional Quarterly
noted:

---

[161]   For precedents regarding conditions, see 8 Deschler,
Chapter 26, Part D ("Provisions as Changing Existing Law:
Appropriations Subject to Conditions"); for precedents
regarding changes in executive duties, see 8 Deschler,
Chapter 26, Part E ("Provisions as Changing Existing Law:
Provisions Affecting Executive Authority; Imposition of New
Duties on Officials").

[162]   House Manual § 842d.   For example, appropriation
provisions could not require the Office of Management and
Budget not "to interfere with" the rulemaking authority of
other agencies, because this language would require OMB to
make determinations about what constituted interference.
Id.

[163]   Contingent appropriations can condition the
availability of appropriations on executive findings (such
as certifications that foreign countries made progress on
human rights) or legislative findings (such as in a nuclear
waste disposal bill saying that some problem has been
resolved).   Moreover, if an authorizing committee can enact
into law some certification requirement, then a rider may be
sound which does not change existing law, but merely adds
muscle to that existing law.

[164]   House Manual § 842b (legislation);   Deschler 26 § 8.15
(non-germane).

>Hundreds of riders on less-controversial
>issues are added to appropriations bills each
>year by the House Appropriations Committee
>and its subcommittees . . . .
>
>In some cases committee riders are the
>result of floor amendments made in earlier
>years. In others, they are staff
>recommendations arising from the subcommittee
>hearings.
>
>A few also are added by committee
>members as special favors to some of the
>folks back home.[165]

For example, the Fiscal Year 1986 defense
appropriation consisted of two parts. One part
was 17 pages of provisions appropriating amounts
of money.[166] The second part was a title 22 pages
in length called "General Provisions," consisting
largely of policy-directing language. The
"General Provisions" included everything from a
host of limitations to elaborate, positively
worded provisions regarding NATO consultation and
international agreements for binary chemical

---

[165]   Murray at 3255. The Democratic Study Group estimated
in 1978 that "[l]ast year the FY 1978 general and
supplemental appropriations bill[s] carried nearly 200 new
limitations and legislative provisions reported by the
Appropriations Committee. These were in addition to
previously enacted general provisions which are carried in
appropriations bills year after year." Democratic Study
Group, The Appropriation Rider Controversy 5 (1978),
reprinted in Final Report of the House Select Committee on
Committees, H.R. Rep. No. 866, 96th Cong., 2d Sess. 79
(1980).

[166]   Even in this part, much of the text consisted of
limitation language with policy effect, such as the
provision accompanying the appropriation of $10.8 billion
for Navy shipbuilding that "none of the funds herein . . . .
shall be expended in foreign shipyards." This part of the
act is at 99 Stat. 1185-1202 (1985). (The defense
appropriation act was included as a discrete part of the
continuing resolution.) The foreign shipyard limitation is
at 99 Stat. 1196.

weapons.[167]

Particular committee riders may provoke turf battles with the authorizing committees, as described above, and occasionally the authorizing committees conduct a general revolt.[168]   However, generally, the Appropriations Committee practices do not provoke disputes.[169]   Most of the provisions represent a settled and accepted resolution of an issue, and do not provoke controversy.[170]

For more controversial legislation that would provoke points of order, the Rules Committee can waive the rule against legislation on appropriations.   This end-runs authorizing committees that bottle up popular legislation, like other end-runs such as germaneness waivers or the discharge procedure.   However, waivers for legislation on appropriations raise fewer hackles than discharge, especially when they can be justified as saving money and thus natural for appropriations bills.

---

[167]   99 Stat. 1202-25 (1985).   The binary weapons language is at 99 Stat. 1217-18.

[168]   In a 1980 incident, the chairs of 17 House committees (and several ranking minority members) wrote the House Select Committee on Committees, asking that such legislative provisions either requiring authorizing committee approval for a Rules waiver or receive a sequential referral to the authorizing committee.   Final Report of the House Select Committee on Committees, H.R. Rep. No. 866, 96th Cong., 2d Sess. 387-88 (1980).

[169]   Technically, a point of order would lie even if a provision has been present year after year.   "The fact that an item has been carried in appropriation bills for many years does not exempt it from a point of order as being legislation."   House Manual § 842a.

[170]   If points of order loom, the Appropriations Committee can ask the Rules Committee for a special rule waiving the points of order.   Alternatively, if a rider is struck, later in conference the Members who put the rider in originally can restore it and then bring the rider back as an amendment in technical disagreement, like the riders accepted from the Senate.

Two examples illustrate such waivers in action. Members desired in 1984 and 1985 to cut back the synfuels program. Rather than try to move legislation through a series of authorizing committees, synfuels opponents asked the Rules Committee for a waiver to allow legislative amendments on the Interior Appropriation.[171] Both years the Rules Committee refused, and both years its special rule for the bill was defeated -- these being two out of the total of six rules defeated in 1981-85[172] -- in order to persuade the Rules Committee to report a second rule with the requisite waiver. In two years the House cut $10 billion this way, wiping the program out.[173] As an even broader example, in 1947-48, when the Republicans briefly regained control of both chambers, they used such waivers, and legislative riders on appropriations, as their principal tool for dismantling large numbers of New Deal programs, much as reconciliation was used in 1981.[174]

Limitations

Although such legislation serves an occasional dramatic role, limitations constituted the heart of the upsurge in riders on the House floor.[175] A surge of limitation riders began with

---

[171] Since synfuels were funded by backdoor contracting authority outside the annual appropriations process, there was no appropriation to cut directly.

[172] Plattner, Rules Under Chairman Pepper Looks Out for the Democrats, 43 Cong. Q. Week. Rep. 1671, 1674 (1985).

[173] 1984 Congressional Quarterly Almanac 348-49; 1985 Congressional Quarterly Almanac 337.

[174] The 1947-48 waivers "enabled the majority party to avoid going through the authorizing committees where members' constituency attachments might make it difficult for them to cut back or abolish programs." House Committee on Rules, 97th Cong., 2d Sess., A History of the Committee on Rules 157 (Comm. Print 1983).

(footnote continued)

the allowance of recorded votes in the Committee of the Whole in 1970 and with opposition to the Vietnam War.[176] The technique quickly spread from foreign to domestic matters and from liberal to conservative use.   A fateful step occurred in 1977, when Representative Henry Hyde (R-Ill.) offered, almost casually, his anti-abortion rider for the first time,[177] with the profound impact of tying up the largest civilian appropriation, the Labor-HEW appropriation, for several months in 1977.   Abortion rider battles prevented enactment of that appropriation bill in 1979 and 1980, and continued in the 1980s on other appropriation bills.[178]

---

[175]   As mentioned above, limitation riders are provisions such as that "none of the funds appropriated herein shall be used for abortions."   Technically, Congress deems them not to be legislation when suitably drafted to restrict spending on the particular bills rather than making any changes in the permanent law.   For example, after expiration of the appropriation bill with that abortion rider, all future appropriation bills could be spent without any restriction regarding abortions, unless new riders are included in those bills.

[176]   Opponents of the Nixon and Ford administration foreign policies used limitation amendments to force cutoffs of funding for the Vietnam War in 1973, and then to cut off aid to unpopular regimes such as the Turkish government after it occupied Cyprus.   By 1979, "21.3 percent (33 of 155) of the foreign policy amendments offered during floor debate [in the House for the entire year] were directed toward the Foreign Assistance Appropriations Bill."   C. Whalen, The House and Foreign Policy 167 (1979).   The author, former ranking minority member on the House Foreign Affairs Committee, presents a case study of the impact on relations with the Turkish government of the limitation rider at 95-99.

[177]   R. H. Davidson, Procedures and Politics in Congress, in The Abortion Dispute and the American System 30, 39 (G.Y. Steiner ed. 1983) (quoting Congressional Quarterly article) (Representative Hyde described: after a chat with a colleague, "We scribbled [the amendment] out in longhand right on the spot.").

[178]   1979 Congressional Quarterly Almanac 236; 1980 (footnote continued)

Limitation riders face two hurdles: drafting and the motion to rise. As for drafting, it would seem easy simply to specify that money not be spent for some objectionable purpose. The catch is that the limitation must not change the duties of federal agencies, for only authorization legislation can do that, and so it must specify a cutoff in a way that creates no administrative duties.[179] The Hyde anti-abortion amendment on the Labor-HEW appropriation in 1977 illustrated this dramatically. As originally proposed, it prohibited use of Medicaid funds in the bill "to perform abortions except where the life of the mother would be endangered if the fetus were carried to term." Although this did not mention changes in agency duties, opponents made the point of order that it created a new duty "to ascertain from some physician that the life of the mother or other pregnant woman would be endangered if the fetus is carried to term."[180]

Congressional Quarterly Almanac 222; 1981 Congressional Quarterly Almanac 357; 1983 Congressional Quarterly Almanac, 507 (Labor-HHS), 533 (Treasury-Postal).

[179] In fact, the limitation must make no changes in many respects, summed up by Walter Kravitz:

> proposals may not give executive officials affirmative directions (even when the law gives them discretion to take such actions), or impose additional specific duties on them, or take away or 'affirmatively interfere' with their discretionary authority, or require them to make new determinations, or implicitly require them to make investigations, compile evidence, or make judgments and determinations not otherwise required of them by law.

Kravitz, Legislation in Appropriation Bills: Procedural Problems in the House of Representatives and Some Options 5 (1983) (Congressional Research Service).

[180] Proponents responded that private physicians make the medical determinations and do so under state rather than federal supervision, but the Chair concluded: "the language in the bill addresses determinations by the Federal Government and is not limited by its terms to determinations by individual physicians or by the respective States."
(footnote continued)

Representative Hyde said he was "forced into this position today by points of order," and offered an absolutist prohibition against funding abortions at all. This raised no point of order because it involved no exercise of discretion. Ultimately, the Senate, and then the conference committee restored some exceptions to the absolute prohibition. The result is that the technical rules force limitations into strange shapes,[181] often making them less useful for legislating than for purposes of sending political signals.

By the early 1980s, the floods of limitation amendments threatened the House majority leadership with loss of its agenda control, mangling of the scheduling on appropriations, and political fallout from never-ending controversial issues reaching the floor unscreened by the legislative committees. Accordingly, in 1983, the House created new machinery regarding limitation amendments. Rule XXI(2)(c) and (d) postpones all limitation amendments during an initial reading of a general appropriation bill for amendment.[182]

Id. Proponents then tried to draft around the problem by restricting discretion unreviewably to physicians, not the government, by prohibiting use of funds for "abortions, except where a physician has certified the abortion is necessary to save the life of the mother." However, the Chair still ruled this out, since some physicians working in federal hospitals receive federal pay, and they would be making decisions.

[181] For another example of it taking three drafts to get past a point of order against a limitation rider, see the debate on a limitation on American contributions to international organizations, aimed at precluding their use for paying off interest charges on borrowing. 128 Cong. Rec. H9238-41 (daily ed. Dec. 9, 1982).

[182] Rule XXI(2)(c) provides: "Except as provided in paragraph (d), no amendment shall be in order during consideration of a general appropriation bill proposing a limitation not specifically contained or authorized in existing law for the period of the limitation." Then, "[a]fter a general appropriation bill has been read for amendment and amendments not precluded by paragraph (a) or (c) of this clause have been considered," Rule XXI(2)(d), the timetable unrolls as discussed in the text.

Then Rule XXI(2)(d) gives an old motion new precedence: "motions that the Committee of the Whole rise and report the bill to the House with such amendments as may have been adopted shall have precedence over motions to further amend the bill."

Pursuant to this rule, a manager steers an appropriation bill through all the amendments dealing with specific amounts of money, and then moves to rise before any limitation amendments can be offered. If the motion carries, the Committee of the Whole rises, and there is no opportunity then or later for limitation amendments. Proponents of a limitation amendment must defeat the motion to rise in order to offer their amendment.[183]

Such proponents have several strikes against them. The motion to rise is not debatable, so they have to use indirect moves to get debate time.[184] More important, the motion to rise offers a procedural out by which the Members can fend off a rider without having to be recorded against something popular. This is like voting for the previous question on a special rule to avoid its being altered to make in order something popular. As Representative Dan Lungren (R-Calif.) said in opposing the new rule, Members would go home and say "I am sorry, that vote never came up. I did not vote on it. I voted on a question of whether we should rise as a committee. It is a

---

[183]   Rule XXI(2)(d) provides:

If any such motion [to rise] is rejected, amendments proposing limitations not specifically contained or authorized in existing law for the period of the limitation or proposing germane amendments which retrench expenditures by reduction of amounts of money covered by the bill may be considered.

[184]   IV Hinds § 4766-68 (nondebatable). To gain debate time, opponents of the motion can speak in advance of the motion, in one-minutes early in the day or during debate on the special rule for the bill (if any) or during general debate, or on pro forma amendments during the reading of the bill for amendment. At the critical junction they can make the preferential motion to strike the enacting clause.

procedural matter."[185]   The rule also allows the manager to gauge tactics nicely, since it can be offered again after one or successive limitation riders so that even if one gets through (with or without a struggle) the manager can block others.[186]

Adoption of that rule immediately cut down on limitation riders.   Members only attempted offering 12 in 1983, a large drop from the scores being offered in previous years, and of these 12, only two were adopted by defeating the motion to rise.   One, adopted after a battle,[187] concerned a limitation on abortions in federal government employee health plans.   On that rider, the motion to rise lost 193-229, and in subsequent years, riders with similar strong support, such as abortion riders, continued to defeat the motion to rise and to be offered and adopted.[188]   Apart from these strong riders, the motion largely cut off attempts at limitation riders, such as in 1984 on the legislative branch appropriation, when it prevented a minority party effort to curb the practice it disliked of televising the emptiness of the chamber during special order speeches.[189]

---

[185]   129 Cong. Rec. H16 (daily ed. Jan. 3, 1983).

[186]   Rule XXI(2)(d) provides that even if the motion is rejected and an amendment is offered, "after the vote on any such amendment, the privileged motion made in order under this paragraph may be renewed."   For example, in 1983, on the HUD Appropriation, although a first motion to rise was defeated, allowing an amendment to be offered against EPA sanctions, a second motion to rise was adopted, preventing a jobs amendment.   1983 Congressional Quarterly Almanac 498.

[187]   Another motion to rise lost 144-225, apparently without much consideration of the procedural posture.   1983 Congressional Quarterly Almanac 498.

[188]   1983 Congressional Quarterly Almanac 535.   See, e.g., 132 Cong. Rec. H4650 (daily ed. July 17, 1986) (motion to rise defeated on abortion rider to State-Justice-Commerce appropropriation).

[189]   1984 Congressional Quarterly Almanac 388.

Senate Rules

The Senate has its own rules against legislation on appropriations. Rule XVI(2) forbids the Appropriations Committee to report any,[190] while Rule XVI(4) forbids any as floor amendments.[191] Both rules expressly forbid limitation riders that contain contingencies.[192]

---

[190]   Rule XVI(2) provides in part:

> The Committee on Appropriations shall not report an appropriations bill containing amendments to such bill proposing new or general legislation . . . and if an appropriation bill is reported to the Senate containing amendments to such bill proposing new or general legislation . . . a point of order may be made against the bill, and if the point is sustained, the bill shall be recommitted to the Committee on Appropriations.

Actually, a point of order against an Appropriations Committee amendment does not cause the bill to be recommitted, but only causes the amendment to fall. The bill falls only if Appropriations reports out an original bill, which is rare, instead of Senate Appropriations' usual practice of reporting the House bill with Senate committee amendments. Riddick, "Appropriations: Points of Order: Bill Recommitted if Point of Order Sustained That Committee Reported with Legislation," at 136-37.

[191]   Rule XVI(3) provides in part: "On a point of order made by any Senator, no amendment offered by any other Senator which proposes general legislation shall be received to any general appropriation bill . . . ." For a description of the nineteenth-century rise of Senate rules curbing legislative riders, see C. H. Kerr, The Origin and Development of the United States Senate 78-80 (1895).

[192]   Rule XVI(2) forbids the Appropriations Committee to report "any restriction on the expenditure of the funds appropriated which proposes a limitation not authorized by law if such restriction is to take effect or cease to be effective upon the happening of a contingency . . . ." Rule XVI(4) contains virtually identical language regarding floor amendments. Rule XVI(6) adds: "When a point of order is made against any restriction on the expenditure of funds appropriated in a general appropriation bill on the ground (footnote continued)

Moreover, Rule XVI(4) even imposes a germaneness rule on floor amendments, in contrast to regular bills on which the Senate freely permits non-germane amendments. These rules do not apply to provisions that the House has already put in the bill before sending it over, but only to Senate amendments; to take out House language requires the Senate to vote a motion to strike, not just for one Senator to make a point of order.[193]

These rules use tests for legislation similar to the House's.[194] As in the House, a key test is whether the amendment gives new directions or imposes new duties on executive officials.[195] Another is whether the amendment contains a contingency, such as "denying funds to any country which thereafter nationalized any industry."[196]

Notwithstanding the rules, the Senate Appropriations Committee, like its House counterpart, routinely reports many noncontroversial legislative provisions on appropriations.[197] As in the House, there may be

---

that the restriction violates this rule, the rule shall be construed strictly and, in case of doubt, in favor of the point of order."

[193] Riddick, "Appropriations: Points of Order: House Language," at 138.

[194] For a long list of amendments struck down as legislation, see Riddick, "Appropriations: Legislation to a General Appropriation Bill Not in Order," at 162-67.

[195] See, e.g., 128 Cong. Rec. S15894 (daily ed. Nov. 10, 1983) (requirement that the President submit a balanced budget out of order); id. S15919 (new duties on Secretaries of Agriculture and Interior out of order).

[196] Riddick, "Appropriations: Amendments to General Appropriation Bills -- When Not in Order: Contingency, Happening or Not Happening of," at 153.

[197] This can be seen most simply by the large number of amendments in technical disagreement that come back from conferences on appropriations, for as discussed in the chapter on conferences, these reflect a House rule regarding legislation and unauthorized appropriations added by the Senate.

an occasional turf fight, but mostly these
provisions pass without challenge, either as old
and settled or because the provisions represent
favors that Senators do not quarrel over.[198]
    On the occasions when a Senator raises a
point of order that a committee or floor amendment
is legislation on an appropriation, the Chair
would rule on the question.   Quite often, an
appeal will be taken, and the Senate may overrule
the Chair -- not because anyone seriously contends
the Parliamentarian made a mistake, but because
the amendment is popular and the Senators want it
notwithstanding the rules.[199]
    A striking example occurred when the Senate
considered a backdoor increasing for its pay, by
an amendment to an appropriation bill letting
Members take larger tax deductions for expenses.
In 1981, the Chair struck such an amendment as
legislation on an appropriation, and the Senate
overruled the Chair and enacted the amendment.
The next year, when an amendment was offered to
repeal the provision, the Chair struck the repeal
as legislation on an appropriation, and this time
the Senate upheld the Chair.[200]
    In 1987 the Chair struck an amendment on the
transportation appropriation to ban smoking on
flights -- not as legislation on an appropriation,
but on the ground of committee jurisdiction (that
the matter was under the legislative juridiction
of the Commerce Committee).   The amendment's
backer offered the proposal as a floor amendment,

---

[198]   In a typical discussion, a 1983 provision on a
continuing resolution was to give a federal island to the
State of Washington.   When Senator Howard Metzenbaum (D-
Ohio) protested, the manager freely conceded that "[w]e did
approve this in the committee.   We are aware that it is
legislation on an appropriations bill . . . . I assume that
it is subject to a point of order."   128 Cong. Rec. S15447
(daily ed. Nov. 4, 1983) (Sen. Theodore Stevens (R-Alaska)).

[199]   Some older examples of such overrulings are in
Riddick, "Appropriations: Legislation to a General
Appropriation Bills Not in Order," at 161.

[200]   1982 Congressional Quarterly Almanac 229-30; 1981
Congressional Quarterly Almanac 293.

obtaining enactment of a compromise version.[201]
As in the House, legislation on an appropriation
serves as a means for end-running an authorizing
committee that bottles up a bill, and Senators may
resist legislative riders out of deference to the
committee system.[202]

When the Senate favors an amendment, its
proponents have a more elegant mechanism for
avoiding a point of order than such crude
overruling, called the "defense of germaneness."
To illustrate with a concrete example, Senator
Wendell Ford (D-Ky.) offered a floor amendment to
a 1983 supplemental appropriation to add
supplemental unemployment benefits for railroad
workers. Senator Don Nickles (R-Okla.) announced,
"I make a point of order that this is legislation
on an appropriation bill and ask for the yeas and
nays."

Senator Ford responded, "Mr. President, I
raise the question of germaneness."[203] At that

---

[201]   1987 Congressional Quarterly Almanac 442.   The
amendment had not been an invalid item of legislation on an
appropriation -- for example, it had been in order in the
House, although protested as an incursion on the authorizing
committee's jurisdiction. Id. at 441. Striking it from the
committee-reported version as a violation of committee
jurisdiction still allowed it to be offered from the floor.

[202]   For years, the Senate Labor and Human Resources
Committee had bottled up legislation to relax the Davis-
Bacon Act, which maintains wages on federal building
projects. In 1985, the military construction appropriation
included a rider to relax Davis-Bacon for Pentagon
construction project. On the floor, the point of order
about legislation on an appropriation was met with a defense
of germaneness, but the Senate rejected the defense 45-49.
1985 Congressional Quarterly Almanac 395.

[203]   Technically, this means Senator Ford had made a point
of order against his own amendment under Rule XVI's
germaneness requirement. He would do so because if he
waited for a ruling on Senator Nickles' point of order, that
ruling would come from the Chair. On the other hand, a
ruling on germaneness to the House language comes by vote of
the chamber. Rule XVI(4) states that "all questions of
relevancy of amendments under this rule, when raised, shall
(footnote continued)

point, the Chair announced the amendment passed a threshold test.[204]   While an opponent of the provision could have moved to table the question of germaneness, none did.[205]   Accordingly, the Senate voted on the question of germaneness and voted to uphold the amendment as germane to House language.   By so voting, the Senate caused the point of order about legislation on an appropriation fall by the wayside.[206]

E. CONTINUING RESOLUTIONS

In the 1980s, Congress made historically unprecedented uses of continuing resolutions.[207]

---

be submitted to the Senate and be decided without debate."

[204]   The Chair announced, after Senator Ford raised his question of germaneness, that it had applied a threshold test as to whether there was "House legislative language to which the amendment could be germane," and that it had found such language.   128 Cong. Rec. S2649 (daily ed. March 11, 1983).   This test was devised by Majority Leader Byrd in 1979, to prevent the defense of germaneness from being raised frivolously when absolutely no language in the House bill even colorably related to the Senate amendment.   The 1979 point of order of Majority Leader Byrd is described in Riddick, "Appropriations: Germaneness of Amendments to General Appropriations Bills," at 130.

[205]   Tabling the question of germaneness is a second technique exploited by Majority Leader Byrd to stem the use of the defense of germaneness.   For a discussion, see Fisher at 93 & n.257; Riddick, "Appropriations: Germaneness of Amendments to General Appropriations Bills," at 130.

[206]   That rule developed because the House inserts items of legislation before sending the bill over, and "[i]f the House of Representatives opens the door by incorporating legislation in a general appropriation bill, the Senate has an inherent right to amend such proposed legislation, and to perfect that language, notwithstanding its rules."   Riddick, "Appropriations: Germaneness of Amendments to General Appropriations Bills," at 133.

[207]   "[S]ince 1979, continuing resolutions have become a (footnote continued)

These resolutions metamorphosed from simple temporary holding patterns into year-long omnibus conglomerations of appropriations bills with contents and procedures all their own. The story of that change, and the new procedures for continuing resolutions, brings together much of congressional procedure in accounting for what became a major annual focus of legislation action.

Rise in Importance

Continuing resolutions date back at least a century, with the first example apparently a ten-day resolution in 1876.[208]   Until recent years they attracted little attention.   In 1965, Professor Fenno's massive study of appropriations could suffice with one brief description of continuing resolutions:

> If no appropriation bill has been passed by [the start of the fiscal year], the practice is for Congress to provide a "continuing resolution" Under this resolution, agencies are allowed to spend at the previous year's rate or, if only the House has passed the appropriation bill, at whichever rate is lower, or, if both Senate and House have passed the bill, at whichever of those two rates is lower.[209]

Although Congress used continuing resolutions

---

principal source of funding for federal programs." Konigsberg, Amending the Congressional Budget Act of 1974, 11 J. Legis. 90, 111 (1984).

[208]   19 Stat. 65 (1876).   There were said to be seven between 1876 and 1894.   52 Cong. Rec. 8532 (1912).

[209]   Fenno at 421.   Even later "[d]uring the 1960s and early 1970s," as Congressional Quarterly noted, "the scope of the continuing resolutions was fairly narrow.   Typically, they funded a few agencies whose programs were controversial or whose appropriations bills had become burdened with controversial amendments."   1982 Congressional Quarterly Almanac 226.

during problems with late appropriations in the early 1970s, the 1974 Congressional Budget Act reduced the need for them, by a unique solution to the scheduling problem -- moving the start of the fiscal year from July 1 to October 1.

However, by the late 1970s, Congress increasingly fell behind in passing appropriations.[210] Moreover, continuing resolutions became increasingly important when the Attorney General issued opinions that agencies could no longer hang on during funding gaps until the next payday, but had to shut down during even brief lapses in funding.[211] Then, in 1981, the continuing resolution occupied the headlines when President Reagan vetoed it as setting too high a spending rate, causing "a dramatic confrontation . . . that forced a temporary shutdown of much of the government."[212] The third continuing

---

[210] In 1979 and 1980, it had to pass second continuing resolutions in November and December to provide funds for five regular appropriations that were behind schedule. 1979 Congressional Quarterly Almanac 280 (five of the regular appropriations -- Interior, Defense, Transportation, military construction, and foreign aid -- were behind schedule, though some were enacted on the eve of signing of the continuing resolution); 1980 Congressional Quarterly Almanac 218 (continuing resolution funded Labor-HHS, Treasury-Postal Service, legislative branch, foreign aid, and State-Justice-Commerce).

[211] In 1979, a funding gap had occurred between October 1, the start of the fiscal year, and October 12, the date the President signed the first continuing resolution, without incident, since the date had not come for paychecks to issue. 1979 Congressional Quarterly Almanac 278. However, Attorney General Benjamin Civiletti subsequently issued two opinions suggesting that most government departments would have to shut down at the outset of a funding gap without awaiting the next payday. These opinions of April 25, 1980, and January 16, 1981, are reprinted as appendices in General Accounting Office, Funding Gaps Jeopardize Federal Government Operations (1981).

[212] 1981 Congressional Quarterly Almanac 294. The shutdown is described at 298-99. Another shutdown occurred in 1984. 1984 Congressional Quarterly Almanac 444.

resolution that year, passed on December 11, took
the place in the end of seven regular
appropriation bills, none of which ever succeeded
in being passed.[213]
   In subsequent years, sharp disagreements
between the administration and Congress,
particularly the House Democrats, over funding
levels and riders guaranteed delays in enactment
of regular appropriations which forced much
funding into the continuing resolution. The
culminations came in 1984, 1986, and 1987, when
the fiscal year 1985, 1987, and 1988 continuing
resolutions appropriated $470, $570, and $604
billion, the largest spending bills up to that
time.[214]
   What added to continuing resolutions'
importance, besides their size and the necessity
for their timely enactment, was the increasing
diversity and complexity of their contents.
Before the 1980s, continuing resolutions had used
simple measures -- some combination of the prior
year's rate, the President's budget's rate, or
what the House or Senate had put in the regular
bill. However, in 1981, the administration used
the leverage of its successful veto of the
continuing resolution to negotiate a complex
series of across-the-board cuts in the final
version of the continuing resolution.[215]
   Whole bills began regularly coming aboard --
not incorporated by reference, but as full texts
on what had become an omnibus vehicle. Battles

---

[213]   1981 Congressional Quarterly Almanac 331.

[214]   1984 Congressional Quarterly Almanac 444 (size of
continuing resolution); 1987 Congressional Quarterly Almanac
401.

[215]   These cut the civilian portions by four percent,
exempted some programs from cuts, and gave the
administration some flexibility "to make a cut of up to 6
percent in spending for any individual program, in achieving
a 4 percent reduction for a whole appropriations account."
1981 Congressional Quarterly Almanac 331. There was also an
across-the-board cut in the military portions of two
percent, but only until enactment of regular bills or the
end of the first congressional session.

loomed in 1981 over the legislative branch appropriation,[216] so "[t]he House put their [legislative branch] appropriation into the continuing resolution so they could maintain as much leverage as possible in conference."[217] In 1982, Congress again put the full year's legislative branch appropriation on the first continuing resolution. Then, it put on the second continuing resolution the entire text of the defense appropriation bill, plus the full texts of appropriations for Labor-HHS, Energy and Water, Foreign Aid, State-Justice-Commerce, and Treasury-Postal.[218]

The continuing resolution soon became the routine omnibus vehicle for hard-to-pass appropriations.[219] By 1986, the foreign aid

---

[216] Congress had failed in 1979 and 1980 to enact an independent legislative branch appropriation, direct and indirect pay raises for Members were at issue, and the Senate subcommittee had deleted from its version of the 1981 legislative branch bill all House budget items.

[217] 1981 Congressional Quarterly Almanac 288. The bill as it emerged from conference also enacted a permanent appropriation for congressional salaries, obviating the need for annual votes on pay (unless a change was made). Id. 289.

[218] "Congress failed for the first time in at least 30 years to pass a separate defense appropriations bill," although appropriations leaders "noted that the defense provisions of H J Res 631 represented completed legislation and, unlike most continuing resolutions, were not based on a mere continuation of spending levels from the previous year." 1982 Congressional Quarterly Almanac 277; see 1982 Congressional Quarterly Almanac 250, 292, 242, 246, 273 (texts of other bills included).

[219] In 1984, Congress "cleared a $470 billion continuing appropriations resolution for fiscal 1985, the largest and most sweeping stopgap funding bill ever approved." 1984 Congressional Quarterly Almanac 444. The resolution "contained the entire texts of five regular fiscal 1985 appropriations bills: Defense, Foreign Assistance, Interior, Military Construction and Transportation," plus the conference reports on three others. 1984 Congressional (footnote continued)

appropriation -- which "often d[id] not come to
the floor for fear that it w[ould] be gutted by
members anxious to shift money to domestic
programs" -- "ha[d] been incorporated into the
continuing resolution seven times since fiscal
1976, and the Labor-HHS bill" -- which "frequently
bec[a]me mired in controversies surrounding
abortion, busing and other social issues" -- had
been incorporated six times.[220]

In 1982, the second continuing resolution
enacted on December 21 provided funding for the
whole fiscal year.[221] The resolution thus became
a true omnibus appropriation rather than an
interim measure. Moreover, the expanded
continuing resolutions tended to pick up other
legislation that would never have come aboard an
appropriation bill even as a rider. A supreme
example was the 1984 continuing resolution. Along
with its $470 billion, it carried "a sweeping
anti-crime package that represented the
culmination of an 11-year effort to make major
changes in the federal criminal code."[222]

Floor Procedure

The rise of the omnibus continuing resolution
produced new procedural patterns in each
chamber. The House tended to channel its
consideration restrictively; the Senate, to open
up the resolution as a "Christmas tree." Along
the way, a number of dramatic procedural incidents
over the years reflected the importance of the
resolution for the party leaderships. As the
Brookings Institution Review observed in 1988,
"the majority party leaders, who broker the
process and shape the rule that governs floor
debate in the House, have the loudest voice"
regarding "what goes into the CR."[223]

Quarterly Almanac 444.

[220]   Gettinger, Diverse Spending Practices Have a Long
History, 44 Cong. Q. Week. Rep. 2060 (1986).

[221]   1982 Congressional Quarterly Almanac 173.

[222]   1984 Congressional Quarterly Almanac 215.
(footnote continued)

Traditional rules treated continuing resolutions oddly, but in a way eased their enactment.[224] The House did not consider continuing resolutions to be general appropriations for purposes of Rule XXI's prohibitions against unauthorized appropriations and legislation on appropriations.[225] This kept the House's strict rule against unauthorized appropriations from holding up interim funding for agencies for which the authorizations had been delayed. On the other hand, the Senate did consider continuing resolutions to be general appropriations.[226] Application of the Senate's porous rule against unauthorized appropriations posed no problem, as it only applied to floor amendments and not to the committee-reported version. The Senate's rule against legislation on an appropriation was a help in keeping disputatious riders off the resolution.

In the House, the rise in importance of the continuing resolution generated sophisticated use of the special rule. At first this was relatively tactical. Cleverly crafted special rules in 1979 and 1981 prevented recorded votes on sensitive issues[227] and in 1980 sidetracked proposals to

---

[223]   White, The Continuing Resolution: A Crazy Way to Govern, 6 Brookings Review, Summer 1988, 28, 34. "Continuing resolutions are tightly controlled by leaders in each chamber." Gettinger, Congress Returns to Tackle Biggest-Ever "CR", 44 Cong. Q. Week. Rep. 2059, 2061 (1986).

[224]   One traditional lack was corrected in 1981, when the House gave continuing resolutions the same privilege for floor consideration as general appropriations, H.R. Rule XI(4)(a), House Manual § 726, so that they only need special rules to waive points of order or to shape floor consideration, not merely to reach the floor as with ordinary bills.

[225]   House Manual § 835; Deschler 25 § 2.

[226]   Riddick, "Appropriations: Continuing Appropriations," and "Appropriations: Definition of General Appropriations Bills" at 127.

[227]   The 1979 special rules had two continuing resolutions (footnote continued)

shorten the resolution's duration.[228]   Then in
1982-1985, with the rise of the continuing
resolutions as true omnibus appropriations, the
special rules played major roles in shaping floor
consideration.

In 1982, the special rule for the key
continuing resolution made only eight amendments
in order, such as an amendment to cut funding for
the Clinch River breeder reactor (which passed).
However, the rule did not make in order a
requested amendment to cut funding for the
Tennessee-Tombigbee waterway, a project with
strong backing among southern Democrats. The rule
thus provided enough choice to be passed, but not
enough to alienate project defenders who might
well otherwise have killed the special rule.[229]

---

considered in the House as in Committee of the Whole, rather
than simply in the Committee of the Whole. The difference
was that a recorded vote required 44 votes for a second in
the House, rather than 25 in Committee of the Whole.
Accordingly, there was an insufficient second for recorded
votes on congressional pay raise proposals, and the votes on
that sensitive issue were unrecorded. 1979 _Congressional
Quarterly Almanac_ 276-77.

The 1981 special rule was closed, preventing dissident
majority members from asking for the continuing resolution
to terminate early. The minority still got to offer its
across-the-board cut proposals as a motion to recommit,
where it lost (leading to a presidential veto and acceptance
of across-the-board cuts on a later version).   1981
Congressional Quarterly Almanac 296.

[228]   The 1980 special rule barred the minority from offering
its proposal for the continuing resolution to terminate
October 18 (before the election, thus forcing pre-election
appropriations votes) as an amendment, so the minority had
to offer it as a motion to recommit. 1980 _Congressional
Quarterly Almanac_ 170.

[229]   Representative Robert W. Edgar (D-Pa.), the opponent of
the waterway, explained what had transpired in the Rules
Committee: "I am the only Member of the House to request an
amendment before the Rules Committee yesterday [t]hat was
denied.   All other amendment requests were accepted.   I
would like to ask just a basic question, and that is: Who in
this House, who of our colleagues, is afraid of an up or
(footnote continued)

In 1983, the special rule for the second continuing resolution[230] made only a few amendments in order, one of which was a major jobs program by Majority Leader Jim Wright (D-Tex.).[231] Clean resolutions were not always acceptable. In 1984, faced with a threatened veto of any costly new programs, the Rules Committee attempted not to allow any amendments and even stripped off new water projects that the Appropriations Committee had put on the resolution. By a rare revolt, the House defeated the proposed special rule, requiring the Rules Committee to turn around and make the continuing resolution "a potential vehicle for nearly every major stalled legislative initiative of the 98th Congress," 11 floor amendments in all.[232] In 1987, House Democratic leaders orchestrated an extraordinary gambit, tying passage of the special rule for the continuing resolution to repeal of a Congressional pay raise. "The result of the procedural gambit was that Republicans, by opposing the rule because of the extraneous amendments it permitted and the virtual lid on GOP amendments, were also voting against repeal of the

---

down vote on the Tennessee Tombigbee Waterway?" 128 Cong. Rec. H9650 (daily ed. Dec. 14, 1982). The rule only passed by 223-163. House floor action is discussed in 1982 Congressional Quarterly Almanac 292.

[230] For the first continuing resolution, although "Rules became the forum for frustrated members and lobbyists who wanted to stick their pet projects on the continuing resolution," the Rules Committee rejected all requests. The House passed a clean continuing resolution in less than half an hour, and the Senate followed suit, so that "[n]either the House nor Senate added any extraneous amendments to the bill on the floor, another departure from tradition." 1983 Congressional Quarterly Almanac 527, 526.

[231] 1983 Congressional Quarterly Almanac 529-530. In 1985, the Rules Committee made only a single amendment in order, concerning offshore oil drilling in order. 1985 Congressional Quarterly Almanac 363.

[232] 1984 Congressional Quarterly Almanac 445. The veto threat evaporated in conference when the House removed all money for water projects. Id. 447.

pay raise,"[233] meaning that Republicans would be recorded voting in favor of higher Congressional pay, and thereby spoiling an issue they wished to use against Democrats.

These various special rules made the continuing resolution a vehicle for House choice much like the budget resolution. They confined -- and focused -- Members' consideration to a few major alternatives. As with the budget resolution, focusing on alternatives meant that the minority party won some major victories when it could summon the votes. One successful minority motion to recommit made large cuts in a continuing resolution: "$3.7 billion in outlay savings from seven domestic spending bills" plus savings in other sectors.[234] Another enacted the whole comprehensive rewrite of the criminal code.[235] In other years, majority party leadership proposals passed the House in this fashion, such as a jobs program in 1982 and the Wright package in 1983.[236]

Often majority party Members revolted against what they were offered, defeating in 1983 the first version of the continuing resolution, in 1984 the special rule stripping off water projects, and in 1985 the first version of the conference report.[237] By 1988, President Reagan

---

[233]   1987 Congressional Quarterly Almanac 485.

[234]   This occurred through a "a revival of the coalition that gave Reagan his major victories earlier in the year" on the budget resolution, reconciliation bill, and tax cut. 1981 Congressional Quarterly Almanac 330.

[235]   1984 Congressional Quarterly Almanac 215.

[236]   1982 Congressional Quarterly Almanac 240; 1983 Congressional Quarterly Almanac 529-30.

[237]   1985 Congressional Quarterly Almanac 366 (defeated because of pro-administration defense figures). The resolution followed an interesting course in 1983. The first time around, it was defeated by a revolt of the Democrats of the Class of 1982, who wanted to signal their frustration at the lack of action on deficit reduction. Having made their point, they passed the resolution the (footnote continued)

could go on national television to denounce
continuing resolutions as depriving him of his
rightful ability to veto individual bills. Under
internal and external pressure, the 1988 Congress
passed all its appropriations before the deadline,
avoiding the need for a continuing resolution.

Still, the structure of consideration built
around continuing resolutions restored to the
Appropriations Committee some of floor control it
had before the 1970s. Continuing resolutions
included whole appropriation bills just as the
Appropriations Ccommittee reported them. Only
Appropriations Committee members went to
conference on them. Only the Appropriations
Committee even knew the ontents as huge
resolutions rushed through under time pressure.
As Congressman David Obey (D-Wis.), an
appropriations subcommittee chair, said of the
huge 1986 continuing resolution, "[t]here may be
10 people in this place who know what's in it."[238]

Moreover, in this fashion the appropriations
committee solved some of its most difficult floor
problems -- enacting its most vulnerable bills.
An example was the foreign aid appropriation. In
the four years 1982-85, the House never had such a
bill on the floor. Essentially the leadership of
the House and the appropriations committee, and
members of the foreign aid subcommittee,
determined the House view and negotiated it on the
continuing resolution with the Senate and the
administration.[239] The situation could not have

---

second time around. 1983 Congressional Quarterly Almanac
529-530.

[238] Gettinger, supra, at 2059 (quoting Representative
Obey). "Members who do not belong to the Appropriations
committees, however, are often left in the dark." Id. at
2061. Representative John Porter (R-Ill.), a Member of the
Appropriations Committee, "polled his House colleagues on
the subject of continuing resolutions. Of the 124 who
responded, two thirds said such bills were irresponsible; 92
percent said they concentrated too much power in the hands
of a few members." Id.

[239] In terms of opportunities for foreign aid floor
amendments, at most, in 1983, the House voted on one
amendment on the continuing resolution to boost military
(footnote continued)

differed more from the mid-1970s, when foreign policy had been considerably affected -- whether for better or for worse depended on one's point of view -- by large numbers of floor amendments to the foreign aid appropriations.

Senate floor procedure on continuing resolutions followed a different course from the House's. Continuing resolutions became, not closed floor vehicles as in the House, but open vehicles, along with supplemental appropriations and debt resolutions, for hosts of floor amendments. The 1980 bill typified the pattern, as Congressional Quarterly described: "Senators found [the continuing resolution] a powerfully attractive magnet for all sorts of legislative provisions they had been unable to enact into law earlier in the year . . . . The Senate acted on 67 amendments to the resolution, after dozens of amendments had been added in the Appropriations Committee."[240] As Congressional Quarterly noted in 1986, "[w]ith virtually no limits on amendments or debate, the [continuing resolution] often becomes bogged down. Senators can use the threat of filibusters to force floor managers to accept amendments that would benefit particular states . . . [and] their favorite social causes . . . ."[241]

Senate adoption of such amendments often had purely symbolic significance, as the party and committee leaderships freely admit in announcing the amendments' likely fate in conference.

---

aid. 1983 Congressional Quarterly Almanac 523. Congressional Quarterly observed in 1986 that: "As in the past, foreign aid was spared even deeper cuts partly because Congress acted on it behind closed doors. A handful of members from the House and Senate Appropriations committees . . . negotiated the final spending figures in those private meetings." Felton, Foreign Aid Cutbacks: Minimizing the Pain, 44 Cong. Q. Week. Rep. 2671 (1986).

[240] 1980 Congressional Quarterly Almanac 220. Similarly, in 1985 "[a]bout 50 amendments were considered, but many were technical, and only a handful of generally non-controversial proposals were adopted." 1985 Congressional Quarterly Almanac 365.

[241] Gettinger, supra, at 2061.

Majority Leader Byrd commented in 1980 that the
Senate actions were "a needless, profane waste of
time"; "What are we doing?   Playing to the
headlines back home.   Ninety percent of these
amendments are going to be dropped in
conference."[242] Similarly, in 1982 Appropriations
Chairperson Hatfield "joked that he had dropped
about 50 of the Senate-approved amendments in the
Capitol Rotunda on his way over from the Senate.
'I admit we have put a lot of garbage in it.'
Hatfield said."[243]   As the House did not load up
its version of the bill with amendments and thus
had no appetite for swapping, and final
postconference Senate adoption was unlikely to
depend on saving the minor amendments, the
conferees had little reason to enact most of the
Senate riders.

     The Senate did use continuing resolutions for
a few significant test votes.   In 1982, the defeat
of an amendment to kill the Clinch River breeder
by the close vote of 48-49[244] presaged the
project's ultimate demise.   In 1984, the
continuing resolution served as the vehicle for
the memorable postcloture struggle over the Grove
City civil rights bill, discussed in detail in the
chapter on filibuster and cloture.   In 1985, the
continuing resolution served as the vehicle for a
compromise on a $7.3 billion defense package on
which the authorizing and appropriations
committees had staked rival claims.[245]   However,
in general, the amendments offered were either
parochial or symbolic and remarkable chiefly for
their large numbers and hasty consideration.

Supplementals

     Besides the regular appropriations and the
continuing resolutions, Congress passes another,

---

[242]   1980 Congressional Quarterly Almanac 220.

[243]   1982 Congressional Quarterly Almanac 228.

[244]   1982 Congressional Quarterly Almanac 227.

[245]   1985 Congressional Quarterly Almanac 365.

rather unique type of appropriation: supplemental appropriations. These are variable bills, typically two or three each fiscal year, providing funds for which Congress will not wait until the next year's regular appropriations.

Supplementals have a rich history in the relationship of the executive branch to the Congress. In the nineteenth and early twentieth centuries, departmental overexpenditures and unauthorized commitments used to force Congress to pass both supplemental appropriations and "deficiency" appropriations ("coercive" deficiencies). It took 150 years of struggle for Congress to succeed, partially, in getting agencies to spend within their instructions.[246]

Modern supplementals include a wide range of unpredictable or urgent matters. Supplementals fund the pay increase for military and civilian employees, since Congress does not determine the size of that pay increase in advance of the fiscal year. They fund wars and extra stimulus in times of recession: large supplementals funded the Korean and Vietnam conflicts and American aid to Nicaraguan contras, and provided stimulus in the recessions of 1977 and in 1982.[247] Supplementals fund agricultural aid, disaster relief, and forest fire fighting, which vary with weather and other unpredictable factors. When new Presidents take office, they serve as vehicles for a quick major shift in priorities, such as in 1977 and in 1981.

Supplemental appropriations also serve as a vehicle for approving or rejecting presidential spending cut proposals (rescissions and deferrals). They provide a convenient occasion for appropriations that may politically do better if not squeezed through the regular appropriations cycle. "Omnibus spending bills traditionally attracted all sorts of pet projects and amendments because small items might pass unnoticed while controversial ones stood a better chance if

---

[246] The key was having the President's budget office police agency "apportionment" of funds into increments for each calendar period. See L. Fisher, Presidential Spending Power 232-38 (1975); L. Wilmerding, The Spending Power (1943).

[247] 1985 Congressional Quarterly Almanac 351 (contras).

embedded in such a package."[248]

To organize the preparation and management of supplemental appropriations, generally the chairs of the appropriations committees refer agency requests for supplementals (previously sifted by the Office of Management and Budget) to the appropriations subcommittee with regular jurisdiction over that agency or program. Once the supplemental appropriation comes to the floor, the full committee leadership manages the bill overall, with each bill portion or floor amendment managed by the leadership of the appropriations subcommittee with regular jurisdiction.

Supplementals generally require that budget act restrictions be waived.[249] By the late date at which supplementals come up, typically the sum total of expenditures has exceeded the budget act's section 311 ceiling, and each subcommittee's expenditures have exceeded Gramm-Rudman's section 302(d) ceiling. This may entice appropriations committees to underfund programs, such as farm price supports, when passing regular appropriations. They thereby meet tight budget ceilings on the regular bills and put off expenditures until a supplemental when the budget ceilings will necessarily be waived anyway. In 1987, Congress attempted to stop this time-honored practice.[250]

---

[248] 1987 Congressional Quarterly Almanac 403 (citing provisions ranging from federal employee drug testing to beekeeper loans).

Long ago, the appropriations committees had subcommittees just for deficiency or supplemental bills, but for lack of specialization this arrangement was abandoned.

[249] 1987 Congressional Quarterly Almanac 406 (Gramm-Rudman budget objections waived for 1987 supplemental).

[250] In OMB Director Stockman's words, "[t]he major defect of the 302(b) process is that, as it has operated to date, it does not account very well for the fact that Spring Supplementals are often used for budget authority increases for programs, as well as pay. There is a tendency to use the full authority provided in the 302(b) allocation in the Fall appropriations season." Hearing at 336-37.
(footnote continued)

Also, supplementals may require waivers of points of order for unauthorized appropriations, which can occasion a major, multi-stage turf and budgeting battle. In 1985, the Rules Committee refused to give a waiver for unauthorized water projects dear to the heart of the Appropriations Committee, allowing the authorizing committee to strike them on a point of order.[251] When, notwithstanding this, the appropriations conferees came back with funding for water projects, the House rejected it in favor of a restrictive compromise.[252] Conversely, in 1984, a floor amendment to fund aid to El Salvador fell on a point of order for unauthorization, after conference the House voted to accept such funding.[253]

Floor consideration may be either open or closed.[254] For a closed example, in 1983 the House took up a supplemental appropriation pairing $15 billion of House-desired housing funding for $8 billion of administration-desired funding for the International Monetary Fund -- in Senator Jake Garn's (R-Utah) words, "like mating a turkey and a camel and hoping it would fly."[255] The House rule

---

For example, in 1983, the agricultural appropriations bill reported in the House was attacked for exceeding the administration request, in terms applicable to a bill exceeding a suballocation: "The bill has funded food stamps, child nutrition, and the WIC program at less -- let me emphasize that -- at less than 12 months in order to fall within the administration's request . . . . We are going to have to have a supplemental to fill out these . . . ." In 1987, a "reconciliation measure provided for an 'indefinite,' open-ended authorization for . . . farm price-support programs . . . . The change was meant to end an annual rite of spring known as supplemental appropriation bills." 1987 Congressional Quarterly Almanac 616.

[251]   1985 Congressional Quarterly Almanac 354.

[252]   1985 Congressional Quarterly Almanac 359.

[253]   1984 Congressional Quarterly Almanac 439, 442.

[254]   Moreover, floor amendments adding funds to a supplemental may not be in order unless the special rule not only is open, but waives relevant points of order.
(footnote continued)

allowed no amendments, limited debate to one hour, and by its self-executing provisions provided that passage of the rule itself passed the bill with no further votes necessary.[256]

In the Senate, supplementals tend, like continuing resolutions, to become omnibus vehicles targeted by legions of floor amendments. In 1983, "Senators spent days slogging through several dozen amendments to the [supplemental] bill -- in the process adding $1.3 billion to the $3.9 billion jobs package reported by the Appropriations Committee."[257] In 1984, a supplemental bill spent nine days on the Senate floor. House Chairperson Whitten called the Senate bill that resulted a "Sears, Roebuck catalog" because of all its amendments.[258]

The Senate has the same issue as the House regarding the lack of authorization for floor amendments to supplemental appropriations. In addition, the Senate's germaneness rule on appropriations comes into play with particular force for supplementals; since, unlike regular appropriations, they are not comprehensive in scope, amendments likely do not pertain to existing provisions. Sometimes the Senate disposes elegantly of such points of order, such as on the 1982 supplemental in which it voted to suspend the rules in order to add a non-germane housing appropriation.[259] Sometimes it just votes not to follow the rules; when the 1982 bill came back from conference, the Chair again held the housing provision non-germane, and this time[260] the Senate voted to overrule that ruling.

---

[255] 1983 Congressional Quarterly Almanac 536.

[256] 1983 Congressional Quarterly Almanac 539.

[257] 1983 Congressional Quarterly Almanac 455.

[258] 1984 Congressional Quarterly Almanac 432-33 (floor consideration), 438 (Whitten remark).

[259] 1982 Congressional Quarterly Almanac 209.

[260] 1982 Congressional Quarterly Almanac 211.

Selected Bibliography

FOR ALL CHAPTERS

Brown, William Holmes, <u>Deschler's Procedure in the House of Representatives</u>. Washington, D.C.: Government Printing Office, 1979 (with periodic supplements).

Congressional Quarterly, 1987 <u>Congressional Quarterly Almanac</u>. Washington, D.C.: Congressional Quarterly Press, 1987 (available each prior year).

<u>Constitution, Jefferson's Manual and Rules of the House of Representatives</u>, H. Doc. No. 279, 99th Cong., 2d Sess., Washington, D.C.: Government Printing Office, 1987 (updated each Congress).

Minority Leader of the House of Representatives, <u>Manual on Legislative Procedure in the United States House of Representatives</u>. Washington, D.C.: Minority Leader, 1986 (periodically updated).

Riddick, Floyd M., <u>Senate Procedure: Precedents and Practices</u>, S. Doc. No. 2, 97th Congress, 1st Sess. Washington, D.C.: Government Printing Office, 1981 (periodically updated).

THE MYSTERY OF CONGRESSIONAL PROCEDURE

Birnbaum, Jeffrey H., and Murray, Alan S.,

Showdown at Gucci Gulch: Lawmakers, Lobbyists, and the Unlikely Triumph of Tax Reform. New York: Random House, 1987.

Berman, Daniel M. A Bill Becomes a Law: Congress Enacts Civil Rights Legislation. New York: The MacMillan Company, 1967 (2d ed.).

Congressional Quarterly. Guide to Congress. Washington, D.C.: CQ Press, 2d ed. 1976 (3d ed. 1982).

Congressional Quarterly. Origins and Development of Congress. CQ Press: Washington, D.C., 1976.

Davidson, Roger H., and Oleszek, Walter J. Congress and its Members. Washington, D.C.: CQ Press, 1981.

Congress Reconsidered (3d ed. by L. C. Dodd & B. I. Oppenheimer 1985).

Galloway, George B. History of the House of Representatives. New York: Thomas Y. Crowell Co., 1976 (Wise, Sidney, rev. ed).

Goehlert, Robert U., and Sayre, John R. The United States Congress: A Bibliograph. New York: The Free Press, 1982.

Green, Mark, Fallows, James M., and Zwick, David R. Who Runs Congress. New York: Bantam Books, 1972.

Gross, Bertram. The Legislative Struggle. New York: McGraw-Hill, 1953.

Luce, Robert. Legislative Procedures. Boston: Houghton Mifflin, 1922.

Oleszek, Walter J. Congressional Procedure and the Policy Process. Washington, D.C.: CQ Press: 3d ed., 1988.

Willett, Edward F. How Our Laws Are Made. H. Doc. No. 158, 99th Cong., 2d Sess. Washington, D.C.: Government Printing Office, 1966.

Young, James Sterling. The Washington Community 1800–1828. New York: Columbia University Press, 1966.

COMMITTEE JURISDICTION, ORGANIZATION, AND PROCEDURE

Alexander, DeAlva Stanwood. History and Procedure of the House of Representatives. Boston: Houghton Mifflin Co., 1916.

Broden, Thomas F. Congressional Committee Reports: Their Role and History, 33 Notre Dame Law. 209

(1958).

Calmes, Jacqueline, and Granat, Diane. Senate Cuts Committee Slots; Members Assigned to Panels. 43 Cong. Q. Week. Rep. 348 (1985).

Calmes, Jacqueline. Seniority System Thriving in Congress . . . Despite Challenges in House, Senate. 45 Cong. Q. Week. Rep. 140 (1987).

Cohen, Richard. The Mysterious Ways Congress Makes Committee Assignments. National Journal (February 3, 1979).

Cohen, William S. Roll Call: One Year in the United States Senate. New York: Simon and Schuster, 1981.

Commission on the Operation of the Senate, Committees and Senate Procedures: A Compilation of Papers. Committee Print. Washington, D.C.: Government Printing Office, 1976.

Commission on the Operation of the Senate, Legislative Activity Sourcebook: United States Senate. Committee Print. Washington, D.C.: Government Printing Office. 1976

Commission on the Operation of the Senate. Toward a Modern Senate. S. Doc. No. 278, 94th Cong., 2d Sess. Washington, D.C.: Government Printing Office, 1976.

Congressional Quarterly. Origins and Development of Congress. Washington, D.C.: CQ Press, 1976.

Cooper, Joseph. The Origins of the Standing Committees and the Development of the Modern House. Houston: Rice University Monograph in Political Science, vol. 56, no. 3, 1970.

Cummings, Frank. Capitol Hill Manual. Washington, D.C.: Bureau of National Affairs, 2d ed. 1984.

Davidson, Roger H., and Oleszek, Walter J. Congress Against Itself. Bloomington: Indiana University Press, 1977.

Eulau, Hans. Legislative Committee Assignments. 9 Legis. Stud. Q. 587 (1984).

Felton, John. In Victory for Seniority System, Helms Wrests Post from Lugar. 45 Cong. Q. Week. Rep. 143 (1987).

Fenno, Richard F. Congressmen in Committees. Boston: Little, Brown & Co., 1973.

Foley, Michael. The New Senate: Liberal Influence on a Conservative Institution 1959-1972. New Haven: Yale University Press, 1980.

Goodwin, George. Subcommittees: the Miniature Legislatures of Congress. 56 Am. Poli. Sci.

Rev. 596 (1962).

Goodwin, George. The Little Legislatures. Amherst: University of Massachusetts Press, 1970.

Haeberle, Hans. The Institutionalization of the Subcommittee in the United States House of Representatives. 50 J. of Politics 1054 (1978).

Hook, Janet. Winning a Budget Seat Can Be a Yearlong Job, 47 Cong. Q. Week. Rep. 18 (1989).

House Select Committee on Committees, 93d Cong., 2d Sess. Monographs on the Committees of the House of Representatives. Committee Print. Washington, D.C.: Government Printing Office, 1974.

Haynes, George H. The Senate of the United States. Boston: Houghton Mifflin Co., 1938. New York: Russell & Russell, 1960.

House Select Committee on Committees. H.R. Rept. No. 866. 96th Cong., 2d Sess. Washington, D.C.: Government Printing Office, 1980.

Kravitz, Walter. Evolution of the Senate's Committee System. 411 Ann. Am. Acad. of Poli. Sci. 27 (1974).

Loomis, Congressional Careers and Party Leadership in the Contemporary House of Representatives, 28 Am. J. Poli. Sci. 180 (1984)

McConachie, Lauros G. Congressional Committees. Thomas Y. Crowell & Co., 1898.

McGeary, Nelson. Congressional Investigations: Historical Development. 18 U. Chi. L. Rev. 425 (1951).

Mikva, Abner J., and Sarris, Patti B. The American Congress. New York: Franklin Watts, 1983.

Morrow, William L. Congressional Committees. New York: Charles Scriber's Sons, 1969.

Munger, Michael C. Allocation of Desirable Committee Assignments: Extended Queues Versus Committee Expansion. 32 Am. J. Poli. Sci. 317 (1988).

Ornstein, Norman, and Rhode, David W. "Shifting Forces, Changing Rules, and Political Outcomes: The Impact of Congressional Change on Four House Committees" in New Perspectives on the House of Representatives. Chicago: Rand McNally, 1977 (ed. by Peabody, Robert L., and Polsby, Nelson W., 3d ed.)

Parris, Judith. The Senate Reorganizes Its Committees, 1977. 94 Poli. Sci. Q. 319 (1979).

Polsby, Nelson W. The Institutionalization of the House of Representatives. 62 Am. Poli. Sci. Rev. 144 (1968).

Price, David E. Who Makes the Laws? Cambridge, Mass.: Schenkman Publishing Co., 1972.

Ray, Bruce A. Federal Spending and the Selection of Committee Assignments in the U.S. House of Representatives, 24 Am. J. Poli. Sci. 494 (1980).

Ray & Smith, Committee Size in the U.S. Congress, 9 Legis. Stud. Q. 679 (1984).

Ripley, Randall P. Congress: Process and Policy. New York: W.W. Norton & Company, 1975.-

Robinson, George L. "The Development of the Senate Committee System." Ph.D. diss. New York: New York University, 1954.

Samuelson, Betsy. "Senate Committee Operations," in Commission on the Operation of the Senate, 94th Cong., 2d Sess., Committees and Senate Procedure. Committee Print. Washington, D.C.: Government Printing Office, 1977.

Schlesinger, Arthur, and Bruns, Roger, eds. Congress Investigates: 1792-1974. New York: Chelsea House Publishers, 1975.

Shepsle, Kenneth A. The Giant Jigsaw Puzzle: Democratic Committee Assignments in the Modern House. Chicago: University of Chicago Press, 1978.

Siff, Todd, and Weil, Alan. Ruling Congress: How the House and Senate Rules Govern the Legislative Process. New York: Grossman, 1975.

Sinclair, Barbara. The Distribution of Committee Positions in the U.S. Senate: Explaining Institutional Change. 32 Am. J. Poli. Sci. 276 (1988).

Smith, Stephen S., and Deering, Christopher J. Committees in Congress. Washington, D.C.: CQ Press, 1984.

Temporary Senate Select Committee to Study the Senate Committee System, 94th Cong., 2d Sess. The Senate Committee System: Jurisdictions, Referrals, Numbers and Sizes, and Limitations on Membership. Committee Print. Washington, D.C.: Government Printing Office, 1976.

Temporary Senate Select Committee to Study the Senate Committee System. S. Prt. No. 254, 98th Cong., 2d Sess. Washington, D.C.: Government Printing Office, 1984.

Van der Slik, Jack R., and Stenger, Thomas C.

Citizen   Witnesses   Before   Congressional
Committees. 92 Poli. Sci. Q. 465 (1977).
Wayne, Stephen J. The Legislative Presidency. New
York: Harper & Row, 1979.
Westefield, Majority Party Leadership and the
Committee System in the House of Representa-
tives, 69 Am. Poli. Sci. Rev. 1593 (1974).
Wilson,   Woodrow. Congressional Government. New
York: Meridian Books, Inc., 1956 ed.
Zwirn, Jerrold. Congressional Committee Reports.
7A Gov. Pub. Rev. 319 (1980)

HOUSE PROCEDURE

Alexander, DeAlva Stanwood. History and Procedure
of   the   House   of   Representatives.   Boston:
Houghton Mifflin Co., 1916.
Bach,   Stanley.   Parliamentary   Strategy & the
Amendment Process: Rules & Case Studies of
Congressional Action. Polity (Summer 1983).
Bach,   Stanley. The Structure of Choice in the
House   of   Representatives: The   Impact   of
Complex Special Rules. 18 Harv. J. Legis. 553
(1981).
Bach,   Stanley. Suspension of the Rules in the
House of Representatives.   Washington, D.C.:
Congressional Research Service, May 12, 1986.
Beth,   Richard   S.   Outline   and   Historical
Development of the Discharge Rule in the House
of   Representatives.   Washington,   D.C.:
Congressional Research Service, Dec. 30, 1982.
Bolling, Richard. Power in the House. New York:
Capricorn Books, 1974 (2d ed.).
Brown, George R.   The Leadership of Congress.
Indianapolis: Bobbs-Merrill, 1922.
Calmes, Jacqueline. The Hill Leaders: Their Places
on the Ladder. 45 Cong. Q. Week. Rep. 5
(1987).
Cannon, Clarence. Cannon's Procedure in the House
of Representatives, H. Doc. No. 122, 86th
Cong., 1st Sess. (1959).
Cheney, Richard B. and Cheney, Lynn V. Kings of
the Hill: Power and Personality in the House
of   Representatives.   New   York: Continuum,
1983.
Chiu, Chang Wei.   The Speaker of the House of
Representatives   Since   1896.   New   York:

Columbia University Press, 1928.

Congressional Quarterly. Origins and Development of Congress. CQ Press: Washington, D.C., 1976.

Cooper, Ann. House Use of Suspensions Grows Drastically, 36 Cong. Q. Week. Rep. 2694 (1978).

Cooper, Joseph, and Brady, David W. Institutional Context and Leadership Style: The House from Cannon to Rayburn. American Political Science Review, March 1965, at 52.

Damon, Richard E. The Standing Rules of the United States House of Representatives. Ph.D. diss., Columbia University. Michigan: University Microfilms, 1971.

Dodd, Lawrence C. The Expanded Roles of the House Democratic Whip System: The 93rd and 94th Congresses. 7 Cong. Studies 27 (1979).

Ehrenhalt, Alan. Media, Power Shifts Dominate O'Neill's House. 44 Cong. Q. Week. Rep. 2131 (1986).

Elder, Shirley, and Clancy, Paul. Tip: A Biography of Thomas P. O'Neill. New York: Macmillan, 1980.

Follett, Mary P. The Speaker of the House of Representatives. New York: Burt Franklin Reprints, 1896.

Froman, Lewis. The Congressional Process: Strategies, Rules and Procedures. Boston: Little, Brown & Co., 1967.

Galloway, George B. History of the House of Representatives. New York: Thomas Y. Crowell Co., 1976 (Wise, Sidney, rev. ed).

Harlow, Ralph V. The History of Legislative Methods in the Period Before 1825. New Haven, Conn.: Yale University Press, 1917.

Hasbrouck, Paul D. Party Government in the House of Representatives. New York: The Macmillan Company, 1927.

Hook, Janet. End-of-Session Vote Spreee Inflames Tempers, 46 Cong. Q. Week. Rep. 2787 (1988).

----------. GOP Chafes Under Restrictive House Rules. 45 Cong. Q. Week. Rep. 2449 (1987).

----------. Lott's Departure Makes Rume for Republicans to Move Up.. 46 Cong. Q. Week. Rep. 3195 (1988).

House Committee on Rules, 97th Cong., 2d Sess. A History of the Committee on Rules. Committee Print. Washington, D.C.: Government Printing Office. 1983.

How Our Laws are Made, H. Doc. No. 97-120, 97th
    Cong., 1st Sess. Washington, D.C.: Government
    Printing Office, 1981.
Jones, Charles O. The Minority Party in Congress.
    Boston: Little, Brown & Co., 1970.
McConachie, Lauros G. Congressional Committees.
    New York: Thomas Y. Crowell & Co., 1898.
Mackaman, Frank H. Understanding Congressional
    Leadership. Washington, D.C.: CQ Press, 1981.
MacNeil, Neil. Forge of Democracy: the House of
    Representatives New York: David McKay, 1963.
Matsunaga, Spark M., and Chen, Ping. Rulemakers of
    the House. Urbana: Univ. of Illinois, 1976.
Oppenheimer, Bruce I. "Policy Implications of
    Rules Committee Reforms," in Legislative
    Reform (L. N. Rieselbach ed. 1978).
O'Neill, Thomas P. Man of the House. New York,
    N.Y.: St Martin's Press, 1987.
Plattner, Andy. Rules Under Chairman Pepper Looks
    Out for the Democrats. 43 Cong. Q. Week. Rep.
    1671 (1985).
Riddick, Floyd M. The United States Congress,
    Organization and Procedure. Manassas, Va.:
    National Capital Publishers, 1949.
Ripley, Randall B. Party Leaders in the House of
    Representatives. Washington, D.C.: Brookings
    Institute, 1967.
Ripley, Randall B. Majority Power Leadership in
    Congress. Boston: Little, Brown & Co., 1969.
Robinson, James A. The House Rules Committee.
    Indianapolis: Bobbs-Merrill, 1963.
Sinclair, Barbara. Majority Leadership in the U.S.
    House. Washington, D.C.: CQ Press, 1983.
Smith, Stephen S., and Deering, Christopher J.
    Committees in Congress. Washington, D.C.: CQ
    Press, 1984.

SENATE PROCEDURE

Asbell, Bernard. The Senate Nobody Knows. Garden
    City: Doubleday, 1978.
Bach, Stanley. Senator and Senate: Influence on
    the Legislative Agenda. Washington, D.C.:
    Congressional Research Service, 1983.
Beeman, Richard R. Unlimited Debate in the Senate:
    The First Phase. LXXXIII Poli. Sci Q. 419
    (1968).

Berman, Daniel M. A Bill Becomes a Law: Congress
    Enacts Civil Rights Legislation. London:
    Macmillan & Co., 1966. (2d ed.)
Burdette, Franklin L. Filibustering in the Senate.
    Princeton, N.J.: Princeton University Press,
    1940.
Calmes, The Hill Leaders: Their Places on the
    Ladder, 45 Cong. Q. Week. Rep. 5 (1987).
Celada, Ray & Bach, Stanley. Treaty Making and the
    INF Treaty in the Senate. CRS Review, March
    1988.
Clark, Joseph S. Congress: The Sapless Branch. New
    York: Harper & Row, 1964.
---------------. The Senate Establishment.   New
    York: Hill & Wang, 1963.
Cohen, William S. Roll Call: One Year in the
    United States Senate.   New York: Simon &
    Schuster, 1981.
Cooper, Ann. The Senate and the Filibuster: War of
    Nerves -- and Hardball.   36 Cong. Q. Week.
    Rep. 2307 (1978).
Davidson, Roger H. Senate Leaders: Janitors for an
    Untidy Chamber?. In Congress Reconsidered (3d
    ed. by Dodd, Lawrence C. and Oppenheimer,
    Bruce I,.) Washington, D.C.: CQ Press: 1985.
Dove, Robert B. Enactment of a Law: Procedural
    Steps in the Legislative Process. S. Doc. No.
    20, 97th Cong., 2d Sess. Washington, D.C.:
    Government Printing Office, 1981.
Drew, Elizabeth. Senator. New York: Simon &
    Schuster, 1979.
Ehrenhalt, Alan. In the Senate of the '80s, Team
    Spirit has Given Way to the Rule of
    Individuals. 40 Cong. Q. Week. Rep. 2175
    (1982).
Elving, Ronald D. Cranston Beats Ford for Whip;
    Pryor Wins Secretary Position. 46 Cong. Q.
    Week. Rep. 3437 (1988).
---------------. Mitchell Will Try to Elevate
    Policy, Predictability. 46 Cong. Q. Week. Rep.
    3423 (1988).
---------------. No Safe Bets in Senate Majority
    Leader's Race. 46 Cong. Q. Week. Rep. 3357
    (1988).
Evans, Rowland, and Novak, Robert. Lyndon Johnson:
    The Exercise of Power. New York: The New
    American Library Co., 1966.
Felton, Senate's Climate of Partisanship Yields an
    Agreement of Unusual Complexity, 44 Cong. Q.

Week. Rep. 1878 (1986).

Foley, Michael. The New Senate: Liberal Influence on a Conservative Institution 1959-1972. New Haven, Conn.: Yale University Press, 1980.

Froman, Lewis A. The Congressional Process: Strategies, Rules, and Procedures. Boston: Little, Brown & Co., 1967.

Galloway, George B. The Legislative Process in Congress. New York: Thomas Y. Crowell Co., 1953.

Gilfry, Henry H. Precedents: Decisions on Points of Order with Phraseology in the United States Senate. S. Doc. No. 129, 61st Cong., 1st Sess. Washington, D.C.: Government Printing Office, 1909.

Glass, Andrew J. Mansfield Reforms Spark 'Quiet Revolution' in Senate. National Journal, March 6, 1971, at 499.

Gold, Martin. Senate Procedure & Practice: An Introductory Manual. Unpublished paper, Washington, D.C. 1981.

Harris, Joseph P. The Advice and Consent of the Senate. Berkeley: University of California Press, 1953.

Hook, Janet. Changes in Senate Rules Suggested -- Again. 46 Cong. Q. Week. Rep. 2657 (1988).

-----------. Senate Rules, Closeness of GOP Margin . . . Keep Democrats Influential in Minority, 44 Cong. Q. Week. Rep. 1394 (1986).

Haynes, George H. The Senate of the United States. New York: Russell & Russell, 1960.

Kerr, Clara Hannah. The Origin and Development of the United States Senate. Ithaca: Andrus & Church, 1895.

Keith, Robert. The Use of Unanimous Consent in the Senate. In Commission on the Operation of the Senate, 94th Cong., 2d Sess. Committees and Senate Procedures. Washington, D.C.: Government Printing Office, 1977.

Matthews, Donald R. U.S. Senators and Their World. New York: W. W. Norton & Co., 1973 ed.

McConachie, Lauros G. Congressional Committees. Thomas Y. Crowell & Co., 1898.

Miller, James A. Running in Place: Inside the Senate. New York: Simon & Schuster Inc., 1986.

Munk, Margaret. Origin and Development of the Party Floor Leadership in the United States Senate. 2 Capitol Studies J. 23 (1974).

Oleszek, Walter. Majority and Minority Whips of the Senate, S. Doc. No. 23, 96th Cong., 1st Sess. Washington, D.C.: Government Printing Office, 1979.

Oppenheimer, Bruce I. "Changing Time Constraints on Congress: Historical Perspectives on the Use of Cloture", in Congress Reconsidered. Washington, D.C.: CQ Press, 1985 (3d ed. by Dodd, Lawrence D., and Oppenheimer, Bruce I.).

Patterson, James T. Congressional Conservatism and the New Deal: The Growth of the Conservative Coalition in Congress, 1933-1939. Lexington: University of Kentucky Press, 1967.

Peabody, Robert L. Leadership in Congress: Stability, Succession, and Change. Boston: Little, Brown, & Co., 1976.

Peabody, Robert L. "Senate Party Leadership: From the 1950s to the 1980s," in Understanding Congressional Leadership (ed. Frank H. Mackaman. Washington, D.C.: CQ Press, 1981.

Redman, Eric. The Dance of Legislation. New York: Simon & Schuster, 1973.

Reid, Thomas R. Congressional Odyssey: The Saga of a Senate Bill. San Francisco: W. H. Freeman, 1980.

Riddick, Floyd M. History of the Senate Committee on Rules and Administration. S. Doc. No. 27, 96th Cong., 1st Sess. Washington, D.C.: Government Printing Office, 1980.

----------------. Majority and Minority Leaders of the Senate. S. Doc. No. 12, 97th Cong., 1st Sess. Washington, D.C.: Government Printing Office, 1981.

----------------. The United States Congress, Organization and Procedure. Manassas, Va.: National Capital Publishers, 1949.

Ripley, Randall B. Power in the Senate. New York: St. Martin's Press, 1969.

Rogers, Lindsay. The American Senate. New York: Alfred A. Knopf, Inc., 1926.

Rothman, David J. Politics and Power: The United States Senate 1869-1901. Cambridge, Mass.: Harvard University Press, 1966.

Russell, Robert W. "Workings of Congress," in Effective Washington Representation. New York: Law & Business, 1983. (Marcuss, Stanley J., editor.)

Senate Committee on Rules and Administration, 96th

Cong., 1st Sess. Senate Cloture Rule. Washington, D.C.: Government Printing Office, 1979.

Shuman, Howard E. Senate Rules and the Civil Rights Bill: A Case Study. Am. Poli. Sci. Rev. 955 (1957).

Smith, Stephen S. and Deering, Christopher J. Committees in Congress. Washington, D.C.: CQ Press, 1984.

S. Prt. No. 254, 98th Cong., 2d Sess. Washington, D.C.: Government Printing Office, 1984.

Swanstrom, Roy. The United States Senate, 1787–1801. S. Doc. No. 19, 99th Cong., 1st Sess. Washington, D.C.: Government Printing Office, 1985.

White, William S. Citadel: The Story of the U.S. Senate . New York: Harper and Brothers, 1957.

Wilson, Woodrow. Congressional Government. Baltimore: Johns Hopkins University Press, 1981 ed.

CONFERENCE PROCEDURE

Fenno, Richard F. The Power of the Purse: Appropriations Politics in Congress. Boston: Little, Brown & Co., 1966.

Ferejohn, John. Who Wins in Conference Committees? Journal of Politics, November 1975, at 1033.

Froman, Lewis A. The Congressional Process: Strategies, Rules, and Procedures. Boston: Little, Brown & Co., 1967.

Gore, Sr., Albert. The Conference Committee: Congress' Final Filter. The Washington Monthly, June 1971.

Hook, Janet. In Conference: New Hurdles, Hard Bargaining, 45 Cong. Q. Week. Rep. 2080 (1986).

Malbin, Michael J. Unelected Representatives: Congressional Staff and the Future of Representatives Government. New York: Basic Books, 1980.

McCown, Ada. The Congressional Conference Committee New York: Columbia University Press, 1927.

Pressman, Jeffrey L. House vs. Senate New Haven, Conn.: Yale University Press, 1966.

Reform Penetrates Conference Committee, 33 Cong.

Q. Week. Rep. 290 (1975).
Siff, Todd, and Weil, Alan. Ruling Congress. New York: Grossman, 1975.
Steiner, Gilbert. The Congressional Conference Committee, Seventieth to Eightieth Congresses. Urbana: University of Illinois Press, 1951.
Strom, Gerald S., and Rundquist, Barry S. A Revised Theory of Winning in House-Senate Conferences. LXXI Am. Poli. Sci. Rev. 448 (1977).
Vogler, David J. The Third House: Conference Committee in the United States Congress. Evanston, Ill. Northwestern University Press, 1971.

BUDGET AND APPROPRIATIONS PROCEDURE

Berger, Raoul. Executive Privilege: A Constitutional Myth. Cambridge: Harvard University Press, 1974.
Committee on Appropriations: 100th Anniversary, 1867-1967. S. Doc. No. 21. 90th Cong., 1st Sess. (1967).
Congressional Quarterly. Origins and Development of Congress. Washington, D.C.: CQ Press, 1976.
Fenno, Richard F. The Power of the Purse: Appropriations Politics in Congress. Boston: Little, Brown & Co. 1966.
Fisher, Louis. The Authorization-Appropriation Process in Congress: Formal Rules and Informal Practices. 29 Cath. U. L. Rev. 51 (1979).
Fisher, Louis. Annual Authorizations: Durable Roadblocks to Biennial Budgeting. Public Budgeting & Finance, Spring 1983.
Fisher, Louis. Presidential Spending Power. Princeton, N.J.: Princeton University Press, 1975.
Granat, Diane. House Appropriations Panel Doles Out Cold Federal Cash, Chafes at Budget Procedures, 41 Cong. Q. Week. Rep. 1209 (1983).
Havemann, Joel. Congress and the Budget. Bloomington: Indiana University Press, 1978.
House Committee on the Budget, 95th Cong., 1st Sess., Congressional Control of Expenditures. Committee Print Washington, D.C.: Government Printing Office, 1977.

House Committee on Rules. Report on the Congressional Budget Act Amendments of 1984. H.R. Rept. No. 1152, 98th Cong., 2d Sess. Washington, D.C.: Government Printing Office, 1984.

Ippolito, Dennis S. Congressional Spending. Ithaca: Cornell University Press, 1981.

LeLoup, Lance T. The Fiscal Congress. Westport: Greenwood Press, 1980.

Murray, Alan. House Funding Bill Riders Become Potent Policy Force, 38 Cong. Q. Week. Rep. 3251 (1980).

Penner, Rudolf G., and Abramson, Alan J. Broken Purse Strings: Congressional Budgeting, 1974-88. Washington, D.C.: The Urban Institute, 1988.

Penner, Rudolf G., ed. The Congressional Budget Process After Five Years. Washington, D.C.: American Enterprise Institute, 1981.

Schick, Allen. Congress and Money: Budgeting, Spending and Taxing. Washington, D.C.: The Urban Institute, 1980.

Schick, Allen. Making Economic Policy in Congress Washington, D.C.: American Enterprise Institute, 1983.

Schick, Allen. Crisis in the Budget Process: Exercising Political Choice. Washington, D.C.: American Enterprise Institute, 1986.

Schick, Allen. "The Three-Ring Budget Process: The Appropriations, Tax, and Budget Committees in Congress," in The New Congress 297. Ed. by Mann, Thomas E., and Ornstein, Norman J. Washington, D.C.: The American Enterprise Institute For Public Policy Research, 1981.

Stith, Kate, Congress' Power of the Purse, 97 Yale L. J. 1343 (1988).

Stith, Kate, Rewriting the Fiscal Constitution: The Case of Gramm-Rudman-Hollings, 76 Calif. L. Rev. 593 (1988).

Stockman, David A. The Triumph of Politics. New York: Harper & Row, 1986.

Wander, W. Thomas; Hebert, F. Ted; and Copeland, Gary W. Congressional Budgeting: Politics, Process, and Power. Baltimore: The Johns Hopkins University Press W. T., 1984.

White, Joe. The Continuing Resolution: A Crazy Way to Govern? Brookings Rev., Summer 1988, at 28.

Wildavsky, Aaron. The New Politics of the Budgetary Process. Glenview: Scott, Foresman,

1988.
Wildavsky, Aaron. <u>The Politics of the Budgetary Process</u>. Boston: Little, Brown & Co., 1984.

INDEX

Index

About the Author

CHARLES TIEFER is the Deputy General Counsel to the Clerk of the House of Representatives, and an adjunct professor at Georgetown University Law Center. He has presented arguments in a number of federal courts of appeals on behalf of the Senate and House, and has contributed articles to the *Harvard Law Review, Labor Law Journal,* and *Boston University Law Review.*